140.00

MISSION COLLEGE
LIBRARY

D0819640

REFERENCE
ONLY

3 1215 00095 0524

Contemporary Authors®

NEW REVISION SERIES

Explore your options!

Gale databases are offered in a variety of formats

 **GALE**

The information in this Gale publication is also available in some or all of the formats described here. Your Gale Representative will be happy to fill you in. Call toll-free 1-800-877-GALE.

 *GaleNet* ᔆᴹ
your information community

GaleNet

A number of Gale databases are now available on GaleNet, our new online information resource accessible through the Internet. GaleNet features an easy-to-use end-user interface, the powerful search capabilities of BRS/SEARCH retrieval software and ease of access through the World Wide Web.

Diskette/Magnetic Tape

Many Gale databases are available on diskette or magnetic tape, allowing systemwide access to your most-used information sources through existing computer systems. Data can be delivered on a variety of mediums (DOS-formatted diskettes, 9-track tape, 8mm data tape) and in industry-standard formats (comma-delimited, tagged, fixed-field).

CD-ROM

A variety of Gale titles are available on CD-ROM, offering maximum flexibility and powerful search software.

Online

For your convenience, many Gale databases are available through popular online services, including DIALOG, NEXIS, DataStar, ORBIT, OCLC, Thomson Financial Network's I/Plus Direct, HRIN, Prodigy, Sandpoint's HOOVER, the Library Corporation's NLightN and Telebase Systems.

ISSN 0275-7176

Contemporary Authors®

A Bio-Bibliographical Guide to Current Writers in Fiction, General Nonfiction, Poetry, Journalism, Drama, Motion Pictures, Television, and Other Fields

DANIEL JONES
JOHN D. JORGENSON
Editors

NEW REVISION SERIES
volume 62

GALE

DETROIT · NEW YORK · TORONTO · LONDON

STAFF

Daniel Jones and John D. Jorgenson, *Editors, New Revision Series*

Thomas Wiloch, *Sketchwriting Coordinator and Online Research Specialist*

Tim Akers, Pamela S. Dear, Jeff Hunter, Jerry Moore, Deborah A. Schmitt, Polly A. Vedder, Tim White and Kathleen Wilson, *Contributing Editors*

Bruce Boston, Linda Cohen, Jason Dobrowski, John Furness, Mary Gillis, Beaird Glover, Joan Goldsworthy, Amanda Hiber, Anne Janette Johnson, Tamara Kendig, Rena Korb, Sarah Madsen-Hardy, Scott Martin, Robert Miltner, Susan Salter, Arlene True, Shanna Weagle, Denise Wiloch, and Tim Winter-Damon, *Sketchwriters*

Emily J. McMurray, Neil Schlager, and Pamela L. Shelton, *Copyeditors*

James P. Draper, *Managing Editor*

Victoria B. Cariappa, *Research Manager*

Julia C. Daniel, Jeffrey Daniels, Tamara C. Nott, Tracie A. Richardson Norma Sawaya, and Cheryl L. Warnock, *Research Associates*

Talitha Dutton, *Research Assistant*

While every effort has been made to ensure the reliability of the information presented in this publication, Gale Research neither guarantees the accuracy of the data contained herein nor assumes any responsibility for errors, omissions, or discrepancies. Gale accepts no payment for listing; and inclusion in the publication of any organization, agency, institution, publication, service, or individual does not imply endorsement of the editors or publisher. Errors brought to the attention of the publisher and verified to the satisfaction of the publisher will be corrected in future editions.

This publication is a creative work copyrighted by Gale Research and fully protected by all applicable copyright laws, as well as by misappropriation, trade secret, unfair competition, and other applicable laws. The authors and editors of this work have added value to the underlying factual material herein through one or more of the following: unique and original selection, coordination, expression, arrangement, and classification of the information.

Gale Research will vigorously defend all of its rights in this publication.

Copyright © 1998 by Gale Research
835 Penobscot Building
Detroit, MI 48226

All rights reserved including the right of reproduction in whole or in part in any form.

This book is printed on acid-free paper that meets the minimum requirements of American National Standard for Information Sciences-Permanence Paper for Printed Library Materials, ANSI Z39.48-1984.

Library of Congress Catalog Card Number 81-640179
ISBN 0-7876-2005-X
ISSN 0275-7176

Printed in the United States of America

10 9 8 7 6 5 4 3 2 1

Contents

Indexing note: All *Contemporary Authors New Revision Series*
entries are indexed in the *Contemporary Authors* cumulative
index, which is published separately and distributed with even-
numbered *Contemporary Authors* original volumes and odd-
numbered *Contemporary Authors New Revision Series* volumes.

**As always, the most recent *Contemporary Authors* cumula-
tive index continues to be the user's guide to the location
of an individual author's listing.**

Preface

The *Contemporary Authors New Revision Series* (*CANR*) provides updated information on authors listed in earlier volumes of *Contemporary Authors* (*CA*). Although entries for individual authors from any volume of *CA* may be included in a volume of the *New Revision Series*, *CANR* updates only those sketches requiring significant change. However, in response to requests from librarians and library patrons for the most current information possible on high-profile writers of greater public and critical interest, *CANR* revises entries for these authors whenever new and noteworthy information becomes available.

Authors are included on the basis of specific criteria that indicate the need for a revision. These criteria include a combination of bibliographical additions, changes in addresses or career, major awards, and personal information such as name changes or death dates. All listings in this volume have been revised or augmented in various ways and contain up-to-the-minute publication information in the Writings section, most often verified by the author and/or by consulting a variety of online resources. Many sketches have been extensively rewritten, often including informative new Sidelights. As always, a *CANR* listing entails no charge or obligation.

The key to locating an author's most recent entry is the *CA* cumulative index, which is published separately and distributed with even-numbered original volumes and odd-numbered revision volumes. It provides access to all entries in *CA* and *CANR*. Always consult the latest index to find an author's most recent entry.

For the convenience of users, the *CA* cumulative index also includes references to all entries in these Gale literary series: *Authors and Artists for Young Adults, Authors in the News, Bestsellers, Black Literature Criticism, Black Writers, Children's Literature Review, Concise Dictionary of American Literary Biography, Concise Dictionary of British Literary Biography, Contemporary Authors Autobiography Series, Contemporary Authors Bibliographical Series, Contemporary Literary Criticism, Dictionary of Literary Biography, Dictionary of Literary Biography Documentary Series, Dictionary of Literary Biography Yearbook, DISCovering Authors, DISCovering Authors: British, DISCovering Authors: Canadian, DISCovering Authors: Modules* (including modules for Dramatists, Most-Studied Authors, Multicultural Authors, Novelists, Poets, and Popular/Genre Authors), *Drama Criticism, Hispanic Literature Criticism, Hispanic Writers, Junior DISCovering Authors, Major Authors and Illustrators for Children and Young Adults, Major 20th-Century Writers, Native North American Literature, Poetry Criticism, Short Story Criticism, Something about the Author, Something about the Author Autobiography Series, Twentieth-Century Literary Criticism, World Literature Criticism, World Literature Criticism Supplement,* and *Yesterday's Authors of Books for Children.*

A Sample Index Entry:

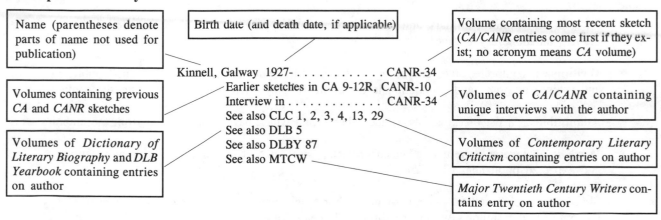

For the most recent *CA* information on Kinnell, users should refer to Volume 34 of the *New Revision Series,* as designated by "CANR-34"; if that volume is unavailable, refer to CANR-10. If CANR-10 is also unavailable, refer to CA 9-12R, published in 1974, for Kinnell's first revision entry.

How Are Entries Compiled?

The editors make every effort to secure new information directly from the authors. Copies of all sketches in selected *CA* and *CANR* volumes previously published are routinely sent to listees at their last-known addresses, and returns from these authors are then assessed. For deceased writers, or those who fail to reply to requests for data, we consult other reliable biographical sources, such as those indexed in Gale's *Biography and Genealogy Master Index,* and biobliographical sources, such as *Magazine Index, Newspaper Abstracts, LC MARC,* and a variety of online databases. Further details come from published interviews, feature stories, book reviews, online literary magazines and journals, author web sites, and often the authors' publishers supply material.

* Indicates that a listing has been compiled from secondary sources but has not been personally verified for this edition by the author under review.

What Kinds of Information Does an Entry Provide?

Sketches in *CANR* contain the following biographical and bibliographical information:

- **Entry heading:** the most complete form of author's name, plus any pseudonyms or name variations used for writing

- **Personal information:** author's date and place of birth, family data, ethnicity, educational background, political and religious affiliations, and hobbies and leisure interests

- **Addresses:** author's home, office, or agent's addresses, plus e-mail and fax numbers, as available

- **Career summary:** name of employer, position, and dates held for each career post; resume of other vocational achievements; military service

- **Membership information:** professional, civic, and other association memberships and any official posts held

- **Awards and honors:** military and civic citations, major prizes and nominations, fellowships, grants, and honorary degrees

- **Writings:** a comprehensive, chronological list of titles, publishers, dates of original publication and revised editions, and production information for plays, television scripts, and screenplays

- **Adaptations:** a list of films, plays, and other media which have been adapted from the author's work

- **Work in progress:** current or planned projects, with dates of completion and/or publication, and expected publisher, when known

- **Sidelights:** a biographical portrait of the author's development; information about the critical reception of the author's works; revealing comments, often by the author, on personal interests, aspirations, motivations, and thoughts on writing

- **Biographical and critical sources:** a list of books and periodicals in which additional information on an author's life and/or writings appears

Related Titles in the *CA* Series

Contemporary Authors Autobiography Series complements *CA* original and revised volumes with specially commissioned autobiographical essays by important current authors, illustrated with personal photographs they provide. Common topics include their motivations for writing, the people and experiences that shaped their careers, the rewards they derive from their work, and their impressions of the current literary scene.

Contemporary Authors Bibliographical Series surveys writings by and about important American authors since World War II. Each volume concentrates on a specific genre and features approximately ten writers; entries list works written by and about the author and contain a bibliographical essay discussing the merits and deficiencies of major critical and scholarly studies in detail.

Available in Electronic Formats

CD-ROM. Full-text bio-bibliographic entries from the entire *CA* series, covering approximately 101,000 writers, are available on CD-ROM through lease and purchase plans. The disc combines entries from the *CA, CANR,* and *Contemporary Authors Permanent Series* (*CAP*) print series to provide the most recent author listing. It can be searched by name, title, subject/genre, nationality/ethnicity, personal data, and as well as advanced searching using boolean logic. The disc is updated every six months. For more information, call 1-800-877-GALE. *CA* is also available on CD-ROM from SilverPlatter Information, Inc.

Online. The *Contemporary Authors* database is made available online to libraries and their patrons through online public access catalog (OPAC) vendors. Currently, *CA* is offered through Ameritech Library Services' Vista Online (formerly Dynix).

GaleNet. *CA* is available on a subscription basis through GaleNet, a new online information resource that features an easy-to-use end-user interface, the powerful search capabilities of the BRS/Search retrieval software, and ease of access through the World Wide Web. For more information, call 1-800-877-GALE.

Magnetic Tape. *CA* is available for licensing on magnetic tape in a fielded format. The database is available for internal data processing and nonpublishing purposes only. For more information, call 1-800-877-GALE.

Suggestions Are Welcome

The editors welcome comments and suggestions from users on any aspects of the *CA* series. If readers would like to recommend authors for inclusion in future volumes of the series, they are cordially invited to write: The Editors, *Contemporary Authors New Revision Series,* 835 Penobscot Bldg., 645 Griswold St., Detroit, MI 48226-4094; call toll-free at 1-800-347-GALE; or fax at 1-313-961-6599.

CA Numbering System and Volume Update Chart

Occasionally questions arise about the *CA* numbering system and which volumes, if any, can be discarded. Despite numbers like "29-32R," "97-100" and "157," the entire *CA* print series consists of only 149 physical volumes with the publication of *CA* Volume 160. The following charts note changes in the numbering system and cover design, and indicate which volumes are essential for the most complete, up-to-date coverage.

CA **First Revision**	• 1-4R through 41-44R (11 books) *Cover:* Brown with black and gold trim. There will be no further First Revision volumes because revised entries are now being handled exclusively through the more efficient *New Revision Series* mentioned below.
CA **Original Volumes**	• 45-48 through 97-100 (14 books) *Cover:* Brown with black and gold trim. • 101 through 160 (60 books) *Cover:* Blue and black with orange bands. The same as previous *CA* original volumes but with a new, simplified numbering system and new cover design.
CA **Permanent Series**	• *CAP*-1 and *CAP*-2 (2 books) *Cover:* Brown with red and gold trim. There will be no further *Permanent Series* volumes because revised entries are now being handled exclusively through the more efficient *New Revision Series* mentioned below.
CA **New Revision Series**	• *CANR*-1 through *CANR*-62 (62 books) *Cover:* Blue and black with green bands. Includes only sketches requiring significant changes; **sketches are taken from any previously published *CA*, *CAP*, or *CANR* volume**.

If You Have: You May Discard:

If You Have:	You May Discard:
CA First Revision Volumes 1-4R through 41-44R **and** *CA* *Permanent Series* Volumes 1 and 2	*CA* Original Volumes 1, 2, 3, 4 Volumes 5-6 through 41-44
CA Original Volumes 45-48 through 97-100 **and** 101 through 160	**NONE:** These volumes will not be superseded by corresponding revised volumes. Individual entries from these and all other volumes appearing in the left column of this chart may be revised and included in the various volumes of the *New Revision Series*.
CA New Revision Series Volumes *CANR*-1 through *CANR*-62	**NONE:** The *New Revision Series* does not replace any single volume of *CA*. Instead, volumes of *CANR* include entries from many previous *CA* series volumes. All *New Revision Series* volumes must be retained for full coverage.

A Sampling of Authors and Media People
Featured in This Volume

Paul Bailey

Usually concerned with elderly or isolated characters who are suffering from a personal catastrophe in their lives, Bailey's novels are, according to one critic, "characterized by extreme compression in an attempt to produce great poetic intensity." *At the Jerusalem,* Bailey's first novel, was described at the time of its release as "probably the most original, and certainly the most accomplished, first novel of the year," by Alan Ross of *London Magazine.* Bailey's other titles include *A Distant Likeness, Gabriel's Lament, An Immaculate Mistake: Scenes from Childhood and Beyond,* and *Sugar Cane.*

Andre Brink

As an Afrikaner novelist, playwright, essayist, and educator, Brink is, according to one reviewer, "a rarity in anti-apartheid literature." A product of South Africa's exclusionary white culture, he repudiated its policies of apartheid during his studies in Paris in 1960 but was drawn back to the land of his birth to witness and record its turmoil and injustice. His works include *File on a Diplomat, The Ambassador, A Dry White Season,* and *Imaginings of Sand.*

Rita Mae Brown

With the 1973 publication of her "exuberantly raunchy" autobiographical novel *Rubyfruit Jungle,* Brown joined the ranks of those in the forefront of the feminist and gay rights movements. However, despite her commitment to depicting gay women in a positive light, Brown balks at being labeled a "lesbian writer." Her works include *Six of One, Southern Discomfort, Sudden Death, Dolley: A Novel of Dolley Madison in Love and War,* and *Riding Shotgun.*

Charles Bukowski

A cult hero, Bukowski was a prolific underground writer who depicted the depraved metropolitan environments of the down-trodden members of American society in his poetry and prose. While some critics find his style offensive, others claim that Bukowski satirized the machismo attitude through his routine use of sex, alcohol abuse, and violence. His works include *Flower, Fist and Bestial Wail, It Catches My Heart in Its Hands, Dangling in the Tournefortia,* and *Betting on the Muse: Poems & Stories.*

Tom Clancy

Known for hugely successful, detailed novels about espionage, the military, and advanced military technology, Clancy was proclaimed by one critic as the "king of the techno-thriller." Since the 1984 publication of his first novel, the acclaimed *Hunt for Red October,* all of his books have become best-sellers and several have been adapted into popular motion pictures. His novels include *Red Storm Rising, Patriot Games, Clear and Present Danger, Debt of Honor,* and *Executive Orders.*

Nelson DeMille

American writer DeMille has written several highly popular novels and has garnered acclaim for his skills in creating fast-moving plots and colorful characters. The settings of his novels range from Vietnam in *Word of Honor* to wealthy Long Island, New York, in *The Gold Coast* and *Plum Island* to small-town Ohio in *Spencerville.* His other titles include *Mayday, Cathedral,* and *The Charm School.*

Annie Dillard

With her carefully-wrought language, keen observations, and original metaphysical insights, Dillard has carved a unique niche for herself in the world of American letters. Her first significant publication, *Pilgrim at Tinker Creek,* drew numerous comparisons to Thoreau's *Walden* and earned Dillard a Pulitzer Prize for general nonfiction. Her other titles include *Encounters with Chinese Writers, An American Childhood, The Writing Life,* and *Mornings Like This: Found Poems.*

Louise Erdrich

Award-winning author Erdrich published her first two books—*Jacklight,* a volume of poetry, and *Love Medicine,* a novel—at the age of thirty. The daughter of a Chippewa Indian mother and a German-American father, Erdrich explores Native American themes in her works, with major characters representing both sides of her heritage. Erdrich is praised by critics for her "mastery of words" and "vividly drawn" characters who "will not leave the mind once they are let in." Erdrich's other works include *The Beet Queen, Baptism of Desire, The Crown of Columbus, The Blue Jay's Dance: A Birth Year,* and *Tales of Burning Love.*

Paula Fox

Fox is best known for her children's books, which have won numerous awards, including the prestigious Hans Christian Andersen Medal, the Newbery Medal, and the American Book Award for Children's Fiction Paperback. She is also the author of novels for adults, and has been described by one critic as "one of the our most intelligent (and least appreciated) contemporary novelists." Her works include *The Stone-Faced Boy, Blowfish Live in the Sea, The Slave Dancer, The God of Nightmares,* and *The Little Swineherd and Other Tales.*

Robert Fulghum

Unlike some writers who struggle for years to become best-selling authors, semi-retired Unitarian minister and art teacher Fulghum struck gold with his first book, a collection of inspirational essays entitled *All I Really Need to Know I Learned in Kindergarten: Uncommon Thoughts on Common Things.* His second work, a similar array of thought-provoking compositions called *It Was on Fire When I Lay Down on It,* experienced comparable popularity, so much so that the author's two books ran for a time in the first and second positions on the *New York Times* bestseller list. His other titles include *Maybe (Maybe Not), True Love,* and *Words I Wish I Wrote.*

Patricia Highsmith

The author of numerous short-story collections and novels, including the well-known *Strangers on a Train,* American-born Highsmith enjoyed greater critical and commercial success in England, France, and Germany than in her native country. According to one reviewer, the art in Highsmith's work springs from her skillful fusion of plot, characterization, and style, with the crime story serving primarily "as a means of revealing and examining her own deepest interests and obsessions." Her titles include *The Snail-Watcher, and Other Stories, People Who Knock on the Door, Mermaids on a Golf Course,* and *Small g: A Summer Idyll.*

S. E. Hinton

Hinton is credited with revolutionizing the young adult genre by portraying teenagers realistically rather than formulaically and by creating characters, settings, and dialogue that are representative of teenage life in America. Her classic *The Outsiders* was the first in her short but impressive list of books to feature troubled but sensitive male adolescents as protagonists. Her other works include *That Was Then, This Is Now, Rumble Fish,* and *The Puppy Sister.*

Evan Hunter

With numerous novels, short stories, plays, and film scripts to his credit, Hunter ranks as one of today's most versatile, prolific and bestselling writers. Known to millions throughout the world under his pseudonym, Ed McBain (originator of the "87th Precinct" detective series), Hunter is also the author under his own name of such thought-provoking best-sellers as *The Blackboard Jungle* and *Last Summer.*

David Leavitt

Lauded for his insightful and empathetic characterizations, Leavitt has been at the leading edge of the gay literature movement in the United States for over a decade. In addition to chronicling what it means to be gay in contemporary society, Leavitt's work also explores more universal issues regarding love and traces the hope, pain, ecstasy, and suffering that are all a part of romantic involvement. His titles include *Family Dancing* and *Arkansas: Three Novellas.*

G. Edward White

White is, according to one critic, "one of the most productive and provocative practitioners of American legal history writing today." He has published books on topics encompassing many aspects of Amercia's legal history, including top-rated biographies of Justices Earl Warren, John Marshall, and Oliver Wendell Holmes. His other titles include *Patterns of American Legal Thought* and *Creating a National Pastime.*

A

Indicates that a listing has been compiled from secondary sources believed to be reliable but has not been personally verified for this edition by the author sketched.

ABBEY, Lynn
  See ABBEY, Marilyn Lorraine

*   *   *

ABBEY, Marilyn Lorraine 1948-
  (Lynn Abbey)

PERSONAL: Born September 18, 1948, in Peekskill, NY; daughter of Ronald Lionel (an insurance manager) and Doris Lorraine (a homemaker; maiden name, DeWees) Abbey; married Ralph Dressler, July 14, 1969 (divorced October 31, 1972); married Robert Asprin (a writer), August 28, 1982 (divorced). *Education:* University of Rochester, A.B., 1969; New York University, M.A., 1971. *Avocational interests:* History (particularly 11th century and the Normans), embroidery.

ADDRESSES: Home—Oklahoma City, OK. *Agent*—Spectrum Literary Agency, 432 Park Ave. S., Suite 1205, New York, NY 10016.

CAREER: Metropolitan Life Insurance Company, New York City, actuarial assistant, 1969-76; Citizens Hanover Insurance, Howell, MI, systems analyst, 1976-80; community resources teacher at public schools in Ann Arbor, MI, 1980-82; American Automobile Association, Dearborn, MI, systems analyst, 1982-84. Writer.

MEMBER: Science Fiction Writers of America.

WRITINGS:

FANTASY NOVELS; UNDER NAME LYNN ABBEY

The Guardians, Ace Books (New York City), 1982.
(With C. J. Cherry and Janet Morris) *The Soul of the City,* Ace Books, 1986.
(With Robert Asprin) *Catwoman,* Warner, 1992; published in England as *Catwoman: Tiger Hunt,* Millennium (London), 1992.
Siege of Shadows, Ace, 1996.
Aquitania, TSR (Lake Geneva, WI), 1997.
The Simbul's Gift, TSR, 1997.

"RIFKIND SAGA"

Daughter of the Bright Moon, Ace Books, 1979.
The Black Flame, Ace Books, 1980.

"UNICORN AND DRAGON" SERIES

Unicorn & Dragon, Avon (New York City), 1987.
Conquest, Avon, 1988, published in England as *The Green Man,* Headline (London), 1989.

"ULTIMA SAGA"

The Forge of Virtue, Warner (New York City), 1991.
The Temper of Wisdom, Warner, 1992.

"WALENSOR SAGA"

The Wooden Sword, Ace, 1991.
Beneath the Web, Ace, 1994.

"DARK SUN" TRILOGY

The Brazen Gambit, TSR, 1994.
Cinnabar Shadows, TSR, 1995.
The Rise and Fall of a Dragonking, TSR, 1996.

"THIEVES' WORLD" SERIES; EDITOR WITH ROBERT ASPRIN

The Face of Chaos (also see below), Ace, 1983.
Wings of Omen (also see below), Ace, 1984.
Cross-Currents (omnibus; includes *Storm Season* [edited solely by Asprin], *The Face of Chaos,* and *Wings of Omen*), Doubleday (New York City), 1984.
The Dead of Winter (also see below), Ace, 1985.
Soul of the City (also see below), Ace, 1986.
Blood Ties (also see below), Ace, 1986.
The Shattered Sphere (omnibus; includes *The Dead of Winter, Soul of the City, Blood Ties*), Doubleday, 1986.
Aftermath (also see below), Ace, 1987.
Uneasy Alliances (also see below), Ace, 1988.
Stealer's Sky (also see below), Ace, 1989.
The Price of Victory (omnibus; includes *Aftermath, Uneasy Alliances,* and *Stealer's Sky*), Doubleday, 1990.

"ELFQUEST" SERIES; EDITOR WITH ROBERT ASPRIN AND RICHARD PINI

The Blood of Ten Chiefs, Tor (New York City), 1986.
Wolfsong: The Blood of Ten Chiefs, Tor, 1988.

OTHER

Adaptor of "Thieves' World Graphics" series, published by Starblaze Graphics (Norfolk, VA), 1985-1987, and Donning Co. (Norfolk, VA), 1986—.

WORK IN PROGRESS: Two sequels to *Siege of Shadows.*

SIDELIGHTS: Lynn Abbey and her former husband, novelist Robert Asprin, made an important contribution to the science fiction/fantasy world with the shared-world concept of their "Thieves' World" series. With it, they joined their own talents with those of other well-known writers to create characters and plots for the imaginary town of Sanctuary, in which the stories are based. "Most of my writing career has been caught up in the development of the 'Thieves' World' anthology concept," Abbey told *CA.* "This project, begun in 1978, has represented an attempt to bring the short story anthology into vigorous compe-

tition with current entertainment such as popular television series. Working with a core group of about ten authors, Robert Asprin and I have produced numerous volumes of interconnected fiction. Certain settings and characters were provided by us at the beginning of the project; each author is responsible for developing new characters. These settings and characters are 'shared' to the extent that, while retaining the author's individual style and outlook in a particular story, each volume of the series presents unified themes and advances along a single, predetermined chronology."

Abbey continued: "Introduced without fanfare in 1979, 'Thieves' World' has become one of the cornerstones of the Ace Books fantasy line. Response to individual stories and characters has led to spin-off novels—full-length works which do not involve the entire group of authors and which focus on events in the lives of specific characters, generally outside the chronology presented in the anthologies (although never in contradiction to it). 'Thieves' World' has also been licensed as a board game, a fantasy role-playing game, and, most recently, as a graphic novel adaptation. There is also a suite of music which is currently under consideration by several record companies and which would serve as the backbone for several MTV-type video clips. In essence, 'Thieves' World' is an attempt by a group of authors to confront the entertainment conglomerates on their own ground. Successful movies and television series have had a measurable impact on the prose publication industry; we are trying to create the same marketing *gestalt* without subordinating the prose to other media. A special 'shared universe anthology' contract was prepared by our lawyers in order to preserve licensing and trademark control. Revenues are divided along mutual funds principles, with shares credited for short stories published in the anthologies.

"If imitation is an indication of success, then 'Thieves' World' has been very successful," Abbey mused. "Within the fantasy and science fiction genre, there are at least a half-dozen 'shared universe' concepts in production from most of the major publishers. Horror and mystery writers have also begun investigating the concept. As editors of 'Thieves' World,' my [former] husband and I feel we have been able to meet the challenge of producing prose literature as entertainment. We have been able to respond to the popular publisher and reader demand for more, without sacrificing any of our creative prerogatives. The reputations (and sales figures) of all our authors have improved through their association with 'Thieves' World.'"

Abbey remarked on the influence her earlier work experience exerted on her writing career: "Prior to becoming an author and editor, I was a systems programmer and analyst for several large insurance companies in New York and the Midwest. The experience gained in the corporate cultures, especially in the handling of large amounts of data, has proven invaluable to me since my husband and I determined that we would try to create something that would make both publishers and readers sit up and take notice. 'Thieves' World' would be impossible for two people to manage without microcomputers."

Aside from her involvement with "Thieves' World," Abbey has written numerous fantasy novels set in widely varying worlds. In *Daughter of the Bright Moon* and *The Black Flame,* the heroine, Rifkind, is a warrior, priestess, healer, and witch. She discovers her destiny and then fulfills it in a world of desert, castle, and the dangerous swamps. The "Ultima Saga," which includes *The Forge of Virtue* and *The Temper of Wisdom,* is set in a more conventional, near-medieval world. Abbey's complex, detailed settings are a key ingredient in her work, according to Mary Corran in *St. James Guide to Fantasy Writers.* The critic reports that they provide "a mood all her books share in common: whether the plot involves a quest, or a conflict of good versus evil, each world displays dirt and squalor and constant perils, both human and magical. These settings are designed to repel, not appeal to, the senses, and the major characters are similarly contrived to lack attractive or sympathetic qualities; Rifkind, a strong and all-powerful heroine, alone possesses the power and knowledge necessary to defeat the evil gods. Yet although she becomes pregnant by her doomed lover, Domnhall, and returns to her own people in the guise of a healer once the battle is won, she is still a woman apart, to be respected but never loved."

Corran concludes: "Lynn Abbey's talent is unmistakable, most particularly in the creation of cheerless terrains peopled by sinister creatures of every type. She has constructed her own type of fantasy, where the endings are not always happy nor the heroes and heroines noble or fulfilled by their quests. . . . Abbey possesses the ability to create dark nightmares, where motives for valour are more complex than simple virtue. Her characters reflect the worlds they inhabit, filled with unsettling, malign emotions. The dismal settings may occasionally irritate; but they are very

well drawn, and filled with a rare depth of detail which is formidably imagined."

BIOGRAPHICAL/CRITICAL SOURCES:

BOOKS

St. James Guide to Fantasy Writers, St. James Press (Detroit), 1996.

PERIODICALS

Booklist, August, 1994, p. 2029.*

* * *

ADAMS, Glenda 1939-

PERSONAL: Born December 30, 1939, in Sydney, Australia; came to the United States, 1964; daughter of Leonard Henry and Elvira (Wright) Felton; children: one daughter. *Education:* University of Sydney, B.A. (honors), 1962; Columbia University, M.S., 1965.

ADDRESSES: Home—New York, NY. *Office*—Department of English, Columbia University, New York, NY 10027. *Agent*—Goodman Associates, 500 West End Ave., New York, NY 10024.

CAREER: Held various writing and editorial jobs in New York, NY, and Europe, 1965-72; associate director, Teachers and Writers Collaborative, 1973-76; fiction writing teacher at University of Technology, Sydney; writing workshop instructor, Columbia University, New York, and Sarah Lawrence College, 1976—.

MEMBER: Australian Society of Authors, Australian Writers Guild.

AWARDS, HONORS: Fellow of New York State Creative Artist Program Service, 1975-76; senior fellow of Australia Council, 1979; Miles Franklin Literary Award, 1987, for *Dancing on Coral; Age* Fiction Book of the Year, 1990; National Book Council award for fiction, 1991.

WRITINGS:

STORY COLLECTIONS

Lies and Stories, Inwood Press, 1976.

The Hottest Night of the Century, Angus and Robertson (Sydney), 1979.

NOVELS

Games of the Strong, Angus and Robertson, 1982, Cane Hill Press (New York City), 1989.
Dancing on Coral, Viking (New York City), 1988.
Longleg, Angus and Robertson, 1990.
The Tempest of Clemenza, Angus and Robertson, 1996.

Also author of television plays *Pride* and *Wrath,* both 1993. Work represented in anthologies, including *Bitches and Sad Ladies, In the Looking Glass,* and *Statements Two.* Contributor of stories to magazines in the United States, England, Australia, Denmark, and the Netherlands, including *Ms., Mother Jones, Transatlantic Review, Sun,* and *Seattle Review.* Manuscripts held at Australian Defense Force Academy, University of New South Wales, Canberra, Australia.

SIDELIGHTS: Glenda Adams is a short-story writer and novelist whose works are better known in her native Australia—where they have received several literary awards—than in the United States. Adams first captured critical attention with her second collection of stories, *The Hottest Night of the Century,* which reprints seven pieces from her first collection, *Lies and Stories.* These brief sketches, most fewer than ten pages in length, share "a note of implicit protest against the mistreatment of women," according to Laurie Clancy in *Contemporary Novelists.* "The strongest stories map the casual cruelty of men toward women," the reviewer for *Publishers Weekly* similarly noted, singling out the author's experiments with style in such pieces as "The Hollow Woman," "Friends," and "A Snake Down Under."

Adams's short stories "are written in a deceptively simple style and marked often by a bizarre kind of humour and almost surreal disconnectedness," noted Clancy, qualities exhibited to varying degrees in the author's novels. *Games of the Strong,* Adams's first novel, is a dystopic vision of a future police state where dissidents are exiled to an island prison colony and left to die. Critics noted an almost surreal quality to the author's narrative, exhibited in the characters' tendency to change their names and their political affiliations, "appear and disappear, rise and fall from power for no apparent reason in almost dreamlike fashion," according to the critic for *Kirkus Reviews.* Unfortunately, this aspect of the book weakens the emotional impact of the characters' problems, this reviewer contended. Adams's next novel, *Dancing on Coral,* which won an award for for the best Australian novel of the year, is considered to be a more successful experiment in style.

Lark Watters, the protagonist of "Summer in France," a story in *The Hottest Night of the Century,* reappears in *Dancing on Coral,* "a very funny and witty novel," Clancy averred, describing the book as "a satire on what the author sees as a decade of silliness." Lark falls in love first with Solomon Blank, a student who wins a scholarship in America, and then with Tom Brown, a man whom she follows—along with a competitor for his affections—to the United States. During the course of the narrative Adams loses both her father and her lover to death and thus is freed for the first time "to be her own person," as Clancy put it. Like Lark, William, the protagonist of Adams's next novel, *Longleg,* is a character whose experiences with the opposite sex provide a series of necessary lessons in personal independence. Though Clancy called this "a brilliantly inventive novel," and William the author's "most sympathetic character," she also dubbed *Longleg* Adams's "most disturbing novel."

Adams is also the author of *The Tempest of Clemenza,* a novel in which Abel Chase relates the events surrounding the death of her thirteen-year-old daughter Clemenza in a narrative that shifts backwards and forwards in time as well as back and forth between Australia and the United States. The ambitious narrative also encompasses diary entries written by a character whose relation to Abel and Clemenza is unclear and chapters from a melodramatic novel written by an unidentified author. "These various narratives give Adams an opportunity to riff on the nature of fiction," remarked the reviewer for *Publishers Weekly,* but ultimately stretch the reader's patience too far as page after page of the "authentically naive and correspondingly tedious" diary provide a too-extensive interruption of the main story. Although Adams is appreciated in her native Australia as a "magical storyteller," the reviewer for *Publishers Weekly* continued, *The Tempest of Clemenza,* "a brave but muddled mishmash of interlocking novels within novels," is not her most successful work to date.

BIOGRAPHICAL/CRITICAL SOURCES:

BOOKS

Contemporary Novelists, St. James Press (Detroit), 1996.

PERIODICALS

Kirkus Reviews, March 15, 1989, p. 394.
Publishers Weekly, April 21, 1989, pp. 84-85; August 12, 1996, pp. 63-64.

*　　*　　*

AIDOO, (Christina) Ama Ata 1942-

PERSONAL: Born March 23, 1942, in Abeadzi Kyiakor, Ghana; daughter of Nana Yaw Fama (a chief of Abeadzi Kyiakor) and Maame Abba Abasema; children: Kinna Likimani. *Education:* University of Ghana, B.A. (with honors), 1964; attended Stanford University.

ADDRESSES: Home—P.O. Box 4930, Harare, Zimbabwe.

CAREER: Writer, educator. Lecturer in English, University of Cape Coast, Ghana, 1970-82; consulting professor, Phelps-Stokes Fund Ethnic Studies Program, Washington, D.C., 1974-75; Minister of Education, Ghana, 1982-83; writer-in-residence, University of Richmond, Virginia, 1989; chair, African Regional Panel of the Commonwealth Writers' prize, 1990, 1991.

AWARDS, HONORS: Short story prize from Mbari Press competition; prize from *Black Orpheus* for story, "No Sweetness Here"; research fellowship, Institute of African Studies, University of Ghana; Fulbright scholarship, 1988.

WRITINGS:

The Dilemma of a Ghost (play; first produced in Legon, Ghana, at Open Air Theatre, March, 1964), Longmans, Green (London), 1965, Macmillan (New York), 1971.
Anowa (play; produced in London, 1991), Humanities Press (New York), 1970.
No Sweetness Here (stories), Longmans, Green (London), 1970, Doubleday (New York), 1971.
Our Sister Killjoy; or, Reflections from a Black-Eyed Squint (novel), Longman (London), 1977, NOK Publishing (New York), 1979.
Dancing Out Doubts, NOK (Engu, Nigeria), 1982.
Someone Talking to Sometime (poetry), College Press (Harare, Zimbabwe), 1985.

The Eagle and the Chickens and Other Stories (for children), Tana Press (Engu, Nigeria), 1986.
Birds and Other Poems (for children), College Press (Harare, Zimbabwe), 1987.
Changes: A Love Story (novel), Women's Press (London), 1991, Feminist Press at the City University of New York (New York), 1993.
An Angry Letter in January and Other Poems, Dangaroo Press (Coventry, England), 1992.

Contributor to anthologies, including *Modern African Stories,* Faber, 1964; *Black Orpheus: An Anthology of New African and Afro-American Stories,* Longmans, 1964, McGraw-Hill, 1965; *Pan African Short Stories,* Thomas Nelson, 1966; *New Sum of Poetry from the Negro World* Presence Africaine, 1966; *African Writing Today,* Penguin, 1967; *African Writing Today,* Manyland Books, 1969; *Political Spider: An Anthology of Stories from 'Black Orpheus,'* Africana Publishing, 1969; and *African Literature and the Arts,* Volume I, Crowell, 1970. Contributor of stories and poems to magazines, including *Okyeame, Black Orpheus, Presence Africaine, Journal of African Literature,* and *New African.*

SIDELIGHTS: Ama Ata Aidoo is a respected Ghanian playwright, short-story writer, novelist, and poet whose works explore the far-reaching effects of sexism and colonialism. Aidoo's "greatest strength," according to Jill Franks in *Contemporary Novelists,* "is her ability to mix humor and hope with the serious issues of gender and social conflict." She is also lauded for her innovative attempts to blend African oral with Western literary traditions. Indeed, in the *Dictionary of Literary Biography,* Aidoo is quoted as stating, "I pride myself on the fact that my stories are written to be heard, primarily." As the daughter of a chief, Aidoo was raised as royalty and given an extensive education; she has worked as an educator in the United States as well as in her native Ghana, where she served for a time as Minister of Education.

Aidoo's career as a writer began with the publication of two plays and a collection of short stories, a trio that shares a concern with female characters at odds with the expectations of their culture. In addition, as Naana Banyiwa Horne noted in her essay in *Dictionary of Literary Biography,* Aidoo's stories rely nearly as extensively as do her plays on dialogue to do the work of characterization. In *The Dilemma of a Ghost,* Aidoo's first play, a young man returns to Ghana from studying in the United States accompanied by an African-American wife, a situation with inherent conflict accentuated by the young woman's "immaturity, ignorance, and exasperating arrogance," according to Horne. Set against the backdrop of Africa's colonial history, which has divided black peoples around the world, the play probes "social conventions as they relate to the roles and identities of women," Horne contended. *Anowa,* Aidoo's second play, is a reworking of a folktale in which a woman's insistence on choosing her own husband ultimately leads to tragedy for both. In her short story collection, *No Sweetness Here,* Aidoo is considered to confront directly the feminist concerns that more obliquely motivate her plays. "This gallery of female portraits offers perceptive images of womanhood, exposing sexism and degradation, and celebrating the physical and intellectual capabilities of women," wrote Horne.

Aidoo's first novel, *Our Sister Killjoy,* was published after a gap of some years during which the author worked as an educator at the University of Cape Coast, Ghana, and as a consultant in Washington, D.C. These were also years marked by grave political upheaval in her homeland of Ghana. Generically, Aidoo's novel is a mixture of prose, poetry, and fictional letters exchanged by the characters; moreover, "its caustic tone and aggressive mood mirror the critical, committed stance of its well-meaning but enraged and politically conscious writer," observed Horne. The narrative follows Sissie as she travels to Germany and England, urging the black students she meets—"willfully blind to the horror they have bought into: soul-destroying white capitalism," Franks noted—to return to Africa. Aidoo expands her feminist concerns in *Our Sister Killjoy,* Horne noted, by universalizing them: "Womanhood becomes a metaphor depicting the condition of oppressed and exploited humankind in general."

The poems collected in Aidoo's first volume of poetry, *Someone Talking to Sometime,* display the range of the author's interests, from acerbic political commentary in such pieces as "From the Only Speech That Was Not Delivered at the Rally" and "Nation Building," to positive love poems such as "Of Love and Commitment," and "Lorisnrudi." Aidoo's works for children, including *The Eagle and the Chickens and Other Stories* and *Birds and Other Poems,* have not been reviewed. However, her second novel, *Changes: A Love Story,* was warmly received and is considered a significant advance over her earlier *Our Sister Killjoy.* In this work, an ambitious Ghanaian careerwoman flouts convention by divorcing her husband and becoming the second wife of a progressive man. Through this woman's struggle for self-respect

within a relationship, "Aidoo explores such issues as marital rape and career choices, and their impact on love and marital relationships, highlighting the role of compromise," explained Horne. *Changes* is "entirely honest in portraying the conflict between the need for love and the need for independence," added Franks. "Aidoo's characters," and presumably Aidoo herself, "are wise about gender differences," Franks concluded; "they do not blame everything on the 'system' but recognize fundamental differences between men and women."

Aidoo is a writer whose concerns with the status of women in her society permeate her works of drama, poetry, and fiction. Although such early works as the play *The Dilemma of a Ghost,* the short fiction collection *No Sweetness Here,* and the novel *Our Sister Killjoy* were sometimes faulted for the author's unabashedly critical stance toward the pattern of sexism and colonialism in Ghanian society, others claimed that her portraits of African women depict the universal condition of womanhood. Later works, such as the novel *Changes: A Love Story,* have received praise for their more mature rendering of theme, including the recognition that while women may choose to reject many aspects of their traditional roles they still need and desire loving relationships.

BIOGRAPHICAL/CRITICAL SOURCES:

BOOKS

Contemporary Novelists, 6th edition, St. James Press (Detroit), 1996.
Dictionary of Literary Biography, Volume 117: *Twentieth-Century Caribbean and Black African Writers,* Gale (Detroit), 1992, pp. 34-40.
Pieterse, Cosmo and Dennis Duerdon, editors, *African Writers Talking,* Africana Publishing, 1972.

*   *   *

ALUKO, T(imothy) M(ofolorunso) 1918(?)-

PERSONAL: Born June 14, 1918 (one source says 1920), in Ilesha, West Nigeria; married Janet Adebisi Fajemisin, 1950; children: six. *Education:* Attended Government College, Ibadan, Nigeria, 1933-38, and Yaba Higher College, Lagos, Nigeria, 1939-42; University of London, England, B.Sc., 1948, Diploma in Town Planning, 1950; University of Newcastle upon

Tyne, England, M.Sc., 1969; University of Lagos, Ph.D., 1976.

ADDRESSES: Home—53 Ladipo Oluwole Rd., Apapa, P.O. Box 1854, Lagos, Nigeria. *Office*—Scott Wilson Kirkpatrick & Partners, P.O. Box 1854, Lagos, Nigeria.

CAREER: Public works department, Lagos, Nigeria, junior engineer, 1943-46; public works departments of Ibadan, Oyo, Oshogbo, and Lagos, all Nigeria, executive engineer, 1950-56; Lagos Town Council, Lagos, town engineer, 1956-60; Ministry of Works and Transport, Western Nigeria, director and permanent secretary, 1960-66; University of Ibadan, Ibadan, Nigeria, senior lecturer, 1966; University of Lagos, Lagos, senior research fellow in municipal engineering, 1966-78, associate professor of public health engineering, 1978; Commissioner for finance, Government of Western Nigeria, 1971-73; Scott Wilson Kirkpatrick & Partners (consulting engineers), partner, 1979 until retired.

MEMBER: Institution of Civil Engineers (fellow), Institution of Municipal engineers (fellow), Institution of Public Health Engineers (fellow), Nigerian Society of Engineers (fellow), Nigerian Institute of Town Planners (fellow), Royal Town Planning Institute.

AWARDS, HONORS: Officer, Order of the British Empire, 1963; Officer, Order of the Niger, 1964.

WRITINGS:

NOVELS

One Man, One Wife, Nigerian Printing and Publishing Co. (Lagos), 1959, revised edition, Heinemann (London & Ibadan), 1967, Humanities Press (New York City) 1968.
One Man, One Matchet, Heinemann, 1964, Verrey (Mystic, CT) , 1965.
Kinsman and Foreman, Heinemann, 1966, Humanities Press (New York City), 1967.
Chief the Honourable Minister, Humanities Press, 1970.
His Worshipful Majesty, Heinemann, 1973.
Wrong Ones in the Dock, Heinemann, 1982.
State of Our Own, Macmillan (London), 1986.
Conduct Unbecoming, Heinemann, 1993.

OTHER

Also author of "The New Engineer," included in *African New Writing,* Lutterworth Press (London &

Redhill, U.K.), 1947. Contributor of essay, "Case for Fiction," and various short stories to *West African Review.* Interviewee with Lee Nichols on radio program "Conversations with African Writers," *Voice of America,* Washington, DC, 1978.

SIDELIGHTS: T. M. Aluko has played a key role in the development of modern Nigerian literature, but his writing has been strongly criticized, and the place he will claim in African literary history remains uncertain. Aluko's first novel, *One Man, One Wife,* has the distinction of being the first African novel written in English to be published by a Nigerian company. It was published in 1959, one year before Nigeria gained independence from Great Britain's colonial rule. Over the next four decades—decades that span Nigeria's history as an independent nation—Aluko has written a total of eight novels. Each one is centrally concerned with the social and cultural transformations that Nigeria has undergone as a postcolonial nation. Aluko incorporates many themes typical to postcolonial literature, such as the struggle between modern and traditional ways of life. However, the African writers and intellectuals who are his peers have not embraced him. His comic approach to social problems and his detached use of satire have put Aluko out of step with the politicized and morally serious West African writers of his generation.

Growing up in colonial Nigeria, Aluko received an excellent British-style education that groomed him to take a place in the leadership class. He launched a successful career in civil engineering, finding time to write on the side. As Aluko told *CA,* he considers writing "a most enjoyable hobby." He says, "I have discovered that, more and more, I need this medium of expression for keeping my sanity in the mad, mad world." Both his wry, ironic style and his realistic subject matter have been shaped by his experiences working in postcolonial Nigeria's public sector. In the *Dictionary of Literary Biography* Patrick Scott writes that Aluko's novels "reflect the realism and perhaps the inevitable elitism of his special vantage point; they certainly reflect a practical man's impatience with more theoretical commentators."

Aluko's debut novel, *One Man, One Wife,* is set in a small village during colonial times and concerns the clash between the traditional Yoruba religion and mission Christianity. He skewers both belief systems as equally superstitious and manipulative, drawing accusations of sensationalism and imperialism from pro-traditionalists. In his next three novels, which are considered his major works, *One Man, One Matchet*

(1964), *Kinsman and Foreman* (1966), and *Chief the Honourable Minister* (1970), Aluko turns away from village life and focuses on the educated but apolitical elite, professional class of which he is part. *One Man, One Matchet* describes with comic exuberance the frustrations of a new government administrator as he faces hypocrisy and corruption in the early days of Nigerian independence. *Kinsman and Foreman* blithely narrates the mixed allegiances and cross-cultural misunderstandings that ensue when a foreign-educated Nigerian returns to his hometown in the official capacity of a public works engineer. With a more tragicomic vision, *Chief the Honourable Minister* explores the break-up of Nigerian civil service upon Nigeria's 1966 military coup.

Aluko's later novels continue to focus on the social reality of life in Nigeria, but according to many critics, they lack the vitality of his major works. *Times Education Supplement* critic Edward Blishen describes Aluko's 1982 *Wrong Ones in the Dock,* for example, as "an account, essentially, of the sheer daily difficulties of living in Lagos." Perhaps due to the critical response to his social satires by Nigerian writers, or perhaps due to his own growing pessimism in regard to his country's future, Aluko's later novels are more somber in tone and present a less hopeful message.

As the particular political situations about which Aluko writes pass into history, it may be easier for critics to reevaluate his best works in terms of their literary merit. He has been lauded for capturing the distinctive qualities of the English language as it is spoken in Nigeria, and his use of satire has been interpreted as part of a tradition of Yoruba storytelling. Furthermore, as Patrick Scott observes, "From his work as a whole . . . there emerge recurring images, of lonely protagonists and nightmarelike breakdowns, of rooted and transplanted trees, of health and disease and contagion, of water and streams and rains, that suggest behind the surface satire a deeper and more poetic imaginative vision."

BIOGRAPHICAL/CRITICAL SOURCES:

BOOKS

Bengu, Sibusiso M. E., *Chasing Gods Not Our Own,* Shuter & Shooter, 1976.
Booth, James, *Writers and Politics in Nigeria,* Africana, 1981, pp. 82-92.
Brown, Susan Windisch, *Contemporary Novelists,* sixth edition, St. James (Detroit), 1996.

Dathorne, Oscar R., *The Black Mind,* University of Minneapolis Press, 1974.
Dictionary of Literary Biography, Volume 117: *Twentieth-Century Caribbean and Black African Writers, First Series,* Gale (Detroit), 1992, pp. 40-48.
Laurence, Margaret, *Long Drums and Cannon,* Macmillan, 1968 and Praeger, 1969, pp. 169-177.
Lindfors, Bernth, *Folklore in Nigerian Literature,* Africana, 1973, pp. 153-75.
Ngugi wa Thiong'o, *Homecoming,* Heinemann, 1973, pp. 55-66.
Obiechina, Emmanuel, *Culture, Tradition and Society in the West African Novel,* Cambridge University Press, 1975.
Palmer, Aztec Taiwo, *Growth of the African Novel,* Heinemann, 1979, pp. 102-23.
Parker, Carolyn, editor, *When the Drumbeat Changes,* Three Continents, 1981, pp. 215-39.
Taiwo, Oladele, *Culture and the Nigerian Novel,* Macmillan/St. Martin's, 1976, pp. 149-80.

PERIODICALS

African Literature Today, Volume 5, 1971, pp. 41-53, 137-42.
Critique, Volume 17, 1975, pp. 81-93.
Horizons, Volume 1, 1981, pp. 45-57.
Ibadan, Volume 10, 1960, pp. 27-30.
Journal of the Nigerian English Studies Association, Volume 8, 1976, pp. 33-39.
Legon Journal of the Humanities, Volume 2, 1976, pp. 28-41.
Literary Half-Yearly, Volume 23, 1982, pp. 115-27.
Modern Fiction Studies, Volume 34, 1988, pp. 45-54.
Nsukka Studies in African Literature, Volume 2, 1979, pp. 3-11.
Studies in Black Literature, Volume 2, 1970, pp. 21-32.
Times Educational Supplement, October 16, 1970, p. 1184; January 28, 1983, p. 26.*

*   *   *

ANDERSON, Jessica (Margaret) Queale 1916-

PERSONAL: Born September 25, 1916, in Gayndah, Queensland, Australia; daughter of Charles James (a stock inspector) and Alice (Hibbert) Queale; married Ross McGill (divorced); married Leonard Culbert Anderson, March 12, 1954 (divorced); children: (first marriage) Laura Rae McGill. *Education:* Attended public schools in Brisbane, Queensland, Australia, and Brisbane Technical College art school.

ADDRESSES: Home—Sydney, Australia. *Agent*—Elaine Markson Literary Agency, 44 Greenwich Avenue, New York, NY 10011.

MEMBER: Australian Society of Authors.

AWARDS, HONORS: Miles Franklin Award and Australian Natives' Association Award, 1979, both for *Tirra Lirra by the River;* Miles Franklin Award, and New South Wales Premier's Award, both 1981; *The Age* Book of the Year Award, 1987.

WRITINGS:

NOVELS

An Ordinary Lunacy, Macmillan (London), 1963, Scribner (New York City), 1964.
The Last Man's Head, Macmillan, 1970.
The Commandant, St. Martin's (New York City), 1975.
Tirra Lirra by the River, Macmillan (Melbourne, Australia), 1978, Penguin (New York City), 1984.
The Impersonators, Macmillan, 1980, published as *The Only Daughter,* Viking (New York City), 1985.
Taking Shelter, Viking, 1990.

STORY COLLECTIONS

Stories from the Warm Zone and Sydney Stories, Viking, 1987.

Also author of radio plays, including *The American,* 1966, *The Aspern Papers,* 1967, *The Maid's Part,* 1967, *Daisy Miller,* 1968, *The Blackmail Caper,* 1972, *Quite Sweet, Really,* 1972, *Tirra Lirra by the River,* 1975, *The Last Man's Head,* 1983, *A Tale of Two Cities* and *Outbreak of Love.* Contributor to Australian and English magazines and to Australian radio prior to 1960. Anderson's papers are housed in permanent collections in the Mitchell Library, Sydney, Australia, and the Australian National Library, Canberra, Australia.

SIDELIGHTS: Jessica Anderson told *Contemporary Novelists:* "The settings of my seven works of fiction relate neatly to the three places where I have spent my life: mostly Sydney, a substantial portion of Brisbane, and a dash of London.

"Now that I intend to write no more fiction, I can appreciate the pleasure I had in writing those seven books, and discount the pain, by realising how disappointed I would be if I had failed to produce them. That is not to say that I am wholly satisfied, but that I worked to my full capacity, and am pleased to have had this chance of deploying my imagination, observation, and experience."

Though not as well known outside Australia as she is in her homeland, where her books are best-sellers, Anderson has received high praise from British and American critics for her storytelling abilities. Some have singled out her acute rendering of the Australian land and people, and the subtlety of her thematic exposition for special praise. Anderson's first novel, *An Ordinary Lunacy,* tells of a confirmed bachelor lawyer who falls for his client, a woman eventually cleared of the charge of murder but driven to suicide by society's condemnation of her for promiscuity. Critics were at pains to warn readers that though elements of the plot are clearly cliched, particularly Anderson's over-the-top characterization her protagonist's domineering mother, the resulting book as a whole "is an acutely sensed, intelligent, and discerning account of a genuinely troublesome, and most important, aspect of the psychosexual relationship between men and women," as Anthony West put it in *The New Yorker.*

Anderson's next book, *The Last Man's Head,* is a murder mystery that has never been published in the United States. Her third novel, *The Commandant,* is a work of historical fiction in which the death of the notorious commandant of the Moreton Bay penal colony, and the official account of it, are reconstructed. "No sketch of its plot can convey the subtlety of this moving novel," wrote Donat Gallagher in *Southerly,* who called *The Commandant* "a novel of character for which historical research has provided a solid and fascinating setting." Similarly, *Tirra Lirra by the River,* Anderson's fourth novel, was credited with "great subtlety in characterization and structure" by Clifford Hanna in *Southerly.* Considered Anderson's most accomplished work, this short novel recounts the life story of an elderly woman whose return to Australia after many years spent in London reveals to her the depth of the illusion under which she has lived her life. Her story, to which Anderson draws frequent parallels to Tennyson's poem "Lady of Shallott," has been championed "by feminist critics as showing the difficulties of women's lives from the point of view of a woman born early in the century," according to Alrene Sykes in an essay on Anderson for *Contemporary Novelists.*

Anderson once told *CA* that, like other authors and artists of Australia, she feels drawn to London and Europe as the center of things, adding that "some return, as I did, feeling that Australia is inescapable, . . . though never at home away from the place, nor ever quite at home in it." Sykes noted evidence of these feelings in the import of travel in several of the author's novels. "Anderson is fascinated by the tug between the old culture (Europe) and the new (Australia)," Sykes remarked, and thus *Tirra Lirra by the River, The Commandant,* and *The Impersonators* each open with a woman arriving in Australia from the Old World. *The Impersonators,* which appeared in the United States as *The Only Daughter,* places the debate between the Old World and the New at the center of its plot, in which a woman's return to Australia after twenty years abroad causes her to doubt the value of European culture, the superiority of which she had heretofore accepted unquestioningly.

Although not widely known outside of her native Australia, Anderson has won respect for the lucid narrative style of her well-crafted novels. Though she is sometimes accused of relying on hackneyed plots, Anderson's talents as a storyteller and the subtlety and depth of her characterization and use of setting are often felt to considerably outweigh this flaw. Rona Berg, for example, asserted in *Village Voice,* "Jessica Anderson is a graceful storyteller with the rare and quirky ability to transcend plot cliches through the emotional fidelity of her writing."

BIOGRAPHICAL/CRITICAL SOURCES:

BOOKS

Contemporary Literary Criticism, Volume 37, Gale (Detroit), 1986.
Contemporary Novelists, 6th edition, St. James Press (Detroit), 1996.

PERIODICALS

Kirkus Reviews, January 15, 1985, pp. 45-46.
Listener, May 1, 1975.
London Times, August 22, 1970, p. 8.
New Yorker, August 8, 1964, pp. 86-90.
New York Times, March 5, 1964, p. 31.

New York Times Book Review, February 19, 1984, p. 24; March 24, 1985, p. 12.
Observer, July 20, 1975.
Southerly, December, 1978, p. 477; September, 1980, pp. 360-363.
Spectator, August 22, 1970.
Village Voice, May 22, 1984, p. 54.

*　　*　　*

ANDRESS, Lesley
  See SANDERS, Lawrence

*　　*　　*

ANIEBO, I(feanyichukwu) N(dubuisi) C(hikezie) 1939-

PERSONAL: Born January 31, 1939, in Port Harcourt, Nigeria; son of Augustine Nwafor and Monica Chiji (a housewife; maiden name, Okafor) Aniebo; married Chiaka Mbakwem (a lecturer), January 30, 1982; children: Ikechukwu, Chinyere, Ijeoma. *Education:* Attended Government College, Umuahia; University of California, Los Angeles, B.A. (cum laude), 1976, M.A., 1977, C.Phil., 1979.

ADDRESSES: Home—Amuda Umunze, Orumba P.A., Anambra State, Nigeria. *Office*—Department of English, University of Port Harcourt, P.M.B. 5523, Port Harcourt, Rivers State, Nigeria. *Agent*—Lou Sison, 1701 South Holt Ave., Los Angeles, CA 90035.

CAREER: Writer. Nigerian Army, career officer, 1959-71; served in United Nations peace-keeping force in the Congo (now Zaire), 1960, and at Command and General Staff College, Fort Leavenworth, KS, 1966; quartermaster general of Biafran Army in Nigerian civil war, 1967-68, became brigade commander, 1968; University of California, Los Angeles, coordinator of Foreign Students Association, 1974-75, financial aid adviser, 1976-79; University of Port Harcourt, Port Harcourt, Nigeria, senior lecturer in English, 1979—.

MEMBER: African Literature Association (United States).

AWARDS, HONORS: Military awards, including Nigerian Independence Medal, United Nations Medal, and Nigerian Republic Medal. Harry Kurnitz Literature Award, 1974-76 and 1979; Shirley Robbins Fiction Award, University of California, Los Angeles, 1978, for *The Journey Within;* Felds/Kelly Award, International Student Center, University of California, Los Angeles, 1978.

WRITINGS:

The Anonymity of Sacrifice (novel), Heinemann (London), 1974.
The Journey Within (novel), Heinemann, 1978.
Of Wives, Talismans and the Dead (stories), Heinemann, 1983.

Contributor of stories to magazines and newspapers in Nigeria and abroad. Editor-in-chief, *Ufahamu: Journal of the African Activist Association,* 1976-77; editor, *Kiabara: Journal of the Humanities,* 1980.

SIDELIGHTS: I. N. C. Aniebo is a Nigerian writer best known for his short stories, collected in the volume *Of Wives, Talismans and the Dead.* In this work, as in his two novels, *The Anonymity of Sacrifice* and *The Journey Within,* the author takes as his primary subject the harmful influence of Western culture, technology, and values on African life. "The acrid taste of defeat is perhaps Aniebo's most distinctive contribution to West African literature in English—his ability to record convincingly instances of human strength wilting and shriveling, usually as the indirect outcome of large social processes," remarked Arthur Ravenscroft in *Contemporary Novelists.* "Aniebo is a neglected Nigerian writer who . . . seems to be overlooked by most critics," Alastair Niven notes in *British Book News.*

Aniebo's first novel, *The Anonymity of Sacrifice,* is set during the Nigerian civil war, and provides a series of sketches "chiefly of betrayals, misunderstandings, personal defeats, frustrations, and distrust" of those who fought in the war, according to Ravenscroft. Though individual scenes are often effective, the author fails to adequately incorporate the estrangement and eventual death of the work's two protagonists "into a firm design," Ravenscroft complained, concluding that "the title promises more significance than the book delivers."

The Journey Within, Aniebo's second novel, focuses on the disintegration of the traditional African institutions of marriage and the family under the pressure of a Europeanizing Nigerian society. Against a portrait of a traditional marriage, the author juxtaposes the marriage of Janet and Christian, who have converted to Christianity. When Christian pursues an adulterous affair with another man's wife, he is beaten up, contracts a venereal disease, and is killed running naked and insane through the streets of Port Harcourt. Janet on the other hand is raped by three soldiers on her way to visit a traditional herbalist about her infertility and becomes pregnant. "The novel's greatest strength—the vitality and variety of the human experience it describes—is also its greatest weakness," wrote Robert L. Berner in *World Literature Today,* who protested that Aniebo's portrait of his Christian characters is particularized in such a way that it fails to serve as an effective critique of the Christianization of Africans.

Unlike his novels, Aniebo's short story collection is considered to display "his particular gift," according to Ravenscroft, that is, "the rapid but accurate sketching of a scene without having to sustain its implications across a large design," a gift that in *Of Wives, Talismans and the Dead* "is revealed as professional and complete in its own right." The stories themselves deal with the strain amounting to despair or spiritual defeat of rural characters struggling to adapt to the urbanization of their society and the onslaught of civil war. "What Aniebo records is the intense pain that afflicts people when social change halts, trips, nonpluses, or defeats them," Ravenscroft observed.

Aniebo once told *CA:* "African countries, as they now exist, are and will continue to be mere geographical entities until western civilization collapses or western economic power declines. No African government can claim that it represents the majority of the people. Each government has been put and kept in power by powerful, and often alien, sectional interests."

BIOGRAPHICAL/CRITICAL SOURCES:

BOOKS

Contemporary Novelists, 6th edition, St. James Press (Detroit), 1996.

PERIODICALS

British Book News, June, 1984, p. 372.
World Literature Today, winter, 1980, p. 161; summer, 1985.

ATCHISON, Sandra Dallas 1939-
 (Sandra Dallas)

PERSONAL: Born June 11, 1939, in Washington, DC; daughter of Forrest Everett and Harriett (Mavity) Dallas; married Robert Thomas Atchison (in public relations field), April 20, 1963; children: Dana Dallas, Kendal. *Education:* University of Denver, B.A., 1960.

ADDRESSES: Home and office—850 Humboldt St., No. 3, Denver, CO 80218-3573.

CAREER: Writer. *Business Week,* Denver, CO, editorial assistant, 1961-63; University of Denver, Denver, affiliated with public relations department, 1965-66; *Business Week,* editorial assistant, 1967-69, bureau chief, 1969-85, senior correspondent, 1985-90. Historic Denver, Inc., member of board of directors, 1979-82, 1984-87; Visiting Nurse Association, Denver, member of board of directors, 1983-85.

MEMBER: Western Writers of America, Women's Forum of Colorado, Denver Woman's Press Club.

AWARDS, HONORS: Wrangler Award, National Cowboy Hall of Fame, 1980; named Exceptional Chronicler of Western History, Women's Library Association and Denver Public Library Friends Foundation, 1986.

WRITINGS:

UNDER NAME SANDRA DALLAS

Gaslights and Gingerbread: Colorado's Historic Homes, Sage Books, 1965, revised edition, Swallow Press (Athens, OH), 1984.
No More Than Five in a Bed: Colorado Hotels in the Old Days, University of Oklahoma Press (Norman, OK), 1967.
Vail, Pruett (Boulder, CO), 1969.
Cherry Creek Gothic: Victorian Architecture in Denver, University of Oklahoma Press, 1971.
Yesterday's Denver, E. A. Seeman, 1974.
Sacred Paint: Ned Jacob, Fenn Galleries (Kansas City, MO), 1979.
Colorado Ghost Towns and Mining Camps, with photographs by son Kendal Atchison, University of Oklahoma Press, 1985.
Colorado Homes, with photographs by Dallas and Atchison, University of Oklahoma Press, 1986.
Buster Midnight's Cafe (novel), Random House (New York City), 1990.

The Persian Pickle Club (novel), St. Martin's (New York City), 1995.
The Diary of Mattie Spenser (novel), St. Martin's, 1997.

Also author of *Gold and Gothic,* 1967. Regional book columnist, *Denver Post,* 1980—. Writer of travel articles for magazines. Book reviewer, *Denver Post,* 1962—.

SIDELIGHTS: Sandra Dallas Atchison's nonfiction focuses on the history and architecture of the western United States. Under the name Sandra Dallas, she writes about historic homes and hotels, ghost towns and mining camps, and cities like Denver and Vail. Her fiction, however, examines small-town America and the intricate relationships of the ordinary people who live there.

Atchison's first novel, *Buster Midnight's Cafe,* explores the background of a fictional movie star named Marion Street and her lover, a boxer named Buster Midnight, both of whom had been exposed in a Hollywood murder case. Effa, the narrator of the novel, attempts to balance published reports of the scandal against her own recollections of growing up with Buster and Marion in Butte, Montana, in the 1920s and 1930s. Effa speaks, according to *Publishers Weekly* reviewer Sybil S. Steinberg, "in a sharp and snappy voice that captures the reader's interest on the very first page." Steinberg praises the author for creating "a remarkable cluster of enduring friendships that . . . accurately reflect the flavor of a small town."

The Persian Pickle Club represents "a colorful exploration of Depression-era Kansas and the meaning of friendship," writes Suzanne Berne in the *New York Times Book Review.* Once a week, in a small town in rural Kansas, a group of farmers' wives gathers to sit and sew, share gossip, and trade scraps of cloth for their handmade quilts. The most treasured pieces of cloth contain a paisley pattern that the quilters call a "Persian pickle," and they have named their sewing circle the Persian Pickle Club. The communal work of quilting draws the women ever closer to one another, and the silence of their activity encourages conversation. Over long hours of stitching and storytelling, they develop bonds of friendship and loyalty that enable them to surmount the sorrows and hardships of country life during the Depression.

The narrator of the tale is quilter Queenie Bean. Steinberg reports in *Publishers Weekly* that the novel is enlivened by "the narrator's humorous down-home voice," and Keddy Ann Outlaw tells *Library Journal* readers that Queenie "narrates the novel with snappy style." Berne compliments the author's "knack for capturing the quirky details of [the quilters'] lives."

The insularity of the circle is pierced by the arrival of Rita Ritter, a lively "city girl" from Denver, who has married a local farmer. Rita joins the club but, unsuited for a sedentary activity that nonetheless requires mechanical precision, patience, and dexterity, she searches for a more exciting form of entertainment. Rita decides to pursue her dream of becoming a newspaper reporter. News stories are scarce in Harveyville, Kansas, however, until a man's body is found buried in a local field. The man is identified as the missing husband of quilter Ella Crook, and Rita determines to solve the mystery of his death by probing the innermost secrets of the Persian Pickle Club. According to a critic for *Kirkus Reviews,* Rita "finds the wall of feminine loyalty unyielding." The same reviewer calls *The Persian Pickle Club* "a tale of pioneer justice and impenetrable loyalty." Steinberg calls it "a simple but endearing story that depicts small-town eccentricities with affection."

BIOGRAPHICAL/CRITICAL SOURCES:

PERIODICALS

American Artist, January-February, 1980, p. 52; April, 1980, p. 29.
Kirkus Reviews, August 1, 1995, p. 1042.
Library Journal, April 15, 1990, p. 122; September 1, 1995, p. 206.
Los Angeles Times, July 20, 1990, p. E-14.
New York Times Book Review, June 3, 1990, p. 39; November 12, 1995.
Publishers Weekly, February 16, 1990, pp. 66-67; July 31, 1995, p. 67.
School Library Journal, November, 1990, p. 149.
Travel-Holiday, October, 1985, p. 107.
Wilson Library Bulletin, November, 1990, p. BT4.

B

BAIL, Murray 1941-

PERSONAL: Born September 22, 1941, in Adelaide, South Australia; married Margaret Wordsworth, 1965. *Education:* Attended a technical high school in Adelaide.

ADDRESSES: Home—39/75 Buckland St., Chippendale, New South Wales 2008, Australia.

CAREER: Writer and art critic. Australian National Gallery, Canberra, trustee, 1976-81.

AWARDS, HONORS: Book of the year award from *The Age* newspaper and National Book Council Award from National Book Council, both 1980, both for *Homesickness;* Victorian Premier's Award, 1988, for *Holden's Performance.*

WRITINGS:

Contemporary Portraits and Other Stories, University of Queensland Press (St. Lucia, Australia), 1975, published as *The Drover's Wife and Other Stories,* University of Queensland Press (New York City), 1984.
Homesickness (novel), Macmillan (London), 1980, Penguin (New York City), 1981.
Ian Fairweather (monograph), Bay Books (Sydney, Australia), 1981.
Holden's Performance (novel), Faber (London), 1987.
(Editor) *The Faber Book of Contemporary Australian Short Stories* (anthology), Faber, 1988.

Longhand: A Writer's Notebook, McPhee Gribble (Fitzroy, Australia), 1989.

Works represented in anthologies, including *Winter's Tales 27,* edited by Edward Leeson, Macmillan, 1981, St. Martin's Press (New York City), 1982. Contributor of short stories to periodicals, including *New Yorker* and *Transatlantic Review.*

SIDELIGHTS: Murray Bail "has established himself as one of the leading prose-writers of the Australian new wave," opined Peter Lewis, writing for the *Times Literary Supplement.* Bail, who has a critically acclaimed collection of short stories and two novels to his credit, is considered a major force in contemporary Australian literature. In addition to advancing the status of the short story during the 1970s, his experiments with language and literary devices earned him the praise of critics, including that of Constance Casey, who claimed in the *Washington Post Book World* that Bail's writings "are carefully and consciously avant-garde."

Bail's 1975 collection, *Contemporary Portraits and Other Stories,* is comprised of innovative stories that expose the absurdity in everyday life and focus on people's eccentricities and peculiar relationships. The story "Heubler" features a photographer who aspires to take a picture of every living person. He begins by shooting the portraits of twenty-three characters—upon whom Bail expounds—who represent various stereotypical personality types. They include a person who believes his experiences would make a great novel, a person who hears voices, and one who always has to have the last word in an argument. The more surrealistic tales of *Contemporary Portraits* offer new perspectives on seemingly ordinary situations. In "The Dog Show" pet owners display themselves alongside their animals, and in "The Silence" a solitary rabbit trapper, so overwhelmed by the great emptiness and silence of the Australian outback, can no longer bear the sound of the human voice.

Another of Bail's *Contemporary Portraits,* "The Drover's Wife," was inspired by Australian artist Russell Drysdale's painting of the same name. The narrator of the tale sees his own wife—who abandoned him thirty years earlier—in the portrait and imagines the events of her life in the years since she has left him. Gaining insight into the drover's personality as well as his wife's, reviewers praised Bail's clever manipulation of what is real and what is imagined. The tale "Portrait of Electricity" provided the basis for Bail's first novel, *Homesickness.* In the story, a museum devoted to a man—its displays ranging from personal trinkets to an example of his excrement—is the only proof of his existence. Randall Stevenson for the *Times Literary Supplement* praised Bail's "lively inventiveness," while a *West Coast Review of Books* contributor applauded the author's "fresh, energetic view of life" and "originality and wit."

Homesickness, Bail's 1980 novel, recounts the adventures of a group of Australians undertaking a world tour. Bail focuses his attention on the travelers as a social group, commenting on the various relationships they forge and break during the journey and on their reactions to the cultural artifacts they encounter. Their sight-seeing is limited, however, to a number of bizarre museums that they visit in Africa, Ecuador, the United States, England, and the Soviet Union. One museum displays human legs preserved in formaldehyde and another features a bathtub with its taps in the Northern Hemisphere and drain in the Southern. On exhibit in an African museum of handicrafts are an old sewing machine, used toothpaste tubes, and an umbrella, while in Lenin's Tomb in Moscow the tourists are asked to prove that his cadaver is real. In New York City the group watches the wildlife in Central Park, and in another brightly lit but empty museum they find themselves on display. Lewis pointed out that "much of the interest of the book, with its off-beat satire and restrained, oddball comedy, lies in these surreal set-pieces."

Bail's 1987 work, *Holden's Performance,* is considered more intricate and stylized than his previous offerings, though Laurie Clancy points out in *Contemporary Novelists* that the novel is "rather less sure of

its direction" than the author's earlier work. The novel focuses on Holden Shadbolt, who was named, we are told, after the automobile produced specifically for the Australian market by General Motors. It was "the most famous car Australia has produced," Clancy writes. Bail uses the car as a vehicle for what the reviewer calls an obsession for "mythologizing what he sees as so far unmythologized and therefore unpossessed country."

Whereas *Homesickness* is a novel "of Australians circling the world looking for themselves and their home," Clancy suggests, the unpossessed country of *Holden's Performance* is Australia itself, from 1932, the year of Holden's birth, through the 1960s to the point where the thirty-four-year-old civil servant leaves his native home for new adventures in America. During these years Holden befriends many eccentric characters who allow the author to inject into the novel the "strange mixture of surrealist fantasy and broad satire of Australian life that characterizes all of Bail's work," Clancy reports. She praises the novel as "a brilliantly inventive work. . . . The motif of the car is carried skillfully through to the final page of the novel, which is a summary of Holden himself," using the terminology of vehicle specifications to describe the man.

Clancy also points to "Bail's abiding concerns, which are strikingly consistent in his . . . works of fiction. His interest in nationality is but part of his larger interest in identity. . . . And in turn concern with identity merges into concern with language and the relationship between language and experience."

BIOGRAPHICAL/CRITICAL SOURCES:

BOOKS

Contemporary Novelists, sixth edition, St. James Press (Detroit), 1996.

PERIODICALS

Listener, September 4, 1980, p. 313.
Observer, August 24, 1980, p. 26; October 18, 1987; June 11, 1989, p. 43.
Spectator, November 7, 1981, p. 41.
Times Literary Supplement, April 9, 1976; September 19, 1980; June 19, 1987; November 27-December 3, 1987.
Washington Post Book World, October 4, 1981.
West Coast Review of Books, July, 1986.

BAILEY, Paul 1937-

PERSONAL: Born Peter Harry Bailey, February 16, 1937, in Battersea, London, England; son of Arthur Oswald and Helen (Burgess) Bailey. *Education:* Attended Central School of Speech and Drama, London, 1953-56. *Politics:* Socialist. *Religion:* Agnostic. *Avocational interests:* Music, literature, tennis.

ADDRESSES: Home—79 Davisville Rd., London W12, England.

CAREER: Actor, 1956-63. University of Newcastle-upon-Tyne and University of Durham, literary fellow, 1972-74; North Dakota State University, Fargo, visiting lecturer, 1977-79. Has been an actor on television and with the Stratford and Royal Court theatres in London, England; left a job "selling at a large Knightsbridge store" to write full-time.

AWARDS, HONORS: Arts Council of Great Britain Award and Somerset Maugham Travel Award, both 1968, both for *At the Jerusalem;* Authors' Club Award, 1970; E. M. Forster Award, National Institute of Arts and Letters, 1974; Bicentennial Arts fellowship, 1976; George Orwell Memorial Prize, 1976; Fellow, Royal Society of Literature, 1982.

WRITINGS:

NOVELS

At the Jerusalem, Atheneum (New York City), 1967.
Trespasses, J. Cape (London), 1970, Harper (New York City), 1971.
A Distant Likeness, J. Cape, 1973.
Peter Smart's Confessions, J. Cape, 1977.
Old Soldiers, J. Cape, 1980.
Gabriel's Lament, J. Cape, 1986, Viking (New York City), 1987.
Sugar Cane, Bloomsbury (London), 1993.

PLAYS

At Cousin Henry's (radio play), 1964.
A Worthy Guest, produced in Newcastle-upon-Tyne, 1973, London, 1974.
Alice, produced in Newcastle-upon-Tyne, 1975.
Crime and Punishment (based on novel by Feodor Dostoevski), produced in Manchester, 1978.
(With Trastram Powell) *We Think the World of You* (television play), 1980.

OTHER

(With others) *Living in London,* London Magazine Editions, 1974.
An English Madam: The Life and Work of Cynthia Payne (biography), J. Cape, 1982.
An Immaculate Mistake: Scenes from Childhood and Beyond (autobiography), Bloomsbury (London), 1990, Dutton (New York City), 1992.
(Editor) *The Oxford Book of London* (anthology of fiction and non-fiction), Oxford University Press (Oxford), 1995.

Contributor to *New Statesman, Listener, Observer, London Magazine, Sunday Times,* and *Daily Telegraph.*

SIDELIGHTS: Paul Bailey's novels are "characterized by extreme compression," Peter Lewis writes in the *Times Literary Supplement,* "in an attempt to produce great poetic intensity." Usually concerned with elderly or isolated characters who are suffering from a personal catastrophe in their lives, Bailey's work is often pessimistic. Yet, Thomas J. Cousineau states in the *Dictionary of Literary Biography,* "Bailey is a writer who possesses a remarkable sensitivity to human relations and an exceptional gift for rendering the inner lives of his characters."

At the Jerusalem, Bailey's first novel, was described at the time of its release as "probably the most original, and certainly the most accomplished, first novel of the year," by Alan Ross of *London Magazine.* It is set at the Jerusalem, the retirement home where Mrs. Gadny has been forced to live. Her struggle against, and eventual failure to adjust to, the loneliness of institutional life is the subject of the novel. "Bailey's social comment," Miles Burrows observes in his *New Statesman* review, "is precise and made with an enviably light touch while never failing to be serious." This blending of the comic and compassionate results, Ross comments, in "a series of portraits remarkable for their insight and tenderness." Because of her inability to adjust to life in the retirement home, and her disturbing memories of past failures to achieve intimacy with others, Mrs. Gadny eventually "breaks and goes from poorhouse to mental institution," J. M. Carroll writes in *Library Journal.* Carroll finds *At the Jerusalem* a "sad, almost clinical account of unhappiness in growing old," while the *Times Literary Supplement* critic praises Bailey for combining "mature understanding with immense control and accomplishment."

Ralph Hicks, the narrator and protagonist of Bailey's second novel, *Trespasses,* is also committed to a mental institution. Following the suicide of his wife, who blames him for her action, Hicks has suffered a breakdown and committed himself. In a series of short narrative fragments, Hicks examines the details of his life as a way to find some sort of sense in it. "He hopes," Cousineau writes, "that the exploration of his past will awaken in him that sense of a strong personal identity which has until now eluded him." As in *Jerusalem,* the principal theme of *Trespasses* is "estrangement: the subtly inevitable process by which parents and children, men and women, draw tragically and uncomprehendingly apart from one another," the *Times Literary Supplement* reviewer maintains. The critic goes on to conclude that with *Trespasses,* Bailey "establishes a firm place among the best of the younger novelists." Cousineau believes *Trespasses* "may well be Bailey's finest novel."

Estrangement is also an important theme in *A Distant Likeness,* the story of police inspector Frank White, recently deserted by his wife for another man. White's efforts to reconcile himself to this loss are interwoven with his daily police work and his memories and presented in a stream-of-consciousness narration. It is written, writes the *Times Literary Supplement* critic, "almost entirely in tiny, cryptic paragraphs collected in short batches separated by blank pages." This method is "probably less effective," Cousineau admits, "than the more explicitly controlled technique of *Trespasses.*" Lewis believes that in this novel Bailey is "aiming at a hyper-concentration of linguistic effect."

The "likeness" of the title refers to the similarity between White and a wife murderer named Belsey who sits silently in his cell and refuses to talk to police. Both men have failed in life and this common failure eventually moves White to give Belsey a knife, hinting to the man that he may want to kill himself with it. Instead, Belsey attacks a guard and White is arrested as his accomplice. Some critics see the novel's short length and minimal plot as its major flaws. "No amount of ingenuity," the *Times Literary Supplement* critic concludes, "in the deployment of symbols, the details which echo meaningfully across the pages, the nice attention to minuscule portrayals of settings, can compensate for the final absence of the full-blooded novel which Mr. Bailey's skills might have provided. *A Distant Likeness* is thin stuff."

As in previous Bailey novels, the protagonist of *Peter Smart's Confessions* is caught in a catastrophic situation. The novel begins with Smart waking up in a hospital intensive care ward after a failed suicide attempt. Like Ralph Hicks of *Trespasses,* Smart then decides to write his autobiography as a means of sorting out his life. The result is an often-humorous book filled with the constant chatter of a host of eccentric characters. In fact, as Paddy Kitchen explains in the *Listener,* the text of this autobiography consists primarily of "the dialogue of [Smart's] motley and intermittently splendid cast of relations, friends, and employers. "*Peter Smart's Confessions,*" Peter Ackroyd observes in *Spectator,* "is a sport, a game constantly threatening to get out of hand as Bailey swoops with horrid glee upon each of his characters as they alternately fumble, strut and moan through their lives." The characters, Ackroyd continues, "address the world about themselves, ferocious and furious, helpless and merciless in turn, lying and hesitating." "Irony and humour are not unwelcome in tragedy," Kitchen states, "but too often here they deteriorate into long-drawn-out badinage. However, there are some brilliant passages." Similarly, Cousineau believes the book's humor "seems to reside more in isolated set pieces . . . than in any underlying novelistic conception."

In *Old Soldiers,* Bailey again deals with elderly characters who are experiencing a painful loss. The novel begins with Victor Harker returning to London for the first time in fifty years. He has come to get away from his hometown for a few days following the recent death of his wife. While visiting St. Paul's Cathedral, Harker meets Harold Standish, another elderly man. Both men served in the First World War, and so they have dinner and share their memories of that time. Harker soon realizes that Standish is not what he first seemed to be. Standish maintains three separate identities—a tramp, an unknown poet, and a retired army officer—and dons each disguise for a few days at a time. Standish's intention is "to escape from himself," Cousineau explains, "and the inevitability of his own death." This need to escape was triggered by an act of cowardice during the war. "I was not entirely persuaded by Paul Bailey's literal explanation of how Standish's protean obsession began," Nicholas Shrimpton of *New Statesman* allows. "But in other respects this is a marvellously skillful book, deftly constructed and full of incidental delights." Writing in the *Listener,* John Naughton focuses his attention on the book's length, calling it "an exercise in compression, a stylistic experiment conducted to see how far a scenario can be cut to the descriptive bone while still remaining credible." Elaine Feinstien notes in her review for the London *Times* that "to bring us into the presence of the dead and dying and then, without the slightest precautionary numbing of ordinary emotions, bewilder us into laughter is a remarkably difficult manoeuvre. [*Old Soldiers*], however, does just this, and gently, without a taint of black farce." Lewis believes that *Old Soldiers* is the "most completely satisfying" Bailey novel since *At the Jerusalem*.

Gabriel's Lament "is by far [Bailey's] longest work of fiction and encompasses over 40 years of English life, from the early years of World War II on," states Lewis in *Contemporary Novelists*. The novel tells the story of Gabriel, a writer whose life "has been profoundly affected by [his mother's] mysterious absence as well as by the overbearing presence of his outrageously eccentric father, Oswald, one of Bailey's most brilliant creations and a comic character of Dickensian stature," noted Lewis, continuing, "Oswald may make Gabriel suffer, but he simultaneously makes the reader laugh. Bailey achieves a delicate synthesis of the tragic and the comic." Identifying similar characteristics, Boyd Tonkin summarizes in *The Listener,* "Bailey's rich comedy and wily narration suggest a link between creation and delusion that places *Gabriel's Lament* squarely inside a Romantic tradition." Jill Johnson comments in the *New York Times Book Review,* "The oppression of Gabriel is so pervasive, so persistent, that his ultimate triumph as a writer, let alone his survival, may be hard to believe," stating also that, "All Mr. Bailey's characters tend to talk like [Oswald], whose speech is mannered and inflated. This blurs the distinctness of the characters and often makes the reading hard going." Neil Philip viewed the novel more positively. He states in his *British Book News* review that "Bailey maintains Gabriel's rather fussy narrative voice with great skill, and within that constraint unerringly manages a cast of almost Dickensian eccentrics."

There are recurring themes in all of Bailey's novels, Cousineau notes. "In each novel," he writes, "the stability of the main character's life is undermined by some painful circumstance. . . . It frequently happens as well that the catastrophe is provoked at last in part by the main character's personal inadequacies . . . [and, in addition,] Bailey's characters are generally isolated from normal human relationships." Bailey's great strength, Lewis observes, is his ability to depict the isolation of his characters. "He exposes the vulnerable core at the heart of all individuals," Lewis writes, "the strategies by which people try to disguise their vulnerability and to protect themselves from the daily assault of reality, including the inevitability of death."

Bailey has produced several non-fiction publications, including *An Immaculate Mistake: Scenes from Childhood and Beyond* and *The Oxford Book of London. An Immaculate Mistake: Scenes from Childhood and Beyond* is a "slim, unpretentious memoir" of Bailey's life, according to Nisid Hajari in *Entertainment Weekly*. A reviewer in *Publishers Weekly* states of the biography, "varying in intensity, the episodes shine with good humor." *The Oxford Book of London* contains various fiction and non-fiction works, ordered chronologically from 1180 to 1994, that detail life in London. In *Observer,* Anthony Quinn describes it as "a fine anthology, that should leave minds as madly divided on the place as they ever were . . . it might be said to unfold a tale of two cities within a single metropolis, one of them home to privilege, the other to privation. Bailey's artful juxtapositions keep this grim divide always before us." Oliver Reynolds faults the book in the *Times Literary Supplement* for failing to include material describing key aspects of London life , such as "sport," "the Long Room," and "twin towers." Reynolds states "considering its subject matter, [it] is relatively slim; rather narrow in its choice of materials, it is one of those rare books that a reviewer might wish were longer." Praising the book, Reynolds comments, "The book reads very easily, and is constantly diverting through its juxtaposition of poetry and prose, factual account and gilded memory . . . [it] is cogently ordered and consistently enjoyable."

In 1991, Bailey commented to *Contemporary Novelists:* "I write novels for many reasons, some of which I have probably never consciously thought of. I don't like absolute moral judgments, the 'placing' of people into types—I'm both delighted and appalled by the mysteriousness of my fellow creatures. I enjoy 'being' other people when I write, and the novels I admire most respect the uniqueness of other human beings. I like to think I show my characters respect and that I don't sit in judgment on them. This is what, in my small way, I am striving for—to capture, in a shaped and controlled form, something of the mystery of life. I am writing, too, to expand and stimulate my own mind. I hope I will have the courage to be more ambitious, bolder and braver in my search for the ultimately unknowable, with each book I write."

BIOGRAPHICAL/CRITICAL SOURCES:

BOOKS

Contemporary Novelists, sixth edition, St. James Press (Detroit), 1996.
Dictionary of Literary Biography, Volume 14: *British Novelists since 1960,* Gale (Detroit), 1983.

PERIODICALS

Antioch Review, spring, 1971.
Booklist, May 1, 1987, p. 1332.
Books and Bookmen, August, 1967.
British Book News, January 19, 1987, p. 43.
Encounter, September, 1973.
Entertainment Weekly, August 14, 1992, p. 56.
Kirkus Reviews, April 1, 1987, p. 486.
Library Journal, April 15, 1967.
Listener, July 6, 1967; April 30, 1970; June 14, 1973; June 2, 1977; March 6, 1980; October 2, 1986, pp. 23-24.
London Magazine, October, 1976.
London Review of Books, October 23, 1986, p. 16.
New Statesman, June 2, 1967; April 17, 1970; June 15, 1973; June 10, 1977; February 29, 1980.
New Statesman & Society, May 28, 1993, p. 38.
New York Times Book Review, May 21, 1967; October 18, 1987, p. 34.
Observer, May 28, 1967; June 17, 1973; May 29, 1977; March 2, 1980; October 22, 1995, p. 14.
Publishers Weekly, January, 13, 1992, p. 39.
Punch, July 5, 1967; October 1, 1986, p. 59.
Spectator, April 18, 1970; June 16, 1973; June 4, 1977; June 14, 1980.
Times (London), February 28, 1980.
Times Literary Supplement, June 8, 1967; April 16, 1970; June 29, 1973; May 27, 1977; November 6, 1982; June 21, 1996, p. 32.
USA Today, August 6, 1987, p. 5D.*

* * *

BALDWIN, Gordo
　See BALDWIN, Gordon C.

* * *

BALDWIN, Gordon C. 1908-
　(Gordo Baldwin, Lew Gordon)

PERSONAL: Born June 5, 1908, in Portland, OR; son of John A. and Pearl E. (Gibbs) Baldwin; married Pauline Farriss (a high school teacher), May 25, 1935; children: Patricia Jane Hutchings, Marjorie Louise Clarkson. *Education:* University of Arizona, B.A., 1933, M.A., 1934; University of Southern California, Ph.D., 1941. *Politics:* Republican. *Religion:* Baptist. *Avocational interests:* Reading mysteries and spy stories; volunteer work in Mountain View library; walking and sightseeing in the Bay area.

ADDRESSES: Home—426 Poppy Pl., Mountain View, CA 94043. *Agent*—William Reiss, Paul R. Reynolds, Inc., 12 East 41st St., New York, NY 10017.

CAREER: University of Arizona, Tucson, instructor in archaeology, 1934-37; Arizona State Museum, Tucson, assistant curator, 1937-40; National Park Service, Boulder City, NV, archaeologist, 1940-48; National Park Service, Omaha, NE, archaeologist, 1948-53; University of Omaha (now University of Nebraska at Omaha), instructor in anthropology, 1953-54; writer, 1954-74.

MEMBER: Westerners International (member of board of directors, 1973-79; vice-president, 1974-76), Western Writers of America (member of board of directors, 1962-63, 1968-70; president, 1968-69), Society of Southwestern Authors (member of board of directors, 1972-76), Tucson Corral of the Westerners (sheriff, 1973), Palo Alto Host Lions Club (member of board of directors, 1979—).

WRITINGS:

NOVELS

Trouble Range, R. Hale (London), 1956, Arcadia (New York City), 1959.
Trail North, R. Hale, 1956, Arcadia, 1957.
Range War at Sundown, R. Hale, 1957, published as *Sundown Country,* Arcadia, 1959.
(Under pseudonym Lew Gordon) *Powdersmoke Justice,* R. Hale, 1957, Avalon (New York City), 1961.
Roundup at Wagonmound, Arcadia, 1960.
(Under pseudonym Gordo Baldwin) *Ambush Basin,* Avalon, 1960, published under pseudonym Lew Gordon, R. Hale, 1965.
Brand of Yuma, Avalon, 1960.
(Under pseudonym Gordo Baldwin) *Wyoming Rawhide,* Avalon, 1961, published under name Gordon C. Baldwin, R. Hale, 1965.

NONFICTION

America's Buried Past: The Story of North American Archaeology, Putnam (New York City), 1962.
The Ancient Ones: Basketmakers and Cliff Dwellers of the Southwest, Norton (New York City), 1963.
The World of Prehistory: The Story of Man's Beginnings, Putnam, 1963.
Stone Age Peoples Today, Norton, 1964.
The Riddle of the Past: How Archeological Detectives Solve Prehistoric Riddles, Norton, 1965.
The Warrior Apaches: A Story of the Chiricahua and Western Apache, Dale Stuart King (Tucson), 1965.
Race against Time: The Story of Salvage Archeology, Putnam, 1966.
Strange People and Stranger Customs, Norton, 1967.
Calendars to the Past: How Science Dates Archeological Ruins, Norton, 1967.
How Indians Really Lived, Putnam, 1967.
Games of the American Indian, Norton, 1969.
Indians of the Southwest, Putnam, 1970.
Talking Drums to Written Word: How Early Man Learned to Communicate, Norton, 1970.
Schemers, Dreamers, and Medicine Men: Witchcraft and Magic among Primitive People, Four Winds Press (New York City), 1970.
Pyramids of the New World, Putnam, 1971.
Inventors and Inventions of the Ancient Worlds, Four Winds Press, 1973.
The Apache Indians: Raiders of the Southwest, Four Winds Press, 1978.

Contributor of articles on anthropology to professional journals. Editor, *The Roundup,* 1962-66. A collection of Baldwin's manuscripts is housed at the University of Arizona Library, Tucson. Many of Baldwin's books have been published in England, Norway, Sweden, Germany, France, and Spain.

ADAPTATIONS: Some of Baldwin's titles have been produced as Talking Books for the blind.

SIDELIGHTS: After writing several Western novels, Gordon C. Baldwin turned to writing nonfiction books focusing on archeological research, the customs and history of Native Americans, and the history of archeology. Many of Baldwin's books are about the American West and Native Americans, utilizing his extensive knowledge of that field from his years of teaching.

Baldwin's first nonfiction book, *America's Buried Past: The Story of North American Archaeology,* traces the history of Native Americans from their early migrations from Asia to the time of Columbus. The critic for *Horn Book* praises the "authority and scientific method" exhibited in the book, while C. M. Turnbull in *Natural History* notes that Baldwin "disposes of some of the wilder theories about America's past" and "gives us a feeling that the scientist's insistence on absolute accuracy is no dull quibble over trivia, but rather an exciting, stimulating challenge."

In *Games of the American Indian* Baldwin describes the various pastimes used by Native peoples for amusement. Toys and games found among the nine major cultural groups of Native Americans are discussed in such detail, according to E. R. Downum in *Library Journal,* that readers are able "to understand how to play some of the games—or, in many cases, how to make the toys discussed."

Baldwin's *The Apache Indians: Raiders of the Southwest* is, according to P. R. Meldrum in *Twentieth-Century Western Writers,* "a carefully researched and scientific approach to American history. . . . Baldwin makes a useful contribution to American history by discrediting images of Apache cruelty and investigating their economic system." Similarly, R. A. Brown in *School Library Journal* praises Baldwin for "properly discrediting the image of the Apache Indian as brutal, cruel, dishonest, and tricky." C. W. Draper in *Horn Book* finds that in Baldwin's book, the Apache ways of life "are described in detail, and a picture emerges very different from that of life on the reservation."

Baldwin told *CA:* "During my years as an archeologist in the Southwest and in the high plains area east of the Rocky Mountains, I had collected notes and information and photographs on all phases of western history. I had also written about 60 articles on Indians and archeology and history, all of which were published in technical and non-technical journals. With this background I had little difficulty in writing and selling eight western novels.

"However, in 1960 my agent discovered that I had a Ph.D. degree in anthropology and convinced me that we could both make more money writing nonfiction books for young readers, 10-12 and up. He was right. I also found it a more challenging field and hoped I was helping youngsters as well as older readers by giving them accurate facts about Indians and archeology."

BIOGRAPHICAL/CRITICAL SOURCES:

BOOKS

Twentieth-Century Western Writers, second edition, St. James Press (Detroit), 1991.

PERIODICALS

Best Sellers, August 1, 1969, p. 29.
Horn Book, April, 1963, p. 39; August, 1978, p. 54.
Library Journal, November 15, 1962, p. 87; September 15, 1963, p. 88; June 15, 1964, p. 89; April 15, 1965, p. 90; June 15, 1966, p. 91; May 15, 1967, p. 92; September 15, 1969, p. 94; September 15, 1970, p. 95.
Natural History, December, 1963, p. 72; November, 1964, p. 73; November, 1965, p. 74; November, 1966, p. 75.
School Library Journal, February, 1978, p. 63.
Young Readers' Review, October, 1967.

*   *   *

BARNES, Linda
  See BARNES, Linda J(oyce)

*   *   *

BARNES, Linda J(oyce) 1949-
  (Linda Barnes)

PERSONAL: Born June 6, 1949, in Detroit, MI; daughter of Irving (a mechanical engineer) and Hilda (a teacher and homemaker; maiden name, Grodman) Appelblatt; married Richard Allen Barnes (a software engineer), June 7, 1970; children: Samuel J. Education: Boston University, B.F.A. (cum laude), 1971. Avocational interests: Blues guitar, film noir.

ADDRESSES: Home—Brookline, MA. Agent—Gina Maccoby, P.O. Box 60, Chappaqua, NY 10514.

CAREER: Writer. Chelmsford High School, Chelmsford, MA, theater teacher, 1971-76; Lexington Pubic Schools, Lexington, MA, drama program director, 1977-78.

MEMBER: International Crime Writers Association, American Crime Writers Association, Mystery Writ-

ers of America (regional vice president, 1982-83), Private Eye Writers of America, Authors Guild.

AWARDS, HONORS: Anthony Award, Bouchercon Mystery Convention, 1986, for short story "Lucky Penny"; Edgar Allan Poe Award nomination, Mystery Writers of America, 1987, and American Mystery Award, Mystery Scene Magazine, 1988, both for A Trouble of Fools.

WRITINGS:

"MICHAEL SPRAGGUE" SERIES; UNDER NAME LINDA BARNES, EXCEPT AS NOTED

(Under name Linda J. Barnes) Blood Will Have Blood, Avon (New York City), 1982.
Bitter Finish, St. Martin's (New York City), 1983.
Dead Heat, St. Martin's, 1984.
Cities of the Dead, St. Martin's, 1986.

"CARLOTTA CARLYLE" SERIES; UNDER NAME LINDA BARNES

A Trouble of Fools, St. Martin's, 1987.
The Snake Tattoo, St. Martin's, 1989.
Coyote, Delacorte (New York City), 1990.
Steel Guitar, Delacorte, 1991.
Snapshot, Delacorte, 1993.
Hardware, Delacorte, 1995.
Cold Case, Delacorte, 1997.

PLAYS

Wings, Baker (Boston), 1973.
Prometheus, Baker, 1974.

OTHER

Also author of a short story, "Lucky Penny."

ADAPTATIONS: Spraggue: Murder for Two, a television movie "loosely based on characters from Blood Will Have Blood," Lorimar Productions, September, 1984.

SIDELIGHTS: Linda J. Barnes is the author of numerous mystery novels which are separated into two series based on their lead characters. The protagonist of her first four works is Michael Spraggue, a wealthy actor and private detective. In latter works, Barnes focuses on a female detective, Carlotta Carlyle, who is a divorced ex-cop who exudes the toughness required of an investigator while bringing "a feminist perspective" to her work, noted *Village Voice* reviewer James Ledbetter. Carlyle has a "tendency to violence" and "pick[s] the wrong man every time" for her personal relationships, stated Ted Hertel in the *St. James Guide to Crime and Mystery Writers*.

Barnes' characters have been the focus of many reviews. "Barnes has made certain that the long term consequences of Carlotta's acts are reflected in subsequent books. The same was true with Spraggue, whose continually building depression ultimately resulted in the end of his series," noted Hertel. Bettina Berch of *Belles Lettres* commented that "most of the characters in *Snapshot* are either stereotypical or improbable or both," and concluded, "On the other hand, our heroine is not rude, and I suppose she *is* politically correct. And that is all some people ask for in what is essentially recreational reading." Shattuck critiqued *Snapshot* as having "a P. I. centerpiece who's been cannily created to wear extremely well with readers."

Within the Carlotta Carlyle series, Hertel commented, "Barnes has shifted the answer to the questions of "whom do you save?' to children [rather than "the dewey-eyed damsel in distress.'] While this is not the theme in every book, there is always an underlying concern for Paolina," the child Carlyle was paired with through Big Sisters. *Snapshot,* the Carlyle mystery investigating the death of a child being treated for leukemia, is "a slickly written, fast moving read," according to *The Armchair Detective*'s Norma J. Shattuck. In the *Times Literary Supplement,* Peter Clarke reviewed *Snapshot* as "showy," stating "verve is more to the point than plot." Ledbetter termed *A Trouble of Fools* as "a well-plotted story" and added that "the novel's real strength is its humanist, unpretentious voice."

The sixth Carlyle mystery, *Hardware,* centers around the bombing of the cab company Carlyle drives for on a part-time basis. When commenting on the novel in *Publishers Weekly,* Sybil S. Steinberg summarized: "The puzzle works well, but mainly it's Carlotta and her interactions with the well-drawn folks around her that make Barnes's story hum." "[*Hardware*] takes a while to unfold, but the humor and the self-reliance of the heroine make the wait worthwhile," stated Wes Lukowsky in *Booklist.*

In the *St. James Guide to Crime and Mystery Writers,* Barnes commented: "I consider my four Spraggue novels to be my apprentice work. At the time I began the series, I was seeking a detective who was neither a wealthy British dilettante nor a tough American woman-hater. I created Michael Spraggue—wealthy, ex-private eye, actor, feminist—a 'mid-Atlantic' detective. Because I had chosen to make Spraggue an amateur, I had the continuing problem of involving him legitimately in his cases. I solved this by killing off many of his friends and relatives. His subsequent depression became difficult to deal with and I sought a new hero.

"I had always wanted to write a female first-person detective novel. I hesitated because I was told by publishing insiders that my envisioned 'semi-tough' woman would never sell. Still, Carlotta Carlyle—ex-cop, part-time cab driver, licensed private eye—was on my mind, and in between Spraggue novels I auditioned her in a short story, 'Lucky Penny,' which languished unsold for over a year. In 1986, I sent it along to my new agent as an afterthought. She promptly sold it, and it quickly garnered more attention and critical acclaim than all the Spraggue books to date.

"I enjoy Carlotta for her voice, her independence, and her relationships with those she loves."

BIOGRAPHICAL/CRITICAL SOURCES:

BOOKS

St. James Guide to Crime and Mystery Writers, fourth edition, St. James Press (Detroit), 1996.

PERIODICALS

Armchair Detective, winter, 1994.
Belles Lettres, fall, 1993; summer, 1995.
Booklist, February 1, 1995.
Observer, January 9, 1994.
Publishers Weekly, January 16, 1995.
Times Literary Supplement, January 7, 1994.
Village Voice, December 15, 1987.*

* * *

BARRY, Jane (Powell) 1925-

PERSONAL: Born July 25, 1925, in New Baltimore, NY; daughter of Levit Clark (self-employed) and Ida (Van der Poel) Powell; married John David Barry (now in advertising and public relations), September 6, 1953. *Avocational interests:* Reading, music, gardening; grows and hybridizes iris and daylilies, and has a small commercial garden.

ADDRESSES: Home—R. D. 3, Lotus Point, Catskill, NY 12414. *Agent*—Harold Matson Co., 22 East 40th St., New York, NY 10016.

CAREER: Writer. *Coxsackie Union News,* Coxsackie, NY, reporter, 1946-48, editor of centennial edition, 1950-51; *Greene County Examiner Recorder,* Catskill, NY, editor, 1952-53.

MEMBER: Western Writers of America, American Iris Society.

AWARDS, HONORS: Award for best single issue of newspaper in New York State, for centennial edition of *Coxsackie Union News,* 1951.

WRITINGS:

The Long March, Appleton (New York City), 1955.
The Carolinians, Doubleday (New York City), 1959.
A Time in the Sun, Doubleday, 1962.
A Shadow of Eagles, Doubleday, 1964.
Maximilian's Gold, Doubleday, 1966.
Grass Roots, Doubleday, 1968.
The Cavendish Face, Collins (London), 1983.
The Conscience of the King, M. Joseph (London), 1987.
Grand Illusions, Avon (New York City), 1988.

SIDELIGHTS: Jane Barry's historical novels draw on the American past for their dramatic situations. In particular, writes Vicki Piekarksi in *Twentieth-Century Western Writers,* Barry is known for "three fine, but little recognized, historical novels about the American Southwest"—*A Time in the Sun, A Shadow of Eagles,* and *Maximilian's Gold.*

In *A Time in the Sun,* the Apaches capture a white girl who falls in love with one of the tribal boys. B. W. Garfield in *Saturday Review* states: "Barry's treatment excels in credible characterizations, smooth style, believable motivations and refreshing plot twists." Piekarski finds the novel "a perceptive historical reconstruction, true to the land, the period, and the people; it rejects the idea of white supremacy and questions white values."

In *A Shadow of Eagles* Barry again addresses interracial issues by picturing a Spanish ranching family and their conflicts with Anglo neighbors. "The cultural questions raised are obscured . . . ," Piekarski writes,

"because much of the story is given over to a trail drive to Montana and the drama of the drive. Yet, notwithstanding this structural incongruity, life both on the trail and on Tres Reyes ranch are vividly described, and the book demonstrates Barry's ability to recreate adeptly the historical past."

Maximilian's Gold concerns a rumored buried treasure in Texas and of the efforts of six men to recover the gold. The novel's characters, Piekarski believes, "are individually, and collectively, among Barry's finer literary portraits." Piekarski concludes that Barry is "a unique and sensitive author" who "presents a balanced view of the southwest in her fiction, one without sentimentality. Her concern is not with heroes triumphing over villains, but rather with what happens when peoples of diverse cultures, traditions, and backgrounds collide. Her meticulously constructed stories are gripping and her characters are almost always credible."

BIOGRAPHICAL/CRITICAL SOURCES:

BOOKS

Twentieth-Century Western Writers, second edition, St. James Press (Detroit), 1991.

PERIODICALS

Library Journal, November 15, 1955, p. 80; August, 1962, p. 87.
New York Herald Tribune Book Review, June 21, 1959, p. 11.
New York Times, May 24, 1959, p. 41.
San Francisco Chronicle, September 16, 1962, p. 28.
Saturday Review, September 1, 1962, p. 45.
Social Studies, March, 1956, p. 47.
Springfield Republican, August 16, 1959, p. 4D.

* * *

BARSTOW, Stan(ley) 1928-

PERSONAL: Born June 28, 1928, in Horbury, Yorkshire, England; son of Wilfred (a coal miner) and Elsie (Gosnay) Barstow; married Constance Mary Kershaw, 1951; children: Richard Neil, Gillian Rosemary.

ADDRESSES: Home—Goring House, Goring Park Ave., Ossett, West Yorkshire WF5 0HX, England.

Agent—Lemon Unna and Durbridge, Ltd., 24 Pottery Lane, London W11 4LZ, England.

CAREER: Employed in engineering industry, 1944-62; writer, 1962—.

MEMBER: Society of Authors, PEN English Centre, Writers' Guild of Great Britain.

AWARDS, HONORS: Best British Dramatization Award, Writers' Guild of Great Britain, and best drama series award, British Broadcasting Press Guild, both 1974, both for *South Riding;* Royal Television Society's Writer's Award, 1975, for dramatizations of *South Riding, A Raging Calm,* and *Joby;* honorary M.A., Open University, 1982; honorary fellowship, Bretton College, 1985.

WRITINGS:

NOVELS

A Kind of Loving (also see below), M. Joseph (London), 1960, Doubleday, 1961.
Ask Me Tomorrow (also see below), M. Joseph, 1962, Black Swan, 1990.
Joby (also see below), M. Joseph, 1964.
The Watchers on the Shore (also see below), M. Joseph, 1966, Doubleday, 1967.
A Raging Calm (also see below), M. Joseph, 1968, published as *The Hidden Part,* Coward, 1969.
The Right True End (also see below), M. Joseph, 1976.
A Brother's Tale (also see below), M. Joseph, 1980.
Just You Wait and See, M. Joseph, 1986.
B-Movie, M. Joseph, 1987.
Give Us This Day, M. Joseph, 1989.
Next of Kin, M. Joseph, 1991.

SHORT STORY COLLECTIONS

The Desperadoes and Other Stories (also see below), M. Joseph, 1961, revised edition published as *The Human Element* (also see below), Longmans, 1969.
A Season with Eros, M. Joseph, 1971.
The Glad Eye and Other Stories, M. Joseph, 1984.

PLAYS

(With Alfred Bradley) *Ask Me Tomorrow* (based on Barstow's novel of same title; produced in Sheffield, Yorkshire, 1964), Samuel French, 1966.

(With Bradley) *A Kind of Loving* (based on Barstow's novel of same title; produced in Sheffield, Yorkshire, 1965; also see below), Blackie & Son, 1970.
(Adapter) Henrik Ibsen, *An Enemy of the People* (produced in Harrogate, Yorkshire, 1969), J. Calder, 1978.
Listen for the Trains, Love, music by Alec Glasgow, produced in Sheffield, Yorkshire, 1970.
(With Bradley) *Stringer's Last Stand* (produced in York, 1971), Samuel French, 1972.

TELEVISION PLAYS

South Riding (based on novel by Winifred Holtby), produced by Yorkshire Television, 1974.
A Raging Calm (based on Barstow's novel of same title), Independent Television (Canada), 1974.
Joby (based on Barstow's novel of same title), 1975.
The Human Element, and Albert's Part (also see below; televised 1977), Blackie, 1984.

Also author of television scripts *The Human Element, The Pity of It All,* 1965, *A World Inside* (with John Gibson; documentary), 1966, *Mind You, I Live Here* (with Gibson; documentary), 1971, *The Cost of Loving,* 1977, *Travellers,* 1978, *A Kind of Loving* (based on Barstow's novels *The Watcher on the Shore, The Right True End,* and *A Kind of Loving;* also see below), 1982, *A Brother's Tale* (based on Barstow's novel of same title), 1983, and *Albert's Part,* 1984.

OTHER

Also author of radio scripts *The Desperadoes,* 1965, *A Kind of Loving, The Watchers on the Shore,* and *The Right True End,* all based on Barstow's novels of the same titles, and of the radio scripts *We Could Always Fit a Sidecar,* 1974, and *Bright Day,* based on J. B. Priestley's novel of the same title.

SIDELIGHTS: In the tradition of the "angry young men"—those politically and socially charged novelists and playwrights who took postwar England by storm—Stan Barstow parlayed his upbringing in coal-mining Yorkshire into a series of well-received novels and short stories that explore working-class issues. It was Barstow's bestselling debut novel, *A Kind of Loving,* that thrust the young author into the literary spotlight and, according to *Contemporary Novelists* writer Trevor Royle, set up an expectation for future novels. "All too often, Royle notes, "publishers demand a sequel, or at the very least another novel written in the same vein, in an attempt to recreate the formula. Stan Barstow is one of the few novelists who has managed to keep intact the mold of their first success and then to have built upon it."

Barstow did follow up on an early success, first by creating a trilogy of stories set in the fictional town of Cressley—an amalgam of Britain's industrial north, a place of "terraced houses, ugly factories, garish cinemas and grubby parts," as critic Frederick Bowers is quoted in the *Dictionary of Literary Biography*. Cressley is also where Barstow's central character, Vic Brown, "finds himself struggling against the odds in a tough and no-nonsense world," as Royle writes. In writing about an area that seems to have been left behind during a period of prosperity, Barstow uses Cressley and the character of Vic to reflect "a sense of proletarian evangelism," according to Royle, "as if [the author] was desperate to write about real lives and real events, things normally ignored by the literary world at the time." In one story, another character sets Vic straight on the facts about his country: "But we're all living in a fool's paradise, that's all. A fools' paradise, Vic. Full employment and business booming? It just isn't possible, lad. Don't say I didn't warn you when the crash comes."

Barstow's short-story collections remain true to his time and place. Citing the way his stories "have become progressively more noteworthy since the 1960s," Grigsby goes on to say that the author's development of his craft springs "from increasingly complex and effective technical artistry and form increasingly profound and complex subjects and themes." In the collection *The Desperadoes and Other Stories*—despite some question about the sophisticated language employed by undereducated sheep farmers—Barstow offers much to recommend, says John L. Grigsby in his *Dictionary of Literary Biography* essay. "The two most noteworthy stories . . . are tragic," he continues. "In them [the author] realizes his special gift for ironic ambiguity and reality (some would say pessimistic) presentation of the tragedy of the working-class world. in his later collections Barstow refines his literary techniques and eschews the comic (at which he rarely succeeds) to present the tragic lives of his people and his region of England in ever more powerful ways."

Grigsby sees in Barstow's works the difficulties of working-class life—which include "how to deal with newly acquired wealth and independence when one is young and lacks guidance and stable values (as in 'The Desperadoes'), and how to survive in a work world in which the money earned is the only positive element." Getting deeper into his characters, Barstow also "focuses on the possibilities and permutations of awareness of others and the growth of love in [an environment] where self-indulgence and destruction of self and others are the overt manifestations."

Despite his ongoing success, Barstow has never been tempted to abandon his home region to join the literary social whirl in more cosmopolitan cities. This son of a coal miner explains in *Contemporary Novelists* that his dedication to the north country reflects his knowledge "that some of the finest novels in the language are 'regional,' [leading] me to the belief that to hoe one's own row diligently, thus seeking out the universal in the particular, brings more worthwhile satisfaction than the frantic pursuit of a largely phony jet-age internationalism."

BIOGRAPHICAL/CRITICAL SOURCES:

BOOKS

Contemporary Novelists, sixth edition, St. James Press (Detroit), 1996.
Dictionary of Literary Biography, Gale (Detroit), Volume 14: *British Novelists since 1960,* 1983, Volume 139: *British Short-Fiction Writers, 1945-1980,* 1994.
Hawthorn, Jeremy, editor, *The British Working Class Novel in the Twentieth Century,* Arnold (London), 1984, pp. 139-150.
Klaus, H. Gustav, editor, *The Socialist Novel in Britain: Towards the Recovery of a Tradition,* St. Martin's (New York City), 1982, pp. 145-165.
Raban, Jonathan, *The Technique of Modern Fiction: Essays in Practical Criticism,* Arnold, 1968.
Vannatta, Dennis, editor, *The English Short Story, 1945-1980: A Critical History,* G. K. Hall (Boston), 1985, pp. 34-74, 75-119.

*　　*　　*

BAUR, Susan 1940-
(Susan Schlee)

PERSONAL: Original name, Susan Whiting Baur; born January 22, 1940, in New York, NY; daughter of John I. H. (the director of the Whitney Museum of American Art) and Louise Chase (a teacher) Baur; married John Schlee (a marine geologist), December, 1969 (divorced, 1984); children: Scott Hubbard, Louisa Schlee. *Education:* Vassar College, A.B.,

1961; attended Florida Atlantic University, 1967, and Duke University, 1968; Harvard University, A.L.M., 1987; Boston College, Ph.D., 1990. *Politics:* Democrat. *Religion:* None. *Avocational interests:* Running, art.

ADDRESSES: Home—P. O. Box 1620, North Falmouth, MA 02556. *Office*—Thorne Clinic, P.O. Box 989, Pocasset, MA 02559. *Agent*—Miriam Altshuler, Russell & Volkening, 50 West 29th St., New York, NY 10001.

CAREER: Thorne Clinic, Pocasset, MA, psychologist, 1989—; writer. Worked variously as a computer programmer, reporter, editor, instructor in marine literature, and investigator at a biological laboratory.

MEMBER: American Psychological Association.

AWARDS, HONORS: Mark Ethridge fellow, Duke University, 1968; Pfizer Award for best book in the history of science, 1974, for *The Edge of an Unfamiliar World;* Thomas Small Prize for academic excellence, Harvard University, 1987.

WRITINGS:

Hypochondria: Woeful Imaginings, University of California Press (Berkeley), 1988.
The Dinosaur Man: Tales of Madness and Enchantment from the Back Ward, HarperCollins (New York City), 1991.
Confiding: A Psychotherapist and Her Patients Search for Stories to Live By, HarperCollins, 1994.
The Intimate Hour: Love and Sex in Psychotherapy, Houghton (Boston), 1997.

UNDER NAME SUSAN SCHLEE

The Edge of an Unfamiliar World: A History of Oceanography, Dutton (New York City), 1973.
On Almost Any Wind: The Saga of the Oceanographic Research Vessel Atlantis, Cornell University Press (Ithaca, NY), 1978.

OTHER

Contributor to periodicals, including *Natural History, Wilson Quarterly,* and *Smithsonian.* Baur's works have been translated into Spanish and German.

SIDELIGHTS: In *Hypochondria: Woeful Imaginings* Susan Baur discusses the condition in which healthy people believe they are suffering from physical ail-

ments. Although reasons for the development of hypochondria vary, the author suggests that one of its primary causes lies in society's tendency to offer sympathy to people who are physically ill over those who might be suffering emotionally or mentally. For example, a person involved in a detrimental marriage might feel safer complaining about arthritis to gain consolation rather than risk revealing the truth about his or her dissatisfaction with the relationship. In Baur's opinion many children are conditioned to become hypochondriacs because they are exposed to habitual complainers and learn that they can receive love and attention for feigning illness. Although some reviewers complained that the book fails to explore the biological reasons for hypochondria to the fullest extent, several critics acknowledged that Baur adeptly explores a number of psychological and sociological issues surrounding the condition.

Throughout her book Baur investigates medical history, providing information about some of the most extreme hypochondriacs and offering anecdotes about figures such as biologist Charles Darwin and singer Enrico Caruso who regularly feared physical illness. Several reviewers felt that *Hypochondria* benefits from the inclusion of quotes from primary-source materials such as the journals of biographer James Boswell, who was obsessed with death and dying. Some commentators, however, felt that Baur's work was not comprehensive. Alex Raksin, writing in the *Los Angeles Times Book Review,* remarked, "Viewed as an incomplete survey of hypochondria . . . this book is singular, intelligent and entertaining." Commenting on Baur's content and style, Mike Oppenheim of the *New York Times Book Review* remarked that "despite its impressive scholarship, the book is gracefully written and accessible."

In *The Dinosaur Man: Tales of Madness and Enchantment from the Back Ward* Baur continues her exploration of psychological phenomena, deriving material from her experiences working with schizophrenic patients. The author focuses on delusions—irrational beliefs held by individuals, usually about themselves and their past experiences. In the author's view, delusions provide mentally unstable people with a sense of identity and a way to cope with their fragmented lives. In this respect they serve a similar function to memories for sane individuals who use episodes from the past to define themselves. At the center of the book is the story of the "Dinosaur Man," who convinces himself that he was once a powerful "Nicodemosauras." Baur also includes encounters with a person who thinks that his mother was once transformed into a bee with huge eyes and a patient who cries when he believes he hears his children telling him to behave. Terri Apter of the *New York Times Book Review* remarked that despite Baur's professional status "what comes through most clearly is not the voice of the psychologist but the many voices of the lovable, comic, tormented patients, who relentlessly try to construct a self out of a mind that continually sabotages itself."

In *Confiding: A Psychotherapist and Her Patients Search for Stories to Live By,* Baur presents a "brilliant and passionate examination of how the stories we tell about ourselves shape our lives," writes Erika Taylor in the *Los Angeles Times Book Review.* Baur argues that our choice of the personal anecdotes we share with others indicate the kind of person we believe ourselves to be. "The qualities that make *Confiding* so effective," Taylor writes, "come largely from [Baur's] unconventional approach to therapy and from the beauty of the writing itself."

In *The Intimate Hour: Love and Sex in Psychotherapy,* Baur explores the quesiton of romantic liaisons within the doctor-patient relationship. Citing actual cases of love affairs between psychiatrists and their patients, Baur argues that a kind of love—"like the pure intimacy of courtly love"—can arise from psychotherapy and be positive and ethical. "Baur," notes Christopher Lehmann-Haupt in the *New York Times,* "is good at characterizing case histories."

Baur told *CA:* "The more I study storytelling, both from a writer's and a psychologist's point of view, the more convinced I become that the continual trading and refining of tales—from the common conversation to the heroic presentation—is the root metaphor for knowing. We think by talking. As [twentieth-century philosopher and author] Hannah Arendt maintained, individuals mature by talking to each other, and groups of people become communities in the same way. As I see it, the goal is to become inclusive. The richest stories, like the richest lives and richest communities, incorporate the most diverse and unexpected viewpoints. Much of my writing tries to capture the hidden gifts of the profoundly mentally ill and sneak them back into the community for the benefit of *all.*"

BIOGRAPHICAL/CRITICAL SOURCES:

PERIODICALS

Booklist, December 15, 1996, p. 700.
Kirkus Reviews, April 15, 1994, p. 512.
Lancet, April 5, 1997, p. 1034.
Library Journal, April 15, 1988, p. 85; May 15, 1994, p. 86; December, 1996, p. 124.
Los Angeles Times Book Review, March 27, 1988, p. 4; September 11, 1994, p. 14.
New Republic, December 26, 1988, p. 28.
New York Times, April 26, 1988; January 20, 1997, p. C18.
New York Times Book Review, March 27, 1988, p. 39; September 1, 1991, p. 7; January 19, 1997.
People, August 29, 1988, p. 81.
Publishers Weekly, March 18, 1988, p. 66; May 2, 1994, p. 292; November 11, 1996, p. 65.
Times Literary Supplement, November 18, 1988, p. 1273.

*　　*　　*

BECKER, Jasper 1956-

PERSONAL: Born May 19, 1956, in London, England; son of Alfred (an electronics engineer) and Ille Becker; married Ruwani Jayewardene (a development consultant), August, 1987. *Education:* Attended University of Munich, 1976-77; University of London, graduated (with honors), 1978.

ADDRESSES: Home—84 Chapel Market, London N1 9ET, England. *Office*—British Broadcasting Corp., Bush House, London, England; *South China Morning Post,* Jianguoweuwai 3-1-43, Beijing, People's Republic of China. *Agent*—A. P. Watt Ltd., 20 John St., London WC1N 2DR, England.

CAREER: Journalist in Brussels, Belgium, 1980-83; Associated Press, Geneva, Switzerland, journalist, 1983-85; *Guardian,* London, England, journalist in London and China, 1985-91; British Broadcasting Corp., London, journalist, 1991—.

WRITINGS:

The Lost Country: Mongolia Revealed, Hodder & Stoughton, 1991.
Hungry Ghosts: China's Secret Famine, The Free Press, 1996.

Work represented in anthologies, including *Reporting the News from China,* Chatham House, 1992.

SIDELIGHTS: Thirty million is an incomprehensible number of human beings, but it is a conservative estimate of how many Chinese peasants died from a state-caused famine between 1958 and 1962. Jasper Becker's *Hungry Ghosts: China's Secret Famine* explores this underreported tragedy.

Mao Zedong's "Great Leap Forward" was an attempt to push China past the Soviet Union, "pass England and catch up with America" all within fifteen years. Through this plan, China would become the leading nation in the world, and Mao would be the greatest leader in the world. Equal parts pseudo-science, sycophantic bureaucracy, and Mao's will-to-power allowed the starvation of so many to occur. The illusion of progress was sustained by false reports, cover-ups, and deceit. For example, reports of better-than-normal weather were falsified to indicate poor weather when news of the famine spread to higher government officials.

Famine was not new to China, but past occurrences of it were largely due to flooding and drought, and relief was impaired due to the great distances that separated villages. This particular famine was not localized but affected all of rural China. Mao would not admit the truth when faced with it, and he apparently did not understand until 1961 that millions had already died. Becker collected eyewitness accounts of cannibalism, stories of people feasting on cats and dogs, mice, insects, bark, leaves, and even dirt long after the peasants' grain ran out. He further noted that the same government was still in power in the late 1990s and still reluctant to admit to all that occurred during those four years.

The world outside China was blind, Becker suggested. He shows how a broad spectrum of Westerners, from economists to Maoist supporters, were misled by Chinese information that asserted there was no starvation and only bad weather was causing slight supply problems. Some Sinophiles even make Mao out as an averter of a famine rather than an instigator.

Many critics found *Hungry Ghosts* to be powerful, if somewhat gruesome. Caroline Moorehead of the *New Statesman* called it a "a painstakingly readable account of the famine that engulfed China. . . . It is as full as possible, given the restrictions on information, lost archives and a continuing attitude of secrecy." "A horrifying but excellent book," she concluded. Writing for the *Wall Street Journal,* Paul G. Pickowicz called *Hungry Ghosts* "an important, sometimes spellbinding, account of this terrible episode." He did, however, disagree with some of Becker's conclusions, namely that "even now in the West the famine is still not accepted as a historical event." Another complaint was voiced by Richard Bernstein in the *New York Times:* "Sometimes he includes information without giving the reasons he found the information credible." Nevertheless, Bernstein admitted the book was "remarkable." A *New York Times Book Review* article by Nicholas Eberstadt claimed that Becker "has offered both a grim tribute to the dead and a challenge to our consciences."

Jasper Becker told *CA:* "My interests are Oriental cultures, Buddhism, Chinese politics, archaeology, central Asia, and international politics. These stem from twelve years as a correspondent in Brussels, Geneva, and especially Peking."

BIOGRAPHICAL/CRITICAL SOURCES:

PERIODICALS

London Review of Books, July 18, 1996, p. 3, 5.
New Statesman, June 14, 1996, pp. 44-45.
New York Times, February 5, 1997, p. C15.
New York Times Book Review, February 16, 1997, p. 6.
Spectator, June 29, 1996, p. 33-34.
Times Literary Supplement, October 25, 1996, p. 3.
Wall Street Journal, February 7, 1997, p. A16.*

*   *   *

BECKER, Stephen (David) 1927-
   (Steve Dodge)

PERSONAL: Born March 31, 1927, in Mount Vernon, NY; son of David (a pharmacist) and Lillian (Kevitz) Becker; married Mary Elizabeth Freeburg, December 24, 1947; children: Keir, Julia, David. *Education:* Harvard University, A.B., 1947; Yenching University, graduate studies, 1947-48. *Politics:* Democrat.

CAREER: Free-lance writer, translator, and editor, 1949—, living in China, France, Alaska, the Guianas, and the United States. Teaching fellow in history, Brandeis University, 1951-52; visiting professor of English, University of Alaska, summer, 1967; teacher in literature, Bennington College, fall, 1971; University of Central Florida, Orlando, professor of English, 1987—. *Military service:* U.S. Marine Corps, 1945.

AWARDS, HONORS: Guggenheim fellowship in creative writing, 1954.

WRITINGS:

NOVELS, EXCEPT AS INDICATED

The Season of the Stranger, Harper (New York City), 1951.

Shanghai Incident, Gold Medal (New York City), 1955.

Juice, Simon & Schuster (New York City), 1959.

Comic Art in America (history), Simon & Schuster, 1960.

Marshall Field III (biography), Simon & Schuster, 1964.

A Covenant with Death, Atheneum (New York City), 1965.

The Outcasts, Atheneum, 1967.

When the War Is Over, Random House (New York City), 1970.

Dog Tags, Random House, 1972.

The Chinese Bandit, Random House, 1975.

The Last Mandarin, Random House, 1979.

The Blue-Eyed Shan, Random House, 1982.

A Rendezvous in Haiti, Norton (New York City), 1987.

Also author of screenplays, short stories, magazine articles and reviews.

TRANSLATOR

Romain Gary, *Colors of the Day,* Simon & Schuster, 1953.

P. D. Gaisseau, *Sacret Forest,* Knopf (New York City), 1954.

Louis Carl and Joseph Petit, *Mountains in the Desert,* Doubleday (New York City), 1954 (published in England as *Tefedest: Journey to the Heart of the Sahara,* D. Allen, 1954).

Andre Dhotel, *Faraway,* Simon & Schuster, 1957.

R. Puissesseau, *Someone Will Die Tonight in the Caribbean,* Knopf, 1958.

A. Schwarz-Bart, *The Last of the Just,* Atheneum, 1960.

Elie Wiesel, *The Town beyond the Wall,* Atheneum, 1964.

Andre Malraux, *The Conquerors,* Holt (New York City), 1976.

Louis-Philippe, *Diary of My Travels in America,* Delacorte (New York City), 1978.

Agustin Gomez-Arcos, *Ana No,* Secker & Warburg, 1980.

Weisel, *The Forgotten,* Schoken (New York City), 1995.

ADAPTATIONS: A Covenant with Death was filmed by Warner Bros. in 1967.

SIDELIGHTS: The details of Stephen Becker's real life are the stuff by which one of his acclaimed novels may be made: a prodigious student (reading by age three); Harvard scholarship winner at 16; U.S. Marine on active duty at age 17; a whirlwind wedding; professor in Peking, China, by age 21; then survived a life-threatening illness to become an acclaimed author and world traveler.

Today, "equally distinguished as a translator, a biographer, a commentator on the popular arts and a novelist" (as William J. Schafer describes him in a *Contemporary Novelists* essay), Becker "brings to his fiction a breadth of experience with world culture and human behavior which yields moral complexity and psychological verity in his work." Becker's first novel, *The Season of the Stranger*—an autobiographical story of a young American professor in the months preceding Peking's liberation—is recalled by the author in his essay for *Contemporary Authors Autobiography Series* as "grotesquely overwritten" but nonetheless "quite well reviewed . . . probably so dense and awkward that the reviewers decided it must be serious."

Becker needn't have justified the favorable reviews of his subsequent works, including *A Covenant with Death, The Outcasts* and *Juice.* As a whole, critics such as Stephen Geller of the *New York Times Book Review* finds the author's style "fluid and graceful," that his language is "acutely and effectively imagistic." *The Outcasts,* which tells of a group of engineers trying to build a bridge deep in the jungle, touches on common Becker themes—"men struggling with themselves, with nature and with circumstances to become fully alive and functioning human beings," as Schafer puts it. In her review of *The Outcasts, Harper's* critic Katherine Gauss Jackson writes: "Mr. Becker is incapable of writing a dull or frivolous book. There is flavor and reason in everything he has to say."

Contemporary Novelists essayist Schafer goes on to call *When the War Is Over* Becker's "most satisfying novel. It is the story of the last victim of the Civil War, a boy executed as a Confederate guerrilla long after hostilities had ceased. The moral struggle is embodied in [the character of] a young career officer caught between a genuine love of peace and justice and a natural inclination toward the arts of war."

Becker's self-admitted favorite among his works is another war story, *Dog Tags.* He wrote in *Contemporary Authors Autobiography Series* that this story "is closest to my own life . . . in theme and event." He adds that he sought to create "the only accurate North Korean prison camp in American fiction. Jewishness [Becker's family is of Jewish extraction] was a minor theme; healing, a major; love and betrayal omnipresent; the marriage, between two invincibly decent people, better than most but eternally wrong. The prose sings, to me anyway—there is scarcely a sentence in the book that does not bear more than its own weight."

BIOGRAPHICAL/CRITICAL SOURCES:

BOOKS

Contemporary Authors Autobiography Series, Volume 1, Gale (Detroit), 1984.
Contemporary Novelists, sixth edition, St. James Press (Detroit), 1996.

PERIODICALS

Chicago Tribune Book World, May 13, 1979.
Harper's, April, 1967.
Kirkus Reviews, May 1, 1987.
Newsweek, March 20, 1967.
New York Times, February 16, 1967; November 7, 1969.
New York Times Book Review, March 19, 1967; November 9, 1969.
Saturday Review, April 1, 1967.
Time, March 17, 1967.
Tribune Books (Chicago), July 5, 1987.*

* * *

BECKHAM, Barry (Earl) 1944-

PERSONAL: Born March 19, 1944, in Philadelphia, PA; son of Clarence and Mildred (Williams) Beckham; married Betty Louise Hope, February 19, 1966 (divorced, 1977); married Geraldine Lynne Palmer, 1979; children: (first marriage) Brian Elliott, Bonnie Lorine. *Education:* Brown University, A.B., 1966; attended Columbia University Law School. *Religion:* Episcopalian.

ADDRESSES: Home—140 Lancaster St., Providence, RI 02906. *Office*—Department of English, Brown University, Brown Station, Providence, RI 02912. *Agent*—William Morris Agency, 1350 Ave. of the Americas, New York, NY 10019.

CAREER: Chase Manhattan Bank, New York City, public relations consultant, 1966-67, urban affairs associate, 1969-70; National Council of Young Men's Christian Associations, New York City, public relations consultant, 1967-68; Western Electric Co., New York City, public relations associate, 1968-69; Brown University, Providence, RI, visiting lecturer, 1970-72, assistant professor, 1972-78, associate professor of English, 1979—, director of Graduate Program in Creative Writing, 1980—. Visiting professor, University of Wyoming, 1972. Member of literature panel, Rhode Island Council on the Arts, 1980—. President, Beckham House Publishers, Inc., Hampton, VA.

MEMBER: Authors Guild, Authors League of America, PEN (member of executive board, American Center, 1970-71).

WRITINGS:

My Main Mother (novel), Walker (New York City), 1969, published in England as *Blues in the Night,* Tandem, 1974.
Runner Mack (novel), Morrow (New York City), 1972.
Garvey Lives! (play), produced in Providence, RI, 1972.
Double Dunk (novel), Holloway House (Los Angeles), 1981.
(Editor and contributor) *The Black Student's Guide to Colleges* (nonfiction), Dutton (New York City), 1982, revised edition, Beckham House (Providence, RI), 1984.
(Editor) *The College Selection Workbook,* 2nd edition, Beckham House, 1987.
(Editor and contributor) *The Black Student's Guide to Scholarships* (nonfiction), 1996.

Contributor to *Black Review, Brown Alumni Monthly, Esquire, Intellectual Digest, New York, New York Times,* and *Novel.* Papers held in permanent collection at Mugar Memorial Library, Boston University.

WORK IN PROGRESS: A portrait of Chase Manhattan Bank; another novel.

SIDELIGHTS: Barry Beckham's reputation rests on two novels written at the end of the 1960s. His first novel, *My Main Mother,* won praise as the probing account of a young black man and the events that lead him to murder his mother. Narrated by its protagonist, Mitchell Mibbs, the novel is "basically . . . a psychological study of the ruinous effect on a child who is either ignored or tormented by a parent," wrote Peter Rowley in the *New York Times Book Review.* Mitchell's beautiful, alcoholic mother, Pearl, who dreams of becoming a rich and famous singer, shuns and abandons the fatherless boy. Mitchell's lone source of support and companionship is a kindly uncle, whose death "and the horror of a sordid squabble over his money spur Mitchell into matricide," Rowley noted. A *Times Literary Supplement* contributor observed that "the single act of violence towards which the book works appropriately underlines the particular, personal anxieties which made it, for Mitchell, an inevitability." Less prominently featured, yet as influential as the psychological devastation of Mitchell's upbringing, are the forces of racism in a white dominant society. "Throughout, racial themes are both present and understated," remarked Frank Campenni in *Contemporary Novelists,* "while authentic portrayal of main characters, skillfull use of point-of-view, and vivid imagery earn our attention."

Unlike most novels featuring black characters published during this period, *My Main Mother* abdures social realism or naturalism for "a blend of verbal impressionism and surrealism," according to Campenni, who nonetheless noted affinities between the plot and thematic concerns of Beckham's first book with such pivotal works of black fiction as *Native Son and Black Boy.* Indeed, remarked Joe Weixlmann in *Dictionary of Literary Biography,* though "Beckham's first novel lacks the ideological breadth and some of the stylistic sophistication" of *Runner Mack,* his second novel, each "is marked by stylistic innovation and the author's ability to hold the comic and the pathetic in equipoise."

"If Barry Beckham's second book is as brilliant as the second half of his first," predicted *New York Times Book Review* critic Rowley, "he may well become one of the best American novelists of the decade." While Beckham's fame has never measured up to such predictions, in *Runner Mack* he "move[s] far beyond the boundaries of his first novel," Mel Watkins contended in the *New York Times Book Review.* The story of the education of Henry Adams, a naive Southern black man who moves to the North to find fortune as a professional baseball player, *Runner Mack* is considered to be more directly critical of an American society permeated with racism. Like Ralph Ellison in

Invisible Man, "Beckham casts his young innocent in a picaresque narrative reprise of black-American history, with emphasis on the absurdity of American rituals and the indecencies of American institutions," noted Campenni. Thus, Adams moves from the world of professional sports, where he is cheated of his chance by a white midget manager, to the world of business, where he finds himself in a dead-end job, and then receives notification from the draft board that he must report for duty in the "Alaska War." These scenes, which comprise the first half of the novel, are interspersed with "dreamlike sequences," according to Campenni, in which the violence and perfidy of the white world are blatant. In the second half of the novel, Adams meets "Runner" Mack, a revolutionary who takes Adams under his wing and convinces him to join in a plan to blow up the White House. Phyllis Rauch Klotman commented in *Another Man Gone: The Black Runner in Contemporary Afro-American Literature* that "each experience in the novel is a kind of education," and notes a disturbing continuity in that "Henry moves from one mad, dehumanizing way of life to another."

"Its humor and burlesque notwithstanding," wrote Watkins in a similar vein, *Runner Mack* ". . . is an unsettling book." Watkins continued: "By creating an ironic verbal world, [Beckham] has produced an allegory that both illuminates the despair and recurring frustration that has characterized blacks' struggle for freedom and brilliantly satirizes the social conditions that perpetuate that frustration." As such, *Runner Mack* has far-reaching implications. "Rather than proposing some simpleminded solution to the ethical dilemmas caused by this country's racial prejudices . . . , Beckham causes the reader of *Runner Mack* to contemplate what he or she might do to ameliorate the deplorable condition of current-day America," concluded Weixlmann. "*Runner Mack* is a tightly wrought masterpiece which probes deeply into the American psyche."

Following the publication of these two works and the successful production of his play, *Garvey Lives!* at Brown University, where Beckham taught, the author began work on a fictionalized biography of basketball player Earl "The Goat" Manigault. The resulting book, *Double Dunk,* manages to avoid being "a maudlin, cautionary tale about the deleterious effects of Harlem ghetto existence," according to Weixlmann, through Beckham's use of a second-person narrator, and the infusion of humor and surrealistic imagery into an otherwise bleak tale of the rapid rise and fall of a basketball star due to drug addiction. Beckham has published no fiction since *Double Dunk,* concentrating his efforts on his publishing company, Beckham House Publishers, and his work on nonfiction projects, including *The Black Student's Guide to Colleges* and *The College Selection Workbook.*

BIOGRAPHICAL/CRITICAL SOURCES:

BOOKS

Beckham, Barry, *Runner Mack,* Morrow, 1972.
Contemporary Novelists, St. James Press (Detroit), 1996.
Dictionary of Literary Biography, Volume 33: *Afro-American Fiction Writers after 1955,* Gale (Detroit), 1984, pp. 17-20.
Klotman, Phyllis Rauch, *Another Man Gone: The Black Runner in Contemporary Afro-American Literature,* Kennikat Press, 1977.

PERIODICALS

Black Images, autumn, 1974.
MELUS, winter, 1981.
Modern Fiction Studies, spring, 1987, p. 73.
New York Times, October 10, 1982.
New York Times Book Review, November 30, 1969; September 17, 1972; November 25, 1984, p. 44.
Studies in Black Literature, winter, 1974.
Times Literary Supplement, February 12, 1971.
Variety, January 14, 1970.

*   *   *

BENNER, Judith Ann 1942-

PERSONAL: Born August 8, 1942, in Herrin, IL; daughter of Herbert, Jr. (in U.S. Air Force) and Dorothy (a federal civil servant; maiden name, Stewart) Benner. *Education:* San Antonio College, A.A., 1963; Southwest Texas State College (now University), B.A., 1965; Trinity University, San Antonio, TX, M.A., 1967; Texas Christian University, Ph.D., 1975. *Avocational interests:* Reading, walking, music, movies, jigsaw puzzles.

ADDRESSES: Office—c/o BCI, 2210 Basse Rd., San Antonio, TX 78213.

CAREER: Trinity University Press, San Antonio, TX, editorial assistant, 1967-68; Bethesda Christian Institute, San Antonio, instructor, 1976-81; *Heritage* (pe-

riodical), Duncan, OK, editor, 1981-84; Bethesda Christian Institute, assistant principal and instructor, 1985-96; BCI Interim Librarian, 1995.

MEMBER: Sigma Tau Sigma, Beta Phi Gamma, Pi Gamma Mu, Alpha Chi, Phi Alpha Theta.

AWARDS, HONORS: Grant from Association of Former Students of Texas A & M University, 1979, for *Sul Ross: Soldier, Statesman, Educator; Sul Ross* was named the "best historical publication of 1983" in local history division by Texas Historical Commission.

WRITINGS:

(With George H. Paschal, Jr.) *One Hundred Years of Challenge and Change: A History of the Synod of Texas of the United Presbyterian Church in Texas,* Trinity University Press (San Antonio, TX), 1968.
Fraudulent Finance: Counterfeiting and the Confederate States, Hill Junior College Press (Hillsborough, TX), 1970.
Lone Star Rebel, John Blair (Winston-Salem, NC), 1971.
(Contributor) W. C. Nunn, editor, *Ten More Texas in Gray,* Hill Junior College Press, 1980.
Sul Ross: Soldier, Statesman, Educator, Texas A & M University Press (College Station), 1983.
Uncle Comanche, Texas Christian University Press (Fort Worth), 1996.

Contributor to the periodical *Military History of Texas and the Southwest* and new *Handbook of Texas.* Editor, *Seventh Trumpet* magazine, 1984—.

WORK IN PROGRESS: "Two sequels to *Uncle Comanche;* a story of a white boy raised by Indians; a juvenile novel about the 'Reservation War' here in Texas; editing Civil War letters of Lawrence S. Ross; a juvenile novel about the Third Crusade; research on the Trojan legends of the Celts."

SIDELIGHTS: Judith Ann Benner told *CA:* "I loved books and stories even before I learned to read, and then I read everything I could get my hands on, especially history, horse, and adventure stories. In middle school I started writing western stories and poetry, although I didn't really become serious about being a writer until I took journalism in high school. At the same time, I became interested in the research and writing of history, and over the years I have tried to combine the two interests. My book-publishing career started in 1968 when I co-authored a book with a blind professor. (My book-writing career began when I was sixteen and wrote my first but never published novel, a Civil War western).

"While working on my master's degree I ran across a mention of counterfeiting and the Confederacy which aroused my curiosity. There was no detailed study of the subject available although it was a serious problem during the Civil War. I made it my thesis topic, and in 1979 Hill Junior College Press published my book on counterfeiting.

"About the same time I became fascinated with the life of a popular nineteenth century Texan, Lawrence Sullivan 'Sul' Ross—Indian fighter and friend, ranger, Confederate general, peace officer, constitutional convention delegate, state legislator, governor, and college president. As in the case of counterfeiting, here was a subject worthy of a detailed study but lacking one. I began serious research on Ross before I entered TCU [Texas Christian University] to work on my Ph.D.

"During this time I combined my background knowledge on counterfeiting and Ross to write my first published novel for young people, *Lone Star Rebel*. It is the story of a fourteen-year-old Texas boy who leaves home during the Civil War to join Sul Ross's Sixth Texas Cavalry and helps to bring a band of counterfeiters to justice. I had a lot of fun doing this book, particularly as I had vowed in high school to write a book someday with dogs and guns and horses in it. It turned out the dogs were in somewhat short supply, but there were plenty of guns, and my own registered Galiceno, Capitan, appeared in it as the young hero's mustang pony. A lot of the fictional Bugler's antics were those pulled by Capitan in the years when I rode almost every day. *Lone Star Rebel* is out of print now but still selling nicely, I understand, on the rare book market. Someday I hope to write the sequel to LSR which brings Rob and Bugler safely home at the end of the war.

"At TCU my major professor's early retirement forced me to limit my projected biography of Ross to his military career. After receiving my Ph.D. I went into teaching, and in 1979 the Association of Former Students of Texas A & M University gave me a grant to complete my biography of Ross. It was published in 1983 and won the Texas Historical Commission award for best historical publication of that year in the local history division.

"My research on Ross's relationship to the Indian tribes here in Texas then opened up a whole new world of information on little known Texan-Indian affairs. For example, in 1860 as a young ranger captain he was threatened with lynching by a lawless white element because he was an 'Indian-lover.' (Ross's father had been an Indian agent, and he had more or less grown up around the friendly reservation tribes). My second young adult novel, *Uncle Comanche,* grew out of this research and also new material about Ross's childhood which came to light after my biography was published.

"At the same time, I wanted to explore the complex white-Indian relations on the pre-Civil War Texas frontier, so in my mind *Uncle Comanche* was only the first of what I hope would be a series of books on the subject. Right now I have at least four others in mind: I have written the immediate sequel to UC which deals with another adventure with Sul's Comanche friend Runs Fast. I am polishing it while I have started the next book in the series which completes the Sul-Runs Fast trilogy and chronicles the deteriorating white-Comanche relations of the time. It is a story of friends from two different worlds wanting to understand each other and yet being pulled apart by events over which they have no control. Since TCU Press is not going to publish any more young adult books after 1998, I am looking for a publisher for my other manuscripts.

"When I write a novel, the important scenes come to me first. (In UC, the first scene I 'saw' was Sul riding slung over Sergeant Mason's saddle saying, 'I'm going to puke.') I write these scenes down and put them in a ring binder along with any notes that come to mind in order in which I think they will appear in the story. The ring binder makes it easy to move the pages around and add to them. Then I join the major scenes with notes and ideas, although these sometimes change during the writing process. What really fascinates me is the way the characters interact, sometimes seemingly on their own, and often change the direction of the story itself.

"What also interests me is the way created characters have of developing a life of their own. Hanse Mason was the hard-bitten sergeant who gave the young hero of LSR a hard time and later friendship. In UC he developed into the boyhood mentor of Sul Ross, and now I am doing research for a novel which is Hanse's own story and chronicles his life with the Comanches. There's a lot of my late father, a career military man, in Sergeant Mason. The relationship is even more special since there are rumors in our family that my father had Choctaw Indian blood through his grandmother who was supposedly a descendant of Chief Greenwood of Mississippi.

"I have several other history monographs for which I am doing research, and I would certainly like to continue writing historical novels for middle school students. One of the reasons I chose to write for this age group was that I wished to avoid the adult themes of so many modern novels. However, I do have a historical novel for adults 'rolling around' in my mind, and perhaps someday I will actually have a chance to write it."

BIOGRAPHICAL/CRITICAL SOURCES:

PERIODICALS

Fort Worth Press, January 9, 1972.
Review of Texas Books, summer, 1996.
Voice of Youth Advocates, October, 1996.

*   *   *

BERNARD, Jay
   See FORBES, Colin

*   *   *

BLAKE, Margaret
   See TRIMBLE, Barbara Margaret

*   *   *

BONDIE, J. D.
   See CUNNINGHAM, Chet

*   *   *

BOYER, Richard Lewis 1943-
   (Rick Boyer)

PERSONAL: Born October 13, 1943, in Evanston, IL; son of Paul Frederick (an attorney) and Betty (Hatton) Boyer; married Elaine Edith Smudsky, June 29, 1968

(divorced, 1983); children: Clayton Paul, Thomas Edward. *Education:* Denison University, B.A., 1965; University of Iowa, M.F.A., 1968. *Politics:* Independent. *Religion:* Roman Catholic.

ADDRESSES: Home—18 Colonial Pl., Asheville, NC 28804. *Office*—Places Rated Partnership, P.O. Box 8040, Asheville, NC 22814. *Agent*—Helen Rees, 308 Commonwealth Ave., Boston, MA 02116.

CAREER: New Trier High School, Winnetka, IL, English teacher, 1968-70; Little, Brown & Co. (publishers), Boston, MA, textbook salesman, 1971-73, acquisitions editor in College Division, 1973-78; Places Rated Partnership, Asheville, NC, founding partner, 1978—; Western Carolina University, Cullowhee, NC, assistant professor of English, 1988—.

MEMBER: Mystery Writers of America, International Crime Writers Association.

AWARDS, HONORS: Chicago Geographic Society publication award, 1981, for *Places Rated Almanac;* Edgar Award for best novel, Mystery Writers of America, 1982, for *Billingsgate Shoal.*

WRITINGS:

The Giant Rat of Sumatra (mystery novel), Warner Books (New York City), 1976.

"DOCTOR CHARLIE ADAMS" SERIES; MYSTERY NOVELS; UNDER NAME RICK BOYER

Billingsgate Shoal, Houghton (Boston, MA), 1982.
The Penny Ferry, Houghton, 1984.
The Daisy Ducks, Houghton, 1986.
Moscow Metal, Houghton, 1987.
The Whale's Footprints, Houghton, 1988.
Gone to Earth, Fawcett (New York City), 1990.
Yellow Bird, Fawcett, 1992.
Pirate Trade, Ivy (New York City), 1995.

"PLACES RATED" SERIES; UNDER NAME RICK BOYER

(With David Savagau) *Places Rated Almanac: Your Guide to Finding the Best Places to Live in America,* Rand McNally (Chicago, IL), 1981, 2nd edition, 1985.
(With Savagau) *Places Rated Retirement Guide,* Rand McNally, 1983.
(With Savagau) *Rand McNally Retirement Places Rated,* Rand McNally, 1987.

SIDELIGHTS: Richard Lewis Boyer is best known as the author of an Edgar Award-winning mystery series featuring amateur detective and oral surgeon Doctor Charlie Adams. Doc Adams, as he is most commonly known, has "a lucrative practice in the well-to-do suburban community of Concord, Massachusetts," explains Jim Huang in the *St. James Guide to Crime and Mystery Writers.* He also owns a private home on Cape Cod, a boat, and an expensive motorcycle—all of which puts him in a very elite group of people. "Doc Adams is my attempt to create a character," says Boyer in the *St. James Guide to Crime and Mystery Writers,* "who . . . mirrors—in his socioeconomic class and in his lifestyle and tastes—the readers of suspense and thriller books (who, surveys show, are the top 2-5% of the population in income, education, and intelligence)."

Boyer's first mystery novel was not in fact part of the Doc Adams series, but was instead a Sherlock Holmes pastiche. He tells *CA* that he began *The Giant Rat of Sumatra* in 1970. "From the time of its conception, it was to be a serious attempt to continue the Sherlockian saga much as Sir Arthur Conan Doyle would have written it were he still alive." "The story, inspired by *The Hound of the Baskervilles,*" says Huang, "offers some intriguing hints of the direction Boyer's writing would take, including, of course, the curious parallel of the two medical men who shun their practices in order to pursue challenging, exciting, and entertaining adventures."

Doc Adam's first outing was in the Edgar Award-winning *Billingsgate Shoal.* It established a pattern that Boyer follows in the rest of his mystery novels. Doc becomes accidentally involved in a mystery (he spots a strange boat stranded on the coast near his Cape Cod residence) which results in the death of a family friend. "Doc feels responsible," explains Huang, and he begins an investigation of his own. "The investigation becomes quite complicated and rather dangerous, but Doc doesn't let go. He must find his friend's killer. His persistence and his sense of justice are powerful. It's also more fun than oral surgery." "The strength of Rick Boyer's novels," concludes Huang, "is that while Doc's lifestyle isn't average, he remains a figure with whom the average person can identify. His adventures are demanding, but for the most part, Boyer successfully puts us in Doc's shoes and allows us to come along as participants rather than mere observers."

This same desire for fun and excitement motivates Doc through a series of seven more adventures. Doc,

says Boyer, "longs for some sort of escape from this tedious treadmill (the parallels with Sherlock Holmes and Doctor Watson might be obvious here). Doc usually gets relief from his boredom; the trouble is, it's usually quite a bit more than he's bargained for." "If he's lucky," writes *New York Times Book Review* contributor Marilyn Stasio in her review of *Gone to Earth,* "some mad-dog killer will stray onto his suburban patch, and before you can say 'Cancel that 2 o'clock root canal, nurse,' he's oiled his service revolver and is tearing off in his BMW after truth, justice, and kicks."

Several reviewers have remarked on the contrast between Doc Adam's vocation and the ease with which he handles himself in dangerous situations. A *Kirkus Reviews* critic, writing about *Moscow Metal,* calls the book's plot "early-Hitchcock" but adds that, with Boyer's "textured characterization, dry humor, and subdued background details," the story resists "becoming silly or cartoonish." "Not for everyone, perhaps," the reviewer concludes, "but an appealing blend of Yankee charm and gritty derring-do nonetheless." "If we never really buy that a dentist could outfight a KGB assassin," writes Bill Ott in his *Booklist* review of the same book, "we return to our own 'dun-colored days' realizing that it doesn't hurt to pretend once in a while."

BIOGRAPHICAL/CRITICAL SOURCES:

BOOKS

St. James Guide to Crime and Mystery Writers, 4th edition, St. James Press (Detroit), 1996.

PERIODICALS

Booklist, June 15, 1987, pp. 1562-63.
Kirkus Reviews, August 1, 1986, p. 1159; June 1, 1987, p. 824; September 1, 1991, p. 1118.
Library Journal, July, 1986, p. 114.
Los Angeles Times Book Review, September 9, 1990, p. 10.
New York Times Book Review, September 21, 1986, p. 37; September 30, 1990, p. 32.
Publishers Weekly, September 13, 1991, p. 66.

*   *   *

BOYER, Rick
See BOYER, Richard Lewis

BRECHT, (Eugen) Bertolt (Friedrich) 1898-1956

PERSONAL: Born February 10, 1898, in Augsburg, Germany; died of a coronary thrombosis in East Berlin, East Germany (now Germany), August 14, 1956; son of Berthold Friedrich (a paper mill manager) and Sofie Brezing Brecht; married Marianne Zoff, November 3, 1922 (divorced, 1927); married Helene Weigel, April 10, 1929; children: (first marriage) Hanne Hiob; (second marriage), Stefan, Marie Barbara. *Education:* Attended Munich University, 1917-21. *Politics:* Marxist. *Religion:* Raised as a Protestant.

CAREER: Playwright, poet, and director. Worked as a dramaturge for the Deutsches Theater during the early 1920s, ending 1925. Founder, Berliner Ensemble. *Military service:* Worked as an orderly in an Augsburg hospital, 1918.

AWARDS, HONORS: First prize, *Berliner Illustrierte Zeitung,* 1928, for short story "Die Bestie"; Stalin Freedom Prize, 1955.

WRITINGS:

PLAYS

Baal (also see below), Kiepenheuer (Potsdam), 1922, translated by Eric Bentley as *Baal* in *Baal, A Man's a Man, and The Elephant Calf,* Grove, 1964, reprinted, 1989.

Trommeln in der Nacht (also see below), Drei Masken (Munich), 1922, edited by Volkmar Sander, Blaisdell, 1969, translated by Anselm Hollo and others as *Drums in the Night* in *Jungle of Cities and Other Plays,* Grove, 1966.

(With Lion Feuchtwanger) *Leben Eduards des Zweiten von England: Nach Marlowe, Histoire* (also see below), Kiepenheuer, 1924, translated by Bentley as *Edward II: A Chronicle Play,* Grove, 1966.

Im Dickicht der Staedte: Der Kampf zweier Maenner in der Riesenstadt Chicago (also see below), Propylaeen (Berlin), 1927, translated by Hollo as *Jungle of Cities* in *Jungle of Cities and Other Plays,* Grove, 1966.

Mann ist Mann: Die Verwandlung des Packers Galy Gay in den Militaerbaracken von Kilkoa im Jahre 1925: Lustspiel (also see below), Propylaeen, 1927, translated by Bentley as *A Man's a Man* in *Baal, A Man's a Man, and The Elephant Calf,* Grove, 1964, reprinted, 1989.

(With Feuchtwanger) *Drei angelsaechsische Stuecke,* Propylaeen-Verlag, 1927.

Aufstieg und Fall der Stadt Mahagonny: Oper in drei Akten (also see below), music by Kurt Weill, Universal-Edition, 1929, translated by Guy Stern as a brochure entitled *Rise and Fall of the City of Mahagonny* accompanying the recorded version, Columbia, 1959, published in book form as *The Rise and Fall of the City of Mahagonny & The Seven Deadly Sins of the Petty Bourgeoisie,* Arcade Publishers (New York City), 1994.

Die Dreigroschenoper (based on John Gay's *The Beggar's Opera;* also see below), music by Weill, Universal-Edition, 1929, translated by Bentley and Desmond Vesey as *The Threepenny Opera,* Grove, 1964, reprinted, 1983.

Der Jasager und der Neinsager (first produced in 1930; also see below), Suhrkamp, 1966.

Das Badener Lehrstueck von Einverstaendnis (also see below), first produced in 1930.

Die Massnahme (first produced in 1931; also see below), translated by Carl Mueller as *The Measures Taken* in *The Measures Taken and Other Lehrstuecke,* Methuen, 1977.

Die heilige Johanna der Schlachthoefe: Schauspiel (first produced in 1932; also see below), Kiepenheuer, 1932, translated by Frank Jones as *Saint Joan of the Stockyards,* Indiana University Press, 1969.

Die Mutter (first produced in 1933; also see below), Kiepenheuer, 1933, translated by Lee Baxandall as *The Mother,* Grove, 1965, reprinted, 1989.

Die Rundkoepfe und die Spitzkoepfe (also see below), first produced in 1936, translated by N. Goold-Vershoyle as *Roundheads and Peakheads* in *Jungle of Cities and Other Plays,* Grove, 1966.

Die Ausnahme und die Regel (also see below), first produced in 1937, translated by Bentley as *The Exception and the Rule: A Play in Nine Scenes,* Boston Publishing, 1961.

Die Gewehre der Frau Carrar (first produced in 1937; also see below), Aufbau (Berlin), 1957, translated by George Tabori as *The Guns of Carrar,* Samuel French, 1971.

(With Margarete Steffin) *Das Verhoer des Lukullus: Oper in 12 Bildern* (first produced in 1940; also see below), music by Paul Dessau, Aufbau, 1951.

Furcht und Elend des Dritten Reichs (also see below), Meshdunarodnaja Kniga (Moscow), 1941, Aurora, 1945, translated as *Fear and Misery in the Third Reich,* Mezhdunarodnaya Kniga, 1942, translated by Bentley as *The Private Life of the Master Race,* New Directions, 1944.

Leben des Galilei (first produced in 1943; revised English version with Charles Laughton produced in California, 1947; second revised version produced in 1957), Suhrkamp, 1955, translated by Vesey as *The Life of Galileo,* Methuen, 1960, reprinted, 1986, translated by Laughton as *Galileo,* Grove, 1966.

(With Ruth Berlau) *Der kaukasische Kreidekreis* (first produced in 1949; also see below), Suhrkamp, 1955, translated by Bentley and Maja Apelman as *The Caucasian Chalk Circle* in *Parables for the Theater: Two Plays by Bertolt Brecht,* University of Minnesota Press, 1948, revised edition, Grove, 1961, published separately as *The Caucasian Chalk Circle,* Grove, 1987, Arcade (New York City), 1994.

Mutter Courage und Ihre Kinder: Eine Chronik aus dem Dreissigjaehrigen Krieg (first produced in 1949; also see below), Suhrkamp, 1949, translated by Bentley as *Mother Courage and Her Children,* Grove, 1949.

Herr Puntila und sein Knecht: Nach Erzaehlungen der Hella Wuolijoki. Volksstueck in 9 Bildern (first produced in 1950; also see below), Desch (Munich), 1948, reprinted as *Herr Puntila und sein Knecht Matti,* edited by Margaret Mare, Methuen, 1962, translated by Gerhard Nellhaus as *Puntila and His Hired Man,* G. Nellhaus, 1960, translated by John Willett as *Mr. Puntila and His Man Matti,* Methuen, 1977.

Die Verurteilung des Lukullus: Oper (also see below), music by Dessau, Aufbau, 1951, translated by H. R. Hays as *The Trial of Lucullus,* New Directions, 1943.

Der Hofmeister (based on the play by Jacob Michael Reinhold Lenz; also see below), edited by Elizabeth Hauptmann, Suhrkamp, 1951, translated by Pip Broughton as *The Tutor,* Applause Theatre Book Publishers, 1988.

(With Berlau and Steffin) *Der gute Mensch von Szechuan* (first produced in 1953; also see below), music by Dessau, Suhrkamp, 1959, translated by Bentley and Apelman as *The Good Woman of Szechuan* in *Parables for the Theater: Two Plays by Bertolt Brecht,* University of Minnesota Press, 1948, revised edition, Grove, 1961, translated by Willett as *The Good Person of Szechuan,* Methuen, 1965.

Die Geschichte der Simone Marchard, first produced in 1956, translated by Arnold Hinchuffe as *The Visions of Simone Marchard,* [London], c. 1961, translated by Mueller, Grove, 1965.

Die Tage der Kommune (also see below), Suhrkamp, 1957, translated by Leonard J. Lehrman as *The Days of the Commune* in *Dunster Drama Review,* Volume 10, number 2, 1971.

Schweyk im Zweiten Weltkrieg, Suhrkamp, 1959, translated by Peter M. Sandler as *Schweyk in the Second World War,* Brandeis University, 1967.

(With Zuckmayer von Verner Arpe) *Aufruhr und Empoerung,* Sveriges Radio, 1959.

Die sieben Todsuenden der Kleinbuerger, Suhrkamp, 1959.

Drums and Trumpets (translation of Brecht's *Pauken und Trompetten* based on *The Recruiting Officer* by George Farquhar), English version by Rose and Martin Kastner, Trinity College, 1963.

Der aufhaltsame Aufstieg des Arturo Ui (also see below), Suhrkamp, 1965, translated by Tabori as *The Resistable Rise of Auturo Ui: A Gangster Spectacle,* Samuel French, 1971.

Turandot oder Der Kongress der Weisswaescher, Suhrkamp, 1967.

Der Brotladen: Ein Stueckfragment, Suhrkamp, 1967.

(With Dorothy Lane) *Happy End,* music by Weill, Routledge, Chapman & Hall, 1983.

POEMS

Taschenpostille: Mit Anleitung, Gesangsnoten und einem Anhange, privately printed, 1926, reprinted, Aufbau, 1958.

Hauspostille: Mit Anleitung, Gesangsnoten und einem Anhang (poems and songs), Propylaeen, 1927, translated by Bentley as *Manual of Piety: A Bilingual Edition,* Grove, 1966.

Lieder, Gedichte, Choere, music by Hanns Eisler, Editions du Carrefour (Paris), 1934.

Svendborger Gedichte; Deutsche Kriegsfibel; Chroniken: Deutsche Satiren fuer den deutschen Freiheitssender, Malik, 1939.

Selected Poems (in German and English), translated and with introduction by Hays, Reynal & Hitchcock, 1947, reprinted, Harcourt, 1975.

Hundert Gedichte, 1918-1950, Aufbau, 1951, reprinted, 1966.

Gedichte, edited by Siegfried Streller, Reclam (Leipzig), 1955.

Gedichte und Lieder, edited by P. Suhrkamp, Suhrkamp, 1956.

Selected Poems, translated by Hays, Grove, 1959.

Ausgewaehlte Gedichte, edited by Siegfried Unseld, Suhrkamp, 1960, reprinted, 1981.

Poems on the Theatre, translated by John Berger and Anna Bostock, Scorpion Press, 1961.

Selected Poems, translated by K. Woelfel, Oxford University Press, 1965.

Liebesgedichte, edited by Hauptmann, Insel Verlag, 1966.

Bertolt Brecht Poems 1913-1956, three volumes, edited by Willett and Manheim, Methuen (London), 1979.

Gedichte fuer Staedtebewohner, edited and with afterword by Franco Buono, Suhrkamp, 1980.

Gedichte aus dem Nachlass, 1913-1956, Suhrkamp, 1982.

COLLECTED WORKS

Versuche, edited by Hauptmann, Volume 1: *Der Flug der Lindberghs; Radiotheorie; Geschichten vom Herrn Keuner; Fatzer, 3,* Kiepenheuer, 1930, Volume 2: *Aufstieg und Fall der Stadt Mahagonny: Oper in drei Akten; Ueber die Oper; Aus dem Lesebuch fuer Staedtebewohner; Das Badener Lehrstueck vom Einverstaendnis,* Kiepenheuer, 1930, Volume 3: *Die Dreigroschenoper; Die Beule: Ein Dreigroschenfilm; Der Dreigroschenprozess,* Kiepenheuer, 1931, Volume 4: *Der Jasager und der Neinsager: Schulopern; Die Massnahme: Lehrstueck,* Kiepenheuer, 1931, Volume 5: *Die heilige Johanna der Schlachthoefe: Schauspiel; Geschichten vom Herrn Keuner,* Kiepenheuer, 1932, Volume 6: *Die drei Soldaten: Ein Kinderbuch,* Kiepenheuer, 1932, Volume 7: *Die Mutter; Geschichte aus der Revolution,* Kiepenheuer, 1933, Volume 9: *Mutter Courage und Ihre Kinder: Eine Chronik aus dem Dreissigjaehrigen Krieg; Anmerkungen; Fuenf Schwierigkeiten beim Schreiben der Wahrheit,* Suhrkamp, 1949, Volume 10: *Herr Puntila und sein Knecht Matti; Chinesische Gedichte; Dis Ausnahme und die Regel,* Suhrkamp, 1950, Volume 11: *Der Hofmeister; Studien: Neue Technik der Schauspielkunst; Uebungsstuecke fuer Schauspieler; Das Verhoer des Lukullus; Anmerkungen ueber die Oper "Die Verurteilung des Lukullus,"* Suhrkamp, 1951, Volume 12: *Der gute Mensch von Sezuan; Kleines Organon fuer das Theater; Ueber reimlose Lyrik mit unregelmaessigen Rhythmen; Geschichten vom Herrn Keuner,* Suhrkamp, 1953, extra volume: *Die Gewehre der Frau Carrar; Der Augsburger Kreidedreis; Neue Kinderlieder,* Volume 13: *Der kaukasische Kreidekreis; Weite und Vielfalt der realistischen Schreibweise; Buckower Elegien,* Suhrkamp, 1954, Volume 14: *Leben des Galilei; Gedichte aus dem Messingkauf; Die Horatier und die Kuratier,* Suhrkamp, 1955, Volume 15: *Die Tage der Kommune; Die Dialektik auf dem Theater; Zu "Leben des Galilei"; Drei Reden; Zwei*

Briefe, Suhrkamp, 1957, Volumes 5-8: *Die heilige Johanna der Schlachthoefe: Schauspiel; Die drei Soldaten: Ein Kinderbuch; Die Mutter; Die Rundkoepfe und die Spitzkoepfe,* one volume, Suhrkamp, 1959.

Gesammelte Werke, two volumes, Malik, 1938.

Erste Stuecke, two volumes, Suhrkamp, 1953.

Fruehe Stuecke (contains *Baal, Trommeln in der Nacht,* and *Im Dickicht der Stadt*), Deutscher Taschenbuch, 1953.

Stuecke fuer das Theater am Schiffbauerdamm, three volumes, Suhrkamp, 1955-57.

Stuecke, Volume 1: *Baal, Trommeln in der Nacht, Im Dickicht der Staedte;* Volume 2: *Leben Eduards des Zweiten von England, Mann ist Mann;* Volume 3: *Die Dreigroschenoper, Aufstieg und Fall der Stadt Mahagonny, Das Badener Lehrstueck vom Einverstaendnis;* Volume 4: *Die heilige Johanna der Schlachthoefe: Schauspiel, Der Jasager und der Neinsager, Die Massnahme,* Aufbau, 1956.

Stuecke aus dem Exil; Die Rundkoepfe und die Spitzkoepfe; Furcht und Elend des Dritten Reiches; Die Gewehre der Frau Carrar; Mutter Courage und ihre Kinder; Das Verhoer des Lukullus; Leben des Galilei; Der gute Mensch von Sezuan; Herr Puntila und sein Knecht Matti; Der aufhaltsame Aufstieg des Arturo Ui; Die Geschichte der Simone Marchard; Schweyk im zweiten Weltkrieg; Der kaukasische Kreidekreis; Die Tage der Kommune, five volumes, Suhrkamp, 1957.

Bertolt Brecht (poetry and play selections), edited by Hans Klaehn and Waldemar Sowade, Deutsche Kulturbund, 1958.

Bearbeitungen: Die Antigone des Sophokles; Der Hofmeister; Coriolan; der Prozess der Jeanne d'Arc zu Rouen 1431; Don Juan; Paulsen und Trompeten (Coriolan based on Shakepeare's *Coriolanus; Der Prozess der Jeanne d'Arc zu Rouen 1431* based on the version by Anna Segher; *Don Juan* based on the play by Moliere), two volumes, Suhrkamp, 1959.

Plays (contains *The Caucasian Chalk Circle, The Threepenny Opera, The Trial of Lucullus,* and *The Life of Galileo*), Methuen, 1960.

Seven Plays (contains *In the Swamp, A Man's a Man, Saint Joan of the Stockyards, Mother Courage and Her Children, The Life of Galileo, The Good Woman of Setzuan,* and *The Caucasian Chalk Circle*), edited and with introduction by Bentley, Grove, 1961.

Die drei Johanna-Stuecke (contains *Die heilige Johanna der Schlachthoefe: Schauspiel Die*

Geschichte der Simone Marchard, and *Der Prozess der Jeanne d'Arc zu Rouen 1431*), Fischer Bucherei, 1964.

Geschichten, Volume 1: *Unveroeffentlichte und nicht in Sammlungen enthaltene Geschichten, Eulenspiegelgeschichten,* Volume 2: *Kalender-geschichten, Geschichten vom Herrn Keuner, Fluechtlingsgespraech* (also see below), Suhrkamp, 1965.

The Jewish Wife, and Other Short Plays, translated by Bentley, Grove, 1965.

Einakter: Die Kleinburgerhochzeit, Der Bettler; oder, der tote Hunde, Er treibt einen Teufel aus, Lux in Tenebris, Der Fischzug, Dansen, Was kostet das Eisen?, Suhrkamp, 1966.

Gesammelte Werke, 22 volumes, Suhrkamp, 1967-69, Volumes 1-7: *Stuecke,* translated and edited by Willett and Ralph Manheim as *Collected Plays,* nine volumes, Random House, 1971-73, Volume 8-10: *Gedichte,* translated by Willett and Manheim as *Poems 1913-1956,* Methuen, 1976, Volume 11: *Prosa I,* translated by Willett and Manheim as *Short Stories 1921-1946,* Methuen, 1983, Volumes 15-17: *Schriften zum Theater,* translated by Willett as *Brecht on Theatre,* Hill & Wang, 1964.

Fuenf Lehrstuecke, edited by Keith A. Dickson, Methuen Educational, 1969.

Die Bibel und andere fruehe Einakter, Suhrkamp, 1970.

Lehrstuecke (contains *Der Jasager und der Neinsager, Die Massnahme, Die Ausnahme und die Regel, Die Rundkoepfe und die Spitzkoepfe, Das Badener Lehrstueck von Einverstaendnis*), Rowohlt, 1970.

Werke, five volumes, Aufbau, 1973.

Der Stuecke von Bertolt Brecht in einem Band, Suhrkamp, 1978.

Plays, Continuum, 1994.

OTHER

Ballade vom armen Stabschef +30: Juni 1934, [Germany], 1934.

Dreigroschenroman (novel), Albert de Lange (Amsterdam), 1934, translated by Vesey and Christopher Isherwood as *A Penny for the Poor,* R. Hale, 1937, published as *Threepenny Novel,* Grove, 1956, reprinted, Ungar, 1984.

(Translator) M. Andersen-Nexoe, *Die Kindheit: Erinnerungen,* Vereinigung "Kultur und Volk," 1945.

Kalendergeschichten, Mitteldeutscher Verlag, 1948, Norton, 1960, translated by Yvonne Kapp and Michael Hamburger as *Tales from the Calendar,* Methuen, 1961.

Das Zukunftslied: Aufbaulied der FDJ, music by Dessau, Thueringer Volksverlag (Weimar), 1949.

Sinn und Form: Beitraege zur Literatur, Ruetten & Loening, 1949.

Antigonemodell 1948; Die Antigone des Sophokles, nach der Hoelderlinschen Uebertragung fuer die Buehne, bearbeitet, Weiss, 1949, translated by Judith Malina as *Antigone: With Selections from Brecht's Model Book,* Applause Theatre Book, 1989.

(Contributor) Feuchtwanger, *Auswahl,* Greifen (Rudolstadt), 1949.

(Editor with Dessau) *Wir singen zu den Weltfestspielen: Herrnburger Bericht,* Verlag Neues Leben (Berlin), 1951.

Offener Brief an die deutschen Kuenstler und Schriftsteller, [Berlin], 1951.

Die Erziehung der Hirse, Nach dem Bericht von G. Frisch: Der Mann, der das Unmoegliche wahr gemacht hat, Aufbau, 1951.

An meine Landsleute, VEB Offizin Haag-Drugulin (Leipzig), 1951.

(Editor with Berlau, C. Hubalek, and others), *Theaterarbeit: Sechs Auffuehrungen des Berliner Ensembles,* Dresdner Verlag, 1952.

Kriegsfibel, edited by Berlau, Eulenspiegel (Berlin), 1955.

Die Geschaefte des Herrn Julius Caesar: Romanfragment, Aufbau, 1957.

Lieder und Gesaenge, Henschel (Berlin), 1957.

Schriften zum Theater: Ueber eine nicht-aristotelische Dramatik, edited by Unseld, Suhrkamp, 1957.

Geschichten vom Herrn Keuner, Aufbau, 1958.

Brecht: Ein Lesebuch fuer unsere Zeit, edited by Hauptmann and Benno Slupianek, Volksverlag Weimar, 1958.

Bertolt Brecht in Selbstzeugnissen und Bilddokumenten, compiled by Marianne Wolf-Kesting, edited by Paul Raabe, Rowohlt (Hamburg), 1959.

Kleines Organon fuer das Theater: Mit einem "Nachtrag zum Kleinen Organon," Suhrkamp, 1960, translated by Willett as "A Short Organum for the Theatre" in *Brecht on Theatre,* Hill & Wang, 1964.

Fluechtlingsgespraeche, Suhrkamp, 1961.

Helene Weigel, Actress: A Book of Photographs, translated by Berger and Bostock, VEB Edition (Leipzig), 1961.

Gespraech auf der Probe, Sanssouci (Zurich), 1961.

Dialoge aus dem Messingkauf, Suhrkamp, 1964.

Ueber Lyrik, Suhrkamp, 1964.

(Contributor) Samuel Weiss, editor, *Drama in the Modern World,* Heath, 1964.

Ein Kinderbuch, illustrated by Elizabeth Shaw, Kinderbuchverlag, c. 1965.

Me-ti; Buch der Wendungen-Fragment, edited by Uwe Johnson, Suhrkamp, 1965.

Ueber Klassiker, edited by Unseld, Insel, 1965.

Ueber Theater, edited by Hecht, Reclam, 1966.

Schriften zur Literatur und Kunst, Suhrkamp, 1967.

Schriften zur Politik und Gesellschaft 1919-1956, Suhrkamp, 1968.

Kuehle Wampe: Protokoll des Films und Materialien, edited by Wolfgang Gersch and Werner Hecht, Suhrkamp, 1969.

Politische Schriften, edited by Hecht, Suhrkamp, 1970.

Ueber den Beruf des Schauspielers, Suhrkamp, 1970.

Ueber experimentelles Theater, edited by Hecht, Suhrkamp, 1970.

Brecht Fibel, edited by Reinhold Grimm and Henry J. Schmidt, Harper, 1970.

Herr Bertolt Brecht sagt, Weismann (Munich), 1970.

Ueber die irdische Liebe und andere gewisse Weltraetsel in Liedern und Balladen, Eulenspiegel Verlag (Berlin), 1971.

Ueber Politik auf dem Theater, edited by Hecht, Suhrkamp, 1971.

Ueber Politik und Kunst, edited by Hecht, Suhrkamp, 1971.

Ueber Realismus, edited by Hecht, Suhrkamp, 1971.

Arbeitsjournal 1938 bis 1955, three volumes, Suhrkamp, 1973.

Der Tui-Roman: Fragment, Suhrkamp, 1973.

Tagebuecher 1920-1922: Autobiographische Aufzeichnungen 1920-1954, edited by Herta Ramthun, Suhrkamp, 1975, translated by Willett as *Diaries 1920-1922,* St. Martin's, 1979.

Brecht in Gespraech, Henschelverlag Kunst und Gesellschaft, 1975.

Und der Haifisch, der hat Zaehne: Die grossen Songs und Kleinen Lieder, Henschelverlag (Berlin), 1977.

Ein gemeiner Kerl: Geschichten, edited by Fritz Hofmann, Aufbau, 1978.

Der Staedtebauer: Geschichten und Anekdoten 1919-1956, edited and with afterword by Hubert Witt, Insel, 1978.

Nordseekrabben, Eulenspiegel, 1979.

Briefe, edited and with commentary by Guenter Glaeser, Suhrkamp, 1981, translated by Willett and Manheim as *Brecht Letters,* Routledge, Chapman & Hall, 1989.

Ich leb so gern, Kinderbuchverlag, 1982.

Ueber die bildenden Kuenste, Suhrkamp, 1983.

Kriegsfibel, Eulenspiegel, 1983.

Brecht-Journal, Suhrkamp, 1983.

Fragen an Brecht, Reclam, 1987.

Brecht Letters, Routledge, 1989.

Bertolt Brecht Journals, Routledge, Chapman & Hall, 1993.

Bad Time for Poetry: 152 Poems and Songs, edited by Willett, Methuen (London), 1995.

Contributor to periodical *Internationale Literatur: Deutsche Blaetter,* and to other German publications.

ADAPTATIONS: Die Dreigroschenoper was adapted as a German film by G. W. Pabst in 1931. David Hare has published *"Mother Courage and Her Children," a Version for the National Theatre,* Arcade (New York City), 1996.

SIDELIGHTS: One of the major playwrights of the twentieth century, Bertolt Brecht was renowned for such works as *The Threepenny Opera, Mother Courage and Her Children, The Life of Galileo,* and *The Caucasian Chalk Circle.* Recognized as one of the main innovators of theatrical technique in modern times, Brecht turned away from conventional dramatic devices in favor of the "epic theater" and the use of the *Verfremdungseffekt* ("estrangement effect"). The purpose of his ground-breaking techniques—distinguished by the use of non-climactic, episodic narrative—was to remind his audiences that what they were seeing was not reality, resulting in a distancing effect that was intended to help them absorb what was being said, rather than what the characters were feeling. His plays are, therefore, didactic, rather than dramatic.

First achieving prominence in 1922 with his play *Trommeln in der Nacht* (*Drums in the Night*), about a soldier who rejects the violent existence of World War I in favor of finding a happy domestic life, the playwright revealed an interest in life's social forces even at the beginning of his career. During the chaotic years of post-World War I Germany, the author turned toward Communism as an answer to the anarchy that surrounded him. Because of his belief in the theories of Marxism, the action in many of his plays is driven by economic and political—rather than psychological or emotional—forces.

Die Dreigroschenoper (*The Threepenny Opera*), based on the eighteenth-century comic opera by John Gay, *The Beggar's Opera,* was a dramatic international success for Brecht, but not for the same reasons that he had intended. Audiences enjoyed the irony of Brecht's dialogue and the catchy jazz music written by Kurt Weill, missing the author's comparisons between capitalists and the gangster characters in the play. "If the businessman is identified with the gangster in *The Threepenny Opera,*" noted Robert Brustein in his *The Theatre of Revolt: An Approach to the Modern Drama,* "then he is identified with the warmaker in *Mother Courage.*" In *Mother Courage and Her Children,* a play set during the Thirty Years' War in which a mother unwittingly destroys her family as a result of her attempts to profit from the war, Brecht portrays war as motivated by economics, rather than politics, religion, or nationalism. This play, too, was often misinterpreted by Brecht's audiences, who viewed the protagonist as a tragic human figure, rather than as an example of the folly of capitalism. Modern critics like Brustein have called *Mother Courage* "the culminating work of Brecht's career."

Another well-known Brecht play that also occurs during the Thirty Years' War is *Der kaukasische Kreidekreis* (*The Caucasian Chalk Circle*). The theme of this play, in which a servant girl proves her superior love for her mistress's child over that of its mother, is that "motherhood is based on the bondage created by work and suffering rather than on biological factors," according to *Dictionary of Literary Biography* contributor Siegfried Mews. "In *Der kaukasische Kreidekreis* this new definition of motherhood is expanded to promote a new kind of thinking with regard to property rights." Marxist undertones are also present in Brecht's *Leben des Galilei* (*The Life of Galileo*), which is largely concerned with the famous scientist's recantation of his belief in a heliocentric universe when he is faced with the prospect of punishment by the Catholic Church. With this subject, Brecht was able to portray how outside forces often interfere with social progress.

Despite Brecht's faithful allegiance to Marxism and the propagandistic value of the renowned Berliner Ensemble that he founded during his final years in East Berlin, the Communist world was suspicious of Brecht's art. The West, on the other hand, tended to try to ignore the author's political message and praise his artistic achievement. Of Brecht's influence as a political commentator, *Theatre Arts* critic Alan Pryce-Jones wrote: "It has never been recorded that [his plays have] had the least influence on the political thinking of either Right or Left—and influence towards the establishment of a Marxist Europe was their primary aim." "Whether or not Brecht wrote what are all too glibly called 'great' plays," concluded Harold Clurman in a *New York Times Magazine* article, ". . . it is my conviction that his plays

are the most important to have been written anywhere" in recent times.

Brecht's Marxist leanings come through in the journals he kept while an exile from the Nazis, first in Scandinavia and later in the United States, and after his return to Berlin after appearance before the House Committee on Un-American Activities in 1947. *Bertolt Brecht Journals* contains edited and translated entries from his original journals and includes the newspaper and magazine clippings and photographs he inserted in relevant places. The entries are factual and contain commentary on professional concerns, but are devoid of analysis and human emotion, even when mentioning lovers. Phillip Brantingham declared in the Chicago *Tribune Books* that the journals chronicle "day by day the barren and self-serving soul of the genius Bertolt Brecht." Yet, noted Ned Chaillet in the *New Statesman & Society,* "The journals . . . take us closer to the process of his creation than anything previously published. And, however carefully he guarded his borders, there are revelations everywhere."

BIOGRAPHICAL/CRITICAL SOURCES:

BOOKS

Abel, Lionel, *Metatheatre: A New View of Dramatic Form,* Hill & Wang, 1963.

Arendt, Hannah, *Men in Dark Times,* Harcourt, 1968.

Barthes, Roland, *Critical Essays,* translated by Richard Howard, Northwestern University Press, 1972.

Bartram, Graham, and Anthony Waine, editors, *Brecht in Perspective,* Longman, 1982.

Bauland, Peter, *The Hooded Eagle: Modern German Drama on the New York Stage,* Syracuse University Press, 1968.

Bentley, Eric, *The Playwright as Thinker: A Study of Drama in Modern Times,* Reynal & Hitchcock, 1946.

Bentley, Eric, *In Search of Theater,* Atheneum, 1953.

Bentley, Eric, *Theatre of War: Comments on 32 Occasions,* Viking, 1972.

Bentley, Eric, *The Brecht Commentaries: 1943-1980,* Grove, 1981.

Block, Haskell M., and Herman Salinger, editors, *The Creative Vision: Modern European Writers on Their Art,* Grove, 1960.

Brustein, Robert, *The Theatre of Revolt: An Approach to the Modern Drama,* Little, Brown, 1964.

Clurman, Harold, *The Naked Image: Observations on the Modern Theatre,* Macmillan, 1966.

Clurman, Harold, *The Divine Pastime: Theatre Essays,* Macmillan, 1974.

Cohn, Ruby, *Currents in Contemporary Drama,* Indiana University Press, 1969.

Cook, Bruce, *Brecht in Exile,* Holt, 1983.

Corrigan, Robert W., *The Theatre in Search of a Fix,* Delacorte, 1973.

Demetz, Peter, editor, *Brecht: A Collection of Critical Essays,* Prentice-Hall, 1962.

Dickson, Keith A., *Towards Utopia: A Study of Brecht,* Clarendon Press, 1978.

Dictionary of Literary Biography, Volume 124: *Twentieth-Century German Dramatists, 1919-1992,* Gale, 1992.

Drama Criticism, Gale, Volume 3, 1993.

Eddershaw, Margaret, *Performing Brecht,* Routledge (New York City), 1996.

Ellis, Lorena B., *Brecht's Reception in Brazil,* P. Lang (New York City), 1995.

Esslin, Martin, *Brecht, a Choice of Evils: A Critical Study of the Man, His Work and His Opinions,* Eyre & Spottiswoode, 1959.

Esslin, Martin, *Brecht: The Man and His Work,* Doubleday, 1960.

Esslin, Martin, *Bertolt Brecht,* Columbia University Press, 1969.

Ewen, Frederic, *Bertolt Brecht: His Life, His Art, and His Times,* Citadel, 1967.

Fuegi, John, *Brecht and Company: Sex, Politics, and the Making of the Modern Drama,* Grove Press (New York City), 1994.

Gass, William H., *The World within the Word,* Knopf, 1978.

Gassner, John, *The Theatre in Our Times: A Survey of the Men, Materials and Movements in the Modern Theatre,* Crown, 1954.

Gilman, Richard, *The Making of Modern Drama: A Study of Buechner, Ibsen, Strindberg, Chekhov, Pirandello, Brecht, Beckett, Handke,* Farrar, Straus, 1974.

Gray, Ronald D., *Brecht the Dramatist,* Cambridge University Press, 1976.

Greenberg, Clement, *Art and Culture: Critical Essays,* Beacon Press, 1961.

Grossvogel, David I., *Four Playwrights and a Postscript,* Cornell University Press, 1962.

Hill, Claude, *Bertolt Brecht,* Twayne, 1975.

Horwich, Cara Mary, *Survival in "Simplicissimus" and "Mutter Courage,"* P. Lang (New York City), 1996.

International Bertolt Brecht Symposium (University of Delaware, 1992) with Lyon and Breuer, *Brecht Unbound,* University of Delaward Press (Newark), 1995.

Jones, David Richard, *Great Directors at Work: Stanislavsky, Brecht, Kazan, Brook,* University of California Press, 1986.

Lyons, Charles R., *Bertolt Brecht: The Despair and the Polemic,* Southern Illinois University Press, 1968.

Mews, Siegried, *A Bertolt Brecht Reference Companion,* Greenwood Press (Westport, CT), 1996.

Nagavajara, Chetana, *Brecht and France,* P. Lang (New York City), 1994.

Nathan, George Jean, *The Theatre Book of the Year, 1947-48: A Record and an Interpretation,* Knopf, 1948.

Reinelt, Janelle G., *After Brecht: British Epic Theater,* University of Michigan Press (Ann Arbor), 1994.

Scott, Nathan A., Jr., *Man in the Modern Theatre,* John Knox, 1965.

Spalek, John M., and Robert F. Bell, *Exile: The Writer's Experience,* University of North Carolina Press, 1982.

Styan, J. L., *Modern Drama in Theory and Practice: Expressionism and Epic Theatre,* Volume 3, Cambridge University Press, 1981.

Szczesny, Gerhard, *The Case against Bertolt Brecht, with Arguments Drawn from His "Life of Galileo,"* translated by Alexander Gode, Ungar, 1969.

Thomson, Peter and Glendyr Sacks, *The Cambridge Companion to Brecht,* Cambridge University Press (New York City), 1994.

Thoss, Michael, *Brecht for Beginners,* Writers and Readers Publishers (New York City), 1994.

Twentieth Century Literary Criticism, Gale, Volume 1, 1978, Volume 6, 1982, Volume 13, 1984, Volume 35, 1990.

Voelker, Klaus, *Brecht: A Biography,* translated by John Nowell, Seabury, 1978.

Weideli, Walter, *The Art of Bertolt Brecht,* translated by Daniel Russell, New York University Press, 1963.

Willett, John, *Brecht in Context: Comparative Approaches,* Methuen, 1984.

Witt, Hubert, editor, *Brecht: As They Knew Him,* translated by John Peet, International Publishers, 1974.

PERIODICALS

Atlantic, January, 1969.

Commonweal, December 19, 1947.

Communications from the International Brecht Society, November, 1984.

Comparative Drama, spring, 1967.

Contemporary Literature, winter, 1970.
Critical Quarterly, summer, 1961.
Drama Review, winter, 1968.
Educational Theatre Journal, March, 1957.
Germanic Review, January, 1966.
Los Angeles Times Book Review, December 19, 1993, p. 3.
Listener, May 6, 1976.
London Review of Books, July 16-August 5, 1981.
Modern Drama, February, 1969.
Modern Language Quarterly, June, 1962; December, 1966.
Nation, May 8, 1967; April 19, 1971; June 7, 1975; May 22, 1976.
New Republic, December 29, 1947.
New Statesman, May 7, 1976.
New Statesman & Society, September 24, 1993; April 15, 1994, p. 33.
New Yorker, September 12, 1959.
New York Review of Books, December 1, 1994, pp. 4-6.
New York Times Book Review, August 7, 1994; December 4, 1994, p. 69.
New York Times Magazine, November 3, 1963.
Observer, January 16, 1994.
Oxford Review, Number 2, 1966.
Parnassus: Poetry in Review, spring/summer/fall/winter, 1980.
Queen's Quarterly, spring, 1994, pp. 49-61.
Theatre Arts, June, 1963.
Tribune Books (Chicago), February 27, 1994.
University of Kansas City Review, October, 1960.
World Review, January, 1951.
yale/theatre, summer, 1968.*

*   *   *

BRINK, Andre (Philippus) 1935-

PERSONAL: Born May 29, 1935, in Vrede, South Africa; son of Daniel (a magistrate) and Aletta (a teacher; maiden name, Wolmarans) Brink; married Estelle Naude, October 3, 1951 (divorced); married Salomi Louw, November 28, 1965 (divorced); married Alta Miller (a potter), July 17, 1970 (divorced); married Maresa de Beer, November 16, 1990; children: Anton (first marriage), Gustav (second marriage), Danie, Sonja. *Education:* Potchefstroom University, B.A., 1955, M.A. (Afrikaans), 1958, M.A. (English), 1959; postgraduate study at Sorbonne, University of Paris, 1959-61.

ADDRESSES: Home—6 Banksia Road, Rosebank, Cape Town 7700, South Africa. *Office*—Department of English, University of Cape Town, Rondebosch 7701, South Africa.

CAREER: Rhodes University, Grahamstown, South Africa, lecturer, 1961-73, senior lecturer, 1974-75, associate professor, 1976-79, professor of Afrikaans and Dutch literature, 1980—; University of Cape Town, professor of English, 1991—. Director of theatrical productions.

MEMBER: South African PEN, Afrikaans Writers' Guild (president, 1978-80).

AWARDS, HONORS: Reina Prinsen Geerlings Prize, 1964; Central News Agency award for Afrikaans literature, 1965, for *Ole,* and for English literature, 1978, for *Rumours of Rain,* and 1982, for *A Chain of Voices;* prize for prose translation from South African Academy, 1970, for *Alice through the Looking Glass, and 1982;* D. Litt., Rhodes University, 1975, Witwatersrand University, 1985, and University of the Orange Free State, 1997; Central News Agency award for English literature, 1978, for *Rumours of Rain;* Martin Luther King Memorial Prize and Prix Medicis Etranger, both 1980, both for *A Dry White Season;* named chevalier de Legion d'Honneur and officier de l'Ordre des Arts et des Lettres, promoted to Commandeur, 1992; Premio Mondello, 1997, for *Imaginings of Sand.*

WRITINGS:

Ik ben er geweest: Gesprekken in Zuid-Afrika, Kok, 1974.
Die wyn van bowe, Buren, 1974.
Die klap van die meul, Buren, 1974.
Die fees van die malles: 'n keur uit die humor, Saayman & Weber, 1981.
Mapmakers: Writing in a State of Siege (essays), Faber, 1983, revised edition published as *Writing in a State of Siege: Essays on Politics and Literature,* Summit, 1983.
Oom Kootjie Emmer en die nuwe bedeling, Taurus, 1983.
(Editor with J. M. Coetzee) *A Land Apart: A South African Reader,* Faber, 1986.
Reinventing a Continent (essays), Secker & Warburg, 1996, revised edition with a preface by Nelson Mandela, Zoland Books, 1998.

FICTION

Eindelose wee, Tafelberg Publishers, 1960.
Lobola vir die lewe (title means "Dowry for Life"), Human & Rousseau, 1962.

Die Ambassadeur, Human & Rousseau, 1963, translation by Andre Brink published as *File on a Diplomat,* Longmans, Green, 1965, revised edition of translation published as *The Ambassador,* Faber, 1985.

Orgie, John Malherbe, 1965.

Die Rebelle: Betoogstuk in nege episodes, Human & Rousseau, 1970.

Die Verhoor: Verhoogstuk in drie bedrywe, Human & Rousseau, 1970.

Kinkels innie kabel: 'n verhoogstuk in elf episodes, Buren, 1971.

A Portrait of Woman as a Young Girl, Buren Publishers, 1973.

Kennis van die aand, Buren Publishers, 1973, translation by Brink published as *Looking on Darkness,* W. H. Allen, 1974, Morrow, 1975.

Die Geskiedenis van oom Kootjie Emmer van Witgratworteldraai, Buren, 1973.

'n Oomblik in die wind, Taurus, 1975, translation published as *An Instant in the Wind,* W. H. Allen, 1976, Morrow, 1977.

Gerugte van Reen, Human & Rousseau, 1978, translation published as *Rumours of Rain,* Morrow, 1978, reprinted as *Rumors of Rain,* Penguin, 1984.

'n Droe wit seisoen, Taurus, 1979, translation published as *A Dry White Season,* W. H. Allen, 1979, Morrow, 1980.

Houd-den-bek (title means "Shut Your Trap"), Taurus, c. 1982, translation published as *A Chain of Voices,* Morrow, 1982.

Miskien nooit, Human and Rousseau, 1982.

Die Muur van die pes, Human & Rousseau, 1984, translation published as *The Wall of the Plague,* Summit, 1984.

Loopdoppies: Nog dopstories, Saayman & Weber, 1984.

States of Emergency, Penguin, 1988, Summit, 1989.

An Act of Terror, Secker & Warburg, 1991, Summit, 1992.

Inteendeel: Roman, Human & Rousseau (Kaapstad), 1993.

On the Contrary: A Novel: Being the Life of a Famous Rebel, Soldier, Traveller, Explorer, Reader, Builder, Scribe, Latinist, Lover, and Liar, Little, Brown (Boston), 1993.

Cape of Storms: The First Life of Adamastor: A Story, Simon & Schuster (New York City), 1993, published as *The First Life of Adamastor,* Secker & Warburg, 1993.

Sandkastele, Human & Rousseau (Kaapstad), 1995.

Imaginings of Sand, Harcourt Brace & Co. (New York City), 1996.

DRAMA

Caesar, Nasionale Boekhandel, 1961.

Bagasie: Triptiek vir die toneel (three one-act plays), Tafelberg Publishers, 1964.

Elders mooiweer en warm (three-act play; title means "Elsewhere Fine and Warm"; first produced in Bloemfontein at Little Theatre, April, 1970), John Malherbe, 1965.

Afrikaners is plesierig (two one-act plays; title means "Afrikaners Make Merry"), Buren Publishers, 1973.

Pavane (three-act play; first produced in Cape Town at Hofmeyr Theatre, 1974), Human & Rousseau, 1974.

Die hamer van die hekse, Tafelberg, 1976.

Die Jogger, Human & Rousseau, 1997.

LITERARY HISTORY AND CRITICISM

Orde en chaos: 'n studie oor Germanicus en die tragedies van Shakespeare, Nasionale Boekhandel, 1962.

Aspekte van die nuwe prosa (title means "Aspects of the New Fiction"), Academica, 1967, revised edition, 1975.

Die Poesie van Breyten Breytenbach, Academica, 1971.

Inleiding tot die Afrikaanse letterkunde, onder redaksie van E. Lindenberg, Academica, 1973.

Aspekte van die nuwe drama (title means "Aspects of the New Drama"), Academica, 1974.

Voorlopige rapport: Beskouings oor die Afrikaanse literatuur van Sewentig, Human & Rousseau, 1976.

Tweede voorlopige rapport: Nog beskouings oor die Afrikaanse literature van sewentig, Human & Rousseau, 1980.

(With others) *Perspektief en profiel: 'n geskiedinis van die Afrikaanse letterkunde,* Perskor, 1982.

Waarom literatuur? (essays; title means "Why Literature?"), Human & Rousseau, 1985.

Literatuur in die strydperk (essays; title means "Literature in the Battle Zone"), Human & Rousseau, 1985.

Vertelkunde: 'n inleiding tot die lees van verhalende tekste, Academica, 1987.

OTHER

Pot-pourri: Sketse uit Parys (travelogue), Human, 1962.

Sempre diritto: Italiaanse reisjoernaal (travelogue), Afrikaanse Pers-Boekhandel, 1963.

Ole: Reisboek oor Spanje (travelogue), Human & Rousseau, 1966.

Midi: Op reis deur Suld-Frankyrk (travelogue), Human & Rousseau, 1969.

Fado: 'n reis deur Noord-Portugal (travelogue), Human & Rousseau, 1970.

Brandy in South Africa, translated by Siegfried Stander, Buren, 1973.

Dessert Wine in South Africa, Buren, 1974.

The Essence of the Grape, Saayman & Weber, 1993.

(Compiler) *SA, 27 April 1994: An Authors' Diary,* Queillerie (Pretoria), 1994.

Also translator into Afrikaans of Lewis Carroll's *Alice through the Looking Glass* and works by other authors, including William Shakespeare, Henry James, Graham Greene, Albert Camus, Marguerite Duras, Georges Simenon, Pavel Kohout, J. M. Synge, and Cervantes.

Author of scenarios for South African films and television series, including *The Settlers.* Contributor to books on Afrikaans literature and to periodicals, including *World Literature Today, Asahi Journal,* and *Theatre Quarterly.* Editor of *Standpunte,* 1985—; cditor of weekly book page in *Rapport.*

ADAPTATIONS: A Dry White Season was adapted for a film of the same title by Euzhan Palcy and Colin Welland, directed by Palcy, Metro-Goldwyn-Mayer, 1989.

SIDELIGHTS: As an Afrikaner, novelist, playwright, essayist, and educator Andre Brink is "a rarity in anti-apartheid literature," says Scott Kraft in the *Los Angeles Times.* A product of his country's exclusionary white culture, he repudiated its policies of apartheid during his studies in Paris in 1960 but was drawn back to the land of his birth to witness and record its turmoil and injustice. Earning both international recognition and governmental censure for his work in the years that followed, "Brink is one of the leading voices in the literary chorus of dissent, and for two decades his tales of black hope and white repression have shamed the nation," remarks Curt Suplee in the *Washington Post.*

Brink writes in both English and Afrikaans, a language derived from that spoken by South Africa's seventeenth- and eighteenth-century Dutch, French, and German settlers. In an interview with *CA,* Brink says: "There is a certain virility, a certain earthy, youthful quality about Afrikaans because it is such a young language, and because, although derived from an old European language like Dutch, it has found completely new roots in Africa and become totally Africanized in the process. . . . One can do almost anything with it. If you haven't got a word for something you want to express, you simply make a word or pluck a word from another language and shape it to fit into yours. Working in this young and very vital language is quite exhilarating, which creates a very special sense of adventure for authors working in it. And if one works in both languages, there is the wonderful experience of approaching the same subject, the same territory, through two totally different media. One is the more or less rigorous English language, the world language, and although one can still do a hell of a lot of new things in it, so much of it has already become standardized: it's almost as if one looks at the African experience through European eyes when one writes English. Through the Afrikaans language, it is a totally different, a more 'immediate,' experience. It's a language that can take much more emotionalism, for instance, whereas English tends toward understatement, Afrikaans is more overt, more externalized, more extroverted in its approach."

Brink translated his 1963 novel, *Die Ambassadeur,* from Afrikaans into English. Published in England as *File on a Diplomat,* and in the United States as *The Ambassador,* the novel relates a story about a French Ambassador to South Africa and his Third Secretary who become involved with the same young, promiscuous female and are drawn into the wild nightlife of Paris until jealousy destroys them both, reports Savkar Altinel in a *Times Literary Supplement* essay. While Fred Pfeil suggests in *Nation* that the novel "sets forth Brink's vision of sexual-existential liberation with nary a nod toward any political considerations," according to Altinel, the novel is "an elegantly tidy creation which, with its trinity of somewhat stylized central characters and its economically evoked setting, seems very much the unified product of a powerful initial vision." In a London *Times* review of the revised version of the novel in 1985, Henry Stanhope writes that despite "something ever so slightly dated about it," the novel "remains a good book, intelligent in its exploration of human behaviour under emotional and political stress."

"In 1968 I left South Africa to settle in Paris with the exiled poet Breyten Breytenbach," Brink explained to *CA,* "but the nature of the student revolt of that year forced me to reassess my situation as a writer and prompted my return to South Africa in order to accept full responsibility for whatever I wrote, believing that, in a closed society, the writer has a specific social and moral role to fill. This resulted in a more committed form of writing exploring the South African political situation and notably my revulsion of apartheid. My first novel to emerge from this experience was *Kennis van die aand,* which became the first Afrikaans book to be banned by the South African censors. This encouraged me to turn seriously to writing in English in order not to be silenced in my own language. Under the title *Looking on Darkness,* it became an international success, with translations into a dozen languages, including Finnish, Turkish, Japanese, Czechoslovakian, and Russian."

In Brink's *Looking on Darkness,* the protagonist, Joseph Malan, murders his white lover, Jessica Thomson, in a mutual pact and then sits in jail, awaiting execution. Calling the 1973 novel "ambitious and disturbing," Jane Larkin Crain concludes in the *Saturday Review* that "a passionately human vision rules here, informed by an imagination that is attuned at once to complex and important abstractions and to the rhythms and the texture of everyday experience." Noting that the "novel is structured in the form of a confessional," Martin Tucker adds in *Commonweal* that its style "is compelling: it is a work that throbs with personal intensity." Because of the novel's explicit treatment of sex, racism, persecution, and the torture of political prisoners in South African jails, C. J. Driver suggests in the *Times Literary Supplement* that it is not difficult to understand why it was banned; however, Driver concludes that "within its context this is a brave and important novel and in any terms a fine one."

Publication of *Looking on Darkness* in Europe coincided with the Soweto riots of 1976, and the novel became something of a handbook on the South African situation. Regarding racism generally, Brink told *CA:* "America seems to be slowly working its way through racism; whereas in South Africa it is entrenched in the whole system and framework of laws on which society has had its base. It is not just a matter of sentiment, of personal resentment, of tradition and custom, but these negative aspects of society are so firmly rooted in the framework of laws that it is very, very difficult to eradicate. *Looking on Darkness* elicited much comment because it is one of the first Afrikaans novels to confront openly the apartheid system. This account of an illicit love between a 'Cape Coloured' man and a white woman evoked, on the one hand, one of the fiercest polemics in the history of that country's literature and contributed, on the other, to a groundswell of new awareness among white Afrikaners of the common humanity of all people regardless of color. In numerous letters from readers I was told that 'for the first time in my life I now realize that 'they' feel and think and react just like 'us.'"

"In *An Instant in the Wind,*" Brink explained to *CA,* "I used essentially the same relationship—a black man and a white woman—but placed it in the midst of the eighteenth century in an attempt to probe the origins of the racial tensions of today. An episode from Australian history in which a shipwrecked woman and a convict return to civilization on foot is here transposed to the Cape Colony with so much verisimilitude that many readers have tried to look up the documentation in the Cape Archives." In the *Spectator,* Nick Totten describes the plot further: "A civilised woman, her husband dead, is lost in the wilderness . . . rescued by an escaped [black] prisoner . . . with whom she experiences for the first time fulfilled sexual love, but whom she betrays after the long trek back to civilisation." Calling it "a frank confrontation with miscegenation in a contemporary South African setting," Robert L. Berner comments in *World Literature Today:* "What Brink has produced is a historical novel with an almost documentary degree of verisimilitude. . . . But more than for its interest as evidence of Brink's artistic development, it is the recognition of the relationship of sex to politics that makes *An Instant in the Wind* a remarkable work of South African literature." And although R. A. Sokolov suggests in the *New York Times Book Review* that "it is important for political reasons that Brink should be published, but doubtful on the evidence of this book that he will be read for his art as a writer," Richard Cima contends in *Library Journal* that "the subject is important and the novelistic achievement impressive."

"*Rumours of Rain,* set on the eve of the Soweto riots, is placed on a much larger stage," Brink remarked to *CA* about his 1978 novel. "The apartheid mind is demonstrated in the account given by a wealthy businessman of the one weekend in which his whole familiar world collapsed through the conviction of his best friend for terrorism, the revolt of his son, the loss of his mistress, and the sale of his family's farm. In spite of his efforts to rigorously separate all the elements of his life, he becomes the victim of his own paradoxes and faces an apocalypse." The novel is about Martin Mynhardt, a mining entrepreneur, whose "only principles are money and safety," observes Phoebe-Lou Adams in the *Atlantic Monthly,* "and for them he betrays friend, colleague, brother, mother, wife, and mistress, and will eventually betray his son." According to C. G. Blewitt in *Best Sellers,*

"Much insight is shed on the life of the Afrikaner, his judicial system and the horrors of apartheid." Similarly, Daphne Merkin comments in *New Republic* that "Brink has taken a large, ideologically-charged premise and proceeds to render it in intimate terms without . . . sacrificing any of its hard-edged 'political' implications." Moreover, Merkin believes that the book "is an ambitious resonant novel that depicts a volatile situation with remarkable control and lack of sentimentality."

"In comparison with the complex structures" of *Rumours of Rain,* Brink commented to *CA* that his 1979 *A Dry White Season* "has a deceptively simple plot: a black man dies while being detained by the security police. In all good faith his white friend tries to find out what really happened, and as a result the whole infernal machinery of the State is turned against him." According to June Goodwin in the *Christian Science Monitor,* "Few novels will speak to the Afrikaner—or to foreigners who want to understand the Afrikaner—as well as this one." *A Dry White Season* is about Afrikaner Ben Du Toit, who helps a black school janitor investigate the questionable circumstances surrounding the death of his son at the hands of the police. Mel Watkins, in a *New York Times Book Review* essay, finds that the novel "demonstrates Andre Brink's continuing refinement of his fictional technique, without sacrificing any of the poignancy that his previous books have led us to expect."

"Brink's writing is built on conviction," remarks Dinah Birch in the London *Times.* "His characters move in a world of absolutes: goodness and truth war with cruelty and greed, and the reader is never left in any doubt as to which is which." Although not considering Brink "a 'great' writer," Eric Redman points out in the *Washington Post Book World* that "he's an urgent, political one and an Afrikaner other Afrikaners can't ignore." Moreover, noting that "big books have sparked change throughout South Africa's recent history," Redman observes that "this much is certain: the era of the trivial South African novel is dead, and courage killed it." Remarking to *CA* that the novel was begun "almost a year before the death in detention of black-consciousness leader Steve Biko in 1976," Brink added: "In fact, the death of Biko came as such a shock to me that for a long time I couldn't go back to writing. I believe that however outraged or disturbed one may be, a state of inner serenity must be obtained before anything meaningful can emerge in writing."

"In *A Chain of Voices* I have tried to extend and expand my field of vision," Brink added. "Using as a point of departure a slave revolt in the Cape Colony in 1825, I used a series of thirty different narrators to explore the relationships created by a society shaped by the forces of oppression and suffering. The 'separateness' of the voices haunted me; masters and slaves, all tied by the same chains, are totally unable to communicate because their humanity and their individuality are denied by the system they live by. I tried to broaden and deepen the enquiry by relating the voices, in four successive sections, to the elements of earth, water, wind, and fire.

Many critics consider Brink's 1982 *A Chain of Voices* to be his best work. Suplee labels it "an incendiary success abroad and a galling phenomenon at home." According to Julian Moynahan in the *New York Times Book Review,* "Like all good historical novels, [it] is as much about the present as the past. . . . Brink searches the bad old times for a key to understanding bad times in South Africa today, and what he sees in the historical record is always conditioned by his awareness of the South African racial crisis now." However, while Jane Kramer suggests in the *New York Review of Books* that "Brink may have an honorable imagination," she thinks that "he has written a potboiler of oppression" in which the "voices" of the novel "end up more caricature than character." On the other hand, Moynahan compares the device of telling a story from multiple viewpoints to the novels of William Faulkner in which he "counts the moral cost of white racism, both before and after Emancipation, in terms of the tragic spoliation of all relationships, not merely those between white oppressors and their nonwhite or partially white victims."

In the 1988 *States of Emergency,* Brink tells a story within a story. A writer's attempt to compose an apolitical love story is marred by the reality of racism, violence, and death. When the narrator receives an impressive but unpublishable manuscript from Jane Ferguson, a young writer who subsequently commits suicide by setting herself on fire, he abandons the historical novel he has been writing about South Africa and begins to compose a love story based on Ferguson's manuscript. The novel he writes is centered around a professor of literary theory and a student with whom he has an affair. According to a *Publishers Weekly* contributor, Brink "demonstrates that neither love nor art offers an escape; even the imagination is determined by political realities." Finding intensity between "reality and the author's idea of just what reality best suits his characters,"

Alfred Rushton comments in the Toronto *Globe and Mail* that the reader becomes aware that "no writer owns his or her characters, just as the state doesn't own people no matter what method is used to justify the attempt."

Not all critics responded positively to *States of Emergency,* though. For example, *Los Angeles Times* book critic Richard Eder suggests: "It is one thing for contemporary theory to come in afterward and argue that the fiction we have read tells us not about real characters but only about how its text was created. It is another for this reductivism to be applied in the moment of creation. It is literary contraception; nothing emerges alive." However, calling the novel "complicated and forceful" as well as "richly developed," Michael Wood maintains in the *Observer* that Brink "does depict, with great compassion and authority, the 'weight and madness of the violence' surrounding individuals." And Rushton concludes that "Brink also successfully challenges those people, writers and artists included, who persist in believing reason will somehow prevail over passion."

In his next novel, *An Act of Terror,* Brink portrays the political tension in South Africa in 1988 during a particularly brutal period of police repression. The narrative centers on Thomas Landman, a member of a guerrila group of blacks and whites who are planning to assassinate the president. When the plan fails, Landman seeks to escape from the police, and revisits the scens of his past life. Reviewers found much to praise in the work. Adam Hochschild writes in the *Los Angeles Times Book Review,* "the meal that Brink cooks up is an intricate, fast-moving story that succeeds in keeping us at the table for more than 600 pages of this 834-page behemoth of a book." *Nation* contributor Jenefer Shute similarly praises the novel's ambition, asserting that it "soars in its aspiration, its revised creation myth for a race 'conceived and born in lies,' its hope for a history that might open out instead of shutting down." Several critics, however, judge that the novel's lengthy, oratorical conclusion, in which Landman chronicles his family's presence in South Africa from the first Dutch settlers in the seventeenth century to the present day, compromises the work as a whole. Hochshild maintains that "Brink's skill as a storyteller collapses" in this "interminable" chronicle. Similarly, Randolph Vigne, commenting in the *San Francisco Review of Books,* characterizes the conclusion as "a heavy dose of cheap magazine fiction."

Brink returned to historical fiction in his next two novels, *Cape of Storms: The First Life of Adamastor* and *On the Contrary.* In the first of these works, Brink draws on Greek mythology and Renaissance European literature to shape an allegorical commentary on the colonial history of southern Africa. The novel is narrated by T'kama, a Khoi who witnesses the arrival of the first Europeans and inadvertently precipitates an attack on his people by frightening a white woman who has come ashore to bathe. Despite the humorous style of the novel, Brink told Laurel Graeber in the *New York Times Book Review* that "under the humor there's a deep and serious concern with the origins of racial animosities in South Africa and everywhere." In reviewing the novel for that same publication, Mario Vargas Llosa echoes this concern, asserting that "however much we enjoy reading the book, Andre Brink's beautiful mythological re-creation leaves us anguished over what appear to be its predictions regarding a society where, after a bloody past of injustice and institutionalized racism, different races and cultures are finally preparing to try co-existence under conditions of equality."

In *On the Contrary* Brink again concentrates on the early racial tensions of South Africa by telling the story of the historical figure Estienne Barbier, who emigrated from France to South Africa in the eighteenth century and who was executed by the Dutch East India Company for his role in fomenting rebellion in the Cape in 1739. The novel is presented as a single letter—comprising over 300 sections interweaving fact and fantasy—that is written to a slave-girl on the eve of the protagonist's execution. Critics gave the work a mixed reception. *New York Times Book Review* contributor Peter S. Prescott, for example, maintains that while novel is "ambitious and imaginative," it nevertheless suffers from a "serious confusion of styles" and a lack of humor and wit. Boyd Tomkin, writing in the *Observer,* notes that "though he conjures up the sun-dried veldt, Brink's prose gorges on a lush glut of ideas. It leaves its readers as drunk as its hero, addled but inspired."

Brink returns to contemporary political concerns in his fiction with his 1996 novel *Imaginings of Sand.* This work concentrates on the experiences of Kristien, a disaffected Afrikaner who has been living in self-imposed exile in England and returns to her native land to care for her dying grandmother during the elections that will bring an end to the apartheid system. Critics were divided in their assessment of Brink's handling of his females characters in this work. *Spectator* reviewer Barbara Trapido asserts that the main character, "who is offered to the reader as the spirit of defiance, a left-hander, a 'witch,' never really rises above drag act and disappoints with her ordinariness." Amanda Hopkinson, commenting in *New Statesman & Society,* registers a dissenting opinion, however, maintaining that "Brink raises even familiar feminist issues in intelligent ways." Similarly, the quality of the writing itself elicited conflicting responses. Hopkinson finds Brink's style "varied and highly accomplished," while *New York Times* reviewer Richard Bernstein characterizes the novel as "a ramshackle, muddled work always threatening to blow apart by virtue of its very extravagace." *Washington Times* contributor Martin Rubin describes *Imaginings of Sand* as Brink's "finest achievement yet. . . . More substantial than Nadine Gordimer's recent novels and more authentically rooted in myth than J. M. Coetzee's work." Alan Cheuse offers similar praise in his review for the *Chicago Tribune,* contending that "Brink presents his kinsmen in the patterns and rhythms of myth and legend, sometimes employing the techniques of magical realism, thus making his novel seem thoroughly African in texture and effect."

"Since my tastes in literature are Catholic," Brink remarked to *CA,* "I have never been a disciple of any one school. The most abiding influence on my work, however, has been Albert Camus, notably in his view of man in a state of incessant revolt against the conditions imposed upon him, and reacting creatively to the challenge of meaninglessness. In much of my work this is linked to an element of mysticism derived from the Spanish writers of the seventeenth century. The other most abiding influence on my writing is the study of history. All my work is pervaded with a sense of 'roots,' whether in the collective history of peoples or in the private history of an individual." Brink added, "However close my work is to the realities of South Africa today, the political situation remains a starting point only for my attempts to explore the more abiding themes of human loneliness and man's efforts to reach out and touch someone else. My stated conviction is that literature should never descend to the level of politics; it is rather a matter of elevating and refining politics so as to be worthy of literature."

BIOGRAPHICAL/CRITICAL SOURCES:

BOOKS

Contemporary Literary Criticism, Gale, Volume 18, 1981, Volume 36, 1986.
Jolly, Rosemary Jane, *Colonization, Violence, and Narration in White South African Writing: Andre Brink, Breyten Breytenbach, and J. M. Coetzee,* Ohio University Press (Athens), 1995.

PERIODICALS

Atlantic Monthly, October, 1978.
Best Sellers, February, 1979.
Canadian Forum, December, 1983.
Chicago Tribune, September 5, 1995; October 16, 1996; November 24, 1996.
Christian Science Monitor, March 10, 1980; July 21, 1982; April 10, 1985; June 4, 1986.
Commonweal, September 12, 1975; July 13, 1984.
Globe and Mail (Toronto), August 20, 1988.
Kirkus Reviews, March 15, 1989.
Library Journal, August, 1975; February 15, 1977; April 1, 1985.
Listener, October 8, 1987.
London Magazine, June, 1979.
London Review of Books, August 4, 1988.
Los Angeles Times, August 19, 1987; May 18, 1989; September 29, 1989; October 7, 1989; October 15, 1989; April 17, 1990; January 26, 1992; August 29, 1993.
Maclean's, May 10, 1982.
Nation, June 21, 1986; April 6, 1992, p. 455.
New Leader, January 14-28, 1985.
New Republic, October 21, 1978; April 30, 1984.
New Statesman, November 17, 1978; October 5, 1979; July 8, 1983; September 28, 1984; December 6, 1985; August 29, 1986.
New Statesman & Society, August 27, 1993, p. 37; February 23, 1996, p. 45.
Newsweek, December 2, 1974.
New Yorker, August 25, 1975.
New York Review of Books, December 2, 1982; April 25, 1985.
New York Times, February 2, 1984; March 6, 1984; September 17, 1989; September 20, 1989; September 25, 1989; December 11, 1996.
New York Times Book Review, February 27, 1977; March 23, 1980; June 13, 1982; March 17, 1985; June 29, 1986; January 12, 1992, p. 6; July 25, 1993, p. 1; August 14, 1994, p. 94.
Observer, May 15, 1988; August 29, 1993.
Publishers Weekly, March 10, 1989.
San Francisco Review of Books, January, 1992.
Saturday Review, August 23, 1975.
Spectator, September 18, 1976; October 6, 1984; February 17, 1996.
Times (London), May 6, 1982; November 14, 1985; March 3, 1990.
Times Literary Supplement, November 15, 1974; September 17, 1976; October 20, 1978; May 14,

1982; September 16, 1983; October 5, 1984; January 10, 1986; February 26, 1993; September 3, 1993; February 9, 1996.

UNESCO Courier, September, 1993, p. 4.

Voice Literary Supplement, November, 1987.

Washington Post, May 28, 1982; July 13, 1989; September 22, 1989; September 26, 1989.

Washington Post Book World, January 20, 1980; February 17, 1985; July 13, 1989; March 15, 1992.

Washington Times, November 24, 1996.

World Literature Today, autumn, 1977; summer, 1984; winter, 1985; summer, 1986; spring, 1989.

*   *   *

BROEG, Bob
See BROEG, Robert M.

*   *   *

BROEG, Robert M. 1918-
(Bob Broeg)

PERSONAL: Surname rhymes with "vague"; born March 18, 1918, in St. Louis, MO; son of Robert M. (a bread salesman) and Alice (Wiley) Broeg; married Dorothy Carr, June 19, 1943 (died November 1, 1975); married Lynette A. Emmenegger, July 23, 1977. *Education:* University of Missouri, B.J., 1941.

ADDRESSES: Home—60 Frontenac Estates, St. Louis, MO 63135. *Office*—St. Louis Post-Dispatch, St. Louis, MO 63101.

CAREER: Reporter for Associated Press in Jefferson City, MO, 1941, and Boston, MA, 1942; *St. Louis Post-Dispatch,* St. Louis, MO, sports writer, 1945-58, sports editor, 1958-77, assistant to publisher, 1977-84; contributing editor, 1984—. Columnist for the *Sporting News,* 1967-77. Member of Baseball Hall of Fame board of directors and veteran's committee, Football Foundation and Hall of Fame honors committee, Pro Football Hall of Fame election committee, and Missouri Sports Hall of Fame. *Military service:* U.S. Marine Corps, 1942-45; became technical sergeant.

MEMBER: Baseball Writers Association of America (president, 1958), Football Writers Association of America, St. Louis Press Club, Sigma Phi Epsilon, Omicron Delta Kappa, Kappa Tau Alpha, Sigma Delta Chi.

AWARDS, HONORS: Sportswriter of the Year Award, Knute Rockne Club, 1964; University of Missouri journalism medal, 1971; elected to writers' wing of Baseball Hall of Fame, 1979; Baseball Writers' meritorious service award, 1980.

WRITINGS:

UNDER NAME BOB BROEG

(With Bob Burrill) *Don't Bring That Up! Skeletons in the Sports Closet,* A. S. Barnes (San Diego, CA), 1946.

Stan Musial: "The Man's" Own Story, Doubleday (New York City), 1964, revised edition published as *The Man, Stan: Musial Then and Now,* Bethany Press (St. Louis, MO), 1977.

Super Stars of Baseball, Spink & Son (St. Louis, MO), 1971, revised and expanded edition published as *Superstars of Baseball: Their Lives, Their Loves, Their Laughs, Their Laments,* Diamond Communications (South Bend, IN), 1994.

Ol' Mizzou: A Story of Missouri Football, Stroud (Huntsville, AL), 1974, revised edition published as *Ol' Mizzou: A Century of Tiger Football,* Walsworth (Marceline, MO), 1990.

(With Stan Musial and Jack Buck) *We Saw Stars,* Bethany Press, 1976.

(With Buck and Weeb Ewbank) *Football Greats,* Bethany Press, 1977.

(With Paula Knoderer and Carole Hollander) *St. Louis Is for Families,* Bethany Press, 1979.

The Pilot Light and the Gas House Gang, Bethany Press, 1980.

Bob Broeg's Redbirds: A Century of Cardinals' Baseball, River City Publishers (St. Louis, MO), 1981, second revised edition, Walsworth, 1992.

(Editor) *Front Page: A Century of Post-Dispatch News and Sports,* River City Publishers, 1982.

My Baseball Scrapbook, River City Publishers, 1983.

(With William J. Miller Jr.) *Baseball from a Different Angle,* Diamond Communications (South Bend, IN), 1988.

Baseball's Barnum: Ray "Hap" Dumont, Founder of the National Baseball Congress, Wichita State University (Wichita, KS), 1989.

Bob Broeg: Memories of a Hall of Fame Sportswriter, Sagamore (Champaign, IL), 1995.

SIDELIGHTS: Bob Broeg was unable to play many sports due to an eye injury sustained at childbirth. He loved the games, however, and he directed his career toward sportswriting from his high school days onward. Based for most of his career at the *St. Louis Post-Dispatch,* Broeg became known nationwide for his coverage of the Cardinals baseball team as well as both professional and college football. *Dictionary of Literary Biography* correspondent James A. Vlasich called Broeg "one of the giants in sportswriting in the generation following World War II. . . . Broeg helped to define American sportswriting in that era."

Broeg was a youngster of nine when he attended his first big-league baseball game at Sportsman's Park in his native St. Louis. He was completely captivated, and he decided soon thereafter to become a sportswriter. He was sports editor of his high school newspaper and attended journalism school at the University of Missouri in Columbia, graduating with honors in 1941. One of his first jobs was a public relations stint for Ray "Hap" Dumont, an entrepreneur whose National Baseball Congress helped bring major league games to new parts of America. Broeg's 1989 book, *Baseball's Barnum: Ray "Hap" Dumont, Founder of the National Baseball Congress,* is a warm recollection of Dumont and the years before television brought big games into every corner of the nation.

After wartime military service and a short stint in Boston, Broeg returned to St. Louis in 1945 and began an association with the *St. Louis Post-Dispatch* that continues to this day. As a writer and editor for one of America's best-known newspapers, he was influential in changing the scope and purpose of press coverage of sports. Vlasich noted that Broeg's emphasis "is on the anecdotal, and his stories are heavily laden with his own opinions; his writing is crisp and sprightly, with a frequent use of alliteration." Broeg thought fans had become bored with newspaper accounts that merely re-told the events of a game. He filled his stories with sidelights and background information, interviewed not only athletes but managers and front office personnel as well, and turned out numerous human-interest pieces that found their way into national magazines. He covered everything from the World Series and the National Football League to such bizarre moments as the night Bill Veeck inserted midget Eddie Gaedel into the second game of a doubleheader.

Broeg's books cover many aspects of baseball and football, especially as played in Missouri. His biography of Musial, *Stan Musial: "The Man's" Own Story,* was first published in 1964 and then significantly revised and re-published in 1977. A *Library Journal*

contributor wrote that the work "has captured the warmth of a man beloved by all," and *Best Sellers* reviewer J. P. McNicholas cited it as "engrossing reading . . . full of good sound advice." The best known of Broeg's titles include *Superstars of Baseball: Their Lives, Their Loves, Their Laughs, Their Laments,* a book that profiles 55 current and past stars; and *Baseball from a Different Angle,* a history of such offbeat baseball topics as equipment, announcers, salaries, and rule changes. Vlasich described the work as "a perfect combination of scholarship and light prose."

Broeg was inducted into the writers' division of the Baseball Hall of Fame in 1979. He was also one of the first sportswriters allowed to cast a ballot for the Pro Football Hall of Fame. Known for his devotion to alliteration (cheating players, for instance, were "cunning cutthroat characters"), he bridged the gap between fans and their heroes by writing in a comfortable, companionable style. "Broeg will always be embraced by the average fan," Vlasich concluded. "He came from their ranks, and his writing shows that he has never forgotten them."

BIOGRAPHICAL/CRITICAL SOURCES:

BOOKS

Dictionary of Literary Biography, Volume 171: *Twentieth-Century American Sportswriters,* Gale (Detroit, MI), 1996, pp. 23-30.

PERIODICALS

Best Sellers, May 15, 1964, p. 89.
Book Week, August 18, 1946, p. 7.
Christian Century, April 22, 1964, p. 523.
Library Journal, April 15, 1964, p. 1772; May 15, 1964, p. 2245.
New York Times, September 22, 1946, p. 20.
New York Times Book Review, June 7, 1964, p. 18.
San Francisco Chronicle, July 7, 1946, p. 150.

* * *

BROWN, George Mackay 1921-1996

PERSONAL: Born October 17, 1921, in Stromness, Orkney Islands, Scotland; died April 13, 1996, in Kirkwall, Orkney Islands, Scotland; son of John and

Mary Jane (Mackay) Brown. *Education:* Attended Newbattle Abbey College, 1951-52, 1956; University of Edinburgh, M.A., 1960, graduate study on the poetry of Gerard Manley Hopkins, 1962-64.

CAREER: Poet and author.

MEMBER: Royal Society of Literature (fellow).

AWARDS, HONORS: Arts Council of Great Britain award for poetry, 1965; Society of Authors Travel Award, 1967; Scottish Arts Council Prize and Katherine Mansfield-Menton Prize, both 1969, for *A Time to Keep, and Other Stories;* officer, Order of the British Empire, 1974; LL.D., University of Dundee, 1977; D.Litt., University of Glasgow, 1985; M.A., Open University; Fletcher of Saltoun (Saltire) Award, 1991; *Beside the Ocean of Time* was shortlisted for the Booker Prize for Literature in 1994.

WRITINGS:

POETRY

The Storm, and Other Poems, Orkney Herald Press, 1954.
Loaves and Fishes, Hogarth, 1959.
The Year of the Whale, Hogarth, 1965.
The Five Voyages of Arnor, K. D. Duval, 1966.
Twelve Poems, Belfast Festival Publications, 1968.
Fishermen with Ploughs: A Poem Cycle, Hogarth, 1971.
Lifeboat, and Other Poems, Gilbertson, 1971.
Poems New and Selected, Hogarth, 1971, Harcourt, 1973, enlarged edition published as *Selected Poems,* Hogarth, 1977.
(With Iain Crichton Smith and Norman MacCaig) *Penguin Modern Poets 21,* Penguin, 1972.
Winterfold, Chatto & Windus, 1976.
Voyages, Hogarth, 1983.
Christmas Poems, illustrations by John Lawrence, Perpetua Press, 1984.
Stone, photographs by Gunnie Moberg, Duval & Hamilton, 1987.
Tryst on Egilsay, Celtic Cross Press, 1988.
Selected Poems, 1954-1983, J. Murray, 1991.
The Lost Village: Poems, Celtic Cross Press (Wetherby, West Yorkshire), 1992.

Contributor with Ted Hughes, Seamus Heaney, and Christopher Fry, to *Four Poets for St. Magnus,* Brockness Press, 1987; contributor to *The Wreck of the Archangel,* J. Murray, 1989.

NOVELS

Greenvoe, Harcourt, 1972.
Magnus, Hogarth, 1973.
Time in a Red Coat, Chatto & Windus, 1984, Vanguard Press, 1985.
Vinland, J. Murray (London), 1992.
Beside the Ocean of Time, J. Murray, 1994.

SHORT FICTION

A Calendar of Love, Hogarth, 1967, published as *A Calendar of Love, and Other Stories,* Harcourt, 1968.
A Time to Keep, and Other Stories, Hogarth, 1969, Harcourt, 1987.
Hawkfall, and Other Stories, Hogarth, 1974.
The Sun's Net, Hogarth, 1976.
Witch, and Other Stories, Longman, 1977.
Andrina, and Other Stories, Chatto & Windus, 1982.
Christmas Stories, illustrations by John Lawrence, Perpetua Press, 1985.
The Hooded Fisherman: A Story, illustrations by Charles Shearer, Duval & Hamilton, 1985.
Selected Stories, Vanguard Press, 1986.
The Golden Bird: Two Orkney Stories, Vanguard Press, 1987.
Winter Tales, J. Murray (London), 1995.

JUVENILE FICTION

The Two Fiddlers: Tales from Orkney (also see below), illustrations by Ian MacInnes, Hogarth, 1974.
Pictures in the Cave, illustrations by MacInnes, Chatto & Windus, 1977.
Six Lives of Fankle the Cat, Chatto & Windus, 1980.
Keepers of the House, illustrations by Gillian Martin, Old Stile Press, 1986.

PLAYS

Witch, first produced in Edinburgh, Scotland, 1969.
A Time to Keep (television play based on three stories by Brown), telecast, 1969.
A Spell for Green Corn (radio play; broadcast, 1967; produced in Edinburgh, 1970; adaptation produced at Perth Theatre, 1972), Hogarth, 1970.
Orkney (television play), telecast, 1971.
The Loom of Light (produced in Kirkwall, 1972; also see below), photographs by Gunnie Moberg, illustrations by Simon Fraser, Balnain Books, 1986.

The Storm Watchers, produced in Edinburgh, 1976.

The Martyrdom of St. Magnus (opera libretto; music by Peter Maxwell Davies; adaptation of novel *Magnus* by Brown; produced in Kirkwall, Vienna, and London, 1977; produced in Santa Fe, 1979), Boosey and Hawkes, 1977.

Miss Barraclough (television play), telecast, 1977.

Four Orkney Plays for Schools (television play), telecast, 1978.

The Two Fiddlers (opera libretto; music by Davies; adaptation of story by Brown; produced in London, 1978), Boosey and Hawkes, 1978.

The Well (also see below), produced at St. Magnus Festival, 1981.

The Voyage of Saint Brandon (radio play; also see below), broadcast, 1984.

Andrina (teleplay), telecast, 1984.

Three Plays (contains *The Loom of Light, The Well,* and *The Voyage of Saint Brandon*), Chatto & Windus, 1984.

The Road to Colonus, broadcast by PTE-Dublin, 1989.

Also author of *A Celebration for Magnus,* son-et-lumiere play performed in Firkwall, 1987.

OTHER

Let's See the Orkney Islands, Thomson, 1948.

Stromness Official Guide, Burrow, 1956.

An Orkney Tapestry (essays), Gollancz, 1969.

Letters from Hamnavoe (essays), Gordon Wright Publishing, 1975.

Edwin Muir: A Brief Memoir, Castlelaw Press, 1975.

From Stone to Thorn, Abingdon, 1975.

George Mackay Brown (sound recording), Claddagh, 1977.

Under Brinkie's Brae (essays), photographs by Gordon Wright, Gordon Wright Publishing, 1979.

Portrait of Orkney, photographs by Werner Forman, Hogarth, 1981, photographs by Gunnie Moberg, drawings by Erlend Brown, J. Murray, 1989.

The Scottish Bestiary, illustrations by John Bellany, Steven Campbell, Peter Howson, Jack Knox, Bruce McLean, June Redfern, and Adrian Wiszniewski, Paragon Press, 1986.

(Editor) *Selected Prose of Edwin Muir,* J. Murray, 1987.

(Editor with Neil Miller Gunn and Aonghas MacNeacail), *A Writers Celidh for Neil Gunn,* Balnain Books (Nairn, Scotland), 1991.

(With Llewellyn Thomas, Old Stile Press, and Press Collection), *In the Margins of a Shakespeare,* Old Stile Press (Monmouth), 1991.

Rockpools and Daffodils: An Orcadian Diary, 1979-1991, G. Wright (Edinburgh), 1992.

(With Peter Maxwell Davies) *Apple-Basket, Apple-Blossom: For Unaccompanied Choir SATB* (musical score), Chester Music (London), 1992.

Also author of television poem *The Winter Islands,* broadcast in 1966. Also collaborator, with composer Peter Maxwell Davies, of musical works, including a cantata, *Solstice of Light.* Brown's manuscripts are collected at the Scottish National Library at the University of Edinburgh.

ADAPTATIONS: The Two Fiddlers was adapted as *The Two Fiddlers: Opera in Two Acts* by Peter Maxwell Davies, with the libretto by Davies published by Boosey & Hawkes in 1978; the story "Andrina" of *Andrina, and Other Stories* was made into a television film by Bill Forsyth in 1982.

SIDELIGHTS: A prolific author of poems, novels, short stories, children's stories, essays, and media pieces, George Mackay Brown wrote of life and nature in his native Orkney Islands, off the coast of Scotland. Brown was once called "probably the greatest living Scottish writer" by *Dictionary of Literary Biography* contributor Thomas J. Starr. In another essay in the *Dictionary of Literary Biography,* Joseph Reino elaborated: "His successes in poetry and the prose narrative are considerable, and the really surprising thing about him is not so much his extensive talents, but rather that he is not more widely known as one of Britain's outstanding contemporary authors." Similarly, poet Seamus Heaney maintained in the *Listener:* "Mackay Brown's imagination is heraldic and formal; it is stirred by legends of Viking warrior and Christian saint; it solemnises the necessary labour of life into a seasonal liturgy; it consecrates the visible survivals of history, and ruins of time, into altars that are decked with the writings themselves. I have never seen his poetry sufficiently praised."

Brown was born in 1921 in the village of Stromness in the Orkney Islands. He left school early to work as a journalist, but he returned at age 30 to work on his degree at Newbattle Abbey College. Under the tutelage of poet Edwin Muir, Brown began composing poetry of his own; his first collection of poems, *The Storm, and Other Poems,* was published in 1954. During this time he continued writing columns for the *Orkney Herald.* It was not until the 1960s and 1970s that he began writing short stories and novels. From this point until his death in 1996, Brown remained a fixture of the Orkney Islands, contributing regularly to the *Orcadian.*

Brown attempted to capture and re-create the reality of his homeland through his prose and verse, using religious, ritualistic themes, especially relating to Orkney living and his fictional Orkney town, Hamnavoe. "George Mackay Brown is a writer in love with the past and with the Orkney Islands where he finds it still precariously lingering," wrote Julia O'Faolain in the *New Review.* A *Times Literary Supplement* reviewer commented that "Brown is a uniquely observant and skillful chronicler of life in his native Orkneys, past and present." Harold Massingham concurred in *Phoenix,* seeing the same approach in Brown's poetry: "His local colour, in fact his total effect, is of a mature distillation and blend by an excellent and unmistakable poet patiently subdued by, and to, the demands of his terrain." Reviewing *Voyages* for the *Times Literary Supplement,* Douglas Dunn maintained that "Brown's idealism is retrospective, fictionalizing a place and its meaning through an affectionate exploration of history which he holds up like a cupped treasure in the hands, and as an offering to the residual innocence of his native Orkney Islands."

According to Reino, "Two aspects of Brown's personal convictions are important to keep in mind: his rejection of nineteenth-and twentieth-century concepts of progress and his personal belief that Scotland . . . is a 'Knox-ruined nation,' that is destroyed by the Calvinist reformer John Knox." Neil Roberts, in a *Cambridge Quarterly* assessment of Brown's work, wrote that "he is interested in art, religion and ritual, their relations to each other and to the agricultural basis of civilisation. He is interested in the relation of pagan to Christian religion, and of the World of Christ to the word of the poet."

Brown's work concentrated on traditional values and time-honored ethics. Dunn observed in *Poetry Nation* that "Brown, as a poet of remote island communities and unindustrial, non-urban landscapes, is at odds with the tradition of modern poetry." Dunn continued: "Brown's best poems are . . . full of names and characters, their typical vulnerabilities, and the virtues of the way of life their personalities prove. He celebrates an ideal of community." In the *Times Literary Supplement,* Dunn remarked upon Brown's traditional qualities in prose as well: "Brown has perfected a narrative style of great simplicity, its virtues drawn more from the ancient art of telling tales than from new-fangled methodologies of fiction." "Cleav-

ing to a collective tradition which rests on the work of old oral tale-tellers," said O'Faolain, "his stories make no concession to contemporary taste."

About Brown's efforts in *Andrina, and Other Stories,* Stuart Evans claimed in the London *Times* that "this superb teller of tales who, whether he is writing in prose or verse, is always the poet, offers in this book a magical selection." Evans added, "[The stories'] common strength, apart from George Mackay Brown's exquisite and unerring way with words, is in their humanity." Dunn also applauded Brown's work in the book, stating in the *Times Literary Supplement,* "In writing so controlled, . . . by a poet perfectly at ease with his imagination and a language natural to it, the effect of that apparent collision of old and new can only be fruitful and challenging, as well as, in this case, profoundly enjoyable."

Similarly, about Brown's final short story collection, *Winter Tales, Times Literary Supplement* reviewer Patrick Crotty commented, "Brown's view of history is familiar from many of his earlier books, as is the maritime imagery he uses to render it. Remarkably, he can still make this imagery sound new-minted." Writing in the *Spectator,* Patricia Craig noted, "Brown's Orkney stories aren't so much sad as stark, all clear-cut edges and elemental feeling. . . . Brown is never too far in spirit from the ballad of folk-tale which accommodates wonders within its boundaries."

Calling Brown a "portent," Jo Grimond suggested in the *Spectator* that "there are not so many poets and some have only a little poetry in them. We should be thankful for Mr. Brown and grateful to Orkney that has fed him." Considering *Fishermen with Ploughs: A Poem Cycle* to be "Brown's most impressive poetic effort," Reino described the work as "a sequence of obscurely connected lyrics based on island 'history' as the author reconceives it." Massingham called the work "a task indeed . . . which is vividly and quietly accomplished with an interesting range of verse-forms and a marvelous prose chorus at the end." Dunn agreed, stating in *Poetry Nation* that "much of Brown's best writing is to be found in *Fishermen with Ploughs.*" Massingham concluded that "all his work to date has been a persistent devotion, not because he is running in runic circles but digging, rooting deeper."

Noting the affinity between Brown's prose and poetry styles, Starr called him "a prose stylist with a poetic vision," and found *Greenvoe,* Brown's novel of an imaginary island town, to be a superb example of his artistry. The novel "describes the destruction of a village by progress in the form of a secret military establishment," wrote Neil Roberts in the *Cambridge Quarterly*. "Most of the novel is devoted to an evocation of the life of the village." Starr found that Brown "successfully weaves all of [his recurring themes] into his own seamless garment." Calling it "the culmination of all of George Mackay Brown's fictional concerns," Starr noted that it "ranks with *The Great Gatsby, Mrs. Dalloway,* and *The Spire* as among the great prose poems of this century." Although Roberts found the novel somewhat "disappointing," suggesting it was overwritten, Ruth Farwell praised Brown for the "beauty and precision of his style," and remarked in the *Washington Post Book World,* "Novels like this don't come along very often."

Brown's final novel, *Beside the Ocean of Time,* was published in 1994 to another wave of critical acclaim. Shortlisted for the prestigious Booker Prize for Literature, the novel follows protagonist Thorfinn Ragnarson from his day-dream-filled childhood in the 1920s to his World War II experiences in the 1940s and finally to his reflections as an author during the 1960s. The novel's narrative is far from linear, however; young Thorfinn's dreams, which carry him back to the middle ages as a Viking explorer and as a squire at the Battle of Bannockburn in 1314, play a vital role in the story. "In addition to nicely juxtaposing two moments in time to expose their essential similarities, the tales are enriched by subtly juxtaposing Thorfinn with other members of the community," commented Richard Henry in *World Literature Today*. Although feeling that "Brown's hand has . . . been lighter, more subtle in his previous work," *New Statesman & Society* reviewer Jane Roscoe remarked that Brown's "poems and stories brilliantly evoke the 'rich and strange' of Orkney history."

Brown did not always garner critical praise, however. About *Six Lives of Fankle the Cat,* Charles Causley suggested in the *Times Literary Supplement* that "Brown's relaxed manner and somewhat loosely constructed narrative lack the cutting edge, the dramatic tension, that we have grown to expect from his brilliant creation and re-creation of Orcadian myth and legend, for children and adults." And Dunn remarked in *Poetry Nation* that "unfortunately, Brown has now put forward a quaintly antithetical notion that there is a certain kind of real life for the good men of the Orkneys, and another kind of life in the cities of the mainland which is so vicious that it brings total punishment." Despite the occasional negative comment,

most reviewers admired Brown's work. In the *Times Literary Supplement,* David Profumo wrote about the unique qualities of Brown's work: "He has kept faith with the same themes—the saving grace of ceremony, the importance of the cycle of the seasons, the past in relation to the present—yet he constantly turns them to fresh advantage, while maintaining a strong sense of tradition." And in the London *Times,* Peter Tinniswood wrote that "if an aspiring writer came to me and asked how to tell a story, plot a book, round a character, make dialogue sing and whisper and bellow, I would say: 'Read George Mackay Brown.'"

In a brief commentary on his own writing, Brown once told *CA:* "Since it seems to me that our civilization will possibly destroy itself before too long, I am interested in the labour and lives of the most primitive people of our civilization, the food-getters (crofters and fishermen) since it is those people living close to the sources of life who are most likely to survive and continue the human story; and since even their lives would be meaningless otherwise, I see religion as an illuminating and stabilising force in the life of a community. Out of these things I make my poems, stories, and plays."

Brown also told *CA* he considered the following "a kind of basic credo": "I believe in dedicated work rather than in 'inspiration'; of course on some days, one writes better than on others. I believe writing to be a craft like carpentry, plumbing, or baking; one does the best one can. Much mischief has been caused by a loose word like 'culture,' which separates the crafts into the higher arts like music, writing, sculpture, and the lowlier workaday arts (those, and the many others like them, that I have mentioned above). In 'culture circles,' there is a tendency to look upon artists as the new priesthood of some esoteric religion. Nonsense—and dangerous nonsense moreover—we are all hewers of wood and drawers of water; only let us do it as thoroughly and joyously as we can."

BIOGRAPHICAL/CRITICAL SOURCES:

BOOKS

Bold, Alan, *George Mackay Brown,* Oliver & Boyd, 1978.

Contemporary Authors Autobiography Series, Volume 6, Gale, 1988.

Contemporary Literary Criticism, Gale, Volume 5, 1976, Volume 48, 1988.

Dictionary of Literary Biography, Gale, Volume 14: *British Novelists since 1960,* 1983, Volume 27:

Poets of Great Britain and Ireland, 1945-1960, 1984, Volume 139: *British Short-Fiction Writers, 1945-1980,* 1994.

Hart, Francis Russell, *The Scottish Novel: From Smollett to Spark,* Harvard University Press, 1978.

Schoene, Berthold, *The Making of Orcadia: Narrative Identity in the Prose Work of George MacKay Brown,* P. Lang (New York City), 1995.

Smith, Iain Chrichton, *Iain Chrichton Smith, Norman MacCaig, George Mackay Brown,* Penguin Books, 1972.

Yamada, Osamu, Hilda D. Spear, and David S. Robb, *The Contribution to Literature of Orcadian Writer George MacKay Brown: An Introduction and a Bibliography,* E. Mellen Press (Lewiston), 1991.

PERIODICALS

Cambridge Quarterly, Volume 6, number 2, 1973.
Chapman (Edinburgh), 1990 (special Brown issue).
Hudson Review, Volume 26, number 4, 1973-74.
Listener, April 17, 1967; August 21, 1969; January 9, 1975.
London Magazine, December, 1959.
London Review of Books, September 17, 1987; March 22, 1990.
New Review, June, 1976.
New Statesman & Society, June 24, 1994, p. 39.
New York Times Book Review, April 28, 1968; July 19, 197; September 9, 1984; March 31, 1996, p. 18.
Observer, October 11, 1989.
Phoenix, winter, 1971.
Poetry Australia, October, 1978.
Poetry Nation, number 2, 1974.
Publishers Weekly, August 29, 1994, p. 63; June 26, 1995, p. 103
Spectator, August 23, 1969; September 16, 1995, p. 38.
Stand Magazine, Volume 13, number 1, 1972.
Times (London), February 13, 1983; July 23, 1987; December 31, 1987; June 8, 1989.
Times Literary Supplement, February 16, 1967; April 27, 1967; September 28, 1973; September 27, 1974; August 13, 1976; February 22, 1980; November 21, 1980; April 10, 1981; April 1, 1983; January 20, 1984; June 15, 1984; October 30, 1987; June 30, 1989; May 11-17, 1990; October 6, 1995, p. 26.
Washington Post Book World, November 26, 1972.
World Literature Today, autumn, 1995, p. 790.

OBITUARIES:

PERIODICALS

Economist, April 20, 1996, p. 78.
Facts on File, April 18, 1996, p. 272.
New York Times, April 16, 1996, p. 11.*

* * *

BROWN, Rita Mae 1944-

PERSONAL: Born November 28, 1944, in Hanover, PA; adopted daughter of Ralph (a butcher) and Julia Ellen (Buckingham) Brown. *Education:* Attended University of Florida; Broward Junior College, A.A., 1965; New York University, B.A., 1968; New York School of Visual Arts, cinematography certificate, 1968; Institute for Policy Studies, Washington, DC, Ph.D., 1973. *Avocational interests:* Polo, fox hunting, horses, gardening.

ADDRESSES: Home—Charlottesville, VA. *Office*—American Artists Inc., P. O. Box 4671, Charlottesville, VA 22905. *Agent*—The Wendy Weil Agency, 232 Madison Ave., New York, NY 10016.

CAREER: Writer. Sterling Publishing, New York City, photo editor, 1969-70; Federal City College, Washington, DC, lecturer in sociology, 1970-71; Institute for Policy Studies, Washington, research fellow, 1971-73; Goddard College, Plainfield, VT, visiting member of faculty in feminist studies, beginning 1973. Founder, Redstockings Radical Feminist Group, National Gay Task Force, National Women's Political Caucus; co-founder, Radical Lesbians; member of board of directors of Sagaris, a feminist school. American Artists Inc., Charlottesville, VA, president, 1980—. Member of literary panel, National Endowment for the Arts, 1978-81; Hemingway judge for first fiction PEN International, 1984; blue ribbon panelist for Prime Time Emmy Awards, 1984, 1986.

MEMBER: PEN International.

AWARDS, HONORS: Shared Writers Guild of America award, 1983, for television special *I Love Liberty;* Emmy Award nominations for *I Love Liberty,* 1982, and *The Long Hot Summer,* ABC miniseries, 1985; Literary Lion Award, New York Public Library, 1986; named Charlottesville Favorite Author.

WRITINGS:

(Translator) *Hrotsvitra: Six Medieval Latin Plays,* New York University Press (New York City), 1971.

The Hand That Cradles the Rock (poems), New York University Press, 1971.

Rubyfruit Jungle (novel; also see below), Daughters, Inc. (Plainfield, VT), 1973, hardcover edition, Bantam (New York City), 1988.

Songs to a Handsome Woman (poems), Diana Press (Baltimore, MD), 1973.

In Her Day (novel), Daughters, Inc., 1976.

A Plain Brown Rapper (essays), Diana Press, 1976.

Six of One (novel), Harper (New York City), 1978.

Southern Discomfort (novel), Harper, 1982.

Sudden Death (novel), Bantam, 1983.

High Hearts (novel), Bantam, 1986.

The Poems of Rita Mae Brown, Crossing Press (Trumansburg, NY), 1987.

Starting from Scratch: A Different Kind of Writer's Manual (nonfiction), Bantam, 1988.

Bingo (novel), Bantam, 1988.

(With Sneaky Pie Brown) *Wish You Were Here* (mystery), Bantam, 1990.

(With Sneaky Pie Brown) *Rest in Pieces* (mystery), Bantam, 1992.

Venus Envy (novel), Bantam, 1993.

Dolley: A Novel of Dolley Madison in Love and War (novel), Bantam, 1994.

(With Sneaky Pie Brown) *Murder at Monticello, or, Old Sins* (mystery), Bantam, 1994.

(With Sneaky Pie Brown) *Pay Dirt, or, Adventures at Ash Lawn,* Bantam, 1995.

Riding Shotgun, Bantam, 1996.

(With Sneaky Pie Brown) *Murder, She Meowed* (mystery), Bantam, 1996.

Also author or co-author of eight screenplays, including *Rubyfruit Jungle* (based on novel of same title) and *Slumber Party Massacre;* contributor to script of television special *I Love Liberty,* ABC-TV, 1982, and author of television filmscripts for *The Long Hot Summer,* a mini-series for NBC, 1985, *The Mists of Avalon,* 1986, *The Girls of Summer,* 1989, *Selma, Lord, Selma,* 1989, *Rich Men, Single Women,* 1989, *Home, Sweet Home,* CBS, 1990, and *Graceland,* Napello County Productions, 1992.

SIDELIGHTS: With the 1973 publication of her "exuberantly raunchy" autobiographical novel *Rubyfruit Jungle,* Rita Mae Brown joined the ranks of those in the forefront of the feminist and gay rights movements. Described by *Ms.* reviewer Marilyn Webb as "an inspiring, bravado adventure story of a female Huck Finn named Molly Bolt," *Rubyfruit Jungle* was at first rejected by editors at the major New York publishing companies due to what they believed to be its lack of mass-market appeal. Eventually published by the small feminist firm Daughters, Inc., it sold an unexpected 70,000 copies. The book's popularity soon brought it to the attention of Bantam Books, which acquired the rights to *Rubyfruit Jungle* in 1977 and printed an additional 300,000 copies. Total sales of the novel number more than one million, and in 1988 Bantam released the book for the first time in hardcover form.

As Webb's comment suggests, *Rubyfruit Jungle* is told in a picaresque, Mark Twain-like fashion, an observation shared by *New Boston Review* critic Shelly Temchin Henze. "Imagine, if you will, Tom Sawyer, only smarter; Huckleberry Finn, only foulmouthed, female, and lesbian, and you have an idea of Molly Bolt," writes Henze. Though some have adopted *Rubyfruit Jungle* as "a symbol of a movement, a sisterly struggle," the critic continues, the plot of the book is basically that of the "classic American success story." Explains Henze: "*Rubyfruit Jungle* is not about revolution, nor even particularly about feminism. It is about standing on your own two feet, creaming the competition, looking out for Number One." The truly original part of the novel, maintains the critic, is Brown's perspective. "While American heroes may occasionally be women, they may not be lesbian. Or if they are, they had better be discreet or at least miserable. Not Molly. She is lusty and lewd and pursues sex with relentless gusto."

Village Voice reviewer Bertha Harris has a few reservations about the authenticity of Brown's portrayal of lesbian life. "Much of Molly's world seems a cardboard stage set lighted to reveal only Molly's virtues and those characteristics which mark her as the 'exceptional' lesbian," remarks Harris. Nevertheless, Harris goes on to state, "it is exactly this quality of *Rubyfruit Jungle* which makes it exemplary (for women) of its kind: an American primitive, whose predecessors have dealt only with male heroes. Although Molly Bolt is not a real woman, she is at least the first real *image* of a heroine in the noble savage, leatherstocking, true-blue bullfighting tradition in this country's literature."

Another *Village Voice* critic, Terry Curtis Fox, views *Rubyfruit Jungle* in a somewhat different light. Like Henze, Fox finds that Brown relies on a well-known theme for her novel, namely, "sensitive member of outside group heads toward American society and lives to tell the tale." Since this portrayal of resilience and triumph in the face of adversity is so familiar and appealing, maintains the reviewer, "you don't have to be gay or female to identify with Molly Bolt—she is one of the outsiders many of us believe ourselves to be." Furthermore, says Fox, Brown "can laugh at herself as well as at others, and make us laugh, too."

Acutely aware of the fact that humor is a quality seldom found in books dealing with homosexual life, Brown attaches special importance to her ability to make readers laugh, regarding it as a means of overcoming offensive stereotypes. "Most lesbians are thought to be ugly, neurotic and self-destructive and I just am not," she explains in a *New York Times* article. "There's no way they can pass me off that way. I'm not passing myself off as gorgeous, and a bastion of sanity, but I'm certainly not like those gay stereotypes of the miserable lesbian, the poor woman who couldn't get a man and eventually commits suicide. . . . I'm funny. Funny people are dangerous. They knock down barriers. It's hard to hate people when they're funny. I try to be like Flip Wilson, who helped a lot of white people understand blacks through humor. One way or another, I'll make 'em laugh, too."

The novel *Six of One* was Brown's second major breakthrough into the mass-market arena. Based once again on the author's own life as well as on the lives of her grandmother, mother, and aunt, *Six of One* (like *Rubyfruit Jungle*) attempts to make its point through ribald humor and an emphasis on the poor and uneducated as sources of practical wisdom. The story chronicles the events in a half-Northern, half-Southern, Pennsylvania- Maryland border town from 1909 to 1980 (focusing on the years between 1911 and 1921) as viewed through the eyes of a colorful assortment of female residents. John Fludas of the *Saturday Review,* noting that *Six of One* is a "bright and worthy successor" to *Rubyfruit Jungle,* writes that Brown "explores the town's cultural psychology like an American Evelyn Waugh, finding dignity and beauty without bypassing the zany and the corrupt. . . . If at times the comedy veers toward slapstick, and if there are spots when the prose just grazes the beauty of the human moment . . . , the novel loses none of its warmth."

Both Eliot Fremont-Smith and Richard Boeth feel that Brown could have done a better job with her material. Commenting in *Village Voice,* for example, Fremont-Smith admits that *Six of One* "does have a winning

cheerfulness," but concludes that "it's mostly just garrulous. . . . As a novel, it doesn't go anywhere; there's no driving edge; and the chatter dissipates. And as a polemical history (the secret and superior dynamics of female relationships), it gives off constant little backfires." *Newsweek* critic Boeth is even less impressed. He states: "It is a major sadness to report that Brown has made her women [in *Six of One*] not only boring but false. . . . Her only verbal tool is the josh—speech that is not quite witty, sly, wry, sardonic, ironic or even, God help us, clever, but only self-consciously breezy. . . . These aren't human beings talking; it's 310 pages of 'Gilligan's Island.'"

Henze also finds fault with Brown's characterization, remarking that the author peoples an otherwise "surprisingly accepting, even celebratory portrait of down-home America" with men and women who exhibit "the simplicity of heroes of a Western." Continues the critic: "Time progresses, measured off in days and years [in *Six of One*], but the characters do not: the two old biddies at the center of the narrative trade off the same scatological insults at seventy as at six; [another personage] acquires political insight but no emotional depth."

In her *New York Arts Journal* review of *Six of One,* Liz Mednick attributes these characterization problems to Brown's determination "to show how wise, witty, wonderful and cute women really are. Her silent competitor in this game is the masculine standard; her method, systematic oneupmanship. The women in *Six of One* buzz around like furies trying to out-curse, out-class, out-wit, out-smart, out-shout, out-smoke, out-drink, out-read, out-think, out-lech, out-number and outrage every man, dead or alive, in history. Needless to say, ambition frequently leads the author to extremes. . . . As if to insure her success, Brown makes her men as flat as the paper on which they're scrawled. The problem with her men is not even so much that they lack dimension as that they don't quite qualify as male." In short, concludes Mednick, *Six of One* "is less a novel than a wordy costume the author wears to parade herself before her faceless audience. Her heroines are presented not for inspection but as subjects for whom the narrative implicitly demands admiration."

Washington Post Book World reviewer Cynthia Macdonald, on the other hand, cites *Six of One* as evidence of a welcome change in women's literature. She writes: "The vision of women we have usually gotten from women novelists is of pain and struggle or pain and passivity; it is seldom joyous and passionate, and almost never funny. And what humor there was has been of the suffering, self-deprecating New York Jewish stand-up comedian type. *Six of One* by Rita Mae Brown is joyous, passionate and funny. What a pleasure! . . . In spite of its spacious time span, this is no historical novel. . . . [It] clicks between the present and the past neatly and precisely. . . . I believe that Brown uses a kind of revisionist history to support her conviction that what was seen in the first half of the 20th century as the life of women was only what was on the surface, not what was underneath. She opens the seams to give us her vision of what was really there. We are shown not the seamy side of life, but a body ready for anything, especially celebration."

Responding to criticism that women of the early 1900s could not possibly have been as liberated, not to mention as raucous, as they are depicted in the novel, Brown told Leonore Fleischer in a *Washington Post Book World* interview: "I grew up with these two almost mythical figures around me, my mother and my aunt, who didn't give a rat's a— what anybody thought. They'd say anything to anybody, and they did as they damn well pleased. We were so poor, who cares what poor people do? Literature is predominantly written by middle-class people for middle-class people and their lives were real different. As a girl, I never saw a woman knuckle under to a man, or a man to a woman, for that matter. . . . The people closest to me were all very dominating characters. The men weren't weak, but somehow the women . . . were the ones you paid attention to."

Though it, too, focuses on the difficulties straight and gay women face in a hypocritical and judgmental society, Brown's novel *Sudden Death* represents what the author herself terms "a stylistic first for me." Written in an uncharacteristically plain and direct manner, *Sudden Death* examines the "often vicious and cold-blooded" world of women's professional tennis; many readers assume that it more or less chronicles Brown's experiences and observations during her involvement with star player Martina Navratilova. As Brown sees it, however, the book is much more than that: it is the fulfillment of a promise to a dying friend, sportswriter Judy Lacy, who had always wanted to write a novel against the background of women's tennis. Just prior to her death from a brain tumor in 1980, Lacy extracted a reluctant promise from Brown to write such a novel, even though Brown "didn't think sports were a strong enough metaphor for literature." "[Judy] tricked me

into writing it," explained the author to Fleischer in a *Publishers Weekly* column. "She knew me well enough to know how I'd feel about my promise, that it would be a deathbed promise. . . . I thought about her all the time I was writing it. It was strange to be using material that you felt belonged to somebody else. It's really Judy's book."

For the most part, critics agree that *Sudden Death* has few of the qualities that make *Rubyfruit Jungle* and *Six of One* so entertaining. In the *Chicago Tribune Book World,* for instance, John Blades notes that despite the inclusion of "intriguing sidelights on how [tennis] has been commercialized and corrupted by sponsors, promoters and greedy players," *Sudden Death* "lacks the wit and vitality that might have made it good, unwholesome fun. Brown seems preoccupied here with extraliterary affairs; less interested in telling a story than in settling old scores."

Anne Chamberlin has a similar reaction to the novel, commenting in the *Washington Post:* "If you thought Nora Ephron's *Heartburn* had cornered the market on true heartbreak, thinly veiled, make room for *Sudden Death*. . . . Don't get mad; get even, as the saying goes, and this novel should bring the score to deuce. It not only chops the stars of women's professional tennis down to size; it tackles the whole pro tennis establishment. . . . Having reduced that tableau to rubble, Brown turns her guns on America's intolerance of lesbians. That's a lot of targets for one bombing run, and all 241 acerbic pages of *Sudden Death* are jammed with as disagreeable a bunch of people doing mean things to each other as you are likely to meet at one time."

"I would like to be able to report without qualification that this novel is a smash, an ace," states *Los Angeles Times Book Review* critic Kay Mills in her article on *Sudden Death*. "But that would be like calling a ball a winner just because you admired the way someone played yesterday." Though Mills does point out that "Brown is devastating to the hype, the fashion shows, [and] the product pimping that now accompany women's tennis," she believes that the protagonist is characterized so flatly "that one is devoid of sympathy for her when a jealous rival seeks to break her."

In short, concludes Elisabeth Jakab in the *New York Times Book Review*, Brown "is not at her best here. The world of tennis does not seem to be congenial terrain for her, and her usually natural and easy style seems cramped. The novel tends to read like the casebook of an anthropologist stranded in the midst of a disappointingly boring tribe. She does what she can, but there's just not that much to work with. In *Sudden Death* we can almost hear the pieces of the plot clanking into their proper slots."

Brown, who says she does not read reviews of her books, is nevertheless aware of the kinds of remarks critics have made about *Sudden Death,* to which she responds: "I don't care; it doesn't matter at all; and anyway, I'm already on the next book. . . . I wrote this because Judy asked me to. . . . I learned a lot, but I can't wait to get back on my own territory." Three years after the publication of *Sudden Death,* Brown produced *High Hearts,* followed by the novel *Bingo* two years later. According to Carolyn See of the *Los Angeles Times, High Hearts* is "a truly wacko novel," while Carolyn Banks of the *Washington Post* calls *Bingo* a "pitch for a comic novel, a run-through rather than at something given us at performance level." While neither book has achieved the popularity and critical respect of *Rubyfruit Jungle,* both have addressed Brown's familiar themes of feminism and relationships—both homosexual and heterosexual—and have satisfied admirers of Brown's glib, often raunchy prose.

In 1990, Brown attempted a literary departure, of sorts. With the "help" of her cat Sneaky Pie Brown, she wrote a mystery entitled *Wish You Were Here.* The plot of the book is rather complicated, full of death by cement and train "squishing." At the center of all the mayhem is postmistress Harry and her pets, a cat named Mrs. Murphy and a Welsh Corgi named Tee Tucker. According to See, *Wish You Were Here* is "a carefree canvas for Rita Mae Brown—who remember, has declared independence from the rest of us—to air certain of her own views on the human, feline, and canine condition. . . . Independence is her great thing. And animals, and nature, and a few friends. Not a bad agenda, come to think of it."

After her first successful attempt at murder mysteries, Brown continued with a second mystery, *Rest in Pieces.* As the title suggests, the murder victim this time is dismembered and dispersed, and, as Marilyn Stasio writes in *The New York Times Book Review,* "turns up in bits and pieces all over town." The point, according to Stasio, is not to shock readers with gruesome detail: "It is the shattering of [the villagers'] intimacy by acts of violence that Ms. Brown examines so thoughtfully, creating such an enchanting world of Crozet that we shudder to see any more of its citizens in their graves. Or caught with red hands."

Brown resumes her focus on a strong lesbian character in her next novel, *Venus Envy.* Published in 1993, the book begins when a successful art dealer, Mary Armstrong Frazier, is misdiagnosed and, under the assumption that her death is immanent, "comes out" through a series of letters to her family and friends. Once she discovers that she will live after all, Frazier must deal with the fall-out of the letters. She also must face a realization the terminal diagnosis first brought to light—that she has never truly been in love. Brown addresses this through the fantastic device of having Frazier suddenly transported to her favorite painting. The painting depicts Mt. Olympus, and while there, Frazier learns from Venus and other deities what true love requires.

Although her forthright treatment of lesbianism first attracted many critics to *Rubyfruit Jungle,* reception of *Venus Envy* has been somewhat less enthusiastic. Carla Tomaso, who finds Frazier to be another of Brown's loveable, "irreverent individualists," suggests in a *Los Angeles Times Book Review* that Brown's tenth novel, focusing as it does on the importance of self-acceptance and self-love, is too didactic: "Rita Mae Brown is pulling too many strings," Tomaso writes, adding that "Brown needs to relax and stop worrying that we won't get the message." Book reviewer Diane Salvatore reaches a similar conclusion, calling the book a "disappointment" due to its "cardboard characters" and "mostly tired observations about the strains of gay life." R. C. Scott of *The New York Times Book Review* goes even further, stating that *Venus Envy* "forsake[s] character for the naive and irksome dogma of guilt-free and munificent sex." Nevertheless, Salvatore finds Brown still capable of acerbic wit, and notes that the message, if somewhat repetitive, is valid.

Brown's 1994 historical work, *Dolley: A Novel of Dolley Madison in Love and War* renewed critical admiration of Brown. The product of eight years of research, *Dolley* stimulated interest in one of America's still-admired though nearly-forgotten women at a time when the current first lady, Hillary Rodham Clinton, was sparking new debates on the roles and rights of presidential wives. A series of journal entries interspersed with third-person chapters, *Dolley* follows history more closely in some areas than others.

The connection between the political power-plays, scandals, and infighting during Madison's presidency and contemporary times is not lost on reviewer Roz Spafford, who notes that Washington during the War of 1812 is "not unfamiliar." He states that "Brown successfully brings to life . . . a woman who up to now has not been redeemed by feminist scholarship. . . . Brown persuasively highlights the tensions Dolley Madison must have felt: She was closely connected to her Quaker heritage, yet committed to the war effort, strongly anti-slavery but, through her husband, the owner of slaves." He notes, however, that the novel becomes rather "bland" as it progresses. A *Publishers Weekly* review voices a similar concern, although the "leisurely pace" does yield an interesting "payoff." *Library Journal* reviewer Mary Ann Parker is pleased: "Brown knows how to combine the personal and the political in an attractive picture of Dolley." The key to the novel's success, asserts Joyce Slater in the *Chicago Tribune,* "is the author's obvious affection for her subject."

After her extensive research on Dolley Madison, Brown published two more murder mysteries. The first, *Murder at Monticello,* was published in 1994. Again detective Mary (Harry) Haristeen, along with Mrs. Murphy and Tee Tucker, heads an investigation, this time at the estate of Thomas Jefferson. *Pay Dirt,* published in 1995, takes place at another historic Virginia location, James Monroe's Ash Lawn. This time, a belligerent biker is murdered and a computer foul-up at the local bank creates a two-million-dollar shortfall. More murders and a rescue (Mrs. Murphy, Tee Tucker, and their friends keep Harry from being the murderer's next victim) precede Mrs. Murphy's eventual solution to the crimes.

Both *Murder at Monticello* and *Pay Dirt,* like the earlier murder mysteries with the feline co-author, run the risk of being cutesy or even inane, but critics have yet to dismiss them as such. Instead, the most frequent description is "cozy," a term used not only by Johnson but by a *Publisher's Weekly* reviewer as well. Although somewhat of a change from earlier works like *Rubyfruit Jungle* or *Southern Discomfort,* Brown's murder mysteries continue to convey what a *Los Angeles Times* book reviewer calls her "acerbic humor." In his 1990 *Quill and Quire* review of *Wish You Were Here,* Mark Gerson compares Brown's efforts to the work of Agatha Christie on the grounds that "Brown uses village life much the same way Agatha Christie did: to illustrate that human emotions are no less complex in a rural backwater than they are in the big city." Three mysteries later, *Publisher's Weekly* considers *Pay Dirt* part of an ongoing series, announcing that it is "the best Mrs. Murphy adventure yet."

With the 1996 publication of *Riding Shotgun,* Brown returns to the literary device of time travel. Newly widowed Cig Blackwood is transported from a present-day Virginia fox hunt to one taking place in 1699, where she joins her ancestors in their struggles with the elements, the natives, and other obstacles encountered in plantation life. The actual purpose of the time travel is to help Cig understand her relationship with her husband and to empower her to find her true love.

An entry in *Kirkus Reviews* states that *Riding Shotgun* "sinks under the weight of its impossible plot." Although somewhat put off by this "high-risk plot device," the reviewer goes on to admire Brown's "meticulously researched descriptions of Virginia's colonial life, as well as her dead-on ridicule of modern-day bad behavior." Seemingly more familiar with Brown's novels, a *Publishers Weekly* review considers the book "every bit as giddily enjoyable as her series of Mrs. Murphy mysteries." *Booklist* reviewer Brad Hopper sees the book in a more positive light, stating that the time travel device "works like a charm in Brown's capable hands" and citing the "delightfully romantic ending" as one of the novel's strong points.

Also in 1996, the Browns published their fifth murder mystery, *Murder, She Meowed.* Marilyn Stasio, in the *New York Times Book Review,* begins her assessment with a firm endorsement. "People who love cats (count me in) but loathe cute cat mysteries (keep counting) have a friend in Rita Mae Brown," writes Stasio, who adds that Brown's "solid storytelling and tart regional voice and the nice satirical edge she gives to her characterizations (human and otherwise) keep her mysteries from congealing in their own cuteness." *Murder, She Meowed* takes place at the annual steeplechase at Montpelier, the former estate of James and Dolley Madison. Someone, it seems, is stabbing jockeys, whose deaths initiate some surprising information about their suspicious backgrounds. Once again, Mrs. Murphy and her animal friends (including some barn mice with whom she strikes a truce) solve the mystery that the humans are too dumb to figure out.

Since her initial publication of *Rubyfruit Jungle*—which remains her best known work—Brown's identity as a writer has developed several facets. Despite her commitment to depicting gay women in a positive light, Brown balks at being labeled a "lesbian writer." In a *Publishers Weekly* interview, she states: "Calling me a lesbian writer is like calling [James] Baldwin a black writer. I say no; he is not: he is a great writer and that is that. I don't understand people who say Baldwin writes about 'the black experience'—as if it is so different from 'the white experience' that the two aren't even parallel. That is so insulting . . . and I really hate it."

In an essay written for the *Publishers Weekly* column "My Say," Brown elaborates on her opposition to the use of such labels. "Classifying fiction by the race, sex or sex preference of the author is a discreet form of censorship," she maintains. "Americans buy books by convicted rapists, murderers and Watergate conspirators because those books are placed on the bestseller shelf, right out in front where people can see them. Yet novels by people who are not safely white or resolutely heterosexual are on the back shelves, out of sight. It's the back of the bus all over again. Is this not a form of censorship? Are we not being told that some novels are more 'American' than others? That some writers are true artists, while the rest of us are 'spokespersons' for our group? What group? A fiction writer owes allegiance to the English language only. With that precious, explosive tool the writer must tell the *emotional* truth. And the truth surely encompasses the fact that we Americans are female and male; white, brown, black, yellow and red; young, old and in-between; rich and poor; straight and gay; smart and stupid. . . . On the page all humans really are created equal. All stories are important. All lives are worthy of concern and description. . . . Incarcerating authors into types is an act of treason against literature and, worse, an assault on the human heart." Therefore, concludes Brown in the *Publishers Weekly* interview, "next time anybody calls me a lesbian writer I'm going to knock their teeth in. I'm a writer and I'm a woman and I'm from the South and I'm alive, and that is that."

BIOGRAPHICAL/CRITICAL SOURCES:

BOOKS

Contemporary Literary Criticism, Gale (Detroit), Volume 18, 1981, Volume 43, 1987.
Ward, Carol Marie, *Rita Mae Brown,* Twayne (Boston), 1993.

PERIODICALS

Advocate, June 15, 1993, p. 68.
Best Sellers, February, 1979, May, 1982.
Booklist, August, 1992, p. 1997; February 15, 1993, p. 1011; March 15, 1994, p. 1302; October 1, 1994, p. 241; February 1, 1996, p. 898.
Chatelaine, May, 1993, p. 12.
Chicago Tribune Book World, July 4, 1982; July 3, 1983; June 26, 1994, p. 6.
Christian Science Monitor, November 22, 1978.
Detroit Free Press, May 15, 1983.
Detroit News, May 8, 1983.
Globe and Mail (Toronto), May 28, 1988; November 5, 1988.
Kirkus Reviews, January 15, 1996, p. 83.
Lambda Book Report, May 1993, pp. 13-14.
Library Journal, November 15, 1987, p. 83; February 1, 1988, p. 64; October 15, 1988, p. 100; November 1, 1990, p. 128; April 15, 1994, p. 108; October 15, 1995, p. 86.
Los Angeles Times, March 10, 1982; April 28, 1986; February 22, 1988; November 10, 1988.
Los Angeles Times Book Review, May 22, 1983; November 27, 1988; April 4, 1993; December 10, 1995, p. 15.
Maclean's, November 13, 1978.
Ms., March, 1974; June, 1974; April, 1977.
Nation, June 19, 1982.
New Boston Review, April-May, 1979.
Newsweek, October 2, 1978.
New York Arts Journal, November-December, 1978.
New York Times, September 26, 1977.
New York Times Book Review, March 21, 1982; June 19, 1983; May 17, 1987, p. 54; December 20, 1987, p. 13; June 5, 1988, p. 13; September 6, 1992, p. 17; June 27, 1993, p. 18; December 8, 1996.
Omni, April, 1988, p. 36; December 16, 1990, p. 33.
People, April 26, 1982; September 6, 1992, p. 17; June 27, 1993, p. 18.
Publishers Weekly, October 2, 1978; February 18, 1983; July 15, 1983; November 20, 1987, p. 66; December 11, 1987, p. 56; September 9, 1988, p. 122; September 21, 1990, p. 66; June 1, 1992, p. 54; February 8, 1993, p. 76; March 28, 1994, p. 81; August 14, 1995, p. 79; October 16, 1995, p. 44; January 22, 1996, p. 57; October 14, 1996, p. 67.
Quill and Quire, December, 1990, p. 24.
Saturday Review, September 30, 1978.
School Library Journal, April, 1991, p. 153.
Times Literary Supplement, December 7, 1979.
Village Voice, September 12, 1977; October 9, 1978.
Washington Post, May 31, 1983; October 27, 1988, p. 11.
Washington Post Book World, October 15, 1978; May 1, 1994.
Wilson Library Bulletin, January, 1991, p. 113.*

BUKOWSKI, Charles 1920-1994

PERSONAL: Born August 16, 1920, in Andernach, Germany; died of leukemia, March 9, 1994, in San Pedro, CA; brought to the United States, 1922; married Barbara Fry, October, 1955 (divorced); married Linda Lee Beighle; children: Marina Louise. *Education:* Attended Los Angeles City College, 1939-41. *Politics:* None. *Religion:* None. *Avocational interests:* Playing the horses, symphony music.

CAREER: Worked as an unskilled laborer, beginning 1941, in various positions, including dishwasher, truck driver and loader, mail carrier, guard, gas station attendant, stock boy, warehouse worker, shipping clerk, post office clerk, parking lot attendant, Red Cross orderly, and elevator operator; also worked in dog biscuit factory, slaughterhouse, cake and cookie factory, and hung posters in New York subways. Former editor of *Harlequin,* and *Laugh Literary and Man the Humping Guns;* columnist ("Notes of a Dirty Old Man"), *Open City* and *L.A. Free Press.*

AWARDS, HONORS: National Endowment for the Arts grant, 1974; Loujon Press Award; Silver Reel Award, San Francisco Festival of the Arts, for documentary film.

WRITINGS:

POETRY

Flower, Fist, and Bestial Wail, Hearse Press, 1959.
Longshot Poems for Broke Players, 7 Poets Press, 1961.
Run with the Hunted, Midwest Poetry Chapbooks, 1962.
Poems and Drawings, EPOS, 1962.
It Catches My Heart in Its Hands: New and Selected Poems, 1955-1963, Loujon Press, 1963.
Grip the Walls, Wormwood Review Press, 1964.
Cold Dogs in the Courtyard, Literary Times, 1965.
Crucifix in a Deathhand: New Poems, 1963-1965, Loujon Press, 1965.
The Genius of the Crowd, 7 Flowers Press, 1966.
True Story, Black Sparrow Press (Santa Rosa, CA), 1966.
On Going out to Get the Mail, Black Sparrow Press, 1966.
To Kiss the Worms Goodnight, Black Sparrow Press, 1966.
The Girls, Black Sparrow Press, 1966.
The Flower Lover, Black Sparrow Press, 1966.
Night's Work, Wormwood Review Press, 1966.

2 by Bukowski, Black Sparrow Press, 1967.
The Curtains Are Waving, Black Sparrow Press, 1967.
At Terror Street and Agony Way, Black Sparrow Press, 1968.
Poems Written before Jumping out of an 8-Story Window, Litmus, 1968.
If We Take. . ., Black Sparrow Press, 1969.
The Days Run Away Like Wild Horses over the Hills, Black Sparrow Press, 1969.
Another Academy, Black Sparrow Press, 1970.
Fire Station, Capricorn Press, 1970.
Mockingbird, Wish Me Luck, Black Sparrow Press, 1972.
Me and Your Sometimes Love Poems, Kisskill Press, 1972.
While the Music Played, Black Sparrow Press, 1973.
Love Poems to Marina, Black Sparrow Press, 1973.
Burning in Water, Drowning in Flame: Selected Poems, 1955-1973, Black Sparrow Press, 1974.
Chilled Green, Alternative Press, 1975.
Africa, Paris, Greece, Black Sparrow Press, 1975.
Weather Report, Pomegranate Press, 1975.
Winter, No Mountain, 1975.
Tough Company, bound with *The Last Poem* by Diane Wakoski, Black Sparrow Press, 1975.
Scarlet, Black Sparrow Press, 1976.
Maybe Tomorrow, Black Sparrow Press, 1977.
Love Is a Dog from Hell: Poems, 1974-1977, Black Sparrow Press, 1977.
Legs, Hips, and Behind, Wormwood Review Press, 1979.
Play the Piano Drunk Like a Percussion Instrument until the Fingers Begin to Bleed a Bit, Black Sparrow Press, 1979.
A Love Poem, Black Sparrow Press, 1979.
Dangling in the Tournefortia, Black Sparrow Press, 1981.
The Last Generation, Black Sparrow Press, 1982.
Sparks, Black Sparrow Press, 1983.
War All the Time: Poems 1981-1984, Black Sparrow Press, 1984.
The Roominghouse Madrigals: Early Selected Poems, 1946-1966, Black Sparrow Press, 1988.
Beauti-ful and Other Long Poems, Wormwood Books and Magazines, 1988.
People Poems: 1982-1991, Wormwood Books and Magazines, 1991.
The Last Night of the Earth Poems, Black Sparrow Press, 1992.
Days Run Away Like Wild Horses over the Hills, Black Sparrow Press, 1993.
(With Kenneth Price), *Heat Wave,* Black Sparrow Graphic Arts (Santa Rosa, CA), 1995.

NOVELS

Post Office, Black Sparrow Press, 1971.
Factotum, Black Sparrow Press, 1975.
Women, Black Sparrow Press, 1978.
Ham on Rye, Black Sparrow Press, 1982.
Horsemeat, Black Sparrow Press, 1982.
Hollywood, Black Sparrow Press, 1989.
Pulp, Black Sparrow Press, 1994.

SHORT STORIES

Notes of a Dirty Old Man, Essex House, 1969, 2nd edition, 1973.
Erections, Ejaculations, Exhibitions, and General Tales of Ordinary Madness, City Lights, 1972, abridged edition published as *Life and Death in the Charity Ward*, London Magazine Editions, 1974; selections, edited by Gail Ghiarello, published as *Tales of Ordinary Madness* and *The Most Beautiful Woman in Town, and Other Stories*, two volumes, City Lights, 1983.
South of No North: Stories of the Buried Life, Black Sparrow Press, 1973.
Bring Me Your Love, illustrated by R. Crumb, Black Sparrow Press, 1983.
Hot Water Music, Black Sparrow Press, 1983.
There's No Business, Black Sparrow Press, 1984.

OTHER

Confessions of a Man Insane Enough to Live with Beasts, Mimeo Press, 1966.
All the Assholes in the World and Mine, Open Skull Press, 1966.
A Bukowski Sampler, edited by Douglas Blazek, Quixote Press, 1969.
(Compiler with Neeli Cherry and Paul Vangelisti) *Anthology of L.A. Poets*, Laugh Literary, 1972.
Art, Black Sparrow Press, 1977.
What They Want, Neville, 1977.
We'll Take Them, Black Sparrow Press, 1978.
You Kissed Lilly, Black Sparrow Press, 1978.
Shakespeare Never Did This, City Lights, 1979.
(With Al Purdy) *The Bukowski/Purdy Letters: A Decade of Dialogue, 1964-1974*, edited by Seamus Cooney, Paget Press (Ontario), 1983.
Under the Influence: A Charles Bukowski Checklist, Water Row Press, 1984.
You Get So Alone at Times That It Just Makes Sense, Black Sparrow Press, 1986.
(Author of Preface) Jack Micheline, *River of Red Wine*, Water Row Press, 1986.

Barfly (screenplay based on Bukowski's life), Cannon Group, 1987, published as *The Movie "Barfly": An Original Screenplay by Charles Bukowski for a Film by Barbet Schroeder*, Black Sparrow Press, 1987.
A Visitor Complains of My Disenfranchise, limited edition, Illuminati, 1987.
Bukowski at Bellevue (video cassette of poetry reading; broadcast on EZTV, West Hollywood, CA, 1988), Black Sparrow Press, 1988.
Septuagenarian Stew: Stories and Poems, Black Sparrow Press, 1990.
(Author of Preface) John Fante, *Ask the Dust*, Black Sparrow Press, 1993.
Run with the Hunted: A Charles Bukowski Reader, edited by John Martin, Harper Collins, 1993.
Screams from the Balcony: Selected Letters 1960-1970 (autobiography), Black Sparrow Press, 1994.
(Author of foreword) Steve Richmond, *Hitler Painted Roses*, Sun Dog Press, 1994.
Confession of a Coward, Black Sparrow Press, 1995.
(Editor) Cooney, Seamus, *Living on Luck: Selected Letters, 1960s-1970s, Volume 2*, Black Sparrow Press, 1995.
Betting on the Muse: Poems & Stories, Black Sparrow Press, 1996.

Also author of the short story "The Copulating Mermaids of Venice, California." Work represented in anthologies, including *Penguin Modern Poets 13,* 1969, *Six Poets,* 1979, and *Notes from the Underground,* edited by John Bryan. Also author of a one-hour documentary film, produced by KCET public television Los Angeles. A collection of Bukowski's papers is housed at the University of California, Santa Barbara.

ADAPTATIONS: Stories from *Erections, Ejaculations, Exhibitions and General Tales of Ordinary Madness* were adapted by Marco Ferreri, Sergio Amidei, and Anthony Foutz into the film *Tales of Ordinary Madness,* Fred Baker, 1983; a film adaptation of *Love Is a Dog from Hell* was produced in 1988; *The Works of Charles Bukowski,* based upon more than thirty of his works published by Black Sparrow Press, was staged by California State University in Los Angeles, 1988; *Crazy Love,* based on *The Copulating Mermaids of Venice, California,* was filmed in 1989.

SIDELIGHTS: Charles Bukowski was a prolific underground writer who depicted the depraved metropolitan environments of the down-trodden members of American society in his poetry and prose. A cult hero, Bukowski relied on experience, emotion, and imagination in his works, often using direct language and violent and sexual imagery. While some critics find his style offensive, others claim that Bukowski satirized the machismo attitude through his routine use of sex, alcohol abuse, and violence. "Without trying to make himself look good, much less heroic, Bukowski writes with a nothing-to-lose truthfulness which sets him apart from most other 'autobiographical' novelists and poets," points out Stephen Kessler in the *San Francisco Review of Books,* adding: "Firmly in the American tradition of the maverick, Bukowski writes with no apologies from the frayed edge of society, beyond or beneath respectability, revealing nasty and alarming underviews." Michael Lally, writing in *Village Voice,* maintains that "Bukowski is . . . a phenomenon. He has established himself as a writer with a consistent and insistent style based on what he projects as his 'personality,' the result of hard, intense living."

Bukowski had "a sandblasted face, warts on his eyelids and a dominating nose that looks as if it were assembled in a junkyard from Studebaker hoods and Buick fenders," describes Paul Ciotti in the *Los Angeles Times Magazine.* "Yet his voice is so soft and bemused that it's hard to take him seriously when he says: 'I don't like people. I don't even like myself. There must be something wrong with me.'" Born in Germany, Bukowski was brought to the United States at the age of two. His father believed in firm discipline and often beat Bukowski for the smallest offenses. A slight child, Bukowski was also bullied by boys his own age, and was frequently rejected by girls because of his bad complexion. "When Bukowski was 13," writes Ciotti, "one of [his friends] invited him to his father's wine cellar and served him his first drink of alcohol. 'It was magic,' Bukowski would later write. 'Why hadn't someone told me?'"

In 1939, Bukowski began attending Los Angeles City College, dropping out at the beginning of World War II and moving to New York to become a writer. The next few years were spent writing and traveling and collecting a pile of rejection slips. By 1946 Bukowski had decided to give up his writing aspirations, and what followed was a binge that took him all over the world and lasted for approximately ten years. Ending up near death, Bukowski's life changed and he started writing again. "If a writer must sample life at its most elemental, then surely Bukowski qualifies as a laureate of poetic preparedness," observes Bob Graalman in the *Dictionary of Literary Biography;* Bukowski's many jobs over the years included stock boy, dishwasher, postal clerk, and factory worker. He did not

begin his professional writing career until the age of thirty-five, and like other contemporaries, Bukowski began by publishing in underground newspapers, especially his local papers *Open City* and the *L.A. Free Press.* "It is tempting to make correlations between [Bukowski's] emergence in Los Angeles literary circles and the arrival of the 1960s, when poets were still shaking hands with Allen Ginsberg and other poets of his generation while younger activist poets tapped on their shoulders, begging for an introduction," explains Graalman. "Bukowski cultivated his obvious link to both eras—the blackness and despair of the 1950s with the rebellious cry of the 1960s for freedom."

"Published by small, underground presses and ephemeral mimeographed little magazines," describes Jay Dougherty in *Contemporary Novelists,* "Bukowski has gained popularity, in a sense, through word of mouth." Many of his fans regard him as one of the best of the Meat School poets, who are known for their tough and direct masculine writing. "The main character in his poems and short stories, which are largely autobiographical, is usually a down-and-out writer [Henry Chinaski] who spends his time working at marginal jobs (and getting fired from them), getting drunk and making love with a succession of bimbos and floozies," relates Ciotti. "Otherwise, he hangs out with fellow losers—whores, pimps, alcoholics, drifters, the people who lose their rent money at the race track, leave notes of goodbye on dressers and have flat tires on the freeway at 3 a.m."

After his first book of poetry was published in 1959, Bukowski wrote over forty others. Ciotti maintains: "Right from the beginning, Bukowski knew that if a poet wants to be read, he has to be noticed first. 'So,' he once said, 'I got my act up. I wrote vile (but interesting) stuff that made people hate me, that made them curious about this Bukowski. I threw bodies off my porch into the night. I sneered at hippies. I was in and out of drunk tanks. A lady accused me of rape.'"

Flower, Fist and Bestial Wail, Bukowski's first book of poetry, covers the major interests and themes that occupy many of his works, the most important being "the sense of a desolate, abandoned world," as R. R. Cuscaden points out in the *Outsider.* In addition to this sense of desolation, Bukowski also filled his free verse with all the absurdities of life, especially in relation to death. "Bukowski's world, scored and grooved by the impersonal instruments of civilized industrial society, by 20th-century knowledge and experience, remains essentially a world in which meditation and analysis have little part," asserts John William Corrington in *Northwest Review.* Among the subjects used to present this bleak world are drinking, sex, gambling, and music. The actual style of these numerous poems, however, has its virtues, including "a crisp, hard voice; an excellent ear and eye for measuring out the lengths of lines; and an avoidance of metaphor where a lively anecdote will do the same dramatic work," maintains Ken Tucker in *Village Voice.*

It Catches My Heart in Its Hands, published in 1963, collects poetry written by Bukowski between the years of 1955 and 1963. "Individual poems merge to form together a body of work unrivalled in kind and very nearly unequalled in quality by Bukowski's contemporaries," states Corrington. The poems touch on topics that were familiar to Bukowski, such as rerolling cigarette butts, the horse that came in, a hundred-dollar call girl, and a rumpled hitchhiker on his way to nowhere. *It Catches My Heart in Its Hands* contains poems which "are energetic, tough, and unnerving," relates Dabney Stuart in *Poetry.* And Kenneth Rexroth asserts in the *New York Times Book Review* that Bukowski "belongs in the small company of poets of real, not literary, alienation."

Bukowski's more recent poetry, such as *Dangling in the Tournefortia,* published in 1982, continues along the same vein as his first collection. "Low-life bard of Los Angeles, Mr. Bukowski has nothing new for us here," observes Peter Schjeldahl in the *New York Times Book Review,* "simply more and still more accounts in free verse of his follies with alcohol and women and of fellow losers hitting bottom and somehow discovering new ways to continue falling." Despite the subject matter, though, Schjeldahl finds himself enjoying the poems in *Dangling in the Tournefortia.* "Bukowski writes well," he continues, "with ear-pleasing cadences, wit and perfect clarity, which are all the more beguiling for issuing from a stumblebum persona. His grace with words gives a comic gleam to even his meanest revelations." William Logan, writing in the *Times Literary Supplement,* concludes: "Life here has almost entirely mastered art."

Similar to his poetry in subject matter, Bukowski's short stories also deal with sex, violence, and the absurdities of life. In his first collection of short stories, *Erections, Ejaculations, Exhibitions, and General Tales of Ordinary Madness,* later abridged and published as *Life and Death in the Charity Ward,*

Bukowski "writes as an unregenerate lowbrow contemptuous of our claims to superior being," describes Thomas R. Edwards in the *New York Review of Books.* On the other hand, Peter Ackroyd maintains in the *Spectator,* "A dull character finally emerges, and it is a dullness which spreads through these stories like a stain." Thomas, however, concludes that "in some of these sad and funny stories [Bukowski's] status as a relic isn't wholly without its sanctity."

The protagonists in the stories in *Hot Water Music,* published in 1983, live in cheap hotels and are often struggling underground writers, similar to Bukowski himself. Bukowski's main autobiographical figure is Henry Chinaski, who appears in a few of these stories and in many of his novels. Among the semi-autobiographical stories in this collection are two which deal with events following the funeral of Bukowski's father. The other stories deal with numerous violent acts, including a jealous wife shooting her husband over an old infidelity, a drunk bank manager molesting young children, a former stripper mutilating the man she is seducing, and a young man who gets over his impotence by raping a neighbor in his apartment elevator. "Lives of quiet desperation explode in apparently random and unmotivated acts of bizarre violence," describes Michael F. Harper in the *Los Angeles Times Book Review,* adding: "There is certainly a raw power in these stories, but Bukowski's hard-boiled fatalism seems to me the flip side of the humanism he denies and therefore just as false as the sentimentality he ridicules." Erling Friis-Baastad, writing in the Toronto *Globe and Mail,* concludes, "In his best work, Bukowski comes close to making us comprehend, if not the sense of it all, then at least its intensity. He cannot forget, and he will not let us forget, that every morning at 3 a.m. broken people lie 'in their beds, trying in vain to sleep, and deserving that rest, if they could find it.'"

Bukowski continues his examination of "broken people" in such novels as *Post Office* and *Ham on Rye.* In *Post Office,* Henry Chinaski is very similar to ex-postman Bukowski; he is a remorseless drunk and womanizer who spends a lot of time at the race track. Chinaski also has to deal with his monotonous and strenuous job, as well as a number of harassing supervisors. Eventually marrying a rich nymphomaniac from Texas, Chinaski is inevitably dumped for another man and finds himself back at the post office. "Bukowski's loser's string of anecdotes, convulsively funny and also sad, is unflagging entertainment but in the end doesn't add up to more than the sum of its parts, somehow missing the novelist's alchemy," asserts a *Times Literary Supplement* contributor. But Valentine Cunningham, also writing in the *Times Literary Supplement,* sees the novel as a success: "Pressed in by Post Office bureaucrats, their mean-minded regulations and their heaps of paperwork, the misfit [Chinaski] looks frequently like an angel of light. His refusal to play respectability ball with the cajoling, abusive, never-take-no-for-an-answer loops who own the mailboxes he attends . . . can make even this ribald mess of a wretch seem a shining haven of sanity in the prevailing Los Angeles grimnesses."

Ham on Rye, published in 1982, features Henry Chinaski as its protagonist. Bukowski travels into new territory with this novel, describing his/Chinaski's childhood and adolescent years. The first part of the book is dominated by Chinaski's brutal and domineering father, focusing more on Henry as he moves into his lonely and isolated adolescent years. Following high school, Chinaski holds a job and attends college for a short period of time before beginning his "real" life of cheap hotels, sleazy bars, and the track. It is also at this time that Henry starts to send stories to magazines and accumulate a number of rejection slips. "Particularly striking is Bukowski's uncharacteristic restraint: the prose is hard and exact, the writer's impulse towards egocentricity repressed," comments David Montrose in the *Times Literary Supplement.* Ben Reuven, writing in the *Los Angeles Times Book Review,* describes the "first-person reminiscences" in *Ham on Rye* as being "taut, vivid, intense, sometimes poignant, [and] often hilarious," concluding that Bukowski's "prose has never been more vigorous or more powerful."

Continuing the examination of his younger years, Bukowski wrote the screenplay for the movie *Barfly,* which was released in 1987, starring Mickey Rourke. The movie focuses on three days in the life of Bukowski at the age of twenty-four. As the lead character, Henry Chinaski, Rourke spends most of these three days in a seedy bar, where he meets the first real love of his life, Wanda, played by Faye Dunaway. While this new romance is developing, a beautiful literary editor takes an interest in Chinaski's writings, and tries to seduce him with success. Chinaski must then choose between the two women. "At first *Barfly* seems merely a slice of particularly wretched life," observes David Ansen in *Newsweek.* "But under its seedy surface emerges a cunning comedy—and a touching love story." Vincent Canby, writing in the *New York Times,* sees the film as dealing "in the continuing revelation of character in a succession of horrifying, buoyant, crazy confronta-

tions of barflies, bartenders, police and other representatives of the world of the sober." And Michael Wilmington concludes in the *Los Angeles Times:* "Whatever its flaws, [*Barfly*] does something more films should do: It opens up territory, opens up a human being. The worst of it has the edge of coughed-up whimsy and barroom bragging. But the best has the shock of truth and the harsh sweet kiss of dreams."

Bukowski's experiences with the making of *Barfly* became the basis of his 1989 novel *Hollywood.* Chinaski is now an old man, married to Sarah, a shrewd woman apt to interrupt him during his many repetitive stories. The couple is off hard liquor, but are faithful drinkers of good red wine, and their life is a peaceful one until a filmmaker asks Chinaski to write a screenplay based upon his previous lifestyle; he agrees, figuring that this new venture will leave him enough time to spend at the track. Entering the world of show business, Chinaski finds himself mingling with famous stars, but must also deal with a number of other things, including a tax man (who advises him to spend his advance money before the government can get it). As the project progresses, its funding becomes shaky, the producer threatens to dismember parts of his body if the movie is not made, there are many rewrites, and Chinaski is hit with a terrible sadness. The movie is about what he used to be—a poetic barfly—and covers a time in his life when he feels he did his best writing. An old man now, Chinaski can watch his life being acted out at the movies, but he cannot jump back into it; he is now a successful man leading a respectable life. "The words often jar and Bukowski is better when he lets his dialogue do his griping for him. But this is still a superb snapshot of what filmmaking at the fag-end of the Hollywood dream is all about," relates Toby Moore in the *Times Literary Supplement.* Gary Dretzka, writing in the *Chicago Tribune,* asserts that "Bukowski offers an often insightful and continually outrageous view of how some movies get made." Dretzka goes on to advise: "Have some fun: Read this book, then go out and rent the *Barfly* video. Grab a beer and offer a toast to Charles Bukowski—survivor."

Like Dretzka, Kessler also believes in Bukowski's survival abilities, concluding that he "is a soulful poet whose art is an ongoing testimony to perseverance. It's not the drinking and f—-ing and gambling and fighting and shitting that make his books valuable, but the meticulous attention to the most mundane experience, the crusty compassion for his fellow losers, the implicit conviction that by frankly telling the unglamorous facts of hopelessness some stamina and courage can be cultivated."

Pulp, published posthumously, is the novel Bukowski worked on just prior to his death in 1994 of leukemia. It is a send-up, Bukowski-style, of the pulp detective novel. His protagonist, not surprisingly a Bukowski-like character, is Nicky Belane, who sometimes wonders if he is Harry Martel. Like any good pulp detective, Belane has a series of clients including Lady Death (looking for Celine, who has been spotted in L.A. bookstores), John Barton (looking for the Red Sparrow, which is a play on Bukowski's publisher John Martin of Black Sparrow Press), and a host of others, whose stories come together in the final pages. George Stade comments in the *New York Times Book Review,* "It does not, of course take much to send up the hard-boiled detective novel. . . . [T]he conventions . . . seem to mock themselves, if you stand back a bit. But *Pulp* does more than stand back from itself." Daniel Woodreli, writing in *Washington Post Book World,* also finds Bukowski's reworking of a time-honored form refreshing: "The hard-boiled form as a framework is nicely utilized, with snappy dialogue that is always off-center, and oddly very honest." He continues, "[Bukowski] treats it with a kind of poignant ridicule that somehow works. *Pulp* is comic and bizarre and sad without a trace of self-pity." "A whimsical and oddly charming (a word not often used in describing Bukowski's work) spoof," declares Dick Lochte in the *Los Angeles Times Book Review. Chicago Tribune* contributor John Litweller similarly offers high praise, "Thriller novel realism never got 'down' like Bukowski's writing usually did. The result is more fun than an ordinary parody." Stade finds deeper significance in the novel beyond its form: "As parody, *Pulp* does not cut very deep. As a farewell to readers, as a gesture of rapprochement with death, as Bukowski's send-up and send-off of himself, this bio-parable cuts as deep as you would want." Litweller concludes, "Maybe some readers hung up on the young, low-life Bukowski will be disappointed. . . . For the rest of us, it's masterly stuff from the old master in his old age."

Run with the Hunted, published in 1993, is an anthology of Bukowski's stories and poetry, placed chronologically in the periods in which they were set (not published) by longtime publisher and editor, John Martin. It provides a solid overview of Bukowski's work and—given its autobiographical nature—his life. "An effective primer for the uninitiated, or a refresher for past readers who, incredibly, have managed to forget," comments a *Publishers Weekly* contributor. Benjamin Segedin, writing for *Booklist* avers of Bukowski's works: "Less celebrations of self-destruction than honest self-portraiture, they reveal him in all his ugliness as an outsider on the verge of respectability." He continues, "Here is a collection of blunt, hard-edged angry stuff as uncompromising as you will ever hope to find." Elizabeth Young, in the *New Statesman & Society* at once lauds and criticizes the anthology, "From the vast vat of Bukowski homebrew, John Martin has distilled a cut-glass decanter of 100-proof literary perfection. . . . [He] has done Bukowski a great service—and a sort of disservice too. After such a brilliantly constructed anthology, who is going to read all the books?" Bukowski's previously unpublished work, introduced posthumously by Black Sparrow Press in *Betting on the Muse: Poems & Stories,* shows him to have continued in the same vein with the character, Henry Chinaski, as well as the verse that made him, as noted by a *Publishers Weekly* contributor, the "original take-no-prisoners poet." Ray Olson, writing for *Booklist,* finds his stories and poems to be "effortlessly, magnetically readable, especially if you are susceptible to their bargain-basement existentialist charm."

Bukowski's life via his letters is chronicled in *Screams from the Balcony: Selected Letters 1960-1970,* rumored to be the first volume in a series. "The honesty, humor and lack of pretension in these letters make them a must for Bukowski fans and an engaging read for anyone interested in literary lives," writes a *Publishers Weekly* critic. Benjamin Segedin in *Booklist,* speaks for occasional readers and fans alike, finding Bukowski "perversely intriguing, attracting the kind of attention one usually reserves for grisly train wrecks."

BIOGRAPHICAL/CRITICAL SOURCES:

BOOKS

Contemporary Literary Criticism, Gale, Volume 2, 1974, Volume 5, 1976, Volume 9, 1978, Volume 41, 1987, Volume 82, 1994.

Contemporary Novelists, 4th edition, edited by D. L. Kirkpatrick, St. James Press, 1986.

Dictionary of Literary Biography, Volume 5: *American Poets since World War II,* Gale, 1980.

Dorbin, Sanford, *A Bibliography of Charles Bukowski,* Black Sparrow Press, 1969.

Fox, Hugh, *Charles Bukowski: A Critical and Bibliographical Study,* Abyss Publications, 1969.

Harrison, Russell, *Against the American Dream: Essays on Charles Bukowski,* Black Sparrow Press (Santa Rosa, CA), 1994.

Richmond, Steve, *Spinning off Bukowski,* Sun Dog Press (Northville, MI), 1996.

Sherman, Jory, *Bukowski: Friendship, Fame, and Bestial Myth,* Blue Horse Press, 1982.

Weinberg, Jeffrey, editor, *A Charles Bukowski Checklist,* Water Row Press, 1987.

PERIODICALS

Booklist, February 15, 1993, p. 1010; January 15, 1994, p. 893; May 15, 1996, p. 1563.

Chicago Tribune, July 18, 1989; August 28, 1994, p. 6.

Globe and Mail (Toronto), January 21, 1984.

Los Angeles Magazine, June, 1994, p. 76.

Los Angeles Times, March 17, 1983; November 3, 1987; November 5, 1987; September 23, 1988.

Los Angeles Times Book Review, October 3, 1982, p. 6; August 28, 1983, p. 6; December 11, 1983, p. 2; March 17, 1985, p. 4; November 3, 1987; June 4, 1989, p. 4; October 30, 1994, p. 11.

Los Angeles Times Magazine, March 22, 1987, pp. 12-14, 17-19, 23.

New Statesman & Society, June 17, 1994, p. 37.

Newsweek, October 26, 1987, p. 86.

New York Review of Books, October 5, 1972, pp. 21-23.

New York Times, September 30, 1987.

New York Times Book Review, July 5, 1964, p. 5; January 17, 1982, pp. 13, 16; June 11, 1989, p. 11; November 25, 1990, p. 19; June 5, 1994, p. 50.

Northwest Review, fall, 1963, pp. 123-29.

Outsider, spring, 1963, pp. 62-65.

People, November 16, 1987, pp. 79-80.

Poetry, July, 1964, pp. 258-64.

Publishers Weekly, March 29, 1993, p. 34; December 20, 1993, p. 62; April 29, 1996, p. 66.

Review of Contemporary Fiction, fall, 1985, pp. 56-59.

San Francisco Review of Books, January-February, 1983, p. 11.

Spectator, November 30, 1974.

Times (London), March 3, 1988; July 8, 1989.

Times Literary Supplement, April 5, 1974, p. 375; June 20, 1980, p. 706; September 4, 1981, p. 1000; November 12, 1982, p. 1251; December 3, 1982, p. 1344; May 4, 1984, p. 486; August 11, 1989, p. 877; September 7, 1990, p. 956.

Village Voice, March 26, 1964, pp. 11-12; February 20, 1978, pp. 89-90; March 23, 1982, pp. 42-43.

Washington Post, November 20, 1987.

Washington Post Book World, July 14, 1994, p. 2.

OBITUARIES:

PERIODICALS

Chicago Tribune, March 11, 1994, p. 12.

Entertainment Weekly, March 25, 1994, p. 49.

Facts on File, March 17, 1994, p. 196.

Los Angeles Times, March 10, 1994, p. 1, 24.

New York Times, March 11, 1994, p. B9.

Time, March 21, 1994, p. 26.

Times (London), March 11, 1994, p. 23.

Variety, March 14, 1994, p. 67.

Washington Post, March 11, 1994, p. B5.*

* * *

BURICK, Si(mon) 1909-1986

PERSONAL: Surname is pronounced *Byoo*-rick; born June 14, 1909, in Dayton, OH; died of a stroke December 10, 1986, in Dayton, OH; son of Samuel F. (a rabbi) and Lillian (Solnitzky) Burick; married Rachel Siegel (a teacher), June 28, 1935; children: Lenore Burick Goldman, Marcia Burick Goldstein. *Education:* Attended University of Dayton, 1926-27. *Politics:* Democrat. *Religion:* Jewish.

CAREER: Dayton Daily News, Dayton, OH, sports writer, 1925-86, sports editor, 1928-86. Notable assignments include every World Series but one between 1934 and 1984, twenty Super Bowl games, all but two Kentucky Derby races between 1929 and 1986, the Olympics five times, numerous college football bowl games, golf championships, and numerous heavyweight title boxing matches since 1931. Member of board of directors of Dayton Newspapers, Inc.; Commissioner of Dayton—Montgomery County Park District; former charter member of local Human Relations Council and Jewish Community Council; former chair of United Jewish Campaign and of National Foundation for Infantile Paralysis, Montgomery County chapter; board member of Dayton Boys' Club.

MEMBER: National Sportswriters and Sportscasters Association (president, 1974), Football Writers Association of America (president, 1973), Basketball Writers Association, Baseball Writers Association, Turf Writers Association, U.S. Golf Writers Association,

Dayton Bicycle Club, Dayton Agonis Club, B'nai B'rith.

AWARDS, HONORS: D.H.L. from University of Dayton, 1977; named Ohio sportswriter of the year by Ohio writers and broadcasters, 1964-75, 1977, 1978; distinguished alumni award from University of Dayton, 1980; J. G. Taylor Spink Award and induction into the writers' wing of the Baseball Hall of Fame, both 1983; Red Smith Award from Associated Press Sports Editors, 1986.

WRITINGS:

Alston and the Dodgers, Doubleday (Garden City, NY), 1966.
The Main Spark: Sparky Anderson and the Cincinnati Reds, Doubleday, 1978.
Byline: Si Burick—A Half Century in the Press Box, Dayton Daily News (Dayton, OH), 1982.

Contributor to sports magazines and local periodicals.

SIDELIGHTS: Si Burick achieved the remarkable feat of earning a national reputation as a sportswriter while living and working in a city that did not have a major league team. From his base at the *Dayton Daily News* in Ohio, Burick wandered the country—indeed, the world—writing sports pieces of national interest with a nod to his home state wherever possible. Burick loved his job and stayed at it for better than sixty years. It is estimated that he wrote thirteen thousand columns in his lifetime—some fifteen million words. "Burick's writing style was never ornate or elaborate," declared Mike Lackey in the *Dictionary of Literary Biography.* "His mature work was distinguished by its sound reporting, gentle wit, and polished storytelling."

Born and raised in Dayton, Burick began his sportswriting career in 1925 as a high school correspondent earning a wage of two dollars a week. Just three years later, at age nineteen, he was named sports editor of the *Dayton Daily News* and was given *carte blanche* to attend all the major sporting events as the newspaper's lead columnist. He attended his first World Series in 1930 and his last in 1984, covered boxing matches from the era of Joe Louis to the days of Muhammad Ali, saw every one of the first twenty Super Bowls, and attended five Olympics. He never shied from controversial pieces—including several that took tempestuous football coach Woody Hayes to task—but he also indulged in gentle humor, often at his own expense.

Burick's duties at the *Dayton Daily News* kept him so busy that he was not able to write many books on the side. Two projects that he did complete were *Alston and the Dodgers,* a biography of manager Walter Alston, and *The Main Spark: Sparky Anderson and the Cincinnati Reds.* Interestingly enough, both subjects of Burick's books had connections to rural Ohio. Lackey characterized the works as "gentle, affectionate portraits of men Burick liked and respected. Written in the first person, each book allowed its subject to tell his own story the way he wanted it told." In the *New York Times Book Review,* Rex Lardner faulted the Alston biography as "somewhat bland and sugary," adding: "One has the feeling that there is more to the story of managing the country's most picturesque ball club than is revealed to us here." On the other hand, *Library Journal* correspondent George Whitbeck called the work "a top-notch baseball book that is sure to delight devotees of the national pastime."

Byline: Si Burick—A Half Century in the Press Box, Burick's final book, appeared four years prior to his death. The book is a collection of his favorite columns, spanning the decades that comprised his career. The work was not a capstone, however, for he continued to write columns until three days before his death in 1986.

At his induction into the writers' wing of the Baseball Hall of Fame, Burick reflected on his singular career. "Joy has been the keynote of my life as a sportswriter and as a baseball writer," he said. "I never considered it hard work. I never considered it work. Else why would I have chosen to stay with it all these years?"

Burick once told *CA:* "Several careers have been offered to me (I left pre-medical courses at University of Dayton for the opportunity to work for *Dayton Daily News*), but printer's ink has gotten under my nails and I've stuck to my typewriter. I enjoy the travel accompanying sports events and feel very fortunate to have done fifty years of sports writing."

BIOGRAPHICAL/CRITICAL SOURCES:

BOOKS

Dictionary of Literary Biography, Volume 171: *Twentieth-Century American Sportswriters,* Gale (Detroit, MI), 1996, pp. 52-7.

PERIODICALS

Editor and Publisher, January 24, 1987.
Library Journal, September 1, 1966, p. 3968.
New York Times Book Review, October 16, 1966, p. 30.
Variety, December 24, 1986.*

C

CALHOUN, Chad
See CUNNINGHAM, Chet

*　　*　　*

CANNON, Curt
See HUNTER, Evan

*　　*　　*

CAPOTE, Truman 1924-1984

PERSONAL: Original name, Truman Streckfus Persons; name legally changed; born September 30, 1924, in New Orleans, LA; died of liver disease complicated by phlebitis and multiple drug intoxication, August 25, 1984, in Los Angeles, CA; son of Archulus Persons (a nonpracticing lawyer) and Lillie Mae (Faulk) Persons Capote; adopted by Joseph G. Capote. *Education:* Attended Trinity School and St. John's Academy, both in New York City, and public schools in Greenwich, CT.

CAREER: Writer. Worked for *New Yorker* magazine as a newspaper clipper and cartoon cataloger, c. 1943-44; also moonlighted as a filmscript reader and freelance writer of anecdotes for a digest magazine. Appeared in motion picture *Murder by Death,* Columbia, 1976.

MEMBER: National Institute of Arts and Letters.

AWARDS, HONORS: Won first literary prize at age ten in Mobile Press Register contest, for short story, "Old Mr. Busybody"; O. Henry Award, Doubleday & Co., 1946, for "Miriam," 1948, for "Shut a Final Door," and 1951; National Institute of Arts and Letters creative writing award, 1959; Edgar Award, Mystery Writers of America, 1966, and National Book Award nomination, 1967, both for *In Cold Blood;* Emmy Award, 1967, for television adaptation *A Christmas Memory.*

WRITINGS:

Other Voices, Other Rooms (novel), Random House, 1948, reprinted with an introduction by the author, 1968.

A Tree of Night, and Other Stories (also see below), Random House, 1949.

Local Color (nonfiction sketches), Random House, 1950.

The Grass Harp (novel; also see below), Random House, 1951.

The Grass Harp, and A Tree of Night, and Other Stories, New American Library, 1956.

The Muses Are Heard: An Account (first published in *New Yorker*), Random House, 1956 (published in England as *The Muses Are Heard: An Account of the Porgy and Bess Visit to Leningrad,* Heinemann, 1957).

Breakfast at Tiffany's: A Short Novel and Three Stories, Random House, 1958 (published in England as *Breakfast at Tiffany's,* Hamish Hamilton, 1959).

(Author of commentary) Richard Avedon, *Observations,* Simon & Schuster, 1959.

Selected Writings, introduction by Mark Schorer, Random House, 1963.

In Cold Blood: A True Account of a Multiple Murder and Its Consequences (nonfiction novel; Book-of-the-Month Club selection; first serialized in *New Yorker*), Random House, 1966.

A Christmas Memory (first published in *Mademoiselle,* December, 1956; also see below), Random House, 1966.

The Thanksgiving Visitor (first published in *McCall's;* also see below), Random House, 1968, published with illustrations by Beth Peck, Knopf (New York City), 1996.

The Dogs Bark: Public People and Private Places, Random House, 1973.

Miriam (first published in *Mademoiselle;* also see below), Creative Education, Inc., 1982.

Music for Chameleons: New Writing, Random House, 1983.

One Christmas (first published in *Ladies Home Journal*), Random House, 1983.

Answered Prayers: The Partial Manuscript (first serialized in *Esquire*), edited by Joseph Fox, Random House, 1986, published as *Answered Prayers: The Unfinished Novel,* Random House, 1987.

I Remember Grandpa, Peachtree, 1987.

"The Thanksgiving Visitor," "One Christmas," & "A Christmas Memory," Modern Library (New York City), 1996.

PLAYS

The Grass Harp: A Play (based on novel of the same title; first produced on Broadway at Martin Beck Theatre, March 27, 1952; produced as a musical on Broadway at Martin Beck Theatre, November, 1971), Random House, 1952.

(With Harold Arlen) *The House of Flowers* (libretto; based on short story of the same title; first produced on Broadway at Alvin Theatre, December 30, 1954; rewritten version first produced Off-Broadway at Theater de Lys, January 24, 1968), Random House, 1968.

SCREENPLAYS

(With John Huston) *Beat the Devil,* United Artists, 1954.

(With William Archibald and John Mortimer) *The Innocents* (based on Henry James's novel of the same title), Twentieth Century-Fox, 1961.

(With Eleanor Perry) *Trilogy* (also see below; adapted from Capote's short stories "Miriam," "Among the Paths to Eden," and the novella *A Christmas Memory*), Allied Artists, 1969.

TELEPLAYS

A Christmas Memory (based on novella of same title), American Broadcasting Co. (ABC-TV), December 21, 1966.

The Thanksgiving Visitor (based on book of same title), ABC-TV, November, 1968.

Also author of teleplays *Among the Paths to Eden* (adapted from short story of the same title), first produced in 1967; *Laura,* 1968; *Behind Prison Walls,* 1972; with Tracy Keenan Wynn and Wyatt Cooper, *The Glass House,* 1972; and *Crimewatch,* 1973.

OTHER

(Author of introduction) *The Collected Works of Jane Bowles,* Farrar, Straus, 1966.

(With E. Perry and Frank Perry) *Trilogy: An Experiment in Multimedia,* Macmillan, 1969.

A Capote Reader, Random House, 1987.

Also author of *Then It All Came Down: Criminal Justice Today Discussed by Police, Criminals, and Correction Officers, With Comments by Truman Capote,* 1976. Contributor to numerous anthologies, including *Five Modern American Short Stories,* edited by Helmut Tischler, M. Diesterweg, 1962. Author of *Esquire* column "Observations," beginning March, 1983. Contributor to national magazines, including *Vogue, Mademoiselle, Ladies Home Journal, Esquire,* and *New Yorker.* Many of Capote's books have been translated into foreign languages, including French, German, Spanish, and Italian.

ADAPTATIONS: Capote made a sound recording of his short story "Children on Their Birthdays" for Columbia in the 1950s; *Breakfast at Tiffany's* was filmed by Paramount, 1961; *In Cold Blood* was filmed by Columbia Pictures, 1967; "Handcarved Coffins" was sold to Lester Persky Productions, 1980.

SIDELIGHTS: A masterful stylist who took great pride in his writing, Truman Capote was also a well-known television personality, openly obsessed with fame. In addition to literary recognition, the flamboyant, Southern-born writer sought social privilege and public celebrity, objectives he achieved in 1948 with the appearance of his first novel, *Other Voices, Other Rooms.* That book—published with a provocative dust-jacket photo of the author that far overshadowed the literary merit of the work—was the start of what Capote later termed "a certain notoriety" that kept step with him over the years. Believing that fame would not affect his art, Capote cultivated an entourage of rich and celebrated friends, observing their foibles with a watchful eye and inspiring confidences he would later betray. By 1959, he had already embarked on *Answered Prayers*—the never-to-be-finished *roman a clef* that precipitated a personal and professional crisis. Then he decided to put it "temporarily" aside while he explored something more serious—"a theme," as he explained to *Newsweek*'s Jack Kroll, "not likely to darken and yellow with time." His idea was to bring "the art of the novelist together with the technique of journalism" to produce a new genre, the nonfiction novel. Over six years in the making, the resulting book was *In Cold Blood: A True Account of a Multiple Murder and Its Consequences,* not only an enormous critical and commercial success, but also a seminal work of new journalism that remains the highlight of Capote's career.

Though the nonfiction novel was his most original contribution to the literary world, Capote also produced conventional writing of top quality. In short stories, plays, straight reportage, television adaptations, and filmscripts, he demonstrated what *Los Angeles Times* contributor Carolyn See called "the uncanny gift of putting a world or a scene together in a few perfect details." Among his other talents were "his patience for fact-collecting, his faithfulness to the true nature of his subject and his consummate gift as a storyteller," according to *New York Times Book Review* contributor Lis Harris. He was, in, the words of David Remnick in the *Washington Post,* "a writer of brilliance, capable of economical, evocative prose. His technique was mature, professional in the best possible sense."

Though his style of writing evolved over the years, falling into what Capote himself considered four different phases, his poetic voice was distinctive right from the start. "Truman had an odd and personal perspective on experience that only real writers have," poet and novelist James Dickey explained in the *New York Times*. "A lot of writers sweat and labor to acquire that, but Truman Capote had it naturally. He was maybe a little heavy on the Southern gothic side of things, a little bit willfully perverse. . . . But at his best, he had a very great sensitivity and linguistic originality." In the same *New York Times* article, novelist John Knowles expressed a similar view, saying of Capote's voice that "it was like no one else's— precise, clear, sometimes fey, lyrical, witty, graceful."

Capote himself often suggested that his originality was pervasive, influencing not just his writing, but every aspect of his life. "The thing about people like me is that we always knew what we were going to do," Capote told *New York Times Magazine* contributor Anne Taylor Fleming. "Many people spend half their lives not knowing. But I was a very special person, and I had to have a very special life. . . . I would have been successful at whatever I did. But I always knew that I wanted to be a writer and that I wanted to be rich and famous." According to Fleming, "looking at the boy he must have been, the slender, pretty, high-voiced boy. . . , it seems easy to see, too easy maybe, how the kind of fame he coveted would someday become too heavy."

Born Truman Streckfus Persons in New Orleans, Louisiana, Capote had a childhood that, by all accounts, was difficult. His mother, a former Miss Alabama who later committed suicide, considered herself temperamentally unsuited to motherhood and sent him off to be raised by relatives in Monroeville, a small Alabama town. When he was four, his parents ended their marriage in a bitter divorce: his mother went north to New York, his father south to New Orleans, and young Truman became "a spiritual orphan," in Fleming's words. Though he frequently summered with his father, traveling up and down the Mississippi on the family-owned Streckfus Steam Boat Line, the two were never close, and Capote considered him "a bounder and a cad." The Monroeville years were difficult for Capote, comprising a time when he felt "like a turtle on its back. You see," he explained to Fleming, "I was so different from every one, so much more intelligent and sensitive and perceptive. I was having fifty perceptions a minute to everyone else's five. I always felt that nobody was going to understand me, going to understand what I felt about things. I guess that's why I started writing. At least on paper I could put down what I thought."

His closest friends at this time were an elderly cousin, Miss Sook Faulk, whom Fleming describes as "the archetype of the aging innocent, the best of the simple people with an inarticulate wisdom and a childlike capacity for joy and strange imaginings," and a neighboring tomboy, Harper Lee, who helped young Truman type his manuscripts and eventually became an award-winning author herself, writing *To Kill a Mockingbird*. Both personalities appear in Capote's early fiction, his cousin in autobiographical stories, such as "A Christmas Memory," and his friend in his first novel *Other Voices, Other Rooms*.

His mother, meanwhile, had remarried a Cuban-born New York businessman, Joe Capote, and when, after a series of miscarriages, she realized she could have no more children, she sent for Truman. He was nine years old. Legally adopted by his stepfather, the young author attended school in Manhattan, then enrolled at Trinity, and, at thirteen, was sent to live at St. John's Academy, a military boarding school. "I was lonely and very insecure," Capote told *Playboy* interviewer Eric Norden about his schooling. "Who wouldn't be? I was an only child, very sensitive and intelligent, with no sense of being particularly wanted by *anybody*. . . . I wasn't neglected financially; there was always enough money to send me to good schools, and all that. It was just a total *emotional* neglect. I never felt I belonged anywhere. All my family thought there was something wrong with me."

His grades were so low that, over the years, his family began to worry that he might be retarded. But when a special group of WPA researchers came to his school to conduct intelligence tests, Capote received the highest score they had ever seen. "I had the highest intelligence of any child in the United States," Capote told *Washington Post* reporter David Remnick, "an IQ of 215." Nonetheless, he had little use for formal schooling and, though he did graduate from high school (a fact which he obscured for many years), Capote told Norden he was "determined never to set foot inside a college classroom. If I was a writer, fine; if I wasn't, no professor on earth was going to make me one."

In place of formal education, Capote substituted experience, landing a job with the *New Yorker* when he was seventeen. "That job wasn't very glamorous, just clipping newspapers and filing cartoons," Capote told Norden, but it marked the beginning of a long association with the magazine that would serialize his best-known work and, to some extent, shape his writing style. Initially, however, his stories were rejected by the magazine. He made his first big sale shortly after leaving the *New Yorker,* when *Mademoiselle* bought a short story, "Miriam," which later garnered an O. Henry Award. According to *Dictionary of Literary Biography* contributor Craig M. Goad, "'Miriam' typifies the early Capote manner. It is a story of isolation, dread, and psychological breakdown told in rich, precisely mannered prose. There is little technical or thematic experimentation in 'Miriam' and the other Capote stories that appeared regularly in the postwar years. The shadow of Edgar Allan Poe floats over the surface of these stories, and

their chief aim often seems to be only to produce a mild *frisson.*"

"Miriam" caught the attention of Random House editor Robert Linscott, who told Capote that he would be interested in publishing whatever he wanted to write. Capote had already begun work on *Summer Crossing,* "a spare, objective story with a New York setting," according to Capote, who acknowledged in the preface to the 1968 reprint of *Other Voices, Other Rooms* that "in order to complete the book . . . I took courage, quit my job, left New York and settled with relatives in a remote part of Alabama." But, once arrived, Capote began having doubts about his novel. "More and more," he wrote, "*Summer Crossing* seemed to me thin, clever, unfelt." While walking in the woods one afternoon, Capote was seized with a new vision, one inspired by childhood memories. He returned home, "tossed the manuscript of *Summer Crossing* into a bottom bureau drawer, collected several sharp pencils and a fresh pad of yellow lined paper and with pathetic optimism, wrote: *Other Voices, Other Rooms*—a novel by Truman Capote."

The novel took two years to complete and was published in 1948 to mostly favorable reviews. But it was the book's packaging rather than its literary merit that titillated the public's attention, for the dust-jacket photo portrayed the twenty-three-year-old author reclining on a couch, looking "as if he were dreamily contemplating some outrage against conventional morality," according to a report in the *Los Angeles Times.* Because Capote, an open homosexual, had focused on the developing relationship between an effete transvestite and his young male cousin, "readers at the time suspected that Capote may have identified with the book's protagonist and that 'Other Voices, Other Rooms' was a confession of sexual deviation," continued George Ramos and Laurie Becklund in the *Los Angeles Times.* In retrospect, Capote was able to identify the book's many autobiographical elements— particularly, as he explained in his 1968 preface, the parallels between protagonist Joel Knox's quest for love and his own search for an "essentially imaginary" father—but he did not make the connection at the time. "Rereading it now, I find such self-deception unpardonable," Capote wrote.

What many conservative critics found "unpardonable" was not Capote's self-deception, but rather his aberrant theme. "For all his novel's gifted invention and imagery, the distasteful trappings of its homosexual theme overhang it like Spanish moss," wrote the *Time* contributor. And, writing in the *Nation,* respected literary critic Diana Trilling expressed a similar view: "Even if Mr. Capote were ten or twenty years older than he is, his powers of description and evocation, his ability to bend language to his poetic moods, his ear for dialect and for the varied rhythms of speech would be remarkable. . . . On the other hand, I find myself deeply antipathetic to the whole artistic moral purpose of Mr. Capote's novel. I would freely trade eighty per cent of his technical virtuosity for twenty per cent more value in the uses to which it is put."

Some critics also reacted against the apparent self-consciousness of the writing. "*Other Voices, Other Rooms* is the novel of someone who wanted, with a fixed and single-minded and burning will, to write a novel," wrote Cynthia Ozick in a *New Republic* critique of the twentieth-anniversary edition. "The vision of *Other Voices, Other Rooms* is the vision of capital-A Art—essence freed from existence." What this artistic preoccupation led to, in the eyes of the *Times Literary Supplement* reviewer, was "the temptation to mystify for the sake of mystification." Noted *Saturday Review* contributor Richard McLaughlin: "If he had selected his material more carefully, shown more restraint, and had been less concerned with terrifying us out of our wits, he might have easily made a real and tenderly appealing story out of the experiences of thirteen-year-old Joel Knox and the people he meets during that long and lonely summer of his approaching maturity."

After the publication of *Other Voices, Other Rooms,* Capote moved for a time to Europe, where he traveled widely with novelist Jack Dunphy, "the only man . . . with whom he has ever been in love," according to Fleming in the *New York Times Magazine.* During this ten-year period, which Capote described as the second phase of his development and which ended in 1958, the author experimented with various kinds of writing. There were nonfiction travel essays and portraits (*Local Color, Observations*), short story collections (*A Tree of Night, A Christmas Memory*), adaptations of two earlier fictions into Broadway plays (*The Grass Harp, House of Flowers*), and the scripting of two original films (*Beat the Devil, The Innocents*). There was also "a great deal of factual reportage, most of it for the *New Yorker,*" Capote recalled in the preface to *Music for Chameleons.* His most memorable assignments included a tongue-in-cheek profile of Marlon Brando and a wry account of a black theatrical troupe's production of "Porgy and Bess" in Russia, later published in book form as *The Muses Are Heard.*

Though Capote's version of the "Porgy and Bess" tour of Russia "didn't quite jibe with the way some other observers of the trip remembered it," according to *Washington Post* reporter Tom Zito, *The Muses Are Heard* was a critical success, which "brilliantly utilized the literary forms of a fiction writer to present factual material." To achieve its effect of "deadpan mockery," the book poked gentle fun at a number of people, leaving "almost everyone touched by Mr. Capote's pen looking a little foolish," according to a review in the *Christian Science Monitor.* But *The Muses Are Heard* had "more to it than entrancing fun," as *Atlantic* contributor C. J. Rolo explained: "While Capote's eye and ear have a radar-like sensitivity to the incongruous and the hilarious, they also dig the significant. What is dingy and nasty in Soviet life is revealed subtly and shrewdly, with a telling selectivity."

That selectivity reflected Capote's approach to his subject. To research his chronicle, he had employed neither tape recorder nor note pad, relying instead upon his photographic memory, which he viewed as the journalist's stock-in-trade. He would write up his impressions at the end of the day, but never during an interview, for he felt note-taking put his subjects on guard. "Taking notes produces the wrong kind of atmosphere," he pointed out to *Newsweek*'s Jack Kroll, explaining how he had trained his memory "by getting a friend to read me the Sears Roebuck catalog. I would have a tape recorder going at the same time. At first I could remember only forty per cent, then after three months sixty per cent. Now I can remember ninety per cent, and who cares about the other ten per cent," he said in 1966.

The Muses Are Heard, which was the first book Capote produced using this method, impressed the *New York Times* reviewer as "a record made by a brilliant writer in a casual, almost flippant manner—but with such freshness, with such light strokes and subtle innuendo, that the book reads like a highly enjoyable, charming story." The technique was so successful that it prompted Capote to envision a new kind of novel—"something on a large scale that would have the credibility of fact, the immediacy of film, the depth and freedom of prose, and the precision of poetry," Capote explained to James Wolcott in the *New York Review of Books.* In his mind, he christened this new genre "the nonfiction novel" and began looking for a suitable theme.

Before Capote found his subject, he published one more conventional novel, *Breakfast at Tiffany's,* later adapted into a popular film starring Audrey Hepburn and George Peppard. The engaging story of Manhattan playgirl Holly Golightly, *Breakfast at Tiffany's* demonstrated a maturity lacking in Capote's early fiction—at least in the opinion of *New Republic* contributor Stanley Kauffmann, who wrote: "It was with *Breakfast at Tiffany's* . . . that . . . Capote began to see enough of life and love to be more interested in his material than himself and to reveal the humor that now seems basic to him." Though Capote conceived of his story as a fiction, he was already drawing heavily from real life incidents, a point not lost on Kauffmann, who observed that "real names might conceivably be affixed to every character in *Breakfast at Tiffany's* and the whole published as a report on Manhattan life in the war years. If this is a restrictive comment, it is not meant to be condemnatory: because from her first appearance Holly leaps to life. Her dialogue has the perfection of pieces of mosaic fitting neatly and unassailably in place. The fey madness and extravagance, character qualities that easily throw fiction off the rails, always seem intrinsic, not contrived. . . . His fiction is strongest, most vital, when it resembles his best non-fiction." In the opinion of the *Times Literary Supplement* critic, the writing in *Breakfast at Tiffany's* "shorn of affection and the too-carefully chosen word," put Capote "in immediate sympathy with his characters" and placed "him at once among the leading American writers of the day."

Capote saw the second phase of his development as a writer come to a close with *Breakfast at Tiffany's,* and, after its publication, he turned his efforts "toward journalism as an art form in itself. I had two reasons," Capote explained in the preface to *Music for Chameleons.* "First, it didn't seem to me that anything truly innovative had occurred in prose writing . . . since the 1920s; second, journalism as an art was almost virgin territory." He began to search in earnest for a suitable subject, experimenting with several different ideas at this time. One project was a Proustian work, according to Baumgold, tentatively entitled *Answered Prayers.* "Capote had the title since the 1950s," wrote Baumgold, and "began in 1958 with notes, a full outline, and an ending." Despite his commitment to the project—which he admittedly envisioned as his masterwork—*Answered Prayers* was "temporarily" shelved when Capote got a brainstorm. "One day," he recalled to Haskel Frankel in the *Saturday Review,* "it suddenly occurred to me that a crime might be an excellent subject to make my big experiment with. . . . Once I had decided on the possibility of a crime . . . I would half-consciously,

when looking through the papers, always notice any item that had a reference to a crime."

On November 16, 1959, Capote found what he had been looking for. Briefly noted in a *New York Times* wire story was the multiple murder of a wealthy wheat farmer, his wife, and their two teenage children in a small Kansas town. "Almost instantaneously I thought, well, this is maybe exactly what I want to do, because I don't know anything about that part of the world," Capote told Frankel. "I've never been to Kansas, much less western Kansas. It all seems fresh to me. I'll go without any prejudices. And so I went."

Three days later, Capote arrived in Holcomb, Kansas, accompanied by his childhood friend Harper Lee, who assisted him with the initial research. The town was in the throes of a brutal unsolved slaying, its residents not only traumatized but also deeply suspicious, and the urbane little dandy from New York City was not well received. Capote recalled that it took about a month for his presence to be accepted and that after the killers, Perry Smith and Dick Hickock, were apprehended, people finally began to open up to him. In addition to interviewing the townspeople, murderers, and anyone else even remotely connected to the Clutter case, Capote retraced the killers' flight, journeying south to Miami and Acapulco, renting rooms in the same cheap hotels. He did months of research on the criminal mind and interviewed a number of death row killers, "solely to give me a perspective on these two boys," Capote told George Plimpton in the *New York Times Book Review.* Before he began writing, he had amassed over six thousand pages of notes, explaining, "Eighty per cent of the research I . . . never used. But it gave me such a grounding that I never had any hesitation in my consideration of the subject." All told, the project, which Capote regarded as the third phase of his writing development, consumed almost six years. When it was over, Capote confessed to Frankel, "I would never do it again. . . . If had known what that book was going to cost in every conceivable way, emotionally, I never would have started it, and I really mean that."

Some people attribute Capote's escalating physical and emotional problems to the acute stress he suffered during the project. Fleming reported that this was the period when he "began to take the tranquilizers to which he later became addicted." But, if he paid a high personal price, the financial compensations for *In Cold Blood* were generous, for the story was a commercial success even before it appeared in book form. Serialized in the *New Yorker* in four consecutive issues, *In Cold Blood* boosted the magazine's sales and netted Capote a rumored $70,000 in serialization rights. New American Library paid a reported $700,000 for paperback rights and Columbia Pictures spent almost a million dollars for filming rights. By 1983, according to the *Washington Post, In Cold Blood* had brought the author $2 million in royalties.

The book was also a critical success, described by *New York Times Book Review* contributor Conrad Knickerbocker as "a masterpiece—agonizing, terrible, possessed, proof that the times, so surfeited with disasters, are still capable of tragedy." *In Cold Blood,* according to the *Time* reviewer, "plays a light that illuminates the interior climate of murder with intense fidelity. Capote has invested the victims with a dignity and reality that life hitherto had confined only to the closed circle of their friends, and he has thrust the act of violence itself before the reader as if it were happening before his very eyes." David Remnick deemed certain "passages in it every bit as rhythmically spellbinding as Hemingway's famous opening to 'A Farewell to Arms,'" while F. W. Dupee extolled it as "the best documentary account of an American crime ever written," in the *New York Review of Books.*

Like any experimental literary work, *In Cold Blood* also had its share of detractors. Fellow novelist Norman Mailer, when asked his reaction to Capote's new genre, glibly dismissed it as "a failure of imagination," though as Capote took great pleasure in pointing out, Mailer later employed the same subject and technique in his Pulitzer Prize-winning *The Executioner's Song.* "Now I see that the only prizes Norman wins are for the very same kind of writing," Capote later quipped to the *Washington Post.* "I'm glad I was of some service to him."

Capote, who told Norden that he had "undertaken the most comprehensive and far-reaching experiment to date in the medium of reportage," never doubted the originality of his contribution. But others, like Diana Trilling, were not convinced. "Works of autobiography such as Isak Dinesen's *Out of Africa,* works of history such as Cecil Woodham Smith's *The Reason Why,* works of journalism like James Agee's *Let Us Now Praise Famous Men* are all at least as close to, or far from, proposing a new nonfiction form as Mr. Capote's *In Cold Blood,*" she wrote in the *Partisan Review.* While admitting that "the form is not new or remarkable," the *Times Literary Supplement* reviewer acknowledged that "it is handled here with a narrative

skill and delicate sensibility that make this re-telling of a gruesome murder story into a work of art." Capote "did not intend to be merely the novelist-as-journalist, writing diversionary occasional pieces," wrote Conrad Knickerbocker in the *New York Times Book Review.* "In the completer role of novelist-as-journalist-as-artist, he was after a new kind of statement. He wanted the facts to declare a reality that transcended reality."

Capote believed that in order for his nonfiction-novel form to be successful, it must be an objective account in which the author himself did not appear. "Once the narrator does appear," he explained to Plimpton, "he has to appear throughout . . . and the I-I-I intrudes when it really shouldn't." Capote's absence from the story was interpreted as a moral cop-out by some critics, including Cynthia Ozick, who complained that *In Cold Blood* "has excised its chief predicament, the relation of the mind of the observer to the mind of the observed, and therefore it cannot be judged, it escapes interpretation because it flees its own essential deed." Diana Trilling accused Capote of "employing objectivity as a shield for evasion. This is what is resented . . . the sense shared in some dim way by virtually all of Mr. Capote's audience of having been unfairly used in being made to take on the burden of personal involvement pridefully put aside by Mr. Capote himself. An unpleasant critical charge leveled against *In Cold Blood* is that it is itself written in cold blood, exploiting tragedy for personal gain."

No one familiar with Capote's involvement with the Clutter case leveled this charge, for he made his personal commitment clear. "I had to surrender my entire life to this experience," he told Norden. "Try to think what it means to totally immerse yourself in the lives of two men waiting to be hanged, to feel the passage of hours with them, to share every emotion. Short of actually living in a death cell myself, I couldn't have come closer to the experience." Though his sympathies were divided between one of the killers, Perry Smith, and the head of the investigation, Alvin Dewey, Capote worked openly to have the murderers' death sentences commuted. He became physically ill when they were hanged.

Writing in the *Dictionary of Literary Biography,* Craig M. Goad concluded that "the controversy about the nature and literary status of *In Cold Blood* can never be wholly resolved, for it hinges on the definition of art that the individual reader accepts, but there is little doubt that the book creates a vivid portrait of western Kansas and captures the manners and speech of the people who live there. . . . It explores the irony of the fact that the murder of the Clutters, apparently exactly the sort of crime that a prosecuting attorney can describe as being committed 'in cold blood,' was essentially a crime of passion, a brief explosion of repressed rage and hate, while the executions of Hickock and Smith were carried out cold-bloodedly after years of legal wrangling. Finally, and perhaps most importantly, *In Cold Blood* contains the detailed portraits of Hickock and Smith which continue to fascinate not only those with literary interests, but students of criminal psychology as well."

After the book was finished, Capote orchestrated a major promotional campaign, prompting further charges of impropriety, which he answered with one of his quips: "A boy has to hustle his book," he said, according to the *Los Angeles Times*. He took a long vacation from writing and resumed his fast-paced social life, hosting a fancy dress ball for 540 friends in November, 1966. According to Fleming, "Capote worked on the party as if it were a book, laboring over flowers, colors, seating, food—which alone cost $12,000—scrawling details in a notebook in his tiny hand." Many of those closest to the author believed his quest for social acceptance was pathological, compensating for the emotional neglect of his childhood years. "It was harder to do than was the writing for him," Norman Mailer told Julie Baumgold in *New York* magazine. "His talent was his friend. His achievement was his social life."

In 1966, Capote had taken a $750,000 writing advance in the form of stocks and was supposed to resume work on *Answered Prayers,* the nonfiction novel he had named from a quote by Saint Therese: "More tears are shed over answered prayers than unanswered ones." Instead, Capote wrote in the preface to *Music for Chameleons,* "for four years, roughly from 1968 through 1972, I spent most of my time reading and selecting, rewriting and indexing my own letters, other people's letters, my diaries and journals . . . for the years 1943 through 1965." Finally, in 1972, he resumed work on the book, entering what he viewed as the fourth and final cycle of his writing. He wrote the last chapter first, then produced several more chapters in random order. In 1975 and 1976, four chapters were published in *Esquire* magazine.

Capote's reasons for releasing a work in progress remain unclear. Fleming theorized that it was "to jolt himself out of his sadness." Albin Krebs hypothesized that he did it "to keep alive the public's interest in the promised work," while Norman Mailer speculated

that it "may have been Capote's deliberate effort to free himself" from the debilitating influence of his cafe society friends. Whatever his reasons, the results, according to Baumgold were "social suicide."

In the work, which Capote likened to a contemporary version of Marcel Proust's *Remembrance of Things Past,* Capote divulged many of the scandalous secrets he had coaxed from his wealthy and powerful friends. "The first excerpt was called '*La Cote Basque,*' after the New York restaurant frequented by many of society's more celebrated members," wrote Tom Zito in the *Washington Post*. "Many of the whispered stories and innuendoes he had heard over the years he now had the audacity to print, either factually or thinly veiled. It was as if he was metaphorically recreating what Perry Smith had said in '*In Cold Blood*' about the murder of Herbert Clutter: 'I thought he was a very nice gentleman. Softspoken. I thought so right up to the moment I cut his throat.'" The reprisals were swift and immediate. Many of the circles in which he'd traveled now became closed to him. His telephone calls went unreturned. Invitations fell off. Perhaps the most deeply felt repercussion was the loss of his relationship with Babe Paley, once an almost constant companion and friend.

This social crisis was paralleled by a creative crisis that struck Capote around 1977. Dissatisfied with the texture of his writing, Capote reread every word he had ever published and "decided that never, not once in my writing life, had I completely exploded all the energy and esthetic excitements that material contained. Even when it was good," Capote continued in *Music for Chameleons,* "I was never working with more than half, sometimes only a third, of the powers at my command."

In a 1978 television interview with Stanley Siegel, Capote appeared on the air under the influence of drugs and alcohol, confessing that he frequently mixed "them together like some kind of cocktail." Before the segment was cut, Capote attributed his substance abuse problems to "free-floating anxiety," developed as a child: "My mother was a very beautiful girl and only seventeen years old, and she used to lock me in these rooms all the time, and I developed this fantastic anxiety." He also alluded to his artistic problems with *Answered Prayers,* admitting "I'm pretty anxious about this new book of mine . . . really a great sense of anxiety about it."

A legendary fabricator, Capote may well have been exaggerating the hardships of his childhood, at least according to his aunt Marie Rudisill, who told Baumgold that "he might have locked his mother in rooms." Capote's penchant for exaggeration was also confirmed by the late playwright Tennessee Williams, who once told a reporter for the *Washington Post,* "Truman's a mythologist, baby, you know that. That's a polite way of saying he does fabricate. I love him too much to say he's a liar. That's part of his profession." In the case of *Answered Prayers,* however, the writer's block he alluded to was real.

The crux of the problem, as Capote explained in *Music for Chameleons,* was that "by restricting myself to the techniques of whatever form I was working in, I was not using everything I knew about writing—all I'd learned from film scripts, plays, reportage, poetry, the short story, novellas, the novel. A writer ought to have all his colors . . . available on the same palette for mingling. . . . But how?" The solution, he decided after months of contemplation, was to reverse the process of invisibility he had mastered for *In Cold Blood* and to set himself at "center stage" in his writing. From this vantage point, using dialogue, stage direction, narrative, and a variety of other literary techniques, he would report his tales. This is the approach Capote employed in most of the selections published in his 1980 work, *Music for Chameleons,* the last major book he would write.

A collection of stories and portraits, *Music for Chameleons* has as its centerpiece "Handcarved Coffins"—a 30,000 word "nonfiction account of an American crime." In an interview with *Los Angeles Times* reporter Wayne Warga, Capote attributed his ability to "get that story at that length" to the innovative techniques he was using. "The entire point of this whole book is stylistic compression. I want everything to be minimal," he explained. But in a *Saturday Review* critique of the work, John Fowles found that "despite [Capote's] claims, the technique is (mercifully) innovatory only in one or two superficial and formal ways; in many more important ones it is a brave step back to older literary virtues. He now writes fiction increasingly near fact, and vice versa. In practice this means that he is very skillfully blending the received techniques of several kinds of writing."

Though *Los Angeles Times Book Review* contributor Thomas Thompson dismissed the book as "fast food coated with snake oil," other reviewers reserved their criticisms for Capote's preface, with its self-conscious posturing about capital-A Art, rather than denouncing the work as a whole. As Anthony Quinton

put it in the *London Times,* "Where he is a detached, neutral observer, as in the main item in this collection, there is brilliant force and economy to his writing." Less attractive, "and more conspicuous, is a kind of nervous blustering, only an inch away from self-pity that afflicts Capote when occupied with the topic of his own importance and achievements." Writing in the *Village Voice,* Seymour Krim also addressed this issue, noting: "Not one of these first-person vignettes is boring or without its humane and unexpected charm. And practically all the writing, it is true, is unstudied simplicity at its best, often so light that you can blow it around the room like a tissue-paper airplane. But as far as its living up to the burn-your-bridges trumpet call at the beginning of *Music for Chameleons. . . ,* one has to conclude that the ringing peptalk is more important to the author than to the reader."

Like *In Cold Blood, Music for Chameleons* also raised the issue of fact versus fiction. Publicized as a true story, in which names and locations had been changed to protect identities, "Handcarved Coffins" was particularly scrutinized. "The details are so fuzzy and the murders so far-fetched that you begin to wonder whether fact and fiction aren't bubbling together in the same pot," wrote James Wolcott in the *New York Review of Books.* Writing in the *Times Literary Supplement,* David Lodge attributed his skepticism to "the inherent implausibility of the discrete events narrated" as well as "the very literary 'feel' of the whole text." Asked *Time*'s R. Z. Sheppard: "How much of this book can be called documentary truth? How much is a masterly synthesis of all the author has learned as a fiction writer, scenarist and journalist? It is impossible to be sure." According to *Washington Post Book World* contributor Noel Perrin, "the proper response is to ignore [Capote's] pronouncements and read his work. D. H. Lawrence's advice, 'Trust the tale and not the teller,' might have been composed with Capote in mind. . . . Trust these tales. They are brilliant renderings of some of the more bizarre aspects of human reality—and if they happen to be literal word-for-word transcriptions, well, no harm in that. Either way, they are superb reading."

Between the appearance of *Music for Chameleons* in 1980 and the author's death in 1984, Capote wrote some magazine pieces and published *One Christmas,* a twenty-one-page short story, packaged as a book. His personal and health problems persisted, but he spoke frequently of the progress he was making on his masterwork *Answered Prayers,* telling *Publishers Weekly* in January, 1984 that he was "finishing my long-lost novel. . . . I hope it will be published in fall 1984." After his death, however, such remarks turned out to have been a smokescreen. Except for the portions published in *Esquire,* no manuscript of *Answered Prayers* was ever found. So convincing had been Capote's fabrications that several obituaries reported that the author was working on his book just hours before his death. Though the exact nature of that prose—whether magazine article, short story, or memoir—has not been determined, consensus is that it does not belong to *Answered Prayers.*

Because Capote had shown bits and pieces of his work in progress to associates and had actually read unpublished passages to friends over the telephone, some people speculate that Capote destroyed what he had written. Baumgold, for instance, alluded to the possibility of whole chapters being "rewritten out of existence in Capote's obsession with getting his work perfect." His editor, Joseph Fox, even remembered receiving an additional excerpt, which Capote subsequently took back and never returned. When asked about the content of *Answered Prayers: A Partial Manuscript,* a representative for Random House explained, "We are publishing the excerpts as they appeared in *Esquire* because, as I understand it, there's nothing else that goes with it."

A final version of the collected excerpts appeared in 1987 under the title *Answered Prayers: The Unfinished Novel.* The slim volume contains only the three previously published parts as chapters entitled "Unspoiled Monsters," "Kate McCloud," and "La Cote Basque." The narrator of each is P. B. Jones, a struggling writer and sometime male prostitute who rises from humble orphan origins in the South to infiltrate the inner circles of the New York social elite. According to John Melmoth in the *Times Literary Supplement,* "*Answered Prayers* can be read as a historical novel bent on dismantling the glitz and depravity of a crummy *ancien regime* whose way of life was built on inconsequential sexual contacts made tolerable by cocaine and liqueurs and is now threatened by AIDS." Commenting on the unusual harshness of Capote's characterizations, Walter Nash wrote in the *London Review of Books,* "there is little innocent laughter in this book. The prevailing tone is the giggling of the vicious." Despite his egregious authorial indiscretion, as R. Z. Sheppard noted in *Time,* "Capote was on his way to a spectacular best seller, an irresistible piece of malicious mischief inspired by the traditional detective thriller and the *National Enquirer.*"

Speculating on the cause of Capote's difficulty finishing the novel, *New York Times Book Review* contributor Christopher Lehmann-Haupt observed, "What he seems really to have wanted was to tell a deeper, more damning truth about himself and the world, a truth that would brand him a criminal and 'put me in prison for life.'" Sadly, as Charles Trueheart remarked in *Washington Post Book World,* "*Answered Prayers* is a coldly accurate memorial to the writer's worst days. It contains isolated examples of Capote at his keen-eared, story-telling best, and of Capote at his pickle-brained, gossip-mongering worst—examples suspended in an aspic of undistinguished other stuff." As Shirley Ann Grau concluded in Chicago *Tribune Books,* "'Answered Prayers' is quirky, annoying, sad, funny, brilliant, exasperating. . . . the sad relic of a talent, a faint echo from the brain of an extraordinary writer."

Despite protestations to the contrary while stalling on *Answered Prayers,* Capote may never have gotten over his writer's block, and that, in turn, may have contributed to his death. According to Norman Mailer, who told Baumgold, "He loved writing so much and had such pride of offering nothing but his best, that when he could no longer deliver, he lost much of his desire to live." Reflecting on Capote's life and work, *Los Angeles Times* contributor Armand S. Deutsch concluded: "The exhausting years of the alcohol and drug battles, the long hospital stays, the illnesses, are behind him. The celebrity, which was such an integral part of him, will soon vanish, but his writing will remain to speak brilliantly and strongly for him."

BIOGRAPHICAL/CRITICAL SOURCES:

BOOKS

Algeo, Ann M., *The Courtroom as Forum: Homicide Trials by Dreiser, Wright, Capote, and Mailer,* P. Lang (New York City), 1996.

Brinnin, John Malcolm, *Truman Capote: Deat Heart, Old Buddy,* Delacourte Press, 1986.

Clarke, Gerald, *Capote: A Biography,* Simon & Schuster, 1986.

Contemporary Literary Criticism, Gale, Volume 1, 1973; Volume 3, 1975; Volume 8, 1978; Volume 13, 1980; Volume 14, 1981; Volume 38, 1986; Volume 58, 1990.

Dictionary of Literary Biography, Volume 2, *American Novelists since World War II,* Gale, 1978.

Dictionary of Literary Biography Yearbook: 1980, Gale, 1981.

Grobel, Lawrence, *Conversations with Capote*, New American Library, 1985.

Hallowell, John, *Between Fact and Fiction: New Journalism and the Nonfiction Novel*, University of North Carolina Press, 1977.

Moates, Marianne M., *A Bridge of Childhood: Truman Capote's Southern Years*, Henry Holt, 1989.

Moates, Marianne M. and Jennings Faulk Carter, *Truman Capote's Southern Years: Stories from a Monroeville Cousin*, University of Alabama Press (Tuscaloosa), 1996.

Nance, William L., *The Worlds of Truman Capote*, Stein & Day, 1970.

Rudisill, Marie, and James C. Simmons, *Truman Capote*, William Morrow, 1983.

Short Story Criticism, Gale, Volume 2, 1989.

PERIODICALS

America, January 22, 1966; October 4, 1980.
American Scholar, winter, 1955-56; summer, 1966.
Atlantic, March, 1948; January, 1957; March, 1966.
Book Week, January 16, 1966.
Canadian Forum, March, 1966.
Chicago Tribune, June 5, 1983; July 5, 1987.
Christian Science Monitor, November 8, 1956.
Commentary, February, 1988, p. 81.
Detroit News, November 27, 1983.
Detroit News Magazine, September 7, 1980.
Esquire, April, 1988, p. 174.
Harper's, February, 1966.
Interview, November, 1989, p. 98.
Listener, March 28, 1968.
London Review of Books, December 18, 1986, p. 19.
Los Angeles Times, August 3, 1980; November 28, 1983; September 2, 1984.
Los Angeles Times Book Review, August 3, 1980.
Nation, February 7, 1966.
New Republic, February 23, 1963; January 22, 1966; January 27, 1973; December 21, 1987, p. 30.
New Statesman, August 30, 1963; March 22, 1968.
Newsweek, January 24, 1966.
New York, October 29, 1984; November 26, 1984.
New Yorker, September 21, 1987, p. 113; November 27, 1989, p. 143.
New York Review of Books, February 3, 1966; September 25, 1980; December 17, 1987, p. 3.
New York Times, December 2, 1956; January 7, 1980; August 5, 1980; September 10, 1987.
New York Times Book Review, January 18, 1948; February 24, 1952; January 16, 1966; October 28, 1973; August 3, 1980; November 13, 1983; September 13, 1987, p. 13.

New York Times Magazine, July 9, 1978; July 16, 1978.
Paris Review, spring-summer, 1957.
Partisan Review, spring, 1966.
Playboy, March, 1968.
Publishers Weekly, January 6, 1984.
Saturday Review, February 14, 1948; February 16, 1963; January 22, 1966; July, 1980.
Spectator, March 18, 1966; March 29, 1968.
Time, January 26, 1948; January 21, 1966; August 4, 1980; September 7, 1987, p. 65.
Times (London), February 19, 1981.
Times Literary Supplement, October 3, 1948; December 19, 1958; March 17, 1966; August 30, 1974; February 20, 1981; December 5, 1986, p. 1369.
Tribune Books (Chicago), October 18, 1987, p. 7.
Village Voice, August 6, 1980; October 20, 1987, p. 57.
Washington Post, December 8, 1973; June 6, 1979; June 7, 1979; March 13, 1983; March 31, 1983; September 20, 1987, p. 1.
Washington Post Book World, July 27, 1980.
Writer's Digest, April, 1990, p. 26.

OBITUARIES:

PERIODICALS

Chicago Tribune, August 27, 1984.
Los Angeles Times, August 26, 1984.
Newsweek, September 3, 1984.
New York Times, August 27, 1984.
Publishers Weekly, September 7, 1984.
Time, September 3, 1984.
Times (London), August 27, 1984.*

* * *

CARRINGTON, G. A.
See CUNNINGHAM, Chet

* * *

CARSON, Clayborne 1944-

PERSONAL: Born June 15, 1944, in Buffalo, NY; son of Clayborne and Louise (Lee) Carson; married Susan Ann Beyer (a librarian), 1967; children: David Malcolm, Temera Lea. *Education:* University of California, Los Angeles, B.A., 1967, M.A., 1970, Ph.D., 1975.

ADDRESSES: Home—884 Boyce St., Palo Alto, CA 94301. *Office*—Department of History, Stanford University, Stanford, CA 94305; Martin Luther King, Jr., Papers Project, Cypress Hall D, Stanford, CA 94305.

CAREER: Los Alamos Scientific Laboratory, Los Alamos, NM, laboratory assistant, summers, 1962-64; Audience Studies, Inc., Los Angeles, CA, editor, 1965-66; Los Angeles Free Press, Los Angeles, staff writer, 1966-67; University of California, Los Angeles, computer programmer at Survey Research Center, 1968-71, acting assistant professor of history, 1971-74; Stanford University, Stanford, CA, assistant professor, 1974-81, associate professor of history, 1981-1990, professor, 1991—.

MEMBER: American Historical Association, Organization of American Historians, Social Science History Association, Association for the Study of Afro-American Life and History, Southern Historical Association.

AWARDS, HONORS: Andrew Mellon fellow at Stanford University, 1977; fellow at Center for the Study of Civil Rights and Race Relations, Duke University, 1978-79; fellow at Center for Advanced Study in the Behavioral Sciences, Stanford, 1993-94.

WRITINGS:

In Struggle: SNCC and the Black Awakening of the 1960s, Harvard University Press (Cambridge, MA), 1981, new edition with introduction and epilogue by Carson, 1995.

(Editor with others) *Eyes on the Prize: America's Civil Rights Years,* Penguin Books (New York City), 1987, revised edition published as *The Eyes on the Prize: Civil Rights Reader: Documents, Speeches, and Firsthand Accounts from the Black Freedom Struggle, 1954-1990,* Penguin Books, 1991.

(Editor with David Gallen) *Malcolm X: The FBI File,* introduction by Spike Lee, Carroll & Graf (New York City), 1991, Ballantine, 1995.

(Senior editor) *The Papers of Martin Luther King, Jr.,* University of California Press (Berkeley), Volume 1: *Called to Serve, January 1929-June 1951,* 1992, Volume 2: *Rediscovering Precious*

Values, July 1951-November 1955, 1994, Volume 3: *Birth of a New Age, December 1955-December 1956,* 1997.

(With Carol Berkin and others) *American Voices: A History of the United States,* Scott Foresman (Glenview, IL), 1992.

Contributor of articles and reviews to scholarly journals and popular magazines, including *Nation* and *New West,* and to newspapers.

WORK IN PROGRESS: The Autobiography of Martin Luther King, Jr., for Warner Books; *The Rise and Fall of the Black Panther Party,* for Bedford Books.

SIDELIGHTS: Clayborne Carson is a faculty member of the history department at Stanford University. He specializes in African-American and civil rights history. Carson's writings document and analyze the civil rights movement and civil rights leaders, including Martin Luther King, Jr., Malcolm X and Stokely Carmichael.

Carson attended the March on Washington in 1963. "The march was a big step for me. I had never even carried a picket sign before," Carson told the *Washington Post.* It was at the march that Carson saw Martin Luther King, Jr.; this was the only time he saw King. He also met Stokely Carmichael, whom he had met earlier at a national student conference in Indiana, and about whom he would later write his Ph.D. dissertation. A year after the march Carson transferred from the University of New Mexico to UCLA. At UCLA he became involved with off-campus civil rights politics.

Carson's career in academia began with a computer programming position at UCLA. Carson then embarked upon graduate studies in history at UCLA and was encouraged by a professor to do his thesis on the civil rights movement. Carson's thesis was about Stokely Carmichael and his Student Nonviolent Coordinating Committee. Carson was teaching at UCLA as the university was making attempts to establish courses in African-American history. An assistant professorship at Stanford was offered to Carson in the mid-1970s, he received tenure and became an associate professor in 1981.

Carson received a call from Coretta Scott King, widow of Martin Luther King, Jr., asking him to be the director and senior editor of an ongoing multivolume project, *The Papers of Martin Luther King, Jr.* project. The goal of the project is to collect and organize King's major writings and sermons. Sponsors of the project include Stanford University and the Martin Luther King, Jr. Center for Nonviolent Social Change. In Carson's words to the *Washington Post,* "It was a job you couldn't say not to."

Although the young Carson admired King, the subject of his doctoral dissertation, Stokely Carmichael and his Student Nonviolent Coordinating Committee, includes criticism of King. The editorship, however, is important according to Carson's statement to the *Washington Post:* "How many times is Coretta King going to come and ask you to take on a project like this? If you're in African-American history there would be no equivalent job that you could take that had as much importance."

Carson's *In Struggle: SNCC and the Black Awakening on the 1960s* provides a history of the Student Nonviolent Coordinating Committee. The book examines SNCC development, the directions taken, the roles of various individuals, and ultimately its demise in the early 1970s. *Malcolm X: The FBI File* is a collection of FBI information about Malcolm X. The book includes Carson's commentary on the larger civil rights movement, as well as Malcolm X and his relation to the FBI.

BIOGRAPHICAL/CRITICAL SOURCES:

PERIODICALS

Los Angeles Times, March 15, 1992.
Los Angeles Times Book Review, May 31, 1981.
New York Times, March 15, 1992.
Washington Post, February 24, 1992.

*   *   *

CENDRARS, Blaise
  See SAUSER-HALL, Frederic

*   *   *

CHOMSKY, (Avram) Noam 1928-

PERSONAL: Born December 7, 1928, in Philadelphia, PA; son of William (a Hebrew scholar) and Elsie (Simonofsky) Chomsky; married Carol Schatz (a linguist and specialist on educational technology),

December 24, 1949; children: Aviva, Diane, Harry Alan. *Education:* University of Pennsylvania, B.A., 1949, M.A., 1951, Ph.D., 1955. *Politics:* Libertarian socialist.

ADDRESSES: Home—15 Suzanne Rd., Lexington, MA 02173. *Office*—Room E39-219, Massachusetts Institute of Technology, 77 Massachusetts Ave., Cambridge, MA 02139.

CAREER: Massachusetts Institute of Technology, Cambridge, assistant professor, 1955-58, associate professor, 1958-62, professor, 1962-65, Ferrari P. Ward Professor of Modern Languages and Linguistics, 1966-76, Institute Professor, 1976—. Visiting professor of linguistics, Columbia University, 1957-58, University of California, Los Angeles, 1966, University of California, Berkeley, 1966-67, and Syracuse University, 1982. Member, Institute of Advanced Study, Princeton University, 1958-59. John Locke lecturer, Oxford University, 1969; Bertrand Russell Memorial Lecturer, Cambridge University, 1971; Nehru Memorial Lecturer, University of New Delhi, 1972; Huizinga Lecturer, University of Leiden, 1977; Woodbridge Lecturer, Columbia University, 1978; Kant Lecturer, Stanford University, 1979.

MEMBER: National Academy of Sciences, American Academy of Arts and Sciences, Linguistic Society of America, American Philosophical Association, American Association for the Advancement of Science (fellow), British Academy (corresponding fellow), British Psychological Society (honorary member), Deutsche Akademie der Naturforscher Leopoldina, Gesellschaft fur Sprachwissenschaft (honorary member), Linguistic Society of America, Royal Anthropological Institute of Great Britain, Royal Anthropological Institute of Ireland, Utrecht Society of Arts and Sciences (honorary member).

AWARDS, HONORS: Junior fellow, Harvard Society of Fellows, 1951-55; research fellow at Harvard Cognitive Studies Center, 1964-67; named one of the "makers of the twentieth century" by the London *Times,* 1970; Guggenheim fellowship, 1971-72; distinguished scientific contribution from American Psychological Association, 1984; Gustavus Myers Center Award, 1986 and 1988; George Orwell Award, National Council of Teachers of English, 1987, 1989; Kyoto Prize in Basic Sciences, 1988; Professional Excellence Award, Association for Education in Journalism and Mass Communication, 1991; James Killian Faculty Award, MIT, 1992; Lannan Literary Award for Nonfiction, 1992; Joel Seldin Peace Award, Psychologists for Social Responsibility, 1993; Homer Smith Award, New York University School of Medicine, 1994; Loyola Mellon Humanities Award, Loyola University, 1994; Helmholtz Medal, Berlin-Brandenburgische Akademie Wissenschaften, 1996. Honorary degrees include D.H.L., University of Chicago, 1967, Loyola University of Chicago and Swarthmore College, 1970, Bard College, 1971, University of Massachusetts, 1973, University of Pennsylvania, 1984, Gettysburg College and University of Maine, 1992, and Amherst College, 1995; D.Litt., University of London, 1967, Delhi University, 1972, Visva-Bharati University (West Bengal), 1980, and Cambridge University, 1995.

WRITINGS:

Syntactic Structures, Mouton & Co., 1957, reprint, 1978.

Current Issues in Linguistic Theory, Mouton & Co., 1964.

Aspects of the Theory of Syntax, MIT Press (Cambridge, MA), 1965, reprint, 1986.

Cartesian Linguistics: A Chapter in the History of Rationalist Thought, Harper (New York City), 1966.

Topics in the Theory of Generative Grammar, Mouton & Co., 1966, reprint, 1978.

(With Morris Halle) *Sound Patterns of English,* Harper, 1968.

Language and Mind, Harcourt, 1968, enlarged edition, 1972.

American Power and the New Mandarins, Pantheon (New York City), 1969.

At War with Asia, Pantheon, 1970.

Problems of Knowledge and Freedom: The Russell Lectures, Pantheon, 1971.

(With George A. Miller) *Analyse formelle des langues naturelles,* Mouton & Co., 1971.

Studies on Semantics in Generative Grammar, Mouton & Co., 1972.

(Editor with Howard Zinn) *The Pentagon Papers, Volume 5: Critical Essays,* Beacon Press (Boston), 1972.

(With Edward Herman) *Counterrevolutionary Violence,* Warner Modular, Inc., 1974.

Peace in the Middle East?, Pantheon, 1974.

The Logical Structure of Linguistic Theory, Plenum (New York City), 1975.

Reflections on Language, Pantheon, 1975.

Essays on Form and Interpretation, North-Holland (New York City), 1977.

Dialogues avec Mitsou Ronat, Flammarion, 1977, translation published as *Language and Responsibility,* Pantheon, 1979.

Human Rights and American Foreign Policy, Spokesman, 1978.

(With Herman) *The Political Economy of Human Rights,* Volume I: *The Washington Connection and Third World Fascism,* Volume II: *After the Cataclysm: Postwar Indochina and the Construction of Imperial Ideology,* South End (Boston), 1979.

Rules and Representations, Columbia University Press (New York City), 1980.

Lectures on Government and Binding, Foris, 1981.

Radical Priorities, Black Rose Books (New York City), 1982.

Towards a New Cold War: Essays on the Current Crisis and How We Got There, Pantheon, 1982.

Noam Chomsky on the Generative Enterprise: A Discussion with Riny Huybregts and Henk van Riemsdijk, Foris, 1982.

(With Jonathan Steele and John Gittings) *Superpowers in Collision: The Cold War Now,* Penguin (New York City), 1982.

Some Concepts and Consequences of the Theory of Government and Binding, MIT Press, 1982.

The Fateful Triangle: The United States, Israel, and the Palestinians, South End, 1983.

Turning the Tide: U.S. Intervention in Central America and the Struggle for Peace, South End, 1985.

Barriers, MIT Press, 1986.

Knowledge of Language: Its Nature, Origins, and Use, Praeger (New York City), 1986.

Pirates and Emperors: International Terrorism in the Real World, Claremont, 1986, reprint, Black Rose Books, 1991.

On Power and Ideology: The Managua Lectures, South End, 1987.

James Peck, editor, *The Chomsky Reader,* Pantheon, 1987.

Language and Problems of Knowledge: The Managua Lectures, MIT Press, 1987

Language in a Psychological Setting, Sophia University (Tokyo), 1987.

Generative Grammar: Its Basis, Development, and Prospects, Kyoto University of Foreign Studies, 1988.

The Culture of Terrorism, South End, 1988.

(With Edward Herman) *Manufacturing Consent,* Pantheon, 1988.

(With C. P. Otero) *Language and Politics,* Black Rose Books, 1988.

Necessary Illusions: Thought Control in a Democratic Society, South End, 1989.

Deterring Democracy, Verso (New York City), 1991.

Terrorizing the Neighborhood: American Foreign Policy in the Post-Cold War Era, Pressure Drop Press (San Francisco), 1991.

Chronicles of Dissent: Interviews with David Barsamian, Common Courage Press (Monroe, ME), 1992.

What Uncle Sam Really Wants, Odonian Press (Berkeley, CA), 1992.

Letters from Lexington: Reflections on Propaganda, Common Courage Press, 1993.

(With David Barsamian) *The Prosperous Few and the Restless Many,* Odonian Press, 1993.

Rethinking Camelot: JFK, the Vietnam War, and U. S. Political Culture, South End, 1993.

Year 501: The Conquest Continues, South End, 1993.

World Orders, Old and New, Columbia University Press, 1994, revised and expanded edition, 1996.

Language and Thought, Moyer Bell (Wakefield, RI), 1994.

Keeping the Rabble in Line: Interviews with David Barsamian, Common Courage Press, 1994.

Secrets, Lies, and Democracy: Interviews with David Barsamian, Odonian Press, 1994.

The Minimalist Program, MIT Press, 1995.

Class Warfare: Interviews with David Barsamian, Common Courage Press, 1996.

Power and Prospects: Reflections on Human Nature and the Social Order, South End, 1996.

Contributor of numerous articles to scholarly and general periodicals.

SIDELIGHTS: "Judged in terms of the power, range, novelty and influence of his thought, Noam Chomsky is arguably the most important intellectual alive today," writes Paul Robinson in the *New York Times Book Review.* Chomsky, a professor of linguistics at the Massachusetts Institute of Technology, has attracted worldwide attention with his ground-breaking research into the nature of human language and communication. As the founder of the "Chomskyan Revolution," the scholar has become the center of a debate that transcends formal linguistics to embrace psychology, philosophy, and even genetics. *New York Times Magazine* contributor Daniel Yergin maintains that Chomsky's "formulation of 'transformational grammar' has been acclaimed as one of the major achievements of the century. Where others heard only a Babel of fragments, he found a linguistic order. His work has been compared to the unraveling of the genetic code of the DNA molecule." Yergin further contends that Chomsky's discoveries have had an impact "on everything from the way children are taught foreign languages to what it means when we say that we are human." Chomsky is also an impassioned critic of American foreign policy, especially as it affects ordinary citizens of Third World nations.

Many of his books since 1969 concern themselves with "the perfidy of American influence overseas," to quote *Atlantic* essayist James Fallows. In *America,* Kenneth J. Gavin finds a unifying strain in all of Chomsky's various writings. The author's goal, says Gavin, is "to highlight principles of human knowledge and indicate the priority of these principles in the reconstruction of a society. His efforts leave us with more than enough to think about."

Chomsky was born in Philadelphia on December 7, 1928. His father was a Hebrew scholar of considerable repute, so even as a youngster Chomsky "picked up a body of informal knowledge about the structure and history of the Semitic languages," according to David Cohen in *Psychologists on Psychology.* While still in high school Chomsky proofread the manuscript of his father's edition of a medieval Hebrew grammar. Yergin notes: "This backdoor introduction to 'historical linguistics' had considerable impact in the future; it helped fuel his later conviction that the explanation of how language worked, rather than categories and description, was the business of linguistic study." The young Chomsky was more interested in politics than grammar, however. He was especially passionate about the rebirth of a Jewish culture and society in what later became the state of Israel, and for a time he entertained the idea of moving there. In 1945 he enrolled at the University of Pennsylvania, where he came under the influence of Zellig Harris, a noted professor of linguistics. John Lyons observes in *Noam Chomsky* that it was the student's "sympathies with Harris's political views that led him to work as an undergraduate in linguistics. There is a sense, therefore, in which politics brought him into linguistics."

The school of linguistics in which Chomsky took his collegiate training held as its goal the formal and autonomous description of languages without wide reference to the meaning-or semantics—of utterances. Lyons elaborates: "Semantic considerations were strictly subordinated to the task of identifying the units of phonology and syntax and were not involved at all in the specification of the rules or principles governing their permissible combinations. This part of the grammar was to be a purely *formal* study, independent of semantics." Chomsky questioned this approach in his early work in generative grammar as a student at the University of Pennsylvania, and broke with it more radically while in the Harvard Society of Fellows from 1951. There he was immersed in new developments in mathematical logic, the abstract theory of thinking machines, and the latest psychological and philosophical debates. These ideas led him to develop further his earlier work on generative grammar and to ask "precise and formal questions about linguistics and language," to quote Justin Leiber in his work *Noam Chomsky: A Philosophical Overview*. Leiber adds: "His results led him to criticize and discard the prevailing views in linguistics."

What Chomsky began to develop in the 1950s was a mathematically precise description of some of human language's most striking features. Yergin contends that the scholar was "particularly fascinated by 'generative systems'—the procedures by which a mathematician, starting with postulates and utilizing principles and inferences, can generate an infinite number of proofs. He thought that perhaps language was 'generated' from a few principles as well." Yergin claims that this line of reasoning led Chomsky to another salient question, namely: *"How is it possible that, if language is only a learned habit, one can be continually creative and innovative in its use?"* This question—and its explication—would provide a novel and compelling critique of two established fields, traditional structural linguistics and behavioral psychology. Leiber concludes that Chomsky's new theory "explained many features of language that were beyond structuralist linguistics and placed the specific data, and many lower-level generalizations, of the structuralists within a richer theory."

Many of Chomsky's new ideas were published in his first book, *Syntactic Structures,* in 1957. Yergin calls the work "the pale blue book . . . which heralded the Chomskyan Revolution." He adds that the volume "demonstrated that important facts about language could not be explained by either structural linguistics or by computer theory, which was then becoming fashionable in the field. In *Syntactic Structures,* Chomsky departed from his mentors in stressing the importance of explaining creativity in language and introduces his own transformational grammar as a more 'powerful' explanation of how we make sentences." Webster Schott offers a similar assessment in the *Washington Post Book World*. In *Syntactic Structures,* writes Schott, "Chomsky [presents] and [seems] to demonstrate the proposition that every human being has an innate ability to acquire language, and this ability to learn language is called into use when one hears, at the right age, language for the first time. He also [offers] a concept—it came to be known as 'generative' or 'transformational-generative' grammar—which [has] made it possible to predict ('generate') the sentence combinations in a language and to describe their structure." Lyons states

that the short and relatively nontechnical *Syntactic Structures* "revolutionized the scientific study of language."

The proofs Chomsky uses for his theories are complex, but his conclusions are readily accessible. Robinson observes that, put as simply as possible, Chomsky's view holds that "the ability to speak and understand a language cannot be explained in purely empirical terms—that is, purely by induction. When we 'learn' a language, he says, we are able to formulate and understand all sorts of sentences that we've never heard before. What we 'know,' therefore, must be something deeper—a grammar—that makes an infinite variety of sentences possible. Chomsky believes that the capacity to master grammatical structures is innate: It is genetically determined, a product of the evolutionary process, just as the organic structures of our bodies are." A strict "stimulus-response" mechanism cannot adequately account for the way young children master language during the first four years of life; the child, to quote Cohen, "learns . . . to extract the more complex rules of grammar needed for speech." Leiber explains that for Chomsky, then, the primary interest of the linguist should be with specifying the "device of some sort" that *generates* an infinite variety of grammatically-correct sentences. "This device will specify what is somehow 'internalized' in the competent speaker-hearer of the language," Leiber writes. "Though the most usual label for Chomsky's general sort of linguistics is 'transformational-generative linguistics,' the most crucial word is 'generative'—as opposed to 'taxonomical'-since the primary concern is with the 'principles and processes by which sentences are constructed in particular languages,' not with the identification and classification of items found in the surface end product of these principles and processes."

One of the mechanisms Chomsky proposes for sentence generation is the "deep structure-surface structure" scenario. According to Yergin, the surface structure "'faces out' on the world and, by certain phonological rules, is converted into the sounds we hear; it corresponds to the parsing of sentences which we all learned from our indefatigable junior high English teachers. The deep structure 'faces inward' toward the hazy region of conceptualization, is more abstract and related to meaning. It expresses the basic logical relations between nouns and verbs." Transformational grammar therefore "consists of a limited series of rules, expressed in mathematical notation, which transform deep structures into well-formed surface structures. The transformational grammar thus relates meaning and sound." Cohen discusses the applications of this concept. "Chomsky has analysed the necessary constituents of the deep structure and the transformations through which this deep structure is turned into the surface structure we recognize and use as sentences. He has, of course, extended his theory from this point into the implications for our knowledge of man that comes from the fact that our knowledge of language is based upon this deep structure, a structure that we cannot guess or divine just from speaking, and upon the necessary transformations."

Chomsky has argued that all natural human languages possess deep and surface structures and cycles of transformations between them. In the *Nation,* Gilbert Harman writes: "These built-in aspects of grammar will be parts of the grammar of every language. They are, in other words, aspects of 'universal grammar.' We must therefore suppose that people have a specific faculty of language, a kind of 'mental organ' which develops in the appropriate way, given appropriate experience, yielding a knowledge of whatever language is spoken in their community." John Sturrock elaborates in the *New York Times Book Review:* "Chomskyism starts with grammar and finishes in genetics. Drill deep enough into the structure of our sentences, he maintains, and you will come to those ultimate abstractions with which we were born, the grammar of any given language being originally determined by the fairly restricted grammatical possibilities programmed in the brain. . . . DNA sets up to master a syntax, the accident of birth determines which one." Needless to say, not everyone agrees with Chomsky's view. *Psychology Today* contributor Howard Gardner calls the human being in Chomsky's formulation "a totally preprogrammed computer, one that needs merely to be plugged into the appropriate outlet." Lyons, conversely, states that Chomsky "was surely right to challenge 'the belief that the mind must be simpler in its structure than any known physical organ and that the most primitive of assumptions must be adequate to explain whatever phenomena can be observed.'"

Obviously, Chomsky's theory has as much to do with psychology and philosophy as it does with linguistics. For instance, the very premises of the scholar's work have made him one of the most trenchant critics of behaviorism, the view that suggests all human responses are learned through conditioning. Sturrock notes: "Chomsky's case is that . . . that fanatical core known as behaviorism, has a theory of learning, all rote and Pavlovian reinforcement, which is deficient and, in the end, degrading. . . . [Behaviorists], given

their sinister theory of learning, must be proponents of the view that human nature is not nature at all, but a social product conditioned from outside. Chomsky finds hope and a decisive guarantee of intellectual freedom in the cognitive structures which sit incorruptibly in the fastness of our brains." Chomsky's work reinforces the philosophical tradition of "rationalism," the contention that the mind, or "reason," contributes to human knowledge beyond what is gained by experience. He is opposed by the "empiricists," who claim that all knowledge derives from external stimuli, including language. In the *Nation,* Edward Marcotte declares: "What started as purely linguistic research . . . has led, through involvement in political causes and an identification with an older philosophic tradition, to no less than an attempt to formulate an overall theory of man. The roots of this are manifest in the linguistic theory. . . . The discovery of cognitive structures common to the human race but only to humans (species specific), leads quite easily to thinking of unalienable human attributes." Leiber concludes: "Mind is the software of human psychology, and thought is individuated as instances of the mind's operations. The behaviorist is seen to be insisting . . . on a very minimal sort of software; the rationalist is out to show that much more powerful and abstract, perhaps in good measure innate, software has to be involved. One can feel unhappy with Chomsky's particular way of putting, or productively narrowing, the issue, but it is not an unreasonable viewpoint. Chomsky has an interesting and important sense of *know* at hand. He is looking at men in a way that has an established and well-defined sense when applied to thinking devices."

While establishing his academic reputation, Chomsky continued to be concerned about the direction of American politics and ideology. His moral indignation was excited in the 1960s and he became "one of the most articulate spokesmen of the resistance against the Vietnam war," to quote Jan G. Deutsche in the *New York Times Book Review.* Chomsky attacked the war in articles, in books, and from the podium; in the process he became better known for his political views than for his linguistic scholarship. In a *New York Times* piece written during that era, Thomas Lask observes: "Unlike many others, even those who oppose the war, Noam Chomsky can't stand it and his hatred of what we are doing there and his shame, as well as his loathing for the men who defend and give it countenance are tangible enough to touch." *Nation* essayist Brian Morton finds "nothing exotic about his critique of the U.S. role in Vietnam: He attempted no analysis of arcane economic or political structures.

All he did was evaluate our government's actions by the same standards that we apply when we evaluate the actions of other governments."

Chomsky's first book-length work on Vietnam, *American Power and the New Mandarins*, offers "a searing criticism of the system of values and decision-making that drove the United States to the jungles of Southeast Asia," according to Michael R. Beschloss in the *Washington Post Book World*. The book's strongest vitriol is directed toward those so-called "New Mandarins"—the technocrats, bureaucrats, and university-trained scholars who defend America's right to dominate the globe. Deutsch states that Chomsky's concern "is not simply that social scientists have participated widely in designing and executing war-related projects. What he finds disturbing are the consequences of access to power by intellectuals; the difficulties involved in retaining a critical stance toward a society that makes the reward of power available as well as the need to be 'constructive,' the recognition as problems of only those difficulties that are soluble by the means at hand." Inevitably, Chomsky's volume has drawn scathing criticism from those who oppose his views and high praise from those who agree with him. *Chicago Tribune Book World* reviewer Arthur Schlesinger, Jr., claims: "Judging by *American Power and the New Mandarins*, one can only conclude that Chomsky's idea of the responsibility of an intellectual is to forswear reasoned analysis, indulge in moralistic declamation, fabricate evidence when necessary and shout always at the top of one's voice. It need hardly be said that, should the intellectual community follow the Chomsky example, it would betray its own traditions and hasten society along the road to unreason and disaster." In the *Nation*, Robert Sklar feels otherwise about the work. The critic contends: "The importance of *American Power and the New Mandarins* lies in its power to free our minds from old perspectives, to stimulate new efforts at historical, political and social thought."

Subsequent Chomsky books on American foreign policy have explored other political hotbeds around the world, drawing the conclusion that U. S. interests in human rights, justice, and morality are inevitably subordinated to the needs of big business. Critics point out that a good introduction to Chomsky's views and main themes is provided by *Chronicles of Dissent: Interviews with David Barsamian*, which collects interviews conducted in a variety of settings from 1984 through 1991. As a *Publishers Weekly* reviewer summarizes them, the interviews "range all over world history," but focus on standard Chomsky themes, such as American imperialism and the corruption of the media and academic elite. Several of the conversations also touch on autobiographical topics, with Chomsky discussing his childhood and the development of his thought. As Beschloss notes, Chomsky's "is a portrait of corporate executives manipulating foreign policy for profit motives, of Third World peoples devastated for drifting away from the American 'grand area' of influence; of handmaiden journalists, politicians, and intellectuals shrouding the darker realities of American statecraft under platitudes about idealism and goodwill with an eye toward their flow of rewards from the Establishment." These, in fact, are the very subjects of Chomsky's and Edward S. Herman's book *Manufacturing Consent: The Political Economy of the Mass Media,* in which they examine the various ways news organizations ultimately serve the ideological aims of the government. Chomsky and Herman propose a "propaganda model" of the mass media in the United States; countering the commonly held belief that the mass media tend to respond to rather than create public opinion, the two authors argue that the major American news organizations actively misinform the public about the activities of the United States government. As Philip Green of *The Nation* puts it, Chomsky and Herman seek to discover how it is "that the major American mass media manage so often to produce accounts of the world that are largely indistinguishable from what a commissar [of information and cultural affairs] would have commanded." The bulk of the book tests the "propaganda model" against events in recent North and South American history, including the reporting of elections in El Salvador and the coverage given to the murders of Polish priest Jerzy Popieluszko and Salvadoran Archbishop Oscar Romero.

Times Literary Supplement correspondent Charles Townshend observes that Chomsky "sees a 'totalitarian mentality' arising out of the mainstream American belief in the fundamental righteousness and benevolence of the United States, the sanctity and nobility of its aims. The publicly tolerated 'spectrum of discussion' of these aims is narrow."

The very narrowness of public discussion is the subject of *Deterring Democracy,* a book in which Chomsky examines how, regardless of the facts, the American mass media and the United States government conspire to limit the range of opinions that can be widely expressed. Chomsky discusses, for example, the fact that mainstream public opinion embraced only specific kinds of debates regarding the Sandanista government and the Contras in Nicaragua; he shows that the vast majority of lawmakers and reporters disagreed only as to which methods should be employed to rid that country of its communist leaders—no serious attention was given to the debate about whether the Sandanistas or the U. S.-backed Contras would best serve the people of Nicaragua. Also, regarding the "war on drugs," Chomsky examines the government's propaganda campaign supporting its various "successes" and describes the positive news coverage these victories receive; the facts that 1) drug use was declining in the United States before President George Bush announced the start of the "war" and that 2) drug use has increased in the meantime receive very little attention. He concludes that no substantial discussion arises about the effects of this war on the countries involved, and he bitterly denounces the ironic policy of the United States government of threatening trade sanctions against those East Asian countries that block the importing of U. S. tobacco, a product that is proven to be deadly. Chomsky himself transcends that narrow spectrum of debate, however, adducing "example after example to illuminate how American policies have led knowingly to large scale human suffering," to quote Beschloss. In the *New York Times Book Review,* Sheldon S. Wolin suggests that the author "is relentless in tracking down official lies and exposing hypocrisy and moral indifference in the high places. . . . Yet the passion of Chomsky's indictment is always controlled, and while he is harsh toward his opponents, he is never unfair or arrogant."

Other critics have been less sanguine about the quality and influence of Chomsky's political views; in fact, some have labeled him a pariah and attempted to discredit him on a number of grounds. "It has been Chomsky's singular fate to have been banished to the margins of political debate," writes Steve Wasserman in the *Los Angeles Times Book Review.* "His opinions have been deemed so kooky—and his personality so cranky—that his writings no longer appear in the forums . . . in which he was once so welcome." Wolin offers one dissenting view: "Chomsky's political writings are curiously untheoretical, which is surprising in a writer renowned for his contributions to linguistic theory. His apparent assumption is that politics is not a theoretical subject. . . . One gets the impression from reading Chomsky that if it were not urgently necessary to expose lies, immorality and the abuse of power, politics would have no serious claim upon the theoretical mind." *New York Times Book Review* contributor Paul Robinson notes that in Chomsky's case,

"the popular or accessible [political] works often seem to belie the intellectual powers unambiguously established in the professional works. . . . Indeed, one might argue that the discrepancy is more extreme in his work than in that of any other important intellectual." Morton feels that the attacks on Chomsky's historical/political scholarship—and more recently the tendency to ignore his work—have affected his level of stridency. "His later tone is that of a man who doesn't expect anything to change," Morton observes. ". . . Chomsky is savagely indignant because the values he cherishes are being strangled. But increasingly, the reasons for his indignation—the values he cherishes—are hard to see in his work. Only the indignation is clear." This is a major characteristic of *Year 501: The Conquest Continues,* in which Chomsky examines what he sees as the U. S. Government's shabby behavior toward its neighbors in the hemisphere. His strident denunciations of U. S. imperialism are often conveyed through striking comparisons, however; *Kirkus Reviews* offers as an example Chomsky's realization that "the logic of [the United States government's] annexation of Texas was essentially [the same as] that attributed to Saddam Hussein by US propaganda after his conquest of Kuwait."

Leiber finds an overriding commitment to freedom in the Chomsky's work—"the freedom of the individual to produce and create as he will without the goad of external force, economic competition for survival, or legal and economic restraint on social, intellectual, or artistic experiment; and the freedom of ethnic and national groups to work out their own destinies without the intervention of one or another Big Brother." "From his earliest writings to his latest, Chomsky has looked with astonishment at what the powerful do to the powerless," Morton declares. "He has never let his sense of outrage become dulled. If his voice has grown hoarse over twenty years, who can blame him? And who can feel superior? No one has given himself more deeply to the struggle against the horrors of our time. His hoarseness is a better thing than our suavity." Deutsch writes: "The most convincing indication of the extent to which Chomsky's wide ranging indictment of United States society and policy must be taken seriously is that a man possessed of these sensibilities should have felt compelled to undertake it." Morton offers a compelling conclusion. "Americans are no longer convinced that our government has the right to destroy any country it wants to," the essayist states. "And to the extent that this is true, Chomsky, along with others like him, deserves much of the credit. He did his job well."

In 1970, the London *Times* named Chomsky one of the thousand "makers of the twentieth century." According to Yergin, his theory "remains the foundation of linguistics today," and "his vision of a complex universe within the mind, governed by myriad rules and prohibitions and yet infinite in its creative potential, opens up vistas possibly as important as Einstein's theories." Yergin adds: "The impact of Chomsky's work may not be felt for years. . . . Yet this beginning has revolutionized the study of language and has redirected and redefined the broad inquiry into intelligence and how it works." Robinson calls the scholar's work "a prolonged celebration of the enormous gulf that separates man from the rest of nature. He seems overwhelmed by the intellectual powers that man contains within himself. Certainly nobody ever stated the case for those powers more emphatically, nor exemplified them more impressively in his own work. Reading Chomsky on linguistics, one repeatedly has the impression of attending to one of the more powerful thinkers who ever lived."

Appreciation has likewise attended Chomsky's political writings. According to Christopher Lehmann-Haupt in the *New York Times,* Chomsky "continues to challenge our assumptions long after other critics have gone to bed. He has become the foremost gadfly of our national conscience." Philip Green in *The Nation* writes that "not to have read his essays . . . is to court genuine ignorance." *New Statesman* correspondent Francis Hope praises Chomsky for "a proud defensive independence, a good plain writer's hatred of expert mystification, a doctrine of resistance which runs against the melioristic and participatory current of most contemporary intellectual life." Hope concludes: "Such men are dangerous; the lack of them is disastrous."

BIOGRAPHICAL/CRITICAL SOURCES:

BOOKS

Achbar, Mark and the Institute of Policy Alternatives, *Manufacturing Consent: Noam Chomsky and the Media: The Companion Book to the Award-Winning Film by Peter Wintonick and Mark Achbar,* Black Rose Books, 1994.

Botha, Rudolf P., *Challenging Chomsky: The Generative Garden Game,* B. Blackwell (New York City), 1989.

Cohen, David, *Psychologists on Psychology,* Taplinger, 1977.

Cohn, Werner, *Partners in Hate: Noam Chomsky and the Holocaust Deniers,* Avukah Press (Cambridge, MA), 1995.

Contemporary Issues Criticism, Volume 1, Gale, 1982.

Cook, V. J. and Mark Newson, *Chomsky's Universal Grammar,* Basil Blackwell, 1996.

Greene, Judith, *Psycholinguistics: Chomsky and Psychology,* Penguin Books, 1972.

Haley, Michael C. and Ronald F. Lunsford, *Noam Chomsky,* Twayne (New York City), 1994.

Harman, Gilbert, editor, *On Noam Chomsky: Critical Essays,* Anchor Press, 1974.

Harris, Randy Allen, *The Linguistics Wars,* Oxford University Press (New York City), 1993.

Huck, Geoffrey J. and John A. Goldsmith, *Ideology and Linguistic Theory: Noam Chomsky and the Deep Structure Debates,* Routledge (New York City), 1995.

Kasher, Asa, *The Chomskyan Turn,* Blackwell, 1991.

Kim-Renaud, Young-Key, *Studies in Korean Linguistics,* Hanshin Publishing, 1986.

Leiber, Justin, *Noam Chomsky: A Philosophical Overview,* Twayne, 1975.

Lyons, John, *Noam Chomsky,* 2nd edition, Penguin Books, 1977, third edition, Fontana Press (London), 1991.

Mehta, Ved, *John Is Easy to Please,* Farrar, Straus, 1971.

Newmeyer, Frederick J., *Generative Linguistics,* Routledge (New York City), 1994.

Osiatynski, Wiktor, *Contrasts: Soviet and American Thinkers Discuss the Future,* Macmillan, 1984.

Otero, Carlos Peregrin, *Noam Chomsky: Critical Assessments,* Routledge, 1994.

Rai, Milan, *Chomsky's Politics,* Verso (New York City), 1995.

Rieber, Robert W., editor, *Dialogues on the Psychology of Language and Thought: Conversations with Noam Chomsky, Charles Osgood, Jean Piaget, Ulric Neisser, and Marcel Kinsbourne,* Plenum, 1983.

Salkie, Raphael, *The Chomsky Update: Linguistics and Politics,* Unwin Hyman (Boston), 1990.

Sampson, Geoffrey, *Liberty and Language,* Oxford University Press, 1979.

Sen Gupta, Kalyan and Jadavpur University, *Mentalistic Turn, A Critical Evaluation of Chomsky,* K. P. Bagchi & Co. (Calcutta) and Jadavpur University, 1990.

Smith, N. V. and Deirdre Wilson, *Modern Linguistics: The Results of Chomsky's Revolution,* Penguin Books (New York City), 1990.

Thinkers of the Twentieth Century, Gale, 1983.

Williams, T. C., *Kant's Philosophy of Language: Chomskyan Linguistics and Its Kantian Roots,* E. Mellen Press (Lewiston, NY), 1993.

PERIODICALS

America, December 11, 1971; July 15, 1989, p. 42; August 27, 1994, p. 30.

Atlantic, July, 1973; February, 1982.

Bloomsbury Review, September, 1993.

Book World, March 23, 1969.

Christian Century, July 23, 1969.

Christian Science Monitor, April 3, 1969; May 14, 1970.

Chronicle of Higher Education, May 12, 1982.

Commentary, May, 1969.

Current Biography, August, 1995, p. 15.

Dissent, January-February, 1970.

Economist, November 29, 1969.

Globe and Mail (Toronto), June 16, 1984; July 5, 1986.

Harvard Education Review, winter, 1969.

Horizon, spring, 1971.

Humanist, November-December, 1990, p. 8.

International Affairs, January, 1971.

London Review of Books, August 20, 1992.

Los Angeles Times Book Review, December 27, 1981; June 8, 1986; August 30, 1987.

Maclean's, August 18, 1980; March 22, 1993.

Nation, September 9, 1968; March 24, 1969; May 17, 1971; May 8, 1976; March 31, 1979; February 16, 1980; December 22, 1984; December 26, 1987-January 2, 1988; May 7, 1988; May 15, 1989, p. 670.

National Review, June 17, 1969; July 8, 1991, p. 40.

New Republic, April 19, 1969; October 26, 1974; March 13, 1976; February 17, 1979; September 6-13, 1980; March 24, 1982; March 23, 1987; January 9, 1989, p. 34.

New Statesman, November 28, 1969; August 17, 1979; April 25, 1980; July 17, 1981; August 14, 1981; September 11, 1981; January 21, 1983.

New Statesman & Society, July 5, 1991, p. 35; November 27, 1992, p. 43; March 12, 1993, p. 14; April 16, 1993, p. 38; June 3, 1994, p. 22.

Newsweek, March 24, 1969.

New Yorker, November 11, 1969; May 8, 1971.

New York Review of Books, August 9, 1973; January 23, 1975; November 11, 1976; October 23, 1980; February 1, 1996, p. 41.

New York Times, March 18, 1969; August 2, 1973; February 5, 1979; March 8, 1982.

New York Times Book Review, March 16, 1969; January 17, 1971; January 9, 1972; September 30, 1973; October 6, 1974; February 15, 1976; February 25, 1979; October 19, 1980; March 21, 1982; April 13, 1986.

New York Times Magazine, May 6, 1968; December 3, 1972.

Observer, June 23, 1991.

Progressive, December, 1982; October, 1991, p. 39; October, 1993, p. 41; January, 1995, p. 39.

Psychology Today, July, 1979.

Rolling Stone, May 28, 1992, p. 42.

Saturday Review, May 31, 1969.

Science and Society, spring, 1970.

Scientific American, May, 1990, p. 40.

Sewanee Review, winter, 1977.

Times Literary Supplement, March 27, 1969; March 31, 1972; December 21, 1973; December 12, 1975; September 10, 1976; November 21, 1980; February 27, 1981; July 23, 1982; July 15-21, 1988.

Utne Reader, November-December, 1993, p. 120.

Village Voice, June 18, 1980; June 23, 1980; July 13, 1982.

Virginia Quarterly Review, summer, 1969.

Washington Post Book World, March 11, 1979; March 7, 1982; February 21, 1988.

* * *

CLANCY, Thomas L. 1947-
(Tom Clancy)

PERSONAL: Born in 1947 in Baltimore, MD; son of a mail carrier and a credit employee; married Wanda Thomas (an insurance agency manager) in August, 1969; children: Michelle, Christine, Tom, Kathleen. *Education:* Graduated from Loyola College, Baltimore, MD, 1969. *Politics:* Conservative. *Religion:* Roman Catholic.

ADDRESSES: Home—P.O. Box 800, Huntingtown, MD 20639-0800. *Agent*—c/o Putnam, 200 Madison Ave., New York, NY 10016.

CAREER: Insurance agent in Baltimore, MD, and Hartford, CT, until 1973; O. F. Bowen Agency (insurance company), Owings, MD, agent, beginning in 1973, owner, beginning in 1980; writer. *Military service:* U.S. Army Reserve Officers Training Corps.

WRITINGS:

NOVELS; UNDER NAME TOM CLANCY

The Hunt for Red October, Naval Institute Press, 1984.

Red Storm Rising, Putnam (New York City), 1986.

Patriot Games, Putnam, 1987.

The Cardinal of the Kremlin, Putnam, 1988.
Clear and Present Danger, Putnam, 1989.
The Sum of All Fears, Putnam, 1991.
Patriot Games (film version), Berkley (New York City), 1992.
Red Storm Rising; The Cardinal of the Kremlin: Two Complete Novels, Putnam, 1993.
Submarine, Berkley, 1993.
Without Remorse, Putnam, 1994.
Debt of Honor, Putnam, 1994.
Three Complete Novels: Patriot Games, Clear and Present Danger, The Sum of All Fears, Putnam, 1994.
Executive Orders, Putnam, 1996.

NONFICTION

Armed Cav: A Guided Tour of an Armored Calvary Regiment, Putnam, 1994.
Fighter Wing: A Guided Tour of an Air Force Combat Wing, Berkley, 1995.
Marine: A Guided Tour of a Marine Expeditionary Unit, Berkley, 1996.
Into the Storm: A Study in Command, Putnam, 1997.
Reality Check: What's Going on Out There? Putnam, 1997.

Also author of foreword to *Silent Chase: Submarines of the U.S. Navy,* by Steve Kaufman, Thomasson-Grant, 1989.

ADAPTATIONS: The Hunt for Red October was adapted as a film for Paramount, directed by John McTiernan and starring Sean Connery and Alec Baldwin, 1990; *Patriot Games* was adapted as a film for Paramount, directed by Phillip Noyce and starring Harrison Ford and Anne Archer, 1992; *Clear and Present Danger* was adapted as a film for Paramount, directed by Phillip Noyce and starring Harrison Ford and Willem Dafoe, 1994.

SIDELIGHTS: Known for hugely successful, detailed novels about espionage, the military, and advanced military technology, Tom Clancy was proclaimed "king of the techno-thriller" by Patrick Anderson in the *New York Times Magazine.* Since the 1984 publication of his first novel, the acclaimed *Hunt for Red October,* all of his books have become best-sellers. Rich Cohen wrote in *Rolling Stone,* "Indeed, Clancy seems to have saturated the national consciousness, creating a new American style, a hybrid of rugged individualism and high technology." Popular with armed forces personnel as well as the public, they have garnered praise from such prominent figures as

former President Ronald Reagan and Secretary of Defense Caspar Weinberger. Clancy's work has also received more negative attention from officials who found his extrapolations from declassified information uncomfortably close to the top-secret reality and from reviewers who criticized his characterizations and too-perfect weaponry. Still, sales in the millions and constant best-seller status attest to his continued popularity as "novelist laureate of the military-industrial complex," as Ross Thomas described him in the *Washington Post Book World.*

The Hunt for Red October, which describes the race between U.S. and Soviet forces to get their hands on a defecting Russian submarine captain and his state-of-the-art vessel, marked a number of firsts. It was a first novel for both its author and its publisher, Naval Institute Press, whose catalogue had previously consisted of scholarly and strategic works and the occasional collection of short stories or poems about the sea. It was the first best-seller for both parties as well, and it became the first of Clancy's books to be made into a motion picture. Conceived before the author, an insurance agent, had ever set foot on a submarine, it is "a tremendously enjoyable and gripping novel of naval derring-do," according to *Washington Post Book World* critic Reid Beddow. The book contains descriptions of high-tech military hardware so advanced that former Navy Secretary John Lehman, quoted in *Time,* joked that he "would have had [Clancy] court-martialed: the book revealed that much that had been classified about antisubmarine warfare. Of course, nobody for a moment suspected him of getting access to classified information." The details were actually based on unclassified books and naval documents, Clancy's interviews with submariners, and his own educated guesses, the author asserts. Admitting that "neither characterization nor dialogue are strong weapons in Clancy's literary arsenal," Richard Setlowe in the *Los Angeles Times Book Review* nonetheless expressed an opinion shared by other reviewers: "At his best, Clancy has a terrific talent for taking the arcana of U.S. and Soviet submarine warfare, the subtleties of sonar and the techno-babble of nuclear power plants and transforming them into taut drama."

In Clancy's second novel, *Red Storm Rising,* U.S.-Soviet conflict escalates to a non-nuclear World War III. Crippled by a Moslem terrorist attack on a major Siberian oil refinery, the Soviet Union plots to defeat the countries in the North Atlantic Treaty Organization (NATO) so that it can dominate oil-rich Arab nations unhindered. The novel covers military action on land and in the air as well as on submarines; its complicated narrative prompted *Chicago Tribune Book World* reviewer Douglas Balz to note that Clancy's "skill with the plot . . . is his real strength." Balz and other critics faulted Clancy's characterization, although in the *New York Times Book Review* Robert Lekachman deemed the problem irrelevant to the book's merits as a "rattling good yarn" with "lots of action" and the "comforting certainty that our side will win." John Keegan, writing in the *Washington Post Book World,* called *Red Storm Rising* "a brilliant military fantasy—and far too close to reality for comfort."

Patriot Games, Clancy's third book, tells how former Marine officer Jack Ryan, a key figure in *The Hunt for Red October,* places himself between a particularly fanatical branch of the Irish Republican Army and the British royal family. Several reviewers criticized it for lack of credibility, lags in the action, simplistic moral lines, and, again, poor characterization, conceding nevertheless that it should appeal to fans of the earlier books. Anderson voiced another perspective: *"Patriot Games* is a powerful piece of popular fiction; its plot, if implausible, is irresistible, and its emotions are universal." Pointing out Clancy's authentic detail, powerful suspense, and relevance to current history, James Idema suggested in a *Tribune Books* review that "most readers [will] find the story preposterous yet thoroughly enjoyable."

Ryan appears again in *The Cardinal of the Kremlin,* which returns to the theme of conflict between the United States and the Soviet Union. In this episode, regarded by critics such as Lekachman as "by far the best of the Jack Ryan series" to date, Clancy focuses on the controversial laser-satellite "strategic defense systems" also known as "Star Wars." According to Lekachman: "The adventure . . . is of high quality. And while [Clancy's] prose is no better than workmanlike . . . , the unmasking of the title's secret agent, the Cardinal, is as sophisticated an exercise in the craft of espionage as I have yet to encounter." Remarked *Fortune* contributor Andrew Ferguson, Clancy "aims not only to entertain but also to let his readers in on the 'inside story,' meanwhile discussing with relish the strategic and technological issues of war and peace." Concluded Ferguson, "It is refreshing to find a member of the literati who is willing to deal with [defense policy] in a manner more sophisticated than signing the latest disarmament petition in the *New York Times.*"

In *Clear and Present Danger* Ryan, in league with the Central Intelligence Agency (CIA), joins the fight against the powerful South American organizations that supply illegal drugs to the U.S. market. After the director of the Federal Bureau of Investigation (FBI) is murdered on a trip to Colombia, the fight becomes a covert war, with foot soldiers and fighter planes unleashed on virtually any target suspected of drug involvement. Reviewing the novel in the *Wall Street Journal,* former Assistant Secretary of State Elliott Abrams wrote, "What helps to make *Clear and Present Danger* such compelling reading is a fairly sophisticated view of Latin politics combined with Mr. Clancy's patented, tautly shaped scenes, fleshed out with colorful technical data and tough talk." Abrams commended Clancy's awareness of the ethical dilemmas that complicate such covert military operations. Some reviewers echoed earlier criticisms of Clancy's characterizations, his focus on technology, and his prose style, but, noted Evan Thomas in *Newsweek,* "it doesn't really matter if his characters are two dimensional and his machines are too perfect. He whirls them through a half dozen converging subplots until they collide in a satisfyingly slam-bang finale." Thomas called the book "Clancy's best thriller since his first" and "a surprisingly successful cautionary tale."

Patrick O'Brian commented in the *Washington Post Book World* that *The Sum of All Fears* "is about four times the length of the usual novel and deals with at least four times the usual number of themes." In the novel, Jack Ryan is Deputy Director of the CIA, a Middle East peacemaker, and out of favor with the White House. Not all of the factions accept the peace he negotiates. Palestinian terrorists and other radicals obtain a nuclear weapon that they explode at the Super Bowl hoping to cause an all-out war between the United States and the Soviet Union. "The scenes of deployment and nuclear hell at the Super Bowl are truly chilling," wrote Les Standford in his review of the novel in the Chicago *Tribune Books.* Standford added, "And Ryan's subsequent attempts to calm a crackpot president and avert a global nuclear war are harrowing. It's just a shame we couldn't get to the plot a bit sooner." Morton Kondracke remarked in *The New York Times Book Review* that "it's [one] of Mr. Clancy's gifts that he can keep several sub-plots and sub-sub-plots in the air at the same time. In this book he has outdone himself."

John Kelly reappears in *Without Remorse.* The former Navy SEAL becomes somewhat of a vigilante, tracking down and killing the drug-smuggling pimps who are after the prostitute he has befriended following the deaths of his wife and unborn child. In addition, the U.S. government dispatches him on a special mission to Vietnam to liberate POWs. In *The Washington Post Book World* Marie Arana-Ward declared, "What Clancy manages to deliver to us armchair warriors . . . is a different kind of virtuosity: a meticulous chronicle of military hardware, a confident stride through corridors of power, an honest-to-God global war game, and a vertiginous plot that dutifully tracks dozens of seemingly disparate strands to a pyrotechnic finish." Gene Lyons, writing in *Entertainment Weekly,* commented, "given his turgid style and psychological absurdities, Clancy still knows how to tell a tale, and millions of would-be warriors who make up his loyal readership will no doubt find themselves thrilled to their toes."

The plot of *Debt of Honor* emanates from a Japanese financier who blames the United States for his parents' deaths during World War II and seeks revenge in the economic markets and through military means. Jack Ryan, White House national security adviser, becomes vice president as result of the way he handles the crisis, and ascends to the presidency when a Japanese airman hits the Capitol with a Boeing 747. *Los Angeles Times Book Review* contributor John Calvin Batchelor remarked, "Clancy's passion is overwhelming. His sense of cliffhanging is state of the art. The close of this book is a five-run homer." *Executive Orders* picks up where *Debt of Honor* concludes-with Jack Ryan facing the burden of running a government whose power holders are now dead. He also is being assailed by domestic and foreign political and military challenges. "Clancy stacks up the enemies and would-be assassins like thrill-seekers waiting to ride the next roller coaster," noted Jason Zappa in *The Weekly Tribune Plus*. Of the weighty ninth Clancy novel, Gina Bellafante said in *Time* that it "is another doozy of laborious plot, bombastic jingoism and tedious detail."

Op-Center is a briefer yet still complex Clancy novel. In the novel, Paul Hood is the director of a new U.S. intelligence agency that must investigate the implications of a terrorist bombing at a celebration in Seoul, South Korea.

Unprecedented knowledge of military technology, plots of rousing adventure and taut suspense, and themes that address current international concerns have combined to make Clancy "one of the most popular authors in the country," in the estimation of *Washington Post Book World* writer David Streitfeld. He is so well liked by military personnel, in particular, that he has been invited to military bases and given tours of ships; reported Evan Thomas in *Newsweek,* "Bluntly put, the Navy realized that Clancy was good for business." Cohen drew the similarities between Clancy and his popular character Jack Ryan. He wrote, "In a way, Tom Clancy has become Jack Ryan: He lectures at the FBI; he dines at the White House; he has been asked on numerous occasions to run for public office; he gives his thoughts on world affairs; he hosts fund-raisers for his friend Oliver North; he attends meetings at the CIA; and like his friends there, he seems almost comically obsessed with leaks and the flow of information." Some critics even credit the author with helping to banish the negative opinion of the military that arose after the United States's controversial involvement in the Vietnam War.

As for criticism of his work, Clancy admitted in a *Washington Post* article: "I'm not that good a writer. I do a good action scene. I handle technology well. I like to think that I do a fair—fairer—job of representing the kind of people we have in the Navy . . . portraying them the way they really are. Beyond that, I'll try to . . . improve what needs improving." The secrets of his success as an entertainer, concluded Anderson, are "a genius for big, compelling plots, a passion for research, a natural narrative gift, a solid prose style, a hyperactive . . . imagination and a blissfully uncomplicated view of human nature and international affairs."

BIOGRAPHICAL/CRITICAL SOURCES:

BOOKS

Bestsellers 89, Issue 1, Gale, 1989.
Bestsellers 90, Issue 1, Gale, 1990.
Clancy, Tom, Martin Harry Greenberg, and Roland J. Green, editors, *The Tom Clancy Companion,* Berkeley Books (New York City), 1992.
Contemporary Literary Criticism, Volume 45, Gale, 1987.
Garson, Helen S., *Tom Clancy: A Critical Companion,* Greenwood Press (Westport, CT), 1996.

PERIODICALS

American Legion, December, 1991, p. 16.
Chicago Tribune Book World, September 7, 1986.
Detroit News, January 20, 1985.

Economist, March 17, 1990, p. 87.
Entertainment Weekly, August 6, 1993, pp. 50-51.
Fortune, July 18, 1988; August 26, 1991.
Globe and Mail (Toronto), September 2, 1989.
Kliatt, November, 1995, p. 6.
Los Angeles Times, July 16, 1989.
Los Angeles Times Book Review, December 9, 1984; July 26, 1987; August 21, 1994, pp. 1, 9.
Magazine of Fantasy and Science Fiction, December, 1991, p. 73.
National Review, April 29, 1988.
Newsweek, August 17, 1987; August 8, 1988; August 21, 1989.
New Yorker, September 16, 1991, p. 91.
New York Times, July 17, 1986; August 12, 1986; February 25, 1990; March 1, 1990.
New York Times Book Review, July 27, 1986; August 2, 1987; July 31, 1988; August 13, 1989; July 28, 1991, pp. 9-10; August 22, 1993, pp. 13-14; October 2, 1994, pp. 28-29.
New York Times Magazine, May 1, 1988.
People, September 8, 1986; September 12, 1988; September 5, 1994, p. 34.
Publishers Weekly, August 8, 1986; July 1, 1988; July 25, 1994, pp. 34-35; August 5, 1996, p. 433.
Rolling Stone, December 1, 1994, p. 114.
School Library Journal, June, 1995, p. 143.
Saturday Evening Post, September-October, 1991, p. 16.
Time, March 4, 1985; August 11, 1986; August 24, 1987; July 25, 1988; August 21, 1989; March 5, 1990; March 12, 1990; September 2, 1996, p. 61.
Tribune Books (Chicago), July 5, 1987; August 11, 1991, p. 7.
Wall Street Journal, October 22, 1984; August 16, 1989.
Washington Post, January 29, 1985; March 17, 1989; March 2, 1990; August 8, 1993, pp. 1, 14.
Washington Post Book World, October 21, 1984; July 27, 1986; May 14, 1989; August 13, 1989; July 28, 1991, pp. 1-2.
Weekly Tribune Plus, September 16, 1994, p. 8.
West Coast Review of Books, November-December, 1984.
Writer's Digest, October, 1987.*

*   *   *

CLANCY, Tom
  See CLANCY, Thomas L.

CLAYTON, Richard Henry Michael 1907-1993
  (William Haggard)

PERSONAL: Born August 11, 1907, in Croydon, Surrey, England; died October 27, 1993; son of Henry James and Mabel Sarah (Haggard) Clayton; married Barbara Myfanwy Sant, 1939; children: Michael Edward, Julia Katharine. *Education:* Attended Lancing College; Christ Church, Oxford, B.A., 1929, M.A., 1947.

CAREER: Indian Civil Service, 1931-39 (magistrate, 1931; sessions judge, 1937); British Civil Service, Board of Trade, 1947-69; controller, Enemy Property Branch of Board of Trade, 1957-69. *Military service:* Indian Army, 1939-45; became lieutenant colonel.

MEMBER: Travellers' Club (London).

WRITINGS:

"COLONEL CHARLES RUSSELL" SERIES; UNDER PSEUDONYM WILLIAM HAGGARD

Slow Burner (also see below), Little, Brown (Boston), 1958.
Venetian Blind (also see below), Washburn (New York City), 1959.
The Arena (also see below), Washburn, 1961.
The Unquiet Sleep (also see below), Washburn, 1962.
The High Wire (Detective Book Club Selection), Washburn, 1963.
The Antagonists, Washburn, 1964.
The Powder Barrel, Washburn, 1965.
The Hard Sell (also see below), Cassell (London), 1965, Washburn, 1966.
The Power House, Cassell, 1966, Washburn, 1967.
The Conspirators, Cassell, 1967, Walker (New York City), 1968.
A Cool Day for Killing, Walker, 1968.
The Doubtful Disciple, Cassell, 1969.
Haggard for Your Holiday: Three Complete Novels by William Haggard (contains *The Arena, The Unquiet Sleep,* and *The Hard Sell*), Cassell, 1969.
The Hard Liners, Walker, 1970.
The Bitter Harvest, Cassell, 1971, published as *Too Many Enemies,* Walker, 1972.
The Old Masters, Cassell, 1973, published as *The Notch on the Knife,* Walker, 1973.
The Scorpion's Tail, Walker, 1975.
Yesterday's Enemy, Walker, 1976.
Visa to Limbo, Cassell, 1978, Walker, 1979.
The Poison People, Walker, 1979.
The Median Line, Cassell, 1979, Walker, 1981.

The Mischief Makers, Hodder & Stoughton (London), 1982, Walker, 1983 (bound with *The Golden Creep* by George Bagby and *Endgame* by Michael Gilbert, W. J. Black, 1982).
The Need to Know, Hodder & Stoughton, 1984.
The Meritocrats, Hodder & Stoughton, 1985.
The Expatriates, Hodder and Stoughton, 1989.
The Vendettists, Hodder and Stoughton, 1990.

SUSPENSE NOVELS; UNDER PSEUDONYM WILLIAM HAGGARD

The Telemann Touch, Little, Brown, 1958.
Closed Circuit (also see below), Washburn, 1960.
The Haggard Omnibus (contains *Slow Burner, Venetian Blind* and *Closed Circuit*), Cassell, 1967.
The Protectors, Walker, 1972.
The Kinsmen, Walker, 1974.
The Money Men, Walker, 1981.
The Heirloom, Hodder & Stoughton, 1983.
The Martello Tower, Hodder & Stoughton, 1986.
The Diplomatist, Hodder & Stoughton, 1987.
The Expatriates, Hodder & Stoughton, 1989.

OTHER

The Little Rug Book (nonfiction), Cassell, 1972.

Contributor to anthologies, including *Blood on My Mind,* Macmillan (London), 1972, *Winter's Crimes No. 4,* edited by George Hardinge, Macmillan, 1972, and *Winter's Crimes No. 8,* edited by Hilary Watson, Macmillan, 1976. .

SIDELIGHTS: Richard Clayton won a reputation as a first-class writer of suspense fiction, which he published under the pseudonym William Haggard. His novels involve nefarious plots and counterplots in the highest levels of government and behind the scenes of international affairs. "The taste of a Haggard book is unique, inimitable . . . and delightful," declared H. R. F. Keating in *St. James Guide to Crime and Mystery Writers.* "His view of the world, his tone of voice, enter almost all his characters' heads and certainly permeate every phrase he writes as narrator or describer. He cannot put pen to paper without showing in every word an unchippable top-level view of the world." Called by Anthony Boucher of the *New York Times Book Review* a "strikingly individual novelist," Haggard most often wrote about Colonel Charles Russell of the Security Executive, a fictional high-level branch of the English intelligence establishment.

Colonel Russell enjoys a great popularity among readers of spy fiction. Writing in the *New York Times,* Anatole Broyard described Russell as "a fine character. . . . Urbane, autocratic, ironical, he carries not a gun but a personality into his work." Jean M. White of the *Washington Post Book World* noted that Russell "operates in a very civilized yet undeniably effective manner. He is an urbane man, having about him the air of a mature James Bond." In a review of *A Cool Day for Killing,* Allen J. Hubin of the *New York Times Book Review* judged Russell as "surely one of the most effectively developed characters in spy fiction."

In later books, such as *The Mischief Makers,* Haggard allowed the senior sleuth to be "very nearly upstaged" by black Englishman Willy Smith, who is "equally urbane," reported Robin W. Winks in the *New Republic.* Smith makes "a perfectly acceptable substitute" for the retired Russell in the suspense novel *The Diplomatist,* said Tim Heald of the London *Times.* Haggard's other books upheld his reputation even without the considerable talents of Colonel Russell. *The Martello Tower,* for example, gave readers two "clever and likable police types" who take the law into their own hands when faced with a terrorist plot, according to a *Kirkus Reviews* writer. The reviewer called *The Martello Tower* "a solid, tight-as-a-drum adventure."

"I always anticipate savouring the delights of William Haggard's writing," Maurice Prior of *Books and Bookmen* stated. Prior appreciated Haggard's "mastery and expertise in handling a plot" and his "skill and positiveness plus an almost indefinable air of assurance and atmosphere-cultivation which keeps one absorbed and fascinated from first to last." Newgate Callender noted in the *New York Times Book Review* that Haggard "has been compared as a stylist to C. P. Snow, and there is indeed something of that admirable author in Haggard's deliberate, British upper-class, stiff lipped understatement." Winks of the *New Republic* esteemed Haggard as "a thoroughgoing professional who writes as he wishes to, convincingly, cleverly, and with acid."

"Whatever story Haggard embarks on," Keating wrote, "he takes you with superb unconcern straight into the highest of high places in the stacked hierarchy of British life (and occasionally into what he sees as the equally hierarchic life of Soviet Russia). It is an entrancing process, because the highest places are of their nature very small places. There is not room at the very top for all of us. But in Haggard we have a proxy in the seats of power." The critic went on to observe that "these highest places are not your mere Cabinet Rooms or Prime Minister's studies. They are the rooms behind these, the rooms occupied by the people who view prime ministers as simply the awkward and temporary holders of an office. They are the less grandiloquent rooms of those who have acquired, or semi-inherited, the duty of protecting the children of Demos from themselves. I do not know whether in drab real life they actually exist, but while I am reading the pages of a book by Haggard they certainly do."

BIOGRAPHICAL/CRITICAL SOURCES:

BOOKS

Dictionary of Literary Biography Yearbook: 1993, Gale (Detroit), 1994.
St. James Guide to Crime and Mystery Writers, 4th edition, St. James Press (Detroit), 1996.

PERIODICALS

Best Sellers, September 1, 1965; August 1, 1968; February 15, 1972.
Books and Bookmen, November, 1968; November, 1969; October, 1970; September, 1973.
Book Week, September 13, 1964, p. 13; September 12, 1965, p. 27.
Globe and Mail (Toronto), April 21, 1984.
Guardian, April 7, 1961, p. 7.
Kirkus Reviews, April 1, 1987, p. 498; May 15, 1988, p. 711.
Library Journal, September 15, 1962; August, 1963; May 1, 1966; October 1, 1971; May 1, 1967; December 15, 1967.
New Republic, March 19, 1977; June 10, 1978; June 13, 1983.
New Statesman, March 24, 1961.
New Yorker, September 22, 1962; February 1, 1969.
New York Herald Tribune Book Review, July 30, 1961, p. 15; September 23, 1962, p. 15; August 18, 1963, p. 11.
New York Times, January 14, 1972; March 10, 1979.
New York Times Book Review, July 23, 1961, p. 22; September 30, 1962, p. 34; August 11, 1963, p. 17; August 30, 1964, p. 14; August 22, 1965, p. 26; March 13, 1966, p. 20; April 9, 1967, p 30; November 17, 1968; January 14, 1972; April 23, 1972, p. 43; September 16, 1973; December 28, 1976.

Observer, August 24, 1969; September 12, 1971; September 10, 1972; November 25, 1979; November 15, 1987, p. 26.
San Francisco Chronicle, August 20, 1961, p. 24.
Saturday Review, November 24, 1962; September 28, 1963; September 26, 1964; September 25, 1965; April 30, 1966; April 29, 1967; June 29, 1968.
Spectator, April 14, 1961, p. 524; September 4, 1971.
Springfield Republican, July 23, 1961, p. 5D.
Times (London), December 24, 1987.
Times Literary Supplement, March 31, 1961, p. 206; March 23, 1962, p. 205; May 17, 1963, p. 361; March 19, 1964, p. 238; April 8, 1965, p. 280; November 11, 1965, p. 1007; November 3, 1966, p. 1008; November 16, 1967, p. 1092; September 18, 1969; October 22, 1971, p. 1340; September 29, 1972.
Washington Post Book World, March 18, 1979.

OBITUARIES:

PERIODICALS

Times (London), November 5, 1993, p. 21.*

*   *   *

CODY, Jess
See CUNNINGHAM, Chet

*   *   *

COLES, Cyril Henry 1899-1965
(Manning Coles, Francis Gaite, joint pseudonyms)

PERSONAL: Born June 11, 1899, in London, England; died October 9, 1965; son of David and Rose Elizabeth (Gaite) Coles; married Dorothy Cordelia Smith, 1934; children: Peter, Michael. *Education:* Attended school in Petersfield, Hampshire, England. *Avocational interests:* Model making, travel, flying.

CAREER: Apprenticed to shipbuilding firm, John I. Thornycroft, Southampton, England, became manager of millfitting department; left in mid-twenties to travel around the world, staying for a long period in Australia where he worked as a garage manager, railway employee, and daily columnist on a Melbourne newspaper; returned to England in 1928, and in 1936 began writing detective stories and thrillers with a neighbor, Adelaide Frances Oke Manning, a partnership that continued until her death in 1959. *Military service:* British Army, Infantry and Intelligence, World War I; served in France and Germany; became major.

WRITINGS:

MYSTERY NOVELS; WITH ADELAIDE FRANCES OKE MANNING, UNDER JOINT PSEUDONYM, MANNING COLES

Drink to Yesterday, Hodder & Stoughton (London), 1940, Knopf (New York City), 1941, reissued with an introduction by James Nelson, Norton (New York City), 1967.

Pray Silence, Hodder & Stoughton, 1940, published under title *A Toast to Tomorrow,* Doubleday (New York City), 1941.

They Tell No Tales, Hodder & Stoughton, 1941, Doubleday, 1942.

This Fortress, Doubleday, 1942.

Without Lawful Authority, Doubleday, 1943.

Green Hazard, Doubleday, 1945.

The Fifth Man, Doubleday, 1946.

Let the Tiger Die, Doubleday, 1947.

With Intent to Deceive, Doubleday, 1947 (published in England as *A Brother for Hugh,* Hodder & Stoughton, 1947).

Among Those Absent, Doubleday, 1948.

Diamonds to Amsterdam, Doubleday, 1949.

Not Negotiable, Doubleday, 1949.

Dangerous by Nature, Doubleday, 1950.

Now or Never, Doubleday, 1951.

Alias Uncle Hugo, Doubleday, 1952.

Night Train to Paris, Doubleday, 1952.

A Knife for the Juggler, Hodder & Stoughton, 1953, Doubleday, 1964, reisued as *The Vengeance Man,* Pyramid Publications (New York City), 1967.

All that Glitters, Doubleday, 1954 (published in England as *Not For Export,* Hodder & Stoughton, 1954).

Brief Candles, Doubleday, 1954 (published in England under pseudonym Francis Gaite, Hodder & Stoughton, 1954).

Happy Returns, Doubleday, 1955 (published in England under pseudonym Francis Gaite as *A Family Matter,* Hodder & Stoughton, 1956).

The Man in the Green Hat, Doubleday, 1955.

The Basle Express, Doubleday, 1956.

Birdwatcher's Quarry, Doubleday, 1956.

The Far Traveller, Doubleday, 1956 (published in England under pseudonym Francis Gaite, Hodder & Stoughton, 1957).

Death of an Ambassador: A Tommy Hambledon Story, Doubleday, 1957.

Three Beans, Hodder & Stoughton, 1957.

Come and Go, Doubleday, 1958 (published in England under pseudonym Francis Gaite, Hodder & Stoughton, 1958).

No Entry, Doubleday, 1958.

Duty Free, Doubleday, 1959 (published in England under pseudonym Francis Gaite, Hodder & Stoughton, 1959).

The Exploits of Tommy Hambledon (includes *Drink to Yesterday, A Toast to Tomorrow,* and *Alias Uncle Hugo*), Doubleday, 1959.

Crime in Concrete, Hodder & Stoughton, 1959, published under title *Concrete Crime,* Doubleday, 1960.

NOVELS WITH TOM HAMMERTON; UNDER JOINT PSEUDONYM MANNING COLES

Search for a Sultan, Doubleday, 1961.

The House at Pluck's Gutter, Hodder & Stoughton, 1963.

OTHER

Half-Valdez, Hodder & Stoughton, 1939.

(With Adelaide Frances Oke Manning, under joint pseudonym Manning Coles) *Great Caesar's Ghost* (juvenile), Doubleday, 1943 (published in England as *The Emperor's Bracelet,* University of London Press, 1947).

(With Adelaide Frances Oke Manning, under joint pseudonym Manning Coles) *Nothing to Declare* (short stories), Doubleday, 1960.

Contributor of articles on engineering, travel, and model making to magazines. The Manning Coles books have been translated into Japanese, Lebanese, and a number of European languages.

SIDELIGHTS: With Adelaide Frances Oke Manning, Cyril Henry Coles was the author of a number of innovative mystery-adventure novels featuring the British Intelligence Service agent Thomas Elphinstone Hambledon—one of the precursors to James Bond. Tommy Hambledon's adventures, explained Elizabeth F. Duke in the *St. James Guide to Crime and Mystery Writers,* "were based on Cyril Coles's own war experiences with the Nazis, and his characterization on a much admired professor of Coles's. Tommy, like Coles, has a talent for emerging unscathed from behind enemy lines. And, like the professor, he has an uncanny knack at mastering foreign languages." Hambledon's first adventures, *Drink to Yesterday* and *Pray Silence,* were set in the period between the World Wars. During World War II and throughout the remainder of the 1940s, his exploits remained among the most popular contemporary spy and adventure stories.

In his first few adventures Tommy Hambledon worked as an espionage agent in Germany, infiltrating the Nazi regime and gaining the confidence of Adolf Hitler himself. By 1942, with the publication of *They Tell No Tales,* he had returned to England and was stalking the German agents who sabotaged battleships in the Portsmouth dockyard. Reviewers noted that, despite the inevitable blood and gore of a spy story set in wartime, Coles managed to retain a sense of humor in the work. A reviewer for the *Times Literary Supplement* celebrated Coles's "refreshingly light touch." "Here," reported *New York Times* contributor Isaac Anderson, "are mystery, adventure and romance as Manning Coles knows so well how to present them."

The Coles team continued Hambledon's adventures after the conclusion of World War II but, reviewers felt, the stories rapidly lost the qualities that had made the earlier work so successful. "As the 1940s ended," explained Duke, "the public taste for spy fiction about Nazis declined, and the team attempted to adapt Tommy's adventures to the international scene of the 1950s. It was at this point that their reputation began to slip, with reviewers commenting on the formulaic nature of both settings and plots." "Thomas Elphinstone Hambledon was the brightest creation of modern espionage fiction—the most audacious and inventive adventurer since Arsene Lupin," stated Anthony Boucher in a 1949 *New York Times* review of *Diamonds to Amsterdam.* "But these weak and piping times of peace proffer few situations worthy of Tommy's peculiar talents; and he has been wasting his time for several books."

With Tommy Hambledon's decline in popularity, the Coles team created a new set of characters and launched a new series. The feature characters, cousins James and Charles Latimer and their pet monkey Ulysses, were dead. In *Brief Candles* they return from their graves in order to help their descendant Richard Scroby out of difficulties. "The publishers call this 'a spoofing spook story' and 'a tale that proves to be considerably quicker than dead,'" declared Boucher in his *New York Times* review of the initial volume.

"And this time it seems they haven't stretched things a bit." *Brief Candles* proved popular enough that it spawned two sequels, *Happy Returns* and *Come and Go.* "All one needs to say is, 'a Coles ghost story, as good as the others,'" stated a *San Francisco Chronicle* reviewer about the third volume. "Unhappy is the reader who couldn't enjoy it."

BIOGRAPHICAL/CRITICAL SOURCES:

BOOKS

St. James Guide to Crime and Mystery Writers, 4th edition, St. James Press (Detroit), 1996.

PERIODICALS

Booklist, December 1, 1942, p. 122.
Books, February 8, 1942, p. 13; September 27, 1942, p. 24.
Boston Globe, March 11, 1942, p. 19.
Chicago Sunday Tribune, August 12, 1956, p. 11.
New York Herald Tribune Book Review, December 18, 1949, p. 25; January 31, 1954, p. 14; July 13, 1958, p. 9.
New York Herald Tribune Weekly Book Review, March 9, 1947, p. 24; July 11, 1948, p. 9.
New York Times, February 8, 1942, p. 20; September 27, 1942, p. 30; March 9, 1947, p. 24; November 16, 1947, p. 53; July 11, 1948, p. 18; December 11, 1949, p. 25; January 10, 1954, p. 26; July 18, 1954, p. 15; August 21, 1955, p. 22; January 22, 1956, p. 30; June 29, 1958, p. 21; July 6, 1958, p. 11; October 15, 1965.
San Francisco Chronicle, August 12, 1956, p. 19; September 15, 1957, p. 23; May 18, 1958, p. 27.
Saturday Review, August 11, 1956, p. 41.
Times Literary Supplement, October 25, 1941, p. 529.*

*   *   *

COLES, Manning
  See COLES, Cyril Henry

*   *   *

COLLINS, Hunt
  See HUNTER, Evan

COOGAN, Tim(othy) Pat(rick) 1935-

PERSONAL: Born in 1935, in County Dublin, Ireland. *Education:* Has earned both B.A. and M.A.

ADDRESSES: Office—Irish Press, Tara House, Tara St., Dublin 2, Ireland.

CAREER: Irish Press (newspaper), Dublin, Ireland, editor; freelance author, 1966—. Has also worked as a television interviewer.

WRITINGS:

Ireland since the Rising, Praeger, 1966.
The I.R.A., Praeger, 1970, revised version, Roberts Rinehart, 1993.
The Irish: A Personal View, Phaidon, 1975.
On the Blanket: The H Block Story, Ward River Press, 1980.
(Editor) *Ireland and the Arts,* Namara Press, 1983.
Disillusioned Decades: Ireland 1966-1987, Gill and Macmillan, 1987.
Michael Collins: A Biography, Hutchinson, 1990, published in the United States as *The Man Who Made Ireland: The Life and Death of Michael Collins,* Roberts Rinehart, 1992.
De Valera: Long Fellow, Long Shadow, Hutchinson, 1993, published in the United States as *Eamon de Valera: The Man Who Was Ireland,* Harper-Collins, 1995.
The Troubles: Ireland's Ordeal, 1966-1995, and the Search for Peace, Hutchinson, 1995.
(Author of Foreword) Michael Collins, *The Path to Freedom,* Roberts Rinehart, 1996.

Editor of *Blackrock* (journal).

SIDELIGHTS: Tim Pat Coogan has been a long-time editor of the *Irish Press,* described by Owen Dudley Edwards in the *New York Times Book Review* as Ireland's "most nationalist daily newspaper." In addition, Coogan has penned or edited numerous books on Ireland and its history, concentrating on the years during and after the southern portion of the island won its independence from Great Britain. The first of these volumes, published in 1966, is *Ireland since the Rising.* The book traces political developments in Ireland after the 1916 Easter Rebellion (the rising by Irish patriots against the British that was swiftly put down but which also generated popular support for the Irish cause). A *Times Literary Supplement* reviewer noted Coogan's perceptive grasp of modern Irish politics, writing that "the atmosphere is chang-

ing. In politics the old hands are going and the fervours of deep green nationalism of the old style are yielding to the pragmatism of the new men at the top. This transformation Mr. Coogan describes from an intimate knowledge of the facts and his book is a useful guide to modern Ireland." Benedict Kelly in the *New York Times Book Review* found that Coogan offers "a good run-of-the-treadmill account" in *Ireland since the Rising,* "enlivened by some illuminating asides." And A. J. P. Taylor, critiquing the book in the *New York Review of Books,* was favorably impressed by the author's impartiality, noting that "he is interested in practical achievements, not in ancient feuds."

One of Coogan's best-known works is 1970's *The I.R.A.* An in-depth study of the terrorist organization which operates in both southern and Northern Ireland, the book examines, among other things, the psychological profile of the men and women who comprise its members. A critic in the *Times Literary Supplement* lauded Coogan's effort, asserting that "his research is as thorough as it could be in the circumstances, his narrative clear, his point of view impeccably neutral." The critic concluded that "no student of Irish history over the past fifty years can afford to ignore this book." Although Owen Dudley Edwards in the *New York Times Book Review* was not quite as enthusiastic, he did declare that *The I.R.A.* "is distinguished by the industry of its research, the wide spectrum of persons interviewed by the author, the blunt—almost ham-handed—readiness to quote any statement, however informal, which might serve to illustrate a point, and the mass of useful factual raw material presented in its pages." An updated version of *The I.R.A.* was published in 1993.

Coogan's next project was *The Irish: A Personal View.* "For those ignorant of but curious about this troubled country it will reveal much," stated D. W. Harkness in the *Times Literary Supplement.* In this volume Coogan examines the everyday lives of his countrymen and discusses the problems that challenge them—which, in his opinion, include the Catholic Church. Harkness reported that the author's "harshest words are reserved for those aspects of the Roman Catholic Church in Ireland which have stunted the development of the people, by discouraging 'individual thought . . . discretion or personal truth other than that revealed by the bishops and priests of Ireland.'" Coogan also discusses issues of alcohol abuse and the rights of women, and advocates a united Ireland. "His book is always interesting," commented

Harkness, "and will surprise even those who think they know Ireland well."

Coogan has also authored a biography of Irish revolutionary leader Michael Collins, published in the United States as *The Man Who Made Ireland: The Life and Death of Michael Collins.* Collins "was the brains behind the Irish revolution," Christopher Matthews explained in the *New York Times Book Review.* "His exploits as the intelligence chief of the Irish Republican Army during the war of 1919-21 are legendary." During this time Collins was so popular that he could ride a bicycle safely through the city of Dublin, despite the fact that the city was full of British agents bent upon his assassination. However, after he negotiated the peace treaty that helped create the Irish Free State of the 1920s, he *was* assassinated—by members of his own organization who felt he had sold out to the British. As Matthews put it, Coogan "shows us an unusual leader, someone ready to use terror in war but equally ready to pay the ultimate price for peace." A *Los Angeles Times Book Review* critic offered praise for *The Man Who Made Ireland;* noting Coogan's use of myriad details about both Collins and the Irish revolution, the reviewer judged that the volume was nonetheless "sufficiently sprightly."

Coogan followed with a biography of Eamon de Valera, the Irish revolutionary who rose to become Ireland's longtime Prime Minister, *Eamon de Valera: The Man Who Was Ireland.* He sets de Valera against Michael Collins, writes Thomas Flanagan in *New York Times Book Review,* as a counterhero, painting "a dark portrait of a man driven, from youth through old age, by lust for power." Flanagan highlights the book's appeal as "colorfully written [and] engagingly robust," but also infers that its author enjoys pointing out de Valera's dishonest and power-hungry tendencies. "The implacability of Mr. Coogan's attack . . . itself merits examination." He and other critics nonetheless find this biography to be another of Coogan's fascinating, well-researched, and well-written historical accounts.

Coogan's next project was the ambitious *The Troubles: Ireland's Ordeal 1966-1995, and The Search for Peace,* in which he documents the political history of the war in Northern Ireland and the attempts made at peace since 1969. He bases his information primarily on his own research and personal experience. "For this insider's account alone," writes Kevin Toolis in *Observer Review, "The Troubles* will be essential reading for any future scholar of Irish

peace-making." The book has also been praised for its readability and sheer abundance of information.

Most criticism, though, has centered around accusations that Coogan is overtly biased in favor of Irish nationalists, blaming only the British government for the recent failed attempts at peace. Malachi O'Doherty of *New Statesman & Society* says, "Tim Pat Coogan's book is a celebration of the increasing power of Irish nationalism, a tradition in which he sees no fault." Peter Finn writes in *Washington Post Book World,* "He has little or no sympathy for Unionist sensitivities or fears. . . . His detailed interviewing is almost entirely among Irish Americans, the Irish government and the nationalist community in Northern Ireland." Others find his actual political analysis of the stalled peace process to be simply askew. "He says the logjam can be broken only by President Clinton," writes Finn, "a suggestion that seems fantastic to a reader on this side of the Atlantic." Toolis agrees, "Coogan at times is in danger of forgetting the dynamie of his own superb earlier work on the IRA; in Irish Republicanism it is not priests or popes or politicians but gunmen who call the shots." Coogan's book is still considered a valuable account of Irish history. Finn admits, "When he finally gets around to it, Coogan provides a worthy account of the guarded, nuanced evolution in Sinn Fein's thinking." Robert Moore notes Coogan's "having an excellent vantage point from which to watch and reflect," in *Library Journal.* Toolis writes that "In others' hands it would be an impossible task." Coogan, however, "maintains a steady canter through the dense boglands of Ulster's sectarian strife. . . . He touches on every issue of significance and enlivens a horrific history with wit."

BIOGRAPHICAL/CRITICAL SOURCES:

PERIODICALS

Library Journal, March 15, 1996, p. 82.
Los Angeles Times Book Review, November 15, 1992, p. 6.
New Statesman and Society, October 20, 1995, p. 41.
New York Review of Books, July 28, 1966, p. 8.
New York Times Book Review, August 21, 1966, p. 6; October 11, 1970, p. 20; April 11, 1993; April 30, 1995.
Observer Review, October 8, 1995.
Publishers Weekly, October 10, 1994, p. 68.
Times Literary Supplement, July 14, 1966, p. 612; July 9, 1970, p. 743; February 20, 1976; December 1, 1995, p. 21.
Washington Post Book World, July 28, 1996, p. 6.*

CRAWFORD, Thomas 1920-

PERSONAL: Born July 6, 1920, in Dundee, Scotland; son of Thomas (a public works foreman) and Margaret Campbell (a teacher; maiden name, Marr) Crawford; married Jean Rennie (a laboratory technician), August 19, 1946; children: Rosemary Margaret Crawford Ulas, Thomas Campbell. *Education:* University of Edinburgh, M.A., 1944; University of Auckland, M.A., 1953. *Politics:* Labour.

ADDRESSES: Home—61 Argyll Place, Aberdeen AB25 2HU, Scotland. *Office*—Department of English, University of Aberdeen, Old Aberdeen AB9 2UB, Scotland.

CAREER: University of Auckland, Auckland, New Zealand, lecturer, 1953-60, senior lecturer, 1961-62, associate professor of English, 1962-65; University of Edinburgh, Edinburgh, England, lecturer in English, 1965; McMaster University, Hamilton, Ontario, Commonwealth research fellow, 1966-67; University of Aberdeen, Aberdeen, Scotland, reader in English, 1967-85; writer.

MEMBER: Association for Scottish Literary Studies (president, 1984-88), Scottish Text Society (member of council, 1975-96), Scots Language Society, Saltire Society.

WRITINGS:

Burns: A Study of the Poems, Oliver & Boyd, 1960, Stanford University Press (Stanford, CA), 1965, Canongate Academic, 1994.

Scott, Oliver & Boyd, 1965, revised edition, Scottish Academic Press, 1982.

(Editor) *Sir Walter Scott: Selected Poems,* Clarendon Press, 1972.

Love, Labour, and Liberty, Carcanet Press, 1976.

Society and the Lyric, Scottish Academic Press, 1979.

Longer Scottish Poems, Volume II, Scottish Academic Press, 1987.

Boswell, Burns, and the French Revolution, Saltire Society, 1990.

(Editor) *The Correspondence of James Boswell and William Johnson Temple 1756-1795,* Volume I: 1756-1777, Yale University Press (New Haven), CT, 1997.

Member of editorial board of "Canongate Classics," 1987-97; editor, *Scottish Literary Journal,* 1974-84.

WORK IN PROGRESS: "Editor with Heather Barkley of *The Correspondence of James Boswell and William Johnson Temple 1756-1795,* Volume II: 1777-1795, to be published by Edinburgh University Press and Yale University Press."

SIDELIGHTS: Thomas Crawford told *CA* that his work reflects "a passionate involvement with the literature of Scotland and a wish to make it more widely known."

*   *   *

CRONKITE, Walter (Leland, Jr.) 1916-

PERSONAL: Born November 4, 1916, in St. Joseph, MO; son of Walter Leland (a dentist) and Helen Lena (Fritsche) Cronkite; married Mary Elizabeth Simmons Maxwell (a journalist), March 30, 1940; children: Nancy Elizabeth, Mary Kathleen, Walter Leland III. *Education:* Attended University of Texas, 1933-35. *Politics:* Independent. *Religion:* Episcopalian. *Avocational interests:* Yachting, dancing, golf, tennis, bowling, and reading.

ADDRESSES: Office—CBS News, 51 West 52nd St., New York, NY 10019.

CAREER: Scripps-Howard Bureau, Austin, TX, reporter on state capitol staff, 1933-35; *Houston Press,* Houston, TX, reporter, 1935-36; KCMO-Radio, Kansas City, MO, news and sports editor and broadcaster, 1936-37; United Press International (UPI), organizer of El Paso (TX) bureau, 1937; WKY-Radio, Oklahoma City, OK, football announcer, 1937; Braniff Airways, Kansas City, executive, 1937; UPI, reporter, 1937-48, war correspondent from Germany, North Africa, British Isles, Normandy, and Belgium, 1941-45, established bureaus in Belgium, the Netherlands, and Luxembourg, 1945, chief correspondent from the Nuremberg trials of Nazi war criminals, 1945-46, chief correspondent from the Soviet Union in Moscow, 1946-48; broadcaster, lecturer, and journalist from Washington, DC, 1948-50; Columbia Broadcasting System (CBS)-News, New York City and Washington, DC, 1950—, discussion chair of *Man of the Week,* 1951, anchor of *The Week in Review,* 1951-62, moderator of *Pick the Winner,* 1952, narrator of *You Are There,* 1953-55, host of *It's News to Me,* 1954, coordinator and master of ceremonies of *Morning Show,* 1955, narrator of *The Twentieth Century,* 1957-67, managing editor and anchor of *CBS*

Evening News with Walter Cronkite, 1962-81, special correspondent, 1981—. Writer, editor, and narrator of television specials for CBS and others, including *The Newsreel Era—Seventy Years of Headlines,* 1972; *Solzhenitsyn,* 1974; *The Rockefellers,* 1974; *Vietnam: A War That Is Finished,* 1975; *The President in China,* 1975; *In Celebration of US,* 1976; *Our Happiest Birthday,* 1977; *Walt Disney . . . One Man's Dream,* 1981; *Walter Cronkite's Universe,* 1981-82; *A Journey of the Mind,* 1983; *1984 Revisited,* 1984; *Walter Cronkite at Large,* 1986-88; *The Cronkite Report,* 1993-96; and *Cronkite Remembers,* 1997. Associated with Interfaith Alliance.

MEMBER: Overseas Press Club, Overseas Writers Club, National Press Club, Academy of Television Arts and Sciences (president, 1959), Association of Radio News Analysts, Chi Phi, Century Association, Players Club, New York Yacht Club, Edgartown Yacht Club, Cruising Club of America.

AWARDS, HONORS: George Foster Peabody Radio and Television Award, 1962; William Allen White Award of Journalistic Merit, 1969; Emmy Award from Academy of Television Arts and Sciences, 1970; George Polk Memorial Award from Long Island University, 1971; Fourth Estate Award from National Press Club, 1973; Emmy Awards, 1973, for "coverage of shooting of Governor Wallace" and for *The Watergate Affair;* Emmy Awards, 1974, for *The Agnew Resignation, The Rockefellers,* and *Solzhenitsyn;* gold medal from International Radio and Television Society and Freedom Award from John Marshall Law School, both 1974; Alfred I. DuPont-Columbia University Award in Broadcast Journalism, 1978; Governor's Award (special Emmy award), 1979; Jefferson Award, Paul White Award, special George Foster Peabody Award, and Presidential Medal of Freedom, all 1981; Distinguished Service Award from National Association of Broadcasters and Trustees Award from National Academy of Television Arts and Sciences, both 1982. Recipient of numerous honorary degrees, including University of Notre Dame, Harvard University, Northwestern University, University of Massachusetts, Bucknell University, Ohio State University, University of Michigan, Duke University, and Dartmouth College.

WRITINGS:

(Contributor) M. Mirkin Stanford, editor, *Conventions and Elections, 1960: A Complete Handbook,* Channel Press, 1960.

Vietnam Perspective: A CBS News Special Report, Pocket Books (New York City), 1965.
Eye on the World, Cowles Book Co., 1971.
The Challenge of Change, Public Affairs Press (Washington, DC), 1971.
(Editor) *South by Southeast: Paintings by Ray Ellis,* Oxmoor House (Birmingham, AL), 1983.
North by Northeast, Oxmoor House, 1986.
Westwind, Oxmoor House, 1990.
(Author of commentary) Irving Haberman, *Eyes on an Era: Four Decades of Photojournalism,* Rizzoli (New York City), 1995.
A Reporter's Life (memoir), Knopf (New York City), 1996.

Also author of *I Can Hear It Now: The Sixties,* 1970.

AUTHOR OF INTRODUCTION

George Orwell, *Nineteen Eighty-Four: Commemorative Edition,* Dutton (New York City), 1950.
Steve Weinberg, *Trade Secrets of Washington Journalists: How To Get the Facts about What's Going on in Washington,* Acropolis (Washington, DC), 1981.
Kathy Cronkite, *On the Edge of the Spotlight,* Warner Books (New York City), 1982.
John Bryson, *The World of Armand Hammer,* Harry N. Abrams (New York City), 1985.
Dennis Conner, *Comeback: My Race for the America's Cup,* St. Martin's (New York City), 1988.
Roger Tory Peterson, *Save the Birds,* Houghton (Boston, MA), 1989.
Register of American Yachts 1988-89: The Yacht Owners Register, Yacht Owners Register, Inc., 1989.
Lorraine Monk, *Photographs That Changed the World,* Doubleday (New York City), 1989.
Register of American Yachts, 1990, Yacht Owners Register, Inc., 1990.

OTHER

Contributor to interactive CD-ROM, *American Presidents: The Most Powerful Men on Earth.*

SIDELIGHTS: Walter Cronkite was voted "the most trusted man in America" in a 1973 opinion poll, a reflection of the respect he earned as anchorman of the *CBS Evening News.* Cronkite joined CBS in 1950 and began broadcasting a nightly news show in 1962. He earned numerous Emmy Awards and other citations from his peers before he retired in 1981. According to Maureen Orth in *Vogue,* Cronkite "has not only been the ultimate witness to history, he has also helped shape our perception of that history by virtue of his role in directing the course of television news." In his reassuring, generally unflappable manner, Cronkite told national television audiences of the first man on the moon, of the assassinations of John F. Kennedy, Robert F. Kennedy, and Martin Luther King, Jr., of the failing Vietnam War, and of the resignation of Richard Nixon. An estimated nineteen million viewers tuned in to his broadcasts each night at the dinner hour.

In a *50 Plus* profile, Dalma Heyn called Cronkite "our most reliable world guide; someone so familiar and real to us he might have been a close friend." Heyn also pinpointed the anchorman's popularity, only now diminishing after more than a decade off the air: "As a constant, someone who was thoroughly professional, believable and honest for so many years, he filled a deeply felt need. He seemed to make the bad news a little more palatable." Cronkite prided himself on his unbiased presentation of national and world events—he often pointed out that he was not a commentator, but a reporter who allowed his viewers to form their own opinions. This philosophy contributed to his reputation for integrity in presenting the news, but most Americans appreciated him more for his steady on-air presence. As Michael Gorkin put it in *50 Plus,* Cronkite's "steady and reassuring voice— 'And that's the way it is . . .'—provided just the soothing we needed. *He,* at least, believed we would muddle through."

Some critics have observed that Cronkite's standing in Middle America was enhanced by the fact that he comes from Midwestern and middle-class origins himself. He was born in St. Joseph, Missouri, in 1916, the son of a dentist. From an early age he felt tugged toward journalism, and his ambitions were nurtured by his public school teachers. After attending high school in Houston, Texas, he enrolled at the University of Texas, but he spent more time stringing for the *Houston Post* and working as a radio announcer than he did attending classes. After two years of college he dropped out and took a full-time reporting job. Within a year he was working as a correspondent for United Press International.

Prior to World War II, Cronkite held a number of positions as a journalist, radio broadcaster, and bureau organizer. He rejoined UPI as war erupted in Europe, and he was sent to cover the fighting from the front lines. Gorkin claimed that Cronkite's associates found him "one of the most daring war-front

reporters. He parachuted into Holland with the 101st Airborne Division, and was with the U.S. Third Army for the Battle of the Bulge. He specialized in the personal story with the hometown angle, and nobody worked harder or wrote faster than he did. He was, they say, simply one of the best American reporters to come out of the war."

Cronkite has insisted that he was never extraordinarily courageous during his years as a war correspondent. "I was scared to death all the time," he told *Playboy.* "I did everything possible to avoid getting into combat. . . . But the truth is that I did everything only once. It didn't take any great courage to do it once. If you go back, and do it a second time—knowing how bad it is—that's courage."

After the war Cronkite stayed with UPI, working in Europe, the Soviet Union, and Washington, DC He joined CBS in 1950 and began appearing on a number of fledgling television shows, most notably *The Week in Review.* Cronkite told *50 Plus:* "There were better speakers, better interviewers, and better-looking people than me, [but] people sensed that I believe in what I am doing." Cronkite's early career at CBS took some unexpected turns. Beginning in 1953 he hosted *You Are There,* a show that re-created historical events and offered imaginary interviews with such luminaries as Joan of Arc and Julius Caesar.

Cronkite proved himself a serious on-air reporter in 1952, when CBS sent him to provide radio coverage of the presidential nominating conventions in Chicago. In an *Atlantic Monthly* expose on CBS, David Halberstam noted that Cronkite "was thoroughly prepared, knew the weight of each delegation, and was able to bind the coverage together at all times. He was a pro in a field short of professionalism. By the end of the first day . . . the other people in the control booth just looked at each other; they knew they had a winner." Subsequently, CBS expanded Cronkite's duties as an on-site television reporter. He especially enjoyed covering rocket liftoffs at Cape Canaveral and elsewhere—a prelude to his longstanding interest in the nation's space program.

A shuffle of personnel at CBS in 1962 made Cronkite the anchorman of the evening news. Throughout the turbulent 1960s the show gained steadily on its competitors, and in the 1970s it led the ratings by a wide margin every year. Cronkite served as managing editor of the show as well as its anchor, taking great responsibility for the content of each program and the wording of each script. Halberstam observed that

Cronkite "was a good synthesizer and clarifier, working hard in the brief time allotted to his program to make the news understandable to millions of people. And his style and character seemed to come through."

"In no small measure," Orth wrote, "Walter Cronkite's success and the esteem in which he is held have helped glamorize television news and invest it with the kind of disturbing power it has today." Eventually Cronkite transcended his role as reporter of the news and began to *make* news himself. After a visit to South Vietnam in 1968, during which he observed the Tet Offensive, Cronkite made a special broadcast and candidly reported that the United States was losing the war. Historians credit that broadcast with helping to turn majority opinion against the effort in Southeast Asia, as well as helping to convince Lyndon Johnson not to seek re-election. In 1977 Cronkite was instrumental in initiating peace talks between Egypt and Israel, when chance comments in an interview led to a live-broadcast dialogue between those countries' leaders.

Cronkite told *Playboy* that he made every effort to remain impartial on every story he reported. "The basic function of the press has to be the presentation of all the facts on which the story is based," he said. "Advocacy is all right in special columns. But how the hell are you going to give people the basis on which to advocate something if you don't present the facts to them? If you go only for advocacy journalism, you're really assuming unto yourself a privilege that was never intended anywhere in the definition of a free press."

Nevertheless, Cronkite's special interest in space exploration and the environment meant that CBS News gave extra precedence to these issues. *Newsweek* contributor Harry F. Waters claimed that Cronkite's "passion for moon shots probably did more to rally the nation behind the U.S. space program than all of NASA's public-relations efforts." Heyn maintained that Cronkite's love of nature "almost certainly helped create the climate for passage of the environmental legislation of the '70s." After retiring from the daily anchor spot in 1981, Cronkite continued to pursue his interests in these fields through a series of specials called *Walter Cronkite's Universe* and *Walter Cronkite at Large*.

Since 1981 Cronkite has remained on the staff at CBS as a consultant and the host of numerous special broadcasts. He has also hosted documentaries for the Public Broadcasting System (PBS) and the Discovery Channel. He has used his spare time to indulge his passion for yachting and other sports and has written several books on boating and its pleasures. Cronkite is still much sought after as a speaker; his positions on broadcast journalism in particular are accorded a great deal of respect. Cronkite told the *Washington Post* that he misses his work as an anchorman, but he relishes the opportunity to enjoy himself. "I've made my contribution over 45 or 50 years of journalism," he said. "I don't know why I shouldn't be entitled to take it easier as well as others. . . . I was tired of the Evening News when I stepped down. I wasn't tired of the job so much as I was tired of the routine. The job I loved. It would be wonderful if I could dip into the Evening News—if I could say, 'Gee, I'm going to go and work this week.' There's no place for individuals with such whimsical ideas."

Late in 1996 Cronkite published a memoir entitled *A Reporter's Life*. The work covers his years as a schoolboy and struggling reporter as well as his rise to prominence in television broadcasting. "The title really tells almost all" about the book, according to *New Leader* correspondent Richard C. Hottelet. "This is not an anchorman's journey or a correspondent's reflections; it is the story of a man who has always seen himself as a working stiff, a reporter. Rubbing elbows with world leaders, sitting first row center at the history of a generation and receiving virtually unanimous acclaim have not softened a core of common sense." Hottelet went on to style the memoir "a serious book by a professional who has mastered his craft. The last chapter should be read in schools of journalism, by all who work in the broadcast industry, and especially by people who want to know how television is informing them."

Many of the reviewers of *A Reporter's Life* noted that the work reflects its author's unassuming personality. *New York Times Book Review* contributor Tom Wicker wrote: "It's the story of a modest man who succeeded extravagantly by remaining mostly himself—succeeded in a demanding new medium, itself part of an exploding technology that made the world more complex by enable peoples to know more about one another. And not unlike journalism itself, [Cronkite's] memoir is a short course on the flow of events in the second half of this century—events the world knows more about because of Walter Cronkite's work, and some of which might not have happened without it." An *Economist* reviewer concluded that *A Reporter's Life* "reflects its author. An old time wire-service reporter who moved on to radio and television, his virtues are decency and reliability. He is neither a deep thinker nor an outstanding writer. But the tale of his career, laced with anecdotes, some of the hilarious, and interspersed with often platitudinous commentary, reveals how Mr. Cronkite presided over what already seems to have been the golden age of television news, and why he is so missed."

The last years of the twentieth century have found Cronkite working hard as ever, producing a television documentary series called *Cronkite Remembers* that mirrored his memoir, and even lending his expertise to an interactive CD-ROM on the American presidents. "The career of Walter Cronkite parallels the evolution of modern media—from newspapers and radio to television, and now on to digital news gathering and distribution," noted a reporter for *Computer Life.* "Perhaps the most respected and identifiable newsman of the twentieth century, Cronkite embodies credibility. His thoughts on history, education, and computers are relevant and inspiring."

Arthur Taylor, former corporate president of CBS, told *50 Plus:* "I think Walter will go down in history for having the character not to exploit the power that was his. Had he not had the character to do that, he might have provoked an enormous change in the rules. . . . And I think life would have become very difficult for the broadcast community." Cronkite told *TV Guide* how he managed to keep his perspective over a twenty-year career in front of the camera. "A good journalist doesn't just *know* the public, he *is* the public," Cronkite concluded. "He feels the same things they do."

BIOGRAPHICAL/CRITICAL SOURCES:

BOOKS

Authors in the News, Gale (Detroit, MI), Volume 1, 1975, Volume 2, 1976.
Contemporary Theatre, Film, and Television, Volume 6, Gale, 1989.
Cronkite, Kathy, *On the Edge of the Spotlight,* Warner Books (New York City), 1982.
Wood, Carlyle, *Television Personalities Biographical Sketch Book,* Television Personalities, 1956.

PERIODICALS

American Heritage, December, 1994, p. 42.
Atlantic Monthly, February, 1976.
Booklist, November 1, 1996, p. 458.
Broadcasting, October 15, 1973.
Chicago Tribune, December 31, 1996, Section 5, p. 1; March 9, 1997, p. 4.
Christian Century, December 14, 1994, p. 1200.
Christian Science Monitor, December 26, 1973.
Computer Life, January, 1997, p. 54.
Current, June, 1980.
Economist, February 15, 1997, p. S8.
Entertainment Weekly, December 20, 1996, p. 67; April 11, 1997, p. 20.
Esquire, April, 1973; December, 1980.
50 Plus, November, 1979; March, 1985.
Forbes, February 10, 1997, p. 28.
Library Journal, December, 1996, p. 106.
Look, August 25, 1964; November 17, 1970; March 26, 1971.
Los Angeles Times Book Review, January 12, 1997, p. 3.
Los Angeles Times Magazine, January 21, 1996, p. 8.
National Review, June 30, 1997, p. 58.
New Leader, December 16, 1996, p. 18.
Newsweek, February 9, 1953; March 11, 1968; November 12, 1973; December 5, 1980; March 9, 1981.
New York, December 16, 1996, p. 62.
New York Post Magazine, March 21, 1954.
New York Times, July 20, 1952; January 18, 1981; April 27, 1988; July 25, 1993, p. 28; December 30, 1996; January 5, 1997, p. 37.
New York Times Book Review, December 30, 1996; January 26, 1997.
People, March 9, 1981; September 22, 1986; June 12, 1995, p. 138; January 13, 1997, p. 27.
Playboy, June, 1973.
Publishers Weekly, May 3, 1971; November 4, 1996, p. 60.
Reader's Digest, December, 1969; June, 1980.
Saturday Evening Post, March 16, 1963.
Saturday Review, November, 1983.
Time, October 14, 1966; November 21, 1969; September 10, 1973; November 11, 1973; April 14, 1997, p. 31.
Today's Health, autumn, 1972.
Tribune Books (Chicago), January 23, 1997, p. 5.
TV Guide, July 11, 1992, p. 14; December 28, 1996, p. 46.
USA Today, January 10, 1997, p. A13.
Vanity Fair, January, 1997, p. 140.
Vogue, April, 1986.
Washington Post, August 28, 1973; November 20, 1983; April 16, 1988; October 25, 1988; March 7, 1997, p. B1.
Washington Post Book World, December 15, 1996, p. 3.

—Sketch by Anne Janette Johnson

CUNNINGHAM, Cathy
  See CUNNINGHAM, Chet

*   *   *

CUNNINGHAM, Chet 1928-
  (J. D. Bondie, Chad Calhoun, G. A. Carrington, Jess Cody, Cathy Cunningham, Kit Dalton, Lionel Derrick, Dirk Fletcher, Don Pendleton)

PERSONAL: Born December 9, 1928, in Shelby, NE; son of Merle Burritt and Hazel (Zedicher) Cunningham; married Rose Marie Wilhoit, January 18, 1953; children: Gregory, Scott, Christine. *Education:* Pacific University, B.A., 1950; Columbia University, M.S., 1954.

ADDRESSES: Home and office—8431 Beaver Lake Dr., San Diego, CA 92119.

CAREER: News-Times, Forest Grove, OR, city editor, 1954-55; Jam Handy, Detroit, MI, writer of educational and church films and sales training materials, 1955-59; General Dynamics Corp., Convair Division, San Diego, CA, writer in motion picture section, 1959-60; Cunningham Press, San Diego, publisher and writer, 1960—. Freelance writer, 1960—. Chair of San Diego Writers Workshop, 1962—. *Military service:* U.S. Army, 1950-52; became sergeant.

WRITINGS:

NOVELS

The Chicom Affair, Powell Books (New York City), 1969.
Bushwhackers at Circle K, Avalon (New York City), 1969.
Killer's Range, Avalon, 1970.
Nick Carter: Night of the Avenger, Award Books (New York City), 1971.
Moscow at High Noon Is the Target, Award Books, 1972.
The Gold Wagon, Pinnacle Books (New York City), 1972, published under pseudonym Jess Cody, Ulcerscroft (Crewe, England), 1989.
Fatal Friday, Venice Books, 1973.

Die of Gold, Pinnacle (New York City), 1973, published under pseudonym Jess Cody, Dorchester (New York City), 1986.
Bloody Gold, Pinnacle Books, 1975, published under pseudonym Jess Cody, Dorchester, 1986.
The Gold and the Glory, Tower (New York City), 1977.
The Power and the Price, Tower, 1977.
The Patriots, Tower, 1977.
Seeds of Rebellion, Tower, 1977.
Beloved Rebel, Tower, 1978.
The Poker Club, Condor Publishing, 1978.
This Splendid Land, Tower, 1979.
Rainbow Saga, Tower, 1979.
Mansion of Dreams, Carousel (New York City), 1979.
Apache Ambush, Carousel, 1979.
Arizona Gunfire, Carousel, 1980.
Man in Two Camps, Carousel, 1980.
The Deadly Connection, Carousel, 1980.
Silent Murder, Carousel, 1980.
Cheyenne Payoff, Dell (New York City), 1981.
The Silver Mistress, Dell, 1981.
Tucson Temptress, Dell, 1981.
Remember the Alamo, Dell, 1981.
Gold Train, Tower, 1981, published under pseudonym Jess Cody, Dorchester, 1987.
Aztec Gold, R. Hale (London), 1982, published under pseudonym Jess Cody, DOrchester, 1987.
Deepwater Showdown, Dell, 1983.
The Avenger, Warner (New York City), 1987.
The Avenger 2, Warner, 1988.
Colombia Crackdown, Warner, 1988.
Manhattan Massacre, Warner, 1988.

"PONY SOLDIERS" SERIES

Slaughter at Buffalo Creek, Dorchester, 1987.
Comanche Massacre, Dorchester, 1987.
Comanche Moon, Dorchester, 1988.
Cheyenne Blood Storm, Dorchester, 1988.
Sioux Showdown, Dorchester, 1988.
Sioux Slaughter, Dorchester, 1988.
Boots and Saddles, Dorchester, 1988.
Renegade Army, Dorchester, 1988.
Battle Cry, Dorchester, 1989.
Fort Blood, Dorchester, 1989.

"JIM STEEL" WESTERN SERIES

Gold Wagon, Pinnacle Books, 1972.
Die of Gold, Pinnacle Books, 1973.
Bloody Gold, Pinnacle Books, 1974.
Devil's Gold, Tower, 1980.
Gold Train, Tower, 1980.

"OUTLAWS" SERIES

Ride Tall or Hang High, Dorchester, 1989.
Six Guns, Dorchester, 1989.
Dead Man's Hand, Dorchester, 1989.
Avengers, Dorchester, 1990.

NONFICTION

Your Wheels: How to Keep Your Car Running, Putnam (New York City), 1973.
Your Bike: How to Keep Your Motorcycle Running, Putnam, 1973.
Baja Bike, Putnam, 1974.
Police Tactics, West Publishing (St. Paul, MN), 1975.
Your First Car, Putnam, 1976.
The New Runners' Running Book, Manor, 1977.
222 Ways to Save Gas and Get the Best Possible Mileage, Prentice-Hall (Englewood Cliffs, NJ), 1981.

JUVENILES

Dead Start Scramble, Scholastic Book Services (New York City), 1973.
You Are Expelled, Fitzhenry & Whiteside (Post Mills, VT), 1974.
Narc One Going Down, Scholastic Book Services, 1975.
The Locked Storeroom Mystery, Scholastic Book Services, 1977.
Apprentice to a Rip-Off, Scholastic Book Services, 1978.

UNDER PSEUDONYM J. D. BONDIE

Red Bluff Revenge, Lynx (New York City), 1989.

UNDER PSEUDONYM G. A. CARRINGTON

The Templeton Massacre, Dell, 1990.

UNDER PSEUDONYM CATHY CUNNINGHAM

The Demons of Highpoint House, Popular Books (New York City), 1973.
Lost Love Found, Pioneer Communications, 1986.
Love's Confession, Pioneer Communications, 1986.
Young Lovers, Pioneer Communications, 1986.
Love's Denial, Pioneer Communications, 1986.

UNDER PSEUDONYM KIT DALTON

Gunpoint, Dorchester, 1986.
Lever Action, Dorchester, 1986.

Scattergun, Dorchester, 1987.
Winchester Valley, Dorchester, 1987.
Gunsmoke Gorge, Dorchester, 1987.
Remington Ridge, Dorchester, 1987.
Shotgun Station, Dorchester, 1987.
Pistol Grip, Dorchester, 1987.
Peacemaker Pass, Dorchester, 1988.
Silver City Carbine, Dorchester, 1988.
California Crossfire, Dorchester, 1988.
Hangfire Hill [and] Crossfire, Dorchester, 1988.
Gunpoint [and] Lever Action, Dorchester, 1989.
Colt Crossing, Dorchester, 1989.
Powder Charge, Dorchester, 1989.
Laramie Showdown, Dorchester, 1989.
Double Action, Dorchester, 1989.
Dead Man's Moon, Dorchester, 1989.
Apache Rifles, Dorchester, 1990.
Return Fire, Dorchester, 1990.

WITH MARK ROBERTS UNDER JOINT PSEUDONYM LIONEL DERRICK; "THE PENETRATOR" SERIES

Blood on the Strip, Pinnacle Books, 1973.
Hijacking Manhattan, Pinnacle Books, 1974.
Tokyo Purple, Pinnacle Books, 1974.
Northwest Contract, Pinnacle Books, 1974.
The Hellbomb Flight, Pinnacle Books, 1975.
Bloody Boston, Pinnacle Books, 1975.
Mankill Sport, Pinnacle Books, 1975.
Deepsea Shootout, Pinnacle Books, 1976.
Countdown to Terror, Pinnacle Books, 1976.
The Radiation Hit, Pinnacle Books, 1976.
High Disaster, Pinnacle Books, 1977.
Cryogenic Nightmare, Pinnacle Books, 1977.
Mexican Brown Death, Pinnacle Books, 1978.
The Skyhigh Betrayers, Pinnacle Books, 1979.
Computer Kill, Pinnacle Books, 1979.
Showbiz Wipeout, Pinnacle Books, 1979.
Death Ray Terror, Pinnacle Books, 1980.
Deadly Silence, Pinnacle Books, 1980.
Hawaiian Trackdown, Pinnacle Books, 1980.
Assassination Factor, Pinnacle Books, 1980.
Deadly Gold Hijackers, Pinnacle Books, 1981.
Deep Cover Cataclysm, Pinnacle Books, 1981.

UNDER PSEUDONYM DIRK FLETCHER; "SPUR WESTERN" SERIES

High Plains Temptress, Dorchester (New York City), 1981.
Arizona Fancy Lady, Dorchester, 1981.
St. Louis Jezebel, Dorchester, 1982.
Rocky Mountain Vamp, Dorchester, 1982.
Cathouse Kitten, Dorchester, 1983.

Indian Maid, Dorchester, 1983.
San Francisco Strumpet, Dorchester, 1983.
Wyoming Wench, Dorchester, 1983.
Texas Tart, Dorchester, 1983.
Montana Minx, Dorchester, 1983.
Santa Fe Floozy, Dorchester, 1984.
Nevada Hussy, Dorchester, 1984.
New Mexico Sisters, Dorchester, 1985.
Hang Spur McCoy, Dorchester, 1985.
Rawhider's Woman, Dorchester, 1985.
Saloon Girl, Dorchester, 1985.
Bald Knobber's Woman, Dorchester, 1986.
San Diego Sirens, Dorchester, 1987.
Frisco Foxes, Dorchester, 1988.
Portland Pussycat, Dorchester, 1989.
Boise Belle, Dorchester, 1989.
Bounty Hunter's Moon, Dorchester, 1989.
Tall Timber Trollop, Dorchester, 1989.

UNDER PSEUDONYM DON PENDLETON; "MACK BOLAN"
   SERIES

Crude Kill, Gold Eagle (Toronto), 1982.
Orbiting Omega, Gold Eagle, 1983.
Skysweeper, Gold Eagle, 1983.
Hellbinder, Gold Eagle, 1983.
Resurrection Day, Gold Eagle, 1984.
Baltimore Trackdown, Gold Eagle, 1984.
Nothing Personal, Gold Eagle, 1984.
Kill Trap, Gold Eagle, 1984.
Motor City Mayhem, Gold Eagle, 1985.

OTHER

Also author of military training and commercial instruction films and film reports for the Department of Defense and the U.S. Air Force. Author of monthly column "Truck Talk," in numerous trade magazines, 1956-79, and of ghost-written column "Your Car," published in numerous weekly and daily newspapers, 1960-82.

SIDELIGHTS: Chet Cunningham is a prolific writer, primarily of adventure and Western novels. In addition to contributing individual novels to a number of ongoing series published under house pseudonyms, Cunningham has also created series of his own, ranging from traditional Western novels of adventure to Westerns with a sophisticated, adult-oriented storyline.

In his early Westerns, Cunningham wrote of Jim Steel, a man obsessed with the pursuit of gold. In a number of novels, all of which feature the word "gold" in their titles, Cunningham chronicled Steel's adventures. Steel, according to David Whitehead in *Twentieth-Century Western Writers,* "is an ex-lawman with a love of (if not a mania for) gold. Indeed, gold is the only currency in which he will trade." In *Die of Gold,* Steel is the guard for a shipment of dies used for minting the 1867 Eagle gold coin. "It's the standard Western plot," as the reviewer for *Publishers Weekly* states, who judges the novel "entertaining."

Cunningham's "Pony Soldiers" series, according to Whitehead, is "possibly his best" work. The fictional saga of a "Lightning Troop" of soldiers trained to fight and move quickly in Indian fashion, the series, Whitehead explains, contains "a wealth of Indian and Army lore (which, if not always totally accurate, is certainly authoritative) adds credibility to the adventures. . . . Cunningham's skill at creating three-dimensional supporting characters is also used to good advantage."

Cunningham has also written two series of Westerns that Whitehead calls "exceptionally pornographic." These books are published under his Kit Dalton and Dirk Fletcher pseudonyms. The Dalton books tell the adventures of Lee Morgan, a gunslinger of the Old West whose adventures take him from Alaska to Argentina. The Fletcher books follow Spur McCoy, "an over-sexed U.S. Secret Service agent who works as a trouble-shooter primarily for the Treasury Department," as Whitehead notes.

BIOGRAPHICAL/CRITICAL SOURCES:

BOOKS

Twentieth-Century Western Writers, second edition, St. James Press (Detroit), 1991.

PERIODICALS

Booklist, September 1, 1975, p. 38; October 15, 1977, p. 370; March 15, 1979, p. 1145.
Publishers Weekly, October 8, 1973, p. 98.

D-E

DAEMER, Will
See MILLER, (H.) Bill(y)

* * *

DAEMER, Will
See WADE, Robert (Allison)

* * *

DAHL, Roald 1916-1990

PERSONAL: Given name is pronounced "Roo-aal"; born September 13, 1916, in Llandaff, South Wales; died November 23, 1990, in Oxford, England; son of Harald (a shipbroker, painter, and horticulturist) and Sofie (Hesselberg) Dahl; married Patricia Neal (an actress), July 2, 1953 (divorced, 1983); married Felicity Ann Crosland, 1983; children: (first marriage) Olivia (deceased), Tessa, Theo, Ophelia, Lucy. *Education:* Graduate of British public schools, 1932.

CAREER: Shell Oil Co., London, England, member of eastern staff, 1933-37, member of staff in Dar-es-Salaam, Tanzania, 1937-39; writer. Host of a series of half-hour television dramas, *Way Out,* during early 1960s. *Military service:* Royal Air Force, fighter pilot, 1939-45; became wing commander.

AWARDS, HONORS: Edgar Award, Mystery Writers of America, 1954, 1959, and 1980; New England Round Table of Children's Librarians award, 1972,

and Surrey School award, 1973, both for *Charlie and the Chocolate Factory;* Surrey School award, 1975, and Nene award, 1978, both for *Charlie and the Great Glass Elevator;* Surrey School award, 1978, and California Young Reader Medal, 1979, both for *Danny: The Champion of the World;* Federation of Children's Book Groups award, 1982, for *The BFG;* Massachusetts Children's award, 1982, for *James and the Giant Peach; New York Times* Outstanding Books award, 1983, Whitbread Award, 1983, and West Australian award, 1986, all for *The Witches;* World Fantasy Convention Lifetime Achievement Award, and Federation of Children's Book Groups award, both 1983; Maschler award runner-up, 1985, for *The Giraffe and Pelly and Me; Boston Globe/Horn Book* nonfiction honor citation, 1985, for *Boy: Tales of Childhood;* International Board on Books for Young People awards for Norwegian and German translations of *The BFG,* both 1986; Smarties Award, 1990, for *Esio Trot.*

WRITINGS:

FOR ADULTS

Sometime Never: A Fable for Supermen (novel), Scribner, 1948.
My Uncle Oswald (novel), M. Joseph, 1979, Knopf, 1980.
Going Solo (autobiography), Farrar, Straus, 1986.

FOR CHILDREN

The Gremlins, illustrations by Walt Disney Productions, Random House, 1943.
James and the Giant Peach: A Children's Story (also see below), illustrations by Nancy Ekholm Bur-

kert, Knopf, 1961, illustrations by Michel Simeon, Allen & Unwin, 1967.

Charlie and the Chocolate Factory (also see below), illustrations by Joseph Schindelman, Knopf, 1964, revised edition, 1973, illustrations by Faith Jaques, Allen & Unwin, 1967.

The Magic Finger (also see below), illustrations by William Pene du Bois, Harper, 1966, illustrations by Pat Marriott, Puffin, 1974.

Fantastic Mr. Fox (also see below), illustrations by Donald Chaffin, Knopf, 1970.

Charlie and the Great Glass Elevator: The Further Adventures of Charlie Bucket and Willy Wonka, Chocolate-Maker Extraordinary (also see below), illustrations by J. Schindelman, Knopf, 1972, illustrations by F. Jaques, Allen & Unwin, 1973.

Danny: The Champion of the World, illustrations by Jill Bennett, Knopf, 1975 (collected with *James and the Giant Peach* and *Fantastic Mr. Fox,* Bantam, 1983).

The Enormous Crocodile (also see below), illustrations by Quentin Blake, Knopf, 1978.

The Complete Adventures of Charlie and Mr. Willy Wonka (contains *Charlie and the Chocolate Factory* and *Charlie and the Great Glass Elevator*), illustrations by F. Jaques, Allen & Unwin, 1978.

The Twits, illustrations by Q. Blake, J. Cape, 1980, Knopf, 1981.

George's Marvelous Medicine, illustrations by Q. Blake, J. Cape, 1981, Knopf, 1982.

Roald Dahl's Revolting Rhymes, illustrations by Q. Blake, J. Cape, 1982, Knopf, 1983.

The BFG (also see below), illustrations by Q. Blake, Farrar, Straus, 1982.

Dirty Beasts (verse), illustrations by Rosemary Fawcett, Farrar, Straus, 1983.

The Witches (also see below), illustrations by Q. Blake, Farrar, Straus, 1983.

Boy: Tales of Childhood, Farrar, Straus, 1984.

The Giraffe and Pelly and Me, illustrations by Q. Blake, Farrar, Straus, 1985.

Matilda, illustrations by Q. Blake, Viking Kestrel, 1988.

Roald Dahl: Charlie and the Chocolate Factory, Charlie and the Great Glass Elevator, The BFG (boxed set), Viking, 1989.

Rhyme Stew (comic verse), illustrations by Q. Blake, J. Cape, 1989, Viking, 1990.

Esio Trot, illustrations by Q. Blake, Viking, 1990.

The Dahl Diary, 1992, illustrations by Q. Blake, Puffin Books, 1991.

The Minpins, Viking, 1991.

Three More from Roald Dahl (includes *The Witches, James and the Giant Peach,* and *Danny: The Champion of the World*), Puffin, 1991.

The Vicar of Nibbleswicke, illustrations by Q. Blake, Viking, 1992.

My Year, illustrations by Q. Blake, Viking Children's, 1994.

Roald Dahl's Revolting Recipes, illustrations by Quentin Blake, Viking (New York City), 1994.

Some of Dahl's works have been translated into French and Spanish.

SHORT FICTION

Over to You: Ten Stories of Flyers and Flying (also see below), Reynal, 1946.

Someone Like You (also see below), Knopf, 1953.

Kiss, Kiss (also see below), Knopf, 1959.

Selected Stories of Roald Dahl, Modern Library, 1968.

Twenty-nine Kisses from Roald Dahl (contains *Someone Like You* and *Kiss, Kiss*), M. Joseph, 1969.

Switch Bitch (also see below), Knopf, 1974.

The Wonderful World of Henry Sugar and Six More, Knopf, 1977 (published in England as *The Wonderful Story of Henry Sugar and Six More,* Cape, 1977).

The Best of Roald Dahl (selections from *Over to You, Someone Like You, Kiss Kiss,* and *Switch Bitch*), introduction by James Cameron, Vintage, 1978.

Roald Dahl's Tales of the Unexpected, Vintage, 1979.

Taste and Other Tales, Longman, 1979.

A Roald Dahl Selection: Nine Short Stories, edited and introduced by Roy Blatchford, photographs by Catherine Shakespeare Lane, Longman, 1980.

More Tales of the Unexpected, Penguin, 1980 (published in England as *More Roald Dahl's Tales of the Unexpected,* Joseph, 1980, and as *Further Tales of the Unexpected,* Chivers, 1981).

(Editor) *Roald Dahl's Book of Ghost Stories,* Farrar, Straus, 1983.

Two Fables (contains "Princess and the Poacher" and "Princess Mammalia"), illustrations by Graham Dean, Viking, 1986.

The Roald Dahl Omnibus, Hippocrene Books, 1987.

A Second Roald Dahl Selection: Eight Short Stories, edited by Helene Fawcett, Longman, 1987.

Ah, Sweet Mystery of Life, illustrations by John Lawrence, J. Cape, 1988, Knopf, 1989.

The Collected Short Stories, Michael Joseph, 1991.

Contributor of short fiction to *Penguin Modern Stories 12,* 1972.

SCREENPLAYS

Lamb to the Slaughter (teleplay), *Alfred Hitchcock Presents,* Columbia Broadcasting System (CBS-TV), 1958.

(With Jack Bloom) *You Only Live Twice,* United Artists, 1967.

(With Ken Hughes) *Chitty Chitty Bang Bang,* United Artists, 1968.

The Night-Digger (based on *Nest in a Falling Tree,* by Joy Crowley), Metro-Goldwyn-Mayer, 1970.

Willie Wonka and the Chocolate Factory (motion picture; adaptation of *Charlie and the Chocolate Factory*), Paramount, 1971.

Also author of screenplays *Oh Death, Where Is Thy Sting-a-Ling-a-Ling?,* United Artists, *The Lightning Bug,* 1971, and *The Road Builder.*

OTHER

The Honeys (play), produced in New York City, 1955.

(With wife Felicity Dahl) *Memories with Food at Gipsy House,* Viking, 1991.

Dahl recorded *Charlie and the Chocolate Factory,* Caedmon, 1975, *James and the Giant Peach,* Caedmon, 1977, *Fantastic Mr. Fox,* Caedmon, 1978, and *Roald Dahl Reads His "The Enormous Crocodile" and "The Magic Finger,"* Caedmon, 1980, as well as an interview, *Bedtime Stories to Children's Books,* Center for Cassette Studies, 1973. Contributor to anthologies and periodicals, including *Harper's, New Yorker, Playboy, Collier's, Town and Country, Atlantic, Esquire,* and *Saturday Evening Post.*

ADAPTATIONS:

MOVIES AND FILMSTRIPS

36 Hours (motion picture; adaptation of Dahl's short story "Beware of the Dog"), Metro-Goldwyn-Mayer, 1964.

Delicious Inventions (motion picture; excerpted from film *Willie Wonka and the Chocolate Factory,* Paramount, 1971), Films, Inc., 1976.

Willie Wonka and the Chocolate Factory—Storytime (filmstrip; excerpted from the 1971 Paramount motion picture of the same name), Films, Inc., 1976.

Willie Wonka and the Chocolate Factory—Learning Kit (filmstrip; excerpted from the 1971 Para-

mount motion picture of the same name), Films, Inc., 1976.

The Witches, screenplay by Allan Scott, Lorimar, 1990.

James and the Giant Peach (animated motion picture; adapted from Dahl's novel of the same name), screenplay by Karey Kirkpatrick, Jonathan Roberts, and Steve Bloom, Walt Disney, 1996.

TELEVISION

Tales of the Unexpected, WNEW-TV, 1979.

PLAYS

George, Richard, *Roald Dahl's Charlie and the Chocolate Factory: A Play,* introduction by Dahl, Knopf, 1976.

George, R., *Roald Dahl's James and the Giant Peach: A Play,* introduction by Dahl, Penguin, 1982.

RECORDINGS

The Great Switcheroo, read by Patricia Neal, Caedmon, 1977.

SIDELIGHTS: Roald Dahl, best known as the author of children's books *Charlie and the Chocolate Factory* and *James and the Giant Peach,* was also noted for his short stories for adults, and his enchanting autobiographical descriptions of growing up in England and flying in World War II. His children's fiction is known for its sudden turns into the fantastic, its wheeling, fast-moving prose, and its decidedly harsh treatment of any adults foolish enough to cause trouble for the young heroes and heroines. Similarly, his adult fiction often relies on a sudden twist that throws light on what has been happening in the story, a trait most evident in *Tales of the Unexpected,* which was made into a television series.

Dahl was born on September 13, 1916, the son of an adventurous shipbroker. He was an energetic and mischievous child and from an early age proved adept at finding trouble. His very earliest memory was of pedaling to school at breakneck speed on his tricycle, his two sisters struggling to keep up as he whizzed around curves on two wheels. In *Boy: Tales of Childhood,* Dahl recounted many of these happy memories from his childhood, remembering most fondly the trips that the entire family took to Norway, which he always considered home. Each summer the family would tramp aboard a steamer for the two-day trip to

Oslo, where they were treated to a Norwegian feast with his grandparents, and the next day board a smaller ship for a trip north to what they called "Magic Island." On the island the family whiled away the long summer days swimming and boating.

Though Dahl's father died when the author was four, his mother abided by her husband's wish to have the children attend English schools, which he considered the best in the world. At Llandaff Cathedral School the young Dahl began his career of mischievous adventures and met up with the first of many oppressive, even cruel, adults. One exploit in particular foretold both the author's career in school and the major themes of his adult work. Each day on the way to and from school the seven-year-old Dahl and his friends passed a sweetshop. Unable to resist the lure of "Bootlace Liquorice" and "Gobstoppers"—familiar candy to *Charlie and the Chocolate Factory* fans—the children would pile into the store and buy as much candy as they could with their limited allowances. Day after day the grubby, grouchy storekeeper, Mrs. Pratchett, scolded the children as she dug her dirty hands into the jars of candy; one day the kids had had enough of her abuse, and Dahl hatched the perfect plan to get back at her. The very next day, when she reached into the jar of Gobstoppers she clamped her hand around a very stiff, dead mouse and flung the jar to the ground, scattering Gobstoppers and glass all over the store floor. Mrs. Pratchett knew whom to blame, and when the boys went to school the next day she was waiting, along with a very angry Headmaster Coombes. Not only did Coombes give each of the boys a severe beating, but Mrs. Pratchett was there to witness it. "She was bounding up and down with excitement," Dahl remembered in *Boy,* "'Lay it into 'im!' she was shrieking. 'Let 'im 'ave it! Teach 'im a lesson!'"

Dahl's mother complained about the beating the boys were given, but was told that if she didn't like it she could find another school. She did, sending Roald to St. Peters Boarding School the next year, and later to Repton, a renowned private school. Of his time at St. Peters, Dahl said: "Those were days of horrors, of fierce discipline, of not talking in the dormitories, no running in the corridors, no untidiness of any sort, no this or that or the other, just rules, rules and still more rules that had to be obeyed. And the fear of the dreaded cane hung over us like the fear of death all the time."

Dahl received undistinguished marks while attending Repton, and showed little sign of his future prowess as a writer. His end-of-term report from Easter term, 1931, which he saved, declared him "a persistent muddler. Vocabulary negligible, sentences mal-constructed. He reminds me of a camel." Nevertheless, his mother offered him the option of attending Oxford or Cambridge when he finished school. His reply, recorded in *Boy,* was, "No, thank you. I want to go straight from school to work for a company that will send me to wonderful faraway places life Africa or China." He got his wish, for he was soon hired by the Shell Oil Company, and later shipped off to Tanganyika (now Tanzania), where he enjoyed "the roasting heat and the crocodiles and the snakes and the log safaris up-country, selling Shell oil to the men who ran the diamond mines and the sisal plantations. . . . Above all, I learned how to look after myself in a way that no young person can ever do by staying in civilization."

In 1939, Dahl's adventures took on a more dangerous cast as he joined the Royal Air Force training squadron in Nairobi, Kenya. World War II was just beginning, and Dahl would soon make his mark as a fighter pilot combating the Germans all around the Mediterranean Sea. While strafing a convoy of trucks near Alexandria, Egypt, his plane was hit by machine-gun fire. The plane crashed to the ground and Dahl crawled from the wreckage as the gas tanks exploded. The crash left his skull fractured, his nose crumpled, and his eyes temporarily stuck shut. After six months of recovery he returned to his squadron in Greece and shot down four enemy planes, but frequent blackouts as a result of his earlier injuries eventually rendered him unable to fly.

Dahl was soon transferred to Washington, D.C., to serve as an assistant air attache. One day C. S. Forester interviewed Dahl over lunch for an article he was writing for the *Saturday Evening Post,* but was too engrossed in eating to take notes himself. The notes that Dahl took for him turned out to be a story, which Forester sent to the magazine under Dahl's name. The magazine paid Dahl one thousand dollars for the story, which was titled "Piece of Cake" and later published in *Over to You: Ten Stories of Fliers and Flying.* Soon his stories appeared in *Collier's, Harper's, Ladies' Home Journal, Tomorrow* and *Town and Country.* Dahl indicated in a *New York Times Book Review* profile by Willa Petschek that "as I went on, the stories became less and less realistic and more fantastic. But becoming a writer was pure fluke. Without being asked to, I doubt if I'd ever have thought of it."

Dahl went on to publish numerous short story collections during the next several decades, some of which—notably 1953's *Someone Like You* and 1959's *Kiss, Kiss*—sold widely in the United States and earned Dahl a measure of fame. After 1960 Dahl's primary focus became children's fiction, although he did produce a short story collection, *Switch Bitch,* in 1974 as well as a novel, *My Uncle Oswald,* in 1979. Both of the latter works are marked by themes of sexual sadism and obsession; both were controversial and received criticism from reviewers for the sexual violence they portrayed. *Dictionary of Literary Biography* contributor John L. Grigsby summarized Dahl's achievements as a short fiction writer: "In his best stories Dahl presents skillfully composed plots that convey powerful insights into the frequently negative depths of the human psyche. . . . In his less effective works, however, Dahl's outsider status results in a kind of cynical condescension toward and manipulation of the reader in surprise-of-plot stories that stereotype characters outside his self-focused realm of psychological experience."

In 1943, Dahl wrote his first children's story, and coined a term, with *The Gremlins.* Gremlins were tiny saboteurs who lived on fighter planes and bombers and were responsible for all crashes. Mrs. Roosevelt, the president's wife, read the book to her children and liked it so much that she invited Dahl to dinner, and he and the president soon became friends. Through the 1940s and into the 1950s Dahl continued as a short story writer for adults, establishing his reputation as a writer of macabre tales with an unexpected twist. A *Books and Bookmen* reviewer called Dahl "a master of horror—an intellectual Hitchcock of the writing world." J. D. O'Hara, writing in *New Republic,* labeled him "our Supreme Master of Wickedness," and his stories earned him three Edgar Allan Poe Awards from the Mystery Writers of America.

In 1953 he married Hollywood actress Patricia Neal, star of such movies as *The Fountainhead* and, later, *Hud,* for which she won an Academy Award. Dahl recalled in *Pat and Roald* that "she wasn't at all movie-starish; no great closets filled with clothes or anything like that. She had a drive to be a great actress, but it was never as strong as it is with some of these nuts. You could turn it aside." Although the marriage did not survive, it produced five children. As soon as the children were old enough, he began making up stories for them each night before they went to bed. These stories became the basis for his career as a children's writer, which began in earnest with the publication of *James and the Giant Peach* in 1961. Dahl insisted that having to invent stories night after night was perfect practice for his trade, telling the *New York Times Book Review:* "Children are a great discipline because they are highly critical. And they lose interest so quickly. You have to keep things ticking along. And if you think a child is getting bored, you must think up something that jolts it back. Something that tickles. You have to know what children like." Sales of Dahl's books certainly attest to his skill: *Charlie and the Chocolate Factory* and *Charlie and the Great Glass Elevator* have sold over one million hardcover copies in America, and *James and the Giant Peach* more than 350,000.

James and the Giant Peach recounts the fantastic tale of a young boy who travels thousands of miles in a house-sized peach with as bizarre an assemblage of companions as can be found in a children's book. After the giant peach crushes his aunts, James crawls into the peach through a worm hole, making friends with a centipede, a silkworm, a spider, a ladybug, and a flock of seagulls that lifts the peach into the air and carries it across the ocean to Central Park. Gerald Haigh, writing in *Times Literary Supplement,* said that Dahl had the ability to "home unerringly in on the very nub of childish delight, with brazen and glorious disregard for what is likely to furrow the adult brow."

One way that Dahl delighted his readers was to exact often vicious revenge on cruel adults who harmed children. In *Matilda,* the Amazonian headmistress Miss Turnbull, who deals with unruly children by grabbing them by the hair and tossing them out windows, is finally banished by the brilliant, triumphant Matilda. *The Witches,* released as a movie in 1990, finds the heroic young character, who has been turned into a mouse, thwarting the hideous and diabolical witches who are planning to kill all the children of England. But even innocent adults receive rough treatment: parents are killed in car crashes in *The Witches,* and eaten by a rhinoceros in *James and the Giant Peach;* aunts are flattened by a giant peach in *James and the Giant Peach;* and pleasant fathers are murdered in *Matilda.* Many critics have objected to the rough treatment of adults. Eleanor Cameron, for example, in *Children's Literature in Education,* found that "Dahl caters to the streak of sadism in children which they don't even realize is there because they are not fully self-aware and are not experienced enough to understand what sadism is." And in *Now Upon a Time: A Contemporary View of Children's Literature,* Myra Pollack Sadker and David Miller Sadker criticized *Charlie and the Chocolate Factory* for its "ageism": "The message with which we close the book is that the needs and desires and opinions of old people are totally irrelevant and inconsequential."

However, Dahl explained in the *New York Times Book Review* that the children who wrote to him "invariably pick out the most gruesome events as the favorite parts of the books. . . . They don't relate it to life. They enjoy the fantasy. And my nastiness is never gratuitous. It's retribution. Beastly people must be punished." Alasdair Campbell, writing in *School Librarian,* argued that "normal children are bound to take some interest in the darker side of human nature, and books for them should be judged not by picking out separate elements but rather on the basis of their overall balance and effect." He found books such as *James and the Giant Peach, Charlie and the Chocolate Factory,* and *The Magic Finger* "ultimately satisfying, with the principles of justice clearly vindicated."

In *Trust Your Children: Voices Against Censorship in Children's Literature,* Dahl contended that adults may be disturbed by his books "because they are not quite as aware as I am that children are different from adults. Children are much more vulgar than grownups. They have a coarser sense of humor. They are basically more cruel." Dahl often commented that the key to his success with children was that he conspired with them against adults. Vicki Weissman, in her review of *Matilda* in the *New York Times Book Review,* agreed that Dahl's books are aimed to please children rather than adults in a number of ways. She thought that "the truths of death and torture are as distant as when the magician saws the lady in half," and delighted that "anarchic and patently impossible plots romp along with no regard at all for the even faintly likely." Just as children are more vulgar than adults, so too do they have more tolerance for undeveloped characters, loose linking of events, ludicrous word play, and mind-boggling plot twists. Eric Hadley, in his sketch of Dahl in *Twentieth Century Children's Writers,* suggested that the "sense of sharing, of joining with Dahl in a game or plot, is crucial: you admire him and his cleverness, *not* his characters." The result, according to Hadley, is that the audience has the "pleasure of feeling that they are in on a tremendous joke."

"The writer for children must be a jokey sort of a fellow. . . ," Dahl once told *Writer.* "He must like simple tricks and jokes and riddles and other childish things. He must be unconventional and inventive. He must have a really first-class plot." As a writer, Dahl encountered difficulty in developing plots. He filled an old school exercise book with ideas that he had jotted down in pencil, crayon, or whatever was handy, and insisted in *The Wonderful World of Henry Sugar and Six More* that every story he had ever written, for adults or for children, "started out as a three-or four-line note in this little, much-worn, red-covered volume." And each book was written in a tiny brick hut in the apple orchard about two hundred yards away from his home in Buckinghamshire, England. The little hut was rarely cleaned, and the walls were lined with "ill-fitting sheets of polystyrene, yellow with age and tobacco smoke, and spiders . . . [making] pretty webs in the upper corners," Dahl once declared. "The room itself is of no consequence. It is out of focus, a place for dreaming and floating and whistling in the wind, as soft and silent and murky as a womb."

Looking back on his years as a writer in *Boy,* Dahl contended that "the life of a writer is absolute hell compared with the life of a businessman. The writer has to force himself to go to work. . . . Two hours of writing fiction leaves this particular writer absolutely drained. For those two hours he has been miles away, he has been somewhere else, in a different place with totally different people, and the effort of swimming back into normal surroundings is very great. It is almost a shock. The writer walks out of his workroom in a daze. He wants a drink. He needs it. It happens to be a fact that nearly every writer of fiction in the world drinks more whisky than is good for him. He does it to give himself faith, hope, and courage. A person is a fool to become a writer. His only compensation is absolute freedom. He has no master except his own soul, and that, I am sure, is why he does it."

BIOGRAPHICAL/CRITICAL SOURCES:

BOOKS

Children's Literature Review, Gale, Volume 1, 1976, Volume 7, 1984.

Contemporary Literary Criticism, Gale, Volume 1, 1973, Volume 6, 1976, Volume 18, 1981, Volume 79, 1993.

Dahl, Lucy, *James and the Giant Peach: The Book and Movie Scrapbook,* Disney Press (New York City), 1996.

Dahl, Roald, *The Wonderful World of Henry Sugar and Six More,* Knopf, 1977.

Dahl, Roald, *Boy: Tales of Childhood,* Farrar, Straus, 1984.

Dahl, Roald, *Going Solo*, Farrar, Straus, 1986.

Dictionary of Literary Biography, Volume 139: *British Short-Fiction Writers, 1945-1980*, Gale, 1994.

Farrell, Barry, *Pat and Roald*, Random House, 1969.

McCann, Donnarae, and Gloria Woodard, editors, *The Black American in Books for Children: Readings in Racism*, Scarecrow, 1972.

Powling, Chris, *Roald Dahl*, Hamish Hamilton, 1983.

Sadker, Myra Pollack, and David Miller Sadker, *Now Upon a Time: A Contemporary View of Children's Literature*, Harper, 1977.

Treglown, Jeremy, *Roald Dahl: A Biography*, Farrar, Straus (New York City), 1994.

Twentieth-Century Children's Writers, 3rd edition, St. James Press, 1989, pp. 255-256.

Warren, Alan with Dale Salwak and Daryl F. Mallett, *Roald Dahl: From the Gremlins to the Chocolate Factory*, second edition, Borgo Press (San Bernadino, CA), 1994.

West, Mark I., interview with Roald Dahl in *Trust Your Children: Voices against Censorship in Children's Literature*, Neal-Schuman, 1988, pp. 71-76.

Wintle, Justin, and Emma Fisher, *Pied Pipers: Interviews with the Influential Creators of Children's Literature*, Paddington Press, 1975.

PERIODICALS

Atlantic, December, 1964.

Best Sellers, January, 1978.

Books and Bookmen, January, 1969; May, 1970.

Chicago Sunday Tribune, February 15, 1960; November 12, 1961.

Chicago Tribune, October 21, 1986.

Chicago Tribune Book World, August 10, 1980; May 17, 1981.

Children's Book News, March-April, 1968.

Children's Literature in Education, spring, 1975; summer, 1976, pp. 59-63.

Christian Century, August 31, 1960.

Christian Science Monitor, November 16, 1961.

Commonweal, November 15, 1961.

Entertainment Weekly, January 24, 1994, p. 57.

Horn Book, October, 1972; December, 1972; February, 1973; April, 1973; June, 1973; January/February, 1989, p. 68; January/February, 1992, p. 64.

Kenyon Review, Volume 31, number 2, 1969.

Library Journal, November 15, 1961.

Life, August 18, 1972.

New Republic, October 19, 1974, p. 23; April 19, 1980.

New Statesman, October 29, 1960; March 5, 1971; November 4, 1977.

New Statesman & Society, November 24, 1989, p. 34.

New York, December 12, 1988.

New Yorker, December 12, 1988, p. 157; November 25, 1991, p. 146.

New York Herald Tribune Book Review, November 8, 1953; February 7, 1960.

New York Review of Books, December 17, 1970; December 14, 1972.

New York Times, November 8, 1953; April 29, 1980.

New York Times Book Review, February 7, 1960; November 12, 1961; October 25, 1964; November 8, 1970; September 17, 1972; October 27, 1974; October 26, 1975; December 25, 1977, pp. 6, 15; September 30, 1979; April 20, 1980; March 29, 1981; January 9, 1983; January 20, 1985; October 12, 1986; January 15, 1989, p. 31; October 27, 1991, p. 27; May 1, 1994, p. 28.

Observer, September 8, 1991.

People, November 3, 1986; May 9, 1988.

Publishers Weekly, June 6, 1980; December 20, 1991, p. 82; January 24, 1994, p. 57; October 10, 1994, p. 69.

Punch, November 29, 1967; December 6, 1978.

Quill & Quire, November, 1991, p. 25.

San Francisco Chronicle, February 15, 1960; December 10, 1961.

Saturday Review, December 26, 1953; February 20, 1960; February 17, 1962; November 7, 1964; March 10, 1973.

School Librarian, June, 1981, pp. 108-114.

School Library Journal, November, 1991, p. 92; May, 1992, p. 112; March, 1993, p. 155; April, 1994, p. 136; March, 1995, p. 210.

Sewanee Review, winter, 1975.

Spectator, December, 1977; December 11, 1993, p. 45.

Springfield Republican, March 13, 1960.

Times (London), December 22, 1983; April 21, 1990.

Times Educational Supplement, November 19, 1982, p. 35.

Times Literary Supplement, October 28, 1960; December 14, 1967; June 15, 1973; November 15, 1974; November 23, 1979; November 21, 1980; July 24, 1981; July 23, 1982; November 30, 1984; September 12, 1986; May 6, 1988; July 12, 1991, p. 21; October 4, 1991, p. 28; November 22, 1991, p. 23.

Vanity Fair, January, 1994, p. 26.

Washington Post, October 8, 1986.

Washington Post Book World, November 13, 1977; April 20, 1980; May 8, 1983; January 13, 1985.

Wilson Library Bulletin, February, 1962; February, 1989; June, 1995, p. 125.
Writer, August, 1976, pp. 18-19.
Young Reader's Review, November, 1966.

OBITUARIES:

PERIODICALS

Los Angeles Times, November 24, 1990.
New York Times, November 24, 1990.
School Library Journal, January, 1991.
Times (London), November 24, 1990; December 19, 1990.
Washington Post, November 24, 1990.*

* * *

DAHLBERG, Edward 1900-1977

PERSONAL: Born July 22, 1900, in Boston, MA; died February 27, 1977, in Santa Barbara, CA; son of Saul Gottdank (a barber) and Elizabeth Dahlberg (a hairdresser); married Fanya Fass, 1926 (divorced); married Winifred Sheehan Moore, 1942; married Rlene LaFleur Howell, 1950; married Julia Lawlor, June 13, 1967; children: (second marriage) Geoffrey, Joel. *Education:* Attended University of California, Berkeley, 1921-23; Columbia University, B.S., 1925.

CAREER: Writer. Teacher at James Madison High School and Thomas Jefferson High School, New York City, 1925-26; New York University, New York City, visiting lecturer in Graduate School, 1950, 1961, lecturer in School of General Education, 1961-62; University of Missouri at Kansas City, Carolyn Benton Cockefair Professor, 1964-65, professor of language and literature, beginning 1966. Visiting professor at Columbia University, 1968. *Military service:* U.S. Army, private.

MEMBER: National Institute of Arts and Letters.

AWARDS, HONORS: Attended McDowell Colony, 1930; National Institute of Arts and Letters grant, 1961; Rockefeller Foundation grant, 1965, 1966; Ariadne Foundation grant, 1970; Cultural Council Foundation award, 1971; National Foundation on Arts and Humanities award; Longview Foundation grant; CAPS grant; National Endowment for the Arts grant.

WRITINGS:

Bottom Dogs (also see below; novel), with introduction by D. H. Lawrence, Putnam (London), 1929, Simon & Schuster, 1930, reprinted, AMS Press, 1976.
From Flushing to Calvary (also see below; novel), Harcourt, 1932.
Kentucky Blue Grass Henry Smith (prose poem), White Horse Press (Cleveland), 1932.
Those Who Perish (also see below; novel), John Day, 1934, reprinted, AMS Press, 1977.
(Author of introduction) Kenneth Fearing, *Poems,* Dynamo (New York City), 1936.
Do These Bones Live (criticism), Harcourt, 1941, revised edition published in England as *Sing O Barren,* Routledge, 1947, 2nd revised edition published as *Can These Bones Live,* New Directions, 1960.
The Flea of Sodom (essays), New Directions, 1950.
The Sorrows of Priapus (also see below; philosophy), New Directions, 1957.
Moby Dick: An Hamitic Dream, Fairleigh Dickinson University, 1960.
(With Herbert Read) *Truth Is More Sacred* (critical exchange on modern literature), Horizon, 1961.
Alms for Oblivion (essays), University of Minnesota Press, 1964.
Because I Was Flesh (autobiography), New Directions, 1964.
Reasons of the Heart (aphorisms), Horizon, 1965.
Cipango's Hinder Door (poems), University of Texas Press, 1966.
The Leafless American, and Other Writings, edited by Harold Billings, Roger Beacham, 1967.
The Edward Dahlberg Reader, edited by Paul Carroll, New Directions, 1967.
Epitaphs of Our Times: The Letters of Edward Dahlberg, edited by Edwin Seaver, Braziller, 1967.
The Carnal Myth: A Look into Classical Sensuality (also see below), Weybright, 1968.
The Confessions of Edward Dahlberg, Braziller, 1971.
(Compiler and contributor) *The Gold of Ophir: Travels, Myths and Legends in the New World,* Dutton, 1972.
The Sorrows of Priapus: Consisting of The Sorrows of Priapus and The Carnal Myth, Harcourt, 1973.
The Olive of Minerva; or, The Comedy of a Cuckold, Crowell, 1976.
Bottom Dogs, From Flushing to Calvary, Those Who Perish, and Hitherto Unpublished and Uncollected Works, Crowell, 1976.

Samuel Beckett's Wake and Other Uncollected Prose, edited by Steven Moore, Dalkey Archive Press, 1989.

In Love, in Sorrow: The Complete Correspondence of Charles Olson and Edward Dahlberg, Paragon House (New York City), 1990.

CONTRIBUTOR

Henry Hart, editor, *American Writers' Congress,* International Publishers, 1935.

Martha Foley and David Burnett, editors, *Best American Short Stories, 1961-1962,* Houghton, 1962.

Stanley Burnshaw, editor, *Varieties of Literary Experience,* New York University Press, 1962.

Louis Filler, editor, *The Anxious Years,* Putnam, 1963.

Also contributor to volumes of *New Directions in Prose and Poetry,* edited by James Laughlin, New Directions.

OTHER

Contributor of short stories, reviews, essays, and articles to *Nation, New Republic, New York Times, Holiday, Poetry, This Quarter, Twentieth Century, Massachusetts Review, New York Review of Books, New York Times Book Review,* and other publications.

WORK IN PROGRESS: At the time of his death in 1977 Dahlberg was reported to have been working on two books: *Rightness Is All* and *Jesus, Man or Apocrypha.*

SIDELIGHTS: Throughout his long and varied literary career, Edward Dahlberg was a puzzle to many American critics. His distinctive, eccentric, and often archaic style caused the literary establishment to either dismiss his work or to praise him as a genius. As Edmund White explained in the *New Republic,* "Dahlberg continues to be one of the most unaccountable forces in American letters, a phenomenon that every critic seeks, in one way or another, either to justify or dismiss." Why Dahlberg chose to write in such a singular manner was also a puzzle to critics. "Even critics who are theoretically quite opposed to examining a man's work as a pendant to his life find themselves worrying over how Dahlberg *got to be this way,*" as White wrote. Dahlberg was also adept at shedding labels that confined his talents. His early books earned him the title of "proletarian novelist," but he later gained critical recognition for his poetry, which was rich in allusion, while his work as an

essayist, philosopher and literary critic earned him yet further accolades. Perhaps his most widely respected work is an autobiography, *Because I Was Flesh.* X. J. Kennedy, writing in the *New York Times Book Review,* called Dahlberg "a rare figure among American writers: a man of letters in the European sense, a versatile performer in more than one genre."

Perhaps the overriding feature of Dahlberg's work, particularly during the 1960s, was his stance as a sophisticated outsider who berated the culture of his day, as a curmudgeon who hurled invective at those whom he thought his inferiors. This attitude did not endear him to many readers. He "is not," Robert M. Adams admitted in the *New York Review of Books,* "an easy writer to like. . . . He is given to vociferous protests about his own genuineness and authenticity; and to make it the more exemplary, he vigorously denigrates almost all his contemporaries and most of his predecessors." Arno Karlen of the *New York Times Book Review* compared Dahlberg to the poet John Donne, "the poet-preacher whose bitterness and warmth were also those of a sensual man alive to regret, whose life's lessons were also burned into his bones, making him somber and sardonic, witty and kind with sensual pessimism. Sometimes Dahlberg sours into misogynous rant, which is ungenerous and thus unbecoming; just as his diction may become labored, so his pessimism may become a truculent pose."

To fashion the raw experience of life into art, Dahlberg employed myth, "which, in his best work, functions as a way of giving depth, perspective, and perhaps order" to life, according to Adams. Raymond Rosenthal, writing in the *Nation,* called Dahlberg "a lone searcher for the true myths of human destiny in our violent, barren, raddled land." Dahlberg himself explained his use of myth in these words: "Until he is connected with the fens, the ravines, the stars, [man] is more solitary than any beast. Man is a god, and kin to men, when he is a river, a mountain, a horse, a moon. . . . The American legend is the mesa and the bison; it is the myth of a tragic terrain stalked by banished men." In his article for the *Dictionary of Literary Biography,* Larry R. Smith quoted Dahlberg as saying: "As for myself, I'm a medievalist, a horse and buggy American, a barbarian, anything, that can bring me back to the communal song of labor, sky, star, field, love."

Much of Dahlberg's fiction was drawn from his troubled childhood. Dahlberg was born illegitimately at a charity hospital in Boston in 1900. His mother was Elizabeth Dahlberg, married and the mother of three other children, and his father was Elizabeth's lover, a Jewish barber named Saul Gottdank. Following Dahlberg's birth, the couple took him and moved to Dallas, Texas. Once there, Gottdank stole Elizabeth's money, left town, and abandoned her. Later reconciliations in Memphis and New Orleans ended with similar betrayals. Elizabeth wandered about the South and Midwest for several years before settling in Kansas City, where she opened a hair salon. But the family's troubles continued. Despite the successful business, Elizabeth was to lose her money to a string of opportunistic men. One of these men suggested that she send Edward to an orphanage so he would not be exposed to the immorality of the Kansas City streets. She did so in 1912, and Edward entered the Jewish Orphan Asylum in Cleveland. With his admission to the orphanage, Smith remarked, "life turned from harsh to grim" for the young boy. Children at the orphanage were called by their numbers instead of their names; the windows in the building were barred; and the boredom and brutality of the place caused Dahlberg to suppress his emotions.

Upon reaching legal age in 1917, Dahlberg left the orphanage and served a brief stint as a Western Union messenger in Cleveland before making his way back to Kansas City and his mother. In the next few years Dahlberg was to work in the stockyards as a drover and serve in the U.S. Army as a private. He also wandered about the American West as a hobo, working as a dishwasher, cook, and day laborer to pay his way. In 1919 he made his home at the Los Angeles YMCA. It was there that he met Max Lewis, an older, self-educated man who taught Dahlberg to appreciate such writers as Friedrich Nietzsche, Samuel Butler, and Ralph Waldo Emerson. Dahlberg developed an interest in learning, and Lewis encouraged him to attend college. In 1921 Dahlberg enrolled at the University of California at Berkeley, where he majored in philosophy and anthropology. He transferred to Columbia University in 1923 to finish his degree. Upon graduation in 1925, Dahlberg taught at James Madison and Thomas Jefferson high schools in New York City.

After marrying Fanya Fass, the daughter of a Cleveland industrialist, in 1926, Dahlberg and his new wife moved to Europe. The couple divorced soon after arriving. For a time Dahlberg was a part of the expatriate group of American writers living in Paris. He became friends with Hart Crane, Robert McAlmon, and Richard Aldington. While living in Brussels in 1928, he completed his first novel, *Bottom Dogs,*

based on his childhood experiences at the orphanage and as a hobo traveling in the American West. The novel was marked by Dahlberg's use of coarse slang and his often graphic descriptions of down-and-out workers, farmers, and wanderers. It was published in England in 1929 and in the United States in 1930.

In his introduction to *Bottom Dogs,* D. H. Lawrence praised Dahlberg as a naturalist writer who successfully recreated the psychological mind-set of society's underclass. The novel's style, Lawrence wrote, "seems to me excellent, fitting the matter. It is sheer bottom-dog style, the bottom-dog mind expressing itself direct, almost as if it barked. That directness, that unsentimental and non-dramatised thoroughness of setting down the under-dog mind surpasses anything I know. I don't want to read any more books like this. But I am glad to have read this one, just to know what is the last word in repulsive consciousness, consciousness in a state of repulsion."

Several critics agreed with Lawrence, finding that *Bottom Dogs* accurately reflected the language and life of the lowest levels of society. Herbert Leibowitz of the *American Scholar* judged the novel's language to be "bare of mythical adornments, a flat morose voice moving over the terrain of memory, never straying from its tone of inert defeat, as the hero, Lorry Lewis, wanders across America. There is no connection among characters, just a drab amnesia, the stylistic counterpart of the Great Depression." Walter Allen, writing in his *The Modern Novel,* maintained that *Bottom Dogs* "communicates hopelessness, the hopelessness of the . . . lives of the bottom dogs, men and women who can sink no lower in the social and economic system."

For writing of society's underclass in the language of the streets, Dahlberg became immensely influential. Other writers adopted the approach, which came to be known during the 1930s as social realism or proletarian writing. In his book *Proletarian Writers of the Thirties,* Jules Chametsky described Dahlberg as a pioneer of proletarian writing: "Dahlberg's language of disgust, his imagery of rot and decay—and most importantly—his pioneering exploration of the bottom-dog milieu of flophouses, hobo jungles, and freight cars certainly places him in the vanguard of that school." J. D. O'Hara in the *New York Times Book Review* credited Dahlberg with having spawned the proletarian school of writing, but "those writers who had seized on his 'Bottom Dogs' style worked it to death in the service of Communism."

In his next two novels, *From Flushing to Calvary* and *Those Who Perish,* Dahlberg continued to write of his early life, garnering a reputation as one of the decade's leading proletarian novelists. Writing in the *Massachusetts Review,* Frank MacShane called these early books "socially committed. . . . More deeply, they were fed by [Dahlberg's] own anger at injustice. They were written in a colloquial style suited, as was thought, to the proletariat." Dahlberg's political inclinations moved him to work with other leftist writers of the 1930s. He helped to organize the communist-dominated American Writers' Congress of 1935, where he delivered a paper entitled "Fascism and Writers." By the late 1930s, however, his novels, although critically accepted, "showed no artistic growth, so Dahlberg, who meanwhile had fallen out with the Communists and who had genuine literary ambitions, ceased writing and began to read," according to MacShane. Dahlberg later repudiated his early novels as "mediocre manipulations of his childhood and young manhood, disfigured by self-pity," as Leibowitz explained. He also referred to the books as "dunghill fiction."

For many years Dahlberg wrote no new fiction, instead devoting his time to an intense study of literature. In this study he rejected most of the authors and books of the twentieth century, preferring such earlier writers as Shakespeare, Cervantes, Melville, Poe, Dickinson, and especially Thoreau. His readings of their works resulted in a writing style drastically different from his proletarian approach of the 1930s. He left behind the "linguistic void and gibbering of robots that he says marked much of the fiction and discourse of the thirties," Leibowitz stated.

Dahlberg's new style, first presented in the essay collection *Do These Bones Live* (later published as *Can These Bones Live*), is rich in biblical cadence, allusions, and aphoristic pronouncements. It is, White maintained, "a new language, an amalgam of 17th-century prose, moralizing in the style of La Rochefoucauld and queer classical learning. The effect of this language is in turn unintelligible, beautiful and ludicrous." Brom Weber in the *Saturday Review* claimed that "Dahlberg's baroque exuberance marks a return to the florid style of Melville and, beyond him in time, of Puritans Cotton Mather and Nathaniel Ward, whose fervid prose, like that of Dahlberg, is rich in rare and archaic diction, allusions to and quotations from more ancient savants, paradoxes, contradictions, factual errors, misinterpretations, impatience with contemporaries, and powerful self-assertiveness."

Do These Bones Live, "a brilliant and profound survey of American literature," as Allen Tate called it in the *Sewanee Review,* also introduced Dahlberg's support for a mythical kind of writing meant to endow ordinary life with greater significance. As John Wain wrote in the *New York Review of Books,* Dahlberg's later work "was largely concerned to transmogrify experience into myth: to give to everyday episodes that range of implication which animates the great anonymous world-explaining stories of mankind." Accordingly, Dahlberg criticized such earlier American writers as Whitman and Poe, citing the limitations of their work in comparison to such writers as Dante, who had used myth more effectively. He also condemned modernist writing, especially the works of Eliot and Pound. *Do These Bones Live,* Weber explained, "is the literary and cultural criticism of an impassioned lyric poet."

During the 1940s and 1950s, Dahlberg published little new work. Then, beginning in the early 1960s, he entered a period of production that was surprising for a middle-aged writer, publishing an average of one new book every year. Perhaps the most important of these later works was the autobiography *Because I Was Flesh,* a book in which Dahlberg came to terms with the circumstances of his early life and, in particular, with his mixed feelings about his mother. Adams described *Because I Was Flesh* as "Dahlberg's extended tribute to his mother" as well as the author's "one sustained achievement."

Critics praised Dahlberg for successfully transforming the story of his life into a form of myth. *Because I Was Flesh,* according to Wain, "succeeds in the tremendous undertaking of mythologizing modern America, as thoroughly as Joyce mythologized Dublin." Smith explained that "the book is a synthesis of Dahlberg's pithy epigrams, his concise realistic detail, and his passages of philosophical reverie. It fuses myth and reality in a flowing style that encompasses emotion, thought, and humor." MacShane noted that in *Because I Was Flesh* the "bare narrative was given substance by the rich prose in which it was written—a prose that incorporated literary, historical and mythical references so as to give the story greater resonance than was possible when accepting the limitations of colloquial English. The danger of the method is that it can be artificially literary and therefore pretentious; but *Because I Was Flesh* is grounded in observed reality." Leibowitz concluded: "*Because I Was Flesh* is a masterpiece of Oedipal obsession, a poetic memoir of primal sunderings and rages."

Although he had been writing poetry for many years, it was only during the 1960s that Dahlberg published his work in book form. *Cipango's Hinder Door* and *The Leafless American, and Other Writings* present thirty of his poems, most of them mythologizing American history as well as Dahlberg's own personal past. Cipango is the name of the mythical Asian land which Columbus believed he had discovered when he landed in the New World, Kennedy explained in his review of *Cipango's Hinder Door.* Thus, "Dahlberg's theme is the discovery of a new world—the rediscovery, to be exact [and] the rediscovery of America is another name for a discovery of himself," Kennedy concluded. "Dahlberg's poetry," Smith observed, "can be described as epigrammatic, lyric, densely mythical in reference . . . , rhythmic, intense, and progressing in associative or lyrical leaps." Donald W. Baker of *Poetry* claimed that "the best of his work, alive with incantatory rhythms and a prophetic tone, generates the power of psalm and prayer."

Much of Dahlberg's later reputation was colored by his often-acrid commentary on contemporary literature and society. O'Hara labeled these comments as being "consistently hostile, vituperative, personally insulting and wrong." Several critics compared Dahlberg to biblical figures like Ishmael and Jeremiah who spoke out against the sinful ways of their time. Benjamin T. Spencer, in an article for *Twentieth Century Literature,* credited Dahlberg with "the stance of an Old Testament prophet" and a "self-appointed mission to cleanse the Augean stables of literature." Saul Maloff remarked in *Commonweal* that "the jeremiad is his characteristic tone. . . . Dahlberg is a crank in a peculiarly American grain, a solitary who sets himself intransigently against all contemporary literary conventions and traditions, and rails against the mainstream and all its tributaries as they churn unheeding past." This later vein in Dahlberg's writing is evident in *Samuel Beckett's Wake and Other Uncollected Prose,* published posthumously in 1989. Containing essays, book reviews, and a handful of short fiction pieces, the collection reflects Dahlberg's unique prose style and his low regard for many of this century's most-renowned writers.

His controversial criticism focused on what Dahlberg saw as contemporary literature's lack of morals, and on the limitations of a rational and scientific worldview. White summarized Dahlberg's "moral analysis" as a belief "that sexuality is permanently at war with man's higher aspirations and must be disciplined; that human companionship is a great good, though difficult to find and keep; that instinct is often more trustworthy than reason; that accumulating wisdom, however, is honorable, if vain practice; that each person's character is so inflexible it cannot be significantly improved; that the machine age is an abomination; and that life is tragic." Rosenthal explained that Dahlberg's "cause, his importance, lie in his ingrained suspicion of the rationalistic, scientific heritage which has imprisoned intellect in our time. He knows, instinctively . . . that above reason and the soul or spirit stands . . . the good of the intellect, the light of wisdom which is a perpetual source of interpretation and transformation. Dahlberg instinctively knows that the method of this form of intellect is the explanation of myths, the presentation of symbols, the search for ancient wisdom."

Dahlberg died in Santa Barbara, California, in 1977. Because of the singular nature of his vision and the sometimes scathing words he had for his contemporaries, Dahlberg's literary standing is still undecided. Dahlberg, Tate believed, "like Thoreau whom he admires more than any other nineteenth-century American, eludes his contemporaries; he may have to wait for understanding until the historians of ideas of the next generation can place him historically. For we have at present neither literary nor historical standards which can guide us into Mr. Dahlberg's books written since *Bottom Dogs.*" Smith called him "a rare American poet of mythography as well as lyric personal verse. His extraordinary prose style is at times of erudite obscurism, and at [other times] personal and poetic. . . . In Edward Dahlberg the writing is the man, and there is much in the experience of that life to make his work tragically, comically, even beautifully unique." August Derleth described Dahlberg as being "as much a genius as anyone of whom I can think, past or present." He credited Dahlberg's sheer talent as the cause of critical resistance to his work: "The world is seldom ready to extend genius a helping hand, but only to salute genius when he who possessed it is safely underground." Writing in the *New York Times Book Review* about his career as a writer, Dahlberg once claimed: "I never put together a shoal of vowels and consonants for mammon or for that other whore, fame. I propose to go along as I always have done, sowing dragon's teeth when necessary, and seeding affections in the souls of my unknown readers if I can."

BIOGRAPHICAL/CRITICAL SOURCES:

BOOKS

Allen, Walter, *The Modern Novel,* Dutton, 1964.
Billings, Harold, editor, *Edward Dahlberg: American Ishmael of Letters,* Roger Beacham, 1968.

Billings, Harold, *A Bibliography of Edward Dahlberg,* University of Texas Press, 1971.

Contemporary Literary Criticism, Gale, Volume 1, 1973, Volume 7, 1977, Volume 14, 1980.

Dahlberg, Edward, *Bottom Dogs,* Putnam, 1929, Simon & Schuster, 1930.

Dahlberg, Edward, *Because I Was Flesh,* New Directions, 1964.

Dahlberg, Edward, *The Confessions of Edward Dahlberg,* Braziller, 1971.

DeFanti, Charles, *The Wages of Expectation: A Biography of Edward Dahlberg,* New York University Press, 1978.

Dictionary of Literary Biography, Volume 48: *American Poets, 1880-1945, Second Series,* Gale, 1986.

Madden, Donald, editor, *Proletarian Writers of the Thirties,* Southern Illinois University Press, 1968.

Moramarco, Fred, *Edward Dahlberg,* Twayne, 1972.

Williams, Jonathan, editor, *Edward Dahlberg: A Tribute,* David Lewis, 1971.

Wilson, Edmund, *The Shores of Light,* Farrar, Straus, 1952.

PERIODICALS

American Scholar, summer, 1975.

Atlantic, March, 1971.

Book World, June 2, 1968; July 21, 1968; February 16, 1969.

Christian Science Monitor, April 13, 1967.

Commonweal, February 19, 1971.

Contemporary Literature, spring, 1977.

Kirkus Reviews, July 1, 1989, p. 964.

Library Journal, September 15, 1989, p. 112.

Massachusetts Review, spring, 1964; spring, 1978.

Nation, November 11, 1968.

National Review, September 19, 1967.

New Republic, August 3, 1968; February 6, 1971.

Newsweek, January 23, 1967.

New York Review of Books, August 24, 1967; January 2, 1969.

New York Times Book Review, December 19, 1965; June 19, 1966; January 15, 1967; March 5, 1967; August 18, 1968; April 18, 1976.

Poetry, March, 1967.

Publishers Weekly, June 23, 1989, p. 48; May 11, 1990, p. 238.

Saturday Review, March 6, 1971.

Sewanee Review, spring, 1961.

Southern Review, spring, 1965; summer, 1967.

Twentieth Century Literature, December, 1975.

Washington Post Book World, September 10, 1989, p. 17.

Western Humanities Review, summer, 1966.*

DALEY, Arthur (John) 1904-1974

PERSONAL: Born July 31, 1904, in New York, NY; died of a heart attack January 3, 1974, in New York, NY; son of Daniel Michael (a sales executive) and Mary (Greene) Daley; married Betty Blake, November 28, 1928; children: Robert, Kevin, Patricia (Mrs. John F. Trout), Katharine. *Education:* Fordham University, B.A., 1926. *Religion:* Roman Catholic.

CAREER: New York Times, New York, NY, sports writer, 1926-74, columnist, "Sports of the Times," 1942-74.

AWARDS, HONORS: Pulitzer Prize for reporting, 1956; Grantland Rice Award, 1961; Sportswriter of the Year Award, 1963.

WRITINGS:

(With John Kieran) *The Story of the Olympic Games,* Stokes Publishing, 1936, revised edition published as *The Story of the Olympic Games, 776 B.C. to 1968,* Lippincott (Philadelphia, PA), 1969, 2nd revised edition published as *The Story of The Olympic Games, 776 B.C. to 1972,* 1973; 3rd revised edition published in 1977.

(Contributor) E. V. McLoughlin, editor, *The Story of Our Time-Encyclopedia Yearbook,* Grolier Society (Danbury, CT), 1947.

Times at Bat: A Half Century of Baseball, Random House (New York City), 1950, published as *Inside Baseball: Times at Bat, A Half Century of Baseball,* Grosset (New York City), 1961.

Sports of the Times, Dutton (New York City), 1959, revised edition published as *Sports of the Times: The Arthur Daley Years,* Quadrangle (New York City), 1975.

Knute Rockne: Football Wizard of Notre Dame, Kenedy (New York City), 1960.

Kings of the Home Run, Putnam (New York City), 1962, also published as *All the Home Run Kings,* 1972.

Pro Football's Hall of Fame: The Official Book, Quadrangle, 1963.

(With John Arlott) *Pageantry of Sport: From the Age of Chivalry to the Age of Victoria,* Hawthorne (New York City), 1968.

Contributor of articles to periodicals, including *Reader's Digest, Collier's, Saturday Review* and *Literary Digest.*

SIDELIGHTS: Arthur Daley spent almost fifty years working for the *New York Times,* principally as the

"Sports of the Times" columnist. Decade after decade, Daley turned out seven columns a week, covering title fights, football, and especially baseball, not only for his New York City audience but for the whole nation as well. Known for his incredible longevity and matchless integrity, Daley "knew sports inside and out and communicated this knowledge with enthusiasm, warmth, and a subtle sense of comedy," to quote *Dictionary of Literary Biography* contributor Scott A. G. M. Crawford.

Daley was an avid athlete who began writing about sports while completing his degree at Fordham University. Soon after earning his bachelor's degree in 1926 he was hired by the *New York Times* as a beat writer for track and field and basketball. He soon moved into other arenas, however, serving as correspondent to New York Giants football games and major league baseball contests. In 1936 he became the first *New York Times* sportswriter to travel abroad when he covered the Berlin Olympics—and the extraordinary feats of Jesse Owens.

Awarded the "Sports of the Times" column in 1942, Daley wrote seven pieces per week and also managed to turn out 61 longer profiles for the *New York Times Magazine*. At the same time he wrote several well-received books and contributed to such periodicals as *Reader's Digest* and the *Saturday Review*. He seemed to revel in the workload, and indeed was quite disconcerted when the *Times* cut him back to six columns a week. "Daley's writing was engagingly uneven," noted Crawford. "It is as if a boyish energy, a youth's overpowering love of athletics, is harnessed by the practical realities of a working journalist who had to produce his column daily." The critic added: "Daley's gifts as a writer were considerable, and his canvas was broad. . . . [He] possessed a vast amount of what could be called 'sports sense'. . . . A review of . . . Daley columns . . . underscores Daley's penchant for varied topics treated thoughtfully without either humbug or pretension."

Among Daley's best known books are *Times at Bat: A Half Century of Baseball* and *Kings of the Home Run*. Both works take an affectionate look at America's pastime and provide profiles of the game's star players. A *Chicago Sunday Tribune* reviewer called *Times at Bat* "something to settle happily down with in an easy chair," and no less than baseball immortal Branch Rickey deemed the work "the most comprehensive book on baseball yet published." In the *New York Times Book Review*, Arnold Hano praised *Kings of the Home Run*, writing: "It is always

Daley's boyish delight we sense rather than any manifestation of a sunny disposition in Ruth or Foxx or Musial or the rest." *Chicago Sunday Tribune* correspondent Tom Fitzpatrick concluded that *Kings of the Home Run* "is probably the most readable book about baseball published this spring."

Two other Daley books had lives almost as long as his column. His title *The Story of the Olympic Games*, co-authored with John Kieran, was revised on seven different occasions. His collection of columns, *Sports of the Times*, was first published in 1959 and revised in 1975, the year after his death. Hano described the latter volume as suggesting "a mellowed Don Quixote, pen at full tilt against those who would have us remove one last illusion left in this material America." Likewise, *Saturday Review* contributor Quentin Reynolds wrote: "This is the best of Arthur Daley, and the best of Arthur Daley is awfully good."

Daley died of a heart attack in front of the New York Giants' office on his way to work one January morning in 1974. He had planned to retire on his seventieth birthday but was still a few months shy of that milestone. "Daley's legacy lies in his common touch. . . . ," Crawford observed. "He wrote all those columns for all those years because he held passionately to the credo that sports was a way of life in which fairness and respect for others prevailed."

BIOGRAPHICAL/CRITICAL SOURCES:

BOOKS

Dictionary of Literary Biography, Volume 171: *Twentieth-Century American Sportswriters,* Gale (Detroit, MI), 1996, pp. 87-94.
Kahn, Roger, *The Era, 1947-1957: When the Yankees, the Giants, and the Dodgers Ruled the World,* Ticknor & Fields (New York City), 1993.

PERIODICALS

Chicago Sunday Tribune, May 7, 1950, p. 8; April 29, 1962, p. 17.
Library Journal, May 1, 1950, p. 779; November 15, 1959, p. 3582; February 15, 1961, p. 875; April 15, 1962, p. 1626.
New York Times, April 16, 1950, p. 7.
New York Times Book Review, December 6, 1959, p. 12; December 11, 1960, p. 44; April 15, 1962, p. 7.
Saturday Review, November 21, 1959, p. 48.*

DALLAS, Sandra
   See ATCHISON, Sandra Dallas

* * *

DALTON, Kit
   See CUNNINGHAM, Chet

* * *

DALY, Mary 1928-

PERSONAL: Born October 16, 1928, in Schenectady, NY; daughter of Frank X. and Anna Catherine (Morse) Daly. *Education:* College of St. Rose, B.A., 1950; Catholic University of America, M.A., 1952; St. Mary's College, Notre Dame, IN, Ph.D., 1954; University of Fribourg, Dr. Theol., 1963, Ph.D., 1965.

ADDRESSES: Office—Department of Theology, Boston College, Chestnut Hill, MA 02167.

CAREER: Cardinal Cushing College, Brookline, MA, teacher of philosophy and theology, 1954-59; Junior Year Abroad programs, Fribourg, Switzerland, teacher of philosophy and theology, 1959-66; Boston College, Chestnut Hill, MA, assistant professor, 1966-69, associate professor of theology, 1969—. Visiting lecturer in English, St. Mary's College, 1952-54.

MEMBER: American Academy of Religion, American Association of University Professors, American Association of University Women, National Organization for Women.

WRITINGS:

Natural Knowledge of God in the Philosophy of Jacques Maritain, Catholic Book Agency (Rome), 1966.
The Church and the Second Sex, Harper, 1968, with a new Feminist Postchristian introduction by the author, 1975, revised edition, Beacon Press, 1985.
Beyond God the Father: Toward a Philosophy of Women's Liberation, Beacon Press, 1973, 2nd revised edition, 1985.

Gyn/Ecology: The Metaethics of Radical Feminism, Beacon Press, 1978, revised edition, 1990.
Pure Lust: Elemental Feminist Philosophy, Beacon Press, 1984, revised edition, HarperCollins, 1992.
(With Jane Caputi) *Websters' First New Intergalactic Wickedary of the English Language,* Beacon Press, 1987.
Outercourse: The Be-Dazzling Voyage: Containing Recollections from My Logbook of a Radical Feminist Philosopher, HarperSanFrancisco, 1992.
Quintessence: Realizing the Outrageous, Contagious Courage of Women, Beacon Press, 1998.

Contributor to numerous anthologies, including *Sisterhood Is Powerful,* edited by Robin Morgan, Random House, 1970, and *A World of Ideas: Essential Readings for College Writers,* edited by Lee A. Jacobus, St. Martin's, 1994. Contributor to *Dictionary of the History of Ideas;* contributor of articles and reviews to *Commonweal, New Yorker, Woman of Power, National Catholic Reporter, Quest, Social Policy,* and other journals.

SIDELIGHTS: Philosopher and theologian Mary Daly's work has evolved from criticism of the antifeminist stance of the Catholic Church—in *The Church and the Second Sex*—to later books of more universal scope, centering on the misogynistic tendencies of society and how to deal with them. Religion is a cornerstone of society, however, and remains the starting point for Daly's theories. She maintains that all religions are patriarchal and thus they legitimize the patriarchal attitudes of the modern world. "All [religions] . . . ," she writes in *Gyn/Ecology: The Metaethics of Radical Feminism,* "are erected as parts of the male's shelter against anomie. And the symbolic message of all the sects of the religion which is patriarchy is this: Women are the dreaded anomie. Consequently, women are the objects of male terror, the projected personifications of 'The Enemy.'"

As the scope of Daly's books widened from a religious to a societal focus so did her interest in what *New York Times Book Review* contributor Demaris Wehr describes as "the role of language in the transformation of consciousness," a theme which Wehr finds throughout Daly's work. In Wehr's review of *Pure Lust: Elemental Feminist Philosophy* the critic notes that, while in *The Church and the Second Sex* Daly focuses on "antifeminism in language" and in *Beyond God the Father* suggests that new non-sexist words need to be created, in *Gyn/Ecology* and *Pure Lust,* Daly offers the reader a new feminist vocabulary. In both of the later books Daly takes derogatory terms for women, such as shrew, hag, or crone, and uses them as words of praise, capitalizing them to emphasize the importance of the women to which they refer. Her *Websters' First New Intergalactic Wickedary of the English Language,* a collaborative effort with Jane Caputi, is a glossary of these old words with new definitions as well as the many new words created by Daly. Commenting on the feminist's vocabulary, Wehr notes, "Whether it is invigorating or arduous to read [these new words] (they are all Very Big) depends on varying factors, such as how alert the reader is at the time. But the point is, new words challenge us to think different thoughts in different ways. This is exciting."

In his *Spectator* review of *Pure Lust* David Sexton elaborates more fully on Daly's unique use of language to express her beliefs. "Daly herself," he observes, "attempts to write a language that is free of unwanted associations—a form of alliterative thought chant, decorated with typographical freaks. Words are given arbitrary new histories—('we are not surprised to hear that *dream* is said to be etymologically related to the Latvian word (dunduris) meaning gadfly, wasp. For Metamorphosing women sting and provoke each other to Change'). . . . Daly's prose is in fact thrillingly horrid; it reads like Carlyle under the influence of *Finnegans Wake.*" In Sara Maitland's *New Statesman* review of the same volume, the critic expresses some doubts about Daly's style but also praises her work, "Daly is probably the most important Radical Feminist thinker around; she is also a writer of flamboyant brilliance—despite the fact that her addiction to alliteration is wearing, she has an unmatched depth of passion, imagination and pure verbal wit."

In addition to receiving both criticism and acclaim for her use of and emphasis on language, Daly has been widely celebrated for her attacks on what she considers patriarchal philosophies. In a review of *Beyond God the Father* for the *Washington Post Book World,* Adrienne Rich explains that "the major and most original portion of the book lies in its delineation of a feminist metaphysics and its closely argued affirmation of feminism as the radical source of vision—and liberation—in this century. . . . [Daly] sees the spiritual revolution of women as requiring not only self-transformation but a conscious resistance to patriarchy which involves collective activism in the world as much as inner travail. She insists upon the process, individual and communal, by which each woman must confront her own nonbeing under patriarchy." Alix Kates Shulman offers further praise in her *Village*

Voice review: "Daly is the ultimate Christian feminist. What other radical feminists have revealed by analyzing patriarchal society's political, economic, social, and sexual institutions, Daly does for the spiritual institution on which Western civilization is founded."

Despite the controversy caused by much of her work, many critics agree that Daly is, in fact, one of today's most significant feminist minds. One such critic is Vicky Cosstick, who, in her review of *Gyn/Ecology,* procalimed it "probably the most important book to come out of the feminist movement since Daly's last book, *Beyond God the Father.* . . . It speaks to the Lesbian imagination in all feminists, to our creativity and to our intelligence, as well as to our fury at the injustices of a patriarchal world." Similarly, Barbara Berman describes *Gyn/Ecology* as "probably the most important book of feminist thought written in the past ten years. . . . What Daly has produced is a brilliant presentation of one woman's passage toward finding out who she—the whole—is."

In *Outercourse: The Be-Dazzling Voyage: Containing Recollections from My Logbook as a Radical Feminist Philosopher,* Daly offers an autobiographical account of the development of her philosophy. The book is divided into four sections, or "Spiral Galaxies." The first galaxy covers her childhood; her collegiate years, during which she earned seven higher degrees; the publication of her landmark book, *The Church and the Second Sex;* and the events surrounding Boston College's refusal to grant her tenure in 1969 (she began teaching there in 1966). The second galaxy covers the writing of *Beyond God the Father,* while the third galaxy includes the writing of her subsequent books, including *Gyn/Ecology* and *Pure Lust.* The fourth galaxy covers the present at the time Daly was writing the book, which was published in 1992.

"Through the medium of one woman's life-her own-Mary Daly invites us into the process of radical feminist philosophy," remarks Carol J. Adams in the *Women's Review of Books.* Adams, however, notes that *Outercourse* is far from being a straightforward autobiography: "Daly is not so much reading her life as an example of her theory or writing in her own voice for the first time . . . but placing herself philosophically within the ontological framework that her books provide in order to help elucidate those books." Mary Jo Weaver, writing in the *New York Times Book Review,* remarks that "Daly presents herself as inhabiting a universe of her own making. Most of her references are to her own work; her reflections on language and wordplay acknowledge neither context nor content beyond herself." Nonetheless, Weaver avers that *Outercourse* "is alive with creative energy, impelled by an urgency of vision and infused with the 'outlandish reality that is present in everyday occurrences.'" Commenting on Daly's legendary forthrightness and startlingly direct language, Adams states that "Daly reminds us that it does none of us any good to mince words, to be humble or hold back speaking the truth." Adams adds, *"Outercourse* will satisfy anyone curious about Mary Daly's life and her writings."

Summarizing her views for *CA,* Daly once wrote: "My fundamental interest is the women's revolution, which I see as the radical source of possibility for other forms of liberation from oppressive structures. I am interested precisely in the spiritual dimension of women's liberation, in its transforming potential in relation to religious consciousness and the forms in which this consciousness expresses itself. This is not 'one area' of theology; rather, it challenges the whole patriarchal religion."

BIOGRAPHICAL/CRITICAL SOURCES:

BOOKS

Contemporary Issues Criticism, Volume 1, Gale, 1982.
Daly, Mary, *Gyn/Ecology: The Metaethics of Radical Feminism,* Beacon Press, 1990.
Daly, Mary, *Outercourse: The Be-Dazzling Voyage: Containing Recollections from My Logbook of a Radical Feminist Philosopher,* HarperSanFrancisco, 1992.
Ratcliffe, Krista, *Anglo-American Feminist Challenges to the Rhetorical Traditions: Virginia Woolf, Mary Daly, Adrienne Rich,* Southern Illinois University Press (Carbondale), 1996.

PERIODICALS

Belles Lettres, summer, 1993, p. 42.
Christianity Today, August 16, 1993, p. 21.
Los Angeles Times Book Review, April 25, 1993, p. 6.
Ms., February, 1979.
National Catholic Reporter, April 7, 1989, p. 5; May 5, 1989, p. 5; May 31, 1996, p. 18.
New Directions for Women, January, 1979.
New Statesman, April 4, 1980, January 18, 1985.
New York Times Book Review, February 4, 1979; July 22, 1984; January 24, 1993, p. 15.
San Francisco Chronicle, January 10, 1993.
Spectator, February 23, 1985.
Village Voice, January 31, 1974.
Washington Post Book World, November 11, 1973; May 17, 1979.
Whole Earth Review, spring, 1989, p. 128; summer, 1995, p. 31.
Women's Review of Books, March, 1993, p. 1.

*   *   *

DANZIG, Allison 1898-1987

PERSONAL: Born February 27, 1898, in Waco, TX; died of a heart attack January 27, 1987, in Ridgewood, NJ; son of Morris (a businessman) and Ethel (Harvith) Danzig; married Dorothy Charlotte Chapman, July 9, 1923; children: Dorothy (Mrs. Shelley Hull), Mimi (Mrs. Charles Christie), Allison C. *Education:* Cornell University, A.B., 1921.

CAREER: Brooklyn Eagle, Brooklyn, NY, sports writer, 1921-23; *New York Times,* New York, NY, sports writer, 1923-68. Member of board of directors, National Tennis Foundation and Hall of Fame; trustee of National Rowing Foundation, National Art Museum of Sport, and Christopher Morley Knothole Association. Chair of war fund sport committee, Greater New York Red Cross, 1944-45; also former member of Roslyn auxiliary police force and former trustee, Village of Roslyn Estates. *Military service:* U.S. Army, Infantry, 1918-19; became second lieutenant.

MEMBER: National Football Foundation and Hall of Fame (member of honors court; member of board of directors), Lawn Tennis Writers Association of America (former president), Rowing Writers Association of America (former president), U.S. Tennis Writers Association (honorary member), U.S. Naval Academy Athletic Association (honorary member), North American Racquets Association (honorary member), U.S. Court Tennis Association, Authors Guild, International Lawn Tennis Club (honorary member), Circumnavigators Club, Royal Tennis Court of Hampton Court Palace (London), Football Writers Association of New York (former president), Cornell Club of New York, West Side Tennis Club of Forest Hills (honorary member).

AWARDS, HONORS: Elected to National Lawn Tennis Hall of Fame and Tennis Museum, 1968; elected to Helms Foundation Rowing Hall of Fame, 1968; received distinguished service awards from National Football Foundation and Hall of Fame, U.S. Lawn Tennis Association, U.S. Professional Lawn Tennis Association, City of New York, and Medical Society of New York; Grantland Rice Award for distinguished sports writings. Also has received awards from Football Writers Association of New York, Philadelphia Sports Writers Association, Yale University Football "Y" Association, National Association of Amateur Oarsmen, Princeton University Athletic Association, West Side Tennis Club, Tennis Umpires Association of the United States, and Cornell Club of New York. Columbia University has instituted Allison Danzig Cup for tennis in his honor; Longwood (Massachusetts) Cricket Club established Allison Danzig Award for tennis writing.

WRITINGS:

The Racquet Game, Macmillan (New York City), 1930.
(With John Doeg) *Elements of Lawn Tennis,* Coward (New York City), 1931.
(Editor with Peter Brandwein) *Sport's Golden Age: A Close-Up of the Fabulous Twenties,* Harper (New York City), 1948, 2nd edition, 1969.
(Editor with Brandwein) *The Greatest Sports Stories from the New York Times: Sport Classics of a Century,* A. S. Barnes (New York City), 1951.
The History of American Football: Its Great Teams, Players, and Coaches, Prentice-Hall (Englewood Cliffs, NJ), 1956.
(With Joe Reichler) *The History of Baseball: Its Great Players, Teams and Managers,* Prentice-Hall, 1959.
Oh, How They Played the Game: The Early Days of Football and the Heroes Who Made It Great, Macmillan, 1971.
(Editor with Peter Schwed) *The Fireside Book of Tennis,* Simon & Schuster (New York City), 1972.
The Winning Gallery: Court Tennis Matches and Memories, United States Court Tennis Association (Philadelphia, PA), 1985.

Sports columnist, *New Yorker,* during 1920s. Contributor to *Encyclopaedia Britannica, Collier's Year Book, Companion to Sports and Games, English Encyclopedia of Tennis,* and *English International Encyclopedia of Sports;* contributor to national periodicals, including *Saturday Evening Post, Collier's,* and *New Yorker.*

SIDELIGHTS: Allison Danzig served on the staff of the *New York Times* for forty-five years, principally as a sportswriter covering tennis, football, and the Olympic Games. Throughout much of the twentieth century, Danzig was considered the leading authority on lawn tennis and its lesser-known indoor cousins such as court tennis, squash racquets, and squash tennis. As the years of his tenure increased at the *New York Times,* Danzig brought a unique perspective to his work—that of an observer who had followed many American sports from their formative years. According to Adam R. Hornbuckle in the *Dictionary of Literary Biography,* Danzig "established a standard in sportswriting that remains a source of guidance and inspiration, especially to tennis correspondents."

Danzing began his sportswriting career after graduating from Cornell University in 1921. His first job was with the *Brooklyn Daily Eagle,* and it consisted of covering baseball, billiards, boxing, golf, football, and tennis for "space rates"—anywhere from eight to twelve dollars per week. A college athlete who, despite his diminutive stature, concentrated on football, Danzig knew little about tennis at first. He educated himself on the sport's refinements after being asked to cover matches. He was soon an authority on the game.

The *New York Times* hired Danzig in 1923 as a tennis correspondent. Hornbuckle wrote: "In his first year with the *Times* Danzig began an annual pattern of sports reporting that he would maintain throughout his tenure at the newspaper. After the outdoor tennis season concluded with the men's United States Lawn Tennis Association (USLTA) Championship in September, Danzig covered college football, traveling to Ithaca to report on his alma mater. In the winter and early spring he wrote about indoor tennis, court tennis, racquets, and squash—obscure sports that were played and followed by the social elite. In the spring he reported on crew, concentrating on the major Ivy League regattas and the intercollegiate championships."

Danzig was the first sportswriter to coin the term "grand slam" for a player's victory in the four major international tennis tournaments (Wimbledon, the U.S. Open, the French Open, and the Australian Open). He is said to have been so authoritative in his coverage that the players themselves often sought out his press reports of their performances in the same way that actors look for their theatrical reviews. This wide-ranging knowledge found its way into Danzig's books on tennis, such as *The Racquet Game, Elements of Lawn Tennis,* and *The Fireside Book of Tennis.* In the *New York Times Book Review,* Fred Tupper called *The Fireside Book of Tennis* "a must for all tennis buffs" and a book in which "all the wonderful matches come alive."

Danzig also contributed to the history of other major sports, with titles such as *The History of American Football: Its Great Teams, Players, and Coaches,* and *The History of Baseball: Its Great Players, Teams and Managers.* In the *New York Herald Tribune Book Review,* I. T. Marsh deemed the football book a "definitive work," adding: "It would be difficult to envision a story of the great American game as complete, as accurate and as full of the romance and the lore of the fall sport as Allison Danzig's effort." Likewise, *Saturday Review* correspondent Al Silverman characterized the book as "a small miracle," concluding that it "must be classified as the definitive work on American football, at least the college end of it." In a *San Francisco Chronicle* review of *The History of Baseball,* William German wrote that Danzig and his co-author Joe Reichler "put together a beauty, one of the mightiest books ever."

Danzig enjoyed reminiscing about what he considered the "golden age" of sports—the 1920s, when the lines between amateur and professional were carefully drawn and when many players gave their all just for the joy of the game. He served as an editor for two essay collections on sports history, *Sport's Golden Age: A Close-up of the Fabulous Twenties* and *The Greatest Sports Stories from the New York Times: Sport Classics of a Century.* The latter title was reviewed by Wilbur Watson in the *New York Times* as a "hilarious and moving history. . . . For the all-round sports-minded reader, the book can be read, with complete pleasure and even fascination, from beginning to end."

Danzig retired from the *New York Times* in 1968. He spent his retirement in Ridgewood, New Jersey, and there died of a heart attack on January 27, 1987. "Danzig . . . distinguished himself from other sportswriters by showing an interest in sports history well before the topic became an acceptable area for academic analysis in the 1970s," wrote Hornbuckle. "Of the twentieth century's tennis correspondents, none has been more revered and respected by fellow reporters and players than Danzig."

BIOGRAPHICAL/CRITICAL SOURCES:

BOOKS

Collins, Bud and Zander Hollander, editors, *Bud Collins' Modern Encyclopedia of Tennis,* Gale (Detroit, MI), 1994.
Dictionary of Literary Biography, Volume 171: *Twentieth-Century American Sportswriters,* Gale, 1996, pp. 95-102.

PERIODICALS

Boston Globe, July 9, 1987, p. 8.
Chicago Sunday Tribune, January 13, 1952, p. 10.
Library Journal, November 15, 1959, p. 3582; September 15, 1972, p. 2857.
New York Herald Tribune Book Review, December 16, 1956, p. 9; February 7, 1960, p. 6.
New York Times, October 3, 1948, p. 34; December 9, 1951, p. 20; December 9, 1956, p. 20.
New York Times Book Review, November 22, 1959, p. 24; October 22, 1972, p. 26.
San Francisco Chronicle, September 19, 1948, p. 21; December 9, 1956, p. 26; November 22, 1959, p. 6.
Saturday Review, December 8, 1956, p. 23.
Springfield Republican, September 19, 1948, p. 17B.
Tennis, September, 1987, pp. 107-08.
Times Literary Supplement, May 1, 1930, p. 375.
World Tennis, March, 1956, p. 15.

OBITUARIES:

PERIODICALS

Detroit Free Press, January 29, 1987.
Newsday, January 29, 1987.
New York Times, January 28, 1987.*

*   *   *

**DeMILLE, Nelson (Richard) 1943-
(Ellen Kay, Kurt Ladner, Brad Matthews)**

PERSONAL: Born August 23, 1943, in New York, NY; son of Huron (a builder) and Antonia (Panzera) DeMille; married Ellen Wasserman (a medical technologist), July 17, 1971 (divorced January, 1987); married Ginny Sindel Witte, 1988; children: (first marriage) Lauren, Alex. *Education:* Hofstra University, B.A., 1970. *Politics:* Libertarian. *Religion:* Roman Catholic.

ADDRESSES: Office—61 Hilton Ave., Ste. 23, Garden City, NY 11530. *Agent*—Nick Ellison, Sanford J. Greenburger Associates Inc., 55 5th Ave., New York, NY 10003.

CAREER: Has worked variously as a carpenter, electrician's apprentice, house painter, men's clothing salesperson, art dealer, stable boy, deck hand, insurance investigator, and editorial assistant; novelist and freelance writer, 1973—. *Military service:* U.S. Army Infantry, 1966-69; became first lieutenant; received Bronze Star Medal, Air Medal, combat infantryman's badge, and Vietnamese Cross of Gallantry.

MEMBER: Mystery Writers of America, Authors Guild, Mensa.

AWARDS, HONORS: Honorary D.H.L., 1989, and Estabrook Award, both from Hofstra University; honorary D.H.L., Long Island University, 1993, and Dowling College, 1997.

WRITINGS:

The Sniper (police novel), Leisure Books (Norwalk, CT), 1974.
The Hammer of God (police novel), Leisure Books, 1974.
The Agent of Death (police novel), Leisure Books, 1974.
The Smack Man (police novel), Manor Publishing (Staten Island, NY), 1975.
The Cannibal (police novel), Manor Publishing, 1975.
Night of the Phoenix (police novel), Manor Publishing, 1975.
Death Squad (police novel), Manor Publishing, 1975.
The Quest (novel), Manor Publishing, 1975.
(Under pseudonym Ellen Kay) *The Five Million Dollar Woman: Barbara Walters* (biography), Manor Publishing, 1976.
(Under pseudonym Kurt Ladner) *Hitler's Children* (World War II novel), Manor Publishing, 1976.
(Under pseudonym Brad Matthews) *Killer Sharks: The Real Story,* Manor Publishing, 1976.
By the Rivers of Babylon (novel), Harcourt (San Diego, CA), 1978.
(With Thomas H. Block) *Mayday,* Richard Marek, 1979, reprint, Warner (New York City), 1998.
Cathedral, Delacorte (New York City), 1981.
The Talbot Odyssey, Delacorte, 1984.
Word of Honor, Warner, 1985.

The Charm School, Warner, 1989.
The Gold Coast, Warner, 1990.
The General's Daughter, Warner, 1992.
Spencerville, Warner, 1994.
Plum Island, Warner, 1997.

Contributor to various periodicals, including *Alfred Hitchcock Magazine, Mystery Monthly,* and *Newsday.* Editor, *Law Officer,* 1975-76.

SIDELIGHTS: American writer Nelson DeMille has written several highly popular novels and has garnered acclaim for his skills in creating fast-moving plots and colorful characters. The settings of his novels range from Vietnam in *Word of Honor* to wealthy Long Island, New York, in *The Gold Coast* and *Plum Island* to small-town Ohio in *Spencerville.*

In an interview with Robert Dahlin for *Publishers Weekly,* DeMille discusses the ease with which he wrote *Word of Honor,* a novel recalling his years in the Army during the Vietnam War. "This book wasn't concocted," explains DeMille, who adds, "It was the easiest and quickest book I've ever done. I just told the story of my own experiences, basically. It was a straight linear plot, and all the characters were based on somebody I'd come across. . . . What I wanted to do was bring out the officer's side of the war. Officers had the worst time of it in many respects." According to Dahlin, "The results are riveting. . . . DeMille's personal experiences and observations do provide *Word of Honor* with a rich texture."

Word of Honor's plot centers on the court-martial of ex-lieutenant Ben Tyson. Eighteen years after the fact, the publication of a book details Tyson's primary role in a civilian massacre. A *Publishers Weekly* contributor asserts, "If fiction can assuage the lingering moral pain of the Vietnam War, it's through the kind of driving honesty coupled with knowledgeability that DeMille . . . employs here." A *Time* critic hails *Word of Honor* as "*The Caine Mutiny* of the '80s, a long, over-the-shoulder look at the time that grows larger as it recedes from sight." Dahlin maintains that DeMille will not be writing on the Vietnam era again: "*Word of Honor* did serve as something of a catharsis for [DeMille], he says, but even if it accomplished nothing else, 'At least it stops people from asking when I'm going to write a Vietnam novel.'"

The Gold Coast examines the life of attorney John Sutter and his heiress wife, Susan, who frequent all the "right" places on Long Island's "old money" North Shore. Sutter, disillusioned with the trappings and superficiality of the moneyed set and concerned with professional dishonesty among his colleagues, feels bored and ready for a change, which occurs when Mafia kingpin Frank Bellarosa moves into the estate next door and Sutter eventually winds up representing him in court. The *Washington Post Book World*'s Consuelo Saah Baehr describes *The Gold Coast* as a "captivating cautionary tale of soul-selling by a Wall Street lawyer seeking release from the stupefying boredom and compromise of upper-crust life." The reviewer continues, "DeMille . . . is a gifted eyewitness and so at home with his material we never doubt that he got it from the source. . . . DeMille observes with a personal involvement and self-deprecating rue that's irresistible. This is a page-turner but we want to linger and re-read."

Joanne Kaufman writes in the *New York Times Book Review* that "what makes *The Gold Coast* glitter is Nelson DeMille's sharp evocation of the vulpine Bellarosa and of Sutter. . . . In his way, Mr. DeMille . . . is as keen a social satirist as Edith Wharton." Joyce Slater comments in *Tribune Books* that "DeMille shares with Dominick Dunne a caustic view of corruption and wealth." Stefan Kanfer of *Time* asserts that *The Gold Coast* exhibits "a smart social eye and an unfailing sense of humor."

The General's Daughter follows the process of the Criminal Investigation Division of the United States Army at fictional Fort Hadley, Georgia, as the C.I.D.'s Paul Brenner investigates the murder of Captain Ann Campbell, daughter of the camp commander. The trail leads to sexual and psychological secrets, which provide numerous suspects with motives for the murder. Chris Petrakos observes in *Tribune Books* that "the author is a solid craftsman with a droll sense of humor." A *Time* reviewer finds the book "two or three levels better than routine," in particular citing DeMille's prose style. Although the *New York Times Book Review*'s Newgate Callendar believes the book lacks sufficient character development, he nevertheless claims, "Mr. DeMille writes well enough, there is some snappy dialogue, [and] the police work is painstakingly thorough."

Spencerville, published in 1994, features a retired government operative, Keith Landry. Finally back home in Ohio after 25 difficult years working for the government, Landry rekindles his love for his high school sweetheart, Annie Baxter. Unfortunately, Annie is married to the town's sadistic police chief, a man who dominates Annie and the rest of the townspeople with his brutal ways. A struggle ensues between Landry and the police chief, with Landry attempting to liberate Annie and the townspeople while staying alive.

About his career as a writer, DeMille once told *CA:* "Having tried other forms of writing, I always return to the novel. The novel is the ultimate test of a writer's skills, the most arduous of writing tasks, and the medium most open to criticism. The novelist reveals a good deal of himself in his story and has the final responsibility for every word written. Neither editors nor publicity people, cover artists nor advertising people should be made to share the responsibility for an unsuccessful novel, nor should they share in the triumph of a successful one. A novel is a long-term commitment with little ego reinforcement along the way, a brief flash of the limelight at publication, then back to the typewriter. It takes a great deal of tenacity to stick with a project for so long a period with no guarantee of anything at the end. Yet, the novelist, who by nature must be an optimist, goes on, year after year. I know very few ex-novelists; I know many working novelists and many aspiring novelists. It must be a good job."

BIOGRAPHICAL/CRITICAL SOURCES:

PERIODICALS

Chicago Tribune Book World, May 24, 1981.
Entertainment Weekly, November 11, 1994, p. 68.
Kirkus Reviews, April 15, 1997.
Library Journal, September 15, 1994, p. 90.
New York Times, July 26, 1978.
New York Times Book Review, May 27, 1990, p. 14; March 31, 1991, p. 28; November 15, 1992, p. 21.
Publishers Weekly, October 4, 1985; November 8, 1985; August 22, 1994, p. 39; April 21, 1997, p. 60.
Time, December 9, 1985; July 2, 1990, p. 66; December 28, 1992, p. 73.
Tribune Books (Chicago), June 17, 1990, p. 4; November 8, 1992, p. 8.
Washington Post, August 7, 1978; June 23, 1981; November 30, 1985.
Washington Post Book World, April 29, 1990, p. 1.

* * *

DERRICK, Lionel
See CUNNINGHAM, Chet

DeSALVO, Louise A(nita) 1942-

PERSONAL: Born September 27, 1942, in Jersey City, NJ; daughter of Louis B. (a machinist) and Mildred (Calabrese) Sciacchetano; married Ernest J. DeSalvo (a physician), December 21, 1963; children: Jason, Justin. *Education:* Rutgers University, B.A., 1963; New York University, M.A., 1972, Ph.D., 1977.

ADDRESSES: Home—1045 Oakland Court, Teaneck, NJ 07666; Stoney Ridge, Sag Harbor, NY. *Office*—Department of English, Hunter College of the City University of New York, 695 Park Ave., New York, NY 10021.

CAREER: High school English teacher in Wood-Ridge, NJ, 1963-67; Fairleigh Dickinson University, Teaneck, NJ, co-ordinator of English education, 1977-83; Hunter College of the City University of New York, New York, NY, professor of English and women's studies, 1983—.

MEMBER: Modern Language Association of America, National Council of Teachers of English, Assembly on Literature for Adolescents, Bronte Society, Virginia Woolf Society (treasurer, 1979-82), Women's Ink, Northeast Victorian Studies Association.

AWARDS, HONORS: National Endowment for the Humanities grant, 1980; seal from Committee on Scholarly Editions from Modern Language Association of America, 1980, for *Melymbrosia: Early Version of "The Voyage Out";* distinguished achievement award from Educational Press Association of America, 1980, for "Writers at Work"; President's Award for scholarship from Hunter College, 1986.

WRITINGS:

Virginia Woolf's First Voyage: A Novel in the Making, Rowman & Littlefield (Towtowa, NJ), 1980.
Melymbrosia: Early Version of "The Voyage Out," New York Public Library (New York City), 1980.
(With Carol Ascher and Sara Ruddick) *Between Women,* Beacon Press (Boston), 1984.
(Editor with Mitchell A. Leaska) *The Letters of Vita Sackville-West to Virginia Woolf,* Morrow (New York City), 1984.
Nathaniel Hawthorne: A Feminist Reading, Humanities Press (Atlantic Highlands, NJ), 1987.

"Children Never Forget": Virginia Woolf on Childhood, Adolescence, and Young Adulthood, Beacon Press, 1988.
Casting Off: A Novel, Harvester, 1988.
Virginia Woolf: The Impact of Childhood Sexual Abuse on Her Life and Work, Beacon Press, 1989.
(Co-editor) *Territories of the Voice: Contemporary Stories by Irish Women Writers,* Beacon Press, 1989.
Between Women: Biographers, Novelists, Critics, Teachers, and Artists Write about Their Work on Women, Routledge (New York City), 1993.
Conceived with Malice: Literature as Revenge in the Lives and Works of Leonard and Virginia Woolf, D. H. Lawrence, Djuna Barnes, and Henry Miller, Dutton (New York City), 1994.
Vertigo: A Memoir, Dutton, 1996.

Contributing editor, *Media and Methods,* 1980-81. Contributor to literature journals.

SIDELIGHTS: Louise DeSalvo has devoted much of her scholarly research and writing to the life and work of writer Virginia Woolf. It is widely known that Woolf was sexually molested by her half-brothers from the time she was six until she left the family home at the age of twenty-three, but DeSalvo was one of the first critics to examine the effect that this extended trauma had on the woman and her writings. She focused on this subject in *Virginia Woolf: The Impact of Childhood Sexual Abuse on Her Life and Work. Washington Post Book World* writer Julia Epstein noted: "DeSalvo attempts, not always successfully, to integrate readings on a variety of Woolf's works with recent research on child sexual abuse." Epstein found that DeSalvo failed to provide an adequate discussion of how Woolf's childhood experiences affected her adult love life, yet the critic concluded that despite some flaws, DeSalvo produced "an important book. She refutes standard notions about the idyllic, secure, affectionate household in which Virginia Woolf grew up, and questions the alleged sexual liberation of the Bloomsbury circle. Most important, she hears and believes Virginia Woolf's testimony to her childhood abuse, and in consequence offers a genuinely new account of her early life and work." *Women's Review of Books* writer Gillian Gill called the book "something of a milestone in women's studies." Woolf was also an important part of *Conceived with Malice: Literature as Revenge in the Lives and Works of Leonard and Virginia Woolf, D. H. Lawrence, Djuna Barnes, and Henry Miller.* In this study, DeSalvo examines the various authors' works and the elements in them that probably sprang from a desire to take revenge on certain people in their lives.

DeSalvo took a look at her own life with *Vertigo: A Memoir.* She applies "a scholarly scalpel to the complex layers of her life," wrote Carolyn Alessio in *Tribune Books.* DeSalvo grew up in a working-class Italian neighborhood—Hoboken, New York—during World War II. It was a woman's world, for most men were in the armed forces at that time. She recalls this as the happiest time in her life, however; when the men returned, "life became grim," as Genevieve Stuttaford put it in a *Publishers Weekly* review. Her mother was institutionalized for depression, her sister took her own life, and DeSalvo herself was repeatedly molested by an aunt. She escaped the horrors of her life by burying herself in books and films, eventually becoming a respected professor of English. Still, depression haunted her as an adult, and part of *Vertigo* is the story of her struggle with this mental illness. In fact, the book was begun as a means of therapy.

"De Salvo clearly has a sense of humor, and although her success in life—she repeatedly stresses the problems of being Italian, working class and a 'girl'—may not be as unique as she seems to think, her clarity of insight and expression makes this an impressive achievement," decided Stuttaford. Carolyn See of the *Los Angeles Times* also endorsed *Vertigo,* declaring: "The writing here is terrific. DeSalvo constructs an inviting, unlikely heaven made up of women and children who have their tenement world to themselves. . . . The kids and their moms break all the old boundaries and rip around through each other's dwellings, laughing and talking. . . . Then the dads come home, reasserting their private territorial rights, slamming all the doors to all the apartments and yelling at their wives and kids until they shut up and stop having fun. Once again, the world is made safe for patriarchal 'democracy,' for brutish, humorless violence." See found the portions of the book covering the author's adult life less "riveting" than those describing her early years, but she concluded: "This is a highly subjective narrative of what it's like to grow up American, reject what's expected of you and then make your own fate."

BIOGRAPHICAL/CRITICAL SOURCES:

PERIODICALS

Booklist, June 1, 1996, p. 1665.
Globe and Mail (Toronto), January 5, 1985.
Journal of American Studies, April, 1989.
Library Journal, July, 1996, p. 126.
Literary Review, spring, 1990.
Los Angeles Times Book Review, December 23, 1984; February 26, 1995, p. 9; August 4, 1996, p. 4.
Modern Fiction Studies, summer, 1991.
New Statesman and Society, October 27, 1989.
New Yorker, November 6, 1989.
New York Review of Books, March 15, 1990.
New York Times, July 9, 1995, p. LI13.
Publishers Weekly, May 9, 1994, p. 27; September 19, 1994, p. 56; May 27, 1996, p. 57.
Times (London), December 20, 1984.
Times Literary Supplement, December 21, 1984.
Tribune Books (Chicago), August 18, 1996, p. 3.
Tulsa Studies in Women's Literature, fall, 1991.
Washington Post Book World, May 14, 1989, p. 4.
Women's Review of Books, March, 1995, p. 14.

*   *   *

DILLARD, Annie 1945-
(Annie Doak)

PERSONAL: Born April 30, 1945, in Pittsburgh, PA; daughter of Frank and Pam (Lambert) Doak; married Richard Dillard (a professor and writer), June 5, 1964 (divorced); married Gary Clevidence (a writer), April 12, 1980 (divorced); married Robert D. Richardson, Jr. (a professor and writer), 1988; children: (with Clevidence) Cody Rose; Carin, Shelly (stepchildren). *Education:* Hollins College, B.A., 1967, M.A., 1968.

ADDRESSES: Agent—Timothy Seldes, Russell & Volkening, 50 West 29th St., New York, NY 10001.

CAREER: Writer. The Wilderness Society, columnist in *The Living Wilderness,* 1973-75; *Harper's Magazine,* editor, 1973-85; Western Washington University, Bellingham, scholar in residence, 1975-79; Wesleyan University, Middletown, CT, distinguished visiting professor, beginning in 1979, full adjunct professor, beginning in 1983, writer in residence, beginning in 1987. Member of U.S. cultural delegation to China, 1982. Board member, Western States Arts Foundation, Milton Center, and Key West Literary Seminar; board member and chair (1991—), Wesleyan Writers' Conference. Member, New York Public Library National Literacy Committee, National Committee for U.S.-China relations, and Catholic Commission on Intellectual and Cultural Affairs.

Member of usage panel, *American Heritage Dictionary.*

MEMBER: International PEN, Poetry Society of America, Society of American Historians, NAACP, Phi Beta Kappa.

AWARDS, HONORS: Pulitzer Prize (general nonfiction), 1975, for *Pilgrim at Tinker Creek;* New York Press Club Award for Excellence, 1975; Washington State Governor's Award for Literature, 1978; grants from National Endowment for the Arts, 1980-81, and Guggenheim Foundation, 1985-86; *Los Angeles Times Book Prize* nomination, 1982, for *Living by Fiction;* honorary degrees from Boston College, 1986, Connecticut College, and University of Hartford, both 1993; National Book Critics Circle award nomination, 1987, for *An American Childhood;* Appalachian Gold Medallion, University of Charleston, 1989; St. Botolph's Club Foundation Award, Boston, 1989; English-speaking Union Ambassador Book Award, 1990, for *The Writing Life;* Best Foreign Book Award (France), 1990, for *Pilgrim at Tinker Creek;* History Maker Award, Historical Society of Western Pennsylvania, 1993; Connecticut Governor's Arts Award, 1993; Campion Medal, 1994; Milton Prize, 1994.

WRITINGS:

Tickets for a Prayer Wheel (poems), University of Missouri Press (Columbia), 1974.
Pilgrim at Tinker Creek (also see below), Harper's Magazine Press, 1974.
Holy the Firm (also see below), Harper (New York City), 1978.
Living by Fiction (also see below), Harper, 1982.
Teaching a Stone to Talk: Expeditions and Encounters (also see below), Harper, 1982.
Encounters with Chinese Writers, Wesleyan University Press (Middletown, CT), 1984.
(Contributor) *Inventing the Truth: The Art and Craft of Memoir,* edited by William Zinsser, Houghton (Boston), 1987.
An American Childhood (also see below), Harper, 1987.
(Editor with Robert Atwan) *The Best American Essays, 1988,* Ticknor & Fields (New York City), 1988.
The Annie Dillard Library (contains *Living by Fiction, An American Childhood, Holy the Firm, Pilgrim at Tinker Creek,* and *Teaching a Stone to Talk*), Harper, 1989.
The Writing Life, Harper, 1989.

Three by Annie Dillard (contains *Pilgrim at Tinker Creek, An American Childhood,* and *The Writing Life*), Harper, 1990.
The Living (novel), HarperCollins (New York City), 1992.
The Annie Dillard Reader, HarperCollins, 1994.
(Editor with Cort Conley) *Modern American Memoirs,* HarperCollins, 1995.
Mornings Like This: Found Poems, HarperCollins, 1995.

Columnist, *Living Wilderness,* 1973-75. Contributing editor, *Harper's,* 1974-81, and 1983-85. Contributor of fiction, essays, and poetry to numerous periodicals, including *Atlantic Monthly, American Scholar, Poetry, New York Times Magazine, New York Times Book Review,* and *Chicago Review.*

SIDELIGHTS: Annie Dillard has carved a unique niche for herself in the world of American letters. Over the course of her career, Dillard has written essays, a memoir, poetry, literary criticism—even a western novel. In whatever genre she works, Dillard distinguishes herself with her carefully wrought language, keen observations, and original metaphysical insights. Her first significant publication, *Pilgrim at Tinker Creek,* drew numerous comparisons to Thoreau's *Walden;* in the years since *Pilgrim* appeared, Dillard's name has come to stand for excellence in writing.

Tickets for a Prayer Wheel was Dillard's first publication. This slim volume of poetry—which expressed the author's yearning for a hidden God—was praised by reviewers. Within months of *Tickets*'s appearance, however, the book was completely overshadowed by the release of *Pilgrim at Tinker Creek.* Dillard lived quietly on Tinker Creek in Virginia's Roanoke Valley, observing the natural world, taking notes, and reading voluminously in a wide variety of disciplines, including theology, philosophy, natural science, and physics. Following the progression of seasons, *Pilgrim* probes the cosmic significance of the beauty and violence coexisting in the natural world.

The book met with immediate popular and critical success. "One of the most pleasing traits of the book is the graceful harmony between scrutiny of real phenomena and the reflections to which that gives rise," noted a *Commentary* reviewer. "Anecdotes of animal behavior become so effortlessly enlarged into symbols by the deepened insight of meditation. Like a true transcendentalist, Miss Dillard understands her task to be that of full alertness." Other critics found fault

Dillard's work, however, calling it self-absorbed or overwritten. Charles Deemer of the *New Leader,* for example, claimed that "if Annie Dillard had not spelled out what she was up to in this book, I don't think I would have guessed. . . . Her observations are typically described in overstatement reaching toward hysteria." A more charitable assessment came from Muriel Haynes of *Ms.* While finding Dillard to be "susceptible to fits of rapture," Haynes asserted that the author's "imaginative flights have the special beauty of surprise."

The author's next book delved into the metaphysical aspects of pain. *Holy the Firm* was inspired by the plight of one of Dillard's neighbors, a seven-year-old child badly burned in a plane crash. As Dillard reflects on the maimed child and on a moth consumed by flame, she struggles with the problem of reconciling faith in a loving god with the reality of a violent world. Only seventy-six pages long, the book overflows with "great richness, beauty and power," according to Frederick Buechner in the *New York Times Book Review. Atlantic* reviewer C. Michael Curtis concurred, adding that "Dillard writes about the ferocity and beauty of natural order with . . . grace."

Elegant writing also distinguishes *Living by Fiction,* Dillard's fourth book, in which the author analyzes the differences between modernist and traditional fiction. "Everyone who timidly, bombastically, reverently, scholastically—even fraudulently—essays to live 'the life of the mind' should read this book," advised Carolyn See in the *Los Angeles Times.* See went on to describe *Living by Fiction* as "somewhere between scholarship, metaphysics, an acid trip and a wonderful conversation with a most smart person." "Whether the field of investigation is nature or fiction, Annie Dillard digs for ultimate meanings as instinctively and as determinedly as hogs for truffles," remarked *Washington Post Book World* contributor John Breslin. "The resulting upheaval can be disconcerting . . . still, uncovered morsels are rich and tasty."

Dillard returned to reflections on nature and religion in a book of essays entitled *Teaching a Stone to Talk: Expeditions and Encounters.* In minutely detailed descriptions of a solar eclipse, visits to South America and the Galapagos Islands, and other, more commonplace events and locations, Dillard continues "the pilgrimage begun at Tinker Creek with an acuity of eye and ear that is matched by an ability to communicate a sense of wonder," stated Beaufort Cranford in the *Detroit News. Washington Post Book World*

contributor Douglas Bauer was similarly pleased with the collection, judging the essays to be "almost uniformly splendid." In his estimation, Dillard's "art as an essayist is to move with the scrutinous eye through events and receptions that are random on their surfaces and to find, with grace and always-redeeming wit, the connections."

Dillard later chronicled her experiences as a member of a Chinese-American cultural exchange in a short, straightforward volume entitled *Encounters with Chinese Writers;* she then looked deeply into her past to produce another best-seller, *An American Childhood.* On one level, *An American Childhood* details Dillard's upbringing in an idiosyncratic, wealthy family; in another sense, the memoir tells the story of a young person's awakening to consciousness. In the words of *Washington Post* writer Charles Trueheart, Dillard's "memories of childhood are like her observations of nature: they feed her acrobatic thinking, and drive the free verse of her prose." Critics also applauded Dillard's keen insight into the unique perceptions of youth, as well as her exuberant spirit. "Loving and lyrical, nostalgic without being wistful, this is a book about the capacity for joy," said *Los Angeles Times Book Review* contributor Cyra McFadden, while Noel Perrin of the *New York Times Book Review* observed that "Ms. Dillard has written an autobiography in semimystical prose about the growth of her own mind, and it's an exceptionally interesting account."

The activity that had occupied most of Dillard's adulthood was the subject of her next book, *The Writing Life.* With regard to content, *The Writing Life* is not a manual on craft nor a guide to getting published; rather, it is a study of a writer at work and the processes involved in that work. Among critics, the book drew mixed reaction. "Annie Dillard is one of my favorite contemporary authors," Sara Maitland acknowledged in the *New York Times Book Review.* "Dillard is a wonderful writer and *The Writing Life* is full of joys. These are clearest to me when she comes at her subject tangentially, talking not of herself at her desk but of other parallel cases—the last chapter, a story about a stunt pilot who was an artist of air, is, quite simply, breathtaking. There are so many bits like this. . . . Unfortunately, the bits do not add up to a book." *Washington Post Book World* contributor Wendy Law-Yone voiced similar sentiments, finding the book "intriguing but not entirely satisfying" and "a sketch rather than a finished portrait." Nevertheless, she wondered, "Can anyone who has ever read Annie Dillard resist hearing what she has to say about writing? Her authority has been clear since *Pilgrim at Tinker Creek*—a mystic's wonder at the physical world expressed in beautiful, near-biblical prose."

Dillard ventured into new territory with her 1992 publication, *The Living,* a sprawling historical novel set in the Pacific Northwest. Reviewers hailed the author's first novel as masterful. "Her triumph is that this panoramic evocation of a very specific landscape and people might as well have been settled upon any other time and place—for this is, above all, a novel about the reiterant, precarious, wondrous, solitary, terrifying, utterly common condition of human life," wrote Molly Gloss in *Washington Post Book World.* Dillard's celebrated skill with words was also much in evidence here, according to Gloss, who noted that Dillard "uses language gracefully, releasing at times a vivid, startling imagery." Carol Anshaw concurred in the *Los Angeles Times Book Review:* "The many readers who have been drawn in the past to Dillard's work for its elegant and muscular language won't be disappointed in these pages."

Following the 1994 publication of *The Annie Dillard Reader,* a collection of poems, stories, and essays that prompted a *Publishers Weekly* reviewer to term Dillard "a writer of acute and singular observation," Dillard produced two works that were published in 1995. *Modern American Memoirs,* which Dillard edited with Cort Conley, is a collection of thirty-five pieces excerpted from various writers' memoirs. Authors whose work appears here include Ralph Ellison, Margaret Mead, Reynolds Price, Kate Simon, and Russell Baker. "Many of these memoirs are striking and memorable despite their brevity," commented Madeline Marget in a *Commonweal* review of the collection.

Mornings Like This: Found Poems, Dillard's other 1995 publication, is an experimental volume of poetry. To create these poems, Dillard culled lines from other writers' prose works—Vincent Van Gogh's letters and a Boy Scout Handbook, for example—and "arranged [the lines] in such a way as to simulate a poem originating with a single author," noted John Haines in *The Hudson Review.* While commenting that Dillard's technique in this book works better with humorous and joyful pieces than with serious ones, a *Publishers Weekly* critic remarked that "these co-op verses are never less than intriguing." Haines expressed serious concern with the implications of Dillard's experiment: "What does work like this say about the legitimacy of authorship?" He concluded,

however, that "on the whole the collection has in places considerable interest."

BIOGRAPHICAL/CRITICAL SOURCES:

BOOKS

Authors and Artists for Young Adults, Volume 6, Gale, 1991.
Contemporary Literary Criticism, Gale, Volume 9, 1978, Volume 60, 1990.
Dictionary of Literary Biography Yearbook: 1980, Gale, 1981.
Ihab, Hassan, *Selves at Risk: Patterns of Quest in Contemporary American Letters,* University of Wisconsin Press, 1991.
Johnson, Sandra Humble, *The Space Between: Literary Epiphany in the Works of Annie Dillard,* Kent State University Press, 1992.
Smith, Linda, *Annie Dillard,* Twayne, 1991.
Something about the Author, Volume 10, Gale, 1976.

PERIODICALS

America, April 20, 1974; February 11, 1978, pp. 363-364; May 6, 1978, pp. 363-64; November 25, 1989, p. 1; November 19, 1994, p. 2.
American Literature, March, 1987.
American Scholar, summer, 1990, p. 445.
Atlantic, December, 1977.
Best Sellers, December, 1977.
Chicago Tribune, October 1, 1987.
Chicago Tribune Book World, September 12, 1982, p. 7; November 21, 1982, p. 5.
Christian Century, November 15, 1989, p. 1063.
Christianity Today, May 5, 1978, pp. 14-9, 30-1; September 14, 1992, p. 46.
Commentary, October, 1974.
Commonweal, October 24, 1975, pp. 495-96; February 3, 1978; March 9, 1990, p. 151; April 5, 1996, p. 32.
Detroit News, October 31, 1982, p. 2H.
English Journal, April, 1989, p. 90; May 1, 1989, p. 69.
Globe and Mail (Toronto), November 28, 1987.
Hudson Review, winter, 1996, p. 666.
Los Angeles Times, April 27, 1982; November 19, 1982.
Los Angeles Times Book Review, October 31, 1982, p. 2; November 18, 1984, p. 11; July 6, 1986, p. 10; September 20, 1987, pp. 1, 14; May 31, 1992, pp. 1, 7.
Ms., August, 1974.

Nation, November 20, 1982, pp. 535-536; October 16, 1989, pp. 435-436; May 25, 1992, p. 692.

New Leader, June 24, 1974; August 10, 1992, p. 17.

New Republic, April 6, 1974.

New Statesmen and Society, December 23, 1988, p. 30; November 9, 1990, p. 34.

Newsweek, June 8, 1992, p. 57.

New Yorker, December 25, 1989, p. 106; July 6, 1992, p. 80.

New York Times, September 21, 1977; March 12 1982, p. C18; November 25, 1982.

New York Times Book Review, March 24, 1974, pp. 4-5; September 25, 1977, pp. 12, 40; May 9, 1982, pp. 10, 22-23; July 1, 1979, p. 21; November 28, 1982, pp. 13, 19; January 1, 1984, p. 32; September 23, 1984, p. 29; September 27, 1987, p. 7; September 17, 1989, p. 15; May 3, 1992, p. 9.

New York Times Magazine, April 26, 1992, p. 34.

People, October 19, 1987, p. 99.

Publishers Weekly, September 1, 1989, pp. 67-68; October 31, 1994, p. 45; April 24, 1995, p. 65.

Reason, April, 1990, p. 56.

South Atlantic Quarterly, spring, 1986, pp. 111-122.

Threepenny Review, summer, 1988.

Time, March 18, 1974; October 10, 1977.

Tribune Books (Chicago), September 13, 1987, pp. 1, 12; December 18, 1988, p. 3; August 27, 1989, p. 6.

Village Voice, July 13, 1982, pp. 40-41.

Virginia Quarterly Review, autumn, 1974, pp. 637-40; spring, 1996, p. 57.

Washington Post, October 28, 1987.

Washington Post Book World, October 16, 1977, p. E6; April 4, 1982, p. 4; January 2, 1983, p. 6; September 9, 1984, p. 6; July 6, 1986, p. 13; September 6, 1987, p. 11; August 14, 1988, p. 12; August 27, 1989, p. 6; September 24, 1989, p. 4, May 3, 1992, pp. 1-2.

Yale Review, October, 1992, p. 102.

* * *

DOAK, Annie
See DILLARD, Annie

* * *

DODGE, Steve
See BECKER, Stephen (David)

DONLEAVY, J(ames) P(atrick) 1926-

PERSONAL: Born April 23, 1926, in Brooklyn, NY; became Irish citizen, 1967; married Valerie Heron (divorced); married Mary Wilson Price, 1970 (divorced); children: (first marriage) Philip, Karen; (second marriage) Rebecca Wallis, Rory. *Education:* Attended Trinity College, Dublin.

ADDRESSES: Home and office—Levington Park, Mullingar, County Westmeath, Ireland.

CAREER: Writer and playwright. Founder with son Philip Donleavy and producer Robert Mitchell of De Alfonce Tennis Association for the Promotion of the Superlative Game of Eccentric Champions. *Military service:* U.S. Navy, served in World War II.

AWARDS, HONORS: Most Promising Playwright Award, *Evening Standard,* 1960, for *Fairy Tales of New York;* Brandeis University Creative Arts Award, 1961-62, for two plays, *The Ginger Man* and *Fairy Tales of New York;* citation from National Institute and American Academy of Arts and Letters, 1975; American Academy of Arts and Letters grantee, 1975; Worldfest Houston Gold Award, 1992; Cine Golden Eagle Award for writer and narrator, 1993.

WRITINGS:

FICTION

The Ginger Man (novel; also see below), Olympia Press (Paris), 1955, published with introduction by Arland Ussher, Spearman (London), 1956, Obolensky (New York City), 1958, complete and unexpurgated edition, Delacorte (New York City), 1965.

A Singular Man (novel), Little, Brown (Boston), 1963.

Meet My Maker the Mad Molecule (short stories; also see below), Little, Brown, 1964, reprinted, Penguin (New York City), 1981.

The Saddest Summer of Samuel S (novel; also see below), Delacorte/Seymour Lawrence (New York City), 1966.

The Beastly Beatitudes of Balthazar B (novel), Delacorte/Seymour Lawrence, 1968.

The Onion Eaters (novel), Delacorte, 1971, reprinted, Penguin/Eyre & Spottiswoode (Andover, England), 1986.

A Fairy Tale of New York (novel; also see below), Delacorte/Seymour Lawrence, 1973.

The Destinies of Darcy Dancer, Gentleman (novel), illustrations by Jim Campbell, Delacorte/Seymour Lawrence, 1977.

Schultz (novel), Delacorte/Seymour Lawrence, 1979.

"Meet My Maker the Mad Molecule" and *"The Saddest Summer of Samuel S,"* Dell (New York City), 1979.

Leila: Further in the Destinies of Darcy Dancer, Gentleman (novel; sequel to *The Destinies of Darcy Dancer, Gentleman*), Delacorte/Seymour Lawrence, 1983, published as limited edition with *A Special Message for the First Edition from J. P. Donleavy*, Franklin Library, 1983, published in England as *Leila: Further in the Life and Destinies of Darcy Dancer, Gentleman*, Allen Lane (London), 1983.

Are You Listening Rabbi Loew (novel; sequel to *Schultz*), Viking (New York City), 1987.

That Darcy, That Dancer, That Gentleman (novel; sequel to *Leila*), Viking, 1990.

The Lady Who Liked Clean Rest Rooms: The Chronicle of One of the Strangest Stories Ever to Be Rumored about around New York (novella), St. Martin's (New York City), 1997.

PLAYS

The Ginger Man (adaptation of his novel of same title; first produced at Fortune Theatre, London, September 15, 1959; produced at Gaiety Theatre, Dublin, October 26, 1959; produced on Broadway at Orpheum Theatre, November 21, 1963; contains introduction "What They Did in Dublin"; also see below), Random House (New York City), 1961, published in England as *What They Did in Dublin with The Ginger Man*, MacGibbon and Kee (London), 1961 (also see below).

Fairy Tales of New York (adaptation of his novel *A Fairy Tale of New York;* first produced at Comedy Theatre, London, January 24, 1961; also see below), Random House, 1961.

A Singular Man (first produced at Comedy Theatre, October 21, 1964; produced at Westport County [CT] Playhouse, September 4, 1967; also see below), Bodley Head (London), 1964.

The Plays of J. P. Donleavy (with a preface by the author; contains *What They Did in Dublin with The Ginger Man, The Ginger Man, Fairy Tales of New York, A Singular Man,* and *The Saddest Summer of Samuel S*), photographs of productions by Lewis Morley, Delacorte/Seymour Lawrence, 1973.

The Beastly Beatitudes of Balthazar B (adaptation of his novel of same title), first produced in London, 1981.

Also author of radio play, *Helen,* 1956.

OTHER

The Unexpurgated Code: A Complete Manual of Survival and Manners, illustrations by the author, Delacorte/Seymour Lawrence, 1975.

De Alfonce Tennis: The Superlative Game of Eccentric Champions, Its History, Accoutrements, Rules, Conduct, and Regimen, Dutton (New York City)/Seymour Lawrence, 1984.

J. P. Donleavy's Ireland: In All Her Sins and in Some of Her Graces, Viking, 1986, published in England as *Ireland: In All Her Sins and in Some of Her Graces,* M. Joseph (London), 1986.

A Singular Country, Ryan (Peterborough, England), 1989, Norton (New York City), 1990.

The History of the Ginger Man, Houghton (Boston), 1994.

Contributor of short fiction and essays to *Atlantic Monthly, Playboy, Queen, Saturday Evening Post,* and *Saturday Review.*

SIDELIGHTS: "If there is an archetypal post-World War II American writer-in-exile it may well be James Patrick Donleavy," writes William E. Grant in a *Dictionary of Literary Biography* essay. The son of Irish immigrant parents, J. P. Donleavy renounced the America of their dreams for an Ireland of his own, and became a citizen when Ireland granted tax-free status to its authors. Although literary success came several years after the publication of his stylistically innovative first novel, *The Ginger Man,* Donleavy is now internationally recognized for having written what many consider to be a modern classic. Referring to the "sense of exile and alienation that seems to haunt his life as well as his work," Grant observes that "even achieving the literary success he thought America would deny him has not lessened his alienation from his country, though it has enhanced the style in which he expresses his exile status." Donleavy now writes at his expansive two-hundred-year-old manor situated on nearly two hundred acres in County Westmeath. "He's a sort of born-again Irishman who enthusiastically embraces the life of a man of letters and leisure, adopting not only an Irish country estate but also the appropriate deportment and brogue," says Peter Ross in the *Detroit News.* "He also happens to be one of the funniest and most audacious writers around."

Donleavy's decision to emigrate, although precipitated by difficulty finding a publisher for his first novel, appears to have been the result of a slowly evolving dissatisfaction with what he refers to in his *Atlantic Monthly* essay, "An Expatriate Looks at America," as "a country corrosive of the spirit." Donleavy explains: "Each time I go to these United States I start anew trying to figure them out. After two weeks I decide that like anywhere, greed, lust and envy make them work. But in America it is big greed, big lust, big envy." Although Donleavy remembers his childhood in the Bronx as peaceful, New York City became an increasingly threatening presence, and the ubiquitous violence made him fearful of death there. He recalls in the *Atlantic Monthly* that "something in one's bowels was saying no to this land. Where my childhood friends were growing up, just as their parents did, to be trapped trembling and terrified in a nightmare." Skeptical of America's treatment of its artists as well, Donleavy felt at the outset of his career that he stood little chance of achieving literary success in a land he describes in the *Atlantic Monthly* as a place "where your media mesmerized brain shuts off when the media does." He adds, "And if I stayed they would, without even trying, or knowing, kill me."

Donleavy was resolved to achieve recognition and relates in a *Paris Review* interview with Molly McKaughan: "I realized that the only way you could ever tackle the world was to write something that no one could hold off, a book that would go everywhere, into everyone's hands. And I decided then to write a novel which would shake the world. I shook my fist and said I would do it." That novel, *The Ginger Man,* is set in post-World War II Dublin and details the hedonistic existence of Sebastian Dangerfield who, according to Alfred Rushton in the Toronto *Globe and Mail,* gave "moral turpitude a new lease on life." While still a student, Donleavy began crafting the novel, but he returned to New York to complete and publish it. He indicates in the *Paris Review* that Scribners, to whom he first took the manuscript, thought it was one of the best ever brought to them; its content, however, prevented them from publishing it. Forty-five publishers rejected the novel because they "thought it was a dirty book—scatological, unreadable, obscene," Donleavy tells David Remnick in the *Washington Post.* "My life literally depended on getting this book into print, and when I couldn't, it just drove me out of America."

In the *Paris Review,* Donleavy recalls his reluctance to edit *The Ginger Man* into acceptability: "I had a sense that the book held itself together on the basis of these scatological parts. That its life was in these

parts. And I was quite aware that cutting them would be severely damaging to it." Brendan Behan, the legendary Irish playwright and patriot with whom Donleavy became friends during his Dublin days, suggested sending the manuscript to the Olympia Press in Paris, where it eventually was accepted. Following its publication as part of an overtly pornographic series, however, a lengthy legal battle ensued in which Donleavy emerged as the owner of the publishing house. Despite "the potential for literary damage, publication by Olympia Press had the generally salutary effect of establishing the unexpurgated edition of *The Ginger Man* as an underground classic before complete editions became available," notes Grant. In order to ensure the novel's publication in England, though, and to get it recognized and reviewed, Donleavy agreed to certain cuts, stating in the *Paris Review:* "It was an act of pure practicality. If someone wanted to read the unexpurgated edition, they could buy it in Paris. I had published it as I had written it, so it wasn't wrong, then, to publish it to establish my reputation."

Although Donleavy's reputation had to endure both court battles and censors, his experience as a litigant proved invaluable in negotiating subsequent contracts with publishers. "He's very courtly, but he's a very sharp businessman," comments Donleavy's longtime publisher Seymour Lawrence, according to Samuel Allis in the *Washington Post.* "He does all of his negotiating and, unlike most authors, he understands copyrights. He drives a hard bargain, but he's the most professional author I've ever known." Donleavy's legal and business dealings have also given him a special sense of his profession. Money, says the author in the *Paris Review,* has a dramatic effect upon his writing: "In fact, I would say that money is everything in my profession. One's mind almost becomes a vast cash register. . . . To sit at a desk and think, and write, you must have peace, and to buy peace costs a fortune."

In 1994 Donleavy's *The History of the Ginger Man* was published. In the book Donleavy chronicles his efforts to publish *The Ginger Man* and recounts his struggles to become a writer while supporting his family. The author also reprints his entire correspondence with Olympia Press publisher Maurice Girodias, with whom Donleavy waged a protracted battle for the rights to the novel. Even before the publication of *The History of the Ginger Man,* critics recognized the autobiographical aspects of Donleavy's best-known novel. Sally Eckhoff, writing in the *Voice Literary Supplement,* observes: "In Dangerfield,

Donleavy created his prototypical diver into Irish society. Like his hero, the author has a history of Olympic pub-crawling—right down there under the rug with Flann O'Brien." Eckhoff also notes that Donleavy's writing exhibits a strong sense of setting. "Most of *The Ginger Man,*" writes Eckhoff, "takes place in Dublin—the world of dreams, populated by gullible shopkeepers, screaming kids, crooked priests, affectionate laundrywomen with time on their hands, and a pub on every corner with a weird name like 'The Bleeding Horse.'"

Critics were unsure at first how to categorize Donleavy and *The Ginger Man.* Grant observes that the critical establishment "debated whether Donleavy belonged with Britain's Angry Young Men, America's black humorists, or France's existentialists." In his *Doings and Undoings,* Norman Podhoretz calls *The Ginger Man* "fundamentally a book without hope." Similarly, in his *Radical Innocence: Studies in the Contemporary American Novel,* Ihab Hassan considers the novel to be "full of gusto, seething with life, but its energy may be the energy of negation, and its vitality has a nasty edge." The nihilism in *The Ginger Man* "refers us to the postwar, existential era," states Hassan. "Traditional values are not in the process of dying, they have ceased entirely to operate, and their stark absence leaves men to shift for themselves as best they can." The "freshness" of the characterization of Sebastian Dangerfield was one of the most critically acclaimed aspects of the novel, notes Grant, who adds that some critics recognized that the character "existed almost totally outside any system of ideas." Eckhoff calls *The Ginger Man* "a hilarious, cruel, compassionate book."

Despite the commercial success of Donleavy's subsequent work, the critics generally consider his reputation to rest solely on *The Ginger Man.* "So far as most critics and reviewers are concerned, the later works have been but pale shadows of the first brilliant success, and the publication of each succeeding novel has seen a decline in critical attention," writes Grant. Some critics believe that Donleavy has run out of ideas, that he is refurbishing old material, reworking or resurrecting earlier work. For instance, in a *Harper's* review of *The Destinies of Darcy Dancer, Gentleman,* Michael Malone compares a Donleavy book to Guinness stout: "It's distinctive, it's carbonated, it's brimmed with what Hazlitt called 'gusto,' and those who like it can drink it forever. The ingredients never change." Donleavy pays attention to the critics only in a "fairly superficial way" because, as he says in the *Paris Review,* "A writer must always

be aware that he has to be a supreme critic. . . . And only his judgement matters." Allis indicates, however, that Donleavy "displays something close to hostility toward academics and the people who review his books and plays," and that he discourages academic interest in his work because he says, "I never want [to] get that self-conscious of my literary position." Grant suggests that "though none individually rivals the first masterpiece, several of these later works deserve wider attention than they have had from the American reading public and critical establishment alike."

Critics point to several characteristics of *The Ginger Man* that surface in Donleavy's later work. Beneath the bawdy humor lies an inherent despondency, with licentiousness masking the more profound search for love; bizarre, eccentric characters, around whom his books revolve, tend to be alienated, victimized by life, and weakened by impending death. "The novels range from variations of the humorous—slapstick, scatological, sardonic—to the sentimental in an idiosyncratic style that conveys the pressure of time on language," writes Thomas LeClair in *Contemporary Literature.* "But such features of Donleavy's work are finally extensions of and returns to death, the test of man's mettle in landscapes made pale by death's presence."

An awareness of death figures significantly in Donleavy's work, and the question Donleavy's heroes "answer in their own, progressively inefficacious ways," writes LeClair in *Twentieth Century Literature,* is, "How does a man weakened by an awareness of death survive in a world experienced as magical with malevolence?" LeClair observes that "to evade his consciousness of mortality, Sebastian Dangerfield . . . lives a hedonistic life in the present and dreams of relaxed ease for the future"; and the rich and reclusive George Smith of Donleavy's *A Singular Man,* who is absorbed with the idea of death and even builds his own mausoleum, "separates himself from the world in a parody of Howard Hughes' and John Paul Getty's attempts to avoid the disease of life." LeClair notes in *Critique: Studies in Modern Fiction* that "the heroes of *The Saddest Summer of Samuel S, The Beastly Beatitudes of Balthazar B,* and *The Onion Eaters* all attempt to overcome their fear of their own death or their sadness about the death of others through love."

According to Grant, the themes of love and loss are also important in much of Donleavy's work. *The Saddest Summer of Samuel S* is about an eminent literary figure in the United States who undergoes psychoanalysis in Vienna in order to live a more conventional life. Of this novel, Grant writes: "Longing for a love he has never had and cannot find because in spite of his need he cannot give, Samuel S is the victim of a life that cannot be lived over and a destiny that cannot be changed." The character, observes Grant, is withdrawn and "trapped in a life-in-death state of mind with neither belief nor passion to motivate him." Similarly, in *The Beastly Beatitudes of Balthazar B,* a novel that details the lonely life of a wealthy young man whose marriage collapses, the hero is "separated from those he loves . . . and seeks completion by loving others, a simple but impossible quest," says Shaun O'Connell in the *Nation.* Robert Scholes observes in the *Saturday Review* that although this "shy and gentle" character seeks love, "it proves elusive, even harder to keep than to find." And O'Connell sees in Donleavy "the joy of the artist who can embody his vision, however bleak, the self-certainty of the writer who can so eloquently move his hero to name his pain."

However, writing in the *Washington Post Book World* about Donleavy's *The Destinies of Darcy Dancer, Gentleman,* a novel in which a young aristocrat is thwarted in several of his attempts at love, Curt Suplee suggests that "Donleavy does not write novels so much as Oedipal fairy tales: semi-realistic fables in which the same patterns are obsessively reenacted. Invariably, a young man finds himself trapped in a society dominated by hostile father-figures and devoid of the uncritical comfort afforded by mothers. . . . Every time the young man attempts to assert his ego in this world, he fails or is beaten, and flees to succour—either to the manic medium of alcohol or the overt mother-surrogates who provide sex and self-esteem, for a while." O'Connell finds, though, that Donleavy's characters "press the possibilities of life with high style and win many tactical victories of great hilarity . . . before they are defeated," and he believes that "Donleavy's vision of sadness seems earned, won by a search of all the possible routes toward happiness."

Focusing on the bawdy humor in Donleavy's work, critics sometimes fault it for what they consider to be gratuitously lewd language and a reliance upon sexual slapstick. A *Times Literary Supplement* reviewer of *The Onion Eaters,* for instance, states that "the scenes of violence and the sexual encounters suggest an attitude to the human body and its functions, weaknesses and pleasures, which is anything but tender, compassionate, or celebratory." The novel is about a young

and handsome character named Clayton Claw Clever Clementine, who in addition to being somewhat freakishly over-endowed sexually, has inherited an Irish manor and must confront what a *New Statesman* contributor refers to as a "bizarre collection of servants and . . . an ever-growing crew of sex-obsessed weirdies." Guy Davenport finds in the *National Review* that "Donleavy is uninterruptedly bawdy, yet his obscenity is so grand and so open, that it rises above giving offense into a realm of its own, unchallenged and wild."

Critics also recognize, however, that Donleavy's humor belies an inherent sadness. "Donleavy writes sad and lonely books," says R. Z. Sheppard in a *Time* review of *The Onion Eaters.* Sheppard finds that Donleavy's fictional worlds are "closed worlds, their boundaries no more distant than the most prominent erectile tissue. Alone, without context or meaning, the flesh is all." Sheppard suggests that the absence of meaning in the novel, as well as its "animal warmth, at once grotesque and touching," is perhaps Donleavy's way of asserting that "this warmth is the only thing about which we can be certain."

Writing in *Newsweek* about Donleavy's nonfiction book *The Unexpurgated Code: A Complete Manual of Survival and Manners,* Arthur Cooper describes Donleavy's humor: "Like Mel Brooks, he knows that bad taste is merely a joke that doesn't get a laugh. And like Brooks, Donleavy's demonic humor is utterly democratic, thrusting the needle into everyone regardless of race, creed, color, or ability to control one's bowels." Referring to the book as "a collection of bilious and often funny rules for living," Melvin Maddocks observes in *Time* that "between the lines, Donleavy's diatribes manage to say more." Maddocks believes that Donleavy's "visions of grace, chivalry and order" reveal the author as "an inverted romantic, profoundly sad beneath his disguise because he and the world are no better than they happen to be."

Similarly, in a *Midwest Quarterly* assessment of *The Unexpurgated Code,* Charles G. Masinton suggests that "Donleavy normally proceeds by means of instinct, inspiration, and intuition—the tools of a romantic artist. He aims to produce belly laughs and . . . a sympathetic response to his chief characters; he does not set out to impose order and rationality on experience. And instead of elevated language (which he often parodies quite effectively), he records with great skill an earthy vernacular full of both comic and lyric possibilities." While Grant believes that Donleavy's "characteristic tone of pessimism, melancholia, alienation, and human failure . . . suggest Jonathan Swift's misanthropic humor," he also finds it reminiscent of Mark Twain's later work, "which combines pessimism and humor in an elegiac, melancholic, and misanthropic voice."

In the *Los Angeles Times Book Review,* David Hirson laments that while a unique blend of lyricism and farce still characterize Donleavy's later novels, his humor has begun to be derived almost exclusively from overkill. An example is *Are You Listening Rabbi Loew.* Despite its "dauntingly energetic prose," Hirson believes that the novel ultimately wears out the reader. Writes Hirson, "Funny though boorishness, bodily functions and excessive profanity can be, the effect, finally, is of a joke that takes too long in the telling, a numbingly protracted jape."

The style and language of Donleavy's fiction has attracted a great deal of critical attention over the years. Notes Thomas Lask, "critics keep citing his first book . . . some saying that nothing after it has equaled that first effort, and objecting to his language, which has a syntax of its own, without connectives or prepositions, shifting tense at will." Stylistically innovative, *The Ginger Man* employs not only a shifting point of view (from first to third person) so that Dangerfield becomes both observer and observed but, according to Grant, it "relies on rapidly moving, nearly staccato sentence fragments which capture brilliantly the chaotic and fragmented qualities of Dangerfield's world." In a *Times Literary Supplement* review of *That Darcy, That Dancer, That Gentleman* (the third volume in the trilogy that began with *The Destinies of Darcy Dancer, Gentleman*), Mark Sanderson observes that Donleavy's unusual use of language masks the thinness of the novel's plot. "The stylistic tics remain," writes Sanderson, "a fondness for the present continuous; hyphens reserved for double-barreled surnames; each chapter rounded off by a homespun haiku; semi-colons and question marks entirely absent."

Donleavy explains that his use of language is "designed to reflect the way the mind works," says Lask in a *New York Times* review of *Schultz,* a novel about the exploits of an American producer of vulgar plays in London. In the *Paris Review,* Donleavy offers a more detailed explanation: "You're trying to get what you've written on your page into a reader's mind as quickly as possible, and to keep them seeing it. That is why I use the short, truncated telegraphic sentences. They are the most efficient use of language,

and I think the brain puts words together the way I do."

Some critics think Donleavy has become a "prisoner of style," says Paul Abelman in the *Spectator,* that "he has never escaped from the prose techniques which he invented for his fine first novel." Abelman believes that "the style of the later books is not really that of *The Ginger Man* at all but simply one that employs superficial aspects of it and neglects the lyrical essence." Unlike *The Ginger Man,* says Abelman, the other books are "monster prose poems founded on the most plodding, leaden metrical foot known to the English language [the spondee—two stressed syllables regularly repeated]." Abelman, though, considers Donleavy "possibly the greatest lyrical humorist to emerge since the war," and adds that he "has that to his credit which few living writers can claim: a modern classic."

Although Donleavy indicates to Thomas Lask in the *New York Times* that he's as "delighted" with *The Ginger Man* as when he first wrote it, he feels that his subsequent books keep *The Ginger Man* alive. Commenting to Remnick that he does not feel *The Ginger Man* represents his "best work," Donleavy states, "When I pick it up and read it now critically as a piece of writing, in technical terms, it doesn't compare to later books." Acknowledging in the *Paris Review* that his subsequent writing has not provided the pleasure that *The Ginger Man* did, Donleavy says: "I don't think you ever have that again. When an author's recognized, all that leaves him, because that's what he's needed to force himself to go through the terrible agony of being unknown and being able to face the world and the fact that it's a giant, vast place where nearly every man is saying: Dear God, hear my tiny voice."

Another point of interest for critics of Donleavy's writing is the effect that leaving the United States for Ireland has had on the author. Grant believes that "Donleavy remains essentially the exile who once wrote of America, 'there it goes, a runaway horse, with no one in control.'" Donleavy recalls in his *Atlantic Monthly* essay, that "each time you arrive anew in America, you find how small you are and how dismally you impress against the giantness and power of this country where you are so obviously, and with millions like yourself, so totally fatally expendable." Grant notes that this vision is often expressed in Donleavy's portrayal of the United States as a nightmare. In *A Fairy Tale of New York,* for instance, the wife of the Brooklyn-born, Bronx-raised, and European-educated Cornelius Christian dies on their way to New York; and without money or friends, Christian is taken advantage of by everyone. "Affection, loathing, nostalgia and fear are the main components of the attitude he brings to bear upon his native place," writes Julian Moynahan in the *Washington Post Book World,* adding that "hidden away in the book for those who can find it is a good deal of personal revelation, a good deal of alembicated and metamorphosed autobiography." As D. Keith Mano states in the *New York Times Book Review,* the book is "about social impotence and despair. Valleys of humiliation, sloughs of despond." The story focuses on the brutality of New York City; and Christian, who lacks the funds to move, sees emigration as the only answer to his liberation. "Yet Donleavy's thunderous, superb humor has the efficacy of grace," says Mano. "It heals and conquers and ratifies." And a *Times Literary Supplement* contributor, who remarks that "few writers know how to enjoy verbal promiscuity like . . . Donleavy," considers that "it is largely because of the confidence of the style, too, that you come out of the welter of failure and misery feeling good—nastiness is inevitably laced with hilarity and sentiment in his telling it."

Moving to Ireland changed his life "utterly," Donleavy says in the *Paris Review,* adding, "It also romanticized the United States for me so that it became a subject for me as a writer." However, in the *Atlantic Monthly,* Donleavy speaks about the indelibility of his American beginnings: "As far away as you may go, or as foreign as your life can ever become, there is something that always stays stained American in you." About living among the Irish, however, Donleavy remarks in a *Publishers Weekly* interview: "Literally, everywhere you go here, they're half nuts. It's very tough to discover real insanity, because the whole race is like that, and, indeed, this is the place to come if you're not right in the head."

John Kelly writes in the *Times Literary Supplement* that "during a disconsolate return to his native America," Donleavy discovered that "Ireland is a state of mind" and his recent *J. P. Donleavy's Ireland: In All Her Sins and in Some of Her Graces* "attempts a description of that state of mind." Donleavy recreates his own first exposure to the postwar Dublin that, says Kelly, provided the "raw material" for "Donleavy's myth-making imagination." In

a Toronto *Globe and Mail* review of the book, Rushton thinks that "Donleavy belongs to the people he describes, and acknowledges their kinship by giving them their full due." As Kevin E. Gallagher comments in the *Los Angeles Times Book Review,* it is "a love story that, I think never ends for anyone who cares, like this, about a place."

Although Donleavy's *The Ginger Man* remains the standard by which the entirety of his work is measured, his writing has generated the full spectrum of critical response. Ken Lawless in an *Antioch Review* of *The Destinies of Darcy Dancer, Gentleman,* for example, writes that "no literary artist working in English today is better than J. P. Donleavy, and few merit comparison with him." On the other hand, in the *New York Times Book Review,* Geoffrey Wolff reacts to similar critical assessments of Donleavy's work with: "Nonsense. He is an Irish tenor who sets his blarney to short songs that are sometimes as soft as velvet or good stout, sometimes plangent, elliptical and coarse." However, Grant suggests that "at the very least, he represents the example of a writer who goes very much his own way, eschewing both the popular success of the best-sellers and the literary acclaim of the academic establishment. At best, a case can be made for a few of his novels as primary expressions within the black humorist tradition of modern literature. Certainly he is a foremost American exponent of the Kafkaesque vision of the modern world, and his better works strongly express that sense of universal absurdity at which we can only laugh."

"After all my years of struggle, it makes me realize that in my own way I have conquered America, totally silently, totally from underground and from within and that television or being interviewed doesn't matter," Donleavy relates in the *Paris Review.* In his *Saturday Review* essay, "The Author and His Image," Donleavy ponders the complexities of an author's image in its various aspects from obscurity through success, and concludes: "But you know no matter what you do the world will always finally turn its face away. Back into all its own troubled lives. . . . Forgetting what you wanted them to see. Silent with what you wanted them to say. And empty with what you wanted them to feel. Except somewhere you know there will be a voice. At least once asking. Hey what happened to that guy, did he die, you know the one, who wrote that book, can't remember his name but he was famous as hell. That was the author. And that was his image."

BIOGRAPHICAL/CRITICAL SOURCES:

BOOKS

Authors in the News, Volume 2, Gale (Detroit), 1976.

Contemporary Fiction in America and England, 1950-1970, Gale, 1976.

Contemporary Literary Criticism, Gale, Volume 1, 1973, Volume 4, 1975, Volume 6, 1976, Volume 10, 1979, Volume 45, 1987.

Dictionary of Literary Biography, Volume 6: *American Novelists since World War II,* Gale, 1980.

Donleavy, J. P., *The Ginger Man,* Olympia Press, 1955, published with introduction by Arland Ussher, Spearman, 1956, Obolensky, 1958, complete and unexpurgated edition, Delacorte, 1965.

Donleavy, J. P., *J. P. Donleavy's Ireland: In All Her Sins and in Some of Her Graces,* Viking, 1986.

Donleavy, J. P., *A Singular Country,* Ryan, 1989, Norton, 1990.

Donleavy, J. P., *The History of the Ginger Man,* Houghton, 1994.

Hassan, Ihab, *Radical Innocence: Studies in the Contemporary American Novel,* Princeton University Press (Princeton, NJ), 1961.

Masinton, Charles G., *J. P. Donleavy: The Style of His Sadness and Humor,* Popular Press, 1975.

Podhoretz, Norman, *Doings and Undoings,* Farrar, Straus (New York City), 1964.

Sharma, R. K., *Isolation and Protest: A Case Study of J. P. Donleavy's Fiction,* Ajanta (New Delhi), 1983.

PERIODICALS

America, May 3, 1969; May 10, 1980.

Antioch Review, winter, 1978; winter, 1980, p. 122.

Architectural Digest, November, 1986.

Atlantic Monthly, December, 1968; December, 1976; December, 1977; June, 1979.

Books, November, 1987, p. 29.

Chicago Tribune, May 25, 1958; May 19, 1985.

Chicago Tribune Book World, October 28, 1979.

Commonweal, August 15, 1958; December 2, 1966; March 7, 1969; September 14, 1990, p. 518.

Contemporary Literature, Volume 12, number 3, 1971.

Critique: Studies in Modern Fiction, Volume 9, number 2, 1966; Volume 12, number 3, 1971; Volume 17, number 1, 1975.

Detroit News, October 2, 1983; June 9, 1985.

Economist, November 10, 1973.

Gentleman's Quarterly, April, 1994, p. 88.

Globe and Mail (Toronto), October 13, 1984; January 17, 1987; April 18, 1987.

Harper's, December, 1977.

Listener, May 11, 1978; December 13, 1984, p. 30; October 29, 1987, p. 32; November 2, 1989, p. 35; November 1, 1990, p. 34.

Los Angeles Times, October 28, 1983.

Los Angeles Times Book Review, October 7, 1979; May 5, 1985, p. 11; November 16, 1986, p. 11; November 13, 1988, p. 7; May 1, 1994, p. 8.

Michigan Academician, winter, 1974; summer, 1976.

Midcontinent American Studies Journal, spring, 1967.

Midwest Quarterly, winter, 1977.

Nation, May 24, 1958; December 14, 1963; January 20, 1969.

National Review, October 18, 1971.

New Leader, December 19, 1977.

New Republic, December 14, 1963; March 1, 1969; July 24, 1971; December 15, 1979.

New Statesman, April 17, 1964; February 7, 1969; July 16, 1971; May 12, 1978; March 28, 1980, p. 483; October 14, 1983.

Newsweek, November 11, 1963; March 21, 1966; November 18, 1968; September 15, 1975.

New Yorker, October 25, 1958; May 16, 1964; October 15, 1966; October 8, 1973; December 19, 1977; July 16, 1990.

New York Herald Tribune Book Review, May 11, 1958.

New York Review of Books, January 2, 1969.

New York Times, May 11, 1958; November 16, 1979; April 17, 1987; October 12, 1988.

New York Times Book Review, November 24, 1963; November 7, 1965; December 5, 1965; March 20, 1966; December 29, 1968; September 5, 1971; September 23, 1973; November 6, 1977; October 7, 1979, p. 14; October 26, 1980; October 11, 1983; October 30, 1983; April 28, 1985, p. 24; November 27, 1988, p. 22; March 4, 1990, p. 38; December 2, 1990, p. 72.

Observer (London), October 28, 1984, p. 25; July 6, 1986, p. 24; November 8, 1987, p.28; November 4, 1990, p. 61.

Paris Review, fall, 1975.

Playboy, May, 1994, p. 34.

Publishers Weekly, October 31, 1986.

Punch, October 21, 1987, p. 64.

Saturday Review, May 10, 1958; November 23, 1963; November 23, 1968; November 12, 1977; January 20, 1979.

Spectator, September 22, 1973; May 13, 1978; April 12, 1980; December 8, 1984, p. 33; July 19, 1986, p. 29; November 28, 1987, p. 36.

Studies in Contemporary Satire, Number 1, 1975.

Time, March 18, 1966; December 6, 1968; July 5, 1971; October 29, 1973; September 22, 1975; November 14, 1977; October 15, 1979.

Times (London), October 13, 1983; July 17, 1986, p. 15; October 29, 1987.

Times Literary Supplement, April 30, 1964; May 6, 1965; May 5, 1967; March 20, 1969; July 23, 1971; September 7, 1973; May 12, 1978; April 4, 1980, p. 382; October 28, 1983, p. 1185; November 16, 1984, p. 1302; December 19, 1986, p. 1433; February 1, 1991, p. 10; June 24, 1994, p. 36.

Tribune Books (Chicago), January 25, 1987, p. 6; October 2, 1988, p. 7; June 5, 1994, p. 5.

Twentieth Century Literature, January, 1968; July, 1972.

Village Voice, September 17, 1979.

Virginia Quarterly Review, spring, 1987, p. 56.

Voice Literary Supplement, October, 1988, p. 28.

Washington Post, October 30, 1979; February 24, 1985.

Washington Post Book World, September 30, 1973; November 13, 1977.

World Literature Today, summer, 1978; summer, 1980, p. 431; spring, 1984.

Yale Review, October, 1966.*

* * *

DOUGLAS, Arthur
See HAMMOND, Gerald (Arthur Douglas)

* * *

DUNCAN, Robert (Edward) 1919-1988
(Robert Edward Symmes)

PERSONAL: Born January 7, 1919, in Oakland, CA; died January 7, 1988, of a heart attack in San Francisco, CA; name at birth, Edward Howard Duncan; son of Edward Howard (a day laborer) and Marguerite (Wesley) Duncan (who died at the time of his birth); adopted, March 10, 1920, by Edwin Joseph (an architect) and Minnehaha (Harris) Symmes; adopted name, Robert Edward Symmes; in 1941 he took the name Robert Duncan; companion of Jess Collins (a painter). *Education:* Attended University of California, Berkeley, 1936-38, 1948-50, studying the civilization of the Middle Ages under Ernst Kantorowicz.

CAREER: Poet. Worked at various times as a dishwasher and typist. Organizer of poetry readings and workshops in San Francisco Bay area; *Experimental Review,* co-editor with Sanders Russell, publishing works of Henry Miller, Anais Nin, Lawrence Durrell, Kenneth Patchen, William Everson, Aurora Bligh (Mary Fabilli), Thomas Merton, Robert Horan, and Jack Johnson, 1940-41; *Berkeley Miscellany,* editor, 1948-49; lived in Banyalbufar, Majorca, 1955-56; taught at Black Mountain College, Black Mountain, NC, spring and summer, 1956; assistant director of Poetry Center, San Francisco State College, under a Ford grant, 1956-57; associated with the Creative Writing Workshop, University of British Columbia, 1963; lecturer in Advanced Poetry Workshop, San Francisco State College, spring, 1965. *Military service:* U.S. Army, 1941; discharged on psychological grounds.

AWARDS, HONORS: Ford Foundation grant, 1956-57; Union League Civic and Arts Foundation Prize, *Poetry* magazine, 1957; Harriet Monroe Prize, *Poetry,* 1961; Guggenheim fellowship, 1963-64; Levinson Prize, *Poetry,* 1964; Miles Poetry Prize, 1964; National Endowment for the Arts grants, 1965, 1966-67; Eunice Tietjens Memorial Prize, *Poetry,* 1967; nomination for National Book Critics Circle Award, 1984, for *Ground Work: Before the War;* first recipient of National Poetry Award, 1985, in recognition of lifetime contribution to the art of poetry; Before Columbus Foundation American Book Award, 1986, for *Ground Work: Before the War;* Fred Cody Award for Lifetime Literary Excellence from Bay Area Book Reviewers Association, 1986.

WRITINGS:

Heavenly City, Earthly City (poems, 1945-46), drawings by Mary Fabilli, Bern Porter, 1947.

Medieval Scenes (poems, 1947), Centaur Press (San Francisco), 1950, reprinted with preface by Duncan and afterword by Robert Bertholf, Kent State University Libraries, 1978.

Poems, 1948-49 (actually written between November, 1947 and October, 1948), Berkeley Miscellany, 1950.

The Song of the Border-Guard (poem), Black Mountain Graphics Workshop, 1951.

The Artist's View, [San Francisco], 1952.

Fragments of a Disordered Devotion, privately printed, 1952, reprinted, Gnomon Press, 1966.

Caesar's Gate: Poems, 1949-55, Divers Press (Majorca), 1956, 2nd edition, Sand Dollar, 1972.

Letters (poems, 1953-56), drawings by Duncan, J. Williams (Highlands, NC), 1958.

Faust Foutu: Act One of Four Acts, A Comic Mask, 1952-1954 (an entertainment in four parts; first produced in San Francisco, CA, 1955; produced in New York, 1959-60), decorations by Duncan, Part I, White Rabbit Press (San Francisco), 1958, reprinted, Station Hill Press, 1985, entire play published as *Faust Foutu,* Enkidu sur Rogate (Stinson Beach, CA), 1959.

Selected Poems (1942-50), City Lights Books, 1959.

The Opening of the Field (poems, 1956-59), Grove, 1960, revised edition, New Directions, 1973.

(Author of preface) Jess [Collins], *O!* (poems and collages), Hawk's Well Press (New York City), 1960.

(Author of preface) Jonathan Williams, *Elegies and Celebrations,* Jargon, 1962.

On Poetry (radio interview, broadcast on WTIC, Hartford, CT, May 31, 1964), Yale University, 1964.

Roots and Branches (poems, 1959-63), Scribner, 1964.

Writing Writing: A Composition Book of Madison 1953, Stein Imitations (poems and essays, 1953), Sumbooks, 1964.

As Testimony: The Poem and the Scene (essay, 1958), White Rabbit Press, 1964.

Wine, Auerhahn Press for Oyez Broadsheet Series (Berkeley), 1964.

Uprising (poems), Oyez, 1965.

The Sweetness and Greatness of Dante's "Divine Comedy," 1263-1965 (lecture presented at Dominican College of San Raphael, October 27, 1965), Open Space (San Francisco), 1965.

Medea at Kolchis; [or] The Maiden Head (play; first produced at Black Mountain College, 1956), Oyez, 1965.

Adam's Way: A Play on Theosophical Themes, [San Francisco], 1966.

(Contributor) Howard Nemerov, editor, *Poets on Poetry,* Basic Books, 1966.

Of the War: Passages 22-27, Oyez, 1966.

A Book of Resemblances: Poems, 1950-53, drawings by Jess, Henry Wenning, 1966.

Six Prose Pieces, Perishable Press (Rochester, MI), 1966.

The Years as Catches: First Poems, 1939-46, Oyez, 1966.

Boob (poem), privately printed, 1966.

Audit/Robert Duncan (also published as special issue of *Audit/Poetry,* Volume 4, number 3), Audit/Poetry, 1967.

Christmas Present, Christmas Presence! (poem), Black Sparrow Press, 1967.

The Cat and the Blackbird (children's storybook), illustrations by Jess, White Rabbit Press, 1967.

Epilogos, Black Sparrow Press, 1967.

My Mother Would Be a Falconress (poem), Oyez, 1968.

Names of People (poems, 1952-53), illustrations by Jess, Black Sparrow Press, 1968.

The Truth and Life of Myth: An Essay in Essential Autobiography, House of Books (New York City), 1968.

Bending the Bow (poems), New Directions, 1968.

The First Decade: Selected Poems, 1940-50, Fulcrum Press (London), 1968.

Derivations: Selected Poems, 1950-1956, Fulcrum Press, 1968.

Achilles Song, Phoenix, 1969.

Playtime, Pseudo Stein; 1942, A Story [and] A Fairy Play: From the Laboratory Records Notebook of 1953, A Tribute to Mother Carey's Chickens, Poet's Press, c.1969.

Notes on Grossinger's "Solar Journal: Oecological Sections," Black Sparrow Press, 1970.

A Selection of Sixty-Five Drawings from One Drawing Book, 1952-1956, Black Sparrow Press, 1970.

Tribunals: Passages 31-35, Black Sparrow Press, 1970.

Poetic Disturbances, Maya (San Francisco), 1970.

Bring It up from the Dark, Cody's Books, 1970.

(Contributor) Edwin Haviland Miller, editor, *The Artistic Legacy of Walt Whitman: A Tribute to Gay Wilson Allen,* New York University Press, 1970.

A Prospectus for the Prepublication of Ground Work to Certain Friends of the Poet, privately printed, 1971.

An Interview with George Bowering and Robert Hogg, April 19, 1969, Coach House Press, 1971.

Structure of Rime XXVIII; In Memoriam Wallace Stevens, University of Connecticut, 1972.

Poems from the Margins of Thom Gunn's Moly, privately printed, 1972.

A Seventeenth-Century Suite, privately printed, 1973.

(Contributor) Ian Young, editor, *The Male Muse: Gay Poetry Anthology,* Crossing Press, 1973.

Dante, Institute of Further Studies (New York City), 1974.

(With Jack Spicer) *An Ode and Arcadia,* Ark Press, 1974.

The Venice Poem, Poet's Mimeo (Burlington, VT), 1978.

Veil, Turbine, Cord & Bird: Sets of Syllables, Sets of Words, Sets of Lines, Sets of Poems, Addressing . . . , J. Davies, c. 1979.

Fictive Certainties: Five Essays in Essential Autobiography, New Directions, 1979.

The Five Songs, Friends of the University of California, San Diego Library, 1981.

Towards an Open Universe, Aquila Publishing, 1982.
Ground Work: Before the War, New Directions, 1984.
A Paris Visit, Grenfell Press, 1985.
The Regulators, Station Hill Press, 1985.
Ground Work II: In the Dark,, New Directions, 1987.
Selected Poems, edited by Robert J. Bertholf, New Directions, 1993.
Selected Prose, New Directions, 1995.

Also author of *The H. D. Book,* a long work in several parts, published in literary journals. Represented in anthologies, including *Faber Book of Modern American Verse,* edited by W. H. Auden, 1956, *The New American Poetry: 1945-1960,* edited by Donald M. Allen, 1960, and many others. Contributor of poems, under the name Robert Symmes, to *Phoenix* and *Ritual.* Contributor to *Atlantic, Poetry, Nation, Quarterly Review of Literature,* and other periodicals.

SIDELIGHTS: Though the name Robert Duncan is not well known outside the literary world, within that world it has become associated with a number of superlatives. Kenneth Rexroth, writing in *Assays,* names Duncan "one of the most accomplished, one of the most influential" of the postwar American poets. An important participant in the Black Mountain school of poetry led by Charles Olson, Duncan became "probably the figure with the richest natural genius" from among that group, suggests M. L. Rosenthal in *The New Poets: American and British Poetry since World War II.* Duncan was also, in Rosenthal's opinion, perhaps "the most intellectual of our poets from the point of view of the effect upon him of a wide, critically intelligent reading." In addition, "few poets have written more articulately and self-consciously about their own intentions and understanding of poetry," reports *Dictionary of Literary Biography* contributor George F. Butterick. The homosexual companion of San Francisco painter Jess Collins, Duncan was also one of the first poets to call for a new social consciousness that would accept homosexuality. Largely responsible for the establishment of San Francisco as the spiritual hub of contemporary American poetry, Duncan has left a significant contribution to American literature through the body of his writings and through the many poets who have felt the influence of the theory behind his poetics.

Duncan's poetics were formed by the events of his early life. His mother died while giving him birth, leaving his father, a day-laborer, to care for him. Six months later, he was adopted by a couple who selected him on the basis of his astrological configuration. Their reverence for the occult in general, and especially their belief in reincarnation, and other concepts from Hinduism, was a lasting and important influence on his poetic vision. Encouraged by a high school English teacher who saw poetry as an essential means of sustaining spiritual vigor, Duncan chose his vocation while still in his teens. Though his parents wanted him to have a European education in Medieval history, he remained in San Francisco, living as a recluse so as not to embarrass the academic figure who was his lover. He continued reading and writing, eventually became the student of Middle Ages historian Ernst Kantorowicz, and throughout his life "maintained a profound interest in occult matters as parallel to and informing his own theories of poetry," Michael Davidson reports in another *Dictionary of Literary Biography* essay.

Minnesota Review contributor Victor Contoski suggests that Duncan's essays in *The Truth and Life of Myth* may be "the best single introduction to his poetry," which, for Duncan, was closely related to mysticism. Duncan, says a London *Times* reporter, was primarily "concerned with poetry as what he called 'manipulative magic' and a 'magic ritual', and with the nature of what he thought of (in a markedly Freudian manner) as 'human bisexuality.'" Reports James Dickey in *Babel to Byzantium,* "Duncan has the old or pagan sense of the poem as a divine form of speech which works intimately with the animism of nature, of the renewals that believed-in ceremonials can be, and of the sacramental in experience; for these reasons and others that neither he nor I could give, there is at least part of a very good poet in him." While this emphasis on myth was an obstacle to some reviewers, critic Laurence Liebermann, writing in a *Poetry* review, said of *The Opening of the Field,* Duncan's first mature collection, that it "announced the birth of a surpassingly individual talent: a poet of mysticism, visionary terror, and high romance."

Duncan wrote some of the poems in *The Opening of the Field* in 1956 when he taught at Olson's Black Mountain College. Olson promoted projective verse, a poetry shaped by the rhythms of the poet's breath, which he defined as an extension of nature. These poems would find their own "open" forms unlike the prescribed measures and line lengths that ruled traditional poetry. "Following Olson's death Duncan became the leading spokesman for the poetry of open form in America," notes Butterick. Furthermore, say some critics, Duncan fulfilled Olson's dictum more fully than Olson had done; whereas Olson projected the poem into a space bounded by the poet's natural breath, Duncan carried this process farther, defining the poem as an open field without boundaries of any kind.

Duncan was a syncretist possessing "a bridge-building, time-binding, and space-binding imagination" in which "the Many are One, where all faces have their Original Being, and where Eternal Love encompasses all reality, both Good and Evil," writes Stephen Stepanchev in *American Poetry since 1945.* A Duncan poem, accordingly, is like a collage, "a compositional field where anything might enter: a prose quotation, a catalogue, a recipe, a dramatic monologue, a diatribe," Davidson explains. The poems draw together into one dense fabric materials from sources as diverse as works on ancient magic, Christian mysticism, and the *Oxford English Dictionary.* Writing in the *New York Times Book Review,* Jim Harrison calls the structure of a typical Duncan poem multi-layered and four-dimensional ("moving through time with the poet"), and compares it to "a block of weaving. . . . *Bending the Bow* is for the strenuous, the hyperactive reader of poetry; to read Duncan with any immediate grace would require Norman O. Brown's knowledge of the arcane mixed with Ezra Pound's grasp of poetics. . . . [Duncan] is personal rather than confessional and writes within a continuity of tradition. It simply helps to be familiar with Dante, [William] Blake, mythography, medieval history, H.D., William Carlos Williams, Pound, [Louis] Zukofsky, Olson, [Robert] Creeley and [Denise] Levertov."

Process, not conclusion, drew Duncan's focus. In some pages from a notebook published in Donald Allen's *The New American Poetry: 1945-1960,* Duncan stated: "A longing grows to return to the open composition in which the accidents and imperfections of speech might awake intimations of human being. . . . There is a natural mystery in poetry. We do not understand all that we render up to understanding. . . . I study what I write as I study out any mystery. A poem, mine or another's, is an occult document, a body awaiting vivisection, analysis, X-rays." The poet, he explained, is an explorer more than a creator. "I work at language as a spring of water works at the rock, to find a course, and so, blindly. In this I am not a maker of things, but, if maker, a maker of a way. For the way is itself." As in the art of marquetry (the making of patterns by enhancing natural wood grains), the poet is aware of the possible meanings of words and merely brings them out. "I'm not *putting* a grain into the wood," he told Jack R. Cohn and Thomas J. O'Donnell in a *Contemporary Literature* interview. Later, he added, "I acquire language lore. What I am supplying is something like . . . grammar of design, or of the possibilities of design." The goal of composition, he wrote in a *Caterpillar* essay, was "not to reach conclusion but to keep our exposure to what we do not know."

Each Duncan poem builds itself by a series of organic digressions, in the manner of outward-reaching roots or branches. The order in his poems is not an imposed order, but a reflection of correspondences already present in nature or language. At times, the correspondences inherent in language become insistent so that the poet following an organic method of writing is in danger of merely recording what the language itself dictates as possible. Duncan was highly susceptible to impressions from other literature—perhaps too susceptible, he said in a *Boundary 2* interview. In several interviews, for example, Duncan referred to specific early poems as "received" from outside agents, "poems in which angels were present." After reading Rainer Marie Rilke's *Duino Elegies,* he came to dread what he called "any angelic invasion"—or insistent voice other than his own. One poem that expresses this preference is "Often I Am Permitted to Return to a Meadow," the first poem in *The Opening of the Field.* He told Cohn and O'Donnell, "When I wrote that opening line, . . . I recognized that this was my permission, and that this meadow, which I had not yet identified, would be the thematic center of the book. In other words, what's back of that opening proposition I understood immediately: twice *you* wanted to compel me to have a book that would have angels at the center, but *now* I am permitted, often you have permitted me, to return to a mere meadow." His originality consisted of his demand that the inner life of the poem be his own, not received from another spiritual or literary source. "Whether he is working from Dante's prose Renaissance meditative poems, or Thom Gunn's *Moly* sequence, he works *from* them and *to* what they leave open or unexamined," explains Thomas Parkinson in *Poets, Poems, Movements.*

At the same time, Duncan recognized his works as derivative literature for several reasons. He said, "I am a traditionalist, a seeker after origins, not an original," reports Herbert Mitgang in the *New York Times.* Often he claimed Walt Whitman as his literary father, seeking in poetry to celebrate the experiences common to all men and women of all times, trying to manifest in words the underlying unity of all things that was essential to his beliefs. Complete originality is not possible in such a cosmos. In fact, the use of language—an inherited system of given sounds and symbols—is itself an imitative activity that limits originality. Even so, the poet, he believed, must be as free as possible "from preconceived ideas, whether structural or thematic, and must allow the internal forces of the composition at hand to determine the final form," Robert C. Weber observes in *Concerning Poetry*. This position, Duncan recognized, was bequeathed to him by Whitman and Pound, who viewed a poet's life work as one continuous "unfinished book," Parkinson notes.

Duncan's works express social and political ideals conversant with his poetics. The ideal environment for the poet, Duncan believed, would be a society without boundaries. In poetry, Duncan found a vocation where there was no prohibition against homosexuality, James F. Mersmann observes in *Out of the Viet Nam Vortex: A Study of Poets and Poetry against the War*. Duncan's theory, he goes on, "not only claims that the poem unfolds according to its own law, but envisions a compatible cosmology in which it may do so. It is not the poem alone that must grow as freely as the plant: the life of the person, the state, the species, and indeed the cosmos itself follows a parallel law. All must follow their own imperatives and volition; all activity must be free of external coercion."

Political commitment is the subject of *Bending the Bow*. Duncan was "one of the most astute observers of the malpractices of Western governments, power blocs, etc., who [was] always on the human side, the *right* side of such issues as war, poverty, civil rights, etc., and who therefore [did] not take an easy way out," though his general avoidance of closure sometimes weakened his case, Harriet Zinnes remarks in a *Prairie Schooner* review. Highly critical of the Vietnam War, pollution, nuclear armament, and the exploitation of native peoples and natural resources, the poems in *Bending the Bow* include "Up-Rising," "one of the major political poems of our time," according to Davidson. For Duncan, the essayist continues, "the American attempt to secure *one* meaning of democracy by eliminating all others represents a massive violation of that vision of polis desired by John Adams and Thomas Jefferson and projected through Walt Whitman." Though such poems voice an "essentially negative vision," says Weber, "it is a critical part of Duncan's search for the nature of man since he cannot ignore what man has become. . . . These themes emerge from within the body of the tradition

of the poetry he seeks to find; politics are a part of the broad field of the poet's life, and social considerations emerge from his concern with the nature of man."

The difference between organic and imposed order, for Duncan, says Mersmann, "is the difference between life and death. The dead matter of the universe science dissects into tidy stacktables; the living significance of creation, the angel with which the poet wrestles, is a volatile whirlwind of sharp knees and elbows thrashing with a grace beyond our knowledge of grace." The only law in a dancing universe, he goes on, is its inherent "love of the dance itself." Anything opposed to this dance of freedom is seen as evil. Both Duncan's poetics and his lifestyle stem from "a truly different kind of consciousness, either a very old or a very new spirituality," Mersmann concludes.

Duncan's method of composition based on this spirituality results in several difficulties for even the sympathetic reader. Duncan's "drifting conglomerations" are an exercise of poetic freedom that sometimes inspires, "but more often I feel suicidal about it," Dickey comments. Davidson notes that Duncan "never courted a readership but rather a special kind of reader, who grants the poet a wide latitude in developing his art, even in its most extreme moments . . . . The number of such readers is necessarily limited, but fierce in devotion." A large number of Duncan's poems are most accessible to an inner circle familiar with the personal and literary contexts of his writings, observes a *Times Literary Supplement* reviewer, who points out that "not everyone can live in California."

Duncan's method of composition presents some difficulties for the critic, as well. The eclectic nature of *Bending the Bow,* for example, remarks Hayden Carruth in the *Hudson Review,* excludes it from "questions of quality. I cannot imagine my friends, the poets who gather to dismember each other, asking of this book, as they would of the others in this review, those narrower in scope, smaller in style, 'Is it good or is it bad?' The question doesn't arise; not because Duncan is a good poet, though he is superb, but because the comprehensiveness of his imagination is too great for us."

After the publication of *Bending the Bow* in 1968, Duncan announced he would not publish a major collection for another fifteen years. During this hiatus he hoped to produce process-oriented poems instead of the "overcomposed" poems he wrote when he thought in terms of writing a book. In effect, this silence kept him from receiving the widespread critical attention or recognition he might otherwise have enjoyed. However, Duncan had a small but highly appreciative audience among writers who shared his concerns. Distraught when *Ground Work: Before the War,* the evidence of nearly twenty years of significant work, did not win the attention they thought it deserved from the publishing establishment, these poets founded the National Poetry Award and honored Duncan by making him the first recipient of the award in 1985. The award, described in a *Sagetrieb* article, was "a positive action affirming the admiration of the poetic community for the dedication and accomplishment of a grand poet."

Duncan concluded the project he began with *Ground Work: Before the War* with *Ground Work II: In the Dark,* which was published shortly before his death. Critics such as Leonard Schwartz in the *American Book Review* notes that while not as groundbreaking in technique as the first, the poems in *In the Dark* are "much more surer and more complete than those in *I* . . . [which] is . . . an exploration of words to find their fullest senses." Schwartz concludes, "*II* is the fruit of that exploration, finished works brought back and thereby bringing to term a specific condition of consciousness." Thom Gunn, writing in the *Times Literary Supplement* finds that Duncan "trusts his spontaneity so completely that he encourages it to *trip up* his conscious intentions." He notes that "It is this current that accounts for the most exciting, and the most exasperating of Duncan's writing."

Selected Poems, published posthumously in 1993, gathers together Duncan's writings from throughout his career, resulting in a comprehensive review of his innovative technical and spiritual poetics. In comparing Duncan to other Black Mountain poets, Mark Ford in the *London Review of Books* remarks, "Duncan's work . . . exhibits a far more nuanced awareness of its own relationship to the traditions of poetry that it aims to modify." A *Publishers Weekly* reviewer praises editor Berthold's work, stating that even readers familiar with the author's poetry will "become more sensitized to his . . . imagery and consistency" after reviewing this collection. Dachine Ranier, contributor to *Agenda,* declaring "[Publisher] Carcanet is to be congratulated," calls the collection "a lovely offering of the work of an American poet, unjustly neglected for decades."

BIOGRAPHICAL/CRITICAL SOURCES:

BOOKS

Allen, Donald M., *The New American Poetry, 1945-1960,* Grove, 1960.

Allen, *The Poetics of the New American Poetry,* Grove, 1973.

Bertholf, Robert J. and Ian W. Reid, editors, *Robert Duncan: Scales of the Marvelous,* New Directions, 1979.

Charters, Samuel, *Some Poems/Poets: Studies in American Underground Poetry since 1945,* Oyez, 1971.

Contemporary Literary Criticism, Gale, Volume 1, 1973, Volume 2, 1974, Volume 4, 1975, Volume 7, 1977, Volume 15, 1980, Volume 41, 1987, Volume 55, 1989.

Dickey, James, *Babel to Byzantium,* Farrar, Straus, 1968.

Dictionary of Literary Biography, Gale, Volume 5: *American Poets since World War II,* 1980, Volume 16: *The Beats: Literary Bohemians in Postwar America,* 1983.

Faas, Ekbert, editor, *Towards a New American Poetics: Essays and Interviews,* Black Sparrow Press, 1978.

Fass, Ekbert, *Young Robert Duncan: Portrait of the Homosexual in Society,* Black Sparrow Press, 1983.

Fauchereau, Serge, *Lecture de la poesie americaine,* Editions de Minuit, 1969.

Foster, Edward Halsey, *Understanding the Black Mountain Poets,* University of South Carolina Press (Columbia), 1995.

Mersmann, James F., *Out of the Viet Nam Vortex: A Study of Poets and Poetry against the War,* University Press of Kansas, 1974.

Parkinson, Thomas, *Poets, Poems, Movements,* University of Michigan Research Press, 1987.

Pearce, Roy Harvey, *Historicism Once More: Problems and Occasions for the American Scholar,* Princeton University Press, 1969.

Rexroth, Kenneth, *Assays,* New Directions, 1961.

Rexroth, *American Poetry in the Twentieth Century,* Herder and Herder, 1971.

Rosenthal, M. L., *The New Poets: American and British Poetry since World War II,* Oxford University Press, 1967.

Stepanchev, Stephen, *American Poetry since 1945,* Harper, 1965.

Tallman, Warren, *Godawful Streets of Man,* Coach House Press, 1976.

Weatherhead, Kingsley, *Edge of the Image: Marianne Moore, William Carlos Williams, and Some Other Poets,* University of Washington Press, 1967.

PERIODICALS

Agenda, autumn/winter, 1970; autumn, 1994, p. 308.
American Book Review, May, 1989, p. 12.
Audit/Poetry (special Duncan issue), Number 3, 1967.
Boundary 2, winter, 1980.
Caterpillar, number 8/9, 1969.
Centennial Review, fall, 1975; fall, 1985.
Concerning Poetry, spring, 1978.
Contemporary Literature, spring, 1975.
History Today, January, 1994, p. 56.
Hudson Review, summer, 1968.
Library Journal, March 1, 1993, p. 81, August, 1994, p. 132.
London Review of Books, March 10, 1994, p. 20.
Maps (special Duncan issue), 1974.
Minnesota Review, fall, 1972.
New York Review of Books, June 3, 1965; May 7, 1970.
New York Times Book Review, December 20, 1964; September 29, 1968; August 4, 1985.
Poetry, March, 1968; April, 1969; May, 1970.
Publishers Weekly, February 15, 1993, p. 232; May 16, 1994, p. 63.
Sagetrieb, winter, 1983; (special Duncan issue) fall/winter, 1985.
Saturday Review, February 13, 1965; August 24, 1968.
School Library Journal, August, 1994, p. 132.
Southern Review, spring, 1969; winter, 1985.
Sulfur 12, Volume 4, number 2, 1985.
Times Literary Supplement, May 1, 1969; July 23, 1971; November 25, 1988, p. 1294.
Unmuzzled Ox, February, 1977.
Voice Literary Supplement, November, 1984.
World Literature Today, autumn, 1988, p. 659; spring, 1994, p. 373.

OBITUARIES:

PERIODICALS

Los Angeles Times, February 4, 1988.
New York Times, February 2, 1988.
Times (London), February 11, 1988.*

*   *   *

EHRENREICH, Barbara 1941-

PERSONAL: Born August 26, 1941, in Butte, MT; daughter of Ben Howes and Isabelle Oxley (Isely) Alexander; married John Ehrenreich, August 6, 1966 (marriage ended); married Gary Stevenson, December 10, 1983; children: (first marriage) Rosa, Benjamin. *Education:* Reed College, B.A., 1963; Rockefeller University, Ph.D., 1968. *Politics:* "Socialist and feminist." *Religion:* None.

CAREER: Health Policy Advisory Center, New York City, staff member, 1969-71; State University of New York College at Old Westbury, assistant professor of health sciences, 1971-74; writer, 1974—; *Seven Days* magazine, editor, 1974—; *Mother Jones* magazine, columnist, 1986-89; Time magazine, essayist, 1990; *The Guardian,* London, columnist, 1992—. New York Institute for the Humanities, associate fellow, 1980—; Institute for Policy Studies, fellow, 1982—. Co-chair, Democratic Socialists of America, 1983—.

AWARDS, HONORS: National Magazine award, 1980; Ford Foundation award for Humanistic Perspectives on Contemporary Issues, 1981; Guggenheim fellowship, 1987.

WRITINGS:

(With husband, John Ehrenreich) *Long March, Short Spring: The Student Uprising at Home and Abroad,* Monthly Review Press (New York City), 1969.

(With J. Ehrenreich) *The American Health Empire: Power, Profits, and Politics, a Report from the Health Policy Advisory Center,* Random House (New York City), 1970.

(With Deirdre English) *Witches, Midwives, and Nurses: A History of Women Healers,* Feminist Press (Old Westbury, NY), 1972.

(With English) *Complaints and Disorders: The Sexual Politics of Sickness,* Feminist Press, 1973.

(With English) *For Her Own Good: One Hundred Fifty Years of the Experts' Advice to Women,* Doubleday (New York City), 1978.

The Hearts of Men: American Dreams and the Flight from Commitment, Doubleday, 1983.

(With Annette Fuentes) *Women in the Global Factory* (pamphlet), South End Press (Boston), 1983.

(With Elizabeth Hess and Gloria Jacobs) *Re-making Love: The Feminization of Sex,* Anchor Press/Doubleday, 1986.

(With Fred Block, Richard Cloward, and Frances Fox Piven) *The Mean Season: An Attack on the Welfare State,* Pantheon (New York City), 1987.

Fear of Falling: The Inner Life of the Middle Class, Pantheon, 1989.

The Worst Years of Our Lives: Irreverent Notes from a Decade of Greed, Pantheon, 1990.

Kipper's Game, Farrar, Straus, (New York City), 1993.

The Snarling Citizen: Essays, Farrar, Straus, 1995.

Contributor to magazines, including *Radical America, Nation, Esquire, Vogue, New Republic,* and *New York Times Magazine.* Contributing editor, *Ms.,* 1981—, and *Mother Jones,* 1988—.

SIDELIGHTS: An outspoken feminist and socialist party leader, Barbara Ehrenreich crusades for social justice in her books. Although many of her early works were shaped by her formal scientific training-she earned a Ph.D. in biology-her later works have moved beyond health care concerns to the plight of women and the poor. In addition to her numerous nonfiction books, Ehrenreich is widely known for her weekly columns in *Time* and *The Guardian.*

Early in her career, while working for the Health Policy Advisory Center, Ehrenreich published a scathing critique of the American health "empire," exposing its inefficiency, inhumanity, and self-serving policies. Then, turning from the population in general to women in particular, Ehrenreich and her co-author Deirdre English unveiled the male domination of the female health care system in *Complaints and Disorders: The Sexual Politics of Sickness* and *For Her Own Good: One Hundred Fifty Years of the Experts' Advice to Women.* In her most controversial book to date, *The Hearts of Men: American Dreams and the Flight from Commitment,* Ehrenreich takes on the whole male establishment, challenging the assumption that feminism is at the root of America's domestic upheaval.

Describing *The Hearts of Men* as a study of "the ideology that shaped the breadwinner ethic," Ehrenreich surveys the three decades between the 1950s and the 1980s, showing how male commitment to home and family collapsed during this time. "The result," according to *New York Times* contributor Eva Hoffman, "is an original work of cultural iconography that supplements—and often stands on its head—much of the analysis of the relations between the sexes that has become the accepted wisdom of recent years." Ehrenreich's interpretation of the evidence led her to the surprising conclusion that anti-feminism evolved not in response to feminism—but to men's abdication of their breadwinner role.

The seeds of male revolt were planted as far back as the 1950s, according to Ehrenreich, when what she calls "the gray flannel dissidents" began to balk at their myriad responsibilities. "The gray flannel nightmare of the commuter train and the constant pressure to support a houseful of consumers caused many men to want to run away from it all," Carol Cleaver writes in the *New Leader.* What held these men in check, says Ehrenreich, was the fear that, as bachelors, they would be associated with homosexuality. Hugh Hefner banished that stigma with the publication of *Playboy,* a magazine whose name alone "defied the convention of hard-won maturity," Ehrenreich says in her book. "The magazine's real message was not eroticism, but escape . . . from the bondage of breadwinning. Sex—or Hefner's Pepsi-clean version of it—was there to legitimize what was truly subversive about *Playboy.* In every issue, every month, there was a Playmate to prove that a playboy didn't have to be a husband to be a man." Around this time, another more openly rebellious group called the Beats came into ascendancy. Rejecting both marriage and job for the glory of the road, Beats like Jack Kerouac embodied a freewheeling lifestyle that appealed to many men, Ehrenreich maintains.

Neither separately nor in conjunction with one another did these dissident groups possess the power to lure large numbers of male breadwinners from their traditional roles. To allow them "comfortable entree into a full-scale male revolt . . . would take the blessing of those high priests of normalcy, psychologists and doctors," writes Judith Levine in the *Village Voice.* "The *deus ex medica*—the 'scientific' justification for a male revolt—was coronary heart disease. The exertion of breadwinning, Ehrenreich writes in the most original section of her book, was allegedly, literally attacking the hearts of men.

In the decades that followed, men's increasing "flight from commitment" was sanctioned by pop psychologists and other affiliates of the Human Potential Movement, who banished guilt and encouraged people to "do their own thing." Unfortunately for women, Ehrenreich concludes that men abandoned the breadwinner role "without overcoming the sexist attitudes that role has perpetuated: on the one hand, the expectation of female nurturance and submissive service as a matter of right; on the other hand a misogynist contempt for women as 'parasites' and entrappers of men." In response to male abdication, women increasingly adopted one of two philosophies: they became feminists, committed to achieving economic and social parity with men, or they became anti-feminists, who tried to keep men at home by binding themselves ever more tightly to them. Despite such efforts, Ehrenreich concludes that women have not fared well, but instead have found themselves increasingly on their own "in a society that never intended to admit us as independent persons, much less as breadwinners for others."

Widely reviewed in both magazines and newspapers, *The Hearts of Men* was hailed for its provocative insights—even as individual sections of the study were soundly criticized. In her *Village Voice* review, for instance, Judith Levine is both appreciative of the work and skeptical of its conclusions: "Barbara Ehrenreich—one of the finest feminist-socialist writers around—has written a witty, intelligent book based on intriguing source material. *The Hearts of Men* says something that needs saying: men have not simply reacted to feminism—skulking away from women and children, hurt, humiliated, feeling cheated of their legal and emotional rights. Men, as Ehrenreich observes, have, as always, done what they want to do. . . . I applaud her on-the-mark readings of *Playboy,* medical dogma, and men's liberation; her insistence that the wage system punishes women and children when families disintegrate; her mordant yet uncynical voice. . . . But I believe *The Hearts of Men* is wrong. When she claims that the glue of families is male volition and the breadwinner ideology—and that a change in that ideology caused the breakup of the family—I am doubtful. The ideology supporting men's abdication of family commitment is not new. It has coexisted belligerently with the breadwinner ethic throughout American history."

Similarly, in a *New York Times Book Review* article, Carol Tarvis describes *The Hearts of Men* as "a pleasure to read, entertaining and imaginative," but goes on to say that "Ehrenreich's analysis falters in its confusion of causes and effects. She continually implies a sequence (first came concerted pressures upon men to conform, then male protest, then scientific legitimization of male protest) when her own evidence shows simultaneity. . . . Further, to suggest that feminism came after the male revolt is to mix what people say with what they do. . . . In arguing that male protest preceded female protest, Miss Ehrenreich succumbs to an unhelpful, unanswerable 'Who started this?' spiral."

While *New York Times* contributor Eva Hoffman echoes Tarvis's concern about the confusion of causes and effects, she points out that "by her own admis-

sion, Miss Ehrenreich is more interested in cultural imagery and ideas than in sociological proof; and to this reader, her narrative makes good, if sometimes unexpected sense." *Los Angeles Times* reviewer Lois Timnick reaches a similar conclusion: "One may take issue with her cause-and-effect pairings, her prescription for cure . . . and her rather gloomy view of the '80s. . . . But Ehrenreich needs especially to be read by those who fear that 'women's libbers' will wrest away the values she shows men tossed out long ago, or who still cling to the notion that we could, if we wanted, go back to the mythical 'Ozzie and Harriet' days."

In the 1986 *Re-making Love: The Feminization of Sex,* co-authored with Elizabeth Hess and Gloria Jacobs, Ehrenreich reports and applauds the freer attitudes towards sex that women adopted in the 1970s and 1980s. The authors assert that women have gained the ability to enjoy sex just for the sake of pleasure, separating it from idealistic notions of love and romance. In her review of *Re-making Love* for the *Chicago Tribune,* Joan Beck noted that the book "is an important summing up of what has happened to women and sex in the last two decades and [that it] shows why the sex revolution requires re-evaluation." Beck, however, argued that the authors ignore the "millions of walking wounded"—those affected by sexually transmitted diseases, unwanted pregnancy, or lack of lasting relationships. *Washington Post Book World* contributor Anthony Astrachan also expresses a wish for a deeper analysis, but nevertheless finds *Re-making Love* "full of sharp and sometimes surprising insights that come from looking mass culture full in the face."

Ehrenreich's next work to attract critical notice, *Fear of Falling: The Inner Life of the Middle Class,* examines the American middle class and its attitudes towards people of the working and poorer classes. Jonathan Yardley writes in the *Washington Post* that what Ehrenreich actually focuses on is a class "composed of articulate, influential people. . . . in fact what most of us think of as the upper-middle class." According to Ehrenreich this group perceives itself as threatened, is most concerned with self-preservation, and has isolated itself—feeling little obligation to work for the betterment of society. This attitude, Ehrenreich maintains, is occurring at a time when the disparity in income between classes has reached the greatest point since World War II and has become "almost as perilously skewed as that of India," Joseph Coates quotes *Fear of Falling* in *Tribune Books.*

Globe and Mail contributor Maggie Helwig, though praising the book as "witty, clever, [and] perceptive," describes as unrealistic Ehrenreich's hope for a future when everyone could belong to the professional middle class and hold fulfilling jobs. Similarly, David Rieff remarks in the *Los Angeles Times Book Review* that Ehrenreich's proposed solutions to class polarization are overly optimistic and tend to romanticize the nature of work. "Nonetheless," Rieff concludes, "'Fear of Falling' is a major accomplishment, a breath of fresh thinking about a subject that very few writers have known how to think about at all." The book elicited even higher praise from Coates, who deems it "a brilliant social analysis and intellectual history, quite possibly the best on this subject since Tocqueville's."

In *The Worst Years of Our Lives: Irreverent Notes from a Decade of Greed,* Ehrenreich discusses in a series of reprinted articles what some consider to be one of the most self-involved and consumeristic decades in American history: the 1980s. Most of these articles first appeared in *Mother Jones,* but some come from such periodicals as *Nation, Atlantic, New York Times,* and *New Republic.* Together, they summarize "what Ms. Ehrenreich sees as the decade's salient features: blathering ignorance, smug hypocrisy, institutionalized fraud and vengeful polarization—all too dangerous to be merely absurd," says H. Jack Geiger in the *New York Times Book Review.* "One of Mrs. Ehrenreich's main themes," observes *New York Times* reviewer Herbert Mitgang, ". . . is that the Reagan Administration, which dominated the last decade, cosmeticized the country and painted over its true condition. The author writes that the poor and middle class are now suffering the results of deliberate neglect."

Several critics have praised *The Worst Years of Our Lives* as a book that, as Michael Eric Dyson avers in *Tribune Books,* "reflect[s] the work of an engaged intellectual for whom mere description of the world, no matter how incisive, will not suffice. Her aim is to change the world, and her persuasive analyses of many of America's most difficult problems makes a valuable contribution toward that end." However, some reviewers have objected to what they see as Ehrenreich's moralistic approach to her subject. Priscilla Painton, a *Time* contributor, comments, "Overall, her observations suffer from a simplistic yearning for a nonexistent era when the poor were not blamed for their poverty, when people did not cram their appointment books and when college graduates pursued ideals instead of salaries." Others like Gei-

ger, however, consider this quality to be a virtue, rather than a flaw. "Ehrenreich is an up-front socialist," Geiger attests, "but—even more centrally—she is an old-fashioned moralist, someone who believes in the sturdy values of truth, honesty, self-knowledge and family, and argues that the really valid moral reference point for the comfortable and affluent is other people's pain."

The Snarling Citizen: Essays collects fifty-seven previously published essays, most of which Ehrenreich contributed to *Time* and *The Guardian.* The essays once again reveal the author's passion for social justice and feminism. Although some reviewers take exception with Ehrenreich's opinions in these pieces, nearly all lavish praise on her well-honed writing style. Writing in the Chicago *Tribune Books,* for example, Penelope Mesic remarks that the pieces in *The Snarling Citizen* "startle and invigorate because those who espouse liberal causes-feminism, day care and a strong labor movement-all too often write a granola of prose: a mild, beige substance that is, in a dull way, good for us. Ehrenreich is peppery and salacious, bitter with scorn, hotly lucid." *Women's Review of Books* contributor Nan Levinson commends the author for her "writing, a hymn to pithiness and wit, and her ear, attuned to the ways in which language redefined becomes thought reconstructed and politics realigned." Andrew Ferguson, however, commenting in *The American Spectator,* takes issue with what he calls the author's habit of building entire essays around "casual misstatements" of fact. In addition, while conceding that Ehrenreich "knows that caricature can be a verbal art," Ferguson maintains that "too often her fondness for exaggeration and hyperbole drags her into mere buffoonery." While noting that the collection's pieces are all so similar in "size, . . . voice and essentially . . . subject" that they "resemble a box of Fig Newtons," Levinson declares: "Ehrenreich is a rare thing in American public life today—a freelance thinker."

Although she has long been known as a journalist and social critic, Ehrenreich in 1993 published her first novel, *Kipper's Game.* Part science fiction novel and part thriller, the work is "set in a futuristic world that bears a decided resemblance to the present-day United States," explains *New York Times* critic Michiko Kakutani. This world features decaying cities plagued by foliage-eating caterpillars, hazardous waste, and unscrupulous computer companies. The complex plot involves Della Markson's search for her missing son, Kipper, a young computer hacker who mysteriously disappears after he creates a revolutionary computer game. As the plot unfolds, Della's unfaithful husband proves to be in cahoots with the forces trying to steal Kipper's game, and the story evolves to a fateful confrontation between father and son. In addition, however, a strange radio evangelist, Sister Bertha, enters the plot as she warns about the imminent arrival of extraterrestrials who may or may not represent God.

The novel elicited mixed reviews from critics. Kakutani, for instance, remarks that "Unfortunately, little of the irreverent wit that animates Ms. Ehrenreich's essays is in evidence in these pages." He does, however, commend those instances where the author describes scenes of "ordinary life." Reviewing the novel for *New Statesman & Society*, however, Vicky Hutchings avers that *"Kipper's Game* is . . . sharp and funny, in a dry sort of way. Sometimes the observations make your hair stand on end." In an interview with Wendy Smith for *Publishers Weekly*, Ehrenreich commented on her reasons for writing about a wide variety of subjects and moving between nonfiction and fiction: "People have sometimes thought I was a sociologist or a historian, but since I have no formal education in any of these things, I'm not tied to a discipline, so I can rampage through any kind of material I want."

BIOGRAPHICAL/CRITICAL SOURCES:

BOOKS

Ehrenreich, Barbara, *The Hearts of Men: American Dreams and the Flight from Commitment*, Doubleday, 1983.
Ehrenreich, *Fear of Falling: The Inner Life of the Middle Class*, Pantheon, 1989.

PERIODICALS

American Spectator, August, 1995, p. 66.
Chicago Tribune, September 25, 1986.
Globe and Mail (Toronto), August 26, 1986.
Humanist, January-February, 1992, p. 11.
Los Angeles Times, July 24, 1983.
Los Angeles Times Book Review, August 20, 1989.
Ms., May-June, 1995, p. 75.
Nation, December 24, 1983.
New Leader, July 11, 1983.
New Republic, July 11, 1983.
New Statesman & Society, May 17, 1991, p. 37, May 20, 1994, p. 37.
New York Review of Books, July 1, 1971.
New York Times, January 20, 1971; August 16, 1983; May 16, 1990; July 13, 1993, p. C18.
New York Times Book Review, March 7, 1971; June 5, 1983; August 6, 1989; May 20, 1990, August 8, 1993, p. 18; May 28, 1996, p. 12.
New York Times Magazine, June 26, 1996, p. 28.
Progressive, January, 1995, p. 47; February, 1995, p. 34.
Publishers Weekly, July 26, 1993, p. 46.
Time, May 7, 1990.
Times Literary Supplement, July 22, 1977.
Tribune Books (Chicago), November 8, 1987; September 24, 1989; May 13, 1990; May 28, 1995, p. 3.
Utne Reader, May-June, 1995, p. 70.
Village Voice, February 5, 1979; August 23, 1983.
Washington Post, August 23, 1989.
Washington Post Book World, August 19, 1979; July 24, 1983; November 9, 1986.
Whole Earth Review, winter, 1995, p. 86.
Women's Review of Books, October, 1995, p. 25.*

* * *

ELIADE, Mircea 1907-1986

PERSONAL: Born March 9, 1907, in Bucharest, Romania; came to United States, 1956; died April 22, 1986, in Chicago, IL; son of Gheorghe and Ioana (Stonescu) Eliade; married Nina Mares, 1935 (some sources say 1933; died in Portugal during World War II); married Georgette Christinel Cottescu, January 9, 1950; children: Adalgiza Tattaresco, a stepdaughter. *Education:* University of Bucharest, M.A., 1928, Ph.D., 1933; graduate study at University of Calcutta, 1928-32.

CAREER: University of Bucharest, Bucharest, Romania, assistant professor of philosophy, 1933-39; Romanian legation, cultural attache in London, England, 1940-41, cultural adviser in Lisbon, Portugal, 1941-45; University of Paris, Sorbonne, Paris, France, visiting professor of history of religion, 1946-48; lecturer at universities in Rome, Lund, Marburg, Munich, Frankfurt, Uppsala, Strasbourg, and Padua, 1948-56; University of Chicago, Chicago, IL, Haskell Lecturer, 1956, professor of history of religions, 1957-62, Sewell L. Avery Distinguished Service Professor, beginning in 1962, professor emeritus until 1985.

MEMBER: American Academy of Arts and Sciences, American Society for Study of Religion (president, 1963-67), British Academy, Centre Roumain de Recherches (Paris; president, 1950-55), Societe Asiatique, Romanian Writers Society (secretary, 1939), Frobenius Institut, Academie Royale de Belgique, Osterreichische Akademie der Wissenschaften.

AWARDS, HONORS: Honorary doctorates from Yale University, 1966, Universidad Nacional de la Plata, 1969, Universidad del Salvador, 1969, Ripon College, 1969, Loyola University, 1970, Boston College, 1971, La Salle College, 1972, Oberlin College, 1972, University of Lancaster, 1975, and Sorbonne, University of Paris, 1976.

WRITINGS:

IN ENGLISH

Metallurgy, Magic, and Alchemy, Geunther, 1938.
Traite d'histoire des religions, Payot, 1948, translation by Rosemary Sheed published as *Patterns in Comparative Religion,* Sheed, 1958, new French edition, Payot, 1964, reprinted, 1974.
Le Mythe de l'eternel retour; Archetypes et repetition, Gallimard, 1949, translation by Willard R. Trask published as *The Myth of the Eternal Return; or, Cosmos and History,* Pantheon, 1954, published as *Cosmos and History,* Pantheon, 1955, published as *Cosmos and History: The Myth of the Eternal Return,* Harper, 1959, reprinted version edited by Robin W. Winks, Garland Publishing, 1985, original Trask edition reprinted, Princeton University Press, 1987.
Le Chamanisme et les techniques archaiques de l'extase, Payot, 1951, translation by Trask published as *Shamanism: Archaic Techniques of Ecstasy,* Pantheon, 1964, 2nd French edition, Payot, 1968, 2nd English edition, Princeton University Press, 1970.
Images et symboles: Essais sur le symbolisme magicoreligieux, Gallimard, 1952, translation by Philip Mairet published as *Images and Symbols: Studies in Religious Symbolism,* Harvill Press, 1961.
Le Yoga: Immortalitie et liberte, Payot, 1954, translation by Trask published as *Yoga: Immortality and Freedom,* Pantheon, 1958, 2nd edition with corrections and notes, Princeton University Press, 1969.
Forgerons et alchemistes, Flammarion, 1956, translation by Stephen Corrin published as *The Forge and the Crucible,* Harper, 1962, 2nd edition, University of Chicago Press, 1978.
Das Heilige und das profane: Vom Wesen des religiosen, Rowohlt, 1957, translation by Trask published as *The Sacred and the Profane: The Nature of Religion,* Harcourt, 1959, reprinted, 1968.
Mythes, reves, et mysteres, Gallimard, 1957, reprinted in two volumes, 1972, translation by Mairet published as *Myths, Dreams, and Mysteries: The Encounter between Contemporary Faiths and Archaic Realities,* Harvill Press, 1960, reprinted, Harper, 1987.
Birth and Rebirth: The Religious Meaning of Initiation in Human Culture, translated by Trask, Harper, 1958, published as *Rites and Symbols of Initiation: The Mysteries of Birth and Rebirth,* 1965.
(Editor with Joseph M. Kitagawa) *The History of Religions: Essays in Methodology,* University of Chicago Press, 1959, reprinted, 1973.
Patanjali et le yoga, Editions du Seuil, 1962, translation by Charles Lam Markmann published as *Patanjali and Yoga,* Funk, 1969, Schocken, 1975.
Mephistopheles et l'androgyne, Gallimard, 1962, translation by J. M. Cohen published as *Mephistopheles and the Androgyne: Studies in Religious Myth and Symbol,* Sheed, 1965, published in England as *The Two and the One,* Harvill Press, 1965, reprinted, University of Chicago Press, 1979.
Myth and Reality, translated by Trask, Harper, 1963.
Aminitiri: I. Mansarda (title means "An Autobiography: I. The Attic"), Editura Destin, 1966, translation from the Rumanian by Ricketts published as *Autobiography,* Volume 1: *Journey East, Journey West: 1907-1937,* Harper, 1981, and Volume 2: *1937-1960, Exile's Odyssey,* University of Chicago Press, 1988.
(Editor) *From Primitives to Zen: A Thematic Sourcebook of the History of Religions,* Collins, 1967, reprinted in four parts, Part 1: *Gods, Goddesses, and Myths of Creation,* Part 2: *Man and the Sacred,* Part 3: *Death, Afterlife, and Eschatology,* Part 4: *From Medicine Man to Muhammad,* Harper, 1974.
(Editor with Kitagawa and Charles H. Long, and contributor) *The History of Religions: Essays on the Problem of Understanding,* University of Chicago Press, 1967.
Pe Strada Mantuleasa (title means "On Mantuleasa Street"), Caitele Inorugului, 1968, translation by Stevenson published as *The Old Man and the Bureaucrats,* University of Notre Dame Press, 1979.

The Quest: History and Meaning in Religion, University of Chicago Press, 1969, reprinted, 1984.

(With Mihai Niculescu) *Fantastic Tales,* translated and edited by Eric Tappe, Dillon's University Bookstore, 1969.

De Zalmoxis a Gengis Khan: Etudes comparatives sur les religions et le folklore de la Dacie et de l'Europe orientale, Payot, 1970, translation by Trask published as *Zalmoxis, the Vanishing God: Comparative Studies in the Religions and Folklore of Dacia and Eastern Europe,* University of Chicago Press, 1972, reprinted, 1986.

Two Tales of the Occult, translation from the Rumanian by William Ames Coates, Herder & Herder, 1970, published as *Two Strange Tales,* Shambhala Publications, 1986.

Religions australiennes (two volumes; translation of lectures originally given in English), translation by L. Jospin, Payot, 1972, published as *Australian Religions: An Introduction,* Cornell University Press, 1973.

Fragments d'un journal, translation from the Rumanian by Luc Badesco, Gallimard, 1973, translation by Fred H. Johnson, Jr., published as *No Souvenirs: Journal, 1957-1969,* Harper, 1977.

Myths, Rites and Symbols: A Mircea Eliade Reader, edited by Wendell C. Beane and William G. Doty, Harper, 1976.

Occultism, Witchcraft, and Cultural Fashions: Essays in Comparative Religions, University of Chicago Press, 1976.

Histoire des croyances et des idees religieuses, Payot, Volume 1: *De l'age de la Pierre aux mysteres d'Eleusis,* 1976, Volume 2: *De Gautama Bouddha au triomphe du christianisme,* 1978, Volume 3: *De Mahomet a l'age des reformes,* 1983, published as *A History of Religious Ideas,* University of Chicago Press, Volume 1: *From the Stone Age to the Eleusinian Mysteries,* translation from French by Trask, 1979, Volume 2: *From Gautama Buddha to the Triumph of Christianity,* translation from French by Trask, 1982, Volume 3: *From Muhammed to the Age of Reforms,* translation by Alf Hiltebeiten and Diane Apostolos-Cappadona, 1985.

La foret interdite (novel; title means "The Forbidden Forest"), translation by MacLinscott Ricketts and Mary P. Stevenson, University of Notre Dame Press, 1978.

L'Epreuve du labyrinthe: Entretien avec Claude-Henri Rocquet, Belfond (Paris), 1978, translation from the French by Derek Coltman published as *Ordeal by Labyrinth: Conversations with Claude-*

Henri Rocquet, with an Essay on Brancusi and Mythology, University of Chicago Press, 1982.

(Editor with David Tracy) *What Is Religion?: An Inquiry for Christian Theology,* T. & T. Clarke, 1980.

Tales of the Sacred and the Supernatural, Westminster Press, 1981.

Imagination and Meaning, Seabury Press, 1982.

The Quest: History and Meaning in Religion, University of Chicago Press, 1984.

Symbolism, the Sacred, and the Arts, edited by D. Apostolos-Cappadona, Crossroad Publishing, 1985.

(Editor) *Encyclopedia of Religion,* sixteen volumes, Macmillan, 1986.

Youth without Youth and Other Novellas, edited by Matei Calinescu, translated by Ricketts, Ohio State University Press, 1988.

The Eliade Guide to World Religions, Harper (San Francisco), 1991.

Mystic Stories: The Sacred and the Profane, East European Monographs (Boulder), 1992.

Bengal Nights, Rupa & Company (New Delhi), 1993, translation from French edition, 1950.

OTHER

Isabel si Apele Diavolului (novel; title means "Isabel and the Devil's Waters"), Editura Nationala-Ciornei (Bucharest), 1930.

Intr'o Manastire din Hamalaya (title means "In a Himalayan Monastery"), Editura Cartea Romaneasca, 1932.

Soliliquii (aphorisms; title means "Soliloquies"), Editura Cartea ce Semne, 1932.

Maitreyi (novel), Editura Nationala-Ciornei, 1933.

India (autobiographical novel), Editura Cugetarea, 1934.

Lumina ce se stinge (title means "The Light that Fails"), Editura Cartea Romaneasca, 1934.

Alchimia Asiatica (title means "Asiatic Alchemy"), Editura Cultura Porporului, 1934.

Oceanographie (essays), Editura Cultura Porporului, 1934.

(Translator) T. E. Lawrence, *Revolt in the Desert,* two volumes, Editura Fundatia Regala pentru Literatura si Arta, 1934.

Intoarcerea din Rai (novel; also see below; first part of trilogy; title means "The Return from Paradise"), Editura Nationala-Ciornei, 1934-54.

Huliganii (novels; two-volume sequel to *Intoarcerea din Rai;* title means "The Hooligans"), Editura Nationala-Ciornei, 1935.

Santier (autobiographical novel; title means "Work in Progress"), Editura Cugetarea, 1935.

Yoga: Essai sur les origines de la mystique indienne (title means "Yoga: Essays on the Origins of Indian Mystic Techniques"), Librairie Orientaliste Geunther (Paris), 1936.

(Editor) Nae Ionescu, *Roza Vanturilor,* Cultura Nationala, 1936.

Domnisoara Christina (novel; title means "Mademoiselle Christina"), Editura Cultura Nationala, 1936.

Sarpele (novel; title means "The Serpent"), Editura Nationala-Ciornei, 1937.

(Editor) *Scrieri Literare, Morlae si Politice de B. P. Hasdeu,* two volumes, Editura Fundatia Regala pentru Literatura si Arta, 1937.

Cosmologie si Alchimie Babiloniana (title means "Babylonian Cosmology and Alchemy"), Editura Vremea, 1937.

Nunta in Cer (novel; title means "Marriage in Heaven"), Editura Cugetarea, 1938.

Mitul Reintegrarii (title means "The Myth of Reintegration"), Editura Vremea, 1938.

Fragmentarium (essays), Editura Vremea, 1939.

(Translator) Pearl S. Buck, *Fighting Angel,* Editura Fundatia Regala pentru Literatura si Arta, 1939.

Secretul Doctoru lui Honigberger (title means "The Secret of Dr. Honigberger"; also see below), Editura Socec, 1940.

Salaza si Revolutia in Portugalia (title means "Salazar and the Revolution in Portugal"), Editura Gorjan, 1942.

Commentarii la Legenda Mesterlui Manole (title means "Commentaries on the Legend of Master Manole"), Editura Publicom, 1943.

Insula lui Euthanasius (title means "The Island of Euthanasius"), Editura Fundatia Regala pentru Literatura si Arta, 1943.

Os Romenos, Latinos do Oriente (title means "The Romanians, Latins of the East"), Livraria Classica Editora, 1943.

Techniques du Yoga (title means "Techniques of Yoga"), Gallimard, 1948, new edition in three volumes, 1975.

Iphigenia (a play), Editura Cartea Pribegiei, 1951.

Minuit a Serampore [suivi de] *Le Secret du Docteur Honigberger* (title means "Midnight at Seramapore" and "The Secret of Dr. Honigberger"), translated from the Rumanian by Albert Marie Schmidt, Stock, 1956.

Nuvele (novellas; includes "La Tiganci," "O fotografie veche de 14 ani," "Ghicitor in pietre," "Un om mare," "Feta capitanului," and "Douasprezece mil de capete de vite"), Editura Destin, 1963.

Aspects du mythe, Gallimard, 1963.

(With others) *Temoignages sur Brancusi,* Arted (Paris), 1967.

La Tiganci si Alte Povestiri, cu un Studiu Introductiv de Sorin Alexandrescu (title means "At the Gypsies and Other Short Stories"), Editura pentru Literatura (Bucharest), 1969.

Die Pelerine (title means "The Cape"), Suhrkamp (Frankfurt), 1970.

In Curte la Dionis, Caitele Inorogului, 1977.

La Colonne sans fin, translation by Florence M. Hetzler, University Press of America, 1984.

Briser le toit de la maison: La Creativite et ses symbols, Gallimard, 1986.

Also author of some twenty volumes published in Romanian, 1933-45. Contributor to many books about religions and religious history, including Joseph Campbell's *Man and Time,* Pantheon, 1957, and *Man and Transformation,* Pantheon, 1964. Founder and editor, *Zalmoxis* (an international journal for history of religions), 1938-42; founder and senior editor, *History of Religions,* 1961-1986. Contributor to journals in his field.

SIDELIGHTS: Romanian novelist and religious historian Mircea Eliade sought a place among the intellectuals of his homeland "who thought of themselves as provincial outposts on the confines of European culture," encyclopedists who "often found a kind of over-compensation in . . . a thirst for universalism, in prodigies of (disorderly) knowledge, and in resorting to an aesthetic management of their material," reports *Times Literary Supplement* contributor Virgil Nemoianu. The reviewer adds that a survey of Eliade's numerous works in a variety of languages reveals "how the mixture of encyclopedic and aesthetic impulses . . . shaped his entire career."

Eliade was a voracious reader and a life-long student. At first fascinated with natural science, he collected rocks, plants and insects and set up a small chemistry lab in his family's home, filling notebooks with his observations. More than 100 articles he wrote were published before he turned twenty. By the time he entered the University of Bucharest, his interests turned to the study of metaphysics and mystical experience. His enthusiasm for the study of primitive and Eastern religions led him to Rome, Geneva, and eventually India, where he became the avid student of Surendranath Das Gupta, a religious historian from whom he learned Yoga. The influence of this religious discipline on his understanding of religious experience appears throughout his writings. Of *Images and Symbols: Studies in Religious Symbolism,* for example, *Hibbert Journal* contributor S. G. F. Brandon remarked that it is "characterized by his . . . implied conviction that the praxis of Yoga is the way par excellence to a proper apprehension of reality."

Eliade relates his visit to India and love affair with a young Indian woman in the autobiographical novel, *Bengal Nights*. It tells the story of a young French engineer, Alain, who is working on a construction project in Calcutta and becomes fascinated by the culture and people of India. When he is taken ill, he accepts the offer of his superior, Narendra Sen, to spend his convalescence in Sen's home where he conducts an illicit affair with Sen's sixteen-year-old daughter, Maitreyi. This mirrors Eliade's own affair with Surendranath Das Gupta's daughter Maitreyi who was "a published poet, devotee of Rabindranath Tagore, and apple of her father's eye," noted K.E. Fleming in *The Nation*. Elaide/Alain and Maitreyi were betrayed by Maitreyi's sister and Elaide/Alain was banished from the household. The affair, told with less amorous details, was the subject of Maitreyi Devi's own book on the romance, *It Does Not Die*.

Critics were mixed in their opinions of Eliade's version of the affair. A contributor to the *Times Literary Supplement* saw the tale as a "metaphor for the narrator's awakening consciousness of a new and radically different culture" and compared Elaide's "intensely poetic prose style, by turns declamatory and confessional" to Marguerite Duras and Elizabeth Smart. Isabel Colegate, writing for the *New York Times Book Review,* reviewed both accounts and cited Elaide's version as "intensely felt and economically written." Fleming declared *Bengal Nights* to be "a romance not just with an Indian but with India herself." Indeed, several critics noted Elaide's feminization of India in this novel. Tilottama Minu Tharoor, writing for *Washington Post Book World,* noted Elaide's depiction of Alain as an engineer who "unabashedly revels in his assumptions of racial superiority and the power he exercises over the Indian landscape." Tharoor continued, "Whenever there is something about [Maitreyi] that eludes his immediate understanding, Alain refers to her as 'primitive.'" Fleming commented on the discrepancies and similarities between Elaide and Devi's versions: "Elaide's offense was not novelistic embellishment but rather its reverse: Had *Bengal Nights* not retained so many truths, it would have been far less damaging."

Eliade's journals and other autobiographical writings, left incomplete at his death, are collected in *Journal, vols. I-IV* and *Autobiography vols. I and II.* The jour-

nals begin in 1945 upon Eliade's arrival in Paris, following the death of his wife and the seizure of Romania by the Soviets and follow his life and career to 1985. The *Autobiography* volumes focus first on Eliade's youth and years in Bucharest (Vol. I), continuing "the account of the agitated and stressful existence of a great 'wandering scholar' (his critics might say, of an itinerant shaman)," noted John L. Brown in *World Literature Today*. Eliade was a zealous recorder of his own life's journey, as evidenced by these works. This slavish devotion may have been somewhat disingenuous, as George Steiner in the *Times Literary Supplement* remarked, "For all their informality of tone . . . for all their relaxed candour, it is difficult to believe that these pages, often daily, were not destined for public perusal. Eliade's sense of his own possible monumentality is a developing motif."

Writing in the *New York Times Book Review,* Gerald Sykes recognized Eliade as "a scientist-artist who [wrote] not only works of scholarship but novels of admirable intensity." The novels reflect his understanding of world cultures, and their themes parallel his findings "as a historian of religions," George Uscatescu writes in *Myths and Symbols: Studies in Honor of Mircea Eliade,* edited by Joseph M. Kitagawa and Charles H. Long. Spiritual crisis is the "central problem" in Eliade's "great novel *Foret Interdite,*" a 700-page work that shows its author "at the fullest unfolding of his epic faculties and establishes for the reader a problematical situation of great literary authenticity and verisimilitude," Uscatescu remarked. Critics praised the novelist for his craftsmanship as much as for his subject matter, Uscatescu notes: "The first long novels, *Isabel si Apele Diavolului* (1930) and *Maitreyi* (1933), draw their inspiration from Indian themes of a strong erotic character and reveal in the hands of a new author both a solid technique and understanding which assures significant success to the works."

Eliade is best known in the United States for his critical and philosophical works on Indian religions, Asiatic alchemy, and mythical thought. However, he felt that his well-received novels—in particular, *La Foret Interdite (The Forbidden Forest)*—more competently conveyed the experience of the power of myth. He continued writing in both forms because he believed that history, philosophy, and fiction are complementary as instruments of expression. Both his fiction and non-fiction are united by their focus on problems which obsessed him from his youth, including the history of religions, the structure of myths, and religious symbolism.

Eliade identified two stances toward reality: the religious stance, in which man and the world are perceived as sacred, inhabited by powers and meanings beyond the mundane; and the profane, in which man denies the existence of the sacred. Eliade cited Rudolph Otto's book *Das Heilige* (title means "The Sacred") for his definition of the sacred as "something 'wholly other'. . . . Confronted with it, man senses his profound nothingness, feels that he is only a creature." This statement in *The Sacred and the Profane* precedes Eliade's observation that man knows the sacred exists only after something from beyond nature reveals itself to man. The history of religions, therefore, can be seen as a series of "manifestations of sacred realities," encounters with "something of a wholly different order, a reality that does not belong to our world, in objects that are an integral part of our natural 'profane' world," he wrote.

The difference between religious and nonreligious man, Eliade observed in *The Sacred and the Profane,* is that "the nonreligious man refuses transcendence. . . . In other words, he accepts no model for humanity outside the human condition," and "desacralizes himself and the world." Yet beyond that, the tragedy of modern nonreligious man is that his "camouflaged myths and degenerated rituals" show that he can never completely desacralize himself and should not try: "Do what he will he is an inheritor. He cannot utterly abolish his past, since he is himself the product of his past. . . . He continues to be haunted by the realities that he has refused and denied. To acquire a world of his own, he has desacralized the world in which his ancestors lived; but to do so he has been obliged to adopt the opposite of an earlier type of behavior, and that behavior is still emotionally present to him, in one form or another, ready to be reactualized in his deepest being."

Eliade contended it is worthwhile to examine the nature of religious experience because it occurs in every culture. To understand religious man, "to understand his spiritual universe, is, in sum, to advance our general knowledge of man," he claimed in *The Sacred and the Profane*. Eliade criticized early ethnologists and philologists for taking an outsider's approach to religious experience. Eliade insisted the historian of religions needs to empathize, if not to participate, with those who claim to encounter the sacred. In *The Sacred and the Profane,* Eliade stated, "There is no other way of understanding a foreign mental universe

than to place oneself *inside* it, at its very center, in order to progress from there to all the values that it possesses." Furthermore, for the historian of religions, scientific study means dealing with religious facts, man's experiences of time and space.

Central to the patterns of Eliade's thought on the history of religions are sacred time and space, problems to which he has returned frequently and about which he has contributed much significant research. As he explains in *The Myth of the Eternal Return; or, Cosmos and History,* some cultures view time as history, as a one-way progression from the irretrievable past into the unknown future. Others view time as cosmos, an infinitely repeatable cycle reactivated by ceremonies preserved in myths. Men who perceive time as cyclical periodically abolish history by reenacting the conquering of chaos and the creation of the world; actions in the present acquire meaning from their similarity to "first things," encounters with the sacred at the beginning of time. Man trapped in history, however, lives in terror, unable to extract himself from meaningless events. In Christian man, Eliade sees components of both views: "Christianity translates the periodic regeneration of the world into a regeneration of the human individual. But for him who shares in this eternal *nunc* of the reign of God, history ceases as totally as it does for the man of the archaic cultures, who abolishes it periodically."

Substantial sections of *The Myth of the Eternal Return, The Sacred and the Profane,* and *Patterns in Comparative Religion* discuss religious man's concepts of sacred space. Any place where "*something that does not belong to this world has manifested itself*" becomes a symbolic foundation of the world, "a fixed point . . . in the chaos," a central point from which religious man draws his orientation to time and space, Eliade writes in *The Sacred and the Profane*. Thus certain landmarks and buildings become, for religious man, gateways to continued communication with the sacred. These three books, particularly *The Myth of the Eternal Return,* provide a wealth of supporting examples from cultures in all nations and time periods.

Critics were consistently impressed by Eliade's encyclopedic mode, but were not uncritical of the role that his personal beliefs played in his studies. "Too great a respect for the intimations of Indian thought (great though its achievement is) can be misleading," Brandon stated. Eliade's "apparent assumption of social evolution" was "a hindrance to acceptance by nonreligious scholars," reported Dorothy Libby in *American Anthropology*. T. J. J. Altizer, writing in the

Journal of Religion, commented that generally speaking, "One expects from Eliade an argument that is clear, precise, comprehensive, and fully documented." However, he adds, when Eliade equates religious man with primitive man, this "romantic" view makes it difficult for him to discuss modern-day religious experience. Apart from this, Altizer calls Eliade a master of the art of describing religions without proposing questionable explanations or claims about their origins.

Eliade's studies of religious experience gave him a permanent place in the history of religious thought. "On the plane of international academic life, Eliade became a kind of prophet of the trans-historical," or timeless common ground shared by members of many cultures, explains Ivan Strenski in the *Los Angeles Times Book Review.* Before he entered the American academic community as a professor at the University of Chicago, the study of religions consisted of pitting belief systems against each other—a process which fell outside the perameters set by the law of separation of church and state in the United States. Eliade saw in the history of religious man a desire for contact with the sacred that transcended cultural boundaries. This new approach helped to establish the study of religion as an academic discipline in American schools. "A true cultural revolutionary to the end, Eliade challenged the whole secular bourgeois world's comforting belief in the adequacy of its own works of science, politics, and economics," Strenski relates. Robert S. Ellwood, Jr. remarks in the *New York Times Book Review,* "Only a few in his often arcane discipline have equaled his broad impact on his age. With C. G. Jung and Joseph Campbell, Mircea Eliade helped create the midcentury vogue for myth and ritual popularized by critics, dramatists and assorted spiritual seekers."

All but Eliade's earliest works are still in print, and many have been translated into more than a dozen languages. Reviewers repeatedly call for more English translations of the Romanian scholar's works. Considering these facts and Eliade's impact on the American academic community, Sykes concluded, "The work of this important scholar gains yearly in effect."

BIOGRAPHICAL/CRITICAL SOURCES:

BOOKS

Allen, Douglas, *Structure and Creativity in Religion: Hermeneutics in Mircea Eliade's Phenomenology and New Directions,* Mouton, 1978.

Allen and Dennis Doeing, *Mircea Eliade: An Annotated Bibliography,* Garland Press, 1980.

Altizer, Thomas J. J., *Mircea Eliade and the Dialectic of the Sacred,* Westminster Press, 1963.

Apostolos-Cappadona, Diane, editor, *Symbolism, the Sacred, and the Arts,* Crossroad Publishing, 1985.

Carrasco, David and Jane Swanberg, editors, *Waiting for the Dawn: Mircea Eliade in Perspective,* Westview Press, 1985.

Cave, David, *Mircea Eliade's Vision for a New Humanism,* Oxford University Press (New York City), 1993.

Contemporary Literary Criticism, Volume 19, Gale 1981.

Dudley, G., *Religion on Trial: Mircea Eliade and His Critics,* Temple University Press, 1977.

Eliade, Mircea, *The Sacred and the Profane: The Nature of Religion,* Harper, 1961.

Eliade, *Two Tales of the Occult,* Herder, 1970.

Eliade, *The Myth of the Eternal Return; or, Cosmos and History,* Princeton University Press, 1974.

Eliade, *Autobiography,* Volume 1: *1907-1937, Journey East, Journey West,* Harper, 1981, Volume 2: *1937-1960, Exile's Odyssey,* University of Chicago Press, 1989.

Eliade, Carrasco, Jane Marie Law; *Waiting for the Dawn: Mircea Eliade in Perspective,* revised edition, University Press of Colorado (Niwot), 1991.

Eliot, Alexander, *The Universal Myths: Heroes, Gods, Tricksters, and Others,* New American Library (New York), 1990.

Encyclopedia of Occultism and Parapsychology, 2nd edition, Gale, 1985.

Girardot, Norman and MacLinscott Ricketts, editors, *Imagination and Meaning: The Scholarly and Literary Worlds of Mircea Eliade,* Seabury, 1982.

Idinopulos, Thomas A., *Religion and Reductionism: Essays on Eliade, Segal, and the Challenge of the Social Sciences for the Study of Religion,* E.J. Brill (New York City), 1994.

Kitagawa, Joseph M. and Charles H. Long, editors, *Myths and Symbols: Studies in Honor of Mircea Eliade,* University of Chicago Press, 1969.

Mason, John R., *Reading and Responding to Mircea Eliade's History of Religious Ideas: The Lure of the Late Eliade,* E. Mellen Press (Lewiston), 1993.

Olson, Carl, *The Theology and Philosophy of Eliade: A Search for the Centre,* St. Martin's Press (New York City), 1992.

Rennie, Bryan S., *Reconstructing Eliade: Making Sense of Religion,* State University of New York Press (Albany), 1996.

Silabu, John A., *"Homo Religiosus" in Mircea Eliade: An Anthropological Evaluation*, Brill, 1976.

PERIODICALS

America, March 10, 1979.
American Anthropologist, August, 1959.
Books Abroad, Volume 49, number 1, 1975.
Booklist, May 15, 1992, p. 1715.
Christian Century, March 1, 1989, p. 234; July 5, 1989, p. 655.
Encounter, March, 1980.
Hibbert Journal, October, 1961.
Journal of Asian Studies, Volume 30, number 3, 1971.
Journal of Bible and Religion, July, 1965.
Journal of Religion, April, 1960; January 1, 1961; April, 1972; October, 1986.
Library Journal, November 15, 1991, p. 73.
Listener, Volume 99, number 2543, January 19, 1978.
Los Angeles Times Book Review, December 22, 1985; January 22, 1989.
Nation, October 10, 1994, p. 390.
New Republic, August 5, 1991, p. 27; August 15, 1994, p. 43.
New Statesman, December 17, 1960; October 16, 1964; March 23, 1990, p. 38.
Newsweek, July 15, 1985.
New York Review of Books, October 20, 1966; September 22, 1994, p. 27.
New York Times Book Review, July 12, 1964; August 11, 1974; April 15, 1979; November 22, 1981; March 5, 1989, p. 24; May 15, 1994, p. 12.
Publishers Weekly, October 12, 1990, p. 50; March 7, 1994, p. 56.
Reason, February, 1989, p. 56.
Religion in Life, spring, 1967.
Religion: Journal of Religion and Religions, spring, 1973.
Religious Studies, 1972, 1974.
Time, February 11, 1966; October 26, 1981.
Times Literary Supplement, November 11, 1960; October 13, 1978; April 2, 1982; September 26, 1986; February 10, 1989, p. 137; September 28, 1990, p. 1015; September 11, 1993, p. 23.
Tribune Books (Chicago), October 9, 1988.
Union Seminary Quarterly Review, winter, 1970; summer, 1970.
Washington Post Book World, May 22, 1996, p. 6.
World Literature Today, Volume 51, number 3, 1977; Volume 52, number 4, 1978; Volume 54, number 1, 1980; winter, 1990, p. 93.

OBITUARIES:

PERIODICALS

Chicago Tribune, April 23, 1986.
Los Angeles Times, April 26, 1986.
New York Times, April 23, 1986.
Time, May 5, 1986.
Times (London), April 29, 1986.*

* * *

ELLIS, Scott
  See SCHORR, Mark

* * *

ERDRICH, Louise 1954-
  (Heidi Louise, Milou North)

PERSONAL: Born Karen Louise Erdrich June 7 (one source says July 6), 1954, in Little Falls, MN; daughter of Ralph Louis (a teacher with the Bureau of Indian Affairs) and Rita Joanne (affiliated with the Bureau of Indian Affairs; maiden name, Gourneau) Erdrich; married Michael Anthony Dorris (a writer and professor of Native American studies), October 10, 1981 (died April 11, 1997); children: Reynold Abel (died in 1991), Jeffrey Sava, Madeline Hannah, Persia Andromeda, Pallas Antigone, Aza Marion. *Education:* Dartmouth College, B.A., 1976; Johns Hopkins University, M.A., 1979. *Politics:* Democrat *Religion:* "Anti-religion." *Avocational interests:* Quilling, running, drawing, "playing chess with daughters and losing, playing piano badly, speaking terrible French."

CAREER: Writer. North Dakota State Arts Council, visiting poet and teacher, 1977-78; Johns Hopkins University, Baltimore, MD, writing instructor, 1978-79; Boston Indian Council, Boston, MA, communications director and editor of *The Circle,* 1979-80; Charles-Merrill Co., textbook writer, 1980. Previously employed as a beet weeder in Wahpeton, ND; waitress in Wahpeton, Boston, and Syracuse, NY; psychiatric aide in a Vermont hospital; poetry teacher at prisons; lifeguard; and construction flag signaler. Has judged writing contests.

MEMBER: International Writers, PEN (member of executive board, 1985-88), Authors Guild, Authors League of America.

AWARDS, HONORS: Johns Hopkins University teaching fellow, 1978; MacDowell Colony fellow, 1980; Yaddo Colony fellow, 1981; Dartmouth College visiting fellow, 1981; First Prize, Nelson Algren fiction competition, 1982, for "The World's Greatest Fisherman"; National Endowment for the Arts fellowship, 1982; Pushcart Prize, 1983; National Magazine Fiction awards, 1983 and 1987; *Love Medicine* received the Virginia McCormack Scully Prize for best book of the year dealing with Indians or Chicanos in 1984, the National Book Critics Circle Award for best work of fiction in 1984, the *Los Angeles Times Award* for best novel, the Sue Kaufman Prize for the Best First Novel from the American Academy and Institute of Arts and Letters, the American Book Award from the Before Columbus Foundation, and was named one of the best eleven books of 1985 by the *New York Times Book Review*; Guggenheim fellow, 1985-86; *The Beet Queen* was named one of *Publishers Weekly's* best books, 1986; First Prize, O. Henry awards, 1987; National Book Critics Circle Award nomination.

WRITINGS:

NOVELS

Love Medicine, Holt (New York City), 1984, expanded edition, 1993.
The Beet Queen, Holt, 1986.
Tracks, Harper, 1988.
(With Michael Dorris) *The Crown of Columbus,* HarperCollins (New York City), 1991.
The Bingo Palace, HarperCollins, 1994.
Tales of Burning Love, HarperCollins, 1996.

POETRY

Jacklight, Holt, 1984.
Baptism of Desire, Harper, 1989.

OTHER

Imagination (textbook), C. E. Merrill, 1980.
(Author of preface) Michael Dorris, *The Broken Cord: A Family's Ongoing Struggle with Fetal Alcohol Syndrome,* Harper, 1989.
(Author of preface) Desmond Hogan, *A Link with the River,* Farrar, Straus, 1989.
(With Allan Richard Chavkin and Nancy Feyl Chavkin) *Conversations with Louise Erdrich and*

Michael Dorris, University Press of Mississippi (Jackson), 1994.
The Falcon: A Narrative of the Captivity and Adventures of John Tanner, Penguin (New York City), 1994.
The Blue Jay's Dance: A Birth Year (memoir), HarperCollins (New York City), 1995.
Grandmother's Pigeon (children's book), illustrated by Jim LaMarche, Hyperion (New York City), 1996.

Author of short story, "The World's Greatest Fisherman"; contributor to anthologies, including the *Norton Anthology of Poetry; Best American Short Stories* of 1981-83, 1983, and 1988; and *Prize Stories: The O. Henry Awards,* in 1985 and 1987. Contributor of stories, poems, essays, and book reviews to periodicals, including *New Yorker, New England Review, Chicago, American Indian Quarterly, Frontiers, Atlantic, Kenyon Review, North American Review, New York Times Book Review, Ms., Redbook* (with her sister Heidi, under the joint pseudonym Heidi Louise), and *Woman* (with Dorris, under the joint pseudonym Milou North).

ADAPTATIONS: The Crown of Columbus has been optioned for film production.

SIDELIGHTS: Award-winning author Louise Erdrich published her first two books—*Jacklight,* a volume of poetry, and *Love Medicine,* a novel—at the age of thirty. The daughter of a Chippewa Indian mother and a German-American father, the author explores Native American themes in her works, with major characters representing both sides of her heritage. The first in a multi-part series, *Love Medicine* traces two Native American families from 1934 to 1984 in a unique seven-narrator format. The novel was extremely well-received, earning its author numerous awards, including the National Book Critics Circle Award in 1984. Since then, Erdrich has gone on to publish *The Beet Queen, Tracks, The Bingo Palace,* and *Tales of Burning Love,* all of which are related through recurring characters and themes.

Erdrich's interest in writing can be traced to her childhood and her heritage. She told *Writer's Digest* contributor Michael Schumacher, "People in [Native American] families make everything into a story. . . . People just sit and the stories start coming, one after another. I suppose that when you grow up constantly hearing the stories rise, break, and fall, it gets into you somehow." The oldest in a family of seven children, Erdrich was raised in Wahpeton, North Dakota.

Her Chippewa grandfather had been the tribal chair of the nearby Turtle Mountain Reservation, and her parents worked at the Bureau of Indian Falls boarding school. Erdrich once told *CA* of the way in which her parents encouraged her writing: "My father used to give me a nickel for every story I wrote, and my mother wove strips of construction paper together and stapled them into book covers. So at an early age I felt myself to be a published author earning substantial royalties."

Erdrich's first year at Dartmouth, 1972, was the year the college began admitting women, as well as the year the Native American studies department was established. The author's future husband and collaborator, anthropologist Michael Dorris, was hired to chair the department. In his class, Erdrich began the exploration of her own ancestry that would eventually inspire her novels. Intent on balancing her academic training with a broad range of practical knowledge, Erdrich told Miriam Berkley in an interview with *Publishers Weekly,* "I ended up taking some really crazy jobs, and I'm glad I did. They turned out to have been very useful experiences, although I never would have believed it at the time." In addition to working as a lifeguard, waitress, poetry teacher at prisons, and construction flag signaler, Erdrich became an editor for the *Circle,* a Boston Indian Council newspaper. She told Schumacher, "Settling into that job and becoming comfortable with an urban community—which is very different from the reservation community—gave me another reference point. There were lots of people with mixed blood, lots of people who had their own confusions. I realized that this was part of my life—it wasn't something that I was making up—and that it was something I *wanted* to write about." In 1978, the author enrolled in an M.A. program at Johns Hopkins University, where she wrote poems and stories incorporating her heritage, many of which would later become part of her books. She also began sending her work to publishers, most of whom sent back rejection slips.

After receiving her master's degree, Erdrich returned to Dartmouth as a writer-in-residence. Dorris—with whom she had remained in touch—attended a reading of Erdrich's poetry there, and was impressed. A writer himself—Dorris would later publish the best-selling novel *A Yellow Raft in Blue Water* and receive the 1989 National Book Critics Circle Award for his nonfiction work *The Broken Cord*—he decided then that he was interested in working with Erdrich and getting to know her better. When he left for New Zealand to do field research and Erdrich went to

Boston to work on a textbook, the two began sending their poetry and fiction back and forth with their letters, laying a groundwork for a literary relationship. Dorris returned to New Hampshire in 1980, and Erdrich moved back there as well. The two began collaborating on short stories, including one titled "The World's Greatest Fisherman." When this story won five thousand dollars in the Nelson Algren fiction competition, Erdrich and Dorris decided to expand it into a novel—*Love Medicine.* At the same time, their literary relationship led to a romantic one. In 1981 they were married.

The titles Erdrich and Dorris chose for their novels—such as *Love Medicine* and *A Yellow Raft in Blue Water*—tended to be rich poetic or visual images. The title was often the initial inspiration from which their novels were drawn. Erdrich told Schumacher, "I think a title is like a magnet: It begins to draw these scraps of experience or conversation or memory to it. Eventually, it collects a book." Erdrich and Dorris's collaborative process began with a first draft, usually written by whoever had the original idea for the book, the one who would ultimately be considered the official author. After the draft was written, the other person edited it, and then another draft was written; often five or six drafts would be written in all. Finally, the two read the work aloud until they agreed on each word. Although the author had the original voice and the final say, ultimately, both collaborators were responsible for what the work became. This "unique collaborative relationship", according to Alice Joyce in *Booklist,* is covered in *Conversations with Louise Erdrich and Michael Dorris,* a collection of 25 interviews with the couple. By 1997, when Dorris committed suicide, the pair had separated and were no longer actively collaborating.

Erdrich's novels *Love Medicine, The Beet Queen, Tracks, The Bingo Palace,* and *Tales of Burning Love* encompass the stories of three interrelated families living in and around a reservation in the fictional town of Argus, North Dakota, from 1912 through the 1980's. The novels have been compared to those of William Faulkner, mainly due to the multi-voice narration and nonchronological storytelling which he employed in works such as *As I Lay Dying.* Erdrich's works, linked by recurring characters who are victims of fate and the patterns set by their elders, are structured like intricate puzzles in which bits of information about individuals and their relations to one another are slowly released in a seemingly random order, until three-dimensional characters—with a future and a past—are revealed. Through her characters' antics, Erdrich explores universal family life cycles while also communicating a sense of the changes and loss involved in the twentieth-century Native American experience.

Poet Robert Bly, describing Erdrich's nonlinear storytelling approach in the *New York Times Book Review,* emphasized her tendency to "choose a few minutes or a day in 1932, let one character talk, let another talk, and a third, then leap to 1941 and then to 1950 or 1964." The novels' circular format is a reflection of the way in which the works are constructed. Although Erdrich is dealing with a specific and extensive time period, "The writing doesn't start out and proceed chronologically. It never seems to start in the beginning. Rather, it's as though we're building something around a center, but that center can be anywhere."

Erdrich published her first novel, *Love Medicine,* in 1984. "With this impressive debut," stated *New York Times Book Review* contributor Marco Portales, "Louise Erdrich enters the company of America's better novelists." *Love Medicine* was named for the belief in love potions which is a part of Chippewa folklore. The novel explores the bonds of family and faith which preserve both the Chippewa tribal community and the individuals that comprise it.

The novel begins at a family gathering following the death of June Kashpaw, a prostitute. The characters introduce one another, sharing stories about June which reveal their family history and their cultural beliefs. Albertine Johnson, June's niece, introduces her grandmother, Marie, her grandfather, Nector, and Nector's twin brother, Eli. Eli represents the old way—the Native American who never integrated into the white culture. He also plays a major role in *Tracks,* in which he appears as a young man. The story of Marie and Nector brings together many of the important images in the novel, including the notion of "love medicine." As a teenager in a convent, Marie is nearly burned to death by a nun who, in an attempt to exorcize the devil from within her, pours boiling water on Marie. Immediately following this incident, Marie is sexually assaulted by Nector. Marie and Nector are later married, but in middle age, Nector begins an affair with Lulu Lamartine, a married woman. In an attempt to rekindle Nector and Marie's passion, their grandson Lipsha prepares "love medicine" for Nector. But Lipsha has difficulty obtaining a wild goose heart for the potion. He substitutes a frozen turkey heart, which causes Nector to choke to death.

Reviewers responded positively to Erdrich's debut novel, citing its lyrical qualities as well as the rich characters who inhabit it. *New York Times* contributor D. J. R. Bruckner was impressed with Erdrich's "mastery of words," as well as the "vividly drawn" characters who "will not leave the mind once they are let in." Portales, who called *Love Medicine* "an engrossing book," applauded the unique narration technique which produces what he termed "a wondrous prose song."

After the publication of *Love Medicine,* Erdrich told reviewers that her next novel would focus less exclusively on her mother's side, embracing the author's mixed heritage and the mixed community in which she grew up. Her 1986 novel, *The Beet Queen,* deals with whites and half-breeds, as well as American Indians, and explores the interactions between these worlds. The story begins in 1932, during the Depression. *The Beet Queen* begins when Mary and Karl Adare's recently-widowed mother flies off with a carnival pilot, abandoning the two children and their newborn brother. The baby is taken by a young couple who have just lost their child. Karl and eleven-year-old Mary ride a freight train to Argus, seeking refuge with their aunt and uncle. When they arrive in the town, however, Karl, frightened by a dog, runs back onto the train and winds up at an orphanage. Mary grows up with her aunt and uncle, and the novel follows her life—as well as those of her jealous, self-centered cousin Sita and their part-Chippewa friend Celestine James—for the next forty years, tracing the themes of separation and loss that began with Mary's father's death and her mother's grand departure.

The Beet Queen was well-received by critics, some of whom found it even more impressive than *Love Medicine.* Many noted the novel's poetic language and symbolism; Bly noted that Erdrich's "genius is in metaphor," and that the characters "show a convincing ability to feel an image with their whole bodies." Josh Rubins, writing in *New York Review of Books,* called *The Beet Queen* "a rare second novel, one that makes it seem as if the first, impressive as it was, promised too little, not too much."

Other reviewers had problems with *The Beet Queen,* but they tended to dismiss the novel's flaws in light of its positive qualities. *New Republic* contributor Dorothy Wickenden considered the characters unrealistic and the ending contrived, but she lauded *The Beet Queen*'s "ringing clarity and lyricism," as well as the "assured, polished quality" which she felt was missing in *Love Medicine.* Although Michiko Kakutani found the ending artificial, the *New York Times* reviewer called Erdrich "an immensely gifted young writer." "Even with its weaknesses," proclaimed Linda Simon in *Commonweal, "The Beet Queen* stands as a product of enormous talent."

After Erdrich completed *The Beet Queen,* she was uncertain as to what her next project should be. The four-hundred-page manuscript that would eventually become *Tracks* had remained untouched for ten years; the author referred to it as her "burden." She and Dorris took a fresh look at it, and decided that they could relate it to *Love Medicine* and *The Beet Queen.* While more political than her previous novels, *Tracks,* Erdrich's 1989 work, also deals with spiritual themes, exploring the tension between the Native Americans' ancient beliefs and the Christian notions of the Europeans. *Tracks* takes place between 1912 and 1924, before the settings of Erdrich's other novels, and reveals the roots of *Love Medicine*'s characters and their hardships. One of the narrators, Nanapush, is the leader of a tribe that is suffering on account of the white government's exploitation. He feels pressured to give up their land in order to avoid starvation. While Nanapush represents the old way, Pauline, the other narrator, represents change. The future mother of *Love Medicine*'s Marie Lazarre, Pauline is a young half-breed from a mixed-blood tribe "for which the name was lost." She feels torn between her Indian faith and the white people's religion, and is considering leaving the reservation. But at the center of *Tracks* is Fleur, a character whom *Los Angeles Times Book Review* contributor Terry Tempest Williams called "one of the most haunting presences in contemporary American literature." Nanapush discovers this young woman—the last survivor of a family killed by consumption—in a cabin in the woods, starving and mad. Nanapush adopts Fleur and nurses her back to health.

Reviewers found *Tracks* distinctly different from Erdrich's earlier novels, and some felt that her third novel lacked the characteristics that made *Love Medicine* and *The Beet Queen* so outstanding. *Washington Post Book World* critic Jonathan Yardley felt that, on account of its more political focus, the work has a "labored quality." Robert Towers stated in *New York Review of Books* that he found the characters too melodramatic and the tone too intense. Katherine Dieckmann, writing in the *Voice Literary Supplement,* affirmed that she "missed [Erdrich's] skilled multiplications of voice," and called the relationship between Pauline and Nanapush "symptomatic of the overall lack of grand orchestration and perspectival interplay

that made Erdrich's first two novels polyphonic masterpieces." According to *Commonweal* contributor Christopher Vecsey, however, although "a reviewer might find some of the prose overwrought, and the two narrative voices indistinguishable . . . readers will appreciate and applaud the vigor and inventiveness of the author."

Other reviewers enjoyed *Tracks* even more than the earlier novels. Williams stated that Erdrich's writing "has never appeared more polished and grounded," and added, "*Tracks* may be the story of our time." Thomas M. Disch lauded the novel's plot, with its surprising twists and turns, in the *Chicago Tribune.* The critic added, "Louise Erdrich is like one of those rumored drugs that are instantly and forever addictive. Fortunately in her case you can *just say yes.*"

Erdrich and Dorris's jointly-authored novel, *The Crown of Columbus,* explores Native American issues from the standpoint of the authors' current experience, rather than the world of their ancestors. Marking the quincentennial anniversary of Spanish explorer Christopher Columbus's voyage in a not-so-celebratory fashion, Erdrich and Dorris raise important questions about the meaning of that voyage for both Europeans and Native Americans today. The story is narrated by the two central characters, both Dartmouth professors involved in projects concerning Columbus. Vivian Twostar is a Native American single mother with eclectic tastes and a teenage son, Nash. Vivian is asked to write an academic article on Columbus from a Native American perspective and is researching Columbus's diaries. Roger Williams, a stuffy New England Protestant poet, is writing an epic work about the explorer's voyage. Vivian and Roger become lovers—parenting a girl named Violet—but have little in common. Ultimately acknowledging the destructive impact of Columbus's voyage on the Native American people, Vivian and Roger vow to redress the political wrongs symbolically by changing the power structure in their relationship. In the end, as Vivian and Roger rediscover themselves, they rediscover America.

Some reviewers found *The Crown of Columbus* unbelievable and inconsistent, and considered it less praiseworthy than the individual authors' earlier works. However, *New York Times Book Review* contributor Robert Houston appreciated the work's timely political relevance. He also stated, "There are moments of genuine humor and compassion, of real insight and sound satire." Other critics also considered

Vivian and Roger's adventures amusing, vibrant, and charming.

Erdrich returned to the descendants of Nanapush with her 1994 novel, *The Bingo Palace*. The fourth novel in the series which began with *Love Medicine, The Bingo Palace* weaves together a story of spiritual pursuit with elements of modern reservation life. Erdrich also provided continuity to the series by having the novel primarily narrated by Lipsha Morrisey, the illegitimate son of June Kapshaw and Gerry Nanapush from *Love Medicine*. After working at a Fargo sugar beet factory, Lipsha has returned home to the reservation in search of his life's meaning. He finds work at his uncle Lyman Lamartine's bingo parlor and love with his uncle's girlfriend, Shawnee Ray Toose. Thanks to the magic bingo tickets provided to him by the spirit of his dead mother, June, he also finds modest wealth. The character of Fleur Pillager returns from *Tracks* as Lipsha's great-grandmother. After visiting her, Lipsha embarks on a spiritual quest in order to impress Shawnee and learn more about his own tribal religious rites. Family members past and present are brought together in his pursuit, which comprises the final pages of the novel.

Reviewers' comments on *The Bingo Palace* were generally positive. While Lawrence Thornton in the *New York Times Book Review* found "some of the novel's later ventures into magic realism . . . contrived," his overall impression was more positive: "Ms. Erdrich's sympathy for her characters shines as luminously as Shawnee Ray's jingle dress." Pam Houston, writing for the *Los Angeles Times Book Review,* was especially taken by the character of Lipsha Morrissey, finding in him "what makes this her most exciting and satisfying book to date."

The Bingo Palace was also reviewed in the context of the series as a whole. *Chicago Tribune* contributor Michael Upchurch concluded, "*The Bingo Palace* falls somewhere between *Tracks* and *The Beet Queen* in its accomplishment." He added, "The best chapters in *The Bingo Palace* rival, as *Love Medicine* did, the work of Welty, Cheever, and Flannery O'Connor."

Erdrich turned to her own experience as mother of six for her next work, *The Blue Jay's Dance*. Her first book of nonfiction, *The Blue Jay's Dance* chronicles Erdrich's pregnancy and the birth year of her child. The title refers to a blue jay's habit of defiantly "dancing" towards an attacking hawk, Erdrich's metaphor for "the sort of controlled recklessness that having children always is," noted Jane Aspinall in

Quill & Quire. Erdrich has been somewhat protective of her family's privacy and has stated the narrative actually describes a combination of her experience with several of her children. Sue Halpern in the *New York Times Book Review* remarked on this difficult balancing act between public and private lives but found "Ms. Erdrich's ambivalence inspires trust . . . and suggests that she is the kind of mother whose story should be told."

Some reviewers averred that Erdrich's description of the maternal relationship was a powerful one: "the bond between mother and infant has rarely been captured so well," commented a *Kirkus Reviews* contributor. While the subject of pregnancy and motherhood is not a new one, Halpern noted that the book provided new insight into the topic: "What makes *The Blue Jay's Dance* worth reading is that it quietly places a mother's love and nurturance amid her love for the natural world and suggests . . . how right that placement is." Although the *Kirkus Reviews* contributor found *The Blue Jay's Dance* to be "occasionally too self-conscious about the importance of Erdrich's role as Writer," others commented positively on the book's examination of the balance between the work of parenting and one's vocation. A *Los Angeles Times* reviewer remarked: "this book is really about working and having children, staying alert and . . . focused through the first year of a child's life."

Erdrich retained her focus on children with her first children's book, *Grandmother's Pigeon*. Published in 1996, it is a fanciful tale of an adventurous grandmother who heads to Greenland on the back of a porpoise, leaving behind grandchildren and three bird's eggs in her cluttered bedroom. The eggs hatch into passenger pigeons, thought to be extinct, through which the children are able to send messages to their missing grandmother. A *Publishers Weekly* reviewer commented, "As in her fiction for adults . . . , Erdrich makes every word count in her bewitching debut children's story."

Within the same year, Erdrich returned to the character of June Kasphaw of *Love Medicine* in her sixth novel, *Tales of Burning Love*. More accurately, it is the story of June's husband, Jack Mauser, and his five (including June) ex-wives. To begin the tale, Jack meets June while they are both inebriated and marries her that night. In reaction to his inability to consummate their marriage, she walks off into a blizzard and is found dead the next day. His four subsequent marriages share the same elements of tragedy and comedy, culminating in Jack's death in a fire in the house he built. The story of each marriage is told by the four ex-wives as they are stranded together in Jack's car during a blizzard after his funeral. Again, Erdrich references her previous work in the characters of Gerry and Dot Nanapush, Dot as one of Jack's ex-wives and Gerry as Dot's imprisoned husband.

Reviewers continued to note Erdrich's masterful descriptions and fine dialogue in this work. According to Penelope Mesic in the *Chicago Tribune*, "Erdrich's strength is that she gives emotional states—as shifting and intangible, as indefinable as wind—a visible form in metaphor." A *Times Literary Supplement* contributor compared her to both Tobias Wolff—"(like him), she is . . . particularly good at evoking American small-town life and the space that engulfs it"—as well as Raymond Carver, noting her dialogues to be "small exchanges that . . . map out the barely navigable distance between what's heard, what's meant, and what's said."

Tales of Burning Love also focuses Erdrich's abilities (and perhaps Dorris's collaborative talents) on the relationship between men and women. The *Times Literary Supplement* reviewer continued, "Erdrich also shares Carver's clear and sophisticated view of the more fundamental distance between men and women, and how that, too, is negotiated." However, Mark Childress in the *New York Times Book Review* commented that while "Jack's wives are vivid and fully realized . . . whenever (Jack's) out of sight, he doesn't seem as interesting as the women who loved him."

While Erdrich covers familiar territory in *Tales of Burning Love*, she seems to be expanding her focus slightly. Roxana Robinson in *Washington Post Book World* remarked, "The landscape, instead of being somber and overcast . . . is vividly illuminated by bolts of freewheeling lunacy: This is a mad Gothic comedy." Or as Verlyn Klinkenborg noted in the *Los Angeles Times Book Review*, "this book marks a shift in (Erdrich's) career, a shift that is suggested rather than fulfilled . . . there is new country coming into (her) sight, and this novel is her first welcoming account of it."

BIOGRAPHICAL/CRITICAL SOURCES:

BOOKS

Authors and Artists for Young Adults, Volume 10, Gale (Detroit), 1993.

Contemporary Literary Criticism, Gale, Volume 39, 1986, Volume 54, 1989.
Dictionary of Literary Biography, Volume 152: *American Novelists since World War II, Fourth Series,* Gale, 1995.
Erdrich, Louise, *Tracks,* Harper, 1988.
Erdrich, Louise, *Baptism of Desire,* Harper, 1989.
Pearlman, Mickey, *American Women Writing Fiction: Memory, Identity, Family, Space,* University Press of Kentucky, 1989, pp. 95-112.

PERIODICALS

America, May 14, 1994, p. 7.
American Indian Culture and Research Journal, 1987, pp. 51-73.
American Literature, September, 1990, pp. 405-22.
Belles Lettres, summer, 1990, pp. 30-1.
Booklist, January 15, 1995, p. 893.
Chicago Tribune, September 4, 1988, pp. 1, 6; January 1, 1994, pp. 1, 9; April 21, 1996, pp. 1, 9.
College Literature, October, 1991, pp. 80-95.
Commonweal, October 24, 1986, pp. 565, 567; November 4, 1988, p. 596.
Kirkus Reviews, February 15, 1996, p. 244; April 15, 1996, p. 600.
Los Angeles Times Book Review, October 5, 1986, pp. 3, 10; September 11, 1988, p. 2; May 12, 1991, pp. 3, 13; February 6, 1994, p. 1, 13; May 28, 1995, p. 8; June 16, 1996, p. 3.
Nation, October 21, 1991, pp. 465, 486-90.
New Republic, October 6, 1986, pp. 46-48; January 6-13, 1992, pp. 30-40.
Newsday, November 30, 1986.
New York Review of Books, January 15, 1987, pp. 14-15; November 19, 1988, pp. 40-41; May 12, 1996, p. 10.
New York Times, December 20, 1984, p. C21; August 20, 1986, p. C21; August 24, 1988, p. 41; April 19, 1991, p. C25.
New York Times Book Review, August 31, 1982, p. 2; December 23, 1984, p. 6; October 2, 1988, pp. 1, 41-42; April 28, 1991, p. 10; July 20, 1993, p. 20; January 16, 1994, p. 7; April 16, 1995, p.14.
People, June 10, 1991, pp. 26-27.
Playboy, March, 1994, p. 30.
Publishers Weekly, August 15, 1986, pp. 58-59; April 22, 1996, p. 71.
Quill & Quire, August, 1995, p. 30.
Time, February 7, 1994, p. 71.
Times Literary Supplement, February 14, 1997, p. 21.
Voice Literary Supplement, October, 1988, p. 37.

Washington Post Book World, August 31, 1986, pp.
    1, 6; September 18, 1988, p. 3; February 6,
    1994, p. 5; April 21, 1996, p. 3.
Western American Literature, February, 1991, pp.
    363-64.
Writer's Digest, June, 1991, pp. 28-31.*

F

FINDER, Joseph 1958-

PERSONAL: Born October 6, 1958, in Chicago, IL; son of Morris (a professor) and Natalie (a professor; maiden name, Stone) Finder. *Education:* Yale University, B.A., 1980; graduate study at Harvard University, 1980-83.

ADDRESSES: Home—Cambridge, MA. *Agent*—Patricia Berens, Sterling Lord Agency, Inc., 660 Madison Ave., New York, NY 10021.

CAREER: Harvard University, Cambridge, MA, teaching fellow at Harvard College, 1983-84.

MEMBER: Phi Beta Kappa.

WRITINGS:

Red Carpet: The Connection Between the Kremlin and America's Most Powerful Businessmen, Holt (New York City), 1983.
The Moscow Club, Viking (New York City), 1991.
Extraordinary Powers, Ballantine (New York City), 1994.
The Zero Hour, Morrow (New York City), 1996.

Contributor to magazines, including *Atlantic, New Republic, Harper's,* and *Publishers Weekly.*

ADAPTATIONS: Film rights to *The Zero Hour* have been sold to Twentieth Century-Fox.

SIDELIGHTS: Joseph Finder began his writing career with *Red Carpet: The Connection Between the Kremlin and America's Most Powerful Businessmen,* a nonfiction account of Western capitalists making profits from trade with the communist world. But it is as a writer of tense, fast-moving espionage thrillers, based in part upon his extensive knowledge of the former Soviet Union, that Finder has earned a critical reputation. As a reviewer for *Publishers Weekly* comments, Finder "rivals the early Frederick Forsyth in his riveting combination of cool prose and hot plot."

Red Carpet, Finder once told *CA,* "is a nonfiction account of how a very few prominent American businessmen (David Rockefeller, Armand Hammer, Averell Harriman, Cyrus Eaton, and Donald Kendall) came to be involved with the Soviet Union and why. It is based on interviews with the principals, with their colleagues, and with government officials and on documents made available under the Freedom of Information Act, in addition to the normal sources."

Finder's research for *Red Carpet* led him to write *The Moscow Club,* a fictional account of a secret plan to reinstall a communist regime in Russia and the efforts of one American agent to stop it. The novel is, Charles Michaud writes in *Library Journal,* a "tale of multiple conspiracies, deception, murder, and deadly pursuit." "If Finder's fiction debut doesn't outdo Frederick Forsyth in grace of style," the critic for *Publishers Weekly* notes, "it surpasses both Forsyth and Ludlum in density of mystery and swirl of action." The critic for *Kirkus Reviews* calls *The Moscow Club* an "overblown, entertaining first novel" and "compulsively readable." Michaud concludes that Finder's story exhibits "a driving what-happens-next readability."

Extraordinary Powers opens with the death of the director of the CIA, a possible murder connected with the director's alleged involvement with a gold smuggling operation. Calling the novel "a wild tale of corruption in the world of espionage," Chris Petrakos in *Tribune Books* concludes that "Finder keeps things lively with heavy doses of paranoia, cunning plot twists and a varied cast of characters, none of whom can be trusted." The critic for *Kirkus Reviews* notes that "the complex story purrs along like a high-powered race car loaded with options."

The Zero Hour concerns a terrorist plot to destroy the computer system which controls most of the world's monetary transactions and stock trading. FBI terrorism expert Sarah Cahill must uncover the persons behind the plot and foil their scheme before the world's economy is dealt a crippling blow. George Needham in *Booklist* finds that "the tale provides lots of surprises, zooming along at breakneck speed to a thrilling climax." *The Zero Hour,* according to Mark Dery in the *New York Times Book Review,* "is goosebump-good fun," while the *Kirkus Reviews* critic praises Finder for keeping "the menace breathlessly exciting rather than grimly scary. The result is as fleet and entertaining as *Black Sunday,* if you don't mind rooting for an international bank."

BIOGRAPHICAL/CRITICAL SOURCES:

PERIODICALS

Armchair Detective, fall, 1991, p. 411.
Booklist, November 15, 1990, p. 578; January 1, 1994, p. 787; March 1, 1996, p. 1076.
Commentary, August, 1983, p. 86.
Insight on the News, March 25, 1991, p. 60.
Kirkus Reviews, November 15, 1990, pp. 1554-1555; November 15, 1993, p. 1410; March 15, 1996, p. 393.
Library Journal, December, 1990, p. 162; April 1, 1996, p. 116.
Los Angeles Times Book Review, August 4, 1996, p. 8.
New Yorker, July 22, 1996, p. 69.
New York Times Book Review, February 27, 1994, p. 20; June 16, 1996.
People Weekly, June 24, 1996, p. 34.
Publishers Weekly, December 21, 1990; April 17, 1995, p. 54; March 25, 1996, p. 59; May 6, 1996, p. 25.
Tribune Books (Chicago), February 17, 1991, p. 7; January 16, 1994, p. 6.
Washington Monthly, July-August, 1983, p. 59.
Washington Post, February 14, 1991, p. B1; March 8, 1994, p. B2; July 18, 1996, p. C2.

FITZGERALD, Judith 1952-

PERSONAL: Born November 11, 1952, in Toronto, Ontario, Canada. *Education:* York University, B.A. (with honors), 1976, M.A., 1977; attended Univeristy of Toronto, 1978-83. *Politics:* New Democrat. *Avocational interests:* Music, film.

ADDRESSES: Home—1805-2285 Lakeshore Blvd. West, Mimico, Ontario M8V 3X9, Canada.

CAREER: University of Toronto, Toronto, Canada, lecturer in modern American and Canadian literature, 1978-81; Laurentian University of Sudbury, Sudbury, Ontario, assistant professor of Canadian literature, creative writing, and linguistics, 1981-83; freelance writer, 1983—.

AWARDS, HONORS: Grants from Ontario Arts Council, 1973-78; 1980-82, Canada Council project grants and arts grants, 1974-78, 1983-84, 1988-89, 1990-91; Toronto Arts Council grants, 1988, 1990; Fiona Mee Literary Journalism Award, 1983; Writer's Choice Award, 1985.

WRITINGS:

POETRY

City Park, Northern Concept, 1972.
Victory, Coach House Press, 1975.
Lacerating Heartwood, Coach House Press, 1977.
Easy Over, Black Moss (Windsor, Ontario) 1981.
Split/Levels, Coach House Press, 1983.
The Syntax of Things, Prototype Press, 1984.
Beneath the Skin of Paradise: The Piaf Poems, Black Moss, 1984.
Heart Attacks, privately printed, 1984.
Given Names: New and Selected Poems, 1972-1985, edited by Frank Davey, Black Moss, 1985.
Diary of Desire, Black Moss, 1987.
Rapturous Chronicles, Mercury Press (Stratford, Ontario), 1991.
Ultimate Midnight, Black Moss, 1992.
Habit of Blues, Mercury Press, 1993.
Walking Wounded, Black Moss, 1993.
River, ECW Press, 1996.

JUVENILE POETRY

My Orange Gorange, Black Moss, 1985.
Whale Waddleby, Black Moss, 1986.

PROSE

Journal Entries, Dreadnaught Press, 1975.

EDITOR

Un Dozen: Thirteen Canadian Poets, Black Moss, 1982.
SP/Elles: Poetry by Canadian Women; Poesie de femmes canandiennes, Black Moss, 1986.
First Person Plural, Black Moss, 1988.

OTHER

Contributor to numerous periodicals, including *Books in Canada, Canadian Forum, Canadian Literature, Dialogue, Island, Nebula,* and *West Coast Review,* and to anthologies, including *Canadian Poetry Now* 1984, *The New Canadian Poets* 1984, *Relations* 1986, and *Poetry by Canadian Women* 1988. Assistant editor, *English Quarterly,* 1967-68, and 1976-77, poetry editor, *Black Moss Press,* 1981-87, poetry critic and columnist, *Toronto Star,* 1984-88, entertainment writer, *Globe and Mail,* 1983-84, and senior writer and contributing editor, *Country,* 1990-91.

SIDELIGHTS: Judith Fitzgerald is a Canadian poet who has received praise for her use of wordplay, her condensed and sophisticated style and her willingness to utilize a variety of poetic techniques. Fitzgerald once told *CA:* "I write because it is one of the few moral decisions available to individuals during these desolate times. It is a decision of conscience, to be, to do, to make, to continue."

Fitzgerald's early poetry, represented by *Given Names: New and Selected Poems, 1972-1985,* has been praised by Lucille King-Edwards in *Books in Canada* for its "passion and linguistic virtuosity." This volume, according to King-Edwards, shows the development of Fitzgerald's poetry "from conventional lyric pattern to a mixture of forms that move from journal-entry prose to the syntactically disjointed by emotionally integrated language of such works as 'Given Names'." Many of the poems deal with the search for the father, and with coming to terms with a difficult childhood ("There is no escape/ except in the refuge/ of this poem").

In another early work, *Beneath the Skin of Paradise: The Piaf Poems,* Fitzgerald takes on the persona of French singer Edith Piaf, producing a book with a confessional tone, continuing an identification with Piaf which she explored earlier in what Libby Scheier

in *Books in Canada* called "the obviously autobiographical poems series "Past Cards" in *Split/ Levels.*"

Diary of Desire (1987), a long poem divided into monthly sections, was described by Phil Hall, writing in *Books in Canada,* as containing "passionate, playful free-association." But Hall criticizes the book for its "trick of saying nothing so succinctly it sounds wise" and its "expropriation of scientific and linguistic jargon." Bruce Whiteman, in *Quill and Quire,* however, sees the collection as "a kind of post-modern *Sheapheardes Calender* in which Rosalind gets her turn to talk," and which is enhanced by "a wit and perceptiveness that are voiced in long, loping lines beautifully and predictably paced."

Rapturous Chronicles (1991), which was short-listed for the 1991 Governor General's Award for poetry, is a set of prose poem elegies written for writer Juan Butler that are, according to David Manicom in *Essays on Canadian Writing,* "set in a moonlit, heartbroken, Leonard Cohenesque Toronto romanesque of summer nights and baseball and suicide." Barbara Carey, reviewing for *Books in Canada,* notes that the book's "organizing principle is not linear logic, but the roller coaster of emotion in coming to terms with loss: longing, grief, wrenching desire," as the poet turns, as in previous works, to writing as a means of adjustment, adaptation, survival: "the language keeps me going, the world I create from/ words and wrap around me. Each new word tastes and smells and feels/ itself into my nervous system. Sounded over and over, each becomes/ exotic bird, flower, place. Each provides transport." While Manicom praises *Rapturous Chronicles* as a "book of considerable energy and ambition," he also notes how its virtues are "gradually absorbed by the conventional, the muddled . . . by the self-contradictory," Carey praises the book as "a virtuoso dance along the tightrope of language; and, like a highwire act, it's both intensely personal and, supremely, a *performance.*" *Ultimate Midnight* (1992) follows closely as a "worthy successor," according to Bruce Whiteman in *Books in Canada,* with its "characteristic" elegiac tone and poems which center upon "loss, despair, and ephemerality." Made up of thirteen shorter poems and the title poem, as well as a longer piece in twelve sections, or "hours," *Ultimate Midnight* is written in what Whiteman calls "an urban sort of rhythm that must be read slowly and with care."

In *River* (1996), Fitzgerald returns to the use of the persona, here offing a feminine Orpheus who explores a "fractured urban world poised on the borderland," writes A. F. Moritz in *Books in Canada,* "between earth and hell, between Canada and the U.S., between the most ancient human aspirations and the 'postmodern' disintegration of hope, thought, and language." Moritz sees three influences upon Fitzgerald in *River*. The first is that of T. S. Eliot's "condensed urban epic" *The Waste Land,* upon which it is partly modelled and to which it makes various allusions. The second influence is that of the romantic movement in culture, especially in poetry, as evidenced by Fitzgerald's "re-envisioning of the isolation of the individual" coupled with pressure for the nonconformist to conform, leading to the experience and meaning of "alienation." The third influence is that of modernism, as Moritz notes that the work is "rooted in the semantic play and stream-of-consciousness of James Joyce, in Proust's search for the living waters of memory, and in the collage of myth and modernity, vision, and the everyday." All of these influences make *River* a fuller, richer book than Fitzgerald had previosuly written.

Fitzgerald also writes children's poetry, though it falls far short of the critical response which her adult poetry receives. While noted for their inventiveness (children creating imaginary characters, in one case a "gorange" so that a young girl can write a poem that requires a rhyme for "orange"), these same books offer poems that are "often uneven and the rhymes, weak," according to Adele Ashby in *Quill and Quire.*

Fitzgerald's work as an editor has received more praise, however, especially for *SP/Elles: Poetry by Canadian Women* (1987), a collection of thirteen women poets, eleven "English" and two "French." Paul Dutton, writing in *Quill and Quire,* praises the book for "encompassing various approaches, thematic concerns, career stages, and generations," so that it is a "discerning and exciting collection." Barbara Carey, writing in *Books in Canada,* calls it "a celebration of sound and more specifically, of a language that Judith Fitzgerald describes as springing from 'an ideology and aesthetic centered in women's consciousness'." The book offers poets like Betsy Warland who work in areas that explore English language and etymology, Quebecoise poets like Nicole Brossard who present the French dimension of current Canadian poetry, as well as poets like Ayanna Black who present "the rhythm of Jamaican patois" to show that Canadian poetry is as diverse as the nation is large, leading Carey to praise *SP/Elles* for its "spirit . . . of plurality and inclusion."

BIOGRAPHICAL/CRITICAL SOURCES:

PERIODICALS

American Book Review, May, 1988, p. 1.
Atlantic Providences Book Review, February, 1989, p. 10; December, 1991, p. 17.
Books in Canada, October, 1983; March, 1985, p. 17; April, 1986, p. 15; December, 1986, p. 15; January/February, 1987, p. 20; April, 1988, p. 34; December, 1991, p. 54; September, 1992, p. 47; February, 1994, p. 45; April, 1994, p. 48; summer, 1996, pp. 16-18.
Canadian Literature, spring, 1990, p. 310.
Essays on Canadian Writing, fall, 1993, p. 203.
Globe and Mail (Toronto), July 9, 1983; November 16, 1985; February 14, 1987; January 2, 1988.
Quill and Quire, July, 1982; September, 1983; February, 1986, p. 22; February, 1987, p. 20; February, 1988, p. 20.
School Library Review, October, 1986, p. 159.
Toronto Star, August 6, 1983.
Windsor Star, July 23, 1983.

—*Sketch by Robert Miltner*

*   *   *

FLETCHER, Dirk
 See CUNNINGHAM, Chet

*   *   *

FLETCHER, Lucille
 See WALLOP, Lucille Fletcher

*   *   *

FORBES, Colin 1923-
 (Jay Bernard, Richard Raine, Raymond H. Sawkins)

PERSONAL: Born in 1923, in Hampstead, England; married Jane Robertson; children: one daughter. *Education:* Attended grammar school in Harrow, England. *Avocational interests:* Foreign travel.

ADDRESSES: Home—Prospect, Elm Rd., Horsell, Woking, Surrey, England. *Agent*—Elaine Greene Ltd., 37 Goldhawk Rd., London W12 8QQ, England.

CAREER: Freelance writer. *Military service:* British Army, 1942-46.

MEMBER: Society of Authors, Crime Writers' Association.

WRITINGS:

(With Alan Fletcher and Bob Gill) *Graphic Design: Visual Comparisons* (nonfiction), Studio Books, 1964.

Tramp in Armour, Collins (London), 1969, published as *Tramp in Armor,* Dutton (New York City), 1970.

The Heights of Zervos, Collins, 1970, Dutton, 1971.

The Palermo Affair, Dutton, 1972 (published in England as *The Palermo Ambush,* Collins, 1972).

(Editor) Robert Welch, *Robert Welch,* Lund, Humphries, 1973.

Target Five, Dutton, 1973.

Year of the Golden Ape, Dutton, 1974.

The Stone Leopard, Collins, 1975, Dutton, 1976.

Avalanche Express, Dutton, 1977.

The Stockholm Syndicate, Collins, 1981, Dutton, 1982.

The Leader and the Damned, Collins, 1981, Atheneum (New York City), 1984.

Double Jeopardy, Collins, 1982.

Terminal, Collins, 1984, Atheneum, 1985.

Cover Story, Collins, 1985, Atheneum, 1986.

The Janus Man, Harcourt, 1988.

Deadlock, Collins, 1988.

The Greek Key, Collins, 1989.

Shockwave, Pan (London), 1990.

Whirlpool, Pan, 1991.

Cross of Fire, Pan, 1992.

By Stealth, Pan, 1992.

The Power, Pan, 1994.

Fury, Macmillan (London), 1995.

Precipice, Macmillan, 1996.

UNDER PSEUDONYM JAY BERNARD

The Burning Fuse, Harcourt, 1970.

UNDER PSEUDONYM RICHARD RAINE

The Corder Index, Harcourt, 1967 (published in England as *A Wreath for America,* Heinemann, 1967).

Night of the Hawk, Harcourt, 1968.

Bombshell, Harcourt, 1969.

UNDER PSEUDONYM RAYMOND H. SAWKINS

Snow on High Ground, Heinemann (London), 1966.

Snow in Paradise, Heinemann, 1967.

Snow Along the Border, Harcourt (New York City), 1968.

ADAPTATIONS: Avalanche Express was filmed in 1979. Film rights have been optioned on five other Forbes titles.

SIDELIGHTS: Colin Forbes feels that his many novels can be read in three different ways: as "whodunnits," as adventure stories, and as espionage thrillers. A writer who began his career by penning World War II action-adventures, Forbes has moved into the realm of international suspense in a series of tightly-plotted books that have proven popular in his native Britain as well as in America. According to Greg Goode in the *St. James Guide to Crime and Mystery Writers,* Forbes's best works "display an expertise in maintaining swift-paced suspense while enlightening you in the arcana of foreign affairs, natural phenomena, history, and science."

Tramp in Armor, an early Forbes title, is a thriller about five British soldiers trapped in a tank behind enemy lines in World War II. In their effort to rejoin their division, they endure such trials as getting stuck in quicksand, nearly being buried alive in a tunnel cave-in, and almost burning to death when a match is thrown in the haystack under which they are hiding. A *Publishers Weekly* reviewer found *Tramp in Armor* "good reading for war buffs" and an "all-action novel." *The Stone Leopard* details policeman Marc Grelle's search for a man called the "Leopard." A World War II hero of the French Resistance, the Leopard is suspected of being a government official bent on orchestrating a coup d'etat in France. *Publishers Weekly* contributor Barbara Bannon called *The Stone Leopard* "an enticing, figure-out-what's-going-to-happen-next novel about politics and the kind of political maneuvering that began back in World War II." *The Palermo Affair* centers on two saboteurs— one British, one American—who enlist the Mafia to thwart a German occupation of Sicily. *Books & Bookmen* correspondent Trevor Allen characterized that novel as "24 hours' suspense drama tensely told."

In the 1980s Forbes moved from classic war dramas to "blockbuster suspense novels," to quote Goode. Among these are *Year of the Golden Ape,* which somewhat predicted the Arab Oil Crisis, and *The*

Leader and the Damned, a "superlative exemplar of that small but persistent subgenre, the speculative Hitler novel," in Goode's words. *The Leader and the Damned* is one of Forbes's best-known and most widely reviewed titles. In *Booklist,* Peter L. Robertson concluded that the premise of a "substitute fuehrer" proves "an interesting point at which to begin a cunning work of research and an adept spy tale."

BIOGRAPHICAL/CRITICAL SOURCES:

BOOKS

St. James Guide to Crime and Mystery Writers, fourth edition, St. James Press (Detroit, MI), 1996.

PERIODICALS

Best Sellers, June, 1976; November 1, 1977.
Booklist, July 15, 1970, p. 1382; September 1, 1972, p. 30; February 1, 1975, p. 559; June 1, 1976, p. 1392; October 1, 1984, p. 190.
Books & Bookmen, December, 1972, p. 120.
British Book News, December, 1983.
Christian Science Monitor, May 5, 1976.
Library Journal, November, 1974, p. 3060.
New York Times Book Review, May 9, 1976; September 4, 1977.
Publishers Weekly, December 29, 1969, p. 60; April 24, 1972, p. 42; March 1, 1976, p. 84; August 24, 1984, p. 73.*

*　　*　　*

FORSTER, Margaret 1938-

PERSONAL: Born May 25, 1938, in Carlisle, Cumberland, England; daughter of Arthur G. (a mechanic) and Lilian (Hind) Forster; married Hunter Davies (a journalist), June 11, 1960; children: Caitlin, Jake, Flora. *Education:* Somerville College, Oxford, B.A., 1960. *Politics:* Socialist. *Religion:* None.

ADDRESSES: Home—11 Boscastle Rd., London N.W.5, England. *Agent*—Tessa Sayle Agency, 11 Jubilee Place, London SW3 3TE, England.

CAREER: Writer. Taught at girls' school in London, England, 1961-63; literary critic for London *Evening Standard,* 1977-80. British Broadcasting Corp., member of advisory committee on the social effects of television, 1975-78.

MEMBER: Royal Society of Literature (fellow).

AWARDS, HONORS: Award for biography from Royal Society of Literature, 1989, for *Elizabeth Barrett Browning: A Biography;* Fawcet Book Prize, 1994, for *Daphne du Maurier: The Secret Life of the Renowned Storyteller.*

WRITINGS:

FICTION

Dames' Delight, J. Cape, 1964.
Georgy Girl (also see below), Berkley, 1965.
The Bogeyman, Putnam, 1965.
The Travels of Maudie Tipstaff, Stein & Day, 1967.
The Park, Secker & Warburg, 1968.
Miss Owen-Owen, Simon & Schuster, 1969, published in England as *Miss Owen-Owen Is at Home,* Secker & Warburg, 1969.
Fenella Phizackerley, Simon & Schuster, 1970.
Mr. Bone's Retreat, Simon & Schuster, 1971.
The Seduction of Mrs. Pendlebury, Secker & Warburg, 1974.
Mother Can You Hear Me?, Secker & Warburg, 1979.
The Bride of Lowther Fell: A Romance, Atheneum, 1980.
Marital Rites, Secker & Warburg, 1981, Atheneum, 1982.
Private Papers, Chatto & Windus, 1986.
Have the Men Had Enough?, Chatto & Windus, 1989.
Lady's Maid, Chatto & Windus, 1990.
The Battle for Christabel, Chatto & Windus, 1991.
Mothers' Boys, Chatto & Windus, 1994.
Shadow Baby, Chatto & Windus, 1996.

NONFICTION

The Rash Adventurer: The Rise and Fall of Charles Edward Stuart, Stein & Day, 1973.
(Editor) *Drawn from Life: The Journalism of William Makepeace Thackeray,* illustrations by Thackeray, Folio Society, 1984.
Significant Sisters: The Grassroots of Active Feminism 1839-1939, Secker & Warburg, 1984, Knopf, 1985.
(Editor) *Elizabeth Barrett Browning: Selected Poems,* Johns Hopkins University Press, 1988.
Elizabeth Barrett Browning: A Biography, Doubleday, 1989.

Daphne du Maurier: The Secret Life of the Renowned Storyteller, Chatto & Windus and Doubleday, 1993.

OTHER

(With Peter Nichols) *Georgy Girl* (screenplay), Columbia, 1966.

Memoirs of a Victorian Gentleman: William Makepeace Thackeray (fictionalized biography), illustrations by Thackeray, Morrow, 1978, published in England as *William Makepeace Thackeray: Memoirs of a Victorian Gentleman,* Secker & Warburg, 1978.

Hidden Lives—A Family Memoir, Viking, 1995.

ADAPTATIONS: Georgy Girl was adapted as the musical *Georgy* with book by Tom Mankiewicz, lyrics by Carole Bayer, and music by George Fischoff, 1970.

WORK IN PROGRESS: Rich Desserts and Captain's Thin: A Family of Their Times, 1831-1931, a social history based on the Carrs of Carlisle, the biscuit manufacturers.

SIDELIGHTS: With a career that spans more than 30 years, Margaret Forster is most noted for her novels and works of literary biography. Her novels tend to focus on family issues, some of which are loosely drawn on Forster's own experiences. Hana Sambrook points out in *Contemporary Novelists* that in all of Forster's novel, she "is preoccupied with human relationships . . . with the impact of one person on another, with the possibility—or impossibility—of any real change in someone's character and outlook on life through emotional involvement with someone else." Forster has also written a number of well-received biographies. David Bordelon writes in the *Dictionary of Literary Biography,* "[Forster] brings to her biographies the dramatic sensibilities of a novelist as well as the analytic insight of a historian."

Forster's second novel, *Georgy Girl,* was a best-seller and was adapted into a screenplay in 1966. Over the next five years, Forster wrote a series of popular-fiction novels. Forster herself referred to her earliest novels as "third rate," but Pamela Marsh writes in the *Christian Science Monitor* that *Miss Owen-Owen* offers "good entertainment." "[O]pportunities for comedy are right at Miss Forster's fingers and she richly exploits them," applauds Marsh. Sambrook further points out that in these early novels, love "remains all-important to women, and Forster acknowledges

this." She notes a change in Forster's "perception of the impact of love" over the years as charted through her novels.

Forster believes that fiction and biography are closely interrelated, that "the similarity is more important than the differences." In 1973, Forster published her first biography, *The Rash Adventurer: The Rise and Fall of Charles Edward Stuart.* Forster differed from other biographers in her focus on the prince's character instead of on his political intrigues. This effort "to fill the gap between a definitive history and a historical novel" was praised as an "accomplished mixture of skillful narrative and psychological insight" by Antonia Fraser in the *Sunday Times.*

Several years later, Forster turned to another format for the exploration of history: a fictional autobiography. She used this technique in *William Makepeace Thackeray: Memoirs of a Victorian Genleman* to mixed critical opinion. Some objected to the work's subjectivity, while others wondered how truthful it was. Bordelon, however, asserts that Forster's book "proved that biography can retain its veracity yet revel in the experimental qualities of fiction and address questions of objective authority posed by contemporary literary theory." Writes J. I. M. Stewart in the *Time Literary Supplement,* "Miss Forster has provided Thackeray with a colorful and entertaining autobiography on a generous scale. It is a remarkable performance and persuasive." Later, Forster edited a collection of Thackeray's journalism.

In the next decade, Forster continued to produce several novels as well as *Significant Sisters: The Grassroots of Active Feminism 1839-1939,* which explores seven influential women who contributed to feminism. Forster became interested in the subject after her mother's death led her to question the status of women in the twentieth century. Bordelon finds that Forster succeeds in "combining historical background with her own opinions and definitions of feminism, Forster creates a new reference work while offering an additional philosophical approach." The novel *Have the Men Had Enough?,* which describes an old woman's descent into senility and the responses of her children and grandchildren to it, also arose from Forster's personal experiences—her visits with her mother-in-law who suffered from senile dementia and was confined in the psychiatric ward of a nursing home. Anne Duchene called this book "a work of grace and charity" in the *Times Literary Supplement.*

Forster published *Elizabeth Barrett Browning* in 1988, a biography in which Forster revises the popular view of the poet's father as a tyrant. While some critics found that Forster did not pay enough attention to Browning's poetry, the majority of the response was positive. Robert Martin writes in the *Times Literary Supplement* that "this new biography is a daring book, for it shows us a far more complex woman than we have seen before." Forster went on to edit a volume of Browning's poetry. She also wrote the novel *Lady's Maid,* a fictionalized account of the life of Barrett's maid, Elizabeth Wilson. Drawn from material found in the Brownings' correspondence, the events in this book, writes Coral Lansbury in the *New York Times Book Review,* are "fully imagined and persuasive fiction."

Forster next turned her skills as a historian and a writer to best-selling author Daphne du Maurier. Subtitled *The Secret Life of the Renowned Storyteller,* Forster's biography—composed in part from previously unknown diaries and letters and unpublished manuscripts—exposes du Maurier's bisexuality and explores her own perception that she harbored two selves; the second was a boy who lived in a self-constructed "boy-in-the-box." Du Maurier perceived of herself as not a lesbian but as "'a half-breed,' someone internally male and externally female." Forster writes, "It may have tortured her to feel she was two distinct people, but it also fuelled her creative powers." Upon the death of Gertrude Lawrence, with whom du Maurier may have had a physical relationship, she used her writing to lift her out of depression. "All her life," writes Carolyn G. Heilbrun in the *New York Times Book Review,* "she identified with boys and men and was infatuated with women, but she concealed these feelings and gave play to them mainly in writing, where her inner conflicts could be expressed in the fictional guises of male power and female dread."

Forster presents a "a brilliant portrait," writes Heilbrun, "of a woman caught in a destiny she loathes but never openly challenges"; but Patricia Beer, writing in the *London Review of Books,* notes that "[T]he emphasis throughout is on du Maurier the writer." Forster writes, "Daphne herself stresses how her work gave her release from thoughts, images and ideas which disturbed her. . . . Her whole life's work was an attempt to defy reality." Though a few critics maintain that du Maurier wasn't enough of a literary figure to merit a literary biography, the majority welcome this new knowledge and the way it elucidates du Maurier's fiction. Julia Braun Kessler writes

in the *Los Angeles Times Book Review,* "Forster has been able to let us see a side of Du Maurier until now closeted away, exposing a whole other emotional dimension to her fiction's compelling fascination." She adds, "[w]hen we learn from Forster the whole picture . . . we understand the dark shadows in her work: the guilt, the terror, the unease."

Amanda Vaill, writing in the *Chicago Tribune,* though finding the work an "extraordinarily sympathetic and compulsively readable biography," poses one point of concern: for Forster leaves certain details—such as the possibility of du Maurier's father having molested Daphne and one of her sisters—to the source notes or sends readers to another source. Vaill concludes that the "source notes turn out to be a kind of secret biography, where the details too hot for the text are discreetly buried." However, Bordelon points to Forster's "matter-of-fact discussion of du Maurier's sexual ambiguity [as a] model for dealing with politically charged issues." Heilbrun and others also commend Forster for her skill in handling the sensationalistic aspects of du Maurier's life. Heilbrun sees in *Daphne du Maurier* "the rarest of marriages: the perfect subject and a gifted biographer."

Forster next turned to more of a personal biography; in *Hidden Lives,* Forster investigates her own family history and particularly tries to find out about the illegitimate daughter of her grandmother. However, Forster's study of three generations of women in her family is really a social history, and through her descriptions of her relationship with her mother—a woman who cries at her death "'It hasn't amounted to much, my life,'"—shows how women's status and expectations have changed over just a few generations. Candice Rodd writes in the *Times Literary Supplement* that Forster uses "personal recollection, anecdote and dogged detective work to piece together a story that [is] simultaneously commonplace and riveting." The following year, Forster again explored the theme of the relationships between illegitimate children and the mother who give them, including actual details from her grandmother's life, in the novel *Shadow Baby.*

Forster's skills and insights as a writer are seen in both her fiction and nonfiction. Sambrook finds a novelistic style that is "plain, deliberately downbeat, letting the pathos and the irony speak for themselves." According to Bordelon, Forster has expanded her talent for fiction-writing to create "biographies that contain flights of literary imagination yet remain grounded in fact." In both her fiction and her biographies, Forster experiments with character, narrative, and point of view in an effort to "catch the essence of the person and the spirit of the times."

Forster told *CA:* "I can't *not* write; it's as natural as breathing. My circumstances for writing are now easier, after the usual two decades of struggle with the rival claims of children."

BIOGRAPHICAL/CRITICAL SOURCES:

BOOKS

Contemporary Novelists, St. James Press (Detroit), 1996.
Dictionary of Literary Biography, Volume 155: *Twentieth-Century British Literary Biographers,* Gale (Detroit), 1995.

PERIODICALS

Chicago Tribune, November 28, 1993, p. 3.
Christian Science Monitor, August 21, 1969.
London Review of Books, June 24, 1993, pp. 20-22.
Los Angeles Times Book Review, March 17, 1985; December 26, 1993, p. 3.
New York Times Book Review, May 6, 1979; February 17, 1985; May 7, 1989; March 17, 1991, pp. 14, 16; October 17, 1993, pp. 37, 46.
Times (London), September 14, 1984; September 20, 1984; March 16, 1989; June 29, 1990; July 5, 1990.
Times Literary Supplement, July 24, 1981; September 28, 1984; March 7, 1986; March 24-30, 1989; July 20-26, 1990; May 31, 1996, p. 24.
Tribune Books (Chicago), February 26, 1989.
Voice Literary Supplement, number 121, December, 1993, pp. 32-33.
Washington Post Book World, April 28, 1985.

*   *   *

FORSYTH, Frederick 1938-

PERSONAL: Born in 1938 in Ashford, Kent, England; son of a furrier, shopkeeper, and rubber tree planter; married, September, 1973; wife's name, Carole ("Carrie"; a model); children: Frederick Stuart, Shane Richard. *Education:* Attended University of Granada. *Avocational interests:* Sea fishing, snooker.

ADDRESSES: Home—St. John's Wood, London, England. *Office*—c/o Hutchinson Publishing Group, 62-65 Chandos Pl., London WC2N 4NW, England.

CAREER: Novelist. *Eastern Daily Press,* Norwich, England, and King's Lynn, Norfolk, reporter, 1958-61; Reuters News Agency, reporter in London, England, and Paris, France, and bureau chief in East Berlin, East Germany, 1961-65; British Broadcasting Corporation (BBC), London, England, reporter, 1965-67, assistant diplomatic correspondent, 1967-68; free-lance journalist in Nigeria, 1968-70. *Military service:* Royal Air Force, pilot, 1956-58.

AWARDS, HONORS: Edgar Allan Poe Award, Mystery Writers of America, 1971, for *The Day of the Jackal.*

WRITINGS:

NOVELS

The Day of the Jackal, Viking (New York City), 1971.
The Odessa File, Viking, 1972.
The Dogs of War, Viking, 1974.
The Shepherd, Hutchinson (London), 1975, Viking, 1976.
The Novels of Frederick Forsyth (contains *The Day of the Jackal, The Odessa File,* and *The Dogs of War*), Hutchinson, 1978, published as *Forsyth's Three,* Viking, 1980, published as *Three Complete Novels,* Avenel Books (New York City), 1980.
The Devil's Alternative, Hutchinson, 1979, Viking, 1980.
The Four Novels (contains *The Day of the Jackal, The Odessa File, The Dogs of War,* and *The Devil's Alternative*), Hutchinson, 1982.
The Fourth Protocol, Viking, 1984.
The Negotiator, Bantam (New York City), 1989.
The Deceiver, Bantam, 1991.
The Fist of God, Bantam, 1994.
Icon, Bantam, 1996.

OTHER

The Biafra Story (nonfiction), Penguin (London), 1969, revised edition published as *The Making of an African Legend: The Biafra Story,* 1977.
(Contributor) *Visitor's Book: Short Stories of Their New Homeland by Famous Authors Now Living in Ireland,* Arrow Books, 1982.

Emeka (biography of Chukwuemeka Odumegwu-Ojukwu), Spectrum Books (Ibadan), 1982.

No Comebacks: Collected Short Stories, Viking, 1982.

(And executive producer) *The Fourth Protocol* (screenplay; based on his novel), Lorimar, 1987.

Chacal, French and European Publications, 1990.

(Editor) *Great Flying Stories,* Norton (New York City), 1991.

I Remember: Reflections on Fishing in Childhood, Summersdale (London), 1995.

Also author of *The Soldiers,* a documentary for BBC. Contributor of articles to newspapers and magazines, including *Playboy.*

ADAPTATIONS: The Day of the Jackal was filmed by Universal in 1973; *The Odessa File* was filmed by Columbia in 1974; *The Dogs of War* was filmed by United Artists in 1981. The Mobil Showcase Network filmed two of Forsyth's short stories ("A Careful Man" and "Privilege") under the title *Two by Forsyth* in 1984; "A Careful Man" was also videotaped and broadcast on Irish television.

SIDELIGHTS: Realism is the key word behind the novels of Frederick Forsyth. Often credited as the originator of a new genre, the "documentary thriller," Forsyth found sudden fame with the publication of his smash best-seller, *The Day of the Jackal,* a book that combines the suspense of an espionage novel with the detailed realism of the documentary novel, first made popular by Truman Capote's *In Cold Blood.* The detail in Forsyth's novels depends not only on the months of research he spends on each book, but also on his own varied personal experiences which lend even greater authenticity to his writing. As *Dictionary of Literary Biography* contributor Andrew F. Macdonald explains, "the sense of immediacy, of an insider's view of world affairs, of all-too-human world figures," as well as quick-paced plots, are the keys to the author's popularity.

Critics, however, have sometimes faulted the novelist for shallow characterization and a simplistic writing style. Forsyth does not deny his emphasis on plotting over other considerations. In a *Los Angeles Times* interview he remarks: "My books are eighty percent plot and structure. The remaining twenty percent is for characters and descriptions. I try to keep emotions out. Occasionally a personal opinion will appear in the mouth of one of my characters, but only occasionally. The plot's the thing. This is how it works best for me." These plots find their resolution in Forsyth's

painstaking attention to detail. "Forsyth's forte, with the added bonus of precise technical description, worth of a science writer," Macdonald explains, ". . . [is] how things work, ranging from the construction of a special rifle (*The Day of the Jackal,* 1971) and improvised car bombs (*The Odessa File,* 1972), to gunrunning (*The Dogs of War,* 1974) and the innards of oil tankers (*The Devil's Alernative,* 1979), to the assembly of miniature nuclear bombs (*The Fourth Protocol,* 1984)."

For Forsyth the road to becoming a best-selling novelist was a long, circuitous route filled with adventurous detours that would later work their way into his writing. Early in his life, Forsyth became interested in becoming a foreign correspondent when his father introduced him to the world news as reported in the London *Daily Express.* In a London *Times* interview with John Mortimer, Forsyth relates how his father "would get out the atlas and show me where the trouble spots were. And, of course, father had been to the Orient, he told me about tiger shoots and the headhunters in Borneo." Impatient to experience life for himself, Forsyth left school at the age of seventeen and went to Spain, where he briefly attended the University of Granada while toying with the idea of becoming a matador. However, having previously trained as a Tiger Moth biplane pilot, Forsyth decided to join the Royal Air Force in 1956. He learned to fly a Vampire jet airplane, and—at the age of nineteen—he was the youngest man in England at the time to earn his wings.

But Forsyth still dreamed of becoming a foreign correspondent, and towards that end he left the service to join the staff of the *Eastern Daily Press.* His talent for languages (Forsyth is fluent in French, German, Spanish, and Russian) later landed him his dream job as a correspondent for Reuters News Agency and then for the British Broadcasting Corporation (BBC). It was during an assignment for the BBC that Forsyth's career took a sudden turn. Assigned to cover an uprising in the Nigerian region of Biafra, Forsyth began his mission believing he was going to meet an upstart rebellious colonel who was misleading his followers. He soon realized, though, that this leader, Colonel Ojukwu, was actually an intelligent man committed to saving his people from an English-supported government whose corrupt leaders were allowing millions to die of starvation in order to obtain their oil-rich lands. When Forsyth reported his findings, he was accused of being unprofessional and his superiors reassigned him to covering politics at home. Outraged, Forsyth resigned, and he tells Henry Allen in a *Washington*

Post article that this experience destroyed his belief "that the people who ran the world were men of good will." This disillusionment is reflected in his writing. Forsyth reveals to Mortimer that he prefers "to write about immoral people doing immoral things. I want to show that the establishment's as immoral as the criminals."

Going back to Africa, Forsyth did free-lance reporting in Biafra and wrote an account of the war, _The Biafra Story,_ which _Spectator_ critic Auberon Waugh asserts "is by far the most complete account, from the Biafran side [of the conflict], that I have yet read." In 1970, when the rebels were finally defeated and Ojukwu went into exile, Forsyth returned to England to find that his position on the war had effectively eliminated any chances he had of resuming a reporting career. He decided, however, that he could still put his journalism experience to use by writing fiction. Recalling his days in Paris during the early 1960s when rumors were spreading that the Secret Organization Army had hired an assassin to shoot President Charles de Gaulle, Forsyth sat down and in just over a month wrote _The Day of the Jackal_ based on this premise.

Forsyth had problems selling the manuscript at first because publishers could not understand how there could be any suspense in a plot about a presidential assassination that had obviously never come to pass. As the author explains to Allen, however, "The point was not whodunit, but how, and how close would he get?" The fascinating part of _The Day of the Jackal_ lies in Forsyth's portrayal of the amoral, ultra-professional killer known only by his code name, "Jackal," and detective Claude Lebel's efforts to stop him. Despite what _New York Times Book Review_ critic Stanley Elkin calls Forsyth's "graceless prose style," and characterization that, according to J. R. Frakes in a _Book World_ review, uses "every stereotype in the filing system," the author's portrayal of his nemesis weaving through a non-stop narrative has garnered acclaim from many critics and millions of readers. By boldly switching his emphasis from the side of the law to the side of the assassin, Forsyth adds a unique twist that gives his novel its appeal. "So plausible has Mr. Forsyth made his implausible villain . . . and so exciting does he lead him on his murderous mission against impossible odds," says Elkin, "that even saintly readers will be hard put not to cheer this particular villain along his devious way." The author, however, notes that he considered the positive response to his villain a distinctly American response. "There is this American trait of admiring efficiency,"

he explains to a _Washington Post_ interviewer, "and the Jackal is efficient in his job."

"_The Day of the Jackal_ established a highly successful formula," writes Macdonald, "one repeated by Forsyth and a host of other writers." Using a tight, journalistic style, Forsyth creates an illusion of reality in his writing by intermixing real-life people and historical events with his fictional characters and plots; "the ultimate effect is less that of fiction than of a fictional projection into the lives of the real makers of history," Macdonald attests. The author also fills his pages with factual information about anything from how to assemble a small nuclear device to shipping schedules and restaurant menus. But the main theme behind the author's novels is the power of the individual to make a difference in the world, and even change the course of history. Macdonald describes the Forsyth protagonist as "a maverick who succeeds by cutting through standard procedure and who as a result often has difficulty in fitting in, [yet he] lives up to his own high professional standards. Forsyth suggests that it is the lone professionals, whether opposed to the organization or part of it, who truly create history, but a history represented only palely on the front pages of newspapers."

Since Forsyth had a three book contract with Viking, he quickly researched and wrote his next two novels, _The Odessa File,_ about a German reporter's hunt for a Nazi war criminal, and _The Dogs of War,_ which concerns a mercenary who orchestrates a military coup in West Africa. Forsyth drew on his experience as a reporter in East Berlin for _The Odessa File,_ as well as interviewing experts like Nazi hunter Simon Weisenthal, to give the novel authenticity. Background to _The Dogs of War_ also came from the author's personal experiences—in this case, his time spent in Biafra. When it comes to details about criminal doings, however, Forsyth goes right to the source. In a Toronto _Globe and Mail_ interview with Rick Groen, Forsyth says, "There are only two kinds of people who really know the ins and outs of illegal activities: those who practice them and those who seek to prevent them from being practiced. So you talk to cops or criminals. Not academics or criminologists or any of those sorts." This tactic has gotten Forsyth into some dangerous situations. In a _Chicago Tribune_ interview the author regales Michael Kilian with one instance when he was researching _The Dogs of War._ Trying to learn more about gun trafficking in the black market, Forsyth posed as a South African interested in buying arms. The ploy worked until one day when the men he was dealing with noticed a copy of *The Day of the Jackal* in a bookstore window. It was "probably the nearest I got to being put in a box," says the author.

The Dogs of War became a highly controversial book when a London *Times* writer accused Forsyth of paying two-hundred-thousand dollars to mercenaries attempting a coup against the President of Equatorial Guinea, Francisco Marcias Nguema. At first, the novelist denied any involvement. Later, however, David Butler and Anthony Collins reported in *Newsweek* that Forsyth admitted to having "organized a coup attempt for research purposes, but that he had never intended to go through with it." The controversy did not hurt book sales, though, and *The Dogs of War* became Forsyth's third best-seller in a row.

After *The Dogs of War* Forsyth did not attempt another thriller for several years. He credits exhaustion to this lengthy hiatus. "Those first three novels had involved a lot of research, a lot of traveling, a half-million words of writing, a lot of promotion," the novelist tells *New York Times Book Review* contributor Tony Chiu. "I was fed up with the razzmatazz. I said I would write no more." To avoid heavy English taxes, Forsyth moved to Ireland, where tax laws are lenient on writers. One explanation as to why he returned to writing has been offered by *New York Times Book Review* critic Peter Maas, who records that when a tax man came to Forsyth's door one day and explained that only actively writing authors were eligible for tax breaks, Forsyth quickly told him that he was working on a novel at that moment. "I hasten to say," Maas writes, "that all this may be apocryphal, but in the interests of providing us a greater truth, I like to think it happened. It's a wonderful thought, the idea of a tax person forcing a writer into more millions."

Forsyth made his comeback with *The Devil's Alternative,* an intricately plotted, ambitious novel about an American president who must choose between giving in to the demands of a group of terrorists and possibly causing a nuclear war in the process, or refusing their demands and allowing them to release the biggest oil spill in history from the tanker they have hijacked. "The vision is somewhat darker than in Forsyth's earlier works, in which a moral choice was possible," notes Macdonald. "Here . . . somebody must get hurt, no matter which alternative is chosen." The usual complaints against Forsyth's writing have been trained against *The Devil's Alternative.* Peter Gorner, for one, argues in the *Chicago Tribune Book World* that "his characters are paper-thin, the pages are stud-

ded with cliches, and the plot is greased by coincidence." But Gorner adds that " . . . things move along so briskly you haven't much time to notice." *Los Angeles Times* critic Robert Kirsch similarly notes that "Forsyth's banal writing, his endless thesaurus of cliches, his Hollywood characters do not interfere with page turning." Nevertheless, *New York Times Book Review* contributor Irma Pascal Heldman expresses admiration for Forsyth's abilities to accurately predict some of the political crises that came to pass not long after the book was published. She also praises the "double-whammy ending that will take even the most wary reader by surprise. *The Devil's Alternative* is a many-layered thriller."

As with *The Devil's Alternative,* Forsyth's *The Fourth Protocol* and *The Negotiator* offer intrigue on a superpower scale. *The Fourth Protocol* is the story of a Soviet plot to detonate a small atomic device in a U.S. airbase in England. The explosion is meant to be seen as an American error and help put the leftist, antinuclear Labour Party into power. Reviews on the novel have been mixed. *Time* magazine reviewer John Skow faults the author for being too didactic: "[Forsyth's] first intention is not to write an entertainment but to preach a political sermon. Its burden is that leftists and peaceniks really are fools whose habitual prating endangers civilization." Michiko Kakutani of the *New York Times* also feels that, compared to Forsyth's other novels, *The Fourth Protocol* "becomes predictable, and so lacking in suspense." But other critics, like *Washington Post Book World* reviewer Roderick MacLeish, maintain a contrary view. MacLeish asserts that it is Forsyth's "best book so far" because the author's characters are so much better developed. "Four books and a few million pounds after *Jackal* Frederick Forsyth has become a well-rounded novelist."

Of *The Negotiator,* Forsyth's tale of the kidnapping of an American president's son, *Globe and Mail* critic Margaret Cannon declares that "while nowhere nearly as good as *The Day of the Jackal* or *The Odessa File,* it's [Forsyth's] best work in recent years." Harry Anderson, writing in *Newsweek,* also calls the novel "a comparative rarity; a completely satisfying thriller." Some critics like *Washington Post* reviewer John Katzenbach have resurrected the old complaints that Forsyth "relies on shallow characters and stilted dialogue," and that while "the dimensions of his knowledge are impressive, rarely does the information imparted serve any greater purpose." Acknowledging that *The Negotiator* has "too many characters and a plot with enough twists to fill a pretzel factory," Cannon nevertheless adds that ". . . the endless and irrelevant descriptive passages are gone and someone has averted Forsyth's tendency to go off on tiresome tangents."

"Perhaps recognizing the need for sharply defined heroes and villains," states Andrew Macdonald in the *St. James Guide to Crime and Mystery Writers,* "Forsyth's next book, *The Deceiver,* is a nostalgic look back to the good old days (at least for field agents and writers) of the Cold War, when political positions seemed eternally frozen and villainy could be motivated simply by nationality." For British agent Sam McCready, those days were a series of successes. With the collapse of the Soviet Union, however, the government is poised to eliminate his position. As part of his protest against the retirement forced on him, McCready recounts four of his most successful exploits. McCready loses the protest and is sent into retirement. Forsyth nonetheless ends the novel on an uncertain note, with Saddam Hussein's invasion of Kuwait. "The notion that international crises are over, that a new and peaceful world order will prevail, is immediately proved wrong," Macdonald notes. "All that has changed is the names, cultures, and ideologies of the players, and there will always be a need for new versions of Sam McCready, Forsyth suggests."

The author revisits this changing world order in *The Fist of God,* which tells of a secret mission to Iraq in an attempt to prevent the use of a catastrophic doomsday weapon. The intelligence situation in Iraq's closed society has become critical, and the western allies recruit a young version of Sam McCready— Major Mike Martin—to obtain the information they need. Martin's mission is to contact an Israeli "mole," a secret agent planted in Iraq by the Mossad, Israel's secret service, years before. In the process he also encounters rumors of Saddam's ultimate weapon—a weapon he must destroy in order to ensure a western victory. "As with his best works," writes Macdonald in the *St. James Guide to Crime and Mystery Writers,* "Forsyth gives a sense of peering behind the curtains created by governments and media, allowing a vision of how the real battles, mostly invisible, were carried out."

In *Icon,* Forsyth turns to contemporary Russian politics for a thriller about a presidential candidate with ties to the Russian mafia and plans for wholesale ethnic cleansing at home and renewed Russian aggression abroad. Jason Monk, ex-CIA agent, is hired by an unlikely group of Russian and American global players to get rid of candidate Igor Komarov before the election. "As usual," writes the reviewer for *Publishers Weekly,* "Forsyth interweaves speculation with historical fact, stitching his plot pieces with a cogent analysis of both Russian politics and the world of espionage." Although Anthony Lejeune in *National Review* believes that "the scale is too large, the mood too chilly, for much personal involvement" with the novel's characters, J. D. Reed in *People* claims that "*Icon* finds the master in world-class form."

It has always been the plots and technical details in his novels that have most fascinated Forsyth, however. "Invention of the story is the most fun," the author tells Peter Gorner in the *Chicago Tribune.* "It's satisfying, like doing a jigsaw or a crossword." He admits to Groen that he loves the research: "I quite enjoy going after the facts. I put into my books a pretty heavy diet of factuality." Recognizing that Forsyth is aiming to entertain his audience with these techniques, Macdonald writes that a "common element in all the criticism [against the author] is a refusal to accept Forsyth's docudrama formula for what it is, but rather to assume it should be more conventionally 'fictional.'" Forsyth has sold over thirty million books to readers who know, as *Detroit News* contributor Jay Carr puts it, that the thrill of the author's books lies not in finding out how "Forsyth is going to defuse the bomb whose wick he ignites, but rather to see how he works out the details."

BIOGRAPHICAL/CRITICAL SOURCES:

BOOKS

Bestsellers 89, Issue 4, Gale (Detroit), 1990.
Contemporary Literary Criticism, Gale, Volume 2, 1974; Volume 5, 1976; Volume 36, 1986.
Dictionary of Literary Biography, Volume 87: *British Mystery and Thriller Writers since 1940, First Series,* Gale, 1989.
St. James Guide to Crime and Mystery Writers, 4th edition, St. James Press (Detroit), 1996.

PERIODICALS

Armchair Detective, May, 1974; winter, 1985.
Atlantic, December, 1972; August, 1974.
Book and Magazine Collector, June, 1989.
Booklist, March 1, 1994, p. 1139.
Book World, September 5, 1971.
Chicago Tribune, October 16, 1984; April 16, 1989; June 14, 1989.
Chicago Tribune Book World, March 2, 1980.

Christian Science Monitor, September 7, 1984.

Daily News (New York), September 30, 1984.

Detroit News, February 10, 1980; August 15, 1982; April 30, 1989.

Economist, December 7, 1996, p. S3.

Entertainment Weekly, May 20, 1994, p. 55.

Globe and Mail (Toronto), September 8, 1984; August 29, 1987; April 29, 1989.

Guardian, August 16, 1994, p. 3.

Insight on the News, July 11, 1994, p. 28.

Life, October 22, 1971.

Listener, June 17, 1971; September 28, 1972; January 10, 1980.

Los Angeles Times, March 19, 1980; March 28, 1980; May 7, 1982; August 28, 1987.

Los Angeles Times Book Review, April 16, 1989.

National Observer, October 30, 1971.

National Review, August 2, 1974; December 23, 1996, p. 56.

New Leader, April 7, 1980.

New Statesman, September 20, 1974; January 15, 1988.

New Statesman & Society, September 6, 1991, pp. 35-36.

Newsweek, July 22, 1974; May 1, 1978; April 24, 1989.

New York Post, September 21, 1974.

New York Times, October 24, 1972; April 18, 1978; January 17, 1980; August 30, 1984; August 28, 1987.

New York Times Book Review, August 15, 1971; December 5, 1971; November 5, 1972; July 14, 1974; October 16, 1977; February 24, 1980; March 2, 1980; May 9, 1982; September 2, 1984; April 16, 1989.

Observer (London), June 13, 1971; September 24, 1972; September 22, 1974.

People, October 22, 1984; July 18, 1994, p. 24; October 21, 1996, p. 40.

Playboy, July, 1989, p. 26; November, 1991, p. 34.

Publishers Weekly, August 9, 1971; September 30, 1974; March 17, 1989; August 9, 1991, p. 43; March 7, 1994, p. 51; August 12, 1996, p. 61.

Saturday Review, September 4, 1971; September 9, 1972.

Spectator, August 2, 1969.

Time, September 3, 1984.

Times (London), August 22, 1982; March 17, 1987; May 13, 1989.

Times Literary Supplement, July 2, 1971; October 25, 1974; December 19, 1975.

Wall Street Journal, April 12, 1989; April 18, 1989.

Washington Post, August 19, 1971; September 26, 1971; December 12, 1978; February 13, 1981; March 28, 1984; August 29, 1987; April 21, 1989.

Washington Post Book World, February 3, 1980; August 26, 1984.

World Press Review, March, 1980; May, 1987.

*   *   *

FOX, Paula 1923-

PERSONAL: Born April 22, 1923, in New York, NY; daughter of Paul Hervey (a writer) and Elsie (de Sola) Fox; married Richard Sigerson in 1948 (divorced, 1954); married Martin Greenberg, June 9, 1962; children: (first marriage) Adam, Gabriel, Linda. *Education:* Attended Columbia University, 1955-58.

ADDRESSES: Home—Brooklyn, NY. *Agent*—Robert Lescher, 67 Irving Pl., New York, NY 10003.

CAREER: Author. Has worked in numerous occupations, including model, saleswoman, public relations worker, machinist, staff member for the British publisher Victor Gollancz, reader for a film studio, reporter in Paris, France, and Warsaw, Poland, for the British wire service Telepress, English-as-a-second-language instructor, and teacher at the Ethical Culture School in New York City and for emotionally disturbed children in Dobbs Ferry, New York; University of Pennsylvania, Philadelphia, professor of English literature, beginning 1963.

MEMBER: PEN, Authors League of America, Authors Guild.

AWARDS, HONORS: Finalist in National Book Award children's book category, 1971, for *Blowfish Live in the Sea;* National Institute of Arts and Letters Award, 1972; Guggenheim fellowship, 1972; National Endowment for the Arts grant, 1974; Newbery Medal, American Library Association, 1974, for *The Slave Dancer;* Hans Christian Andersen Medal, 1978; National Book Award nomination, 1979, for *The Little Swineherd and Other Tales; A Place Apart* was selected one of *New York Times*'s Outstanding Books, 1980, and received the American Book Award, 1983; Child Study Children's Book Award from the Bank Street College of Education and one of *New York Times*'s Notable Books, both 1984, Christopher Award and Newbery Honor Book, both 1985, and International Board on Books for Young People Honor List for Writing, 1986, all for *One-Eyed Cat;*

Brandeis Fiction Citation, 1984; Rockefeller Foundation grant, 1984; *The Moonlight Man* was selected one of the *New York Times*'s Notable Books, 1986, and one of the Child Study Association of America's Children's Books of the Year, 1987; Silver Medallion, University of Southern Mississippi, 1987; *Boston Globe/Horn Book* Award for fiction and Newbery Honor Book, 1989, for *The Village by the Sea.* Empire State Award for children's literature, 1994.

WRITINGS:

FOR CHILDREN

Maurice's Room, illustrated by Ingrid Fetz, Macmillan, 1966.

A Likely Place, illustrated by Edward Ardizzone, Macmillan, 1967.

How Many Miles to Babylon?, illustrated by Paul Giovanopoulos, David White, 1967.

The Stone-Faced Boy, illustrated by Donald A. Mackay, Bradbury, 1968.

Dear Prosper, illustrated by Steve McLachlin, David White, 1968.

Portrait of Ivan, illustrated by Saul Lambert, Bradbury, 1969.

The King's Falcon, illustrated by Eros Keith, Bradbury, 1969.

Hungry Fred, illustrated by Rosemary Wells, Bradbury, 1969.

Blowfish Live in the Sea, Bradbury, 1970.

Good Ethan, illustrated by Arnold Lobel, Bradbury, 1973.

The Slave Dancer, illustrated by Keith, Bradbury, 1973.

The Little Swineherd and Other Tales, Dutton, 1978, new edition illustrated by Robert Byrd, Dutton Children's Books, 1996.

A Place Apart, Farrar, Straus, 1980.

One-Eyed Cat, Bradbury, 1984.

(Author of introduction) Marjorie Kellogg, *Tell Me That You Love Me, Junie Moon,* Farrar, Straus, 1984.

The Moonlight Man, Bradbury, 1986.

Lily and the Lost Boy, Orchard Books, 1987, published in England as *The Lost Boy,* Dent, 1988.

The Village by the Sea, Orchard Books, 1988.

In a Place of Danger, Orchard Books, 1989.

Monkey Island, Orchard Books, 1991.

(With Floriano Vecchi) *Amzat and His Brothers: Three Italian Tales,* illustrated by Emily Arnold McCully, Orchard Books, 1993.

Western Wind, Orchard Books, 1993.

The Eagle Kite, Orchard Books, 1995.

Also author of *Radiance Descending,* 1997.

FOR ADULTS

Poor George, Harcourt, 1967.

Desperate Characters, Harcourt, 1970, reprinted with an afterword by Irving Howe, Nonpareil, 1980.

The Western Coast, Harcourt, 1972.

The Widow's Children, Dutton, 1976.

A Servant's Tale, North Point Press, 1984.

The God of Nightmares, North Point Press, 1990.

ADAPTATIONS: Desperate Characters was adapted as a motion picture by Paramount, 1970; a cassette and a film strip accompanied by cassette have been produced of *One-Eyed Cat* by Random House.

SIDELIGHTS: Paula Fox is best known for her children's books, which have won numerous awards, including the prestigious Hans Christian Andersen Medal, the Newbery Medal, and the American Book Award for Children's Fiction Paperback. She is also the author of novels for adults, and has been described by *Nation* contributor Blair T. Birmelin as "one of our most intelligent (and least appreciated) contemporary novelists." Fox, however, does not feel the need to distinguish between these two types of writing. She comments in John Rowe Townsend's *A Sense of Story: Essays on Contemporary Writers for Children,* "I never think I'm writing for children, when I work. A story does not start *for* anyone, nor an idea, nor a feeling of an idea; but starts more for oneself." "At the core of everything I write," she explains to *Publishers Weekly* interviewer Sybil S. Steinberg, "is the feeling that the denial of the truth imprisons us even further in ourselves. Of course there's no one 'truth.' The great things, the insights that happen to you, come to you in some internal way."

Fox spent her childhood moving from place to place and school to school. Her father was what Fox describes in the *New York Times* as "an itinerant writer." Working in New York City, he earned a living by rewriting plays by other authors, as well as writing several of his own, and later he went to Hollywood and England to work for film studios. While her parents were traveling about, Fox was sent to live with a minister and his invalid mother in New York's Hudson valley. An avid reader, poet, and history buff, the minister had a profound influence on Fox. He taught her to read and to appreciate the works of authors such as Rudyard Kipling, Eugene Field, Mark Twain, Washington Irving, and Walt

Whitman; and he also told her tales of the Revolutionary War and other historical events. All these stories inevitably rubbed off on the young Fox. "When I was 5, I had my first experience of being a ghost writer—of sorts," Fox relates, recalling how the minister once accepted her suggestion to write a sermon about a waterfall. For "an instant," she later adds, "I grasped consciously what had been implicit in every aspect of my life with the minister—that everything could count, that a word, spoken as meant, contained in itself an energy capable of awakening imagination, thought, emotion." It was this experience that first inspired Fox to become a writer.

When Fox was six years old, she left the minister's home to live in California for two years, and in 1931 she moved again, this time to live with her grandmother on a sugar plantation in Cuba. Here, Fox quickly picked up Spanish from her fellow students while attending classes in a one-room schoolhouse. Three years after her arrival, the revolution led by Batista y Zaldivar forced Fox to return to New York City. By this time in her life, Fox had attended nine schools and had hardly ever seen her parents; she found solace and stability by visiting public libraries. "Reading was everything to me," Fox reveals to Steinberg. "Wherever I went—except in Cuba—there was a library. Even though my schools changed, I'd always find a library."

Fox worked several different jobs after finishing high school, ranging from machinist to working for a publishing company and a newspaper. Her desire to travel led her to a position with a leftist British news service that assigned her to cover Poland after World War II. Later, she returned to the United States, married, and had children, but the marriage ended in divorce. Afterwards, Fox resolved to finish her education, attending Columbia University for four years, until she could no longer afford the expense and had to leave before receiving her diploma. Despite the lack of a degree, Fox's knowledge of Spanish helped her find a job as an English teacher for Spanish-speaking children. She also found other teaching positions, including one as a teacher for the emotionally disturbed. In 1962, Fox married an English professor and moved to Greece for six months where her husband—recipient of a Guggenheim fellowship—studied and wrote. All this time she harbored hopes of one day becoming a writer, "but for a long time it remained a shining, but elusive, goal," she tells *Something about the Author* (*SATA*) interviewer Marguerite Feitlowitz.

It was not until her trip to Greece that Fox finally began to realize her dream. "I remember when I was finally able to quit my teaching job and devote myself full-time to writing. People asked me, 'But what will you do?' 'I'm going to write books,' I would say. And they would reply, 'Yes, but what will you DO?' People have this idea that a life spent writing is essentially a life of leisure. Writing is tremendously hard work. There is nothing more satisfying, but it is work all the same." For Fox, the same reason for reading books applies to her desire to write them: books help both reader and writer to experience and understand—if not necessarily sympathize with-the lives of other people. In her acceptance speech for the Newbery award, reprinted in *Newbery and Caldecott Medal Winners, 1966-1975,* she declares that writing helps us "to connect ourselves with the reality of our own lives. It is painful; but if we are to become human, we cannot abandon it."

Fox's juvenile novels have a complexity and sincerity that make them popular with readers and critics alike. These books cover a wide range of subjects, including parental conflict, alcoholism, and death. Frequently, her young protagonists are emotionally withdrawn children who undertake a journey that is symbolic of their emotional development. In *Blowfish Live in the Sea,* for example, nineteen-year-old Ben travels from New York to Boston to see his estranged, alcoholic father after a twelve-year absence. Because of a past trauma involving a lie his father told him, Ben has withdrawn into himself to the point where he no longer speaks to anyone. His sister Carrie is the only family member who tries to reach out to Ben. The importance of Ben and Carrie's journey to Boston, explains a *Horn Book* reviewer, is that "each step . . . relays something further in their tenuous gropings towards an understanding of themselves and of others."

Other award-winning children's novels by Fox, such as *A Place Apart, One-Eyed Cat,* and *The Village by the Sea,* are similarly concerned with relationships, strong characterization, and emotionally troubled protagonists. *New Statesman* contributor Patricia Craig, for instance, remarks that *A Place Apart* is a book that "depends on subtleties of characterisation . . . rather than on an arresting plot." The novel concerns Victoria Finch, a thirteen-year-old girl whose comfort and security are shaken when her father dies suddenly. Victoria's grief, writes *Washington Post Book World* contributor Katherine Paterson, "is the bass accompaniment to the story. Sometimes it swells, taking over the narrative, the rest of the time it subsides into a dark, rhythmic background against which the main story is played." Victoria must also come to terms with her infatuation with Hugh, a manipulative boy who "exerts . . . a power over her spirit," according to Paterson. This relationship compels Victoria "to explore the difficult terrain between the desire for closeness and the tendency to 'make ourselves a place apart,'" observes Jean Strouse in *Newsweek.*

One-Eyed Cat, declares *Dictionary of Literary Biography* contributor Anita Moss, "is one of Fox's finest literary achievements." The title refers to a stray cat which the main character Ned accidentally injures with an air rifle. The guilt Ned feels afterwards plagues him through most of the rest of the book, even making him physically ill at one point, until at last he confesses his thoughtless act to his mother, who in turn confesses that she had once deserted Ned and his father when he was younger. Recognizing these flaws leads Ned to a reconciliation with his parents and himself.

A typical Fox device is to put a main character in an unfamiliar and hostile setting. In *The Village by the Sea,* for example, Emma is sent to live with her uncle and neurotic, alcoholic aunt for two weeks when her father has to go to the hospital for heart surgery. Unable to cope with her hateful aunt and troubled about her father's health, Emma finds some solace in creating a make-believe village on the beach. But, as Rosellen Brown relates in the *New York Times Book Review,* "Emma's miniature haven is ultimately beyond her protection. She can only cherish the building of it, and then the memory."

Of all her books, the controversial yet highly acclaimed *The Slave Dancer,* winner the 1974 Newbery Medal, is the work for which Fox is best known. It is the story of a New Orleans boy who is kidnapped and placed on a slave ship bound for West Africa. The boy, Jessie Bollier, is chosen for his ability to play the fife; his task aboard ship is to "dance" the slaves so they can exercise their cramped limbs. Eventually, Jessie escapes when the ship's crew is drowned in a storm, but he is forever scarred by his experience. Despite the praise *The Slave Dancer* has received, a number of critics have complained that Fox's portrayal of the slaves made them appear to be merely dispirited cattle, and they accused the author of excusing the slave drivers as being victims of circumstance. Binnie Tate, for example, comments in *Interracial Books for Children:* "Through the characters' words, [Fox] excuses the captors and places the blame for the slaves' captivity on Africans themselves. The author slowly and systematically excuses almost all the whites in the story for their participation in the slave venture and by innuendo places the blame elsewhere."

Other reviewers, however, regard *The Slave Dancer* as a fair and humane treatment of a sensitive subject. In a *Horn Book* essay, Alice Bach calls the book "one of the finest examples of a writer's control over her material. . . . With an underplayed but implicit sense of rage, Paula Fox exposes the men who dealt in selling human beings." *The Slave Dancer,* concludes Kevin Crossley-Holland in the *New Statesman,* is "a novel of great moral integrity. . . . From start to finish Miss Fox tells her story quietly and economically; she is candid but she never wallows."

The selection of *The Slave Dancer* for the Newbery caused a number of protests, including demonstrations during the awards ceremony. "I was a total wreck when I found out what was going on," Fox tells Feitlowitz. "And on the evening of the Newbery Award, when I learned that there were plans for a sort of demonstration, I literally thought I would die. There I was in my evening gown, shaking like a leaf. But I gave my speech, and afterwards one or two of the previously hostile critics approached me, to let me know I was 'forgiven.'"

Continuing her practice of placing her young protagonists in difficult circumstances, Fox, in *Monkey Island,* examines the issue of homelessness and explores the more general childhood fear of abandonment. The story concerns an eleven-year-old boy named Clay Garrity. His father loses his job as a magazine art director and abandons his family; because his mother is eight months pregnant and can't work, Clay fears the social services department will take him away and put him in a foster home. Clay decides to leave home and live on the streets, where he is eventually befriended by two kindly homeless men. Jim Naughton writes in *The Washington Post Book World* that "Fox does a wonderful job of evoking Clay's world-from the stark hopeless room where he lived with his mother to the stairway shooting galleries of their welfare hotel." He concludes, however, that Fox's realism has limits: "Clay's good fortune [in being watched over and instructed by two kindly homeless men] strikes me as the book's chief flaw. Fox conveys the hardship of life on the street, but she does not convey the horror." Naughton does note, though, that in "conveying the bottomless dread of abandonment, [*Monkey Island*] shines."

In *Western Wind,* Fox has been praised for taking a rather well-worn premise in children's literature—a lonely young girl is sent by her parents to live with an elderly relative who proves to be quite wise—and making it original and interesting. This is achieved mainly by Fox's depiction of the young heroine's grandmother, an eccentric painter who lives on a remote island off the coast of Maine in house without indoor plumbing. Patricia J. Wagner in *The Bloomsbury Review* lauds Fox's literary skills and concludes that both "adult and junior fiction writers should study her work with care." Ilene Cooper, on the other hand, writing in *Booklist,* offers the following oblique criticism of this novel and much of Fox's writing: "Fox's work can be like a piece of fine lace. You admire its beauty and the delicate craftsmanship that went into its making, but you don't always know what to do with it. And sometimes you just get tired of so much lace."

Homosexuality and AIDS are the issues that Liam Cormac and his family must come to terms with in *The Eagle Kite.* Young Liam's father is dying from the HIV virus. The fact of his immanent mortality and the circumstances under which he contracted the disease cause the family almost unbearable grief; they also provide the narrative struggles through which some memorable characters are defined. In *The Washington Post Book World,* Elizabeth Hand calls the book "beautifully written."

Although Fox has not received as much recognition for her adult novels as she has for her children's books, she has nevertheless been widely praised for works like *Desperate Characters.* Her adult novels are "concerned with the cataclysmic moments of private lives, and the quiet desperation of ordinary people," writes Linda Simon in *Commonweal. Desperate Characters* portrays the lives of Sophie and Otto Bentwood, a childless couple in their mid-forties "facing the abstract menace of a world perhaps they helped through inadvertence to create," writes John Leonard in the *New York Times.* The Bentwoods live in a renovated Brooklyn townhouse amid the squalor of a slum. While the Bentwoods' marriage is described by *New York Times Book Review* contributor Peter Rowley as "if not dead, at best warring," they are content with their orderly, comfortable lives. As the novel progresses, however, their security is gradually encroached upon. "Sophie and Otto . . . are slowly revealed to be menaced by forces . . . giving off a growl of danger all the more ominous for being so essentially nameless and faceless and vague," observes Pearl K. Bell in the *New Leader.* Bell con-

cludes that *"Desperate Characters* is a small masterpiece, a revelation of contemporary New York middle-class life that grasps the mind of the reader with the subtle clarity of metaphor and the alarmed tenacity of nightmare."

In both Fox's children's and adult novels, her characters suffer through tragic situations for which there are no simple solutions, and this has led some critics to categorize her as an author of serious and depressing works. Fox has at times been frustrated by this label. "People are always saying my work is 'depressing,'" she tells Feitlowitz. "But what does that mean? They said *Desperate Characters* was depressing too, and it's been reissued twice. I'm so used to having the word *'depressing'* tied to me I feel like a dog accustomed to the tin can around its neck. The charge can still make me angry, not because of how it might reflect on my work, but because of what it tells me about reading in this country. Is *Anna Karenina* depressing? Is *Madame Bovary?* 'Depressing,' when applied to a literary work is so narrow, so confining, so impoverished and impoverishing. This yearning for the proverbial 'happy ending' is little more than a desire for oblivion."

A number of critics have defended Fox's approach to fiction, and have praised her ability to address her younger audience frankly. "What sets [Fox] above the gaudy blooms-the social workers and fortunetellers—who are knocking out books as fast as kids can swallow them," writes *Horn Book* contributor Alice Bach, "is her uncompromising integrity. Fox is nobody's mouthpiece. Her unique vision admits to the child what he already suspects: Life is part grit, part disappointment, part nonsense, and occasionally victory. . . . And by offering children no more than the humanness we all share—child, adult, reader, writer—she acknowledges them as equals."

For Fox, writing for children is, except for a few considerations, not that different from writing for adults. "Children have everything adults have," the author tells Feitlowitz, "with the exception of judgment, which comes only over the course of time." While she avoids writing detailed scenes for children involving sex, extreme violence, or subjects outside their experience like teenage pregnancy, Fox adds that "children know about pain and fear and unhappiness and betrayal. And we do them a disservice by trying to sugarcoat dark truths. There is an odd kind of debauchery I've noticed, particularly in societies that consider themselves 'democratic' or 'liberal': they display the gory details but hide meaning, especially if it is ambiguous or disturbing." And so, above all else, Fox strives for honesty and integrity in her writing. She concludes, "We must never, ever try to pull the wool over children's eyes by 'watering down' powerful stories."

BIOGRAPHICAL/CRITICAL SOURCES:

BOOKS

Children's Literature Review, Volume 1, Gale, 1976.
Contemporary Literary Criticism, Gale, Volume 2, 1974, Volume 8, 1978.
Dictionary of Literary Biography, Volume 52: *American Writers for Children since 1960: Fiction,* Gale, 1986.
Kingman, Lee, editor, *Newbery and Caldecott Medal Winners, 1966-1975,* Horn Book, 1975.
Something about the Author, Volume 60, Gale, 1990.
Townsend, John Rowe, *A Sense of Story: Essays on Contemporary Writers for Children,* Lippincott, 1971.

PERIODICALS

Bloomsbury Review, March-April, 1994.
Booklist, October 15, 1993, p. 432.
Chicago Tribune, April 9, 1995, p. 7.
Children's Book Review, December, 1972; winter, 1974-75.
Commonweal, January 11, 1985.
Globe and Mail (Toronto), February 6, 1988.
Horn Book, August, 1969; April, 1970; December, 1970; August, 1974; October, 1977; October, 1978; April, 1984; September-October, 1991, p. 596; July-August, 1993, p. 468; March-April, 1994, p. 198; September-October, 1995, p. 608.
Hudson Review, winter, 1972-73.
Interracial Books for Children, Volume 5, number 5, 1974.
Los Angeles Times, November 21, 1987.
Los Angeles Times Book Review, September 25, 1988.
Ms., October, 1984.
Nation, January 15, 1977; November 3, 1984.
New Leader, July 3, 1967; February 2, 1970.
New Republic, March 18, 1967; January 15, 1977.
New Statesman, November 8, 1974; December 4, 1981.
Newsweek, March 16, 1970; September 27, 1976; December 1, 1980.
New Yorker, February 7, 1970; November 1, 1976.
New York Review of Books, June 1, 1967; October 5, 1972; October 28, 1976; June 27, 1985.

New York Times, February 10, 1970; September 22, 1972; September 16, 1976.
New York Times Book Review, February 1, 1970; October 8, 1972; January 20, 1974; October 3, 1976; November 9, 1980; July 12, 1981; November 11, 1984; November 18, 1984; February 5, 1989; July 8, 1990; November 10, 1991, p. 52; November 10, 1993, p. 52; April 10, 1994, p. 35.
Publishers Weekly, April 6, 1990; April 12, 1993, p. 64; August 23, 1993, p. 73; April 10, 1994, p. 35; February 20, 1995, p. 207.
Saturday Review, October 22, 1966; July 19, 1969; January 23, 1971; October 16, 1976.
School Library Journal, August, 1991, p. 164; April, 1992, p. 42; July, 1993, p. 90; December, 1993, p. 111; April, 1995, p. 150.
Time, October 4, 1976.
Times Literary Supplement, June 6, 1968; February 21, 1986; November 28, 1986; January 15, 1988.
Washington Post, June 7, 1990.
Washington Post Book World, September 24, 1972; October 31, 1976; February 8, 1981; September 23, 1984; March 24, 1991; December 1, 1991; May 7, 1995.

*   *   *

FULGHUM, Robert (L.) 1937-

PERSONAL: Surname is pronounced "*ful*-jum;" born June 4, 1937; raised in Waco, TX; son of Lee (a department store manager) and Eula (Howard) Fulghum; married Marcia McClellan, 1957 (divorced, 1973); married Lynn Edwards (a physician), 1975; children: (first marriage) Christian, Hunter, Molly Jencks (adopted). *Education:* Attended University of Colorado, Baylor University, 1957, and Starr King (Unitarian) Seminary, 1961; studied at Zen Buddhist monastery, 1972. *Religion:* Unitarian. *Avocational interests:* Observing nature, traveling, singing, dancing, sailing, eating chicken-fried steak, and playing the guitar, bass, and mando'cello.

ADDRESSES: Home—Houseboat on Lake Union, WA. *Office*—c/o Random House Inc., 31st Floor, 201 E. 50th St., New York, NY 10022.

CAREER: Ordained a Unitarian minister, 1961; part-time Unitarian minister, Bellingham, WA, beginning in 1961; Edmonds Unitarian Church, Edmonds, WA, part-time minister, 1966-85, minister emeritus,

1985—; Lakeside School (independent), Seattle, WA, art teacher, 1971-88; painter, writer, and lecturer. Worked variously as a sales trainee for International Business Machines (IBM), a singing cowboy and amateur rodeo performer at guest ranches in Montana, Colorado, and Texas, a counselor to mental patients and prison inmates, a creator of motel art, a bartender, and a folk music teacher. Founder of wilderness camp in Canada.

MEMBER: Human Rights Watch, Volunteers of America, American Civil Liberties Union, Planned Parenthood, Sierra Club.

WRITINGS:

All I Really Need to Know I Learned in Kindergarten: Uncommon Thoughts on Common Things (essays), Villard Books, 1988, title narrative reissued as *All I Really Need to Know I Learned in Kindergarten: The Essay that Became a Classic, with a Special Commentary by Robert Fulghum*, Villard Books, 1990.
It Was on Fire When I Lay Down on It, Villard Books, 1989.
Uh-Oh: Some Observations from Both Sides of the Refrigerator Door, Villard Books, 1991.
Maybe (Maybe Not), Villard Books, 1993.
From Beginning to End: The Rituals of Our Lives, Villard Books, 1995.
True Love, HarperCollins, 1997.
Words I Wish I Wrote, HarperCollins, 1997.

All I Really Need to Know I Learned in Kindergarten has been published in ninety-three countries and twenty-seven languages. All of Fulghum's proceeds from *True Love* are being donated to Habitat for Humanity and from *Words I Wish I Wrote* to Human Rights Watch.

ADAPTATIONS: Gail Forman has adapted a number of Fulgham's works, including *Burning Beds and Mermaids,* Prentice Hall Regents, 1994, and *It All Started in Kindergarten: Unforgettable Stories for Listening and Conversation,* Prentice Hall Regents, 1994. Ernest Zulia has adapted a stage production of Fulghum's writings. The adaptation, entitled *All I Really Need to Know I Learned in Kindergarten,* draws upon material from Fulghum's first five works. It has been produced nationally in Chicago, Kansas City, Los Angeles, Louisville, Phoenix and Washington, DC, and internationally in Manila, Singapore, and Kuala Lumpur and is scheduled to open in Prague in 1998.

SIDELIGHTS: Unlike some writers who struggle for years to become best-selling authors, semi-retired Unitarian minister and art teacher Robert Fulghum struck gold with his first book, a collection of inspirational essays entitled *All I Really Need to Know I Learned in Kindergarten: Uncommon Thoughts on Common Things.* The volume—which delves into topics ranging from childhood and adult-life lessons, to the joys of laundry, to the shared experience of a neighbor and the spider that webbed her front porch—won immediate public acclaim and appeared on several bestseller charts. Fulghum's second work, a similar array of thought-provoking compositions called *It Was on Fire When I Lay Down on It,* experienced comparable popularity, so much so that the author's two books ran for a time in the first and second positions on the *New York Times* bestseller list.

In an effort to understand Fulghum's popular appeal, various critics have suggested that the themes explored in the author's essays touch readers with their simplicity, humor, insight, and universal nature. "Fulghum's essays reaffirm the sanctity of the ordinary," explained Patricia Leigh Brown in a review of *All I Really Need to Know I Learned in Kindergarten* for the *New York Times.* "He does not preach, and rarely mentions God, but his book has a strong spiritual component. He focuses on the transcendental stuff of everyday life." Asserting that Fulghum is "not quite preacher, not quite regional humorist," Brown concluded that the author is "a hybrid folk fabulist," a cross between "positive-thinking" American cleric Dr. Norman Vincent Peale and humorist Erma Bombeck.

Fulghum was raised in Waco, Texas in a strict Southern Baptist home. Feeling rebellious after his high school graduation, he embarked on a journey to discover himself and the world around him. He studied at the University of Colorado, obtained a degree in history and philosophy at Baylor University, and a degree in divinity at The Starr King (Unitarian) Seminary. Fulghum held a number of unusual jobs, such as singing cowboy and amateur rodeo performer. Along the way he married his first wife, Marcia McClellan. In 1972 he ventured to Japan to study at a Zen Buddhist monastery and met Lynn Edwards, who, after a divorce from McClellan in 1973, would became his second wife in 1975.

In conjunction with his ministry, from which he retired in 1985, Fulghum began jotting down daily insights for use in sermons and church newsletter articles. These inspirational essays formed the foundation of 1988's *All I Really Need to Know I Learned in Kindergarten.* Publishing these ruminations in book form, however, took some twenty years of grassroots evolution. Apparently, one of Fulghum's columns—about the invaluable life lessons learned in kindergarten—sparked interest in the Unitarian community. According to Beth Ann Krier of the *Los Angeles Times,* the essay "was derived from a personal credo [Fulghum's] been writing and rewriting every spring." Krier added that "people liked the piece, photocopied it at the office, hung it on their refrigerators and sent it to friends, who also photocopied it, hung in on their refrigerators and passed it on." Eventually Fulghum's affirmations made it beyond the Unitarian circuit and into the mainstream. The article was read into the Congressional Record by then-Senate Majority Leader Jim Wright, was broadcast by radio commentators Paul Harvey and Larry King, and appeared in advice writer Abigail Van Buren's "Dear Abby" column. The essay also appeared in *Reader's Digest* magazine and in the *Kansas City Times.*

Finally, Fulghum's kindergarten credo meandered into the home of a Connecticut literary agent via her daughter's school bookbag—the girl's teacher had sent copies home with all her students. The agent was impressed with the writing and contacted its author. The end result was the publication of the well-traveled essay and Fulghum's other writings in the 196-page *All I Really Need to Know I Learned in Kindergarten.* The title piece is typical of the reflections contained in the volume. In the essay, Fulghum urges readers to follow some basic principles: "Share everything. Play fair. Don't hit people. Put things back where you found them. Clean up your own mess. Don't take things that aren't yours. Say you're sorry when you hurt somebody. Wash your hands before you eat. Flush. Warm cookies and milk are good for you. Live a balanced life—learn some and think some and draw and paint and sing and dance and play and work every day some. Take a nap every afternoon." He adds, "Take any one of those items and extrapolate it into sophisticated adult terms and apply it to your family life or your work or your government or your world and it holds true and clear and firm. Think what a better world it would be if we all . . . had cookies and milk about three o'clock every afternoon. . . . Or if all governments had a basic policy to always put things back where they found them and to clean up their own mess."

Other commentaries in the book include Fulghum's description of a truck driver's unusual flying feat, the author's disclosure about the real joys associated with transportation, his discussion of the simple pleasures derived from using crayons, and his observation of a neighbor who walks straight into a spider web and runs away screaming. He also retells the experience from the insect's perspective. For the reprint rights of his volume, Fulghum was awarded $2.1 million, a record amount for a nonfiction paperback at that time. Although the public received the volume with considerable enthusiasm, various critics reviewed the book with skepticism. Commentators variously labeled the essays as homespun wisdom, inspired observations, and "philosophical tofu"—a reference to the soybean food product that is trendy, bland, and fairly insubstantial. Brown, acknowledging Fulghum's unabashed sentimentality, noted that "reading Robert Fulghum at times can be like drinking 5-cent lemonade; it is only after you've downed the Dixie Cup that you realize how much sugar is at the bottom." Jeff Danziger, writing in the *Christian Science Monitor,* called the essays "extremely well written with a friendly and economical prose." He added, "Several of the essays will give you the ever-popular lump in the throat."

Fulghum, who has also written the as-yet-unpublished parody *All I Really Wanted to Know I Learned in the Alley behind My House,* remarked about *Kindergarten*'s success and its impact on his further ministries in *Bestsellers 89:* "I realize now that I'm still in a position of ministry in the sense that one has an opportunity to add to the culture, to be influential, to shape what people think and feel—the size of the congregation has changed, but the task has not." He also remarked, "To be a good steward . . . and to use [fame] well—that's a big concern of mine. On the wall of my studio I put in huge letters a quotation from the book of Matthew that said: 'What does it profit a man if he gain the whole world and lose his own soul?' And I think about that a lot because fame and fortune are very destructive and to be a good steward would be a mighty accomplishment. It would not only set some good examples for people but it would be using what one had for good."

On the heels of *Kindergarten*'s success, Fulghum collected commentaries for a second book, *It Was on Fire When I Lay Down on It,* published in 1989. Also a bestseller soon after publication, the volume contains the author's thoughts on various subjects, including parenting, traveling, joy, and sorrow. The title narrative sets the tone for the diverse discussions that follow. The essay begins, "A tabloid newspaper carried the story, stating simply that a small-town emergency squad was summoned to a house where smoke was pouring from an upstairs window. The crew broke in and found a man in a smoldering bed. After the man was rescued and the mattress doused, the obvious question was asked: 'How did this happen?' 'I don't know. It was on fire when I lay down on it.'" Fulghum goes on to explain his perception of the story, "I thought, there's the story of my life. I've known most of my life what I was getting into and I went ahead and did it anyhow. And that's kind of the story of the human race. Like Adam and Eve, you know, God said 'Don't eat the apple.' And the snake says, 'Try it, you'll like it,' and so they ate it. What I do with the story is introduce the book by saying a lot of us run our lives that way. That sense of why do we do what we know we shouldn't and *why* don't we do what we know we should. There's the great mystery for me of being human."

Critical reception to *It Was on Fire When I Lay Down on It* was mixed, although the public response was enthusiastic. While some reviewers deemed the book slightly sugar-coated and mundane, others praised the author's witty stories, remarking on Fulghum's valuable insights. Fulghum's third book of narratives, titled *Uh-Oh: Some Observations from Both Sides of the Refrigerator Door,* also received similar critical treatment. The work begins by discussing the situations that begin with someone saying "uh-oh," and the ways in which those scenarios can be reversed and overcome.

Fulghum produced more of his crackerbarrel philosophical musings and pithy anecdotes in *Maybe (Maybe Not),* which includes essays on ironing a shirt, selling chocolate, and conducting Ludwig van Beethoven's Ninth Symphony. Similar, but perhaps with a more narrow focus, is *From Beginning to End: The Rituals of Our Lives,* a book that examines the ways in which humans create meaning and give structure to their lives through public rituals. Fulghum examines public events such as weddings, funerals, school reunions, church services, and the like, and he writes about his own reunion with the daughter he had given up for adoption in 1958. Again, critical opinion suggests that these books will more than satisfy Fulghum's many admirers.

Reviewing Fulghum's work for the Toronto *Globe and Mail* Sarah Harvey surmised, "Fulghum specializes in the celebration of the everyday event, the little domestic epiphany, the miracle of the meatloaf, the cosmic significance of jelly beans, the fickle finger of fate." And Fulghum's fate, since his rise to bestseller status, has included more writings, numerous interviews, and various television appearances. "I've always made a clear distinction between making a life and making a living," Fulghum told Andrea Chambers and Priscilla Turner of *People* magazine. He added, "Any fool can make enough money to survive. It's another thing to keep yourself consistently entertained. It's a lot of work, and a lot of fun, to make a life."

BIOGRAPHICAL/CRITICAL SOURCES:

BOOKS

Fulghum, Robert, *All I Really Need to Know I Learned in Kindergarten: Uncommon Thoughts on Common Things,* Villard Books, 1988, pp. 4-6.
Fulghum, *It Was on Fire When I Lay Down on It,* Villard Books, 1989, p. 3.

PERIODICALS

Bestsellers 89: Books and Authors in the News, issue 2, 1989, pp. 37-39.
Booklist, August, 1993, p. 2010.
Christian Science Monitor, October 24, 1988, p. 22.
Current Biography, July, 1994, p. 10.
Globe and Mail (Toronto), September 7, 1991, p. C10.
Kirkus Reviews, July 1, 1993, p. 852; March 1, 1995, p. 316.
Los Angeles Times, November 26, 1989.
New York Times, December 21, 1988; July 23, 1989, pp. 26-30, 32-33.
People, February 27, 1989, pp. 91-92; November 20, 1989, p. 49; March 7, 1994, p. 83.
Publishers Weekly, August 2, 1993, p. 73; March 13, 1995, p. 54.

G

GAITE, Francis
See COLES, Cyril Henry

* * *

GALINDO, P.
See HINOJOSA(-SMITH), Rolando (R.)

* * *

GEORGE, Elizabeth 1949-

PERSONAL: Born February 26, 1949, in Warren, OH; daughter of Robert Edwin (a conveyor salesman) and Anne (a registered nurse; maiden name, Rivelle) George, married Ira Jay Toibin (a business manager), May 28, 1971 (divorced, November, 1995). *Education:* Foothill Community College, A.A., 1969; University of California, Riverside, B.A., 1970; California State University, M.S., 1979. *Politics:* Democratic. *Religion:* "Recovering from Catholicism." *Avocational interests:* Reading, theater, movies, skiing, photography, gardening.

ADDRESSES: Home—611 13th St., Huntington Beach, CA 92648. *Agent*—Deborah Schneider, John Farquharson Ltd., 157 West 57th Street, New York, New York 10107; Vivienne Schuster, John Farquharson Ltd., 162-168 Regent Street, London W1R 5TB, England.

CAREER: Mater Dei High School, Santa Ana, CA, teacher of English, 1974-75; El Toro High School, El Toro, CA, teacher of English, 1975-87; Coastline College, Costa Mesa, CA, teacher of creative writing, 1988—; Irvine Valley College, Irvine, CA, teacher of creative writing, 1989; University of California, Irvine, teacher of creative writing, 1990.

AWARDS, HONORS: Award for teacher of the year, Orange County Department of Education, 1981; Anthony and Agatha awards for best first novel, both 1989, both for *A Great Deliverance;* Le Grand Prix de Litterature Policiere, 1990; MIMI award (Germany).

WRITINGS:

A Great Deliverance, Bantam (New York City), 1988.
Payment in Blood, Bantam, 1989.
Well-Schooled in Murder, Bantam, 1990.
A Suitable Vengeance, Bantam, 1991.
For the Sake of Elena, Bantam, 1992.
Missing Joseph, Bantam, 1993.
Playing for the Ashes, Bantam, 1994.
In the Presence of the Enemy, Bantam, 1996.
Deception on His Mind, Bantam, 1997.

Contributor to *Sisters in Crime,* Volume 2.

SIDELIGHTS: American writer Elizabeth George has won wide acclaim with her popular crime novels featuring a team of Scotland Yard sleuths. The author's depiction of British life is so accurate that even many of her readers in Great Britain have assumed that she is British, but in fact, she was born in Ohio and raised in California. Her fascination with the classic British mystery genre led her to try her own hand at it. Her first book, *A Great Deliverance,* featured an aristocratic inspector, Thomas Lynley; his aggressive, working-class assistant, Detective Sergeant Barbara Havers; and Lynley's best friend, independent forensic pathologist Simon St. James, who team together to investigate the beheading of a wealthy family's patriarch. In a *Publishers Weekly* article by Lisa See, George was quoted as saying that *A Great Deliverance* "wasn't a good book. . . . It was a clunky, old-fashioned, Agatha Christie-style mystery where St. James took everyone into the library and explained the crime. But it *was* a finished book." Many reviewers looked more kindly on the finished product, however, including London *Times* reviewer Marcel Berlins, who proclaimed it "an exciting debut." *A Great Deliverance* also won the prestigious Anthony and Agatha awards.

George followed *A Great Deliverance* with *Payment in Blood,* in which Lynley and Havers are sent to a Glasgow estate to investigate the death of a playwright pierced through the neck with a lengthy dagger. Lynley and Havers discover that the murderer must have passed through a neighboring room, one occupied on that fateful evening by an aristocratic woman with whom Lynley is in love. With Lynley distracted by romance, Havers assumes responsibility for their inquiry, which points to yet another aristocrat, an aging stage director of great prominence. Carolyn Banks, in her review of *Payment in Blood* in the *Washington Post,* noted the novel's "wonderfully drawn tensions and bonds between the characters," and she hailed George for her skilled manipulation of crime-story conventions such as "the isolated old house [and] the tangled histories of the players."

In George's next mystery, *Well-Schooled in Murder,* Lynley and Havers must investigate the murder of a young boy found nude at a churchyard near his prestigious public school. The duo's probe leads to the uncovering of various criminal and scandalous activities, including blackmail, sadism, and suicide. *Washington Post Book World* contributor Jean M. White proclaimed *Well-Schooled in Murder* "a bewitching book, exasperatingly clever, and with a plot that must be peeled layer by layer like an onion." Marilyn Stasio, in her assessment of crime fiction for the *New York Times Book Review,* noted the "sensationalistic plot" of *Well-Schooled in Murder* and proclaimed George "a gifted storyteller."

In *A Suitable Vengeance,* George casts protagonist Lynley into a setting of domestic conflict. He has arrived at his mother's home in Cornwall to introduce his fiance to her. Accompanying the couple are some

of Lynley's friends, including a scientist coworker, Simon St. James, and his sister, Sidney St. James. Shortly into the novel Sidney engages in a surprisingly violent clash with her lover, Justin. Lynley's brother, a drug addict, soon arrives to further disturb matters. Then a newspaper editor is found dead. Lynley, while trying to resolve a long estrangement from his mother, must begin an investigation into the death. That inquiry leads to the uncovering of further drug use and the particularly malicious activities of a London woman. Margaret Cannon, writing in the Toronto *Globe and Mail,* deemed *A Suitable Vengeance* "a superior story," and lauded George as "an elegant craftswoman." Another enthusiast, Charles Champlin, wrote in the *Los Angeles Times Book Review* that with *A Suitable Vengeance* George gives readers a "sumptuous, all-out reading experience."

George continued to develop her characters with each new book. Her skill in plotting also became more finely honed with each successive title, according to numerous reviewers. Discussing *For the Sake of Elena,* the author's fifth book, *Los Angeles Time Book Review* writer Charles Champlin noted that "like P. D. James, whom she comes as close to resembling as anyone now writing, [George] concocts an intricate timetable plot with a guess-again finale." He further noted, however, that "her larger interests are in character delineation, relationships closely observed, and social issues exposed. . . .. the new book sustains the high standard Elizabeth George has set for herself." *Belles Lettres* reviewer Jane Bakerman called *For the Sake of Elena* "suspenseful, literate but readily accessible to a wide range of readers, thoughtful and thought provoking . . . an elegant novel." *Playing for the Ashes,* about the mysterious death of a star cricket player, drew raves from Emily Melton in *Booklist:* "George is a gifted writer who spins rich, colorful, mesmerizing, multifaceted stories that combine an absorbing mystery with provocative insights into her characters' innermost thoughts and emotions. . . . Readers will be astounded by the ease with which she weaves complex relationships and provocative moral, emotional, and ethical questions into the compelling plot. Another tour de force from one of today's best storytellers."

"Elizabeth George is arguably the finest writer working in the mystery genre today," declared Margo Kaufman in a *Los Angeles Times Book Review* assessment of *In the Presence of the Enemy,* George's eighth and longest novel. The plot concerns the kidnaping of the illegitimate daughter of a conservative politician. Yet this book also drew negative comment from James Hynes, who complained in the *Washington Post* that *In the Presence of the Enemy* "is the longest, slowest, dullest book" he had ever read.

George remarked on her work in *St. James Guide to Crime and Mystery Writers:* " My novels tend to harken back to the Golden Age of the detective story in that they attempt to reflect the glamour of Dorothy L. Sayers's type of writing rather than the grim reality of present day dissections of murder. Nonetheless, the issues they revolve around are very much part of contemporary life." In that same book, Jane S. Bakerman summarized that George's popularity results from her skillful use of "an intriguing range of continuing characters who are interesting individually as well as in their interactions with one another, gripping plots, well-drawn descriptive passages, and plenty of gore. The crimes depicted in these novels are horrific not only in physical detail but also in their psychological impact upon the cast of characters—and upon the readers. Strongly sexual undercurrents color and inform all these factors. With sharp realism but without exploitation, then, George notes and capitalizes upon the human fascination with sex and violence. Crime writers often focus on these subjects, of course, but not many display the control George commands."

A collection of George's manuscripts is housed at the Mugar Memorial Library, Boston University.

BIOGRAPHICAL/CRITICAL SOURCES:

BOOKS

St. James Guide to Crime and Mystery Writers, 4th edition, edited by Jay P. Pederson, St. James Press (Detroit), 1996.

PERIODICALS

Atlanta Constitution, March 28, 1996, p. E7.
Atlanta Journal-Constitution, June 16, 1991, p. N9; July 19, 1992, p. N7; July 18, 1993, p. N9.
Belles Lettres, fall, 1992, p. 28.
Booklist, May 15, 1994, p. 1645.
Globe and Mail (Toronto), August 4, 1990; June 22, 1991.
Los Angeles Times, June 28, 1988; June 9, 1996, p. E1.
Los Angeles Times Book Review, August 13, 1989, p. 8; June 9, 1991; July 12, 1992, p. 8; July 10, 1994, p. 8; May 12, 1996, p. 11.
New Yorker, August 23, 1993, p. 165.

New York Times, August 26, 1992, p. C17; July 14, 1993, pp. C13, C18.
New York Times Book Review, November 12, 1989, p. 58; August 12, 1990, p. 21; June 20, 1993, p. 21; April 21, 1996.
Publishers Weekly, May 23, 1994, p. 80; March 11, 1996, pp. 38-39.
Times (London), February 4, 1989.
Tribune Books (Chicago), July 1, 1990, p. 6; June 2, 1991, p. 7.
Washington Post, August 29, 1989; February 29, 1996, p. C2.
Washington Post Book World, July 15, 1990, p. 11.*

*   *   *

GILL, B. M.
    See TRIMBLE, Barbara Margaret

*   *   *

GILMOUR, Barbara
    See TRIMBLE, Barbara Margaret

*   *   *

GINGRICH, Newt(on Leroy) 1943-

PERSONAL: Born June 17, 1943, in Harrisburg, PA; son of Robert Bruce and Kathleen (Daugherty) Gingrich; married Jacqueline Battley, 1962 (divorced); married Marianne Ginther, 1981; children: Linda Kathleen, Jacqueline Sue. *Education:* Emory University, B.A., 1965; Tulane University, M.A., 1968, Ph.D., 1971. *Religion:* Baptist.

ADDRESSES: Office—U.S. House of Representatives, 2438 Rayburn House Office Building, Washington, DC 20515.

CAREER: West Georgia College, Carrollton, professor of history and environmental studies, 1970-78; U.S. House of Representatives, Washington, DC, representative from Sixth District of Georgia and member of Administrative Committee and Public Works and Transportation Committee, 1979-89, House Republican Whip, 1989, Speaker of the House, 1995—. Member of Congressional Clearinghouse on the Future; co-founder of Congressional Military Reform Caucus. Reinhardt College, Waleska, adjunct professor, 1994-95.

MEMBER: American Academy of Arts and Letters, World Future Society, Conservative Opportunity Society (co-founder), Sierra Club, Georgia Conservancy, Kiwanis Club.

AWARDS, HONORS: Time magazine Man of the Year, 1995.

WRITINGS:

(Author of preface) Alfred Balitzer, *A Nation of Associations,* American Society of Association Executives and American Medical Political Action Committee, 1981.

(With wife, Marianne Gingrich, and David Drake) *Window of Opportunity: A Blueprint for the Future,* Tor (New York City), 1984.

(Author of foreword) Teresa Donovan, Marcella Donovan, and Joseph Piccione, *Voluntary School Prayer: Judicial Dilemma, Proposed Solutions,* Free Congress Research and Education Foundation, 1984.

(Author of foreword) David Dean, editor, *Low Intensity Conflict and Modern Technology,* Air University Press, 1986.

(Author of introduction) Perry Smith and others, *Creating Strategic Vision,* National Defense University Press, 1987.

(Author of foreword) Gordon Jones and John Marini, editors, *Imperial Congress,* Pharos Books, 1988.

Quotations from Speaker Newt: The Little Red, White, and Blue Book of the Republican Revolution, Workman (New York City), 1995.

(With Bill Tucker) *To Renew America,* HarperCollins (New York City), 1995.

(With William R. Forstchen) *1945,* Baen Publishing Enterprises (New York City), 1995.

Contributor to books, including *Liberal Cliches/Conservative Solutions,* edited by Phil Crane, Green Hill (Ottawa, IL), 1984; *Nuclear Arms: Ethics, Strategy, Politics,* edited by Jim Woolsey, ICS Press (San Francisco), 1984; and *House of Ill Repute,* edited by Dan Renberg, Princeton University Press (Princeton, NJ), 1987.

SIDELIGHTS: Whatever one's political viewpoint, politician, writer, and orator Newt Gingrich may go down in history as a symbol of the state of America during the 1990s. Beginning his political career as a Republican congressman from Georgia in a hotly Democratic House of Representatives, Gingrich parlayed both the power of his party and his personal fortitude over the next sixteen years, becoming Speaker of the House in 1995. Working under the shadow of the popular administration of Democratic president Bill Clinton, Gingrich proposed to do battle with the political status quo. His mission, according to *Newsweek* reporter Howard Fineman, has been clear from the beginning of his career: to fight "corruption, bloated government and a decaying social order." To Gingrich, Fineman explains, "politics really is a matter of life or death, of good or evil, of domination or loss. He has spent a career trying to prove that politics is as tough as war, as important to freedom."

Gingrich was born into the transient world occupied by many military families. As the stepson of a career officer in the U.S. military, young Newt attended five schools over an eight-year period during his childhood, and lived in three states and two countries in the process. In 1956 thirteen-year-old Gingrich and his family witnessed the Hungarian Uprising while stationed in that area of the Eastern European shatterzone. The family lived under the constant threat of violence during their stay there. A visit to the battlefield at Verdun the following spring further impressed the young student of the importance of history, and of political power. "All that summer I kept thinking to myself, 'This is crazy,'" Gingrich revealed to Fineman. "'People really do bad things to each other.'" The realization that politics was the vehicle for such evil, and that political power in the hands of those dedicated to "right" could make a positive difference for society, would remain his guiding principle, fueling his interest in military history and setting his later course in U.S. politics.

While making his views clear to members of his Georgia constituency during his early tenure as congressman, Gingrich enlightened U.S. readers as to his vision for a "very different, more optimistic, decentralized, growth-oriented, safer American future" in *Window of Opportunity: A Blueprint for the Future,* published in 1985 by science-fiction publisher Tor Books and promoted through funding by various special interest groups. Written while Gingrich was a member of the executive committee of the Clearinghouse of the Future and was actively involved in the formation of the Congressional Space Caucus, *Win-*

dow of Opportunity presents ways in which U.S. social and political ills can be solved by technology. Addressing such diverse issues as social security, space exploration, and traditional values, the volume also contained the conservative back-slapping and anti-welfare state rhetoric that have since become characteristic of its author. The book was hailed as "offering a hopeful political and social strategy to realize the American dream" by fellow congressman Jack Kemp in the staunchly conservative *American Spectator.*

1995 found Gingrich an almost ubiquitous presence in the media—from the cover of *Time,* where he was pronounced 1995's Man of the Year, to CNN, C-SPAN, and the nightly news, Gingrich's leadership of the Republican freshman congress in its efforts to balance the federal budget received constant coverage. Gingrich's visibility on television was matched by his appearance on bookstore shelves, smiling from the dustjacket of his second book, titled *To Renew America* and co-written by Bill Tucker.

A manifesto of Gingrich's beliefs, the book is divided into five parts: "Visions and Strategies"; "The Six Challenges"; "The Contract with America"; "The Ongoing Revolution"; and the forward-looking "A New Beginning: The America We Will Create." While praising Gingrich for addressing the issue of spending reforms with regard to both the Senate and the House of Representatives, Kevin Philips notes that, like *Window of Opportunity, To Renew America* "is stuffed with Pollyannaish views of how technology will uplift politics, culture and public policy." Reviewing the work in the *Washington Post Book World,* Philips also states that, while Gingrich "has his strong points as a historian. . . . he didn't get tenure in his years [teaching] at West Georgia College, and his book is sure to inspire a competition among snickering history professors to scalp the speaker in professional journals." Michael Lind agrees in the *New York Times Book Review,* calling Gingrich's philosophical underpinnings "the antiseptic high-tech future familiar to those of us who grew up between the 1939 World's Fair and the Apollo missions," and calling into question the speaker's use of *"Reader's Digest* and *The Saturday Evening Post* from around 1955" as a realistic baseline from which to judge the failure of modern society.

The fictional work *1945,* also published in 1995, takes another futuristic look at contemporary society, this time from a viewpoint created though an alternate history of World War II. In the novel, Nazi leader Adolf Hitler is severely injured in a plane crash in late 1941, the day before the actual Japanese bombing of Pearl Harbor, leaving others to orchestrate the war. Under the leadership of Nazis such as Albert Speer, war is never declared on the United States, nor is Russia invaded. Instead, Germany focuses on the conquest of Western Europe, while the United States is left to quickly defeat Japan. By 1943 most of Europe is in the hands of the Germans. The States, with no threat of a Communist menace, take arms development—including the atomic bomb—at a more leisurely pace, leaving themselves open to German attack. While noting that the scenario is a credible one, Donald E. Westlake criticizes the lack of setting and character development, noting that "There isn't a scene in the book in which the characters aren't in uniform." "There is no discernible theme and scant literary ambition," Westlake cheekily adds in his review in the *New York Times Book Review,* "though some of the descriptions of military equipment have a certain poetry about them."

Although Gingrich's forte might not be fiction, literary critics would argue, his accomplishments as a politician loom large. "A tough operator, a master of the workings of modern representative politics, a man of ideas and a subversively high level of culture" is how David Frum, with the objectivity of an observer an ocean away from the hotbed of U.S. politics, characterizes Gingrich in Frum's review of *To Renew America* in the *Times Literary Supplement.* Unlike other U.S. politicians, Frum observes, "he is not a man to confuse feeling with doing. Which is why," the critic notes, "unlike the soon to be forgotten Bill Clinton, Newt Gingrich . . . is poised to dominate American politics for a decade."

BIOGRAPHICAL/CRITICAL SOURCES:

BOOKS

Andersen, Alfred F., *Challenging Newt Gingrich: Chapter by Chapter,* Tom Paine Institute (Eugene, OR), 1996.

Bentley, P. F., *Newt: Inside the Revolution,* Collins (San Francisco), 1995.

Drew, Elizabeth, *Showdown: The Struggle between the Gingrich Congress and the Clinton White House,* Simon & Schuster (New York City), 1996.

Gingrich, Newt, Marianne Gingrich, and David Drake, *Window of Opportunity: A Blueprint for the Future,* Tor, 1984.

Maraniss, David, *"Tell Newt to Shut Up!": Prize-winning Washington Post Journalists Reveal How Reality Gagged the Gingrich Revolution,* Simon & Schuster (New York City), 1996.

Warner, Judith, *Newt Gingrich: Speaker to America,* Signet (New York City), 1995.

Wilson, John K., *Newt Gingrich: Capitol Crimes and Misdemeanors,* Common Courage (Monroe, ME), 1996.

PERIODICALS

American Spectator, December 1984.

Business Week, June 12, 1995, p. 34, May 20, 1996, p. 32.

Commonweal, October 6, 1995, p. 26.

Economist, July 8, 1995, p. 83.

Gentlemen's Quarterly, January, 1996, p. 120.

Harper's, September, 1995, p. 5.

Insight on the News, January 30, 1995, p. 13, July 17, 1995, p. 8.

Ladies Home Journal, November, 1995, p. 144.

Meet the Press, June 17, 1990, p. 1, December 1, 1991, p. 1.

Nation, August 14, 1995, p. 174.

National Review, October 9, 1995, p. 62, October 23, 1995, p. 62.

New Republic, January 23, 1995, p. 6; August 14, 1995, p. 34.

Newsweek, January 9, 1995, pp. 28-34.

New York Review of Books, August 10, 1995, p. 7.

New York Times Book Review, July 9, 1995, p. 10, July 23, 1995, p. 3.

Rolling Stone, December 29, 1994, p. 164.

Saturday Review, November, 1984.

Time, December 25, 1995, pp. 4, 48, 84.

Times Literary Supplement, September 22, 1995, p. 7; December 8, 1995, p. 21.

U.S. News & World Report, April 10, 1995, p. 26.

Vanity Fair, September, 1995, p. 147.

Village Voice, November 27, 1984.

Voice of Youth Advocates, April 1985, p. 62.

Washingtonian, July, 1995, p. 37.

Washington Monthly, September, 1995, p. 44.

Washington Post Book World, July 23, 1995, pp. 1, 14.*

* * *

GIROUX, E. X.
   See SHANNON, Doris

GOELDNER, Charles R. 1932-

PERSONAL: Born March 21, 1932, in Fort Dodge, IA; son of Leslie (a publisher) and Beulah (a teacher; maiden name, Bohrer) Goeldner; married Jacquelyn R. Anderson (a teacher), December 31, 1954; children: Jo Lynn, Bradley Allen, Deborah Kay. *Ethnicity:* "USA." *Education:* University of Iowa, B.A. (with high distinction), 1954, M.A., 1958, Ph.D., 1961.

ADDRESSES: Home—3147 Westwood Court, Boulder, CO 80304. *Office*—Division of Marketing, College of Business and Administration, Campus Box 419, University of Colorado, Boulder, CO 80302. *E-mail*—goeldner@colorado.edu; fax 303-492-3620.

CAREER: University of Iowa, Iowa City, instructor in principles of marketing, 1958-59; San Fernando Valley State College (now California State University, Northridge), assistant professor, 1959-63, associate professor of marketing and director of Bureau of Business Services and Research, 1963-67; University of Colorado, Boulder, professor of marketing, 1968—, director of Business Research Division, 1967-90, head of Marketing Division, 1976-79, 1993-97, associate dean of undergraduate studies, 1984-87, associate dean of graduate programs and research, 1985-90. Member of summer faculty at University of California, Los Angeles, 1963 and 1965; lecturer at University of Southern California, 1963-66; member of academic council of Institute of Certified Travel Agents, 1975-90. Publisher of *Journal of Marketing Education,* 1978—, and *Journal of Macromarketing,* 1979—. U.S. Travel Data Center, trustee, 1973-94, secretary, 1977-94; member of board of directors of National Tour Association Foundation, 1981-85. *Military service:* U.S. Army, 1954-56; served in Germany.

MEMBER: International Association of Scientific Experts in Tourism, International Society of Travel and Tourism Educators (member of board of directors, 1980-85, 1997-98), International Academy for the Study of Tourism, Travel and Tourism Research Association (member of board of directors, 1972—; second vice-president, 1972; first vice-president, 1973; president, 1974; chair of board of directors, 1975), American Marketing Association (reprints editor, 1970-73; national placement chair, 1971-75), Association for University Business and Economic Research (vice-president, 1974; president, 1975; member of board of directors, 1982-84), American Academy of Advertising, Travel Industry Association of America, National Recreation and Parks Association,

Leisure Studies Association, Western Marketing Educators Association (member of board of directors, 1979-82), Western Regional Science Association, Colorado Marketing Association, Denver Business Economists Association, Phi Beta Kappa, Beta Gamma Sigma, Kappa Tau Alpha.

AWARDS, HONORS: Ford Foundation grant, 1964; Meritorious Service Award from Travel and Tourism Research Association, 1974; Society of Travel and Tourism Educators Achievement Award, 1990; Colorado Tourism Board Individual Achievement Award, 1990; Travel and Tourism Research Association Achievement Award, 1992; induction into the Travel Industry Association of America Hall of Leaders, 1992; and Marketing Educator of the Year Award by the Western Marketing Educators Association, 1994.

WRITINGS:

(With Robert W. McIntosh) *Tourism: Principles, Practices, and Philosophies,* fifth edition, Wiley (New York City), 1986, sixth edition, 1990, seventh edition, 1995.
(Editor with J. R. Brent Ritchie) *Travel, Tourism, and Hospitality Research: A Handbook for Managers and Researchers,* Wiley, 1987, second edition 1994.

Author of several dozen monographs on travel and tourism. Editor of *Journal of Travel Research,* 1967—, and *Colorado Business Review,* 1972-74; resources editor of *Annals of Tourism Research,* 1980—; member of editorial board of *Journal of Travel and Tourism Marketing,* 1991—; member of editorial policy board of *Leisure Sciences,* 1976-87; member of editorial board of *Journal of Sustainable Tourism,* 1996—; member of the editorial advisory board of *Progress in Tourism and Hospitality Research,* 1995—; member of the editorial board of *Tourism Economics,* 1995—; member of the editorial board of *Tourism Analysis,* 1996—.

CONTRIBUTOR

Charles J. Dirksen, Arthur Kroeger, and Lawrence C. Lockley, editors, *Readings in Marketing,* Irwin (Homewood, IL), 1962.
William J. Schultz and Edward M. Mazza, editors, *Marketing in Action,* Wadsworth (Belmont, CA), 1963.
Taylor W. Meloan and Charles M. Whitie, editors, *Competition in Marketing,* University of Southern California (Los Angeles), 1964.

Hiram C. Barksdale, editor, *Marketing in Progress,* Holt (New York City), 1964.
Encyclopedia of Hospitality and Tourism, Van Nostrand, Reinhold (New York City), 1993.
Tourism Marketing and Management Handbook, Prentice Hall (Englewood Cliffs, NJ), 1994.

Contributor to professional journals.

WORK IN PROGRESS: Research on tourism marketing and skiing.

*   *   *

GORDON, Lew
    See BALDWIN, Gordon C.

*   *   *

GORDON, Noah 1926-

PERSONAL: Born November 11, 1926, in Worcester, MA; son of Robert and Rose (Melnikoff) Gordon; married Claire Lorraine Seay, August 25, 1951; children: Lise Ann, Jamie Beth, Michael Seay. *Education:* Boston University, B.Sc. (journalism), 1950, M.A., 1951. *Politics:* Democrat. *Religion:* Jewish. *Avocational interests:* Fishing, tennis, gardening.

ADDRESSES: Home—23 Savoy Rd., Framingham, MA 01701. *Office*—39 Cochituate Rd., Framingham, MA 01701. *Agent*—Particia Schartle, McIntosh & Otis, Inc., 18 East 41st St., New York, NY 10017.

CAREER: Avon Book, Inc., New York City, assistant editor, 1951-53; Magazine Management, Inc., New York City, associate editor, later managing editor, 1953-56; *Worcester Telegram,* Worcester, MA, reporter, 1957-59; *Boston Herald,* Boston, MA, science editor, 1959-63; Opinion Publications, Inc., Framingham, MA, publisher of *Psychiatric Opinion,* 1964—, editor, 1964-66, 1968—, president and later director of company, 1966—. Writer, 1964—. Member of national advisory board, Center for Psychological Studies on Death, Dying and Lethal Behavior, 1970; member of board of directors, Framingham Writers Workshop; vice-chair of board of trustees, Framingham Public Libraries. *Military service:* U.S. Army, 1945-46.

MEMBER: National Association of Science Writers, Authors Guild, Authors League of America, American Association for the Advancement of Science, B'nai B'rith, Massachusetts Library Trustees Association, Sigma Delta Chi, Sudbury River Tennis Club.

AWARDS, HONORS: Distinguished Achievement Award, Boston University School of Public Communication, 1966.

WRITINGS:

The Rabbi (novel), McGraw (New York City), 1965.
The Death Committee (novel), McGraw, 1969.
The Jerusalem Diamond, Random House (New York City), 1979.
The Physician, Simon and Schuster (New York City), 1986.
Shaman, Dutton (New York City), 1992.
Matters of Choice, Dutton, 1996.

Contributor of fiction and articles to *Saturday Evening Post, Redbook, Reporter, Ladies' Home Journal, Saturday Review,* and other magazines. Member of editorial board, *Omega,* 1970.

SIDELIGHTS: Noah Gordon has managed to write books that are both popular—many have been bestsellers—and which critics have lauded for over thirty years. He works into his novels his own special areas of interest and knowledge, such as science, in *The Death Committee,* and Jewish history, in *The Jerusalem Diamond.* Gordon has worked as a reporter and editor for several publishers and publications, including the *Boston Herald.* He continues, though, to be foremost a novelist.

Gordon's writing career got off to a successful start with *The Rabbi,* a best-seller that chronicles the family life surrounding Michael Kind. A rabbi, Kind constantly balances himself between a Orthodox grandfather who is never satisfied, and a Protestant-convert wife who must endure the anti-gentilism of her husband's congregation. W. G. Rogers writes in *The New York Times Book Review,* "Enough of it is common to us all to convince us; enough is different to supply a flavorsome novelty and keep our interest at a high pitch." Critics were very pleased with the book, many concurring that it is a highly moving and realistic account of a Jewish family. Rogers compares it with Myron Kaufman's *Remember Me to God,* as it is another such account "rich with meaningful experiences."

Gordon's next novel, *The Death Committee,* was also a bestseller. It delves into the workings of Suffolk County General Hospital's mortality committee, an institution before which a doctor who has lost a patient must defend his treatment. At the center of the story are three young surgeons and the leader of the committee, a brilliant doctor who is slowly dying of kidney failure. Frank G. Slaughter writes of the book in *New York Times Book Review,* "This book is a moving re-creation of the personal problems of the major characters, their victories, their defeats—and, most important of all, the evolution of young doctors from cocksure graduate to adult physician."

The only one of Gordon's novels to date which was largely negatively reviewed was *The Jerusalem Diamond.* The general critical consensus was that Gordon had a good idea, but tried to accomplish far too much. The novel's protagonist is Harry Hopeman, a Manhattan Jew who is carrying on a 500-year family legacy in the diamond business. His life changes dramatically when he is asked to represent Israel in an international rivalry for the purchase of the "Jerusalem diamond," a hidden treasure from King Solomon's temple. Hopeman's quest for the gem leads him to his ancestors' homeland, where he experiences a personal, spiritual, and political catharsis.

"Gordon has enough notions here for two or three novels," writes a *Library Journal* critic, "but none of them is fully realized." Newgate Callendar in the *New York Times Book Review* notes that the book's premise is "exciting," but writes, "The author takes off on so many tangents that one wonders what kind of book he originally had in mind." Both critics find the tangents themselves fairly interesting, but put together, as *Library Journal* writes, "the pieces of the mosaic never grip together in a pattern, and the book never gathers much momentum." Both critics, as well, conclude that the book could *and* should "have been so much better."

Gordon bounced back to critical popularity, however, with his next book, *The Physician.* This book begins a trilogy which follows the Cole family of physicians. *The Physician* is set in the 11th century and follows an orphan boy named Rob Cole throughout the English countryside with the barber-surgeon to whom he is apprentice. In his travels, Rob meets all the right people and winds up a student (in Jewish disguise) at a renowned Persian teaching hospital, friend to rulers, and worldly adventurer and philosopher.

Critics note both the book's readability and serious treatment of some critical and timely issues. Jonathan

Fast writes in the *New York Times Book Review,* "One should not mistake this wonderfully conceived time machine of a novel for mere escapism. Mr. Gordon's depiction of the medical profession sheds a harsh light on doctors of today. And his treatment of a Christian living among Jews and Moslems in a foreign land . . . seems surprisingly relevant. . . ." The book is praised primarily for its powerful storyline, characterizations, and prose. Genevieve Stuttaford of *Library Journal* writes, "The reader is propelled through . . . several hundred pages by a tidal wave of vivid imagination and authentic detail." Fast summarizes, "Populated by engaging characters, rich in incident and vivid in historic detail, the . . . novel . . . is a pleasure."

The second book in the Cole trilogy is *Shaman,* set several centuries later. Robert Jefferson Cole, or "Shaman," is another smart young doctor. The novel begins in 1864 with his discovery of his deceased father's diary. The life of this man, his son's life, and the interweaving of the two, are at the center of the novel. Peter Blauner in the *New York Times Book Review* calls the book's passing of stories between generations a "clumsy framing device," and acknowledges that the book's plot is "the stuff of countless mini-series and blockbuster novels," but, like other critics, finds that Gordon still pulls off a powerful story. "The difference," he writes, "is that Mr. Gordon . . . writes with the skill and patience of a good doctor. Instead of swinging for the fences with big overwrought scenes, he builds atmosphere with the careful accretion of detail. . . . He also invests his characters with true complexity." Sybil S. Steinberg of *Publishers Weekly* agrees: "In serviceable, if curiously unemotional prose, Gordon tells a quietly absorbing story. . . ."

Gordon finishes the trilogy with *Matters of Choice,* which focuses on a modern-day female physician, R. J. Cole. Cole is a middle-aged doctor in Boston whose marriage is crumbling and who has just been turned down for a high-level hospital post because of her part-time work at an abortion clinic. In step with the other members of this fictional family, Cole moves her practice to the rural Berkshires, where she develops relationships with a Jewish real estate agent and his 17-year old daughter. Critics, again, are impressed with Gordon's ability to tell an emotionally stirring, complex, and convincing story. A *Booklist* reviewer calls it a "delightful and moving story." Sybil S. Steinberg writes in *Publishers Weekly,* "Gordon's greatest strength is his ability to seamlessly meld his characters' emotional dilemmas and medical crises to dramatic effect." A *Kirkus Reviews* reviewer calls the book, "Perhaps Gordon's best work so far; the pace is even, and R. J. is a heroine worth caring about."

BIOGRAPHICAL/CRITICAL SOURCES:

PERIODICALS

Booklist, April 1, 1996, p. 1342.
Book World, June 28, 1970.
Kirkus Reviews, January 15, 1979, p. 77; February 1, 1996, p. 158.
New York Times Book Review, August 1, 1965, section 7; June 15, 1969, section 7; May 13, 1979, section 7, p. 28; August 17, 1986, section 7, p. 22; January 3, 1993.
Publishers Weekly, June 20, 1966, p. 80; April 20, 1970, p. 63; July 4, 1986, p. 55; July 13, 1992; February 19, 1996, p. 203.*

*   *   *

GULIK, Robert H(ans) van
See van GULIK, Robert Hans

H-K

HAGGARD, William
See CLAYTON, Richard Henry Michael

* * *

HALL, Frederic Sauser
See SAUSER-HALL, Frederic

* * *

HAMMOND, Gerald (Arthur Douglas) 1926-
(Dalby Holden, Arthur Douglas)

PERSONAL: Born March 7, 1926, in Bournemouth, Hampshire, England; son of Frederick Arthur Lucas (a physician) and Maria Birnie (a nursing sister; maiden name, Thomson) Hammond; married Gilda Isobel Watt (a nurse), August 20, 1952; children: Peter, David, Steven. *Education:* Aberdeen School of Architecture, Diploma in Architecture, 1952. *Politics:* Conservative. *Religion:* Atheist.

ADDRESSES: Home—Corrienearn Cottage, Aboyne, Aberdeenshire AB3 5HY, Scotland. *Office*—Livingston Development Corp., Livingston, Scotland. *Agent*—Michael Thomas, A. M. Heath & Co. Ltd., 79 St. Martin's Lane, London WC2N 4AA, England.

CAREER: Navy, Army, and Air Force Institutes, Claygate, Surrey, England, assistant architect, 1952-53; Aberdeen County Council, Aberdeen, Scotland, assistant architect, 1953-60; University of Dundee, Dundee, Argus, Scotland, assistant to resident architect, 1960-69; Livingston Development Corp., Livingston, Scotland, deputy chief architect and planning officer for Livingston New Town, 1969-83; full-time writer, 1983—. *Military service:* British Army, 1944-45.

MEMBER: Royal Institute of British Architects, Chartered Institute of Arbitrators (fellow; past chair of Scottish branch), Crime Writers Association, Muzzle Loaders Association, Shooting Club (founder; president).

WRITINGS:

CRIME NOVELS

Fred in Situ, Hodder & Stoughton (London), 1965.
The Loose Screw, Hodder & Stoughton, 1966.
Mud in His Eye, Hodder & Stoughton, 1967.
(Under pseudonym Dalby Holden) *Doldrum,* Hale (London), 1987.
Cash and Carry, Macmillan (London), 1992.

"KEITH CALDER" SERIES

Dead Game, Macmillan, 1979.
The Reward Game, St. Martin's (New York City), 1980.
The Revenge Game, Macmillan, 1981.
Fair Game, St. Martin's, 1982.
The Game, Macmillan, 1982.
Cousin Once Removed, St. Martin's, 1984.
Sauce for the Pigeon, St. Martin's, 1984.
Pursuit of Arms, St. Martin's, 1985.
Silver City Scandal, St. Martin's, 1986.
The Executor, St. Martin's, 1986.

The Worried Widow, Macmillan, 1987, St. Martin's, 1988.
Adverse Report, Macmillan, 1987.
Stray Shot, Macmillan, 1988.
A Brace of Skeet, Macmillan, 1989.
Let Us Prey, Macmillan, 1990.
Home to Roost, Macmillan, 1990.
In Camera, Macmillan, 1991.
Snatch Crop, Macmillan, 1991.
Thin Air, Macmillan, 1993.
Hook or Crook, Macmillan, 1994.
Carriage of Justice, Macmillan, 1995.
Sink or Swim, Macmillan, 1996.

"CAPTAIN JOHN CUNNINGHAM" SERIES

Dog in the Dark, Macmillan, 1989.
Doghouse, Macmillan, 1989.
Whose Dog Are You?, Macmillan, 1990.
Give a Dog a Name, Macmillan, 1992.
The Curse of the Cockers, Macmillan, 1993.
Sting in the Tail, Macmillan, 1994.
Mad Dogs and Scotsmen, Macmillan, 1995.

NOVELS; UNDER PSEUDONYM ARTHUR DOUGLAS

The Goods, Macmillan, 1985.
Last Rights, Macmillan, 1986, St. Martin's, 1987.
A Very Wrong Number, Macmillan, 1987.
A Worm Turns, Macmillan, 1988, St. Martin's, 1989.

OTHER

Author of "The Abominable Dog," a monthly column in *Sporting Gun.* Contributor to magazines.

SIDELIGHTS: Gerald Hammond has used his profound knowledge of firearms and hunting dogs to create two unique mystery series, one featuring a Scottish gunsmith, Keith Calder, and the other focusing on John Cunningham, a retired soldier turned dog breeder.

Hammond originally set out to write humor, but found that publishers had little interest in humorous novels. Still, his first three books—*Fred in Situ, The Loose Screw,* and *Mud in His Eye*—had a somewhat humorous bent. Their protagonist is Beau Pepys, an architect and amateur race driver who becomes involved in mysteries. *St. James Guide to Crime and Mystery Writers* contributor Judith Rhodes described them as "light-hearted" and "fairly implausible" but "nevertheless pleasant." Hammond related to *St.*

James Guide to Crime and Mystery Writers that after writing those books, he began trying to come up with a new set of characters and a background he would not have to research much: "I was (and am) deeply involved with gundogs and shooting, generally, and was irritated by the stereotypes of the shooting fraternity which seemed to be universal. I set out to depict the shooting scene (particularly in Scotland) as I knew it, most of [it] centered around the character of Keith Calder, a gunsmith of unreliable habits and an enquiring mind" and "a randy but loveable rogue."

Numerous critics have found the Calder series to be unique in the mystery genre because of its heavily detailed lore about dogs and hunting. Rhodes explained: "Keith Calder burst upon the scene in *Dead Game,* bombarding the reader, and any character in the book who will pay him any attention, with intricate details of firearms and firearm history. Calder, in his capacity as gunsmith, shooting instructor, and poacher, is in his younger days none too choosey about which side of the law he operates on. As the series progresses . . . he marries, sets up a gunshop, and as the years pass becomes a relatively respectable figure, upon whom his former adversary Chief Inspector Munro comes unwillingly to rely." Reviewing one title in the series, *Pursuit of Arms,* a *Booklist* contributor approved of its "interesting gun lore, subtle characterization, smashing action, and . . . taut suspense." As the series unfolded, Calder frequently relinquished his role as narrator to other characters. Three of the later novels are written in the voice of Simon Parbitter, a London-born writer who moves in next to Calder; others are narrated by Calder's daughter Deborah, his partner Wallace James, or by Ian Fellowes, a detective who eventually marries Deborah.

Hammond's special knowledge of the hunting world figures prominently in another mystery series, this one featuring John Cunningham, a soldier who was invalided out of the army after contracting a debilitating tropical disease. He takes up a career as a professional breeder and trainer of Springer spaniels, working with kennelmaid Beth Cattrell and hard-drinking veterinarian Isobel Kitts. This trio finds themselves repeatedly drawn into mysteries, and as Rhodes pointed out, "The joint expertise of the three partners (Cunningham's in guns, Isobel's in dog-breeding and Beth's in sheer commonsense) helps in solving murders and associated canine and ballistic puzzles." Rhodes noted that the Cunningham books are more formulaic than the Calder efforts, but concedes that each one "provides an interesting and entertaining read."

Hammond commented to *CA:* "I try very hard to be technically accurate, and this may be why my novels bring me correspondence from all over the world. Americans, in particular, send me supporting material which I wish I had while writing that particular book. A fictional incident in one of my novels recently suggested to a detective in San Francisco the solution to a real crime, and convictions followed.

"I never set out to become a propagandist for the shooting man but this, again, happened without my conscious volition. In Britain, perhaps more than the States, an attitude is growing that shooting must *ipso facto* be cruel and that wildlife would achieve a delightful balance, patterned on Walt Disney, if left severely alone. My series of novels has proved ideal (and, I hope, useful) in putting across, one piece at a time, the facts that the balance of nature (in Britain) is entirely man-made or man-influenced, that it owes a major debt to shooting interests and that the withdrawal of hunting pressures would spell disaster to wildlife as we know it here."

BIOGRAPHICAL/CRITICAL SOURCES:

BOOKS

St. James Guide to Crime and Mystery Writers, St. James Press (Detroit), 1996.

PERIODICALS

Armchair Detective, winter, 1987, p. 17.
Booklist, December 15, 1985, p. 608; August, 1989, p. 1948; April 15, 1991, p. 1626; October 15, 1991, p. 413; February 15, 1992, p. 1091.
British Book News, September, 1985.
Kirkus Reviews, March 15, 1985, p. 252; August 15, 1989, p. 1201; March 15, 1991, p. 362; March 15, 1992, p. 355.
Listener, July 5, 1979; August 20, 1981.
Observer, April 22, 1979; June 15, 1980; July 13, 1980; May 10, 1981.
Times Literary Supplement, April 17, 1981.

*   *   *

HANNON, Ezra
See HUNTER, Evan

HAYMON, S. T.
See HAYMON, Sylvia (Theresa)

*   *   *

HAYMON, Sylvia (Theresa) 1918(?)-1995
(S. T. Haymon)

PERSONAL: Born c. 1918 in Norwich, Norfolk, England; died December, 1995; married Mark Haymon; children: two daughters.

CAREER: Writer. Also worked in farming, public relations, broadcasting, and journalism.

AWARDS, HONORS: Silver Dagger Award from Crime Writers Association, 1982, for *Ritual Murder.*

WRITINGS:

Television and Radio As a Career (nonfiction), Batsford (London), 1963.
The Loyal Traitor: A Story of Kett's Rebellion (novel), Chatto & Windus (London), 1965.
Bonnie Prince Charlie (nonfiction), illustrated by Peter Bailey, Macdonald (London), 1969.
King Monmouth (nonfiction), Macdonald, 1970.
Norwich (nonfiction), illustrated by Joanna Worth, Longman Young Books (London), 1973.
Opposite the Cross Keys: An East Anglian Childhood (autobiography), St. Martin's (New York City), 1988.
The Quivering Tree (autobiography), St. Martin's, 1990.

CRIME NOVELS; UNDER NAME S. T. HAYMON

Death and the Pregnant Virgin, St. Martin's, 1980.
Ritual Murder, St. Martin's, 1982.
Stately Homicide, St. Martin's, 1984.
Death of a God, St. Martin's, 1987.
A Very Particular Murder, St. Martin's, 1989.
Death of a Warrior Queen, Constable (London), 1991, St. Martin's, 1992.
A Beautiful Death, Constable, 1993, St. Martin's, 1994.
Death of a Hero, St. Martin's, 1996.

SIDELIGHTS: Although Sylvia Haymon also wrote nonfiction, she achieved success mainly as a writer of mystery novels under the name S. T. Haymon. As an explorer of the themes of British tradition, nationalism, and religion, Haymon is often compared to other British writers in the mystery genre, including P. D. James and Dorothy Sayers. In her two volumes of autobiography, *Opposite the Cross Keys: An East Anglian Childhood* and *The Quivering Tree,* Haymon described growing up in Norfolk, England. She remembered how her brother and father taught her to read and instilled in her a love of the English language when she was very young. She described herself as "an eclectic reader, generous in her assessments of books, looking primarily for tales which held her interest," according to Carol M. Harper in *St. James Guide to Crime and Mystery Writers.*

In addition to her memoirs, Haymon published a historical novel, a history of Norwich, and biographies of Prince Charles and Geoffrey of Monmouth, a twelfth-century figure who popularized the legend of King Arthur. Yet she was undoubtedly best known for her mysteries featuring Detective Inspector Ben Jurnet. Like the author, Jurnet is a native of Norfolk, and Haymon's love of her homeland is evident in these mysteries. Sensitive, witty, and thoughtful, Jurnet often faces conflict between his professional and emotional lives. In *Ritual Murder,* he investigates the gruesome murder of a choirboy. He discovers that the crime is similar to a twelfth-century killing that had provoked intense anti-Semitic feelings in Norfolk because it was viewed as a Jewish ritual. Those same racial tensions boil over after the modern-day crime, and Jurnet—who is in love with a Jewish woman and contemplating his own conversion to Judaism—finds his work complicated by religious intolerance and the prospect of violence directed against the town's Jewish population. "History serves as an eerie backdrop to present-day terror in this ably plotted tale," asserted a *Booklist* contributor.

Many of these same themes, including the violence provoked by religious tension and Jurnet's ambivalence about his own religious identity, continue throughout the series. In *Death and the Pregnant Virgin,* an attendant at a religious shrine is murdered. In *Death of a God,* a rock star, the leader of a group named Second Coming, is found crucified in the Norfolk village square. A *Booklist* reviewer rated that mystery as "a canny mix of history, police procedure, psychology, and horror." In *A Very Particular Murder,* Haymon shifted the emphasis to the world of academia, spinning a plot that concerned an eminent physicist who is poisoned at an honorary banquet.

Reviewers of Haymon's mystery novels have praised her skill in constructing carefully unfolding, me-thodically paced stories, which are set in motion only after the characters are well established. *Washington Post Book World* critic Jean M. White, for example, lauded *Ritual Murder* as "richly textured in character and atmosphere, elegantly written, and beautifully paced until its chilling finale." Likewise, *New York Times Book Review* critic Newgate Callendar, in a review of *Death of a God,* commended the author's "delicate probings into human behavior" and called the book "an unusually rich, sensitive piece of work." Other reviewers praised Haymon's ability to transcend the boundaries of the mystery genre and craft believable, complex novels. As White noted, Haymon is a writer who can "turn murder into stylish, serious fiction."

Reviewing *Stately Homicide,* a *Books & Bookmen* reviewer applauded Ben Jurnet as "an excellent pivotal character, bright without being brilliant; human in understanding but completely professional in the performance of his duty. In two words, he is credible and sympathetic." Harper concurred that the character study of Jurnet is one of the most engaging aspects of Haymon's mystery series. She noted: "As the series progresses, it is enlightening to compare the Jurnet of *Ritual Murder* with the Jurnet of the later books. . . . [Haymon created] a policeman with very human problems."

BIOGRAPHICAL/CRITICAL SOURCES:

BOOKS

Haymon, Sylvia, *Opposite the Cross Keys: An East Anglian Childhood,* St. Martin's, 1988.
Haymon, Sylvia, *The Quivering Tree,* St. Martin's, 1990.
St. James Guide to Crime and Mystery Writers, fourth edition, James Press (Detroit), 1996.

PERIODICALS

Belles Lettres, winter, 1989, p. 17.
Booklist, September 15, 1982, p. 92; March 15, 1987, p. 1096; August, 1989, p. 1948; December 15, 1990, p. 797.
Books & Bookmen, October, 1984, p. 33.
British Book News, March, 1985, p. 137.
New York Times Book Review, February 13, 1983; April 26, 1987; August 27, 1989.
Spectator, September 26, 1987.
Times Literary Supplement, June 15, 1973.
Washington Post Book World, December 19, 1982.*

HEINZ, W(ilfred) C(harles) 1915-
   (Richard Hooker, a joint pseudonym)

PERSONAL: Born January 11, 1915, in Mount Vernon, NY; son of Frederick Louis Sylvester (a salesman) and Elizabeth (Thielke) Heinz; married Elizabeth Bailey, January 18, 1941; children: Gayl Bailey. *Education:* Middlebury College, A.B., 1937.

ADDRESSES: Home—Dorset, VT. *Agent*—William Morris Agency, Inc., 1350 Avenue of the Americas, New York, NY 10019.

CAREER: New York Sun, New York City, successively copy boy, reporter, feature writer, war correspondent, sports columnist, 1937-50; freelance writer, 1950—.

MEMBER: Authors Guild.

AWARDS, HONORS: E. P. Dutton Award for best magazine sports story, 1948, 1950, 1952, 1954, 1959.

WRITINGS:

The Professional, Harper (New York City), 1958.
(Editor) *The Fireside Book of Boxing,* Simon & Schuster (New York City), 1961.
The Surgeon (Literary Guild selection), Doubleday (Garden City, NY), 1963.
(With Vince Lombardi) *Run to Daylight!,* Prentice-Hall (Englewood Cliffs, NJ), 1963.
(With H. Richard Hornberger under pseudonym Richard Hooker) *M.A.S.H.,* Morrow (New York City), 1968.
Emergency (Book-of-the-Month Club selection), Doubleday, 1974.
Once They Heard the Cheers (Book-of-the-Month Club alternate selection; *Sports Illustrated* Book Club selection), Doubleday, 1979.
American Mirror, Doubleday, 1982.

Work has been published in more than fifty anthologies. Contributor of articles and short stories in *Saturday Evening Post, Collier's, Cosmopolitan, Esquire, Life, Look, Reader's Digest, True, Argosy, Sport,* and *Coronet.*

ADAPTATIONS: Run to Daylight! was filmed as a television special for the American Broadcasting Company (ABC) in 1964.

SIDELIGHTS: W. C. Heinz's journalistic career included work as a war correspondent, a medical reporter, a novelist, and—especially—a sportswriter with emphasis on boxing. Heinz served as a reporter for the *New York Sun* from 1939 until 1950, and when that newspaper closed he chose to be a freelancer, selling his nonfiction pieces to top magazines and his fiction to major publishers. Calling Heinz "one of the best pure writers of his time," *Dictionary of Literary Biography* contributor Edward J. Tassinari declared that the author "was an introspective writer who plumbed the depths of his own experience to better understand himself and capture the essence of his subjects."

Born and raised in Mount Vernon, New York, Heinz went to work as a messenger boy at the *New York Sun* soon after graduating from Middlebury College. He worked his way up through the ranks and soon found himself on the city desk, covering a variety of local stories. In 1943 the *Sun* sent him abroad as a war correspondent. Heinz sent dispatches from the Normandy invasion and followed the Allies through Europe as they struggled to defeat the Germans. The experience was at once self-revealing and tremendously beneficial for him. Later, as quoted in the *Dictionary of Literary Biography,* he described the war as "a patsy for learning writers . . . the perfect foil, the perfect sparring partner. It was so dramatic, you couldn't write it badly."

When he returned from the front at the end of World War II, Heinz asked the editors at the *Sun* to put him in the sports department. There he prepared feature stories and athlete profiles, concentrating on boxing and its colorful characters. In one of his best-known stories from that era, he spent an evening with Norma Graziano as her husband, Rocky, was appearing in a prize fight. Heinz charted Mrs. Graziano's nervousness and the strains that her husband's profession put on their married life. "This innovative article . . . was one of many in which Heinz emphasized the human qualities of the athlete and the concerns of the athlete's wife," to quote Tassinari.

Tassinari observed: "Heinz was a perfectionist constantly striving to enhance his craft and was influenced, as were so many World War II correspondents, by Ernest Hemingway. Heinz viewed sport as a means of self-expression. At its height, he saw it as an art form in which courage, craftsmanship, wisdom, and professionalism—an amalgam of study, effort, imitation, and adaptation—could be found. Heinz thought it was the writer's task to present the scene, locate the character, and convey an understanding through the eyes of the subject."

The *Sun* closed its doors in 1950 and, although he had other newspaper offers, Heinz decided to become a freelance writer. He wrote sports stories for magazines, but he also began to concentrate on full-length books. His first, *The Professional,* is a novel that follows a fictitious middleweight named Eddie Brown as he prepares for the most important fight of his career. The action is seen through the eyes of Frank Hughes, a sportswriter who is profiling Brown for a magazine. *The Professional* was cited for its authenticity and for its unsentimental ending, in which the hero endures a first-round knockout. As C. A. Fenton put it in the *Saturday Review, The Professional* "is a novel that one can look forward to reading several times with profit and pleasure." In the *New York Herald Tribune Book Review,* Herbert Kupferberg wrote: "Although 'The Professional' is anything but an impersonal story, it derives much of its impact and interest from the authenticity of its background." *The Professional* sold 14,000 copies in its initial hardcover edition and is still in print.

In 1961 Heinz wrote a *Life* magazine story about lung surgery, which he used as inspiration for his second novel, *The Surgeon.* Once again an authentic, if fictional, tale—this time about an operating room staff—*The Surgeon* covers one working day in the life of Dr. Matthew Carter, a superb technical surgeon whose troubles begin when he has to deal with his patients' emotions. A *Newsweek* contributor noted of the book: "Heinz spins his narrative with understated assurance, and with mercifully little bravado or sentimentality."

Heinz returned to sportswriting for his next, and arguably best-known book, *Run to Daylight!* The book, which was co-authored by Green Bay Packers coach Vince Lombardi, presents the life of a pro football coach from Lombardi's viewpoint, concentrating on the preparation for an early-season showdown between the Packers and the Detroit Lions. Tassinari wrote of the work: "Heinz, while deftly explaining the technical jargon, was most effective in revealing the roots of Lombardi's coaching philosophy and the coach's often piercing observations of the personalities, strengths, and weaknesses of his players and how, as a coach, teacher, and psychologist, he strove to exact the utmost from each player every Sunday." *Run to Daylight!* has gone through fifteen printings and was also filmed as a television special in 1964. *New York Times Book Review* contributor Rex Lardner wrote: "Tightly written and sharply focused. . . . The book gives splendid insights into the complexity of the pro game."

Heinz's association with the novel *M.A.S.H.* has been obscured, but he did indeed help surgeon H. Richard Hornberger with the well-known tale of field doctors working near the front lines in Korea. The book was published under the pseudonym Richard Hooker and has always been credited to Hornberger, but according to Tassinari, "Heinz's touch is evident in the pacing and characterization and in the depiction of the surgeons as effective teachers, having not only displayed their talents at 'meatball' surgery but in passing on their techniques to their replacements before they depart for the United States and a return to civilian life."

Once They Heard the Cheers and *American Mirror,* Heinz's two most recent books, reveal an author who is able to reminisce without becoming maudlin or judgmental about modern sports. In *Once They Heard the Cheers,* Heinz re-connects with some of his sports heroes of former eras, especially the boxers he followed as a *Sun* reporter. In his review, *New York Times Book Review* critic Robert Lipsyte wrote that "Mr. Heinz, now in his 60's, observing 'society go soft all around me,' revisits or recalls 19 sports figures he had met earlier in an attempt to redefine the nobility that he no longer finds in or out of the modern arena. . . . Mr. Heinz's then-and-now portraits are vivid, informative, subtle and often moving." *American Mirror* collects thirteen of Heinz's best magazine and newspaper pieces, including a number that were anthologized in the *Best Sports Stories* series. Nine of the thirteen stories concern sports, and seven of those nine are about boxing. According to Tassinari, "*American Mirror* was well received critically and benefitted from a typically perceptive Red Smith foreword, describing Heinz as 'a dedicated craftsman and a penetrating observer who never gives half measure.'"

Heinz once wrote *CA:* "What I attempt to do in my writing is to set the scene and put the characters in it and let them talk. When I can do this with sufficient accuracy and sensitivity the reader experiences the impression, very real, that I have not been telling him something and that he is getting it second-hand, but that he himself saw it and heard it for he was there. That, it seems to me, should be the aim of all writing that goes beyond the solely instructional or informational."

BIOGRAPHICAL/CRITICAL SOURCES:

BOOKS

Cosell, Howard, *Cosell on Cosell,* Playboy Press (Chicago, IL), 1973, pp. 99-101, 152.

Dictionary of Literary Biography, Volume 171: *Twentieth-Century American Sportswriters,* Gale (Detroit), 1996, pp. 132-44.

Halberstam, David, editor, *The Best American Sportswriting 1991,* Houghton (Boston, MA), 1991.

PERIODICALS

Best Sellers, April 1, 1963, p. 10.

Newsweek, March 11, 1963, p. 100; February 28, 1983, p. 101.

New Yorker, September 28, 1946, pp. 50-61.

New York Herald Tribune Book Review, January 5, 1958, p. 3.

New York Times Book Review, October 27, 1963, p. 52; July 29, 1979, p. 8.

San Francisco Chronicle, January 9, 1958, p. 21.

Time, January 13, 1958, p. 95; March 8, 1963, p. 105.

* * *

HENSLEY, Joe L.
　See **HENSLEY, Joseph Louis**

* * *

HENSLEY, Joseph Louis 1926-
　(Joe L. Hensley)

PERSONAL: Born March 19, 1926, in Bloomington, IN; son of Ralph Ramon and Frances Mae (Wilson) Hensley; married Charlotte Ruth Bettinger, June 18, 1950; children: Michael Joseph. *Education:* Indiana University, A.B., 1950, LL.B., 1955. *Politics:* Democrat. *Religion:* Presbyterian.

ADDRESSES: Home—2315 Blackmore, Madison, IN 47250. *Office*—Fifth Judicial Circuit Courthouse, Madison, IN 47250. *Agent*—Virginia Kidd, Box 278, Milford, PA 18337.

CAREER: Admitted to State Bar of Indiana, 1955; Metford & Hensley, Attorneys at Law, Madison, IN, associate, 1955-71; Ford, Hensley & Todd, Attorneys at Law, Madison, partner, 1971-73; Hensley, Todd & Castor, Madison, partner, 1973-75; Eightieth Judicial Circuit, Indiana, judge pro-tempore, 1975-76; Fifth Judicial Circuit, Indiana, judge, 1977-

88; Hensley, Walro, Collins & Hensley, Madison, partner, 1988—. Member of Indiana General Assembly, 1961-62; prosecuting attorney of Fifth Judicial Indiana Circuit, 1963-66. *Military service:* U.S. Navy, hospital corpsman, 1944-46, journalist in Korea, 1951-52.

MEMBER: Mystery Writers of America, Science Fiction Writers of America, Indiana State Bar Association, Indiana Judges Association (president, 1983-84), Jefferson County Bar Association.

WRITINGS:

The Color of Hate, Ace (New York City), 1961, published as *Color Him Guilty,* Walker (New York City), 1987.

The Poison Summer, Doubleday (New York City), 1974.

The Black Roads, Laser (Toronto), 1976.

Rivertown Risk, Doubleday, 1977.

Final Doors (short stories), Doubleday, 1981.

Fort's Law, Doubleday, 1988.

Grim City, St. Martin's (New York City), 1994.

"DONALD ROBAK" SERIES

Deliver Us to Evil, Doubleday, 1971.

Legislative Body, Doubleday, 1972.

Song of Corpus Juris, Doubleday, 1974.

A Killing in Gold, Doubleday, 1978.

Minor Murders, Doubleday, 1980.

Outcasts, Doubleday, 1981.

Robak's Cross, Doubleday, 1985.

Robak's Fire, Doubleday, 1986.

Robak's Firm (short stories), Doubleday, 1987.

Robak's Run, Doubleday, 1991.

Robak's Witch, St. Martin's, 1997.

OTHER

Contributor of more than fifty stories to magazines.

SIDELIGHTS: Joe L. Hensley, a judge and former attorney in Indiana, is creator of a series of whodunits featuring Don Robak. With a background similar to the author's, lawyer Robak defends the innocent and tries to identify the guilty in Indiana. Hensley "always uses his knowledge [of the state and its judicial system] . . . to enhance his well-woven novels of chicanery and murder," stated Alice Cromie in the *Chicago Tribune Book World.* Numerous reviewers have commented favorably on his evocation of small-town, Midwestern life, including its dark side. Even in his non-Robak books, such as *The Color of Hate, The Poison Summer,* and *Fort's Law,* Hensley usually features a small-town lawyer who closely resembles Robak.

In one of the earliest titles in the Robak series, *Legislative Body,* the lawyer investigates the mysterious death of a state senator who has fallen out of a window—apparently with some help. A *Library Journal* reviewer rated it "good entertainment," while Newgate Callendar, writing in the *New York Times Book Review,* called it "a well-written, snappily-plotted book." Francis M. Nevins commented on the author's style in *St. James Guide to Crime and Mystery Writers:* "Hensley's tone is quiet and low-key, his pace unhurried and unfrenetic, his plots rather loose and not terribly involuted. He has a nice talent for character-drawing and for describing how mid-America functions and much empathy with blacks, Jews, rebellious young people, and others outside the corn-fed mainstream. Most of his books are solidly satisfying." Nevins rated *Robak's Cross* as one of Hensley's best efforts as well as the book which has "more courtroom action than all the other Robaks put together."

Hensley's largest and most ambitious novel is *Grim City,* in Nevins's opinion. Its central character, Jim Carlos Singer, is quite a bit different from Robak. He is a former intelligence agent who quit his post with a CIA-like agency after being tortured and sexually mutilated by terrorists while on a spy mission in Mexico. He becomes a lawyer, and while working to establish his practice, he must cope with the hit-and-run death of his father and harassment that may come from his old associates in the spy business. "*Grim City* suffers from minimal action outside of court, a crucial coincidence wild enough to pop the eyeballs, and rather cavalier resolution of some plot problems," admitted Nevins. "But even at less than his best Hensley offers complex characterizations, knowing depictions of political and sexual intrigue in the fishbowl of a small midwest community, and more than enough legal shenanigans to satisfy devotees of the courtroom whodunit."

Hensley told *CA:* "I'm a former judge who retired from the bench unbeaten and unbowed. Time is still difficult, but these days I try to find more of it for writing. My books and stories are part of my legal life. Although they usually take the suspense form, my books are about people who must live in this complicated and devious world all of us try our best to exist within. I find that I can't easily stop writing.

So I get up earlier, work harder, and hope to get more done. It isn't fun anymore, but it's something I do. I'm glad I do it and I doubt that anything could make me stop."

A collection of Hensley's manuscript is housed at the Lilly Library, Indiana University, Bloomington.

BIOGRAPHICAL/CRITICAL SOURCES:

BOOKS

St. James Guide to Crime and Mystery Writers, fourth edition, St. James Press (Detroit), 1996.

PERIODICALS

Armchair Detective, winter, 1987, p. 76; summer, 1988, p. 318; winter, 1988, p. 37; spring, 1991, p. 168.
Best Sellers, August 15, 1982.
Booklist, April 15, 1977, p. 1243.
Chicago Tribune Book World, June 21, 1981.
Library Journal, October 1, 1972; March 1, 1974, p. 682; April 1, 1977, p. 837; March 1, 1978, p. 589.
New York Times Book Review, October 8, 1972, p. 46; March 1, 1981; November 30, 1986.
Saturday Review, September 9, 1982.
Washington Post Book World, February 15, 1981; January 17, 1988.*

*   *   *

**HIGHSMITH, (Mary) Patricia 1921-1995
(Claire Morgan)**

PERSONAL: Born January 19, 1921, in Fort Worth, TX; daughter of Jay Bernard Plangman and Mary (Coates) Highsmith; died February 4, 1995, in Locarno, Switzerland. *Education:* Barnard College, B.A., 1942. *Avocational interests:* Drawing, painting, carpentering, snail watching, traveling by train.

CAREER: Writer, 1942-95.

MEMBER: Detection Club.

AWARDS, HONORS: Mystery Writers of America Scroll and Grand Prix de Litterature Policiere, both 1957, both for *The Talented Mr. Ripley;* Silver Dagger Award for best crime novel of the year, Crime

Writers Association of England, 1964, for *The Two Faces of January;* Officer l'Ordre des Arts es des Lettres, 1990.

WRITINGS:

NOVELS

Strangers on a Train (also see below), Harper (New York City), 1950.

(Under pseudonym Claire Morgan) *The Price of Salt,* Coward-McCann (New York City), 1952, reprinted as *Carol* under the name Patricia Highsmith with a new afterword by the author, Naiad Press (Tallahassee, FL), 1984.

The Blunderer (also see below), Coward-McCann, 1954, published as *Lament for a Lover,* Popular Library, 1956, reprinted under original title, Hamlyn (London), 1978.

The Talented Mr. Ripley (also see below), Coward-McCann, 1955.

Deep Water, Harper, 1957, published in England as *Deep Water: A Novel of Suspense,* Heinemann (London), 1957.

A Game for the Living, Harper, 1958.

This Sweet Sickness (also see below), Harper, 1960.

The Cry of the Owl, Harper, 1962.

The Two Faces of January, Doubleday (New York City), 1964.

The Glass Cell, Doubleday, 1964.

The Story-Teller, Doubleday, 1965, published in England as *A Suspension of Mercy,* Heinemann, 1965.

Those Who Walk Away, Doubleday, 1967.

The Tremor of Forgery, Doubleday, 1969.

Ripley under Ground (also see below), Doubleday, 1970.

A Dog's Ransom, Knopf (New York City), 1972.

Ripley's Game (also see below), Knopf, 1974.

Edith's Diary, Simon & Schuster (New York City), 1977.

The Boy Who Followed Ripley, Crowell, 1980.

People Who Knock on the Door, Heinemann, 1983, Mysterious Press, 1985.

The Mysterious Mr. Ripley (contains *The Talented Mr. Ripley, Ripley under Ground,* and *Ripley's Game*), Penguin, 1985.

Found in the Street, Heinemann, 1986, Atlantic Monthly Press (New York City), 1987.

Mermaids on a Golf Course, Mysterious Press, 1988.

Ripley under Water, Knopf, 1991.

The Boy Who Followed Ripley, Vintage (New York City), 1993.

Small g: A Summer Idyll, Bloomsbury, 1995.

SHORT STORIES

(With Doris Sanders) *Miranda the Panda Is on the Veranda* (juvenile), Coward-McCann, 1958.

The Snail-Watcher, and Other Stories, Doubleday, 1970 (published in England as *Eleven: Short Stories,* Heinemann, 1970).

Little Tales of Misogyny (in German), Diogenes Verlag (Zurich), 1974, English language edition, Heinemann, 1977, Mysterious Press, 1987.

The Animal-Lover's Book of Beastly Murder (young adult), Heinemann, 1975.

Slowly, Slowly in the Wind, Heinemann, 1979, Mysterious Press, 1987.

The Black House, David & Charles, 1979, published in England as *The Black House, and Other Stories,* Heinemann, 1981.

Mermaids on the Golf Course, and Other Stories, Heinemann, 1985, Mysterious Press, 1988.

OTHER

Plotting and Writing Suspense Fiction, Writers Inc., 1966, enlarged and revised edition, St. Martin's (New York City), 1981.

Tales of Natural and Unnatural Catastrophes, Heinemann, 1987, Atlantic Monthly Press, 1989.

Also author of material for television, including the "Alfred Hitchcock Presents" series.

ADAPTATIONS: Strangers on a Train was made into a film directed by Alfred Hitchcock, produced by Warner Brothers in 1951, and it also served as the basis for another Warner Brothers movie in 1969, entitled *Once You Kiss a Stranger; The Talented Mr. Ripley* was filmed as *Purple Noon* by Times Film Corp. in 1961; *The Blunderer* was first filmed as *Le Meurtrier* in 1963 and then as *Enough Rope* by Artixo Productions in 1966; *This Sweet Sickness* inspired the French film *Tell Her That I Love Her* in 1977; and *Ripley's Game* was filmed as *The American Friend* in 1978. Many other novels by Highsmith have been optioned for film.

SIDELIGHTS: The author of numerous short story collections and novels, including the well-known *Strangers on a Train,* American-born Patricia Highsmith enjoyed greater critical and commercial success in England, France, and Germany than in her native country. As Jeff Weinstein speculates in the *Village Voice Literary Supplement,* the reason for this is that Highsmith's books have been "misplaced"—relegated to the mystery and suspense shelves instead of being allowed to take their rightful place in the literature section. As far as her ardent admirers in the United States and abroad are concerned, Highsmith was more than just a superb crime novelist. In fact, declares Brigid Brophy in *Don't Never Forget: Collected Views and Reviews,* "there's the injustice. . . . As a novelist *tout court* [Highsmith is] excellent. . . . Highsmith and Simenon are alone in writing books which transcend the limits of the genre while staying strictly inside its rules: they alone have taken the crucial step from playing games to creating art."

The art in Highsmith's work springs from her skillful fusion of plot, characterization, and style, with the crime story serving primarily "as a means of revealing and examining her own deepest interests and obsessions," according to a *Times Literary Supplement* reviewer. Among her most common themes are the nature of guilt and the often symbiotic relationship that develops between two people (almost always men) who are at the same time fascinated and repelled by each other. Highsmith's works therefore "dig down very deeply into the roots of personality," says Julian Symons in the *London Magazine,* exposing the darkside of people regarded by society as normal and good. Or, as Thomas Sutcliffe explains in the *Times Literary Supplement,* Highsmith wrote "not about what it feels like to be mad, but what it feels like to remain sane while committing the actions of a madman."

Also in the *Times Literary Supplement,* James Campbell states that "the conflict of good and evil—or rather, simple decency and ordinary badness—is at the heart of all Highsmith's novels, dramatized in the encounters between two characters, often in an exotic locale, where it is easier to lose one's moral bearings. Usually, we see events from the point of view of the innocent, the blind, as they stumble towards doom."

Highsmith's preoccupations with guilt and contrasting personalities surfaced as early as her very first novel. *Strangers on a Train* chronicles the relationship between Guy Haines, a successful young architect, and Charles Bruno, a charming but unstable man slightly younger than Haines. The two men first meet on a train journey when Bruno repeatedly tries to engage his traveling companion in conversation. He eventually persuades Haines to open up and talk about feelings he usually keeps to himself—including the fact that he harbors resentment toward his wife. Bruno, who has long fantasized about killing his

much-hated father, then suggests to Haines that they rid themselves of the "problems" once and for all: Bruno will kill Haines's wife for him, and Haines in turn will kill Bruno's father. Since there is no connection between the victims and their killers, Bruno theorizes, the police will be at a loss to solve the murders. With more than a hint of reluctance, Haines rejects the plan, but to no avail; Bruno remains intrigued by it and proceeds to carry out his part.

As Paul Binding observes in a *Books and Bookmen* article, "the relation of abnormal Bruno to normal [Haines] is an exceedingly complex one which is to reverberate throughout Patricia Highsmith's output. On the one hand Bruno is a *doppelgaenger* figure; he embodies in repulsive flesh and blood form what [Haines's] subconscious has long been whispering to him. . . . On the other hand Bruno exists in his own perverse right, and [Haines] can have no control over him. . . . As a result of [Bruno's] existence, and of its coincidence with [Haines's] own, the rational, moral [Haines] becomes entangled in a mesh which threatens to destroy his entire security of identity. . . . [Haines is a man] tormented by guilt—guilt originally inspired by interior elements. Yet [he becomes], in society's eyes, guilty for exterior reasons." With the exception of the Ripley books (*The Talented Mr. Ripley, Ripley under Ground, Ripley's Game, The Boy Who Followed Ripley,* and *Ripley under Water*), which focus on the activities of the opportunistic and amoral Tom Ripley, a man incapable of feeling guilt, these themes are at the heart of Highsmith's fiction.

According to Symons, Highsmith typically launched her stories with the kind of "trickily ingenious plot devices . often used by very inferior writers." He hastens to add, however, that these serve only as starting points for the "profound and subtle studies of character that follow." As Burt Supree observes in the *Village Voice Literary Supplement,* most of Highsmith's characters—none of whom are "heroes" in the conventional sense—are likely to be "obsessive, unquestioning, humdrum men with no self-knowledge, no curiosity, and Byzantine fantasy-lives—respectable or criminal middle-class, middle-brow people of incredible shallowness. Nowhere else will you find so many characters you'd want to smack. . . . Like lab animals, [they] come under careful scrutiny, but [Highsmith] doesn't care to analyze them or beg sympathy for them. They go their independent ways with the illusion of freedom. Contact seems only to sharpen their edges, to irk and enrage." Yet as Craig Brown points out in the *Times*

Literary Supplement, "it is a rare villain or psychopath [in Highsmith's fiction] whom the reader does not find himself willing toward freedom, a rare investigator whom the reader is unhappy to see dead. Those she terms her 'murderer-heroes' or 'heropsychopaths' are usually people whose protective shells are not thick enough to deaden the pain as the world hammers at their emotions. . . . Some live, some die, some kill, some crack up."

Sutcliffe echoes this assessment of Highsmith's characters as basically sane people who commit apparently insane acts, usually while under considerable strain. "What she observes so truthfully is not the collapse of reason but its persistence in what it suits us to think of as inappropriate conditions," Sutcliffe assesses. He continues: "Even Ripley, the least scrupulous and likeable of her central characters, has motives for his actions, and though they are venal and vicious they are not irrational. Her suburban killers remain calculatingly evasive until the end. . . . They don't hear voices and they don't have fun. Indeed in the act of killing their attitude is one of dispassionate detachment, of a sustained attempt to rationalize the intolerable. . . . In all the books death is contingent and unsought, almost never meticulously planned and very rarely the focus for our moral indignation."

In the eyes of most critics, it is Highsmith's skill at depicting a character's slide into derangement or death that distinguishes her "in a field where imitative hacks and dull formula-mongers abound," remarks a *Times Literary Supplement* reviewer. Symons declares, "The quality that takes her books beyond the run of intelligent fiction is not [the] professional ability to order a plot and create a significant environment, but rather the intensity of feeling that she brings to the problems of her central figures. . . . From original ideas that are sometimes far-fetched or even trivial she proceeds with an imaginative power that makes the whole thing terrifyingly real." The world she creates for her characters has a "relentless, compulsive, mutedly ominous quality," asserts Hermione Lee in the *Observer,* one that leaves the reader "in a perpetual state of anxiety and wariness."

The prose Highsmith uses to communicate a sense of chilling dread and almost claustrophobic desperation is flat and plain, devoid of jargon, cliches, and padding. Some find it reminiscent of a psychological case history—a detailed and dispassionate account of a life moving out of control. According to Reg

Gadney in *London Magazine,* "It is a characteristic skill of Miss Highsmith to convey unease and apprehension with an understated narrative style and painstaking description of domestic practicalities. Her characters often seem to counterbalance their expectation of fear by entrenching themselves in domestic routines. . . . [Their] tenacious efforts . . . to keep hold of everyday reality and logic serve to heighten the menace and chaos." *New Statesman* reviewer Blake Morrison, in fact, believes Highsmith is "at her most macabre when most mundane."

In Brown's opinion, "her style, on the surface so smooth and calm, underneath so powerful and merciless," is precisely what "entices the reader in and then sends him, alongside the 'psychopath-hero,' tumbling against the rocks." Weinstein agrees that "the reader has no choice but to follow the work, nothing could go another way. You are trapped in the very ease of the reading. The result is like suffocation, losing breath or will." Orhan Pamuk, reviewing the "Ripley" books in the *Village Voice,* describes the fascination: "To know that people really will be hurt bonds the reader, with an almost self-destructive joy, to Highsmith's novels. For the reader has already discovered that the banality and pettiness, which spread like an epidemic in every one of her books, are those of his own life. He might as well begin to loathe himself. We rediscover, in each novel, the vulnerability of our existence."

Symons identifies several qualities in Highsmith's work that make her, in his words, "such an interesting and unusual novelist." He has particular praise for "the power with which her male characters are realized" as well as for her ability to portray "what would seem to most people abnormal states of minds and ways of behavior." Symons continues: "The way in which all this is presented can be masterly in its choice of tone and phrase. [Highsmith's] opening sentences make a statement that is symbolically meaningful in relation to the whole book. . . . The setting is also chosen with great care. . . . [She seems to be making the point that] in surroundings that are sufficiently strange, men become uncertain of their personalities and question the reason for their own conduct in society." In short, remarks Symons, Highsmith's work is "as serious in its implications and as subtle in its approach as anything being done in the novel today."

Curiously, Highsmith's final novel before her death in 1995 departed from her successful formula of suspense. *Small g: A Summer Idyll* features almost no mystery, death, or intrigue. Set in Zurich, Switzerland, the novel revolves around a group of characters who frequent Jacob's Bierstube-Restaurant, known in gay travel-book parlance as a "small g": a place frequented by both straight and gay patrons. Rickie is a middle-aged gay man who is mourning his dead lover and coping with recent news that he is HIV-positive. He becomes friends with Luisa, a young woman stuck in the unpleasant employ of Renate, a crippled fashion designer who controls Luisa's life and actions. Eventually, Luisa inherits a fortune and gets away from Renate, while Rickie finds out that he is not HIV-positive after all. Many critics expressed disappointment with the novel, noting that Highsmith's trademark strengths were simply missing in this work. *New Statesman & Society* reviewer Julie Wheelwright, for instance, notes that "the plot moves along pleasantly enough; but for a writer so skilled in creating suspense and insightful portraits, these qualities seem distinctly lacking in *Small g*. One wishes that, for her final novel, Highsmith had left a more lasting work than this light 'summer idyll.'" While praising the author's "limpid prose" and "deft characterization," *Times Literary Supplement* contributor James Campbell remarks that "if [*Small g*] can be read as a final utterance, Patricia Highsmith died having made peace with her demons. Good triumphed over bad. Too bad for her readers."

Despite this final work, Highsmith's reputation as a top-notch suspense writer remains secure. A *Times Literary Supplement* reviewer reflects on the dilemma facing those who attempt to evaluate Highsmith's work, explaining that, in essence, "it is difficult to find ways of praising [her] that do not at the same time do something to diminish her. . . . With each new book, she is ritually congratulated for outstripping the limitations of her genre, for being as much concerned with people and ideas as with manipulated incident, for attempting a more than superficial exploration of the psychopathology of her unpleasant heroes—for, in short, exhibiting some of the gifts and preoccupations which are elementarily demanded of competent straight novelists." According to the same reviewer, Highsmith can best be described in the following terms: "She is the crime writer who comes closest to giving crime writing a good name." And J. M. Edelstein in a *New Republic* article sums up: "Low-key is the word for Patricia Highsmith. . . . Low-key, subtle, and profound. It is amazing to me that she is not better known for she is superb and is a master of the suspense novel. . . . [The body of her work] should be among the classics of the genre."

BIOGRAPHICAL/CRITICAL SOURCES:

BOOKS

Brophy, Brigid, *Don't Never Forget: Collected Views and Reviews,* Holt, 1966.
Contemporary Literary Criticism, Gale (Detroit), Volume 2, 1974, Volume 4, 1975, Volume 14, 1980, Volume 42, 1987.
Symons, Julian, *Mortal Consequences: A History—From the Detective Story to the Crime Novel,* Harper, 1972.

PERIODICALS

Books and Bookmen, March, 1971; March, 1983.
Entertainment Weekly, February 11, 1994, p. 50.
Globe and Mail (Toronto), January 21, 1984.
Listener, July 9, 1970; February 17, 1983.
London Magazine, June, 1969; June-July, 1972.
Los Angeles Times Book Review, November 1, 1987; March 13, 1988; February 5, 1989; January 17, 1993.
New Republic, May 20, 1967; June 29, 1974.
New Statesman, May 31, 1963; February 26, 1965; October 29, 1965; January 25, 1969; March 30, 1979; October 2, 1981.
New Statesman & Society, March 17, 1995, p. 38.
Newsweek, July 4, 1977.
New Yorker, May 27, 1974.
New York Herald Tribune Books, February 7, 1960.
New York Review of Books, September 15, 1974; March 31, 1988, pp. 36-37.
New York Times Book Review, January 30, 1966; April 1, 1967; April 30, 1967; July 19, 1970; July 7, 1974; April 6, 1986; July 19, 1987; November 1, 1987; April 3, 1988; December 18, 1988; January 29, 1989; September 17, 1989; December 24, 1989; October 18, 1992.
Observer, February 12, 1967; January 19, 1969; July 12, 1970; January 9, 1983; March 12, 1995, p. 19.
Playboy, May, 1994, p. 34.
Publishers Weekly, November 2, 1992, pp. 46-47.
Punch, January 29, 1969; March 10, 1971; June 2, 1982.
Spectator, February 21, 1969; December 5, 1981; February 12, 1983; October 13, 1990, p. 33; December 7, 1991, p. 34; March 18, 1995, p. 34.
Times (London), February 24, 1983; April 3, 1986.

Times Literary Supplement, June 1, 1967; September 24, 1971; April 25, 1980; October 2, 1981; February 4, 1983; September 27, 1985; April 18, 1986; December 6, 1987, p. 1227; October 4, 1991, p. 26; February 24, 1995, p. 32.
Tribune Books (Chicago), October 4, 1992.
Village Voice, November 17, 1992.
Village Voice Literary Supplement, August, 1982.
Washington Post, June 28, 1980.
Washington Post Book World, September 15, 1985; October 6, 1985; October 18, 1992.
Washington Star-News, November 25, 1973.

OBITUARIES:

PERIODICALS

Los Angeles Times, February 5, 1995, p. A22.
New York Times, February 6, 1995, p. B8.
Times (London), February 6, 1995, p. 21.
Washington Post, February 6, 1995, p. B4.*

* * *

HINOJOSA(-SMITH), Rolando (R.) 1929-
(Rolando R. Hinojosa-S., Rolando (R.) Hinojosa Smith, Rolando Hinojosa-Smith; P. Galindo, a pseudonym)

PERSONAL: Born January 21, 1929, in Mercedes, TX; son of Manuel Guzman (a farmer) and Carrie Effie (a homemaker; maiden name, Smith) Hinojosa; married Patricia Mandley, September 1, 1963 (divorced, 1989); children: Clarissa Elizabeth, Karen Louise. *Education:* University of Texas at Austin, B.S., 1953; New Mexico Highlands University, M.A., 1963; University of Illinois, Ph.D., 1969. *Politics:* Democrat. *Religion:* Catholic.

ADDRESSES: Office—Department of English, University of Texas at Austin, Austin, TX 78712.

CAREER: High school teacher in Brownsville, TX, 1954-56; Trinity University, San Antonio, TX, assistant professor of modern languages, 1968-70; Texas A & I University, Kingsville, associate professor of Spanish and chair of modern language department, 1970-74, dean of College of Arts and Sciences, 1974-76, vice president for academic affairs, 1976-77; University of Minnesota—Minneapolis, chair of department of Chicano studies, 1977-80, professor of Chicano studies and American studies, 1980-81;

University of Texas at Austin, professor of English, 1981-85, E. C. Garwood Professor, 1985—, Mari Sabusawa Michener Chair, 1989-93. Consultant to Minneapolis Education Association, 1978-80, to U.S. Information Agency, 1980 and 1989, and to Texas Commission for the Arts and Humanities, 1981-82. Texas Center for Writers, University of Texas, Austin, 1989-93. *Military service:* U.S. Army Reserves, 1956-63; became second lieutenant.

MEMBER: Modern Language Association (chair of Commission on Languages and Literature in Ethnic Studies, 1978-80), PEN, Academia de la Lengua Espanola en Norteamerica, Hispanic Society, Fellow Society of Spanish and Spanish American Studies (fellow), Texas Institute of Letters.

AWARDS, HONORS: Best in West Award for foreign language radio programming from the state of California, 1970-71; Quinto Sol Literary Award for best novel, 1972, for *Estampas del valle y otras obras;* Casa de las Americas award for best novel, 1976, for *Klail City y sus alrededores;* Southwest Studies on Latin America award for best writing in the humanities, 1981, for *Mi querido Rafa;* distinguished alumnus award from University of Illinois College of Liberal Arts, 1988.

WRITINGS:

NOVELS

Estampas del valle y otras obras (first novel in "Klail City Death Trip" series), Quinto Sol, 1972, bilingual edition with translation by Gustavo Valadez and Jose Reyna published as *Sketches of the Valley and Other Works,* Justa Publications, 1980, revised English language edition published as *The Valley,* Bilingual Press (Ypsilanti, MI), 1983.
Klail City y sus alrededores (second novel in "Klail City Death Trip" series), bilingual edition with translation by Rosaura Sanchez, Casa de las Americas, 1976, published under name Rolando R. Hinojosa-S. as *Generaciones y semblanzas* (title means "Biographies and Lineages"), Justa Publications, 1977, translation by Hinojosa published as *Klail City,* Arte Publico Press (Houston, TX), 1987.
Korean Love Songs from Klail City Death Trip (novel in verse form; third in "Klail City Death Trip" series), illustrations by Rene Castro, Justa Publications, 1978.

Claros varones de Belken (fourth novel in "Klail City Death Trip" series), Justa Publications, 1981, bilingual edition with translation by Julia Cruz published as *Fair Gentlemen of Belken County,* Bilingual Press, 1987.

Mi querido Rafa (fifth novel in "Klail City Death Trip" series), Arte Publico Press, 1981, translation by Hinojosa published as *Dear Rafe,* 1985.

Rites and Witnesses (sixth novel in "Klail City Death Trip" series), Arte Publico Press, 1982.

Partners in Crime, Arte Publico Press, 1985.

Los amigos de Becky (seventh novel in "Klail City Death Trip" series), Arte Publico Press, 1990, translation published as *Becky and Her Friends,* 1990.

The Useless Servants (eighth novel in "Klail City Death Trip" series), Arte Publico Press, 1993.

OTHER

Generaciones, notas, y brechas/Generations, Notes, and Trails, (nonfiction; bilingual edition), translation by Fausto Avendano, Casa, 1978.

(Author of introduction) Carmen Tafolla, *Curandera,* M & A Editions, 1983.

(Contributor under name Rolando Hinojosa-Smith) Alan Pogue, *Agricultural Workers of the Rio Grande and Rio Bravo Valleys,* Center for Mexican American Studies, University of Texas at Austin, 1984.

(Translator from the Spanish) Tomas Rivera, *This Migrant Earth,* Arte Publico Press, 1985.

(Contributor) Jose David Saldivar, editor, *The Rolando Hinojosa Reader: Essays Historical and Critical,* Arte Publico Press, 1985.

Also author, under pseudonym P. Galindo, of *Mexican American Devil's Dictionary.* Work represented in anthologies, including *Festival de flor y canto: An Anthology of Chicano Literature,* edited by F. A. Cervantes, Juan Gomez-Quinones, and others, University of Southern California Press, 1976. Contributor of short stories, articles, and reviews to periodicals, including *Texas Monthly, Texas Humanist, Los Angeles Times,* and *Dallas Morning News.*

SIDELIGHTS: The first Chicano author to receive a major international literary award, Rolando Hinojosa won the prestigious Premio Casa de las Americas for *Klail City y sus alrededores* (*Klail City*), part of a series of novels known to English-speaking readers as "The Klail City Death Trip." Hinojosa's fiction, often infused with satire or subtle humor, is widely admired for its blending of diverse plot lines and narrative styles. The individual perspectives of many characters come together in his works to form a unique collective voice representative of the Chicano people. Hinojosa has also produced essays, poetry, and a detective novel titled *Partners in Crime.*

Hinojosa was born in the Lower Rio Grande Valley in Texas to a family with strong Mexican and American roots: his father fought in the Mexican Revolution while his mother maintained the family north of the border. An avid reader during childhood, Hinojosa was raised speaking Spanish until he attended junior high school, where English was the primary spoken language. Like his grandmother, mother, and three of his four siblings, Hinojosa became a teacher; he has held several professorial posts and has also been active in academic administration and consulting work. Although he prefers to write in Spanish, Hinojosa has also translated his own books and written others in English.

Hinojosa entered the literary scene with the 1973 *Estampas del valle y otras obras,* which was translated as *Sketches of the Valley and Other Works.* The four-part novel consists of loosely connected sketches, narratives, monologues, and dialogues, offering a composite picture of Chicano life in the fictitious Belken County town of Klail City, Texas. The first part of *Estampas* introduces Jehu Malacara, a nine-year-old boy who is left to live with exploitative relatives after the deaths of his parents. Hinojosa synthesizes the portrait of Jehu's life through comic and satiric sketches and narratives of incidents and characters surrounding him. The second section is a collection of pieces about a murder, presented through newspaper accounts, court documents, and testimonials from the defendant's relatives. A third segment, narrated by an omniscient storyteller, is a selection of sketches depicting people from various social groups in Klail City, while the fourth section introduces the series' other main character, Jehu's cousin Rafa Buenrostro. Also orphaned during childhood, Rafa narrates a succession of experiences and recollections of his life. Hinojosa later rewrote *Estampas del valle y otras obras* in English, publishing it as *The Valley* in 1983.

Hinojosa's aggregate portrait of the Spanish southwest continues in *Klail City y sus alrededores,* published in English as *Klail City.* Like its predecessor, *Klail City* is composed of interwoven narratives, conversations, and anecdotes that portray fifty years in the town's collective life. Winner of the 1976 Premio Casa de las Americas, the book was cited for its "richness of imagery, the sensitive creation of dialogues, the collage-like structure based on a pattern of converging individual destinies, the masterful control of the temporal element and its testimonial value," according to Charles M. Tatum in *World Literature Today*. Introducing more than one hundred characters and developing further the portraits of Rafa and Jehu, *Klail City* prompted *Western American Literature* writer Lourdes Torres to praise Hinojosa for his "unusual talent for capturing the language and spirit of his subject matter."

Korean Love Songs from Klail City Death Trip and *Claros varones de Belken* are Hinojosa's third and fourth installments in the series. A novel comprised of several long poems originally written in English and published in 1978, *Korean Love Songs* presents protagonist Rafa Buenrostro's narration of his experiences as a soldier in the Korean War. In poems such as "Friendly Fire" and "Rafe," Hinojosa explores army life, grief, male friendships, discrimination, and the reality of death presented through dispassionate, often ironic descriptions of the atrocity of war. *Claros varones de Belken* (*Fair Gentlemen of Belken County*), released three years later, follows Jehu and Rafa as they narrate accounts of their experiences serving in the Korean War, attending the University of Texas at Austin, and beginning careers as high school teachers in Klail City. The book also includes the narratives of two more major characters, writer P. Galindo and local historian Esteban Echevarria, who comment on their own and others' circumstances. Writing about *Fair Gentlemen of Belken County*, Tatum commented that Hinojosa's "creative strength and major characteristic is his ability to render this fictional reality utilizing a collective voice deeply rooted in the Hispanic tradition of the Texas-Mexico border." Also expressing a favorable opinion of the book was *Los Angeles Times Book Review* writer Alejandro Morales, who concluded that "the scores of names and multiple narrators at first pose a challenge, but quickly the imagery, language and subtle folk humor of Belken County win the reader's favor."

Hinojosa continued the "Klail City Death Trip" series with *Mi querido Rafa*. Translated as *Dear Rafe*, the novel is divided into two parts and consists of letters and interviews. The first half of the work is written in epistolary style, containing only letters from Jehu—now a successful bank officer—to his cousin Rafa. Between the novel's two parts, however, Jehu suddenly leaves his important position at the Klail City First National Bank, and in the second section Galindo interviews twenty-one community members about possible reasons for Jehu's resignation. The two major characters are depicted through dialogue going on around and about them; the reader obtains a glimpse of Rafa's personality through Jehu's letters, and Jehu's life is sketched through the opinions of the townspeople. *San Francisco Review of Books* writer Arnold Williams compared the power of Hinojosa's fictional milieu, striking even in translation, to that of twentieth-century Jewish writer Isaac Bashevis Singer, noting that "Hinojosa is such a master of English that he captures the same intimacy and idiomatic word play in his re-creations."

After writing *Rites and Witnesses*, the sixth novel in the "Klail City Death Trip" series, Hinojosa turned to a conventional form of the novel with the 1985 *Partners in Crime*, a detective thriller about the murder of a Belken County district attorney and several Mexican nationals in a local bar. Detective squads from both sides of the border are called to investigate the case; clues lead to an established and powerful cocaine smuggling ring. Jehu and Rafa reappear in the novel as minor characters who nevertheless play important parts in the mystery's development. "Those who might mourn the ending of the ['Klail City Death Trip' series] and their narrative experimentation and look askance at Hinojosa's attempting such a predictable and recipe-oriented genre as the murder mystery need not worry," concluded Williams. "He can weave a social fabric that is interesting, surprising, realistic and still entertaining."

In *Becky and Her Friends* Hinojosa continues his attempt to capture the many voices of the Hispanic community. Twenty-six characters from previous novels in the "Klail City Death Trip" series (including Becky) are each given a chapter here to discuss Becky's divorce from Ira Escobar and her subsequent marriage to Jehu Malacara. The novel has been praised for its evocation of the American-Hispanic ethos, one that is simultaneously deeply traditional, Catholic, and superstitious. However, writing in *Western American Literature*, R. L. Streng noted that "the characters' voices are difficult to differentiate one from another, and since each character falls into a camp for or against Becky and her escapades, there is very little difference between what we hear from Lionel Villa and Viola Barragan in one camp or Elvira Navarrete and Ira Escobar in the other." Streng concluded that *Becky and Her Friends* "fails in its attempt to corral a variety of characters and establish a lively vocal forum. Instead, the novel is tedious and requires readers to wade through extensive and unnecessary redundancies."

More recently, Hinojosa has extended the "Klail City Death Trip" series with *The Useless Servants,* a novel—unlike many others in the series—with only one narrative voice. A kind of novelization of his previous book of poems *Korean Love Songs from Klail City Death Trip, The Useless Servants* is the diary kept by Rafe Buenrostro when he was an infantryman in the U. S. Army during the Korean war. It is written very much in the manner of personal diaries, employing clipped phrases, few pronouns, and little explanation of the objects in the writer's daily routine—in this case, military jargon, acronyms, etc. Thematically, the book presents Rafe's experience of warfare and army life as a Hispanic-American. Critical reaction to the novel has been mixed. B. Adler, writing in *Choice,* felt that the work "is curious in the lack of insight it demonstrates, its flatness overall, with no reaching toward even stylistic significance." Dismayed by Rafe's apparent detachment from his own experiences, Adler concluded: "Perhaps Hinojosa is trying to make a point about the essentially boring nature of the average human being, even when placed in an extraordinary situation such as war. The dilemma is how realistic to make dullness. Hinojosa is too successful here." On the other hand, while William Anthony Nericcio in *World Literature Toady* also found Hinojosa's use of military jargon and acronyms rather unrelenting, he lauded the author's allusions to Plato's *Republic,* stating that "Plato's cave fire and the Korean battlefield illuminate each other nicely." Nericcio also noted that *The Useless Servants* further enriches the thematic texture of its series, writing: "The studied effort at intertextual dialectics set up between volumes in the Klail City Death Trip Series is as dense and electric as some to be found in Faulkner's oeuvre."

Hinojosa told *CA:* "I enjoy writing, of course, but I enjoy the re-writing even more: four or five rewritings are not uncommon. Once finished, though, it's on to something else. At this date, every work done in Spanish has also been done in English with the exception of *Claros varones de Belken,* although I did work quite closely on the idiomatic expressions which I found to be at the heart of the telling of the story.

"I usually don't read reviews; articles by learned scholars, however, are something else. They've devoted much time and thought to their work, and it is only fair I read them and take them seriously. The articles come from France, Germany, Spain, and so on, as well as from the United States. I find them not only interesting but, at times, revelatory. I don't know how much I am influenced by them, but I'm sure I am, as much as I am influenced by a lifetime of reading. Scholars do keep one on one's toes, but not, obviously, at their mercy. Writing has allowed me to meet writers as diverse as Julio Cortazar, Ishmael Reed, Elena Poniatowski and George Lamming.

"My goal is to set down in fiction the history of the Lower Rio Grande Valley. . . . A German scholar, Wolfgang Karrer, from Osnabrueck University has a census of my characters; they number some one thousand. That makes me an Abraham of some sort.

"Personally and professionally, my life as a professor and as a writer inseparably combines vocation with avocation. My ability in both languages is most helpful, and thanks for this goes to my parents and to the place where I was raised."

BIOGRAPHICAL/CRITICAL SOURCES:

BOOKS

Bruce-Novoa, Juan, *Chicano Authors: Inquiry by Interview,* University of Texas Press, 1980.
Dictionary of Literary Biography, Volume 82: *Chicano Writers,* First Series, Gale, 1989.
Saldivar, Jose David, editor, *The Rolando Hinojosa Reader: Essays Historical and Critical,* Arte Publico Press, 1985.

PERIODICALS

Choice, December, 1993.
Hispania, September, 1986.
Hispanic, September, 1990, p. 48.
Los Angeles Times Book Review, April 12, 1987; October 10, 1993.
Publishers Weekly, November 28, 1986; July 12, 1993, p. 69.
San Francisco Review of Books, spring, 1985; fall/winter, 1985.
Western American Literature, fall, 1988; summer, 1991.
World Literature Today, summer, 1977; summer 1986; winter, 1995.*

HINOJOSA-S., Rolando R.
See **HINOJOSA(-SMITH), Rolando (R.)**

* * *

HINOJOSA-SMITH, Rolando
See **HINOJOSA(-SMITH), Rolando (R.)**

* * *

HINTON, S(usan) E(loise) 1950-

PERSONAL: Born in 1950, in Tulsa, OK; married David E. Inhofe (in mail order business), September, 1970; children: Nicholas David. *Education:* University of Tulsa, B.S., 1970.

ADDRESSES: Home—Tulsa, OK.

CAREER: Writer. Consultant on film adaptations of her novels; minor acting roles in some film adaptations of her novels.

AWARDS, HONORS: New York Herald Tribune best teenage books citation, 1967, *Chicago Tribune Book World* Spring Book Festival Honor Book, 1967, *Media & Methods* Maxi Award, American Library Association (ALA) Best Young Adult Books citation, both 1975, and Massachusetts Children's Book Award, 1979, all for *The Outsiders;* ALA Best Books for Young Adults citation, 1971, *Chicago Tribune Book World* Spring Book Festival Honor Book, 1971, and Massachusetts Children's Book Award, 1978, all for *That Was Then, This Is Now;* ALA Best Books for Young Adults citation, 1975, *School Library Journal* Best Books of the Year citation, 1975, and Land of Enchantment Award, New Mexico Library Association, 1982, all for *Rumble Fish;* ALA Best Books for Young Adults citation, 1979, *School Library Journal* Best Books of the Year citation, 1979, New York Public Library Books for the Teen-Age citation, 1980, American Book Award nomination for children's paperback, 1981, Sue Hefly honor book, Louisiana Association of School Libraries, 1982, California Young Reader Medal nomination, California Reading Association, 1982, and Sue Hefly Award, 1983, all for *Tex;* Golden Archer Award, 1983; Recipient of first ALA Young Adult Services Division/*School Library Journal* Author Award, 1988, for body of work.

WRITINGS:

YOUNG ADULT NOVELS

The Outsiders, Viking (New York City), 1967.
That Was Then, This Is Now, Viking, 1971.
Rumble Fish (also see below), Delacorte (New York City), 1975.
Tex, Delacorte, 1979.
Taming the Star Runner, Delacorte, 1988.

The Outsiders and *That Was Then, This Is Now* have been published in bilingual English/Spanish editions.

OTHER

(With Francis Ford Coppola) *Rumble Fish* (screenplay; adapted from her novel), Universal, 1983.
Big David, Little David, illustrated by Alan Daniel, Doubleday (New York City), 1994.
The Puppy Sister, Delacorte, 1995.

ADAPTATIONS: Film adaptations of Hinton's novels include *Tex,* starring Matt Dillon, Walt Disney Productions, 1982; *The Outsiders,* starring C. Thomas Howell and Matt Dillon, Warner Bros., 1983; and *That Was Then, This Is Now,* starring Emilio Estevez and Craig Sheffer, Paramount, 1985. *The Outsiders* was adapted as a television series by Fox-TV, 1990. Current Affairs and Mark Twain Media adapted *The Outsiders* and *That Was Then, This Is Now* as filmstrips with cassettes, both 1978. *Rumble Fish* was adapted as a record and cassette, Viking, 1977.

SIDELIGHTS: Novelist S. E. Hinton is credited with revolutionizing the young adult genre by portraying teenagers realistically rather than formulaically and by creating characters, settings, and dialogue that are representative of teenage life in America. Her classic, *The Outsiders* (published in 1967 when she was seventeen years old), was the first in her short but impressive list of books to feature troubled but sensitive male adolescents as protagonists. Hinton's subjects include social-class rivalry, poverty, alcoholism, drug addiction, and the cruelty teenagers often inflict on each other and on themselves. Film rights to all five of her novels have been acquired, and four have been adapted as major motion pictures.

Hinton was born and raised in Tulsa, Oklahoma, the setting of most of her novels. She was an avid reader as a child and soon began writing stories about cowboys, horses, and other topics of interest to her. While a student at Will Rogers High School, she began writing *The Outsiders* and saw the novel evolve through four drafts before submitting it to Curtis Brown literary agent Marilyn Marlow. A publication contract with Viking arrived during her high school graduation ceremony. Loosely based on her own experiences and those of friends and acquaintances, the book is about the ongoing rivalry and conflict that leads to a deadly confrontation between two gangs—the lower-class "greasers" and their upper-middle-class counterparts, the "socs" (short for "socials"). *The Outsiders* was an instant hit among teenagers and sold more than four million copies in the United States.

Hinton's unique understanding of her subjects allows her to create believable characters. Ponyboy Curtis, the fourteen-year-old narrator in *The Outsiders,* has warranted comparison to J. D. Salinger's Holden Caulfield of *Catcher in the Rye*: "He watches sunsets and looks at the stars and aches for something better," wrote critic William Jay Jacobs in *Record*. "But as much as the sensitive, thoughtful Ponyboy resembles Holden, his milieu is irrevocably different. All around him are hostility and fear, along with distrust for the 'system.'"

With the money she earned from *The Outsiders*, Hinton attended the University of Tulsa and earned a degree in education in 1970. She met her future husband, David Inhofe, while in school, and it was he who encouraged her to write her second novel, *That Was Then, This Is Now,* published in 1971. After suffering for several years from writer's block—"I couldn't even write a letter," she told Carol Wallace of the *Daily News*—Hinton eventually produced a novel she considers superior to her first. The story focuses on two foster brothers who move in different directions: one becomes involved with school and girls while the other sinks into a world of drugs and crime. "The phrase 'if only' is perhaps the most bittersweet in the language," wrote Michael Cart in the *New York Times Book Review*. "And Miss Hinton uses it skillfully to underline her theme: growth can be a dangerous process."

Hinton continued her pattern of producing a novel every four years with the publication of *Rumble Fish* in 1975 and *Tex* in 1979. The former centers on a delinquent youth struggling to gain a tough reputation, and the latter (set in California) on two teenage brothers left in each other's care by their traveling father. As with her previous works, the characters are skillfully drawn and the plots are fast-paced and exciting.

Some critics, like Michael Malone of *The Nation,* have chastised Hinton for "mythologizing the tragic beauty of violent youth" and "avoiding the problem of parental authority and conflict" by placing her characters outside of their families. She has also been criticized for creating too-similar plots in consecutive books. But librarians cite Hinton as one of the most popular authors among "reluctant readers" in the junior-high age group, as well as among teachers, who regularly use her novels as assigned reading. "Teen-agers should not be written down to," Hinton said in *The New York Times Book Review*. "Anyone can tell when his intelligence is being underestimated. Those who are not ready for adult novels can easily have their love of reading killed by the inane junk lining the teen-age shelf in the library."

In 1988 Hinton's fifth novel, *Taming the Star Runner,* was published. The fifteen-year-old protagonist is a "young hood, desperately tough and desperately vulnerable," according to *New York Times Book Review* critic Patty Campbell. Young Travis is a budding writer forced to move to his uncle's Oklahoma horse ranch in order to stay out of trouble.

During the nearly ten-year interim between the publication of *Tex* and *Taming the Star Runner,* Hinton started a family and worked as a consultant on the film adaptations of her novels. Involved in the casting, scriptwriting, directing, and even acting, Hinton found the experience pleasurable but still preferred writing to consulting. "Once I sold the books I expected to be asked to drop off the face of the earth," Hinton told Dave Smith of the *Los Angeles Times*. "But that didn't happen. I know that I had extremely rare experiences for a writer."

In the 1990s, Hinton has written the text for two children's picture books, *Big David, Little David* and *The Puppy Sister*. In the former, it is Nick's first day at kindergarten and he notices a boy who looks remarkably like his father—he has the same color hair, he wears glasses, and his name is the same, David. Nick tells his father about this boy and asks, "He's not you, is he?" Nick's father jokes and says it is: he makes himself small everyday so they can go to school together. The situation comes to a head during parent's day at school, and Nick gets the last laugh. *The Puppy Sister* concerns Nick and his family again, only this time the story is narrated by the female puppy Nick's parents give him. Because Nick wants a sister, and because his parents really want a daughter, the puppy—Aleasha—slowly makes herself human for them. The story shows how the family must hide Aleasha from their neighbors while she is in her "transitional" period. The books for the most part have been well reviewed.

Through her popular novels and their equally popular film adaptations, Hinton has developed a reputation as a perceptive writer of young adult fiction. In 1988, she was honored with the first American Library Association/*School Library Journal* Author Achievement award for her body of work. "I don't think I have a masterpiece in me, but I do know I'm writing well in the area I choose to write in," Hinton explained to Smith. "I understand kids and I really like them. And I have a very good memory. I remember exactly what it was like to be a teenager that nobody listened to or paid attention to or wanted around."

BIOGRAPHICAL/CRITICAL SOURCES:

BOOKS

Authors and Artists for Young Adults, Volume 2, Gale, 1989, pp. 65-76.
Children's Literature Review, Gale, Volume 3, 1978, Volume 23, 1991.
Contemporary Literary Criticism, Volume 30, Gale, 1984.
Daly, Jay, *Presenting S. E. Hinton,* Twayne, 1987.

PERIODICALS

American Film, April, 1983.
Book World, May 9, 1971.
Bulletin for the Center for Children's Books, February, 1995, p. 200; November, 1995, p. 92.
Children's Book Review, December, 1971.
Daily News, September 26, 1982.
English Journal, September, 1989, p. 86.
Growing Point, May, 1980.
Horn Book, January-February, 1989, p. 78.
Kirkus Reviews, August 15, 1988.
Los Angeles Times, July 15, 1982; October 14, 1983.
Nation, March 8, 1986, p. 276.
Newsweek, October 11, 1982.
New York Times, March 20, 1983; March 23, 1983; October 7, 1983; October 23, 1983.
New York Times Book Review, August 27, 1967; August 8, 1971, p. 8; April 2, 1989, p. 26; November 19, 1995, p. 37.
Publishers Weekly, December 12, 1994, p. 62; July 17, 1995, p. 230.
Quill & Quire, April, 1995, p. 37.
Record, November, 1967, pp. 201-02.

Saturday Review, May 13, 1967; January 27, 1968.
School Library Journal, May, 1967; June-July, 1988, p. 4; October, 1988, p. 161; December, 1993, p. 70; April, 1995, p. 102; October, 1995, p. 104; May, 1996, p. 76.
Signal, May, 1980.
Times Literary Supplement, October 30, 1970; October 22, 1971; April 2, 1976; March 20, 1980.
Village Voice, April 5, 1983.
Washington Post, October 8, 1982; October 18, 1983.
Washington Post Book World, February 12, 1989.*

*   *   *

HOLDEN, Dalby
    See HAMMOND, Gerald (Arthur Douglas)

*   *   *

HOOKER, Richard
    See HEINZ, W(ilfred) C(harles)

*   *   *

HOWARD, Elizabeth Jane 1923-

PERSONAL: Born March 26, 1923, in London, England; daughter of David Liddon and Katharine Margaret (Somervell) Howard; married Peter M. Scott, 1942 (divorced, 1951); married James Douglas-Henry, 1960 (divorced); married Kingsley Amis (an author), 1965 (divorced, 1983); children: (first marriage) Nicola Scott. *Education:* Privately educated; trained as an actress at the London Mask Theatre School and with the Scott Thorndike Student Repertory.

ADDRESSES: Home—Suffolk, England. *Agent*—Jonathan Clowes Ltd., Iron Bridge House, Bridge Approach, London NW1 9BD, England.

CAREER: Writer. Actress in Stratford-on-Avon, England, and in repertory theater in Devon, England; model and broadcaster for British Broadcasting Corp., 1939-46; secretary, Inland Waterways Association, London, 1947-50; editor, Chatto & Windus Ltd., London, 1953-56, and for Weidenfeld &

Nicolson Ltd., London, 1957; book critic, *Queen* magazine, London, 1957-60. Honorary artistic director, Cheltenham Literary Festival, 1962; co-artistic director, Salisbury Festival, 1973. Member of awards committee for John Llewelyn Rhys Memorial Prize and for Somerset Maugham Award. *Military service:* Served as an air raid warden in London during World War II.

MEMBER: Royal Society of Literature, fellow.

AWARDS, HONORS: John Llewelyn Rhys Memorial Prize, 1951, for *The Beautiful Visit.*

WRITINGS:

NOVELS

The Beautiful Visit, Random House (New York City), 1950, reprinted, Penguin, 1976.
The Long View, Reynal (New York City), 1956, reprinted, Penguin, 1976.
The Sea Change, Cape (London), 1959, Harper (New York City), 1960, reprinted, Penguin, 1975.
After Julius, Cape, 1965, Viking (New York City), 1966.
Something in Disguise, Cape, 1969, Viking, 1970.
Odd Girl Out, Viking, 1972.
Getting It Right, Viking, 1982.
The Light Years (Cazalet Chronicle), Pocket Books (New York City), 1990.
Marking Time (Cazalet Chronicle), Pocket Books, 1991.
Confusion (Cazalet Chronicle), Pocket Books, 1993.
Casting Off (Cazalet Chronicle), Macmillan, 1995.

SHORT STORIES

(With R. Aickman) *We Are for the Dark: Six Ghost Stories,* Cape, 1951.
Mr. Wrong, Cape, 1975, Viking, 1976.

OTHER

(With Arthur Helps) *Bettina: A Portrait* (biography), Chatto & Windus (London), 1957.
(Editor) *The Lover's Companion: The Pleasures, Joys, and Anguish of Love,* David & Charles (Newton Abbott, England), 1978.
(With Fay Maschler) *Howard and Maschler on Food,* Joseph (London), 1987.

(Editor) *Green Shades: An Anthology of Plants, Gardens, and Gardeners,* Aurum (London), 1990.
(With Maschler) *Cooking for Occasion,* Macmillan (London), 1994.

Also author of screenplays *The Very Edge* (1963) and *Getting It Right* (1989), and television plays *After Julius* (1979) and *Something in Disguise* (1980), both from her novels, as well as scripts for the television series *Upstairs Downstairs, Victorian Scandals,* and *She.* Contributor to *Encounter, Sunday Times, Daily Express, New Yorker,* and *Town and Country.*

SIDELIGHTS: Elizabeth Jane Howard has had a varied career in the arts, beginning as a theater actress and model, moving on to work as an editor at London publishing houses, and culminating in a career as a novelist, short story writer, and nonfiction writer on cooking and gardening. In 1970, the *National Observer*'s Robert Ostermann placed Howard in the same class with "Rosamond Lehmann and Elizabeth Bowen: female novelists of impressive intelligence and sensibilities that respond to every nuance in human relationships." Howard's award-winning first novel, *The Beautiful Visit,* was followed by such critically acclaimed works as *The Long View* and *After Julius,* marking her as a perceptive writer whose scrupulous eye for the details of dress and decor often provide the fuel for her acerbic wit. In a review of *Mr. Wrong,* Howard's second collection of short fiction, Victoria Glendinning observed in *New Statesman* that "Howard writes most confidently and touchingly at very close range, about momentary doubts, unspoken anxieties, fleeting perceptions, intense good moments and equally intense bad ones, all inextricably bound up with a natural or domestic setting."

Howard's early novels demonstrated her ability to combine sympathetic portrayals of female characters with satirical set pieces, poking fun at the characters. In *The Long View,* Howard told the story of a marriage by following its participants backwards in time, from a 1950 party given in honor of their son, to their first meeting in 1926. "It is, simply, a brilliant book," said Michele Slung in a *Washington Post* review of the novel's 1990 reissue. "And it amounts to something of a sacred object among those who have read it, many of us more than once." Similarly, at the time of its original publication, Daniel George wrote in the *Spectator* that "not many novels deserve to be read twice. This one does—preferably, the second time, from finish to start." *The Long View* was followed by *The Sea Change,* a narrative told alternatingly by its four protagonists. Again, Howard's writing elicited ardent responses from critics who admired her delicate handling of her characters' relationships. The novel's theme, stated a *Times Literary Supplement* reviewer of *The Sea Change,* is "the flux of relationships at a level of intimacy which demands the most delicate investigation if we are to discover truth, and the most intricate selection of situations that will appear both complete and natural."

"Events as much as background seem merely devices used to aid her in discovering more about the human heart," said the *Times Literary Supplement* critics, but this technique came to be seen as old-fashioned by the turbulent 1970s. Some reviewers began to detect an unaccustomed element of uncertainty in the author herself. In a review of *After Julius,* a novel centered on a weekend party during which the death of Julius twenty years earlier finally catches up with his wife and two daughters, a contributor to the *Times Literary Supplement* noted: "It is as though, unsure of the contemporary relevance of the central situation she has chosen, Miss Howard has forced herself to provide entertainment for all readers—cosy sentiment, earthy passion, proletarian protest, fastidious respect for convention, in-jokes and authentic factual detail. The mixture does not jell."

Getting It Right, in which a morbidly shy male hairdresser is transformed by a sexual encounter with an overdressed, upper middle-class woman, was generally well received, but garnered similar complaints. The novel "seems to have been written under some odd and regrettable compulsions towards up-to-dateness, from which [Howard] should feel herself honourably absolved," wrote Anne Duchene in the *Times Literary Supplement.* Such criticisms were not levied, however, at Howard's collection of short stories, *Mr. Wrong,* six pieces in which, according to Jerome Charyn in the *New York Times Book Review,* Howard displays her "special grace": "delineating the little corrosions of tight family structures—the bickering husbands and wives, the cruel, secretive world of children in a country house, the territorial squabbles of mothers and daughters, the bonds of jealousy between a beautiful girl and her grandmother."

Likewise, the shift in critical prejudice toward a more democratic approach in literature stood Howard in good stead as she entered the 1990s with the first installment of the Cazalet Chronicle, *The Light*

Years. Patrick Parrinder noted in the *London Review of Books* that Howard included the trials and tribulations of the wealthy Cazalet family's servants in her minutely detailed history of the family. "This is a shrewd move, and a sign of our own times rather like the recent opening-up to visitors of the kitchens and pantries of National Trust houses," Parrinder observed. In addition to the servants, there are the Cazalets themselves: Brig and Duchy, the mother and father of the clan; Edward, their philandering son, and his brothers Hugh, who was injured in the First World War, and Rupert, who longs to be a painter, their respective wives, and their unmarried sister Rachel, who may or may not be a lesbian. Of the many children produced by this generation, three daughters, Louise, Polly, and Clary, capture the majority of the narrative attention and reader interest, critics noted.

The Cazalet Chronicle extends to four volumes. *The Light Years* was followed by *Marking Time, Confusion,* and *Casting Off.* The Chronicle begins before the onset of World War II, continues through the war, and concludes with the early postwar years in England as experienced by three generations of a family made wealthy by the timber industry. Despite the scrupulously detailed time period, these four works are not war novels, according to reviewers, but rather novels of the home front that focus on the lives of the women and children of the Cazalet family. "Somehow, Elizabeth Jane Howard crams it all in: the births, marriages, deaths, love affairs; the ageing grandparents, the rheumaticky servants, the young children in their Sussex Arcadia," observed J. K. L. Walker in a *Times Literary Supplement* review of *Confusion.* "On its level, it is a flawless, busy, yet ultimately sentimental performance."

Though readers of the installments following the first noted the need to keep track of Howard's large cast of characters, it was generally acknowledged that the author did a good job of aiding the reader in this task. Susan Dooley, a contributor to the *Washington Post Book World* noted this effort in her review of *Marking Time* and concluded: "Howard is a delightful writer, giving each of the multitude a distinctive voice, and by the second chapter I was mostly in control of the characters." As installments of the Cazalet Chronicle continued to appear, the critical response to the series was generally enthusiastic. A complaint registered by Muriel Spanier in the *New York Times Book Review* about the lack of "dramatic tension" in *The Light Years,* became praise for the third novel's "persuasive melancholy" through which the author sets the stage for postwar revelations and "the implications of peace," according to Judy Cooke in *New Statesman & Society.* Indeed, Cooke continued, "What is so extraordinarily deft is the author's ability to focus on that moment when the public and private concerns [of her characters] are brought to bear upon each other." Thus, as in her early works, Howard's novels of the 1990s are primarily about relationships. "Howard is not interested in writing about society or history, but about relationships, and specifically sex. She does this extremely well, and with bleak humour," observed Claire Harman in her *Times Literary Supplement* review of *Casting Off.*

BIOGRAPHICAL/CRITICAL SOURCES:

BOOKS

Contemporary Literary Criticism, Gale (Detroit), Volume 7, 1977, pp. 164-65; Volume 29, 1984, pp. 242-47.
Contemporary Novelists, sixth edition, St. James Press (Detroit), 1996, pp. 496-99.

PERIODICALS

Antioch Review, fall, 1992, p. 782.
Best Sellers, February 1, 1966, p. 418; February 15, 1970, p. 430; February 15, 1972, p. 515; March, 1976, p. 367.
Booklist, February 1, 1966, p. 519; March 1, 1976, p. 959; September 1, 1982, p. 28; July, 1990, p. 2042; June 15, 1992, p. 1787.
Books, July, 1987, p. 10; November, 1992, p. 17; November, 1993, pp. 4, 23.
Books & Bookmen, January, 1970, p. 45.
Book Week, January 30, 1966.
British Book News, September, 1982, p. 576.
Christian Science Monitor, February 3, 1966, p. 11; January 29, 1970, p. 7; July 1, 1994, p. 10.
Contemporary Review, April, 1972, p. 213; July, 1982, p. 45.
Guardian Weekly, November 15, 1969, p. 18; January 15, 1972, p. 19; July 19, 1975, p. 20.
Hudson Review, spring, 1966, p. 124; summer, 1983, p. 373.
Illustrated London News, May, 1982, p. 82; December 25, 1989, p. 98; vol. 709, 1990, p. 98; vol. 710, 1991, p. 98; Christmas, 1992, p. 98; winter, 1993, p. 82.

Kirkus Reviews, November 1, 1965, p. 1137; November 15, 1969, p. 1223; November 15, 1971, p. 1227; November 1, 1975, p. 1251; September 1, 1982, p. 1012; July 1, 1990, p. 900; June 15, 1992, p. 739.
Kliatt, September, 1994, p. 58.
Library Journal, January 1, 1966, p. 128; February 1, 1970, p. 513; January 15, 1972, p. 215; December 1, 1975, p. 2264; September 15, 1982, p. 1769; August, 1990, p. 141; July, 1992, p. 124.
Life, January 7, 1966, p. 19.
Listener, November 6, 1969, p. 636; March 30, 1972, p. 428; September 18, 1975, p. 386; June 3, 1982, p. 22; July 12, 1990, p. 29.
London Review of Books, May 20, 1982, pp. 18-19; July 26, 1990, pp. 19-20.
Los Angeles Times Book Review, November 14, 1982, p. 3.
Ms., April, 1976, p. 39; July, 1979, p. 28; March, 1983, p. 33
Nation, December 4, 1982, pp. 598-600.
National Observer, February 23, 1970, p. 19; June 17, 1972, p. 21; March 13, 1976, p. 21.
National Review, March 24, 1970, p. 314.
New Leader, February 21, 1972, p. 16.
New Statesman, November 12, 1965, p. 740; November 7, 1969, p. 665; March 24, 1972, p. 398; July 11, 1975, p. 60; May 14, 1982, p. 25.
New Statesman & Society, November 29, 1991, p. 33; December 3, 1993, p. 40.
Newsweek, December 29, 1975; November 15, 1982, p. 108.
New Yorker, April 16, 1966, p. 199; February 26, 1972, p. 102; December 29, 1975, p. 56; November 15, 1982, p. 203.
New York Herald Tribune Book Review, August 30, 1950, p. 8.
New York Times, December 4, 1988, sec. 2, p. 24.
New York Times Book Review, January 31, 1960; January 9, 1966, p. 36; February 1, 1970, p. 5; January 30, 1972, p. 26; February 22, 1976, p. 36; March 6, 1983, pp. 28-29; September 16, 1990, p. 21; July 19, 1992, p. 20.
Observer (London), November 7, 1965, p. 27; November 9, 1969, p. 34; August 15, 1971, p. 18; March 26, 1972, p. 37; August 3, 1975, p. 21; March 12, 1978, p. 33; May 16, 1982, p. 30; December 5, 1982, p. 25; July 22, 1990, p. 52; November 10, 1991, p. 58; November 28, 1993, p. 3.
Publishers Weekly, November 24, 1969, p. 36; November 15, 1971, p. 66; November 17, 1975, p. 95; September 24, 1982, p. 61; July 20, 1990, p. 49; July 12, 1991, p. 64; July 15, 1992, p. 84; February 28, 1994, pp. 73, 82.

Punch, November 17, 1965, p. 741; November 12, 1969, p. 803; February 15, 1978, p. 289; July, 1987, p. 66.

Saturday Review, February 20, 1960, p. 32; February 14, 1970, p. 49.

Spectator, March 16, 1956, p. 352; November 12, 1965, p. 626; November 1, 1969, p. 682; April 8, 1972, p. 549; July 26, 1975, p. 113; May 15, 1982, p. 26; July 14, 1990, p. 28; November 16, 1991, p. 44; November 23, 1991, p. 39; December 14, 1991, p. 45; November 13, 1993, p. 32; November 4, 1995, p. 52.

Time, May 4, 1970, p. 99.

Times Educational Supplement, December 29, 1995, p. 12.

Times Literary Supplement, March 23, 1956; November 20, 1959, p. 673; November 4, 1965, p. 973; November 6, 1969, p. 1273; March 24, 1972, p. 326; July 11, 1975, p. 753; May 14, 1982, p. 536; March 9, 1984, p. 259; July 27, 1990, p. 804; November 8, 1991, p. 30; October 29, 1993, p. 20; November 10, 1995, p. 23.

Tribune Books, September 27, 1992, p. 6.

Village Voice, December 18, 1990, p. 103.

Virginia Quarterly Review, spring, 1983, p. 58.

Wall Street Journal, August 2, 1996.

Washington Post Book World, February 1, 1970, p. 5; January 30, 1972, p. 10; January 2, 1983, p. 12; September 30, 1990, p. 8; April 28, 1992, p. C3.

Woman's Journal, December, 1995, p. 16.*

*   *   *

HUNTER, Evan 1926-
(Curt Cannon, Hunt Collins, Ezra Hannon, Richard Marsten, Ed McBain)

PERSONAL: Born October 15, 1926, in New York, NY; son of Charles and Marie (Coppola) Lombino; married Anita Melnick, October 17, 1949 (divorced); married Mary Vann Finley, June, 1973 (divorced); married Drasica Dimitrijevic, September 4, 1997; children: (first marriage) Ted, Mark, Richard; (second marriage) Amanda Eve Finley (stepdaughter). *Education:* Attended Cooper Union, 1943-44; Hunter College (now Hunter College of the City University of New York), B.A., 1950. *Politics:* Democrat.

ADDRESSES: Agent—c/o Gelfman Schneider, 250 W. 57th St., New York, NY 10107.

CAREER: Writer. Taught at a vocational high school in New York City, 1950; held various jobs, including answering the telephone at night for American Automobile Association and selling lobsters for a wholesale lobster firm, both New York City; worked for Scott Meredith Literary Agency, New York City, for about eighteen months. *Military service:* U.S. Navy, 1944-46.

MEMBER: Phi Beta Kappa.

AWARDS, HONORS: Mystery Writers of America Award, 1957, for short story "The Last Spin"; Grand Master Award, Mystery Writers of America, 1986, for lifetime achievement.

WRITINGS:

The Evil Sleep, Falcon, 1952.

The Big Fix, Falcon, 1952, published under pseudonym Richard Marsten as *So Nude, So Dead,* Fawcett, 1956.

Find the Feathered Serpent, Winston, 1952, reprinted, Gregg, 1979.

Don't Crowd Me, Popular Library, 1953, published in England as *The Paradise Party,* New English Library, 1968.

(Under pseudonym Hunt Collins) *Cut Me In,* Abelard, 1954, published as *The Proposition,* Pyramid, 1955.

The Blackboard Jungle, Simon & Schuster, 1954, reprinted, Avon, 1976.

(Contributor) David Coxe Cook, editor, *Best Detective Stories of the Year 1955,* Dutton, 1955.

(Under pseudonym Hunt Collins) *Tomorrow's World,* Bouregy, 1956, published as *Tomorrow and Tomorrow,* Pyramid Books, 1956, published in England under pseudonym Ed McBain, Sphere, 1979.

Second Ending, Simon & Schuster, 1956, published as *Quartet in H,* Pocket Books, 1957.

The Jungle Kids (short stories), Pocket Books, 1956.

(With Craig Rice, under pseudonym Ed McBain) *April Robin Murders* (crime novel), Random House, 1958.

(Under pseudonym Curt Cannon) *I'm Cannon—For Hire* (crime novel), Fawcett, 1958.

Strangers When We Meet (also see below), Simon & Schuster, 1958.

(Under pseudonym Curt Cannon) *I Like 'Em Tough* (short stories), Fawcett, 1958.

A Matter of Conviction, Simon & Schuster, 1959, reprinted, Avon, 1976, published as *The Young Savages,* Pocket Books, 1966.

The Remarkable Harry (juvenile), Abelard, 1960.

The Last Spin and Other Stories, Constable, 1960.

The Wonderful Button (juvenile), Abelard, 1961.

Mothers and Daughters, Simon & Schuster, 1961.

Happy New Year, Herbie, and Other Stories, Simon & Schuster, 1963.

Buddwing, Simon & Schuster, 1964.

(Under pseudonym Ed McBain) *The Sentries* (crime novel), Simon & Schuster, 1965.

The Paper Dragon, Delacorte, 1966.

A Horse's Head, Delacorte, 1967.

(Editor under pseudonym Ed McBain) *Crime Squad*, New English Library, 1968.

(Editor under pseudonym Ed McBain) *Homicide Department*, New English Library, 1968.

Last Summer, Doubleday, 1968.

(Editor under pseudonym Ed McBain) *Downpour*, New English Library, 1969.

(Editor under pseudonym Ed McBain) *Ticket to Death*, New English Library, 1969.

Sons, Doubleday, 1969.

Nobody Knew They Were There, Doubleday, 1971.

The Beheading and Other Stories, Constable, 1971.

Every Little Crook and Nanny, Doubleday, 1972.

The Easter Man (a Play), and Six Stories (also see below), Doubleday, 1972.

Seven, Constable, 1972.

Come Winter, Doubleday, 1973.

Streets of Gold, Harper, 1974.

(Under pseudonym Ed McBain) *Where There's Smoke* (crime novel), Random House, 1975.

(Under pseudonym Ezra Hannon) *Doors* (crime novel), Stein & Day, 1975.

The Chisholms: A Novel of the Journey West (also see below), Harper, 1976.

(Under pseudonym Ed McBain) *Guns* (crime novel), Random House, 1976.

Me and Mr. Stenner (juvenile), Lippincott, 1977.

Walk Proud (also see below), Bantam, 1979.

Love, Dad, Crown, 1981.

(Under pseudonym Ed McBain) *The McBain Brief* (short stories), Hamish Hamilton, 1982, Arbor House, 1983.

Far From the Sea, Atheneum, 1983.

Lizzie, Arbor House, 1984.

(Under pseudonym Ed McBain) *Another Part of the City*, Mysterious Press, 1987.

(Under pseudonym Ed McBain) *Downtown*, Morrow, 1989.

(Under pseudonym Ed McBain) *Gangs*, Avon, 1989.

Criminal Conversation, Warner (New York City), 1995.

Privileged Conversation, Warner, 1996.

(Under pseudonym Ed McBain), *Gladly the Cross-Eyed Bear*, Warner, 1996.

UNDER PSEUDONYM ED McBAIN; "87TH PRECINCT" SERIES

Cop Hater (also see below), Simon & Schuster, 1956.

The Mugger (also see below), Simon & Schuster, 1956.

The Pusher (also see below), Simon & Schuster, 1956.

The Con Man (also see below), Simon & Schuster, 1957.

Killer's Choice, Simon & Schuster, 1957.

Killer's Payoff, Simon & Schuster, 1958.

Lady Killer, Simon & Schuster, 1958.

Killer's Wedge, Simon & Schuster, 1958.

'Til Death, Simon & Schuster, 1959.

King's Ransom, Simon & Schuster, 1959.

Give the Boys a Great Big Hand, Simon & Schuster, 1960.

The Heckler, Simon & Schuster, 1960.

See Them Die, Simon & Schuster, 1960.

Lady, Lady, I Did It!, Simon & Schuster, 1961.

Like Love, Simon & Schuster, 1962.

The Empty Hours (three novellas), Simon & Schuster, 1962.

Ten Plus One, Simon & Schuster, 1963.

Ax, Simon & Schuster, 1964.

He Who Hesitates, Delacorte, 1965.

Doll, Delacorte, 1965.

Eighty Million Eyes, Delacorte, 1966.

The 87th Precinct (includes *Cop Hater*, *The Mugger*, *The Pusher*, and *The Con Man*), Boardman, 1966.

Fuzz (also see below), Doubleday, 1968.

Shotgun, Doubleday, 1969.

Jigsaw, Doubleday, 1970.

Hail, Hail, the Gang's All Here, Doubleday, 1971.

Sadie When She Died, Doubleday, 1972.

Let's Hear It for the Deaf Man, Doubleday, 1972.

87th Precinct: An Ed McBain Omnibus, Hamish Hamilton, 1973.

Hail to the Chief, Random House, 1973.

Bread, Random House, 1974.

The Second 87th Precinct Omnibus, Hamish Hamilton, 1975.

Blood Relatives, Random House, 1975.

So Long as You Both Shall Live, Random House, 1976.

Long Time No See, Random House, 1977.

Calypso, Viking, 1979.

Ghosts, Viking, 1980.

Heat, Viking, 1981.

Ice, Arbor House, 1983.
Lightning, Arbor House, 1984.
Eight Black Horses, Avon, 1985.
Poison, Morrow, 1987.
Tricks, Morrow, 1987.
McBain's Ladies: The Women of the 87th Precinct, Mysterious Press, 1988.
Lullaby, Morrow, 1989.
McBain's Ladies, Too, Mysterious Press, 1989.
Vespers, Morrow, 1990.
Widows, Morrow, 1991.
Kiss, Morrow, 1992.
Mischief, Morrow, 1993.
Romance, Warner, 1995.
Nocturne, Warner, 1997.

UNDER PSEUDONYM ED McBAIN; "MATTHEW HOPE" SERIES; CRIME NOVELS

Goldilocks, Arbor House, 1978.
Rumpelstiltskin, Viking, 1981.
Beauty and the Beast, Hamish Hamilton, 1982, Holt, 1983.
Jack and the Beanstalk, Holt, 1984.
Snow White and Rose Red, Holt, 1986.
Cinderella, Holt, 1986.
Puss in Boots, Holt, 1987.
The House That Jack Built, Holt, 1988.
Three Blind Mice, Mysterious Press, 1991.
Mary, Mary, Warner, 1993.
All through the House, Warner, 1994.
There Was a Little Girl, Warner, 1994.
Gladly, the Cross-Eyed Bear, Warner, 1996.

UNDER PSEUDONYM RICHARD MARSTEN

Rocket to Luna (juvenile), Winston, 1953.
Danger: Dinosaurs (juvenile), Winston, 1953.
Runaway Black (crime novel), Fawcett, 1954.
Murder in the Navy (crime novel), Fawcett, 1955, published under pseudonym Ed McBain as *Death of a Nurse,* Pocket Books, 1968.
The Spiked Heel (crime novel), Holt, 1956.
Vanishing Ladies (crime novel), Pocket Books, 1957.
Even the Wicked (crime novel), Permabooks, 1957, published in England under pseudonym Ed McBain, Severn House, 1979.
Big Man (crime novel), Pocket Books, 1959, published in England under pseudonym Ed McBain, Penguin, 1978.
(Contributor) Leo Marguiles, editor, *Dames, Danger, and Death,* Pyramid, 1960.

PLAYS; UNDER NAME EVAN HUNTER

The Easter Man, produced in Birmingham, England, at Birmingham Repertory Theatre, 1964, produced under title *A Race of Hairy Men!* on Broadway at Henry Miller's Theater, April, 1965.
The Conjuror, produced in Ann Arbor, MI, at Lydia Mendelssohn Theatre, November 5, 1969.
Stalemate, produced in New York City, 1975.

SCREENPLAYS AND TELEVISION SCRIPTS; UNDER NAME EVAN HUNTER

Strangers When We Meet (based on author's novel of same title), Columbia Pictures Industries, Inc., 1960.
The Birds (based on short story by Daphne du Maurier), Universal Pictures, 1963.
Fuzz (based on author's novel of same title), United Artists Corp., 1972.
Walk Proud (based on author's novel of same title), Universal, 1979.
The Chisholms (Columbia Broadcasting System miniseries and weekly television series), Alan Landsburg Productions, 1979-80.

OTHER

Also author of *Appointment at Eleven* for *Alfred Hitchcock Presents,* 1955-61. The Mugar Memorial Library of Boston University holds Hunter's manuscripts.

ADAPTATIONS: Several of Hunter's novels have been made into movies, including *The Blackboard Jungle,* Metro-Goldwyn-Mayer, Inc., 1955; *Cop Hater,* United Artists Corp., 1958; *The Muggers* (based on *The Mugger*), United Artists, 1958; *The Pusher,* United Artists, 1960; *The Young Savages* (based on *A Matter of Conviction*), United Artists, 1961; *High and Low* (based on *King's Ransom*), Toho International, 1963; *Mr. Buddwing* (based on *Buddwing*), Metro-Goldwyn-Mayer, 1967; *Last Summer,* Twentieth Century-Fox Film Corp., 1969; *Sans Mobile apparent* (title means "Without Apparent Motive"; based on *Ten Plus One*), President Films, 1971; *Le Cri du cormoran le soir au-dessus des jonques* (title means "The Cry of the Cormorant at Night over the Junks"; based on *A Horse's Head*), Gaumont International, 1971; and *Every Little Crook and Nanny,* Metro-Goldwyn-Mayer, 1972.

SIDELIGHTS: With numerous novels, short stories, plays, and film scripts to his credit, Evan Hunter ranks as one of today's most versatile, prolific and bestselling writers. Known to millions throughout the world under his pseudonym, Ed McBain (originator of the "87th Precinct" detective series), Hunter is also the author (under his own name) of such thought-provoking best-sellers as *The Blackboard Jungle, Strangers When We Meet, Mothers and Daughters,* and *Last Summer.* He prefers to keep these two identities strictly separate, he explains, because "I don't like to confuse critics who are very easily confused anyway. I also do not like to confuse readers. I wouldn't like a woman, for example, who had read *Mothers and Daughters* by Evan Hunter, to pick up *The Heckler* by Evan Hunter and find that it's about mayhem, bloodshed and violence. I think this would be unfair to her and unfair to me as well."

Though it appeared four years after Hunter made his first serious attempts to write for publication, *The Blackboard Jungle* caused the twenty-eight-year-old author to be labeled an "overnight" success. A semi-autobiographical work, *The Blackboard Jungle* tells the story of an idealistic young man who confronts the often violent realities of trying to teach a group of sullen, illiterate, delinquent teenagers in a big-city vocational high school. Written in what was then politely termed the "vernacular," Hunter's dramatic indictment of both the inadequacies of teacher training colleges and of the New York City school system is "a nightmarish but authentic first novel," according to a *Time* critic. The *New York Herald Tribune Book Review*'s Barbara Klaw points to Hunter's "superb ear for conversation," "competence as a storyteller," and "tolerant and tough-minded sympathy for his subject" as some of the book's best features, while Nathan Rothman of the *Saturday Review* feels that it is free of the "distortions and dishonesty" of many newspaper articles on the same topic. And even though the *Nation*'s Stanley Cooperman believes that Hunter "makes only cursory attempts to probe the wellsprings of the action he photographs so well," he concludes that the ex-substitute teacher "succeeds in dramatizing an area heretofore neglected in fiction."

Hunter is frequently praised for the consistently high standard of professionalism evident in his writing. He told *CA:* "When I was beginning to write, I wrote a great many detective stories for the pulp magazines. I wrote not only police stories, but private eye and man-on-the-run and woman-in-jeopardy, the whole gamut. After *The Blackboard Jungle* was pub-

lished, Pocket Books did the reprint of it. I had an old mystery novel kicking around that I had not yet sold, and there was a pseudonym on it, but not Ed McBain. We sent it to Pocket Books as a possibility for a paperback original. The editor there at the time, a man named Herbert Alexander, was a very bright guy. He recognized the style and called my agent and said, 'Is this our friend Hunter?' My agent said, 'Yes, it is,' and Alexander said, 'Well, I'd like to talk to him.'

"We had lunch one day," Hunter continues, "and the gist of the conversation was that the mainstay of Pocket Books was Erle Stanley Gardner; he had sold millions of books and they would just republish each title every three or four years with new jackets. They kept selling as if they were new books all the time. But he was getting old and they were looking for a mystery writer who could replace him, so they asked me if I had any ideas about a mystery series. I said I would think about it. I got back to them and I said that it seemed to me—after all the mysteries I'd written—that the only *valid* people to deal with crime were cops, and I would like to make the lead character, rather than a single *person,* a *squad* of cops instead—so it would be a *conglomerate* lead character. They said, 'OK, we'll give you a contract for three books and if it works we'll renew it.' I started writing the series."

Hunter's "87th Precinct" novels are known as "police procedurals" in the mystery trade. "The nice thing about the '87th Precinct' is that I can deal with any subject matter so long as it's criminally related," Hunter told Gale. "With the Ed McBain novels, I only want to say that cops have a tough, underpaid job, and they deal with murder every day of the week, and that's the way it is, folks. With the Hunters, the theme varies and I'll usually ponder the next book for a long, long time—until it demands to be written."

Kiss, an example of one of Hunter's "87th Precinct" novels, concerns Steve Carella, a police detective in Isola, a city that bears a striking resemblance to New York. Carella winds his way through a series of events that lead him to being involved with his father's killer. The plot also twists around Carella investigating the attempted murder of a stockbroker's wife.

Criminal Conversation, a novel written under Hunter's own name, was purchased by Tom Cruise's production company for use as a potential motion picture starring Nicole Kidman. In the book, Michael Welles is an assistant district attorney whose assignment is to find incriminating evidence on mobster Andrew Faviola. During video surveillance of Faviola, Welles discovers that his wife is having an affair with the crime boss. Welles is then torn between his dedication to his job and his love of his wife. Chris Petrakos of the *Chicago Tribune* complains that the "characters seem a little thin," but overall commends the novel's fast pace and interesting plot. Michael Anderson, writing in the *New York Times Book Review*, feels that some of the story is derivative, but he praises the storytelling and pacing, commenting that Hunter "unfolds them like the master he is."

There Was a Little Girl is one of Hunter's Matthew Hope mysteries. Hope, however, is unconscious through most of the action of the novel. His condition remains a mystery until his colleagues are able to untangle the events leading up to his coma. The trail of evidence leads them to Hope's most recent job, looking for land for a circus. Part of the problem with this novel, claims Richard Gid Powers in the *New York Times Book Review*, is that by getting Hope out of the action "you have to identify with the supporting characters and, frankly, they are not of star caliber." Yet, he concludes that "this is an amazingly accomplished, richly enjoyable three-ring circus of a book directed by a ringmaster at the top of his form, action everywhere, with color, noise and confusion all suddenly resolving themselves into perfect logical order." John Skow comments in *Time* that "the author's secret appears to be the steadiness of his gaze. He looks straight at whatever he is describing, concentrating utterly . . . on, say, why bears are more dangerous than tigers in animal acts."

Most of Hunter's other novels exhibit definite thematic concerns, occasionally inspired by biographical or autobiographical material, but often just "intellectual concepts that come to me and take a while to develop before they're put down on paper." He has written a great deal about young people, especially the relationship between the young and the old (usually parents). "I don't know why I've been attracted to writing about young people," he once remarked to a *Publishers Weekly* interviewer. "I guess from *Blackboard Jungle*, it's been a situation that's always appealed to me, the idea of adults in conflict with the young. I think part of my fascination is with America as an adolescent nation and with our so- called adult responses that are sometimes adolescent."

Often these same novels contain elements of current topical interest as well—the state of the American educational system in *The Blackboard Jungle,* the emptiness of post-World War II middle-class life in *Mothers and Daughters,* the Vietnam War in *Sons,* and the anti-Establishment "hippie" movement of the late 1960s and early 1970s in *Love, Dad.* The *New York Times Book Review*'s Ivan Gold concludes, "Mr. Hunter is a serious and honorable writer trying to entertain us, and also trying to tell us, now and again, some useful things about our lives." As Hunter himself once explained to the *Publishers Weekly* interviewer, "The whole reason I write anything is so that someone somewhere will say, 'Oh, yeah. I feel that way too. I'm not alone.'"

BIOGRAPHICAL/CRITICAL SOURCES:

BOOKS

Contemporary Literary Criticism, Gale, Volume 11, 1979, Volume 31, 1985.
Newquist, Roy, *Conversations,* Rand McNally, 1967.

PERIODICALS

Armchair Detective, summer, 1992, p. 282; spring, 1995, p. 104.
Best Sellers, June 15, 1968; August 15, 1969; March 15, 1971.
Books, June, 1970.
Books and Bookmen, January, 1969.
Catholic World, August, 1958.
Chicago Sunday Tribune, January 22, 1956; June 8, 1958; May 28, 1961.
Choice, June, 1970.
Detroit News, January 16, 1983.
Globe and Mail (Toronto), October 19, 1985; June 21, 1986; February 28, 1987.
Harper's, December, 1967; June, 1968.
Kirkus Reviews, February 15, 1993, p. 175; June 15, 1993, p. 745.
Los Angeles Times, May 14, 1981; February 4, 1983.
Los Angeles Times Book Review, May 8, 1994, p. 11.
Nation, December 4, 1954.
New Statesman, January 10, 1969.
Newsweek, March 8, 1971.
New Yorker, January 13, 1975.
New York Herald Tribune Book Review, October 17, 1954; January 15, 1956; July 20, 1958.
New York Herald Tribune Lively Arts, May 21, 1961.

New York Times, January 8, 1956; June 15, 1958; June 12, 1968; April 10, 1981; April 19, 1985; February 20, 1987; July 3, 1987.

New York Times Book Review, May 28, 1961; October 20, 1968; July 16, 1969; September 28, 1969; September 19, 1976; May 6, 1979; May 10, 1981; May 22, 1994, p. 35; October 2, 1994, p. 27; February 16, 1996, p. 27; April 16, 1995, p. 29; April 14, 1996, p. 21.

Observer (London), April 5, 1970.

People, December 19, 1977; April 3, 1995, p. 97.

Publishers Weekly, April 3, 1981; November 29, 1991, p. 48; March 21, 1994, p. 53; December 18, 1995, p. 39.

San Francisco Chronicle, July 9, 1961.

Saturday Review, October 9, 1954; January 7, 1956; April 24, 1971; September 9, 1972.

Springfield Republican, July 9, 1961.

Time, October 11, 1954; June 9, 1958; March 8, 1971; April 26, 1993, p. 65; October 17, 1994, p. 84.

Times (London), August 20, 1981; September 11, 1982; July 11, 1985.

Times Literary Supplement, November 21, 1958; July 28, 1961; January 25, 1968; May 28, 1970; July 13, 1973.

Tribune Books (Chicago), February 2, 1992; May 15, 1994, p. 7.

Virginia Quarterly Review, summer, 1968.

Washington Post Book World, March 29, 1981; January 19, 1983; June 24, 1984; March 15, 1992, p. 10; April 16, 1995, p. 6.

Writer, April, 1969.

Writer's Digest, April, 1971.

*　*　*

JAMES, C(yril) L(ionel) R(obert) 1901-1989
(J. R. Johnson)

PERSONAL: Born January 4, 1901, in Chaguanas, Trinidad and Tobago; died of a chest infection, May 31, 1989, in London, England; son of a schoolteacher; divorced from first wife; married Constance Webb (marriage ended); married Selma Weinstein, 1955; children: (first marriage) one. *Education:* Graduated from Queen's Royal College secondary school, Port of Spain, 1918.

CAREER: Member of the Maple cricket team, Port of Spain, Trinidad and Tobago; *Trinidad* (literary magazine), Port of Spain, editor, 1929-30; Queen's

Royal College, Port of Spain, teacher, until 1932; *Manchester Guardian,* London, England, correspondent, 1932-38; *Fight* (later *Workers' Fight;* Marxist publication), London, editor, until 1938; trade union organizer and political activist in the United States, 1938-53; West Indian Federal Labor Party, Port of Spain, secretary, 1958-60; *Nation,* Port of Spain, editor, 1958-60. Lecturer at colleges and universities, including Federal City College, Washington, DC; commentator for the British Broadcasting Corporation (BBC); cricket columnist for *Race Today.*

AWARDS, HONORS: Honorary Doctor of Literature, University of the West Indies.

WRITINGS:

The Life of Captain Cipriani: An Account of British Government in the West Indies, Nelson, Lancashire, Coulton, 1932, abridged edition published as *The Case for West-Indian Self-Government,* Hogarth, 1933, University Place Book Shop, 1967.

(With L. R. Constantine) *Cricket and I,* Allan, 1933.

Minty Alley (novel), Secker & Warburg, 1936, New Beacon, 1971.

Toussaint L'Ouverture (play; first produced in London, 1936; revised version titled *The Black Jacobins* and produced in Ibadan, Nigeria, 1967), published in *A Time and a Season: Eight Caribbean Plays,* edited by Errol Hill, University of the West Indies (Port of Spain), 1976.

World Revolution, 1917-1936: The Rise and Fall of the Communist International, Pioneer, 1937, Hyperion Press, 1973, Humanities Press, 1993.

A History of Negro Revolt, Fact, 1938, Haskell House, 1967, revised and expanded edition published as *A History of Pan-African Revolt,* Drum and Spear Press, 1969.

The Black Jacobins: Toussaint L'Ouverture and the San Domingo Revolution, Dial, 1938, Random House, 1963.

(Translator from the French) Boris Souvarine, *Stalin: A Critical Survey of Socialism,* Longman, 1939.

State Capitalism and World Revolution (published anonymously), privately printed, 1950, Facing Reality, 1969.

Mariners, Renegades, and Castaways: The Story of Herman Melville and the World We Live In, privately printed, 1953, Bewick Editions, 1978.

Modern Politics (lectures), PNM (Port of Spain), 1960.

Beyond a Boundary, Hutchinson, 1963, Pantheon, 1984.

The Hegelian Dialectic and Modern Politics, Facing Reality, 1970, revised edition published as *Notes on Dialectics: Hegel, Marx, Lenin,* Lawrence Hill, 1980.

The Future in the Present: Selected Writings of C. L. R. James, Lawrence Hill, 1977.

(Under pseudonym J. R. Johnson) *The Books of American Negro Spirituals,* edited by James Weldon Johnson, Da Capo Press, 1977.

Nkrumah and the Ghana Revolution, Lawrence Hill, 1977, revised edition, Allison & Busby, 1982.

(With Tony Bogues and Kim Gordon) *Black Nationalism and Socialism,* Socialists Unlimited, 1979.

(With George Breitman, Edgar Keemer, and others) *Fighting Racism in World War II,* Monad, 1980.

Spheres of Existence: Selected Writings, Lawrence Hill, 1981.

Eightieth Birthday Lectures, Race Today, 1983.

At the Rendezvous of Victory: Selected Writings, Lawrence Hill, 1985.

Cricket, Allison & Busby, 1986.

The C. L. R. James Reader, edited by Anna Grimshaw, Blackwell, 1992.

American Civilization, edited by Grimshaw and Keith Hart, Blackwell, 1993.

Special Delivery: The Letters of C. L. R. James to Constance Webb, 1939-1948, Blackwell, 1995.

C. L. R. James on the "Negro Question," edited by Scott McLemee, University Press of Mississippi, 1996.

Contributor of short stories to the collections *The Best Short Stories of 1928,* Cape, 1928, and *Island Voices,* Liveright, 1970; author, sometimes under pseudonym J. R. Johnson, of numerous political pamphlets; contributor of articles to newspapers and magazines.

WORK IN PROGRESS: An autobiography.

SIDELIGHTS: C. L. R. James was a leading political and literary figure from Trinidad and Tobago whose interests and values were profoundly shaped by his experiences growing up in this British West Indian colony at the beginning of the century. James, whose father was a schoolteacher, was raised in the capital of Port of Spain in a middle-class, somewhat puritanical, black family suffused in British manners and culture. The James family home faced the back of a cricket field, and young Cyril developed a lifelong passion for the baseball-like sport watching matches from his living room window. He also grew up with an intense love for English literature—at age ten he had memorized long passages of William Makepeace

Thackeray's *Vanity Fair*—and both his reading and his cricket playing often distracted him from his studies at the elite Queen's Royal College in Port of Spain. Dashing his parents' hopes that he would pursue a political career with the colonial administration, James chose instead to play professional cricket and teach at the Queen's Royal College in the 1920s. At the same time, he began documenting the conditions under which his nation's lower-class citizens lived; the resulting series of naturalistic short stories shocked his peers and foreshadowed his future interest in Marxism. James's firsthand study of the Port of Spain slums also furnished background for his only novel, *Minty Alley,* an affecting but unsentimental look at the complex personal relationships and humble aspirations of the denizens of a rundown boarding house.

In 1932, chafing under the placid routines of a life in a colonial backwater, James accepted an invitation to go to London to help the great black cricketer Learie Constantine of Trinidad and Tobago write his autobiography. With Constantine's help, James secured a job as a cricket correspondent with the *Manchester Guardian* and published his first nonfiction book, *The Life of Captain Cipriani: An Account of British Government in the West Indies* (later abridged and published as *The Case for West-Indian Self-Government*). This influential treatise—one of the first to urge full self-determination for West Indians—introduced James to leading figures in the two political movements that were to profoundly shape his thinking in the years to come: Pan Africanism and Marxism.

James first developed his Pan Africanist ideas while working in activist George Padmore's London-based African Bureau, where he joined future African independence leaders Jomo Kenyatta and Kwame Nkrumah as a political propagandist in the mid-1930s. James emphasized the importance of West Indians' coming to terms with their African heritage in order to help forge a sense of national identity in their racially and culturally diverse society. He also came to regard the struggle to liberate and politically unify colonial Africa as a way of inspiring and mobilizing oppressed people of color around the world to seize control of their destinies. James later examined Pan Africanist theory and practice in two historical works, *A History of Negro Revolt* (later revised and published as *A History of Pan-African Revolt*), which surveys nearly two centuries of the black liberation struggle against European colonialism, and *Nkrumah and the Ghana Revolution,* an analysis of the first successful independence movement in modern Africa.

While participating in the vanguard of the African liberation movement, James also became a committed Marxist during his sojourn in London in the 1930s. He sided with the Trotskyists during the great dispute over Stalinism that split the world communist movement during those years, and he wrote a history book from that perspective in 1937 titled *World Revolution, 1917-1936: The Rise and Fall of the Communist International.* James's Marxism also informed his 1938 historical study *The Black Jacobins: Toussaint L'Ouverture and the San Domingo Revolution.* In this book, generally regarded as his masterwork, James analyzes the socioeconomic roots and leading personalities of the Haitian revolution of 1791 to 1804, the first and only slave revolt to achieve political independence in world history.

At the center of the revolution and the book stands Toussaint L'Ouverture. The self-taught black slave turned charismatic political leader and redoubtable military commander organized and led a disciplined army of former slaves, who defeated crack French and British expeditionary forces mustered to crush the insurgency. Of particular interest in *The Black Jacobins,* critics noted, is the author's success in relating the Haitian events to the course of the French Revolution, whose ideals inspired Toussaint even as he fought first Maximilien Robespierre and then Napoleon Bonaparte to free France's most important Caribbean sugar colony, then known as Saint Domingue. The democratic ideals of the Haitian revolution, which culminated in full political independence a year after Toussaint's death in 1803, touched off a wave of slave revolts throughout the Caribbean and helped inspire anti-slavery forces in the southern United States. *New York Herald Tribune Books* reviewer Clara Gruening Stillman judged *The Black Jacobins* as gripping as the events it recounted: "Brilliantly conceived and executed, throwing upon the historical screen a mass of dramatic figures, lurid scenes, fantastic happenings, the absorbing narrative never departs from its rigid faithfulness to method and documentation." A stage version of the book was first performed in 1936, with renowned actor Paul Robeson cast as Toussaint. In the mid-1980s, the play was revived by Yvonne Brewster's Talawa company.

Shortly after publishing *The Black Jacobins,* James moved to the United States, where he joined the Trotskyist Socialist Workers Party (SWP) and became a full-time political activist, organizing auto workers in Detroit, Michigan, and tenant farmers in the South. He broke with the SWP in the late 1940s over the question of the nature of the Soviet Union, which he dubbed "state capitalist," and co-founded a new Detroit-based Trotskyist political organization with Leon Trotsky's former secretary Raya Dunayevskaya. James's political activities eventually provoked the wrath of the McCarthy-era U.S. government, which denied him American citizenship and deported him to Great Britain in 1953. While awaiting his expulsion on Ellis Island, the ever-resourceful James managed to write a short study of Herman Melville, *Mariners, Renegades, and Castaways: The Story of Herman Melville and the World We Live In,* that drew a parallel between Ahab's pursuit of the great white whale in Melville's classic, *Moby Dick,* and left-wing intellectuals' infatuation with Soviet political leader Joseph Stalin.

After five years in London, James returned to Trinidad and Tobago in 1958 to join the movement for political independence there. In Port of Spain he edited *Nation* magazine and served as secretary of the West Indian Federal Labor Party, whose leader, Eric Williams, became the island nation's first premier in 1960. Like the United States authorities, however, Williams found James's outspoken Marxism politically threatening and soon compelled James, who had once been Williams's schoolmaster, to go back to England. James left Trinidad and Tobago aggrieved that the emerging Caribbean nations had failed to achieve a lasting formula for political federation, which he believed necessary to further their social and economic development.

Back in London, James returned to political writing and lecturing, particularly on the Pan Africanist movement, West Indian politics, and the issue of racism in the United States. He also rekindled his passion for cricket after leading a successful campaign to have Frank Worrell of Trinidad and Tobago named the first black captain of the West Indian international cricket team. Worrell's spectacular playing at the Australian championship competition in 1961 galvanized a sense of national pride and identity among the emerging West Indian nations and partly inspired James to write *Beyond a Boundary,* his much-praised 1963 survey of cricket's social and cultural significance in Great Britain and the Caribbean. The book's title refers both to the game's objective of driving a ball beyond a marked boundary and James's thesis that this gentleman's sport can help overcome certain false cultural, racial, and political boundaries within society. On a purely aesthetic level, James argues, cricket has "the perfect flow of motion" that defines the essence of all great art; he holds that a good cricket match is the visual and dramatic equivalent of so-called "high art" and that the sport should be recognized as a genuinely democratic art form. Cricket's high standards of fairness and sportsmanship, on the other hand, illustrate "all the decencies required for a culture" and even played a historic role by showing West Indian blacks that they could excel in a forum where the rules were equal for everyone. The integrated Caribbean cricket teams, James believes, helped forge a new black self-confidence that carried the West Indian colonies to independence. The author renders these observations in an anecdotal style that includes both biographical sketches of great cricketers and personal reminiscences from his own lifelong love affair with the sport. "*Beyond a Boundary* is one of the finest and most finished books to come out of the West Indies," remarked novelist V. S. Naipaul in *Encounter.* "There is no more eloquent brief for the cultural and artistic importance of sport," added *Newsweek*'s Jim Miller.

Before his death in 1989, James published two well-received collections of essays and articles that display his broad literary, cultural, and political interests. *The Future in the Present: Selected Writings of C. L. R. James* contains the author's short story "Triumph," about women tenants in a Port of Spain slum, along with essays ranging from critical interpretations of Pablo Picasso's painting "Guernica" and Melville's *Moby Dick* to a political analysis of workers' councils in Hungary and a personal account of organizing a sharecroppers' strike in Missouri in 1942. "The writings are profound, sometimes; cranky, occasionally; stimulating, always," remarked *Village Voice* critic Paul Berman. *Times Literary Supplement* reviewer Thomas Hodgkin found the book "a mine of richness and variety." *At the Rendezvous of Victory: Selected Writings,* whose title James took from a verse by the great West Indian poet Aime Cesaire, includes an essay on the Solidarity union movement in Poland and critical discussions of the work of black American novelists Toni Morrison and Alice Walker. The more than eighty-year-old James "show(ed) no diminution of his intellectual energies," wrote Alastair Niven in his review of the collection for *British Books News.* "Throughout this book James's elegant but unmannered style, witty and relaxed when lecturing, reflective and analytical when writing for publication, always conveys a sense of his own robust, humane, and giving personality. Was there ever a less polemical or more persuasive radical?"

In 1992, James's secretary, Anna Grimshaw, published *The C. L. R. James Reader,* a 450-page anthology of James's numerous unpublished letters and other documents. The book includes letters to James's wife Constance during his 1940s' residence in the United States, and a stage version of *The Black Jacobins.* Clive Davis, in *New Statesman & Society,* observes that "the book is broadly divided between political, literary and cultural analysis." And in 1993, Grimshaw and Keith Hart edited and published James's *American Civilization.* Written in 1950, this text is an extensive (over 300 pages) prose outline for a larger book James had planned to write but never finished. As it stands, the volume presents James's thoughts on the state of democracy in the United States—he recognizes the excessive power and influence of corporations, yet is optimistic about the possibilities for democratic change—and on the effects of popular culture in America, which he sees as generally positive. Ethan Casey, writing in *Callaloo,* lauded James's body of work and stated that "*American Civilization* shows vividly and indisputably that America is a unique phenomenon in world history, with at least latent potential—perhaps even today—to be a genuinely free and benign society."

BIOGRAPHICAL/CRITICAL SOURCES:

BOOKS

Contemporary Literary Criticism, Volume 33, Gale, 1983.

Cudjoe, Selwyn Reginald, and William E. Cain, *C. L. R. James: His Intellectual Legacies,* University of Massachusetts Press, 1995.

Farred, Grant, *Rethinking C. L. R. James,* Blackwell, 1996.

Grimshaw, Anna, editor, *The C. L. R. James Reader,* Blackwell, 1992.

Henry, Paget, and Paul Buhle, *C. L. R. James Caribbean,* Duke University Press, 1992.

James, C. L. R., *The Future in the Present: Selected Writings of C. L. R. James,* Lawrence Hill, 1977.

James, C. L. R., *Beyond a Boundary,* Pantheon, 1984, reprinted, Duke University Press, 1993.

Mackenzine, Alan and Paul Gilroy, *Visions of History,* Pantheon, 1983.

Mclemee, Scott, and Paul Le Blanc, *C. L. R. James and Revolutionary Marxism: Selected Writings of C. L. R. James 1939-1949,* Humanities Press, 1994.

Worcester, Kent, *C. L. R. James: A Political Biography,* State University of New York Press, 1995.

PERIODICALS

American Scholar, summer, 1985.
British Books News, May, 1984.
Callaloo, fall, 1994.
CLA Journal, December, 1977.
Encounter, September, 1963.
Library Journal, March 15, 1994.
Nation, May 4, 1985.
Newsweek, March 26, 1984.
New Statesman & Society, June 26, 1992, p. 40.
New Yorker, June 25, 1984.
New York Herald Tribune Books, November 27, 1938.
New York Times Book Review, March 25, 1984; November 15, 1992, p. 28.
Radical America, May, 1970.
Times Literary Supplement, December 2, 1977; January 20, 1978; September 25, 1987.
Village Voice, February 11, 1981; July 10, 1984.
Washington Post Book World, April 22, 1984.

OBITUARIES:

PERIODICALS

Los Angeles Times, June 3, 1989.
New York Times, June 2, 1989.
Times (London), June 2, 1989.
Washington Post, June 3, 1989.*

*   *   *

JOHNSON, Diane 1934-

PERSONAL: Born April 28, 1934, in Moline, IL; daughter of Dolph and Frances (Elder) Lain; married B. Lamar Johnson, Jr., July, 1953; married second husband, John Frederic Murray (a professor of medicine), May 31, 1968; children: (first marriage) Kevin, Darcy, Amanda, Simon. *Education:* Attended Stephens College, 1951-53; University of Utah, B.A., 1957; University of California, M.A., 1966, Ph.D., 1968.

ADDRESSES: Home—24 Edith Pl., San Francisco, CA 94133. *Office*—Department of English, University of California, Davis, CA 95616. *Agent*—Lynn Nesbitt, Nesbit-Janklow, New York, NY 10019.

CAREER: Author. University of California, Davis, assistant professor, then professor of English, 1968-87; held Harold and Mildred Strauss Living stipend from the American Academy of Arts and Letters, 1988-92.

MEMBER: International PEN.

AWARDS, HONORS: National Book Award nomination, 1973, for *Lesser Lives,* and 1979, for *Lying Low;* Guggenheim fellowship, 1977-78; Rosenthal Award, American Academy and Institute of Arts and Letters, 1979; Pulitzer Prize nomination in general nonfiction, 1983, for *Terrorists and Novelists; Los Angeles Times* book prize nomination in biography, 1984, for *Dashiell Hammett: A Life;* Pulitzer Prize nomination, 1987, for *Persian Nights;* and a *Los Angeles Times* medal, 1994.

WRITINGS:

NOVELS

Fair Game, Harcourt (New York City), 1965.
Loving Hands at Home, Harcourt, 1968.
Burning, Harcourt, 1971.
The Shadow Knows (also see below), Knopf (New York City), 1974.
Lying Low, Knopf, 1978.
Persian Nights, Knopf, 1987.
Health and Happiness, Knopf, 1990.
Le Divorce, Dutton (New York City), 1997.

BIOGRAPHY

Lesser Lives: The True History of the First Mrs. Meredith, Knopf, 1973, published in England as *The True History of the First Mrs. Meredith and Other Lesser Lives,* Heinemann (London), 1973.
Dashiell Hammett: A Life (also see below), Random House (New York City), 1983.

SCREENPLAYS

(With Stanley Kubrick) *The Shining* (based on the Stephen King novel of the same title), Warner Brothers, 1980.

Also author of unproduced screenplays *Grand Hotel, The Shadow Knows* (based on her novel of the same title), and *Hammett* (based on her biography *Dashiell Hammett: A Life*).

OTHER

(Author of preface) John Ruskin, *King of the Golden River* [and] Charles Dickens, *A Holiday Romance* [and] Tom Hood, *Petsetilla's Posy,* Garland Publishing (New York City), 1976.

(Author of preface) Margaret Gatty, *Parables of Nature,* Garland Publishing, 1976.

(Author of preface) George Sand, *Mauprat,* Da Capo Press (New York City), 1977.

Terrorists and Novelists (collected essays), Knopf, 1982.

(Author of preface) *Tales and Stories of E. A. Poe,* Vintage, 1991.

Natural Opium: Some Travelers' Tales, Knopf, 1993.

Also author of preface to *Frankenstein* by Mary Shelley, c. 1979, and to *Josephine Herhst: Collected Works,* 1990. Contributor of essays and book reviews to periodicals, including the *New York Times, New York Review of Books, San Francisco Chronicle,* and *Washington Post.*

WORK IN PROGRESS: "A novel set in France."

SIDELIGHTS: In an age when writers tend to be pigeonholed, Diane Johnson remains a difficult author to categorize. Perhaps best known as an essayist and biographer, she got her start as a novelist and continues to write successfully in this vein. She is a teacher and scholar, with expertise in nineteenth-century literature, yet she also lent a hand in writing the screenplay for *The Shining,* a popular horror film. And while her initial focus was on women and their problems in society, she has since written sympathetically of a man who faced similar difficulties in *Dashiell Hammett: A Life.* Even her early works, which have been claimed as the province of feminists, were intended to cast a wider net, as Johnson explained to Susan Groag Bell in *Women Writers of the West Coast:* "The kinds of crises, the particular troubles that I assign to my women characters, these are not necessarily meant to be feminist complaints. . . . In my mind, they may be more metaphysical or general. That sounds awfully pretentious, but I guess what I mean is that I'm not trying to write manifestos about female independence, but human lives."

Like many artists, Johnson sees herself as a craftsperson whose work should be judged on its merits as literature, not—as is often the case with women writers—on moral or extraliterary grounds. In her highly acclaimed collection of book reviews and essays, *Terrorists and Novelists,* Johnson addresses the particular problems faced by female novelists, chiding those male critics who "have not learned to read books by women and imagine them all to be feminist polemics." She told Bell, "The writer wants to be praised for the management of formal and technical aspects of the narrative and wide-ranging perceptions about society and perhaps the quality of her sensibility, not her own character, and, mainly you want your book to be a success on its own terms."

Though several of her novels and one of her biographies have California settings, Johnson was born and raised in Moline, Illinois. Her childhood was untroubled: the first child of middle-aged parents, she lived in the same house surrounded by neighboring aunts and uncles until she went away to college at seventeen. She describes herself as a "puny, bookish little child, with thick glasses," and told *Los Angeles Times* reporter Beverly Beyette that she was "the kind of whom you say, 'Let's take her to the library on Saturday.' I was typecast, but I was a type." When she was nineteen, Johnson married her first husband, then a UCLA medical student, and relocated to the West Coast where she has remained.

Despite her long residence in California, Johnson told Bell that "a certain view of life, which I very much obtained from my Illinois childhood, does inform my work. In a couple of my books I have put a middle-western protagonist, always somebody who's displaced like I am, looking at the mess of today. This person remembers an orderly society from which subsequent events have seemed to depart." She maintains that it is the turmoil of modern society, rather than a personal preoccupation with disorder, that leads to the prevalence of violence in her books. "She is not sensational, sentimental, nor simple-minded," suggests *Critique: Studies in Modern Fiction* contributor Marjorie Ryan, who points out that Johnson writes in "the satiric-comic-realistic tradition, in a mode that may not appeal to readers nurtured on the personal, subjective, and doctrinaire."

In her early fiction, *Fair Game, Loving Hands at Home,* and *Burning,* Johnson employs "a comic tone" as well as "a central female character who is uncertain about how to conduct her life," according to Judith S. Baughman in the *Dictionary of Literary Biography Yearbook*. In each of these novels, a woman who has ventured outside the boundaries of convention "has a shocking experience which sends her back inside, but only temporarily until another experience . . . either sends her outside again or changes her whole perspective," Ryan explains.

As is often the case with a writer's first fruits, these early novels largely escaped the notice of critics—at least initially. By the time *Burning* appeared, there were flickers of interest, though it was Johnson's potential as a novelist rather than the work at hand that attracted praise. Much criticism was leveled at Johnson's choice of subject. A Southern California story of disaster, *Burning* was viewed as a genre novel that had been approached in the same fashion many times before. As R. R. Davies put it, "Group therapy and the drug-induced self-analysis of depressed citizens have been done to death as satirical material." Though *Newsweek*'s Peter Prescott finds Johnson "witty and serious," he contends that she "tries to be both at once and doesn't make it. Her book should have been either much funnier, or much grimmer or, failing that, she should have been much better." *Book World* contributor J. R. Frakes compares the crowded canvas of Johnson's apocalyptic tale to "a twelve ring circus" and welcomes its disastrous ending "almost as a relief," but then goes on to praise Johnson's style, noting that she "superintends this asylum with cool disdain and a remarkable neo-classic elegance of phrase, sentence, and chapter. It is comforting to know that someone competent is in charge."

Her competence established, Johnson began to attract more serious attention, and her fourth novel, *The Shadow Knows,* was widely reviewed. Originally set in Los Angeles, the story was relocated to Sacramento because, as the author explained to Bell, "I decided after the reception of *Burning* that Los Angeles was too loaded a place in the minds of readers." The novel takes its title from an old radio melodrama (which featured the line, "Who knows what evil lurks in the hearts of men? The Shadow knows.") and focuses on one terror-filled week in the life of a young divorcee and mother of four known simply as N. When someone slashes her tires, leaves a strangled cat on her doorstep, threatens her over the telephone, and beats up her babysitter in the basement laundry room, N. becomes convinced that she is marked for murder. But who is the assailant? Her spiteful former husband? The wife of her mar-

ried lover? The psychotic black woman who used to care for her children? Her jealous friend Bess, who comes to visit with a hunting knife in her purse? Or, worst of all, is it some nameless stranger, an embodiment of evil she does not even know? N.'s attempt to identify her enemy, and her imaginary dialogue with the Famous Inspector she conjures up to help her, make up the heart of the book.

Writing in the *New Statesman,* A. S. Byatt describes the novel as a "cunning cross between the intensely articulate plaint of the under-extended intelligent woman and a conventional mystery, shading into a psychological horror-story." *Nation* contributor Sandra M. Gilbert calls it "a sort of bitter parody of a genre invented by nineteenth-century men: the detective novel." Though it masquerades as a thriller, most reviewers acknowledge that *The Shadow Knows* is really a woman's story in which N. abandons what she calls her "safe" life to follow one that is "reckless and riddled with mistakes."

"In her attempts to create a fresh, true identity unconfined by the usual social and familial influences, N. must penetrate the evils which lurk in the hearts of men, even in her own heart in order to find her 'way in the dark,'" writes Baughman. "Thus, she has not only to uncover her potential murderer but also to deal with her own considerable problems and confusions. . . . Because the pressures upon her are so great, the possibility arises that N.'s terrors are powerful projections of her own sense of guilt and confusion rather than appropriate responses to the malevolent acts of an outside aggressor." Some reviewers go so far as to suggest that N.'s problems are more imagined than real. "Understandably, N. would like to know who's doing all these bad things to her, if only to be sure that she's not making it all up," writes Thomas R. Edwards in the *New York Review of Books*. "And since we also wonder if she may not be doing that, we share her desire for knowledge."

In her interview with Bell, Johnson asserted that such disbelief stems more from readers' biases than from the way the protagonist is portrayed. "There's [a] problem that comes from having as your central character a female person," said Johnson. "The male narrative voice is still accorded more authority. The female narrative voice is always questioned—is she crazy? Are the things she's saying a delusion, or reality? The narrator in *The Shadow Knows* was intended as an exact and trustworthy reporter of what was happening to her. But many reviewers, while in general liking her, also questioned her about her hysteria, her paranoia, her untrustworthiness. Is she mad or sane? So I began to notice that female narrators, if they're of a sexual age, of a reproductive age, of an age to have affairs, aren't considered trustworthy. . . . Nonetheless, I write about women of childbearing age, because I like to fly in the face of these prejudices and hope that I can make them authoritative and trustworthy reporters."

While women still figure prominently in Johnson's next novel, *Lying Low,* the focus has shifted from psychological to political concerns and from one protagonist to several. The book, which covers four days in the lives of four characters who inhabit a boarding house in Orris, California, is a "mosaic-like juxtaposition of small paragraphs, each containing a short description, a bit of action, reflections of one of the principal characters, or a mixture of all three," according to Robert Towers in the *New York Times Book Review.* Praising its artful construction, elegant style, and delicate perceptions, Towers calls *Lying Low* "a nearly flawless performance. . . . Despite the lack of any headlong narrative rush, one's interest in the working out of the story is maintained at a high level by the skillful, unobtrusive distribution of plot fragments." *Newsweek's* Peter Prescott says it "represents a triumph of sensibility over plot" and observes that, like other feminist novels, it is "most convincing when least dramatic. Condition, not action, is [its] true concern: the problems of women confronting, or trying to ignore, their desperate lot."

Johnson's skill at rendering domestic crises makes *Saturday Review* contributor Katha Pollitt "wish Diane Johnson had kept her canvas small, a comedy or tragicomedy of manners for our decade of extreme political bewilderment. . . . When Johnson aims for a grander drama, though, she is not convincing. . . . The end [in which a bomb explodes, killing one of the main characters], seems a failure of imagination, an apocalypse produced ex machina so that we all get the point about the violence that smolders beneath the American surface." A *New Yorker* critic pronounces the conclusion "an awkward attempt to endow a cerebral narrative with the action of a thriller." And the *New Republic* likens the ending to "one of those simple-minded 1960s films in which the source of all evil is 'Amerika'" and concludes that it "seems much too jarring in a novel as full of subtleties of observation and atmosphere as this one."

Johnson was nominated for a Pulitzer Prize for her 1987 novel *Persian Nights*. This book chronicles the story of Chloe Fowler, a woman who accidentally finds herself traveling in Iran just prior to the revolution. Fowler is a physician's wife, and the couple looks forward to a trip to Iran where he will teach in a local hospital. Just before they arrive, he is called away on an emergency and Fowler decides to continue to Iran without him. Alone in a country where single women are suspect, she finds herself the target of government attention. Fowler gets involved in trying to help an unsatisfied Iranian woman leave the country, and in several affairs, before she is forced to leave the country.

Critics noted Johnson's success in portraying a deeply flawed protagonist. Paul Gray of *Time* believes that "in creating such a selfish, flawed heroine, Johnson took a calculated risk: readers might not be able to see themselves and their prejudices through Chloe and make the appropriate adjustments toward the truth." However, he concludes that the book is "neither a bodice ripper nor a treatise on the Iranian revolution, but an intriguing compromise: an attempt to show major upheavals as a progress of small shocks." Joyce Johnson, writing in the *Washington Post Book World,* also remarks on the flawed central character: "Chloe Fowler reflects a peculiarly American malaise of the spirit. A certain emptiness, a feeling of never having been tested." The reviewer praises Johnson's ability to delve into the life of such an unsympathetic character, calling the book "a social comedy deftly played out in the shadows of an historical tragedy," yet finds fault with some of the writing: "Johnson is such a witty and accomplished novelist that one wishes she had produced a more polished book." Reviewer Rosemary Dinnage of the *New York Review of Books* commends Johnson for her ability to create a complex and clever novel where "nothing much, in the plotty, fictional way, really happens." She concludes that "I find this the best of Diane Johnson's novels; it has the unobtrusively good writing, the gripping readability . . . but with a broader, more expansive canvas."

In addition to novels, Johnson has written two biographies. Her portrait of the first Mrs. George Meredith, *Lesser Lives: The True History of the First Mrs. Meredith,* grew out of her doctoral dissertation. "In biographies of Meredith, there would always be this little paragraph about how he was first married to Mary Ellen Peacock who ran off and left him and then, of course, died, deserted and forlorn—like the woman in a Victorian story," Johnson told Bell. "I always thought, I bet there is her side of it too. This was when my own marriage was breaking up, and I was particularly interested in the woman's side of things."

Working from evidence she exhumed from letters and diaries, Johnson hypothesizes that the real Mary Ellen was a strong-willed, intelligent, free spirit, whose main sin was being out of step with her times. Raised by her father in the tradition of eighteenth-century individualism, she incited the wrath of her decidedly Victorian second husband, the famous novelist George Meredith, when she abandoned their loveless marriage to lead a life of her own. The portrait that survives of her as a crazed adulterer who lured a much younger man into marriage is more a reflection of George Meredith's vindictiveness than an indication of who Mary Ellen was.

Though some critics felt the biography was lacking in evidence, many praised its artful style. "Jump cutting from scene to scene, she shows what she thinks to be true, what she thinks might be true, and what, in all candor, she thinks no one can prove to be either true or false," writes Catharine R. Stimpson in *Ms*. "Like a historian, she recovers pellets of the past. Like a psychologist, she applies theory and common sense to human behavior. Like a novelist, she takes imaginative liberties and worries about the internal coherence of her work of art. . . . *Lesser Lives* has the buoyant vitality of a book in which a writer has taken risks, and won."

Even when her subject is a contemporary figure, about whom concrete facts and anecdotes are readily available, Johnson prefers an artistic to an exhaustive approach. "A biography has a responsibility which is to present the facts and get all of them straight, so that people can get the basic outlines of a person's life," Johnson explained to Miriam Berkley in *Publishers Weekly*. "And then, I think, it has to have a point of view and a shape which has to come out of the biographer as artist. I guess I am arguing for the interpretive biography, you might call it an art biography, as opposed to a compendious . . . presentation of a lot of facts."

Johnson's commitment to biography as art presented special challenges in her study of mystery writer Dashiell Hammett and the writing of *Dashiell Hammett: A Life*. The first "authorized" Hammett biographer, Johnson had access to all his personal papers and the cooperation of his family and friends. But in exchange for these privileges, Hammett's ex-ecutrix and long-time companion Lillian Hellman insisted that she be shown the final manuscript and granted the right to decide whether or not the quoted material could stand.

"She set out to be pleasant and wonderful, then, when she stopped being wonderful, I stopped going to see her," Johnson told Beverly Beyette in the *Los Angeles Times*. The problem was one of vision: "She saw him very much as her guru, this wonderfully strong, terrifically honest, fabulously intelligent dream man. I saw him as an intelligent, troubled man, an alcoholic with terrible writer's block. She didn't like to think of his life having been painful, unsuccessful." Johnson eventually obtained Hellman's permission to use Hammett's letters in her own way. "She had to agree, I guess, that it *was* the best way of presenting Hammett," Johnson told Berkley. "He was a difficult man and not entirely sympathetic, but he was certainly at his most sympathetic in his own voice."

Using a novelistic approach, Johnson intersperses excerpts from Hammett's letters with short stretches of narrative that sometimes reflect her viewpoint, sometimes that of his family and friends. *New York Times Book Review* contributor George Stade compares the technique to one Hammett perfected in his own novels, "the method of the camera eye. We see what the characters do, hear what they say, note their gestures and postures, watch them assume positions toward each other, record their suspect attempts to account for themselves and each other." But just as Hammett's readers had to decipher for themselves his protagonists' motives, so, too, must Johnson's readers "decide for themselves what made Hammett tick."

Because so much is left to the reader, some critics suggest that Johnson is withholding judgment; others conclude that she cannot reveal what she does not know. As *New York Times* reviewer Christopher Lehmann-Haupt puts it: "Silence was Hammett's weapon—silence turned against all bullies and lovers, against his readers and himself. At the bottom of that silence was an ocean of anger: that much this biography makes very clear. The mystery that remains—that will probably remain forever—is the true source of that anger." Characterizing Hammett as "a fundamentally passive individual who drifted through life with no clear motivations or deep impulses," *Washington Post Book World* critic Jonathan Yardley wonders if Johnson's inability to "penetrate through to the inner man" might just reflect the fact that there was nothing there. "Perhaps," Yardley speculates, "when you come right down to it, the 'mystery' lies within us rather than him: for expecting more of him, since he wrote good books, than was actually there, and for feeling frustrated when those expectations go unmet."

Ralph B. Sipper, on the other hand, finds Johnson's "tracking of Hammett's inner life . . . the most revealing to date" and speculates in the *Los Angeles Times Book Review* that perhaps her "most delicate accomplishment is the fine line between iffy psychologizing and creative analysis." Describing the interpretative approach to biography as one in which the writer "studies the facts and filters them through her own sensibility," Sipper concludes that "Diane Johnson has done just that with her multifaceted subject and the result is pure light."

Johnson, a woman who has reluctantly traveled all over the globe with her husband, a physician, published the autobiographical work *Natural Opium* in 1993. The book is narrated by D., a character conspicuously similar to Johnson, who travels the globe while her husband J., an expert in infectious diseases, conducts his research. Critics have praised the book for its realistic feel, writer's attention to detail, and humor and intelligence. "What Ms. Johnson describes is not merely what the place was like, but—far more interesting—what it was like to be there," claims Roxana Robinson in the *New York Times Book Review*. A tragic sled ride following a dinner in Switzerland, ethical physicians being drawn into the heart of corruption, and trying to visit her children who live at opposite ends of the globe are some of the topics she explores; disaster and destruction are almost always the themes. As Francine Prose observes in *Yale Review,* "what animates these stories is their intelligence and humor, their freshness of observation, and the tension between our hope that things will be all right—and our near-certainty that they won't." Robinson concludes that "any traveler would be fortunate to have D as a companion, through the crowded streets of Beijing, the strange plains of Tanzania or the crowded and strange states of one's own mind."

BIOGRAPHICAL/CRITICAL SOURCES:

BOOKS

Contemporary Literary Criticism, Gale, Volume 5, 1976, Volume 13, 1983.

Dictionary of Literary Biography Yearbook: 1980, Gale, 1981.

Johnson, Diane, *Terrorists and Novelists,* Knopf, 1982.

Johnson, *Natural Opium: Some Travelers' Tales,* Knopf, 1993.

Yalom, Marilyn, editor, *Women Writers of the West Coast: Speaking of Their Lives and Careers,* Capra, 1983.

PERIODICALS

America, March 19, 1983.

Best Sellers, September 1, 1971.

Book World, October 13, 1968; September 5, 1971.

Chicago Tribune Book World, January 9, 1983.

Critique: Studies in Modern Fiction, Volume 16, number 1, 1974.

Harper's, September, 1995, p. 66.

Los Angeles Times, October 6, 1982; April 27, 1983.

Los Angeles Times Book Review, October 30, 1983; April 5, 1987, p. 1; May 22, 1988, p. 18; October 7, 1990, p. 1; January 3, 1993, p. 3, 7.

Ms., May, 1974; November, 1978.

Nation, June 14, 1975; November 11, 1978; December 17, 1983.

New Republic, November 11, 1972; November 18, 1978; April 20, 1987, p. 45.

New Statesman, November 19, 1971; June 6, 1975.

Newsweek, December 23, 1974; May 5, 1975; October 16, 1978; October 17, 1983; March 30, 1987, p. 69.

New Yorker, March 3, 1975; November 13, 1978; November 14, 1983.

New York Review of Books, November 2, 1972; February 20, 1975; November 23, 1978; April 23, 1987, p. 14; January 31, 1991, p. 18.

New York Times, November 27, 1974; May 23, 1980; October 16, 1982; October 5, 1983.

New York Times Book Review, September 5, 1971; December 31, 1972; December 22, 1974; November 19, 1978; October 31, 1982; October 16, 1983; April 5, 1987, p. 8; July 26, 1987, p. 24; May 29, 1988, p. 20; September 30, 1990, p. 18; December 15, 1991, p. 32; January 24, 1993, p. 8.

Playboy, March, 1993, p. 30.

Publishers Weekly, September 9, 1983.

Saturday Review, October 28, 1978.

Time, November 7, 1983; March 23, 1987, p. 83.

Times Literary Supplement, June 6, 1975; November 23, 1979; July 3, 1987, p. 714; February 15, 1991, p. 17.

Village Voice, January 8, 1979; June 30, 1987, p. 57.

Vogue, January, 1993, p. 72.

Washington Post Book World, December 22, 1975; November 26, 1978; September 29, 1982; October 9, 1983; March 22, 1987, p. 1; May 1, 1988, p. 12; September 30, 1990, p. 6.

Yale Review, July, 1993, pp. 122-33.

* * *

JOHNSON, J. R.
  See JAMES, C(yril) L(ionel) R(obert)

* * *

JOHNSON, Paul (Bede) 1928-

PERSONAL: Born November 2, 1928, in Barton, England; son of William Aloysius and Anne Johnson; married Marigold Hunt (a book reviewer), 1957; children: Daniel, Cosmo, Luke, Sophie. *Education:* Attended Stonyhurst College; Magdalen College, Oxford, B.A. (honors in history), 1950. *Politics:* Labour. *Religion:* Roman Catholic. *Avocational interests:* Collecting books and paintings, with emphasis on eighteenth-century paintings; painting, mountaineering.

ADDRESSES: Home—29 Newton Rd., London W2 5JR, England. *Office*—*New Statesman,* 10 Great Turnstile, London WC1, England.

CAREER: Realities, Paris, assistant executive editor, 1952-55; *New Statesman,* London, assistant editor, 1955-60, deputy editor, 1960-64, director, 1965, editor, 1965-70; freelance writer. Chair, Iver Village Labour Party, 1966. Member of Royal Commission on the Press, 1974-77. DeWitt Wallace professor of communications, American Enterprise Institute, Washington, DC, 1980. Has done extensive television work, mainly in the field of current affairs broadcasts.

MEMBER: National Union of Journalists.

AWARDS, HONORS: First Prize, Yorkshire Post Book of the Year Award, 1975, for *Pope John XXIII;* Francis Boyer Award for Services to Public

Policy, 1979; King Award for Excellence (Literature), 1980.

WRITINGS:

The Suez War, MacGibbon & Kee, 1957.
Journey into Chaos, MacGibbon & Kee, 1958.
Left of Centre, MacGibbon & Kee, 1960.
Merrie England, Macmillan, 1964.
Statesmen and Nations, Sidgwick & Jackson, 1971.
The Offshore Islanders: From Roman Occupation to European Entry, Weidenfeld & Nicolson, 1972, published as *The Offshore Islanders: England's People from Roman Occupation to the Present,* Holt (New York City), 1972.
(With George Gale) *The Highland Jaunt,* Collins, 1973.
The Life and Times of Edward III, with an introduction by Antonia Fraser, Weidenfeld & Nicolson, 1973.
Pope John XXIII, Little, Brown (Boston), 1974.
Elizabeth I: A Study in Power and Intellect, Weidenfield & Nicolson, 1974, published as *Elizabeth I: A Biography,* Holt, 1974.
A Place in History, Weidenfeld & Nicolson, 1974, Drake (New York City), 1975.
A History of Christianity, Atheneum (New York City), 1976.
Enemies of Society, Atheneum, 1977.
The Civilization of Ancient Egypt, Atheneum, 1978.
The National Trust Book of British Castles, Putnam (New York City), 1978.
Britain's Own Road to Serfdom (monograph), Conservative Political Centre, 1978.
Civilizations of the Holy Land, Atheneum, 1979.
(Contributor) *Will Capitalism Survive?,* Ethics and Public Policy Center, Georgetown University (Washington, DC), 1979.
A Tory Philosophy of Law, Conservative Political Centre, 1979.
The Things That Are Not Caesar's, American Enterprise Institute for Public Policy Research, 1980.
(With Irving Kristol and Michael Novak) *The Moral Basis of Democratic Capitalism,* American Enterprise Institute, 1980.
Ireland: Land of Troubles, Eyre Methuen, 1980, new edition published as *Ireland: A History from the Twelfth Century to the Present Day,* Eyre Methuen, 1981, published as *Ireland: Land of Troubles; A History from the Twelfth Century to the Present Day,* Holmes & Meier (New York City), 1981, new edition published as *Ireland: A Concise History from the Twelfth Century to the Present Day,* Academy Chicago (Chicago), 1982.

The Recovery of Freedom, Basil Blackwell, 1980, Biblio Distributors, 1981.

(With Irving Kristol and Michael Novak) *The Moral Basis of Democratic Capitalism: Three Essays,* American Enterprise Institute, 1980.

British Cathedrals, Morrow (New York City), 1980.

Pope John Paul II and the Catholic Restoration, St. Martin's (New York City), 1982.

A History of the Modern World from 1917 to the 1980s, Weidenfeld & Nicolson, 1983, published as *Modern Times: The World from the Twenties to the Eighties,* Harper (New York City), 1983, revised edition, HarperPerennial (New York City), 1992.

A History of the English People, Harper, 1985.

Saving and Spending: The Working-Class Economy in Britain, 1870-1939, Oxford University Press, 1985.

(Editor) *The Oxford Book of Political Anecdotes,* Oxford University Press, 1986.

(With others) *Unsecular America,* edited by Richard J. Neuhaus, Eerdmans, 1986.

A History of the Jews, Weidenfeld & Nicolson, 1987, Harper, 1988.

Intellectuals, Weidenfeld & Nicolson, 1988.

(Editor with Ethan Haimo) *Stravinsky Retrospectives,* University of Nebraska Press (Lincoln), 1988.

Castles of England, Scotland and Wales, Harper, 1989.

(Coeditor) *Workers versus Pensioners: Intergenerational Justice in an Ageing World,* St. Martin's, 1990.

(Editor with others) *American Government: People, Institutions and Policies* (text edition; with test bank and instructor's manual), second edition (Johnson not associated with earlier edition), Houghton (Boston), 1990.

The Birth of the Modern: World Society, 1815-1830, HarperCollins (New York City), 1991.

The Quotable Paul Johnson: A Topical Compilation of His Wit, Wisdom, and Satire, edited by George J. Marlin, Richard P. Rabatin, and Heather Richardson Higgins, Noonday Press (New York City), 1994.

The Quest for God: A Personal Pilgrimage, HarperCollins, 1996.

SIDELIGHTS: British historian, journalist, broadcaster, and world traveler Paul Johnson is "one of the most passionate and eloquent journalists of his generation," David Wood reports in the London *Times.* The editor of *New Statesman* during the late 1960s, Johnson once defended socialism. However, his disappointment with the results of trade unionism and other current events together with his study of social history eventually convinced him that "collectivist societies simply don't work." *The Recovery of Freedom* chronicles his conversion. Johnson cites recent encroachments of the British state on individual's freedoms in defense of his new distaste for collectivist policies. "No anti-socialist will want to diminish, as no socialist will be able to dismiss, the importance of Paul Johnson's rather repetitive fundamental argument," Wood comments.

Enemies of Society further expresses Johnson's conviction that the combined forces of irrationalism and violence pose a fatal threat to Western civilization. Like *The Recovery of Freedom, Enemies of Society* elicited a wide range of critical response. Tom Stoppard comments in the *Times Literary Supplement,* "The prose is lucid, the tone is forthright—which may be a polite way of saying that there is something to infuriate almost everybody. . . . One does not have to be an expert on anything to know that in one of his themes—the defence of objective truth from the attacks of Marxist relativists—Johnson has got hold of the right end of the right stick at the right time. For this alone, *Enemies of Society* is an important and aptly titled book."

Johnson is the author of a number of well-received studies of British history, including *Ireland: Land of Troubles* and a biography of Elizabeth I. His ventures into world history, however, have brought him more critical attention. *The History of Christianity* and *The History of the Jews* have been widely reviewed in the United States and Europe. Johnson's view is that of the historian moreso than the theologian; both books attend more to historical events and social movements than to the belief systems that fostered them. *Critic* contributor Philip Toynbee remarks that readers looking to *The History of Christianity* for the essence of the Christian faith will find instead "a very able history of Christianity in relation to the political and intellectual history of Western Europe." In the *New York Times Book Review,* Martin E. Marty concurs: "'A History of Christianity' is . . . a reliable if hard-edged story of the public church. Never for a sentence does Johnson get inside the home or heart of simple believers, who outnumber his characters by thousands to one." Though an *Economist* reviewer finds much in the book to criticize, he allows, "Johnson's final analysis of Christianity may, perhaps, be fair. He admits that mankind has not behaved too well under the faith's influence, but that a future without that influence . . . is grim to contemplate."

Johnson's immersion in research on the Christian church allowed him to see that the Christian faith is very closely related to Judaism. In a *Publishers Weekly* interview, Johnson explains, "When I was writing the *History of Christianity* I found that the debt Christianity owed to Judaism was much greater than I'd supposed and, I think, much greater than most . . . people realize. I thought then that if I got the chance I would like to write a history of the Jews, too." Johnson focuses on the many significant exchanges between Judaism and Western culture. Experts in the field of Jewish history comment that Johnson's position as a newcomer to Judaism is evident in the book. But Todd Endelman, writing in the *Times Literary Supplement,* found this to be an asset: "Precisely because he is a relative newcomer to the field, he is not hampered by reigning orthodoxies in matters of interpretation and thus occasionally offers a dissenting view that is fresh, stimulating, and possibly . . . correct."

Critics deemed *The History of the Jews,* like Johnson's other books, eminently readable. "Johnson writes with a fluency that is almost conversational, as though he can describe 4000 years in the course of a dinner party," Field comments. Merle Rubin of the *Christian Science Monitor* feels that though he cannot recommend it as the definitive text on the subject, *The History of the Jews* "is an absorbing, provocative, well-written, often moving book, an insightful and impassioned blend of history and myth, story and interpretation."

Critics generally take issue with many of the author's judgments in *The History of the Jews,* but pronounce his efforts praiseworthy. *New York Times Book Review* contributor Arthur Hertzberg, for example, concludes, "Some of Mr. Johnson's generalizations are overbold and glib. . . . Nonetheless, this book is a remarkable achievement. . . . Johnson's continuing self-education in Jewish history keeps moving the author, chapter by chapter, away from seeing Jewish experience as a function of Christianity and toward understanding Jews in their own terms. . . . Mr. Johnson's account of the Holocaust," Hertzberg declares, "is the best short summary of contemporary scholarship I have read."

Johnson's *Modern Times: The World from the Twenties to the Eighties* combines his aptitude for writing history with the well-founded social criticism he demonstrated in books such as *Enemies of Society,* Robert Nisbet remarks in the *New York Times Book Review.* Johnson aims his presentation of world

events since the failed treaty of Versailles in 1919 to expose the ill effects of moral relativism, social engineering, fascism and totalitarianism on the modern world. "This is a work of intellect and imagination, in which the author shows a strong grasp of complex material and a remarkable ability to fit into a unity the interacting forces of political and social movements all over the world during what is effectively the whole post-1914 period," Stephen Spender observes in the *Atlantic.* "What stands out," Spender adds, "is his dark, almost apocalyptic, . . . vision of what he regards as perhaps the most terrible century (if measured by its inhumanity and acts of violence) in the history of mankind." When individuals began to delegate the role of conscience to domineering institutions and despotic political leaders, civilization became inhumane, Johnson suggests. Yet he concludes that the survival of morality, religious belief, and sustained commitments to individual liberty despite dehumanizing forces leaves a door open to optimism.

When asked in a *Publishers Weekly* interview if he sees himself as an intellectual, Johnson replied, "I've often criticized the whole concept of intellectuals. Their tendency as a class is to put ideas before people, and that is very dangerous. I don't want to be an intellectual of any kind." Elaborating his case, Johnson tests a number of the century's prominent thinkers for moral integrity and finds them wanting in *Intellectuals.* Often violating the standards they professed in public, a dozen historical personages including Jean-Jacques Rousseau and Karl Marx behaved in ways that should cause others to question the viability of their ideals, Johnson asserts. "Those who insisted that they spoke for 'the workers' had never known any. Sponging when they were poor, grasping when they were rich, these gurus were consistently cruel and egocentric. Promising to build a variety of heavens on earth, they paved the way to a good many hells," an *Economist* reviewer summarizes. Johnson's own aspect toward his subjects is a "fascinated disapproval," Joseph Sobran writes in the *National Review.*

The same phrase describes the general response the best seller received from the critics, who largely indicted Johnson for suspending his characteristic depth and objectivity. Writing in the *Times Literary Supplement,* Jaroslav Anders explains, "Johnson is right to warn us that intellectuals are as prone to conformity, self-interest and error as other mortals. They do, sometimes, form self-promoting coteries and act as censors against those who dare to oppose their ideas." Anders feels with many other critics, however, that "Although [Johnson] allows some of his heroes talent, greatness, even genius, his portraits are more like caricatures than serious studies of human character."

Despite these and other criticisms, some commentators claim that to read *Intellectuals* is a valuable experience. Although "caustic" and "skewed," Johnson's profiles are "thought-provoking and thoroughly engaging," comments a *Publishers Weekly* reviewer. *New York Times Book Review* contributor Wendy Doniger O'Flaherty finds that Johnson's revelling in his subjects' "lying, fornicating, and dishonesty about money" is "great fun to read." London *Times* contributor Peter Ackroyd finds other laudable features in the book: "There are . . . occasions when [Johnson] displays a fine grasp of cultural context. . . . His account of Edmund Wilson's tax evasions, and his brief attack on Noam Chomsky, are outstanding. He is also on firm ground when he condemns those writers who feel it necessary to pontificate on public affairs without any apparent qualifications for such a role."

Workers versus Pensioners: Intergenerational Justice in an Ageing World collects essays that look at the impending social conflict between the growing ranks of the elderly (who are either financially secure, having made the most of post-war economic opportunities, or are supported by welfare programs) and the generation of relatively disadvantaged youth. The underemployed and overtaxed working-class youth in Western Europe, the United States and New Zealand may pose a threat to the establishment unless these programs are reevaluated, Johnson maintains.

One of Johnson's most ambitious projects is *The Birth of the Modern: World Society 1815-1830*. A "mammoth tome" of more than 1000 pages, according to *New Republic* writer Lawrence Stone, it proposes that the modern world's foundation was laid in the years between the battle of Waterloo and the overthrow of the restored French monarchy. Critical response to the book is as varied as the subjects the author treats within it. At one extreme is Stone, who allows that *The Birth of the Modern* has "some virtues" but goes on to condemn it as a fatally flawed work. He concedes that "it is very readable, if one is prepared to accept its unbelievably rambling organization," credits the author with extensive research, and allows that "some topics are treated with real brilliance. If anyone wants to know, for example, about the full horrors of traveling in the early nine-

teenth century, and about how things improved, he could not do better than read Johnson's forty pages on the subject. The account is lively, personalized, sensible, and well informed." Yet Stone goes on to say that the theme of Johnson's book is unacceptably vague; the author fails "at any point to define what he means by 'modern.' The reader is left to guess by examining those persons, innovations, events, or ideas" covered in the book. The critic charges that "it is safe to conclude . . . that Johnson does not really know what 'modern' is."

Stone also charges that Johnson "insists on embroidering his lively pen-portraits" of historical figures "with wholly irrelevant detail, frequently erotic in nature, that bears no relation whatever to his argument." He concludes that while "*The Birth of the Modern* is a mine of gossipy information about famous personalities, . . . it is structurally incapable of asking any profound questions. . . . Let the reader be warned. If he tries to read this cozy-looking book in bed, it will crush his ribs, addle his brains, and fill him with much misinformation about the birth of the modern world." *New Statesman & Society* reviewer Stephen Howe concurs that *The Birth of the Modern* "carries an utterly fraudulent title and preface," yet declares that with a more appropriate title, the book could be "appreciated and enjoyed for what it is,"—a "narrative of political, cultural, social and, to a very limited extent, economic changes in the world of the north Atlantic and western Europe, centered overwhelmingly on Britain." *The Birth of the Modern* is also praised as "a savory social history, spiced with lively gossip. . . . In many ways a tour de force" by *New York Times Book Review* contributor Eugen Weber and as a "huge and absorbing book" to be "admired and enjoyed" by Alethea Hayter in *Spectator*.

Norman Gall is unreservedly enthusiastic about the book in his *Commentary* review: "With its masterful weaving of portraits and episodes into long chapters, *The Birth of the Modern* takes on some of the qualities of an epic poem." He admits that Johnson does not completely analyze all aspects of change in society, but states that to expect him to do so "is to require too much of one who has already done an almost unbelievably great deal." He commends "the intellectual resources, the enthusiasm, [and] the narrative gifts displayed in this book" and credits the author with helping readers to "understand the dynamics of modernization as they really were." In conclusion, Gall declares: "*The Birth of the Modern* celebrates the brilliance of modernity's first great burst in the sky; reading it should make us aware of how much courage, understanding, and cooperation will be necessary if the modern enterprise is to be sustained and to develop."

Johnson returned his attention to religion in *The Quest for God: A Personal Pilgrimage.* In it, he attempts to convince readers that God exists and that organized religion is vitally important. A lifelong Roman Catholic, he finds the authority and discipline of that church to be ideal. *New York Times Book Review* critic Kenneth L. Woodward writes: "At a time when the religion bookshelf sags with self-dramatizing 'spiritual journeys,' it is a relief to hear from a writer who feels serenely secure in the faith he received as a child and has practiced all his life." However, he ultimately finds Johnson's religious beliefs "surprisingly unsophisticated" and rather narrow-minded. Rosalind Miles states a similar view more vehemently in the *Spectator,* calling *The Quest for God* "a deeply disappointing book, the more so as its avowed aim is 'to help' both the writer and 'other people.' What could have been an intellectually rigorous, thought-provoking and fascinating journey of spiritual exploration proves to come straight from the 'What-I-tell-you-three-times-is-true' school of bashing the brainless and educating the great unwashed. . . . If you enjoy arrogance for an appetiser, muddle for main course, dullness for dessert and absurdity for afters, this is the dish for you." Ian Buruma concurs in the *New Yorker* that the book "gives off a distinct smell of bigotry. Overexcited opinions fleck his prose like spittle around a fanatic's mouth. . . . One comes away . . . feeling that, if the author is right, one is destined to go straight to Hell."

"Rather like the God he describes, [Johnson] always has the last word," admits Peter Stanford in *New Statesman & Society.* Yet he also has kind words for *The Quest for God* and its author, whom he describes as "expansive, unafraid to tackle huge subjects that span millennia." In Standford's view, *The Quest for God* is "a powerful, colourfully argued and intensely personal study of humankind's desire for something 'other' than the here and now—for a remote, often indiscernible power that created and now guides our world. . . . Every page drips with information, history and anecdote."

BIOGRAPHICAL/CRITICAL SOURCES:

PERIODICALS

Atlantic, August, 1983.
Chicago Tribune, July 10, 1991, section 5, p. 3.

Christian Science Monitor, June 23, 1991, p. 13; September 12, 1996, p. 13.
Commentary, July, 1992, pp. 54, 56.
Economist, October 8, 1988; October 7, 1989.
Harpers, September, 1977.
Insight, June 1, 1987.
London Review of Books, September 12, 1991.
Los Angeles Times Book Review, July 17, 1983; November 10, 1985; April 19, 1987; March 19, 1989; June 9, 1991, p. 1.
Nation, September 17, 1977.
National Review, April 21, 1989.
New Republic, August 12, 1991, pp. 36-40.
New Statesman, October 7, 1988.
New Statesman & Society, September 20, 1991, pp. 44-45; March 15, 1996, pp. 32-33.
Newsweek, August 22, 1983.
New Yorker, September 6, 1976; November 26, 1979; June 10, 1991, p. 112; May 20, 1996, pp. 93-96.
New York Review of Books, August 5, 1976; October 27, 1983.
New York Times, April 14, 1987.
New York Times Book Review, January 28, 1973; October 20, 1974; July 16, 1976; October 17, 1976; June 26, 1983; April 19, 1987; March 12, 1989; June 23, 1991, p. 3; February 27, 1994, p. 20; June 2, 1996, p. 22.
Publishers Weekly, May 1, 1987; January 13, 1989; February 23, 1990.
Saturday Review, September 17, 1977.
Spectator, September 21, 1991, pp. 37-38; March 30, 1996, pp. 29-31.
Time, October 11, 1976; June 6, 1983; January 1, 1990.
Times (London), December 4, 1980; December 22, 1980; June 23, 1983; March 26, 1987; October 7, 1988.
Times Literary Supplement, May 28, 1971; September 15, 1972; May 11, 1973; July 12, 1974; October 11, 1974; June 3, 1977; April 21, 1978; July 8, 1983; May 30, 1986; October 17, 1986; April 22, 1988; October 7, 1988; January 26, 1990; February 23, 1990.
Wall Street Journal, June 11, 1991; May 10, 1996.
Washington Post Book World, November 20, 1977; August 21, 1983; May 24, 1987; February 26, 1989; June 9, 1991, p. 1.*

*   *   *

JORDAN, Robert
See RIGNEY, James Oliver, Jr.

KASSEM, Lou 1931-

PERSONAL: Surname is accented on the first syllable; born November 10, 1931, in Elizabethton, TN; daughter of Edgar Roscoe (in sales) and Dorothy (a nurse; maiden name, Graham) Morrell; married Shakeep Kassem (a financial consultant), June 17, 1951; children: Cherrie, Dottie (Mrs. Cliff Riviera), Lisa (Mrs. Anthony Kummerl), Amy-Leigh (Mrs. Thomas Kubicki). *Ethnicity:* "White." *Education:* Attended East Tennessee State College (now University), 1949-51, University of Virginia, 1982, and Vassar College, 1984. *Politics:* Independent. *Religion:* Methodist. *Avocational interests:* Golf, hiking, travel.

ADDRESSES: Home and office—715 Burruss Dr., Blacksburg, VA 24060. *Agent*—Ruth Cohen, P.O. Box 7626, Menlo Park, CA 94025.

CAREER: Virginia Polytechnic Institute (now Polytechnic Institute and State University), Blacksburg, laboratory technician, 1951-52; Montgomery-Floyd Regional Library, Blacksburg, librarian, 1971-84; writer, 1984—. Lecturer at Roanoke College, Christopher Newport College, East Tennessee Writers Conference, and Litfest of the Ozarks. Member of Blacksburg Town Council, 1978-84; president of Armed Forces Officers' Wives, 1955, Junior Woman's Club, 1961, and Friends of the Library, 1965.

MEMBER: Society of Children's Book Writers, Women's National Book Association, Writers in Virginia, National League of American Pen Women.

AWARDS, HONORS: Notable Book Award from American Library Association, 1986, for *Listen for Rachel;* Virginia State Reading Association Award, 1996, for *A Haunting in Williamsburg,* Avon Camelot, 1990.

WRITINGS:

JUVENILE

Dance of Death, Dell (New York City), 1984.
Middle School Blues, Houghton (Boston), 1986.
Listen for Rachel, Margaret K. McElderry, 1986.
Secret Wishes, Avon (New York City), 1989.
Summer for Secrets, Avon, 1989.
A Haunting in Williamsburg, Avon Camelot, 1990.
The Treasures of Witch Hat Mountain, Avon Camelot, 1992.

Odd One Out, Fawcett Juniper (New York City), 1993.
The Druid Curse, Avon Camelot, 1994.
The Innkeeper's Daughter, Avon Flare, 1996.
Sneeze on Monday, Avon Camelot, 1997.
The Deadly Secrets of Thornhill Manor, in press.

WORK IN PROGRESS: "Research on Montgomery White Sulphur Springs, a resort used as a hospital during the Civil War. Working title: *Ride the Wind.* A young girl's life and adventures during this trying time in our history."

SIDELIGHTS: Lou Kassem told *CA:* "For me, writing is like breathing: absolutely necessary. Reading is the bread that sustains me. Speaking about writing is my pleasure. *Listen for Rachel* is the book of my heart, because it gives a true picture of the proud, independent people who settled the Appalachians. That this book was selected for a cultural exchange program with Russia pleases me immensely.

"With no apologies, I am a writer for young people. The laughter and tears associated with growing up have always fascinated me. Jane Yolen described our profession best when she said, 'An author's real job is to tell a whopping good tale.' Telling a whopping good tale in my mystery, humorous, historical, and contemporary novels is my primary goal.

"A secondary goal, almost as much fun, is speaking in schools, libraries, and workshops about writing. I firmly believe more authors should get out among their reading public. I do more than forty of these lectures and workshops every year and learn far more than I teach. Kids are great! And our teachers need all the help we can give them to promote reading and writing. Try it. I'll bet you like it.

"As for the writing process, it doesn't just take place at my desk or computer. I am always writing, collecting ideas, characters and conversations. Visiting schools isn't a completely altruistic endeavor! Paper and pen are always at hand. But once I have a story line and a main character in my head, I write from 9 to 12 and from 1 to 3 . . . as often as routine chores (housecleaning, cooking, shopping, and laundry) allow. I admit these mundane tasks get a-lick-and-a-promise while I'm 'with book.' Somehow my family and home survive these births!

"My first advice for aspiring writers is: Read, read, read. Read the good, the bad, and the ugly. Read for fun and read critically. See how other authors do things. Would you have handled the situation differently? How? Why? Books are excellent teachers.

"My second and best advice is: Just do it! No book was ever written by simply thinking about it. As H. L. Mencken said, 'Apply butt to chair.'

"May the Muse be with you."

*   *   *

KAY, Ellen
See DeMILLE, Nelson (Richard)

*   *   *

KIERAN, John Francis 1892-1981

PERSONAL: Surname is pronounced *Keer*-un; born August 2, 1892, in New York, NY; died December 10, 1981, in Rockport, MA; son of James Michael (an educator and administrator) and Kate (a teacher and musician; maiden name, Donahue) Kieran; married Alma Boldtmann, May 14, 1919 (died June, 1944); married Margaret Ford (a journalist), September 5, 1947; children: (first marriage) James Michael, John Francis, Beatrice. *Education:* Attended College of the City of New York (now City College of the City University of New York), 1908-11; Fordham University, B.S. (cum laude), 1912; Clarkson College of Technology, D.Sc., 1941; Wesleyan University, M.A., 1942.

CAREER: Held a variety of jobs during his early career, including teaching in a country school in Dutchess County, NY, running a poultry business, and working as a timekeeper for a sewer construction project; *New York Times,* sports writer, 1914-17, 1919-22; *New York Tribune,* baseball writer, 1922-25; *New York American,* columnist, 1925-26; *New York Times,* columnist, 1927-41; *New York Sun,* columnist, 1941-44; freelance writer, 1944-81. Elector, Hall of Fame for Great Americans, beginning 1945; member of the board of experts on radio program, *Information, Please,* 1938-48. *Military service:* Served with the 11th Engineers of the American Expeditionary Forces during World War I.

AWARDS, HONORS: Burroughs Medal, John Burroughs Memorial Association, 1960, for recognition of an outstanding book on natural science.

WRITINGS:

The Story of the Olympic Games: 776 B.C.-1936 A.D., Frederick A. Stokes (New York City), 1936, revised editions (with Arthur Daley) published quadrennially, Lippincott (Philadelphia, PA), 1948-77.
The American Sporting Scene, illustrations by Joseph W. Golinkin, Macmillan (New York City), 1941.
John Kieran's Nature Notes, illustrations by Fritz Kredel, Doubleday, Doran (Garden City, NY), 1941, reprinted, Books for Libraries, 1969.
(Compiler) *Poems I Remember,* Doubleday, Doran, 1942.
Footnotes on Nature, wood engraving by Nora S. Unwin, Doubleday, 1947, reprinted, 1971.
(Editor with Dan Golenpaul) *Information Please Almanac, Atlas and Yearbook,* Simon & Schuster (New York City), 1947.
An Introduction to Birds, illustrations by Don Eckelberry, Garden City Publishing (Garden City, NY), 1950.
An Introduction to Wildflowers, illustrations by Tabea Hofmann, Hanover House, 1952.
An Introduction to Trees, illustrations by Michael H. Bevans, Hanover House, 1954.
(With Margaret Kieran) *John James Audubon,* illustrations by Christine Price, Random House, 1954.
An Introduction to Nature: Birds, Wild Flowers Trees, illustrations by D. Eckelberry, T. Hofmann, and M. Bevans, Hanover House, 1955.
(Editor) *Treasure of Great Nature Writing,* Hanover House, 1957.
A Natural History of New York City, illustrations by Henry Bugbee Kane, Houghton (Boston, MA), 1959, revised and abridged edition, Natural History Press (Garden City, NY), 1971.
Not Under Oath: Recollections and Reflections, Houghton, 1964.
Books I Love: Being a Selection of 100 Titles for a Home Library, Doubleday, 1969.

Contributor of articles to periodicals, including *Saturday Evening Post, Woman's Home Companion, American Magazine, Literary Digest, Collier's,* and *Audubon Magazine.*

SIDELIGHTS: John Kieran was affectionately known as America's "walking encyclopedia." A noted journalist—and first author of the "Sports of the Times" column in the *New York Times*—Kieran made use of his wide-ranging knowledge on the popular radio show *Information, Please.* His radio work made him famous beyond the bounds of sportswriting and helped to create an audience for the numerous books on natural history he wrote later in life. "At the popular level Kieran enjoyed a national reputation not only as an authority on sports but also as the man who knew something about almost everything. . . . ," noted William Curran in the *Dictionary of Literary Biography.* "His explanation for the extraordinary breadth of knowledge was simple: 'I read a lot and I am interested in many things.'"

A native of the Bronx, Kieran began working at the *New York Times* in 1914, after serving as a gentleman farmer and a civil engineer. He stayed at the *Times* continuously between 1927 and 1941 after having been offered the newspaper's first by-lined sports column, "Sports of the Times." Enormously erudite with a keen sense of humor, Kieran was known to lace his columns with mock sonnets and learned references that introduced a new sophistication into sportswriting. Curran observed: "For all the playful interjection of classical references and literary allusions, Kieran's prose offered a refreshing change from the baroque excesses and blizzard of cliches that marked much of American sportswriting even as late as the 1930s. Long before Kieran had taken up the considerable challenge of writing a daily column in the country's most prestigious daily newspaper, he had arrived at a plain, clear, and easy manner of reporting, a style that won him ardent readers."

In 1938 Kieran was asked to join a panel of "experts" for a radio game show called *Information, Please.* Listeners were invited to submit questions in an effort to stump the panel, which also included Franklin P. Adams, Oscar Levant, and moderator Clifton Fadiman. Topics included everything from sports and current events to such esoteric fields as botany, archeology, law, ecology, and language. "Kieran answered correctly thousands of questions submitted by listeners to *Information, Please,*" Curran noted. ". . . There seemed to be no field to which he was a stranger, and he became a national celebrity."

America's "walking encyclopedia" left the *New York Times* in 1941 and accepted a position as a natural history columnist for the *New York Sun.* This job change marked a significant turning point in Kieran's life. Long interested in the natural world, he devoted the rest of his career to writing about the nation's flora and fauna, publishing no less than nine titles on nature themes. In a review of *Footnotes on Nature,* *Commonweal* correspondent Alan Devoe wrote: "John Kieran shows himself a real naturalist, in the best sense: a man with a deep, intelligent and lifelong devotion to the wonder of the natural world, and a man who knows how to write about his nature adventures with a winning enthusiasm." In the *New York Times,* R. G. Davis concluded: "'Footnotes on Nature' is a genuine act of love, and like all the best books of its kind, it gives the reader a very exciting impulse to go out and take for himself these pleasures which are so near, so costless and so inexhaustibly rich."

Kieran must have surprised the citizens of Manhattan when he published *A Natural History of New York City* in 1960. Odd as it may sound, the book explored the fantastic variety of wildlife found in the city, from butterflies and flowers to migratory waterfowl in the region's tidal estuaries. *New York Times Book Review* contributor E. W. Teale cited the work for its "exact and often surprising information," adding: "The volume is one long delightful trip in the company of a charming and erudite companion. . . . [The book] is John Kieran's finest work, in many ways the best treatment the natural history of a great city has ever received."

From 1952 until his death in 1981, Kieran lived quietly in Rockport, Massachusetts. His memoir, *Not Under Oath: Recollections and Reflections,* was published in 1964. "'Information, Please' has passed into the realm of pleasant memories," wrote *Saturday Review* correspondent R. L. Perkin, "but the man with the Spitzenburg voice . . . has brightened and warmed the fall book season with a most delightful memoir. *Not Under Oath* has the richness, the color, and the zest of autumn weather, and it explains why so many men and women love John Kieran." The man who Curran called "perhaps the best and most literate sportswriter of his generation" died in Rockport at the age of 89, having inaugurated a nationally-recognized newspaper column that continues to this day.

BIOGRAPHICAL/CRITICAL SOURCES:

BOOKS

Dictionary of Literary Biography, Volume 171: *Twentieth-Century American Sportswriters,* Gale (Detroit, MI), 1996, pp. 164-72.

PERIODICALS

Books, December 20, 1936, p. 17; December 14, 1941, p. 10.
Book Week, November 1, 1964.
Chicago Sunday Tribune, September 27, 1959, p. 3.
Christian Science Monitor, July 19, 1947, p. 14.
Commonweal, August 1, 1947, p. 387.
Coronet, March, 1949.
Life, June 16, 1941.
New York Herald Tribune Book Review, July 20, 1947, p. 2; September 27, 1959, p. 3.
New York Times, November 8, 1936, p. 29; March 16, 1941, p. 8; November 23, 1941, p. 11; July 20, 1947, p. 6; April 9, 1950, p. 15.
New York Times Book Review, September 27, 1959, p. 1; October 11, 1964, p. 16.
Readers Digest, June, 1939.
San Francisco Chronicle, July 10, 1955, p. 16; September 27, 1959, p. 17.
Saturday Evening Post, June 18, 1949.
Saturday Review, October 24, 1964, p. 75.
Saturday Review of Literature, July 12, 1947, p. 9.
Time, January 4, 1943.

OBITUARIES:

PERIODICALS

Newsweek, December 21, 1981.
New York Times, December 11, 1981.
Time, December 21, 1981.*

*   *   *

KOGAWA, Joy Nozomi 1935-

PERSONAL: Born June 6, 1935, in Vancouver, British Columbia, Canada; daughter of Gordon Goichi (a minister) and Lois (a kindergarten teacher; maiden name, Yao) Nakayama; married David Kogawa, May 2, 1957 (divorced, 1968); children: Gordon, Deidre. *Education:* Attended University of Alberta, 1954, Anglican Women's Training College, 1956, Conservatory of Music, 1956, and University of Saskatchewan, 1968.

ADDRESSES: Home—845 Semlin Dr., Vancouver, British Columbia V5L 4J6, Canada.

CAREER: Office of the Prime Minister, Ottawa, Ontario, staff writer, 1974-76; freelance writer, 1976-78; University of Ottawa, Ottawa, writer in residence, 1978; freelance writer, 1978—.

MEMBER: League of Canadian Poets, Writers Union of Canada, Order of Canada, 1986.

AWARDS, HONORS: Books in Canada First Novel Award, 1981, Canadian Authors Association Book of the Year Award, 1982, Before Columbus Foundation American Book Award, 1982, and American Library Association notable book citation, 1982, all for *Obasan;* Periodical Distributors Best Paperback Fiction Award, 1983.

WRITINGS:

NOVELS

Obasan (novel), Lester and Orphen Dennys (Toronto), 1981, David Godine (New York City), 1982.
Naomi's Road (juvenile fiction), Oxford University Press (Toronto), 1986.
Itsuka (sequel to *Obasan*), Viking Canada (Toronto), 1992, Anchor Books, 1993.
The Rain Ascends, Knopf (Toronto), 1995.

POETRY

The Splintered Moon, University of New Brunswick (st. John), 1967.
A Choice of Dreams, McClelland & Stewart (Toronto), 1974.
Jericho Road, McClelland & Stewart, 1977.
Woman in the Woods, Mosaic Press (Oakville, Ontario), 1985.

OTHER

Contributor of poems to magazines in the United States and Canada, including *Canadian Forum, West Coast Review, Queen's Quarterly, Quarry, Prism International,* and *Chicago Review.*

SIDELIGHTS: Joy Kogawa is best-known for the novel *Obasan,* a fictionalization of her own experiences as a Japanese-Canadian during World War II. Like *Obasan*'s narrator, Kogawa was torn from her family by government officials and exiled into a detention camp in the Canadian wilderness. She published her first book of poetry, *The Splintered Moon,* in 1967. After two follow-up volumes, she received national acclaim for *Obasan.* With *Obasan,* writes Gurleen Grewal in *Feminist Writers,* "Kogawa proved herself to be among the finest of feminist-humanist writers." Out of *Obasan* came the sequel, *Itsuka,* and *Naomi's Road,* a version of the story for children. In addition to pursuing her career as a writer, Kogawa has turned her attention to political work on behalf of Japanese-Canadian citizens.

Before turning to fiction, Kogawa was a "seasoned poet," writes Grewal. Gary Willis writes in *Studies in Canadian Literature* that her first three volumes of poetry are filled with "lyric verse" and poems that often "express feelings that emerge from a narrative context that is only partly defined." A poem from Kogawa's third collection, *Jericho Road,* for example, centers on "a striking surrealistic image" that never makes clear who the protagonist's enemies are. Kogawa explained to Janice Williamson in *Sounding Differences: Covnersations with 17 Canadian Women Writers* that her poems often arise out of her dreams: "The practice of poetry . . . ," she says, "is the sweeping out of debris between the conscious and the unconscious." Grewal maintains that, "[I]n fiction too, her endeavor is the same. Through protagonists Naomi Nakane's recollection of her painful childhood, *Obasan* lays bare the inter-generational pain of Japanese Canadians affected by the Canadian government's relocation and internment of its citizens during World War II."

Obasan was the first Canadian novel to deal with the internment of its citizens of Japanese heritage. The novel focuses on 36-year-old Naomi. She and brother Stephen were separated from their loving parents during World War II. Their mother, visiting relatives in Japan, was not allowed to return to Canada, and their father was shipped to a labor camp. Naomi and Stephen were sent to a frontier town along with their Uncle Isamu and Aunt Obasan. When their parents never returned, they were raised by their aunt and uncle in a house filled with silence. One of the mysteries of Naomi's childhood was yearly pilgrimages. As a child, Naomi continually asked "Why do we come here every year?", and as an adult, Naomi has lost the ability to communicate; as Kogawa writes, she is a victim of "the silence that will not speak." *Obasan* explores Naomi's search for the answer to her childhood question and shows her long-awaited acknowledgment of, writes Grewal, "life's imperative to heal."

At the beginning of the novel, Naomi's uncle has just died, and the rest of the novel, writes Erika Gottleib in *Canadian Literature,* "takes shape as a mourner's meditation during a wake, a framework well suited to the novel's central metaphor of a spiritual journey." Urged by her Aunt Emily, an activist seeking justice for internment victims, Naomi relives her past, thus enabling her to learn about the secrets long held by her family. Naomi reviews documents about the Japanese internment to understand what happened to her and her family. And at the end of the novel, Naomi learns the truth that has been kept from her, that her mother suffered and died in Nagasaki, a victim of the "other holocaust," as Grewal calls it. Naomi, through her examination of the past and her examination of the truth, at last is free and learns to speak again.

Throughout the course of the novel, Naomi realizes her estrangement from mainstream Canadian society as well as from traditional Japanese culture. Kogawa explores the differences of these two groups. Writes Willis of *Obasan,* "[it is] expressive of a sensibility that wishes to define, in relation to each other, Japanese and Canadian ways of seeing, and even to combine these divergent perceptions in an integrated and distinctive vision." In one scene, Naomi muses on carpentry: "There is a fundamental difference in Japanese workmanship—to pull with control rather than push with force." The contrast between the "restrained" Japanese and the "forceful" Canadians is also apparent in the difference between the Issei—those born in Japan—and the Nisei—those born abroad, as represented by Naomi's two aunts. Neither of their models works for Naomi who "like Kogawa," writes Willis, "has roots in both traditions." By the end of the her own exploration, "Naomi blends a Japanese attention to silence with a Western attention to words. Indeed, it is this blending that gives rise to the distinctive beauties and subtleties of *Obasan.*"

Kogawa further enriches her text with documentation of this era of Canadian history. *Obasan* ends with the widely ignored memorandum sent by the Co-operative Committee on Japanese Canadians to the Canadian government in 1946, pointing out that the deportation of Japanese Canadians was "wrong and indefensible" and "an adoption of the methods of Nazism." Kogawa also includes among Aunt Emily's diaries and notes "a series of chilling nonfictional official papers and newspaper accounts," points out Edmund M. White in the *Los Angeles Times Book Review.* These elements serve to emphasize what White calls "systematic outrages inflicted by the Canadian government on its own citizens [which] echo the Nazi treatment of the Jews." Edith Milton in the *New York Times Book Review* writes that

Obasan "grows into a quietly appalling statement about how much hatred can cost when it is turned into a bureaucratic principle." White also finds that "the novel, in turn, shares some of the tone of *The Diary of Anne Frank* in its purity of vision under the stress of social outrage."

Obasan's political implications have been noted by many critics, including Grewal who writes, "this beautifully crafted novel with is moving resonances has done invaluable service to its varied readers. It has opened necessary dialogue; it has healed." Yet, *Obasan* always remains, according to Milton, "a tour de force, a deeply felt novel, brilliantly poetic in its sensibility." Willis notes that the message of Kogawa's poetry is more fully realized in *Obasan*, "an imaginative triumph over the forces that militate against expression of our inmost feelings." White points out that the novel has "a magical ability to convey suffering and privation, inhumanity and racial prejudice, without losing in any way joy in life and in the poetic imagination."

Itsuka is generally thought of as the sequel to *Obasan* but Sandra Martin writes in *Quill and Quire* that "Kogawa is not so much writing a sequel as reclaiming themes and characters from *Obasan*. In *Itsuka*, Naomi goes to Toronto where she works on a multicultural journal and takes her first lover, Father Cedric, a French Canadian priest. With his help, Naomi turns to activism in her desire to win redress for the victims of Canada's internment policies. In *Itsuka*, the political and erotic plots become intertwined. The book, using a similar technique as *Obasan*, closes with an apology from the Canadian government, in which it admits to instituting policies "influenced by discriminatory attitudes" toward Japanese Canadians and also to its own "unjust" actions.

Grewal maintains that *Itsuka* allows "the reader to witness Naomi's growth and personal fulfillment" and that it "openly bears the message of hope and trust implicit in *Obasan*." Yet, Martin compares *Itsuka* unfavorably to the first novel, finding that "Kogawa seems too close to the partisan squabbling that accompanies any such [political] movement. She hasn't yet absorbed the facts and translated them into fiction." Janice Kulyk Keefer, writing in *Books in Canada*, also admits to "a certain disappointment" with the book, one centering on "the absence in *Itsuka* of the kind of poetically charged language and intensity of perception that give *Obasan* its extraordinary power and beauty." But Keefer also realizes that "it would be wrong to fault *Itsuka* for not being

Obasan Revisited." She writes, "What Kogawa has done in her new novel is to move into a different kind of imaginative territory, exposing the politics of multiculturalism that has in may ways abetted rather than eradicated the racism that she presents as an institutionalized aspect of Canadian life."

Kogawa turned back to poetry after publication of her novels. The "insight found [in *Woman in the Woods*]," writes Frank Manley in *Books in Canada*, "is enlightening." He also lauds its "passion for life" along with "its ability to say volumes with only a few words." These attributes are apparent in all of Kogawa's work. Writes Martin, "Through her poetry, her sublime novel *Obasan*, her children's story *Naomi's Road*, and now *Itsuka*, Kogawa has written poignantly about how innocent and loyal Japanese Canadian were stripped of their home and their possessions, interned, and dispersed." Grewal further sees a more universal message in Kogawa's work: an emphasis on "compassion and arduous work of healing."

BIOGRAPHICAL/CRITICAL SOURCES:

BOOKS

Cheung, King-Kok, *Articulate Silences: Hisaye Yamamoto, Maxine Hong Kingston, Joy Kogawa*, Cornell University Press (Ithaca, NY), 1993.
Contemporary Literary Criticism, Volume 78, Gale (Detroit), 1994.
Feminist Writers, St. James Press (Detroit), 1996.
Hogan, Robert and others, editors, *Memory and Cultural Politics: New Essays in American Ethnic Literatures*, North Eastern University Press (Boston), 1996.
Kreiswirth, Martin and Mark A. Cheetham, editors, *Theory between the Disciplines: Authority/Vision/Politics*, University of Michigan Press (Ann Arbor), 1990, pp. 213-229.
Ling, Amy and others, editors, *Reading the Literatures of Asian America*, Temple University Press (Philadelphia), 1992.
Pearlman, Mickey, editor, *Canadian Women Writing Fiction*, University Press of Mississippi (Jackson), 1993.
Williamson, Janice, *Sounding Differences: Conversations with 17 Canadian Women Writers*, University of Toronto Press (Toronto), 1993.

PERIODICALS

Booklist, January 1, 1994, p. 806.
Books in Canada, May, 1986; April, 1992.

Canadian Forum, February, 1982, pp. 39-40; December, 1992, p. 38.

Canadian Literature, summer, 1986, pp. 34-53; spring, 1988, pp. 58-66, 68-82; winter, 1990, pp. 41-57.

Feminist Studies, summer, 1990, pp. 288-312.

Kunapipi, Volume 16, number 1, 1994.

Los Angeles Times Book Review, July 11, 1982. p. 3.

Melus, fall, 1985, pp. 33-42.

Mosaic: A Journal for the Interdisciplinary Study of Literature, spring, 1988, pp. 215-226.

New York Times Book Review, September 5, 1982; March 13, 1994, p. 18.

Quill and Quire, March, 1992, p. 57.

Studies in Canadian Literature, Volume 12, number 2, 1987, pp. 239-249.

L

LADNER, Kurt
See DeMILLE, Nelson (Richard)

* * *

LANEY, Al 1896-1988

PERSONAL: Born January 11, 1896, in Pensacola, FL; died January 31, 1988, in Spring Valley, NY; son of an attorney; married, wife's name Irene; children: Michael.

CAREER: Reporter for *Pensacola Journal, Dallas Dispatch,* and *Minneapolis News,* 1910-14; *New York Evening Mail,* New York City, reporter, 1918-24; New York Herald, New York City, staff member of European edition, *Paris Herald,* 1925-34; *New York Herald Tribune,* New York City, reporter and columnist, 1934-66.

AWARDS, HONORS: Danzig Trophy for outstanding tennis reporting, 1965; gold writers' pass from United States Tennis Writers Association, 1977; Distinguished Service Award from the Metropolitan Golf Association, 1978, for over forty years of golf coverage; inducted into International Tennis Hall of Fame, 1979.

WRITINGS:

Paris Herald: The Incredible Newspaper, Appleton-Century (New York City), 1947.
(Contributor) *Wake Up the Echoes: From the Sports Pages of the New York Herald Tribune,* edited by Bob Cooke, Hanover House (Garden City, NY), 1956.

(Author of text) Edward A. Hamilton and Charles Preston, editors, *Golfing America,* Doubleday (Garden City, NY), 1958.
Prep Schools: Profiles of More Than Fifty American Schools, Doubleday, 1961.
Covering the Court: A Fifty-Year Love Affair with the Game of Tennis, Simon & Schuster (New York City), 1968.
(Contributor) *The Twentieth Century Treasury of Sports,* edited by Al Silverman and Brian Silverman, Viking (New York City), 1992.

Contributor to *Best Sports Stories of 1944, Best Sports Stories of 1945,* and *Best Sports Stories of 1960,* all published by Dutton (New York City). Contributor to periodicals, including *Literary Digest, Scholastic, Popular Science,* and *Saturday Evening Post.*

SIDELIGHTS: "Al Laney was one of the premier golf and tennis writers in the United States from the mid 1930s to the mid 1960s," wrote Joel Sternberg in the *Dictionary of Literary Biography.* "During a career of more than fifty years he developed a reputation as a sensitive, graceful writer capable of beautifully crafted prose. An insightful reporter and master interviewer, Laney had an unerring ability to capture the style and character of the sports he covered and the athletes who played them." Laney is best known for his long years of service to the *New York Herald Tribune,* including nearly a decade he spent at the paper's Paris edition. In the pages of the *Herald Tribune* he covered not only golf and tennis but also the human interest side of sports. According to Sternberg, Laney "never had a job other than on a newspaper, and he wrote about the games and the people he loved."

Laney began working as a reporter in his native Pensacola, Florida, while still in his early teens. He eventually dropped out of high school when the local newspaper offered him a full-time job. By the time he entered the military service at the outset of World War I, he had finished an apprenticeship that had taken him to the *Dallas Dispatch* and the *Minneapolis News.* Even then he was most interested in sports, especially baseball and tennis. At the end of the war—in which he served as an officer and was wounded in the Argonne Forest—Laney returned to New York City in search of another newspaper job.

The *New York Evening Mail* took Laney's sports stories on a piece-by-piece basis, and the editors there encouraged him to specialize in tennis. This he did gladly, having played the game enthusiastically before being wounded in the war. By the time the *Evening Mail* merged with another paper in 1924, Laney was able to use his savings and severance pay to finance a trip to Paris. His first position there was as a reader to writer James Joyce, who was blind by that time. The job was short-lived: Joyce fired Laney because Laney could not read Italian.

In 1925 Laney hired on at the *Paris Herald,* the French edition of the *New York Herald.* His duties included night editor, reporter, copyreader, headline writer, and re-write man. Nevertheless he managed to read widely and to travel between England and France covering the Davis Cup, Wimbledon, and other important tennis tournaments. He returned to America permanently in 1934 and was assigned to the sports department at the *New York Herald Tribune.*

Laney worked briefly as a sports columnist but soon discovered that his talents and proclivities lay more toward longer stories and specific coverage of the sports he most enjoyed. According to Sternberg, "Laney's reputation for reporting, for conducting interviews and writing special stories, was unsurpassed." His reputation as a tennis and golf specialist intact, Laney also drew notice for his thoughtful feature stories on retired sports heroes, some as famous as Babe Ruth and Smokey Joe Wood, and some as forgotten as boxer Sam Langford, who was living in a Harlem tenement. Laney's coverage of Langford's plight was so moving that readers from New York and across the country flooded the newspaper office with donations for the former pugilist, enabling Laney to set up an annuity for Langford.

Laney stayed with the *New York Herald Tribune* until the paper closed in 1966, principally working the tennis and golf beats. "The sources of Laney's success lie not just in the technical aspects of his writing but also in his understanding that any writing about a particular sport should have its unique style," noted Sternberg.

In *Covering the Court,* one of his full-length books, Laney recounted a half-century of tennis reportage, beginning with the summer of 1914. As a teenager, he saw the great Maurice McLoughlin play the game—and decided to dedicate himself to recording the evolution and nuances of tennis. "It is a decision for which many of us who subsequently learned about the game through Laney's penetrating analyses in the columns of the *New York Herald Tribune* will be forever grateful," John Quinn commented in the *Chicago Tribune Book World.* "[Laney] has seen just about all the great players and most of the great matches. . . . The book is in the main a delightfully written and tonically candid exercise in pure nostalgia." *Harper's* reviewer K. G. Jackson wrote of the same book: "This is not just history. It is intelligent firsthand reporting of great matches and great moments in the game with vivid character sketches of the players and descriptions of their games, many of which have become legend."

Laney died in a retirement home on January 31, 1988 at the age of 92. Sternberg quotes sports editor Herbert Warren Wind, who declared: "Many of his colleagues consider Laney as good a sportswriter as ever lived, and they are probably right."

BIOGRAPHICAL/CRITICAL SOURCES:

BOOKS

Dictionary of Literary Biography, Gale (Detroit, MI), Volume 4: *American Writers in Paris, 1920-1939,* 1980, Volume 171: *Twentieth-Century American Sportswriters,* 1996, pp. 179-85.
Holtzman, Jerome, *No Cheering in the Press Box,* Holt (New York City), 1974.
Kluger, Richard, *The Paper: The Life and Death of the New York Herald Tribune,* Vantage (New York City), 1986.
Wind, Herbert Warren, editor, *The Realm of Sport,* Simon & Schuster (New York City), 1966.
Woodward, Stanley, *Sports Page,* Simon & Schuster, 1949.

PERIODICALS

Chicago Tribune Book World, September 15, 1968, p. 12.

Harper's, July, 1968, p. 107.

Newsweek, October 27, 1947, pp. 68, 70; April 4, 1960, pp. 106, 108.

New York Herald Tribune Weekly Book Review, November 16, 1947, p. 4.

New York Times, November 2, 1947, p. 31; December 3, 1978, p. 3.

New York Times Book Review, November 2, 1947, p. 31.

Saturday Review of Literature, December 6, 1947, p. 74.*

*   *   *

LARKIN, Philip (Arthur) 1922-1985

PERSONAL: Born August 9, 1922, in Coventry, Warwickshire, England; died following surgery for throat cancer, December 2, 1985, in Hull, England; son of Sydney (a city treasurer) and Eva Emily (Day) Larkin. *Education:* St. John's College, Oxford, B.A. (with first class honors), 1943, M.A., 1947.

CAREER: Wellington Public Library, Wellington, England, librarian, 1943-46; University College Library, Leicester, England, librarian, 1946-50; Queen's University Library, Belfast, Northern Ireland, sublibrarian, 1950-55; Brynmor Jones Library, University of Hull, Hull, England, librarian, 1955-85. Visiting fellow, All Souls College, Oxford, 1970-71; honorary fellow, St. John's College, Oxford, 1973; chair of judges for Booker Prize, 1977; member, British Library Board, 1984-85; member of standing conference of national and university libraries.

MEMBER: Arts Council of Great Britain (chair of National Manuscript Collection of Contemporary Writers Committee, 1972-79; member of literature panel, 1980-82), Royal Society of Literature (fellow), Royal Society of Arts, Poetry Book Society (former chair), American Academy of Arts and Sciences (honorary member).

AWARDS, HONORS: Arts Council prize, 1965; Queen's Gold medal for Poetry, 1965; Cholmondeley award, 1973; Loines Award, National Institute and American Academy of Arts and Letters, 1974;

Benson medal, 1975; Commander, Order of the British Empire, 1975; Shakespeare prize, FVS Foundation (Hamburg, Germany), 1976; Companion of Literature, Royal Society of Literature, 1978; Coventry Award of Merit, 1978; W. H. Smith & Son Literary Award, 1985, for *Required Writing: Miscellaneous Pieces 1955-82.* Honorary degrees include D.Lit. from Queen's University, 1969, New University of Ulster, Coleraine, 1983, and Oxford University, 1984; D.Litt. from University of Leicester, 1970, University of Warwick, 1973, University of St. Andrews, Fife, 1974, and University of Sussex, Brighton, 1974.

WRITINGS:

The North Ship (poems), Fortune Press, 1946, new edition, Faber, 1966.

Jill (novel), Fortune Press, 1946, revised edition, St. Martin's, 1964, reprinted, Overlook Press, 1984.

A Girl in Winter (novel), Faber, 1947, St. Martin's, 1957.

XX Poems, [Belfast], 1951.

[Poems], Fantasy Press, 1954.

The Less Deceived (poems), Marvell Press, 1955, 4th edition, St. Martin's, 1958.

Listen Presents Philip Larkin Reading "The Less Deceived" (recording), Marvell Press, 1959.

The Whitsun Weddings (poems), Random House, 1964.

Philip Larkin Reads and Comments on "The Whitsun Weddings" (recording), Marvell Press, c. 1966.

All What Jazz: A Record Diary 1961-1968 (essays), St. Martin's, 1970, updated edition published as *All What Jazz: A Record Diary 1961-1971,* Farrar, Straus, 1985.

(Editor and contributor) *The Oxford Book of Twentieth-Century English Verse,* Oxford University Press, 1973.

High Windows (poems), Farrar, Straus, 1974.

British Poets of Our Time, Philip Larkin: "High Windows," Poems Read by the Author (recording), Arts Council of Great Britain, c. 1975.

(Author of introduction) Llewelyn Powys, *Earth Memories,* State Mutual Book and Periodical Service, 1983.

Required Writing: Miscellaneous Pieces 1955-1982 (essays), Faber, 1983, Farrar, Straus, 1984.

Collected Poems, edited with an introduction by Anthony Thwaite, Marvell Press, 1988, Farrar, Straus, 1989.

Selected Letters: 1940-1985, edited by Thwaite, Farrar, Straus, 1993.

Also author of other poetry collections, including *The Explosion,* 1970, *Femmes Damnees,* 1978, and *Aubade,* 1980; author of *A Lifted Study-Storehouse: The Brynmor Jones Library, 1929-1979,* 1987; editor, with Louis MacNeice and Bonamy Dobree, of *New Poets 1958: A PEN Anthology.* Contributor to numerous anthologies; contributor of poetry and essays to periodicals. Jazz critic for *Daily Telegraph* (London), 1961-71.

ADAPTATIONS: Some of Larkin's poetry and a *Paris Review* interview were adapted for stage by Ron Hutchinson and produced as *Larkin* in Los Angeles, CA, 1988.

SIDELIGHTS: Philip Larkin, an eminent writer in postwar Great Britain, was commonly referred to as "England's *other* Poet Laureate" until his death in 1985. Indeed, when the position of laureate became vacant in 1984, many poets and critics favored Larkin's appointment, but the shy, provincial author preferred to avoid the limelight. An "artist of the first rank" in the words of *Southern Review* contributor John Press, Larkin achieved acclaim on the strength of an extremely small body of work—just over one hundred pages of poetry in four slender volumes that appeared at almost decade-long intervals. These collections, especially *The Less Deceived, The Whitsun Weddings,* and *High Windows,* present "a poetry from which even people who distrust poetry, most people, can take comfort and delight," according to X. J. Kennedy in the *New Criterion.* Larkin employed the traditional tools of poetry—rhyme, stanza, and meter—to explore the often uncomfortable or terrifying experiences thrust upon common people in the modern age. As Alan Brownjohn notes in *Philip Larkin,* the poet produced without fanfare "the most technically brilliant and resonantly beautiful, profoundly disturbing yet appealing and approachable, body of verse of any English poet in the last twenty-five years."

Despite his wide popularity, Larkin "shied from publicity, rarely consented to interviews or readings, cultivated his image as right-wing curmudgeon and grew depressed at his fame," according to J. D. McClatchy in the *New York Times Book Review.* To support himself, he worked as a professional librarian for more than forty years, writing in his spare time. In that manner he authored two novels, *Jill* and *A Girl in Winter,* two collections of criticism, *All What Jazz: A Record Diary 1961-1968* and *Required Writing: Miscellaneous Pieces 1955-1982,* and all of his verse. *Phoenix* contributor Alun R. Jones sug-

gests that, as a wage earner at the remote University of Hull, Larkin "avoided the literary, the metropolitan, the group label, and embraced the nonliterary, the provincial, and the purely personal." In *Nine Contemporary Poets: A Critical Introduction,* Peter R. King likewise commends "the scrupulous awareness of a man who refuses to be taken in by inflated notions of either art or life." From his base in Hull, Larkin composed poetry that both reflects the dreariness of postwar provincial England and voices "most articulately and poignantly the spiritual desolation of a world in which men have shed the last rags of religious faith that once lent meaning and hope to human lives," according to Press. McClatchy notes Larkin wrote "in clipped, lucid stanzas, about the failures and remorse of age, about stunted lives and spoiled desires." Critics feel that this localization of focus and the colloquial language used to describe settings and emotions endear Larkin to his readers. *Agenda* reviewer George Dekker notes that no living poet "can equal Larkin on his own ground of the familiar English lyric, drastically and poignantly limited in its sense of any life beyond, before or after, life today in England."

Throughout his life, England was Larkin's emotional territory to an eccentric degree. The poet distrusted travel abroad and professed ignorance of foreign literature, including most modern American poetry. He also tried to avoid the cliches of his own culture, such as the tendency to read portent into an artist's childhood. In his poetry and essays, Larkin remembered his early years as "unspent" and "boring," as he grew up the son of a city treasurer in Coventry. Poor eyesight and stuttering plagued Larkin as a youth; he retreated into solitude, read widely, and began to write poetry as a nightly routine. In 1940 he enrolled at Oxford, beginning "a vital stage in his personal and literary development," according to Bruce K. Martin in the *Dictionary of Literary Biography.* At Oxford Larkin studied English literature and cultivated the friendship of those who shared his special interests, including Kingsley Amis and John Wain. He graduated with first class honors in 1943, and, having to account for himself with the wartime Ministry of Labor, he took a position as librarian in the small Shropshire town of Wellington. While there he wrote both of his novels as well as *The North Ship,* his first volume of poetry. After working at several other university libraries, Larkin moved to Hull in 1955 and began a thirty-year association with the library at the University of Hull. He is still admired for his expansion and modernization of that facility.

The author's *Selected Letters,* edited by Larkin's longtime friend Anthony Thwaite, reveals much about the writer's personal and professional life between 1940 and 1985. *Washington Post Book World* reviewer John Simon notes that the letters are "about intimacy, conviviality, and getting things off one's heaving chest into a heedful ear." He suggests that "these cheerful, despairing, frolicsome, often foulmouthed, grouchy, self-assertive and self-depreciating missives should not be missed by anyone who appreciates Larkin's verse."

In a *Paris Review* interview, Larkin dismissed the notion that he studied the techniques of poets that he admired in order to perfect his craft. Most critics feel, however, that the poems of both William Butler Yeats and Thomas Hardy exerted an influence on Larkin as he sought his own voice. Martin suggests that the pieces in *The North Ship* "reflect an infatuation with Yeatsian models, a desire to emulate the Irishman's music without having undergone the experience upon which it had been based." Hardy's work provided the main impetus to Larkin's mature poetry, according to critics. A biographer in *Contemporary Literary Criticism* claims "Larkin credited his reading of Thomas Hardy's verse for inspiring him to write with greater austerity and to link experiences and emotions with detailed settings." King contends that a close reading of Hardy taught Larkin "that a modern poet could write about the life around him in the language of the society around him. He encouraged [Larkin] to use his poetry to examine the reality of his own life. . . . As a result Larkin abandoned the highly romantic style of *The North Ship,* which had been heavily influenced by the poetry of Yeats, and set out to write from the tensions that underlay his own everyday experiences. Hardy also supported his employment of traditional forms and technique, which Larkin [went] on to use with subtlety and variety." In his work *Philip Larkin,* Martin also claims that Larkin learned from Hardy "that his own life, with its often casual discoveries, could become poems, and that he could legitimately share such experience with his readers. From this lesson [came Larkin's] belief that a poem is better based on something from 'unsorted' experience than on another poem or other art."

Not surprisingly, this viewpoint allied Larkin with the poets of The Movement, a loose association of British writers who "called, implicitly in their poetry and fiction and explicitly in critical essays, for some sort of commonsense return to more traditional techniques," according to Martin in *Philip Larkin.* Mar-

tin adds that the rationale for this "antimodernist, antiexperimental stance is their stated concern with clarity: with writing distinguished by precision rather than obscurity. . . . [The Movement urged] not an abandonment of emotion, but a mixture of rationality with feeling, of objective control with subjective abandon. Their notion of what they felt the earlier generation of writers, particularly poets, lacked, centered around the ideas of honesty and realism about self and about the outside world." King observes that Larkin "had sympathy with many of the attitudes to poetry represented by The Movement," but this view of the poet's task antedated the beginnings of that group's influence. Nonetheless, in the opinion of *Washington Post Book World* contributor Chad Walsh, Larkin says "seemed to fulfill the credo of the Movement better than anyone else, and he was often singled out, as much for damnation as for praise, by those looking for the ultimate Movement poet." Brownjohn concludes that in the company of The Movement, Larkin's own "distinctive technical skills, the special subtlety in his adaptation of a very personal colloquial mode to the demands of tight forms, were not immediately seen to be outstanding; but his strengths as a craftsman have increasingly come to be regarded as one of the hallmarks of his talent."

Those strengths of craftsmanship and technical skill in Larkin's mature works receive almost universal approval from literary critics. London *Sunday Times* correspondent Ian Hamilton writes: "Supremely among recent poets, [Larkin] was able to accommodate a talking voice to the requirements of strict metres and tight rhymes, and he had a faultless ear for the possibilities of the iambic line." David Timms expresses a similar view in his book entitled *Philip Larkin.* Technically, notes Timms, Larkin was "an extraordinarily various and accomplished poet, a poet who [used] the devices of metre and rhyme for specific effects. . . . His language is never flat, unless he intends it to be so for a particular reason, and his diction is never stereotyped. He [was] always ready . . . to reach across accepted literary boundaries for a word that will precisely express what he intends." As King explains, Larkin's best poems "are rooted in actual experiences and convey a sense of place and situation, people and events, which gives an authenticity to the thoughts that are then usually raised by the poet's observation of the scene. . . . Joined with this strength of careful social observation is a control over tone changes and the expression of developing feelings even within a single poem . . . which is the product of great craftsmanship. To these virtues must be added the fact that in all the poems there is a lucidity of language which invites understanding even when the ideas expressed are paradoxical or complex." *New Leader* contributor Pearl K. Bell concludes that Larkin's poetry "fits with unresisting precision into traditional structures, . . . filling them with the melancholy truth of things in the shrunken, vulgarized and parochial England of the 1970s."

If Larkin's style is traditional, the subject matter of his poetry is derived exclusively from modern life. Press contends that Larkin's artistic work "delineates with considerable force and delicacy the pattern of contemporary sensibility, tracing the way in which we respond to our environment, plotting the ebb and flow of the emotional flux within us, embodying in his poetry attitudes of heart and mind that seem peculiarly characteristic of our time: doubt, insecurity, boredom, aimlessness and malaise." A sense that life is a finite prelude to oblivion underlies many of Larkin's poems. King suggests that the work is "a poetry of disappointment, of the destruction of romantic illusions, of man's defeat by time and his own inadequacies," as well as a study of how dreams, hopes, and ideals "are relentlessly diminished by the realities of life." To Larkin, Brownjohn notes, life was never "a matter of blinding revelations, mystical insights, expectations glitteringly fulfilled. Life, for Larkin, and, implicitly, for all of us, is something lived mundanely, with a gradually accumulating certainty that its golden prizes are sheer illusion." Love is one of the supreme deceptions of humankind in Larkin's worldview, as King observes: "Although man clutches at his instinctive belief that only love will comfort, console and sustain him, such a hope is doomed to be denied. A lover's promise is an empty promise and the power to cure suffering through love is a tragic illusion." Stanley Poss in *Western Humanities Review* maintains that Larkin's poems demonstrate "desperate clarity and restraint and besieged common sense. And what they mostly say is, be beginning to despair, despair, despair."

Larkin arrived at his conclusions candidly, concerned to expose evasions so that the reader might stand "naked but honest, 'less deceived' . . . before the realities of life and death," to quote King. Many critics find Larkin withdrawn from his poems, a phenomenon Martin describes in the *Dictionary of Literary Biography* thus: "The unmarried observer, a staple in Larkin's poetic world, . . . enjoys only a curious and highly limited kind of communion with those he observes." Jones likewise declares that

Larkin's "ironic detachment is comprehensive. Even the intense beauty that his poetry creates is created by balancing on a keen ironic edge." King writes: "A desire not to be fooled by time leads to a concern to maintain vigilance against a whole range of possible evasions of reality. It is partly this which makes Larkin's typical stance one of being to one side of life, watching himself and others with a detached eye." Although *Harvard Advocate* contributor Andrew Sullivan states that the whole tenor of Larkin's work is that of an "irrelevant and impotent spectator," John Reibetanz offers the counter suggestion in *Contemporary Literature* that the poetry records and reflects "the imperfect, transitory experiences of the mundane reality that the poet shares with his readers." Larkin himself offered a rather wry description of his accomplishments—an assessment that, despite its levity, links him emotionally to his work. In 1979 he told the *Observer:* "I think writing about unhappiness is probably the source of my popularity, if I have any. . . . Deprivation is for me what daffodils were for Wordsworth."

Critics such as *Dalhousie Review* contributor Roger Bowen find moments of affirmation in Larkin's poetry, notwithstanding its pessimistic and cynical bent. According to Bowen, an overview of Larkin's oeuvre makes evident "that the definition of the poet as a modern anti-hero governed by a sense of his own mortality seems . . . justified. But . . . a sense of vision and a quiet voice of celebration seem to be asserting themselves" in at least some of the poems. Brownjohn admits that Larkin's works take a bleak view of human existence; at the same time, however, they contain "the recurrent reflection that others, particularly the young, might still find happiness in expectation." *Contemporary Literature* essayist James Naremore expands on Larkin's tendency to detach himself from the action in his poems: "From the beginning, Larkin's work has manifested a certain coolness and lack of self-esteem, a need to withdraw from experience; but at the same time it has continued to show his desire for a purely secular type of romance. . . . Larkin is trying to assert his humanity, not deny it. . . . The greatest virtue in Larkin's poetry is not so much his suppression of large poetic gestures as his ability to recover an honest sense of joy and beauty." The *New York Times* quotes Larkin as having said that a poem "represents the mastering, even if just for a moment, of the pessimism and the melancholy, and enables you—you the poet, and you, the reader—to go on." King senses this quiet catharsis when he concludes: "Although one's final impression of the poetry is certainly that the chief emphasis is placed on a life 'unspent' in the shadow of 'untruth,' moments of beauty and affirmation are not entirely denied. It is the difficulty of experiencing such moments after one has become so aware of the numerous self-deceptions that man practices on himself to avoid the uncomfortable reality which lies at the heart of Larkin's poetic identity."

Timms claims that Larkin "consistently maintained that a poet should write about those things in life that move him most deeply: if he does not feel deeply about anything, he should not write." Dedicated to reaching out for his readers, the poet was a staunch opponent of modernism in all artistic media. Larkin felt that such cerebral experimentation ultimately creates a barrier between an artist and the audience and provides unnecessary thematic complications. Larkin's "demand for fidelity to experience is supported by his insistence that poetry should both communicate and give pleasure to the reader," King notes, adding: "It would be a mistake to dismiss this attitude as a form of simple literary conservatism. Larkin is not so much expressing an anti-intellectualism as attacking a particular form of artistic snobbery." In *Philip Larkin,* Martin comments that the poet saw the need for poetry to move toward the "paying customer." Therefore, his writings concretize "many of the questions which have perplexed man almost since his beginning but which in modern times have become the province principally of academicians. . . . [Larkin's poetry reflects] his faith in the common reader to recognize and respond to traditional philosophical concerns when stripped of undue abstractions and pretentious labels." Brownjohn finds Larkin eminently successful in his aims: "It is indeed true that many of his readers find pleasure and interest in Larkin's poetry for its apparent accessibility and its cultivation of verse forms that seem reassuringly traditional rather than 'modernist' in respect of rhyme and metre." As Timms succinctly notes, originality for Larkin consisted "not in modifying the medium of communication, but in communicating something different."

"Much that is admirable in the best of [Larkin's] work is felt [in *Collected Poems*]: firmness and delicacy of cadence, a definite geography, a mutually fortifying congruence between what the language means to say and what it musically embodies," asserts Seamus Heaney in the *Observer.* The collection contains Larkin's six previous volumes of poetry as well as eighty-three of his unpublished poems gleaned from notebooks and homemade booklets. The earliest poems (which reflect the style and social concerns of W. H. Auden) date from his schooldays and the latest close to his death. Writing in the Chicago *Tribune Books,* Alan Shapiro points out, "Reading the work in total, we can see how Larkin, early and late, is a poet of great and complex feeling." Larkin "[endowed] the most commonplace objects and occasions with a chilling poignancy, [measuring] daily life with all its tedium and narrowness against the possibilities of feeling," adds Shapiro.

Larkin's output of fiction and essays is hardly more extensive than his poetry. His two novels, *Jill* and *A Girl in Winter,* were both published before his twenty-fifth birthday. *New Statesman* correspondent Clive James feels that both novels "seem to point forward to the poetry. Taken in their chronology, they are impressively mature and self-sufficient." James adds that the fiction is so strong that "if Larkin had never written a line of verse, his place as a writer would still have been secure." Although the novels received little critical attention when they first appeared, they have since been judged highly successful. Brownjohn calls *Jill* "one of the better novels written about England during the Second World War, not so much for any conscious documentary effort put into it as for Larkin's characteristic scrupulousness in getting all the background details right." In the *New York Review of Books,* John Bayley notes that *A Girl in Winter* is "a real masterpiece, a quietly gripping novel, dense with the humor that is Larkin's trademark, and also an extended prose poem." Larkin's essay collections, *Required Writing* and *All What Jazz,* are compilations of critical pieces he wrote for periodicals over a thirty-year period, including the jazz record reviews he penned as a music critic for the London *Daily Telegraph.* "Everything Larkin writes is concise, elegant and wholly original," Bayley claims in the *Listener,* "and this is as true of his essays and reviews as it is of his poetry." Elsewhere in the *New York Review of Books,* Bayley comments that *Required Writing* "reveals wide sympathies, deep and trenchant perceptions, a subterraneous grasp of the whole of European culture." And in an essay on *All What Jazz* for Anthony Thwaite's *Larkin at Sixty,* James concludes that "no wittier book of criticism has ever been written."

Larkin stopped writing poetry shortly after his collection *High Windows* was published in 1974. In an

Observer obituary, Kingsley Amis characterized the poet as "a man much driven in upon himself, with increasing deafness from early middle age cruelly emphasizing his seclusion." Small though it is, Larkin's body of work has "altered our awareness of poetry's capacity to reflect the contemporary world," according to *London Magazine* correspondent Roger Garfitt. A. N. Wilson draws a similar conclusion in the *Spectator:* "Perhaps the reason Larkin made such a great name from so small an *oeuvre* was that he so exactly caught the mood of so many of us. . . . Larkin found the perfect voice for expressing our worst fears." That voice was "stubbornly indigenous," according to Robert B. Shaw in *Poetry Nation.* Larkin appealed primarily to the British sensibility; he remained unencumbered by any compunction to universalize his poems by adopting a less regional idiom. Perhaps as a consequence, his poetry sells remarkably well in Great Britain, his readers come from all walks of life, and his untimely cancer-related death in 1985 has not diminished his popularity. Andrew Sullivan feels that Larkin "has spoken to the English in a language they can readily understand of the profound self-doubt that this century has given them. He was, of all English poets, a laureate too obvious to need official recognition."

BIOGRAPHICAL/CRITICAL SOURCES:

BOOKS

Aisenberg, Katy, *Ravishing Images: Ekphrasis in the Poetry and Prose of William Wordsworth, W.H. Auden, and Philip Larkin,* P. Lang (New York), 1995.

Alvarez, A., *All This Fiddle: Essays 1955-1967,* Random House, 1969.

Bayley, John, *The Uses of Division,* Viking, 1976.

Bedient, Calvin, *Eight Contemporary Poets,* Oxford University Press, 1974.

Bloomfield, B. C., *Philip Larkin: A Bibliography,* Faber, 1979.

Booth, James, *Philip Larkin, Writer,* St. Martin's Press (New York), 1992.

Brownjohn, Alan, *Philip Larkin,* Longman, 1975.

Contemporary Literary Criticism, Gale, Volume 3, 1975; Volume 5, 1976; Volume 8, 1978; Volume 9, 1978; Volume 13, 1980; Volume 18, 1981; Volume 33, 1985; Volume 39, 1986; Volume 64, 1991; Volume 81, 1994.

Cookson, Linda, and Bryan Loughrey, *Critical Essays on Philip Larkin,* Longman (Harlow, England), 1989.

Davie, Donald, *Thomas Hardy and British Poetry,* Oxford University Press, 1972, pp. 63-82.

Dictionary of Literary Biography, Volume 27: *Poets of Great Britain and Ireland, 1945-1960,* Gale, 1984.

Dodsworth, Martin, editor, *The Survival of Poetry: A Contemporary Survey,* Faber, 1970.

Enright, D. J., *Conspirators and Poets: Reviews and Essays,* Dufour, 1966.

Hartley, Jean, *Philip Larkin, the Marvell Press and Me,* Carcanet (Manchester), 1989.

Jones, Peter, and Michael Schmidt, editors, *British Poetry since 1970: A Critical Survey,* Carcanet, 1980.

King, Peter R., *Nine Contemporary Poets: A Critical Introduction,* Methuen, 1979.

Kuby, Lolette, *An Uncommon Poet for the Common Man: A Study of Philip Larkin's Poetry,* Mouton, 1974.

Latre, Guido, *Locking Earth to the Sky: A Structuralist Approach to Philip Larkin's Poetry,* Peter Lang, 1985.

Martin, Bruce K., *Philip Larkin,* Twayne, 1978.

Motion, Andrew, *Philip Larkin,* Methuen, 1982.

Motion, Andrew, *Philip Larkin: A Writer's Life,* 1993.

O'Connor, William Van, *The New University Wits and the End of Modernism,* Southern Illinois University Press, 1963.

Petch, Simon, *The Art of Philip Larkin,* Sydney University Press, 1981.

Regan, Stephen, *Philip Larkin,* Macmillan (Houndmills, Hampshire, England), 1992.

Rosenthal M. L., *The Modern Poets: A Critical Introduction,* Oxford University Press, 1960.

Rosenthal, M. L., *The New Poets: American and British Poetry since World War II,* Oxford University Press, 1967.

Salwak, Dale, editor, *Philip Larkin: The Man and His Work,* University of Iowa Press, 1989.

Schmidt, Michael, *A Reader's Guide to Fifty Modern British Poets,* Barnes & Noble, 1979.

Swarbrick, Andrew, *Out of Reach: The Poetry of Philip Larkin,* St. Martin's Press, 1995.

Thwaite, Anthony, editor, *Larkin at Sixty,* Faber, 1982.

Timms, David, *Philip Larkin,* Barnes & Noble, 1973.

Tolley, A. T., *My Proper Ground: A Study of the Work of Philip Larkin and Its Development,* Edinburgh University Press (Edinburgh), 1991.

Whalen, Terry, *Philip Larkin and English Poetry,* University of British Columbia Press, 1986.

PERIODICALS

Agenda, autumn, 1974; summer, 1976.
American Scholar, summer, 1965.
Atlantic, January, 1966.
Bucknell Review, December, 1965, pp. 97-105.
Chicago Review, Volume 18, number 2, 1965.
Commentary, April, 1994, p. 39.
Contemporary Literature, summer, 1974, pp. 331-43; autumn, 1976.
Critical Inquiry, number 3, 1976-77, pp. 471-88.
Critical Quarterly, summer, 1964; summer, 1981.
Dalhousie Review, spring, 1968; spring, 1978.
ELH, December, 1971, pp. 616-30.
Encounter, June, 1974; February, 1984.
Harvard Advocate, May, 1968.
Iowa Review, fall, 1977.
Journal of English Literary History, December, 1971.
Listener, January 26, 1967; March 26, 1970; December 22, 1983.
London Magazine, May, 1964, pp. 71-7; November, 1964; June, 1970; October-November, 1974; April-May, 1980, pp. 81-96.
Los Angeles Times, June 13, 1984; October 1, 1988.
Los Angeles Times Book Review, December 1, 1985; July 30, 1989.
Michigan Quarterly Review, fall, 1976.
New Criterion, February, 1986.
New Leader, May 26, 1975.
New Republic, March 6, 1965; November 20, 1976.
New Review, June, 1974, pp. 25-9.
New Statesman, June 14, 1974; July 26, 1974; March 21, 1975.
Newsweek, June 25, 1984.
New Yorker, December 6, 1976.
New York Review of Books, January 28, 1965; May 15, 1975.
New York Times, June 23, 1984; August 11, 1984.
New York Times Book Review, December 20, 1964; January 12, 1975; May 16, 1976; December 26, 1976; August 12, 1984; November 10, 1985; May 21, 1989; January 30, 1994, p. 18.
Observer (London), February 8, 1970; December 16, 1979, p. 35; November 20, 1983; October 9, 1988, p. 44.
Paris Review, summer, 1982, pp. 42-72.
Phoenix, autumn and winter, 1973-74; spring, 1975.
PN Review, Volume 4, number 2, 1977.
Poetry Nation, number 6, 1976.
Poetry Review, Volume 72, number 2, 1982.
Prairie Schooner, fall, 1975.
Review, June-July, 1962; December, 1964.
Southern Review, winter, 1977.

Stand, Volume 16, number 2, 1975.
Time, July 23, 1984.
Times (London), December 8, 1983; June 20, 1985; October 22, 1988.
Times Literary Supplement, January 6, 1984; October 23, 1992, p. 13.
Tribune Books (Chicago), April 16, 1989, p. 4.
Virginia Quarterly Review, spring, 1976.
Washington Post, June 3, 1989.
Washington Post Book World, January 12, 1975; May 7, 1989; December 12, 1993, p. 1.
Western Humanities Review, spring, 1962; autumn, 1975.
Yale Review, July, 1995, p. 136.

OBITUARIES:

PERIODICALS

Chicago Tribune, December 4, 1985.
Detroit Free Press, December 3, 1985.
Globe and Mail (Toronto), December 14, 1985.
Listener, December 12, 1985.
Los Angeles Times, December 3, 1985.
New Criterion, February, 1986.
New Republic, January 6 and 13, 1986.
New York Review of Books, January 16, 1986.
New York Times, December 3, 1985.
Observer (London), December 8, 1985.
Spectator, December 7, 1985.
Sunday Times (London), December 8, 1985.
Times (London), December 3, 1985; December 14, 1985.
Times Literary Supplement, January 24, 1986.
Washington Post, December 3, 1985.*

*   *   *

LEAVITT, David 1961-

PERSONAL: Born June 23, 1961, in Pittsburgh, PA; son of Harold Jack (a professor) and Gloria (a homemaker; maiden name, Rosenthal) Leavitt. *Education:* Yale University, B.A., 1983.

ADDRESSES: Agent—Andrew Wylie, The Wylie Agency, 250 W. 57th Street, Suite 2114, New York, NY, 10107-2199.

CAREER: Writer. Viking-Penguin, Inc., New York City, reader and editorial assistant, 1983-84.

MEMBER: PEN, Authors Guild, Phi Beta Kappa.

AWARDS, HONORS: Willets Prize for fiction, Yale University, 1982, for "Territory"; O. Henry Award, 1984, for "Counting Months"; nomination for best fiction, National Book Critics Circle, 1984, and for PEN/Faulkner Award for best fiction, PEN, 1985, both for *Family Dancing;* National Endowment for the Arts grant, 1985; Visiting Foreign Writer, Institute of Catalan Letters, Barcelona, Spain, 1989; Guggenheim Fellow, 1990.

WRITINGS:

Family Dancing (short stories), Knopf (New York City), 1984.
The Lost Language of Cranes (novel), Knopf, 1986.
Equal Affections (novel), Weidenfeld & Nicolson (London), 1989.
A Place I've Never Been (short stories), Viking (New York City), 1990.
While England Sleeps (novel), Viking, 1993, reprinted with a new preface by the author, Houghton (Boston), 1995.
(Co-editor Mark Mitchell) *Penguin Book of Gay Short Stories,* Viking, 1994.
(With Mark Mitchell) *Italian Pleasures,* Chronicle Books (San Francisco), 1996.
Arkansas: Three Novellas (includes "The Term Paper Artist," "The Wooden Anniversary," and "Saturn Street"), Houghton, 1997.

Contributor to periodicals, including *Esquire, Harper's, New Yorker, New York Times Book Review, New York Times Magazine,* and *Village Voice.*

ADAPTATIONS: The Lost Language of Cranes was made into a film by the British Broadcasting Corp. (BBC) in 1991.

WORK IN PROGRESS: A novel tentatively titled *The Page Turner.*

SIDELIGHTS: Lauded for his insightful and empathetic characterizations, author David Leavitt has been at the leading edge of the gay literature movement in the United States for over a decade. Daniel J. Murtaugh noted in *Dictionary of Literary Biography:* "While Leavitt has converted the experiences of gay men and women into a matter of interest for the mainstream reader, he remains one of the most poignant and subjective tellers of what it means to be gay and how a gay person survives in a world of family, education, or business not necessarily re-

ceptive to sexual difference." Leavitt published his first story, "Territory," in the *New Yorker* at the age of twenty-one. The story of a mother and her homosexual son, it was the first of its kind to be published in that magazine, and it created "a small stir in the city's more conservative circles," according to an *Interview* writer. Leavitt also published pieces in other various periodicals, including *Esquire* and *Harper's,* and in 1984 published his first book, a collection of short stories entitled *Family Dancing.*

Family Dancing showcased Leavitt's insights into some of the more offbeat, troubling aspects of domestic life. Among the stories noted by critics are "Radiation," about a slowly dying cancer victim, "Out Here," which concerns sibling guilt, and "Aliens," in which a young girl believes herself to be an extraterrestrial creature. The story "Territory" is included in this collection, and several other works in the volume also address homosexual concerns, including "Dedicated," and "Out Here," in which one of the characters is a lesbian.

Family Dancing earned acclaim as an impressive debut volume. *Newsweek*'s David Lehman, hailing the 1980s boom in short story writing, called Leavitt's book "a first collection of unusual finesse," and Michiko Kakutani wrote in the *New York Times* that *Family Dancing* is "an astonishing collection" with "the power to move us with the blush of truth." In a review for the *Washington Post,* Dennis Drabelle praised Leavitt as "remarkably gifted," and reserved particular commendation for Leavitt's tales of homosexuality. Leavitt, Drabelle contended, "captures the deep-rooted tensions between adult gays and their families and the efforts of childless gays to carve out families among their peers." Drabelle concluded that Leavitt's insights had "only just been tapped."

Leavitt devoted his first novel, *The Lost Language of Cranes,* to a further depiction of homosexual life. While the main character's romantic experiences are rather typical—he falls in love, loses his lover, and finds a more suitable mate—a subplot involving the protagonist's father delves into traumas specific to homosexuality. The father is a married man who spends Sunday afternoons indulging in his passion for patronizing pornography theaters. After learning that his son is a homosexual, he too makes his own difficult confession.

The Lost Language of Cranes, however, chronicles more than just the elements of a homosexual life. It also addresses more universal issues regarding love and traces the hope, pain, ecstasy, and suffering that are all a part of romantic involvement. Other issues explored in the novel include the notion of family life, and Leavitt narratively delineates the tensions and disappointments of the family as it is altered by the son's and the father's revelations. In addition, the anguish of the wife and mother is also evoked through her increased withdrawal from familial crises. Her disappointment, together with the father's anguish and the son's alternately exhilarating and crushing experiences with love, adds another dimension to Leavitt's work.

The Lost Language of Cranes garnered much critical acclaim. Susan Wood wrote in the *Washington Post* that Leavitt's novel "has much to recommend it," and Philip Lopate noted in the *New York Times Book Review* that the book is "readable and literate." An enthusiastic reviewer for Chicago *Tribune Books* described the novel as "well-written and frankly interesting," and added that "Leavitt's style is compelling, and the subject matter . . . is equally elucidative." Similarly, Dorothy Allison wrote in the *Village Voice* that "Leavitt catches beautifully the terror and passion of new love" and shows a profound understanding of love's "tentativeness." She further declared that *The Lost Language of Cranes* "places David Leavitt firmly among the best young authors of his generation," and concluded that his novel gave her "new hope for modern fiction."

Critics of *The Lost Language of Cranes* were especially impressed with Leavitt's skill in portraying compelling characters and his ability to evoke the tension and turmoil, as well as the fulfillment and ecstasy, of love. The reviewer for *Tribune Books* declared that "Leavitt opens up the gay world to readers" and added that the narrative is "mature, quick-paced and fascinating." Likewise, Allison wrote that the novel's various characters are "so fully realized" that she found herself "tense with fear for each of them." Allison commended Leavitt for his artistry in evincing such a response from readers. "It is David Leavitt's strength that he could inspire that kind of fear in me and win me back when his characters did not find true love or happiness," Allison noted. "At every moment I believed in them, and these days that is so rare as to suggest genius."

Leavitt's second novel, *Equal Affections,* which *Listener* reviewer John Lahr called a "tale of the extraordinariness of ordinary family suffering," centers around Louise Cooper, who is dying of cancer, and

the members of her family who must deal with this reality. Louise's husband, Nat, is a computer visionary whose visions have never amounted to much. Her son Danny is a gay lawyer living in bland, immaculate monogamy in the suburbs with Walter, who has not fully committed to the relationship. Daughter April is a famous folk singer who "discovers" her true lesbian nature and turns her singing to feminist issues. Louise's bitterness over lost opportunities, her crisis of faith, and her impending death color her interactions with her husband and family. As Louise's twenty-year bout with cancer draws to a close, the family deals with this strain as well as their individual problems: Nat is having an affair with another woman, Danny endures Walter's on-line computer philandering, and April is artificially inseminated with donor sperm from a culturally aware San Francisco homosexual.

Equal Affections received mixed reviews. Acknowledging her disappointment in Leavitt's first novel, *The Lost Language of Cranes,* Beverly Lowry wrote in the *New York Times Book Review* that "*Equal Affections* does not compromise itself with easy answers. It is a gritty, passionate novel that should settle the question of David Leavitt's abilities. . . . He has the talent for a lifelong career." Lahr called the novel "adroit," while a *New York* writer found it to be "limp, dreary business." The *Washington Post Book World*'s Alan Hollinghurst praised Leavitt's characterizations but observed that the "emotional drama . . . is distinctly soggy. Leavitt's characters are notoriously lachrymose, but here there's really too much tearful sentiment, spunky goodness and curtain-line corniness: this is a sleepie that turns into a weepie." The London *Observer*'s Candia McWilliam, however, called it an "attentive, unsparing book."

Leavitt followed *Equal Affections* with a second collection of short stories, *A Place I've Never Been,* in which a majority of the stories include gay characters dealing with relationships. "When You Grow to Adultery" finds the protagonist leaving an old lover for a new one, and in "My Marriage to Vengeance," a lesbian character's former lover marries a man. In the title story, a woman finally realizes that her gay friend Nathan is too wrapped up in his own self-pity to contribute to their friendship. A mother tests the limits of her AIDS-stricken son's waning strength in "Gravity," and a heterosexual couple who have lost their respective spouses to cancer begin an affair in "Spouse Night."

Many critics praised *A Place I've Never Been.* Charles Solomon of the *Los Angeles Times Book Review* called Leavitt's writing "fine, polished prose that is refreshingly free of the drip-dry nihilism of his Brat Pack contemporaries." James N. Baker of *Newsweek* summarized that "Leavitt is not an oracle nor is he a groundbreaker. . . . He remains what he has always been: a writer of conventional stories who casts an incisive, ironic eye on families and lovers, loyalty and betrayal." Reviewer Harriet Waugh wrote in the *Spectator:* "Short stories, unlike novels, have to be perfect. *A Place I've Never Been . . .* very nearly is." Waugh further declared, "I do not think I have read short stories that have given me greater pleasure or satisfaction in the last couple of years than *A Place I've Never Been.*" Wendy Martin of the *New York Times Book Review* called the book a "fine new collection of short fiction," and Clifford Chase described the stories as "at once wrenching and satisfying" in his review for the *Village Voice Literary Supplement.*

Leavitt's third novel, *While England Sleeps,* is set in the 1930s against the backdrop of the Spanish Civil War, and follows the love story between Brian Botsford, a literary aristocrat, and Edward Phelan, a lower-class ticket-taker on the London Underground. Brian ends the affair, and in an attempt to deny his homosexuality marries a woman whom his wealthy aunt thinks is suitable. Distraught, Edward joins the fight in Spain, but soon deserts the military and lands in prison. Brian follows his lover to Spain and secures Edward's release, but Edward dies of typhoid on the voyage home.

While England Sleeps borrowed a segment of its plot from Sir Stephen Spender's 1948 autobiography, *World within World,* a fact first revealed by Bernard Knox in his review for the *Washington Post.* Leavitt admitted using an episode from Spender's life as a springboard for his novel and wrote in the *New York Times Magazine* that he had initially included an acknowledgment to Spender, "but had been advised by an in-house lawyer at Viking to omit the reference." He also defended his book on the basis that it is a historical novel and maintained that it "diverged from Spender's account in many more ways than it converged with it." Spender brought suit in London against Leavitt for copyright infringement. Viking agreed to withdraw the book until Leavitt had revised some seventeen points cited in the Spender suit; once this had been done, however, Viking declined to publish the revised version. But in the fall of 1995, Houghton-Mifflin released the new version

with an added preface by Leavitt that addressed the book's legal controversy.

Despite this controversy, the *Los Angeles Times* shortlisted the book for its fiction prize after it had been withdrawn from its initial publication, and *While England Sleeps* continued to receive much publicity from reviewers. In a *New York Times* review, Christopher Lehmann-Haupt lauded the book's authentic portrayal of the pre-war European era and its depiction of divergent social classes. In the scenes which take place in Spain, Lehmann-Haupt added that "the theme of sexual deception is chillingly replicated in the way the Communist leaders treat their followers," and concluded that *While England Sleeps* should be credited for "[climbing] out of its preoccupation with sex and [making] a significant comment on the political issues of its time." Conversely, Jeremy Treglown noted in the *Times Literary Supplement* that "style is one thing about which Spender hasn't complained, yet the book's main offence lies in its novelettishness." D. T. Max concluded in the *Los Angeles Times Book Review* that "A careful reading of *World within World* shows Spender's charge of plagiarism to be over the top—all the novel's words seem Leavitt's own—but a charge of laziness would be far harder to disprove, and the knowledge of it mars an otherwise graceful, romantic novel."

In his next foray into fiction, *Arkansas: Three Novellas,* Leavitt once again explored issues of gay love and life, this time mixing directly autobiographical elements into the work. In "The Term Paper Artist," a young writer—named David Leavitt—tries to break through a case of writer's block caused by an accusation of plagiarism by an English poet. In an interview with Celestine Bohlen in the *New York Times,* Leavitt described his intent with this novella: "It is so common to write autobiographical fiction in which your own experience is thinly disguised. I thought it could be very interesting to do the opposite with a story where even a tiny amount of research into my life would prove it did not happen, . . . and thereby turn the convention inside out." The volume's other two novellas, "The Wooden Anniversary" and "Saturn Street," both deal with characters whose lovers have died and who are struggling with moving on with their lives. "The Wooden Anniversary" is set in Italy, where Leavitt himself now lives. Despite receiving some favorable critical reception, *New York Times* reviewer Michiko Kakutani termed the work "disappointing," criticizing the author's handling of sexual events as "repetitious, tiresome and sophomoric" and noting that "this sort of adolescent writing is unworthy of the richly talented Mr. Leavitt."

In addition to his own writing, Leavitt has edited, with his companion Mark Mitchell, the *Penguin Book of Gay Short Stories*. The collection consists of pieces that focus on gay men and includes a wide variety of writers, both contemporary and historical, among them Larry Kramer, D. H. Lawrence, Graham Greene, Christopher Isherwood, Edna O'Brien, and James Purdy. Writing in *New Statesman & Society,* Richard Canning bemoaned the omission of non-American and non-English writers as well as pre-1900 writers and questioning the inclusion of pieces that seem at odds with the authors' stated criteria. "Leavitt's preference for 'self-contained, autonomous works' rather than novel extracts is shelved for particular favourites." Nonetheless, Canning recommended the anthology as "no less comprehensive than any work subject to such criteria could be." Peter Parker of the *Observer* similarly questioned the scope of the pieces included, noting that the volume reflects Leavitt's own writing terrain— conservative, mainstream, "suburban-sensitive"—at the expense of literature angrier and more raunchy. But Peter Parker, while admitting some reservations about inclusion criteria in his *Times Literary Supplement* review, commended Leavitt and Mitchell for choosing "so many stories of such high literary quality."

Leavitt's success has made him one of the few mainstream writers whose work deals primarily with homosexual themes. As Martin explained in the *New York Times Book Review:* "Leavitt has the wonderful ability to lead the reader to examine heterosexist assumptions without becoming polemical. In prose that is often spare and carefully honed, he sensitizes us to the daily difficulties of homosexual life—of negotiating public spaces, for example, where holding hands or a simple embrace becomes problematic." She added: "Leavitt's insight and empathy serve . . . to enlighten, to make us realize that human sexuality is a continuum of possibilities that encompasses the subtle as well as the sensational." Leavitt once told *CA:* "I think the labeling as a gay writer can be a form of ghettoizing, of saying that now the work will only be read by gay people. That hasn't happened to me. The work has had a larger appeal. . . . More aptly, perhaps, I would say that the sexuality of the characters is less important than the situation that they're in, which may be caused by their sexuality but is ultimately more interesting than that fact itself."

BIOGRAPHICAL/CRITICAL SOURCES:

BOOKS

Contemporary Literary Criticism, Volume 34, Gale (Detroit), 1985.
Dictionary of Literary Biography, Volume 130: *American Short Story Writers since World War II,* Gale, 1993.

PERIODICALS

Advocate, October 19, 1993, pp. 51-55; December 28, 1993, p. 76.
Esquire, May, 1985.
Harper's, April, 1986.
Interview, March, 1985.
Library Journal, June 1, 1995.
Listener, June 15, 1989, p. 25.
London Review of Books, May 23, 1991, pp. 22-23.
Los Angeles Times Book Review, March 5, 1989, p. 6; August 4, 1991, p. 1991; October 3, 1993, pp. 3, 12.
National Review, December 27, 1993, p. 72.
New Statesman & Society, November 12, 1993, p. 38; March 11, 1994, p. 41.
Newsweek, January 14, 1985; February 13, 1989, p. 78; September 3, 1990, p. 66; November 8, 1993, p. 81.
New York, January 30, 1989; October 18, 1993, pp. 139-140.
New York Times, October 30, 1984; October 14, 1993, p. C20; February 20, 1994, p. D14; February 25, 1997, p. B1; March 11, 1997, p. B2.
New York Times Book Review, September 2, 1984; October 5, 1986; February 12, 1989, p. 7; August 26, 1990, p. 11; October 3, 1993, p. 14; September 4, 1994, p. 10.
New York Times Magazine, July 9, 1989, pp. 28-32; April 3, 1994, p. 36.
Observer (London), May 28, 1989, p. 46; February 6, 1994, p. 21.
Partisan Review, winter, 1994, pp. 80-95.
Publishers Weekly, August 24, 1990, pp. 47-48; February 21, 1994.
Spectator, March 9, 1991, p. 28.
Time, November 8, 1993, p. 27.
Times Literary Supplement, June 9-15, 1989, p. 634; October 29, 1993, p. 20; February 4, 1994, p. 20.
Tribune Books (Chicago), September 21, 1986.
Village Voice, October 14, 1986.
Village Voice Literary Supplement, December, 1990, pp. 10-11.

Washington Post, November 19, 1984; March 2, 1985; October 7, 1986; February 17, 1994, p. A1.

Washington Post Book World, January 22, 1989, p. 4; October 7, 1990, p. 7; September 12, 1993, p. 5.

* * *

LIEB, Fred(erick George) 1888-1980

PERSONAL: Born March 5, 1888, in Philadelphia, PA; died June 3, 1980, in Houston, TX; son of George August and Theresa (Zigler) Lieb; married Mary Ann Peck; children: Marie Theresa (Mrs. R. Leslie Pearsall). *Education:* Attended high school in Philadelphia, PA. *Politics:* Republican. *Religion:* "Unity."

CAREER: Norfolk & Western Railway, Philadelphia, PA, clerk, 1904-10; *New York Press,* New York City, baseball writer, 1911-16; *New York Morning Sun,* New York City, baseball writer, 1916-20; *New York Evening Telegram,* New York City, baseball writer, 1920-27; *New York Post,* New York City, baseball writer, 1927-33; *Sporting News,* St. Louis, MO, baseball writer, 1935-67; writer, 1967-80. Official scorer for World Series, 1922-24, 1945; covered sixty World Series.

MEMBER: Masons.

AWARDS, HONORS: J. G. Taylor Spink Award from Baseball Hall of Fame, 1972; inducted into writers' wing of Baseball Hall of Fame, 1973; award from *St. Petersburg Times,* 1975.

WRITINGS:

Sight Unseen: A Journalist Visits the Occult, Harper (New York City), 1939.

Healing Mind, Body, and Purse, privately printed, 1941.

The St. Louis Cardinals: The Story of a Great Baseball Club, Putnam (New York City), 1944, revised edition, 1945.

Connie Mack: Grand Old Man of Baseball, Putnam, 1945, revised edition, 1948.

The Detroit Tigers, Putnam, 1946, revised edition, 1950.

The Boston Red Sox, Putnam, 1947.

The Pittsburgh Pirates, Putnam, 1948.

The Story of the World Series: An Informal History, Putnam, 1949, second revised edition, 1965.

The Baseball Story, Putnam, 1950.

(With Stan Baumgartner) *The Philadelphia Phillies,* Putnam, 1953.

The Baltimore Orioles: The History of a Colorful Team in Baltimore and St. Louis, Putnam, 1955.

(With Bob Burnes, J. G. Taylor Spink, and Les Biederman) *Comedians and Pranksters of Baseball,* C. C. Spink (St. Louis, MO), 1958.

Baseball as I Have Known It, Coward (New York City), 1977.

Author of articles "Hits Are My Bread and Butter," in *Saturday Evening Post,* and "Strictly Screw Ball," in *Collier's.* Also author of columns "Hot Stove League" and "Cutting the Plate." Contributor to *Encyclopedia Americana.* Contributor of stories to *Baseball* and *Railroad Man.*

SIDELIGHTS: Few people could have been more enthusiastic about their work than Fred Lieb. A lifelong baseball enthusiast, Lieb was also one of the most prominent national writers on the sport. His long career included newspaper, magazine, and book-length work—and the heady honor of rubbing elbows with the likes of Babe Ruth, Lou Gehrig, and Connie Mack. Lieb, who wrote almost constantly until his death at ninety-two, is quoted in the *Dictionary of Literary Biography* as having said: "I love baseball. I could watch it every day, every year. And to think I get paid for watching it."

Born and raised in Philadelphia, Lieb set out to find a newspaper job after graduating from high school in 1904. At first he had to settle for publishing in pulp magazines while working in a railroad office, but by 1909 he had a regular assignment from *Baseball Magazine,* and by 1911 he had landed a job as baseball writer at the *New York Press.* All told, Lieb worked for four different New York newspapers between 1911 and 1934. According to J. Douglas English in the *Dictionary of Literary Biography,* Lieb was a superb stylist who considered much popular sportswriting to be vulgar. Rejecting both the "Gee Whiz" and the "aw shucks" angles many writers adopted, he instead "reported as if the audience was composed of readers such as he—as if they wanted what he had wanted as a young connoisseur of sportswriting in Philadelphia."

In 1935 Lieb became a national correspondent for *The Sporting News,* and he earned a reputation for his continuous coverage of the World Series and the

All-Star Games. By the time his career ended, he had sat in the press box for the Fall Classic sixty times, and he was widely respected as one of the foremost historians of major league baseball. It was also during this period that Lieb began his series of book-length team profiles for Putnam, including *The Detroit Tigers, The Boston Red Sox,* and *The Philadelphia Phillies.* His more wide-ranging books, *The Story of the World Series* and *The Baseball Story,* "still serve as foundational references for baseball research, and it is difficult to find any historical work on baseball that does not contain Lieb's name either in its bibliography or index," to quote English.

Another best-selling Lieb book was *Connie Mack: Grand Old Man of Baseball.* The colorful Mack was a manager of the Athletics for fifty years and was much beloved in the hearts of his fans. Lieb's account of Mack's life "should be a welcome addition to the libraries of many of those who are interested in the whys and the wherefores of what has come to be known as America's national pastime," noted a *Book Week* correspondent. According to Al Horwits in the *New York Times,* "For the majority of the sporting world who know much about Connie Mack this biography will serve chiefly to refresh memories of him and of his great players, and of those events in baseball which never become dull no matter how many times they are repeated."

Among Lieb's accomplishments are a few permanent additions to sporting lore. His piece "Hits Are My Bread and Butter" is considered a classic of magazine journalism, and it was he who coined the sobriquet "House that Ruth Built" to describe Yankee Stadium. Lieb was inducted into the writers' wing of the Baseball Hall of Fame in 1973, long after he had "retired" to St. Petersburg, Florida. He died in a nursing home in Houston, Texas, about one month after his last by-line appeared in *The Sporting News.* English quotes Lieb as once having commented: "When I walked into the New York press box for the first time, I couldn't have been happier, not if I'd made it to the Oval Office of the White House."

BIOGRAPHICAL/CRITICAL SOURCES:

BOOKS

Dictionary of Literary Biography, Volume 171: *Twentieth-Century American Sportswriters,* Gale (Detroit, MI), 1996, pp. 218-26.
Holtzman, Jerry, editor, *No Cheering in the Press Box,* Holt (New York City), 1973.

PERIODICALS

Best Sellers, February 15, 1965, p. 455.
Book Week, May 6, 1945, p. 9.
New York Herald Tribune Book Review, November 5, 1950, p. 21.
New York Times, May 27, 1945, p. 12; September 22, 1946, p. 35; April 27, 1947, p. 28; August 1, 1948, p. 19; October 22, 1950, p. 30; April 19, 1953, p. 28.
Saturday Review of Literature, April 29, 1939, p. 27.
Washington Post, December 11, 1977, p. E7.

OBITUARIES:

PERIODICALS

New York Times, June 5, 1980.
Washington Post, June 5, 1980.*

*   *   *

LIVINGSTON, Nancy 1935-1994

PERSONAL: Born November 18, 1935, in Stockton-on-Tees, County Cleveland, England; died, 1994; daughter of Harry William (a tax inspector) and Frances (a homemaker; maiden name, Hewitt) Woolsey; married David Edward Foster (a television director and producer), May, 1975. *Education:* London Academy of Music and Dramatic Art, ALAM (honours); Miss Wilkinson's Academy for Gentlewoman, 1954.

CAREER: Actress, Harry Hanson's Court Players, and television, 1952-54; secretary, Manchester *Guardian,* and F. Smith's Copper Wire Factory, Salford, 1954-60; airline stewardess, BOAC, 1960-66; television production assistant, Tyne Tees Television, Newcastle, 1966-68, ATV, Elstree, Hertfordshire, 1968-83, and freelance producer for independent television companies, London, 1983-89; writer, 1985-94.

MEMBER: Crime Writers Association (vice chair, 1991-92).

AWARDS, HONORS: Poisoned Chalice Award, Crime Writers Association, 1985, for *The Trouble at Aquitaine;* Punch Award, 1988, for *Death in a Distant Land.*

WRITINGS:

"MR. G. D. H. PRINGLE" MYSTERY SERIES

The Trouble at Aquitaine, St. Martin's (New York City), 1985, Chivers Press (Bath, England) and J. Curley (South Yarmouth, MA), 1987.

Fatality at Bath and Wells, St. Martin's, 1986, Chivers Press and J. Curley, 1987.

Incident at Parga, St. Martin's, 1987, Chivers Press and J. Curley, 1988.

Death in a Distant Land, St. Martin's, 1988, Chivers Press and J. Curley, 1989.

Death in Close-Up, St. Martin's, 1989, Chivers Press and J. Curley, 1990.

Mayhem in Parva, St. Martin's, 1991, Chivers Press and J. Curley, 1992.

Unwillingly to Vegas, St. Martin's, 1992.

Quiet Murder, Gollancz (London, England), 1992, St. Martin's, 1993.

OTHER NOVELS

The Far Side of the Hill (generational saga), Macdonald (London, England), 1987, St. Martin's, 1988.

The Land of Our Dreams (generational saga), Macdonald, 1988, St. Martin's, 1989.

Never Were Such Times (generational saga), Macdonald, 1990, St. Martin's, 1991, Thorndike-Magna (Thorndike, ME), 1992.

Two Sisters (historical saga), Little Brown (London), 1992, St. Martin's Press, 1994.

OTHER

Author of radio plays, including *Alice's Ashes,* 1979, and *Slimming Down,* 1984. Author of television script *The Work of Giants,* 1968.

SIDELIGHTS: Nancy Livingston once told *CA:* "The motivation to become a writer stemmed from an overwhelming desire to leave television and 'do my own thing.' The desire continues."

Judith Rhodes said in the *St. James Guide to Crime and Mystery Writers* that "Livingston's series character Mr. G. D. H. Pringle (H.M. Tax Inspector, retired) makes his sedate way into the annals of crime fiction halfway through *The Trouble at Aquitaine.* Accustomed to supplementing his pension by inves-

tigating fraud, Mr. Pringle is here called in to detect a murder at Aquitaine, a 12th-century castle now turned into a health farm; the tools of his investigative trade are buff envelopes, quantities of homemade forms and a calligrapher's pen. But readers should not be deceived by this prim, old-fashioned figure for Mr. Pringle . . . has hidden depths." Rhodes further noted that "the novel is enlivened by the crisply-drawn cast of suspects, some of them sympathetic and some of them downright obnoxious. . . . By far the most endearing character in Livingston's novels appears only briefly in this first book—we see much more of her in subsequent novels. Mavis Bignell is G. D. H. Pringle's lady-friend, whom he first met when she stepped in at the last minute as a nude model at the art class he was attending. They make an incongruous couple—both are widowed, but there, apparently, the similarity ends. Mr. Pringle is 'a man over medium height but stooping slightly, of spare build, with a soft grey moustache, a worried look on his face, and National Health spectacles. . . . Mavis Bignell, on the other hand, is physically well-endowed and given to wearing bright colours and floral designs. . . . Their relationship is summed up in *Fatality at Bath and Wells*—'both of them valued their independence, so Mr. Pringle made weekly visits to the Bricklayers where Mavis worked part-time behind the bar because she enjoyed a bit of company. After closing-time he accompanied her home for what she described as 'a bit of supper and what have you.' . . . His physical relationship with Mavis is always dealt with very tastefully, and it is left to the reader to imagine his participation in the pleasures of the flesh—although we are left in no doubt as to the quality and quantity of Mrs. Bignell's flesh. A never-failing source of comfort and sound common sense, and yet possessed of an endearing naivety, Mavis Bignell is the perfect foil to Mr. Pringle—whose first name we never do learn."

In conclusion, Rhodes stated: ". . . As a detective, Mr. Pringle approaches his cases methodically, and takes a modest, low-key approach. His status is never more than semi-official, and yet suspects are usually surprisingly willing to answer his questions. It is sometimes hard to maintain one's belief in this fictional investigator, and yet had he a more flamboyant personality the other character in the books would not be shown up in such sharp relief."

A *Publishers Weekly* reviewer said of *Mayhem in Parva,* "Livingston skillfully and humorously depicts life in a contemporary English village, and her geriatric detective and his barmaid lady love are a delight." Stuart Miller, reviewing in *Booklist,* termed the book "A light-hearted and amusing mystery using the grand old tradition of murder-in-the-English-village to hilarious effect." Marilyn Stasio, writing in *New York Times Book Review,* assessed: "For all the amusement she takes in the eccentric customs of the country, Ms. Livingston does not neglect craft for charm. . . . Mr. Pringle unravels the well-knotted plot with as much intelligence as humor."

In addition to her detective novels, Livingston also wrote family sagas. One of these, *Two Sisters,* prompted Cynthia Johnson of *Library Journal* to comment that the "richly detailed work . . . nonetheless might have been better had the author subtly revealed—rather than stated—the psychology of her characters." A *Publishers Weekly* review said of *Never Were Such Times,* a generational saga about working-class English family of Victorian times, that Livingston "writes a vivid and lively historical novel about ordinary people affected by changing times." A *Kirkus Reviews* writer said, "In spite of an extravagance in coincidence and a heavy underlining of Good and Evil, Livingston offers a convincing energetic appreciation of the times and the poisoning wells of poverty." Cynthia Ogorek, writing in *Booklist,* said the novel's principal characters, Albert, Esther and Chas possess "dignity and the wisdom to believe in their own self-worth no matter who or what threatens their well-being."

BIOGRAPHICAL/CRITICAL SOURCES:

BOOKS

St. James Guide to Crime and Mystery Writers, fourth edition, St. James Press (Detroit, MI), 1996.

PERIODICALS

Booklist, September 15, 1991, p. 125.
Kirkus Reviews, June 1, 1991, p. 1860; July 15, 1991, p. 893.
Library Journal, August, 1994, p. 130.
New York Times Book Review, September 29, 1991, p. 30.
Publishers Weekly, May 10, 1991, p. 271; July 5, 1991, p. 60.*

LOCKRIDGE, Richard 1898-1982
(Francis Richards, a joint pseudonym)

PERSONAL: Born September 26, 1898, in St. Joseph, MO; died of a series of strokes, June 19, 1982, in Tryon, NC; son of Ralph David L. and Mary Olive (Notson) Lockridge; married Frances Davis (a writer), March 4, 1922 (died, 1963); married Hildegarde Dolson (a writer), May 26, 1965. *Education:* Attended Kansas City Junior College, 1916-18, and University of Missouri, 1920.

CAREER: Writer. *Kansas City Kansas,* Kansas City, KS, reporter, 1921-22; *Kansas City Star,* Kansas City, reporter, 1922; *New York Sun,* New York, NY, reporter, 1923-29, drama critic, 1929-42. *Military service:* U.S. Naval Reserve Force, 1918. U.S. Naval Reserve, 1942-45; became lieutenant.

AWARDS, HONORS: Edgar Allan Poe Award, Mystery Writers of America, 1945, for radio play; special award, Mystery Writers of America, 1962.

WRITINGS:

Darling of Misfortune: Edwin Booth, 1833-1893, Century Co. (New York City), 1932, reprinted, Benjamin Blom, 1971.
Mr. and Mrs. North, Stokes (New York City), 1936.
(With George Hoben Estabrooks) *Death in the Mind,* Dutton (New York City), 1945.
A Matter of Taste, Lippincott (Philadelphia), 1949.
Cats and People, Lippincott, 1950.
The Proud Cat, Lippincott, 1951.
The Lucky Cat, Lippincott, 1953.
The Nameless Cat, Lippincott, 1954.
The Cat Who Rode Cows, Lippincott, 1955.
The Empty Day, Lippincott, 1964.
Squire of Death, Lippincott, 1965.
Encounter in Key West, Lippincott, 1966.
Murder for Art's Sake, Lippincott, 1967.
One Lady, Two Cats, Lippincott, 1967.
Murder in False-Face, Lippincott, 1968.
A Plate of Red Herrings, Lippincott, 1968.
Die Laughing, Lippincott, 1969.
Troubled Journey, Lippincott, 1970.
Twice Retired, Lippincott, 1970.
Preach No More, Lippincott, 1971.
Death in a Sunny Place, Lippincott, 1971.
Write Murder Down, Lippincott, 1972.
Death on the Hour, Lippincott, 1974.
Or Was He Pushed?, Lippincott, 1975.
A Streak of Light, Lippincott, 1976.
The Tenth Life, Lippincott, 1977.

"MERTON HEIMRICH" SERIES

Murder Can't Wait, Lippincott, 1964.
Murder Roundabout, Lippincott, 1966.
With Option to Die, Lippincott, 1967.
A Risky Way to Kill, Lippincott, 1969.
Not I, Said the Sparrow, Lippincott, 1973.
Dead Run, Lippincott, 1976.

"MERTON HEIMRICH" SERIES; WITH WIFE, FRANCES LOCKRIDGE

I Want to Go Home, Lippincott, 1948.
Spin Your Web, Lady!, Lippincott, 1949.
Foggy, Foggy Death, Lippincott, 1950.
A Client Is Cancelled, Lippincott, 1951.
Death by Association, Lippincott, 1952.
Stand Up and Die, Lippincott, 1953.
Death and the Gentle Bull, Lippincott, 1954.
Burnt Offering, Lippincott, 1955.
Let Dead Enough Alone, Lippincott, 1956.
Practice to Deceive, Lippincott, 1957.
Accent on Murder, Lippincott, 1958.
Show Red for Danger, Lippincott, 1960.
With One Stone, Lippincott, 1961.
First Come, First Kill, Lippincott, 1962.
The Distant Clue, Lippincott, 1963.

"MR. AND MRS. NORTH" SERIES; WITH WIFE, FRANCES LOCKRIDGE

The Norths Meet Murder, Stokes, 1940.
Murder Out of Turn, Stokes, 1941.
A Pinch of Poison, Stokes, 1941.
Death on the Aisle, Lippincott, 1942.
Death Takes a Bow, Lippincott, 1943.
Hanged for a Sheep, Lippincott, 1944.
Killing the Goose, Lippincott, 1944.
Murder Within Murder, Lippincott, 1946.
Untidy Murder, Lippincott, 1947.
Payoff for the Banker, Lippincott, 1948.
Murder Is Served, Lippincott, 1948.
Death of a Tall Man, Lippincott, 1949.
The Dishonest Murder, Lippincott, 1949.
Murder in a Hurry, Lippincott, 1950.
Murder Comes First, Lippincott, 1951.
Dead as a Dinosaur, Lippincott, 1952.
Death Has a Small Voice, Lippincott, 1953.
Curtain for a Jester, Lippincott, 1953.
A Key for Death, Lippincott, 1954.
Voyage into Violence, Lippincott, 1956.
The Long Skeleton, Lippincott, 1958.
Murder Is Suggested, Lippincott, 1959.
The Judge Is Reversed, Lippincott, 1960.

Murder Has Its Points, Lippincott, 1961.
Murder by the Book, Lippincott, 1963.

OTHER; WITH WIFE, FRANCES LOCKRIDGE

Think of Death, Lippincott, 1947.
The Dishonest Murder, Lippincott, 1949.
Cats and People, Lippincott, 1950.
Murder in a Hurry, Lippincott, 1950.
The Lucky Cat, Lippincott, 1953.
Death Has a Small Voice, Lippincott, 1953.
A Key to Death, Lippincott, 1954.
The Nameless Cat, Lippincott, 1954.
Death of an Angel, Lippincott, 1955.
The Cat Who Rode Cows, Lippincott, 1955.
(Co-editor) Crime for Two, Lippincott, 1955.
The Faceless Adversary, Lippincott, 1956.
Murder! Murder! Murder!, Lippincott, 1956.
Voyage Into Violence, Lippincott, 1956.
The Tangled Cord, Lippincott, 1957.
Catch as Catch Can, Lippincott, 1958.
The Innocent House, Lippincott, 1959.
Murder and Blueberry Pie, Lippincott, 1959.
Murder Is Suggested, Lippincott, 1959.
The Golden Man, Lippincott, 1960.
And Left for Dead, Lippincott, 1961.
The Drill Is Locked, Lippincott, 1961.
The Ticking Clock, Lippincott, 1962.
Night of Shadows, Lippincott, 1962.
Murder by the Book, Lippincott, 1963.
The Devious Ones, Lippincott, 1964.
Quest of the Bogeyman, Lippincott, 1964.

Also author of the biography *Sergeant Mickey and General Ike,* about Dwight D. Eisenhower's valet. With his wife, Frances Lockridge, author of many mystery radio plays in the 1940s, generally featuring the Mr. and Mrs. North characters; author of a television series in the 1950s, a motion picture, and a Broadway play, all featuring the Norths. The radio series based on the Mr. and Mrs. North books ran for thirteen years, the television series for two years, and the Broadway play for 162 performances.

SIDELIGHTS: In a career spanning close to fifty years, both solo and in collaboration with his first wife Frances Davis, Richard Lockridge published nearly ninety books. Lockridge's work included biographies, children's books, and even books about cats, but mystery novels always remained his prime focus, in particular mysteries with series detectives. Although Lockridge created several popular detective series, by far the most popular were those books featuring the amateur sleuths Mr. and Mrs. North.

The characters of Pam and Jerry North appeared not only in print, but became the subjects of radio and television series, motion pictures, and a Broadway play.

The Norths debuted in short stories that Lockridge penned for the *New Yorker* in the early thirties. These stories gained an immediate following and were soon collected as *Mr. and Mrs. North.* Reviewing the collection for *Books,* Marian Sturges-Jones stated: "The book gains in impressiveness as one reads on, and one closes it with the definite sense of having read an unobtrusive but far from negligible contribution to current Americana." E. H. Walton in the *New Yorker* found the Norths to be "delectable," but believed that some readers would be disappointed because the book was "not a novel." If so, such disappointment was to be short-lived.

Within a few years Lockridge, now in collaboration with his wife Francis (writing as Frances Lockridge), published the first Pam and Jerry North novel, *The Norths Meet Murder.* E. R. Punshon in the *Manchester Guardian* praised the book's characterization and felt that its humor made "it a real success," while Will Cuppy in *Books* dubbed it "a civilized and exciting volume." Although Lockridge continued writing on his own throughout his life, his collaborations with Frances, both on the North series, other mystery novels, and children's books, lasted until her death in 1963. These volumes sometimes appeared under both their names and sometimes under the joint pseudonym of Francis Richards.

Reviewers describing the many Mr. and Mrs. North books (as well as other Lockridge collaborations) that followed *The Norths Meet Murder* often fell back on the same or similar adjectives: charming, delightful, amusing, witty, urbane . . . even delicious. Likewise, critics of the North books often lodged the same complaint, namely that their mystery elements were too simple and transparent, though many also dismissed this failing as inconsequential in light of the books' other virtues. As James Sandoe put it in the *New York Herald Tribune Book Review* of one of the later books in the series, *Murder Has Its Points:* "The Lockridges, sure and delicately wry, continue to outwit time less because they bother with any dazzling ingenuities of plot than because of their dry martini style."

Summing up the Lockridge's work for the *St. James Guide to Crime and Mystery Writers,* Guy M. Townsend agrees that the strength of the Mr. and Mrs. North series lies not in its plotting. Instead, he credits the success of the books to their characteriza-

tions, their skillful descriptions of both urban and rural settings, and to a lesser degree, their clever dialogue. According to Townsend, although the popularity of the North series "is well deserved," it "also possesses characteristics which have put off a number of readers." Among these he includes Pam's uncanny intuitions, the pervasiveness of the North's cats, and "the practice of ending each novel with a terror-filled chase in which the mysterious murderer is in hot pursuit of Mrs. North." Townsend finds other mystery series by the Lockridges, notably the books featuring Merton Heimrich of the New York State Police, more substantial both in terms of plot *and* characterization.

Nearly all of the Lockridges' novels take place in New York City or the New York State countryside. As well as recurring settings, their books are peopled with a large cast of recurring characters, some of whom turn up in other Lockridge collaborations and also in solo novels by each author. New York City Police Officer Bill Wiegand, a constant fixture in the North novels, appears prominently in the series featuring the Jewish homicide detective Bernie Shapiro. Shapiro, in turn, teams up with Merton Heimrich in *Murder Can't Wait.* According to Townsend, "The Lockridge regulars are all people one would like to know, and getting to know them through numerous novels is much like acquiring real friends."

Richard Lockridge also wrote a number of nonseries mysteries, some of which demonstrated a different side to his talent. *A Matter of Taste* tells the story of a man who decides to commit a murder solely so he can experience the sensation of it. E. F. Wallbridge in *Library Journal* described the book as a "slightly Jamesian, well-written exercise in morbidity and suspense" and went on to point out that "its inhumanity and cold-bloodedness are a far cry from the warmth and humor of . . . Mr. and Mrs. North." *Death in the Mind,* written in collaboration with George Hoben Estabrooks, is a thriller about Nazi spies and hypnotism. Will Cuppy in *Weekly Book Review* called it an "unusual espionage tale. . . . A necessity for spy fanciers and a nice bet for all mysteryites interested in oddities."

BIOGRAPHICAL/CRITICAL SOURCES:

BOOKS

St. James Guide to Crime and Mystery Writers, fourth edition, St. James Press (Detroit, MI), 1996.

PERIODICALS

Books, September 27, 1936, p. 3; December 31, 1939, p. 9.
Chicago Sun, December 9, 1949, p. 73.
Kirkus, September 15, 1950; September 1, 1951.
Library Journal, August, 1949; August, 1950.
Manchester Guardian, April 29, 1940, p. 7.
New Republic, April 30, 1945.
New Yorker, April 24, 1943; April 7, 1945, December 13, 1947.
New York Herald Tribune Book Review, March 16, 1958, p. 12; June 22, 1958, p. 9; June 26, 1960, p. 11; October 30, 1960, p. 15; October 15, 1961, p. 15; January 21, 1962, p. 11.
New York Times, September 20, 1936, p. 4; December 31, 1939, p. 7; May 2, 1943, p. 10; April 3, 1949, p. 28; May 13, 1951, p. 24.
New York Times Book Review, March 19, 1961, p. 32.
San Francisco Chronicle, April 13, 1958, p. 28; February 19, 1961, p. 29; May 21, 1961, p. 32.
Saturday Review of Literature, January 3, 1940; April 21, 1945.
Weekly Book Review, May 2, 1943, p. 16; April 8, 1945, p. 19; August 26, 1945, p. 24.

OBITUARIES:

PERIODICALS

Chicago Tribune, June 22, 1982.
Newsweek, July 5, 1982.
New York Times, June 21, 1982.
Publishers Weekly, July 9, 1982.
Time, July 5, 1982.
Washington Post, June 22, 1982.*

* * *

LOWRY, (Clarence) Malcolm 1909-1957

PERSONAL: Born July 28, 1909, in Liscard, Cheshire, England; died of an overdose of barbiturates and alcohol, June 27, 1957, in London, England; buried in churchyard of St. John the Baptist, Ripe, East Sussex, England; son of Arthur Osborne (a cotton broker) and Evelyn (Boden) Lowry; married Jan Gabrial (an American writer), January 6, 1934 (divorced, 1940); married Margerie Bonner (an actress and secretary), December 2, 1940. *Educa-* *tion:* Received degree from Cambridge University, 1932. *Avocational interests:* Jazz; playing ukulele.

CAREER: Writer. Deckhand on the British freighter *S.S. Pyrrhus,* 1927; lived and wrote in England, Spain, and Mexico during the late 1930s, and Canada throughout most of the 1940s and early 1950s.

WRITINGS:

Ultramarine (novel), J. Cape, 1933, revised, Lippincott, 1962.
Under the Volcano (novel), Reynal & Hitchcock, 1947, reprinted with an introduction by Stephen Spender, Lippincott, 1965, reprinted, Harper, 1984, reprinted as *The 1940 Under the Volcano,* MLR Editions (Canada), 1994.
Hear Us O Lord from Heaven Thy Dwelling Place (short stories), Lippincott, 1961.
Selected Poems, edited by Earle Birney and Margerie Bonner Lowry, City Lights Books, 1962.
Selected Letters of Malcolm Lowry, edited by Harvey Breit and Margerie Bonner Lowry, Lippincott, 1965.
Dark As the Grave Wherein My Friend Is Laid (incomplete novel), edited by Douglas Day and Margerie Bonner Lowry, preface by Day, New American Library, 1968.
Lunar Caustic (novella), edited by Birney and Margerie Bonner Lowry, foreword by Conrad Knickbocker, J. Cape, 1968, World, 1970.
October Ferry to Gabriola (incomplete novel), edited by Margerie Bonner Lowry, World, 1970.
(With wife, Margerie Bonner Lowry) *Notes on a Screenplay for F. Scott Fitzgerald's Tender Is the Night,* introduction by Paul Tiessen, Bruccoli Clark, 1976.
The Letters of Conrad Aiken and Malcolm Lowry, edited by Cynthia Conchita Sugars, ECW Press, 1992.
The Collected Poetry of Malcolm Lowry, edited by Kathleen Dorothy Scherf, UBC Press, 1992.
Sursum Corda! The Collected Letters of Malcolm Lowry, Volume 1: 1926-1946, edited by Sherrill E. Grace, University of Toronto Press, 1995.
Malcolm Lowry's "La Mordida," scholarly edition, edited by Patrick A. McCarthy, The University of Georgia Press, 1996.

Works also collected in other editions and represented in anthologies. Contributor to periodicals, including *Paris Review, Partisan Review,* and *Leys Fortnightly,*

SIDELIGHTS: Malcolm Lowry was an experimental English writer who produced a small but important body of writings. Influenced by the introspective, stream-of-consciousness literature of such authors as James Joyce, Lowry is remembered for his intense and highly personal brand of fiction. Only two of his works—the novels *Ultramarine* and *Under the Volcano*—reached publication before his death in 1957 at the age of forty-eight. Although several of the author's unfinished works have been edited and published posthumously, *Under the Volcano,* the largely autobiographical story of the final day in the life of an alcoholic, remains his crowning literary achievement.

Lowry was the youngest child born to an upper-class English family. Sent to a private boarding school at an early age, he failed to develop a close relationship with his parents and would later disregard his claims to the family cotton business. Lowry endured additional isolation for four of his preteen years, suffering a substantial loss of vision in both eyes due to ulcerations of his corneas. Following his recovery, however, he went on to become an avid and accomplished athlete. After a brief stint as a crewhand aboard a British freighter—a diversion frowned upon by his father—Lowry placated his parents by agreeing to attend Cambridge University. Remaining remote and detached during his college years, he chose to cultivate his interest in literature and writing. During this time, Lowry's increasing reliance on alcohol began to surface. As Douglas Day noted in *Malcolm Lowry: A Biography,* alcohol served as "a source of spiritual strength, even of mystical insights [for the writer]. . . . He *liked* to drink." Lowry's drinking addiction would overshadow both his personal life and his fiction, and it would eventually lead to his death.

Biographers have described Lowry as a tormented and self-absorbed individual plagued by feelings of inadequacy, melancholia, detachment, and despair. Yet, in spite of the flaws in his character, the author is said to have possessed an unfailing charm: Day related that a barroom friend once said of Lowry, "The very sight of the old bastard makes me happy for five days. No bloody fooling." Lowry's fiction mirrors his feelings of alienation, frustration, and internal turmoil. He intended to organize his writings under the general title "The Voyage That Never Ends," but the sequence never materialized as Lowry planned. His tendency to write and rewrite numerous drafts of each of his works resulted in the realization of few projects. The works that were edited and

published after his death, then, must be viewed as unpolished representations of Lowry's literary vision.

Lowry's first full-length publication, *Ultramarine,* appeared in his native England in 1933. Written when the author was in his early twenties, *Ultramarine* concerns refined young sailor Dana Hilliot's psychological and social development while journeying to the Far East. An outcast among a crew of lower-class men, Hilliot undergoes a gradual assimilation into the ship's subculture, achieving the acceptance he craves. The story is reportedly based on Lowry's own experience as a restless youth aboard the *S.S. Pyrrhus* in late 1920s, although the author failed to realize the triumph of integration that the fictional Hilliot experienced.

Ultramarine received mixed reviews. Faulted mainly for its lack of cohesiveness, the novel has been described as the rough-edged work of a promising young voice in fiction. In a letter to his agent reprinted in *Selected Letters,* Lowry himself described *Ultramarine* as "an altogether unmentionable early novel . . . that I would like in every way to forget." But *Ultramarine* is now generally regarded as a preface to *Under the Volcano,* Lowry's most enduring work. As *New Republic* contributor J. M. Edelstein wrote, *Ultramarine* represents only "traces of the brilliance and the power which Malcolm Lowry possessed and which he used to create his masterpiece."

Shortly after completing *Ultramarine*—while traveling across Europe with such friends as American writer Conrad Aiken—Lowry met his first wife, American writer Jan Gabrial, whom he married after a brief courtship. Their years together were marred by alternating periods of disagreement and reconciliation. Lowry's drinking problem worsened during this time and eventually led to his two-week treatment at Bellevue Hospital's psychiatric ward in 1935.

Lowry began work on *Under the Volcano* the following year, while living with Gabrial in Cuernavaca, Mexico. They separated permanently in 1937 and were finally divorced three years later. Between 1937 and 1940, Lowry wrote three drafts of *Under the Volcano,* met his second wife, Margerie Bonner, and relocated to Vancouver, British Columbia. The couple was married in December of 1940, one month after Lowry's divorce from Gabrial was finalized. As noted in the *Atlantic* by Clarissa Lorenz, wife of Aiken, Lowry's marriage to Bonner seemed to provide him with the only joy he had ever known. As quoted by Lorenz, Lowry later referred to the relationship as "the only thing holding me to life and sanity."

Lowry and Bonner rented a squatter's shack at Dollarton on a harbor known as Burrard Inlet (near Vancouver), where they would live for the better part of the next fifteen years. There, Lowry worked for nearly four years completing the fourth draft of *Under the Volcano*. After the shack was destroyed in a 1944 fire, Lowry and his wife returned to Dollarton the next winter and, with the help of friends, rebuilt it.

Lowry began to drink heavily over the next year as he awaited word on *Under the Volcano* from publishers in New York and London. Several months passed before he heard from London publisher Jonathan Cape, who requested that Lowry condense and revise the novel extensively. In a thirty-one-page response, later printed in *Selected Letters of Malcolm Lowry*, Lowry advanced a detailed defense of the book: "I have tried . . . to conceal in the *Volcano* as well as possible the deformities of my own mind. . . . [The novel] can be regarded as a kind of symphony, or in another way as a kind of opera. . . . It is hot music, a poem, a song, a tragedy, a comedy, a farce. . . . It is superficial, profound, entertaining and boring, according to taste. . . . It is also I claim a work of art [that focuses on] the forces in man which force him to be terrified of himself. It is also concerned with the guilt of man, with his remorse, with the ceaseless struggling toward the light under the weight of the past."

Under the Volcano was published in New York by Reynal & Hitchcock and in London by Jonathan Cape in 1947. Set against the political unrest of 1938 Mexico, *Under the Volcano* is a dramatic account of one man's inevitable downfall. The novel chronicles the last twelve hours in the life of Geoffrey Firmin, a divorced alcoholic and former British Consul in Quauhnahuac, Mexico. Firmin's ex-wife, Yvonne, returns to him on the festive Day of the Dead to attempt a reconciliation; her efforts, though, are hampered by Firmin's continued abusiveness and drinking, combined with the presence in Mexico of two of her past lovers: Firmin's half-brother, Hugh, and longtime friend Jacques Laurelle, a film producer. Firmin spends his final hours in a bar—drinking and musing over his life as an outcast—and is shot to death by a Mexican fascist who mistakes him for a murderer and thief.

Day has suggested that Firmin's decline is the inexorable result of his "failure to experience love." The critic further noted that the character "never succeeds in escaping from what he calls 'this dreadful tyranny of self' enough to exist in any real way for others. . . . [Firmin] is in hell and the hell is himself." Lowry explained in his letter to Cape the significance of his character's destruction: "The drunkenness of the Consul is used on one plane to symbolize the universal drunkenness of mankind during the [Second World] war, or during the period immediately preceding it, . . . and what profundity and final meaning there is in his fate should be seen also in its universal relationship to the ultimate fate of mankind."

Some reviewers decried the erudite and overly introspective nature of the work. According to Denis Donoghue in the *New York Review of Books*, "*Under the Volcano*, remarkable as it is, gives the impression of being overwritten. After a few chapters we long for something casual, even a mistake, anything to relieve the pressure of deliberate significance." Other critics have deemed the novel a classic—the work of a genius. In a review of *Under the Volcano* for the *New York Herald Tribune Book Review*, Mark Schorer claimed that he knew of few other literary works "which convey so powerfully the agony of alienation, the internal suffering of disintegration." And H. R. Hays, writing in the *New York Times Book Review*, asserted: "It is cause for rejoicing when one encounters a novel which achieves a rich variety of meaning on many levels, which is written in a style both virile and poetic, which possesses profundity of insight, which is, in short, literature."

Having struggled eight years with *Under the Volcano*, Lowry seemed to have expended most of his creative energies. "Then," as Day put it, "he was finished, with ten years of life still left. What remained to him was only the inevitable deterioration of his art, and the analogous deterioration of his self." The frustrated writer's drinking increased in ensuing years, and in 1955 he underwent psychiatric treatment at Atkinson Morley's Hospital. Lowry spent the last year and a half of his life with his wife in the picturesque town of Ripe, Sussex. On the night of June 27, 1957—the culmination of a period of intense depression for the writer—Lowry and his wife argued. Fearing he might do her physical harm, she ran from their house, only to discover his corpse when she returned the next morning. A broken gin bottle was on the floor beside him, and a bottle of Bonner's sleeping tablets had been emptied.

CONTEMPORARY AUTHORS • *New Revision Series, Volume 62*

In the first dozen or so years following Lowry's death, several of his works in progress were edited—by his wife and others—and published in the United States and England. *Hear Us O Lord from Heaven Thy Dwelling Place* is a collection of seven short stories that Lowry had started in the late 1940s. Phoebe-Lou Adams, writing in the *Atlantic,* suggested that the pieces in this volume are not really stories, but "rather elaborations of mood and revelations of the workings of the author's disintegrating mind, with the intensity and egocentricity of lyric poetry." While five of the pieces in the collection garnered little attention, the remaining two—"Through the Panama" and "The Forest Path to the Spring"—are said to be among Lowry's finest compositions after *Under the Volcano.* "Through the Panama" traces a tormented writer's rise from the depths of self-consciousness. "The Forest Path to the Spring," the most poetic of the volume's stories, alludes to the psychic development Lowry experienced during his years with his wife at Dollarton. As a whole, *Hear Us O Lord from Heaven Thy Dwelling Place* presents a rare vision of change and even growth in Lowry's otherwise bleak canon.

Following the completion of *Under the Volcano,* Lowry returned to Mexico in an apparent attempt to recapture his past. Bonner had not experienced the Cuernavaca of the late 1930s, and, captivated by the country's intrigue and beauty, she wanted to explore the areas of Mexico that her husband had immortalized in his novel. Lowry was anxious to visit with Juan Fernando Marquez, a Mexican revolutionary and drinking companion who appears briefly in *Under the Volcano* as the character of Juan Cerillo. The author later learned, though, that his friend had been killed in a brawl more than five years earlier. Lowry then began writing a fictionalized account of his search for Marquez. Published more than a decade after the author's death, the novel *Dark As the Grave Wherein My Friend Is Laid* was compiled by Lowry's widow and Day from Lowry's notes. In the book, Lowry's protagonist Sigbjorn Wilderness, a reformed alcoholic, travels to Mexico in an attempt to put his past behind him. But as Day noted in a preface to *Dark As the Grave Wherein My Friend Is Laid,* "Sigbjorn learns that he really does not *want* to lay the ghosts, but to rejoin them—and this is what makes his descent into the Mexican hell truly perilous."

Because of its setting and subject matter, *Dark As the Grave Wherein My Friend Is Laid* generally drew comparisons to *Under the Volcano.* Elizabeth Janeway, writing in the *New York Times Book Review,* deemed the work "in itself an astounding performance," but several other critics faulted its loose structure, lack of action, and obscure language and allusions. Day defended Lowry's works against such criticism: "If there is no external action, there is almost a surfeit of movement internally; and there is enough tension within the mind of [one of Lowry's] protagonist[s] to render any other conflict superfluous. . . . Whenever he lets his protagonist think, Lowry becomes a great writer." Day went on to call *Dark As the Grave Wherein My Friend Is Laid* "a work of embryonic greatness," noting that although it exists in an "imperfect state," readers should "be glad to have it even as it is."

Another thinly veiled autobiography, the posthumously published *Lunar Caustic* is viewed as a partial record of the time Lowry spent in Bellevue in 1935. Lowry began writing *Lunar Caustic* immediately after his release from Bellevue, and he revised the work many times over the last two decades of his life. The slim and unusual volume takes its title from a silver nitrate treatment for syphilis. (As a child, the impressionable Lowry developed an obsessive fear of contracting syphilis. According to Day, this fear may have stemmed from his religious upbringing, feelings of sexual inadequacy, and guilt.) Published for the first time in 1968, eleven years after Lowry's death, *Lunar Caustic* centers on disoriented alcoholic Bill Plantagenet, who one day finds himself confined to Bellevue's psychiatric wing. Plantagenet encounters three other patients in the ward. Although he eventually equates elements of their insanity with aspects of his own character, he realizes that he is not mad; he is instead a sane drunk.

Dale Edmonds, writing in *Tulane Studies in English,* theorized that "*Lunar Caustic* fails as a work of fiction because of Lowry's uncertainty of intention and inconsistency of style." But several other critics judged the work a striking and insightful study of nothingness, a frightening depiction of a psychic limbo, and a painful reminder of the horrors of earthly life. Day speculated that Lowry may have viewed his own alcoholic degeneration as a source of literary inspiration; in destroying himself, he was better able to fathom—and therefore articulate in his writings—the disintegration of the world. Assessed in these terms, *Lunar Caustic* is a success, since it offers a stunning view of human destruction and disillusionment.

Lowry's last published novel, *October Ferry to Gabriola,* was edited by Bonner Lowry for release in 1970. The story concerns a criminal lawyer who, reacting to apparent omens, moves with his family to British Columbia in search of peace and solitude. A thin and rather formless work, *October Ferry to Gabriola* is generally considered more valuable as an idea than as a fully developed piece of fiction.

In 1995 many of Lowry's private letters from the period between 1926 and 1946 were collected and published in *Sursum Corda! The Collected Letters of Malcolm Lowry.* The letters show Lowry's alcoholism and his numerous other personal troubles but also his comic perspective on his odd life. Writing in the *Times Literary Supplement,* Phil Baker noted, "Lowry dramatizes and hyperbolizes his misadventures throughout, making them extremely funny in the process." *Observer Review* contributor Valentine Cunningham remarked that "these letters are repetitious. Lowry is an adept word recycler." But Cunningham also averred that "these epistolary distress-rockets" are ". . . a marvelously cheering read."

In addition to his narrative fiction, Lowry also produced a sizable amount of poetry, although he did not publish a single volume of poetry during his life. In 1992 much of this poetry was gathered and published as *The Collected Poetry of Malcolm Lowry.* "Lowry . . . left his verse manuscripts in heaped disarray, thereby ensuring that much of the task of deciphering, editing, and ordering his poems would fall to other hands," explained Brad Leithauser in the *New York Review of Books.* Leithauser concluded that in his poetry Lowry "never found the manner—the sure-pitched voice—that would allow him to embark with confidence on a new poem. He's hit and miss." *Times Literary Supplement* reviewer David Bromwich declared that "[Lowry's] poems have wit, dryness, and, occasionally, grace. Yet they utterly lack personal resonance. There is scarcely a phrase to suggest the care and the cadence of accurate feeling that one hears in the sentences of his stories." Most critics admitted that Lowry will remain better known for his narrative writings, especially *Under the Volcano.*

In evaluating Lowry's contributions to modern English fiction, Richard Hauer Costa surmised that without *Under the Volcano,* "it would be easy to conclude that Lowry was incapable of transmuting vision into viable fiction." Day ascertained that "Lowry was . . . in no sense a 'natural' writer—compulsive, yes, but not natural," adding, "He was a writer not because words flowed effortlessly from him, but because he was damned if he were going to be anything else." "To Lowry," Day concluded, "not to write was unimaginable; not to write was death. Genius . . . was something which Lowry had to labor, often frantically, to attain. And attain it he did: for there is before us, after all, the monolithic and undeniable fact of *Under the Volcano. . . .* Such achievement transcends the realm of mere talent."

Portions of the novel *Under the Volcano* are recited in the documentary *Volcano,* released by the National Film Board of Canada, 1976; *Under the Volcano* was adapted by Guy Gallo for a film of the same title, directed by John Huston, released by Universal Pictures, 1984.

BIOGRAPHICAL/CRITICAL SOURCES:

BOOKS

Asals, Frederick, *The Making of Malcolm Lowry's "Under the Volcano,"* University of Georgia Press, 1996.
Barns, Jim, *Fiction of Malcolm Lowry and Thomas Mann: Structural Tradition,* T. Jefferson University Press, 1990.
Bowker, Gordon, *Pursued by Furies: A Life of Malcolm Lowry,* HarperCollins, 1993, reprinted, St. Martin's Press, 1995.
Bradbrook, M. C., *Malcolm Lowry: His Art and Early Life, A Study in Transformation,* Cambridge University Press, 1974.
Bradbury, Malcolm, *Possibilities: Essays on the State of the Novel,* Oxford University Press, 1973.
Cross, Richard K., *Malcolm Lowry: A Preface to His Fiction,* University of Chicago Press, 1980.
Day, Douglas, *Malcolm Lowry: A Biography,* Oxford University Press, 1973.
Dictionary of Literary Biography, Volume 15, *British Novelists, 1930-1959,* Gale, 1983.
Dodson, Daniel B., *Malcolm Lowry,* Columbia University Press, 1970.
Epstein, Perle S., *The Private Labyrinth of Malcolm Lowry: "Under the Volcano" and the Cabbala,* Holt, 1969.
Grace, Sherrill, *Swinging the Maelstrom: New Perspectives on Malcolm Lowry,* McGill-Queen's University, 1992.
Hauer Costa, Richard, *Malcolm Lowry,* Twayne, 1972.

Lowry, Malcolm, *Selected Letters of Malcolm Lowry*, edited by Harvey Breit and Margerie Bonner Lowry, Lippincott, 1965.

Lowry, Malcolm, *Under the Volcano*, introduction by Stephen Spender, Lippincott, 1965.

Lowry, Malcolm, *Dark As the Grave Wherein My Friend Is Laid*, edited by Douglas Day and Bonner Lowry, preface by Day, New American Library, 1968.

Lowry, Margerie, editor, *Malcolm Lowry: Psalms and Songs*, New American Library, 1975.

Markson, David, *Malcolm Lowry's "Volcano": Myth, Symbol, Meaning*, Times Books, 1978.

McCarthy, Patrick A., *Forests of Symbols: World, Text & Self in Malcolm Lowry's Fiction*, University of Georgia Press, 1994.

Porteous, J. Douglas, *Landscapes of the Mind: Worlds of Sense and Metaphor*, University of Toronto Press, 1990.

Singh, Ravindra Prasad, *Malcolm Lowry, Novelist*, Commonwealth (New Delhi), 1992.

Tiessen, Paul and Gordon Bowker, *Apparently Incongruous Parts: The Worlds of Malcolm Lowry*, Scarecrow Press, 1990.

Twentieth-Century Literary Criticism, Volume 6, Gale, 1982.

Wood, Barry, editor, *Malcolm Lowry: The Writer and His Critics*, Tecumseh Press, 1980.

Woodcock, George, editor, *Malcolm Lowry: The Man and His Work*, University of British Columbia Press, 1971.

PERIODICALS

Atlantic, August, 1961; June, 1970.
Canadian Literature, spring, 1963; spring, 1971; winter, 1995, p. 202.
Modern Fiction Studies, summer, 1958.
London Review of Books, January 27, 1994, p. 16.
New York Herald Tribune Book Review, February 23, 1947.
New York Review of Books, March 3, 1966; February 15, 1996, p. 31.
New York Times Book Review, February 23, 1947; November 8, 1964; August 4, 1968; July 27, 1969.
Observer Review, April 9, 1995, p. 18.
Saturday Review, December 4, 1965; July 6, 1968.
Spectator, June 23, 1933.
Studies in the Novel, fall, 1974.
Times Literary Supplement, January 26, 1967; March 21, 1968; July 3, 1969; December 11, 1992, p. 23; May 19, 1995, p. 4.
Tulane Studies in English, Volume 15, 1967.*

LUKACS, Georg
See LUKACS, Gyorgy (Szegedy von)

* * *

LUKACS, George
See LUKACS, Gyorgy (Szegedy von)

* * *

LUKACS, Gyorgy (Szegedy von) 1885-1971
(Georg Lukacs, George Lukacs)

PERSONAL: Given name sometimes transliterated as Georg or George; Born April 13, 1885, in Budapest, Hungary; died June 4, 1971, in Budapest, Hungary; son of a titled banker. *Education:* University of Budapest, Ph.D., 1906; attended University of Heidelberg and University of Berlin.

CAREER: Philosopher, writer, and critic. Minister of education during Bela Kun communist regime in Hungary, 1919; Marx-Engels Institute, Moscow, U.S.S.R. (now Russia), staff member, 1930; affiliated with Philosophical Institute of Academy of Sciences in U.S.S.R., c. 1933-45; University of Budapest, Budapest, Hungary, professor of philosophy, 1945-56; minister of culture during Imre Nagy regime in Hungary, 1956.

AWARDS, HONORS: Goethe Prize, 1970, for *Goethe and His Age*.

WRITINGS:

IN ENGLISH

Die Seele and die Formen (essays), E. Fleischel, 1911, translation by Anna Bostock published as *Soul and Form*, MIT Press (Cambridge, MA), 1974.

Die Theorie des Romans: Ein geschichtsphilosophischer Versuch uber die Formen der grossen Epik, P. Cassirer, 1920, reprinted, Luchterhand, 1971, translation by Bostock published as *The Theory of the Novel: A Historico-Philosophical Essay on the Forms of Great Epic Literature*, MIT Press, 1971.

Geschichte und Klassenbewusstsein: Studien uber Marxistische Dialektik, Malik Verlag, 1923, reprinted, Luchterhand, 1968, translation by Rodney Livingstone published as *History and Class Consciousness: Studies in Marxist Dialectics,* MIT Press, 1971.

Goethe und seine Zeit, A. Francke, 1947, translation by Robert Anchor published as *Goethe and His Age,* Merlin Press, 1968, Grosset & Dunlap, 1969.

Essays uber Realismus (see also below), Aufbau Verlag, 1948, reprinted, Luchterhand, 1971, translation by Edith Bone published as *Studies in European Realism: A Sociological Survey of the Writings of Balzac, Stendhal, Zola, Tolstoy, Gorki, and Others,* Hillway, 1950, Grosset & Dunlap, 1964, Howard Fertig (New York City), 1996.

Der junge Hegel: Uber die Beziehungen von Dialektik und Oekonomie, Europa Verlag, 1948, also published as *Der junge Hegel und die Probleme der kapitalistischen Gesellschaft,* Aufbau Verlag, 1954, translation by Livingstone published as *The Young Hegel: Studies in the Relations Between Dialectics and Economics,* Merlin Press, 1975, MIT Press, 1976.

Thomas Mann, Aufbau Verlag, 1949, translation by Stanley Mitchell published as *Essays on Thomas Mann,* Merlin Press, 1964, Grosset & Dunlap, 1965.

Der historische Roman, Aufbau Verlag, 1955, translation by Hannah Mitchell and Stanley Mitchell published as *The Historical Novel,* Merlin Press, 1962, Humanities Press, 1965.

Wider den missverstandenen Realismus (2nd edition of original *Die Gegenwartsbedeutung des kritischen Realismus*), Claassen, 1958, translation by John Mander and Necke Mander published as *The Meaning of Contemporary Realism,* Merlin Press, 1963, published as *Realism in Our Time: Literature and the Class Struggle,* Harper, 1964.

Lenin: Studie uber den Zusammenhang seiner Gedanken, Luchterhand, 1967, translation by Nicholas Jacobs published as *Lenin: A Study on the Unity of His Thought,* NLB (England), 1970, MIT Press, 1971.

(Contributor) Theo Pinkus, editor, *Gesprache mit Georg Lukacs, Hans Heinz Holz, Leo Kotler, Wolfgang Abendroth,* Rowolt, 1967, translation by David Fembach published as *Conversations With Lukacs,* Merlin Press, 1974, MIT Press, 1975.

Solschenizyn, Luchterhand, 1970, translation by William David Graf published as *Solzhenitsyn,* Merlin Press, 1970, MIT Press, 1971.

Writer and Critic, and Other Essays, translation from the original edited by Arthur D. Kahn, Grosset & Dunlap, 1971.

Political Writings, 1919-1929: The Question of Parliamentarianism and Other Essays, translated by Michael McColgan from the original *Taktika es Ethika,* NLB, 1972, published as *Tactics and Ethics: Political Essays, 1919-1929,* Harper, 1975.

Marxism and Human Liberation: Essays on History, Culture, and Revolution, translation from the original edited by E. San Juan, Jr., Dell, 1973.

Revolution und Gegenrevolution, Luchterhand, 1976, translation by Victor Zitta published as *Revolution and Revelation,* 1976.

Essays on Realism, translation by David Fernbach, edited by Rodney Livingstone, MIT Press, 1981.

Record of a Life: An Autobiography, translation by Rodney Livingstone, edited by Istvan Eorsi, NLB/Verso, 1984.

Georg Lukacs: Selected Correspondence 1902-1920, translated and edited by Judith Marcus and Zoltan Tar, Columbia University Press, 1986.

The Process of Democratization, translation by Susanne Bernhardt and Norman Levine, State University of New York Press, 1991.

German Realists in the Nineteenth Century. translation by Jeremy Gaines and Paul Keast, edited by Rodney Livingstome, MIT Press, 1993.

The Lukacs Reader, edited by Arpad Kadarkay, Blackwell (Oxford), 1995.

Studies in European Realism, translation by Edith Bone, H. Fertig, 1996.

IN GERMAN; ALL PUBLISHED BY AUFBAU VERLAG, UNLESS OTHERWISE NOTED

Alte und neue Kultur (title means "Old and New Culture"), Jungarbeiter Verlag, 1921, reprinted, 1970.

Deutsche Literatur im Zeitalter des Imperialismus: Ein Ubersicht ihrer Hauptstroemungen, 1945.

Gottfried Keller, 1946.

Fortschritt und Reaktion in der deutschen Literatur, 1947.

Karl Marx und Friedrich Engels als Literaturhistoriker, 1947.

Schicksalswende: Beitrage zu einer neuen deutschen Ideologie, 1948, 2nd edition, 1956.

Der russische Realismus in der Weltliteratur, 1949, 3rd edition, 1952.

Existentialismus oder Marxismus?, 1951.

Deutsche Realisten des 19. Jahrhunderts, 1951.

Skizze einer Geschichte der neuen deutschen Literatur (title means "An Outline of the History of Modern German Literature"), 1953.

Beitrage zur Geschichte der Aesthetik, 1954.

Die Zerstorung der Vernunft (title means "The Destruction of Reason"), 1954.

(Author of introduction) Georg Wilhelm Friedrich Hegel, *Aesthetik*, 1955.

(With Franz Mehring) *Friedrich Nietzsche*, 1957.

Tolstoi und die westliche Literatur, J. Fladung, c. 1959.

Schriften zur Literatursoziologie, Luchterhand, 1961.

Aesthetik, four volumes, Luchterhand, 1963.

Die Eigenart des Aesthetischen (title means "The Specific Nature of the Aesthetic"), Luchterhand, 1963.

Deutsche Literatur in zwei Jahrhunderten, Luchterhand, 1964.

Der junge Marx: Seine philosophische Entwicklung von 1840-1844, Neske, 1965.

Von Nietzsche bis Hitler; oder, Der Irrationalismus in der deutschen Politik, Fischer Bucherei, 1966.

Uber die Besonderheit als Kategorie der Aesthetik, Luchterhand, 1967.

Schriften zur Ideologie und Politik, Luchterhand, 1967.

Die Grablegung des alten Deutschland: Essays zur deutschen Literatur des 19. Jahrhunderts, Rowolt, 1967.

Faust und Faustus: Vom Drama der Menschengattung zur Tragoedie der modernen Kunst, Rowolt, 1967.

Frueheschriften, Luchterhand, 1968.

Werke, fourteen volumes, Luchterhand, 1968-69.

Probleme der Aesthetik, Luchterhand, 1969.

Russische Literatur, russische Revolution: Puschkin, Tolstoi, Dostojewskij, Fadejew, Makarenko, Scholochow, Solschenizyn, Luchterhand, 1969.

(Author of afterword) Hegel, *Phaenomenologie des Geistes*, Ullstein, 1970.

Die ontologischen Grundlagen des menschlichen Denkens und Handelns, [Vienna], 1970.

Marxismus und Stalinismus, Rowohlt, 1970.

Zur Ontologie des gesellschaftlichen Seins (title means "The Ontology of Social Existence"; also see below), Luchterhand, 1971.

Die ontologischen Grundprinzipien von Marx (selection from *Zur Ontologie des gesellschaftlichen Seins*), Luchterhand, 1972.

Die Arbeit (selection from *Zur Ontologie des gesellschaftlichen Seins*), Luchterhand, 1973.

(Contributor) Ruediger Bubner, Konrad Cramer, and Reiner Wiehl, editors, *Ist eine philosophische Aesthetik moeglich?*, Vandenhoeck & Ruprecht, 1973.

(Contributor) Johann Wollgang von Goethe, *Die Leiden des jungen Werther*, Insel Verlag, 1973.

Fruehe Schriften zur Aesthetik, Luchterhand, Volume I: *Heidelberger Philosophie der Kunst, 1912-1914*, 1974, Volume II: *Heidelberger Aesthetik, 1916-1918*, 1975.

(With others) *Individuum und Praxis Positionen der budapester Schule*, Suhrkamp, 1975.

Politische Aufsatze, 1918, Luchterhand, 1975.

Kunst und obiektive Warheit: Essays zur Literaturtheorie und Geschichte, P. Reclam, 1977.

(With Arnold Hauser) *Im Gespraech mit Georg Lukacs*, Beck, 1978.

Eine Autobiographie im Dialog, Suhrkamp (Frankfurt), 1981.

IN HUNGARIAN

A Modern Drama fejlodesenek tortenete: Kiadja a kisfaludy-tarsasag, two volumes, Franklin Tarsulet, 1911.

Kristorii realizma, [Hungary], 1939.

Irastudok felelossege, Idegennyelvii irodalmi kiado, 1944.

Irodalom es demokracia, Szikra, 1947.

A Polgari filozofia valsaga, [Hungary], 1947.

A Realizmus problemai: Nemet eredetibol forditotta, Atheneum (Budapest, Hungary), 1948.

Balzac, Stendhal, Zola, Hungaria eloszo, 1949.

Nagy orosz realistak, Szikra, 1949.

Az esz tronfosztasa: Az irracionalista ftlozofia kritikaja, Akademiai Kiado, 1956.

A Kulonosseg mint esztetika katagoria, Akademiai Kiado, 1957.

Istoriski roman, Kultura, 1958.

Prolegomena za marksisticku estetiku: Posebnost kao centralna kategorija estetike, Nolit, 1960.

Az esztetikum sajatossaga, Akademiai Kiado, 1965.

Lukacs Gyorgy valogatott muvei, Gondolat, 1968.

Muveszet es tarsadalom: Valogatott esztetikai tanulmanyok, Gondolat, 1968.

Vilagirodalom: Valogatott vilagirodalmi tanulmanyok, two volumes, Gondolat, 1969.

Magyar irodalom—magyar kultura: Valogatott tanulmanyok, Gondolat, 1970.

Utam Marxhoz: Valogatott filozofiai tanulmanyok, Magveto Konyvkiado, 1971.

Adalekok az esztetika tortenetenez, two volumes, Magveto Konyvkiado, 1972.

Ifjukori muvek, 1902-1918, Magveto Konyvkiado, 1977.

SIDELIGHTS: In *Language and Silence,* George Steiner extrapolated two principal beliefs from Georg Lukacs's works: "First, that literary criticism is not a luxury, that it is not what the subtlest of American critics has called 'a discourse for amateurs.' But that it is, on the contrary, a central and militant force toward shaping men's lives. Secondly, Lukacs affirms that the work of the critic is neither subjective nor uncertain. The truth of judgment can be verified." With such a basis for his writings, Lukacs has been credited with three major contributions to modern philosophical thought, defined by Alden Whitman in the *New York Times:* "A defense of humanism in Communist letters; elaboration of Marx's theory of the alienation of man by industrial society; and formulation of a system of esthetics that repudiated political control of Socialist artists while emphasizing what Mr. Lukacs termed the 'class nature' of beauty."

Although Lukacs was, as Alfred Kazin wrote in the introduction to Lukacs's *Studies in European Realism,* "an individual thinker who is fascinated by and thoroughly committed to Marxism as a philosophy, and who uses it for the intellectual pleasure and moral satisfaction it gives him," he was throughout his life in conflict with the Communist International. From the appearance of *History and Class Consciousness* in 1923, he was forced in and out of political life by charges of "revisionism." Because in his theories he considered the classics and "bourgeois" writers of the eighteenth and nineteenth centuries, he came under frequent attack and was often compelled to publicly recant his own views. Still, he remained an opponent of the party line in literature and disparaged, as Whitman observed, "writers who were Socialists first and writers second."

After his university studies and travels in Italy, Lukacs lived in Heidelberg for a time, where he associated with Max Weber and his circle. Weber, Lukacs's former teacher, was a sociologist and historian in the tradition of Georg Wilhelm Friedrich Hegel, whose philosophical idealism, dialectical method, and concern with history were an early influence on both Lukacs and Marxism itself; Hegel's conception of the historical development of artistic form provided the basis of much of Lukacs's aesthetic.

In 1918 Lukacs joined the Communist party. With his international reputation as a literary critic already established with the appearance of *Soul and Form* in 1911, he was made Hungarian minister of culture and public education in the Communist regime of Bela Kun. Kun remained in power briefly, from March to August of 1919, and upon his overthrow, Lukacs went into hiding. Lukacs spent the next ten years in exile in Vienna, where he was granted asylum.

From Vienna, Lukacs carried on a struggle with Kun for control of the Hungarian underground movement. Official denunciation of Lukacs's writing settled the issue against him, but following statements of "self-criticism" he was granted refuge in the Soviet Union during Hitler's rise to power. When he returned to Budapest after World War II, ending a twenty-five-year period of exile, he joined the coalition government as a member of the National Assembly of Hungary. In 1949 the Communist party again took control, establishing the People's Republic of Hungary, which was overthrown in October, 1956, by an anti-Soviet revolt. As a leader of the insurrectionist Petofi circle and then minister of culture in Imre Nagy's regime, Lukacs was deported to Romania when Soviet troops returned the Communists to power. Allowed to return to Hungary in 1957, Lukacs retired from political activity and devoted his last years to teaching and writing.

Lukacs's early publications, which he renounced after joining the Communist party, strongly influenced existential thought. The neo-Kantian aesthetic of *Soul and Form* and *The Theory of the Novel* saw literature as an expression of man's inwardness. The former, for example, is concerned with the relationship between human life and absolute values. Lucien Goldmann pointed out in *TriQuarterly* that with *Soul and Form* Lukacs was "the first to pose in all its acuteness and force the problem of the relation between the individual, authenticity, and death, . . . affirming the absolute nonvalue of the social world." In *The Theory of the Novel,* on the other hand, Lukacs examined the epic genre as "the expression of complex and multiple relationships between the soul and the world."

Often considered his most important work, *History and Class Consciousness* is marked by a neo-Hegelian idealism, what George Lichtheim called a "belief in the possibility of objective insight into reality." To unify philosophical theory with political practice and to unite Marx's interpretation of history with Hegel's concept of totality, Lukacs here asserted, according to Lichtheim, "that the totality of history could be apprehended by adopting a particular 'class standpoint': that of the proletariat." Lukacs was moving away from his earlier, western humanist conception of literature toward his theory of the "great realism," from his portrayal of man as alienated and alone to his anticipation of a mankind freed from alienation by a consciousness of the historical process.

Although Lukacs eventually repudiated *History and Class Consciousness* along with his first two books, the work contains the seeds of his later orthodoxy, mainly in "its identification of 'true consciousness' with a particular doctrine and a particular class, and its faith in the party as the repository of the doctrine and the vanguard of the class," noted Steven Lukes in the *Washington Post.* Tibor Szamuely, moreover, saw *History and Class Consciousness* as "the best, the frankest, the most wide-ranging and powerful exposition of the philosophy of totalitarianism ever written."

Lukacs's subsequent critical work often ran counter to party position, however. His reading of literature took into account sociology, history, and politics, and he advocated realism as the highest mode of fiction while condemning formalism. But he distinguished realism both from psychological novels and from naturalism, which led him to praise Honore de Balzac, for example, and disparage Emile Zola, in direct opposition to party line. Moreover, he valued the realism of such writers as Sir Walter Scott and Leo Tolstoy as manifestations of the dialectical relationship between historical reality and literature. He was opposed, however, to "proletarian realism" and party control of the literary process. He contended, as Whitman explained, that in a Communist society, "noble art would emerge from the artist's interaction with his environment; but works of art could not be summoned forth in a predetermined pattern."

Essays on Realism contains selected writings that support Lukacs's argument for the supremacy of literary realism. Denis Donoghue observed in the *New York Review of Books,* "Lukacs believed that reality is objective, concrete, and socially determined: in a novel, content determines form." Donoghue continued, "While the modern psychological novel deals with the individual in his solitariness, the realistic novel presents the human type," or, as Lukacs asserts, "'a peculiar synthesis which organically binds together the general and the particular both in characters and situations.'" In this view Lukacs championed writers such as Tolstoy, Balzac, Daniel Defoe, Jonathan Swift, Thomas Mann, and Maxim Gorky, while chastising the likes of Fyodor Dostoyevsky, Franz Kafka, James Joyce, Virginia Woolf, Samuel Beckett, and William Faulkner. According to Donoghue, "For Lukacs, the great achievement of novelists like Tolstoy and Balzac is their vision of 'the contradictions, struggles and conflicts of social life . . . as these appear in the mind and life of actual human beings.' A true narrative also 'dissolves into the processes that they really are.'" However, as George Woodcock noted in *Sewanee Review,* "the dialectical process Lukacs favors very often involves not only his review of a book, but an answer from the writer, and then the final comments of the critic—a process that ends all too often in a display of theoretical one-upmanship that takes one far away from the work itself."

In *The Historical Novel* Lukacs employs Hegelian dialectics to further distinguish between realism and naturalism—the former he favorably regards as historically accurate, the latter he condemns as ahistorical and abstract. Noting the conservatism of Lukacs's perspective, Peter Demetz wrote in the *Yale Review,* "Lukacs conceives the work of art, as any traditionalist would, as a concrete universal which, in its immanent structure of character and situation, offers a reflection of human history moving toward Paradise Planned and Regained; by creating types the writer crystallizes selected details into portraits of general if not prophetic meaning that opens the way to the future." Citing Lukacs's tendency to elevate ideology at the expense of aesthetic consideration, Woodcock contended that *The Historical Novel* "is a justification of nineteenth-century classic realism that parallels the Stalinist reversion to high bourgeois standards in painting, sculpture, music, architecture, and all the other arts." Demetz concludes, "His substantial book on the historical novel clearly reflects Lukacs' double genius for literary history and political terrorism."

Although the occasion of Lukacs's death in 1971 was scarcely acknowledged in the eastern European Communist press, he was buried with customary party honors, having refrained from personal involvement in politics after 1957. It was only after his death that his works began to be widely available to English-speaking audiences. Despite the limited circulation of Lukacs's works, Lucien Goldmann, as early as 1967, deemed Lukacs to be "one of the most influential figures in the intellectual life of the 20th century." Within fifteen years of his death, the publication of Lukacs's autobiographic interviews and a collection of correspondence reaffirmed continuing interest in his life and thought.

Georg Lukacs: Selected Correspondence 1902-1920 consists of 161 letters selected from more than 1600 letters posthumously discovered in a German bank where Lukacs deposited them in 1917. "The contents," according to Edward Timms in the *London Review of Books*, "place his early intellectual development in a radically new light." The volume is divided into two sections; the first represents Lukacs's Hungarian correspondence, the second his involvement in German academia and the Max Weber Circle, including letters between Lukacs and Weber, Karl Mannheim, Martin Buber, Georg Simmel, and Karl Jaspers. The *Selected Correspondence*, according to Hans H. Rudnick in *World Literature Today*, "is an exciting treasure of documents relating to European intellectual history during the first twenty years of this century." The letters also contain important references to Lukacs's generous bourgeois father, who supported his intellectual pursuits; his uneasy maternal relationship; unsuccessful attempts to obtain a professorship; and his failed romance with Irma Seidler, who committed suicide in 1911. Timms noted, "There is no class struggle in Lukacs's early writings, nor even a sense of an awakening social conscience. The dialectic which unfolds is that dividing 'self' from 'other,' 'understanding' from 'life.'"

Eine Autobiographie im Dialog was hastily produced shortly before Lukacs died. The volume is based on a series of interviews and sketchy autobiographic notes, interspersed with excerpts from his writings, in which Lukacs comments on his theoretical views and defends his participation in communist politics. George Steiner wrote in the *Times Literary Supplement*, "Lukacs's self-portrait is that of a 'hardliner.'" Lukacs justifies with scant remorse Stalin's brutality and political executions in his postwar homeland. He once proclaimed, as Rudnick quoted in *World Literature Today*, "the worst socialism will always be better than the best capitalism." Steiner added, "In these conversations, Lukacs scorns the teutonic-bourgeois notion of a *Lebenswerk*, of an *opera omnia* leather-bound for ages to come. Books, he rules, are provisional acts in the validating or, more often, negating context of historical-social-material conditions."

Record of a Life: An Autobiography contains translations of these conversations and late writings. In the *London Review of Books* Raymond Williams commented on the significance of Lukacs's self-reflection: "It is from this project of a 'synthesis of individual aspirations'—not any aspirations, but those learned from and centered in changing reality—that his important work in ethics and aesthetics and literary history, but also his more general philosophical and political theories can be best seen to proceed." While somewhat dissatisfied with the rather unchallenging questions posed by Lukacs's interviewer, Nicholas Jacobs remarked in *New Statesman*, "this unusual book is of great importance in presenting us with the only self-portrait we have of one of the great Marxist thinkers of the century." As James H. Kavanagh concluded in *Choice*, "One cannot study Marxist literary theory without knowing the seminal work of Georg Lukacs, the Hungarian philosopher who has dominated 20th-century Marxist literary studies."

BIOGRAPHICAL/CRITICAL SOURCES:

BOOKS

Bahr, Ehrhard, and Ruth Kunzer, *Georg Lukacs*, Ungar, 1972.
George Lukacs, Boorberg, 1973.
Kadarkay, Arpad, *Georg Lukacs: Life, Thought, and Politics*, B. Blackwell, 1991.
Lichtheim, George, *George Lukacs*, Viking, 1970.
Marcus, Judith, *Georg Lukacs and Thomas Mann: A Study in the Sociology of Literature*, Humanities Press, 1993.
Marcus, and Zoltaan Tarr, *Georg Lukacs: Theory, Culture, and Politics*, Transaction, 1989.
Parkinson, G. H. R., editor, *Georg Lukacs: The Man, His Work, and His Ideas*, Random House, 1970.
Rockmore, Tom, *Irrationalism: Lukas and the Marxist View of Reason*, Temple University Press, 1992.
Rockmore, editor, *Lukacs Today: Essays in Marxist Philosophy*, D. Reidel, 1988
Sim, Stuart, *Georg Lukas*, Harvester Wheatsheaf, 1994.
Steiner, George, *Language and Silence*, Faber, 1967.
Ungar, Frederick, editor, *Handbook of Austrian Literature*, Ungar, 1973.

PERIODICALS

Books and Bookmen, September, 1969.
Canadian Forum, August, 1968.

Choice, October, 1981, p. 203; May, 1992, p. 1466.

Commonweal, November 27, 1970.

Contemporary Literature, summer, 1968; winter, 1968.

Encounter, May, 1963; April, 1965.

Library Journal, October 15, 1986, p. 98; November 1, 1995, p. 67.

Listener, September 5, 1968.

London Review of Books, May 17-June 6, 1984, p. 14; February 19, 1987, p. 8.

Nation, July 14, 1969; December 27, 1971.

National Review, June 1, 1971.

New Statesman, December 17, 1971; March 16, 1984, p. 24.

New York Review of Books, November 19, 1981, p. 44.

New York Times, June 11, 1968.

New York Times Book Review, May 10, 1964; July 18, 1971.

Saturday Review, June 13, 1964; November 6, 1965; December 4, 1971.

Sewanee Review, summer, 1985, p. 457.

Times Literary Supplement, September 25, 1969; November 6, 1970; June 11, 1971; January 22, 1982.

TriQuarterly, spring, 1967; spring, 1968.

Washington Post, July 24, 1971.

World Literature Today, winter, 1983, p. 141; summer, 1987, p. 473.

Yale Review, spring, 1965, p. 435.

OBITUARIES:

PERIODICALS

Antiquarian Bookman, July 19-26, 1971.

New York Times, June 5, 1971.

Time, June 14, 1971.*

* * *

LUNG, Chang
  See RIGNEY, James Oliver, Jr.

M-N

MALAMUD, Bernard 1914-1986

PERSONAL: Born April 28, 1914, in Brooklyn, NY; died of natural causes, March 18, 1986, in New York, NY; son of Max (a grocery store manager) and Bertha (Fidelman) Malamud; married Ann de Chiara, November 6, 1945; children: Paul, Janna. *Education:* City College of New York (now City College of the City University of New York), B.A., 1936; Columbia University, M.A., 1942. *Religion:* Jewish. *Avocational interests:* Reading, travel, music, walking.

CAREER: Worked for Bureau of Census, Washington, DC, 1940; Erasmus Hall High School, New York City, evening instructor in English, beginning 1940; instructor in English, Harlem High School, 1948-49; Oregon State University, 1949-61, began as instructor, became associate professor of English; Bennington College, Bennington, VT, Division of Language and Literature, member of faculty, 1961-86. Visiting lecturer, Harvard University, 1966-68. Honorary consultant in American letters, Library of Congress, 1972-75.

MEMBER: National Institute of Arts and Letters, American Academy of Arts and Sciences, PEN American Center (president, 1979).

AWARDS, HONORS: Partisan Review fellow in fiction, 1956-57; Richard and Hinda Rosenthal Foundation Award, and Daroff Memorial Award, both 1958, both for *The Assistant;* Rockefeller grant, 1958; National Book Award in fiction, 1959, for *The Magic Barrel,* and 1967, for *The Fixer;* Ford Foundation fellow in humanities and arts, 1959-61; Pulitzer Prize in fiction, 1967, for *The Fixer;* O.

Henry Award, 1969, for "Man in the Drawer"; Jewish Heritage Award of the B'nai B'rith, 1976; Governor's Award, Vermont Council on the Arts, 1979, for excellence in the arts; American Library Association Notable Book citation, 1979, for *Dubin's Lives;* Brandeis University Creative Arts Award in fiction, 1981; Gold Medal for fiction, American Academy and Institute of Arts and Letters, 1983; Elmer Holmes Bobst Award for fiction, 1983; honorary degree from City College of the City University of New York.

WRITINGS:

NOVELS

The Natural, Harcourt (New York City), 1952.
The Assistant, Farrar, Straus (New York City), 1957.
A New Life, Farrar, Straus, 1961.
The Fixer, Farrar, Straus, 1966.
The Tenants, Farrar, Straus, 1971.
Dubin's Lives, Farrar, Straus, 1979.
God's Grace, Farrar, Straus, 1982.

SHORT STORIES

The Magic Barrel (includes "The Magic Barrel" and "The First Seven Years"), Farrar, Straus, 1958.
Idiots First (includes "Idiots First" and "The Maid's Shoes"), Farrar, Straus, 1963.
Pictures of Fidelman: An Exhibition (includes "The Last Mohican," "A Pimp's Revenge," and "Glass Blower of Venice"), Farrar, Straus, 1969.
Rembrandt's Hat (includes "The Silver Crown" and "Man in the Drawer"), Farrar, Straus, 1973.

The Stories of Bernard Malamud, Farrar, Straus, 1983.

The People, and Uncollected Stories, edited by Robert Giroux, Farrar, Straus, 1989.

OTHER

(Contributor) John Fisher and Robert B. Silvers, editors, *Writing in America,* Rutgers University Press (Rutgers, NJ), 1960.

A Malamud Reader, edited by Philip Rahv, Farrar, Straus, 1967.

Talking Horse: Bernard Malamud on Life and Work, edited by Alan Cheuse and Nicholas Delbanco, Columbia University Press (New York City), 1996.

Contributor of short stories to various magazines, including *American Preface, Atlantic, Commentary, Harper's, New Threshold,* and *New Yorker.* Contributor of articles to the *New York Times* and the *New York Times Book Review.* Manuscripts, typescripts, and proofs of *The Natural, The Assistant, A New Life, The Fixer, Pictures of Fidelman,* and various stories from *The Magic Barrel* and *Idiots First* are in the collection of the Library of Congress.

ADAPTATIONS: *The Fixer* was filmed by John Frankenheimer for Metro-Goldwyn-Mayer and released in 1969. *The Angel Levine* starred Zero Mostel and Harry Belafonte and was adapted by William Gunn for United Artists in 1970. *A New Life* and *The Assistant* were both optioned in the early 1970s, and producer Sidney Glazier planned a filmscript based on *Black Is My Favorite Color. The Natural,* starring Robert Redford as Roy Hobbs, Robert Duvall as Max Mercy, Glenn Close as Iris Gaines, and Kim Basinger as Memo Paris, was directed by Barry Levinson for Tri-Star Pictures and released in 1984.

SIDELIGHTS: Esteemed novelist and short story writer Bernard Malamud grew up on New York's East Side where his Russian-Jewish immigrant parents worked in their grocery store sixteen hours a day. Malamud attended high school and college during the height of the Depression. His own and his family's experience were clearly echoed in his fiction, much of which chronicled, as Mervyn Rothstein declares in the *New York Times,* "simple people struggling to make their lives better in a world of bad luck." His writings were also strongly influenced by classic nineteenth-century American writers such as Nathaniel Hawthorne, Henry David Thoreau,

Herman Melville, and Henry James. In addition, Malamud's works reflected a post-Holocaust consciousness in addressing Jewish concerns and employing literary conventions drawn from earlier Jewish literature.

The first major period of Malamud's work extended from 1949 to 1961 when he was teaching composition at Oregon State College. Producing three novels and a collection of short stories during this period, he won several fiction prizes, including the National Book Award. Each of the first three novels feature a schlemiel figure who tries to restore a Wasteland to a Paradise against a Jewish background. The setting varies in the novels, but in the short fiction is most often the East Side of New York. "The Prison" portrays a small New York grocery store based on that of Malamud's parents, in which a young Italian, Tommy Castelli, is trapped. Similarly "The Cost of Living"—a predecessor of *The Assistant*—and "The Bill" both present the grocery store as a sort of prison. As Leslie and Joyce Field observe in *Bernard Malamud: A Collection of Critical Essays,* "In Malamud's fictional world, there is always a prison," and in an interview with the Fields given a decade before his death, the author noted: "Necessity is the primary prison, though the bars are not visible to all." Beneath most Malamudian surfaces would lie similar moral and allegorical meanings.

Malamud's first novel, *The Natural,* would serve, as Earl R. Wasserman declares in *Bernard Malamud and the Critics,* "the necessary reference text for a reading of his subsequent fiction." The 1952 work is a mythic novel, based on the Arthurian legends, in which the Parsifal figure, Roy (King) Hobbs, restores fertility to the Fisher King, Pop Fisher, the manager of a baseball team called the Knights. Pitcher Roy appears as an Arthurian knight modeled in part on Babe Ruth, but his character also probably is drawn from Chretien de Troye's medieval tale, *Lancelot of the Cart,* featuring a Lancelot who is most often unhorsed and frequently humiliated. As Peter L. Hays has said in *The Fiction of Bernard Malamud,* "Like Lancelot, Malamud's heroes are cut to ribbons in their quests for love and fortune."

The novel's title is baseball slang for a player with natural talent, but it can also mean, as it did in the Middle Ages, an innocent fool. As Philip Roth has said in *Reading Myself and Others,* this is "not baseball as it is played in Yankee Stadium, but a wild, wacky game." Roy thinks of himself as "Sir Percy lancing Sir Maldemer, or the first son (with a rock in his paw) ranged against the primitive papa." Even more Freudian is Roy's lancelike bat, Wonderboy, which droops when its phallic hero goes into a slump and finally splits at the novel's conclusion.

In an echo of the Black Sox scandal of 1919, Roy is bribed to throw the pennant game by evil-eyed Gus Sands, whose Pot of Fire nightclub and chorus girls wielding pitchforks suggest hell itself. Though there are few obvious Jewish traces in *The Natural,* the prank Roy plays on Gus is a retelling of a Yiddish prankster tale, with the challenge by the prankster, the foil or victim's reaction, and the retort or prank—here Roy's pulling silver dollars out of Gus's ears and nose. Yet Roy's success is only temporary. As Glenn Meeter notes in *Bernard Malamud and Philip Roth: A Critical Essay,* "From the grail legend also we know that Roy will fail; for the true grail seeker must understand the supernatural character of his quest, and Roy does not." In the end Roy, defeated, throws his bribe money in the face of Judge Banner, who is a dispenser of "dark wisdom, parables and aphorisms which punctuate his conversation, making him seem a cynical Poor Richard," as Iska Alter remarks in *The Good Man's Dilemma: Social Criticism in the Fiction of Bernard Malamud.* This dramatic scene, and others in Malamud's work, accords with the statement he once made that his novels were akin to plays.

Other influences were also clearly at work in Malamud's first novel. *The Natural* contains significant references to birds and flowers and steady reminders of the passage of the seasons. The simplicity of this pastoral style at its best allowed the presentation of complex ideas in a natural way. A second influence, as Malamud acknowledged, was film technique. For example, there are quick, movie-like changes of scene—called jump cuts—when Roy and Memo Paris are tricked into sleeping with each other. In addition, the portrayal of Roy has a Chaplinesque quality of humor to it. Though Malamud would never again write non-Jewish fiction, *The Natural* was a treasure house of reusable motifs and methods for all his subsequent work.

In 1954 Malamud published one of his greatest short stories, "The Magic Barrel," which Sanford Pinsker, in *Bernard Malamud: A Collection of Critical Essays,* calls "a nearly perfect blend of form and content." In this story, collected in the 1958 volume of the same name, the matchmaker Pinye Salzman, using cards listing eligible women and drawn from his magic barrel, tricks student rabbi Leo Finkle into a

love match with Salzman's daughter, Stella, a streetwalker. In *Judaism,* Marcia Booher Gealy describes the structural essence of such Hasidic-influenced stories: (1) the inward journey; (2) the older man tutoring the younger; (3) the triumph of love; (4) the reality of evil; and (5) transformation through the tale itself. This structure merges with another influence, that of nineteenth-century American romanticism, for Malamud often joined the Hasidic and Hawthornian in his fables. As Renee Winegarten comments in *Bernard Malamud: A Collection of Critical Essays,* "His magic barrels and silver crowns, whatever their seal, firmly belong in the moral, allegorical realm of scarlet letters, white whales and golden bowls."

Concerning protagonist Salzman, as Irving Howe has said in *World of Our Fathers,* "The matchmaker, or *shadkhn,* is a stereotypical Yiddish figure: slightly comic, slightly sad, at the edge of destitution." Such confidence men reappear in Malamud's fiction, in "The Silver Crown," for example. And Salzman shows Malamud's early perfection of a Jewish-American speech, which was neither pure Yiddish dialect nor mere literary chat, but an imaginative combination of both. Kathryn Hellerstein observes in *The State of the Language* that Yiddish speakers in Malamud's works are "elderly, static, or declining" and concludes that for Malamud, Yiddish figures were "a spectral presence of the constraining, delimited, stultified past."

What many critics would refer to as Malamud's finest novel, *The Assistant,* appeared in 1957. As Ihab Hassan has said in *The Fiction of Bernard Malamud,* "*The Assistant,* I believe, will prove a classic not only of Jewish but of American literature." Frank Alpine, "the assistant," suggests St. Francis of Assisi, whose biography, *The Little Flowers,* is Alpine's favorite book and whose stigmata he at one point seems to emulate. Like Roy in *The Natural,* Frank is the Parsifal figure who must bring fertility, or at least new life, to the Fisher King, here the grocery store owner Morris Bober. Some critics have contended that Bober may parallel philosopher Martin Buber, whose I-THOU philosophy of human relations Bober seems, however instinctively, to share, though Malamud himself denied any use of Buber in this novel.

When he stands under a "No Trust" sign, Bober also recalls Melville's novel, *The Confidence Man.* Giving food to a drunk woman who will never pay, Morris teaches Frank to have compassion for others.

Yet Frank cannot control his passion for Morris's daughter, Helen. Thus when Frank saves Helen from an attempted rape, he fails the trial of the Perilous Bed, rapes her just as she is about to admit her love for him, and loses her.

Frank and Morris represent a familiar motif found throughout Malamud's works: that of the father-son pair, the schlemiel-schlimazel twins. Malamud liked these doublings and included three other father/son pairs in the novel. A favorite definition of these types is that the schlemiel spills his teacup, and the schlimazel is the one he spills it on. Norman Leer, thinking perhaps of Russian novelist Feodor Dostoevsky's *Crime and Punishment,* writes in *Mosaic: A Journal for the Comparative Study of Literature and Ideas* of "the notion of the divided self, and the attraction of two characters who mirror a part of each other, and are thereby drawn together as doubles."

Another recurrent feature of Malamudian narrative, the Holocaust, remains never far from the surface, though it appears almost always in an oblique way. Morris, in despair over his luckless grocery store/prison, turns on the gas to commit suicide, a reminder of the gas chambers of the Holocaust. And here Malamud introduced from the world of fantasy a professional arsonist who is like a figure from hell—recalling the night club women and their pitchforks in *The Natural.* In *The Assistant,* at Morris's funeral, Frank halts the ceremony by falling into the open grave while trying to see the rose Helen had thrown into it. The characters in Malamud's fiction frequently dream, and in Frank's dream, St. Francis successfully gives Frank's rose to Helen. Rachel Ertel declares in *Le Roman juif americain: Une Ecriture minoritaire,* "By going constantly from the real to the supernatural, Bernard Malamud deadens, nullifies the disbelief of the reader and gives himself elbow room to narrate the fables, the parables that make up his novels and short stories."

In 1958, with the publication of his first volume of short stories, *The Magic Barrel,* Malamud received national recognition and in 1959 won the National Book Award for the collection. All the stories in the volume display Malamud's continuing debt to Hawthorne; as Jackson J. Benson says in *The Fiction of Bernard Malamud,* the two writers "possess[ed] the ability to combine, with great skill, reality and the dream, the natural and supernatural." Thus a kinship can be perceived between Malamud's "Idiots First," "The Silver Crown," and "The Magic Barrel" and Hawthorne's short stories "My Kinsman, Major Molineux," "Young Goodman Brown," and "The Birthmark." Moreover, "The First Seven Years"—featuring Feld, a Polish immigrant shoemaker who refuses to speak Yiddish and who wants his daughter Miriam to marry a rising young suitor, Max, rather than his middle-aged but devoted helper, Sobel—is reminiscent of Hawthorne's "Ethan Brand," with its warning about "hardness of the heart." However, "The First Seven Years" was Hawthorne plus Holocaust, for Sobel had barely escaped Hitler's incinerators.

In the years from 1949 to 1961 Malamud slowly became "one of the foremost writers of moral fiction in America," as Jeffrey Helterman comments in *Understanding Bernard Malamud.* Of his last work in this first period, Sheldon J. Hershinow remarks in *Bernard Malamud* that "*A New Life* is Malamud's first attempt at social satire, and much of the novel is given over to it." Its hero, marginal Jew Sy Levin, shows the complexity behind the names Malamud would give to practically all his major characters. In *City of Words: American Fiction 1950-1970,* Tony Tanner explains that the name Levin means the east, or light; it is also associated with lightning. Tanner writes: "I have it direct from Mr. Malamud that by a pun on 'leaven' he is suggesting what the marginal Jew may bring in attitude to the American scene." Levin, whose fictional career resembled that of his creator, is a former high school teacher who joins the faculty at Cascadia University in Easchester, Oregon, a name that suggests a castle of ease. According to Mark Goldman, in a *Critique* review, "Early in the novel, Levin is the tenderfoot Easterner, the academic sad sack, or schlimazel of Yiddish literature, invoking nature like a tenement Rousseau." Levin, then is the schlemiel as lecturer, who teaches his first class with his fly open, then bumbles his way into an affair with coed Nadalee, a lady of the lake who has written an essay on nude bathing. As Sandy Cohen says in *Bernard Malamud and the Trial by Love,* "Malamud's favorite method of portraying a protagonist's struggle to overcome his vanity is to symbolize it in terms of the Grail myth. Thus Levin's journey to meet Nadalee takes on certain aspects of the grail quest." Indeed, Levin journeys "in his trusty Hudson, his lance at his side."

Later Levin makes love in the woods to Pauline Gilley; in an echo of English novelist D. H. Lawrence's *Lady Chatterley's Lover,* Pauline also has an impotent husband, Gerald Gilley, future chairman of the English Department. Against this pastoral background, complete with the passage of the seasons, Levin is also the American Adam: as Hershinow observes, "Immersed in the writings of Emerson, Thoreau, and Whitman, Levin believes wholeheartedly the metaphors about America as a New-World Garden of Eden. By going west he feels he can recapture his lost innocence and escape the past—become the New-World Adam."

This major love affair is also Hawthornian: as Paul Witherington notes in *Western American Literature,* "Levin's affair with Pauline matures in Hawthorne fashion to an inner drama of the ambiguities of paradise." In fact, Levin sees himself as "Arthur Dimmesdale Levin, locked in stocks on a platform in the town square, a red A stapled on his chest." From Levin's point of view, Pauline, whose love earned him his scarlet letter "A", is also the tantalizing *shiksa,* the Gentile temptress of so many Jewish-American novels, not only those of Malamud but also of Saul Bellow and Philip Roth among others. As Frederick Cople Jaher points out in the *American Quarterly,* to Jewish men, such women seem to be "exotic insiders" and so represent "tickets of admission into American society."

At the conclusion of the novel, Gilley asks Levin why he wants to take on two adopted children and Gilley's apparently barren wife. Levin replies, "Because I can, you son of a bitch." And Levin, defeated in academe, but having impregnated the barren Pauline, whose flat breasts are beginning to swell, drives away with his new family, having agreed with Gilley never again to teach in a university. This ending, as so often in Malamud, is ambiguous, for Levin is no longer in romantic love with Pauline. Here is what *Critique* contributor Ruth B. Mandel calls "ironic affirmation"—"The affirmation itself is ironic in that the state of grace is unaccompanied by paradise."

After Malamud's move back East to Bennington College, his second period (roughly 1961-1970) began, and both his stories and his next two novels took a more cosmopolitan and international direction. In *Bernard Malamud,* Sidney Richman perceptively observes that the title story in 1963's *Idiots First* is "a morality [play] *a la* Everyman in which the sense of a real world (if only the sense of it) is utterly absorbed by a dream-landscape, a never-never-land New York City through which an elderly Jew named Mendel wanders in search of comfort and aid." Mendel is indeed a Jewish Everyman, who tries to

dodge the Angel of Death (here named Ginzburg) to arrange for the future of his handicapped son, Isaac.

Another short story, "The Maid's Shoes," reveals the new subject matter and style. Professor Orlando Krantz, who plays the part of the comparatively wealthy American as Everyman, tries to give a small gift to his poor Italian maid, Rosa, but it is a gift without the understanding that the impoverished European needs: "But though they shared the same roof, and even the same hot water bottle and bathtub, they almost never shared speech." Here, failures of the heart, common to the fiction of the first period, are extended to complete failures of empathy. Furthermore, the story is no longer fantastic, as in Malamud's first period, but realistic. Of Rosa, Malamud wrote: "She was forty-five and looked older. Her face was worn but her hair was black, and her eyes and lips were pretty. She had few good teeth. When she laughed she was embarrassed around the mouth." Finally, the story has a single, consistent point of view instead of the omniscient point of view of the earlier stories. Yet since that omniscient narration contained Malamud's often compassionate comments that were characteristic of his first period manner, these newer stories have a bleaker cast to them.

Next to *The Assistant* in critical reputation would come *The Fixer,* winner of the Pulitzer Prize and the National Book Award in 1967. In a search for a suffering Everyman plot, Malamud had thought of several subjects—the trial of Alfred Dreyfus and the Sacco-Vanzetti case, among others—before deciding on a story he had heard from his father as a boy, that of the trial of Mendel Beiliss for ritual bloodletting and murder in 1913 in Russia. Through this story, Malamud also tried to answer the question of how the death camps in Germany had been possible. Hero Yakov Bok's last name suggests a scapegoat, and also the goat mentioned in the song chanted for the end of the Passover Seder as a symbol of Jewish survival. As Malamud once said in an interview with Christopher Lehmann-Haupt in the *New York Times Book Review,* it was necessary "to mythologize—that is, to make metaphors and symbols of the major events and characters."

The novel itself covers two years, spring 1911 to winter 1913, during which Bok is imprisoned after being falsely accused of the ritual murder of a Gentile boy. Without legal counsel Bok suffers betrayal, gangrene, poison, and freezing cold, and finally turns inward to develop a sense of freedom. In prison this Everyman fixer learns through suffering to overcome, at least in part, his initial agnosticism, and his doubts of what is meant by the Chosen People. He rejects both suicide and a pardon, and accepts his Jewishness. Finally, in a dream encounter with Tsar Nicholas II, Bok shoots the Tsar. As John F. Desmond writes in *Renascence: Essays on Values in Literature,* "Yakov has come to understand that no man is apolitical, especially a Jew; consequently, if his chance came, as it does in the imaginary meeting with the Tsar, he would not hesitate to kill the ruler as a beginning step towards purging that society of its agents of repression and injustice, and thus strike a blow for freedom and humanity." Bok, at least in his dream, is no longer the passive, suffering servant of Isaiah portrayed in many of Malamud's first-period fictions, but one who seeks revenge. Has Bok lost more important values? The dream setting leaves the ending ambiguous, but Malamud's real subject was never so much Bok himself as those—like the Germans, other Europeans, and Americans did during the Holocaust—who either participate in, or passively observe, the treatment of Everyman as victim. As the Fields remark, Malamud repeatedly tried to make clear, especially in this second period, that Jewish victims are Everyman as victim, for history, sooner or later, treats all men as Jews.

The final major work of this second period was *Pictures of Fidelman: An Exhibition.* As Leslie A. Field has written in *Bernard Malamud: A Collection of Critical Essays,* "Of all the Malamud characters, early and late, one must return to Arthur Fidelman as the Malamud *schlemiel par excellence.*" The Fidelman stories appeared both separately in magazines and in two story collections from 1958 to 1969, and they were not originally thought of as a unit. But the last three stories are tightly linked, and as Robert Ducharme asserts in *Art and Idea in the Novels of Bernard Malamud: Toward "The Fixer,"* Malamud deliberately saved the last story for the book because he didn't want to let readers know the ending. Three genres merge in *Pictures of Fidelman,* that of the *Kunstlerroman* or artist novel, the *Bildungsroman* or education novel, and the *Huckleberry Finn*-like picaresque novel, in which the main character wanders through a series of adventures. Fidelman (faith man) encounters Susskind (sweet child) in the first story or chapter, "Last Mohican." Susskind is a Jewish folktale type, a *chnorrer,* or as Goldman terms him, "a beggar with style," who wants the second of Fidelman's two suits. Rebuffed, Susskind steals the first chapter of Fidelman's book on Italian artist Giotto di Bondone. Hershinow suggests that

"Susskind becomes for Fidelman a kind of dybbuk (demon) who inhabits his conscience, destroying his peace of mind." As Cohen remarks, "So Fidelman begins an active search for Susskind who begins to take on the roles of alter-ego, superego, and symbol for Fidelman's true heritage and past." Here again would be the familiar Malamud motif of the journey that changes a life.

In pursuit, Fidelman visits a synagogue, a Jewish ghetto, and a graveyard that contains victims of the Holocaust. Both at the cemetery and in his crazy pursuit of Susskind, Schlemiel Fidelman recalls Frank Alpine in *The Assistant,* for Fidelman too is linked to St. Francis. In a dream Fidelman sees Susskind, who shows him a Giotto fresco in which St. Francis gives his clothing to a poor knight. As Sidney Richman affirms in *Bernard Malamud and the Critics,* "In the same fashion as Frankie Alpine, Fidelman must discover that the way to the self is paradoxically through another; and the answer is heralded by a sudden alteration of the pursuit." At the end of this artistic pilgrim's progress, "against his will, Fidelman learns what the ancient rabbis taught and what Susskind has always known: Jews—that is, human beings, *menschen,* in Malamud's terms—are responsible for each other. That is the essence of being human," Michael Brown relates in *Judaism.*

Fidelman would learn in the next stories what makes a great artist. For example, in the fourth story, "A Pimp's Revenge," he returns his mistress, Esmeralda, to prostitution to pay for his constantly repainted masterwork, a portrait of her, first as Mother and Son, then as Brother and Sister, and finally as Prostitute and Procurer. "The truth is I am afraid to paint, like I might find out something about myself," Fidelman says. Esmeralda knows the secret: "If I have my choice, I'll take life. If there's not that there's no art." Barbara Lefcowitz justly argues in *Literature and Psychology,* "Where Malamud excels is in his subtle and nearly always comical juxtaposition of a neurotic character against a deeper and wider moral and historical context." Fidelman finally produces a masterpiece, but, second-rate artist that he is, can't let it alone, and mars it. The genius knows when to stop, but Everyman does not, and Esmeralda calls him a murderer.

In the final story, "Glass Blower of Venice," Fidelman tries to play artist once more, under the reluctant teaching of his homosexual lover Beppo, but at last gives up art for craftsmanship and returns to America. Fidelman, the craftsman, no longer the inadequate artist, has finally achieved the goals toward which Susskind—and later Esmeralda—pointed him. Samuel I. Bellman argues in *Critique* that "more than any other Malamudian character Fidelman is constantly growing, realizing himself, transforming his unsatisfactory old life into a more satisfactory new one." In *Bernard Malamud: A Collection of Critical Essays,* Sheldon N. Grebstein praises the juxtaposition of "the coarsely sexual and the sublimely aesthetic." Indeed, no other work of Malamud would show so much appetite for life; as Helterman has argued: "[Fidelman] also seeks, and occasionally participates in, a richness of passion not typical of Malamud's urban heroes." The epigraph for *Pictures of Fidelman* is from Yeats: "The intellect of man is forced to choose Perfection of the life or of the work." However, the new Fidelman chooses "both."

The Tenants inaugurated Malamud's third and final period. In the works of this period the heroic structuring of the first period would vanish, as would the Wandering Jews and the Everyman motifs of the second. Beneath differing surface plots, though, a new structural likeness would appear. Before 1971 Malamud's typical Jewish characters tended to move towards responsibility rather than towards achievement; from 1971 on, they became extraordinary achievers, or *machers.*

In 1971's *The Tenants* Harry Lesser, a minor Jewish novelist, is writing a novel about being unable to finish a novel, in a kind of infinite regression. He keeps on living in the apartment building that landlord Levenspiel (leaven game) wants to tear down; then a squatter, black writer Willie Spearmint (Willie Shakespeare), moves into the building. Willie and Harry are the kind of doubled pair (drawn from Edgar Allan Poe and Dostoevsky) that Malamud was fond of, for Harry's writing is all form, and Willie's is all vitality. Harry takes over Irene, Willie's Jewish girl; Willie burns Harry's manuscript; Harry axes Willie's typewriter; and in a final burst of overachievement, Willie brains Harry and Harry castrates Willie. *The Tenants* "ends in a scream of language," reports Malcolm Bradbury in *Encounter.* Though the novel hints at two other possible endings—by fire, or by Harry's marriage to Irene—Levenspiel has the last word, which is *Rachmones,* or mercy.

Though *The Tenants* did little for Malamud's reputation, he would continue to publish short fiction in top

U.S. magazines up until his death in 1983; as he would tell *New York Times* critic Mervyn Rothstein near the end of his life, "With me, it's story, story, story." In Malamud's 1973 collection, *Rembrandt's Hat,* only one story, "The Silver Crown," is predominantly Jewish, in sharp contrast to his first collection, while other stories are more reminiscent of Chekhov. There is even a visit to the Chekhov Museum in "Man in the Drawer," a story that shows the fascination with achievement so dominant in Malamud's final period. Howard Harvitz, an intellectual tourist in Russia and a marginal Jew, has changed his name from Harris back to Harvitz. Hardly a creative writer himself, he is doing a piece on museums. A Russian writer, Levitansky—also a marginal Jew, but a determined achiever in spite of official opposition—intends to smuggle his stories out of Russia. Harvitz at first doesn't want this charge, but discovers that four of the stories show heroes not taking responsibility. After reading them, Harvitz timorously takes the stories out of Russia.

The 1979 novel *Dubin's Lives* took Malamud over five years to write, twice as long as any previous novel. Ralph Tyler in the *New York Times Book Review* reports that Malamud referred to the work as "his attempt at bigness, at summing up what he . . . learned over the long haul." In the novel, the biographer Dubin is an isolated achiever, no mere recorder of biographical facts but a creative, even fictionalizing biographer: "One must transcend autobiographical detail by inventing it after it is remembered." Dubin is trying to write a biography of D. H. Lawrence, a writer who made passion his religion, yet was impotent. There had been a glancing counterpointing of Lawrence's career in *A New Life,* but here this motif is much enlarged; as David Levin observes in *Virginia Quarterly Review,* "The complexities of Dubin's subsequent adventures often run parallel to events in Lawrence's life."

In the kind of psychomachia, or inner struggle, which some critics see as the essence of American fiction, Dubin, as Helterman notes, "loses his memory, his sexual powers, his ability to work, even his ability to relate to his family. At first, the only compensation for these losses is a kind of high-grade nostalgia brought about by a process called reverie." These reveries lead Dubin to a liaison with young Fanny Bick, whose first name comes from English novelist Jane Austen's heroine in *Mansfield Park,* Fanny Price; Fanny Bick is an Austen heroine with glands. Like a number of heroines in Malamud's fiction, she is significantly associated with wildflowers, fruit, and bird flights. Chiara Briganti remarks in *Studies in American Jewish Literature* that "all the female characters in Malamud's fiction share a common shallowness and common values: they all respect marriage and family life, and, whatever their past, they all seek fulfillment through a permanent relationship with a man." But Fanny breaks this stereotypical pattern, for at the end of *Dubin's Lives* she ambitiously intends to become a lawyer.

Dubin's affair in Venice, where the youthful Fanny almost immediately betrays him with their gondolier, is that of the schlemiel lover seen before in Frank Alpine and Sy Levin. Barbara Quart, in *Studies in American Jewish Literature,* has seen a further problem: "While Malamud's central characters try to break out of their solitude, they appear to fear love and women as much as they long for them." But dominant among familiar motifs is the character of Dubin as the isolated overachiever, who moves his study from his country house into the barn to devote all possible energy and space to his biography. Dubin even begrudges time wasted thinking about Fanny, with whom he is genuinely in love.

Malamud's last finished novel, 1982's *God's Grace,* would treat both the original Holocaust and a new, imagined Holocaust of the future. In *Immigrant-Survivors: Post-Holocaust Consciousness in Recent Jewish-American Literature,* Dorothy Seldman Bilik has pointed out that the question of why God permitted the Holocaust was a central issue in Malamud's fiction for thirty years; indeed, for Malamud the Holocaust was the ultimate mark of inhumanity, and *God's Grace* treats the Holocaust not only as man's inhumanity to man, but as God's inhumanity to man. The novel is a wild, at times brilliant, at times confusing description of a second Great Flood. Calvin Cohn, a paleologist and the son of a rabbi-cantor, had been doing underseas research when the Djanks and the Druzhkies (Yanks and Russians) launched an atomic Holocaust and destroyed every other human. Calvin recalls many Biblical and literary figures: Parsifal, Romeo, Prospero, Robinson Crusoe, Gulliver, and Ahab. His Eve and Juliet is Mary Madelyn, a chimpanzee. An albino ape appears (possibly an oblique reference to Moby Dick) with other apes as Yahoos from Jonathan Swift's *Gulliver's Travels,* and the chimpanzee Buz serves as Cohn's Isaac, Caliban, and man Friday. There is even an Arthurian spear used to harpoon the albino ape.

On Cohn's Island Calvin turns into an overachiever, and even an un-Job-like defier of God, in spite of God's pillars of fire, showers of lemons, and occasional warning rocks. The foundation of *God's Grace* is Biblical in part, but also characteristically American, for it is the story of the Americanized—and reversed—Fortunate Fall. The idea conveyed by the Fortunate Fall is that Adam and Eve, driven from Paradise by eating of the tree of Knowledge, in fact obtained benefits from their fall, notably free will and a consciousness of good and evil. Cohn has treated the chimpanzees as his inferiors; as a schlemiel lecturer he has imposed his admonitions and teachings on them, rather than encouraging them to learn for themselves. He has promised but never given Mary Madelyn the marriage she has wanted, and he has prevented the marriage or mating of Buz and Mary Madelyn, which could have been just as desirable for the future gene stock as Cohn's half-chimpanzee child Rebekah. In short, over-achieving Calvin Cohn has eaten from the tree of hubris, or sinful pride, rather than knowledge.

This complex novel baffled its first reviewers; for example, Joseph Epstein writes in *Commentary:* "Much of the humor in the novel is of the kind known as faintly amusing, but the chimp humor, on the scale of wit, is roughly three full rungs down from transvestite jokes." Part of the difficulty in the novel is that *God's Grace* does not fall into a clear genre category; in a 1982 *Christian Science Monitor* article, Victor Howes called it "somewhat east of sci-fi, somewhat west of allegory." However, like much of Malamud's work, *God's Grace* not only reflects the Jewish Old Testament but also partakes of an American colonial genre, the Jeremiad, or warning of future disaster.

After Malamud's sudden death in the winter of 1986, he left behind him sixteen chapters of a twenty-one-chapter novel tentatively titled *The People.* The novel, which concerns the adventures of a Russian Jewish peddlar named Yozip in the American West, would be included in its draft form in *The People, and Uncollected Stories,* in 1989. As Nan Robertson explains the work in the *New York Times,* the schlemiel hero Yozip becomes a marshal, is kidnapped by a tribe of Native American Indians, and has a dialogue with an Indian chief about obtaining his freedom. In addition to *The People,* the collection also contains fourteen short stories written between 1943 and 1985, six of which had never before been published. While critics noted that the collection has interest for Malamud scholars, the author's decision not to collect these works was made due to their relative merits. While noting that the unfinished state of Malamud's posthumously published novel precludes any serious discussion of its merits, Jonathan Yardley comments in the *Washington Post Book Review* that "Of the stories, one . . . has merit, and the apprenticework is mildly interesting for the foreshadowing it offers of Malamud's mature writing; but the world would not be the poorer had these tales been allowed to go undisturbed."

During his life, Malamud proved to be a reclusive writer, giving few interviews. However, those he did grant provide perhaps the most illuminating commentary on his work. After his death, several collections of interviews, speeches, and lectures were published. In 1991's *Conversations with Bernard Malamud,* part of the "Literary Conversations" series, thirty interviews transcribed from various sources represent the bulk of the public disclosure of this private literary figure. Within his brief, to-the-point responses to questions regarding his life, Malamud reflected his belief that the tale was far more important than the teller. "He was definite in asserting that to be a writer one must have talent and discipline," Daniel Walden explains in *Modern Fiction Studies.* Calling *Conversations* "an exceptionally useful book," Walden adds of the late author: "What he saw in the writing act was a moral act, in constantly seeking the highest opportunities to do well. . . . Indeed, Malamud as moralist, although not as preacher, comes through the body of his work. The daring writer . . . who reinvented himself with each book, despite the occasional dark vision, never wavered from his positive [humanist] premise."

Another volume of assorted non-literary works by Malamud was published in 1996 under the title *Talking Horse: Bernard Malamud on Life and Work.* Compiled by Alan Cheuse and Nicholas Delbanco, both friends of the late writer, *Talking Horse* contains numerous notes, anecdotes, and other information taken from such sources as an interview published in the *Paris Review* and a lecture given at Bennington College shortly before his death, all of which would be likely to interest aficionados of Malamud's fiction. From reminiscences about his experiences teaching high school and college students, to the stages of development of many of his well-known works of fiction, the collection "will inspire and challenge all readers, especially those interested in the craft of writing," according to *Library Journal* reviewer Nancy R. Ives.

"People say I write so much about misery," Malamud once confided to Michiko Kakutani in a rare interview for the *New York Times,* "but you write about what you write best. As you are grooved, so you are grieved. And the grieving is that no matter how much happiness or success you collect, you cannot obliterate your early experience." Reflecting on the author's life, Malamud's contribution can be seen most clearly in his greatest invention, his Jewish-American dialect, comic even at the height of tragedy. Recall Calvin Cohn, sacrificed in *God's Grace* by the chimpanzee Buz in a wild inversion of the story of Abraham and Isaac, as he reflects that God after all has let him live out his life. Cohn then asks himself—forgetting his educated speech and reverting to the Yiddish rhythms of his youth—"Maybe tomorrow the world to come?" In such comic-serious questioning, Malamud captured the voice of the past and gave it relevance to our present.

BIOGRAPHICAL/CRITICAL SOURCES:

BOOKS

Alter, Iska, *The Good Man's Dilemma: Social Criticism in the Fiction of Bernard Malamud,* AMS Press, 1981.

Astro, Richard, and Jackson J. Benson, editors, *The Fiction of Bernard Malamud,* Oregon State University Press, 1977.

Avery, Evelyn G., *Rebels and Victims: The Fiction of Richard Wright and Bernard Malamud,* Kennikat, 1979.

Baumbach, Jonathan, *The Landscape of Nightmare: Studies in the Contemporary American Novel,* New York University Press, 1965.

Bilik, Dorothy Seldman, *Immigrant-Survivors: Post-Holocaust Consciousness in Recent Jewish-American Literature,* Wesleyan University Press, 1981.

Bloom, Harold, *Bernard Malamud,* Chelsea House, 1986.

Cohen, Sandy, *Bernard Malamud and the Trial by Love,* Rodopi (Amsterdam), 1974.

Concise Dictionary of American Literary Biography: The New Consciousness, 1941-1968, Gale, 1987.

Contemporary Authors Bibliographical Series, Volume 1: *American Novelists,* Gale, 1986.

Contemporary Literary Criticism, Gale, Volume 1, 1973, Volume 2, 1974, Volume 3, 1975, Volume 5, 1976, Volume 8, 1978, Volume 9, 1978, Volume 11, 1979, Volume 18, 1981, Volume 27, 1984, Volume 44, 1987, Volume 78, 1994, Volume 85, 1995.

Dictionary of Literary Biography, Gale, Volume 2: *American Novelists since World War II,* 1978, Volume 28: *Twentieth-Century American-Jewish Fiction Writers,* 1984, Volume 152: *American Novelists since World War II, Fourth Series,* 1995.

Dictionary of Literary Biography Yearbook, Gale, 1980, 1981, 1986, 1987.

Ducharme, Robert, *Art and Idea in the Novels of Bernard Malamud: Toward "The Fixer,"* Mouton, 1974.

Ertel, Rachel, *Le Roman juif americain: Une Ecriture minoritaire,* Payot (Paris), 1980.

Fiedler, Leslie, *Love and Death in the American Novel,* Criterion, 1960.

Field, Leslie A., and Joyce W. Field, editors, *Bernard Malamud and the Critics,* New York University Press, 1970.

Field, Leslie A., and Joyce W. Field, editors, *Bernard Malamud: A Collection of Critical Essays,* Prentice-Hall, 1975.

Helterman, Jeffrey, *Understanding Bernard Malamud,* University of South Carolina Press, 1985.

Hershinow, Sheldon J., *Bernard Malamud,* Ungar, 1980.

Howe, Irving, *World of Our Fathers,* Harcourt, 1976.

Kosofsky, Rita Nathalie, *Bernard Malamud: An Annotated Checklist,* Kent State University Press, 1969.

Lasher, Lawrence M., editor, *Conversations with Bernard Malamud,* University Press of Mississippi, 1991.

Meeter, Glen, *Bernard Malamud and Philip Roth: A Critical Essay,* Eerdmans, 1968.

Michaels, Leonard, and Christopher Ricks, editors, *The State of the Language,* University of California Press, 1980.

Radical Innocence: Studies in the Contemporary American Novel, Princeton University Press, 1961.

Richman, Sidney, *Bernard Malamud,* Twayne, 1966.

Roth, Philip, *Reading Myself and Others,* Farrar, Straus, 1975.

Salzburg, Joel, *Bernard Malamud: A Reference Guide,* G. K. Hall & Co., 1985.

Salzburg, Joel, editor, *Critical Essays on Bernard Malamud,* G. K. Hall, 1987.

The Schlemiel as Metaphor: Studies in the Yiddish and American Jewish Novel, Southern Illinois University Press, 1971.

Short Story Criticism, Gale, Volume 15, 1994.

Tanner, Tony, *City of Words: American Fiction 1950-1970,* Harper, 1971.

PERIODICALS

American Quarterly, Volume 35, number 5, 1983.

American Scholar, winter, 1990, p. 67.

Centennial Review, Volume 9, 1965; Volume 13, 1969.

Chicago Tribune Book World, February 11, 1979; September 5, 1982; October 30, 1983.

Christian Science Monitor, September 10, 1982.

Commentary, October, 1982.

Commonweal, October 28, 1966.

Critique, winter, 1964/65.

Detroit News, December 25, 1983.

Encounter, Volume 45, number 1, 1975.

English Journal, April, 1991, p. 67.

Essays in Literature, spring, 1988, pp. 87-101.

Journal of Ethnic Studies, winter, 1974.

Judaism, winter, 1979; fall, 1980.

Library Journal, May 1, 1996, p. 94.

Linguistics in Literature, fall, 1977.

Literature and Psychology, Volume 20, number 3, 1970.

Los Angeles Times Book Review, September 12, 1982; December 25, 1983; November 26, 1989.

Midstream, winter, 1961.

Modern Fiction Studies, winter 1991, pp. 752-53.

Mosaic: A Journal for the Comparative Study of Literature and Ideas, spring, 1971.

New Leader, May 26, 1969.

New Republic, November 6, 1989, p. 116; September 20, 1982; September 27, 1982.

New Statesman & New Society, January 26, 1990, p. 34.

Newsweek, September 6, 1982; October 17, 1983.

New Yorker, November 8, 1982.

New York Review of Books, September 30, 1973.

New York Times, May 3, 1969; February 2, 1979; July 15, 1980; August 23, 1982; October 11, 1983; February 23, 1985; July 15, 1985; November 14, 1989.

New York Times Book Review, September 4, 1964; May 4, 1969; October 3, 1971; February 18, 1979; August 29, 1982; August 28, 1983; October 16, 1983; April 20, 1986; March 20, 1988, p. 15; November 5, 1989, p. 1; November 19, 1989, p. 7; March 18, 1986, p. 35.

Paris Review, spring, 1975.

Partisan Review, winter, 1962; summer, 1964.

Playboy, January, 1990, p. 31.

Polish Review, Volume XXVII, Nos. 3-4, 1982, pp. 35-44.

Publishers Weekly, April 8, 1996, p. 49.

Renascence: Essays on Values in Literature, winter, 1975.

Saturday Review, May 10, 1969.
Studies in American Fiction, spring, 1986, pp. 93-98.
Studies in American Jewish Literature, spring, 1978, number 3, 1983.
Studies in Short Fiction, spring, 1981, pp. 180-183.
Tikkun, March-April, 1989, p. 32.
Time, May 9, 1969; September 13, 1982; October 17, 1983; November 20, 1989, p. 106.
Times Literary Supplement, October 16, 1969; October 29, 1982; February 24, 1984; February 9, 1990.
Tribune Books (Chicago), November 26, 1989.
USA Today Magazine, May, 1990, p. 95.
Virginia Quarterly Review, winter, 1980.
Washington Post, August 27, 1982.
Washington Post Book World, February 25, 1979; August 29, 1982; October 16, 1983; November 26, 1989, p. 3.
Western American Literature, August, 1975.
Western Humanities Review, winter, 1968; winter, 1970.
Writer's Digest, July, 1972; April, 1995, p. 40.

OBITUARIES:

PERIODICALS

Chicago Tribune, March 20, 1986.
Detroit News, March 23, 1986.
Los Angeles Times, March 19, 1986.
New Republic, May 12, 1986.
Newsweek, March 31, 1986.
New York Times, March 20, 1986.
Times (London), March 20, 1986.
Washington Post, March 20, 1986.*

*   *   *

MARSHALL, William
   See MARSHALL, William Leonard

*   *   *

MARSHALL, William Leonard 1944-
   (William Marshall)

PERSONAL: Born in 1944, in Sydney, Australia; married Mary Fahy; children: one daughter.

ADDRESSES: Agent—c/o Secker and Warburg Ltd., Michelin House, 81 Fulham Road, London SW3 6RB, England.

CAREER: Writer. Worked as a playwright, journalist, proofreader, morgue attendant, and as a teacher at an Irish prison

WRITINGS:

NOVELS

The Fire Circle, Macmillan (London), 1969.
The Age of Death, Macmillan, 1970, Viking (New York City), 1971.
The Middle Kingdom, Macmillan, 1971.
(Under name William Marshall) *Shanghai,* Holt (New York City), 1979.

CRIME NOVELS; "YELLOWTHREAD STREET" SERIES; AS WILLIAM MARSHALL

Yellowthread Street, Hamish Hamilton (London), 1975, Holt, 1976.
Gelignite, Hamish Hamilton, 1976, Holt, 1977.
The Hatchet Man, Hamish Hamilton, 1976, Holt, 1977.
Thin Air, Hamish Hamilton, 1977, Holt, 1978.
Skullduggery, Hamish Hamilton, 1979, Holt, 1980.
Sci Fi, Holt, 1981.
Perfect End, Hamish Hamilton, 1981, Holt, 1983.
War Machine, Hamish Hamilton, 1982, Mysterious Press (New York City), 1988.
The Far Away Man, Secker and Warburg (London), 1984, Holt, 1985.
Roadshow, Holt, 1985.
Head First, Holt, 1986.
Frogmouth, Mysterious Press, 1987.
Out of Nowhere, Mysterious Press, 1988.
Inches, Mysterious Press, 1994.
Nightmare Syndrome, Mysterious Press, 1997.

CRIME NOVELS; "MANILA BAY" SERIES; AS WILLIAM MARSHALL

Manila Bay, Viking (New York City), 1986.
Whisper, Viking, 1988.

CRIME NOVELS; "NEW YORK DETECTIVE" SERIES; AS WILLIAM MARSHALL

The New York Detective, Mysterious Press, 1989.
Faces in the Crowd, Mysterious Press, 1991.

OTHER

King Edward (play), produced in Sydney, Australia, 1971.

ADAPTATIONS: The "Yellowthread Street" novels were adapted for a thirteen-episode series on British television, broadcast in 1990.

SIDELIGHTS: William Marshall has enjoyed substantial success as the creator of various detective series. Best known among his crime-fighting chronicles are the fast-paced "Yellowthread Street" novels featuring the tireless—but not particularly brilliant—Hong Kong inspector Harry Feiffer. In this series, which mixes broad—even slapstick—humor with often extraordinary violence, Feiffer and his beleaguered but ever-resourceful cohorts are inevitably pitted against a gallery of singularly deranged and bizarre villains. The series' first volume, itself entitled *Yellowthread Street,* culminates in a showdown where a relentless moron duels with hoodlums at Yellowthread Street police headquarters. Newgate Callendar, in his regular appraisal of crime fiction for the *New York Times Book Review,* characterized *Yellowthread Street* as "a bit off the usual run of things."

In ensuing "Yellowthread Street" volumes, Marshall has bombarded his hapless Hong Kong cops with all manner of foe and folly. In an early entry, *Gelignite,* Inspector Feiffer and his Yellowthread Street friends try to placate an irate citizen—greatly disturbed by the disappearance of his beloved toucan—while scrambling to capture an apparent lunatic who has already exploded several businessmen and now threatens to bomb a cemetery. *Thin Air,* another early volume, finds Hong Kong's lucrative tourist trade jeopardized when a madman annihilates a planeload of passengers, then threatens to similarly undo other flights unless paid a substantial sum by the airlines. Here Feiffer himself is suspected—by a particularly ignorant police officer—of having committed the wholesale slaughter. And in *Skullduggery,* Feiffer and company must contend with the sudden appearance of a skeleton aboard a raft replete with sweet potatoes, dentures, and a blue drainpipe. *New Republic* reviewer Robin Winks informed readers that *Skullduggery* shared "the same mix as before: rather mad, frequently gruesome."

Further volumes in the "Yellowthread Street" series have managed to sustain Marshall's reputation as a masterful iconoclast within the detective genre. For *Sci Fi,* where a deranged spaceman immolates vari-

ous participants at a science-fiction festival, Marshall was hailed in the *Washington Post Book World* as one "who has the rare gift of juggling scary suspense with wild humor and making both work." *Roadshow,* where one lunatic menaces the Hong Kong public with exploding parking meters while another crazed fellow occasionally fires a hand cannon at a monastery, brought similar recognition for Marshall as a writer skilled at merging "expert police procedures with ludicrous insanities." And *Head First,* where Feiffer struggles to stop the dismembering of unearthed corpses, earned Marshall still further acclaim for his utterly original work. "There's nothing quite like [*Head First*] anywhere else on the crime menu," declared Christopher Wordsworth in the *Times Literary Supplement.*

Out of Nowhere (1988), the thirteenth entry in the "Yellowthread Street" series, sustains the status established by preceding volumes. Here Feiffer and his fellow lawmen are plagued by a range of problems, including a shootout-auto mishap, an armed child, and a dog that periodically steals from the precinct. Marietta Denniston, in her *Armchair Detective* review, speculated that *Out of Nowhere* is "possibly the most bizarre ['Yellowthread Street' mystery] yet," and concluded that it is "one of the best in the series."

Inches and *Nightmare Syndrome,* however, earned mixed reviews from critics. *Nightmare Syndrome* is a "grim and goofy" story, according to a *Publishers Weekly* review which concluded that the "mystery provides less sure footing than the slime-filled basement of the police station." In *Mostly Murder,* Karl Kunkel remarked "the subplots don't mesh readily with one another, and the reader is never quite sure what is real and what is not." Kunkel also stated that Marshall wrote the story in a "disjointed, choppy stream-of-concious writing style that oftentimes grinds the action to a halt." Alan Moores' review of *Inches* in *Booklist* criticized Marshall for "losing touch with his Hong Kong milieu" and being too silly during the middle of the story. However, Moores stated the story has a strong finish. *Publishers Weekly*'s Sybil S. Steinberg positively reviewed *Inches,* commenting that Marshall successfully misleads his readers into thinking "they know more than the coppers." Steinberg praised the book for "perfect timing and trenchant humor," and noted it as "a surefire nominee for best mystery of the year." Philip Plowden and David K. Jeffery in the *St. James Guide to Crime and Mystery Writers* judged *Inches* to be "one of the best of [the "Yellowthread Street"] series."

Although most widely-known for his "Yellowthread Street" mysteries, Marshall has also enjoyed success with the "Manila Bay" detective novels set in the Philippines. The first entry, *Manila Bay,* pits kindly cop Felix Elizalde against the killers of a celebrity gamecock's owners. Prominent among the supporting characters is the equally occupied Sergeant Ambrosio, who is trying to identify, and then capture, whoever is fouling the Manila streets with particularly malodorous fruit remains. Carolyn See, writing in the *Los Angeles Times Book Review,* deemed *Manila Bay* "fun." In *Whisper,* the second volume in the series, Elizalde investigates a psychic dentist's murder and uncovers a CIA operation involving dwarves and illicit skeleton sales. Kevin Moore, in his regular mysteries assessment for *Tribune Books,* noted that *Whisper* "delivers some fascinating insights into Philippine life." Plowden and Jeffery summarized both *Manila Bay* and *Whispers,* stating "The style, the distinctive blend of farce and tragedy, and the complex plotting remain familiar, while the new characters are as finely drawn as in the Yellowthread series. However, some of the frenetic comic energies of that series are missing."

In the late-1980s Marshall also published *The New York Detective,* the first volume of a series set in late-nineteenth-century New York City. In a 1989 interview with *CA,* Marshall described, "The first of the New York series, is probably less of a mystery set against something than a story of New York which happens to have a mystery running through it. . . . There are two main characters in the series—the chief character and his sidekick. . . . The main character is a man called Virgil Tillman, who is a city detective. His sidekick, Ned Muldoon, is a uniformed patrolman from the Strong-Arm Squad, which existed here in the 1880s." According to Plowden and Jeffery, "The first of the two novels is an exceptional one—outrageous, gripping, poignant, and hilarious—and Marshall's recreation of the New York City of 1883 is wonderful. . . . The second of the New York novels [*Faces in the Crowd*] was not as good as the first."

Aside from his various mysteries series, Marshall has produced several relatively mainstream novels. The first of these works, most of which date from the beginning of his literary career, is *The Fire Circle,* about a beleaguered construction worker who finds redemption in the Australian desert. In *The Age of*

Death Marshall delineates the dehumanizing aspects of warfare by focusing on characters fighting in various twentieth-century conflicts, and in *The Middle Kingdom* he focuses on the efforts of a concentration camp survivor's son to fathom events leading to his father's incarceration in China. *Shanghai,* another of Marshall's more-or-less conventional novels, concerns last days in the international settlement in Shanghai, China, preceding the Japanese attack on Pearl Harbor.

For a complete interview with Marshall, please see *Contemporary Authors* Volume 133.

BIOGRAPHICAL/CRITICAL SOURCES:

BOOKS

St. James Press Guide to Crime and Mystery Writers, St. James Press (Detroit), 1996.

PERIODICALS

Armchair Detective, spring, 1990.
Booklist, April 15, 1994.
Listener, November 26, 1987; August 10, 1989.
Los Angeles Times Book Review, February 16, 1986; December 22, 1986.
Mostly Murder, May/June, 1997.
New Republic, June 10, 1978; August 30, 1980.
New Statesman, May 21, 1971.
New York Times Book Review, March 14, 1976; January 30, 1977; November 20, 1977; May 21, 1978; January 27, 1980; April 17, 1983; February 8, 1987; August 16, 1987; April 24, 1988; December 10, 1989.
Observer, May 30, 1971; June 17, 1984; March 23, 1986.
Publishers Weekly, July 17, 1981; April 11, 1994; May 26, 1997.
Spectator, August 8, 1970.
Time, August 8, 1988.
Times Literary Supplement, January 29, 1970; August 28, 1970; August 27, 1971; May 28, 1976; March 4, 1977; April 17, 1981; October 29, 1982; August 24, 1984; September 6, 1985; October 17, 1986.
Tribune Books (Chicago), April 24, 1988.
Washington Post Book World, May 16, 1976; February 20, 1977; January 20, 1980; September 20, 1981.*

MARSTEN, Richard
  See HUNTER, Evan

* * *

MARTINEZ, Tomas Eloy

PERSONAL: Born in Argentina; immigrated to United States, 1975.

ADDRESSES: Office—Carpender Hall, Room 204, 105 George St., Douglass Campus, Rutgers University, New Brunswick, NJ 08903.

CAREER: Worked as professor of Latin American literature at University of Maryland, College Park; journalist; writer; currently director of Latin American program, Rutgers University.

WRITINGS:

La obra de Ayala y Torre Nilsson en las estructuras del cine argentino, Culturales Argentinas, Ministerio de Educacion y Justicia, Direccion General de Cultura, 1961.
Sagrado, Sudamericana, 1969.
La pasion segun Trelew, Granica, 1973.
Los testigos de afuera, M. Neumann, 1978.
Lugar comun la muerte, Monte Avila (Caracas), 1979.
(With Julio Aray and others) *Sadismo en la ensenanza,* Monte Avila, 1979.
La novela de Peron, translation by Asa Zatz published as *The Peron Novel,* Pantheon (New York City), 1987.
La mano del amo, Planeta (Buenos Aires), 1991.
Santa Evita, English translation by Helen Lane, Knopf (New York City), 1996.

SIDELIGHTS: Argentine writer Tomas Eloy Martinez is the acclaimed author of *The Peron Novel,* a provocative blend of fact and fiction centering on Argentina's turbulent political history under the leadership of President Juan Domingo Peron. Peron rose to power in 1946, three years after the military overthrow of the Argentine government. But economic troubles led to his 1955 exile to Madrid and the restoration of civilian rule in Argentina. A decade later, however, the military government was reinstated, and in 1973, Peron reassumed power. Through a series of flashbacks comprising *The Peron Novel,* Martinez offers three varying perspectives on Peron: the president's own cloudy memoirs, his secretary Jose Lopez Rega's tainted version of events, and a journalist's report—based on interviews—spanning the president's childhood, his early career as an army officer, and his eventual fall from power. Furthermore, Martinez illuminates Peron's ambiguous nature: appealing to the conflicting political ideals of both right-and left-wing forces, the president fostered discord among his people and, after his death in 1974, left a legacy of violence and disorder in Argentina. Critics generally applauded *The Peron Novel* as a sharp and stunning portrait of an enigmatic man. Jay Cantor, writing in the *New York Times Book Review,* deemed the book "a brilliant image of a national psychosis."

Martinez continued his exploration of the Peron myth with *Santa Evita,* in which he mingled fact and fiction about Eva Peron, the wife of the Argentine dictator. "Evita," as she was known, was arguably the most powerful woman in the world during her term as first lady. The illegitimate daughter of a provincial politician and a servant woman, she traveled to Buenos Aires as a teenager and pulled herself up by her bootstraps, becoming first a radio actress, then a minor screen star, and finally, as Peron's wife, a figure adored and reviled by various factions of the Argentine citizenry. She was notable for her fanatical speaking style, her childish grasp of politics, her insatiable hunger for power, and her erratic displays of generosity toward the lowest social classes. After her death from cancer at the age of 33, she became a mythical figure to many Argentineans. Her impeccably embalmed body—along with several decoy copies of it—was shuffled around Argentina and even to Europe and back.

Santa Evita is really the story of Eva Peron's body—its indestructible nature, unbelievable journeys, and the powerful effect it had on the people who searched for and hid it. The book begins during the last days of Evita's life, then focuses on a military colonel's mission to find the real corpse and destroy it so that it can never be used as a rallying point by the remaining Peronists. "In the process, he and his men become obsessed by the body's magically hypnotic qualities, and their lives are unalterably changed. It is all a long way from the easy sentimentality of the Broadway musical. . . . This is . . . a captivating study of how magic and politics sometimes surrealistically merge," stated Sybil Steinberg of *Publishers Weekly.* Brad Hooper, a writer for *Booklist,* described *Santa Evita* as "a complex, challenging novel that lovers of Latin American fiction will applaud."

Not all reviewers were so enthusiastic. "It's a pity the novel isn't better," complained Michiko Kakutani in the *New York Times.* "Although Mr. Martinez's narrative is enlivened by some magical and highly perverse set pieces, though it possesses moments that genuinely illuminate the bizarre intersection of history, gossip and legend, the novel as a whole feels leaden and earthbound. In the end, it gives the reader neither a visceral sense of Evita's life nor an understanding of the powerful hold she has exerted on her country's imagination." Yet a *New York Times Book Review* contributor, Nicolas Shumway, extolled *Santa Evita* as "brilliant," and Martinez's insight as "bold and troubling." He found the books to be "a profound meditation on the nature and meaning of memory, the relationship between authors and subjects, and the anarchic drive of popular mythology. . . . A superb craftsman, Mr. Martinez moves through stories of Evita's life and death—and the peregrinations of her body—with a dazzling array of literary devices, including imagined interviews and memoirs, even fake screenplays. He himself plays a central role in the novel, as the obvious narrator and as a character who scrutinizes himself as he grapples with what it means to have come of age under Peronism."

Shumway concluded that Martinez's fictions of the Perons had earned him a prominent place in the literary world. "In recent years, few Latin American writers have confronted their countries' past with the wit, style and candor that Mr. Martinez shows in *Santa Evita* and its earlier companion piece, *The Peron Novel.* With these two books, he affirms his place among Latin America's best writers."

BIOGRAPHICAL/CRITICAL SOURCES:

PERIODICALS

Atlanta Journal-Constitution, October 27, 1996, p. L11.
Booklist, August, 1996, p. 1855.
Chicago Tribune, November 3, 1996, section 14, p. 3.
Christian Science Monitor, May 6, 1988, p. 20.
Hispania, March, 1971.
Library Journal, August, 1996, p. 113.
Nation, August 27, 1988, p. 173; October 28, 1996, pp. 50-52.
New York Times, September 20, 1996, p. C31.
New York Times Book Review, April 15, 1988; May 22, 1988, p. 16; July 30, 1995, section 1, p. 3; September 29, 1996, p. 27.

Publishers Weekly, July 29, 1996, pp. 70-71.
Village Voice, April 26, 1988, pp. 54, 56.
Wall Street Journal, November 14, 1996.
Washington Post, September 27, 1996, p. D2.*

* * *

MARTINI, Steve(n Paul) 1946-

PERSONAL: Born February 28, 1946, in San Francisco, CA; son of Ernest R. and Rita M. Martini; married April 3, 1976; wife's name, Leah; children: one. *Education:* University of California, Santa Cruz, B.A., 1968; University of the Pacific, McGeorge School of Law, J.D., 1974.

ADDRESSES: Agent—John Hawkins & Associates, 71 West Twenty-third St., Suite 1600, New York, NY 10010.

CAREER: Los Angeles Daily Journal, journalist and State House correspondent in Sacramento, CA, 1970-75; lawyer in private practice, Sacramento, 1975-80; state attorney for various agencies, including State Department of Consumer Affairs, also served as deputy director of the State Office of Administrative Hearings and as special counsel for California Victims of Violent Crimes Program, all 1980-91; full-time writer, 1991—.

WRITINGS:

MYSTERIES

The Simeon Chamber, Donald I. Finc, 1988.
Compelling Evidence (Book-of-the-Month Club selection), Putnam, 1992.
Prime Witness, Putnam, 1993.
Undue Influence, (Literary Guild selection, Doubleday Book Club main selection) Putnam, 1994.
The Judge, (Literary Guild main selection, Mystery Guild selection, Doubleday Book Club main selection) Putnam, 1995.
The List, Putnam, 1997.

SIDELIGHTS: Former journalist and attorney Steve Martini is a writer of suspense fiction that is influenced by his professional experience. His expertise and ability to write winning courtroom scenes have led reviewers such as Emily Melton of *Booklist* to call him "one of the leading practitioners of the courtroom drama." Since publication of his first novel, *The Simeon Chamber,* Martini has a won a legion of fans and favorable reviews. Writes B. Jo Bauer Farley in the *St. James Guide to Crime and Mystery Writers,* "Plots are widely varied and always interesting . . . all of Martini's work stands on its own considerable merit." He points out that Martini's novels were "commercially enhanced by favorable comment from author John Grisham and has since enjoyed a wider popularity."

The Simeon Chamber concerns a San Francisco, California, lawyer, Sam Bogardus, who discovers that one of his clients, Jennifer Davies, possesses pages that may be from the long lost diaries of sixteenth-century explorer Sir Francis Drake. Not long after this discovery, Bogardus and Davies find themselves in considerable danger. Pursued by unsavory characters eager to gain possession of the documents, the attorney and his client embark on a wild chase that takes them throughout the San Francisco Bay Area. Their trail eventually leads to the San Simeon castle built by publishing magnate William Randolph Hearst. At San Simeon, Bogardus uncovers a secret black market agenda from World War II and its relationship to Jennifer's documents. A contributor for *Kirkus Reviews* called the novel "generally rousing," and a *Publishers Weekly* reviewer described *The Simeon Chamber* as a "fast read" that features a "stunning finale."

Martini then authored *Compelling Evidence,* a novel about love and murder among law professionals. The novel's hero and narrator is Paul Madriana, an attorney who lost his position with a major firm after it was discovered that he was having an affair with the wife of Ben Potter, his boss and mentor. When Potter is found dead on the eve of his appointment to the U.S. Supreme Court, the police suspect murder. Potter's wife—and Madriana's former lover—is arrested and charged with her husband's death. The plot thickens when Madriana is recruited as a member of the woman's defense team. When the chief defense counsel fumbles the inquest and subsequently bails out of the case, Madriana is left as the woman's sole lawyer. Matters become worse for the attorney as he realizes he has become a pawn in a much larger game, with stakes that are higher than a prison term. While a *Publishers Weekly* reviewer found the author's technical language stifling at times, Martini was applauded for writing a "refreshingly candid legal procedural." *Los Angeles Times* reviewer Charles Champlin praised *Compelling Evidence* for its "sheer storytelling professionalism." Commend-

ing the author's skill in evoking courtroom drama, *New York Times Book Review* contributor Marilyn Stasio opined that "on his feet and in front of a jury, Mr. Martini speaks in a commanding voice."

All of Martini's book since *Compelling Evidence* have featured Madriani as well as, writes Farley in the *St. James Guide to Crime and Mystery Writers,* "a continuum of characters, all well drawn and easy to keep straight." In *Prime Witness,* Madriani takes on the temporary role of district attorney as a favor for a friend. His assignment is to prosecute a Russian national who is accused of two serial killings. Matters are complicated from the beginning—the accused killer was caught in Canada and then abducted and returned to the United States by the father of one of the victim's. Then a third victim is found, evidently murdered by a copy cat killer. To make matters worse, the defense attorney holds a grudge against Madriani for once getting him disbarred. The novel abounds with 80 pages of courtroom actions, and a contributor to *Armchair Detective* found that Martini's "prosecution strategy of using the Grand Jury in lieu of a preliminary hearing is fascinating as are all the legal ins and outs." The same reviewer asserts, "Martini ranks near the top of the fictional tree, and he richly deserves attaining the bestseller status of Scott Turow and John Grisham."

By the time of publication of *Undue Influence,* "Martini's track record as a best-selling thriller writer . . . is well established," writes Emily Melton in *Booklist, Undue Influence* finds Madriani's wife has died of cancer, leaving the grieving widower to raise their seven-year-old daughter alone. Before his wife died, she asked Madriani to look after her sister, Laurel, who is undergoing a bitter custody battle with her ex-husband, one she is on the verge of losing. When the ex-husband's new wife turns up murdered, all evidence points to Laurel. Madriani rushes to her defense but finds a number of obstacles in his way—a cop with a vendetta against him, the mysterious disappearance of potential defense witnesses, and his growing suspicion that Laurel is hiding something. All of the twists and turns "through a brilliant series of trial scenes" lead to a "rousing climax," writes Sybil S. Steinberg in a starred review in *Publishers Weekly.* "Martini's plot is inventive," writes Melton, "the courtroom scene are dazzling, and the climax is guaranteed to shock." In *Library Journal,* Robert H. Donahugh commends *Undue Influence* as "a slam-bang narrative complete with astonishingly good trial scenes." He also points out that "Martini's dialog and characterizations are first-rate."

Martini's fourth Madriani book, *The Judge,* "seems certain to add to [Martini's] renown," writes Melton in *Booklist.* Judge Armando Acosta, who has appeared as Madriani's nemesis in earlier novels, is currently in charge of a grand jury investigating police corruption. In the midst of this, he gets arrested for soliciting an undercover vice operator masquerading as a prostitute. Matters get worse for the judge when the key witness against him turns up murdered. The judge declares that he was set up. Circumstances lead Madriani to accept the job as Acosta's defender, even though the two are longtime enemies. Challenges abound in Madriani's defense—physical and slanderous attacks, uncooperative witnesses, mounting evidence against the judge, and an abnormally aggressive prosecutor. Madriani races to find the real motive and killer, making *The Judge,* according to Melton, "A keep-'em-guessing page-turner that will keep readers riveted." She finds Martini's courtroom scenes "suspenseful," and Madriani's defense "tenuous but ultimately brilliant." Writes Sybil S. Steinberg in a starred *Publishers Weekly* review, Madriani "once again proves [to be] a sophisticated, good-humored hero who tells a suspenseful tale, right up to the perfectly satisfying climax." She adds, "Legal thrillers don't get much better than this."

Martini told *CA:* "Full-time fiction writing had been my dream for many years, since college and particularly since my days as a journalist twenty years ago. For those who wish to make such a career for themselves there is only one known formula: consistent and diligent effort over an extended period of time. For me the mix of law and fiction was natural as I had been writing in the field during my career as a journalist, covering the courts, the legislature, and various other governmental agencies. Later, having engaged in the practice of law, I was able to bring to bear that experience in order to craft credible trial and courtroom fiction. For me, a good courtroom story must cut very close to the bone of reality to have true value."

BIOGRAPHICAL/CRITICAL SOURCES:

BOOKS

St. James Guide to Crime and Mystery Writers, fourth Edition, St. James Press, 1996.

PERIODICALS

Armchair Detective, winter, 1994, pp. 85-87.
Booklist, June 1, 1994, p. 1725; December 1, 1995, p. 587.
Entertainment Weekly, January 19, 1996, p. 47; November 29, 1996, p. 85; March 21, 1997, p. 68.
Kirkus Reviews, August 1, 1988, p. 1089.
Library Journal, June 15, 1994, p. 96; January, 1996, p. 144.
Los Angeles Times Book Review, March 8, 1992, p. 8.
New York Times Book Review, March 22, 1992, p. 22.
People Weekly, July 4, 1994, p. 29; March 3, 1997, p. 35.
Publishers Weekly, September 2, 1988, p. 90; November 29, 1991, p. 43; June 20, 1994, p. 96; December 11, 1995, p. 58; January 20, 1997, p. 394.

* * *

MASTERSON, Whit
See MILLER, (H.) Bill(y)

* * *

MASTERSON, Whit
See WADE, Robert (Allison)

* * *

MATTHEWS, Brad
See DeMILLE, Nelson (Richard)

* * *

McBAIN, Ed
See HUNTER, Evan

McGIVERN, William P(eter) 1922-1982

PERSONAL: Born December 6, 1922, in Chicago, IL; died November 18, 1982, in Palm Desert, CA; sn of Peter Francis (a banker) and Julia (Costello) McGivern; married Maureen Daly (a writer), December 28, 1948; children: Megan (daughter), Patrick. *Education:* Attended University of Birmingham, 1945-46. *Politics:* Democrat.

CAREER: Philadelphia Evening Bulletin, Philadelphia, PA, reporter and book reviewer, 1949-51; writer. *Military service:* U.S. Army, 1943-46; became master sergeant.

MEMBER: Mystery Writers of America (president), Writers Guild of America, Authors League of America, Players Club (New York), Garrick Club and Savage Club (both London).

AWARDS, HONORS: Edgar Allan Poe Award, Mystery Writers of America, 1953, for *The Big Heat.*

WRITINGS:

But Death Runs Faster, Dodd (New York City), 1948.
Heaven Ran Last, Dodd, 1949.
Very Cold for May, Dodd, 1950.
Shield for Murder, Dodd, 1951.
The Crooked Frame, Dodd, 1952.
The Big Heat, Dodd, 1953.
Margin of Terror, Dodd, 1953.
Rogue Cop (also see below), Dodd, 1954.
The Darkest Hour (also see below), Dodd, 1955.
The Seven File (also see below), Dodd, 1956.
Night Extra, Dodd, 1957.
Odds against Tomorrow, Dodd, 1957.
(With wife, Maureen Daly McGivern) *Mention My Name in Mombasa: The Unscheduled Adventures of an American Family Abroad* (nonfiction), Dodd, 1958.
Savage Streets, Dodd, 1959.
Seven Lies South, Dodd, 1960.
The Road to the Snail, Dodd, 1961.
Police Special (includes *Rogue Cop, The Seven File,* and *The Darkest Hour*), Dodd, 1962.
A Pride of Place, Dodd, 1962.
A Choice of Assassins, Dodd, 1963.
The Caper of the Golden Bulls, Dodd, 1966.
Lie Down, I Want to Talk to You, Dodd, 1967.
Caprifoil, Dodd, 1972.
Reprisal, Dodd, 1973.

Night of the Juggler (also see below), Putnam (New York City), 1974.
Soldiers of '44 (Book-of-the-Month Club alternate selection), Arbor House (New York City), 1979.
Summitt, Arbor House, 1982.
War Games, Arborn House, 1984.
A Matter of Honor (completed by Maureen Daly McGivern), Arbor House, 1984.

SCREENPLAYS

Chicago 7 (based on novel *The Seven File*), 1968.
The Wrecking Crew, 1968.
The Man from Nowhere, 1968.
Lie Down, I Want to Talk to You (based on the novel), 1968.
Caprifoil (based on the novel), 1973.
Joe Battle, 1974.
Brannigan, 1974.
Night of the Juggler (based on the novel), 1977.

TELEVISION SCRIPTS

San Francisco International Airport, 1970.
The Young Lawyers, 1970.
Banyon, 1972.

ADAPTATIONS: Nine of McGivern's novels have been made into motion pictures, including *The Big Heat, Odds against Tomorrow, Seven Lies South,* and *The Caper of the Golden Bulls.* Two novels were adapted for the television series *Studio One.*

SIDELIGHTS: Soldiers of '44, a novel on World War II set in the Ardennes during the Battle of the Bulge, represented more than just a departure in theme for William P. McGivern. Best known to his readers as the author of some two dozen "tough" crime novels, McGivern struggled for over thirty years to write, as a *Publishers Weekly* interviewer described it, "a book that would represent with the authenticity of a Mailer or a Shaw or a Jones how the war was actually fought on a human level." Based on a true incident which occurred in then-Sergeant McGivern's fifteen-man gun section, *Soldiers of '44* for the most part focuses on the lives of American Sergeant Buell 'Bull' Docker and German SS Colonel Karl Jaeger during the bitterly cold winter of 1944. Parallel themes and stories involving racism, fascism, homosexuality, and morality emerge as Docker and his men attempt to defend an isolated hill and Jaeger and his men attempt to capture it.

Though he admitted to beginning the entire project with "a compulsion to write something very significant, something as important as a global war," McGivern insisted he did not deliberately set out to create a moral balance in which each instance of prejudice or authoritarianism on the German side is met with a corresponding example on the American side. Nevertheless, he says, "too often you see the war used as a easy target—the Americans were the Good Guys, the Germans were the Bad Guys, period. I think that's just irresponsible—I mean if you're going to condemn the racism in Germany, you also have to comment on the fact that, while it was not acted out so virulently in the Army of the White Hats, it certainly was there."

In general, however, McGivern avoided discussing the "significance" of his book, choosing instead to draw attention to his characterizations and to the atmosphere he creates. One of his major goals, he explained, was to find the words which would convey "the Wagnerian feeling of eerie, weird, terrible silence; of swirling snow, tanks appearing and disappearing in the drifts; of night and day melded into grayness." In such a place, the author recallrd, "you could get trapped in a mental labyrinth if you started thinking about moral questions, and besides, nobody had the time."

Critical reaction to *Soldiers of '44* ranged from the *Atlantic's* assessment of it as "a remarkably fine book" to the *New Statesman's* claim that it is a "pale reflection" of war novels by other writers. The *Los Angeles Times Book Review's* Grover Sales, for instance, believed that in addition to including "obvious and sometimes disquieting snatches of Norman Mailer, James Jones, Irwin Shaw and *The Caine Mutiny* court-martial" in his novel, McGivern displayed "a recurrent weakness for tipping his hand. . . . *Soldiers of '44* would have been a more suspenseful book if [the author's] assault on his readers contained 'the four essential elements' of the German Bulge offensive—'secrecy, surprise, a massive concentration of strength against weakness and terror.' [He] is least convincing when he departs from straight action and aims for profundity."

Describing *Soldiers of '44* as a "creaky, leaden American melodrama" in which the author "turns the real into the incredible," the *New Republic's* Paul Fussel faulted the book for its simplicity and implausibility. According to the reviewer, "the audience McGivern assumes requires elementary instruction about the war and expects diagramatic simplification of all human emotions and motives. . . . The *frissions* and the yards of unreal dialogue and dying speeches are from one of those adolescent war films made for TV." As for the characterization, Fussell disputed the dust-jacket description of Sergeant Docker as "perhaps the most memorable hero in all World War II fiction." Observed the critic: "If your conception of a hero is Superman, you'll buy [the publisher's description.] Otherwise you will find Yossarian, Billy Pilgrim and Tyrone Slothrop more memorable. Docker is simply Burt Lancaster, but simplified." Ironically enough, concludes Fussell, "because it is so false, so corny and so shallow, and because it misrepresents so optimistically the emotional conditions of the war, *Soldiers of '44* is going to be popular. . . . It will carry on the work of rationalizing and romanticizing the war begun by Herman Wouk in *The Winds of War* and *War and Remembrance.*"

Rationalization and romanticization are the very qualities that Christopher Lehmann-Haupt of the *New York Times* also found disconcerting in *Soldiers of '44.* "For a while," he began, "it looks as if [McGivern] will have something fresh to say. . . . [But] *Soldiers of '44* settles down to become a shoot-out. . . . And while there are other developments hinting that Mr. McGivern may be up to something unusual . . . the novel ends celebrating the familiar verities." Admitting that it is often entertaining and well-written, Lehmann-Haupt nevertheless believed that *Soldiers of '44* cannot be excused for its dangerously deceptive nostalgia, a nostalgia that continues to idealize World War II as "the last conflict in which the issues of right and wrong were clear-cut."

Other critics, however, did not seem to be aware of, or at least are not disturbed by, any traces of nostalgia present in *Soldiers of '44.* The *Washington Post's* Robert Sherrod, for example, called it "a tautly told tale" and "the best novel about the military since Anton Myrer's *Once an Eagle.* . . . McGivern, whose gift is story-telling, weaves a tale that is hard to put down. . . . He is a craftsman. *Soldiers of '44* sometimes sounds as though it might have been written from the author's diaries. . . . His characters are sharply etched, and they talk like soldiers." The *New Yorker* critic agreed with this latter remark, stating that "although they do not entirely escape the familiar . . . , they emerge a cut or two above the stereotype. . . . The result is an effective, and an affecting, depiction—a first-class melodrama." Even Sales decided that "for all its derivations and flaws, *Soldiers of '44* remains a vastly readable novel with flashes of accurate soldier talk and some rousing wire-tight battle scenes. Most of all, World War II historians and buffs will relish McGivern's exhaustive labor-of-love research on the Battle of the Bulge."

McGivern was better known for his work in the mystery genre. He produced more than twenty novels "covering the gamut of crime—homicide detection, espionage, political corruption, the world of the psychopath, the crooked cop," according to Katherine M. Restaino in the *St. James Guide to Crime and Mystery Writers.* "A number of his novels deal with the metaphor of the jungle—the jungle of crime."

One of McGivern's most popular protagonists was Dave Bannion, "the detective who refuses to compromise," according to Restaino. A contemplative sleuth who favors intellectual pursuits (quoting St. John's *Ascent of Mount Carmel* is not unusual for him), Bannion nonetheless is a man of the streets who "feels the big heat of racketeers and corrupt politicians and law enforcers." Indeed, the novel *The Big Heat* finds Bannion turning up the heat himself as he searches for clues in the murder of both his wife and a colleague. The book won the Edgar Allan Poe award from the Mystery Writers of America.

Given the warm reception for *The Big Heat,* McGivern had to prove that he could sustain the level of depth in further works. *Rogue Cop* (1954), which sets up a conflict between two brothers-one an honest police officer, the other an easily corrupted sergeant-was hailed by several critics as an outstanding entry in the crime genre. To the *New York Herald Tribune,* the work was "a savage little thriller quite as good as The Big Heat," while in the view of *New York Times* critic Anthony Boucher, McGivern made "classic study in guilt, retribution and atonement—without for an instant forgetting to tell an exciting story of swift action."

By 1957 the *Times'* Boucher had praise for McGivern, whose *Night Extra* the critic called "very nearly a serious novel on character and ethics." Timely themes highlighted *Odds against Tomorrow* (1957), in which "two men involved in a bank job operate in a jungle of fear," as Restaino put it. The fear is based on raw prejudice, as white Earl Slater and black John Ingram are forced by circumstance to take refuge together in an isolated farmhouse and learn to depend on one another's strength and cunning to survive. Boucher, in his *Times* review, called *Odds against Tomorrow* "a powerfully exciting ac-

tion melodrama and a novel of no little subtlety. The shifting relationship between the two focal characters is developed with great sensitivity and conviction." Agreed the *San Francisco Chronicle,* this McGivern work had "the usual wallop, compelling plot and people."

One of several McGivern books to be adapted for the movies, *Night of the Juggler* is "an engrossing study of a psychopathic killer," said Restaino. Gus Soltik is a "demented inhabitant of the South Bronx who cannot read or write but who instinctively knows when the anniversary of his mother's death arrives. As the anniversary nears, Gus prepares for his commemoration [by preparing] to kill a young girl." The action is played out in New York's Central Park as a pair of detectives conduct a frantic search before Gus can kill again.

To Restaino, "the characters in all of McGivern's novels are developed precisely. The reader participates in the twistings of the psychopathic mind in *Night of the Juggler* and *A Choice of Assassins* where a man agrees to kill for the price of a drink. The tightrope mentality of McGivern's rogue cops in not merely understood, but actually experienced by the reader." The author, she continued, "is not given to excesses in characterization or action. Consequently, his work does not lend itself to stereotypes."

BIOGRAPHICAL/CRITICAL SOURCES:

BOOKS

St. James Guide to Crime and Mystery Writers, 4th edition, St. James Press (Detroit), 1996.

PERIODICALS

Atlantic, April, 1979.
Chicago Tribune Book World, March 18, 1979.
Los Angeles Times Book Review, March 25, 1979.
New Republic, March 3, 1979.
New Statesman, August 17, 1979.
New Yorker, April 9, 1979.
New York Times, May 2, 1954; May 13, 1956; April 7, 1957; November 3, 1957; April 17, 1979.
New York Times Book Review, June 25, 1961; March 6, 1966; September 24, 1967; March 25, 1973; March 25, 1979.
Publishers Weekly, March 12, 1979.
San Francisco Chronicle, May 23, 1954; June 10, 1956; December 8, 1958.
Washington Post, April 5, 1979.

OBITUARIES:

PERIODICALS

Chicago Tribune, November 20, 1982.
Detroit Free Press, November 22, 1982.
New York Times, November 21, 1982.*

*   *   *

MICHAELS, Leonard 1933-

PERSONAL: Born January 2, 1933, in New York, NY; son of Leon (a barber) and Anna (Czeskies) Michaels; married former wife, Priscilla Older, June 30, 1966; married third wife, Brenda Lynn Hillman (a poet), August 10, 1977; married fourth wife, Katharine Ogden (a general contractor in Italy), February 3, 1995; children: (first marriage) Ethan, Jesse; (third marriage) Louisa. *Education:* New York University, B.A., 1953; University of Michigan, M.A., 1956, Ph.D., 1966.

*ADDRESSES: Home—*409 Boynton Ave., Kensington, CA 94707; 06060 Lisciano Niccone, Casella 19, P.G., Italy. *Office—*Department of English, University of California, Berkeley, CA 94720. *Agent—*Lynn Nesbit, International Creative Management, 40 West 57th St., New York, NY 10019.

CAREER: Paterson State College (now William Paterson State College of New Jersey), Wayne, instructor, 1961-62; University of California, Davis, assistant professor of English, 1966-69; University of California, Berkeley, professor of English, 1970—, editor of *University Publishing* review, 1977—. Visiting professor at many universities, including Johns Hopkins University and University of Alabama. Guest lecturer in institutions in the United States and abroad.

AWARDS, HONORS: Quill Award, Massachusetts Review, 1964, for "Sticks and Stones" (short story), and 1966, for "The Deal" (short story); National Book Award nomination, 1969, for *Going Places;* Guggenheim fellow, 1969; National Endowment for the Humanities fellow, 1970; American Academy Award in Literature, National Institute of Arts and Letters, 1971, for published work of distinction; *New York Times Book Review* Editor's Choice Award,

1975, for *I Would Have Saved Them If I Could;* American Book Award nomination and National Book Critics Circle Award nomination, both in 1982, for *The Men's Club;* National Foundation on the Arts and Humanities prize, for short story in *Transatlantic.*

WRITINGS:

Going Places (short stories; also see below), Farrar, Straus, 1969.
I Would Have Saved Them If I Could (short stories; also see below), Farrar, Straus, 1975.
(Contributor) Theodore Solotaroff, editor, *American Review 26,* Bantam, 1977.
(Contributor) William Abrahams, editor, *Prize Stories, 1980: The O. Henry Awards,* Doubleday, 1980.
(Editor with Christopher Ricks) *The State of the Language,* University of California Press, 1980.
The Men's Club (novel; also see below), Farrar, Straus, 1981, expanded edition, Mercury House, 1993.
City Boy (play adapted from short stories in *City Boy* (play adapted from short stories in (play adapted from short stories in *Going Places* and *I Would Have Saved Them If I Could*), produced in New York City at The Jewish Repertory Theater, 1985.
The Men's Club (screenplay based on his novel of the same title), Atlantic Releasing Corporation, 1986.
(Editor with Raquel Sheer and David Reid) *West of the West: Imagining California* (essays), North Point Press, 1989, reprinted, University of California Press, 1995.
(Editor with Ricks) *The State of the Language* (new essays on English), University of California Press, 1990.
Shuffle, Farrar, Straus & Giroux, 1990.
Sylvia: A Fictional Memoir, Mercury House, 1992.
To Feel These Things: Essays, Mercury House, 1993.
A Cat, illustrated by Frances Lerner, Riverhead Books, 1995.

Also contributor of short stories to *The American Literary Anthology / One,* sponsored by the National Endowment for the Arts, and to numerous literary journals and popular magazines, including *Esquire, Paris Review, Evergreen Review, Partisan Review, Vogue, New Yorker,* and *Tri-Quarterly.* Contributing editor, *Threepenny Review,* 1980; corresponding editor, *Partisan Review.*

WORK IN PROGRESS: "A collection of short stories and a collection of essays."

SIDELIGHTS: With several award-winning short stories placed in prestigious literary magazines, Leonard Michaels became known as an impressive writer—a reputation that was extended when *Going Places,* his first book-length collection, was nominated for the National Book Award in 1969. Reviews of his second collection, *I Would Have Saved Them If I Could,* named Michaels a master of short fiction forms. "The hallmarks of these stories," David Reid summarizes in the *Threepenny Review,* "are an amazing rapidity of image, incident, and idea and a deftness of rhythm and phrasing that, quite simply, confirm, sentence by sentence, his status as one of the most original, intelligent, and stylistically gifted writers of his generation." Critics praise the blend of horror and humor in the stories which are unified by their New York settings, often noting that Michaels's descriptions of urban brutality strike the reader with an almost physical impact. After *I Would Have Saved Them If I Could* was named by the *New York Times Book Review* staff as one of the six outstanding works of fiction published in 1975, Michaels co-edited three popular essay collections (*The State of the Language,* a 600-page anthology of essays and poems; a second tome on the English language also entitled *The State of the Language;* and *West of the West: Imagining California,* about California's unique role in history as "the New World's New World") and wrote the controversial novel *The Men's Club.* Though not prolific, Michaels sustains critical favor by pressing on to new territory and larger forms, while reducing his use of literary allusions.

Michaels grew up in the Lower East Side of New York City, the son of immigrant Polish Jews. "I spoke only Yiddish until I was about five or six years old," he tells *Washington Post* contributor Curt Suplee. At that time, his mother bought a complete set of Charles Dickens, providing Michaels's introduction to English prose: "If you can imagine a little boy . . . listening to his mother, who can hardly speak English, reading Dickens hour after hour in the most extraordinary accent, it might help to account for my peculiar ear." Interested in literature, but feeling that his heritage placed him outside "The Tradition" as defined by T. S. Eliot, Michaels studied painting in high school and then entered New York University as a premed student. There he met and became the protege of Austin Warren, a respected critic who encouraged Michaels to cultivate his literary interests.

After two failed attempts at graduate school at the University of Michigan and the University of California, Berkeley, Michaels moved to New York City, where he began to write stories. During this time, he met and married his first wife, Sylvia, who eventually committed suicide after the pair separated; she figures prominently in Michaels's later writings. Michaels returned to the University of Michigan to work on his Ph.D. He also wrote two novels that were never published. Though he eventually reshaped the second novel into the series of stories in *I Would Have Saved Them If I Could,* he incinerated the first one, Helen Benedict reports in the *New York Times Book Review,* "because of the 'severe' ideas he then held about the writer's obligation to art." "It's true," Michaels told *Threepenny Review* contributor Mona Simpson, "I wrote it in a very short period of time and I threw it into the incinerator. It was absolutely horrible. I wrote it . . . to show I could write a novel any time I wanted to, even in two weeks. But I wasn't about to really *do* anything like that. . . . I was more interested in forms of writing that seemed to me closer to the high ideals of art." Michaels found the short story form more demanding and better suited to his artistic ideals. He was twenty-nine when *Playboy* magazine bought the first story he sent them for $3,000, making him, as Suplee remarks, "an instant success." This assessment of Michaels's talent proved to be no exaggeration when stories published in literary journals such as the *Massachusetts Review* brought him two Quill Awards, the O. Henry Prize, and a National Foundation on the Arts and Humanities prize.

Going Places contains several of the prize winners. "The key events in [these] stories—usually holocausts in the lives of his protagonists—are indistinguishable from the settings in which they occur," Laurence Lieberman notes in the *Atlantic.* They are set in New York City, which is itself "a crucial protagonist in each story," according to *Village Voice* contributor Stephan Taylor. Taylor sees the city in these stories as a "laboratory" in which "human beings are the only remaining manifestations of nature," a condition that makes their relationships more intense, more sexual, and more prone to culminate in violence. More imposing than the city's skyline, the urban population is presented as a "monster" that brutally rapes or beats its victims. In "The Deal," an attractive woman's trip across the street to buy cigarettes puts her into a confrontation with "twenty Puerto Rican boys congregated into the shape of a great bird of prey on a banistered front stoop in Spanish Harlem," Lieberman notes; and in the title story, an aimless cab driver's fares beat him with such force that it leaves him near death, and—for the first time in his life—conscious of his will to live. In "Crossbones," an unmarried couple fight and maim each other in the tension provoked by an impending visit from the girl's father, making it clear to Taylor that "while we've controlled natural disasters like plague and drought and famine in our cities, we may simply have freed people to perpetrate personal disasters that are just as harrowing." This view is shared by Christopher Lehmann-Haupt in the *New York Times:* "Mr. Michaels creates a hostile, violent, and absurd world in which people grope for each other longingly, yet can only touch one another by inflicting damage."

Horrors such as "orgies, rapes, mayhem and suicide in city scenes and subwayscapes" keep the reader's attention while Michaels explores the familiar themes of love and death, Lore Segal remarks in a *New Republic* review. Segal believes the author "makes these horrors horrible again and funny." For instance, in "City Boy," Phillip and his girlfriend are caught in a carnal embrace on the girl's living room floor by her father. Phillip escapes into the street without his clothes, and tries to disguise his nakedness by walking on his hands. The nude Phillip fails to establish enough trust with the subway conductor to secure his ride home. As he leaves the subway station, his girlfriend greets him with his clothing and the news that her father has suffered a heart attack.

Taylor concedes that the stories are comic, "not funny," since "their comedy takes place on a tightrope, a high wire beneath which there's broken glass instead of nets. And the laughter, ranging everywhere from booming to tittery, is flung in the teeth of despair." "The balance between the plaintively humorous and the grotesquely sad is what gives full dimension to Michaels's fiction," Ronald Christ suggests in a *Commonweal* review. Segal summarizes, "If [*Going Places*] poses that old chestnut of a question, How is it possible to read about what is bleak and hideous and be reading something hilarious and beautiful and pleasurable, the answer is the old one: It is at the miraculous point where this transformation happens that literature has occurred."

In 1970, Michaels began teaching at the University of California, Berkeley, where he is still professor of English. His second collection of stories, *I Would Have Saved Them If I Could,* published in 1975, "is a useful reminder that the rich complexity of a suc-

cessful novel can, in the hands of a master, be achieved within the limitations of smaller forms," Thomas R. Edwards comments in the *New York Times Book Review,* adding that he considers the book "an important literary event." These stories trace Phillip Liebowitz's social and sexual development as a second-generation Jew during the fifties. In one story, the adolescent Phillip and his friends climb a water tower from which they have an unobstructed view of their young rabbi enjoying sex with his voluptuous wife, until the youngest boy falls to his death. In this, as in the other stories, Edwards notes that Phillip "finds his sexuality a source of continuous humiliation and self-betrayal, and the fine comic flair of these stories doesn't obscure their gloomy appraisal of past postrevolutionary life." The book measures the development of Phillip's mind as well as his body. Edwards concludes, "I know of few writers who can so firmly articulate intensity of feeling with the musculature of cool and difficult thinking, and 'I Would Have Saved Them If I Could' . . . should be read by anyone who hopes that fiction can still be a powerful and intelligent art."

Michaels discusses the relationship between creativity and death through his character Phillip in the title story, which "identifies the personal history of the narrator with the history of modern European Jewry," Lehmann-Haupt writes in the *New York Times.* He feels that the story raises the question, "By what right do we go on living and creating when our forefathers have been slaughtered?" Phillip's reflections include a quote from Wallace Stevens ("Death is the mother of beauty"), and an extended quote from Lord Byron. In a letter describing the execution of three robbers in Rome, Byron admits that, after the first decapitation, the next two failed to move him as horrors, though he would have rescued them if he could. Lehmann-Haupt paraphrases Byron to put the story's thesis, as he sees it, into simple terms: "I would have saved them if I could. But I couldn't, so I rescued art from them." Moreover, the reviewer concludes, "This is Mr. Michaels's achievement. . . . He has rescued art from the horror."

"Leonard Michaels's stories established him as a master phenomenologist of dread and desire. *The Men's Club* will confirm and enlarge that reputation," Dave Reid comments in the *Threepenny Review.* In the novel, a group of men assemble in the Berkeley home of a psychiatrist to form a club. The club's purpose, they discover, is "to make women cry," and to tell their life stories—tales of sexual conquest, marital frustration, and insatiable appetite. "It is a little as if Golding's *Lord of the Flies* had been transposed to middle-class, middle-aging California," Carol Rumens remarks in the *Times Literary Supplement*. "As the night progresses," David Evanier summarizes in his *National Review* article, "the men fight, throw knives, destroy furniture, and howl together in unison." At that point, the host's wife returns to find the feast she had prepared for her women's group devoured and her home demolished. While she gives her husband a serious head injury with an iron frying pan, his guests escape into the early morning, offering no answer when one of them shouts "Where are we going?" Evanier remarks that "on its own terms it is a considerable novel. Nothing in Michaels's two previous books of short stories . . . prepared me for the relentlessly dark and brilliant strength of these pages. Here is a middle-aged predatory Berkeley inferno of loss and chaos."

Some critics view *The Men's Club* as an antifeminist novel; others contend it is feminist. A review in the *New Yorker* claims that the men in the novel amount to "one married misogynist split seven ways." Robert Towers concedes, "*The Men's Club* might at first glance seem to be part of an anti-feminist backlash, to draw its energies from male fantasies of revenge against the whole monstrous regiment of women. As an ostensible *cri de coeur* from a small herd of male chauvinist pigs, it will thrive upon the outrage it provokes and the rueful yearnings it indulges." Nonetheless, Towers suggests, the book's subtler implications become apparent during a more careful reading. *Newsweek* magazine contributor Peter S. Prescott believes that since the men reveal themselves to be at fault in their failed relationships, the book takes on "a distinctly feminist cast that is far more appealing than what we find in most novels written by angry women today." Michaels is surprised by both interpretations. He tells Suplee, "[*The Men's Club*] is not in any sense propaganda, pro or con feminism, pro or con male sensibility. . . . It is, I hope, believe it or not, a description of reality."

Another debate among critics is the attempt to link Michaels with literary influences. "From [Franz] Kafka and [Jorge Luis] Borges . . . and more immediately [Donald] Barthelme, Michaels has learned how to dissolve the conventions of 'rational' narrative, replacing continuity with a collage of intensely rendered moments, so that reading feels like taking a number of hard blows to the head and groin," Edwards remarks in his review of Michaels's second book. A *Chicago Tribune Book World* review by

Joyce Carol Oates and a review in *Atlantic* also name Barthelme as an influence and add Philip Roth. However, Larry Woiwode argues in the *Partisan Review* that Michaels's works were completed before Roth's; and, regarding the Barthelme connection, Woiwode maintains, "In terms of influence, it seems surely possible that Michaels has touched on Barthelme as much as Barthelme on Michaels, especially since Barthelme didn't really delve deeply into anguish, Michaels's prime subject, until *The Dead Father* [published in 1975]." Rather, the major influences on Michaels, Woiwode believes, are not his contemporaries: "[Isaac] Babel is obviously Michaels's literary mentor, but it often seems that [Ernest] Hemingway is a favorite sounding board, the Americanized side of Michaels's fascination with violence, suicide, and death (which has 'eat' at its center), and perhaps a bit of patriarchal scourge, being anti-intellectual, a tyrant in most matters, and a fellow practitioner of the short sentence with the kick-back of a pistol-shot."

Allusions to Michaels's favorite writers appear often in the stories, which Towers believes are "excessively literary in their inspiration." An *Atlantic* contributor muses that "One piece [in the second book] pays homage to Borges so efficiently that there is hardly any Michaels in it." In the novel, Michaels deliberately adopts a different approach. "I think of *The Men's Club* as a descent into the human," the author told Simpson. In another interview, he told Benedict, "By that I mean the considerations of literary art in this book are supposed to seem minimal. Everything I talk about, I try to talk about in regard to human reality, which is a much sloppier thing than art." Towers's comment on the novel indicates that Michaels succeeds: "The literary influences so evident in the stories have now been largely assimilated. Leonard Michaels has become his own man, with his own voice and a subject substantial enough to grant his talents the scope they have needed all along."

In 1985, Michaels worked with director Edward M. Cohen to produce several of the Phillip Liebowitz stories as a play. "Leonard writes splendid dialogue," Cohen told *New York Times* contributor Samuel G. Freedman. "He writes short, concise stories. So there is a dramatic compression already there." Speaking to Freedman, Michaels described the experience of working with other artists to adapt the stories for theater as "wrenching," "frightening," and "exhilarating." Michaels also wrote the screenplay for the film based on *The Men's Club,* condensing its long monologues and adding a new ending in which the men finish their evening out with prostitutes instead of breakfast. Janet Maslin's review in the *New York Times* states that "the lengthy whorehouse sequence" which makes up the film's second half "wasn't in Mr. Michaels's book and didn't need to be." A *Los Angeles Times* review concurs that the film's "porno ambiance is doubly unfortunate," and adds that the film does not reach the potential promised in the "stinging, smart, abrasive dialogue from scenarist Leonard Michaels." Still, Evanier commends the author for his foray into yet another genre: "Leonard Michaels breaks new ground, in the tradition of the artist who does not stand still."

Michaels's next two works found him back in the realm of fiction—at least marginally. *Shuffle,* described by its dust-jacket blurb as autobiographical fiction, comprises several parts, including the narrator's "Journal"; a narrative piece entitled "Sylvia" that discusses the narrator's marriage and divorce; and four short stories. Throughout, Michaels interweaves fact and fiction, examining the familiar terrain of "anomie and cigarette smoke and literary referents and sex," notes Nicholas Delbanco in the Chicago *Tribune Books.* Reviewers struggled with *Shuffle*'s structure, generally criticizing the work as self-indulgent and aimless. Anatole Broyard, writing in the *New York Times Book Review,* avers that *Shuffle* "is a shockingly bad book for a man of Mr. Michaels's stature. All the wryness [evident in his previous work] has dried up and left him with a bad taste in his mouth." *Times Literary Supplement* reviewer Roz Kaveney, while praising the four short stories in the collection for their "artful authenticity," characterizes the prose as "tinny through and through" and avers that the work as a whole lacks "the ring of truth."

Sylvia: A Fictional Memoir similarly confounded critics trying to determine what was fiction and what was not. In fact, as Tom Clark notes in the *Los Angeles Times Book Review,* the work was "advertised in the publicity copy as a rewrite" of the narrative section in *Shuffle* titled "Sylvia." In this "rewrite," Michaels offers the story of a young writer's combustible love affair and marriage with a troubled woman who eventually commits suicide—events that mirror Michaels's own life. Set in Greenwich Village during the 1960s, the book details the "moral chaos and social confusion" of the decade's "counterculture landscape," comments Clark. A *New Yorker* reviewer calls *Sylvia* "stylish" and "hard to put down." "There is an airless, claustrophobic, solipsistic qual-

ity to Michaels's book," writes Clancy Sigal in a *Washington Post Book World* review. While critical of the author's portrayal of Sylvia as possibly hostile and one-sided, Sigal avers that the book "rings with awful truth."

The 1993 publication *To Feel These Things* brings together fourteen previously published essays. While reviewers continued to wonder at the labels attached to Michaels's work—fiction or nonfiction?—several greeted the book with praise. Peggy Constantine, writing in the *New York Times Book Review,* terms the author's style "evocative" and "gloriously relaxed." Calling Michaels "a superb stylist," Corrine Robins in *American Book Review* states that "Michaels's prose achieves the beauty of a physical feat."

BIOGRAPHICAL/CRITICAL SOURCES:

BOOKS

Contemporary Literary Criticism, Gale, Volume 6, 1976, Volume 25, 1983.
Dictionary of Literary Biography, Volume 130, *American Short-Story Writers since World War II,* Gale, 1993.
Michaels, Leonard, *Going Places,* Farrar, Straus, 1969.
Michaels, *I Would Have Saved Them If I Could,* Farrar, Straus, 1975.
Michaels, *The Men's Club,* Farrar, Straus, 1981, expanded edition, Mercury House, 1993.

PERIODICALS

American Book Review, June-July, 1994, p. 8.
Antaeus, summer, 1979.
Atlantic, April, 1969.
Chicago Tribune, January 31, 1990.
Chicago Tribune Book World, March 30, 1969.
Commonweal, September 19, 1969; July 11, 1975.
Contemporary Review, April, 1980.
Esquire, May, 1981.
Harper's, September, 1975.
Hudson Review, autumn, 1981.
Kenyon Review, Volume 31, number 3, 1969.
Los Angeles Times, May 10, 1981; May 28, 1981; September 22, 1986; January 18, 1990.
Los Angeles Times Book Review, November 26, 1989; October 11, 1992, p. 3.
Nation, November 15, 1975, November 27, 1989, p. 638.
National Review, September 18, 1981.

New Republic, July 19, 1969; August, 1978; May 2, 1981.

New Statesman & Society, January 12, 1990, p. 33.

Newsweek, March 2, 1970; April 27, 1981; September 10, 1990, p. 56.

New Yorker, May 4, 1981; October 26, 1992, p. 139.

New York Review of Books, July 10, 1969; November 11, 1975; July 16, 1981.

New York Times, April 14, 1969; July 30, 1975; April 7, 1981; February 8, 1985; September 21, 1986; September 28, 1986.

New York Times Book Review, May 25, 1969; August 3, 1975; January 6, 1980; April 12, 1981; September 9, 1990, p. 14; September 20, 1992, p. 11; August 8, 1993, p. 20.

Observer, January 27, 1980; September 1, 1991, p. 54.

Partisan Review, winter, 1977.

Playboy, December, 1989, p. 30.

Publishers Weekly, March 13, 1981; September 1, 1989; p. 72; July 13, 1990, p. 40; May 24, 1993, p. 81.

Saturday Review, August 2, 1969; April, 1981.

Spectator, February 16, 1980.

Threepenny Review, summer, 1981.

Time, April 27, 1981.

Times Literary Supplement, April 23, 1970; February 22, 1980; October 16, 1981; October 18, 1985; February 2, 1990; August 30, 1991, p. 19.

Tribune Books (Chicago), August 19, 1990, p. 6.

Village Voice, February 19, 1970; October 20, 1975; March 10, 1980; April 8, 1981.

Washington Post, May 26, 1981; October 3, 1989.

Washington Post Book World, February 17, 1980; April 26, 1981; February 25, 1990; December 20, 1992, p. 6.

*   *   *

MILLER, (H.) Bill(y) 1920-1961
(Will Daemer, Whit Masterson, Wade Miller, Dale Wilmer, joint pseudonyms)

PERSONAL: Born in 1920 in Garrett, IN; died August 21, 1961, in San Diego, CA; married Enid Elena Edwards; children: Mark, Lloyd (daughter). *Education:* Attended San Diego State College (now San Diego State University), 1938-42.

CAREER: Writer. *East San Diego Press,* East San Diego, CA, coeditor, 1939-42; scriptwriter for Mu-

tual Broadcasting Co., 1940-41, 1946-48. *Military service:* U.S. Army Air Forces, 1942-46; served in the Pacific; became master sergeant.

AWARDS, HONORS: Second prize in *Ellery Queen's Mystery Magazine* contest, 1955, for short story "Invitation to an Accident"; Edgar Allan Poe special award from Mystery Writers of America, 1956.

WRITINGS:

MYSTERY NOVELS

(With Robert Wade) *Pop Goes the Queen,* Farrar, Straus (New York City), 1947 (published in England as *Murder—Queen High,* W. H. Allen [London], 1958).

WITH ROBERT WADE, UNDER JOINT PSEUDONYM WILL DAEMER

The Case of the Lonely Lovers, Farrell (New York City), 1951.

WITH ROBERT WADE, UNDER JOINT PSEUDONYM WHIT MASTERSON

All Through the Night, Dodd, 1955, published as *A Cry in the Night,* Bantam (New York City), 1956.

Dead, She Was Beautiful, Dodd, 1955.

Badge of Evil, Dodd, 1956, published as *Touch of Evil,* Bantam, 1958.

A Shadow in the Wild, Dodd, 1957.

The Dark Fantastic, Dodd, 1959.

A Hammer in His Hand, Dodd, 1960.

Evil Come, Evil Go, Dodd, 1961.

WITH ROBERT WADE, UNDER JOINT PSEUDONYM WADE MILLER

Deadly Weapon, Farrar, Straus, 1946.

Guilty Bystander, Farrar, Straus, 1947.

Fatal Step, Farrar, Straus, 1948.

Uneasy Street, Farrar, Straus, 1948.

Devil on Two Sticks, Farrar, Straus, 1949, published as *Killer's Choice,* New American Library (New York City), 1950.

Calamity Fair, Farrar, Straus, 1950.

Devil May Care, Fawcett, 1950.

Murder Charge, Farrar, Straus, 1950.

Stolen Woman, Fawcett, 1950.

The Killer, Fawcett (New York City), 1951.

Shoot to Kill, Farrar, Straus, 1951.

The Tiger's Wife, Fawcett, 1951.
Branded Woman, Fawcett, 1952.
South of the Sun, Fawcett, 1953.
The Big Guy, Fawcett, 1953.
Mad Baxter, Fawcett, 1955.
Kiss Her Goodbye, Lion (New York City), 1956.
Kitten with a Whip, Fawcett, 1959.
Sinner Take All, Fawcett, 1960.
Nightmare Cruise, Ace (New York City), 1961, published in England as *The Sargasso People,* W. H. Allen (London), 1961.
The Girl from Midnight, Fawcett, 1962.

Also author, under joint pseudonym Wade Miller, of two screenplays, 200 radio scripts, several novelettes, and numerous short stories, including "Invitation to an Accident."

WITH ROBERT WADE, UNDER JOINT PSEUDONYM DALE WILMER

Memo for Murder, Graphic Publications (Hasbrouck Heights, NJ), 1951.
Dead Fall, Bouregy & Curl (New York City), 1954.
Jungle Heat, Pyramid (New York City), 1954.

ADAPTATIONS: Guilty Bystander was filmed by Film Classics, 1950; *A Cry in the Night* was filmed by Warner Brothers, 1956; *Touch of Evil* was filmed by Universal, 1958; *Kitten with a Whip* was filmed by Universal, 1964; *Evil Come, Evil Go* was filmed under the title *The Yellow Canary. South of the Sun, Invitation to an Accident,* and *Women in His Life* have been adapted for television. *The Killer* was adapted for television under the title *The Man Hunter.*

SIDELIGHTS: Bill Miller and Robert Wade began writing together after meeting at a San Diego junior high school, and the collaborative effort continued through high school and during their years at San Diego State College, when both men edited the *East San Diego Press.* During World War II they continued to work together through the mail, and *Deadly Weapon,* the first of several novels published under their joint pseudonym Wade Miller, appeared soon after their return to the United States.

Deadly Weapon follows detective Walter James as he probes a murder at a San Diego burlesque house. The reviewer for *Saturday Review of Literature* called the book "very tough stuff . . . that delivers real surprises." Edward D. Hoch in the *St. James Guide to Crime and Mystery Writers* found "some-

thing of the pace and violence of [Dashiell] Hammett here, together with an ending unique in the private eye genre. Though praised at the time of its publication, the book is too little known today."

Six early Wade Miller novels concern San Diego private eye Max Thursday. "Thursday's career," wrote Hoch, "begins as a house detective in a cheap hotel. He is divorced and drinking too much. He is drawn into a case when his child is kidnapped. The solving of it rehabilitates him and he becomes a successful private eye—though one with a hair-trigger temper that often flares into violence. The first few books end in a burst of violence, until finally he becomes reluctant to carry a gun." Hoch concluded that Thursday "is still someone worth knowing, and his six cases, . . . are still a pleasure to read."

BIOGRAPHICAL/CRITICAL SOURCES:

BOOKS

St. James Guide to Crime and Mystery Writers, 4th edition, St. James Press (Detroit), 1996.

PERIODICALS

Book Week, August 25, 1946, p. 6.
New York Times, August 11, 1946, p. 20.
San Francisco Chronicle, August 18, 1946, p. 14.
Saturday Review of Literature, August 17, 1946, p. 28.
Weekly Book Review, August 11, 1946, p. 15.

OBITUARIES:

PERIODICALS

New York Times, August 23, 1961.
Publishers Weekly, September 11, 1961.*

*　　*　　*

MILLER, Wade
　See MILLER, (H.) Bill(y)

*　　*　　*

MILLER, Wade
　See WADE, Robert (Allison)

MORGAN, Claire
  See HIGHSMITH, (Mary) Patricia

*   *   *

MORRIS, Desmond (John) 1928-

PERSONAL: Born January 24, 1928, in Purton, Wiltshire, England; son of Harry Howe (a writer) and Dorothy Marjorie Fuller (Hunt) Morris; married Ramona Baulch (a writer), July 30, 1952; children: Jason. *Education:* Birmingham University, B.Sc., 1951; Magdalen College, Oxford, D.Phil., 1954. *Politics:* None. *Religion:* None. *Avocational interests:* Painting, archaeology.

ADDRESSES: Agent—c/o Jonathan Cape, 20 Vauxhall Bridge Road, London SW1V 25A, England.

CAREER: Oxford University, Oxford, England, researcher in animal behavior in department of zoology, 1954-56; Zoological Society of London, London, England, head of Granada TV and Film Unit, 1956-59, curator of mammals, 1959-67; Institute of Contemporary Arts, London, director, 1967-68; full-time writer, 1968—. Oxford University, research fellow at Wolfson College, 1973-81. Paintings exhibited in numerous shows throughout England, first in one-man show, London, 1950. Former host of *Zootime* television series, Granada TV.

MEMBER: Zoological Society of London (scientific fellow).

AWARDS, HONORS: Statuette with Pedestal, World Organization for Human Potential, 1971, for *The Naked Ape* and *The Human Zoo.*

WRITINGS:

The Reproductive Behaviour of the Ten-Spined Stickleback, E. J. Brill, 1958.
(Editor with Caroline Jarvis) *The International Zoo Yearbook,* Zoological Society of London, Volume 1, 1959-60, Volume 2, 1960-61, Volume 3, 1961-62, Volume 4, 1962-63.

Introducing Curious Creatures, Spring Books, 1961.
The Biology of Art: A Study of the Picture-Making Behaviour of the Great Apes and Its Relationship to Human Art, Knopf (New York City), 1962.
(With wife, Ramona Morris) *Men and Snakes,* McGraw, 1965.
The Mammals: A Guide to the Living Species, Harper, 1965.
(With R. Morris) *Men and Apes,* McGraw, 1966.
(With R. Morris) *Men and Pandas,* Hutchinson, 1966, McGraw, 1967, revised edition published as *The Giant Panda,* Penguin, 1981.
(Editor) *Primate Ethology,* Aldine, 1967.
The Naked Ape: A Zoologist's Study of the Human Animal, J. Cape, 1967, McGraw, 1968, revised edition published as *The Illustrated Naked Ape,* J. Cape, 1986.
The Human Zoo, McGraw, 1969.
Patterns of Reproductive Behaviour: Collected Papers (all previously published in journals), J. Cape, 1970, McGraw, 1971.
Intimate Behavior, J. Cape, 1971, Random House, 1972.
Manwatching: A Field Guide to Human Behavior, Abrams, 1977.
(With Peter Collett, Peter Marsh, and Marie O'Shaughnessy) *Gestures: Their Origins and Distributions,* Stein & Day, 1979.
Animal Days, Perigord Press, 1979.
The Soccer Tribe, J. Cape, 1981.
Inrock (fiction), J. Cape, 1983.
The Book of Ages, Viking, 1983.
The Art of Ancient Cyprus, Phaidon, 1985.
Bodywatching: A Field Guide to the Human Species, J. Cape, 1985.
Dogwatching, J. Cape, 1986, Crown, 1987.
Catwatching, Crown, 1987.
The Secret Surrealist: The Paintings of Desmond Morris, Salem House, 1987.
Catlore, Crown, 1988.
(With the Roadshow Team) *The Animals Roadshow,* J. Cape, 1988.
Horsewatching, Crown, 1988.
Animalwatching: A Field Guide to Animal Behavior, Crown, 1990.
The Animal Contract: Sharing the Planet, Warner, 1990.
Babywatching, Crown, 1992.
The Human Animal: A Personal View of the Human Species, Crown, 1994.
Bodytalk: The Meaning of Human Gestures, Crown, 1995.

FOR CHILDREN

The Story of Congo, Batsford, 1958.
Apes and Monkeys, Bodley Head, 1964, McGraw, 1965.
The Big Cats, McGraw, 1965.
Zoo Time, Hart-Davis, 1966.
The World of Animals, illustrated by Peter Barrett, Viking, 1993.

OTHER

Author of *The Human Nestbuilders,* 1988. Contributor to journals, including *Behavior, British Birds, New Scientist,* and *Zoo Life.*

ADAPTATIONS: The Naked Ape was filmed by Universal and released in 1973.

WORK IN PROGRESS: Research in human ethology; planning another exhibit of paintings.

SIDELIGHTS: Desmond Morris first came to public attention as the host of *Zootime,* a British Broadcasting Corporation (BBC) television series featuring the animals of the London Zoo, and as the author of *The Naked Ape,* in which he examines humans from a zoologist's perspective. Morris's fascination with animals began in early childhood, when he spent hours at a time in close observation of worms and beetles near his home. As a student, he was drawn to the science of ethology—the study of natural animal behavior. His teachers were some of the founders of this young science, including Konrad Lorenz and Niko Tinbergen. Morris's research in this discipline uncovered such phenomena as homosexuality among the ten-spined stickleback fish and the "divorce" of mated pairs of zebra finches.

His work won him the respect of his peers, but when the opportunity came to trade his academic career for a stint as a television-show host, Morris accepted. *Zootime* was shown live and its animal stars were known for their unpredictable—and often embarrassing—antics. Morris's own popularity was built largely upon his deft, humorous handling of his misbehaving co-stars. In his book *Animal Days,* Morris explains the appeal that a public role holds for him. He was a very shy child and admits that upon entering boarding school, "I often overcompensated and became almost painfully extroverted, as if determined to obliterate my inner relish for privacy. I became a joker, an entertainer. If I am honest, it is a struggle I have never fully resolved, the 'ham'

and the academic in me doing battle with one another, with first one, then the other getting the upper hand." When the program ended, Morris resumed academic "respectability" by becoming curator of mammals at the London Zoo and holding that post for eight years. He left to become director of the Institute of Contemporary Arts in London, but resigned a year later when publication of *The Naked Ape* made him wealthy.

In *The Naked Ape,* Morris brings the methods of observation he learned as an ethologist to bear upon his fellow man. He states that humans are merely one of many variations within the ape family, and then attempts to explain humankind's complex behavior by relating it to that of the lesser apes. The result proved fascinating to the general public; the book quickly became a best-seller. Many scientists, however, particularly anthropologists (whose domain is specifically the study of man), have reserved harsh criticism for Morris and *The Naked Ape.*

Saturday Review contributor Morton Fried, for example, believes that Morris is unqualified to write a book on human behavior. Morris, he writes, "has simply given us a naive and scientifically reactionary book. . . . Clearly, he never took even a freshman course in [anthropology], or he flunked it." J. Z. Young similarly faults the book, suggesting that Morris deliberately emphasizes the most provocative aspects of his subject in order to ensure his book's popularity. Young points out in the *New York Review of Books* that while more than one-fourth of *The Naked Ape* describes man's sexual habits, there is no mention whatsoever of language or learning. "It is not fair for any biologist to describe only those aspects of an animal that interest him and titillate his readers, especially if the ones omitted are the essential biological foundations of the success of the species." Other reviewers, however, praise Morris for making scientific material accessible to a wide audience. Peter Williams applauds *The Naked Ape* in *Natural History* for its "brilliant insights" and a *Times Literary Supplement* critic calls it "not only a thoughtful and stimulating book, but also an extremely interesting one." Readers agreed, for *The Naked Ape* was eventually published in twenty-three countries and sold over 8 million copies.

Publication of *Animal Days* marked a change in tone. "This time, Morris doesn't try to shock or titillate with . . . theories," notes Peter Gwynne of *Newsweek.* "[*Animal Days*] is a straightforward, unpretentious memoir of his encounters with animals and fellow scientists. And it is a delightful book." Writing in the *New York Times,* Christopher Lehmann-Haupt likewise praises the book for its "gallery of arresting portraits of Mr. Morris's fellow animal behaviorists—the first great generation of them, really." *Animal Days* is "a visit with an engaging raconteur who has spent his life in a fascinating field," a *New York Times Book Review* critic concludes.

Morris's books have continued to bring the more intriguing aspects of animal nature to a broad readership. In the highly readable *Bodytalk: The Meaning of Human Gestures,* published in 1995, the naturalist examines the vast number of meanings attached to hand gestures. Among the six hundred gestures Morris discusses are the "thumbs up" and "high five" familiar to most Americans, as well as the German convention of signaling someone as an idiot by slapping one's elbow with the palm of one's hand. Not only adults, but children as well have benefited from Morris's books. Illustrated with watercolor paintings by Peter Barrett, *The World of Animals* finds the author contrasting the real nature of a variety of species from their cartoon and stuffed-animal counterparts. Not only lions, tigers, and bears, but koalas, platypus, and beavers are described in a prose style accessible to younger readers that is as engaging as "the narration of a zoo tour led by an enthusiastic and expert guide," according to *Booklist* reviewer Elizabeth Bush. Other Morris books geared towards inspiring younger readers with the joy of nature include *The Story of Congo* and *The Big Cats.*

In books such as *Dogwatching* and *Catwatching,* Morris applies his ethologist's eye to some of man's favorite pets. The books offer a variety of information about animals, answering questions from why cats seem to prefer women to why dogs bark. "The author turns his attention to animal behavior in just the right tone for pet lovers," notes *Los Angeles Times Book Review* contributor Mordecai Siegal, who commends the books' question-and-answer format as "quite appropriate for the curator of a zoo." Nevertheless, the critic echoes former criticisms of Morris's work, faulting the books for "the absence of information sources." The author refutes this charge in a *Chicago Tribune* interview with Kathy Hacker, explaining that the popular nature of his books precludes the use of extensive citations: "A lot of the statements I make have this huge backup of quantified field work. . . . [Some] do not and are simply based on intuition and anecdotal observation. The agony of writing a pop book is that you can't say which is which. The text has got to flow," Morris continued. "If you put down every detail and every chart and every figure, I suspect people wouldn't read it at all."

Morris's works don't suffer from lack of readers, however. His popularity extends to his other books, which encompass a variety of subjects, from art to soccer. His wide range of interests prompts Gwynne to write of him, "Zoologist Desmond Morris is the epitome of the scholar with interests too lively to hide under an academic bushel." Of himself, Morris told William Overend of the *Los Angeles Times:* "I describe myself as a senile 14-year-old. . . . I get more foolish and frivolous each year. I confess to cultivating immaturity. I don't aspire to maturity because it's so often connected with rigid thought. . . . I really don't want to ever take things too seriously, least of all myself."

BIOGRAPHICAL/CRITICAL SOURCES:

BOOKS

Morris, Desmond, *Animal Days,* Perigord Press, 1979.

PERIODICALS

Best Sellers, December 15, 1969.
Booklist December 13, 1993, pp. 751-52.
Book World, October 12, 1969; February 27, 1972.
Chicago Tribune, January 9, 1986.
Los Angeles Times, March 9, 1984; May 21, 1984.
Los Angeles Times Book Review, June 24, 1979; May 31, 1987; April 9, 1995.
Natural History, February, 1968; January, 1970.
Newsweek, August 4, 1980.
New York Review of Books, March 14, 1968.
New York Times, July 18, 1980.
New York Times Book Review, February 4, 1968; November 30, 1969; March 5, 1972; November 13, 1977; December 30, 1979; August 10, 1980; May 14, 1995, p. 16.
Observer (London), October 20, 1996.
Publishers Weekly, October 18, 1993, p. 74.
Saturday Review, February 17, 1968; March 4, 1972; July, 1980.
School Library Journal, January, 1994, pp. 126-27.
Spectator, October 16, 1971; November 5, 1977.
Time, January 26, 1968; March 13, 1972; January 16, 1978; December 9, 1985.
Times Literary Supplement, November 9, 1967; October 30, 1969; December 7, 1979.

Washington Post, December 8, 1981; March 20, 1984.
Washington Post Book World, August 12, 1979.
Yale Review, summer, 1968.

*   *   *

MULLER, Marcia 1944-

PERSONAL: Born September 28, 1944, in Detroit, MI; daughter of Henry J. (a marketing executive) and Kathryn (Minke) Muller; married Frederick T. Guilson, Jr. (in sales), August 12, 1967 (divorced, 1981); married Bill Pronzini, 1992. *Education:* University of Michigan, B.A. (English), 1966, M.A. (journalism), 1971.

ADDRESSES: Home—P.O. Box 2536, Petaluma, CA 94953. *Agent*—Molly Friedrich, Aaron M. Priest Literary Agency Inc., 708 Third Avenue, 23rd Floor, New York, NY 10017-4103.

CAREER: Sunset magazine, Menlo Park, CA, merchandising supervisor, 1967-69; University of Michigan Institute for Social Research, Ann Arbor, field interviewer in the San Francisco Bay area, 1971-73; freelance writer and novelist, 1973—; Invisible Ink, San Francisco, partner (with Julie Smith), 1979-83.

MEMBER: Mystery Writers of America, Sisters in Crime, Women in Communications.

AWARDS, HONORS: Private Eye Writers of America Shamus award, 1991; Private Eye Writers of America Life Achievement award, 1993; Anthony Boucher award, 1994.

WRITINGS:

CRIME NOVELS; "SHARON McCONE" SERIES

Edwin of the Iron Shoes, McKay (New York City), 1977.
Ask the Cards a Question, St. Martin's (New York City), 1982.
The Chesire Cat's Eye, St. Martin's, 1983.
Games to Keep the Dark Away, St. Martin's, 1984.
Leave A Message for Willie, St. Martin's, 1984.
(With Bill Pronzini) *Double,* St. Martin's, 1984.
There's Nothing to Be Afraid Of, St. Martin's, 1985.
(With Pronzini) *Eye of the Storm,* Mysterious Press (New York City), 1988.
The Shape of Dread, Mysterious Press, 1989.

There's Something in a Sunday, Mysterious Press, 1989.
Trophies and Dead Things, Mysterious Press, 1990.
Where Echoes Live, Mysterious Press, 1991.
Pennies on a Dead Woman's Eyes, Mysterious Press, 1992.
Wolf in the Shadows, Mysterious Press, 1993.
Till the Butchers Cut Him Down, Mysterious Press, 1994.
A Wild and Lonely Place, Mysterious Press, 1995.
The Broken Promise Land, Mysterious Press, 1996.
Both Ends of the Night, Mysterious Press, 1997.

CRIME NOVELS; "ELENA OLIVEREZ" SERIES

The Tree of Death, Walker & Company (New York City), 1983.
The Legend of Slain Soldiers, Walker & Company, 1985.
(With Pronzini) *Beyond the Grave,* Walker & Company, 1986.

CRIME NOVELS; "JOANNA STARK" SERIES

The Cavalier in White, St. Martin's, 1986.
There Hangs the Knife, St. Martin's, 1988.
Dark Star, St. Martin's, 1989.

OTHER CRIME NOVELS

(With Pronzini) *The Lighthouse,* St. Martin's, 1987.

COLLECTIONS; EDITED WITH PRONZINI

The Web She Weaves; An Anthology of Mystery and Suspense Stories by Women, Morrow (New York City), 1983.
Child's Play, Macmillan (New York City), 1984.
Witches' Brew: Horror and Supernatural Stories by Women, Macmillan, 1984.
Chapter and Hearse: Suspense Stories about the World of Books, Morrow, 1985.
Dark Lessons: Crime and Detection on Campus, Macmillan, 1985.
Kill or Cure: Suspense Stories about the World of Medicine, Macmillan, 1985.
She Won the West: An Anthology of Western and Frontier Stories by Women, Morrow, 1985.
The Wickedest Show on Earth: A Carnival of Circus Suspense, Arbor House (New York City), 1985.
The Deadly Arts: A Collection of Artful Suspense, Arbor House, 1985.
1001 Midnights: The Aficionado's Guide to Mystery and Detective Fiction, Arbor House, 1986.

(Also with Martin H. Greenberg) *Lady on the Case,* Bonanza (New York City), 1988.
Detective Duos, Oxford University Press, 1997.

CRIME SHORT STORIES

Deceptions, Mystery Scene Press, 1991.
The Wall (novella; in *Criminal Intent I*), Dark Harvest, 1993.
The McCone Files: The Complete Sharon McCone Stories (collection of short stories), Norfolk, Crippen and Landru, 1995.

OTHER

(Author of preface) *Hard-Boiled Dames: A Brass-Knuckled Anthology of the Toughest Women from the Classic Pulps,* St. Martin's, 1986.

Manuscript collection is held at the Popular Culture Library, Bowling Green State University, Bowling Green, Ohio.

SIDELIGHTS: Novelist Marcia Muller has been credited with helping revolutionize the depiction of female private eyes. "When Marcia Muller introduced Sharon McCone in 1977 [in *Edwin of the Iron Shoes*], the author created the first contemporary female hard-boiled private investigator to feature in a series of American crime fiction novels," according to Adrian Muller of the *St. James Guide to Crime and Mystery Writers.* Sharon McCone, perhaps Muller's most popular character, is an ace San Francisco legal investigator who differs from some of her more hard-boiled counterparts in that she is more apt to use her wits than her gun. The author once explained that in creating McCone, her aim was "to use the classical puzzle form of the mystery to introduce a contemporary female sleuth, a figure with surprisingly few counterparts in the world of detective fiction."

"Following *Edwin of the Iron Shoes* however, publishers felt that female protagonists held little appeal for readers of crime fiction and it wasn't until 1982 that McCone reappeared in *Ask the Cards a Question,*" noted Adrian Muller. In a *Booklist* review, Connie Fletcher stated that *Ask the Cards a Question* was a "perfectly plotted follow-up to Muller's first novel." *Publishers Weekly*'s Barbara A. Bannon also praised the book, commenting that "fans . . . won't be disappointed with this."

Since introducing McCone, Muller has been praised for both the realistic depiction of her heroine and for giving readers vivid descriptions of the series' Bay area locales. Fletcher noted the presence of "San Francisco atmosphere, fast action, and Muller's usual witty dialogue," in her *Booklist* review of *Leave a Message for Willie,* the fifth McCone mystery. In a review of *There's Something in a Sunday* for the *Los Angeles Times Book Review,* Charles Champlin noted that "as before, Muller's strength is in her characters—McCone is likable and believable—and her ability to convey places and atmospheres." Adrian Muller commented that "it is the supporting characters that make these novels stand out from many other crime fiction series. Not only do many of the secondary characters continue to reappear, so do many of the minor characters; newly introduced or hovering in the background, they occasionally play larger parts in the books. Once established they rarely disappear without a given reason. The effect is that each new McCone novel is like coming back to a cast of well-loved characters. . . . Throughout the novels McCone's character is constantly evolving, both personally and professionally."

Muller's other female detectives are Elena Oliverez and Joanna Stark. Elena Oliverez is a Hispanic curator in an American Mexican arts museum. She has been featured in three of Muller's novels, beginning with *The Tree of Death,* in which Elena must prove that she had nothing to do with the murder of her boss. The novel is "a tale with an appealing and unusual setting, some well drawn characters and a heroine one wouldn't mind meeting again," according to Bannon's *Publishers Weekly* review. Rosemary Herbert recommended the book in a *Library Journal* review, calling it "an excellent power struggles with a small group."

Muller has edited many short story collections with her husband, Bill Pronzini, including *The Web She Weaves: An Anthology of Mystery and Suspense Stories by Women* and *Kill or Cure: Suspense Stories about the World of Medicine.* In *Publishers Weekly,* Bannon critiqued *The Web She Weaves* as an "eminently entertaining and worthwhile collection." "Pronzini and Muller have unearthed some genuine gems," Margaret Cannon wrote of *Kill or Cure* for the Toronto *Globe and Mail,* "there are no turkeys in the collection."

Muller has also collaborated with Pronzini to produce a number of novels. *The Lighthouse,* a tale of yuppies and murder in a small town on the Oregon coast, "combines both authors' strengths . . . and avoids their weaknesses" in a setting that is "excellent," according to Cannon in her Toronto *Globe and Mail* review. "*Double* . . . [is] noteworthy for the fact that the point of view alternates from chapter to chapter between Muller's Sharon McCone and Pronzini's series character, the 'Nameless' detective," stated Adrian Muller of the *St. James' Guide to Crime and Mystery Writers.*

Marcia Muller told *St. James' Guide to Crime and Mystery Writers:* "In my detective fiction I am attempting to explore various problems of contemporary American society through the eyes of women who become involved in situations which compel them to seek the solutions to various crimes. In the cases of amateur detectives Elena Oliverez and Joanna Stark, these circumstances are more or less thrust upon them, and the women have a strong personal stake in seeing the perpetrators of the crimes brought to justice. Private investigator Sharon McCone's involvement is professional, but more often than not she becomes deeply involved with her clients and/or crimes' victims. McCone, the character upon whom I will be concentrating in the future, is a woman with day-to-day problems and a fully developed personal life, who must deal with the increasingly complex pressures and issues posed by modern society. While not a superwoman, when forced to confront extraordinary situations, she reaches beyond her normal capabilities and grows and changes accordingly. In recent years, McCone has left her rather confining position at All Souls Legal Cooperative and established her own agency in a new location—thus allowing for the series to change in scope and direction."

BIOGRAPHICAL/CRITICAL SOURCES:

BOOKS

St. James Guide to Crime and Mystery Writers, fourth edition, St. James Press (Detroit), 1996.

PERIODICALS

Booklist, August, 1982, p. 1510; January 15, 1984, p. 718; October 1, 1984, p. 192.
Globe and Mail (Toronto), December 7, 1985; April 11, 1987.
Library Journal, October 1, 1977; October 1, 1983, p. 1890; October 1, 1984, p. 1865.
Los Angeles Times, August 14, 1985; June 6, 1986.

Los Angeles Times Book Review, October 10, 1982, p. 7; February 12, 1989, p. 6.
New York Times Book Review, November 7, 1982, p. 39; October 6, 1985; March 12, 1989, p. 24; December 24, 1989, p. 23; November 4, 1990, p. 30.
Publishers Weekly, April 30, 1982, p. 48; December 24, 1982, p. 49; September 9, 1983, p. 51; September 23, 1983, p. 63.
USA Today, July 27, 1987.*

*　　*　　*

NICHOLS, (John) Beverley 1898-1983

PERSONAL: Born September 9, 1898, in Bristol, England; died after a fall, September 15, 1983, in Kingston-upon-Thames, England; son of John (a solicitor) and Pauline (Shalders) Nichols. *Education:* Attended Marlborough College; Balliol College, Oxford, B.A., 1921.

CAREER: Journalist, novelist, playwright, and composer. Gossip columnist for *Sunday Chronicle,* London, England, for fourteen years; press correspondent in India, 1939-45.

MEMBER: Oxford Union Debating Society (president, c. 1922).

WRITINGS:

NOVELS

Prelude, Chatto & Windus (London), 1920.
Patchwork, Chatto & Windus, 1921, Holt (New York City), 1922.
Self, Chatto & Windus, 1922.
Crazy Pavements, G. H. Doran (New York City), 1927.
Evensong (also see below), Doubleday (New York City), 1932.
Revue, Doubleday, 1939.

CRIME NOVELS; "HORATIO GREEN" SERIES

No Man's Street, Dutton (New York City), 1954.
The Moonflower Murder, Dutton, 1955, published as *The Moonflower,* Hutchinson (London), 1955.
Death to Slow Music, Dutton, 1956.

The Rich Die Hard, Hutchinson, 1957, Dutton, 1958.
Murder by Request, Dutton, 1960.

PLAYS

Picnic (revue; composer only), produced in London, 1927.
Many Happy Returns (revue; composer only; by Herbert Farjeon) produced in London, 1928.
The Stag (also see below; first produced in London, England, in 1929), Peter Smith (New York City), 1933.
Cochran's 1930 Revue, (music by Nichols and Vivian Ellis), produced in London, 1930.
Avalanche (also see below; first produced in Edinburgh, Scotland, in 1931; produced in London in 1932), Peter Smith, 1933.
(With Edward Knoblock) *Evensong* (three-act; based on own novel of the same title; first produced in London in 1932; produced in New York City, in 1933), Samuel French (New York City), 1933.
(With Alma Reveille and John Paddy Carstairs) *Nine Till Six* (screenplay), 1932.
When the Crash Comes (also see below; first produced in Birmingham, England, in 1933), Peter Smith, 1933.
Failures: Three Plays (contains *The Stag, Avalanche,* and *When the Crash Comes*), Peter Smith, 1933.
Mesmer (first produced in London in 1938), J. Cape, 1937.
Floodlight (revue; music by Nichols), produced in London, 1937.
(With Rupert Croft-Cooke) *You Bet Your Life* (radio play), 1938.
Shadow of the Vine (three-act; first produced in London in 1954), J. Cape, 1949.
La Plume de Ma Tante, produced in Bromley, Kent, 1953.

Also author of *Song on the Wind* (operetta), 1948, and *Lady's Guide,* 1950.

JUVENILE

The Tree That Sat Down (also see below), J. Cape, 1945.
The Stream That Stood Still (also see below), J. Cape, 1948.
The Mountain of Magic, J. Cape, 1950.
The Wickedest Witch in the World, W. H. Allen (London), 1971.

NONFICTION

Twenty-five: Being a Young Man's Candid Recollections of His Elders and Betters, G. H. Doran (New York City), 1926.
Are They the Same at Home? Being a Series of Bouquets Diffidently Distributed, G. H. Doran, 1927.
The Star Spangled Manner, Doubleday, 1928.
Women and Children Last, Doubleday, 1931.
Down the Garden Path, Doubleday, 1932, reprinted, Norwood Editions, 1978.
For Adults Only, J. Cape, 1932, Doubleday, 1933.
Cry Havoc!, Doubleday, 1933.
A Thatched Roof, Doubleday, 1933.
A Village in a Valley, Doubleday, 1934, reprinted, Arden Library (Darby, PA), 1980.
(With others) *How Does Your Garden Grow?* (broadcast talks), Doubleday, 1935.
The Fool Hath Said, Doubleday, 1936, reprinted, Norwood Editions, 1978.
No Place Like Home (travel), Doubleday, 1936.
News of England; or, A Country without a Hero, Doubleday, 1938.
Green Grows the City: A Story of a London Garden, Harcourt, 1939.
Verdict on India, Harcourt, 1944.
All I Could Never Be: Some Recollections, J. Cape, 1949, Dutton (New York City), 1952.
(With Monica Dickens) *Yours Sincerely* (*Woman's Own* articles), G. Newnes (London), 1949.
Uncle Samson (on America), Evans Brothers (London), 1950.
Merry Hall (also see below), J. Cape, 1951, Dutton, 1953.
A Pilgrim's Progress, J. Cape, 1952.
Laughter on the Stairs (also see below), J. Cape, 1953, Dutton, 1954, reprinted, Dynamic Learning Corp., 1979.
The Queen's Coronation Day: The Pictorial Record of the Great Occasion, Pitkin Pictorials (London), 1953.
Beverley Nichols' Cat Book, T. Nelson (London), 1955.
Sunlight on the Lawn (also see below), Dutton, 1956.
The Sweet and Twenties, Weidenfeld & Nicolson (London), 1958.
Cats A. B. C. (also see below), Dutton, 1960.
Cats X. Y. Z. (also see below), Dutton, 1961.
Garden Open Today, Dutton, 1963.
Forty Favourite Flowers, Studio Vista (London), 1964, St. Martin's (New York City), 1965.
Powers That Be, St. Martin's, 1966.

A Case of Human Bondage (on Somerset Maughan), Award Books (New York City), 1966.

The Art of Flower Arrangement, Viking (New York City), 1967.

Garden Open Tomorrow, Heinemann (London), 1968, Dodd (New York City), 1969.

The Sun in My Eyes; or, How Not to Go Around the World, Heinemann, 1969.

Father Figure (autobiography), Simon & Schuster (New York City), 1972.

Down the Kitchen Sink (autobiography), W. H. Allen (London), 1974.

The Unforgiving Minute: Some Confessions from Childhood to the Outbreak of the Second World War, W. H. Allen, 1978.

The Romantic Garden, Gordon-Cremonesi (New York City), 1980.

COLLECTIONS

The Tree That Sat Down [and] *The Stream That Stood Still,* St. Martin's, 1966.

The Gift of a Garden; or, Some Flowers Remembered, edited by John E. Cross, W. H. Allen, 1971, Dodd, 1972.

The Gift of a Home (contains condensed versions of *Merry Hall, Laughter on the Stairs,* and *Sunlight on the Lawn*), W. H. Allen, 1972, Dodd, 1973.

Beverley Nichols' Cats A-Z (contains *Cats A. B. C.* and *Cats X. Y. Z.*), W. H. Allen, 1977.

OTHER

(Author of introduction) Charles Sedley, *The Faro Table; or, The Gambling Mothers,* Nash & Grayson, 1931.

In the Next War I Shall Be a Conscientious Objector, Friends' Peace Committee (London), 1932.

(Contributor) *Puck at Brighton: The Offical Handbook of the Corporation of Brighton,* Corporation of Brighton (Brighton), 1933.

(Compiler) *A Book of Old Ballads,* Loring and Mussey (New York City), 1934.

(Author of foreword) *The Making of a Man,* Nicholson & Watson, 1934.

The Valet as Historian, Forsyth (London), 1934.

Men Do Not Weep (short stories), J. Cape (London), 1941, Harcourt (New York City), 1942.

(Author of preface) Jan Styczynski, *Cats in America,* A. Deutsch (London), 1962.

(Author of preface) *Receipt Book,* Woolf (London), 1968.

Twilight: First and Probably Last Poems (poetry), Bachman & Turner (Maidstone, Kent), 1982.

Founder and editor of *Oxford Outlook;* editor of *American Sketch,* 1928-29, and *Isis;* contributor to newspapers and periodicals. Manuscript collection is held at Humanities Research Center, University of Texas, Austin.

SIDELIGHTS: Precocious and multi-faceted talent made Beverley Nichols a celebrity by the time he was old enough to attend Oxford University. His first Novel, *Prelude,* was written before his eighteenth birthday; his second, *Patchwork,* was published before he finished his degree. While in school he founded a literary magazine, the *Oxford Outlook,* and edited it along with an already-established magazine, *Isis.* He was president of the famous Oxford Union Debating Society and was also known as a gifted pianist. Following school, he quickly established a reputation as a brilliant and daring interviewer and journalist. "Witty, elegant, and ruinously good-looking," according to the London *Times,* he was an intimate of Noel Coward, Winston Churchill, George Bernard Shaw, D. H. Lawrence, and Somerset Maugham, among others. His sparkling wit and his connections made him a natural candidate for the job of columnist for the *Sunday Chronicle,* and for fourteen years he filled page two of that newspaper with "glossy gossip and name-dropping anecdotes," according to Victoria Glendinning in the *Times Literary Supplement.*

Nichols's books and plays were consistent best-sellers, and thanks to his column he was known to millions, but "as the years went by he never quite developed as a writer in the way forecast by his contemporaries in the 1920s," noted a London *Times* writer. "His was the kind of success, showy and obviously remunerative, which it was easy to denigrate, and Nichols had his share of denigration where a comparable talent exercised in diligent obscurity would have earned approval. His readers had to wait more than 50 years for the key to what had struck some of the author's contemporaries as a compulsive seeking after success rather than a more serious reputation."

That key was found in Nichols's 1972 autobiography, *Father Figure.* It describes a desperately unhappy childhood dominated by a sadistic, alcoholic father, who constantly mistreated his wife, humiliated his family, and ridiculed his son's musical abilities. A London *Times* contributor suggested that Beverley Nichols's adult life was made up of "running . . . from the squalor and unhappiness of his home . . . from seediness, and from poverty. He had an overwhelming desire to make money, and make money he did," but perhaps at the cost of fully realizing his considerable gift for writing.

Publication of *Father Figure* caused some scandal because of Nichols's confession in it that he had made three sincere but unsuccessful efforts to murder his father. At age fifteen, Nichols had dissolved a bottle of aspirin in his father's soup; some months later, upon finding his father sprawled at the bottom of a steep hill, he climbed to the top of the slope, aimed a heavy lawn roller at the unconscious body below, and gave it a push. Years later, at the age of thirty-one, Nichols returned to his own home one winter night to find that his hated parent had let himself in, become dead drunk, wrecked the house, and passed out. The younger Nichols dragged his father outside and dumped him in a snowbank to freeze. But the man survived, eventually dying quite peacefully of natural causes. Commenting in the *New York Times Book Review,* Guy Davenport called *Father Figure* a "painful but wholly interesting confession."

Nichols' sentimental, witty musings on gardening, country life, and cats have proved to be his most enduring books. His style is personal and highly tangential; an essay about gardens may lead to an anecdote about a backstage encounter with an opera diva, then to an impassioned statement on pacifism, and then back to the garden. This style prompted a *New York Times Book Review* writer to call Nichols' most famous book, *Down the Garden Path,* "a charming and amusing book that you can read with much enjoyment, whether or not you care anything about gardens."

Thirty years into his writing career, Nicholas wrote five novels within the crime genre. In the *St. James Guide to Crime and Mystery Writers,* B. A. Pike noted that Nichols "abandoned the form, discouraged by hostile criticism." Pike remarks, "It is hard to see why the books were ill-received, since they were accomplished and alluring mysteries in the classic mode, intricate, ingenious, shapely, and continually absorbing: alibis seem impregnable, suspicion spreads impartially, red herrings proliferate, and the great detective sums up at the end. They are remarkably elegant novels, meticulously contrived and controlled, and stylishly written, with a relative austerity unexpected in a writer so avowedly romantic."

In his first mystery, *No Man's Street,* Nichols introduces his protagonist Horatio Green, a famous but retired detective that "conducts himself in the time-honoured manner of the great fictional detectives, uttering 'cryptic remarks,' indulging in 'unaccountable behaviour,' blinking furiously at moments of 'cerebral activity,' and outstripping the police with prodigies of perception and deduction. His insights are invariably subtle, deriving from 'scraps of dialogue—shadows on faces—fleeting gestures,'" according to Pike.

Despite not receiving overwhelming praise from critics, the crime series was not dismissed by reviewers either. *The Moonflower Murder,* the second "Horatio Green" entry, was described by Anthony Boucher in the *New York Times* as "conventional and old-fashioned . . . but mildly pleasant, with glints of sly humor, up to a wholly preposterous and unfair solution." H. H. Holmes described it in the *New York Herald Tribune Book Review* was "long-winded but rather agreeable soporific and genteel as anything. Engagingly foolish." Boucher wrote in his *New York Times'* review of *Death to Slow Music,* "This third Nicholas mystery is hardly apt to appeal to most American readers. Yet there is a great deal of leisurely charm." Of the same novel, Ralph Partridge wrote in *New Statesman & Nation,* "Mr. Nichols appears to make up his own rules for detection as he goes along, but he is a careful workman; and his prose, if one can stomach a complacent style verging on the unctuous, cannot be impeached. His facts are less reliable." A *Times Literary Supplement* reviewer stated that in *The Rich Die Hard,* "imagination to some extent triumphs over the grim convention . . . complex plot is well controlled and Mr. Green's curious sensitivity produces some quaint and striking reflections." Drexal Drake in the *Chicago Sunday Tribune* described the novel as "remarkably literate, grotesque stage setting, blandly developed until final 50 pages." *Murder by Request* is "not without charm and rather sweetly fussy," according to James Sandoe in *New York Herald Tribune Book Review.* Boucher commented that "the solution of the plot is an old and obvious one but unusually well-clued," in *New York Times Book Review.*

BIOGRAPHICAL/CRITICAL SOURCES:

BOOKS

Nichols, Beverley, *Twenty-five: Being a Young Man's Candid Recollections of His Elders and Betters,* G. H. Doran (New York City), 1926.

Nichols, *Father Figure* (autobiography), Simon & Schuster (New York City), 1972.

Nichols, *Beverley Nichols' Cats A-Z,* W. H. Allen (London), 1977.

Nichols, *The Unforgiving Minute: Some Confessions from Childhood to the Outbreak of the Second World War,* W. H. Allen, 1978.

St. James Guide to Crime and Mystery Writers, fourth edition, St. James Press (Detroit), 1996.

PERIODICALS

Chicago Sunday Tribune, May 18, 1958.

New Statesman & Nation, September 8, 1956.

New York Herald Tribune Book Review, October 30, 1955; April 13, 1958; September 25, 1960.

New York Times, October 16, 1955; September 23, 1956.

New York Times Book Review, February 28, 1923; October 23, 1932; December 17, 1944; September 18, 1960; October 8, 1972.

Times Literary Supplement, October 18, 1957; March 10, 1972; September 8, 1978.

OBITUARIES:

PERIODICALS

London Times, September 17, 1983.

Los Angeles Times, September 17, 1983.

Washington Post, September 17, 1983.*

* * *

NORTH, Milou
   See ERDRICH, Louise

O

O'CASEY, Sean 1880-1964
(Sean O'Cathasaigh)

PERSONAL: Born John Casey; name Gaelicized to Sean O'Cathasaigh, c. 1909; surname Anglicized to O'Casey, 1923; born March 30, 1880, in Dublin, Ireland; self-exiled to England, 1926; died September 18, 1964, in Torquay, Devon, England; son of Michael (a clerk) and Susan (Archer) Casey; married Eileen Carey Reynolds (an actress; stage name, Eileen Carey), 1928; children: two sons, Breon, Niall Ayamonn (died, 1956); one daughter, Shivaun. *Education:* Self-educated. *Religion:* Church of Ireland.

CAREER: Playwright. Worked in ironmongery and hardware store, c. 1895-98; worked at clerical jobs intermittently; railroad worker, Great Northern Railway, Ireland, 1901-11; laborer, 1911-23; secretary of Irish Citizen Army, 1913-14; full-time writer, 1924-64. Associated with Abbey Theatre, London, 1923-28.

MEMBER: Gaelic League, St. Laurence O'Toole Pipers' Band (founding member).

AWARDS, HONORS: Hawthornden Prize, 1926, for *Juno and the Paycock.*

WRITINGS:

PLAYS

The Shadow of a Gunman (also see below; two-act; first produced in Dublin at the Abbey Theatre, April 9, 1923).
Cathleen Listens In (one-act), first produced in Dublin at the Abbey Theatre, October 1, 1923.

Juno and the Paycock (also see below; three-act; first produced in Dublin at the Abbey Theatre, March 3, 1924).
Nannie's Night Out (one-act), first produced in Dublin at the Abbey Theatre, September 29, 1924.
The Plough and the Stars (four-act; first produced in Dublin at the Abbey Theatre, February 8, 1926), Macmillan (New York City), 1926.
The Silver Tassie (four-act; first produced on the West End at Apollo Theatre, October 11, 1929), Macmillan (New York City), 1928.
Within the Gates (four-scene; first produced on the West End at Royalty Theatre, February 7, 1934), Macmillan (London), 1933, Macmillan (New York City), 1934.
The End of the Beginning (also see below; one-act; first produced in Dublin at the Abbey Theatre, February 8, 1937).
A Pound on Demand (also see below; one-act; first produced in London at the Q Theatre, October 16, 1939).
Purple Dust (three-act; first produced in Newcastle upon Tyne, England, at People's Theatre, December 16, 1943), Macmillan (London), 1940, Dramatists Play Service (New York City), 1957.
The Star Turns Red (one-act; first produced in London, at Unity Theatre, March 12, 1940), Macmillan (London), 1940.
Red Roses for Me (four-act; first produced in Dublin at Olympia Theatre, March 15, 1943), Macmillan (London), 1942, Macmillan (New York City), 1943.
Oak Leaves and Lavender; or, A World on Wallpaper (first produced in Sweden at Helsingborgs Stadsteater, November 28, 1946), Macmillan (London), 1946, Macmillan (New York City), 1947.

Cock-a-Doodle Dandy (three-scene; first produced in Newcastle upon Tyne, England, at People's Theatre, December 11, 1949), Macmillan (London), 1949.

Hall of Healing, Bedtime Story, and *Time to Go* (also see below; one-act plays; all first produced in New York City at Yugoslav-American Hall, May 7, 1952).

The Bishop's Bonfire: A Sad Play within the Tune of a Polka (first produced in Dublin at Gaeity Theatre, February 28, 1955), Macmillan (New York City), 1955.

The Drums of Father Ned (first produced in Lafayette, IN, at Little Theatre, April 25, 1959), St. Martin's (New York City), 1960.

Behind the Green Curtains, Figuro in the Night, and *The Moon Shines on Kylenamoe* (three plays; all first produced Off-Broadway at Theatre de Lys, 1962), St. Martin's, 1961.

The Harvest Festival: A Play in Three Acts, New York Public Library, 1979.

AUTOBIOGRAPHIES

I Knock at the Door: Swift Glances Back at Things That Made Me, Macmillan (New York City), 1939.

Pictures in the Hallway, Macmillan (New York City), 1942.

Drums Under the Windows, Macmillan (London), 1945, Macmillan (New York City), 1946.

Inishfallen, Fare Thee Well, Macmillan (New York City), 1949.

Rose and Crown, Macmillan (New York City), 1952.

Sunset and Evening Star, Macmillan (New York City), 1954.

Mirror in My House: The Autobiographies of Sean O'Casey, two volumes (Volume 1 contains *I Knock at the Door: Swift Glances Back at Things That Made Me, Pictures in the Hallway,* and *Drums Under the Windows;* Volume 2 contains *Inishfallen, Fare Thee Well, Rose and Crown,* and *Sunset and Evening Star*), Macmillan (New York City), 1956, published as *Autobiographies,* two volumes, Macmillan (London), 1963.

OMNIBUS VOLUMES

Two Plays: Juno and the Paycock and The Shadow of a Gunman, Macmillan (New York City), 1925.

Five Irish Plays (contains *Juno and the Paycock, The Shadow of a Gunman, The Plough and the Stars, The End of the Beginning,* and *A Pound on Demand*), Macmillan (London), 1935.

Collected Plays (contains *Juno and the Paycock, The Shadow of a Gunman, The Plough and the Stars, The End of the Beginning, A Pound on Demand, The Silver Tassie, Within the Gates, The Star Turns Red, Purple Dust, Red Roses for Me, Halls of Healing, Oak Leaves and Lavender, Cock-a-Doodle Dandy, Bedtime Story,* and *Time to Go*), four volumes, Macmillan (London), 1949-52, St. Martin's, 1958.

Selected Plays of Sean O'Casey (contains *The Shadow of a Gunman, Juno and the Paycock, The Plough and the Stars, The Silver Tassie, Within the Gates, Purple Dust, Red Roses for Me, Bedtime Story,* and *Time to Go*), introduction by John Gassner, Braziller (New York City), 1954.

Juno and the Paycock and The Plough and the Stars, Macmillan, 1957.

Three Plays: Juno and the Paycock, The Shadow of a Gunman, The Plough and the Stars, Macmillan (London), 1957, St. Martin's, 1960.

Five One-Act Plays (contains *The End of the Beginning, A Pound on Demand, Hall of Healing, Bedtime Story,* and *Time to Go*), St. Martin's, 1958.

Three More Plays (contains *The Silver Tassie, Purple Dust,* and *Red Roses for Me*), introduction by J. C. Trewin, St. Martin's, 1965.

The Complete Plays of Sean O'Casey (includes all 15 plays in *Collected Plays,* plus *The Harvest Festival, Cathleen Listens In, Nannie's Night Out, The Bishop's Bonfire: A Sad Play within the Tune of a Polka, The Drums of Father Ned, Behind the Green Curtains, Figuro in the Night,* and *The Moon Shines on Kylenamoe*), five volumes, Macmillan (London), 1984.

Seven Plays by Sean O'Casey: A Student's Edition (includes *The Shadow of a Gunman, Juno and the Paycock, The Plough and the Stars, The Silver Tassie, Red Roses for Me, Cock-a-Doodle Dandy,* and *The Bishop's Bonfire*), St. Martin's, 1985.

UNDER NAME SEAN O'CATHASAIGH

Lament for Thomas Ashe, Fergus O'Connor (Dublin), 1917.

The Story of Thomas Ashe, Fergus O'Connor, 1917.

Songs of the Wren, two volumes, Fergus O'Connor, 1918.

More Wren Songs, Fergus O'Connor, 1918.

The Story of the Irish Citizen Army, Maunsel (Dublin and London), 1919.

OTHER

Windfalls: Stories, Poems, and Plays, Macmillan (New York City), 1934.

The Flying Wasp, Macmillan (London), 1937, B. Blom (New York City), 1971.

The Green Crow, Braziller, 1956.

Feathers from the Green Crow, edited by Robert Hogan, University of Missouri Press (Columbia), 1962.

Under a Colored Cap: Articles Merry and Mournful with Comments and a Song, St. Martin's, 1963.

Blasts and Benedictions (articles and stories), edited with an introduction by Ronald Ayling, St. Martin's, 1967.

The Sean O'Casey Reader: Plays, Autobiographies, Opinions, edited with an introduction by Brooks Atkinson, St. Martin's, 1968.

The Sting and the Twinkle: Conversations with Sean O'Casey, compiled by H. H. Mikhail, Barnes & Noble (New York City), 1974.

The Letters of Sean O'Casey, edited by David Krause, Macmillan, 1975.

Niall, Riverrun Press (New York City), 1992.

Work represented in numerous anthologies, including *Six Great Modern Plays,* Dell (New York City), 1956, and *One Act: Eleven Short Plays of the Modern Theater,* edited by Samuel Moon, Grove/Atlantic (New York City), 1987. Wrote for Irish nationalist and labor journals in the early 1900s; drama critic, *Time and Tide,* during the 1930s.

ADAPTATIONS: Pictures in the Hallway was adapted by Paul Shyre and published by Samuel French as the two-act play under the same title, 1956; *I Knock at the Door: Swift Glances Back at Things That Made Me* was adapted by Shyre and published by Dramatists Play Service as the two-act play *I Knock at the Door,* 1958; *Drums under the Windows* was adapted by Shyre and published by A. Meyerson under the same title, 1960.

SIDELIGHTS: Sean O'Casey rose from the Dublin slums to become one of the most esteemed dramatists of the twentieth century. When O'Casey was six years old his father died, leaving a Protestant family of thirteen to fend for themselves in predominantly Catholic Dublin. O'Casey, the youngest child in the family, suffered from a chronic eye disease that threatened him with blindness throughout his life. Because of this he was seldom able to attend school, but taught himself to read and write by the age of thirteen. He then became a drama enthusiast, reading

works by Shakespeare and Dion Boucicault, and began performing in local theatre groups.

During his early years O'Casey supported himself by working as a common laborer. He continued his self-education and joined the Gaelic League, learned to speak, read, and write fluent Gaelic, and Gaelicized his name from John Casey to Sean O'Cathasaigh, under which his writings of that time were published. He soon became involved with the Irish struggle for freedom from England, joining the Irish Republican Brotherhood, an underground group which went on to help plan the Easter Rising in 1916. At the age of thirty, O'Casey began to devote his energies to the Irish labor movement headed by Jim Larkin, helping to fight the appalling living and working conditions of his fellow workers. He served under Larkin as the first secretary of the Irish Citizen Army, wrote articles for the labor union's newspaper, and helped organize a transport strike in 1913. He resigned his post, however, in 1914 when he was unable to prevent a rival group, the Irish Volunteers, from weakening the labor union.

In his mid-thirties O'Casey returned to his previous interest in drama and began writing plays to express his concern for the effects of the Irish rebellion on average Dubliners like himself. His first play to be produced was *The Shadow of a Gunman,* followed by *Juno and the Paycock* and *The Plough and the Stars.* Critic Kevin Sullivan remarked that O'Casey's "reputation for genius begins, and I think ends," with these three plays. "That in any event is the commonly accepted critical judgment on O'Casey which only his most fervent admirers . . . would care to dispute." In Robert Hogan's critical view, the negative reception of O'Casey's later plays may be attributed to most critics' unquestioning acceptance of the belief that "when O'Casey left for England, he left his talent behind on the North Circular Road." Yet, Hogan himself argued that "you can only prove the worth of a play by playing it," and having staged or performed in five of O'Casey's later plays, he asserted that "most of O'Casey's late work is eminently, dazzlingly good."

O'Casey submitted several of his first playwriting attempts to the Abbey Theatre, which was headed by William Butler Yeats and Lady Gregory. The Abbey finally accepted *The Shadow of a Gunman* for production in 1923. The play is a tragic story of a poet and a peddler who become inadvertently involved in the guerrilla warfare of the Irish Republican Army (IRA) and the British soldiers in Dublin during the

1920s. Seumas Shields, a peddler, allows Donal Davoren, a struggling poet, to stay in his tenement room. Donal is mistaken by the neighbors for an IRA fighter and one of them, Minnie Powell, falls in love with the image of Donal as a romantic poet-gunman. An actual patriot hides explosives in Seumas's room and, when guards raid the tenement, Minnie moves the bombs to her own room in order to save Seumas and Donal. As a result, Minnie is arrested and then accidentally killed in a cross-fire between Irish patriots and British guards.

Seumas's room, cluttered with religious icons, pots and pans, a typewriter, flowers, and books, is the setting for both acts of *The Shadow of a Gunman*. Bernice Schrank noted that "the setting creates an atmosphere of chaos congenial to the theme of breakdown which runs throughout the play." O'Casey's explicit stage directions call for a messy room to imply the confused psychological states of Donal and Seumas, as well as the confusion of the country.

O'Casey's second play, *Juno and the Paycock*, was considered by T. E. Kalem to be "one of the granitic masterworks of modern dramatic art." This tragicomedy studies the effects of Dublin's post-war disturbances on a tenement family in 1922. The head of the family is Captain Jack Boyle, who struts about from pub to pub like a peacock (paycock) while his wife Juno struggles to make ends meet at home. The family is without income because the Captain is unemployed, his son Johnny has been injured in the fight for independence, and his daughter Mary has joined the workers strike. The family rejoices when Mary's suitor, lawyer Charlie Bentham, informs the Boyles that they are to inherit half the property of a rich relative. They begin to buy lavishly on credit and the Captain promises to give up drinking and look for work. When the interpretation of the will turns out to be erroneous, Bentham skips town, creditors repossess the new merchandise, and Mary discovers that she is pregnant.

William A. Armstrong noted that the family's reaction to these events provides "a continuous contrast between the masculine and the feminine personages, from which the women emerge as far superior to the men because of their capacity for love, altruism, and wisdom. The men in the play are all deluded, self-centered, and hypocritical." The Captain and Johnny turn viciously against Mary when they learn of her pregnancy, while Bentham and another boyfriend both desert her. Juno, on the other hand, is supportive and gives Mary sensible advice in her time of need.

Among the play's most noteworthy aspects, according to Armstrong, are its "modulated movement from the apparently comic to the grievously catastrophic," and the paralleling of domestic and national themes as represented by the treachery, desertion, and dissolution occurring both among the Boyles and the Irish people. Bernard Benstock also praised the characterization of the Captain as "probably O'Casey's finest achievement," and the first presentation of a character type that he used in many of his later plays: "the indolent, self-indulgent braggart whom he saw at the crux of the paralytic condition in Irish life, but whose boisterous wit and elan always brought him at least halfway back to redemption."

The final drama of O'Casey's tragicomic trilogy about the Irish struggle for independence is *The Plough and the Stars,* whose title was taken from the symbols on the Irish Citizen Army flag. The play occurs in 1916, just before and during the Easter Rebellion. The plot revolves around Nora Clitheroe, a young bride who is expecting a baby. She unsuccessfully tries to prevent her husband, Jack, from leaving to become a troop commander in the IRA. In his absence, chaos ensues. The tenement neighbors join in the looting of Dublin. Nora loses her baby and goes mad; when word comes that Jack has died in the fighting, she cannot even be told. The play closes as a neighbor is fatally shot trying to protect Nora from stray bullets as she cries for Jack's help, still unaware of his death.

During the fourth Abbey performance of this play, a riot erupted in the audience. Benstock observed that "the same Dubliners who were being dissected and lampooned in . . . O'Casey's first two comic tragedies sat in the theatre and roared at themselves, until the full brunt of O'Casey's satire struck home in *The Plough and the Stars*." The blunt realism of O'Casey's depiction of sex and religion even offended some of the actors, and several refused to speak their lines. Another reason for the uproar was that the people were accustomed to viewing Ireland as a fair land with the national fighters as hero-figures. But in *The Plough and the Stars* and his other plays, the heroes are noncombatants, usually women who manage to survive the tragedies of war. "For O'Casey the essential reality of war, revolutionary or otherwise, no matter how splendid the principle for which it is fought, is pain, and pain dominates the last half of *The Plough and the Stars:*

fear, madness, miscarriage, and death," noted Julius Novick. "No wonder the Nationalists rioted when the play was new; they did not want to see the seamy side of their glorious struggle."

Disturbed by the rioting, O'Casey moved to London in 1926. He continued to write, but his next play, *The Silver Tassie,* was rejected by Yeats for production at the Abbey Theatre. Although most of the play is written in a naturalist style, O'Casey used an expressionistic dream structure, a distorted setting, and stylized action in the second act. "Yeats told O'Casey that the play suffered from both inadequate technical prowess and imaginative unconvincingness," Richard Gilman related. O'Casey was bitter about the rejection and kept up a feud with Yeats for years because of it. He even published the correspondence concerning the rejection, claiming that Yeats had decided not to accept the play before he ever saw it. Denis Donoghue asserted: "Yeats made a critical error in rejecting the play, but the published correspondence shows that he was scrupulously honorable in reaching his decision. . . . The strongest argument against Yeats . . . is that *The Silver Tassie,* whatever its faults, was demonstrably superior to many of the plays that the Abbey had already accepted. But Yeats' critique of the play is formidable, and not all foolish or shallow."

After the rioting over *The Plough and the Stars* and Yeats's rejection of *The Silver Tassie,* O'Casey was convinced that he could never achieve artistic freedom in Ireland. He remained in London, living "in stubborn exile a far remove from the people and places that fed his imagination and stirred his deepest feelings," reflected Sullivan. Although O'Casey never returned to Ireland, he and Yeats reconciled after several years, and his plays were once again produced at the Abbey Theatre.

When O'Casey began to write for the theatre he was a dedicated socialist, but Benstock said that despite this, "the early tenement plays are devoid of propagandistic evidence. He concentrated on real events, their complexities and their multiple effects on the people he knew, rarely showing his hand to his audience." Armstrong noted that "the topical and the local elements in O'Casey's early plays are so strong that some critics belittled him as nothing more than a photographic realist who merely shuffled together for the stage familiar details of life in the Dublin slums during the time of the Troubles. This criticism is invalid, for O'Casey . . . has the myth-maker's great gift of discerning archetypal characters and situations, of distilling from everyday elements a quintessence of life far superior to the products of any documentary form of realism."

Even after his exile to England, O'Casey's "subject matter remained almost exclusively Irish, with only one or two exceptions, and for over thirty years he kept in touch with political and social changes in Ireland, mirroring them in his new plays and remaining a persistent critic of essential elements of Irish life under the Republic," Benstock noted. He continued to experiment with Expressionism in everything from morality plays to comic fantasies. Although his stylization did not succeed in *The Silver Tassie,* Joan Templeton declared that "the techniques of Expressionism figure significantly in the success of the late comedies."

Among his more successful later plays are *Purple Dust* and *Cock-a-Doodle-Dandy.* Most of these plays are comic pastorals containing the message that "merriment and joy are the primary virtues in a world that has denounced them too long," stated Templeton. O'Casey often attempted to present a serious message through the comic mode, but this method did not always fare well. Benstock noted that the "technique in these late comedies parallels that of the Dublin plays in their blend of the tragic and the pathetic with the wildly comic, but with strong elements of fantasy for leavening. Supernatural birds, superhuman heroes, mysterious priests who stir the youth to rebellion—all embodiments of the Life Force—take command in the more optimistic of the plays. . . . But in the more somber dramas, despite the many flashes of hilarity and song, the mood of bitterness predominates." Hogan said of the late plays that "by their verve, vitality, and brilliance, they and not the early masterpieces may ultimately prove to be O'Casey's great contribution to the theatre."

Written in 1918, O'Casey's *The Harvest Festival* prefigured much of the playwright's later works, including *Juno and the Paycock, Red Roses for Me,* and *The Star Turns Red.* The only survivor of three plays the playwright submitted to the Abbey Theatre early in his career, *Harvest Festival* takes place in the city of Dublin during the 1913 labor uprising. The drama, which was rejected by the Abbey, later abandoned by its author, and resigned to an archive until its publication in 1980, incorporates a dramatic irony grounded in O'Casey's characteristic realism as the violence of the streets is carried into the homes of the urban poor, and from there into the sanctuary of the Church. While noting that the work, which O'Casey wrote while he himself was employed as a member of the laboring class, is mature in its view of the world, *Booklist* reviewer Penelope Mesic noted that *Harvest Festival* "is strident, inartistic, and obvious in its juxtaposition of laborer and lord." However, the work is valuable to students of O'Casey, who can see the foundations of many of his later characters, settings, and themes. Of additional interest to O'Casey scholars is his partial revision of the first act, which is included as an appendix.

In 1939 O'Casey published the first book of his six-volume, part-fictional autobiography. The autobiographies have been said to contain many literary faults and have often been brushed aside as the work of an established writer's old age. But Gilman claimed that they were "perhaps the most durable of O'Casey's contributions." In addition to providing valuable insight into O'Casey's personality and writing methods, these volumes contain many fascinating passages about important figures such as Yeats, Lady Gregory, T. P. O'Connor, and George Bernard Shaw, and serve as important social documents of the period.

The Letters of Sean O'Casey supplements the autobiographies with numerous letters to, from, and about O'Casey. Sullivan noted that the letters emphasize O'Casey's "generosity, his incredible energy and resilience," as well as his "perverse affection" for poverty "because it was *his* way of life," and his impatience "with any opinion that is not his own and, we suspect, precisely *because* it is not his own." Donoghue thought the letters presented O'Casey as "the most quarrelsome writer in Ireland, a notoriously quarrelsome country. . . . O'Casey brought his Ireland with him, and held on to its rancor wherever he happened to be; London, Devon, New York." Nevertheless, a *New Yorker* critic concluded that "his grievances were, for the most part, real, and they are, even now, heartbreaking to read about."

Some critics have recently questioned O'Casey's place in literary history as one of the great modern playwrights. Gilman contended that "O'Casey can't bear the weight of such an apotheosis. . . . There are too many bad and even deeply embarrassing plays in his oeuvre (*Within the Gates, The Star Turns Red, The Bishop's Bonfire*, et al.) and too many esthetic sins of naivete, rhetorical excess, sentimentality and tendentiousness in all but his very best work." Gilman suggested that O'Casey's reputation has less to do with his art than with other circumstances: "the sterility of the English-speaking theater in the twenties when he came to prominence with his 'Dublin' plays at the Abbey Theatre; his ferocious battle with censorship; his own 'dramatic' story—slum childhood, self-education, lifelong nearblindness, self-exile."

Denis Donoghue declared that O'Casey's "career as an important dramatist came and went within five years. A man who writes *The Shadow of a Gunman* in 1923, *Juno and the Paycock* in 1924, *The Plough and the Stars* in 1926 and *The Silver Tassie* in 1928 should have the luck to continue writing good plays or the prudence to withdraw into dignity and silence. . . . But O'Casey lapsed into bad plays, hysterical essays, hectic reminiscences, blasts against the world, benedictions lavished upon communism, atheism, Welsh nationalism." Sullivan agreed, claiming that "the experimental plays . . . are interesting as experiments but hardly memorable as works of art. Sean O'Casey was above all a passionate man and his genius, if granted, is concentrated in this quality of his life which only occasionally carried over into the work."

Despite this criticism, Irma S. Lustig reminds us that "it is unjust to obscure O'Casey's farsightedness . . . by recalling only the strident means by which he was driven to express his views. . . . Politically a realist as well as a humanitarian, he predicted the global successes of socialism, especially if there were repeated wars. He foresaw the consequences of dividing Ireland, and the impossibility of 'classless' nationalist struggle. He challenged the exaltation of reckless violence." According to Benstock, O'Casey developed "a voice of his own, a style of his own, and a body of artistic work that reflected his personality and thinking with flair and color." Benstock concluded that, "Sean O'Casey stands as Irish drama almost by himself—and one of the best dramatists writing in the English language in his time in any country."

BIOGRAPHICAL/CRITICAL SOURCES:

BOOKS

Armstrong, William A., *Sean O'Casey*, Longman (New York City), 1967.

Benstock, Bernard, *Sean O'Casey*, Bucknell University Press (Cranbury, NJ), 1970.

Contemporary Literary Criticism, Gale (Detroit), Volume 1, 1973, Volume 5, 1976, Volume 9, 1979, Volume 11, 1979, Volume 15, 1980, Volume 88, 1995.

Dictionary of Literary Biography, Volume 10: *Modern British Dramatists, 1900-1945,* Gale, 1982.

Kilroy, Thomas, editor, *Sean O'Casey: A Collection of Critical Essays,* Prentice-Hall (Englewood Cliffs, NJ), 1975.

O'Casey, Eileen, *Cheerio, Titan: The Friendship between George Bernard Shaw and Sean O'Casey,* Scribner (New York City), 1989.

Schrank, Bernice, *Sean O' Casey: A Research and Production Sourcebook,* Greenwood, 1996.

PERIODICALS

Booklist, June 15, 1980, p. 1464.
British Book News, September 1980, pp. 562-63.
Choice, July/August, 1980, p. 674.
Modern Drama, May, 1971; March, 1974.
MOSAIC, fall, 1977.
Nation, March 20, 1972; July 19, 1975.
New Republic, April 26, 1975.
Newsweek, January 15, 1973; March 31, 1975.
New Yorker, March 11, 1972; January 13, 1973; May 5, 1975.
New York Times Book Review, March 16, 1975.
South Atlantic Quarterly, summer, 1976.
Time, March 27, 1972; November 18, 1974.
Times Literary Supplement, Muly 17, 1969, p. 771; January 2, 1976; August 14, 1981; April 19, 1985.
Village Voice, November 29, 1976.
Virginia Quarterly Review, summer, 1975.*

* * *

O'CATHASAIGH, Sean
See O'CASEY, Sean

* * *

ODETS, Clifford 1906-1963

PERSONAL: Born July 18, 1906, in Philadelphia, PA; died August 14, 1963, in Los Angeles, CA; son of Louis J. (a printer and company vice-president) and Pearl (Geisinger) Odets; married Luise Rainer (an actress), January 8, 1937 (divorced May, 1940); married Bette Grayson (an actress), May 14, 1943 (died, 1954); children: (second marriage) Nora, Walt. *Education:* Attended secondary school in New York, New York. *Religion:* Jewish.

CAREER: Playwright. Left school at age fourteen; worked as actor in local New York City theatre groups, vaudeville performer, radio play and gag writer, and as radio broadcaster; acted character parts in traveling stock theatre productions and small parts in Broadway plays, 1923-28; played juvenile roles in New York Theatre Guild productions, 1928-30; founding member and actor with Group Theatre, New York City, 1930-35; screenwriter in Hollywood, California, 1935-37; returned to New York and remained associated with Group Theatre, 1937-41; screenwriter and producer in Hollywood, 1941-61; worked in television, beginning 1961. Theatre director.

MEMBER: League of American Writers, Actors' Equity Association, Dramatists Guild, Screen Writers Guild.

AWARDS, HONORS: New Theatre League award and Yale Drama Prize, both 1935, both for *Waiting for Lefty;* Award of Merit Medal from American Academy of Arts and Letters, 1961.

WRITINGS:

PLAYS

Awake and Sing! (three-act; first produced on Broadway at Belasco Theatre, February 19, 1935; copyrighted in 1933 under title *I Got the Blues*), Covici-Friede, 1935 (also see below).

Waiting for Lefty [and] *Till the Day I Die: Two Plays* (the former, one-act; the latter, seven scene; both first produced on Broadway at Longacre Theatre, March 26, 1935), Covici-Friede, 1935 (also see below).

Paradise Lost (three-act; first produced on Broadway at Longacre Theatre, December 9, 1935), Random House, 1936 (also see below).

Golden Boy (three-act; first produced on Broadway at Belasco Theatre, November 4, 1937), Random House, 1937 (also see below).

Rocket to the Moon (three-act; first produced on Broadway at Belasco Theatre, November 24, 1938), Random House, 1939 (also see below).

Night Music: A Comedy in Twelve Scenes (three-act; first produced on Broadway at Broadhurst Theatre, February 24, 1940), Random House, 1940.

Clash by Night (two-act; first produced on Broadway at Belasco Theatre, December 27, 1941), Random House, 1942.

The Russian People (three-act; adapted from the play by Konstantin Simonov), first produced in New York at Guild Theatre, December 29, 1942.

The Big Knife (three-act; first produced on Broadway at American National Theatre and Academy, February 24, 1949), Random House, 1949 (also see below).

The Country Girl (three-act; first produced on Broadway at Lyceum Theatre, November 10, 1950), Viking, 1951, published as *Winter Journey,* Samuel French, 1955.

The Flowering Peach (three-act), first produced on Broadway at Belasco Theatre, December 28, 1954.

Also author of *I Can't Sleep,* 1936, and of the unproduced plays *9-10 Eden Street, The Silent Partner, The Law of Flight, By the Sea, The Seasons,* and *The Tides of Fundy.*

OMNIBUS VOLUMES

Three Plays (contains *Awake and Sing!, Waiting for Lefty,* and *Till the Day I Die*), Covici-Friede, 1935.

Six Plays of Clifford Odets (contains *Awake and Sing!, Waiting for Lefty, Till the Day I Die, Paradise Lost, Golden Boy,* and *Rocket to the Moon*), Modern Library, 1939, reprinted, 1963.

Golden Boy, Awake and Sing, [and] The Big Knife, Penguin, 1963.

Waiting for Lefty: And Other Plays, Grove, 1993.

SCREENPLAYS

The General Died at Dawn (adapted from the novel by Charles G. Booth), Paramount, 1936.

(And director) *None but the Lonely Heart* (adapted from the novel by Richard Llewellyn), RKO, 1944.

Deadline at Dawn (adapted from the novel by William Irish), RKO, 1946.

(With Zachary Gold) *Humoresque* (adapted from the short story by Fannie Hurst), Warner Brothers, 1946.

(With Ernest Lehman) *The Sweet Smell of Success* (adapted from the novella, *Tell Me About It Tomorrow,* by Lehman), United Artists, 1957.

(And director) *The Story on Page One,* Twentieth Century-Fox, 1960.

Wild in The Country (adapted from the novel *The Lost Country,* by J. R. Salamanca), Twentieth Century-Fox, 1961.

Also author of unproduced screenplays, *Gettysburg* and *The River Is Blue.*

OTHER

Also author of *The Time Is Ripe: The 1940 Journal of Clifford Odets,* 1988. Work included in *Famous American Plays of the Nineteen Thirties,* Dell, 1980 and *Awake and Singing: Seven Classic Plays from the American Jewish Repertoire,* Mentor, 1995.

SIDELIGHTS: A writer of the depression, Clifford Odets became an idol of the proletariat in the mid-1930s. Yet his own roots in the working class he treated so sympathetically in his works were not very deep: "I was a worker's son until the age of twelve," Odets once recalled. His father originally worked as a printer but eventually came to own his own printing plant. When he moved his family to Philadelphia, the senior Odets continued to prosper in business. In contrast, young Clifford remained intent on pursuing a less conventional life by writing, giving poetry recitals, and acting in various companies. His refusal to pursue the family business combined with his devotion to writing at times provoked conflict in his family. Once, Odets's obviously irate father smashed Clifford's typewriter. (Later, he replaced it.)

By 1930, Odets lived alone in New York City. There he grew increasingly aware of the destructive impact of the Great Depression as he observed the city's suffering masses. R. Baird Shuman reported that "as the depression continued, Odets grew more and more concerned about the plight of the working and middle classes. He looked about him for ways of ameliorating the widespread suffering and privation of the masses." Drawing on this sympathy, a sympathy he claimed first developed after reading Hugo's *Les Miserables* in 1918, Odets wrote his first play, *9-10 Eden Street.* Upon reading the play, Group Theatre associate Harold Clurman noticed most of the pain emitted from the work came from Odets himself. "Something in his past life had hurt him," Clurman speculated. "He was doubled up in pain, now, and in his pain he appeared to be shutting out the world." Whatever the source of his pain, Odets could not have been too encouraged about succeeding in acting or in writing—he "was not generally considered a gifted actor"; *9-10 Eden Street* was never produced.

Even Odets's association with the Group Theatre did not provide him enough influence to get his next play, *Awake and Sing,* staged. Despite its interest in the work, the financially weak organization could not risk the chance of introducing an unproven play-wright. Undaunted by this rejection, Odets wrote his next play, *Waiting for Lefty,* for a New Theatre League play contest. It won, and was soon being played by the awarding organization on Sunday nights. This brief exposure precipitated a glorious introduction into the New York Theatre world: within a year the most-talked-about playwright since Eugene O'Neill had three plays running on Broadway.

Waiting for Lefty is "undoubtedly the most angry play which Clifford Odets had ever produced," claimed Shuman. Based on the incidents of the 1934 New York City cab strike, it is set on a practically bare stage, a meeting hall where the taxi drivers' union is gathered to take a strike vote. As the strike talks progress the union members, who have been seated among the audience, come forth to defend their position. In the process, flashback reveals the hardship in each of their financially desperate lives. With word that the absent Lefty, their militant representative, has been killed by an assailant, the workers fervently join together in chanting "Strike! Strike! Strike!" The play's impact is made even more shattering by Odets's skillful manipulation of events as they lead to a climax. As Joseph Wood Krutch pointed out, "The pace is swift, the characterization is for the most part crisp, and the points are made, one after another, with bold simplicity."

In judging *Waiting for Lefty,* Krutch felt "there is no denying its effectiveness in achieving all it sets out to achieve." He conceded, however, that the play's "simplicity must be paid for at a certain price. The villains are mere caricatures and even the very human heroes occasionally freeze into stained glass attitudes. . . . No one, however, expects subtleties from a soap-box, and the interesting fact is that Mr. Odets invented a form which turns out to be a very effective dramatic equivalent of soap-box oratory."

Encouraged by the success of *Waiting for Lefty,* the Group Theatre finally decided to run *Awake and Sing.* Their decision was hardly a mistake: many critics include it among Odets's finest plays. *Awake and Sing* presents, with an "extraordinary freshness," the story of Ralph Berger as he frees "himself from his obsession with a purely personal rebellion against poverty which separates him from his girl and determines to throw himself with enthusiasm into the class struggle." Odets's ability in bringing life into his play fascinated Alfred Kazin: "In Odets's play there was a lyric uplifting of blunt Jewish

speech, boiling over and explosive, that did more to arouse the audience than the political catch words that brought the curtain down. Everybody on that stage was furious, kicking, alive—the words, always real but never flat, brilliantly authentic like no other theater speech on Broadway, aroused the audience to such delight that one could feel it bounding back and uniting itself with the mind of the writer."

The Broadway success of Odets's proletariat themes brought him sudden critical attention. One critic called him "one of the few American playwrights who is worth thinking about at all." Many did think about him, but not so receptively; *Waiting for Lefty* was banned in seven cities. His suspected affiliations with the Communist party only increased the controversy surrounding him. Although Odets had belonged to the party for an eight-month span in 1934, he later quit, claiming it interfered with his freedom to write. He also joined in a delegation traveling to Cuba in 1935 to investigate conditions there. The group was deported by the Cuban government after the first day. Such activities helped create a "Communist" stigma around Odets which continued for many years: in the 1950s he testified at the Senate McCarthy hearings.

The much-anticipated fourth Odets's play, *Paradise Lost,* marked an unexpected turning point in his career. It failed miserably, but not before the success of his earlier works had made him an attractive candidate for a Hollywood screenwriting job. The decision racked Odets; he saw the lure of Hollywood and its promise of financial success shadowed by his devotion to the Group Theatre and its atmosphere of artistic freedom. Moved by the reasoning that he could help finance the Theatre with his Hollywood earnings, Odets decided to leave. In doing so, he incurred the scorn of many who accused him of abandoning his proletarian ideals for Hollywood's big money. Response to his first screenplay, *The General Died at Dawn,* was made in the light of his plays. One disappointed critic asked, "Odets, where is thy sting?"

While the impact of the Hollywood move on Odets's career has been debated, at least one change is certain: his next plays gained a much broader audience. In *Golden Boy,* Odets continued to probe the themes of his previous plays but kept his political and economic theories in the background. The story of a young Italian boy who abandons the fiddle for a fighting career, *Golden Boy* re-established Odets's reputation as a leading dramatist. Stark Young felt "his theatrical gift most appears . . . in the dialogue's avoidance of the explicit. The explicit, always to be found in poor writers trying for the serious, is the surest sign of a lack of talent. . . . Mr. Odets is the most promising writer our theatre can show." Viewing his career in retrospect, Walter Kerr affirmed that Hollywood had at least not stolen Odets's playwriting sting: "Odets wrote *Golden Boy* at the height of his powers as an angry, moralizing neo-realist, and it remains his most successful play."

Drawing on his belief that "the more talented the Marxian dramatist the less sharply his plays are set from the best work of writers holding different political opinions," Krutch felt that in many respects Odets's next play, *Rocket to the Moon,* was his finest. It was the last play to evoke major comparisons with his earlier Marxist works and their view of American life. Barry Hyams felt it similar to *Waiting for Lefty* and *Golden Boy,* for these plays "did not attempt to speak *for* America. They spoke *of* America, of its indestructible good nature. . . . The shipping clerk could feel like Paul Bunyan. His nature was wedded to Walt Whitman. . . . His testament was that the human being not be nullified."

In 1940 Odets began keeping a journal, recording his thoughts and feelings on his work, career, and the people he worked with. Called *The Time Is Ripe,* the diary was intended to be published the following year, and was meant to be instructive to young writers. In it he documents his wonder at the success he was enjoying, writes of socializing with the country's elite artists and literary figures, and comments candidly about the difficulties he was having writing and about his worries for the future of his career. Critic Richard Christiansen wrote in the Chicago *Tribune Books* in 1988 (when the journal was finally published) that the work "shows us a writer cut loose from his moorings and drifting. The first great burst of talent that rocketed Odets to fame was over, and it was never to be equaled." Christiansen stated, however, that there "isn't a page in the journal that doesn't have something interesting to say about the times, the manners and the people Odets knew." Harold Cantor, though, writing in the *American Book Review,* averred that *The Time Is Ripe* "is the work of a writer with an instinctive knack for the telling phrase, apt descriptions of people and places, the singular anecdote and significant generalization."

Nonetheless, just as he feared when he was keeping the journal, Odets's later plays were marked by moments of genuine praise but failed to capture the critical acclaim of the earlier works. *Night Music* was a "lyric improvisation . . . on the basic homelessness of the little man in the big city," wrote Harold Clurman. "It is charmingly sentimental, comically poetic, airy and wholly unpretentious." But, Clurman continued, "in *Night Music* Odets is far more wistful than angry." In *The Big Knife,* a portrait of life in Hollywood, John Gassner thought Odets proved he "had lost none of his theatrical vigor and that no one writing realistic drama . . . can surpass his power to write with an explosive force and with a wild and swirling poetry of torment and bedevilment. . . . If *The Big Knife* is not a successfully realized play. . . , it is because Odets, a product of the agitated left-wing theatre of the 1930s, is heir to its major faults—to the tendency to put too much of the blame on society and too little on the individual." Another play, *The Country Girl,* enjoyed tremendous success on Broadway and had "a certain honesty and considerable power." But still, said Clive Barnes, it was "by no means, a great play."

The Flowering Peach, Odets's last play, marked a significant conclusion to his playwriting career, as it confronted the author's declining political commitment. Shuman found in the play, a retelling of the Noah's ark story, evidence that "Odets seemed to find again the proper vehicle for what he wanted to say: . . . beyond hope and despair lies the desperate idea of *hope.*" Gassner, on the other hand, expressed disappointment in these "doubts and vacillations. . . . It seemed as if Odets, with the example of generations of men before him, had given up hopes for a better world and is ready to accept humanity on its own second best terms." Gerald Rabkin demonstrated, however, that the tone of acceptance inherent in *The Flowering Peach* can be interpreted differently. He believed "the significance of the play lies in the fact that Odets finally attempted to come to terms with the esthetic consequences of the loss of his political commitment. . . . The essence of *The Flowering Peach* is the acceptance of the loss of political faith. . . . Odets is basically concerned with man's reaction to cosmic injustice, his attempt to construct a means whereby he can *accept* this injustice. It is this concept of acceptance which dominates *The Flowering Peach.*"

In general, whatever faults there have been in Odets's plays have been transcended by his writing skill, especially in character presentation and language. "What has been impressive in Mr. Odets's plays," declared *Commonweal* reviewer Grenville Vernon, "has not been their ideas, which are pretty confused, or their structure, which has been pretty melodramatic, but the fact that the characterizations and the dialogue have a bite and an originality of turn which set them apart from the somewhat pallid characters and dialogues of most modern plays." Edith Isaacs, too, noticed "each of Odets's faults has almost its counterpart in creative quality. Against his extreme subjectiveness can be placed his wise desire to express the nature and the problems of the people that he knows. . . . Against the fact that he himself does most of the talking in his plays, there is the fact that the talk is exceptionally alive and theatrical, speech for an actor's tongue. Against the fact that the majority of his characters are cliches, the recognition that in almost every play there is at least one that is a real creation . . . one that has three dimensions and a soul."

While most critics at least respect Odets's contribution to the American theatre, there are some who feel he barely deserves that. John Simon called Odets "a well-meaning, mildly skillful hack, like the rest of our thirties dramatists. A hack who had lost his nerve." In a similar opinion, Brendan Gill declared: "The fact is that Odets has always been an absurdly overpraised playwright, and it is odd, looking back over his career, to recall the wringing of hands that took place when he seemed to abandon a lofty purpose on Broadway for the fleshpots of Hollywood; the dream factory was his proper milieu, and if he did not prosper there as an artist it is because there was little of the artist in him capable of prospering anywhere."

Undoubtedly, the events of the 1930s spurred Odets to write his plays of social impact. In a time when America thirsted for some sort of hope, his romanticism in plays offering hope for the individual mattered more than the inconsistencies inherent in them. As Allan Lewis noted, "These final exhilarating but inconsistent affirmations were requirements of the play of the depression, for actuality was full of heartbreak and terror." Inevitably, then, as the despair of the depressed thirties faded, a force that had provided the impact for Odets's plays was lost. "It is true that Odets took up other issues in certain works," admitted Malcom Goldstein, "particularly in his late plays; but whether subsidiary or paramount, class-consciousness is never absent, regardless of the year and remoteness of his characters' concerns from money worries. Having taken a stand with the destitute proletariat, he could not recognize the fact of a rising employment index. After the first six plays. . . . Odets's work dwindled in relevance to the age, until

finally, after 1954, he could give the stage nothing at all."

BIOGRAPHICAL/CRITICAL SOURCES:

BOOKS

Clurman, Harold, *The Fervent Years,* Knopf, 1945, Harcourt, 1975.
Contemporary Literary Criticism, Gale, Volume 2, 1974, Volume 28, 1984.
Downer, Alan S., editor, *American Drama and Its Critic,* Chicago University Press, 1965.
Dusenbury, Winifred Loesch, *The Theme of Loneliness in American Drama,* University of Florida Press, 1960.
Gassner, John, *Theatre at the Crossroads,* Holt, 1960.
Gould, Jean, *Modern American Playwrights,* Dodd, 1966.
Kazin, Alfred, *Starting Out in the Thirties,* Little, Brown, 1965.
Krutch, Joseph Wood, *The American Drama Since 1918: An Informal History,* Braziler, 1957.
Lewis, Allan, *American Plays and Playwrights of the Contemporary Theatre,* Crown, 1965.
Mendelsohn, Michael J., *Clifford Odets: Humane Dramatist,* Everett/Edwards, 1969.
Rebkin, Gerald, *Drama and Commitment,* Indiana University Press, 1964.
Shuman, R. Baird, *Clifford Odets,* Twayne, 1962.
Simon, John, *Singularities: Essays on the Theatre, 1964-73,* Random House, 1975.

PERIODICALS

American Book Review, January, 1989, p. 4.
American Film, May, 1988, p. 28.
American Quarterly, winter, 1963.
Chicago Tribune—Books, August 21, 1988, p. 5.
Commentary, May, 1946.
Commonweal, December 16, 1938; March 28, 1952; December 3, 1971.
Drama Survey, fall, 1963.
Forum, May, 1949.
Library Journal, May 1, 1988, p. 88.
Nation, March 13, 1935; April 3, 1972.
New Republic, November 17, 1937; September 27, 1939; April 30, 1951.
New York, January 21, 1991, p. 55; April 4, 1994, p. 74.
New Yorker, January 22, 1938; March 25, 1972; January 21, 1991, p. 77; October 26, 1992, p. 119; May 31, 1993, p. 68; April 4, 1994, p. 94.

New York Review of Books, September 29, 1988, p. 37.

New York Times, December 24, 1971; March 16, 1972.

New York Times Book Review, October 30 1988, p. 40.

Publishers Weekly, May 13, 1988, p. 259.

Saturday Review of Literature, December 9, 1950.

South Atlantic Quarterly, winter, 1970; spring, 1972.

Theatre Arts, April, 1939; October, 1954; September, 1955.

Time, June 8, 1970.

Variety, July 20, 1988, p. 92; January 14, 1991, p. 118; March 21, 1994, p. 64.*

* * *

O'NEAL, Reagan
See RIGNEY, James Oliver, Jr.

* * *

O'REILLY, Jackson
See RIGNEY, James Oliver, Jr.

* * *

OSBORNE, Mary Pope 1949-

PERSONAL: Born May 20, 1949, in Fort Sill, OK; daughter of William P. (a U.S. Army colonel) and Barnette (Dickens) Pope; married Will Osborne (an actor and writer), May 16, 1976. *Education:* University of North Carolina at Chapel Hill, B.A., 1971.

ADDRESSES: Home and office—325 Bleecker St., New York, NY 10014.

CAREER: Writer. Has worked as a medical assistant in Monterey, CA, and as a travel agent in Washington, DC, and New York City; *Scholastic News Trials,* New York City, assistant editor, 1973-79.

WRITINGS:

JUVENILES

Run, Run as Fast as You Can (novel), Dial (New York City), 1982.

Love Always, Blue (novel), Dial, 1984.

Best Wishes, Joe Brady (novel), Dial, 1984.

Mo to the Rescue, Dial, 1985.

Last One Home (novel), Dial, 1986.

Beauty and the Beast, Scholastic, Inc. (New York City), 1987.

Christopher Columbus, Admiral of the Ocean Sea, Dial, 1987.

Pandora's Box, Scholastic, Inc., 1987.

(With husband, Will Osborne) *Jason and the Argonauts,* Scholastic, Inc., 1987.

(With W. Osborne) *The Deadly Power of Medusa,* Scholastic, Inc., 1988.

Mo and His Friends, Dial, 1989.

Favorite Greek Myths (Book-of-the-Month Club selection), Scholastic, Inc., 1989.

A Visit to Sleep's House (picture book), Knopf (New York City), 1989.

Moon-Horse (picture book), Knopf, 1990.

George Washington: Leader of a New Nation, Dial, 1990.

The Many Lives of Benjamin Franklin, Dial, 1990.

(Adaptor) *American Tall Tales,* Knopf, 1991.

Spider Kane and the Mystery under the May-Apple, Knopf, 1992.

Dinosaurs before Dark, Random House (New York City), 1992.

Spider Kane and the Mystery at Jumbo Nightcrawler's, Knopf, 1993.

(Adaptor) *Mermaid Tales from around the World,* Scholastic, Inc., 1993.

Mummies in the Morning, Random House, 1994.

Haunted Waters, Candlewick Press, 1994.

Molly and the Prince (picture book), Knopf, 1994.

(Adaptor) *Favorite Norse Myths,* Scholastic, Inc., 1996.

SIDELIGHTS: Mary Pope Osborne has distinguished herself as a versatile author for young readers. She has written novels for several different age groups, as well as produced picture book texts and nonfiction titles. Her novels for young adults frequently focus on the problems, conflicts, and difficult situations encountered by many adolescents. *Run, Run as Fast as You Can,* for example, relates the story of Hallie, who wants to join a group of popular girls at school; facing the clique's rejection as well as her younger brother's fatal illness, however, forces Hallie to reexamine her values. It is Osborne's treatment of this self-analysis that transforms the novel into what London *Times* contributor Jennie Ingham calls "a compulsively gripping story." Osborne presents similarly well-developed characters in her novel *Last One Home,* the story of Bailey, a young girl torn between her alcoholic mother and her father, who has just remarried. A *Publishers Weekly* writer notes that "all the characters, including the heedless mother whose abuses Bailey forgets in her wistful dreams, are skillfully humanized," while Phyllis Graves comments in *School Library Journal* that the author's "finely crafted characterization enhances this affecting story about the difficulties of coping."

In addition to her realistic fiction, Osborne has written more fantastic tales, such as *Haunted Waters,* a romance based on the nineteenth-century tale "Undine," by Baron de La Motte-Fouque. Undine, a daughter of the sea kingdom, is left as a baby on a fisherman's doorstep by her father, who wishes to bind his world with humanity. As an adult, Undine is the picture of innocent beauty, and she captures the heart of dashing Lord Huldebrand of Ringstetten. They marry, but are doomed by the spirits who rule her. Osborne's retelling of the fairy tale was well received. Sally Estes remarks in *Booklist,* "This quiet tale is eerily atmospheric and will appeal to the special reader." A *Publishers Weekly* writer calls it a "sweepingly romantic novel" with "irresistible momentum" and a "lush narrative. . . . Lustrous as a pearl."

Osborne's picture books have also been praised by many reviewers. In *Molly and the Prince,* the author created a fantasy involving a girl and her dog, who travel through a forest wonderland to discover the dog's hidden identity. "Unlike Disney-eque frog-prince stories, Osborne's . . . original tale touches the deep ground where children find secrets hidden from adult knowledge. Elegant prose and deceptively simple dialogue couch the rare accomplishment of a genuinely childlike voice," enthuses a *Publishers Weekly* reviewer. "Dog lovers and lovers of magic will respond to this brief but intense idyll," observes a writer for *Kirkus Reviews.* Another picture book, *Moonhorse,* was singled out by a *Kirkus* reviewer for its "gracefully phrased text."

Biography is another area in which Osborne has made a significant contribution, with her books on Benjamin Franklin and George Washington. *The Many Lives of Benjamin Franklin* "presents a clear picture of a man of his period," notes a *Kirkus Reviews* contributor. "Osborne gives a broader sense of Franklin's achievements by carefully setting them in their historical context." Phillis Wilson credits Osborne with conveying "a copious amount of infor-

mation on Franklin's multi-faceted life," but remarks that "a slightly less glowing tone and some insight into her subject's quirks and foibles would have rendered a more human account." And *George Washington: Leader of a New Nation* is lauded by Deborah Abbott in *Booklist* as "a pithy biography" that "reveals the human side of a man who set precedents still in effect 200 years after."

Osborne once told *CA:* "My childhood was spent on different Army posts with my parents, two brothers, and sister. We lived mostly in the southern United States with a three-year stay in Salzburg, Austria. When I was fifteen my father retired and my family settled permanently in North Carolina." After a series of jobs and travels, the author married actor Will Osborne, and "the day after our wedding we took off on a theatre tour. While on the road with Will, I began writing," Osborne relates. "In 1979, I wrote a young adult novel, *Run, Run as Fast as You Can,* about a girl whose family retires from the military and settles in the South. Dial Press bought the manuscript and my editor, Amy Ehrlich, helped me develop it. Amy has also been a big influence on my other [novels], *Love Always, Blue,* about a southern teenager who travels to Greenwich Village to visit her playwright father, and *Best Wishes, Joe Brady,* about a North Carolina girl who falls in love with an actor performing in a local dinner theatre—and *Last One Home,* a novel inspired by a scene I witnessed on the Florida Coast: a young girl leading a disheveled mother down a fishing pier. The girl became Bailey, and the book revolved around her coming to terms with the loneliness of having an alcoholic mother.

More recently, Osborne's work has taken several new directions. As the author noted, "I've been concentrating on mythology and fairy tale retellings, picture books and biographies," adding: "I've been very lucky in that I've been able to channel so many different interests into books for children and young people. I imagine I'll probably focus next on the natural world. After having lived exclusively in New York City for [over a decade], my husband and I now spend part of each week in a cabin in Pennsylvania, and as a result of this, I feel a new passion developing for animals and nature. The wonderful thing about a career as a children's book writer is that there are so many different forms in which to fill different sorts of content. Choosing the vehicle that will carry a new story or passion out into the world is half the fun."

BIOGRAPHICAL/CRITICAL SOURCES:

PERIODICALS

Baltimore Sun, May 16, 1982.
Booklist, October 15, 1985, p. 342; June 1, 1989, p. 1728; June 1, 1990, p. 1900; August, 1991, p. 2143; March 15, 1993, p. 1319; October 15, 1993, p. 436; April 1, 1994, p. 1466; November 1, 1994, p. 492; March 1, 1996, p. 1177.
Kirkus Reviews, May 15, 1990, p. 733; May 15, 1991, p. 678; July 1, 1991, p. 865; April 15, 1992, p. 541; August 1, 1992, p. 993; May 15, 1993, p. 667; August 1, 1993, p. 1006; August 15, 1994, p. 1137; January 1, 1996, p. 72.
New York Times Book Review, March 17, 1991, p. 27; June 7, 1992, p. 22.
Publishers Weekly, November 29, 1985, p. 49; March 21, 1986; June 21, 1991, p. 66; October 18, 1991, p. 62; March 23, 1992, p. 72; June 28, 1993, p. 77; January 10, 1994, p. 63; August 15, 1994, pp. 94, 96; January 22, 1996, p. 73.
School Library Journal, May, 1986.
Times (London), August 23, 1983.
Times Literary Supplement, September 30, 1983.
Washington Post Book World, April 7, 1996, p. 6.

*   *   *

OSTRIKER, Alicia (Suskin) 1937-

PERSONAL: Born November 11, 1937, in New York, NY; daughter of David (a civil service employee) and Beatrice (Linnick) Suskin; married Jeremiah P. Ostriker (a professor of astrophysics), December, 1958; children: Rebecca, Eve, Gabriel. *Education:* Brandeis University, B.A., 1959: University of Wisconsin, M.A., 1961, Ph.D., 1964. *Religion:* Jewish.

ADDRESSES: Home—33 Phillip Dr., Princeton, NJ 08540. *Office*—Department of English, Rutgers University, New Brunswick, NJ 08903.

CAREER: Rutgers University, assistant professor, 1965-68, associate professor, 1968-72, professor of English, 1972—.

AWARDS, HONORS: National Council on the Humanities summer grant, 1968; National Endowment for the Arts fellowship, 1976-77; Pushcart Prize, 1979; New Jersey Arts Council fellowship, 1980-81; Rockefeller Foundation fellowship, 1982; Guggenheim Foundation fellowship, 1984-85; William Carlos Williams Prize, Poetry Society of America, 1986, for *The Imaginary Lover;* Strousse Poetry Prize, *Prairie Schooner,* 1986; Edward Stanley Award, *Prairie Schooner,* 1994; Anna David Rosenberg Poetry Award, 1994; faculty fellow Rutgers Center for Historical Analysis, 1995-96.

WRITINGS:

POETRY

Songs, Holt (New York City), 1969.
Once More Out of Darkness, and Other Poems, Smith/Horizon Press (New York City), 1971, enlarged edition, Berkeley Poets Cooperative (Berkeley, CA), 1974.
A Dream of Springtime, Smith/Horizon Press (New York City), 1979.
The Mother/Child Papers, Momentum (Santa Monica, CA), 1980.
A Woman under the Surface: Poems and Prose Poems, Princeton University Press (Princeton, NJ), 1982.
The Imaginary Lover, University of Pittsburgh Press (Pittsburgh, PA), 1986.
Green Age, University of Pittsburgh Press, 1989.
The Crack in Everything, University of Pittsburgh Press, 1996.

OTHER

Vision and Verse in William Blake, University of Wisconsin Press (Madison), 1965.
(Editor) *William Blake: Complete Poems,* Penguin (New York), 1977.
Writing Like a Woman, University of Michigan Press (Ann Arbor), 1983.
Stealing the Language: The Emergence of Women Poets in America, Beacon, 1986.
Feminist Revision and the Bible, Blackwell (Cambridge, MA), 1992.
The Nakedness of the Fathers: Biblical Visions and Revisions, Rutgers University Press, 1994.

Contributor of poems and essays to literary reviews and magazines, including *American Poetry Review, Connotations: A Journal for Critical Debate, Emily Dickinson Journal, New Yorker,* and *Wallace Stevens Journal.*

SIDELIGHTS: Feminist critic Alicia Ostriker has published eight books of poetry and several books of feminist literary criticism that examine the relationship between gender and literature. In a comment that applies to both Ostriker's poetry and criticism, Amy Williams in *Dictionary of Literary Biography* notes how Ostriker "consistently challenges limitations. For discovery to take place there must be movement, and Ostriker refuses to stand still; each volume tries to uncover anew what must be learned in order to gain wisdom, experience, and identity. She is a poet who breaks down walls."

In Ostriker's feminist criticism, she argues that literature written by women is fundamentally different from that written by men. In *Stealing the Language: The Emergence of Women Poets in America* (1986), Ostriker asserts that women writers have produced poetry that is "explicitly female in the sense that the writers have chosen to explore experiences central to their sex." Furthermore, in their search to find an aesthetic that accommodates this expression, Ostriker claims that women poets are "challenging and transforming the history of poetry. They constitute a literary movement comparable to romanticism or modernism in our literary past."

These claims have evoked a wide range of response from reviewers. Frieda Gardner, writing in the *Women's Review of Books,* agrees that women have brought new subject matter to American poetry; the "thematic landscape" of literature now includes poems on "women's quests for self-definition, on the uses and treachery of anger, . . . female eroticism and, most impressively, on women poets' sweeping revision of Western mythology," Gardner relates. However, "lots of male poets grew fat on the 'butter and sugar' Ostriker calls peculiarly feminine," Mary Karr points out in a *Poetry* review. Daisy Aldan, writing in *World Literature Today,* concurs, taking exception to Ostriker's assumptions that women's poetry is naturally more visceral and necessarily less sophisticated in form and thought than that of men. Reviewers also question if poetry by women is unified by the concentrated "drive for power" that Ostriker sees in it. Nonetheless, states Karr, "those predisposed to feminist criticism will eagerly take up these pages. At the other extreme, certain critics and philosophers will shudder at the very thought of women generating language, a practice they interpret as exclusively masculine."

The Nakedness of the Fathers: Biblical Visions and Revisions (1994), offers "an imaginative and spiritual dialogue with characters and narratives of the Old Testament," writes Lynn Garrett in *Publishers Weekly.* By exploring the women's stories from the Bible—Sarah, Rachel, Esther, Ruth, Miriam—and speaking through their voices, Ostriker attempts to offer a more humanized and modernized reading of the Bible, and in doing so, she attempts to reconcile the revisionism of feminism with the traditions of Judaism. She presents Esther as a nice girl who uses her beauty to make her way in the world, and shows Job's wife as a bystander who must accept the "casual brutality of this world," according to Enid Dame in *Belles Lettres.* Ostriker's book is as grand and comprehensive as her subject, offering, notes Dame, "a retelling-with-commentary of Jewish scripture intertwined with a brilliant web of poems, stories, personal memoirs, scholarly observations, and speculative meditations." Ultimately, it is "in the reclamation of the Shekhina, or female aspect of God," states Dame, that Ostriker finds a reconciliation between Judaism and feminism.

In addition to her reputation as a feminist literary critic, Ostriker is also an accomplished poet. In 1986, the Poetry Society of America gave this recipient of numerous fellowships and grants the William Carlos Williams Prize for *The Imaginary Lover.* Ostriker "is at her best when most urbane and ironic" in these poems that look back at marriage from the perspective of mid-life, says *Times Literary Supplement* contributor Clair Wills. "The actions are melodramatic, but the recording consciousness is steady," Patricia Hampl relates in the *New York Times Book Review.* Since the poems often reflect on disappointment or loss, they have an elegiac tone. More noticeable, however, "is Mrs. Ostriker's tendency to locate a sustaining force for the rest of life—a force that is both passionate and honorable," Hampl observes. "This is evident in lines from 'Everywoman Her Own Theology,' in which Ostriker declares: 'Ethically, I am looking for / An absolute endorsement of loving-kindness.' At times, says Hampl, the poems lack music, but charm the reader with their "candor and thoughtfulness."

Green Age (1989) is a book of poems which blends "personal time, history and politics, and inner spirituality," writes Williams. As Robyn Selman notes in *Village Voice,* Ostriker's title denotes "the stage in a woman's life—after her children have left home, after the death of her parents—when her sense of herself is clear and muscular: a time of loss, but also of heightened awareness and passion." Ostriker offers love poems, poems which are forceful and persuasive, and poems which, according to a *Publishers Weekly* reviewer, "sympathize and nurture, affirming life," as when the poet states: "Friend, I could say / I've been alive a half a dozen moments / but that's not true / I've been alive my entire time / on this earth / I've been alive."

The poems in *The Crack in Everything* (1996) are "accomplished poems," writes a *Publishers Weekly* reviewer, which are "grounded in the details of a woman's daily life and speak with the appeal of an intelligent, sympathetic friend," making the poems feel as if they possess "a quality of being over-heard," writes Patricia Monaghan in *Booklist,* so that "reading them can seem like finding an especially lyrical journal." The topics of some of Ostriker's poems range from the rape of a mentally retarded girl by her high school classmates to the bombing of MOVE in Philadelphia, so that her poems feel, according to *Publishers Weekly,* as though "a broad-based politics enters this work routinely, like the morning news." The long sequence, "The Mastectomy Poems," which concludes the collection movingly address the poet's successful treatment for cancer, "in a frank and liberating clarity," states Steven Ellis in *Library Journal,* as Ostriker refers to how "cells break down, their membranes crushed / Where the condemned / Beg for forgetfulness."

According to Williams, Ostriker's voice is "personal, honest, and strong; her poetry incorporates family experiences, social and political views, and a driving spirit that speaks for growth and, at times, with rage."

BIOGRAPHICAL/CRITICAL SOURCES:

BOOKS

Contemporary Authors Autobiography Series, Volume 24, Gale (Detroit), 1996.
Dictionary of Literary Biography, Volume 120: *American Poets since World War II,* third series, Gale, 1992.

PERIODICALS

American Literature, October, 1987, p. 464.
American Poetry Review, July/August, 1981; July, 1986, p. 12.

Belle Lettres, summer, 1990, p. 30; fall, 1993, p. 56; spring, 1995, p. 44.
Booklist, April 15, 1986, p. 1176; February 15, 1987, p. 871; March, 1988, p. 25; September 1, 1989, p. 29; December 1, 1994, p. 1546; May 1, 1996, p. 1485.
Borderlands: The Texas Poetry Review, spring, 1993, pp. 80-6.
Choice, December, 1986, p. 627; July, 1987, p. 871; March, 1990, p. 1146.
Contemporary Literature, summer, 1988, pp. 305-10.
Criticism, fall, 1989, pp. 505-7.
Georgia Review, fall, 1987, p. 631.
Hiram Poetry Review, fall/winter, 1982.
Hudson Review, autumn, 1985, p. 516.
Iowa Review, spring, 1982.
Kliatt Young Adult Paperback Book Guide, fall, 1986, p. 34; April, 1988, p. 26.
Library Journal, May 1, 1986, p. 121; November 15, 1986, p. 100; January 1987, p. 57; September 15, 1989, p. 114; April 1, 1996, p. 87.
Literature and Psychology, 1992, pp. 71-83.
Michigan Quarterly Review, spring, 1991, pp. 354-66.
Ms., August, 1986, p. 75.
National Forum, summer, 1987, p. 45.
New Directions for Women, January, 1988, p. 17.
New York Times Book Review, July 20, 1986, p. 21; June 7, 1987, p. 15.
Poetry, March, 1983; February, 1987, p. 294; July, 1990, p. 226.
Poets and Writers, November-December, 1989, pp. 16-26.
Publishers Weekly, October 24, 1984; March 21, 1986, p. 79; October 24, 1986, p. 69; October 6, 1989, p. 94; November 14, 1994, p. 34; April 26, 1996, p. 63.
Religious Studies Review, April, 1989, p. 141.
San Francisco Chronicle, September 6, 1983.
Signs, winter, 1984, p. 384; autumn, 1988, p. 220; autumn, 1989, pp. 220-2.
Times Educational Supplement, August 28, 1987, p. 15.
Times Literary Supplement, July 10, 1987, p. 748.
Village Voice, February 6, 1990, p. 59.
Virginia Quarterly Review, spring, 1990, p. 65.
Wilson Library Bulletin, September, 1986, p. 85.
Women's Review of Books, April, 1987, p. 14.
World Literature Today, spring, 1987, p. 291.

—*Sketch by Robert Miltner*

P-Q

PAUL, Barbara 1931-

PERSONAL: Born June 5, 1931, in Maysville, KY. *Education:* Bowling Green State University, A.B., 1953; University of Redlands, M.A., 1957; University of Pittsburgh, Ph.D., 1969.

ADDRESSES: Home and office—5433 Elmer St. No. 1, Pittsburgh, PA 15232. *Agent*—Dominick Abel, 146 West 82nd St. 1-B, New York, NY 10024.

CAREER: Berry College, Mt. Berry, GA, instructor, 1957-61; Erskine College, Due West, SC, assistant professor and drama director, 1961-65; University of Pittsburgh, Pittsburgh, PA, part-time instructor, 1969-73; writer.

MEMBER: American Crime Writers League (former treasurer), Science Fiction Writers of America, Sisters in Crime (founder and first president, Genie Chapter), Novelists, Inc.

WRITINGS:

SCIENCE FICTION

An Exercise for Madmen, Berkley Publishing (New York City), 1978.
Pillars of Salt, Signet (New York City), 1979.
Bibblings, Signet, 1979.
Under the Canopy, Signet, 1980.
The Three-Minute Universe ("Star Trek" novel), Pocket Books (New York City), 1988.

MYSTERIES

The Fourth Wall, Doubleday (New York City), 1979.

Liars and Tyrants and People Who Turn Blue, Doubleday, 1980.
First Gravedigger, Doubleday, 1980.
Your Eyelids Are Growing Heavy, Doubleday, 1981.
The Renewable Virgin, Scribners (New York City), 1984.
A Cadenza for Caruso, St. Martin's (New York City), 1984.
Kill Fee, Scribners, 1985.
Prima Donna at Large, St. Martin's, 1985.
But He Was Already Dead When I Got There, Scribners, 1986.
A Chorus of Detectives, St. Martin's, 1987.
He Huffed and He Puffed, Scribners, 1989.
Good King Sauerkraut, Scribners, 1989.
In-Laws and Outlaws, Scribners, 1990.
You Have the Right to Remain Silent, Scribners, 1992.
The Apostrophe Thief, Scribners, 1993.
Fare Play, Scribners, 1995.

ADAPTATIONS: Story "All the Dogs of Europe" adapted as "Dream Girl" for television series *Tales from the Darkside,* January 19, 1986; novel *Kill Fee* adapted as *Murder C.O.D.* for National Broadcasting Co. (NBC-TV), September 21, 1990.

SIDELIGHTS: Barbara Paul's numerous mysteries reflect their author's lifelong interests in theatre and the fine arts. Paul was a drama instructor before turning to writing, and some of her best known mysteries revolve around staged plays, the theatrical community, or the world of opera in the early decades of the twentieth century. In Paul's debut mystery, *The Fourth Wall,* for instance, a sadistic prankster haunts the cast of a Broadway production, attacking everyone from the stage manager to the actors themselves. Three other novels, *A Cadenza for Caruso, Prima Donna at Large,* and *A Chorus of Detectives,* offer mysteries featuring notable American and French opera stars—including Caruso and Geraldine Ferrar.

Yet another of Paul's interests, antiques, informs the plot of her novel *First Gravedigger.* The narrator, a dishonest dealer named Earl Sommers, resorts to plotting murder when some of his spurious deals come to light. While never officially tied to the death of his superior, Amos Speer, Earl finds that the profit he expected to take by Speer's demise is littered with pitfalls that ultimately lead him into mortal danger. A *Publishers Weekly* reviewer called *First Gravedigger* "one for the must-read list," and a *Booklist* contributor cited the work for its "innovative, surprising narrative."

Beginning with *The Renewable Virgin* in 1984, Paul has written a series of novels featuring Marian Larch, a New York homicide detective who brings aspects of the feminine to her work solving crimes. Once again the theatre world provides venues for Paul's plots, as Larch teams with an actress friend, Kelly Ingram, to solve homicides in the theatrical community. According to Janice M. Bogstad in the *St. James Guide to Crime and Mystery Writers,* Paul's novels are exceptional for their "analysis of the darker facets of the human personality. She does not include whimsical elements, amusing turns of phrase, or individuals who provide comic relief for the grim plots. She creates in their stead brooding characters whose lives are made miserable by the circumstances of each case."

Paul, who has been described in *Publishers Weekly* as a "highly literate and witty author," is known for producing gripping plots with elements of revenge and musings on social and international issues. Bogstad concluded that the author "is not afraid to experiment with her writing style and her characters, in a time when the series novel predominates. Paul has created some memorable focal characters but gives us the promise of more variety to come."

BIOGRAPHICAL/CRITICAL SOURCES:

BOOKS

St. James Guide to Crime and Mystery Writers, St. James Press (Detroit, MI), 1996.

PERIODICALS

Best Sellers, March, 1981, p. 431.
Booklist, March 15, 1980, p. 1031; January 1, 1981, p. 615.
Library Journal, May 1, 1981, p. 996.
Publishers Weekly, November 5, 1979; October 31, 1980, p. 78; April 17, 1981, p. 51.

* * *

PEGLER, (James) Westbrook 1894-1969

PERSONAL: Born August 2, 1894, in Minneapolis, MN; died of cancer June 24, 1969, in Tucson, AZ; son of Arthur James (a journalist) and Frances (Nicholson) Pegler; married Julia Harpman (a reporter), August 28, 1922 (died, 1955); married Pearl W. Doane, 1959 (divorced, 1961); married Maud Towart, 1962. *Education:* Attended school in Illinois.

CAREER: United Press (now United Press International), telephone reporter in Chicago, IL, reporter and bureau manager in Texas, Des Moines, Iowa, and St. Louis, MO, 1912-16, correspondent in London, England, 1916-17, war correspondent with American Expeditionary Force, 1917-18, sports editor in New York City, 1919-25; *Chicago Tribune,* Chicago, IL, eastern sports correspondent, 1925-33; *New York World-Telegram and Sun,* New York City, syndicated columnist, 1933-44; King Features Syndicate, New York City, syndicated columnist, 1944-62; freelance writer and journalist, Tucson, AZ, 1962-69. *Military service:* U.S. Navy, 1918-19.

MEMBER: National Press Club (Washington, DC), Jonathan Club (Los Angeles).

AWARDS, HONORS: Pulitzer Prize for reporting, 1941, for expose of labor union racketeering; LL.D. from Knox College, 1943; Gold Medal award from Nassau County Bar Association, 1944; American Legion Award; two National Headliners Club awards, both for achievement in journalism; and numerous other citations.

WRITINGS:

(Contributor) *The Omnibus of Sport,* edited by Grantland Rice and Harford Powel, Harper (New York City), 1932.

'T Ain't Right, Doubleday (New York City), 1936.

The Dissenting Opinions of Mister Westbrook Pegler, Scribner (New York City), 1938.

George Spelvin, American, and Fireside Chats, Scribner, 1942, reprinted, Arno, 1972.

(Contributor) *The Fireside Book of Baseball,* edited by Charles Einstein, Simon & Schuster (New York City), 1956.

Contributor of articles to newspapers and journals, including *Jacksonville Chronicle* and *American Opinion.*

SIDELIGHTS: Westbrook Pegler's was one of the most recognizable names in journalism throughout much of the twentieth century. He began as a sportswriter in the years following the First World War and then, at the height of the Great Depression, became a nationally syndicated political columnist for whom no target was too dangerous or publicly revered. Pegler developed an outspoken, caustic style that he later used in "Fair Enough," his popular syndicated column on national affairs. According to a *Washington Post* reporter, Pegler established his reputation as "one of the most controversial Americans of his time" by using his typewriter "like a meat ax" on a long list of well known personalities and institutions.

Pegler's journalistic career began at age sixteen when United Press hired him to telephone short news stories to small dailies. By 1914 he had found work with the Scripps-Howard newspaper chain in cities as far-flung as New York, St. Louis, Dallas, and London. After brief service as a war correspondent—and a short stint in the Navy—he returned to America in 1919 and began writing sports wire stories for United Press. Soon he had developed his own column, "Six Short Pegs from Pegler," which drew him a national audience, and in 1925 the *Chicago Tribune* doubled his already hefty $125-per-week salary to be that paper's eastern sports editor. The *Tribune* was soon syndicating Pegler's offerings as "The Sporting Goods."

Among his other talents, Pegler gained national attention with his sports commentaries on the funny or unusual side of athletics. He also found plenty of targets for his sharp wit, either when he used a sporting event as a metaphor for social ills, or when he detected corruption and malfeasance in the proceedings. "Readers increasingly began to see that

Pegler's columns referred to matters beyond the realm of sports," observed Richard Orodenker in the *Dictionary of Literary Biography.* "Pegler touched on larger issues that were personal, moral, and controversial, and he began offering analysis rather than straightforward reporting. Sports in his view was more than the event itself; ultimately, what happened on the field of competition could affect people's consciences as well as their pocketbooks. Pegler believed that sports fulfilled an important moral function in American life, and he saw himself as the gadfly of the sports pages."

By the mid-1930s the fledgling "gadfly" was ready to strike at larger targets on the national stage. Writing first for the Scripps-Howard chain, and then for King Features syndicate, he created a controversial political column called "Fair Enough." For the next three decades Pegler ranked among America's best known newspaper columnists, with fans and foes alike paying heed to his observations. "Pegler took pleasure in exposing frauds and phonies, fools and dupes," declared Orodenker. "He lampooned any sort of hero worship—of athletes as well as presidents—and he saved his most potent venom for men in power who let themselves be corrupted by that power."

Favorite Pegler targets included Franklin and Eleanor Roosevelt, Huey Long, Upton Sinclair, Nazis, Frank Sinatra, Drew Pearson, the Newspaper Guild, communism, gambling, and the national income tax. Pegler was especially virulent in his treatment of labor union officials, whom he regarded as either gangsters or Communists. His 1940 investigation into racketeering involving George Scalise, head of the Building Service Employees International Union, resulted in a prison sentence for Scalise and a Pulitzer Prize for Pegler. Another of Pegler's targets, Hollywood union official William Bioff, was exposed by Pegler as an extortionist; Bioff also went to jail.

Even Pegler's employers were not immune from his assaults. In 1962 his contract with King Features was canceled when he made statements attacking the syndicate's owner, William Randolph Hearst, Jr., and other members of the Hearst organization. He then began working as a freelance journalist and writing articles for the John Birch Society's publication *American Opinion.* A dispute with the society's founder, Robert Welch, over an article on Chief Justice Earl Warren prompted Pegler to quit, saying,

"I had enough of that with Hearst. I don't have to take it any more."

Pegler was involved in two widely publicized law suits, both resulting from a 1949 column in which he attacked magazine writer Quentin Reynolds. Reynolds brought a libel suit against the journalist claiming that Pegler had falsely accused him of cowardice and of being a Communist sympathizer. Pegler lost the suit and Reynolds was awarded $175,000 in punitive damages—the largest award ever at that time. A Broadway play, *A Case of Libel,* was based on the Pegler-Reynolds lawsuit. Pegler was so incensed by the caricature of himself in the play that he sued after segments of *A Case of Libel* were aired on the *Ed Sullivan Show.* The suit was still pending at the time of Pegler's death.

As he became older and infirm, Pegler began to lose his audience. The latter years of his life were spent working for two right-wing parochial publications, the *Jacksonville Chronicle* and the *Councilor,* based in Shreveport, Louisiana. He died on June 24, 1969 after a long battle with stomach cancer.

Orodenker, for one, believes that Pegler made an important contribution to two realms of journalism—sportswriting and political commentary. Pegler's contemporaries were certainly cognizant of his stature. In a *Books* review published in 1938, Stanley Walker called the columnist "a tough man who calls them as he sees them," and a *Springfield Republican* correspondent hailed him for having "mental grasp and a considerable range of ideas." In a *Saturday Review of Literature* piece on Pegler's *George Spelvin, American, and Fireside Chats,* Irwin Edman offered a dissenting—but still respectful—opinion. "It is difficult to write about Westbrook Pegler without being as unfair, as intolerant, and as rambunctious as he is," Edman maintained. "One is tempted to try to imitate his epithets, which would not be easy, and to emulate his intellectual morals, which would be nothing short of scandalous."

Orodenker concluded: "While some scholars will think it politically incorrect to resurrect Pegler (finding his spirit alive and well in the prose of combative conservatives such as Pat Buchanan and Joseph Sobran), those individuals willing to overlook ideological differences or Pegler's failings in character will discover a masterful writer who played a significant role in two distinct fields of American journalism, of which his sportswriting is the more enduring."

BIOGRAPHICAL/CRITICAL SOURCES:

BOOKS

Dictionary of Literary Biography, Volume 171: *Twentieth-Century American Sportswriters,* Gale (Detroit, MI), 1996, pp. 264-74.
Farr, Finis, *Fair Enough: The Life of Westbrook Pegler,* Arlington House (New Rochelle, NY), 1975.
Frank, Stanley, editor, *Sports Extra,* Barnes (New York City), 1944.
Pilat, Oliver, *Pegler: Angry Man of the Press,* Beacon (Boston, MA), 1963.
Smith, Red, *To Absent Friends,* Atheneum (New York City), 1982, pp. 185-87.
Weiner, Richard, *Syndicated Columnists,* 3rd edition, Richard Weiner, 1979.

PERIODICALS

Books, October 25, 1936, p. 17; October 23, 1938, p. 20; September 27, 1942, p. 6.
New York Times, October 11, 1936, p. 4; October 16, 1938, p. 4; September 13, 1942, p. 3.
Saturday Review of Literature, October 10, 1936, p. 5; September 26, 1942, p. 9.
Springfield Republican, October 7, 1938, p. 10.

OBITUARIES:

PERIODICALS

New York Times, June 25, 1969.
Times (London), June 25, 1969.
Variety, July 2, 1969.
Washington Post, June 25, 1969.*

*   *   *

PENDLETON, Don
   See CUNNINGHAM, Chet

*   *   *

PETIEVICH, Gerald 1944-

PERSONAL: Born October 15, 1944, in Los Angeles, CA; son of Zarko (a police officer) and Dorothy (an artist; maiden name, Hibbert) Petievich; married

Pamela Lentz (a teacher), December 23, 1968; children: Emma. *Education:* California State University, Los Angeles, B.A., 1966.

ADDRESSES: Office—Charles Carr Production Inc., 948 Winston Ave., San Marino, CA 91108. *Agent*—Knox Burger, 39 Washington Sq., New York, NY 10012.

CAREER: Associated with U.S. Secret Service, beginning 1970. *Military service:* U.S. Army, 1967-70; in intelligence corps; became sergeant.

MEMBER: Society for Investigative and Forensic Hypnosis, Mystery Writers of America, Authors Guild.

WRITINGS:

NOVELS

Money Men/One Shot Deal (two novellas), Pinnacle (New York City), 1981.
To Die in Beverly Hills, Arbor House (New York City), 1983.
To Live and Die in L.A. (also see below), Arbor House, 1984.
The Quality of the Informant, Arbor House, 1985.
Shakedown, Simon & Schuster (New York City), 1988.
Earth Angels, New American Library (New York City), 1989.
Paramour, Dutton (New York City), 1991.

SCREENPLAYS

(With William Friedkin) *To Live and Die in L.A.,* 1985.
C.A.T. Squad (television play), 1986.

OTHER

Contributor to *Writer.*

SIDELIGHTS: The grim horizons of organized crime in the nation's biggest cities have provided grist for the novels of Gerald Petievich. Himself a U.S. Secret Service agent and investigator for the Treasury Department, Petievich informs his fiction with profiles of successful counterfeiters and blackmail artists, juxtaposed against a corps of detectives who are hobbled by bureaucracy and the political ambitions of their superiors. According to Robert E. Skinner in the *St. James Guide to Crime and Mystery Writers,*

Petievich "is the only modern writer to examine the world of the counterfeiter, and he brings a genuine sense of reality to his descriptions of both the art of counterfeiting and the underworld network which enables this crime to flourish."

Petievich's *Money Men/One Shot Deal* contains two mystery novellas centering on a United States Treasury agent named Charles Carr. In both tales, Carr hunts counterfeiters, though in the second story there is also an element of swindling. A commentator in *New York Times Book Review* called the tales "unusually good," and noted that "nothing about the writing suggests that they are first novelettes." The reviewer also declared that "Petievich goes about it all with a good deal of confidence, a sure hand, a fine ear for dialogue and canny feel for plot." In *Best Sellers,* Charles J. Keffer characterized Petievich's debut work as "straightforward, interesting, realistic, hard hitting, and suspenseful."

Detective Carr is also featured in two of Petievich's other novels, *To Die in Beverly Hills* and *The Quality of the Informant.* In these works he is joined by an imaginative and somewhat unscrupulous partner named Jack Kelly who shares his singleminded dedication to the pursuit of criminals. Skinner found these protagonists as "similar to many of the tough, world-weary heroes who populate much of modern crime fiction, but they are set apart from other such characters by the absolute . . . ruthlessness with which they pursue their quarry."

In *To Die in Beverly Hills,* Carr and Kelly are lured into a fake stakeout that ends in bloodshed. Carr makes it his mission to nail the crooked Beverly Hills detective who organized the stakeout. A *Publishers Weekly* reviewer cited the book for its details, noting that Petievich's "background as a treasury agent himself intensifies the reality of this superthriller." A *New Yorker* contributor especially liked the portrait of Carr, observing that—although Carr is a familiar figure for his cynicism and devotion to his job—"Mr. Petievich has charged him with abundant life, and even a kind of charm."

Petievich's best known work is *To Live and Die in L.A.,* which was also made into a feature film. In this outing, Treasury agents Vukovich and Chance, finding themselves pitted against an intelligent and wily counterfeiter, decide to bend the rules to catch their man. Their efforts are juxtaposed against those of an older agent named Jim Hart, who follows correct procedure as he pursues the same criminal.

"Petievich's description of the fine line that these men must walk in order not to fall into criminal behavior themselves is brutally frank," Skinner declared. "The ease with which a lawman can slip over the edge is grimly and realistically depicted in . . . *To Live and Die in L.A.*" A *New Yorker* reviewer observed that *To Live and Die in L.A.* shows Petievich "at his gritty, gripping best—strong on plausibility and character and vigorous storytelling."

More recent Petievich novels have focused on gang activity in Los Angeles and top-secret chicanery in the White House. Whatever his setting, however, he focuses on the crime fighter as a man beset on one side by ruthless criminals and on the other by self-serving superiors. "Petievich has shown a genuine knack for projecting not only the intensity of the policeman's life, but also the loneliness and emotional emptiness that accompanies it," concluded Skinner. "He has skillfully blended Elmore Leonard's colorful underworld milieu with Joseph Wambaugh's bleak vision of the cop's personal and professional life. . . . His unique picture of the fight against counterfeiters will endure far past his writing life."

Petievich told *CA:* "In my novellas, I've tried to draw the milieu in which cops and crooks thrash about as I have seen it—from street level. I have always been fascinated by the atmosphere of violence and self interest which governs the underworld. There, the extreme is normal. Perfidy is custom. A touch of bad luck means time in the penitentiary or perhaps death. Success is measured by the yardstick of evil. It's society's distorted reflection in a fun house mirror."

BIOGRAPHICAL/CRITICAL SOURCES:

BOOKS

St. James Guide to Crime and Mystery Writers, fourth edition, St. James Press (Detroit, MI), 1996.

PERIODICALS

Best Sellers, August, 1981, p. 174; May, 1984, p. 47.
Booklist, February 15, 1984, p. 847.
Library Journal, June 1, 1981, p. 1247.
Los Angeles Times, July 23, 1981.
New Yorker, July 4, 1983; June 4, 1984, pp. 136-137.

New York Times Book Review, July 12, 1981.
Publishers Weekly, February 25, 1983, p. 82; January 13, 1984, p. 62.

* * *

POESCH, Jessie (J.) 1922-

PERSONAL: Born in 1922 in Postville, IA; daughter of Edward H. and Vina Meier Poesch. *Ethnicity:* "Caucasian." *Education:* Antioch College, B.A., 1944; University of Delaware, M.A., 1956; University of Pennsylvania, Ph.D., 1966.

ADDRESSES: Home—5807 Tchoupitoulas, New Orleans, LA 70115. *Office*—Department of Art, Tulane University, New Orleans, LA 70118; fax 504-862-8710.

CAREER: Curatorial Assistant at Winterhur Museum in Delaware, 1956-58; Tulane University, New Orleans, LA, assistant professor, 1963-67, associate professor, 1967-75, professor, 1975—; Maxine and Ford Graham Professor of History of Art, 1987-92. Member of board of directors of Louisiana Endowment for the Humanities, 1984-90. Guest curator at Virginia Museum of Fine Arts, 1983; lecturer.

MEMBER: College Art Association of America, Victorian Society of America (member of board, 1988-90), American Antiquarian Society, Society of Architectural Historians (member of board, 1986-89).

WRITINGS:

Titian Ramsay Peale, 1799-1885, and His Journals of the Wilkes Expedition, American Philosophical Society (Philadelphia), 1961.
The Early Furniture of Louisiana, Louisiana State Museum (Baton Rouge), 1972.
The Art of the Old South: Painting, Sculpture, Architecture, and the Products of Craftsmen, 1560-1860, Knopf (New York City), 1983.
Newcomb Pottery: An Enterprise for Southern Women, 1895-1904, Schiffer (Exton, PA), 1984.
Will Henry Stevens, 1881-1949, Greenville County Museum of Art (Greenville, SC), 1987.

Also co-author with John Cuthbert of *David Hunter Strother, "One of the Best Draughtsmen the Country Possesses,"* [Morgantown, WV], 1997.

WORK IN PROGRESS: Research on the art and architecture of the American South.

SIDELIGHTS: Jessie Poesch once told *CA:* "I love research. As an art historian I try to place art in context and to have some familiarity with the whole range of creativity—the 'minor' arts and the so-called fine arts appeal to me equally."

* * *

POWELL, Anthony (Dymoke) 1905-

PERSONAL: Surname rhymes with "Noel"; born December 21, 1905, in London; son of Philip Lionel William (an army officer) and Maude Mary (Wells-Dymoke) Powell; married Lady Violet Pakenham, daughter of fifth Earl of Longford, December 1, 1934; children: Tristram, John. *Education:* Balliol College, Oxford, B.A., 1926, M.A., 1944.

ADDRESSES: Home—The Chantry, near Frome, Somerset, England.

CAREER: Writer, 1930—. Affiliated with Duckworth & Co., Ltd. (publishing house), London, 1926-35; scriptwriter for Warner Brothers of Great Britain, 1936. Trustee of National Portrait Gallery, London, 1962-76. *Military service:* Welch Regiment, Infantry, 1939-41, Intelligence Corps, 1941-45; served as liaison officer at War Office; became major; received Order of the White Lion (Czechoslovakia), Order of Leopold II (Belgium), Oaken Crown and Croix de Guerre (both Luxembourg).

MEMBER: American Academy of Arts and Letters (honorary member), Travellers' Club (London), Modern Language Society (honorary member).

AWARDS, HONORS: Named Commander of Order of the British Empire, 1956, named Companion of Honor, 1988; James Tait Black Memorial Prize, 1958, for *At Lady Molly's;* W. H. Smith Fiction Award, 1974, for *Temporary Kings;* Bennett Award from *Hudson Review* and T. S. Eliot Award from Ingersoll Foundation, both 1984, both for body of work; D.Litt., University of Sussex, 1971, University of Leicester and University of Kent, 1976, Oxford University, 1980, and Bristol University, 1982.

WRITINGS:

(Editor) *Barnard Letters, 1778-1884,* Duckworth, 1928.
Afternoon Men (novel), Duckworth, 1931, Holt, 1932, reprinted, Popular Library, 1978.
Venusberg (novel; also see below), Duckworth, 1932, Popular Library, 1978.
From a View to a Death (novel), Duckworth, 1933, reprinted, Popular Library, 1978, published as *Mr. Zouch, Superman: From a View to a Death,* Vanguard, 1934.
Agents and Patients (novel; also see below), Duckworth, 1936, Popular Library, 1978.
What's Become of Waring? (novel), Cassell, 1939, Little, Brown, 1963, reprinted, Popular Library, 1978.
(Editor and author of introduction) *Novels of High Society from the Victorian Age,* Pilot Press, 1947.
John Aubrey and His Friends, Scribner, 1948, revised edition, Barnes & Noble, 1963, reprinted, Chatto & Windus, 1988.
(Editor and author of introduction) John Aubrey, *Brief Lives and Other Selected Writings,* Scribner, 1949.
(Author of introduction) E. W. Hornung, *Raffles,* Eyre & Spottiswoode, 1950.
Two Novels: Venusberg [and] Agents and Patients, Periscope-Holliday, 1952.
(Author of preface) *The Complete Ronald Firbank,* Duckworth, 1961.
(Contributor) *Burke's Landed Gentry,* Burke's Peerage Publications, 1965.
Two Plays: The Garden God [and] The Rest I'll Whistle, Heinemann, 1971, Little, Brown, 1972.
(Contributor) Richard Shead, *Constant Lambert,* Simon Publications, 1973.
To Keep the Ball Rolling: The Memoirs of Anthony Powell, Volume 1: *Infants of the Spring,* Heinemann, 1976, published as *Infants of the Spring: The Memoirs of Anthony Powell,* Holt, 1977, reprinted, Penguin, 1984, Volume 2: *Messengers of Day,* Holt, 1978, Volume 3: *Faces in My Time,* Heinemann, 1980, Holt, 1981, Volume 4: *The Strangers Are All Gone,* Heinemann, 1982, Holt, 1983, abridged edition of all four volumes published as *To Keep the Ball Rolling,* Penguin, 1983.
(Author of introduction) Jocelyn Brooke, *The Orchid Trilogy,* Secker & Warburg, 1981.
O, How the Wheel Becomes It! (novella), New American Library, 1985.
The Fisher King (novel), Norton, 1986.

Miscellaneous Verdicts: Writings on Writers, 1946-1989, Heinemann, 1990, reprinted, University of Chicago Press, 1992.

Under Review: Further Writings on Writers, 1946-1990, University of Chicago Press, 1994.

Journals 1982-1986, Heinemann, 1995.

"A DANCE TO THE MUSIC OF TIME" SERIES; NOVELS; ALSO SEE BELOW

A Question of Upbringing, Scribner, 1951, reprinted, Warner Books, 1985.

A Buyer's Market, Heinemann, 1952, Scribner, 1953, reprinted, Warner Books, 1985.

The Acceptance World, Heinemann, 1955, Farrar, Straus, 1956, reprinted, Warner Books, 1985.

At Lady Molly's, Heinemann, 1957, Little, Brown, 1958, reprinted, Warner Books, 1985.

Casanova's Chinese Restaurant, Little, Brown, 1960, reprinted, Warner Books, 1985.

The Kindly Ones, Little, Brown, 1962, reprinted, Warner Books, 1985.

The Valley of Bones, Little, Brown, 1964, reprinted, Warner Books, 1985.

The Soldier's Art, Little, Brown, 1966, reprinted, Warner Books, 1985.

The Military Philosophers, Heinemann, 1968, Little, Brown, 1969, reprinted, Warner Books, 1985.

Books Do Furnish a Room, Little, Brown, 1971, reprinted, Warner Books, 1986.

Temporary Kings, Little, Brown, 1973, reprinted, Warner Books, 1986.

Hearing Secret Harmonies, Heinemann, 1975, Little, Brown, 1976, reprinted, Warner Books, 1986.

"A DANCE TO THE MUSIC OF TIME" OMNIBUS VOLUMES

A Dance to the Music of Time: First Movement (contains *A Question of Upbringing, A Buyer's Market,* and *The Acceptance World*), Little, Brown, 1963.

A Dance to the Music of Time: Second Movement (contains *At Lady Molly's, Casanova's Chinese Restaurant,* and *The Kindly Ones*), Little, Brown, 1964.

A Dance to the Music of Time: Third Movement (contains *The Valley of Bones, The Soldier's Art,* and *The Military Philosophers*), Little, Brown, 1971.

A Dance to the Music of Time: Fourth Movement (contains *Books Do Furnish a Room, Temporary Kings,* and *Hearing Secret Harmonies*), Little, Brown, 1976.

A Dance to the Music of Time (complete collection), University of Chicago Press, 1995.

SIDELIGHTS: Novelist Anthony Powell has spent more than forty years chronicling the changing fortunes of Great Britain's upper class in the twentieth century. He is best known for his twelve-volume series *A Dance to the Music of Time,* the longest fictional work in the English language. Published in installments over almost twenty-five years, *A Dance to the Music of Time* follows a number of characters from adolescence in 1914 to old age and death in the late 1960s. *New Yorker* contributor Naomi Bliven calls the series "one of the most important works of fiction since the Second World War," and *New Republic* reviewer C. David Benson describes the novels as "the most sophisticated chronicle of modern life we have." In the Toronto *Globe and Mail,* Douglas Hill observes that Powell "has had the good fortune to be in the right place at the right time and among the right people, and to be able to watch all this passing scene and transform the most apparently insignificant moments into the fabric of his fiction."

Newsweek correspondent Gene Lyons notes that Powell is "entirely provincial, yet not at all a snob, . . . an aristocratic man of letters in the best British tradition." Lyons continues: "He is a contemporary of that extraordinary group of English writers who were born during the first decade of this century." Indeed, Powell enjoyed close friendships with Evelyn Waugh, Cyril Connolly, and George Orwell, and he knew numerous other important writers, including Dylan Thomas and F. Scott Fitzgerald. Powell grew up in comfortable circumstances—he is a descendent of nobility—and was educated at Eton and Oxford. As Benson notes, however, the author's entire generation "was marked by having experienced the extinction of the privileged England of their childhoods which was replaced by a completely different post-war world." In his fiction Powell explores the extinction, or rather the metamorphosis, of the British upper class.

Powell graduated from Oxford in 1926 and took a job with Duckworth, a major publishing house in London. While he served as an editor at Duckworth, Powell began to write fiction of his own; eventually, Duckworth published four of his five early novels. *Dictionary of Literary Biography* contributor James Tucker describes Powell's first few books as "entertaining, light, but not lightweight." Tucker also observes that in his early works Powell "appears to be interested in societies under threat, either from their own languor and foolishness or from huge political reverses or from calculated infiltration by arrivistes."

Powell's first novel, *Afternoon Men,* has become his best known pre-war work. A satire of the upper-middle-class penchant for aimlessness, *Afternoon Men* begins and ends with party invitations. Tucker contends that, in the novel, Powell "expertly depicts the banality of the lives under scrutiny by having characters talk with a remorseless, plodding simplicity, as if half-baked, half-drunk, or half-asleep after too many nights on the town."

Even though Powell's first five novels sold only several thousand copies apiece, by the 1930s the author "had come to be recognized as one of several significant novelists who had emerged in Britain since World War I," to quote Tucker. Like most Englishmen his age, however, Powell faced a cessation of his career when the Second World War began. He enlisted in the Welsh Regiment and then served four years with the Intelligence Corps as liaison to the War Office. When the war ended, Powell still did not return to fiction for some time. Instead, he wrote a comprehensive biography on John Aubrey, a seventeenth century writer and antiquary of Welsh descent. Only when *John Aubrey and His Friends* was completed did Powell return to fiction—but he did so in a grand way. Tucker writes: "Believing that many authors went on producing what were virtually the same characters in book after book, though with different names and in fresh circumstances, [Powell] wanted to break out from the confines of the 80,000 word novel. The *roman-fleuve* would allow him to recognize the problem openly and continue with established characters through successive volumes. During the late 1940s, while visiting the Wallace Collection in London, he saw Nicolas Poussin's painting *A Dance to the Music of Time* and felt he had at last found the theme and title of his work."

The Poussin painting depicts the four seasons as buxom young maidens, dancing under a threatening sky to music provided by a wizened, bearded man—Father Time. Powell's work, too, involves "dancers," a coterie of interrelated men and women living in modern Britain, whose lives intersect on the whims of fate. As Tucker notes, "scores of major characters dance their way in and out of one another's lives—and especially one another's beds—often in seemingly random style; yet when the whole sequence is seen together there is some sort of order. To put it more strongly than that would be wrong; but music and dance do imply a system, harmony, pattern."

Kerry McSweeney describes *A Dance to the Music of Time* in a *South Atlantic Quarterly* essay. According to McSweeney, the book's subject "is a densely populated swathe of upper-class, upper-middle-class, artistic, and Bohemian life in England from the twenties to the seventies. The vehicle of presentation is the comedy of manners. Attention is consistently focused on the nuances of social behavior, the idiosyncracies of personal style, and the intricacies of sexual preference. All of the characters in the series . . . are seen strictly from the outside—that is, in terms of how they choose to present themselves to the world." In the early volumes, the characters leave school to establish careers which are often less important than the whirl of social obligations. The middle volumes concern the years of the Second World War, and the later volumes send many of the characters to their deaths. In *The Situation of the Novel,* Bernard Bergonzi notes that *A Dance to the Music of Time* is "a great work of social comedy in a central English tradition" that "also conveys the cumulative sense of a shabby and dispirited society." A *Washington Post Book World* reviewer calls the series "an addictive social fantasy, strictly controlled by the author's sense of the ambiguity of human relationships and an indispensable literary style."

The action in *A Dance to the Music of Time* is revealed by Nicholas Jenkins, a non-participant observer who is happily married, urbane, and loyal to his values. From his vantage point in society, Jenkins describes the ascent of several power-hungry men—chief among them Kenneth Widmerpool—who become consumed by the perfection of their public images. Bliven contends that the series "subtly but ever more insistently contrasts the quest for power with the urge to create. The power seekers are killers and lovers of death, and the defenses against them are disinterestedness, playfulness, and, above all, artistic dedication." Tucker sees the tension between Jenkins and Widmerpool as "the difference between a man who is nothing but ambition, a sort of burlesque Faust, and another who represents enduring standards of humaneness, creativity, and artistic appreciation in a shoddy world."

A Dance to the Music of Time does not provide a continuous narrative; rather, it presents a series of minutely-observed vignettes, described with an understated prose. "What strikes one first about [the series]," Tucker writes in *The Novels of Anthony Powell,* "is its elaborate texture and seemingly cast-iron poise, qualities suiting the narrator's wisdom, favoured status, knowledge and assurance. . . . The prose is largely appositional: to borrow the mode, plain statement followed by commentary or modification or conjecture, so that the reader feels himself presented with a very wide choice of possible responses; the uncertainties of real life are caught. . . . This modulated dignity, mandarin with the skids under it, gives Powell's style its distinction." In the *New York Review of Books,* Michael Wood concludes that the most "persistent pleasure" to be gained from Powell's masterwork "is that of having your expectations skillfully and elegantly cheated: the musician plays a strange chord, or an old chord you haven't heard for a long time, even a wrong note now and then." Lyons makes the observation that *A Dance to the Music of Time* provides a remarkable steadfastness of vision—"the novel's closing pages, written 25 years after the opening, make so perfect a fit they might have been the product of a single morning's work."

Powell's series has found numerous champions in both Great Britain and the United States. Chicago *Tribune Books* reviewer Larry Kart, for one, calls *A Dance to the Music of Time* the "century's finest English-language work of fiction." In *The Sense of Life in the Modern Novel,* Arthur Mizener writes that the effect of the work "is a very remarkable one for the mid-twentieth century. It is as if we had come suddenly on an enormously intelligent but completely undogmatic mind with a vision of experience that is deeply penetrating and yet wholly recognizable, beautifully subtle in ordination and yet quite unostentatious in technique, and in every respect undistorted by doctrine." *Commonweal* contributor Arnold Beichman praises Powell's novels for their "great cosmic sadness about our lives," adding: "It is Powell's skill and power in depicting man's helplessness that makes [his] novels so unforgettable, so wonderfully sad." Speaking to the universality of *A Dance to the Music of Time, National Review* correspondent Anthony Lejeune concludes that Powell "makes us see not only his world, but ours, through his eyes. Not only his characters, but our own lives and the lives which are constantly weaving and unweaving themselves around us, become part of the pattern, part of the inexplicable dance."

Powell has not been idle since the completion of *A Dance to the Music of Time.* Since 1975 he has written a four-volume memoir, a novella entitled *O, How the Wheel Becomes It!,* and a novel, *The Fisher King. The Fisher King* involves passengers on an educational cruise around the British Isles, particularly the character Saul Henchman, a renowned photographer and emasculated veteran of the Second World War who loses the devotion of his beautiful companion, Barberina Rookwood, to another passenger. Powell incorporates significant mythical allusions—Henchman represents the impotent "Fisher King" of Arthurian legend, and the cruise ship is named "Alecto" after one of the Furies from Greek mythology. A departure from his "stylized" and "basically realistic" narrative of *A Dance to the Music of Time, The Fisher King* "gives us a fresh chance to savor Mr. Powell's irony and urbanity, and his dexterous turns of phrase," comments *New York Times* reviewer John Gross. According to John Bayley in the *Los Angeles Times Book Review,* "*The Fisher King* is a rare work of art for a number of reasons, not least because of the skill and economy with which it makes an absorbing narrative out of the simplest daily materials—gossip, vanity, curiosity, the routine ways in which consciousness works on the situations that intrigue it." John Espey concludes in the *New York Times Book Review,* "Mr. Powell remains the master storyteller, ever quick to catch the conscience of the king, not to mention that of his reader."

Powell has also produced several collections of criticism. *Miscellaneous Verdicts: Writings on Writers, 1946-1989* is an assemblage of Powell's literary reviews over four decades, divided into four sections that offer appraisal of classic English writers, Marcel Proust, Powell's contemporaries, and American writers. *Washington Post Book World* reviewer Daniel Max writes, "Powell, like all his literary friends, reviewed constantly. And although he does not make any claim to have particularly enjoyed it or having gotten much more on paper than the sort of comments that people find useful in deciding whether to buy a book or not, he has the innate respect for any professional, competent job done without complaint." Though some critics view Powell's analysis as uninspired and relatively conservative, Anthony Burgess concludes in an *Observer* review, "This is an urbane book, quietly erudite, very sensible, highly civilized, remarkably useful."

Under Review: Further Writings on Writers, 1946-1990 is another collection of Powell's literary journalism dealing with British, Irish, and Continental writers, passing over their American counterparts altogether. This collection, more biographical than critical, includes portraits of a wide range of authors in four sections entitled "The Nineties," "Bloomsbury and Non-Bloomsbury," "Some Novels and Novelists," and "The Europeans"—the latter section featuring Victor Hugo, Leo Tolstoy, and Fyodor Dostoyevsky, among others. According to Merle Rubin in Chicago's *Tribune Books,* "Powell also happens to be a model book reviewer: an elegantly understated critic more inclined to err on the side of kindness than of severity. Straightforward, focused, seldom if ever using a review as an excuse to sound off on pet topics, demonstrate his superiority to the book's author or write up a storm of showy prose, he is not only erudite but also genuinely wise—the kind of passionate, informed and discriminating reader that other writers dream of."

In *The Novels of Anthony Powell,* James Tucker suggests that one feels "a plea throughout Powell's books for the natural warmth and vitality of life to be allowed their expression. . . . The distinction of Powell's novels is that they engagingly look at surfaces and, at the same time, suggest that this is by no means enough. They will continually disturb the surface to show us much more. In their quiet way they direct us towards a good, practical, unextreme general philosophy of life." *Voice Literary Supplement* contributor Ann Snitow observes that Powell can be recommended "for his long, honorable battle with language, his unavoidable anxieties, his preference for kindness over gaudier virtues. If he's brittle, it's because he knows things break; he's never complacent in either his playfulness or his hauteur." Snitow concludes: "Powell's a writer who values humility—antique word—a virtue now so necessary, and even more rare and obscure, perhaps, than Powell himself."

BIOGRAPHICAL/CRITICAL SOURCES:

BOOKS

Allen, Walter, *The Modern Novel,* Dutton, 1965.

Bergonzi, Bernard, *The Situation of the Novel,* University of Pittsburgh Press, 1970.

Bergonzi, Bernard, *Anthony Powell,* Longman, 1971.

Brennan, Neil Francis, *Anthony Powell,* Prentice Hall, 1995.

Contemporary Literary Criticism, Gale, Volume 1, 1973; Volume 3, 1975; Volume 7, 1977; Volume 9, 1978; Volume 10, 1979; Volume 31, 1985.

Dictionary of Literary Biography, Volume 15: *British Novelists, 1930-1959,* Gale, 1983.

Felber, Lynette, *Gender and Genre in Novels without End,* University Press of Florida, 1996.

Gorra, Michael Edward, *The English Novel at Mid-Century: From the Leaning Tower,* St Martin's, 1990.

Hall, James, *The Tragic Comedians,* Indiana University Press, 1963.

Joyau, Isabelle, *Investigating Powell's "A Dance to the Music of Time",* St. Martin's, 1994.

Karl, Frederick R., *A Reader's Guide to the Contemporary English Novel,* Farrar, Straus, 1962.

Lilley, George P., *Anthony Powell, A Bibliography,* Oak Knoll, 1993.

McEwan, Neil, *Anthony Powell,* St Martin's, 1991.

Mizener, Arthur, *The Sense of Life in the Modern Novel,* Houghton, 1964.

Morris, Robert K., *The Novels of Anthony Powell,* University of Pittsburgh Press, 1968.

Ries, Lawrence R., *Wolf Masks: Violence in Contemporary Poetry,* Kennikat, 1977.

Russell, John, *Anthony Powell, A Quintet, Sextet and War,* Indiana University Press, 1970.

Selig, Robert L., *Time and Anthony Powell: A Critical Study,* Associated University Presses, 1991.

Shapiro, Charles, *Contemporary British Novelists,* Southern Illinois University Press, 1965.

Spurling, Hilary, *Invitation to the Dance: A Guide to Anthony Powell's "Dance to the Music of Time,"* Little, Brown, 1978.

Symons, Julian, *Critical Occasions,* Hamish Hamilton, 1966.

Tucker, James, *The Novels of Anthony Powell,* Columbia University Press, 1976.

PERIODICALS

American Scholar, autumn, 1993, p. 619.

Atlantic, March, 1962.

Best Sellers, March 15, 1969.

Books and Bookmen, April, 1971; March, 1976; January, 1977.

Book Week, April 9, 1967.

Chicago Tribune Book World, July 19, 1981.

Christian Science Monitor, October 6, 1960; January 25, 1967; March 16, 1967; March 9, 1981.

Commonweal, July 31, 1959; May 12, 1967; May 30, 1969.

Contemporary Literature, spring, 1976.

Critique, spring, 1964.

Economist, February 18, 1995, p. 89.

Encounter, February, 1976.

Globe and Mail (Toronto), March 31, 1984.

Hudson Review, summer, 1967; spring, 1976; winter, 1981-82; autumn, 1984.

Kenyon Review, winter, 1960.

Listener, October 14, 1968; September 11, 1975; May 11, 1978.

London Magazine, January, 1969.

London Review of Books, May 18, 1983.

Los Angeles Times Book Review, May 22, 1983; November 6, 1983; April 17, 1986, p. 16.

Nation, May 29, 1967; December 10, 1973; June 19, 1976.

National Review, December 7, 1973; June 11, 1976; January 11, 1985.

New Leader, November 26, 1973.

New Republic, September 24, 1962; April 22, 1967; October 27, 1973; June 11, 1977.

New Review, September, 1974.

New Statesman, June 25, 1960; July 6, 1962; May 19, 1980; May 21, 1982.

New Statesman & Society, February 3, 1995, p. 39.

Newsweek, March 24, 1969; October 29, 1973; April 5, 1976; April 25, 1983; September 2, 1985.

New Yorker, July 3, 1965; June 3, 1967; May 10, 1976; December 18, 1995, p. 106.

New York Herald Tribune Books, February 11, 1962.

New York Review of Books, May 18, 1967; November 1, 1973.

New York Times, March 14, 1968; March 13, 1969; September 8, 1971; February 17, 1972; February 4, 1981; November 16, 1984; September 23, 1986.

New York Times Book Review, January 21, 1962; September 30, 1962; March 19, 1967; March 9, 1969; October 14, 1973; November 1, 1973; April 11, 1976; February 8, 1981; June 26, 1983; January 22, 1984; October 19, 1986; February 21, 1988.

Observer, October 10, 1967; October 13, 1968; February 14, 1971; May 20, 1990.

Publishers Weekly, April 5, 1976.

Saturday Review, March 18, 1967; March 8, 1969; November 11, 1973; April 17, 1976.

Sewanee Review, spring, 1974.

South Atlantic Quarterly, winter, 1977.

Spectator, June 24, 1960; September 16, 1966; October 18, 1968; September 13, 1975; October 9, 1976; June 5, 1982.

Time, August 11, 1958; March 3, 1967; March 28, 1969; March 9, 1981.

Times (London), April 3, 1980; May 13, 1982; June 16, 1983; April 3, 1986.

Times Literary Supplement, October 17, 1968; March 28, 1980; June 24, 1983; September 21, 1984; April 4, 1986; May 18-24, 1990, p. 524; March 20, 1992, p. 22.

Tribune Books (Chicago), September 28, 1986; July 12, 1992, p. 1; September 25, 1994, p. 6.

Twentieth Century, July, 1961.

Virginia Quarterly Review, summer, 1976; spring, 1978; autumn, 1985.

Voice Literary Supplement, February, 1984.

Washington Post Book World, April 4, 1976; May 30, 1976; October 9, 1977; September 17, 1978; January 18, 1981; October 12, 1986; December 13, 1987; July 26, 1992.

World Literature Today, summer, 1979.*

* * *

PROCTER, Maurice 1906-1973

PERSONAL: Born February 4, 1906, in Nelson, Lancashire, England; died following a long illness, 1973, in England; son of William and Rose (Wilson) Procter; married Winifred Blakey, 1933; children: Noel. *Education:* Attended grammar school, Nelson, England. *Politics:* Conservative. *Religion:* Church of England. *Avocational interests:* Gardening, travel.

CAREER: Halifax Borough Police, Halifax, England, constable, 1927-46; writer, 1946-69.

MEMBER: Mystery Writers of America, Crime Writers Association, Press Club (London), Royal Overseas Club, Albany Club (Halifax).

WRITINGS:

No Proud Chivalry, Longmans, Green (London), 1946.

Each Man's Destiny, Longmans, Green, 1947.

The End of the Street, Longmans, Green, 1948.

The Chief Inspector's Statement, Hutchinson (London), 1949 (published in America as *The Pennycross Murders,* Harper [New York City], 1951).

Hurry the Darkness, Harper, 1950.

Rich Is the Treasure, Hutchinson, 1952.

Hell Is a City, Hutchinson, 1953 (published in America as *Somewhere in This City,* Harper, 1954).

The Midnight Plumber, Harper, 1955.

The Pub Crawler, Harper, 1956.

The Ripper, Harper, 1956 (published in England as *I Will Speak Daggers,* Hutchinson, 1956).

Three at the Angel, Harper, 1957.

Killer at Large, Harper, 1958.

Man in Ambush, Harper, 1960.

Devil's Due, Harper, 1961.

The Spearhead Death, Hutchinson, 1961.

The Devil Was Handsome, Harper, 1961.

Devil in Moonlight, Hutchinson, 1962.

A Body to Spare, Harper, 1962.

The Graveyard Rolls, Harper, 1963 (published in England as *Moonlight Flitting,* Hutchinson, 1963).

Two Men in Twenty, Harper, 1965.

Homicide Blonde, Harper, 1965 (published in England as *Death Has a Shadow,* Hutchinson, 1965).

His Weight in Gold, Harper, 1966.

Rogue Running, Harper, 1966.

Exercise Hoodwink, Harper, 1967.

Hideaway, Harper, 1968.

The Dog Man, Hutchinson, 1969.

Procter's books were translated into Norwegian, Swedish, Finnish, German, Dutch, French, Italian, Portuguese, Japanese, and Spanish.

SIDELIGHTS: The late Maurice Procter is considered an important figure in the development of the police procedural novel. Procter, himself a nineteen-year veteran of the Halifax Police Department in Yorkshire, England, called upon his own experiences to write novels that often combined classic detective fiction with the more modern procedural. In the *St. James Guide to Crime and Mystery Writers,* George N. Dove called Procter's early work "transitional," pointing in a direction soon taken by John Creasey and Ed McBain.

Through two decades of writing, Procter worked frequently with two favorite protagonists: the well-known and gentlemanly Harry Martineau, a chief inspector, and Philip Hunter, a conniving and abrasive detective superintendent. Martineau made his debut in *Hell Is a City*—also Procter's first procedural. Hunter took the stage even earlier, in the 1951 title *The Chief Inspector's Statement.* For his settings Procter turned to the milieu he knew best, northern England, which fictionalizes in his work as the towns of "Granchester" and "Yoreborough."

Procter died after a long illness in 1973, having published his last novel, *The Dog Man,* in 1969. Dove noted that the police methods in the author's stories "are based somewhat less on modern forensic science than on common sense and an understanding of human nature." Procter was hardly a sedate writer, however. A *Publishers Weekly* reviewer of one of his last novels, *Hideaway,* praised the work as "a slam-bang, action packed British cops and robbers tale" that "meshes together convincingly."

BIOGRAPHICAL/CRITICAL SOURCES:

BOOKS

St. James Guide to Crime and Mystery Writers, fourth edition, St. James Press (Detroit, MI), 1996.

PERIODICALS

Publishers Weekly, September 11, 1967, p. 68; September 23, 1968, p. 92.*

*   *   *

QUARRINGTON, Paul (Lewis) 1953-

PERSONAL: Born July 22, 1953, in Toronto, Ontario, Canada; son of Bruce Joseph (a psychologist) and Mary Ormiston (a psychologist; maiden name, Lewis) Quarrington; married Dorothie Bennie; children: Carson Lara, Flannery. *Education:* Attended University of Toronto, 1970-72. *Politics:* Green party of Canada. *Religion:* Anglican. *Avocational interests:* Fishing, weight lifting, competing in the Toronto Inquisition Pub Trivia League.

ADDRESSES: Home—221 Springdale Blvd., Toronto, Ontario M4C 1Z8, Canada. *Agent*—David Johnston, Peter Livingston Associates, 120 Carlton St., Suite 304, Toronto, Ontario M5A 4K2, Canada.

CAREER: Writer, 1975—. Musician with group Joe Hall and the Continental Drift, 1973-83; Book Cellar, Yorkville, Toronto, Ontario, sales clerk, 1983-86.

MEMBER: Trout Unlimited, Scarborough Fly & Bait Casting Association, Canadian Sportfishing Club.

AWARDS, HONORS: Stephen Leacock Award for Humor, 1987, for *King Leary;* Governor's General Literary Award for English-Language Fiction in Canada, 1990, for *Whale Music;* Genie Award for best screenplay, for *Perfectly Normal;* Periodical Distributors of Canada Authors Award.

WRITINGS:

NOVELS

The Service, Coach House Press (Toronto), 1978.

Home Game, Doubleday (New York City), 1983.

The Life of Hope, Doubleday, 1985.
King Leary, Doubleday, 1987.
Whale Music, Doubleday, 1989.
Logan in Overtime, Doubleday, 1990.
Civilization and Its Part in My Downfall, Random House (New York City), 1994.

OTHER

Hometown Heroes: On the Road with Canada's National Hockey Team, Doubleday, 1988.
Fishing with My Old Guy, Greystone Books, 1996.

Also author of screenplays, including *Perfectly Normal* (with Eugene Lipinski), 1990, *Camilla,* 1994, and *Whale Music* (with Richard J. Lewis; an adaptation of Quarrington's novel of the same name), Alliance Productions, 1994. Author of two unpublished plays, *The Second,* 1982, and *The Invention of Poetry,* 1987.

SIDELIGHTS: The work of Canadian writer Paul Quarrington has been favorably compared with that of Robertson Davies, Henry David Thoreau, Herman Melville, and Francois Rabelais. Toronto *Globe and Mail* critic William French proclaimed Quarrington "a fresh and zany voice" in Canadian fiction, and his novel *The Life of Hope,* a "first-class farce of the absurd." *The Life of Hope* is narrated by a novelist named Paul who visits a professor friend near the town of Hope. Paul becomes engrossed with the history of the town, which was founded by Joseph Benton Hope, a man described by French as a "randy leader of a utopian religious sect that believed in communal living and communal sex." The Perfectionists, as the sect was known, were nudists who later became rich from their fishing gear inventions.

Quarrington followed *The Life of Hope* with his novel *King Leary,* for which he received the Stephen Leacock Medal for Humor in 1987. Protagonist Percival Leary, an aging hockey great, leaves South Grouse Nursing Home to make a ginger ale commercial in Toronto. During the trip he experiences flashbacks of his life. *New York Times Book Review* contributor Ron Carlson observed that "what starts out to be the life story of the King of Ice changes into something more like a mystery." Quarrington begins "tormenting King Leary with memory," wrote Carlson, and "as the layers of memory peel away, Leary is wide-eyed at what he finds his life has been, and he moves toward atonement." Leary remembers

his early years learning how to play hockey at the Brothers of St. Albans Reformatory, where the monks' motto is "To keep a boy out of hot water, put him on ice," and where he met his friend and rival, Manny Oz. Leary repeatedly recalls the household accident that ended his own career, and the uncertain circumstances of Manny's death and funeral fifty years in the past. Leary's discoveries—about himself, the death of Manny, and of Leary's son—"make this novel rueful and zany, full of wonder and regret," Carlson concluded.

According to an article in the *New York Times Book Review,* the voice of Leary was inspired by the colorful speech of the late hockey star and vice president of the Toronto Maple Leafs, Francis Michael "King" Clancy. In a phone interview for the *New York Times Book Review,* Quarrington said that the process of writing *King Leary* was similar to that of a character actor learning his role. As he sat down to write each morning, the author found himself "a little more like Percival Leary—irritable, cantankerous, more likely to lash out." Quarrington's familiarity with hockey would also serve him in the nonfiction work *Hometown Heroes,* which details his experiences on the road to the 1988 Olympic Games with the Canadian hockey team.

Quarrington's 1990 novel, *Logan in Overtime,* also takes hockey as its milieu. A one-time National Hockey League goalic, Logan has returned to his hometown where he plays for what Doug Bell, writing in *Quill & Quire,* dubbed "a dubious team in a dubious league," and is often drunk. Bell praised the book, asserting that Quarrington's fiction shines when it spotlights "the hilarity and heroism of eccentricity and failure."

Quarrington is also the author of the novel *Whale Music,* a comic treatment of the disturbing life of Desmond Howell, lead singer for the fictional rock group The Howls. In the 1960s, Desmond explains as he retraces his own history, The Howls crested the wave of success, rivaling even the Beatles, before crashing into a roiling surf littered with the debris of drugs, alcohol, sex, and excess. The ride ended when Desmond's brother Danny launched himself and his car into the Pacific Ocean on an explosive suicide mission, with no audience at the grand finale save a group of curious whales.

Desmond's story begins where Danny's lies submerged. Desmond's response to the loss of the brother he idolized is a retreat to the solitude and security of his oceanside mansion. He acquires a powerful electronic keyboard synthesizer and commits himself, in honor of Danny, to compose a rock symphony for the last creatures to see Danny alive—the whales. What occupies more of his time, however, is lethargy, complicated by junk food, alcohol, and drugs, and avoidance of the outside world. The overweight, aging musician never achieves the insulated life he seeks. As Jack MacLeod wrote in *Books in Canada,* "Intruders and the sharp teeth of life keep snapping at him." Desmond is surrounded by what *Quill & Quire* contributor Paul Kennedy calls "Rabelaisian figments of Quarrington's vivid imagination." One of these is an escaped mental patient named Claire, who revives Desmond's interest in life and love and lays the groundwork for what could prove to be his salvation.

Critical response to *Whale Music* has been mixed. John Gault wrote in *Maclean's* that "*Whale Music* is very much a novel of character," and Margot Mifflin reported in the *New York Times Book Review* that "Quarrington is an exceptionally inventive writer [with an] ability to create rounded and colorful characters." Yet Mifflin was disturbed by the novel's "infuriatingly happy ending," as was Tom Schnabel of the *Los Angeles Time Book Review.* Both reviewers were also critical of Desmond Howell's apparent likeness to Brian Wilson of the Beach Boys, who similarly retreated into a solitary and unhealthy lifestyle after the suicide of his brother Dennis. A high point of the novel for some critics, and a frustration for some others, was the elusive theme of the whale music itself. "Deftly and seductively," Gault commented, "Quarrington has the reader straining to hear the chords, anticipating the concert," but Kennedy wrote: "[B]y the final page . . . most readers will sincerely want to know, and try to imagine just how wonderful Whale Music sounds." Critics like MacLeod praised the author's craftsmanship: "*Whale Music* demonstrates that Quarrington can write a lean, spare prose. There is comic capering and a rush of epiphany, but there is also taut control evident here, an artistic restraint and even a suggestion of wisdom." Even Schnabel, who admitted to "plenty of problems" with the novel, concluded: "*Whale Music* is dazzling prose. . . . At times . . . the narrative resembles an existential portrait out of Heidegger." Julian Mason told *Canadian Forum* readers that "*Whale Music* is immensely likeable. It's impossible to resist the perverse charm of . . . Des Howell and his eccentric cast of hangers-on."

Quarrington adapted *Whale Music* for film with co-writer Richard J. Lewis during a five-year period in which the novelist devoted much of his time to writing screenplays. Remarking in *Maclean's* on this period and the difference between writing novels and writing screenplays, Quarrington stated that for him, screenplays are akin to concertos rather than symphonies: "Beethoven, Brahms and those other people, they would never say, 'Well I only write symphonies.' But they saved that part of them that was most important for the symphonies. I feel a little bit that way. I can save what's most important for the novels. . . . [Screenplays] are important; they're just not symphonies."

Among Quarrington's screenplay credits is *Camilla,* a movie about a young musician who meets an aging violinist, played by the late Jessica Tandy in her last film role. In his *Maclean's* review, Brian D. Johnson called the screenplay "quirky" and notes that its "whimsical tone—and its concern with the theme of musical ambition—is highly reminiscent of Quarrington's *Whale Music.*"

Fittingly, Quarrington's next published novel concerns the industry he worked in for half a decade. *Civilization and Its Part in My Downfall* tells the story of Thom Moss, a former star of movie Westerns from the 1920s. Moss narrates his rags-to-riches story from his prison cell, where he is imprisoned for a crime not immediately apparent to the reader. The novel, stated Carole Giangrande in *Books in Canada,* is "a wild and woolly look at our confusion of image and reality" which takes "dead aim at . . . our obsessions with media and stardom." Peter Oliva, in his *Quill & Quire* review, called it "a thoroughly engaging novel, full of 1920s vocabulary and Shakespearean street slang" and "a raucous adventure along a tale well told."

Commenting on the author's efforts as a novelist and a screenwriter, Smallbridge stated: "Quarrington tempers a mordant wit with sympathy and affection." The critic added that the writer's "ability to inhabit the souls of [his] protagonists is what initially attracted filmmakers to his work." Smallbridge included the comment of Steven DeNure, president of production for Alliance Pictures: "'Paul Quarrington has an unparalleled ability with character and voice. . . . Nobody creates characters like his. They're quirky, they're unique, and there's been some tragedy in their lives.'"

BIOGRAPHICAL/CRITICAL SOURCES:

BOOKS

Contemporary Literary Criticism, Volume 65, Gale (Detroit), 1991.

PERIODICALS

Books in Canada, June-July, 1989, pp. 25-26; November, 1994, p. 48; February, 1996, p. 24.
Canadian Forum, July-August, 1990, pp. 28-29.

Canadian Geographic, January/February, 1996, p. 85.
Globe and Mail (Toronto), September 21, 1985; October 22, 1988.
Los Angeles Times Book Review, April 15, 1990, p. 8.
Maclean's, May 29, 1989, p. 61; October 3, 1994, pp. 52-53; November 28, 1994, p. 86.
New York Times Book Review, May 1, 1988; February 25, 1990, p. 12.
Publishers Weekly, August 19, 1996, p. 46.
Quill & Quire, May, 1989, p. 20; February, 1990, p. 24; October, 1994, p. 33.*

R

RADLEY, Sheila
See ROBINSON, Sheila Mary

*   *   *

RAINE, Richard
See FORBES, Colin

*   *   *

RAND, Peter 1942-

PERSONAL: Born February 23, 1942, in San Francisco, CA; son of C(hristopher) T. (a journalist) and M(argaret) A(aldridge) (maiden name, Demott) Rand; married M. Bliss Inui (a researcher and reporter), December 19, 1976: children: one son. *Education:* Johns Hopkins University, M.A., 1976.

ADDRESSES: Agent—Phoenix Literary Agency, 150 East 74th St., New York, NY 10021.

CAREER: Antaeus, New York City, advisory fiction editor, 1970-72; *Washington Monthly,* Washington, DC, editor, 1973-74; Johns Hopkins University, teaching fellow, 1975; New York University, New York City, lecturer, 1976-77; Columbia University, New York City, lecturer, 1977-91.

MEMBER: PEN, Poets and Writers, Authors Guild.

AWARDS, HONORS: Creative Artists Public Service Award, 1977.

WRITINGS:

NOVELS

Firestorm, Doubleday (New York City), 1969.
The Time of the Emergency, Doubleday, 1977.
Gold from Heaven, Crown (New York City), 1988.

NONFICTION

China Hands: The Adventures and Ordeals of the American Journalists Who Joined Forces with the Great Chinese Revolution, Simon & Schuster (New York City), 1995.

Also author of *The Private Rich,* a novel (1984); co-editor and co-translator, with Nancy Liu and Lawrence R. Sullivan, of *Deng Xiaoping: Chronicle of an Empire,* by Ruan Ming. Contributor to *New York Times, Washington Post, Penthouse,* and other periodicals.

SIDELIGHTS: The son of journalist Christopher Rand, Peter Rand is an educator, novelist, and nonfiction writer who was inspired to write his book *China Hands: The Adventures and Ordeals of the American Journalists Who Joined Forces with the Great Chinese Revolution* by the discovery of his father's writings on China. In an attempt to learn more about the parent who in a sense had been stolen from him by his passionate involvement in the communist revolutionary movement in China, Rand decided to examine the lives of a number of similarly obsessed Western journalists. The resulting book offers portraits of a number of reporters, from Christopher Rand to Edgar Snow and Theodore White, along with several lesser-known lights, all of whom went to China to report on a story and ended up becoming participants in the political struggles which consumed that country during the first half of the twentieth century. Though Rand was faulted by some for failing to delve more deeply into the commonalities between his subjects, apart from their passionate interest in China—an interest which took widely divergent forms—others praised the author for providing what Martin Walker called in the *Washington Post Book World* "a solid account of the American reporters who covered China in the long years before 1950."

Many of the reporters Rand covers in his book had already told their own stories in books published in the first years after their return to the West, as Emily MacFarquhar pointed out in the *New York Times Book Review.* Rand's account was nonetheless deemed "lively," by *Chicago Tribune* reviewer John Maxwell Hamilton, who added that the book "offers valuable portraits of journalists who have not previously received the attention they deserve." "Rand is long on personal stories about his characters," Hamilton observed, a comment echoed both positively and negatively by other critics, who disagreed about the effectiveness of the author's incorporation of personal information about his subjects. "Rand could have hacked a clearer path through the dense political underbrush of his period," complained MacFarquhar, "but he does a good job of tracing relationships among his colorful characters and brings in personal detail from unpublished letters and interviews." On the other hand, the *Nation*'s Carol Brightman considered Rand's "flashes of insight into the byzantine politics of the Kuomintang" of more value than his treatment of his ostensible subjects, whose "portraits are tarted up with trivia." Brightman conceded, however, that "there is just enough offbeat history in *China Hands,* and several unforgettable sketches . . . make the book worth reading."

Rand is also the author of *Gold from Heaven,* a novel that details "the dazzling trappings and bizarre activities of a filthy rich family," according to a critic for *Kirkus Reviews,* who added that Rand's story is "lewd, luxe, amusing, and without any redeeming social value." "A strange and quirky stable of characters" populate *Gold from Heaven,* according to Lydia Burruel Johnson in *Library Journal;* in the lead are Ivan and Ann Albrecht, twins whose plot to wrest control of the family firm from their mother—who runs the vast business in the prolonged absence of her husband, whom her children know to be dead

at her hands, though everyone pretends he is merely somewhere else—propels the action of Rand's story. Though some reviewers found it difficult to be amused by Rand's "cardboard" characters, who are "distinguished mainly by degrees of moral turpitude," as the critic for *Publishers Weekly* put it, others took a lighter approach to the novel. A reviewer for *Booklist* predicted that "readers will be irresistibly drawn into this clever, slightly macabre caper."

BIOGRAPHICAL/CRITICAL SOURCES:

PERIODICALS

Booklist, May 1, 1988, pp. 1477-1478; November 15, 1995, p. 517.
Far Eastern Economic Review, May 23, 1996, p. 46.
Journal of American History, June, 1996, p. 245.
Kirkus Reviews, March 15, 1988, p. 397; September 15, 1995, p. 1335.
Kliatt, winter, 1995, p. 34.
Library Journal, June 1, 1988, p. 144; December, 1995, p. 128.
Nation, January 1, 1996, pp. 27-29.
New York Times Book Review, December 10, 1995, p. 24.
Publishers Weekly, April 8, 1988, p. 78; October 9, 1995, p. 73.
Tribune Books (Chicago), February 11, 1996, p. 5.
Washington Post Book World, November 5, 1995, p. 2.

*   *   *

REYNOLDS, William J. 1956-

PERSONAL: Born December 17, 1956, in Omaha, NE; son of William J. (in public relations) and Rose (a retailer; maiden name, Caliendo) Reynolds; married Peggy Blankenfeld (an artist and teacher), September 5, 1981. *Education:* Creighton University, B.A., 1979. *Avocational interests:* The American private-eye novel and its practitioners, Mark Twain ("the greatest American writer"), photography, motion pictures, music ("as a listener, not a player"), travel, board games, electronics, computers and computer games.

ADDRESSES: Home—2601 South Minnesota Ave., Suite 105-118, Sioux Falls, SD 57105. *E-mail*—

wjreynolds@aol.com. *Agent*—Lescher & Lescher, 155 East 71st St., New York, NY 10021.

CAREER: TWA Ambassador (Trans World Airlines magazine), St. Paul, MN, associate editor, 1979-80, senior editor, 1980-83, managing editor, 1983-84. Writer, 1979—.

MEMBER: Mystery Writers of America, Authors Guild.

AWARDS, HONORS: Gavel Award Certificate of Merit from American Bar Association, 1981, 1982, and 1983, for legal column in *TWA Ambassador;* nominated for Shamus Award from Private Eye Writers of America, 1985, for *The Nebraska Quotient;* Journalism Award from Aviation/Space Writers Association, 1985; ADDY Awards from South Dakota Advertising Federation, 1985 and 1986.

WRITINGS:

The Nebraska Quotient (novel), St. Martin's (New York City), 1984.
Moving Targets (novel), St. Martin's, 1986.
Money Trouble, Putnam (New York City), 1988.
Things Invisible, Putnam, 1989.
The Naked Eye, Putnam, 1990.
Drive-by, Ex Machina, 1995.

OTHER

Sioux Falls: The City and the People, American & World Geographic (Helene, MT), 1994.

Contributor of articles to periodicals, including *South Dakota, Link-Up,* and *Corporate Report.*

SIDELIGHTS: All of William J. Reynolds' mystery novels are set in Omaha, Nebraska, a city that Dale Carter in the *St. James Guide to Crime and Mystery Writers* admits "does possess a certain charm [but] it is difficult to imagine many places less glamorous. . . . Lacking the instant glamour of place, Reynolds relies upon character development, meticulous plotting, interesting situations, and realistic, witty dialogue to provide the variety necessary to sustain the reader's interest." All of Reynolds' mysteries feature a private detective known by the nickname Nebraska whose cases are humorous renderings of the classic hard-boiled detective story.

Reviewing Reynolds's first novel, *The Nebraska Quotient,* the *Washington Post Book World*'s Jean

M. White calls it "hardboiled detective fiction with a twist of self-deprecating humor." The novel concerns a senator's daughter who has posed for pornographic pictures and Nebraska's efforts to foil the blackmail plot launched against her. Nebraska finds himself ranged against mobsters, corrupt politicians, sleazy pornographers, and, of course, a murderer. While a *New York Times Book Review* critic finds *The Nebraska Quotient* to be too "conventional," White praises Reynolds for the way he "dangerously but deftly skirts parody without betraying the tough-guy tradition." The critic for *Publishers Weekly* notes that Reynolds takes his "hardboiled detective and turns him into a hardboiled punster guaranteed to elicit either a smile or a groan." The *Booklist* reviewer judges *The Nebraska Quotient* "an absorbing, fast-moving, and mostly convincing first novel."

The major strengths of the Nebraska series, according to Carter, are "the main characters and the sprightly dialogue," although the essayist notes that "Reynolds is also adept at plot construction. [The plots] are complex, yet there are sufficient clues to enable the observant reader to arrive at the solution almost as soon as Nebraska." Carter concludes that the Nebraska "books are fast-paced, exciting, and with a humor that often borders on parody, yet never quite goes that far. Reynolds is a serious practitioner of the hard-boiled detective genre, and each of his books is better than the last. He has polished his craft to a fine sheen, and deserves all the critical praise that has come his way."

Reynolds once told *CA:* "My desire to write, and particularly to write fiction, has always been strong, yet so too was the notion that writing was something to be done in one's spare time. In other words, one learned a 'real' profession, and one wrote on weekends. Consequently, I studied political science with an eye toward law school. However, a 'temporary' position as a magazine editor turned into something other, and I realized that being a writer was better than being something else in order to finance a writing life. I 'retired' from the magazine in order to write full time.

"My choice of genre was greatly influenced by the works of Dashiell Hammett. Hammett—and later, Raymond Chandler—proved that 'genre' is a meaningless concept. Merit is inherent in the work—any work—regardless of what label others choose to give the work. In my view, genres exist for the convenience of publishers, booksellers, and lazy shoppers. A novel is a novel. I find the private-eye novel a convenient format in which to treat serious themes in a less-than-heavy-handed manner.

"After a lifetime spent in various parts of the Midwest, I am only now developing much interest in the history of this region of the country, and lately I have been toying with the possibility of using the travels of Lewis and Clark as the basis for a novel. By inclination and by training (as an editor of a general-interest magazine), I am something of a generalist. I read widely and somewhat indiscriminately in a variety of subjects—science, politics, literature, the arts, popular culture, and more—and can honestly claim to have at least a mild interest in virtually every area. Except sports."

BIOGRAPHICAL/CRITICAL SOURCES:

BOOKS

St. James Guide to Crime and Mystery Writers, fourth edition, St. James Press (Detroit), 1996.

PERIODICALS

Best Sellers, October, 1984, p. 257.
Booklist, July, 1984, p. 1523.
Los Angeles Times Book Review, August 10, 1986.
New York Times Book Review, November 18, 1984.
Publishers Weekly, June 1, 1984, p. 58.
Washington Post Book World, August 19, 1984.

* * *

RHYS, Jean 1890(?)-1979

PERSONAL: Original name Ella Gwendolen Rhys (sometimes spelled Rees) Williams; born August 24, 1890 (some sources say 1894), in Roseau, Dominica, West Indies; died May 14, 1979, in Exeter, England; daughter of William Rhys (a doctor) and Minna (Lockhart) Williams; married Jean Lenglet (a poet, journalist, and singer; divorced); married Leslie Tilden Smith (a literary agent and reader for a publishing company; deceased, 1945), 1934; married Max Hamer (a poet and retired naval officer; deceased), 1947; children: Maryvonne (Mrs. Moerman). *Education:* Attended The Convent, Roseau; studied at Royal Academy of Dramatic Art, London.

CAREER: Writer. Immigrated to England, c. 1906; toured England as a chorus-girl during World War I; moved to Paris and traveled throughout Europe; worked as a ghost-writer, Juan-les-Pins, France; returned to England.

MEMBER: Royal Society of Literature (fellow).

AWARDS, HONORS: W. H. Smith Award and Heinemann Award, both 1967, for *Wide Sargasso Sea;* Arts Council of Great Britain Award for Writers, 1967; named Commander of the British Empire, c. 1979, for service to literature.

WRITINGS:

The Left Bank, and Other Stories, preface by Ford Madox Ford, J. Cape, 1927.
Postures (novel), Chatto & Windus, 1928, published as *Quartet,* Simon & Schuster, 1929.
After Leaving Mr. Mackenzie (novel), J. Cape, 1930, Knopf, 1931.
Voyage in the Dark (novel), Constable, 1934, Morrow, 1935.
Good Morning, Midnight (novel), Constable, 1939, Harper, 1970.
Wide Sargasso Sea (novel), introduction by Francis Wyndham, Deutsch, 1966, Norton, 1967.
Tigers Are Better-Looking (stories, including selections from *The Left Bank, and Other Stories*), Deutsch, 1968.
(With William Sansom, Bernard Malamud, and David Plante) *Penguin Modern Stories I,* Penguin, 1969.
My Day, F. Hallman, 1975.
Sleep it Off, Lady, Harper, 1976.
Smile Please: An Unfinished Autobiography, Harper, 1980.
The Letters of Jean Rhys, edited by Francis Wyndham and Diana Melly, Viking, 1984, published in England as *Jean Rhys Letters 1931-1966,* Deutsch, 1984.
The Complete Novels, Norton, 1985.
The Collected Short Stories, Norton, 1987.

Contributor to *Art and Literature* and *London Magazine.*

ADAPTATIONS: Good Morning, Midnight was adapted into a radio play by Selma Vaz Dias and broadcast in 1957; *Quartet* was adapted into a motion picture by James Ivory and Ruth Prawer Jhabvala and released in 1981; *Wide Sargasso Sea* was adapted as a motion picture.

SIDELIGHTS: Jean Rhys, with five novels, three collections of short stories, and an unfinished autobiography all to her credit, was neglected by critics until relatively late in her life. The rediscovery, during the 1960s and 1970s, of her highly personal fictions prompted Alfred Alvarez of the *New York Times Book Review* to deem her "one of the finest British writers of this century." "When she wrote a novel," wrote her former editor, Diana Athill, in the foreword to *Smile Please,* "it was because she had no choice, and she did it—or 'it happened to her'—for herself, not for others." Reviewers noted that Rhys frequently wrote with powerful insistence and control, drawing the reader relentlessly into her startling language that, according to David Plante in *Difficult Women: A Memoir of Three,* consists of "intense events which occur in space and silence."

Born Ella Gwendolen Rhys Williams in Roseau, Dominica, on August 24, 1890, she was the daughter of Rhys Williams, a Welsh doctor trained in London, and Minna Lockhart, a third-generation Dominican Creole. Although she was the fourth of five children, Rhys spent a rather lonely childhood. According to her unfinished autobiography *Smile Please,* her two older brothers were sent to school abroad, her older sister went to live with an aunt in St. Kitts, and a baby sister born seven years after Rhys "supplanted" her; she had few friends, finding herself "alone except for books" and voices that, as she later reported to Plante, "'had nothing to do with me. I sometimes didn't even know the words. But they wanted to be written down, so I wrote them down.'"

At the Catholic convent school she attended, Rhys experienced what she described in *Smile Please* as a "religious fit." Immersed in and fascinated by the "movements," "sounds," and "smells" of the service, she wished for a time to convert from Anglicanism to Catholicism and become a nun. The convent school influenced Rhys's writing in many ways, including through her exposure to a particular nun, Mother Sacred Heart: "I date all my love of words, especially beautiful words, to her half-ironical lessons."

Smile Please documents yet another appeal of Catholicism to Rhys: "Instead of the black people sitting in a different part of the church, they were all mixed up with the white and this pleased me very much." The split between black and white preoccupied Rhys, who was herself of mixed heritage, throughout her life; although her feelings about the racial division of her native island were often am-

bivalent, she always felt a nostalgia for the blacks of her homeland. Part of that longing resulted from her affinity with native nurses and servants. Despite the racial strife on the island, including riots and violence, black women in particular offered Rhys access to a mysterious sphere of sorcery and patois that, both frightening and seductive, reappears throughout her novels. Her attraction to both the ritual of Catholicism and the subversiveness of island magic is an example of the polarities caught in her work. There is often a double language going on in Rhys—the bourgeois, white, English discourse of survival and control, and the secret, private, primitive subtext of incantation, sexuality, and madness.

Another appeal of the black women in Rhys's life was perhaps the contrast they provided to her own mother, who was distant and distracted. "She drifted away from me," Rhys recalled in her autobiography, "and when I tried to interest her she was indifferent." Her mother, however, seemed to love babies, and Rhys once heard her remark that black ones were prettier than white ones: "Was this the reason why I prayed so ardently to be black, and would run to the looking-glass in the morning to see if the miracle had happened?" Although the "My Mother" chapter of *Smile Please* concludes with the dismissive statement "Gradually I came to wonder about my mother less and less until at last she was almost a stranger and I stopped imagining what she felt or what she thought," the motif of the indifferent mother permeates much of Rhys's work. As Ronnie Scharfman noted in an article appearing in *Yale French Studies,* there is great damage caused in Rhys's fiction by the "distant, inaccessible, depressed, rejecting mother" and by the "yearning, . . . [the] desire for this present-absent figure."

In 1907 Rhys (still known as Gwen Williams) left her native island for England, where she was to be under the care of her aunt, Clarice Williams. At first drawn by the promise of adventure, Rhys soon discovered that England was cold, alien, and hostile and that she was an outsider. As Thomas Staley pointed out in *Jean Rhys: A Critical Study,* "The drastic climatic change becomes a constant metaphor in her work to dramatise the parallel, chilling psychological effects of England," which often leave transplanted women like Julia Martin's mother in *After Leaving Mr. Mackenzie* "sickening for the sun." In the autumn of 1907 Rhys was enrolled in the Perse School, where she was tormented by English girls who, according to Carole Angier's *Jean Rhys,* appreciated neither

her Creole background nor her "flashing, instinctive
. . . mind." Although she was incompetent in many
aspects of English life, Rhys's early affinity for language stood her in good stead: the *Persean Magazine,* Angier reported, wrote that "she expressed her
views fearlessly" against a debate resolution "that
'The popularity of modern literature, to the exclusion
of standard works, is unreasonable and deplorable.'"
Rhys was still years from discovering herself to be a
writer, but this anecdote presages both the intensity
and the style of her later work, described by Francis
Wyndham in the introduction to *Wide Sargasso Sea*
as a "mixture of quivering immediacy and glassy
objectivity." Rhys's unhappy time at Perse reinforced impulses that would later become motifs in
her writing; as Staley observed, "Her sense of dis-
placement and cultural rift created a . . . racial identity with blacks and an affinity for the exile."

After Rhys left the Perse school she entered the
Academy of Dramatic Art in 1909 to become an
actress. There, too, she met with disappointment,
and when her father died, she found herself, with
little money, forced to drop out. Shortly afterwards
she found a job in a musical chorus and for two
years, under the stage name Ella (sometimes Emma)
Gray, toured the provinces while living in shabby
hotels, eating meagerly, and beginning the habit of
drinking against which she struggled until her death.
Between runs she took odd jobs, working as an
artist's model and posing for advertisements. As
Staley observed, her early experiences provided
"scenes she was later to recreate so well in her novels."

During this period Rhys lived with women who eventually served as prototypes for characters in her
books: disenfranchised women who depended financially on men, fatalistic and satiric "tarts," as Angier
reported, whose slang drew Rhys to them. According
to Angier, they spoke a "secret language, like the
ones at home—the servants' patois, or the Carib
women's language, which the men didn't know."

Despite the rats in the dressing room, her almost
paralyzing shyness, and her pervasive sense of herself as an outsider, Rhys had not yet succumbed to
the depression and rage that would ultimately permeate her novels and her life. In 1910 she began an
affair with a distinguished and respectable Englishman named Lancelot Hugh Smith, who seemed to
engage her not just through love but through language, "a secret language . . . a male language of
upper-class cliche," Angier wrote. When the affair

ended, Rhys was devastated: desperate, disillusioned,
and suicidal. However, as Staley observed, "It was
in the aftermath of this loss that she began to record
her experiences and feelings in a notebook. This was
the first writing she had done since childhood, and as
she painfully recorded her feelings, she was, un-
knowingly, embarking on another career which
would allow her to transform the bitter experiences
of her life into art." The transformation was still a
long time coming, however; after the initial purging,
as Athill reported in her introduction to *Jean Rhys:
The Complete Novels,* Rhys buried her notebooks in
the bottom of a suitcase where they remained untouched for years although she continued writing
diaries and lived on an allowance from Smith.

In 1917 she met the half-French, half-Dutch, Jean
Lenglet in the London boarding house where she
lived. Within a few weeks she was engaged to a man
she barely knew, a singer, painter, and sometimes
author who wrote under the name Edouard de Neve.
By 1919 Rhys and Lenglet were married and living
in Holland, where she worked in a pensions office.
Shortly afterwards they moved to Paris, reinforcing
the pattern of transit and upheaval that was to mark
Rhys's life. In Paris Rhys became an English tutor
while Lenglet pursued clandestine espionage activities of which Rhys apparently knew little if anything.
In late December 1919, Rhys gave birth to a son,
William Owen, who died within a few weeks. Accounts of his birth and death appear in thinly veiled
autobiographical sections of *After Leaving Mr.
Mackenzie* and *Good Morning, Midnight.* When she
was finally able, Rhys joined Lenglet in Vienna,
where he had taken a post as secretary-interpreter but
was also dealing in the black-market currency exchange. A time of relative wealth, this period was
followed by a transfer to Budapest, where Rhys
found herself pregnant again with her daughter,
Maryvonne, who was born in 1922 in Brussels after
the Lenglets fled Budapest, in Angier's words, "like
hunted animals" following revelation of Lenglet's
illegal activities.

Leaving the baby at a clinic in Brussels (she was
later cared for by a family in Paris), Rhys and
Lenglet returned to Paris where he attempted a career as a journalist. Rhys, working in a dress shop,
tried to help her husband sell his rejected articles,
which she translated into English, by calling on an
old acquaintance, Pearl Adam, the wife of a London
Times correspondent in Paris. Adam, who was more
interested in Rhys's language than in Lenglet's ideas,

asked whether Rhys had written anything herself. Reluctantly, Rhys gave her access to the old notebooks, which Adam tried to unify into a narrative she called "Triple Sec." Although the two women never succeeded as author and editor and the work was abandoned, Adam effected a turning point in Rhys's life by introducing her to Ford Madox Ford, then editor of the *Transatlantic Review.*

Ford became Rhys's mentor, helping her with her writing, exposing her to contemporary literature, introducing her to writers, and publishing some of the stories she began to write. When they were collected in 1927 as her first book, *The Left Bank, and Other Stories,* Ford wrote the introduction, in which he described her "terrifying insight and a terrific—an almost lurid!—passion for stating the case of the underdog." Ironically, while Ford launched Jean Rhys the writer, he also exploited Jean Rhys the woman. In 1923, after the police finally arrested and extradited Lenglet, Rhys, desperate and penniless, turned to Ford, who drew her into a short-lived menage a trois with his live-in mistress, Stella Bowen. In *Drawn from Life: Reminiscences* Bowen later described Rhys as a "tragic person" with a "gift for prose" and a "personal attractiveness," which, however, "were not enough to ensure her any reasonable life, for on the other side of the balance were bad health, destitution, shattered nerves, an undesirable husband, lack of nationality, and a complete absence of any desire for independence." With the exception of the last observation, Bowen probably accurately reports the state in which she and Ford found Rhys, who thought she had discovered in Ford a patron and protector but found instead, as Staley declared, confirmation of "her deepest suspicions about her own feminine vulnerability and male exploitation." Lenglet, who returned to Paris about the time Ford was disentangling himself from Rhys, harbored suspicions about the nature of the Ford-Rhys relationship, suspicions that led to the breakup of the Lenglet-Rhys marriage. Nonetheless, the couple returned for a time to Amsterdam where they lived again with Maryvonne. Rhys translated Francis Carco's *Perversite,* a translation that was later attributed to Ford, who had negotiated with its American publisher, Pascal Covici. In Amsterdam Rhys also completed the final version of her first published novel, *Quartet.* By the time Rhys left Lenglet and Maryvonne together in Holland and returned to England as the writer now known as Jean Rhys, all the central plots and motifs—the divisions, disappointments, and conflicts—of her future work had been irrevocably established.

The abusive, shattering relationship with Ford, which reinforced the bitterness and despair Rhys felt after the breakup with Lancelot Smith, is the basis of *Quartet* (1928), which details the involvement of art-dealer H. J. Heidler and his wife with the young Marya Zelli, whose husband is in prison. Jonathan Cape, the first publisher to whom Rhys submitted the barely disguised roman a clef, was afraid of a libel suit from Ford. Chatto & Windus eventually published the book, requiring first that Rhys change the title to *Postures* (her original title—and the one by which the novel is generally known—was restored in the 1929 American edition). Although there were some encouraging reviews, neither *The Left Bank* nor *Postures* was a financial success. Staley stated, "Her work . . . would seem relentlessly depressing. . . . However well-wrought and deeply felt, her subject matter would seem narrow, confining, and even suffocating."

Critics for many years have tended to focus on Rhys's subject matter and to judge—rather than attempt to understand—her characters from psychological, economic, racial, or feminist perspectives. In his Twayne study Peter Wolfe, for example, wrote of *Voyage in the Dark,* "Single women who live alone do not always become prostitutes or drunkards. Anna might have supported herself honorably. Somebody with more fiber would not have slid so easily into her groove of sameness." Plante felt that Rhys herself failed to understand the women about whom she wrote: "There is about [Rhys's female characters] a great dark space in which they do not ask themselves, removing themselves from themselves in the world in which they live: Why do I suffer?"

Critics have noted that *Quartet,* Rhys's first major attempt to manipulate material for a reading audience, is the least polished, the least aesthetically distanced of her novels, betraying "uncertainties," as Wyndham wrote, "that were later eliminated from her style" as she gained a sense of the shape of her work. According to Plante, "Jean often talked of the 'shape' of her books: she imagined a shape, and everything that fit into the shape she put in, everything that didn't she left out, and she left out a lot." Forged during the modernist period, Rhys's art, as Staley suggested, "shares many of [the] characteristics and impulses of literary modernism, but she was unaware of or removed from many of its preoccupations. . . . [H]er work was never very closely attuned to the technical innovations of modernism; her art developed out of an intensely private world—a world whose sources of inspiration were neither literary nor intellectual." Rhys's isolation from the intellectual and literary sources of modernism, along with her position as an economically and culturally disenfranchised woman, may partially explain the longtime critical neglect of her work.

Despite the technical weaknesses noted by critics, *Quartet* introduces at least two devices characteristic of all of Rhys's work: her style, described by Staley as "carefully modulated, terse, frequently flat, always understated," and interior monologues resulting from her female protagonists' inability to posit themselves as speaking selves, particularly to men who, according to Judith Kegan Gardiner, in her *boundary 2* essay, deny Rhys's women "the freedom of language and therefore the freedom to define [themselves]" and then despise them for their failures. But Judith Thurman averred in *Ms.* that "one of the strongest impressions . . . one gets from *Quartet* is that Jean Rhys mistrusts other women." Thurman perceived Rhys's otherness as genderless in a world where women, as exemplified by Heidler's mistress Lois, are "even more treacherous than men." Although many feminist critics have been drawn to Rhys, she herself did not embrace feminism; Rhys, in fact, was impatient with and pessimistic about most -isms, including those associated with the women's movement: according to Angier, "Whenever she read a review that was even mildly feminist, she laughed and tore it up."

Another important aspect of *Quartet* is its blending of realism with what Staley calls "open-ended images and dreamlike flights" that initially are "rigidly controlled by the direct and simple style" and then give way to the protagonist's "horror, fear, dislocation, and desperation," producing a "stylisation of consciousness." In later works this control vanishes, and much of the language and behavior of Rhys's characters exhibit qualities of schizophrenia, as Elizabeth Abel described it in her *Contemporary Literature* essay: "impoverished affect, apathy, obsessive thought and behavior coupled with the inability to take real initiative, a sense of the unreality of both the world and self, and a feeling of detachment from the body." Accordingly, Rhys's second novel, *After Leaving Mr. Mackenzie,* was labeled by Thurman "a vision, in slow motion, of a woman coming apart." Again taking up the story of a woman abandoned by a lover, it also draws material from Rhys's Caribbean childhood and her ambivalent relationship to her dying mother.

Between the publication of *Quartet* and *After Leaving Mr. Mackenzie,* Rhys met Leslie Tilden Smith, a literary agent who was instrumental in placing her novels; Rhys moved in with him in 1929, and they married in 1934. The years of their relationship, during which Rhys wrote virtually all of her early work were, however, far from happy. Smith apparently indulged Rhys with great kindness, took on most of the household chores, and endured her drinking and her periodic rages, but according to Angier, "He had come too late. Instead, she went over and over the loss of love, the loss of hope." Nonetheless, Smith supported her in her work, typing and reading manuscripts and borrowing money (which he mismanaged) to subsidize her trips to Paris, the setting of so much of her work. For Rhys writing was apparently an arduous process during which she seemed to need to relive her own pain, bitterness, and desperation through that of the women about whom she wrote. She also was unable to end work on a book; as Angier noted, "she wrote and rewrote, in an obsessive search for perfection that would not allow her to let anything go. When Leslie knew that a manuscript was finished, he simply took it away from her. There would be a terrible row, but at least it was done; and soon Jean would forget her anguish and feel relieved."

In 1934, *Voyage in the Dark* was completed and published: derived from notebooks written more than a decade before *Quartet,* this third novel combined the urgency of a journal with the more developed craft of an experienced writer, and it remained for Rhys, despite years of critical neglect, her favorite work. *Voyage in the Dark* reworks the familiar Rhysian plot of a destitute chorus girl, abandoned by lovers and left alone and pregnant; stylistically, however, it develops more fully the preoccupations established in her earlier published work: flashbacks to Dominica, floating memories that disrupt the text, syntactical aberrations, and finally, following Anna Morgan's abortion, a kind of delirious discourse in which all boundaries between past and present, hallucination and reality, disappear. Rhys's publishers insisted she change the "morbid" ending in which Anna died. In a June 1934 letter printed in Francis Wyndham and Diana Melly's collection of Rhys's correspondence, Rhys confided: "I minded more than I would have believed possible. . . . I suppose I shall have to give in and cut the book and I'm afraid it will make it meaningless. The worst is that it is precisely the last part which I am most certain of that will have to be mutilated." She was haunted by this revision for more than thirty years.

The last of Rhys's early novels, *Good Morning, Midnight,* which appeared in 1939, confirmed, as Staley observed, that "her fiction was not a literature of social engagement. . . . [H]er writing seemed untouched by the devastating political and military events which had occurred and by the even more horrendous ones which were on the horizon." *Good Morning, Midnight* centers on the oldest of Rhys's protagonists, Sasha Jansen, wandering the streets of Paris and trying to avoid the psychological and physical threats that surround her. Gardiner, in her *boundary 2* essay, characterized the novel as "a sustained critique of polarizations about sex, class and moral value that oppress women and the poor."

If the earlier novels are marked by a kind of defeated passivity, *Good Morning, Midnight* is characterized by fear and violence. "I'm very much afraid of men," Sasha says. "And I'm even more afraid of women. And I'm very much afraid of the whole bloody human race." At another moment, when she feels a woman is staring at her in a bar, she declares, "One day, quite suddenly, when you're not expecting it, I'll take a hammer from the folds of my dark cloak and crack your little skull like an egg-shell. Crack it will go, the egg-shell; out they will stream, the blood, the brains. One day, one day. . . . One day the fierce wolf that walks by my side will spring on you and rip your abominable guts out. One day, one day. . . . Now, now, gently, quietly, quietly. . . ." The elliptical style is characteristic of Rhys's novels, as Gardiner observed in her *boundary 2* essay: "She uses [ellipses] often, as through she is quoting herself incompletely, deliberately leaving gaps that we must fill in." The ending of the novel involves a rather sadistic, surreal sexual encounter with a traveling salesman whose presence and function for Sasha, as she both seduces and submits to him, remain complex and ambiguous. Whether her final affirmation "Yes—yes—yes . . ." is masochistic or enlightened remains unclear, reflecting the precarious state of consciousness that structures this last novel before Rhys retreated into years of heavy drinking and emotional instability.

After *Good Morning, Midnight,* Rhys became depressed and unsettled. According to Angier, Leslie Smith gave his wife a copy of Charlotte Bronte's nineteenth-century novel *Jane Eyre,* and by the end of 1939, by which time Smith had volunteered for the war effort and was traveling a great deal, Rhys had finished part if not all of a version of *Wide Sargasso Sea,* called at the time "Le Revenant" and based on *Jane Eyre.* Apparently, however, in one of

the rages to which she was increasingly prone, she burned the typescript and, during a move, lost most of the manuscript. Angier reported that "many years later [Rhys] found 'two chapters (in another suitcase),' and used them for *Wide Sargasso Sea.* But she had to undergo much more suffering before she could create the final version of Antoinette," the novel's protagonist.

During the war, with her husband gone much of the time, Rhys did, in Angier's words, "cross a line between anguish and breakdown." Stories such as "The Insect World" reflect her wartime paranoia and her sense that "almost any book was better than life," as she declared in *Sleep It Off, Lady,* her final collection of short stories; the suicidal Teresa of "A Solid House" confirms, as does much of the writing of this period, Rhys's own precarious state. As Angier noted, Rhys struggled to transform her own fragile and violent states into art, but the emotions became again "too raw, too close to breakdown and delusion. Her notebooks and drafts for the stories show how close they were. They are wild, obsessive, almost illegible. . . ." When *Tigers Are Better-Looking* finally appeared in 1968, two of its most disturbing stories had been removed; they were printed separately in *Penguin Modern Stories 1.*

Leslie Smith died suddenly in 1945, and Rhys's condition worsened. In 1947 she married Max Hamer, Smith's cousin and estate executor, who, like Rhys's first husband, was apparently involved in illegal financial dealings. In 1949 she "cracked" and was prosecuted for having raged at and assaulted a neighbor. She spent almost a week in the hospital wing of Holloway Prison and then was sent home on probation. She began to write the story "Let Them Call It Jazz," with which she struggled for over a decade; her fears that she was losing her ability to sustain either herself or her work seemed well founded. In 1950 Hamer was arrested for stealing checks, and Rhys, supported anonymously during her husband's imprisonment, was truly desperate and incapacitated. When she began to work again, Angier commented, "it was [a] return to the very first form she had used, to lift the blackness of her first big 'smash': a diary. . . . The part of it she kept (for later she tore out most of its pages) was published in her autobiography, *Smile Please.*"

By now all of Rhys's books were out of print, and she had been virtually forgotten. She wrote erratically, more concerned with her health and finances than with her work; her novel based on *Jane Eyre* had been abandoned. In November 1949, however, an advertisement had appeared in the *New Statesman* seeking Jean Rhys or anyone who knew her whereabouts. It had been placed by Selma Vaz Dias, an actress who was familiar with Rhys's work and who wanted permission to adapt *Good Morning, Midnight* for a radio monologue. Vaz Dias and Rhys, who had seen the ad, corresponded, and the actress gave an initial performance at the Anglo-French Art Centre in London. The production was rejected by the BBC, but Vaz Dias had initiated a kind of resurrection of Rhys. In 1957 the adaptation was finally broadcast and well received, starting a chain of events that would change the direction of Rhys's last years.

Francis Wyndham, an editor with Andre Deutsch, had long been an admirer of Rhys's work but had, like many others, presumed her dead. Wyndham and another Deutsch editor, Diana Athill, secured for Rhys an option on the novel that would become *Wide Sargasso Sea.* However, her depression, ill health, continued heavy drinking, and sporadic attention to the stories that would later comprise *Sleep It Off, Lady* delayed her completion of the novel. It took her eight years to finish a manuscript she had promised to have done in six to nine months. Moreover, *Wide Sargasso Sea* was more demanding than her other work had been. Structurally it was complicated because it was written in the context of another novel, *Jane Eyre,* retelling the story from the madwoman Bertha Mason's point of view and creating a history for the inarticulate Creole locked in the attic of an English mansion; psychologically it was complicated because of the obvious similarities between Rhys's own life and that of Antoinette/Bertha.

In 1936 Rhys and Smith had visited Dominica, the only time she returned to her homeland. Despite the troubling nature of Rhys's journey, Staley credited it with "enabl[ing] her to integrate the experience of her childhood with a mature sensibility in order to inform [*Wide Sargasso Sea*] with the deep and complex feelings that arose within her." But the problem involved more than coming to terms with one's past; as Athill declared in her introduction to *Jean Rhys: The Complete Novels:* "Nowhere else did [Rhys] write with more poignancy about what it is like to be rejected, and nowhere else did she go so deeply into something which filled her with a special terror because . . . there had been times when she felt it happening to herself: what it is like to be driven beyond your psychic strength, and go mad. At a hidden level the story of Antoinette and her mother is that of Jean and her own mother, and the story of

Antoinette and Mr. Rochester is that of Jean and England; and it is from this hidden level that its vibrancy springs."

Narratively, *Wide Sargasso Sea* is constructed around Antoinette's and Rochester's alternating voices, his discourse punctuated by a strange section in the middle of the novel where Antoinette returns to her old nurse; as Angier observed, "Whenever she was hurled most low, Jean found a black woman from her islands to speak for her." What is important in this last novel is not that Christophine speaks for Rhys and Antoinette, but that it is through the black woman that Rhys can speak with the most power, can disturb and disrupt the control Rochester has over her protagonist economically, physically, and linguistically. At the end of the novel, the two stories merge, Antoinette having been taken to England where she replays in the last section Bertha Mason's suicide as she leaps from the burning roof of Thornfield. In Rhys's version, the conclusion is open-ended, as Antoinette/Bertha dreams Bronte's ending and then takes off down a dark passageway thinking, "Now at last I know why I was brought here and what I have to do." Whether or not she acts out the dream is left unclear; in either case, Rhys has transformed the madwoman into a woman who has taken control of her own narrative despite the presumably predetermined outcome. As Staley pointed out, working within the framework of an already written story allowed Rhys to concentrate on "the tale of the telling rather than the telling of the tale."

Wide Sargasso Sea, which in 1967 won the W. H. Smith literary award and an award from the Royal Society of Literature, brought Rhys the success that had eluded her for so long. Yet despite moderate fame and the reissuance of all her earlier novels, Rhys was uncertain, unhappy, and ill; scholars and students plagued her, she was helpless when faced with legal or financial decisions, and she signed away artistic control and fifty percent of her profits to Vaz Dias. According to Angier, Rhys "retreated further and further into self-absorption, self-pity, and anger. She had always remembered feelings more than facts: now that she was old, and ill, and dying, she confused them utterly."

The years following *Wide Sargasso Sea* saw the publication of three more volumes of Rhys's work. In 1968 appeared the short story collection *Tigers Are Better-Looking,* which includes nine selections from *The Left Bank* and eight previously published but theretofore uncollected pieces. In 1975 *My Day,* a trio of autobiographical sketches, was privately printed, followed in 1976 by *Sleep It Off, Lady,* mostly unpublished work, much of which predates the newer stories of *Tigers Are Better-Looking.* Staley considered this third volume "a kind of thematic code, or retrospective chorus, to all of Rhys's previous work" with a "clarity of focus" and "certainty of feeling within that narrow world she draws upon for her subject matter." Rhys herself, however, confessed that she regarded these last pieces "no good, no good, magazine stories."

All thirty-six stories in Rhys's three published collections, as well as three previously unpublished works, were later released as 1987's *The Collected Short Stories.* With an introduction by editor and friend Anthill, the volume provides an excellent overview of the writer's career, spanning as it does the three main periods of her work: the 1920s, 1960s, and the 1970s. "The result . . . ," noted Linda Barrett Osborne in the *Washington Post Book World,* "is singular, an intense and disturbing reading experience." "Reading such stories as a group, so remarkably consistent in tone and theme, can be overwhelming," Osborne continued. "Yet it is precisely this intense immersion in experience that is the essence of Rhys's art. The force of her stories lies in the fusion of elegant prose with an uncanny penetration into the darker reaches of the soul."

In the last years before her death, Rhys worked on compiling her autobiography from scribbles, abandoned fragments of novels, diaries, and an increasingly unreliable memory. As Plante described in *Difficult Women,* this was a grueling process during which Rhys despaired of the project, her life, and her previous work. She had always viewed writing as "a way of getting rid of something, something unpleasant especially" and considered herself "'a pen . . . nothing but a pen'" through which a story told itself: "'I think and think for a sentence, and every sentence I think for is wrong, I know it. Then, all at once, the illuminating sentence comes to me. Everything clicks into place.'" In her last work, the autobiography *Smile Please,* which Rhys felt compelled to do to set the record straight—"everything they say about me is wrong"—fewer and fewer illuminations were coming to her. Never finished, the book is abruptly divided into two major sections: the first, reflections on Rhys's childhood in Dominica, and the second, pre-1923, "first major drafts, or notes towards first drafts" dealing with her life in England, which Athill arranged and titled "It began to grow

cold." The volume, which was published six months after its author's death, also contains an appendix, "From a diary," drawn from entries Rhys had made over a period of some thirty years.

On May 14, 1979, Rhys died, a lonely, angry woman who, despite being honored shortly before her death as Commander of the British Empire for her service to literature, saw herself finally only as part of something much greater than her own work. "'All of writing is a huge lake,'" she told Plante several years previous. "'There are great rivers that feed the lake, like Tolstoy and Dostoevsky. And there are trickles, like Jean Rhys. All that matters is feeding the lake. I don't matter. The lake matters. You must keep feeding the lake.'"

BIOGRAPHICAL/CRITICAL SOURCES:

BOOKS

Angier, Carole, *Jean Rhys,* Viking, 1985.

Angier, Carole, *Jean Rhys: Life and Work,* Little, Brown, 1990.

Brown, Stella, *Drawn from Life,* Mann, 1974.

Carr, Helen, *Jean Rhys,* Northcote House, 1996.

Contemporary Literary Criticism, Gale, Volume 2, 1974, Volume 4, 1975, Volume 6, 1976, Volume 14, 1980, Volume 19, 1981, Volume 51, 1989.

Dictionary of Literary Biography, Gale, Volume 36: *British Novelists, 1890-1929: Modernists,* 1985, Volume 117: *Twentieth-Century Caribbean and Black African Writers,* first series, 1992, Volume 162: *British Short-Fiction Writers, 1915-1945,* 1996.

Gardiner, Judith Kegan, *Rhys, Stead, Lessing, and the Politics of Empathy,* Indiana University Press, 1989.

Gregg, Veronica Marie, *Jean Rhys's Historical Imagination: Reading and Writing the Creole,* University of North Carolina Press, 1995.

Malcolm, Cheryl Alexander, and David Malcolm, *Jean Rhys: A Study of the Short Fiction,* Prentice Hall, 1996.

Plante, David, *Difficult Women: A Memoir of Three,* Atheneum, 1983.

Raiskin, Judith L., *Snow on the Cane Fields: Women's Writing and Creole Subjectivity,* University of Minnesota Press, 1996.

Short Story Criticism, Gale, 1996.

Wolfe, Peter, *Jean Rhys,* Twayne, 1980.

PERIODICALS

Atlantic Monthly, June 1980.
English Journal, March 1994, p. 97.
Listener, December 6, 1979.
Los Angeles Timse Book Review, March 8, 1987, p. 4.
New Republic, February 17, 1992.
New Statesman, February 15, 1980.
New Yorker, August 11, 1980, December 2, 1991.
Times Literary Supplement, December 21, 1979.
Washington Post Book World, June 28, 1987.
World Literature Today, summer, 1988, p. 497.
Yale Review, summer, 1980.

OBITUARIES:

PERIODICALS

Newsweek, May 28, 1979.
New York Times, May 17, 1979.
Time, May 28, 1979.
Washington Post Book World, May 18, 1979.*

*   *   *

RICHARDS, Francis
  See LOCKRIDGE, Richard

*   *   *

RICHLER, Mordecai 1931-

PERSONAL: Born January 27, 1931, in Montreal, Quebec, Canada; son of Moses Isaac and Lily (Rosenberg) Richler; married Florence Wood, July 27, 1960; children: Daniel, Noah, Emma, Martha, Jacob. *Education:* Attended Sir George Williams University, 1949-51. *Religion:* Jewish.

ADDRESSES: Home and office—1321 Sherbrooke St. W., Apt. 80C, Montreal, Quebec, Canada H3G 1J4. *Agent*—Lynn Nesbit, International Creative Management, 40 West 57th St., New York, NY 10019; (for films) William Morris Agency, 1350 Avenue of the Americas, New York, NY 10019.

CAREER: Writer. Freelance writer in Paris, France, 1952-53, London, England, 1954-72, and Montreal, 1972—. Sir George Williams University, writer-in-residence, 1968-69; Carleton University, visiting professor of English, 1972-74. Member of editorial board, Book-of-the-Month Club, 1972—.

MEMBER: Montreal Press Club.

AWARDS, HONORS: President's medal for nonfiction, University of Western Ontario, 1959; Canadian Council junior art fellowships, 1959 and 1960, senior arts fellowship, 1967; Guggenheim Foundation creative writing fellowship, 1961; *Paris Review* humor prize, 1967, for section from *Cocksure* and *Hunting Tigers under Glass;* Governor-General's Literary Award, Canada Council, 1968, for *Cocksure* and *Hunting Tigers under Glass,* and 1971, for *St. Urbain's Horseman; London Jewish Chronicle* literature awards, 1972, for *St. Urbain's Horseman;* Berlin Film Festival Golden Bear, Academy Award nomination, and Screenwriters Guild of America award, all 1974, for the screenplay *The Apprenticeship of Duddy Kravitz;* ACTRA Award for best television writer—drama, Academy of Canadian Cinema and Television, 1975; Book of the Year for Children Award, Canadian Library Association, and Ruth Schwartz Children's Book Award, Ontario Arts Council, both 1976, for *Jacob Two-Two Meets the Hooded Fang; London Jewish Chronicle* H. H. Wingate award for fiction, 1981, for *Joshua Then and Now;* named a Literary Lion, New York Public Library, 1989; Commonwealth Writers Prize, Book Trust, 1990, for *Solomon Gursky Was Here.*

WRITINGS:

NOVELS

The Acrobats, Putnam, 1954, published as *Wicked We Love,* Popular Library, 1955.
Son of a Smaller Hero, Collins (Toronto), 1955, Paperback Library, 1965.
A Choice of Enemies, Collins, 1957.
The Apprenticeship of Duddy Kravitz, Little, Brown (Boston), 1959.
The Incompatible Atuk, McClelland & Stewart (Toronto), published as *Stick Your Neck Out,* Simon & Schuster (New York City), 1963.
Cocksure, Simon & Schuster, 1968.
St. Urbain's Horseman, Knopf (New York City), 1971.
Joshua Then and Now, Knopf, 1980.
Solomon Gursky Was Here, Viking (New York City), 1989.

FOR CHILDREN

Jacob Two-Two Meets the Hooded Fang, Knopf, 1975.

Jacob Two-Two and the Dinosaur, Knopf, 1987.

Jacob Two-Two's First Spy Case, Farrar, Straus (New York City), 1997.

SCREENPLAYS

(With Nicholas Phipps) *No Love for Johnnie,* Embassy, 1962.

(With Geoffrey Cotterell and Ivan Foxwell) *Tiara Tahiti,* Rank, 1962.

(With Phipps) *The Wild and the Willing,* Rank, 1962, released in the United States as *Young and Willing,* Universal, 1965.

Life at the Top, Royal International, 1965.

The Apprenticeship of Duddy Kravitz (adapted from his novel of the same title), Paramount, 1974.

(With David Giler and Jerry Belson) *Fun with Dick and Jane,* Bart/Palevsky, 1977.

Joshua Then and Now (adapted from his novel of the same title), Twentieth Century-Fox, 1985.

TELEVISION AND RADIO PLAYS

The Acrobats (based on his novel of the same title), Canadian Broadcasting Company (CBC), 1956 (radio), 1957 (television).

Friend of the People, CBC-TV, 1957.

Paid in Full, ATV (England), 1958.

Benny, the War in Europe, and Myerson's Daughter Bella, CBC-Radio, 1958.

The Trouble with Benny (based on a short story), ABC (England), 1959.

The Apprenticeship of Duddy Kravitz (based on his novel of the same title), CBC-TV, 1960.

The Spare Room, CBC-Radio, 1961.

Q for Quest (excerpts from his fiction), CBC-Radio, 1963.

The Fall of Mendel Krick, British Broadcasting Corp. (BBC-TV), 1963.

It's Harder to Be Anybody, CBC-Radio, 1965.

Such Was St. Urbain Street, CBC-Radio, 1966.

The Wordsmith (based on a short story), CBC-Radio, 1979.

OTHER

Hunting Tigers under Glass: Essays and Reports, McClelland & Stewart, 1969.

The Street: Stories, McClelland & Stewart, 1969, New Republic, 1975.

(Editor) *Canadian Writing Today* (anthology), Peter Smith (Magnolia, MA), 1970.

Shoveling Trouble (essays), McClelland & Stewart, 1973.

Notes on an Endangered Species and Others (essays), Knopf, 1974.

The Suit (animated filmstrip), National Film Board of Canada, 1976.

Images of Spain, photographs by Peter Christopher, Norton (New York City), 1977.

The Great Comic Book Heroes and Other Essays, McClelland & Stewart, 1978.

(Editor) *The Best of Modern Humor,* Knopf, 1984.

Home Sweet Home: My Canadian Album (essays), Knopf, 1984, published as *Home Sweet Home,* Penguin (New York City), 1985.

(Author of book) *Duddy* (play; based on his novel *The Apprenticeship of Duddy Kravitz,*) first produced in Edmonton, Alberta, at the Citadel theatre, April, 1984.

Broadsides: Reviews and Opinions, Viking, 1990.

(Editor) *Writers on World War II: An Anthology,* Knopf, 1991.

Oh Canada! Oh Quebec! Requiem for a Divided Country, Knopf, 1992.

The Language of Signs, McKay (New York City), 1992.

This Year in Jerusalem, Knopf, 1994.

Contributor to Canadian, U.S., and British periodicals. Richler's papers are collected at the University of Calgary Library in Alberta.

ADAPTATIONS: Richler's children's book *Jacob Two-Two Meets the Hooded Fang* was filmed by Cinema Shares International and recorded by Christopher Plummer for Caedmon Records, both 1977; film rights have been sold for both *Stick Your Neck Out* and *Cocksure.*

SIDELIGHTS: "To be a Canadian and a Jew," as Mordecai Richler wrote in his book *Hunting Tigers under Glass: Essays and Reports,* "is to emerge from the ghetto twice." He referred to the double pressures of being in both a religious minority and the cultural enigma that is Canada. Yet in his decades as a novelist, screenwriter, and essayist, Richler has established himself as one of the few representatives of Canadian Jewry known outside his native country.

That many of his fictional works feature Jewish-Canadian protagonists in general (most notably in his best-known book, *The Apprenticeship of Duddy Kravitz*), and natives of Montreal in particular, denotes the author's strong attachment to his early years. Richler was born in the Jewish ghetto of Montreal to a religious family of Russian emigres. "In his teens, however, he abandoned Orthodox customs, gradually becoming more interested both in a wider world and in writing," related R. H. Ramsey in the *Dictionary of Literary Biography*. After a stint at a university, Richler cashed in an insurance policy and used the money to sail to Liverpool, England. Eventually he found his way to Paris, where he spent some years emulating such expatriate authors as Ernest Hemingway and Henry Miller, then moved on to London, where he worked as a news correspondent.

During those early years, Richler produced his first novel, *The Acrobats,* a book he later characterized as "more political than anything I've done since, and humorless," as he told Walter Goodman in a *New York Times* interview, adding that the volume, published when he was twenty-three, "was just a very young man's novel. Hopelessly derivative. Like some unfortunate collision of [Jean-Paul] Sartre and Hemingway and [Louis-Ferdinand] Celine, all unabsorbed and undigested. I wasn't writing in my own voice at all. I was imitating people." But Richler found his voice soon after, with novels like *Son of a Smaller Hero, A Choice of Enemies,* and *The Incomparable Atuk.* Ramsey found that from these efforts on, "two tendencies dominate Richler's fiction: realism and satire. [Many of the early stories are] realistic, their plots basically traditional in form, their settings accurately detailed, their characters motivated in psychologically familiar ways." At the other extreme, Ramsey continued, there is "pure satiric fantasy, [with] concessions to realism slight. In [such works] Richler indulges the strong comic vein in his writing as he attacks Canadian provincialism and the spurious gratifications of the entertainment medium."

Richler gained further notice with three of his best-known titles, *The Apprenticeship of Duddy Kravitz, St. Urbain's Horseman,* and *Joshua Then and Now.* These books share a common theme—that of a Jewish-Canadian protagonist at odds with society—and all three novels revolve around the idea of the way greed can taint success. *The Apprenticeship of Duddy Kravitz* presents its eponymous hero as a ghetto-reared youth on a never-ending quest to make a name for himself in business. It is also "the first of Richler's novels to exhibit fully his considerable comic talents, a strain that includes much black humor and a racy, colloquial, ironic idiom that be-

comes a characteristic feature of Richler's subsequent style," according to Ramsey.

Comparing *The Apprenticeship of Duddy Kravitz* to other such coming-of-age stories as James Joyce's *Portrait of the Artist as a Young Man* and D. H. Lawrence's *Sons and Lovers,* A. R. Bevan, in a new introduction to Richler's novel, found that the book, "in spite of its superficial affinity with the two novels mentioned above, ends with [none of their] affirmation." The character of Duddy, "who has never weighted the consequences of his actions in any but material terms, is less alone in the physical sense than the earlier young men, but he is also much less of a man. . . . He is a modern 'anti-hero' (something like the protagonist in Anthony Burgess's *A Clockwork Orange*) who lives in a largely deterministic world, a world where decisions are not decisions and where choice is not really choice." In *Modern Fiction Studies,* John Ower saw *The Apprenticeship of Duddy Kravitz* as "a 'Jewish' novel [with] both a pungent ethnic flavor and the convincingness that arises when a writer deals with a milieu with which he is completely familiar." For the author, Ower continued, "the destructive psychological effects of the ghetto mentality are equalled and to some extent paralleled by those of the Jewish family. Like the society from which it springs, this tends to be close and exclusive, clinging together in spite of its intense quarrels. The best aspect of such clannishness, the feeling of kinship which transcends all personal differences, is exemplified by Duddy. Although he is in varying degrees put down and rejected by all of his relatives except his grandfather, Duddy sticks up for them and protects them."

For all its success, *The Apprenticeship of Duddy Kravitz* was still categorized by most scholars as among Richler's early works. By the time *St. Urbain's Horseman* was published in 1971, the author had all but sealed his reputation as a sharp cultural critic. In this work, a character named Jacob Hersh, a Canadian writer living in London, questions "not only how he rose to prominence but also the very nature and quality of success and why, having made it, [he] is dissatisfied," as Ramsey put it. Hersh's success as a writer "brings with it a guilt, a sense of responsibility, and an overwhelming paranoia, a belief that his good fortune is largely undeserved and that sooner or later he will be called to account," Ramsey added. In his guilt-based fantasies, Hersh dreams that he is a figure of vengeance protecting the downtrodden, a character based on the Horseman, a shadowy figure from Hersh's past.

"Richler prefaces *St. Urbain's Horseman* with a quotation from [British poet W. H.] Auden which suggests that he does not wish to be read as a mere entertainer, a fanciful farceur," noted David Myers in *Ariel*. "What is there in the *Horseman* that would justify us as regarding it as such a[n affirming] flame? Certainly the despair that we find there is serious enough; the world around Jake Hersh is sordid and vile." The author accords sympathy "to only two characters in his novel, Jake and his wife Nancy," Myers said. "They are shown to feel a very deep love for one another and the loyalty of this love under duress provides the ethical counterbalance to the sordidness, instability, lack of integrity, injustice, and grasping materialism that Richler is satirizing in this book."

In the opinion of Kerry McSweeney, writing in *Studies in Canadian Literature,* the novel "gives evidence everywhere of technical maturity and full stylistic control, and combines the subjects, themes and modes of Richler's earlier novels in ways that suggest—as does the high seriousness of its epigraph—that Richler was attempting a cumulative fictional statement of his view on the mores and values of contemporary man. But while *St. Urbain's Horseman* is a solid success on the level of superior fictional entertainment, on the level of serious fiction it must be reckoned a considerable disappointment. It doesn't deliver the goods and simply does not merit the kind of detailed exegesis it has been given by some Canadian critics." Elaborating on this thesis, McSweeney added that everything in the novel "depends on the presentation of Jake, especially of his mental life and the deeper reaches of his character, and on the intensity of the reader's sympathetic involvement with him. Unfortunately, Jake is characterized rather too superficially. One is told, for example, but never shown, that he is charged with contradictions concerning his professional life; and for all the time devoted to what is going on in his head he doesn't really seem to have much of a mental life. Despite the big issues he is said to be struggling with, *St. Urbain's Horseman* can hardly claim serious attention as a novel of ideas."

Robert Fulford offered a different view. In his *Saturday Night* article, Fulford lauded *St. Urbain's Horseman* as "the triumphant and miraculous bringing-together of all those varied Mordecai Richlers who have so densely populated our literary landscape for so many years. From this perspective it becomes clear that all those Richlers have a clear purpose in mind—they've all been waiting out there, working

separately, honing their talents, waiting for the moment when they could arrive at the same place and join up in the creation of a magnificent *tour de force,* the best Canadian book in a long time."

The third of Richler's later novels, *Joshua Then and Now,* again explores a Jewish-Canadian's moral crises. Joshua Shapiro, a prominent author married to a Gentile daughter of a senator, veers between religious and social classes and withstands family conflicts, especially as they concern his father Reuben. It is also a novel full of mysteries. Why, asked *Village Voice* critic Barry Yourgrau, "does the book open in the present with this 47-year-old Joshua a rumple of fractures in a hospital bed, his name unfairly linked to a scandalous faggotry, his wife doped groggy in a nuthouse and he himself being watched over by his two elderly fathers?" The reason, Yourgrau continued, "is Time. The cruelest of fathers is committing physical violence on Joshua's dearest friends (and crucial enemies)."

Joshua, sometimes shown in flashback as the son of the ever-on-the-make Reuben and his somewhat exhibitionist mother (she performed a striptease at Joshua's bar mitzvah), "is another one of Richler's Jewish *arrivistes,* like Duddy Kravitz [and] Jacob Hersh," said *New Republic* critic Mark Shechner. After noting Joshua's unrepentant bragging, Shechner called the character "a fairly unpleasant fellow, and indeed, though his exploits are unfailingly vivid and engaging—even fun—they rarely elicit from us much enthusiasm for Joshua himself. He is as callow as he is clever, and, one suspects, Richler means him to be an anti-type, to stand against the more common brands of self-congratulation that are endemic to Jewish fiction. From Sholom Aleichem and his Tevye to [Saul] Bellow and [Bernard] Malamud, . . . Jewish fiction has repeatedly thrown up figures of wisdom and endurance, observance and rectitude. . . . Richler, by contrast, adheres to a tradition of dissent that runs from Isaac Babel's Odessa stories through Daniel Fuchs's *Williamsburg Trilogy* and Budd Schulberg's *What Makes Sammy Run?,* which finds more color, more life, and more fidelity to the facts of Jewish existence in the demimonde of hustlers, heavies, strong-arm types and men on the make than in the heroes of *menschlichkeit* [Yiddish slang for the quality of goodness]."

But whatever message *Joshua Then and Now* might deliver, the lasting appeal of the novel, to John Lahr, is that "Richler writes funny. Laughter, not chicken soup, is the real Jewish penicillin. . . . Richler's characters enter as philosophers and exit as stand-up comics, firing zingers as they go," as Lahr explained in a *New York* article. On the other hand, *New York Times Book Review* writer Thomas R. Edwards, while acknowledging the novel's humor, found it "dangerously similar in theme, situation and personnel to a number of Mordecai Richler's other novels— 'Son of a Smaller Hero,' 'The Apprenticeship of Duddy Kravitz,' 'Cocksure' and 'St. Urbain's Horseman.' It's as if a rich and unusual body of fictional material had become a kind of prison for a writer who is condemned to repeat himself ever more vehemently and inflexibly." *Joshua Then and Now* brought much more critical debate. Mark Harris, on one hand, faulted the novel for its style, "resplendent with every imaginable failure of characterization, relevance, style or grammar," in his *Washington Post Book World* review. An *Atlantic* critic, on the other hand, saw the book as "good enough to last, perhaps Richler's best novel to date."

Nine years would pass before Richler published another novel. When he broke the silence in 1989 with *Solomon Gursky Was Here,* several reviewers welcomed the novel as worth the wait, and England's Book Trust honored it with a Commonwealth Writers Prize. The story focuses on Moses Berger, an alcoholic Jewish writer whose life's obsession is to write a biography of the legendary Solomon Gursky. Gursky, of a prominent Jewish-Canadian family of liquor distillers, may have died years ago in a plane crash, but Berger finds numerous clues that suggest he lived on in various guises, a trickster and meddler in international affairs. Jumping forward and backward in time, from events in the Gursky past to its present, Richler "manages to suggest a thousand-page family chronicle in not much more than 400 pages," observed Bruce Cook in Chicago *Tribune Books.* The critic lauded the novel's humor and rich texture, concluding, "Page for page, there has not been a serious novel for years that can give as much pure pleasure as this one." Acknowledging the inventiveness of Richler's narrative, Francine Prose in the *New York Times Book Review* nonetheless found the book somewhat marred by predictable or flat characters. Other critics suggested that there was too much going on in the novel, and for some its humor seemed a bit too black. *Village Voice* writer Joel Yanofsky affirmed the book despite its weaknesses: "If the structure of Richler's story is too elaborate at times, if the narrative loose ends aren't all pulled together, it's a small price to pay for a book this beguiling and rude, this serious, this fat and funny."

Jonathan Kirsch, writing in the *Los Angeles Times Book Review,* called it "a worthy addition" to Richler's canon, the work "of a storyteller at the height of his powers."

In addition to his adult fiction, Richler has also penned a series of popular books for younger readers. *Jacob Two-Two Meets the Hooded Fang,* first published in 1976, has become something of a children's classic in the author's native Canada. After a space of ten years, Richler produced two sequels: 1987's *Jacob Two-Two and the Dinosaur* and *Jacob Two-Two's First Spy Case,* published in 1995. In *Jacob Two-Two and the Dinosaur,* eight-year-old Jacob, who is still constantly battling his sibling's barrage of teasing remarks, has moved with his family from England to Montreal. When his parents return from a safari in Kenya, they give Jacob a small green lizard, which they discovered near an ancient block of ice recently dislodged by an earthquake. He dubs his new pet Dippy, and Dippy becomes his best friend. Dippy also becomes larger, having a voracious appetite for food that Jacob can hardly satisfy. It soon becomes clear that Dippy is in fact a diplodocus, one of the larger varieties of vegetarian dinosaurs that inhabited the Earth during the Jurassic period. Jacob and Dippy's adventures truly begin when the Canadian government authorities realize that there is a dinosaur in their midst and attempt to combat it through the usual channels. "The range and bite of this novel's hilarity will come as no surprise to fans of Mordecai Richler's adult fiction," noted *New York Times Book Review* critic Francine Prose, adding that the novel was as entertaining to adults as it was to children. That conclusion was also made by Howard Engel, reviewing Richler's third children's book, *Jacob Two-Two's First Spy Case,* for *Books in Canada.* Engel dubbed Jacob's attempt to outsmart local bully Loathsome Leo Louise and give his private school principle and nasty geography teacher their comeuppance a "wonderfully funny and cunning tale." "It is the trick of the clever writer of children's stories to engage both parent-reader and child-listener in his lines," Engel added. "The humour and the passion of the adventure are snapped up by the one, while the other catches the sly social comment and satire."

Among his nonfiction works, Richler's *Home Sweet Home: My Canadian Album, Oh Canada! Oh Quebec! Requiem for a Divided Country, This Year in Jerusalem,* and *Broadsides: Reviews and Opinions* have all drawn attention. While these works focus on Richler's native country and his identity as a Canadian, they have distinctly different styles and purposes. *Home Sweet Home,* for example, focuses on Canadian culture, addressing subjects from nationalism to hockey, while in *Oh Canada! Oh Quebec!* Richler turns his considerable intellect and wit to the problem of Quebec separatism, and *This Year in Jerusalem* focuses more personally on Richler's identity as a Canadian Jew—a theme also present in *Oh Canada! Oh Quebec! Broadsides* focuses on both the writing life and modern literature. Richler's interest in early twentieth-century literature, in particular, resulted in his editorship of *Writers on World War II,* a compendium of war writing by some of North America and Europe's most eminent authors.

A Toronto *Globe and Mail* writer called *Home Sweet Home* "a different sort of book, but no less direct and pungent in its observations about what makes a society tick," and in another *Globe and Mail* article, Joy Fielding saw the book as "a cross-country tour like no other, penetrating the Eastern soul, the Western angst, and the French-Canadian spirit." *Home Sweet Home* drew admiring glances from American as well as Canadian critics. Peter Ross, of the *Detroit News,* wrote, "Wit and warmth are constants and though Richler can temper his fondness with bursts of uncompromising acerbity, no reader can fail to perceive the depth of his feelings as well as the complexities of Canada." And *Time*'s Stefan Kanfer observed that "even as he celebrates [Canada's] beauties, the author never loses sight of his country's insularity: when Playboy Films wanted to produce adult erotica in Toronto, he reports, officials wanted to know how much Canadian content there would be in the features. But Richler also knows that the very tugs and pulls of opposing cultures give the country its alternately appealing and discordant character."

It is precisely these tugs and pulls of opposing cultures that Richler sets out to expose in *Oh Canada! Oh Quebec!,* and the resulting book set off a furor among Canadian politicians and press—one Canadian MP even called for a banning of the book (to no avail). Anthony Wilson-Smith summed up the controversy in *Maclean's:* "The objection in each case: that Richler's view of Quebec and its nationalist movement is overly harsh and unfair—particularly his assertion that the province's history reflects a deep strain of anti-Semitism." And in fact, while Richler's earlier works abound with wit and humour, in *Oh Canada! Oh Quebec!,* "his mood . . . hovers much closer to exasperation," wrote Wilson-Smith, and Robin W. Winks, writing in the *New York Times*

Book Review, stated more bluntly: "he is, for the most part, simply angry."

Winks declared that in the book Richler is "concerned, above all, with the Condition of Canada," and called the book "an unsystematic but powerful examination of what Mr. Richler regards as the idiocy of the day"—the legislation and organizations which enforce and oversee the exclusive use of the French language on all public signage in the province of Quebec. But even more compelling is Richler's claim that many of Quebec's leading politicians and intellectuals have been anti-Semitic, and, as Winks reported, that this anti-Semitism is linked to the Quebec separatist movement through the figure of Abbe Lionel-Adolphe Groulx. As Wilson-Smith reported, Richler makes the damaging claim that Groulx's paper, *Le Devoir,* "'more closely resembled *Der Sturmer* [a German Nazi newspaper of the same period] than any other newspaper I can think of.'"

Both Wilson-Smith and Winks, who was himself the chairman of the Committee on Canadian Studies at Yale University, question Richler's scholarship and accuracy in *Oh Canada! Oh Quebec!.* Winks claimed the book "is not always as informative as it might be," and questioned Richler's decision not to examine the original sources for his assertions. Wilson-Smith suggested that Richler's assertions are "debatable, largely because dislike and suspicion of Jews was widespread in Canada then among both anglophones and francophones." These problematic assertions led Winks to term the book "very readable" but "something of a missed opportunity."

Still, as Wilson-Smith reported, Richler does evince affection for his native province: "'There is nowhere else in the country as interesting, or alive.'" And it is this sentiment—love for his native land and all of the contradictory impulses that make for a Canadian Jew—that haunts *This Year in Jerusalem.* Louis Simpson quotes Richler's account of his hybrid identity in his review of the volume for the *New York Times Book Review:* Richler described himself as "'a Canadian, born and bred, brought up not only on Hillel, Rabbi Akiba and Rashi, but also on blizzards, Andrew Allan's CBC Radio "Stage" series, a crazed Maurice Richard skating in over the blue line . . . the Dieppe raid.'"

This Year in Jerusalem is a nonfiction account of a year Richler spent in Israel and is, for Morton Ritts, writing in *Maclean's,* "less a study of the character of politics than the politics of character." What makes this a book not just about Israel, but about Canada and Richler as well, is that Richler connects his journey to Israel with his own personal history of growing up as a young Zionist in Canada with a grandfather who was both a rabbi and a "celebrated Hasidic scholar," according to Louis Simpson in the *New York Times Book Review: "This Year in Jerusalem* is history made personal."

By telling the tale of his own spiritual journey whereby Richler became, in Ritts' words, "more rebel than rebbe (spiritual leader)," by giving his real-life young Zionist companions pseudonyms and tracing their stories over several decades, by talking to Israelis and Palestinians from all walks of life, and by examining, as Ritts also put it, the "trouble between Jew and gentile, French and English, the Orthodox and secular, Arab and Israeli, hawk and dove, Israeli Jew and North American Jew," Richler infuses the book with his novelist's craft. Simpson called the book "lively reporting" and "interesting," but Ritts' praise was higher. In *This Year in Jerusalem,* Ritts claimed, Richler is "at the top of his own game."

The collected reviews and articles included in *Broadsides* cover a thirty-year span in the life of the author. Richler, who has dedicated himself to writing since his early years, professes his lack of understanding, in the essay "Hemingway Set His Own Hours," as to why he was one of the few students at school to chose a writer's life. "What I find more intriguing than why anybody became a writer is how some of the boys at school grew up to be caterers, or frozen-chicken-breast packagers." Critical reaction to the volume was mixed, as several critics deemed the pieces in the volume not up to the written quality of the author's fiction. While noting that the essay collection "is not nearly as abusive or denunciatory as its title implies," Morton Ritts noted in his *Maclean's* review that "Richler is always worth the price of admission." Jim Cormier found more to enjoy in his review of *Broadsides* for *Quill and Quire,* commenting that each of the volume's selections "are marked by a terse, colloquial, and sardonic style that is invariably engaging and occasionally laugh-out-loud funny."

"Throughout his career Richler has spanned an intriguing gulf," concluded Ramsey in his *Dictionary of Literary Biography* piece. "While ridiculing popular tastes and never catering to popular appeal, he has nevertheless maintained a wide general audience.

Though drawing constantly on his own experience, he rejects the writer as personality, wishing instead to find acceptance not because of some personal characteristic or because of the familiarity of his subject matter to a Canadian reading public but because he has something fresh to say about humanity and says it in a well-crafted form, which even with its comic exuberance, stands firmly in the tradition of moral and intellectual fiction."

BIOGRAPHICAL/CRITICAL SOURCES:

BOOKS

Authors in the News, Volume 1, Gale, 1976.
Children's Literature Review, Volume 1, Gale, 1989.
Contemporary Literary Criticism, Gale, Volume 3, 1975; Volume 5, 1976; Volume 9, 1978; Volume 13, 1980; Volume 18, 1981; Volume 46, 198; Volume 70, 1992.
Dictionary of Literary Biography, Volume 53: *Canadian Writers since 1960, First Series,* Gale, 1986.
Klinck, Carl F., and others, editors, *Literary History of Canada: Canadian Literature in English,* University of Toronto Press, 1965.
New, W. H., *Articulating West,* New Pres, 1972.
Northey, Margot, *The Haunted Wilderness: The Gothic and Grotesque in Canadian Fiction,* University of Toronto Press, 1976.
Ramraj, Victor J., *Mordecai Richler,* Twayne, 1983.
Richler, Mordecai, *The Apprenticeship of Duddy Kravitz,* introduction by A. R. Bevan, McClelland & Stewart, 1969.
Richer, Mordecai, *Hunting Tigers under Glass: Essays and Reports,* McClelland & Stewart, 1969.
Richler, Mordecai, *Broadsides: Reviews and Opinions,* Viking, 1990.
Sheps, G. David, editor, *Mordecai Richler,* McGraw-Hill/Ryerson, 1971.
Woodcock, George, *Mordecai Richler,* McClelland & Stewart, 1970.

PERIODICALS

Ariel, January, 1973.
Atlantic, July 1980; May, 1990, p. 132.
Books in Canada, August-September, 1984; August-September, 1987, pp. 35-36; November, 1990, pp. 35-56; January-February, 1991, pp. 18-20; December, 1995, p. 34.

Canadian Children's Literature, Volume 49, 1988, pp. 43-44.

Canadian Literature, spring, 1973; summer, 1973.

Commentary, October, 1980; June, 1990.

Detroit News, July 29, 1984.

Esquire, August, 1982.

Globe and Mail (Toronto), May 5, 1984; June 24, 1985; June 13, 1987.

Insight on the News, June 25, 1990, pp. 62-63.

Los Angeles Times Book Review, August 19, 1984; June 17, 1990, p. 4.

Maclean's, May 7, 1984; November 13, 1989, pp. 64-67; November 26, 1990, pp. 78-79; December 31, 1990, pp. 18-19; December 30, 1991, p. 26; March 30, 1992, pp. 66-67; April 13, 1992, pp. 28-30; September 12, 1994, p. 66.

Modern Fiction Studies, autumn, 1976.

Nation, July 5, 1980; June 4, 1990, pp. 785-86, 788-91.

National Review, December 19, 1994, p. 56.

New Republic, may 18, 1974; June 14, 1980; December 5, 1983; May 7, 1990, pp. 42-44.

Newsweek, June 16, 1980; February 3, 1986.

New York, June 16, 1980; April 16, 1990, pp. 95-96.

New York Review of Books, July 17, 1980.

New York Times, June 22, 1980.

New York Times Book Review, May 4, 1975; October 5, 1975; June 22, 1980; September 11, 1983; February 5, 1984; June 3, 1984; October 18, 1987; April 8, 1990, p. 7; April 27, 1990, p. 7; May 24, 1992; November 13, 1994, p. 64.

Publishers Weekly, April 27, 1990, pp. 45-46; August 15, 1994, p. 83.

Queen's Quarterly, summer, 1990, pp. 325-27.

Quill and Quire, September 1990, p. 62; November 1995, p. 45.

Saturday Night June 1971; March 1974.

Spectator, August 25, 1981; July 25, 1992, pp. 33-34.

Studies in Canadian Literature, summer, 1979.

Time, June 16, 1980; November 7, 1983; April 30, 1984; May 14, 1990, p. 91.

Times Literary Supplement, April 2, 1976; September 26, 1980; August 3, 1984; December 21, 1984; June 15-21, 1990, p. 653; April 10, 1992, p. 5.

Tribune Books (Chicago), April 8, 1990, p. 6.

Village Voice, June 2, 1980; May 1, 984; May 1, 1990, p. 86.

Washington Post, November 9, 1983.

Washington Post Book World, June 29, 1980; May 10, 1987.

World Literature Today, autumn, 1990, pp. 639-40.

RIGNEY, James Oliver, Jr. 1948-
(Robert Jordan, Chang Lung, Reagan O'Neal, Jackson O'Reilly)

PERSONAL: Born October 17, 1948, in Charleston, SC; son of James Oliver and Eva May (Grooms) Rigney; married Harriet Stoney Popham McDougal, March 28, 1981; children: William Popham McDougal. *Education:* The Citadel, B.S., 1974.

ADDRESSES: Office—c/o Tor Books, 175 FIfth Ave., New York, NY 10010.

CAREER: U. S. Civil Service, nuclear engineer, 1974-78; freelance writer, 1978—.

MEMBER: Science Fiction Writers of America.

WRITINGS:

UNDER PSEUDONYM ROBERT JORDAN; "CONAN" SERIES

Conan the Invincible, Tor Books (New York City), 1982.

Conan the Defender, Tor Books, 1982.

Conan the Unconquered, Tor Books, 1983.

Conan the Triumphant, Tor Books, 1983.

Conan the Magnificent, Tor Books, 1984.

Conan the Destroyer, Tor Books, 1984.

Conan the Victorious, Tor Books, 1984.

The Conan Chronicles (omnibus; contains *Conan the Invincible, Conan the Defender,* and *Conan the Unconquered*), Tor Books, 1995.

UNDER PSEUDONYM ROBERT JORDAN; "WHEEL OF TIME" SERIES

The Eye of the World, Tor Books, 1990.

The Great Hunt, Tor Books, 1990.

The Dragon Reborn, Tor Books, 1992.

The Shadow Rising, Tor Books, 1992.

The Fires of Heaven, Tor Books, 1993.

Lord of Chaos, Tor Books, 1994.

A Crown of Swords, Tor Books, 1996.

OTHER

Also author, under pseudonym Reagan O'Neal, of *the Fallon Blood,* 1980, *The Fallon Pride,* 1981 (published under pseudonym Robert Jordan, Forge [New York City], 1996), and *The Fallon Legacy,* 1982. Also author, under pseudonym Jackson O'Reilly, of *Cheyenne Raiders,* 1982. Contributor, sometimes under the pseudonym Chang Lung, to periodicals, including *Library Journal.*

SIDELIGHTS: James Oliver Rigney, Jr. has enjoyed success in two areas of fantasy writing: as a writer of novels in the continuing saga of the popular sword-and-sorcery character Conan the Barbarian and as the creator of the Wheel of Time series, set in a complex fantasy world of his own creation. Speaking of Rigney's work on the Conan books, Wendy Bradley writes in the *St. James Guide to Fantasy Writers* that "his additions to the best-known of all sword-and-sorcery saga are vigorous, lusty, and full of excellent scene setting." Of the Wheel of Time series, Bradley reports that "this saga is turning into a really impressive piece of work." Roland Green, writing in *Booklist,* calls the Wheel of Time series a "major fantasy epic."

Conan, a wandering warrior of the ancient land of Hyperborea whose adventures lead him into battle with monsters, magicians and underworld demons, is the invention of Robert E. Howard, a pulp writer of the 1930s. Following Howard's death in 1936, the Conan character faded from view until revived in paperback reprints during the 1960s. The character's renewed popularity spawned an entire fantasy subgenre known as sword-and-sorcery, stories in which barbarian warriors armed with swords, courage and strength battle otherworldly opponents in exotic settings. The continuing Conan saga has been written in the past thirty years by a number of different writers. Under the pseudonym Robert Jordan, Rigney tried his own hand at the series in the early 1980s, adding a total of seven novels to the ongoing adventure saga. Eleanor Klopp in *Voice of Youth Advocates,* in her review of *The Conan Chronicles,* praises the lush nature of Jordan's Conan adventures: "Devotees of Margaret Weiss and Tracy Hickman will delight in the profuse description: tempestuous weather, ornate decoration, forbidding architecture, jewels, gold, mosaics, marble barbarian splendor. . . . Conan comes out a hero who saves damsels in distress and fights evil." Of those who have written stories featuring Conan, "none [have done so] with more consistency or better technique than Jordan," according to a critic for *Kirkus Reviews.*

Under the Jordan pseudonym, Rigney began his own fantasy series of novels in 1990 with *The Eye of the World.* Set in a world where two kinds of magic exist, one female and the other male, the Wheel of Time series features the hero Rand. Rand is on an epic quest to unite the diverse peoples of his planet against the Dark One, who threatens to destroy their world. His quest takes him through a series of complex and well-delineated alien cultures. Jo-Ann Goodwin in *New Statesman and Society* calls the Wheel of Time books "high fantasy that demands to be taken seriously. . . . [Jordan] has been rightly praised for creating an entirely convincing and compelling alternative world, complete with social systems, cultural differences and competing motivations."

The Wheel of Time books are noted for their complex plotting, vivid characters and realistically portrayed fantasy world. But several critics have noted that, because of the saga's enormous length and huge cast of characters, new readers to the series can be easily overwhelmed. A *Kirkus Reviews* critic describes the Wheel of Time books, for example, as "enormous, imaginative, uncontrolled, and utterly unintelligible to outsiders." Still, as Green notes in *Booklist,* "no one should expect to start a work of this size except at the beginning." If followed from the beginning, the series can be rewarding. A *Library Journal* reviewer calls it a "richly detailed and vividly imagined series." Bradley particularly praises Jordan's talent with the many characters in the multi-book saga: "His strength is in how he juggles with the multiple and multiplying field of characters without losing any of the depth of characterization or pace of plotting." A *Publishers Weekly* critic claims that "Jordan's talent for sustaining the difficult combination of suspense and resolution, so necessary in a multivolume series such as this one, . . . is nothing short of remarkable."

BIOGRAPHICAL/CRITICAL SOURCES:

BOOKS

St. James Guide to Fantasy Writers, St. James Press (Detroit), 1996.

PERIODICALS

Booklist, October 1, 1989, p. 218; October 15, 1990, p. 394; October 1, 1992, p. 242; October 1, 1993, p. 195; October 15, 1994, p. 372; June 1, 1996, p. 1630.
Fantasy Review, August, 1984, p. 12; September, 1984, p. 30.
Kirkus Reviews, December 15, 1989, p. 1791; November 1, 1990, p. 1502; October 1, 1993, p. 1234; October 1, 1994, p. 1318; May 1, 1995, p. 596.

Library Journal, November 15, 1990, p. 95; November 15, 1992, p. 104; November 15, 1993, p. 103; November 15, 1994, p. 89; June 15, 1996, p. 96.

Locus, August, 1989, p. 15; November, 1990, p. 27; December, 1992, p. 29; November, 1993, p. 29; November, 1994, p. 33.

New Statesman and Society, November 26, 1993, p. 44.

Publishers Weekly, October 19, 1992, p. 64; November 1, 1993, p. 71; October 17, 1994, p. 67; July 3, 1995, p. 52; August 7, 1995, p. 447; June 10, 1996, p. 90; September 9, 1996, p. 65.

Science Fiction Chronicle, March, 1989, p. 36; March, 1991, p. 30; August, 1995, p. 48.

Science Fiction Review, February, 1983, p. 31; May, 1983, p. 55.

Voice of Youth Advocates, June, 1990, p. 116; August, 1991, p. 181; April, 1993, p. 41; June, 1995, p. 106; February, 1996, p. 384; April, 1996, p. 23.

*   *   *

RILKE, Rainer Maria 1875-1926

PERSONAL: Born (Rene Karl Wilhelm Johann Josef Maria Rilke) December 4, 1875, in Prague, Austria (now the Czech Republic); changed his name to Rainer Maria Rilke, 1897; died of leukemia, December 29, 1926, in Montreaux, Switzerland; son of Josef (a railway official) and Sophie Entz Rilke; married Clara Westhoff (a sculptress), 1901 (separated, 1902); children: Ruth. *Education:* Attended Handelsakademie, Linz, Austria, 1891-92, and University of Prague, 1895-96. *Religion:* Raised Roman Catholic.

CAREER: Poet, novelist, short story writer, and translator. Traveled extensively throughout Europe. Joined the Worpswede artists' colony, 1900-02; worked as a secretary for sculptor Auguste Rodin in Paris, France, 1905-06. *Military service:* Austro-Hungary Army, First Infantry Regiment; served in the War Department, 1916.

WRITINGS:

Leben und Lieder: Bilder und Tagebuchblaetter (poems; main title means "Life and Songs"), Kattentidt, 1894.

Larenopfer (poems; title means "Offering to the Lares"), Dominicus (Prague), 1896.

Todtentaenze: Zwielicht-Skizzen aus unseren Tagen, Loewit & Lamberg (Prague), 1896.

Traumgekroent: Neue Gedichte (title means "Crowned with Dreams: New Poems"), Friesenhahn (Leipzig), 1896.

Wegwarten (poems), Selbstverlag (Prague), 1896.

In Fruehfrost: Ein Stueck Daemmerung, Drei Vorgaenge (play), Theaterverlag O. R. Eirich (Vienna), 1897.

Advent (poems), Friesenhahn, 1898.

Ohne Gegenwart: Drama in zwei Akten, Entsch (Berlin), 1898.

Am Leben hin: Novellen und Skizzen, Bonz (Stuttgart), 1898.

Zwei Prager Geschichten, Bonz, 1899, translation by Angela Esterhammer published as *Two Stories of Prague,* University Press of New England, 1994.

Mir zur Feier: Gedichte (poems), Meyer (Berlin), 1899, reprinted as *Die fruehen Gedichte,* Insel (Germany), 1909, Ungar, 1943.

Vom lieben Gott und Anderes: An Grosse fuer Kinder erzaehlt (short stories), Schuster & Loeffler, 1900, published as *Geschichten vom lieben Gott,* Insel, 1904, translation by Nora Purtscher-Wydenbruck and M. D. Herter Norton published as *Stories of God,* Norton, 1932, revised edition, 1963.

Das taegliche Leben: Drama in zwei Akten (play; first produced in Berlin at the Residenz Theater, December, 1901), Langen (Munich), 1902.

Zur Einweihung der Kunsthalle am 15. Februar 1902: Festspielszene, [Bremen], 1902.

Buch der Bilder (poems), Juncker (Berlin), 1902, enlarged edition, 1906, Ungar, 1943.

Die Letzten, Juncker, 1902.

Worpswede: Fritz Mackenses, Otto Modersohn, Fritz Overbeck, Hans am Ende, Heinrich Vogeler, Velhagen & Klasing, 1903.

Auguste Rodin (biography), Bard (Berlin), 1903, translation by Jesse Lemont and Hans Trausil published as *Auguste Rodin,* Sunwise Turn (New York), 1919, published as *Rodin,* Haskell Booksellers, 1974.

Das Stundenbuch enthaltend die drei Buecher: Vom moenchischen Leben; Von der Pilgerschaft; Von der Armuth und vom Tode (poems), Insel, 1905, translation by Babette Deutsch published as *Poems from the Book of Hours,* New Directions, 1941, translation by A. L. Peck published as *The Book of Hours; Comprising the Three Books: Of the Monastic Life, Of Pilgrimage, Of Poverty and Death,* Hogarth, 1961, published as *Rilke's Book of Hours: Love Poems to God,* Riverhead, 1996.

Die Weise von Liebe und Tod des Cornets Christoph Rilke (prose poem), Juncker, 1906, translation by B. J. Morse published as *The Story of the Love and Death of Cornet Christopher Rilke,* Osnabrueck, 1927, translation by Herter Norton published as *The Tale of the Love and Death of Cornet Christopher Rilke,* Norton, 1932, translation by Stephen Mitchell published as *The Lay of the Love and Death of Cornet Christopher Rilke,* Arion, 1983, new edition, Graywolf Press, 1985.

Neue Gedichte (poems), two volumes, Insel, 1907-08, translation by J. B. Leishman published as *New Poems,* New Directions, 1964, translation by Edward Snow, North Point Press, Volume 1: *New Poems (1907),* 1984, Volume 2: *New Poems: The Other Part (1908),* 1987.

Requiem (poems), Insel, 1909.

Die Aufzeichnungen des Malte Laurids Brigge (novel), Insel, 1910, translation by John Linton published as *The Journal of My Other Self,* Norton, 1930, translation by Norton published as *The Notebooks of Malte Laurids Brigge,* Norton, 1964, translation by Mitchell published as *The Notebooks of Malte Laurids Brigge,* Random House, 1983.

Erste Gedichten, Insel, 1913, Ungar, 1947.

Das Marien-Leben, Insel, 1913, translation by R. G. L. Barrett published as *The Life of the Virgin Mary,* Triltsch (Wuerzburg), 1921, translation by Stephen Spender published as *The Life of the Virgin Mary,* Philosophical Library, 1951.

Poems, translation by Lemont, Wright, 1918.

Aus der Fruehzeit Rainer Maria Rilke: Vers, Prosa, Drama (1894-1899), edited by Fritz Adolf Huenich, Bibliophilenabend (Leipzig), 1921.

Mitsou: Quaranto imagos par Baltusz, Rotapfel, 1921.

Puppen, Hyperion (Munich), 1921.

Duineser Elegien (poems; also see below), Insel, 1923, Ungar, 1944, translation by V. Sackville-West and Edward Sackville-West published as *Duineser Elegien: Elegies from the Castle of Duino,* Hogarth, 1931, translation by Leishman and Spender published as *Duino Elegies,* Norton, 1939, translation by Robert Hunter and Gary Miranda published as *Duino Elegies,* Breitenbush, 1981.

Die Sonette an Orpheus: Geschrieben als ein Grab-Mal fuer Wera Ouckama Knoop (poems; also see below), Insel, 1923, Ungar, 1945, translation by Leishman published as *Sonnets to Orpheus, Written as a Monument for Wera Ouckama Knoop,* Hogarth, 1936, translation by Norton published as *Sonnets to Orpheus,* Norton, 1942, translation by Mitchell published as *The Sonnets to Orpheus,* Simon & Schuster, 1986, published as *Os Sonetos a Orfeu,* Quetzal Editores, 1994.

Vergers suivi des Quatrains Valaisans, Editions de la Nouvelle Revue Francaise (Paris), 1926, translation by Alfred Poulin, Jr., published as *Orchards,* Graywolf Press (Port Townsend, Wash.), 1982.

Gesammelte Werke, six volumes, Insel, 1927.

Les Fenetres: Dix Poemes, Officina Sanctandreana (Paris), 1927, translation by Poulin published as *The Windows* in *The Roses and the Windows,* Graywolf Press, 1979.

Les Roses, Stols (Bussum, Netherlands), 1927, translation by Poulin published as *The Roses* in *The Roses and the Windows,* Graywolf Press, 1979.

Erzaehlungen und Skizzen aus der Fruehzeit, Insel, 1928.

Ewald Tragy: Erzaehlung, Heller (Munich), 1929, Johannespresse (New York City), 1944, translation by Lola Gruenthal published as *Ewald Tragy,* Twayne, 1958.

Verse und Prosa aus dem Nachlass, Gesellschaft der Freunde der Deutschen Buecherei (Leipzig), 1929.

Gesammelte Gedichte, four volumes, Insel, 1930-33.

Ueber den jungen Dichter, [Hamburg], 1931.

Gedichte, edited by Katharina Kippenberg, Insel, 1931, Ungar, 1947.

Rainer Maria Rilke auf Capri: Gespraeche, edited by Leopold von Schloezer, Jess (Dresden), 1931.

Spaete Gedichte, Insel, 1934.

Buecher, Theater, Kunst, edited by Richard von Mises, Jahoda & Siegel (Vienna), 1934.

Der ausgewaehlten Gedichten anderer Teil, edited by Kippenberg, Insel, 1935.

Ausgewaehlte Werke, two volumes, edited by Ruth Sieber-Rilke, Carl Sieber, and Ernst Zinn, Insel, 1938.

Translations from the Poetry of Rainer Maria Rilke, translation by Norton, Norton, 1938, reprinted, 1962.

Fifty Selected Poems with English Translations, translation by C. F. MacIntyre, University of California Press, 1940.

Selected Poems, translation by Leishman, Hogarth, 1941.

Tagebuecher aus der Fruehzeit, edited by Sieber-Rilke, Insel, 1942, translation by Edward Snow and Michael Winkler published as *Diaries of a Young Poet,* Norton, 1997.

Briefe, Verse und Prosa aus dem Jahre 1896, two volumes, Johannespresse, 1946.

Thirty-one Poems, translation by Ludwig Lewisohn, Ackerman, 1946.

Freundschaft mit Rainer Maria Rilke: Begegnungen, Gespraeche, Briefe und Aufzeichnungen mitgeteilt durch Elga Maria Nevar, Zuest (Buempliz), 1946.

Five Prose Pieces, translation by Carl Niemeyer, Cummington Press (Cummington, MA), 1947.

Gedichte, edited by Hermann Kunisch, Vandenhoeck & Ruprecht (Goettingen), 1947.

Gedichte in franzoesicher Sprache, edited by Thankmar von Muenchhausen, Insel, 1949.

Aus Rainer Maria Rilkes Nachlass, four volumes, Insel, 1950, Volume 1: *Aus dem Nachlass des Grafen C. W.,* translation by Leishman as *From the Remains of Count C. W.,* Hogarth, 1952.

Werke: Auswahl in zwei Baenden, two volumes, Insel, 1953.

Gedichte, 1909-26: Sammlung der verstreuten und nachgelassenen Gedichte aus den mittleren und spaeteren Jahren, translation, with additions, by Leishman published as *Poems 1906 to 1926,* Laughlin (Norfolk, CT), 1953, reprinted, Knopf, 1996.

Selected Works, two volumes, translation by G. Craig Houston and Leishman, Hogarth, 1954, New Directions, 1960.

Saemtliche Werke, six volumes, edited by Zinn, Insel, 1955-66.

Angel Songs/Engellieder (bilingual), translation by Rhoda Coghill, Dolmen Press (Dublin), 1958.

Die Turmstunde und andere Novellen (novella collection), edited by Fritz Froehling, Hyperion, 1959.

Selected Works: Prose and Poetry, two volumes, 1960.

Poems, edited by G. W. McKay, Oxford University Press, 1965.

Werke in drei Baenden, three volumes, Insel, 1966.

Gedichte: Eine Auswahl, Reclam (Stuttgart), 1966.

Visions of Christ: A Posthumous Cycle of Poems, translation by Aaron Kramer, edited by Siegfried Mandel, University of Colorado Press, 1967.

Das Testament, edited by Zinn, Insel, 1975.

Holding Out: Poems, translation by Rika Lesser, Abbatoir Editions (Omaha, NE), 1975.

Possibility of Being: A Selection of Poems, translation by Leishman, New Directions, 1977.

The Voices, translation by Robert Bly, Ally Press, 1977.

Duino Elegies [and] *The Sonnets to Orpheus,* translation by Poulin, Houghton, 1977.

Werke: In 3 Baenden, three volumes, edited by Horst Nalewski, Insel, 1978.

Where Silence Reigns: Selected Prose, New Directions, 1978.

Nine Plays, translation by Klaus Phillips and John Locke, Ungar, 1979.

I Am Too Alone in the World: Ten Poems, translation by Bly, Silver Hands Press, 1980.

Selected Poems of Rainer Maria Rilke, translation by Bly, Harper, 1980.

Requiem for a Woman, and Selected Lyric Poems, translation by Andy Gaus, Threshold Books (Putney, Vt.), 1981.

An Unofficial Rilke: Poems 1912-1926, edited and with translation by Michael Hamburger, Anvil Press, 1981.

Selected Poetry of Rainer Maria Rilke, edited and with translation by Mitchell, Random House, 1982.

The Astonishment of Origins: French Sequences, translation from the French by Poulin, Graywolf Press, 1982.

Selected Poems, translation by A. E. Flemming, Golden Smith (St. Petersburg, Fla.), 1983.

The Unknown Rilke: Selected Poems, translation by Franz Wright, Oberlin College, 1983.

The Migration of Powers: French Poems, translation by Poulin, Graywolf Press, 1984.

Between Roots: Selected Poems, translation by Lesser, Princeton University Press, 1986.

The Complete French Poems of Rainer Maria Rilke, translation by Poulin, Graywolf Press, 1986.

Die Briefe en Karl und Elisabeth von der Heydt (letters), Frankfurt a.M. Insel, 1986.

Rodin and Other Prose Pieces, translation by G. Craig Houston, Salem House, 1987.

Shadows on the Sundial (selected poems), edited by Stanley H. Barkan, translation by Norbert Krapf, Cross-Cultural Communications, 1989.

The Best of Rilke, translation by Walter Arndt, University Press of New England, 1989.

The Book of Images (selected poems), translation by Edward Snow, North Point, 1991.

Rilke: Poisia-Coisa, edited by Augusto de Campos, Imago, 1994.

Selected Poems of Rainer Maria Rilke: The Book of Fresh Beginnings, translated by David Young, Oberlin College, 1994.

Two Stories of Prague: "King Bohush" and "The Siblings" (stories), translation by Angela Estherhammer, University Press of New England, 1994.

Uncollected Poems, translated by Edward A. Snow, North Point Press, 1995.

Ahead of All Parting: The Selected Poetry and Prose of Rainer Maria Rilke, edited by Stephen Mitchell, Modern Library, 1995.

TRANSLATOR

Elizabeth Barrett Browning, *Sonette nach dem Portugiesischen,* Insel, 1908.

Maurice de Guerin, *Der Kentaur,* Insel, 1911.

Die Liebe der Magdalena: Ein franzoesischer Sermon, gezogen durch den Abbe Joseph Bonnet aus dem Ms. Q I 14 der Kaiserlichen Bibliothek zu St. Petersburg, Insel, 1912.

Marianna Alcoforado, *Portugiesische Briefe,* Insel, 1913.

Andre Gide, *Die Rueckkehr des verlorenen Sohnes,* Insel, 1914.

Die vierundzwanzig Sonette der Louise Labe, Lyoneserin, 1555, Insel, 1918.

Paul Valery, *Gedichte,* Insel, 1925.

Valery, *Eupalinos oder Ueber die Architektur,* Insel, 1927.

Uebertragungen, Insel, 1927.

Dichtungen des Michelangelo, Insel, 1936.

Gedichte aus fremden Sprachen, Ungar, 1947.

Maurice Maeterlinck, *Die sieben Jungfrauen von Orlamuende,* Dynamo (Liege), 1967.

LETTERS

Briefe an Auguste Rodin, Insel, 1928.

Briefe aus den Jahren 1902 bis 1906, edited by Sieber-Rilke and Sieber, Insel, 1929.

Briefe an einen jungen Dichter, Insel, 1929, translation by Norton published as *Letters to a Young Poet,* Norton, 1934, translation by K. W. Maurer published as *Letters to a Young Poet,* Langley (London), 1943, revised edition, Norton, 1963, translation by Mitchell, Random House, 1984.

Briefe an eine junge Frau, Insel, 1930, translation by Maurer published as *Letters to a Young Woman,* Langley, 1945.

Briefe aus den Jahren 1906 bis 1907, edited by Sieber-Rilke and Sieber, Insel, 1930.

Briefe und Tagebuecher aus der Fruehzeit, edited by Sieber-Rilke and Sieber, Insel, 1931.

Briefe aus den Jahren 1907 bis 1914, edited by Sieber-Rilke and Sieber, Insel, 1933.

Ueber Gott: Zwei Briefe, Insel, 1933.

Briefe an seinen Verleger 1906 bis 1926, edited by Sieber-Rilke and Sieber, Insel, 1934.

Briefe aus Muzot 1921 bis 1926, edited by Sieber-Rilke and Sieber, Insel, 1935.

Gesammelte Briefe, six volumes, edited by Sieber-Rilke and Sieber, Insel, 1936-39.

Lettres a une Amie Venitienne, Asmus, 1941.

Briefe an eine Freundin, edited by Herbert Steiner, Wells College Press, 1944.

Briefe, Oltener Buecherfreunde (Olten), 1945.

Briefe an Baronesse von Oe, edited by von Mises, Johannespresse, 1945.

Letters of Rainer Maria Rilke, translation by Jane Bannard Greene and Norton, Norton, Volume 1: *1892-1910,* 1945, reprinted, 1969, Volume 2: *1910-1926,* 1948, reprinted, 1969.

Briefe an eine Reisegefaehrtin: Eine Begegnung mit Rainer Maria Rilke, Ibach (Vienna), 1947.

Briefe an das Ehepaar S. Fischer, edited by Hedwig Fischer, Classen (Zurich), 1947.

La derniere amitie de Rainer Maria Rilke: Lettres inedites de Rilke a Madame Eloui Bey, edited by Edmond Jaloux, Laffont (Paris), 1949, translation by William H. Kennedy published as *Rainer Maria Rilke: His Last Friendship; Unpublished Letters to Mrs. Eloui Bey,* Philosophical Library, 1952.

"So lass ich mich zu traeumen gehen," Mader, 1949, translation by Heinz Norden published as *Letters to Benvenuta,* Philosophical Library, 1951.

Briefe an seinen Verleger, two volumes, edited by Sieber-Rilke and Sieber, Insel, 1949.

Briefe, two volumes, edited by Sieber-Rilke and Karl Altheim, Insel, 1950.

Die Briefe an Graefin Sizzo, 1921 bis 1926, Insel, 1950, enlarged edition, edited by Ingeborg Schnack, Insel, 1977.

Briefwechsel in Gedichten mit Erika Mitterer 1924 bis 1926, Insel, 1950, translation by N. K. Cruickshank published as *Correspondence in Verse with Erika Mitterer,* Hogarth, 1953.

Lettres francaise a Merline 1919-1922, du Seuil (Paris), 1950, translation by Violet M. Macdonald published as *Letters to Merline, 1919-1922,* Methuen, 1951.

Rainer Maria Rilke/Marie von Thurn und Taxis: Briefwechsel, two volumes, edited by Zinn, Niehans & Rokitansky (Zurich), 1951, translation by Nora Wydenbruck published as *The Letters of Rainer Maria Rilke and Princess Marie von Thurn and Taxis,* New Directions, 1958.

Rainer Maria Rilke/Lou Andreas-Salome, Briefwechsel, edited by Ernst Pfeiffer, Insel, 1952, revised and enlarged edition, 1975.

Rainer Maria Rilke/Andre Gide: Correspondance 1909-1926, edited by Renee Lang, Correa (Paris), 1952.

Briefe ueber Cezanne, edited by Clara Rilke, Insel, 1952, translation by Joel Agee published as *Letters on Cezanne,* Fromm, 1985.

Die Briefe an Frau Gudi Noelke aus Rilkes Schweizer Jahren, edited by Paul Obermueller, Insel, 1953, translation by Macdonald published as *Letters to Frau Gudi Noelke during His Life in Switzerland,* Hogarth, 1955.

Rainer Maria Rilke/Katharina Kippenberg: Briefwechsel, edited by Bettina von Bomhard, Insel, 1954.

Briefwechsel mit Benvenuta, edited by Kurt Leonhard, Bechtle (Esslingen), 1954, translation by Agee published as *Rilke and Benvenuta: An Intimate Correspondence,* Fromm, 1987.

Rainer Maria Rilke et Merline: Correspondance 1920-1926, edited by Dieter Basserman, Niehans (Zurich), 1954, reprinted, Paragon House, 1988.

Lettres milanaises 1921-1926, edited by Lang, Plon (Paris), 1956.

Rainer Maria Rilke/Inge Junghanns: Briefwechsel, edited by Wolfgang Herwig, Insel, 1959.

Selected Letters, edited by Harry T. Moore, Doubleday, 1960.

Wartime Letters of Rainer Maria Rilke, 1914-1921, translation by Norton, Norton, 1964.

Briefe an Sidonie Nadherny von Borutin, edited by Bernhard Blume, Insel, 1973.

Ueber Dichtung und Kunst, edited by Hartmut Engelhardt, Suhrkamp (Frankfurt), 1974.

Rainer Maria Rilke on Love and Other Difficulties: Translations and Considerations of Rainer Maria Rilke, edited by John J. L. Mood, Norton, 1975.

Rainer Maria Rilke/Helene von Nostitz: Briefwechsel, edited by Oswalt von Nostitz, Insel, 1976.

Briefe an Nanny Wunderly-Volkart, two volumes, edited by Niklaus Bigler and Raetus Luck, Insel, 1977.

Lettres autour d'un jardin, La Delirante (Paris), 1977.

Hugo von Hofmannsthal/Rainer Maria Rilke: Briefwechsel, edited by Rudolph Hirsch and Schnack, Suhrkamp, 1978.

Briefe an Axel Juncker, edited by Renate Scharffenberg, Insel, 1979.

Briefwechsel mit Rolf Freiherrn von Ungern-Sternberg, edited by Knorad Kratzsch, Insel Verlag Anton Kippenberg (Leipzig), 1980.

Rainer Maria Rilke/Anita Forrer: Briefwechsel, edited by Magda Kerenyi, Leipzig (Frankfurt am Main), 1982.

Rainer Maria Rilke/Marina Zwetajewa/Boris Pasternak: Briefwechsel, edited by Jewgenij Pasternak, Jelena Pasternak, and Konstantin M. Asadowski, Insel, 1983, translation by Margaret Wettlin and Walter Arndt published as *Letters Summer 1926,* Harcourt, 1985.

Rainer Maria Rilke: Briefe an Ernst Norlind, edited by Paul Astroem, Paul Astroems Forlag (Partille), 1986.

Rilke und Russland: Briefe, Erinnerungen, Gedichte, edited by Asadowski, Russian text translation by Ulrike Hirschberg, Insel, 1986.

Rainer Maria Rilke: Briefwechsel mit Regina Ullman und Ellen Delp, edited by Walter Simon, Insel, 1987.

Rainer Maria Rilke/Stefan Zweig: Briefe und Dokumente, edited by Donald Prater, Insel, 1987.

Briefe an Schweizer Freunde, Insel, 1994.

Briefwechsel mit Anton Kippenberg 1906 bis 1926, edited by Ingeorg Schnack and Renate Scharffenberg, Insel, 1995.

SIDELIGHTS: Of the poetry composed by the three major German poets writing during the early twentieth century—Stefan George, Hugo von Hofmannsthal, and Rainer Maria Rilke—the lyrical intensity of Rilke's verses is generally considered to represent the highest artistic achievement. Rilke was unique in his efforts to expand the realm of poetry through new uses in syntax and imagery and in the philosophy that his poems explored. With regard to the former, W. H. Auden declared in *New Republic,* "Rilke's most immediate and obvious influence has been upon diction and imagery." Rilke expressed ideas with "physical rather than intellectual symbols. While Shakespeare, for example, thought of the non-human world in terms of the human, Rilke thinks of the human in terms of the non-human, of what he calls Things (Dinge)." Besides this technique, the other important aspect of Rilke's writings is the evolution of his philosophy, which reached a climax in *Duineser Elegien* (*Duino Elegies*) and *Die Sonette an Orpheus* (*Sonnets to Orpheus*). Rejecting the Catholic beliefs of his parents as well as Christianity in general, the poet strove throughout his life to reconcile beauty and suffering, life and death into one philosophy. As C. M. Bowra observed in *Rainer Maria Rilke: Aspects of His Mind and Poetry,* "Where others have found a unifying principle for themselves in religion or morality or the search for truth, Rilke found his in the search for impressions and the hope these could be turned into poetry. . . . For him Art was what mattered most in life."

Rilke was the only child of a German-speaking family in Prague, then part of the Austro-Hungarian empire. His father was a retired officer in the Austrian army who worked as a railroad official; his mother, a socially ambitious and possessive woman. At age eleven, Rilke began his formal schooling at a military boarding academy, and in 1891, less than a year after transferring to a secondary military school, he was discharged due to health problems, from which he would suffer throughout his life. He immediately returned to Prague, to find that his parents had divorced in his absence. Shortly thereafter, he began receiving private instruction toward passing the entrance exams for Prague's Charles-Ferdinand University. In 1894 his first book of verse, *Leben und Lieder: Bilder und Tagebuchblatter,* was published.

By 1895 Rilke had enrolled in the philosophy program at Charles-Ferdinand University, but soon became disenchanted with his studies and left Prague for Munich, ostensibly to study art. In Munich Rilke mingled in the city's literary circles, had several of his plays produced, published his poetry collections *Larenopfer* and *Traumgelkront,* and was introduced to the work of Danish writer Jens Peter Jacobsen, a decisive influence during Rilke's formative years. Visiting Venice in 1897, Rilke met Lou Andreas-Salome, a married woman fifteen years his senior who stimulated radical personal changes in Rilke. After spending the summer of 1897 with her in the Bavarian Alps, Rilke accompanied Salome and her husband to Berlin in late 1897 and to Italy the following year.

Rilke's early verse, short stories, and plays are characterized by their romanticism. His poems of this period show the influence of the German folk song tradition and have been compared to the lyrical work of Heinrich Heine. The most popular poetry collections of Rilke's during this period were *Vom lieben Gott und Anderes* (*Stories of God*) and the romantic cycle *Die Weise von Liebe und Tod des Cornets Christoph Rilke* (*The Story of the Love and Death of Cornet Christoph Rilke*), which remained the poet's most widely recognize book during his lifetime. *Dictionary of Literary Biography* contributor George C. Schoolfield called Rilke's first poetry collection, *Leben und Lieder* ("Life and Songs"), "unbearably sentimental," but later works such as *Larenopfer* ("Offering to the Lares") and *Traumgekroent* ("Crowned with Dreams") demonstrate "considerably better proof of his lyric talent." Although none of Rilke's plays are considered major works, and his short stories, according to Schoolfield, demonstrate the author's immaturity, the latter do show "his awareness of language and a certain psychological refinement," as well as "flashes of brilliant satiric gift" and "evidence of a keen insight into human relations." Schoolfield also observed that "some of Rilke's best tales are autobiographical," such as "Pierre Dumont," which features a young boy saying

goodbye to his mother at the gates to a military school, and "Ewald Tragy," a two-part story about a boy who leaves his family and hometown of Prague for Munich, where he fights loneliness but enjoys a new sense of freedom.

In 1899 Rilke made the first of two pivotal trips to Russia with Salome, discovering what he termed his "spiritual fatherland" in both the people and the landscape. There Rilke met Leo Tolstoy, L. O. Pasternak (father of Boris Pasternak), and the peasant poet Spiridon Droschin, whose work Rilke translated into German. These trips provided Rilke with the poetic material and inspiration essential to his developing philosophy of existential materialism and art as religion. Inspired by the lives of the Russian people, whom the poet considered more devoutly spiritual than other Europeans, Rilke's work during this period often featured traditional Christian imagery and concepts, but presented art as the sole redeemer of humanity. Soon after his return from Russia in 1900, he began writing *Das Stundenbuch enthaltend die drei Buecher: Vom moenchischen Leben; Von der Pilgerschaft; Von der Armuth und vom Tode,* a collection that "marked for him the end of an epoch," according to Bowra and others. This book, translated as *The Book of Hours; Comprising the Three Books: Of the Monastic Life, Of Pilgrimage, Of Poverty and Death,* consists of a series of prayers about the search for God. Because of this concern, *Hound and Horn* critic Hester Pickman noted that the book "might have fallen out of the writings of Christian contemplatives," except that "the essential pattern is an inversion of theirs. God is not light but darkness—not a father, but a son, not the creator but the created. He and not man is our neighbor for men are infinitely far from each other. They must seek God, not where one or two are gathered in His name, but alone."

Whenever Rilke writes about God, however, he is not referring to the deity in the traditional sense, but rather uses the term to refer to the life force, or nature, or an all-embodying, pantheistic consciousness that is only slowly coming to realize its existence. "Extending the idea of evolution," Eudo C. Mason explained in an introduction to *The Book of Hours,* "and inspired probably also in some measure by Nietzsche's idea of the Superman, Rilke arrives at the paradoxical conception of God as the final result instead of the first cause of the cosmic process." Holding in contempt "all other more traditional forms of devoutness, which . . . merely 'accept God as a given fact,'" Rilke did not deny God's existence, but insisted that all possibilities about the nature of life be given equal consideration.

The real theme of *The Book of Hours,* concluded Mason, is the poet's "own inner life," his struggles toward comprehension, and, "above all . . . his perils *as a poet*"; the second major concept in *The Book of Hours,* then, is Rilke's apotheosis of art. "Religion is the art of those who are uncreative," Mason quoted Rilke as having said; the poet's work is often concerned with the artist's—especially poet's—role in society and with his inner doubts about his belief in poetry's superiority. Because of the firm establishment of these two themes in *The Book of Hours,* the collection "is essential to the understanding of what comes afterwards" in Rilke's writing, attests Pickman. *The Book of Hours* was also another of the poet's most popular works, second only to *The Story of the Love and Death of Cornet Christoph Rilke* during his lifetime. But despite being a "very beautiful" book, it also "remains too constantly abstract. It lacks the solid reality of great poetry," according to Pickman.

Rilke fixed his verse more firmly in reality in his next major poetry collection, *Neue Gedichte (New Poems).* The major influence behind this work was Rilke's association with the famous French sculptor, Auguste Rodin. Working as Rodin's secretary from 1905 to 1906, Rilke gained a greater appreciation of the work ethic. More importantly, however, the poet's verses became objective, evolving from an impressionistic, personal vision to the representation of this vision with impersonal symbolism. He referred to this type of poetry as *Dinggedichte* (thing poems). These verses employed a simple vocabulary to describe concrete subjects experienced in everyday life. Having learned the skill of perceptive observation from Rodin, and, later, from the French painter Paul Cezanne, Rilke "sustained for a little while the ability to write without inspiration, to transform his observations—indeed his whole life—into art," according to Nancy Willard, author of *Testimony of the Invisible Man.* The "'thingness' of these poems," explained Erich Heller in his *The Artist's Journey into the Interior and Other Essays,* "reflects not the harmony in which an inner self lives with its 'objects'; it reflects a troubled inner self immersing itself in 'the things.'" But although this objective approach innovatively addressed subjects never before recognized by other poets and created "dazzling poems," Rilke realized, reported Willard, that it "did not really open the secret of living things."

By this point in his career, Rilke was reaching a crisis in his art that reveals itself both in *New Poems* and his only major prose work, the novel *Die Aufzeichnungen des Malte Laurids Brigge (The Notebooks of Malte Laurids Brigge).* These works express the poet's growing doubts about whether anything existed that was superior to mankind and his world. This, in turn, brought into question Rilke's very reason for writing poetry: the search for deeper meanings in life through art. E. M. Butler elucidated in her *Rainer Maria Rilke:* "[*The Notebooks of Malte Laurids Brigge*] marks a crisis in Rilke's attitude to God, a crisis which might be hailed as the loss of a delusion, or deplored as the loss of an ideal. [His concept of the] future artist-god had never been more than a sublime hypothesis, deriving from Rilke's belief in the creative and transforming powers of art." Having failed, in his mind, to accurately represent God in his poetry, Rilke attempted to "transform life into art" in his *New Poems.* "What he learnt," Butler continued, ". . . is what every artist has to face sooner or later, the realisation that life is much more creative than art. So that his mythological dream, the apotheosis of art, appeared to be founded on delusion. Either art was not as creative as he had thought, or he was not such a great artist. Both these doubts were paralyzing, and quite sufficient to account for the terrible apprehension present in every line of *Malte Laurids Brigge.* For this skepticism struck at the roots of his reason and justification for existence. Either he was the prophet of a new religion, or he was nobody."

Some critics, however, felt that Butler's interpretation overanalyzed Rilke's novel. In *Rainer Maria Rilke: The Ring of Forms,* for example, author Frank Wood granted that Butler had devised an "ingenious theory," but added that her interpretation "does less than justice to its artistic importance. Though no one would claim the *Notebooks* to be a completely achieved work of art, Malte's story nonetheless provides a valuable commentary on [Rilke's] Paris poetry and that yet to come, interpreting and enlarging still nuclear ideas. More than that, Malte allows us an inside view, as the poetry itself rarely does, into the poetic mind in process, with all its variety and even confusion."

"*The Notebooks of Malte Laurids Brigge* were supposed to be the coherent formulation of the insights which were formulated disjointly in the *New Poems,*" wrote *Phases of Rilke* author Norbert Fuerst. The book is a loosely autobiographical novel about a student who is the last descendant of a noble Danish family (Rilke believed, erroneously according to his biographers, that he was distantly related to Carinthian nobility), and follows his life from his birth to a grim, poverty-stricken life as a student in Paris. Images of death and decay (especially in the Paris scenes) and Malte's fear of death are a continuous presence throughout the narrative. The novel concludes with a retelling of the story of the Prodigal Son that represents, according to a number of critics like Schoolfield, "Rilke's long search for the freedom that would enable him to apply his artistic will to the fullest."

Because Rilke never finished *The Notebooks of Malte Laurids Brigge* (in one of his letters, the author told a friend he ended the book "out of exhaustion," reported Schoolfield) Malte's ultimate fate is left ambiguous. Ronald Gray commented in his *The German Tradition in Literature: 1871-1945:* "Malte seems to have come to terms with suffering not so much by enduring it as by cutting himself off from contact with all others. But does Rilke present this as an ideal or as a deplored end? His own comments . . . are inconclusive, and in part this was due to his own uncertainty as to the extent to which Malte's life could be identified with his own." In one of Rilke's letters translated in the collection *Letters of Rainer Maria Rilke: 1910-1926,* the author remarked that the most significant question in *The Notebooks of Malte Laurids Brigge* is: "[How] is it possible to live when after all the elements of this life are utterly incomprehensible to us?" Some authorities, summarized Wood, concluded that the answer to this question is that it is not possible to live; therefore, Malte is doomed. Others believed that Malte's answer lies in finding God. Wood, however, held that both these interpretations are too extreme. The solution, he proposed, can instead be found in Rilke's poetry collection, *Requiem,* which was written about the same time as his novel and "emphasizes that not victory but surviving is everything." As William Rose determined in *Rainer Maria Rilke: Aspects of His Mind and Poetry, The Notebooks of Malte Laurids Brigge* actually was kind of a catharsis for the author in which "Rilke gave full vent . . . to the fears which haunted him." "Without the *Notebooks* behind him," Wood concluded, "the poet would hardly have ventured to" write the *Duino Elegies* in 1912.

Duino Elegies "might well be called the greatest set of poems of modern times," averred Colin Wilson, author of *Religion and the Rebel.* Wilson added, "They have had as much influence in German-speaking countries as [T. S. Eliot's] *The Waste Land* has in England and America." Having discovered a dead end in the objective poetry with which he experimented in *New Poems,* Rilke once again turned to his own personal vision to find solutions to the questions about the purpose of human life and the poet's role in society. *Duino Elegies* finally resolved these puzzles to Rilke's own satisfaction. Called *Duino Elegies* because Rilke began writing them in 1912 while staying at Duino Castle on the Italian Adriatic coast, the collection took ten years to complete due to an inspiration-stifling depression the poet suffered during and after World War I. When his inspiration returned, however, the poet wrote a total of eleven lengthy poems for the book; later this was edited down to ten poems.

The unifying poetic image that Rilke employs throughout *Duino Elegies* is that of angels, which carry many meanings except for the usual Christian denotation. The angels represent a higher force in life, both beautiful and terrible, completely indifferent to mankind; they represent the power of poetic vision, as well as Rilke's personal struggle to reconcile art and life. Butler elaborates: "[The] Duino angels are truly a poetical creation to be completely susceptible of rational interpretation, and too complex to stand for any one idea. Rilke's idolatry of art as the supreme creative power became incarnate in them; a more mysterious and less ambiguous piece of symbolism than his previous use of the word God to represent an emergent aesthetic creator. These angels had more of the protean nature of the God of *The Book of Hours;* they were far more arresting and terrible in their utter aloofness, and self-sufficiency, as befitting beings who were not in a state of becoming but of eternal and immortal existence. Their absolute beauty annihilated human standards; and Rilke could only avert his personal destruction as a poet by accepting the challenge implicit in their very being. This is the drama inherent in *Duino Elegies.*" The Duino angels thus allowed Rilke to objectify abstract ideas as he had done in *New Poems,* while not limiting him to the mundane materialism that was incapable of thoroughly illustrating philosophical issues.

Duino Elegies, according to E. L. Stahl, a contributor to *Rainer Maria Rilke: Aspects of His Mind and Poetry,* "begin with lament, but end with praise." Beginning in the first elegy with what Butler called "a bitter confession of poetical and emotional bankruptcy," Rilke steadily develops his reasons for lamenting our existence, until the seventh elegy, where the discovery of a means to solving life's puzzles first turns lament into praise. The "lesson of the seventh elegy," wrote Butler, is "that the only real world is within us, and that life is one long transformation. Rilke had at last found the formula for his cosmic mission and a connecting link between himself and the angel." However, it is not until the ninth elegy that this formula is used. "We exist," said Stahl in his clarification of Rilke's revelation, "because existence is in itself of value and because everything which exists apparently appeals to us and depends on us for its future existence, though in this world we are the most fleeting creatures of all. But we pass on into another world, and it is our task to ensure for other beings a form of continued existence. We accomplish this task by expressing their hidden and inner meaning and by taking this possession 'across' with us. The purpose of our existence is to praise and extol the simple things of existence."

This conclusion allowed Rilke to accept life's suffering and death because he realized the purpose of life was not to avoid these destructive forces in favor of happiness. Instead, as the poet explains in the tenth elegy, the "principle of the whole of our life, in this world and the next, is sorrow." Having reconciled himself to the belief that man's existence by necessity involves suffering, Rilke concluded, according to Stahl, that the poet's function is to project "the world into the angel, where it becomes invisible." "Then the angels," Butler finished, "who can only apprehend what is invisible, will marvel at this hymn of praise to humble, simple things. They will receive them and rescue them from oblivion." This complex explanation of life's purpose, which Rilke developed slowly over many years, is not one that lends itself to a "rational explanation," Stahl pointed out. "It is a matter of Rilke's personal belief."

Nevertheless, the revolutionary poetic philosophy that Rilke proposes in *Duino Elegies* is considered significant to many literary scholars. "No poet before him had been brave enough to accept the *whole* of [the dark side of the] world, as if it were unquestionably valid and potentially universal," asserted Conrad Aiken in his *Collected Criticism*. Like the German philosopher Friedrich Nietzsche, who lived about the same time as Rilke, the poet determined his objective to be "[praise] and celebration in the face of and in full consciousness of the facts that had caused other minds to assume an attitude of negativity," wrote *Emergence from Chaos* author Stuart

Holroyd. But even though the final purpose of *Duino Elegies* is to praise existence, the "predominant note . . . is one of lament." But by overcoming his quandaries in this collection, Rilke was completely free to devote his poetry to praise in his *Sonnets to Orpheus*.

"The *Sonnets* are the songs of his victory," affirmed Bowra in his *The Heritage of Symbolism*. "In the *Sonnets*," Bowra also wrote, "Rilke shows what poetry meant to him, what he got from it and what he hoped for it. The dominating mood is joy. It is a complement to the distress and anxiety of the *Elegies*, and in Rilke's whole performance the two books must be taken together." Aiken similarly commented that the "*Sonnets to Orpheus* . . . is, with the *Elegies*, Rilke's finest work—the two books really belong together, shine the better for each other's presence."

In the last few years of his life, Rilke was inspired by such French poets as Paul Valery and Jean Cocteau, and wrote most of his last verses in French. Always a sickly man, the poet succumbed to leukemia in 1926 while staying at the Valmont sanatorium near Lake Geneva. On his deathbed, he remained true to his anti-Christian beliefs and refused the company of a priest. Hermann Hesse summed up Rilke's evolution as a poet in his book, *My Belief: Essays on Life and Art*: "Remarkable, this journey from the youthful music of Bohemian folk poetry . . . to *Orpheus*, remarkable how . . . his mastery of form increases, penetrates deeper and deeper into his problems! And at each stage now and again the miracle occurs, his delicate, hesitant, anxiety-prone person withdraws, and through him resounds the music of the universe; like the basin of a fountain he becomes at once instrument and ear." Without his parents' religious ideals to comfort him, Rilke found peace in his art. As Holroyd concluded, the "poetry which Rilke wrote to express and extend his experience . . . is one of the most successful attempts a modern man has made to orientate himself within his chaotic world."

Rilke is among the most widely translated of modern poets, a distinction that promotes varied interpretations of his poetry resulting from the disparate readings of various translators. Walter Arndt's translation of a selection of Rilke's poems in his 1989 publication *The Best of Rilke*, for example, attempts to translate Rilke's unique idiom into English while simultaneously attempting to maintain the original rhythm and rhyme scheme of the poet's verse. While noted as an ambitious and difficult endeavor, the translation has received mixed reviews. "Unfortunately Professor Arndt, for all his commendable intentions, does not bring out new strengths [in Rilke's poetry] and often falls wide of the mark," argued Walter Tonetto in *Modern Language Notes*. Edward Snow's translation of Rilke's *Uncollected Poems*, in contrast, has received high praise from several critics. Michael Dirda of *Washington Post Book World*, for example, asserted that "Snow is, with Stephen Mitchell and David Young, among the most trustworthy and exhilarating of Rilke's contemporary translators." While noted for the quality of the English translation, the volume is also significant in its presentation of some of Rilke's lesser-known verse, which, some argue, has been overshadowed by the *Duino Elegies*. Writing in *The Nation*, William H. Gass commented: "Snow's splendid selection supports his contention that these late poems—as occasional as lit matches in a crowd, and so different, in their quick responsive character, from the vatic seriousness of the *Elegies* and *Sonnets*—have their own high value and importance."

BIOGRAPHICAL/CRITICAL SOURCES:

BOOKS

Aiken, Conrad, *Collected Criticism*, Oxford University Press, 1968.

Baron, Frank, Ernst S. Dick, and Warren R. Maurer, eds., *Rainer Maria Rilke: The Alchemy of Alienation*, Regents Press of Kansas, 1980.

Borkowska, Ewa, *From Donne to Celan: Logo(theo)logical Patterns in Poetry*. Uniwersytet Slaskiego, 1994.

Bowra, C. M., *The Heritage of Symbolism*, Macmillan, 1943.

Burnshaw, Stanley, ed., *The Poem Itself*, Holt, 1960.

Butler, E. M., *Rainer Maria Rilke*, Macmillan, 1941.

Casey, Timothy J., *Rainer Maria Rilke: A Centenary Essay*, Macmillan, 1976.

Dictionary of Literary Biography, Volume 81: Austrian Fiction Writers, 1874-1913, Gale, 1989.

Feste-McCormack, Diana, *The City as Catalyst: A Study of Ten Novels*, Fairleigh Dickinson University Press, 1979.

Freedman, Ralph, *Life of a Poet: A Biography of Rainer Maria Rilke*, Farrar, 1995.

Fuerst, Norbert, *Phases of Rilke*, Indiana University Press, 1958.

Graff, W. L., *Rainer Maria Rilke: Creative Anguish of a Modern Poet*, Princeton University Press, 1956.

Gray, Ronald, *The German Tradition in Literature: 1971-1945*, Cambridge at the University Press, 1965.

Guardini, Romano, *Rilke's "Duino Elegies": An Interpretation*, translated by K. G. Knight, Henry Regnery, 1961.

Heep, Hartmut, *A Different Poem: Rainer Maria Rilke's American Translators Randall Jarrell, Robert Lowell, and Robert Bly*, P. Lang, 1996.

Heller, Erich, *The Artist's Journey into the Interior and Other Essays*, Random House, 1965.

Hesse, Hermann, *My Belief: Essays on Life and Art*, Farrar, Straus, 1974.

Holyroyd, Stuart, *Emergence from Chaos*, Houghton, 1957.

Komar, Kathleen L., *Transcending Angels: Rainer Maria Rilke's "Duino Elegies,"* University of Nebraska Press, 1987.

Lewisohn, Ludwig, *Cities and Men*, Harper & Brothers, 1927.

Mandel, Siegfried, *Rainer Maria Rilke: The Poetic Instinct*, edited by Harry T. Moore, Southern Illinois University Press, 1965.

Olivero, Federico, *Rainer Maria Rilke: A Study in Poetry and Mysticism*, W. Heffer & Sons, 1931.

Peters, H. F., *Rainer Maria Rilke: Masks and the Man*, University of Washington Press, 1960.

Poetry Criticism: Volume 2, Gale, 1991.

Pollard, Percival, *Masks and Minstrels of New Germany*, Johw W. Luce and Company, 1911.

Prater, Donald, *A Ringing Glass: The Life of Rainer Maria Rilke*, Clarendon Press, 1986.

Rilke, Rainer Maria, *Letters of Rainer Maria Rilke: 1910-1926*, Volume 2, Norton, 1948.

Rilke, Rainer Maria, *The Book of Hours: Comprising the Three Books, Of the Monastic Life, Of Pilgrimage, Of Poverty and Death*, Hogarth Press, 1961.

Rilke, Rainer Maria, *Nine Plays*, Ungar, 1979.

Rilke, Rainer Maria, *The Notebooks of Malte Laurids Brigge*, Vintage Books, 1985.

Rose, William, and G. Craig Houston, eds., *Rainer Maria Rilke: Aspects of His Mind and His Poetry*, Gordian, 1970.

Sword, Helen, *Engendering Inspiration: Visionary Strategies in Rilke, Lawrence, and H. D.*, University of Michigan Press, 1995.

Tavis, Anna A., *Rilke's Russia: A Cultural Encounter*, Nothwestern University Press, 1994.

Twentieth Century Literary Criticism, Gale, Volume 1, 1978; Volume 6, 1982; Volume 19, 1986.

Van Heerikhuizen, F. W., *Rainer Maria Rilke: His Life and Work*, translated by Fernand G. Renier and Anne Cliff, Routledge and Kegan Paul, 1951.

Willard, Nancy, *Testimony of the Invisible Man,* University of Missouri Press, 1970.

Wilson, Colin, *Religion and the Rebel,* Houghton, 1957.

Wood, Frank, *Rainer Maria Rilke: The Ring of Forms,* University of Minnesota Press, 1958.

Ziolkowski, Theodore, *Dimensions of the Modern Novel: German Texts and European Contexts,* Princeton University Press, 1969.

PERIODICALS

Booklist, April 15, 1994, p. 1516.

Choice, November, 1989, p. 490.

Commonweal, March 9, 1990, pp. 153-54.

Comparative Literature, Volume 35, no. 3 (summer), 1983, pp. 215-46.

Hound and Horn, April-June, 1931.

Library Journal, June 15, 1991, p. 81; April 1, 1994, p. 136.

Listener, December 18, 1975.

Modern Austrian Literature, Volume 15, nos. 3 and 4, 1982, pp. 71-90; Volume 15, nos. 3 and 4, 1982, pp. 291-316.

Modern Language Notes, January, 1991, p. 255.

Modern Language Review, April, 1979.

Nation, December 17, 1930; September 26, 1987, pp. 316-18; April 1, 1996, p. 27.

New Republic, September 6, 1939; January 3, 1994, p. 31; July 1, 1996, p. 32.

New Yorker, September 9, 1991, pp. 96-7.

New York Herald Tribune Books, December 14, 1930.

New York Times Book Review, January 17, 1988, p. 15; April 28, 1996, p. 16.

PMLA, October, 1974.

Publishers Weekly, February 28, 1994, p. 73.

Small Press, February, 1990, p. 51.

Times Literary Supplement, December 12, 1975; July 27-28, 1988, p. 795; May 29, 1992, p. 23.

University of Dayton Review, spring, 1981.

Washington Post Book World, March 31, 1996, p. 5.

World Literature Today, winter, 1988, p. 122.*

*　　*　　*

ROBERTS, Les 1937-

PERSONAL: Original surname Roubert; surname legally changed, 1968; born July 18, 1937, in Chicago, IL; son of Lester Nathaniel (a dentist) and Eleanor Sybil (Bauch) Roubert; married Gail Medland, September 19, 1957 (divorced, 1980); children: Valerie Lynne, Darren Jon. *Education:* Attended University of Illinois at Urbana-Champaign and Roosevelt University, 1954-56. *Avocational interests:* Gourmet cooking, reading.

ADDRESSES: Office—3244 Hyde Park Ave., Cleveland Heights, OH 44118. *Agent*—Dominick Abel, 146 West 82nd St., New York, NY 10024.

CAREER: Television writer and producer; jazz pianist and singer. Owner of Les Roberts Productions and Roberts Two, 1970-81; Delta Audio-Visual Services, director, 1984-85; executive producer and creator of *Cash Explosion* (weekly television game show for the Ohio Lottery), 1987, and for lottery programs in other states. Notre Dame College of Ohio, adjunct faculty; Case Western Reserve University, lecturer; teacher of novel, screenplay, and mystery writing at Glendale Community College, Learning Tree, and Everywoman's Village. Producer of television programs, including *The Jackie Gleason Show; The Andy Griffith Show, The Man from U.N.C.L.E.,* and *The Lucy Show,* all 1967; and *When Things Were Rotten,* 1975. *Military service:* U.S. Army, Signal Corps, 1960-62.

MEMBER: International Association of Crime Writers, Writers Guild of America, Mystery Writers of America, Private Eye Writers of America (president, 1992-94), American Crime Writers League.

AWARDS, HONORS: Best First Private Eye Novel award, Private Eye Writers of America/St. Martin's Press, 1986, for *An Infinite Number of Monkeys;* Cleveland Arts Prize for Literature, 1992; grant from Ohio Arts Council, 1993.

WRITINGS:

DETECTIVE NOVELS; "SAXON" SERIES

An Infinite Number of Monkeys, St. Martin's Press (New York City), 1987.

Not Enough Horses, St. Martin's Press, 1988.

A Carrot for the Donkey, St. Martin's Press, 1989.

Snake Oil, St. Martin's Press, 1990.

Seeing the Elephant, St. Martin's Press, 1992.

The Lemon Chicken Jones, St. Martin's Press, 1994.

DETECTIVE NOVELS; "MILAN JACOVICH" SERIES

Pepper Pike, St. Martin's Press, 1988.

Full Cleveland, St. Martin's Press, 1989.

Deep Shaker, St. Martin's Press, 1991.
The Cleveland Connection, St. Martin's Press, 1993.
The Lake Effect, St. Martin's Press, 1994.
The Duke of Cleveland, St. Martin's Press, 1995.
Collision Bend, St. Martin's Press, 1996.
Cleveland Local, St. Martin's Press, 1997.

OTHER

Foxbat (screenplay), Bang Bang Films (Hong Kong), 1977.
(With Gail Roberts) *Those Little White Lies* (two-act play), produced in Los Angeles, 1985.
A Carol for Cleveland (novella), Cobham-Hatherton (Cleveland, OH), 1991.

Author of screenplays, including *Solar Plexus,* 1981, and *Crooked River* (based on his novel *Pepper Pike*). Also author of unproduced two-act play *Writer's Block.* Producer of and writer for television programs, including *Hollywood Squares, It Takes Two, The Memory Game,* and *Runaround.* Restaurant reviewer for *Today,* 1984-86, and other local magazines; mystery book reviewer, *Cleveland Plain Dealer,* 1989—.

SIDELIGHTS: The crime novels of Les Roberts fall naturally into two series, each of which reveals facets of the author's personal experience. One series follows the slick private eye Saxon through the entertainment world, where Roberts himself spent several years writing screenplays and television scripts. The other traces the adventures of private investigator Milan Jacovich through the streets of Cleveland, Ohio, where Roberts now lives. The author's evident affection for the Midwestern "city on the lake" is noted by several reviewers and acknowledged by the city itself, which in 1992 awarded Roberts the Cleveland Arts Prize for Literature.

Saxon emerges as an almost stereotypical Los Angeles investigator and sometime actor in *An Infinite Number of Monkeys,* which earned Roberts a "best first novel" award in 1986. His character deepens somewhat in *Not Enough Horses,* in which the detective adopts Marvel, a street kid who figures in a later novel, *The Lemon Chicken Jones.* In fact, writes Barry W. Gardner in the *St. James Guide to Crime and Mystery Writers,* "[o]ne of the most appealing aspects of the series is the evolution of Saxon's attitudes as he and Marvel both age and grow." Gardner's choice for "[t]he deepest and best of the Saxon books" is *Seeing the Elephant,* which moves away from Los Angeles into the Midwest, where

Saxon has gone to attend a funeral. Though Gardner praises the series for "novelistic strength," he suggests that a potential weakness may be "Roberts's own ambivalence toward their [Hollywood-style] milieu," which nonetheless the author "brings sharply to life in all its grime and glory."

"The Jacovich books seem the darker of Roberts's two series," Gardner reports, "and the strongest." Milan Jacovich provides a genial, if somewhat strait-laced, contrast to Saxon. A detective of Slovenian descent with a master's degree in journalism, Milan plies his trade in Cleveland's variegated neighborhoods, on grimy city streets peopled with blue-collar laborers, organized crime bosses, and young people at risk. "Roberts is obviously at home in [Cleveland's] ethnic neighborhoods," Gardner comments, "and in his hands their inhabitants achieve a solid reality."

Beginning with *Pepper Pike,* Roberts reveals Jacovich as a man of what Gardner calls "a stern and demanding *personal* morality . . . one of the best-characterized of today's P.I.'s." Whether Milan is chasing a scam artist who stole mob money in *Full Cleveland,* tackling a gang of drug dealers who target his friend's teenage son in *Deep Shaker,* or sleuthing among artists, art galleries, and his mob pals to locate a valuable ceramic vase in *The Duke of Cleveland,* Gardner states that "the broad themes of morality, of obligation and loyalty and responsibility, and what they cost and what they're worth, are the bones beneath the skin of all Roberts's fiction." Yet, he adds, "they are never dealt with in a simplistic fashion . . . [or] allowed to become obtrusive. . . ." Commenting on *The Duke of Cleveland* in *Armchair Detective,* Don Sandstrom remarks that "Jacovich tells his story convincingly, smoothly, and interestingly. . . . He does it exceedingly well this time."

Roberts's 1996 novel, *Collision Bend,* blends the author's experiences as a television and film writer with his evident comfort in a Cleveland setting. In what Sybil S. Steinberg of *Publishers Weekly* calls a "solid, keep-you-guessing mystery," Milan assists a former lover to save her current partner from arrest for the murder of a local television newscaster.

Overall Gardner calls Roberts "one of the consistently best writers of private detective novels practicing today," one whose work "has steadily improved over the course of his literary career, and one who will eventually attain the recognition he merits."

Les Roberts once told *CA:* "I began writing books almost by accident. A producer asked me to come up with a private eye story for a film, and although he and the film's backers liked it, we couldn't come to terms. That story became *An Infinite Number of Monkeys* and changed the direction of my life. Although 95% of my income has come from writing or related fields, I have now realized, at a relatively advanced age, that writing novels is what I was born to do.

"My advice to aspiring writers is simple: read good writing. My own influences will surprise no one— John Steinbeck, for the raw emotion his work engenders; F. Scott Fitzgerald, for his glorious use of the language and his uncanny knack for describing the milieu in which he lived; Ernest Hemingway, who should be required reading for any writer tempted to use twelve overblown words where one perfect one will do; and the writers of the mystery genre: Raymond Chandler, Dashiell Hammett, Ross Macdonald, John D. McDonald. My second piece of advice is: write! 'Wannabees' talk about the book they are going to write; real writers do it!

"Writers of fiction, no matter what the genre, share a commonality. We write about people in crisis, in transition. I've chosen to deal with the greatest crisis of all—life or death. If along the way I can peel back a few layers of gunk and expose corruption, if I can comment on the human condition and provoke a thought, or give a reader a chuckle or two, why, so much the better. But I write because I have to—it's addictive, like heroin, beautiful women, or Big Macs.

"I plan to continue writing, at least two books a year, until (a) I get tired of them or (b) the public does."

BIOGRAPHICAL/CRITICAL SOURCES:

BOOKS

St. James Guide to Crime and Mystery Writers, fourth edition, St. James Press (Detroit), 1996.

PERIODICALS

Armchair Detective, summer, 1990, p. 277; spring, 1996.
Booklist, November 1, 1989, p. 28; June 15, 1991, p. 1937.

Kirkus Reviews, May 1, 1991, pp. 568-69; September 1, 1995; August 1, 1996, p. 1103.
Library Journal, November 1, 1989, p. 114.
Los Angeles Times Book Review, August 9, 1987.
Mystery News, September/October, 1997, p. 29.
Publishers Weekly, July 29, 1996, p. 74.
Romance Forever, June-July, 1997, pp. 64-65.
Washington Post, March 20, 1988.

*   *   *

ROBINSON, Sheila Mary 1928-
   (Sheila Radley, Hester Rowan)

PERSONAL: Born November 18, 1928, in Cogenhoe, Northamptonshire, England; daughter of Wallace (a village postman) and Mabel Elizabeth (Labrum) Robinson. *Education:* Bedford College, University of London, B.A. (honours, history), 1951. *Politics:* "Right of center." *Religion:* Church of England.

ADDRESSES: Home—Cyder Orchard, Church Lane, Banham, Norwich NR16 2HR, England. *Agent*— Curtis Brown, Curtis Brown Ltd., 162-168 Regent St., London W1R 5TB, England.

CAREER: Technical College, Northampton, assistant lecturer, 1960-61; National Savings, Shropshire, district commissioner, 1961-62; Institute of Practitioners in Advertising, London, education officer, 1962-64; Banham, Norfolk, assistant sub-postmistress, 1964-78; writer, 1978—. Owned and worked in village store and post office. *Military service:* Women's Royal Air Force, 1951-60.

WRITINGS:

UNDER PSEUDONYM HESTER ROWAN

Overture in Venice, Collins (London), 1976.
The Linden Tree, Collins, 1977.
Snowfall, Collins, 1978.

"INSPECTOR DOUGLAS QUANTRILL" SERIES; UNDER PSEUDONYM SHEILA RADLEY

Death and the Maiden, Hamilton (London), 1978, published as *Death in the Morning,* Scribner (New York City), 1979.
The Chief Inspector's Daughter, Scribner, 1980.
A Talent for Destruction, Scribner, 1982.

Blood on the Happy Highway, Constable (London), 1983, published as *The Quiet Road to Death,* Scribner, 1984.
Fate Worse Than Death, Constable, 1985, Scribner, 1986.
Who Saw Him Die?, Constable, 1987, Scribner, 1988.
This Way Out, Constable, 1989, Scribner, 1990.
Cross My Heart and Hope to Die, Scribner, 1992.
Fair Game, Constable, 1994.

SIDELIGHTS: Sheila Robinson published her first books, romantic thrillers, under the name Hester Rowan. After writing several books within that genre, Robinson began publishing her "Inspector Douglas Quantrill" crime novels under the pseudonym Sheila Radley. In an interview with *CA,* Radley explained why she changed writing genres: "I wasn't too keen on the romantic angle, or very good at it, so eventually I realized that it would be more sensible to try to write the kind of books that I enjoy reading. I'd always liked reading crime novels, and there again you've got a good framework on which to hang a story. That's what I need, that kind of structure to work with." Radley further explained her interest in crime writing, stating "Character and motive. Motive arising from character. My murderers aren't psychopaths, they're not villainous or violent, they're perfectly ordinary people under some kind of extraordinary stress, and what fascinates me is what it is that finally drives them to commit murder. That's what I think is the really interesting thing, not whodunit but why."

Radley writes within "the realistic tradition that has dominated crime writing since the 1960's," according to Robert Barnard in the *St. James Guide to Crime and Mystery Writers.* Barnard described Radley as "one of the most distinctive of the new crime fiction writers . . . her fingerprints are firm plotting, a vigorous style that can rise to brilliance when her emotions are involved, and a cunning eye for the minutiae of 20th-century living. Characterization is her other great strength, for she is both sharp-eyed and compassionate, and her novels are peppered with a gallery of believable people who are caught up in present-day dilemmas. . . . What principally strikes one is a probing, intense intelligence that gives the reader a sense that what is being written about is thoroughly understood." Barnard believes that Radley's murder motives are sometimes flawed, he stated, "Only in the motive for the murder . . . is credulity stretched unduly."

The "Quantrill" crime stories are set in rural Suffolk. The first novel of the series, *Death in the Morning,* introduces the series' detective team, Inspector Quantrill and Martin Tait. Quantrill, "late-promoted, rural, and bogged down in a dull marriage," and Tait, a "young, university-educated high-flyer," are "not an original combination," but are "sensitively and dramatically done," according to Barnard.

The Chief Inspector's Daughter, the second "Quantrill" entry, is "an intelligent, ironic British thriller," according to *Publishers Weekly*'s Barbara A. Bannon. In this "superior thriller," stated Connie Fletcher of *Booklist,* "envy, self-loathing," "cruelty," and "murder" are uncovered when Quantrill and Tait investigate the brutal murder of a romance novelist. Robins Winks commented in the *New Republic* that "structurally the book is fascinating, for it operates on three levels: as a quiet satire of romantic fiction, as an inquiry into the range of attacks on such fiction, and as an example of such writing at its most able. The cost is a lost puzzle, for few readers will fail to solve the mystery well before [the story's detectives]."

Following *The Chief Inspector's Daughter, A Talent for Destruction* was published. Barnard remarked that this is "perhaps Radley's most original and satisfying work. . . . The detective element is compelling, but the real interest is not in who committed the murders but in how they came about. There is a feeling of spiritual and personal desolation in the novel that is extremely compelling." The story involves the investigation of a skull found by two children. It is "brilliantly plotted and paced, and filled with vivid characters," according to Fletcher's *Booklist* review. The plot's unraveling, according to Bannon's review in *Publishers Weekly,* "show[s] considerable psychological insight and leave[s] us torn by pity for all of those involved."

A *Kirkus Reviews* critic implied the plotting was flawed in *A Talent for Destruction,* for the critic's review of Radley's next thriller, *The Quiet Road to Death,* stated, "plotting and motivation continue to be weak points in the Chief Inspector Quantrill's Suffolk mystery series." The critic, however, praised *The Quiet Road to Death* for a "[sharp] sense of character and milieu." In contrast, Fletcher claimed in a *Booklist* review that *The Quiet Road to Death* was "masterfully plotted" and contained "halting suspense" and "wry humor." Lynette Friesen remarked in *Library Journal* that the novel was "among the best of contemporary English village mysteries."

In her interview with *CA,* Radley described her seventh "Quantrill" novel, *This Way Out.* She stated, "It's slightly different in that it's not so much of a police procedural novel as the others. It's looking at the commission of a murder from the point of view of the person who does it. . . . It's a different approach, though, which I think is interesting. It was quite a change for me to get away from the police procedural formula, and it makes for a stronger plot."

In a summary of Radley's work, Barnard wrote, "Each novel has a different feel to it, due to the wide spectrum from which she draws her characters, her mastery of the specifics of differing lifestyles, and her concern to make each plot slightly different from the run-of-the-mill whodunnit. She has an eye for detail, for the significant gesture, for symptoms of the times we live in, all at the service of a large and compassionate understanding of people and their personal crises."

Radley comments to the *St. James Guide to Crime and Mystery Writers:* "Murder is essentially an amateur crime, committed for the most part not by psychopaths but by otherwise ordinary, decent people who would never dream of robbing a till. My concern in writing crime fiction is to explore the stresses and tensions that can drive such ordinary decent people to commit the ultimate crime of murder. I set my books in the English countryside because this is my own background, one that I understand and love."

BIOGRAPHICAL/CRITICAL SOURCES:

BOOKS

St. James Guide to Crime and Mystery Writers, fourth edition, St. James Press (Detroit), 1996.

PERIODICALS

Booklist, January 15, 1981; November 1, 1982; June 1, 1984.
Kirkus Reviews, April 1, 1984.
Library Journal, June 1, 1984.
New Republic, February 7, 1981.
New Yorker, August 27, 1984.
Publishers Weekly, November 28, 1980; August 27, 1982; May 4, 1992.*

ROSEN, R. D.
See ROSEN, Richard (Dean)

*   *   *

ROSEN, Richard (Dean) 1949-
(R. D. Rosen)

PERSONAL: Born February 18, 1949, in Chicago, IL; son of Sol A. and Carolyn (Baskin) Rosen; married Diane McWhorter (a journalist); children: Lucy. *Education:* Attended Brown University, 1967-68; Harvard University, B.A., 1972. *Religion:* Jewish.

ADDRESSES: Home—166 E. 96th St., Apt. 10-B, New York, NY 10128. *Agent*—(literary) Robert Lescher, 155 E. 71st St., New York, NY 10021; (television) Arthur Kaminsky, Athletes & Artists, 421 Seventh Ave., New York, NY 10001.

CAREER: Writer. *Boston Phoenix,* Boston, MA, staff writer and arts editor, 1972-76; *Boston Magazine,* Boston, staff writer and columnist, 1977-78; WGBH-TV, Boston, television news reporter and columnist, 1978-79; *The Real Paper,* Boston, editor-in-chief, 1979-80; WGBH-TV, Boston, television reporter, writer, actor-producer of national humor special, *The Generic News,* and director-producer of *Enterprise* documentary, 1982-84; National Broadcasting Company (NBC-TV), New York, NY, staff writer for *Saturday Night Live* comedy series, 1985; Home Box Office (HBO), Los Angeles, CA, cast member and writer for *Not Necessarily the News,* 1989-90. Associate, "I Have a Dream" Project, East Harlem, NY, 1986-87.

MEMBER: Writers Guild of America, Mystery Writers of America.

AWARDS, HONORS: Academy of American Poets prize, 1970; three Emmy Awards (New England region), 1984; Edgar Allan Poe Award for best first mystery novel, from Mystery Writers of America, 1985, for *Strike Three, You're Dead.*

WRITINGS:

(Under name R. D. Rosen) *Me and My Friends, We No Longer Profess Any Graces: A Premature Memoir,* Macmillan (New York City), 1971.

(Under name R. D. Rosen) *Psychobabble: Fast Talk and Quick Cure in the Era of Feeling,* Atheneum (New York City), 1977.
Not Available in Any Store: The Complete Catalog of the Most Amazing Products Never Made!, Pantheon (New York City), 1990.

MYSTERIES

(Under name R. D. Rosen) *Strike Three, You're Dead,* Walker (New York City), 1984.
Fadeaway, Harper (New York City), 1986.
Saturday Night Dead, Viking (New York City), 1988.
World of Hurt, Walker, 1994.

SCRIPTS

(Under name R. D. Rosen) *The Generic News,* Public Broadcasting System (PBS), 1983.
(Under name R. D. Rosen) *Workout,* Public Broadcasting System (PBS), 1984.

OTHER

Contributor to numerous periodicals, including *New York Times, New York, Sports Illustrated, New Republic, New Times,* and *Psychology Today.*

SIDELIGHTS: R. D. Rosen, whose first novel *Strike Three, You're Dead* won the prestigious Edgar Allan Poe Award, is a veteran journalist, television writer, producer, and performer. Rosen's career has included stints with WGBH-TV, Boston's public broadcasting station, and the popular *Saturday Night Live* comedy series on NBC. He has also authored several books of nonfiction (in one of which he coined a new term, "psychobabble"), and even penned some poetry. Since 1984, he has become known for his mystery novels, featuring a ballplayer-turned-detective named Harvey Blissberg.

According to Marvin Lachman in the *St. James Guide to Crime and Mystery Writers,* Rosen "has used two subjects enormously popular with millions of people, sports and television, and combined them with vivid descriptions of how people talk and what they buy. The historians and sociologists of the future may turn to his books to find, in addition to the freshness and vigor of the mysteries, graphic descriptions of life in New England and New York during the 1980s."

Strike Three, You're Dead introduces Blissberg, an aging center fielder for the fictitious Providence Jewels. When his roommate is found murdered, Blissberg undertakes his own investigation, during which he himself becomes a target for murder. Rosen drew upon his extensive knowledge of major league baseball—and his own experiences as a player—in order to add realism to the novel. To quote Bob Wiemer in *Newsday,* the resulting work is "the literary equivalent of an in-the-park home run." *New York Times Book Review* columnist Newgate Callendar called *Strike Three, You're Dead* "an entertaining and well-written book," adding: "Mr. Rosen can write. His dialogue is smart and sophisticated and his characters altogether three-dimensional. Clearly the author loves baseball, but he does not get sentimental about it. His approach is entirely professional." The Mystery Writers of America found *Strike Three, You're Dead* the best first mystery novel of the year in 1985.

In subsequent books, Blissberg has retired from baseball and is a full-time gumshoe. *Fadeaway* concerns the violent deaths of two professional basketball players, both found in Boston's Logan Airport. Called in to track the murderer, Blissberg uncovers a sordid trail of drug abuse and recruiting violations. *Washington Post Book World* contributor Jean M. White noted that in *Fadeaway* Rosen "writes with a light, sure touch. He has done his homework on the drug problem and recruiting pressures in basketball. . . . The ending is a corker." To quote Lachman, both *Strike Three, You're Dead* and *Fadeaway* "authentically report those sensational aspects [of sports], especially the drug and alcohol addictions of young millionaire athletes." Likewise, concluded Lachman, "Rosen conveys the hypocrisy in college recruiting and the operation of lucrative professional franchises."

Saturday Night Dead follows Blissberg onto the set of a late-night comedy show where the reigning executive is suddenly killed. The fictitious show, *Last Laughs,* is based upon *Saturday Night Live,* a long-running comedy series that Rosen worked for briefly in 1985. A *Publisher's Weekly* reviewer wrote of the mystery: "The story's skillful contrasts of edged satire and pathos make it irresistible, the third triumph for Blissberg and his creator." While Lachman contended that the solution of *Saturday Night Dead* is "overly melodramatic," he nonetheless observed that the novel "has many strengths, notably its New York atmosphere and the behind-the-scenes look at television, especially its comedy programs."

Rosen told *CA* that he conceived Harvey Blissberg by observing the age-old rule "that you should write about what you know." He added: "When I sat down to plan my first mystery, I thought about what I knew, and I know a lot about baseball. In fact, when I think about the things I've written over the years, I realize that baseball has found its way into almost every form. I've written journalism and poetry about baseball. I've written pieces that were odes to Fenway Park. I've drawn baseball parks. Baseball was sewn into my character at an early age, so I wasn't surprised when baseball popped into my head as the setting for my first novel."

Reflecting on the source of his inspirations, Rosen told *CA:* "Having experience in other professions is very valuable for a writer. You always want to be writing about something. You don't want to be writing about different versions of yourself or different versions of what the inside of your brain looks like. The things I find most fascinating about novels sometimes are what they have to say about what other people do for a living. . . . I think what people do is very interesting, so my experience in journalism, although it's clearly related to being a writer, gave me a larger frame of reference. I'm afflicted, and blessed, by curiosity about what people *do."*

BIOGRAPHICAL/CRITICAL SOURCES:

BOOKS

Contemporary Literary Criticism, Volume 39, Gale (Detroit, MI), 1987.
St. James Guide to Crime and Mystery Writers, fourth edition, St. James Press (Detroit, MI), 1996.

PERIODICALS

Change, April, 1978.
Chicago Tribune Books, July 3, 1988.
Eagle [Providence], October 21, 1984.
Kirkus Reviews, June 15, 1984, p. 554.
New Republic, August 22, 1981; August 29, 1981.
Newsday, August 19, 1984.
New Yorker, November 24, 1986.
New York Times Book Review, October 28, 1984.
Publishers Weekly, May 11, 1984, p. 263; April 22, 1988.
Sports Illustrated, April 18, 1985.
Washington Post Book World, January 20, 1985; November 16, 1986.
Wilson Library Bulletin, November, 1984.

ROSENBERG, Nancy Taylor 1946-

PERSONAL: Born July 9, 1946, in Dallas, TX; daughter of William Hoyt (an "oil man") and Ethel LaVerne (a homemaker) Taylor; married Calvin Skyrme (divorced, 1984); married Jerry Rosenberg (an investor); children: (first marriage) Forrest Blake, Chessly Lynn Nesci, Gerald Hoyt; (second marriage) Amy Laura, Nancy Beth. *Education:* Attended Gulf Park College and University of California, Los Angeles. *Politics:* "Non-partisan." *Religion:* Jewish.

ADDRESSES: Home—Niguel, CA. *Agent*—Peter Miller, 220 West 19th St., Suite 220, New York, NY 10011.

CAREER: Dallas Police Department, Dallas, TX, police officer, 1971-75; Ventura Police Department, Ventura, CA, community service officer, 1978-81; Ventura County Probation Department, Ventura, deputy probation officer, 1981-84; Video Movie Wholesalers, vice president and owner. Has also worked as a police officer in New Mexico and Arizona, a criminal investigator, and a model.

WRITINGS:

NOVELS

Mitigating Circumstances, Dutton (New York City), 1993.
Interest of Justice, Dutton, 1993.
First Offense, Dutton, 1994.
California Angel, Dutton, 1995.
Trial by Fire, Dutton, 1995.

SIDELIGHTS: Nancy Taylor Rosenberg has carved a successful niche for herself writing thrillers that feature strong, savvy women who use their wits and courage to save themselves and others. From her bestselling debut *Mitigating Circumstances* onward, Rosenberg has crafted legal thrillers in which her heroines must overcome their vulnerabilities in mostly hostile, mostly male environments. According to Richard G. La Porte in the *St. James Guide to Crime and Mystery Writers,* "Each of [Rosenberg's] protagonists, from the probation caseworker to the judge on the bench, has her secure seeming world shattered by a violation of the fabric of her life. . . . Rosenberg's books have their crises and conflicts welded into coherent scenarios with meaningful dialogue and gritty action."

Having herself worked in law enforcement in several states, Rosenberg has brought her own experiences to bear on her novels. Most of her heroines have shaky marriages and children to raise, as well as stressful jobs in the legal industry. In *Mitigating Circumstances,* for instance, the protagonist, Lily Forrester, is a district attorney with a teenage daughter. Laura Sanderstone, in *Interest of Justice,* is a judge who is also faced with the task of raising an unruly nephew. These and other Rosenberg protagonists face dangerous affronts to their lives—both professional and personal—and the stories revolve around their efforts to diffuse the terror.

Los Angeles Times Book Review columnist Charles Champlin has called Rosenberg "a ring-a-ding story teller whose tricky plotting was buttressed by the authenticity of the courtroom and police environments she has experienced." In the *Library Journal,* Dawn L. Anderson likewise credited Rosenberg with creating "riveting [stories] with a strong feminine center." Concluded La Porte: "Some of [Rosenberg's] emotional scenes smolder darkly in the heat of the southern California night."

Rosenberg told *CA:* "All my life, I planned to become an author. After studying English in college, however, I found myself in many different careers. I was a model, a police officer, a probation officer, and a criminal investigator. These experiences served me well, as I write thrillers set in the criminal justice system. I am also the mother of five children. Young people appear many times as characters in my novels.

"At the age of forty-five, I decided to pursue my dream by studying writing at the University of California, Los Angeles. One year later my first novel was purchased during a fierce bidding war for what I considered an enormous sum of money. A few days later, the movie rights were sold to Tri Star Pictures and targeted to be Jonathan Demme's next project. The book was also a main selection of the Literary Guild, and it will be printed in thirteen different countries throughout the world. For a writer, this was a dream come true. For me, it was a miracle. It only got better. Approximately six months later, New American Library/Dutton signed me to a four-book contract.

"Many people ask me how I made it as a novelist in such economically poor times, and how any new writer manages to become published. My belief is that any terrific piece of work will find its way into print, but I also believe that hard work and perseverance are the mainstay of the writer. This is not something you can approach as a hobby. You must be as serious and focused with your writing as you would be if you were a surgeon stitching delicate arteries and nerves. Being able to accept criticism, listen to worthwhile suggestions, and tirelessly rewrite are some of the best attributes. Young or unpublished writers of all ages tend to become seduced by their own writing and stubbornly reject suggestions on how they can improve.

"On the specific side, I packaged myself and my work to be commercially attractive and easily assimilated by agents, the first step toward publishing. I included a chapter-by-chapter outline of my novel, enabling agents to follow the plot line without taking the time to read the entire manuscript, and I enclosed sample chapters, allowing them to review my prose and listen to my voice. In addition, I enclosed a photograph of myself, a biography, and comments other fledgling writers had made about my manuscript.

"If you feel compelled to write, you are probably a writer. This driving need to express yourself and tell stories is the distinctive mark of talent. In today's publishing world, however, if you want to produce more than one publishable work, you must discover a niche. Then, as in any business venture, you must examine the work of others in your selected niche. Listen closely to any and all comments made by rejecting agents or publishers. Even though agents are constantly deluged with unsolicited manuscripts to the point where they sometimes let a talented beginner slip right through their fingers, most of them know their stuff. Do not be discouraged. I was rejected by fifteen literary agents long after my novel had been sold, articles had appeared in numerous trade journals and magazines, and the checks were in the bank. Fasten your seat belts, burn the midnight oil, and listen to your inner voice. Good luck!"

BIOGRAPHICAL/CRITICAL SOURCES:

BOOKS

St. James Guide to Crime and Mystery Writers, fourth edition, St. James Press (Detroit, MI), 1996.

PERIODICALS

Armchair Detective, fall, 1993, pp. 43-44; winter, 1994, p. 87.

Kirkus Reviews, May 15, 1994, p. 658; November 15, 1994, p. 1492; October 15, 1995, p. 1453.

Library Journal, May 15, 1994, p. 101; December 1994, p. 134; December 1995, p. 159.

Los Angeles Times Book Review, October 10, 1993, p. 12.

Publishers Weekly, May 30, 1994, p. 34; November 28, 1994, p. 42; November 13, 1995, p. 48.

*   *   *

ROWAN, Hester
  See **ROBINSON, Sheila Mary**

S-V

SANDERS, Lawrence 1920-
(Lesley Andress, Mark Upton)

PERSONAL: Born 1920, in Brooklyn, NY. *Education:* Wabash College, B.A., 1940.

ADDRESSES: Home—Pompano Beach, FL. *Agent*—Putnam Publishing Group, 200 Madison Ave., New York, NY 10016.

CAREER: Macy's (department store), New York City, staff member, 1940-43; feature editor, *Mechanix Illustrated,* New York City; editor, *Science and Mechanics,* New York City; Magnum-Royal Publications, New York City, writer for men's magazines, 1967-68. *Military service:* U.S. Marine Corps, 1943-46; became sergeant.

AWARDS, HONORS: Edgar Allan Poe Award for best first mystery novel, Mystery Writers of America, 1970, for *The Anderson Tapes.*

WRITINGS:

MYSTERY NOVELS

The Anderson Tapes, Putnam (New York City), 1970.
The First Deadly Sin, Putnam, 1973.
The Tomorrow File, Putnam, 1975.
The Tangent Objective, Putnam, 1976.
The Second Deadly Sin, Putnam, 1977.
The Tangent Factor, Putnam, 1978.
The Sixth Commandment, Putnam, 1978.
The Tenth Commandment, Putnam, 1980.
The Third Deadly Sin, Putnam, 1981.
The Case of Lucy Bending, Putnam, 1982.

The Seduction of Peter S., Putnam, 1983.
The Passion of Molly T., Putnam, 1984.
The Fourth Deadly Sin, Putnam, 1985.
The Loves of Harry Dancer, Berkley Publishing (New York City), 1986, published as *The Loves of Harry D,* New English library (London), 1986.
The Eighth Commandment, Putnam, 1986.
Tales of the Wolf, Avon (New York City), 1986.
The Dream Lover, Berkley Publishing, 1987.
The Timothy Files, Putnam, 1987.
Timothy's Game, Putnam, 1988.
Capital Crimes, Putnam, 1989.
Stolen Blessings, Berkley Publishing, 1989.
Sullivan's Sting, Putnam, 1990.
McNally's Secret, Putnam, 1992.
McNally's Luck, Putnam, 1992.
McNally's Risk, Putnam, 1993,
Private Pleasures, Berkley Publishing, 1994.
McNally's Caper, Putnam, 1994.
Three Complete Novels (contains *The Sixth Commandment, The Seventh Commandment,* and *The Eighth Commandment*), Putnam, 1994.
McNally's Trial, Putnam, 1995.
Three Complete Novels (contains *The Anderson Tapes, The Fourth Deadly Sin,* and *The Tenth Commandment*), Putnam, 1996.
McNally's Puzzle, Putnam, 1996.

OTHER

(Editor) *Thus Be Loved: A Book for Lovers,* Arco, 1966.
(With Richard Carol) *Handbook of Creative Crafts* (nonfiction), Pyramid Books, 1968.
The Pleasures of Helen, Putnam, 1971.
Love Songs, Putnam, 1972.

The Marlow Chronicles, Putnam, 1977.
(Under pseudonym Mark Upton) *Dark Summer,* Coward, McCann, 1979.
(Under pseudonym Lesley Andress) *Caper,* Putnam, 1980.

Also author of books under pseudonyms and of several "purse books" for Dell. Contributor of more than one hundred stories and articles to various publications.

ADAPTATIONS: Films based on Sanders's books include *The Anderson Tapes,* Columbia Pictures, 1971, and *The First Deadly Sin,* Filmways, 1980.

SIDELIGHTS: Lawrence Sanders produces thrillers that combine international intrigue with high-tech detail. "In his best work," according to George Grella, writing in the *St. James Guide to Crime and Mystery Writers,* Sanders "combines with great adroitness the necessary ingredients for commercial success—sex, violence, and sensationalism, distinctive characterization, and sociological observation, all packaged with a slick and attractive wrapping of glossy style and suspenseful narrative."

A former editor of pulp magazines, Sanders has said that during this early career he "got to the point where a lot of editors get—I said to myself that I could write the stuff better myself." And so he produced his first novel, *The Anderson Tapes,* in 1970, at age 50.

The Anderson Tapes is the story of a Mafia-backed effort to rob an entire luxury apartment building. Foreshadowing the role electronics were to play in the political scandal known as Watergate during the early 1970s, this plot is thwarted when several governmental agencies wiretap "everything from a candy-store pay phone to Central Park itself." Christopher Lehmann-Haupt, writing in the *New York Times,* speculated that those "fashionably paranoiac and willing to believe that the whole world is plugged into a tape recorder" would "have a zippy time" with this novel. *The Anderson Tapes* was a best seller upon publication and was made into a Columbia motion picture soon thereafter.

To Grella, *The Anderson Tapes* "is one of the most technically innovative thrillers of recent years, an outstanding big caper novel" whose plot "meshes perfectly with its subject, since the big caper itself is a kind of technologically sophisticated crime, depending on split-second timing, careful planning, clockwork routine, and so forth. The novel draws a powerful picture of a criminal world and a pervasively corrupt society; besides its unique narrative use of electronic eavesdropping, the book clearly indicates . . . the threat to freedom and privacy posed by the enormous amount of technological advances in legal and illegal snooping."

Sanders' *The Tomorrow File,* written in 1975 and set in the distant future of 1998, presents an America ruled by a bureaucratic elite. Any new ideas are placed in a "tomorrow file" until the general public can accept such advanced concepts. A member of the government's Department of Bliss (Satisfaction Section) formulates a complex plan to bring down a corrupt system. Sanders "knows how to construct a story," notes John Deck in a *New York Times Book Review* article. "This book begins with a murder and, in finding the killer and causes, Sanders reveals a number of heartaches in Utopia." Less impressed was Robbin Ahrold of *Library Journal,* who dismissed *The Tomorrow File* as "practically unreadable"; to *Best Sellers* critic Robert McGeehin, "the novel is full of people who are just not believable. Dialogue is rather clumsily handled, and the plot is too predictable."

A considerably warmer reception greeted *The Sixth Commandment,* published in 1979. *Library Journal* assessed the plot—concerning a doctor who uses humans in his experiments to achieve immortality—as "complex and brilliant," while a *New Yorker* review calls the novel brimming "with juice and excitement, with some insight and much foolishness—a genuinely riveting diversion."

BIOGRAPHICAL/CRITICAL SOURCES:

BOOKS

Bestsellers 89, Issue 4, Gale (Detroit), 1989.
Contemporary Literary Criticism, Volume 41, Gale, 1987.
St. James Guide to Crime and Mystery Writers, fourth edition, St. James Press (Detroit), 1996.

PERIODICALS

Best Sellers, October, 1975.
Booklist, February 15, 1993, p. 1011; November 1, 1993, p. 559; July, 1994, p. 1965.
Chicago Tribune Book World, September 19, 1982.
Globe and Mail (Toronto), January 12, 1985; August 10, 1985; June 7, 1986; July 4, 1987; June 10, 1989.

Library Journal, January 1989, p. 103; October 15, 1975; January 1, 1979; September 1, 1990, p. 278; June 1, 1992, p. 208.

Los Angeles Times, November 5, 1982.

Los Angeles Times Book Review, October 12, 1980; November 5, 1982; July 31, 1983; October 28, 1984; November 24, 1985; July 10, 1988; May 14, 1989; July 1, 1990.

New Yorker, August 30, 1976; February 5, 1979.

New York Times, February 20, 1970; October 20, 1973; August 25, 1977; March 24, 1978; May 5, 1988.

New York Times Book Review, November 16, 1975; August 21, 1977; August 29, 1977; October 9, 1977; February 11, 1979; September 28, 1980; October 5, 1980, July 26, 1981; September 6, 1981; August 22, 1982; July 24, 1983; September 30, 1984; July 28, 1985; August 10, 1986; July 31, 1988; August 13, 1989; March 3, 1996, p. 18.

People, November 28, 1977; September 16, 1985; July 13, 1987.

Publishers Weekly, August 2, 1976; May 15, 1987, p. 264; October 7, 1988, p. 87; November 3, 1989, p. 86; August 3, 1990, p. 50; February 15, 1991, p. 76; March 7, 1992, p. 28; September 7, 1992, p. 29; January 23, 1995, p. 63.

Time, April 27, 1979; August 29, 1977.

Tribune Books (Chicago) July 10, 1988; January 21, 1990.

Washington Post, May 4, 1978; August 6, 1981; September 2, 1984.

Washington Post Book World, August 18, 1985.

*   *   *

SATTERTHWAIT, Walter 1946-

PERSONAL: Born March 23, 1946, in Philadelphia, PA; son of Walter, Jr. (a club manager) and Jeanne (Woodruff) Satterthwait. *Education:* Attended Reed College. *Politics:* None. *Religion:* Buddhist.

ADDRESSES: Home and office—Albuquerque, NM. *Agent*—Dominick Abel, 498 West End Ave., No. 12C, New York, NY 10024.

CAREER: Writer. Worked as a bartender and bar manager, beginning 1968.

MEMBER: Mystery Writers of America.

WRITINGS:

FICTION

Cocaine Blues, Dell (New York City), 1979.

The Aegean Affair, Dell, 1981.

Wall of Glass, St. Martin's (New York City), 1987.

Miss Lizzie, St. Martin's, 1989.

At Ease with the Dead, St. Martin's, 1990.

Wilde West, St. Martin's, 1991.

A Flower in the Desert, St. Martin's, 1992.

The Hanged Man, St. Martin's, 1993 (published in England as *The Death Card,* Collins [London], 1994).

Escapade, St. Martin's, 1995.

The Gold of Mayani (short stories), Buffalo Medicine Books (Gallup), 1995.

Accustomed to the Dark, St. Martin's, 1996.

Work represented in anthologies, including *Hitchcock's Most Wanted.* Contributor of stories to magazines, including *Alfred Hitchcock's Mystery Magazine* and *Magazine of Fantasy and Science Fiction.*

NONFICTION

Sleight of Hand: Conversations with Walter Satterthwait, with Ernie Bulow, University of New Mexico (Albuquerque), 1993.

SIDELIGHTS: Walter Satterthwait's writing career has blossomed since the late 1980s, when he introduced character Joshua Croft into a series of mystery novels. Satterthwait, himself based in New Mexico, uses that locale—and the West in general—to give an authentic regional flavor to both his detective novels and his historical mystery tales. To quote Barry W. Gardner in the *St. James Guide to Crime and Mystery Writers,* Satterthwait "is a natural storyteller with a smooth, readable prose style, qualities evidenced in everything he writes. . . . While his tales have their subtexts and messages, as any but the shallowest of fiction does, these are not his focus. He tells stories, and so far he has told them very well indeed."

Born in Philadelphia, Satterthwait published his first novel, a paperback entitled *Cocaine Blues,* when he was 33. His early works, which he himself has characterized as "forgettable," were soon upstaged by a series of five detective novels set in Santa Fe, as well as several historical mysteries. The historicals offer intriguing situations, including an unlikely visit to the American West by Oscar Wilde (in *Wilde West)* and an equally imaginative pairing of Harry Houdini and Arthur Conan Doyle (in *Escapade*). Gardner declared Satterthwait's historical mysteries "the most appealing of his works," featuring his "most ambitious" writing.

Perhaps better known, however, are the Joshua Croft novels, including *Wall of Glass, At Ease with the Dead,* and *Accustomed to the Dark.* These are set in Santa Fe and its environs, making liberal use of the desert locale and the particular eccentricities of the city itself. According to Gardner, the Croft books "are among the better of the current private eye series regardless of locale. . . . Satterthwait has excellent narrative skills, striking a good balance between straightforward narration and occasional passages that approach the lyrical." Reflecting on the series title character, Gardner noted: "Croft can fire off his share of the mandatory PI wisecracks, but Satterthwait succeeds in making him a sensitive character without being either pretentious or maudlin."

Satterthwait has indicated that the fifth Joshua Croft book may be the last in that series, and that he may move on to other projects and characters. Gardner concluded that readers need not fear any change the author cares to make. "While many writers are comfortable using only voice, writing only one type of fiction, the record shows that Satterthwait has a versatility that would seem to allow him to go anywhere he chooses with his craft."

Satterthwait told *CA:* "In general I write books and short stories about people who attempt to determine why, and by whom, certain other people were killed. I like mysteries because writing them gives me—theoretically, at least—an opportunity to demonstrate how clever I am. (Which, I suspect, is part of the reason why anyone writes anything for publication. Plumage, Nathanael West called it.) But also because along the way, maybe I can actually learn a little something about the way specific people in a specific locale might react to a specific, potentially dangerous situation. I've invented—and to some extent been invented by—ivory smugglers in Malindi, Kenya; gallery owners in Santa Fe; restaurant owners in Greece; and Lizzie Borden on the Massachusetts shore in 1921. And I think that in order for any of them to have worked as characters, I needed to understand them first as people: to recognize the complicated—sometimes sloppy—uniqueness of their individual lives. And I think that doing this, in the act of fiction or the act of living, is kind of a nifty thing, and may even be important."

BIOGRAPHICAL/CRITICAL SOURCES:

BOOKS

St. James Guide to Crime and Mystery Writers, fourth edition, St. James Press (Detroit), 1996.

PERIODICALS

West Coast Review of Books, September, 1982, p. 63.
Wilson Library Bulletin, May, 1988.

*   *   *

SAUSER-HALL, Frederic 1887-1961
(Blaise Cendrars)

PERSONAL: Listed in some sources as Frederic Sauser or Frederic Sauserhall; born September 1, 1887, in La Chaux-de-Fonds, Switzerland; died January 21, 1961, in Paris, France; son of an inventor and businessman; married Fela Poznanska, 1914 (divorced); married wife, Raymone (an actress), 1946; children: (first marriage) Miriam, two sons. *Education:* Attended University of Berne, 1907-09.

CAREER: Writer. Worked variously in business, horticulture, journalism, juggling, prospecting, and directing, producing, and acting in motion pictures in France, Italy, and Hollywood; traveled extensively around the world, including Egypt, Italy, the United States, and countries in Africa and South America; worked briefly as editor of literary review, *Les Hommes Nouveaux; Paris Soir,* Paris, France, reporter, 1934-40. *Military service:* Served with French Foreign Legion during World War I; became corporal; wounded in Champagne, France, 1915.

WRITINGS:

UNDER PSEUDONYM BLAISE CENDRARS

La Legende de Novgorode, [France], 1909.
Sequences, [France], 1912.
Les Paques a New York (poem), [France], 1912.
La Prose du trans-siberien et la petite Jehanne de France (poem), [France], 1913, published as *Le Trans-siberien,* P. Seghers, 1957.
Profound aujourd'hui, LaBelle, 1917.
J'ai tue, [France], 1918.

Du Monde entier au coeur du monde (poems), Editions de la Nouvelle Revue Francaise, 1919.

(With Abel Gance) *J'accuse* (screenplay), [France], 1919.

Dix-neuf Poemes elastiques, [France], 1919.

La Fin du monde (novel; also see below), Editions de la Sirene, 1919.

J'ai saigne, [France], 1920.

(With Gance) *La Roue* (screenplay), [France], 1922.

Feuilles de route (poems), Au Sans Pareil, 1924.

ABC du cinema, [France], 1926.

L'Eloge de la vie dangereuse, [France], 1926.

Rhum: L'Aventure de Jean Galmot (nonfiction), B. Grasset, 1930, reprinted, 1991..

Aujourd'hui, B. Grasset, 1931.

Vol a voiles (autobiographical), Payot, 1932.

(Translator) O. Henry, *Hors la loi!: La Vie d'outlaw american racontee par lui-meme,* [France], 1936.

Histoires vraies (stories), B. Grasset, 1938.

La Vie dangereuse, B. Grasset, 1938.

D'Oultremer a indigo, B. Grasset, 1940.

Poesies completes, Denoel, 1944.

Blaise Cendrars, Nouvelle Revue Critique, 1947.

Oeuvres choisies, [France], 1948.

La Banlieue de Paris, La Builde du Livre, 1949.

Le Lotissement du ciel (autobiographical novel), Denoel, 1949.

Blaise Cendrars vous parle (radio interviews with Michel Manoll), Denoel, 1952.

Le Bresil: Des Hommes sont venus, Documents d'Art, 1952.

Trop c'est trop, Denoel, 1957.

A L'Aventure, Denoel, 1958.

Films sans images, Denoel, 1959.

Saint Joseph de Cupertino, Club de Livre Chretien, 1960.

Amours (poems), P. Seghers, 1961.

Blaise Cendrars, 1887-1961, Mercure de France, 1962.

Serajevo, Theatre Universitaire, 1963.

Oeuvres completes, eight volumes, Club Francais du Livre, 1968-71.

Dites-nous, Monsieur Blaise Cendrars, edited by Hughes Richard, Editions Recontre, 1969.

Inedits secrets (journals), edited by daughter, Miriam Cendrars, Club Francais du Livre, 1969.

J'ecris. Ecrivoz-moi (correspondence), Denoel (Paris), 1991.

Correspondance, 1934-1979: 45 Ans D'Anitie, Denoel, 1995.

Also author of movie screenplay, *La Fin du monde,* 1931, based on his novel of the same title.

UNDER PSEUDONYM BLAISE CENDRARS; IN ENGLISH TRANSLATION

Le Panama; ou, Les Aventures de mes sept oncles (poem), [Paris], 1918, translation by John Dos Passos published as *Panama; or, The Adventures of My Seven Uncles,* Harper, 1931.

(Compiler) *L'Anthologie negre,* Editions de la Sirene, 1921, revised edition, Correa, 1947, translation by Margery Bianco published as *The African Saga,* Payson & Clarke, 1927.

Kodak (poems), Stock, 1924, translation by Ron Padgett published under same title, Adventures in Poetry, 1976.

L'Or: La Merveilleuse histoire du General Johann August Suter (novel), B. Grasset, 1925, translation by Henry Longan Stuart published as *Sutter's Gold,* Harper, 1926, translation by Nina Rootes published as *Gold: Being the Marvelous History of General John Augustus Sutter,* Michael Kesend, 1984, reprinted, Marlowe & Company, 1996..

Moravagine (novel), B. Grasset, 1926, translation by Alan Brown published under same title, P. Owen, 1968, Projection Books, 1970.

Dan Yack (novel), Volume 1: *Le Plan de l'aiguille,* Au Sans Pariel, 1927, translation by Rootes published as *Dan Yack,* Michael Kesend, 1987, Volume 2: *Les Confessions de Dan Yack,* [Paris], 1929, translation by Rootes published as *Confessions of Dan Yack,* P. Owen, 1990, single-volume edition, [Paris], 1946, translation published as *Antarctic Fugue,* Pushkin Press, 1948.

Petite contes negres pour les enfants des blancs, [Paris], 1928, translation by Bianco published as *Little Black Stories for Little White Children,* Payson & Clarke, 1929.

Une Nuit dans la foret (autobiographical), [France], 1929, translation published by Margaret K. Ewing as *Night in the Forest,* University of Missouri Press, 1985.

(Editor) Hans Bringolf, *I Have No Regrets: Being the Memoirs of Lieutenant Bringolf,* translation from the original French by Warre B. Wells, Jarrolds, 1931.

Hollywood: La Mecque du cinema, B. Grasset, 1936, translation by Garrett White published as *Hollywood: Mecca of the Movies,* University of California Press, 1995.

L'Homme foudroye (autobiographical novel), Denoel, 1945, abridged translation by Rootes published as *The Astonished Man,* Owen, 1970.

La Main coupee (autobiographical novel), Denoel, 1946, abridged translation by Rootes published as *Lice,* Owen, 1973.

Bourlinguer (autobiographical novel), Denoel, 1948, abridged translation by Rootes published as *Planus,* Owen, 1972.

Emmene-moi au bout du monde! (novel), Denoel, 1956, translation by A. Brown published as *To the End of the World,* P. Owen, 1967.

Selected Writings of Blaise Cendrars, translation from the original French edited by Walter Albert, preface by Henry Miller, New Directions, 1962.

Complete Postcards from the Americas: Poems of Road and Sea, translation from the original French, University of California Press, 1976.

Pathe Baby, translation from the original French, City Lights, 1980.

Knockabout, Scarborough House, 1982.

Shadow (juvenile), translation and illustrations by Marcia Brown, Scribner's, 1982, reprinted, Aladdin, 1996.

Modernities and Other Writings, University of Nebraska Press, 1992.

Sky: Memoirs, Paragon House, 1992.

Complete Poems translation by Ron Padgett, University of California Press, 1992.

Christmas at the Four Corners of the Earth, BOA, 1994.

ADAPTATIONS: *L'Or: La Merveilleuse histoire du General Johann August Suter* was filmed in 1936 as *Sutter's Gold,* directed by James Cruze.

SIDELIGHTS: Frederic Sauser-Hall, who is best known under his pen name, Blaise Cendrars, was remarkable not only as a poet and novelist, but also as an adventurous personality whose Bohemian lifestyle was as renowned in the early twentieth century as his writings. As a poet, Cendrars was influenced by the styles of the Cubists, Dadaists, and Surrealists, to which he applied techniques of the cinema and musical composition. As a novelist, his stories were picaresque tales that combined fantasy and personal experience. Because of this mixture, critics have intermittently faulted Cendrars for being too realistic or too incredible in his writings; they have also criticized him for being verbose, reportorial, and undisciplined. To these claims, Cendrars admirer Henry Miller replied in his *The Books in My Life:* "To me [Cendrars's] books reflect his lack of fixed habits, or better yet, his ability to break a habit. (A sign of real emancipation!) In those swollen paragraphs . . . Cendrars reveals his oceanic spirit." It was Cendrars's spirit that distinguished him from many of his contemporaries. He had a voracious appetite for life,

and the simple joy of living was what he tried to portray in his writings.

Just as Cendrars combined reality and myth in his writings, the true story of his life has been obscured by the writer's fondness for fabrications. "Cendrars was one of the greatest liars of all time," according to one *Times Literary Supplement* writer. "Always situating himself at the centre of his own universe, he felt it necessary to protect this universe by a perpetual smoke-screen of exaggeration, invention, and, above all, contradiction." Thus, Cendrars's biography was as tainted by fictions as his fiction was by biography. "To read anything that he has written," observed Sven Birkirts in the *New Boston Review,* "is to be implicated, present at the joining point of life and art. The two are intimately interfused."

It was not until Cendrars's daughter Miriam and wife Raymone discovered the writer's notebooks after his death that some myths about the man were dispelled. Edited by Miriam Cendrars, *Inedits secrets* reveals that the real story of Cendrars's life was not any less fascinating than the versions he told other people while he was alive. Born in Switzerland (on different occasions he claimed to have been born in Paris, Italy, and Egypt), Cendrars came from Swiss-French parentage. He left home in 1904 to be an apprentice watchmaker in Russia (he did not, as he later contended, run away from home), and was in that country during the 1905 revolution. Because of what he witnessed in Russia, he "acquired his lifelong sympathy for anarchism," according to a *Times Literary Supplement* reviewer. In 1907 he studied medicine at the University of Berne, where he met Fela Poznanska. It was while he was living with Fela in New York City two years before their marriage in 1914 that Cendrars wrote his first notable poem, *Les Paques a New York* ("Easter in New York"), an appeal to Christ to save the poor from their plight. Cendrars sent a copy of the poem to his friend Guillaume Apollinaire, and the question of whether this manuscript influenced Apollinaire's poem, "Zone," still remains an issue in literary circles.

Embarrassed that Fela was supporting him while he spent his time reading in libraries, Cendrars returned to Paris where he wrote *Prose du Transsiberien et de la petite Jeanne de France,* a lengthy poem upon which "Cendrars's reputation as a poet will, undoubtedly, rest," according to Walter Albert in his *Texas Studies in Literature and Language* article. Jay

Bochner described *Prose de Transsiberien* in his *Blaise Cendrars: Discovery and Re-creation* as "a poem concerned with travelling through the modern, . . . devastated world and searching out one's frail identity in terms of that disintegrating world." That the poem's narrative describes a long train journey reflects Cendrars's belief that, as Mary Ann Caws related in the *Kentucky Romance Quarterly,* his life was "in perpetual motion, that it has been measured out by train tracks."

Cendrars did indeed lead a restless life. Two years after his arrival in Paris in 1912, he joined the French Foreign Legion and a year later was wounded in the right arm; the arm was amputated above the elbow as a result. The injury did not end his writing career, however. In his 1920 book, *Carte blanche,* Jean Cocteau attested that just the opposite happened: "It seems as if the war removed [Cendrars's] writing arm only to have his poems blossom in even more dazzling colors." But a number of critics did not favor the poet's approach to verse, usually complaining about his use of cataloguing and colloquial—sometimes scatological—language. *Nation* contributor Matthew Josephson, for one, argued that Cendrars's "poems seldom touch a great music which would hypnotize us into reading them over and over again"; and Henri Clouard, writing in *Histoire de la litterature francaise, du symbolisme a nos jours,* commented: "His verse gathers enough material to create living beings, but never gives them life." Clouard did however complement Cendrars for improvising with "bold skill."

In Bochner's view, such gripes against Cendrars miss the point of what the poet was trying to accomplish. "Cendrars's care cannot be emphasized too often," asserted Bochner, "for many critics take exception primarily to the 'disorder' in his writing, whereas the truth is simply that his imaginative and associative reach is longer than what we are accustomed to." Discussing *Dix-neuf Poemes elastiques,* Bochner explained that Cendrars's verse style is the result of his Cubist technique. "Each poem brings together, as did the [Pablo] Picasso and [Georges] Braque collages of the time, the everyday materials at hand. . . . In Cendrars' nineteen poems [in this collection] we are called upon, through the style, to trust that the grab bag will make sense, that there is a sense, a circumstance behind the pieces. The frankness, virility, elan, often plain friendliness of the language suspends our doubting until closer or repeated reading or reflection puts things together."

After World War I, Cendrars produced, directed, wrote, and acted in movies in France, Italy, and Hollywood. But, true to his character, he abandoned this career in the movies to resume his travels around the world. "[It] was during this period," according to a *Times Literary Supplement* article, "that he published three of his most important prose works:" *Gold: Being the Marvelous History of General John Augustus Sutter, Moravagine,* and *Dan Yack. Gold,* Cendrars's first and most successful novel, is the somewhat fictionalized story of how Sutter, an ambitious and adventurous Swiss immigrant, established an agricultural empire in California only to see it destroyed when gold was discovered at his mill in 1849, causing his labor force to leave him and seek their own fortunes. A perfect example of the American dream gone awry (Joseph Stalin once said it was his favorite book), *Gold* "remains a minor masterpiece," according to *Times Literary Supplement* contributor Patrick Lindsay Bowles. The novel was similarly praised by other critics like *Newsweek* reviewer Jim Miller, who calls the book "[w]ise, weird, and poignant, . . . [a] wonderful modernist fable."

Moravagine and the two books comprising *Dan Yack* (*Dan Yack* and *The Confessions of Dan Yack*) have been viewed by some critics as counterparts to each other. *Moravagine* follows the path of the title character, a misogynistic anarchist who murders for pleasure, as he travels the world accompanied by the narrator, a doctor who studies Moravagine and discovers a bond between the murderer and his own darker side. In Moravagine's destructive character, Cendrars thus created a man who, as Bochner stated, "takes upon himself the primitive revenge of twentieth-century man entangled in a plethora of superficial and demeaning conventions and institutions." But Moravagine's misanthropy eventually leads to his death and that of the doctor. The title character of *Dan Yack,* however, is a man who loves the world and people. Yack's loss of his first love, Hedwiga, leads to his determination to experience life to the fullest, and this eventually leads him to his second love, Mireille. Even after an illness takes Mireille away from him, at the end of *Confessions of Dan Yack* Yack finds comfort and love by adopting a child.

The plots of both *Moravagine* and *Dan Yack* are filled with adventurous, bizarre, and implausible episodes that take their characters all around the world, which is typical of Cendrars's novels. His books are also filled with wit and humor, and the highly entertaining tales related in them sometimes led critics to believe that there was not much depth to his novels. "Cendrars is not an ideas man, a novelist-philosopher," according to one *Times Literary Supplement* reviewer. "A good many of his intellectual generalizations, while entertaining, are embarrassing to read on a serious level." However, as another *Times Literary Supplement* critic pointed out in a review of *Confessions of Dan Yack,* Cendrars's "dominant concern, in art as in life, seems to have been an investigative pursuit of life's richness—like Dan Yack, sating both idle curiosity and earthy appetite while causing enjoyment for others." Furthermore, the author's desultory plotting structures reflect the similar disdain he had for form in his cubist poetry; like his verses, his novels jump from image to image, presenting a deluge of associated scenes. Cendrars never allowed the pictures to dictate some profound message. His books, as Bochner explains, "do no more than match the truth. They stand beside it, and within it, not substituting for weakness, but translating the same power from different angles."

During World War II, Cendrars settled in France and did not write for three years. At the urging of one of his friends, however, he returned to writing and produced four autobiographical novels, *L'Homme foudroye* (*The Astonished Man*), *La Main coupee* (*Lice*), *Bourlinguer* (*Planus*), and *Le Lotissement du ciel* ("Heaven in Lots"). Although none of these books accurately depicts Cendrars's life (even *Une Nuit dans la foret* and *Vol a voile,* books that the writer averred to be truly autobiographical, are considered to be "at least partly fiction," according to Bochner), they present the essence of his experiences in a manner similar to his picaresque novels. "Cendrars's autobiography," Peter Reading also remarked in the *Times Literary Supplement,* "contains . . . real-life anecdotes as hair-raisingly memorable as any in his fiction."

In the 1990s Cendrars's writings continued to be collected and published in varying forms, including a number in English translation. *Hollywood: Mecca of the Movies,* originally published in France in 1936, is a book-length journal written by Cendrars during his two-week stay in Hollywood in 1936. The journal records the author's fascination with the intrigues of Hollywood: studio executives, stars, movies, and filmmaking technology. "In just two weeks, Cendrars felt the pulse of a magical, mythical place whose axis spun around the movie makers and their

stars," noted Ellen Lampert-Greaux in the *French Review.*

Modernities and Other Writings is a collection of nonfiction essays, a novella, and a movie treatment. The essays discuss Cendrars's interest in painting and in science and technology; the novella describes a trip by the author in a spaceship that he designed. And 1992's *Complete Poems* contains virtually all of the author's poetry. *American Book Review* critic Harriet Zinnes commented, "It is certainly remarkable that this astonishing poet, this great memoirist and novelist, it not better known in the Unites States." With the substantial number of works being produced in English more than thirty years after Cendrars's death, however, his profile in the U.S. may be rising.

To Cendrars, the experience of life took precedence over all else. He began his life believing that his destiny was to become a writer, but, as a *Times Literary Supplement* revealed, he later came to feel that writing was "an evil that shut him away from his fellow men and prevented him from getting on with the far more important business of living." When Cendrars did write, this conviction came out in his characters. He described Dan Yack this way, for example: "Everything he did was so spontaneous and topsy-turvy that his life seemed to have something of the miraculous about it, and all his days were filled with precious moments." "This seems to have applied no less to Cendrars himself than to Dan Yack," observed Reading. Eugenio Montale went even further in describing Cendrars when he wrote in *Atlas:* "A man who by himself is a whole epoch, perhaps the last great epoch of modern French art, Blaise was the quintessence of cosmopolitanism filtered through the sharpest Gallic wit."

BIOGRAPHICAL/CRITICAL SOURCES:

BOOKS

Albert, Walter, editor, *Selected Writings of Blaise Cendrars,* New Directions, 1962.
Bochner, Jay, *Blaise Cendrars: Discovery and Re-Creation,* University of Toronto Press, 1978.
Cendrars, Blaise, *Dan Yack,* translation by Nina Rootes, Michael Kesend, 1987.
Clouard, Henri, *Histoire de la litterature francaise, du symbolisme a nos jours,* Volume 1, Albin Michel, 1949.

Cocteau, Jean, *Carte blanche,* Editions de la Sirene, 1920.

Contemporary Literary Criticism, Volume 18, Gale, 1981.

Dos Passos, John, *Orient Express,* Harper & Brothers, 1927.

Lovey, Jean-Claude, *Situation de Blaise Cendrars,* Editions de la Baconniere, 1965.

Miller, Henry, *The Books in My Life,* New Directions, 1952.

PERIODICALS

American Book Review, August-September, 1993, p. 10.

Atlas, March, 1961.

Chicago Tribune Book World, August 1, 1982.

French Review, May, 1996, p. 1033.

Kentucky Romance Quarterly, Volume 17, number 4, 1970.

Los Angeles Times, November 24, 1987.

Nation, December 2, 1931.

New Boston Review, June-July, 1980.

New Republic, April 17, 1995, p. 35.

Newsweek, April 9, 1984.

New Yorker, September 7, 1992, p. 95.

New York Times Book Review, October 9, 1966; August 4, 1968; October 3, 1982; March 18, 1984; March 13, 1988; July 12, 1992, p. 29; May 28, 1995, p. 12.

Paris Review, April, 1966.

Publishers Weekly, July 27, 1990, p. 224; March 2, 1992, p. 54; May 18, 1992, p. 53; June 8, 1992, p. 53; August 29, 1994, p. 66; February 13, 1995, p. 70.

Review of Contemporary Fiction, summer, 1993, p. 251.

Spectator, January 24, 1987.

Texas Studies in Literature and Language, autumn, 1962.

Times Literary Supplement, February 16, 1967; March 13, 1969; February 26, 1971; April 14, 1972; July 13, 1973; February 4, 1983; May 29, 1987; January 26, 1990.

Tribune Books (Chicago), February 22, 1987.

Washington Post Book World, February 13, 1983; October 26, 1986.

OBITUARIES:

PERIODICALS

New York Times, January 22, 1961.

Publishers Weekly, February 13, 1961.*

* * *

SAUTER, Eric 1948-

PERSONAL: Born November 1, 1948, in Bay City, MI; son of Ernest, Jr., and Dorothy (Weiss) Sauter; married Beth Olanoff (an attorney), November 26, 1982. *Education:* Michigan State University, B.A., 1971.

ADDRESSES: Home—P.O. Box 112, Pineville, PA 18946. *Agent*—Adele Leone Agency, Inc., 52 Riverside Dr., Suite 6A, New York, NY 10024.

CAREER: Freelance writer and editor, 1972-75; *Trenton Times,* Trenton, NJ, reporter, 1975-77; freelance writer, 1977-79; U.S. Senate, Washington, DC, speechwriter, 1979-80; freelance writer, 1980-82; Squibb Corp., Princeton, NJ, publications manager, 1982-84; freelance writer, 1984—.

MEMBER: Mystery Writers of America.

WRITINGS:

Hunter, Avon (New York City), 1983.

Hunter and the Ikon, Avon, 1984.

Hunter and Raven, Avon, 1984.

Predators, Pocket Books (New York City), 1986.

Skeletons, Dutton (New York City), 1990.

Backfire, Dutton, 1992.

SIDELIGHTS: Eric Sauter brings to his fiction a variety of themes and influences based on the counterculture of the 1960s. Some of his detective novels feature a disaffected writer-hippy named Robert E. Lee Hunter, who "pokes his nose in where it's not wanted, manipulates, makes things happen," to quote Jack Adrian in the *St. James Guide to Crime and Mystery Writers.* Other Sauter novels feature environmental concerns—among them the slaughter of wildlife—as well as the more common conventions of mystery writing. "Sauter is a writer to be watched. . . . ," declared Adrian. "That he chooses to explore other avenues in the mystery/suspense genres is refreshing; that he deliberately threads dark and disturbing themes—obsession, betrayal, bitter disillusionment . . . —into his rarely less than riveting entertainments is wholly admirable."

Sauter, who was born in Michigan, currently resides in eastern Pennsylvania, the setting for his Hunter novels. Hunter lives on an island in the Delaware River, a home base that also functions as his office when he is called in to investigate a case. Obsession of one sort or another looms large in all the Hunter novels, and the character himself demonstrates a lion's share of it. Adrian observed that Sauter's plots "are complex, all built intelligently on the 'out of the past' principle and all containing convincingly rabid villains and, at times, outbursts of extraordinary violence." Like many of his generation, Hunter is aggressively anti-Establishment and suspicious of the federal government. He speaks, to quote Adrian, "with just a touch of the contemporary lunacy of the deranged gonzo journalist Hunter (no coincidence?) S. Thompson . . . to add extra spice to the pungent one-liners with which all [the books] are liberally stuffed." *Los Angeles Times Book Review* correspondent Kristiana Gregory concluded that Hunter "is charming, funny and probably a better lover than spy."

Sauter published three Hunter titles which, at least in Adrian's view, "have a preeminence over just about every other series of private investigator paperback originals (and a good many hardbacks, too) published in the past 20 years." Rather than staying with that character, however, Sauter has moved on to other thrillers, including *Predators, Skeletons,* and *Backfire,* set in such far-flung locales as western Canada, Manhattan, and Philadelphia. These works too highlight Sauter's storytelling ability and his interest in extreme personalities. Adrian called *Predators* "an engrossing and brilliantly crafted journey into the world of hunters and the hunted. . . . A large cast of characters is efficiently handled."

Eric Sauter told *CA:* "I'm writing full time and find it the best way to live. It's also the worst. As a consequence of this paradoxical life-style, I listen to a lot of rock 'n' roll—loud."

BIOGRAPHICAL/CRITICAL SOURCES:

BOOKS

St. James Guide to Crime and Mystery Writers, fourth edition, St. James Press (Detroit, MI), 1996.

PERIODICALS

Los Angeles Times Book Review, April 4, 1984.
West Coast Review of Books, September, 1983, p. 47.

*   *   *

SAWKINS, Raymond H.
  See FORBES, Colin

SCHERF, Margaret 1908-1979

PERSONAL: Born April 1, 1908, in Fairmont, WV; died May 12, 1979; daughter of Charles Henry and Miriam (Fisher) Scherf; married Perry E. Beebe, December 9, 1965. *Education:* Attended Antioch College, 1925-28. *Politics:* Democrat. *Religion:* Episcopalian. *Avocational interests:* Antiques, travel.

CAREER: Robert M. McBride & Co. (publishers), New York City, secretary to the editor, 1928-29; Wise Book Co., New York City, secretary and copywriter, 1932-34; reader for publisher in New York City, 1934-39; writer, 1940-79. Member of House of Representatives, Montana State Legislature, 1965.

MEMBER: Authors Guild.

WRITINGS:

MYSTERY NOVELS

The Corpse Grows a Beard, Putnam (New York City), 1940.
The Case of the Kippered Corpse, Putnam, 1941.
They Came to Kill, Putnam, 1942.
The Owl in the Cellar, Doubleday (New York City), 1945.
Always Murder a Friend, Doubleday, 1948.
Murder Makes Me Nervous, Doubleday, 1948.
Gilbert's Last Toothache, Doubleday, 1949, published as *For the Love of Murder,* Spivak (New York City), 1950.
The Gun in Daniel Webster's Bust, Doubleday, 1949.
The Curious Custard Pie, Doubleday, 1950, published as *Divine and Deadly,* Spivak, 1953.
The Green Plaid Pants, Doubleday, 1951, published as *The Corpse with One Shoe,* Detective Book Club (Rosyn, NY), 1951.
The Elk and the Evidence, Doubleday, 1952.
Dead: Senate Office Building, Doubleday, 1953, published as *The Case of the Hated Senator,* Ace Books (New York City), 1954.
Glass on the Stairs, Doubleday, 1954.
The Cautious Overshoes, Doubleday, 1956.
Judicial Body, Doubleday, 1957.
Never Turn Your Back, Doubleday, 1959.
The Diplomat and the Gold Piano, Doubleday, 1963 (published in England as *Death and the Diplomat,* R. Hale [London], 1964).
The Corpse in the Flannel Nightgown, Doubleday, 1965.
The Banker's Bones, Doubleday, 1968.
The Beautiful Birthday Cake, Doubleday, 1971.

To Cache a Millionaire, Doubleday, 1972.
If You Want a Murder Well Done, Doubleday, 1974.
Don't Wake Me Up While I'm Driving, Doubleday, 1977.
The Beaded Banana, Doubleday, 1978.

OTHER

Wedding Train (historical novel), Doubleday, 1960.
The Mystery of the Velvet Box (juvenile), F. Watts (New York City), 1963.
The Mystery of the Empty Trunk (juvenile), F. Watts, 1964.
The Mystery of the Shaky Staircase (juvenile), F. Watts, 1965.

A collection of Scherf's manuscripts is housed at the University of Oregon Library, Eugene.

SIDELIGHTS: "My theory," Margaret Scherf once told the *St. James Guide to Crime and Mystery Writers,* "is that mysteries appeal to people because the central problem is soluble, unlike most of the problems in the real world." In Scherf's world, mystery is imbued with wisecracking and even slapstick humor; as she remarked: "My idea was to write amusing books, without too much gore but with sufficient suspense to carry the reader on."

Scherf, a former copy reader and writer who also served in the Montana State Legislature, published through four decades. She remains best known for lighthearted mystery as evidenced by such titles as *Murder Makes Me Nervous* and *The Banker's Bones.* Scherf's debut work, *The Corpse Grows a Beard* (1940), was lauded by a *New York Times* critic of the era, who noted that "this is Miss Scherf's first mystery story, but one would never guess it. She writes with all the skill of an old hand at vicarious homicide and bafflement."

A "fast, tough story with plenty of dead people" is the dubious praise bestowed by *New Yorker* magazine on Scherf's 1941 novel *The Case of the Kippered Corpse.* It wasn't until the following year, however, that readers came to meet Dr. Mitton, "one of the most entertaining amateur detectives in the fiction roster," according to a *New York Times* review of Scherf's *They Came to Kill.* "There are indications that we are to hear from him again, and it can't be too soon."

The occasion of a new Scherf novel, in fact, was invariably greeted with kudos for the author's hu-

mor, if not her sleuthing style. Beginning with her first book, which the *Boston Transcript* found "takes the cake" for "utter goofiness," Scherf collected such citations as "one of the funniest whodunits" (from *Weekly Book Review* for *The Owl in the Cellar*) to "undoubtedly [her] funniest mystery to date" (*New York Herald Tribune Weekly Book Review*'s Will Cuppy on *Gun in Daniel Webster's Bust*). Cuppy went on to say that even if Scherf "does seem a bit too free and easy at times with quips about the casualties, . . . her dialog contains a high percentage of bulls-eyes."

Scherf continued writing into the 1970s. That decade brought such titles as *To Cache a Millionaire* and *Don't Wake Me Up While I'm Driving.* The latter book was assessed by Kathleen Gregory Klein, in her essay on Scherf for the *St. James Guide to Crime and Mystery Writers. Driving,* wrote Klein, "is the most exaggerated example of [the author's] unusual characters. Almost slapstick in the Laurel and Hardy vein, the plot is more concerned with whether Hal Brady will again postpone his luckless brother's wedding than with the investigation of a bank robbery in which he is accused. Scherf goes almost too far as the threads of detection are lost in local color, only to appear unexpectedly in the end. The characters are vividly drawn: even a dog, a blue chair, and Hal's car are thoroughly characterized."

BIOGRAPHICAL/CRITICAL SOURCES:

BOOKS

St. James Guide to Crime and Mystery Writers, 4th edition, St. James Press (Detroit), 1996.

PERIODICALS

Boston Transcript, August 24, 1940, p. 2.
Chicago Sunday Tribune, August 30, 1953, p. 10; June 24, 1956, p. 11; April 12, 1959, p. 8.
New Yorker, August 30, 1941, p. 17; July 7, 1951, p. 27.
New York Herald Tribune Book Review, June 1, 1952, p. 12; August 23, 1953, p. 9; May 6, 1956, p. 11; October 13, 1957, p. 10.
New York Herald Tribune Weekly Book Review, September 18, 1949, p. 15.
New York Times, August 18, 1940, p. 17; August 10, 1941, p. 17; August 9, 1942, p. 15; September 18, 1949, p. 29; July 29, 1951, p. 13; June 1, 1952, p. 21; July 12, 1953, p. 21; May 16,

1954, p. 25; May 20, 1956, p. 31; September 22, 1957, p. 43.

New York Times Book Review, February 15, 1959, p. 44.

San Francisco Chronicle, June 24, 1956, p. 25; October 13, 1957, p. 24.

Saturday Review of Literature, September 14, 1940, p. 22; August 7, 1948, p. 31.

Springfield Republican, April 12, 1959, p. 4D.

Weekly Book Review, September 9, 1945, p. 16.*

*   *   *

SCHLEE, Susan
See BAUR, Susan

*   *   *

SCHORR, Mark 1953-
(Scott Ellis)

PERSONAL: Born September 6, 1953, in New York, NY; son of Bernard (an accountant) and Vera (a homemaker; maiden name, Zernik) Schorr; married Sima Epstein (a nurse), May 15, 1973; children: one daughter, one son. *Education:* Attended State University of New York at Binghamton, until 1973; Lewis and Clark College, M.A., 1993.

ADDRESSES: Agent—Michael Carlisle, William Morris Agency, 1350 Avenue of the Americas, New York, NY 10019.

CAREER: Los Angeles Herald Examiner, Los Angeles, CA, reporter, 1980-82; KNXT-TV, Los Angeles, producer in investigations unit, 1983; University of California, Los Angeles, instructor in journalism, 1983—; psychotherapist, 1993—. Worked as bookstore manager, nightclub bouncer, private investigator, photographer, and international courier.

MEMBER: American Counseling Association, Mystery Writers of America (member of regional board of directors), Association of Former Intelligence Officers, National Intelligence Study Center, Oregon Group Psychotherapy Association (board member, 1996—).

AWARDS, HONORS: Journalism awards from Associated Press and Valley Press Club, both 1982, both

for a series on drug dealing; nominated for Edgar Allan Poe Award of the Mystery Writers of America, 1983, for *Red Diamond, Private Eye.*

WRITINGS:

Red Diamond, Private Eye, St. Martin's (New York City), 1983.

Ace of Diamonds, St. Martin's, 1984.

Diamond Rock, St. Martin's, 1985.

Bully!, St. Martin's, 1985.

(Under pseudonym Scott Ellis) *The Borzoi Control,* St. Martin's, 1986.

Overkill, Pocket Books (New York City), 1987.

Seize the Dragon, Pocket Books, 1988.

Blindside, St. Martin's, 1989.

An Eye for an Eye, St. Martin's, 1989.

Gunpowder, Pocket Books, 1990.

Contributor to periodicals, including *New York, Esquire, Argosy,* and *American Lawyer.*

SIDELIGHTS: Mark Schorr's first three novels feature a private detective named Red Diamond. A hero in the Sam Spade school, Diamond is hard-bitten and seems cast straight from old-time pulp fiction—which indeed he is, since he's the alter ego of a mild-mannered New York City cabby named Simon Jaffe. Schorr's tongue-in-cheek parodies featuring Red Diamond have drawn praise for their innovative style and their comic examination of the private eye mythos. *Red Diamond, Private Eye* broke new ground in many ways," observed George Kelley in the *St. James Guide to Crime and Mystery Writers.* "It allowed Schorr to create a tough talking, macho private eye typical of the 1940s, but having to deal with the psychological problems of the 1980s. It showed readers that maybe what the 1980s needed was a few more guys like Red Diamond to take care of business." *Booklist* reviewer Connie Fletcher praised Red Diamond for his "hilarious, time-warped results," noting that his stories pack "a Walter Mitty punch."

Diamond's adventures have been likened to the whimsical quest of Don Quixote, and reviewers credit the author's sense of humor for the success of what is both a parody and an affectionate tribute to the pulp writers of decades past. To quote Kelley: "What Schorr has done is to use the Clark Kent/ Superman, David Banner/Incredible Hulk model and apply it to private-eye fiction. Take an average guy and give him superpowers. But what makes the Simon Jaffe/Red Diamond combination work is the sophistication and feeling Schorr gives his characters. Jaffe is a wimp, but he is also a good guy, a father who loves his kids, and a husband who loves his shrewish wife. Red Diamond is brutal but he is a good guy too—he's always willing to help the defenseless, the little people who can't defend themselves from the bullies and thugs."

After completing three Red Diamond novels, Schorr took his imagination into other spheres, including spy fiction and political thrillers. *Bully!* is a mystery featuring none other than President Theodore Roosevelt. *The Borzoi Control,* which appeared under the pseudonym Scott Ellis, is a novel about geopolitical spying, as is *Overkill.*

In recent years Schorr has taken a hiatus from writing to complete his master's degree and work as a psychotherapist. He may return to fiction, he says, with a psychological thriller.

Schorr told *CA:* "My first job was as a photographer for a string of weekly newspapers. My responsibilities included writing the captions. The captions became longer and longer, and the photographs became fewer. Soon I had metamorphosed into a reporter.

"When I was growing up in Brooklyn, I had a passing familiarity with street life. As a reporter, I focused on organized crime and criminal conspiracies. Naturally, the characters I met and the scams I was told about come in handy as background for the novels I write.

"Along the way, I held low-level film production jobs in New York, worked as a bouncer at Studio 54, was a licensed private investigator for six months, and managed a bookstore. I have studied Japanese philosophy and language. This interest was sparked early when I went to judo school as a boy. I recently returned from a trip to Japan, and I have plans for another trip to Hong Kong and the People's Republic of China. I studied fencing for one novel, scuba diving for another. One of the advantages of being a writer is that it allows you to explore whatever areas intrigue you—all in the name of research.

"I enjoy reading private eye fiction for the strong moral code that private eyes (at least in fiction) adhere to. The limitation is that generally the private detective novel is focused on an individual's crime or crimes, i.e. blackmail, kidnapping, murder. I've switched genres recently to spy fiction, since that allows scenarios with more geopolitical issues, as well as multiple viewpoints and exotic locales."

BIOGRAPHICAL/CRITICAL SOURCES:

BOOKS

St. James Guide to Crime and Mystery Writers, fourth edition, St. James Press (Detroit, MI), 1996.

PERIODICALS

Booklist, May 15, 1984, p. 1296.
Kirkus Reviews, April 1, 1984, pp. 328-329.
Los Angeles Daily News, January 26, 1986.
Los Angeles Times, December 6, 1985.
San Diego Evening Tribune, March 21, 1985.
Washington Post, August 19, 1985.

* * *

SHANNON, Doris 1924-
(E. X. Giroux)

PERSONAL: Born August 7, 1924, in Elmira, NY; daughter of Edwin (an engineer) and Elizabeth (a telephone operator; maiden name, Graham) Giroux; married Frank Shannon (a customs officer), August 1, 1947; children: Patricia Anne, Deborah Elizabeth. *Education:* Attended Napanee Collegiate Institute, 1939-42.

ADDRESSES: Home—16268 Southglen Place, Surrey, British Columbia, Canada.

CAREER: Writer, 1969—. Royal Bank of Canada, teller in Napanee, Ontario, 1942-47, in Vancouver, British Columbia, 1948-49.

AWARDS, HONORS: Writer's Digest creative writing award, 1969, for short story "And Then There Was the Youngest."

WRITINGS:

The Whispering Runes, Lenox Hill (New York City), 1972.
Twenty-two Hallofield, Fawcett (New York City), 1974.
The Seekers, Fawcett, 1975.
Hawthorn Hill, St. Martin's (New York City), 1976.

The Lodestar Legacy, Popular Library (New York City), 1976.
Cain's Daughters, St. Martin's, 1978.
Beyond the Shining Mountains, St. Martin's, 1979.
The Punishment, St. Martin's, 1981.
Little Girls Lost, St. Martin's, 1981.
Family Money, St. Martin's, 1984.

"ROBERT FORSYTHE MYSTERY" SERIES; UNDER PSEUDONYM E. X. GIROUX

A Death for Adonis, St. Martin's, 1984.
A Death for a Darling, St. Martin's, 1985.
A Death for a Dancer, St. Martin's, 1985.
A Death for a Doctor, St. Martin's, 1986.
A Death for a Dilettante, St. Martin's, 1987.
A Death for a Dietitian, St. Martin's, 1988.
A Death for a Dreamer, St. Martin's, 1989.
A Death for a Dancing Doll, St. Martin's, 1991.
A Death for a Dodo, St. Martin's, 1993.
The Dying Room, St. Martin's, 1993.

SIDELIGHTS: Under the pseudonym E. X. Giroux, Doris Shannon has created a series of detective novels featuring a well-knit pair of sleuths, Robert "Robby" Forsythe and Abigail "Sandy" Sanderson. Forsythe is an ex-attorney who begins his detective career as a means to stave off boredom, but the serious nature of the pursuit soon helps him to salvage his own dubious reputation and rebuild his life. His sidekick Sandy is an able crime-solver as well, and the two team their resources in nearly every volume. To quote Carol M. Harper in the *St. James Guide to Crime and Mystery Writers,* Robby and Sandy "have special knowledge, special skills, which make them a fascinating team, respected by the police and lionized by the press."

All of the Giroux novels are set in Great Britain, and a number of them bear more than a passing resemblance to the classic thrillers of Agatha Christie. In the debut novel, *A Death for Adonis,* Robby actually assembles all the murder suspects for a final showdown, and in *A Death for a Dietitian,* Sandy finds herself stranded on an island with a group of hotel guests—one of whom has committed murder. *Best Sellers* contributor Lawrence A. Howard has noted that the Giroux novels "delight and satisfy the most rigorous fan of who-dunnits" through stories that "[succeed] in making the reader's acquaintance, growing on him, and making fast friends."

Throughout the Robert Forsythe series, the title character has evolved from a failed barrister with a shady past and ruined reputation to a respected sleuth dubbed "Mission Impossible Forsythe" by the British tabloid press. Harper found this aspect of the series the most admirable. "Forsythe, his reputation damaged by a past indiscretion, has recovered over the span of the series, primarily as a result of his taking up detection," the critic writes. ". . . He has learned to face his past mistakes, and with the help of his secretary, regain self esteem. In the course of this series, he has built a reputation as a successful detective." If success can be charted by a character's ability to sustain interest through multiple volumes, then Forsythe and his trusty secretary are very successful indeed.

Shannon told *CA* that at the age of forty, "without quite realizing my own motivation I turned to writing. Much to my surprise . . . editors expressed . . . confidence in a talent I had never realized I possessed. . . . Writing appears to be a profession where gray hair and age are not signals that one's working life is over. I share with many writers the desire to write that special book, the fine one, and also eventually I should like to teach creative writing."

BIOGRAPHICAL/CRITICAL SOURCES:

BOOKS

St. James Guide to Crime and Mystery Writers, fourth edition, St. James Press (Detroit, MI), 1996.

PERIODICALS

Best Sellers, June, 1984, pp. 94-95.
Library Journal, August, 1984, p. 1469.
Publishers Weekly, December 5, 1980, p. 45; September 4, 1981, p. 47; February 3, 1984, p. 398; June 15, 1984, p. 73.

*   *   *

SIMPSON, Dorothy 1933-

PERSONAL: Born Dorothy Preece, June 20, 1933, in Blaenavon, Monmouthshire, Wales; daughter of Robert Wilfrid (a civil servant) and Gladys (a teacher of elocution; maiden name, Jones) Preece; married Keith Taylor Simpson (a barrister), July 22, 1961; children: Mark Taylor, Ian Robert, Emma Morag.

Education: University of Bristol, B.A. (with honors), 1954, teaching diploma, 1955. *Religion:* Christian.

ADDRESSES: Home—Kent, England. *Agent*— Peter Robinson, Curtis Brown, Haymarket House, 28/29 Haymarket, London SW1Y 4SP, England.

CAREER: Teacher of English and French at Dartford Grammar School for Girls, Dartford, England, 1955-59, and Erith Grammar School, Erith, England, 1959- 61; Senacre School, Maidstone, Kent, England, teacher of English, 1961-62; marriage guidance counselor, 1969-82; writer, 1975—.

MEMBER: Crime Writers Association, Society of Authors, Mystery Writers of America.

AWARDS, HONORS: Silver Dagger Award from Crime Writers Association of Great Britain, 1985, for *Last Seen Alive.*

WRITINGS:

"INSPECTOR THANET" SERIES

The Night She Died, Scribner (New York City), 1981.
Six Feet Under, Scribner, 1982.
Puppet for a Corpse, Scribner, 1983.
Close Her Eyes, Scribner, 1984.
Last Seen Alive, Scribner, 1985.
Dead on Arrival, M. Joseph (London), 1986, Scribner, 1987.
Element of Doubt, M. Joseph, 1987, Scribner, 1988.
Suspicious Death, Scribner, 1988.
Dead by Morning, Scribner, 1989.
Doomed to Die, Scribner, 1991.
Wake the Dead, Scribner, 1992.
No Laughing Matter, Scribner, 1993.
A Day for Dying, M. Joseph, 1995, Scribner, 1996.

OTHER

Harbingers of Fear (suspense novel), Macdonald & Janes (London), 1977.

Contributor of novella *Just Deserts* to *Dead Giveaway,* Little, Brown (London), 1995. Contributor to *Ellery Queen's Mystery Magazine* and *Alfred Hitchcock's Mystery Magazine.* Manuscript collection held at Mugar Memorial Library, Boston University.

SIDELIGHTS: It was mid-life for Dorothy Simpson before she wrote her first book, *Harbingers of Fear.*

Accepted by the first publisher it was submitted to, this suspense novel was generally well-received by British readers. Although her husband sensed her literary ability and for years urged her to try her hand at writing, Simpson felt uninspired to toil away on a book. However, as she explained to *CA:* "I began to write after a long illness in 1975, which gave me plenty of time for reflection and reassessment. I was fortunate in that my first book found an agent immediately, and a publisher and serialization in a major women's magazine."

Following this initial success, Simpson wrote three books that were all rejected by various publishers. As a result, Simpson took a serious look at her talents, assessed her strengths, and decided to devote her next efforts to creating an intriguing murder mystery staged around an engaging sleuth. After months of molding and planning, Inspector Luke Thanet and his loyal assistant, Sergeant Lineham were created to solve the murder in *The Night She Died.*

Described as "an absolutely first rate mystery" by *Publishers Weekly, The Night She Died* was greeted enthusiastically by reviewers and readers not only in Simpson's homeland of England but in the United States as well. In a *Washington Post Book World* review of *The Night She Died,* Jean M. White states that "Simpson neatly interweaves past and present with deft double-plotting. Her characters take on real-life dimension, notably Inspector Thanet, a policeman with a bad back, an interesting wife, and a compassionate curiosity about human beings. This is a first-rate job from a writer with subtlety and an unobtrusive literate style." Since *The Night She Died,* Simpson has added many more books to her "Inspector Thanet" series and has built a following of loyal readers who eagerly await each new book.

Much of the reason for her success can be attributed to the popularity of Inspector Thanet himself. Simpson portrays Thanet as an average British policeman. Although he seems blessed with great detective skills, he still is very human—besieged with the problems of everyday life, such as experiencing and coping with a chronic bad back, the joys and tribulations of fatherhood, and the efforts needed to maintain a good marriage. "Detective Inspector Luke Thanet [is] a man of gentle mien, he is inclined to use psychology and tact, rather than showboat heroics, when pursuing his murder inquiries," comments a critic for the *New York Times Book Review.* Douglas Hill remarks in Toronto's *Globe and Mail:*

"Thanet comes across as gentle, human, civilized; his approach to [a] particular crime [and] specific people, leads to a rewarding psychological synthesis. Just don't read Simpson after a dose of the neo-Hammett, shoot-'em-up, down-and-dirty school of detective writing. Then you may be disappointed with Luke Thanet and his quiet ways. That would be a pity."

Using her thirteen years as a marriage guidance counselor as a stepping stone, Simpson anchors her characters and storyline in realistic psychology according to both critics and Simpson herself. "Though very directly focused, Simpson's puzzles are satisfyingly knotty because the motives of criminal, witnesses, victim, and sleuth are grounded in sound psychology," Jane S. Bakerman states in the *St. James Guide To Crime and Mystery Writers*. In a *Booklist* review of *No Laughing Matter*, Emily Melton remarks, "shrewd understanding of what makes humans tick results in a story that is both entertaining and though-provoking." Simpson stated in an interview with *Contemporary Authors*, "I decided to give Luke Thanet a good marriage but with the sort of problems that readers of the books would be able to identify with, and this would apply to the children as well . . . [marriage and] the relationships between people and their motivations . . . were all things I very much wanted to bring in." Simpson continues, "I particularly wanted to show Thanet and his wife working through these problems that afflict everybody. Also, in the Thanets' marriage, I hoped to deal with something which I think is one of the big changes in marriage in this century, the fact that so many more women work and how this affects their relationships with their husbands . . . this was something I tried to deal with in the books, coming to a crisis in *Element of Doubt*."

Reviewers have frequently compared Simpson's mystery novels with those of fellow countrywomen Agatha Christie and Margery Allingham. Like these two detective novelists, Simpson presents a meticulously designed mystery with a cast of characters and vividly detailed local settings as developed and integral as her plot. Charles Champlin writes in the *Los Angeles Times Book Review*: "The country village murder cases as Christie and Allingham used to write them, complete with manor house, eccentric vicar and a map for a frontispiece, are an endangered species. But Dorothy Simpson writes them fondly and well." In an interview with *Contemporary Authors*, Simpson described her settings, stating: "The county in which I live, Kent, is the setting for my

books. The town of Sturrenden is entirely imaginary. But, because the architecture and the way I write about it is based on Kentish towns and Kentish buildings and Kentish building materials and so on."

No Laughing Matter and *A Day for Dying*, the twelfth and thirteenth "Inspector Thanet" entries, received mixed reviews. In contrast to the "usually reliable Inspector," *No Laughing Matter* contained "piddling contrivances, dull character, and somnolent pace," remarks a *Kirkus Reviews* critic. A *Publishers Weekly* review stated that the novel was "an absorbing tale," adding that "much of the action takes place off stage." *A Day for Dying* is "solid, cleverly crafted . . . an engaging plot with intriguing characters," according to Melton's *Booklist* review. In *Kirkus Reviews*, the novel was described as "thoughtful, readable, slightly tepid." A *Library Journal* critic praised the story for it's "dialog and characterizations."

"Because [Simpson] keeps murder to a minimum, and mayhem generally occurs offstage, the impact of Dorothy Simpson's neatly crafted mysteries is more of an aftershock than an initial jolt. Even the gentrified grittiness of most English procedurals is softened, for the cerebral quality of the investigations, like Detective Inspector Luke Thanet's conversational interrogations and intuitive leaps, remind one of amateur detectives' methods. In a sense, these qualities are the most sophisticated red herrings Simpson creates, for, framed by the calm tone, the decency of her continuing characters, and the attractiveness of the Kentish setting, these crimes send a fearful message [that murder can happen anywhere]," summarized Bakerman.

Dorothy Simpson comments, as written in the *St. James Guide to Crime and Mystery Writers:* "It takes me about a year to write a book. I'm often asked where my ideas come from, but it really is very difficult to say. Occasionally, as in *Six Feet Under* or *Suspicious Death*, it is from a newspaper story or headline. Sometimes it is from a theme which has been floating around in my mind for many years before I see how to use it in a novel, as in *Last Seen Alive* or *Close Her Eyes*. But it usually starts with an idea of who the victim is, and why he or she has been killed. The victim is almost invariably the central character in my books even though he is dead before the story begins, because everything revolves around him. Thanet's method of solving the crime is usually by reconstructing the victim's emotional past.

"Once I have an idea of who that victim is I spend two or three months working outwards from him, so to speak, building up a sound idea of his character, circumstances, past history, and especially his relationships with other people, one of which has resulted in the present tragedy. At this stage I also work systematically through the many other decisions I have to make at the beginning of every book, so that by the time I begin to write I have a very detailed synopsis to work with. It then takes about five months to write the first draft, and I revise very heavily, page by page, chapter by chapter, so that by the end of it I have a reasonably polished version. I write for three or four hours each morning and consider it a good morning's work if I produce around a thousand words in that time.

"When I've finished the first draft I put it away for about a month to distance myself from it before reading it straight through as a reader might, and noting alterations and insertions I want to make. The final polishing then takes me about another month, by which time I'm ready for a long break before starting another book. I know that many of my fellow crime writers are far more prolific than this, and I am full of admiration for them.

"My chief interest is in character, and these books might perhaps be called Whydunnits. rather than Whodunnits. I try to play fair with the reader and the mystery is solvable with the information he is given, and for me that solution must be psychologically sound. The reader must be able to look back at the end and see that the murderer's behaviour is entirely consistent with his having committed the crime."

BIOGRAPHICAL/CRITICAL SOURCES:

BOOKS

St. James Guide to Crime and Mystery Writers, fourth edition, Gale (Detroit), 1996.

PERIODICALS

Belles Lettres, winter, 1993-94, p. 54.
Booklist, December 1, 1986; May 15, 1996, p. 1573; November 15, 1993, p. 1606; May 15, 1996, p. 1573.
Kirkus Reviews, October 1, 1993, p. 1232; April 1, 1996, p. 492.
Library Journal, January, 1987; May 1, 1996, p. 136.
Listener, July 2, 1987.

Los Angeles Times Book Review, January 1, 1989.
New York Times Book Review, January 1, 1989, p. 23; October 15, 1989, p. 50; December 22, 1991, p. 21; November 22, 1992, p. 28; November 28, 1993, p. 24.
Publishers Weekly, May 1, 1981; August 2, 1985; January 29, 1988; July 21, 1989, p. 53; September 20, 1993, p. 65; March 25, 1996, p. 64.
Times, April 25, 1986.
Times Literary Supplement, May 28, 1982; April 5, 1985.
Washington Post Book World, June 21, 1981; November 17, 1985.
Wilson Library Bulletin, January, 1993, p. 94.*

*   *   *

SMITH, Red
  See SMITH, Walter W(ellesley)

*   *   *

SMITH, Rolando (R.) Hinojosa
  See HINOJOSA(-SMITH), Rolando (R.)

*   *   *

SMITH, Walter W(ellesley) 1905-1982
  (Red Smith)

PERSONAL: Born September 25, 1905, in Green Bay, WI; died of vascular complications from heart disease, January 15, 1982, in Stamford, CT; son of Walter Philip (in wholesale produce) and Ida (Richardson) Smith; married Catherine Cody, February 11, 1933 (died February 19, 1967), married Phyllis Warner Weiss (an artist), November 8, 1968; children: (first marriage) Catherine (Mrs. J. David Halloran), Terence Fitzgerald, (second marriage) five stepchildren. *Education:* University of Notre Dame, A.B., 1927. *Politics:* "Liberal?" *Religion:* Roman Catholic. *Avocational interests:* Fishing.

CAREER: Milwaukee Sentinel, Milwaukee, WI, cub reporter, 1927-28; *St. Louis Star,* St. Louis, MO, copyreader and sports writer, 1928-36; *Philadelphia Record,* Philadelphia, PA, sports reporter and columnist, 1936-45; *New York Herald Tribune,* New York

City, author of "Views of Sport" column, 1946-67; author of "Views of Sport" column for Publishers Hall Syndicate (now Field Newspapers Syndicate), 1967-71; *New York Times,* New York City, syndicated sports columnist, 1971-82.

MEMBER: Society of Silurians, Players Club.

AWARDS, HONORS: Journalism award, National Headliners Club, 1945; Grantland Rice Memorial Award, Sportsmanship Brotherhood of New York, 1956; LL.D., University of Notre Dame, 1968; Pulitzer Prize for Commentary, 1976; recipient of many awards for sportswriting.

WRITINGS:

ALL UNDER NAME RED SMITH

(With Dick Fishel) *Terry and Bunky Play Football,* Putnam (New York City), 1945.
(Editor) *Selected Sports Stories* (from *Saturday Evening Post),* A. S. Barnes (New York City), 1949.
Out of the Red (collected columns), Knopf (New York City), 1950.
(Editor with Joseph Hill Palmer) *This Was Racing,* A. S. Barnes, 1953.
Views of Sport (collected columns), Knopf, 1954.
Red Smith's Sports Annual, Crown (New York City), 1961.
The Best of Red Smith, edited by Verna Reamer, F. Watts (New York City), 1963.
Red Smith on Fishing around the World, Doubleday (Garden City, NY), 1963.
Strawberries in the Wintertime: The Sporting World of Red Smith, Quadrangle (New York City), 1974.
Press Box: Red Smith's Favorite Sports Stories, Norton (New York City), 1976, reprinted, Avon, 1983.
The Red Smith Reader, edited by Dave Anderson, Random House (New York City), 1982.
To Absent Friends from Red Smith, Atheneum (New York City), 1982.

Contributor of essays on sports to periodicals, including *Saturday Evening Post, Collier's, Reader's Digest, Holiday, Harper's Bazaar, New York Times Magazine,* and *American Heritage.*

SIDELIGHTS: In 1928, the managing editor of the *St. Louis Star* fired the sports department and Red Smith, a young copyeditor, became a sportswriter.

Knowing little more about sports than the average fan, he came back from a night football game with a story from the point of view of a glowworm overcome by floodlights. For the next fifty years, Smith entertained and informed readers with his highly literate and personable columns, becoming the most famous sportswriter in America. He reached a readership numbering in untold millions through syndication and book-length collections of his work. At the time of his death in 1982, his sports column was carried by 275 newspapers in America and 225 abroad. "To Red Smith readers, a good many of whom were not, even by loose definition, sports fans, he was first a clever and careful writer, a craftsman of the English language," noted S. M. W. Bass in the *Dictionary of Literary Biography.* "Smith, however, saw himself primarily as a spectator and commentator. He had a good ear for conversation, a full appreciation for the vagaries of human nature, and a relish for the absurd in everything. He rarely failed to see, and to share, the humor in any given situation."

The excellence of Smith's writing was recognized with the Pulitzer Prize for commentary in 1976. A passage in Ernest Hemingway's novel *Across the River and into the Trees* says of a character: "He was reading Red Smith, and he liked him very much." John Leonard wrote in the *New York Times* that Smith "was to sports what Homer was to war." Bass concludes simply that Smith's readers "followed his reports and columns not only because of what he had to say but also because he could say it so well."

Born in Green Bay, Wisconsin, Smith settled on becoming a writer in his late teens. Inspired by an older friend, he worked in a hardware store until he had enough money put away for a year of college. Then he went off to Notre Dame University, which at the time had one journalism professor. Notre Dame was an exciting place to be for a future sportswriter in the mid-1920s, as Knute Rockne fielded championship-calibre teams year after year. Interestingly enough, however, Smith—who was himself never very good at competitive sports—was more interested in working as a news reporter than as a sportswriter.

After graduating in 1927, Smith went to work as a cub reporter at the *Milwaukee Sentinel* at a salary of twenty-five dollars per week. He later said that his years as a general assignment reporter helped to equip him for his future newspaper work. After a year in Milwaukee he moved on to the *St. Louis*

Star, where he was thrust into sportswriting almost by default. Smith discovered that he liked sportswriting, especially when he was sent to cover the Browns and the Cardinals, St. Louis's two baseball teams. When he found himself covering winter sports, however, he grew bored and asked to be sent back into general assignment reporting. Nevertheless, when he was hired by the *Philadelphia Record* in 1936 to write a sports column, he moved east and settled into a long and notable career.

For the next thirty years Smith wrote six—and sometimes seven—sports columns a week, ranging over every sport and recounting major and minor events with equal enthusiasm. In 1945 he moved to the *New York Herald Tribune,* which syndicated his "Views of Sport" column to papers nationwide. When the *Tribune* folded in 1967, he was syndicated by Publishers-Hall, and in 1971—at the age of sixty-six—he went to work at the *New York Times* as the "Sports of the Times" columnist. "Red Smith enjoyed a lifetime of sports that included forty-five World Series games," Bass observed. "Part of what made Smith good was his vast personal history and his staggering memory of all that history's events and characters. He absorbed, rarely to forget, the people, the games, the bust plays, and the spectacular finishes, and all of this added depth and breadth to his reporting."

Writing did not come easy to Smith. While he referred to the sports section as "the fun and games department," he considered himself on a mission to entertain and enlighten his readers. Smith "wanted to get the facts straight, but how he wrote was as important to him as what he wrote," according to Lawrence Baldassaro in the *Dictionary of Literary Biography.* "He constantly worked to polish his style, to find the right word. It was not a painless struggle. Smith admitted that the preparation for writing—watching the event and talking to the athletes—was more enjoyable than the act of writing. He referred to his office as 'The Torture Chamber.'" Nevertheless, Smith was often buoyed by his perception of his place in the journalistic scheme of things. In *No Cheering in the Press Box,* he was quoted as saying: "I think sports constitute a valid part of our culture, our civilization, and keeping the public informed and, if possible, a little entertained about sports is not an entirely useless thing."

Smith served as the mentor for an entire generation of sports writers. Jerry Green commented in the *Detroit News,* "All of us wanted to write as Red did, with the same purity of style. We tried to imitate the marching verbs and paint-palette adjectives which made Red's sentences flow and pulsate." Leonard recalled that Smith "wrote each column as a sort of short story, with a tantalizer and a punch line." The critic added: "The poet who was Mr. Smith had sometimes to make up his own lines. Thus, for the Dallas Cowboys in the Super Bowl, Duane Thomas and Walt Garrison and Calvin Hill 'operated like infuriated beer trucks.' . . . Who could resist an article that described Lefty Grove as 'the only player ever traded for an outfield fence,' or Cliff Mooers as 'the man who bet his tonsil on a horse?'. . . . This is the Smith who, like Doc Greene, bought balloons instead of drinks for the house."

In addition to their wit and poetry, Smith's columns were valued for their outspoken political viewpoints. He had many criticisms of baseball's labor-management relations, at one point referring to the sport as "the slave trade." Smith was the first columnist to propose a boycott of the 1980 Moscow Olympics to protest the Soviet presence in Afghanistan; President Carter officially adopted the boycott soon after Smith's column on the subject was printed.

Smith was intrepid in his search for professional growth. At the age of seventy-four he traveled to Africa to cover a heavyweight championship fight, passing up the World Series because Africa was the only continent he had not yet seen. He worked virtually until the last day of his life, filing his final column just four days before he died. The entire sportswriting community mourned his passing. In the *New York Times,* Ira Berkow cited the newspaper's editor A. M. Rosenthal's comment that Smith "embodied the spirit, vigor and youth of sports. We remember him with affection and pride as a wonderful writer and a wonderful man."

Today Smith's work can be found in numerous collections of his columns and in omnibus volumes of historic journalism. In a *New York Times Book Review* piece on *The Red Smith Reader,* Donald Hall commented: "Red Smith was a good reporter, a brilliant phrase-maker, on occasion a fierce moralist—and he was best at telling a story. . . . The sports column—as Red Smith did it—becomes a wildlife refuge for metaphor and all liveliness, where language lives and breathes." To quote S. M. W. Bass, "The reader always had a friend in Red Smith. Smith was a writer the reader could rely on, a writer who would speak plainly, and with whom, on occasion, the reader could have great fun."

BIOGRAPHICAL/CRITICAL SOURCES:

BOOKS

Berkow, Ira, *Red: A Biography of Red Smith,* Times Books (New York City), 1986.

Dictionary of Literary Biogrpaphy, Gale (Detroit, MI), Volume 29: *American Newspaper Journalists, 1926-1950,* 1984, pp. 329-34; Volume 171: *Twentieth-Century American Sportswriters,* 1996, pp. 308-17.

Holtzman, Jerome, *No Cheering in the Press Box,* Holt (New York City), 1974.

PERIODICALS

Coronet, February, 1953, p. 33.
Esquire, October, 1974, p. 176.
Harper's, March, 1955, pp. 82-86.
Mademoiselle, May, 1957, p. 149.
Newsweek, October 10, 1949, p. 62; April 21, 1958, pp. 77-80; May 17, 1976, p. 87; August 9, 1982, p. 63.
New York Review of Books, September 23, 1982, pp. 45-48.
New York Times, July 15, 1982.
New York Times Book Review, July 18, 1982, p. 3.
New York Times Magazine, September 16, 1973, pp. 42-44.
Style, fall, 1982, pp. 414-35.
Time, May 15, 1950, p. 55; July 26, 1982, p. 161.

OBITUARIES:

PERIODICALS

New York Times, January 16, 1982.
Time, January 25, 1982.*

* * *

SPALDING, Linda 1943-

PERSONAL: Born June 25, 1943, in Topeka, KS; daughter of Jacob Alan (an attorney) and Edith Virginia (a homemaker; maiden name, Senner) Dickinson; married Philip Edmunds Spalding, 1964 (divorced, 1972); children: Esta Alice, Kristin Edith. *Education:* University of Colorado, B.A., 1965; graduate study at University of Hawaii at Manoa, 1970-72.

ADDRESSES: Home—447 Ontario St., Toronto, Ontario, Canada M5A 2V9. *Email*—linbrick@aol.com; fax: 416-921-1411.

CAREER: Child care and related social services administrator for low-income families in Hawaii, 1972-82; former program development manager for public television station in Honolulu, Hawaii; co-editor of *Brick, a Literary Journal,* Toronto, Canada; writer.

WRITINGS:

Daughters of Captain Cook (novel), Lester & Orpen Dennys, 1988, Ecco Press (New York City), 1997.
The Paper Wife, (novel), Knopf (Canada), 1994, Ecco Press, 1996.

Contributor of short stories and reviews to numerous periodicals, including *Canadian Forum, Now,* and the *Malahat Review,* and to various anthologies for PEN and Macmillan. Editor of *InterChange,* a collection of essays and interviews on regionalism and ethnicity.

WORK IN PROGRESS: "A travel memoir set in Borneo expected in 1998. Titled *The Follow,* it explores Spalding's meditations on themes of female heroines, primate-style mothering and life in the rainforest, focusing on the life of Birute Galdikas and her orangutans."

SIDELIGHTS: Linda Spalding once told *CA:* "I lived in Hawaii for fourteen years. I've lived, as well, in New England, the Midwest, Mexico, and Canada. I am interested in contemporary life as it reflects and denies traditional belief. Perhaps everything I write is about the tension between inner and outer reality."

BIOGRAPHICAL/CRITICAL SOURCES:

PERIODICALS

Globe and Mail (Toronto), March 26, 1988.
Publishers Weekly, May 3, 1996.
Toronto Star, March 13, 1988.

* * *

STARRETT, (Charles) Vincent (Emerson) 1886-1974

PERSONAL: Born October 26, 1886, in Toronto, Ontario, Canada; died January 5, 1974; son of Robert Polk and Margaret Deniston (Young) Starrett. *Education:* Attended public schools in Toronto and Chicago, IL.

CAREER: Journalist and novelist. *Chicago Inter-Ocean,* journalist, 1905-06; *Chicago Daily News,* Chicago, journalist, 1906-16, war correspondent in Mexico, 1914-15; *Chicago Wave,* Chicago, editor, 1921-22; *Chicago Tribune,* Chicago, author of "Books Alive" column in Sunday edition, beginning 1942. Northwestern University, instructor at Medill School of Journalism, 1922-23.

MEMBER: Society of Midland Authors (president, 1933-34), Mystery Writers of America (president, 1961), Arthur Machen Society, Sherlock Holmes Society of England, Baker Street Irregulars (founding member).

AWARDS, HONORS: Award for nonfiction, Friends of Literature, 1966, for *Born in a Bookshop;* Grand Master Award, Mystery Writers of America, 1957; received first Edgar Award, Mystery Writers of America.

WRITINGS:

FICTION

The Escape of Alice: A Christmas Fantasy, privately printed, 1919.
The Unique Hamlet: A Hitherto Unchronicled Adventure of Mr. Sherlock Holmes, privately printed, 1920.
Coffins for Two (stories), Covici-McGee (Chicago), 1924.
Seaports in the Moon: A Fantasia on Romantic Themes (novel), Doubleday, Doran (New York City), 1928.
Murder on "B" Deck (novel), Doubleday, Doran, 1929.
The Blue Door: Murder, Mystery, Detection in Ten Thrill-Packed Novelettes, Doubleday, Doran, 1930.
Dead Man Inside (novel), Doubleday, Doran, 1931.
The End of Mr. Garment (novel), Doubleday, Doran, 1932.
The Great Hotel Murder (novel; originally serialized in *Redbook* magazine under title *Recipe for Murder*), Doubleday, Doran, 1935.
Snow for Christmas (stories), privately printed (Glencoe, IL), 1935.
Midnight and Percy Jones (novel), Covici Friede, 1936.

The Laughing Buddha (novel), Magna (Mount Morris, IL), 1937, published as *Murder in Peking,* Lantern Press (New York City), 1946.
The Case Book of Jimmie Lavender (stories), Gold Label Books (New York City), 1944.
The Great All-Star Animal League Ball Game (juvenile), illustrated by Kurt Wiese, Dodd (New York City), 1957.
The Quick and the Dead (stories), Arkham House (Sauk City, WI), 1965.

POETRY

Rhymes for Collectors, privately printed, 1921.
Ebony Flame, Covici-McGee, 1922.
Banners in the Dawn: Sixty-Four Sonnets, W. M. Hill (Chicago), 1923.
Flame and Dust, Covici, 1924.
Fifteen More Poems, privately printed, 1927.
Autolycus in Limbo, Dutton (New York City), 1943.
Sonnets, and Other Verse, Dierkes Press, 1949.

Also author of *Brillig,* 1949, and *Poems,* 1951.

NONFICTION

Arthur Machen: A Novelist of Ecstasy and Sin, W. M. Hill, 1918.
Ambrose Bierce, W. M. Hill, 1920.
A Student of Catalogues, privately printed, 1921.
Stephen Crane: A Bibliography, Centaur (Philadelphia), 1923, revised with Ames W. Williams, J. Valentine (Glendale, CA), 1948.
Buried Caesars: Essays in Literary Appreciation, Covici-McGee, 1923.
Ambrose Bierce: A Bibliography, Centaur, 1929.
Penny Wise and Book Foolish, Covici Friede (New York City), 1929.
All about Mother Goose, Apellicon Press, 1930.
The Private Life of Sherlock Holmes, Macmillan (New York City), 1933, revised and enlarged edition, 1960.
Persons from Porlock, and Other Interruptions (essays), Normandie House (Chicago), 1938.
Oriental Encounters: Two Essays in Bad Taste, Normandie House, 1938.
Books Alive, Random House (New York City), 1940.
Bookman's Holiday: The Private Satisfactions of an Incurable Collector, Random House, 1942.
Books and Bipeds, Argus (New York City), 1947.
Best-Loved Books of the Twentieth Century, Bantam (New York City), 1955.
Book Column, Caxton Club (New York City), 1958.

Born in a Bookshop: Chapters from the Chicago Renascence (autobiography), University of Oklahoma Press (Norman), 1965.

Late, Later and Possibly Last: Essays, Autolycus Press (St. Louis, MO), 1973.

Sincerely Tony/Faithfully Vincent: The Correspondence of Anthony Boucher and Vincent Starrett, edited by Robert W. Hahn, Catullus Press (Chicago), 1975.

An Essay on Limited Editions, Black Cat Press, 1982.

Also author of *The Old Dog and Other Essays,* reissued, 1971.

EDITOR

In Praise of Stevenson, Bookfellows (Chicago), 1919.

(And author of introduction) Stephen Crane, *Men, Women, and Boats,* Boni & Liveright (New York City), 1921.

Arthur Machen, *The Shining Pyramids,* Covici McGee, 1923.

Machen, *The Glorious Mystery,* Covici McGee, 1924.

Et Cetera: A Collector's Scrap-Book, Covici, 1924.

George Gissing, *Sins of the Fathers and Other Tales,* Pascal Covici (Chicago), 1924.

Fourteen Great Detective Stories, Modern Library (New York City), 1928.

Crane, *Maggie, a Girl of the Streets, and Other Stories,* Modern Library, 1933.

A Modern Book of Wonders: Amazing Facts in a Remarkable World, University of Knowledge (Chicago), 1938.

(With Christopher Morley, Elmer Davis, and others) *221B: Studies in Sherlock Holmes,* Macmillan, 1940.

Charles Dickens, *The Mystery of Edwin Drood,* Heritage Press (New York City), 1941.

World's Great Spy Stories, World Publishing (Cleveland, OH), 1944.

Wilkie Collins, *The Moonstone,* Limited Editions Club (New York City), 1959.

OTHER

Contributor to periodicals, including *Real Detective Tales.*

ADAPTATIONS: *The Great Hotel Murder* was produced as a film of the same title by the Fox Film Corp., 1935.

SIDELIGHTS: Born in Toronto of Scottish-Irish parentage, Vincent Starrett was the grandson of famous Canadian publisher and bookseller John Young. Starrett wanted to be an illustrator, but began writing stories instead, a $75 check from *Collier's Weekly* for the publication of a mystery story ultimately deciding his future. An authority on Sherlock Holmes, Starrett wrote prolifically, including poetry, short stories, detective novels, humorous sketches, biographies, and novels.

Commenting on Starrett's *Books Alive,* a *Commonweal* critic noted: "Mr. Starrett has, apparently, written without any serious intent: he succeeds admirably in giving us an entertaining book. It is a volume of literary gossip, a book not for students or bibliographers, but for those literary ladies—and gentlemen—who appreciate a fund of anecdote and chatty comment. The anecdotes are not, by any means, new; in fact, their familiarity is the chief charm of some: known trivia have a power of solacing by again distracting, which, especially today, many a reader will find welcome."

About *221B: Studies in Sherlock Holmes,* a *Books* reviewer observed: "In this branch of biography nobody ever uses the word definitive. It is an appetite that grows as it eats, and Holmesians will not only feed upon but fall upon this feast, opening the book with a gesture like tucking a napkin under the chin." A *Books* writer also commented upon Starrett's *The Private Life of Sherlock Holmes,* describing the original edition as "a book for pleasure, for such peaceful slippered contentment as the two friends found together in Baker Street." A *Chicago Tribune* review of the 1960 revised edition of *The Private Life of Sherlock Holmes* noted, "The volume is rich with enlightenment on every aspect of the lore of Holmes and the period in which he flourished as the world's only consulting detective. The author's scholarship in Holmesiana is supreme, and he writes as if communicating a happy sense of enchantment."

It is not surprising that a Holmes scholar of Starrett's literary stature would turn to writing mystery and crime fiction of his own. In fact, he wrote several novels and dozens of short stories throughout his career, many of them reflecting the analytical depth of his Holmes research. One early work was *The Unique Hamlet: A Hitherto Unchronicled Adventure of Mr. Sherlock Holmes,* which critic Elmer Pry reported "is generally considered the best Holmes pastiche." Pry continued in an essay published in the *St. James Guide to Crime and Mystery Writers:* "This story, detailing Holmes's search for a missing inscribed first edition of Shakespeare's famous tragedy, is not only a masterful Sherlockian burlesque—it is also an amusing satire on both book collecting and Shakespeare scholars."

Starrett's fiction often features the series character Jimmie Lavender, a Chicago sleuth who moves freely in high society and the underworld, against a noisy backdrop of speakeasies, mob violence, and urban corruption that typified the Windy City in the 1920s. Another notable but less familiar Starrett creation is detective Walter Ghost, who appears in *Murder on "B" Deck* with his Watsonesque partner Mollock, and, according to Pry, "solves the murder of the exotic Countess Fogartini . . . by awaiting the answers to several cablegrams." A third memorable character is G. Washington Troxell, "who unfortunately appears in only a few scattered tales," Pry lamented. Troxell is a bookstore owner who solves mysteries as a favor to police reporter Fred Dellabough. Overweight and virtually sedentary, Troxell employs the process of deductive reasoning to uncover leads, which the young reporter then attempts to verify.

Notwithstanding the recurring appearances of these investigators, Pry suggested that Starrett's strength lay, not in characterization, but in his skill "as a deft creator of plots" and as a successful adapter of the classic Holmesian formula. Starrett's tales tend to feature an "amateur" detective, usually linked with a less clever partner who did much of the leg work. They reflect the "whodunit" puzzle-solving style popular in the pulp fiction of their day, and the mysteries are ultimately solved by meticulous deductive analysis of minute shreds of evidence.

Pry also compared Starrett's work to that of Edgar Alan Poe, especially his story collection *The Quick and the Dead,* which leans toward the bizarre and macabre, elements of horror fiction. Pry concluded, however, that Starrett "was a studious critic and reviewer of detective literature. . . . [H]is greatest achievements and his ultimate reputation rest upon his eminence as an imaginative Sherlock Holmes reader and scholar."

A leading member of the Chicago Literary Renaissance, Starrett lived all over the world, including in such cities as St. Louis, Reno, New York, London, Paris, Rome, and Peking. When he died at age eighty-seven, he was interred in Chicago's well-known Victorian resting place Graceland Cemetery, which holds the remains of numerous Chicago lumi-naries. *AB Bookman's Weekly* remarked in a retrospective on the centennial anniversary of his birth that he was "one of the most dedicated bookmen of this century—in the finest sense of Eugene Field's acronym, a DOFAB—a 'damned old fool about books.'" The *Bookman's* critic concluded by commending Starrett's "bookworld dedication and achievements, his personal generosity, gentle nature and his consuming lifelong focus on literature and scholarship."

BIOGRAPHICAL/CRITICAL SOURCES:

BOOKS

Hahn, Robert W., editor, *Sincerely Tony/Faithfully Vincent: The Correspondence of Anthony Boucher and Vincent Starrett,* Catullus Press, 1975.

Rubber, Peter A., *Last Bookman: A Journey into the Life and Times of Vincent Starrett, Author, Journalist, Bibliophile,* Candlelight Press, 1968.

St. James Guide to Crime and Mystery Writers, fourth edition, St. James Press (Detroit), 1996.

Starrett, Vincent, *Born in a Bookshop: Chapters from the Chicago Renascence,* University of Oklahoma Press, 1965.

PERIODICALS

AB Bookman's Weekly, January 28, 1974; October 20, 1986.

Books, October 22, 1933; March 31, 1940.

Chicago Sunday Tribune, May 1, 1960.

Commonweal, December 6, 1940.

New York Times, January 6, 1974.

Publishers Weekly, February 4, 1974.

Washington Post, January 13, 1974.*

*   *   *

SYMMES, Robert Edward
  See DUNCAN, Robert (Edward)

*   *   *

TRIMBLE, Barbara Margaret 1921-
  (B. M. Gill; Margaret Blake, Barbara Gilmour, pseudonyms)

PERSONAL: Born February 15, 1921, in Holyhead, Wales; daughter of Henry John (a master mariner) and Edith (Jones) Gill; married Henry John Trimble, December, 1942 (divorced, 1948); children: Roger Blakely. *Education:* Attended Salford School of Chiropody, 1948-50, and Redland Teacher Training College, 1957-59.

ADDRESSES: Home—Holyhead, Wales.   *Agent*—Patricia Robertson, 87 Caledonian Rd., London N1 9BT, England.

CAREER: Writer. Worked as a clerk/typist for Trinity House Service in Holyhead, Wales; private practice of chiropody in Holyhead, Wales, 1950-56; primary schoolteacher in Bristol, England, 1960-74; National Health Service, Bristol, chiropodist, 1975-81.

MEMBER: Crime Writers Association, Mystery Writers of America.

AWARDS, HONORS: Gold Dagger Award from Crime Writers Association, for *The Twelfth Juror;* Edgar Allan Poe Award nominations from Mystery Writers of America, for *Death Drop, The Twelfth Juror,* and *Nursery Crimes.*

WRITINGS:

THRILLER ROMANCES UNDER PSEUDONYM MARGARET BLAKE

Stranger at the Door, R. Hale (London), 1966.
Bright Sun, Dark Shadow, R. Hale, 1967.
The Rare and the Lovely, R. Hale, 1969.
The Elusive Exile, R. Hale, 1971.
Flight from Fear, R. Hale, 1973.
Courier to Danger, R. Hale, 1973.
Apple of Discord, R. Hale, 1974.
Walk Softly and Beware, R. Hale, 1977.

ROMANTIC FICTION UNDER PSEUDONYM BARBARA GILMOUR

You Can't Stay Here, Mills & Boon (London), 1967.
Pattern of Loving, Mills & Boon, 1969.
Threads of Fate, Mills & Boon, 1971.
Question the Wind, Mills & Boon, 1973.

CRIME FICTION UNDER NAME B. M. GILL

Target Westminster, R. Hale, 1977.
Death Drop, Scribner (New York City), 1979.
Suspect, Scribner, 1981 (published in England as *Victims,* Hodder & Stoughton [London], 1981).

The Twelfth Juror, Scribner, 1984.
Seminar for Murder, Hodder & Stoughton, 1985, Scribner, 1986.
Nursery Crimes, Scribner, 1986.
Dying to Meet You, Hodder & Stoughton, 1988, Doubleday (New York City), 1990.
Time and Time Again, Scribner, 1989.
The Fifth Rapunzel, Hodder & Stoughton, 1991.

SIDELIGHTS: "My books are whydunits, rather than whodunits," Barbara Margaret Trimble once told *CA.* "They are concerned with behavior in stressful situations, each character reacting according to his temperament. Most have some redeeming features, and it is possible to feel a degree of compassion for them."

True to this stated mission, the Welsh author, who writes under the name B. M. Gill, has won praise for her ability "to depict the effects of emotional disturbance with both power and sensitivity," as Martin Edwards observes in the *St. James Guide to Crime and Mystery Writers.* Those emotional disturbances often involve murder, from the slayings of two young nurses and an anesthesiologist in *Victims* to the "locked room" killing of a despised mystery writer in *Seminar for Murder.* The violence provides Trimble's books with their traditional mystery structure, though in her later novels this undergirding becomes increasingly tenuous.

Often compared to her contemporaries P. D. James and Ruth Rendell, Trimble routinely eschews the conventional mystery trappings in favor of character study and cultural commentary. Indeed, Trimble seems more and more occupied by her characters' inner struggles than with the knife-in-the-back plot twists and focus on legal procedure that lard most modern crime novels.

"Physical violence," she writes in the *St. James Guide to Crime and Mystery Writers,* "is inevitably part of all crime stories—emotional violence strikes deeper. I am interested in the circumstances leading up to the act, and in the consequences." Trimble's willingness to take risks with her fiction has pleased some but disappointed others, with some critics claiming her more traditional early novels stand head and shoulders above her later experimentations.

After an apprenticeship spent writing romantic suspense novels under the name Margaret Blake, Trimble published her first B. M. Gill work, *Target Westminster,* in 1977. The political thriller concerned a conspiracy to overthrow the British government and seems a transitional work in light of what followed.

Death Drop was a striking departure, heralding the arrival of a major new talent. The story of a man who searches for the truth in the "accidental" death of his 12-year-old son during a boarding school excursion, the novel is a textbook execution of Trimble's stated intention to explore "people and their reactions to horrifying situations."

Victims, published in the U.S. as *Suspect,* continues in the same vein. A murder mystery set in a hospital community, the book marks the first appearance of Trimble's unobtrusive character, Detective Chief Inspector Tom Maybridge. A courtroom thriller, *The Twelfth Juror,* completed a trifecta of critically-acclaimed early novels and earned Trimble a Golden Dagger Award from the British Crime Writers Association. The book chronicles twin conflicts: that of a television host on trail for murdering his wife; and the flawed, compromised jury that must decide his fate. Readers cheered Trimble's grasp of character and disdain for mystery formula, while a few critics, like Jon L. Breen of the *Armchair Detective,* chide her for plot contrivance and a lack of knowledge about courtroom procedure.

Another Maybridge mystery, *Seminar for Murder,* is set at a convention of crime fiction writers and met with a less favorable reception. Jacques Barzun, writing in *Armchair Detective,* laments the author's "slackening of control over form and content" while Jessica Mann of *British Book News* finds it "a little too obviously contrived."

Nursery Crimes, a striking change of pace, ushered in a period of experimentation for the author. The blackly comic study of a homicidal young girl, the novel is a puzzling mix of social satire, Freudian analysis, and conventional detective devices. "Gill's ironic tone edges so close to cynicism that her message may be missed," opines Barry Gewen in the *New Leader,* capturing the general critical consensus. *Dying to Meet You,* Trimble's next novel, is another macabre character piece. About a crippled pianist's strange obsession with a young girl, the book takes Trimble even further afield from traditional crime fiction. That trend continued with *Time and Time Again,* concerning Maeve Barclay, an anti-nuclear protester who finds it hard to adjust to her "normal" life following an eighteen-month stay in prison. An unsolved murder lends a mystery element to the plot,

though this remains largely a character study. Lamenting the novel's turgid pace, Marilyn Stasio, writing in the *New York Times Book Review,* finds it "a murkier read than its predecessors."

The Fifth Rapunzel, Trimble's eighth novel as B. M. Gill, reintroduced Inspector Maybridge in telling the tale of Simon Bradshaw, a teenager who becomes involved with a female journalist in the wake of the death of his father, a pathologist who had just sent a serial killer off to prison. Writing in *Booklist,* Peter Robertson expresses praise for the novelist's ambition: "By virtually dispensing with the traditional role of a detective, Gill may offend some, but she will win over just as many by deftly whipping up a lush palate of narrative colors, essaying bit parts with panache, and blending the whole with exacting detail." That reaction could serve as a summary to the career of this versatile and adventurous novelist, who has distinguished herself by her willingness to push the boundaries of conventional crime fiction.

BIOGRAPHICAL/CRITICAL SOURCES:

BOOKS

St. James Guide to Crime and Mystery Writers, fourth edition, St. James Press (Detroit), 1996.

PERIODICALS

Armchair Detective, summer, 1986, pp. 262-63; winter, 1987, p. 106.
Booklist, October 15, 1991, p. 413.
Book News from Wales, summer, 1985.
British Book News March, 1986 p. 140.
Globe and Mail (Toronto), December 21, 1985.
New Leader, June 1-15, 1987, p. 18.
New York Times Book Review, March 18, 1990, p. 33.

* * *

TUNIS, John R(oberts) 1889-1975

PERSONAL: Born December 7, 1889, in Boston, MA; died February 4, 1975, in Essex, CT; married Lucy Rogers. *Education:* Harvard University, A.B., 1911.

CAREER: Sportswriter, *New York Evening Post,* 1925-32, and Universal Service, 1932-35; broadcaster of tennis matches for National Broadcasting Co.; writer. *Military service:* Served in France during World War I.

AWARDS, HONORS: New York Herald Tribune spring festival prize, 1938, for *The Iron Duke;* junior book award from Boys' Clubs of America, 1949, for *Highpockets.*

WRITINGS:

$Port$, Heroics, and Hysterics, John Day (New York City), 1928.
American Girl (novel), Brewer & Warren (New York City), 1930.
Was College Worth While?, Harcourt (New York City), 1936.
Choosing a College, Harcourt, 1940.
Sport for the Fun of It, A.S. Barnes (New York City), 1940, 2nd revised edition, Ronald, 1958.
Democracy and Sport, A.S. Barnes, 1941.
This Writing Game: Selections from Twenty Years of Free-Lancing, A.S. Barnes, 1941.
Lawn Games, A.S. Barnes, 1943.
The American Way in Sport, Duell, Sloan & Pearce (New York City), 1958.
A Measure of Independence (autobiography), Atheneum (New York City), 1964.

YOUNG ADULT LITERATURE

The Iron Duke, Harcourt, 1938.
The Duke Decides, Harcourt, 1939.
Champion's Choice, Harcourt, 1940.
The Kid from Tomkinsville, Harcourt, 1940.
World Series, Harcourt, 1941.
All-American, Harcourt, 1942.
Million-Miler: The Story of an Air Pilot, Messner (New York City), 1942.
Keystone Kids, Harcourt, 1943.
Rookie of the Year, Harcourt, 1944.
Yea! Wildcats!, Harcourt, 1944.
A City for Lincoln, Harcourt, 1945.
The Kid Comes Back, Morrow (New York City), 1946, reprinted, 1967.
Highpockets (also see below), Morrow, 1948.
Son of the Valley, Morrow, 1949.
Young Razzle, Morrow, 1949.
The Other Side of the Fence, Morrow, 1953.
Go, Team, Go! (also see below), Morrow, 1954.
Buddy and the Old Pro, Morrow, 1955.
Schoolboy Johnson, Morrow, 1958.
Silence Over Dunkerque, Morrow, 1962.

His Enemy, His Friend, Morrow, 1967.
Two by Tunis: Highpockets [and] Go, Team, Go!, Morrow, 1972.
Grand National, Morrow, 1973.

Contributor of more than two thousand articles to magazines, including *Collier's, Esquire, Reader's Digest, New Yorker,* and *Saturday Evening Post.*

SIDELIGHTS: John R. Tunis held very strong opinions and was able to defend them in both fiction for young adults and essays in magazines and books. Tunis was a lifelong observer of American sports, and much of what he saw dismayed him: rampant professionalism, the bureaucratization of college athletics, sports as business, and the dubious ethic of victory at all costs. Tunis inveighed against all these evils, instead promoting the ideals of good sportsmanship, amateurism, and character-building through athletic pursuit. As Ken Donelson noted in the *Dictionary of Literary Biography,* Tunis "believed in clean-cut, intelligent, clean-living, honest young men, not perfect heroes, but honest and good people trying hard to find the truth and the right way to act. Because of this belief, he was less concerned with the outward excitement of sports and much more concerned with the inner struggles of young people involved in games and life."

A graduate of Harvard who played tennis and ran track-and-field events, Tunis began his writing career after serving in the First World War. By the mid-1920s he was contributing sports pieces to such periodicals as *The New Yorker, The Saturday Evening Post, Collier's,* and *Harper's.* Tennis and baseball were Tunis's favorite sports. He not only wrote about tennis but was also a pioneering radio broadcaster for major tournaments in America and Europe.

His position as a prominent journalist allowed Tunis to view big-time sports from an intimate angle, and he became dismayed by the direction he felt American sports were taking. From his first full-length book onward—and in almost all of his periodical pieces—he crusaded against the moneymaking aspects of athletics in every realm from tennis to college football. Among his earliest efforts was his only novel for adults, *American Girl,* which portrayed the corrupting influences on an American tennis player at the championship level.

Tunis's career reached a turning point in 1935 when he sent a manuscript entitled *The Iron Duke* to

Harcourt, Brace publishers. The editors at Harcourt accepted the story as a young adult novel and encouraged Tunis to write more in the same vein. This assignment suited Tunis perfectly. Novels turned out to be suitable vehicles for his ardent principles, and sporting events served as perfect backdrops for his tenets on racism, democracy, character, maturity, and morality. To quote Donelson, Tunis's books "were never 'rah-rah' sports novels, though they did extol the life of sports, but Tunis disliked so intensely what he felt was wrong with sports—the increasing professionalism and the increasing commercialism and the rising idolatry of athletes by fans—that his books are both detailed accounts of games and moral comments about the place of games in life. He had an abiding faith in common decency and in democracy, and that ultimately led, in his case, to novels that were didactic and political."

"Didactic" and "political" they might have been, but Tunis's books for the young were also popular with both critics and readers. *New York Times Book Review* contributor Ellen Lewis Buell was one observer who found much to praise in Tunis's work. In a review of *All-American,* for instance, she commented: "No one writing for boys today can describe a touchdown or a home run with more photographic clarity than John Tunis, but [he] always has a good deal more to say than just sports talk." Likewise, *Saturday Review* correspondent Raymond Swing noted that the author's best books "take up such issues as racial discrimination and individual integrity, and no boy can read them without sharpened perceptions about his own values and without realizing that Americanism is something that begins inside himself in his relations with his comrades."

Tunis continued writing for both the young adult and the adult market through the 1960s, completing a memoir entitled *A Measure of Independence* in 1964 and his last novel, *Grand National,* two years prior to his death. In a *Horn Book* retrospective published later in the writer's career, William Jay Jacobs concluded: "The reader of the Tunis books learns that one really can be a success—possibly more of a success—after failing to make The Circle at Harvard or being cut from the freshman football squad. He learns that there is a world of bigger things than victory in the high-school basketball game; that a substantial outlay of honest, sometimes unpleasant self-examination may be required before one develops a proper sense of proportion; that becoming a man is not an easy process."

BIOGRAPHICAL/CRITICAL SOURCES:

BOOKS

Children's Literature Review, Volume 12, Gale (Detroit, MI), 1980, pp. 592-99.
Dictionary of Literary Biography, Gale, Volume 22: *American Writers for Children, 1900-1960,* 1983, pp. 321-26; Volume 171: *Twentieth-Century American Sportswriters,* 1996, pp. 326-36.
Umphlett, Wiley Lee, editor, *The Achievement of American Sport Literature: A Critical Appraisal,* Fairleigh Dickinson University Press (Rutherford, NJ), 1991, pp. 46-61.

PERIODICALS

Aethlon: The Journal of Sport Literature, fall, 1992, pp. 9-27.
Elementary English Review, March 22, 1945, pp. 77-80, 93.
Horn Book, November-December, 1943, pp. 394-400; January-February, 1945, pp. 55-61; February, 1967, pp. 48-54; December, 1977, pp. 48-50.
Journal of Popular Culture, winter, 1983, pp. 146-49.
New Republic, September 13, 1943, p. 370.
New York Times Book Review, November 1, 1942; October 28, 1945; September 18, 1949, p. 34; October 29, 1967; April 6, 1975, p. 43.
SABR Review of Books, Volume 1, 1986, pp. 85-97; Volume 5, 1990, pp. 110-20.
Saturday Review, June 19, 1954, p. 40.
Yankee Magazine, December, 1989, pp. 77-81, 116-19.

OBITUARIES:

PERIODICALS

AB Bookman's Weekly, February 24, 1975.
New York Times, February 5, 1975.
Publishers Weekly, March 24, 1975.*

* * *

UPTON, Mark
See SANDERS, Lawrence

VALIN, Jonathan Louis 1948-

PERSONAL: Born November 23, 1948, in Cincinnati, OH; son of Sigmund and Marcella (Fink) Valin; married Katherine Brockhaus (a poet), January 3, 1971. *Education:* University of Chicago, M.A., 1974; doctoral study at Washington University, St. Louis, MO, 1976-79.

ADDRESSES: Agent—Dominick Abel Literary Agency, 498 West End Ave., New York, NY 10024.

CAREER: Writer, 1979—. University of Cincinnati, Cincinnati, OH, lecturer in English, 1974-76; Washington University, St. Louis, MO, lecturer in English, 1976-79.

MEMBER: Mystery Writers of America, Modern Language Association of America.

AWARDS, HONORS: Norma Lowry Memorial Fund Prize, 1978, for "Replay"; Shamus Award, Private Eye Writers of America, 1990, for *Extenuating Circumstances.*

WRITINGS:

"HARRY STONER" MYSTERY NOVELS

The Lime Pit, Dodd (New York City), 1980.
Final Notice, Dodd, 1980.
Dead Letter, Dodd, 1981.
Day of Wrath, Congdon & Weed (New York City), 1982.
Natural Causes, Congdon & Weed, 1983.
Life's Work, Delacorte (New York City), 1986.
Fire Lake, Delacorte, 1987.
Extenuating Circumstances, Delacorte, 1989.
Second Chance, Doubleday, 1991.
The Music Lovers, Delacorte, 1993.
Missing, Delacorte, 1995.

OTHER

Living Stereo: The RCA Bible, a Compendium of Opinion on RCA Living Stereo Records, Music Lovers Press (Cincinnati), 1993.

Work represented in anthologies, including *Subject to Change,* 1978. Contributor to *Writer.*

SIDELIGHTS: Author Jonathan Louis Valin dislikes mystery writers, even though he is one. "I don't read many mysteries," he told *Los Angeles Times* reporter Dick Lochte. The author added, "They're poorly written and even the good ones are predictable. And mystery writers as a whole don't seem to be interested in the same things I'm interested in." Two exceptions to Valin's criticism are Raymond Chandler and Ross Macdonald, authors he admires.

Harry Stoner, private eye, the protagonist in Valin's novels, was created in the tradition of Chandler's Philip Marlowe and Macdonald's Lew Archer. "I've tried to give him a little more character than you normally find in hard-boiled American detectives," Valin told Lochte. "Usually they're just wisecracking voices. I wanted him to be more rounded, to have some sensitivity, not to be just a tough guy. I wanted him to be a recognizable human being rather than a pure type." Jane S. Bakerman and David K. Jeffrey, writing in the *St. James Guide to Crime and Mystery Writers,* explain that "Stoner, Jonathan Valin's protagonist, is a Cincinnati private detective very much in the American Hard-boiled tradition; he is, therefore, very much his own man, and while the tight, vigorous plots, crisply delineated characters, and precise settings are particularly Valin's, his novels fit into a well-established, clearly defined genre. A loner like most of his colleagues, Stoner nevertheless tunes in his Zenith Globemaster constantly, just to be within sound of a human voice. One of several ways in which Harry Stoner reveals his vulnerability rather more than do many of his counterparts, this small tough is typical of Valin's sophisticated manipulation of the form."

Stoner's cases involve American families which are disintegrating under the pressures of modern society. Valin, explain Bakerman and Jeffrey, "takes social decay as symbolized by the ruin of the American family for his theme. By treating immediate families—husbands and wives, parents and children—against the backdrop of the extended families, Valin broadens his portrait of the contemporary scene. By concentrating primarily on ordinary folk (rather than on the rich) and by exploiting the Ohio Valley, an area he knows well, he suggests that corruption festers in America's heartland."

In *Dead Letter* Stoner is hired to locate a missing daughter who may have stolen classified papers from her father, a physics professor at a local university. When the professor turns up dead, Stoner's investigation leads him to an underground group of radicals who are plotting violence. Although James Kaufmann in *Christian Science Monitor* admits that "Valin is a very fine writer," he finds that in *Dead Letter,* "he attempts to juggle more characters than can successfully be kept in the air." The critic for the *Times Literary Supplement* calls *Dead Letter* "a solid, intelligent work which achieves a nice balance between action and ratiocination."

"Harry Stoner takes his work very seriously," *New York Times Book Review*'s Marilyn Stasio says in a review of *Second Chance*. The novel follows Stoner on his search for an emotionally disturbed college student he has been hired to find. To complicate the search, the psychopath who murdered the young woman's mother has just been released from prison and may be after her as well. "Mr. Valin is very good at turning the screws on a tense situation like this one," Stasio comments. The *Globe and Mail*'s Margaret Cannon finds, "As always, Valin's story is skillfully crafted and the pace keeps the pages flapping to the last paragraph."

In *Missing* Stoner investigates the suspicious suicide of a bisexual man in a seedy downtown hotel. His inquiries lead him into the gay community and into run-ins with the uncooperative police department. "Readers are left," the *Publishers Weekly* critic notes, "with an unexpected solution and an unusually affecting portrait of the victim and his times."

Valin's interest in music finds an outlet in two of his publications, the mystery novel *The Music Lovers* and the nonfiction book *Living Stereo: The RCA Bible, a Compendium of Opinion on RCA Living Stereo Records*. In *The Music Lovers* private eye Stoner finds himself in the specialized world of record collectors when some valuable LP records go missing and he must track them down. Chief suspect is Sherwood Leoffler, a "stereophile club member and all-around bigot," as the *Publishers Weekly* critic notes. But Stoner's investigation uncovers other crimes besides record theft and leads to "a powerful conclusion that satisfyingly caps the story's gentler start," the *Publishers Weekly* critic concludes. Mark L. Lehman in *American Record Guide* claims that *The Music Lovers* has "a hilarious plot. . . . It's nice to know Valin can make fun of his own obsession!"

In his study *Living Stereo*, Valin looks at the recording history of RCA records, one of the earliest companies to record in stereo and whose early recordings in this medium are considered among the finest ever done. Lehman terms *Living Stereo* "the definitive tract on the glory years 1958-1964 of RCA's 'Living Stereo' classical recordings. . . . Not only is it

packed with fascinating information, the book is beautifully written."

BIOGRAPHICAL/CRITICAL SOURCES:

BOOKS

St. James Guide to Crime and Mystery Writers, 4th edition, St. James Press (Detroit), 1996.

PERIODICALS

American Record Guide, May-June, 1993, p. 187.
Armchair Detective, winter, 1990, p. 27.
Christian Science Monitor, March 3, 1982, p. 17.
Globe and Mail (Toronto), May 11, 1991, p. C6.
Library Journal, October 1, 1981, p. 106.
Los Angeles Times, June 9, 1983, pp. 1, 17.
New Republic, August 2, 1982, p. 37.
Newsweek, June 7, 1982, p. 71; April 16, 1989, p. 31.
New York Times Book Review, January 25, 1981, p. 26; April 26, 1981, p. 43; January 17, 1982, p. 29; September 4, 1983, p. 20; November 16, 1986, p. 38; November 1, 1987, p. 34; February 12, 1989, p. 32; April 16, 1989, p. 31; July 29, 1990, p. 32; May 19, 1991, p. 45.
Observer, February 26, 1989, p. 47.
Publishers Weekly, February 8, 1993, p. 79; December 5, 1994, p. 69.
Time, April 3, 1989, p. 81.
Times (London), February 4, 1989.
Times Literary Supplement, October 29, 1982, p. 1196; March 30, 1984, p. 354.
Washington Post Book World, July 17, 1983, p. 10; September 21, 1986, p. 6; March 19, 1989, p. 12; April 16, 1989, p. 8; May 19, 1991, p. 8.*

*   *   *

van de WETERING, Janwillem 1931-

PERSONAL: Born February 12, 1931, in Rotterdam, Netherlands; son of Jan Cornelius (a businessman) and Catharina van de Wetering; married Edyth Stewart-Wynne, 1954 (divorced); married Juanita Levy, December, 1960; children: Thera. *Education:* Attended Delft University, 1948, College for Service Abroad, 1949-51, Cambridge University, 1951, and University of London, 1957-58.

ADDRESSES: Home—Maine (summer).   *Agent*—c/o Smith Skolnik Literary Agents, 23 East 10th Street, New York, New York 10003.

CAREER: Writer. Salesman in Dutch companies located in South Africa, 1952-58; layman in Buddhist monastery in Kyoto, Japan, 1958-59; director of companies in Bogota, Colombia, 1959-62, and Lima, Peru, 1963; land salesman in Brisbane, Australia, 1964-65; director of textile company in Amsterdam, Netherlands, 1965-75; member of Buddhist group in Maine, 1975-80. Amsterdam Reserve Police, beginning 1965, began as constable, became sergeant.

AWARDS, HONORS: Grand Prix de litterature Policiere, 1984.

WRITINGS:

"AMSTERDAM COP" SERIES

Outsider in Amsterdam, Houghton (Boston), 1975.
Tumbleweed, Houghton, 1976.
The Corpse on the Dike, Houghton, 1976.
Death of a Hawker, Houghton, 1977.
The Japanese Corpse, Houghton, 1977.
The Blond Baboon, Houghton, 1978.
The Maine Massacre, Houghton, 1979.
The Mind Murders, Houghton, 1981.
The Streetbird, Putnam (New York City), 1984.
The Rattle-Rat, Pantheon (New York City), 1985.
Hard Rain, Pantheon, 1986.
Just a Corpse at Twilight, Soho Press (New York City), 1994.
The Hollow-Eyed Angel, Soho Press, 1996.
The Perfidious Parrot, Soho Press, 1997.

CRIME NOVELS

The Butterfly Hunter, Houghton, 1982.
Seesaw Millions, Ballantine (New York City), 1988.

CRIME SHORT STORIES

Inspector Saito's Small Satori, Putnam, 1985.
The Sergeant's Cat and Other Stories, Pantheon, 1987.
Mangrove Mama and Other Tropical Tales of Terror, McMillan (Tucson, AZ), 1995.

OTHER

De Lege Spiegel (nonfiction), Driehoek (Amsterdam), 1971, translation published as *The Empty Mirror: Experiences in a Japanese Zen Monastery* (Book-of-the-Month Club alternate selection), Houghton, 1974.
A Glimpse of Nothingness: Experiences in an American Zen Community (nonfiction), Houghton, 1975.
Little Owl (for children), Houghton, 1978.
Hugh Pine (for children), Houghton, 1980.
[Hugh Pine] and the Good Place, and Something Else (for children), three volumes, Houghton, 1980-89.
Bliss and Bluster; or, How to Crack a Nut (for children), Houghton, 1982.
Robert van Gulik: His Life, His Work, McMillan (Palm Beach, CA), 1988.
Murder by Remote Control (cartoons), Available Press (New York City), 1989.

Also author of screenplays for Dutch television. Author of column on American art for Dutch newspapers. Contributor to numerous magazines in the United States and the Netherlands. Van de Wetering's books have been translated into fifteen languages.

ADAPTATIONS: Tumbleweed was filmed in 1981; *Outsider in Amsterdam* has also been produced as a motion picture. Van de Wetering plans to produce *The Maine Massacre* himself.

SIDELIGHTS: Janwillem van de Wetering is a former beatnik, policeman, and businessman and a practicing Zen Buddhist and mystery writer. He told *CA* that his first two books, *The Empty Mirror* and *A Glimpse of Nothingness,* "are realistic accounts of Zen Buddhist training, respectively in a Japanese monastery and [an American] Zen hermitage." Paul Kazan of the *New York Times Book Review* states that *A Glimpse of Nothingness* merits "serious attention, in spite (and partly because) of a slightly resume quality of reporting ordinary subjective impressions." Kazan praises the book, describing it as "fascinating" and "eminently readable."

Van de Wetering is perhaps best known for his "Amsterdam Cop" crime novels. These "mystery thrillers" are in part based on his work with the Amsterdam Reserve Police, which he was allowed to join in lieu of being drafted into the military. Although van de Wetering's police experience provides the basic material for his detective novels, his Buddhist training is also a strong influence. This unusual combination gives his fiction a special appeal. Dulcy Brainard writes in a *Publishers Weekly* article, "[van de Wetering's] Zen practice informs his fiction . . . surfacing in the way circumstances propel his plots in nonlinear, occasionally illogical directions." In a review of *The Maine Massacre,* John Leonard of the *New York Times* notes "Wetering's cool prose, serene mind, impish wit" and states that "there are in each of his mysteries moments of transcendence, binges of Zen." Peter Gardner in *Publishers Weekly* contends that "it's not crimes that count so much [in van de Wetering's stories] as the mentalities of criminal and policeman, and not the moral perspective so much as the esthetic." Gardner detects a "distinctive flavor" in van de Wetering's novels, "a flavor primarily composed of mutually enriching strains of Dutch sense and Buddhist sensibility." And the *Chicago Tribune Book World*'s Peter Gorner finds that "[the author] peoples his books with memorable characters, flavored by Zen and fleshed out by his own police experiences."

Van de Wetering's "Amsterdam Cop" stories center on three Amsterdam policemen: Adjutant Grijpstra, Sergeant de Gier, and the commissaris (Jan). J. K. Van Dover in the *St. James Guide to Crime and Mystery Writers* describes the characters: "The senior member of the team [Grijpstra] is a heavy, stolid Dutchman, unhappily married to a fat, stolid Dutchwoman, yet he is capable of original insights into events. De Gier, slim and attractive, is more of a romantic; he pursues originality, yet he is capable of practical judgments and actions. The odd harmony between the two is epitomized in their regular drumand-flute duets . . . the third principal member of the team, the commissaris (known only as Jan) . . . [is] Elderly, married, afflicted with rheumatism, devoted to a pet turtle, the commissaris functions as the spiritual center of the series. He enjoys passive observation of the spectacles of life; he is also committed to appropriate moral intervention in the situations that confront his murder brigade."

Critics credit van de Wetering's characters for the success of the series. Dover states "the real virtue of the series lies in the development of his police detectives and their aesthetic and moral responses to their world." According to Julian Symons in the *New York Times Book Review,* "the series depends largely" on the interrelationship of these three. Van de Wetering's plots, the critic adds, are "fairly conventional" and almost always secondary to his characters. Leonard echoes this belief in his review of *The Maine Massacre,* reporting that while "the puzzle, a real-estate scam, is not particularly absorbing, . . . the people . . . enthrall." Of *The Corpse on the*

Dike, H. C. Viet notes in *Library Journal,* "Van de Wetering keeps his closely controlled characters in the sharpest focus, but his plots are a little untidy. Nevertheless, fresh and interesting." A *Critic* review of *The Japanese Corpse,* remarks, "the plot is not at all credible; there is little mystery, less suspense and few surprises. And yet it is intensely interesting because the author has created three fascinating policemen."

Van de Wetering has published many works outside his "Amsterdam Cop" series of crime novels. He has authored short stories, nonfiction books on Zen, cartoons, and several books for children. However, Dover summarizes, "Van de Wetering's major achievement clearly lies in his Amsterdam series. The novels are more than advertisements for Zen, but the qualities of humor and detachment give the investigations a special character; aesthetic awareness seems to matter as much as moral judgment. Even when the action and characters become too offbeat for some tastes, van de Wetering's original worldview makes his novels worth reading." Symons asserts that although van de Wetering may not be "a superlative mystery writer," as some of his more ardent fans insist, his stories "are written with an alertness and a genuine feeling for amusing dialogue that keep them constantly lively. Janwillem van de Wetering," Symons concludes, "is a considerable asset to the criminal-entertainment industry."

BIOGRAPHICAL/CRITICAL SOURCES:

BOOKS

Contemporary Literary Criticism, Volume 47, Gale (Detroit), 1988.
St. James Guide to Crime and Mystery Writers, fourth edition, St. James Press (Detroit), 1996.

PERIODICALS

Chicago Tribune Book World, October 18, 1979; May 24, 1981.
Critic, winter, 1976; spring, 1978.
Kirkus Reviews, June 1, 1996.
Library Journal, May 15, 1975; August, 1976; November 1, 1977.
Mystery News, September/October, 1997.
New York Times, September 3, 1976; February 24, 1977; March 13, 1978; January 30, 1979.
New York Times Book Review, June 29, 1975; November 7, 1976; February 18, 1979; May 3, 1981.

Publishers Weekly, September 26, 1977; November 7, 1994; May 13, 1996; August 4, 1997.*

* * *

van GULIK, Robert Hans 1910-1967

PERSONAL: Born August 9, 1910, in Zutphen, Netherlands; died September 24, 1967, of cancer, in The Hague, Netherlands; son of William Jacobus and Bertha (de Ruyter) van Gulik; married Shui Shih-fang (Frances Shui), 1943; children: Willem Robert, Pieter Anton, Pauline Frances, Thomas Mathys. *Education:* Attended University of Leyden; University of Utrecht, Ph.D. (with honors), 1935.

CAREER: Joined Netherlands Foreign Service in 1935, posted in China, Japan, and India, interned in Japan during World War II, released through diplomatic exchange in 1942, served as first secretary to Netherlands Embassy in Chungking, China, 1943-46, counselor of Netherlands Embassy and political delegate to Far Eastern Commission in Washington, DC, 1946-47, counselor of Netherlands Embassy in Tokyo, Japan, 1948-52, director of the Middle East with Netherlands Ministry of Foreign Affairs, 1953-56, minister to Lebanon and Syria, 1956-59, ambassador to the Federation of Malaya, 1959-62, director of research with Ministry of Foreign Affairs in The Hague, Netherlands, 1962-65, and ambassador to Japan and the Republic of Korea, 1965-67. Lecturer in ancient Chinese history, University of Malaya, 1960-61. *Wartime service:* Seconded to Allied Headquarters in Cairo and New Delhi, 1942.

AWARDS, HONORS: Grand Cross, Order of the Cedars of Lebanon; Officer, Order of Orange Nassau; Knight of the Netherlands Lion; Order of Merit of Syria; commander, Order of Menelik, Ethiopia; Grand Cross, Order of the Rising Sun, Japan; Order of Culture, Republic of Korea.

WRITINGS:

NONFICTION

(With C. C. Uhlenbeck) *An English-Blackfoot Vocabulary,* Royal Netherlands Academy of Arts and Sciences, 1930, reprinted, AMS Press (New York City), 1977.

(Translator from the Sanskrit) *Urvaci,* [The Hague], 1932.

(With Uhlenbeck) *A Blackfoot-English Vocabulary,* Royal Netherlands Academy of Arts and Sciences, 1934, reprinted, AMS Press, 1977.

Hayagriva, the Mantrayanic Aspect of Horse-Cult in China and Japan, E. J. Brill (Long Island City, NY), 1935.

(Translator) Mi Fei, *On Ink Stones,* Kelly & Walsh, 1938.

The Lore of the Chinese Lute, Monumenta Nipponica Monographs, 1940, revised edition, Tuttle (Rutland, VT), 1969.

Hsi K'ang and His Poetical Essay on the Lute, Monumenta Nipponica Monographs, 1941, revised edition, Tuttle, 1968.

(Translator from the Chinese into Japanese) *Shukaihen,* [Tokyo], 1941.

(Editor) *Tung-kao chan-shih chi-kan,* Commercial Press, 1944.

(Editor) *Trifling Tale of a Spring Dream,* [Tokyo], 1950.

Erotic Colour Prints of the Ming Period, three volumes, privately printed, 1951.

Siddham, [Nagpur, India], 1956.

(Translator from the Chinese) Wan-jung Kuei, *Parallel Cases from under the Pear Tree,* E. J. Brill, 1956.

(Translator from the Chinese) Shih-hua Lu, *Scrapbook for Chinese Collectors,* [Beirut], 1958.

Chinese Pictorial Art as Viewed by the Connoisseur, Istituto Italiano per il Medio ed l'Estremo Oriente, 1958.

Sexual Life in Ancient China, E. J. Brill, 1961.

The Gibbon in China, E. J. Brill, 1967.

FICTION

(Self-illustrated) *Een Gegeven Dag: Amsterdams Mysterie,* W. van Hoeve, 1963, translated as *The Given Day,* Macmillan (New York City), 1964.

De Nacht van de Tijger: Een Rechter Tie Verhaal, W. van Hoeve, 1963.

Vier Vingers: Een Rechter Tie Verhaal, [Amsterdam], 1964.

"JUDGE DEE" MYSTERY SERIES; SELF-ILLUSTRATED

(Translator) *Dee Goong An* (novellas; English translation of *Wu-ze-tian-se-da-gi-an*), limited edition, [Tokyo], 1949, reprinted, Arno, 1976, reprinted as *Celebrated Cases of Judge Dee,* Dover (New York City), 1976.

The Chinese Maze Murders (novellas; also see below), W. van Hoeve, 1956, M. Joseph (London), 1961.

New Year's Eve in Lan-fang (short stories), [Beirut], 1958.

The Chinese Bell Murders, M. Joseph, 1958, Harper (New York City), 1959.

The Chinese Gold Murders, M. Joseph, 1959, Harper, 1961.

The Chinese Lake Murders, Harper, 1960.

The Chinese Nail Murders, M Joseph, 1961, Harper, 1962.

The Red Pavilion, Art Printing Works (Kuala Lumpur, Malaya), 1961, Heinemann (London), 1963, Scribner (New York City), 1970.

The Haunted Monastery (also see below), Art Printing Works, 1962, Heinemann, 1963, Scribner, 1969.

The Lacquer Screen, Art Printing Works, 1962, Scribner, 1970.

The Emperor's Pearl, Heinemann, 1963, Scribner, 1964.

The Willow Pattern, Scribner, 1965.

The Monkey and the Tiger, Heinemann, 1965, Scribner, 1966.

The Phantom of the Temple, Scribner, 1966.

Murder in Canton, Heinemann, 1966, Scribner, 1967.

Judge Dee at Work (short stories), Heinemann, 1967.

Necklace and Calabash, Heinemann, 1967, Scribner, 1971.

Poets and Murder, Heinemann, 1968, Scribner, 1972 (published in England as *The Fox-Magic Murders,* Panther Books, 1973).

The Haunted Monastery and The Chinese Maze Murders: Two Chinese Detective Novels, Dover, 1976.

OTHER

Contributor of articles and reviews to Orientalist journals. Co-editor, *Monumenta Nipponica* (Tokyo), beginning 1938. The Judge Dee mysteries have been translated into French, Swedish, Spanish, Finnish, Yugoslavian, Japanese, Italian, and German. Van Gulik's manuscript collection is housed at Muger Memorial Library, Boston University.

ADAPTATIONS: The Haunted Monastery was adapted for television as *Judge Dee and the Monastery Murders,* 1974.

SIDELIGHTS: A Dutch diplomat and noted Sinologist, Robert Hans van Gulik's interest in Eastern culture and language began with his first glimpse of the Chinese script on his father's porcelain collection. He began studying the Chinese language in the Chinatown section of Batavia (in the Dutch East Indies), where his father was stationed with the Army. Later, at the University of Leyden, van Gulik expanded his studies to include Japanese and Tibetan. In addition, he privately studied Sanskrit, Russian, and comparative philology.

In 1949 van Gulik published a translation of *Dee Goong An,* an eighteenth-century Chinese mystery novel which related the exploits of a detective named Judge Dee. Although Dee's adventures in the novel were fictitious, his character was based on a actual figure in Chinese history, Dee Jen-djieh, a famous detective-judge of the seventh century Tang Dynasty who had served the Empress Wu and whose exploits were idealized in both popular imagination and Chinese folk tales and plays. Van Gulik's translation drew considerable interest, revealing for the first time to many Western readers that China possessed a significant detective literature.

Van Gulik began to write historical Chinese mysteries of his own, featuring the Judge Dee character and aimed initially at contemporary Eastern audiences. The first two books in the Judge Dee series, *The Chinese Bell Murders* and *The Chinese Maze Murders,* were written in English and translated for publication in Japan. However, once the books appeared in English they not only drew critical praise but soon gained a following. With *The Chinese Bell Murders* van Gulik shifted his aim to Western audiences, introducing more of a puzzle element into the plot. Yet throughout the Judge Dee series, which reached eighteen books before van Gulik's death in 1967, he continued to draw heavily on his background in Chinese culture and history, basing many of his stories on actual Chinese court cases and generally retaining the Chinese literary tradition of taking three seemingly unrelated tales and dovetailing them into one.

The Judge Dee books received consistent praise for their originality, their characterizations, and their vivid portrayals of Chinese culture. Writing in the *New York Times,* Anthony Boucher stated: "Van Gulik's Judge Dee books are unique entertainment: excellent as somewhat picaresque detection, and even more enthralling as pictures of an alien culture, at once more subtle and more barbaric than our own." Ralph Partridge in the *New Statesman* compared Judge Dee's "shrewd methods of deduction and the unscrupulous suavity of his procedure" to those of Sherlock Holmes. A reviewer for the *Springfield Republican,* commenting on *The Chinese Gold Mur-*

ders, noted: "This fascinatingly unusual suspense story, spiced richly with the full exotic flavor of ancient Chinese ways and customs, is the complete equal of the best of modern detective tales and has the added advantage of being uniquely different from almost anything else being offered in this genre."

Van Gulik illustrated all of the Judge Dee books himself, in a style reminiscent of Chinese art, and also appended essays which discussed the aspects of Chinese history and culture relevant to each particular novel. A reviewer for London's *Times Literary Supplement* observed that "the commentary which this author is in the habit of appending to his stories must be by no means the least interesting part of the book." On a less positive note, some of the later books in the Judge Dee series were criticized for the introduction of perverse erotic elements that in no way reflected the flavor of classical Chinese mysteries. And some critics found the Dutch van Gulik's use of English to be less than perfect, or as a reviewer for *Time* put it, "lacking professional sheen."

Summing up van Gulik's fiction for the *St. James Guide to Crime and Mystery Writers* E. F. Bleiler pointed out that van Gulik's Judge Dee was based more on the fictional detective of the *Dee Goong An* than on the actual historical figure of Di Jen-djieh. Bleiler also noted that the backdrop for the novels, although authentically rendered, more closely resembled "a generalized medieval China" than the period of the Tang dynasty when Di Jen-djieh actually lived. Nevertheless, Bleiler regarded the Judge Dee mysteries as "certainly the finest ethnographic detective novels in English," and van Gulik as "the person most responsible for introducing the classical Chinese detective story to the West."

BIOGRAPHICAL/CRITICAL SOURCES:

BOOKS

St. James Guide to Crime and Mystery Writers, 4th edition, St. James Press (Detroit, MI), 1996.
van de Wetering, Janwillem, *Robert van Gulik: His Life, His Work,* Macmillan Publications (Miami Beach, FL), 1987.

PERIODICALS

Best Sellers, August 1, 1964.
Guardian, April 29, 1960, p. 11.
Kirkus, January 15, 1959; March 15, 1961; December 1, 1961.
New Statesman, March 29, 1958.
New York Times, April 5, 1959, p. 32.
New York Times Book Review, October 14, 1962, p. 39; September 6, 1964, p. 16; May 23, 1965; April 24, 1966, p. 44; March 12, 1967; February 9, 1969.
San Francisco Chronicle, March 4, 1962, p. 30.
Springfield Republican, June 11, 1961, p. 5D.
Time, August 18, 1967.
Times Literary Supplement (London), March 21, 1958, p. 157; March 31, 1961, p. 206; March 31, 1963; May 17, 1964; July 15, 1965, p. 593.*

W

WADE, Bob
  See WADE, Robert (Allison)

* * *

WADE, Robert (Allison) 1920-
  (Bob Wade; Will Daemer, Whit Masterson,
  Wade Miller, Dale Wilmer, joint pseudonyms)

PERSONAL: Born June 8, 1920, in San Diego, CA; son of Wilson R. and Camille A. Wade; married Jeanne Florence Cioe, June 10, 1951; children: Robert, Timothy, Sari, Winke. *Education:* Attended San Diego State College (now San Diego State University), 1938-42.

ADDRESSES: Home—San Diego, CA. *Office*—7368 Casper Dr., San Diego, CA 92119. *Agent*—Curtis Brown Ltd., 575 Madison Ave., New York, NY 10022.

CAREER: Writer. *East San Diego Press,* East San Diego, CA, co-editor, 1939-42; script writer for Mutual Broadcasting System, 1940-41 and 1946-48; *Mission Beach Californian,* San Diego, editor, 1948; *San Diego Union,* San Diego, book critic and columnist, 1977—; member of advisory board of San Diego Zoo and Wild Animal Park. *Military service:* U.S. Army Air Forces, 1942-45; served in North Africa and Europe; became sergeant; earned Bronze Star and Croix de Guerre.

AWARDS, HONORS: Second prize in *Ellery Queen's Mystery Magazine* contest, 1955, for short story "In-vitation to an Accident"; Private Eye Writers of America lifetime achievement award, 1988.

WRITINGS:

MYSTERY NOVELS

(With Bill Miller) *Pop Goes the Queen,* Farrar, Straus, 1947 (published in England as *Murder—Queen High,* W.H. Allen [London], 1958).
The Stroke of Seven, Morrow (New York City), 1965.
Knave of Eagles, Random House (New York City), 1969.

WITH BILL MILLER, UNDER JOINT PSEUDONYM WILL DAEMER

The Case of the Lonely Lovers, Farrel, 1951.

WITH BILL MILLER, UNDER JOINT PSEUDONYM WHIT MASTERSON

All Through the Night, Dodd (New York City), 1955, published as *A Cry in the Night,* Bantam (New York City), 1956.
Dead, She Was Beautiful, Dodd, 1955.
Badge of Evil, Dodd, 1956, as *Touch of Evil,* Bantam, 1958.
A Shadow in the Wild, Dodd, 1957.
The Dark Fantastic, Dodd, 1959.
A Hammer in His Hand, Dodd, 1960.
Evil Come, Evil Go, Dodd, 1961.

SOLE AUTHOR UNDER PSEUDONYM WHIT MASTERSON

Man on a Nylon String, Dodd, 1963.
711—Officer Needs Help, Dodd, 1965, published as *Killer with a Badge,* W. H. Allen, 1966, pub-

lished as *Warning Shot,* Popular Library (New York City), 1967.
Play Like You're Dead, Dodd, 1967.
The Last One Kills, Dodd, 1969.
The Death of Me Yet, Dodd, 1970.
The Gravy Train, Dodd, 1971, published as *The Great Train Hijack,* Pinnacle (New York City), 1976.
Why She Cries, I Do Not Know, Dodd, 1972.
The Undertaker Wind, Dodd, 1973.
The Man with Two Clocks, Dodd, 1974.
Hunter of the Blood, Dodd, 1977.
The Slow Gallows, Dodd, 1979.

WITH BILL MILLER, UNDER JOINT PSEUDONYM WADE MILLER

Deadly Weapon, Farrar, Straus, 1946.
Guilty Bystander, Farrar, Straus, 1947.
Fatal Step, Farrar, Straus, 1948.
Uneasy Street, Farrar, Straus, 1948.
Devil on Two Sticks, Farrar, Straus, 1949, published as *Killer's Choice,* New American Library (New York City), 1950.
Calamity Fair, Farrar, Straus, 1950.
Devil May Care, Fawcett, 1950.
Murder Charge, Farrar, Straus, 1950.
Stolen Woman, Fawcett, 1950.
The Killer, Fawcett (New York City), 1951.
Shoot to Kill, Farrar, Straus, 1951.
The Tiger's Wife, Fawcett, 1951.
Branded Woman, Fawcett, 1952.
South of the Sun, Fawcett, 1953.
The Big Guy, Fawcett, 1953.
Mad Baxter, Fawcett, 1955.
Kiss Her Goodbye, Lion (New York City), 1956.
Kitten with a Whip, Fawcett, 1959.
Sinner Take All, Fawcett, 1960.
Nightmare Cruise, Ace (New York City), 1961, published in England as *The Sargasso People,* W. H. Allen (London), 1961.
The Girl from Midnight, Fawcett, 1962.

Also author, with Bill Miller under joint pseudonym Wade Miller, of two screenplays, two hundred radio scripts, several novelettes, and numerous short stories, including "Invitation to an Accident."

WITH BILL MILLER, UNDER JOINT PSEUDONYM DALE WILMER

Memo for Murder, Graphic Publications (Hasbrouck Heights, NJ), 1951.

Dead Fall, Bouregy & Curl (New York City), 1954.
Jungle Heat, Pyramid (New York City), 1954.

ADAPTATIONS: Guilty Bystander was filmed by Film Classics, 1950; *A Cry in the Night* was filmed by Warner Brothers, 1956; *Touch of Evil* was filmed by Universal, 1958; *Kitten with a Whip* was filmed by Universal, 1964; *Evil Come, Evil Go* was filmed under the title *The Yellow Canary; 711—Officer Needs Help* was filmed under the title *Warning Shot. South of the Sun, Invitation to an Accident, Women in His Life* and *The Death of Me Yet* have been adapted for television. *The Killer* was adapted for television under the title *The Man Hunter.*

SIDELIGHTS: Robert Wade and Bill Miller began writing together after meeting at a San Diego junior high school, and the collaborative effort continued through high school and during their years at San Diego State College, when both men edited the *East San Diego Press.* During World War II they continued to work together through the mail, and the first of several Wade Miller novels, *Deadly Weapon,* was published soon after their return to the United States. Wade and Miller adopted their second pseudonym, Whit Masterson, in 1955, and Wade has continued to write under the name since Miller's death in 1961.

Deadly Weapon follows detective Walter James as he probes a murder at a San Diego burlesque house. The reviewer for *Saturday Review of Literature* called the book "very tough stuff . . . that delivers real surprises." Edward D. Hoch in the *St. James Guide to Crime and Mystery Writers* found "something of the pace and violence of [Dashiell] Hammett here, together with an ending unique in the private eye genre. Though praised at the time of its publication, the book is too little known today."

Six early Wade Miller novels concern San Diego private eye Max Thursday. "Thursday's career," wrote Hoch, "begins as a house detective in a cheap hotel. He is divorced and drinking too much. He is drawn into a case when his child is kidnapped. The solving of it rehabilitates him and he becomes a successful private eye—though one with a hair-trigger temper that often flares into violence. The first few books end in a burst of violence, until finally he becomes reluctant to carry a gun." Hoch concluded that Thursday "is still someone worth knowing, and his six cases, . . . are still a pleasure to read."

BIOGRAPHICAL/CRITICAL SOURCES:

BOOKS

St. James Guide to Crime and Mystery Writers, 4th edition, St. James Press (Detroit), 1996.

PERIODICALS

Best Sellers, November 15, 1965, p. 328; October 1, 1967, p. 256; August 15, 1969, p. 190; September 1, 1970, p. 216; July 1, 1973, p. 171; October 15, 1974, p. 331; June, 1979, p. 85.

Booklist, October 15, 1969, p. 257; June 15, 1977, p. 1557; April 15, 1979, p. 1274.

Book Week, August 25, 1946, p. 6.

Kirkus Reviews, June 1, 1967, p. 668; July 15, 1974, p. 767; February 1, 1977, p. 116; February 1, 1979, p. 147.

Library Journal, February 1, 1966, p. 719; October 1, 1969, p. 3472; August, 1971, p. 2551; November 1, 1972, p. 3620; June 1, 1973, p. 1846; December 1, 1974, p. 3150.

New Yorker, November 27, 1965, p. 248; September 26, 1970, p. 143.

New York Times, August 11, 1946, p. 20.

New York Times Book Review, November 21, 1965, p. 92; September 10, 1967, p. 60; September 6, 1970, p. 24; June 27, 1971, p. 29; October 15, 1972, p. 42; June 17, 1973, p. 32; October 27, 1974, p. 56.

Publishers Weekly, June 29, 1970, p. 100; March 8, 1971, p. 66; August 14, 1972, p. 45; April 9, 1973, p. 64; February 12, 1979, p. 119.

San Francisco Chronicle, August 18, 1946, p. 14.

Saturday Review, February 26, 1966, p. 40; October 28, 1967, p. 37; October 25, 1969, p. 63.

Saturday Review of Literature, August 17, 1946, p. 28.

Weekly Book Review, August 11, 1946, p. 15.

* * *

WALLOP, Lucille Fletcher 1912-
(Lucille Fletcher)

PERSONAL: Born March 28, 1912, in Brooklyn, NY; daughter of Matthew Emerson (a marine draftsman) and Violet (Anderson) Fletcher; married Bernard Herrmann, 1939; married John Douglass Wallop III (a writer), January 6, 1949; children: (first marriage) Dorothy Louise Herrmann, Wendy Elizabeth Herrmann. *Education:*Vassar College, B.A., 1933.

ADDRESSES: Home and office—Avon Light, Oxford, MD 21654. *Agent*—William Morris Agency, 1350 Avenue of the Americas, New York, NY 10019.

CAREER: Writer. Worked as music librarian, copyright clerk, and publicity writer for Columbia Broadcasting System, 1934-39.

WRITINGS:

NOVELS UNDER NAME LUCILLE FLETCHER

(With Allan Ullman) *Sorry, Wrong Number,* Random House (New York City), 1949.

(With Ullman) *Night Man,* Random House, 1951.

The Daughters of Jasper Clay, Henry Holt (New York City), 1958.

Blindfold, Random House, 1960.

And Presumed Dead, Random House, 1963.

The Strange Blue Yawl, Random House, 1964.

The Girl in Cabin B54, Random House, 1968.

Eighty Dollars to Stamford, Random House, 1975.

Mirror Image, Morrow (New York City), 1988.

PLAYS UNDER NAME LUCILLE FLETCHER

Sorry, Wrong Number (broadcast, 1944; includes *The Hitch-Hiker*), Dramatists Play Service (New York City), 1952.

Night Watch (produced at Morosco Theatre, Broadway, February 28, 1972), Dramatists Play Service, 1972.

Also author of radio plays, including *My Client Curley,* 1940, *The Hitch-Hiker,* 1941, *Remodeled Brownstone, The Furnished Floor, The Diary of Sophronia Winters, The Search for Henri Le Fevre, Badm Dreams Fugue in C Minor, Someone Else, Night Man, Dark Journey* and *The Intruder.* Writer of radio plays for *Suspense, Mercury Theatre on the Air, Chrysler Theatre,* and *Lights Out* series.

ADAPTATIONS: Blindfold was adapted for film in 1966, *Night Watch* was adapted for film in 1973, *Eighty Dollars to Stamford* was adapted for film under the title *Hit and Run* in 1982 and was also released under the title *Revenge Squad; And Presumed Dead* has also been adapted for film.

SIDELIGHTS: Best known for her novel *Sorry, Wrong Number*—made into a successful play and film—Lucille Fletcher Wallop, writing under the name Lucille Fletcher, focuses on suspenseful stories which are "less concerned with the solution of a mystery than with the anticipation and fear which the protagonist and the reader experience," as Kathleen Gregory Klein writes in the *St. James Guide to Crime and Mystery Writers*. Klein explains that "the hallmark of Fletcher's work is that the solution of the mystery is only the first part of a twofold conclusion. The second climax of each story provides an unexpected twist—a new murder is committed, a disguise penetrated, a motive revealed. Even with foreknowledge of Fletcher's style, the reader becomes absorbed in the tension of the plot and is unlikely to anticipate the specific ending."

In *Sorry, Wrong Number* Fletcher tells the story of a bedridden woman who overhears an apparent murder plot being discussed and unsuccessfully tries to convince someone in authority of the danger. Her isolation only adds to the woman's fears when it becomes obvious that a killer is stalking her. "The rejection of requests for assistance, the anticipation of a rejection, or the fear of being disbelieved and suspected often traumatizes Fletcher's protagonists," Klein writes. "They become increasingly isolated from society, suspicious of others, and easily frightened by their lack of knowledge. As a consequence they often reject safe and trustworthy assistance which could save them from the problems they fear. This reversal is the dramatic twist at the conclusion of *Sorry, Wrong Number* where ironically every attempt to cope with the terror has contradictory results."

In *And Presumed Dead* a woman who has lost her son in World War II is led to believe that he may still be alive. Along the way, the reader begins to doubt the protagonist's sanity as she insists against the evidence that her son survived a wartime plane crash. Brigid Brophy in *New Statesman* finds that Fletcher scares "us out of our wits by making us wonder if the characters are out of theirs," while K. G. Jackson in *Harper* states: "You can't wait to see (and can't guess either) what happens next."

The Strange Blue Yawl follows a husband and wife who curiously investigate the apparent murder of a neighbor woman. "It is the narrator," Klein explains, "who solves the mystery in one instant of inspiration. As in Fletcher's other novels, this is only the apparent climax for, while strange as the discovery is, it is followed by a predictable but shocking twist."

Anthony Boucher in the *New York Times Book Review* calls the novel "one of the finest jobs of bamboozling the reader, in the best fair-play tradition, in many long years." M. K. Grant in *Library Journal* concludes that "Fletcher has done another challenging job."

BIOGRAPHICAL/CRITICAL SOURCES:

BOOKS

St. James Guide to Crime and Mystery Writers, 4th edition, St. James Press (Detroit), 1996.

PERIODICALS

Chicago Sunday Tribune, March 2, 1958, p. 5.
Harper, May, 1963, p. 114.
Kirkus, December 15, 1957, p. 914.
Library Journal, August, 1964, p. 3037.
New Statesman, May 10, 1963, p. 717.
New York Herald Tribune Book Review, April 1, 1951, p. 14; April 24, 1960, p. 12.
New York Times, March 16, 1958, p. 41.
New York Times Book Review, April 24, 1960, p. 43; July 19, 1964, p. 25.
San Francisco Chronicle, March 30, 1958, p. 27; May 15, 1960, p. 30.
Saturday Review, July 19, 1958.

* * *

WATKINS, Paul 1964-

PERSONAL: Born February 23, 1964, in Redwood City, CA; son of Norman David (a geophysicist) and Patricia (de Luly) Watkins; married, wife's name, Cath; children: Emma. *Education:* Attended Eton College, 1977-82; Yale University, B.A., 1986; graduate study at Syracuse University, 1986-88.

ADDRESSES: Home—New Jersey. *Agent*—Amanda Urban, International Creative Management, 40 West 57th St., New York, NY 10019.

CAREER: Writer.

WRITINGS:

NOVELS

Night over Day over Night, Knopf (New York City), 1988.

Calm at Sunset, Calm at Dawn, Houghton (Boston), 1989.

In the Blue Light of African Dreams, Houghton, 1990.

The Promise of Light, Faber (London), 1992, Random House (New York City), 1993.

Archangel, Random House, 1995.

OTHER

Stand before Your God (memoir), Random House, 1994.

SIDELIGHTS: American author Paul Watkins has quickly gained a reputation for his dedication to research and for his vivid, detailed prose. His first novel, *Night over Day over Night,* tells the story of Sebastian Westland, a seventeen-year-old German who enlists in the Nazi SS in 1944 and witnesses the horrors of the Third Reich's last, frenzied assaults on the Allied forces at the close of World War II. Michiko Kakutani wrote in the *New York Times* that "Watkins's orchestration of the combat scenes attests to a remarkably assured command of narrative and a journalistic instinct for the telling detail." In a *Chicago Tribune* review, John Blades praised the book's "crystalline prose" and compared it to the works of Stephen Crane and Ernest Hemingway. "The similarities are real," wrote Blades, "but Watkins has a style and angle of vision that are distinctly his own, and . . . his virtuosic first novel won't easily be forgotten."

In preparation for writing *Night over Day over Night* Watkins studied German army equipment both in museums and at flea markets, read long-out-of-print volumes on the Ardennes Campaign, toured the battle area near Rockerath, and spoke with both German and American war veterans. Inspiration for the book came from Watkins's stay in Germany as a student at age sixteen. "I stayed with a family of old Prussian aristocrats," the novelist explained in *Contemporary Literary Criticism,* "who fled the Russians at the end of [World War II]. The father of the family found himself, in the closing stages of the war, in a similar situation to the book's main character."

Watkins's second novel, *Calm at Sunset, Calm at Dawn,* is the result of his experiences working for several seasons on a New England scallop trawler. The story centers on twenty-year-old James Pfeiffer—the restless son of a scallop trawler captain—who, after being expelled from college, decides to go to sea, despite his father's protests. The novel follows Pfeiffer, first to a run-down Portuguese ship, then to a better trawler, as he experiences the difficulties of life at sea and learns that life on the ocean is not immune to the problems which drove him from the land. Reviews of the book were generally favorable. In the *Los Angeles Times,* Carolyn See noted that sections of the plot seemed "contrived and artificial" but added that the author's evocations of life on the sea "are dazzlingly rendered." See concluded, "Paul Watkins is not a dilettante but a human being who takes life seriously, an author whose work should be read with great respect." John Casey in Chicago *Tribune Books* called *Calm at Sunset, Calm at Dawn* "a book that will have value and appeal for more than sea-story lovers," adding "it is written out of acute feeling and experience, in the voice of an artful storyteller."

In *The Promise of Light,* Watkins created Ben Sheridan, a young man who, on the eve of his college graduation, sees his father seriously injured while fighting a fire. The trauma of his father's accident causes Ben to abandon his promising job as a bank teller and go instead to Ireland, where he eventually joins that country's struggle for independence. James Hynes, writing in *Washington Post Book World,* noted that the plot was a bit melodramatic, but he added that it was "melodrama done with such conviction and such a light touch that it is noticeable only in the retelling. . . . Watkins's evocation of a small Irish town at war with itself is so skillfully and unsentimentally rendered. He captures the rage and bitter wit of men and women who have known each other all their lives, but are ready at a moment's notice to slit each other's throats over politics." Hynes concluded that *The Promise of Light* was "part coming-of-age story, part political thriller, part historical novel, and part blood-and-thunder adventure tale."

In the novel *Archangel,* Watkins created another dramatic adventure tale, this time set in the woods of Maine. Jonah Mackenzie, one of the central characters, chainsaws his own leg off after being trapped beneath a tree deep in the woods. The incident leaves him with a hatred for the forces of nature, and later in life, he arranges a government contract that will allow him to clear-cut the forest of his youth. He is opposed by Adam Gabriel, a young environmental activist who resorts to extreme means to protect the trees he loves. Writing in *Spectator,* D. J. Taylor noted that Watkins's style "looks unforced while intermittently hinting that a great deal of care and attention has been lavished on it." Donna Seaman, a reviewer for *Booklist,* noted that "Watkins adeptly orchestrates a thoroughly believable escalation of tension, madness, and violence, all conveyed with bone-chilling accuracy. As taut and expressive as a violin string, this is an outstandingly intelligent and significant novel." And a *Publishers Weekly* writer remarked, "Watkins evokes the grandeur of the woods as well as the wild unpredictability of both natural and social violence. His vision of rural New England refracts through the interactions of multifaceted characters, most notably of the willful Mackenzie, who is no stock villain but a wonderfully complex and often sympathetic creation." The writer concluded that in addition to creating a multitude of memorable characters, Watkins had also captured "the tortured spirit of a place."

In an article about Watkins written at the time *The Promise of Light* was published, *Publishers Weekly* contributor Gary M. Kramer called the author "an expert in creating characters burdened by their pasts" who "describes his protagonists as men who must confront their demons before they can move on with their lives. Typically, his heroes are driven by deep-rooted obsessions, from which Watkins creates what he calls 'a sense of urgency' in his works. His characters' emotional crusades . . . make his fiction convincing and compelling."

"The work of Paul Watkins is refreshingly old fashioned," mused Hynes. "Watkins is not fixated upon the minutiae of the contemporary 20-something experience but ranges farther afield than most young writers. . . . There's nothing self-indulgent about [his protagonists]; they are passionate and engaged, defining themselves by action rather than by narcissistic introspection. . . . Watkins appears to have immersed himself in the work of Hemingway, Remarque and Stephen Crane. As a result, his books are lucid, intelligent and shamelessly entertaining, written in lean, evocative prose and displaying an uncommon delight in storytelling."

BIOGRAPHICAL/CRITICAL SOURCES:

BOOKS

Contemporary Literary Criticism, Volume 55, Gale (Detroit), 1989.

PERIODICALS

Atlanta Journal-Constitution, February 7, 1993, p. N12.

Booklist, December 1, 1995, p. 610.
Christian Science Monitor, September 12, 1989, p. 12.
Entertainment Weekly, January 26, 1996, p. 50.
Esquire, March, 1994, p. 57.
Kirkus Reviews, February 1, 1988, pp. 157-58; October 15, 1995, p. 1455.
Library Journal, November 1, 1995, p. 108.
London Review of Books, September 24, 1992, pp. 18-20; October 7, 1993, pp. 18-19.
Los Angeles Times, September 25, 1989, section IV, p. 1; March 10, 1994, p. E4.
Los Angeles Times Book Review, December 30, 1990, p. 8; February 28, 1993, p. 8.
New Statesman & Society, August 20, 1993.
New York, January 25, 1993.
New York Times, March 26, 1988, p. 18.
New York Times Book Review, December 23, 1990, p. 7; April 11, 1993, p. 29; March 6, 1994, p. 8; February 18, 1996, p. 17.
Observer, September 13, 1992, p. 54; August 22, 1993, p. 47.
Publishers Weekly, February 12, 1988, p. 72; January 4, 1993, p. 55; October 23, 1995, p. 58.
Sewanee Review, fall, 1990.
Spectator, September 4, 1993, p. 30; July 8, 1995, p. 37.
Times Literary Supplement, August 10, 1990; September 4, 1992, p. 19; September 17, 1993, p. 24.
Tribune Books (Chicago), March 20, 1988, p. 3; September 10, 1989, p. 6; September 9, 1990, p. 6.
Vogue, March, 1994, p. 282.
Wall Street Journal, April 4, 1994, p. A10.
Washington Post, September 25, 1990, p. C2; March 2, 1994, p. B2.
Washington Post Book World, April 24, 1988, pp. 5, 14; September 3, 1989, p. 10; January 24, 1993, p. 5; March 21, 1996, p. D2.

*   *   *

WATSON, Lyall 1939-

PERSONAL: Born April 12, 1939, in Johannesburg, South Africa; son of Douglas (an architect) and Mary (Morkel) Watson. *Education:* University of Witwatersrand, B.S., 1958; University of Natal, M.S., 1959; University of London, Ph.D., 1963. *Politics:* "Absolutely none." *Religion:* "Animist."

ADDRESSES: Home—Ballplehob, County Cork, Ireland. *Office*—BCM-Biologic, London WC1, England. *Agent*—Bruce Hunter, 5-8 Lower John Street, Golden Square, London W1R 4HA.

CAREER: Zoological Garden of Johannesburg, Johannesburg, South Africa, director, 1964-65; British Broadcasting Corp., London, England, producer of documentary films, 1966-67; BCM-Biologic (consultants), London, founder and director, 1967—. Expedition leader and researcher in Antarctica, Amazon River area, the Seychelles, and Indonesia, 1968-72.

WRITINGS:

The Omnivorous Ape, Coward (New York City), 1971.

Supernature, Doubleday (New York City), 1973, published as *Supernature: The Natural History of the Supernatural,* Hodder & Stoughton (London), 1973.

The Romeo Error: A Matter of Life and Death, Doubleday, 1974.

Gifts of Unknown Things, Simon & Schuster (New York City), 1976, published as *Gifts of Unknown Things: A True Story of Nature, Healing, and Initiation from Indonesia's Dancing Island,* Destiny Books (Rochester, VT), 1991.

Lifetide: The Biology of the Unconscious, Simon & Schuster, 1979.

Sea Guide to Whales of the World, illustrated by Tom Ritchie, Dutton (New York City), 1981.

Lightning Bird: The Story of One Man's Journey into Africa's Past (biography), Dutton, 1982.

Heaven's Breath: A Natural History of the Wind, Morrow (New York City), 1985.

Earthworks: Ideas on the Edge of Natural History, Hodder & Stoughton, 1986.

The Dreams of Dragons: Riddles of Natural History, Morrow, 1987, published as *The Dreams of Dragons: An Exploration and Celebration of the Mysteries of Nature,* Destiny Books, 1992.

Beyond Supernature: A New Natural History of the Supernatural, (sequel to *Supernature*), Bantam (New York City), 1988.

The Water Planet: A Celebration of the Wonder of Water, Crown (New York City), 1988.

Sumo, Sidgwick & Jackson (London), 1988.

The Nature of Things: The Secret Life of Inanimate Objects, Hodder & Stoughton, 1990, Destiny Books, 1992.

Neophilia, Sceptre (London), 1993.

Dark Nature: A Natural History of Evil, Harper-Collins (New York City), 1995.

By the River of the Elephants: An African Childhood, Kingfisher (New York City), 1997.

Also author of screenplays for feature films *Gifts of Unknown Things* and *Lifetide: The Biology of the Unconscious.* Contributor to Reader's Digest Services' *Living World of Animals* series, 1970. Contributor to professional journals.

WORK IN PROGRESS: Research on the building of a bridge between scientific investigation and mystic revelation.

SIDELIGHTS: "Since 1967 I have traveled constantly," writes biologist Lyall Watson, "looking and listening, collecting bits and pieces of apparently useless and unconnected information, stopping every two years to put the fragments together into some sort of meaningful pattern. Sometimes it works out. And so far, enough people have enjoyed the results to justify publishing several million copies in fourteen languages."

Gifts of Unknown Things is an account of Watson's brief visit to Nus Tarian, a small Indonesian island, and the seemingly supernatural occurrences he witnessed there. Many of the paranormal phenomena in the book center on a young girl named Tia, and several of the book's reviewers find the events incredible. John Naughton, for example, writes in the *New Statesman* that Watson's "chronicle of [Tia's] more spectacular exploits stretches the reader's credulity to breaking point and beyond." Christopher Lehmann-Haupt of the *New York Times* elaborates: "I don't believe that Tia, the young orphan girl of the island, learned to heal burns by touching them with her hand, to cure schizophrenia by drawing out bad chemicals, to raise a man from the dead, and, finally, when the Muslim natives begin to find Tia's powers too disturbing to their orthodoxy, to transform herself into a porpoise. . . . Now it may well be, as Mr. Watson argues, that my Western rationalism is woefully limited—that it fails to perceive what children and poets and Eastern mystics and with-it physicists see with the greatest of ease, which is that 'There are levels of reality far too mysterious for totally objective common sense. There are things that cannot be known by exercise only of the scientific method.' Fair enough. But just because Newton has turned out to be wrong doesn't make *all* things possible. . . . Yet this is how Mr. Watson reasons."

In *Lifetide: The Biology of the Unconscious,* Watson attempts to construct a unified model of life and the universe that accounts for phenomena currently unexplained by modern science. Using a plethora of examples from biology—his own area of expertise—as well as such disciplines as physics, anthropology, medicine, psychology, and paleontology, Watson argues that evolution and everything else in the cosmos is deliberately directed by a kind of collective unconscious of all living things (including biological components). He calls this "contingent system" the Lifetide and describes it as "the whole panoply of hidden forces that shape life in all its miraculous guises, . . . the eddies and vortices of nature that flow together to form the living stream." Reviewing the book in the *Washington Post Book World,* Dan Sperling declares: "Watson builds an admirable case in favor of the existence of such a contingent system, and believes that the eventual discovery of its parameters and properties will reveal it to be the source of much that we now call the paranormal, . . . [though] even this, he feels, will not solve the underlying mysteries of the Lifetide." Sperling also points out that Watson's description of this system contains "language so rich and lively that at times the book seems as though it were written by a poet rather than a scientist."

Dark Nature: A Natural History of Evil examines the nature of evil from the perspective of that which upsets the natural order of a society. Evil, Watson explains in the book, is anything "that is bad for ecology." As the *Kirkus Reviews* critic explains, "evil is anything that disrupts the integrity of the ecological moment—the sense of place and community—anything that disturbs diversity, relative abundance, and communication." Evil, as Watson defines the term, is a force of nature. For example, headhunters in Indonesia are ethically sound from this point of view because their killings are done with cultural purpose and serve as population controls in an area with limited resources. Serial killers in America are evil because there are no apparent societal or ecological benefits. As Charles C. Mann writes in the *Washington Post Book World,* Watson examines the "baffling intersection of morality and biology" and "the apparent ethical implications of genetics and evolutionary theory." In examining the nature of evil, Watson "ranges through philosophy, psychology, anthropology, history, ecology, and especially biology," the *Publishers Weekly* critic writes.

Watson acknowledges that genes play the major role in determining individual behavior and that aggression and violence seem genetically inherent in human beings. He confronts the idea of natural selection and finds it at great odds with morality and aesthetics. "Natural selection," Watson writes, "is extraordinarily good at maximising immediate genetic interests, but it is uncommonly bad at long-term planning." He calls natural selection "a blind man married to a beautiful woman; and we are the products of that union."

Robert Edgerton writes in *National Review* that, with "admirable judgement and superb craftsmanship, Watson ranges widely over such topics as the nature of ecology, genetic fitness, the selfish and deceptive behavior of gorillas, the premeditated violence of chimpanzees, and the altruism of false killer whales." Mann admits that "most nonfiction has small factual errors of the sort that reviewers cite to demonstrate their own superiority. But *Dark Nature* has an astonishing number of them." He also cites several "odd lapses in logic and tone," but concludes that "buried within the factual and logical muddle is an energetic, thoughtful discussion of an important issue."

BIOGRAPHICAL/CRITICAL SOURCES:

BOOKS

Watson, Lyall, *Lifetide: The Biology of the Unconscious,* Simon & Schuster, 1978.
Watson, Lyall, *Dark Nature: A Natural History of Evil,* HarperCollins, 1995.

PERIODICALS

Booklist, February 15, 1996, p. 967.
Cruising World, September, 1982, p. 146.
Earth Science, winter, 1988, pp. 32-33.
Fate, January, 1980, p. 106; March, 1983, p. 93.
Globe and Mail (Toronto), December 8, 1984; October 4, 1986.
Kirkus Reviews, December 15, 1995, pp. 1760-1761.
National Review, September 2, 1996, p. 92.
New Statesman, July 2, 1976.
New Yorker, July 22, 1996, p. 62.
New York Times, April 13, 1977.
New York Times Book Review, June 3, 1979; April 18, 1982; May 10, 1987.
Oceans, September-October, 1982, p. 60.
Parabola, February, 1986, p. 104.
Publishers Weekly, January 15, 1996, p. 456.
Sea Frontiers, March-April, 1982, p. 121.
Skeptical Inquirer, fall, 1993, pp. 76-79.
Spectator, October 26, 1974.

Times Literary Supplement, December 20, 1974; August 20, 1982.

Washington Post Book World, April 10, 1977; July 15, 1979; May 23, 1982; March 31, 1996, p. 9.

Wilson Library Bulletin, February, 1982, p. 464; December, 1985, p. 70.

Yachting, May, 1982, p. 32.

*   *   *

WETERING, Janwillem van de
  See van de WETERING, Janwillem

*   *   *

WHITE, Edmund (Valentine III) 1940-

PERSONAL: Born January 13, 1940, in Cincinnati, OH; son of Edmund Valentine II (an engineer) and Delilah (a psychologist; maiden name, Teddlie) White. *Education:*University of Michigan, B.A., 1962.

ADDRESSES: Agent—Maxine Groffsky, Maxine Groffsky Literary Agency, 2 Fifth Ave., New York, NY 10011.

CAREER: Time, Inc., Book Division, New York City, writer, 1962-70; Saturday Review, New York City, senior editor, 1972-73; Johns Hopkins University, Baltimore, MD, assistant professor of writing seminars, 1977-79; Columbia University School of the Arts, New York City, adjunct professor of creative writing, 1981-83; Brown University, Providence, RI, professor, 1990-92; writer. Instructor in creative writing at Yale University, New York University, and George Mason University, Fairfax, VA. Executive director of New York Institute for the Humanities, 1982-83.

AWARDS, HONORS: Hopwood Awards, University of Michigan, 1961 and 1962, for fiction and drama; Ingram Merrill grants, 1973 and 1978; Guggenheim fellow, 1983; American Academy and Institute of Arts and Letters award for fiction, 1983; citation for appeal and value to youth from Enoch Pratt Free Library's Young Adult Advisory Board, 1988, for *The Beautiful Room Is Empty;* Chevalier de l'ordre des arts et lettres, 1993; National Book Critics Circle award for biography, 1994, for *Genet: A Biography.*

WRITINGS:

NONFICTION

(With Peter Wood) *When Zeppelins Flew,* Time-Life (Alexandria, VA), 1969.

(With Dale Browne) *The First Men,* Time-Life, 1973.

(With Charles Silverstein) *The Joy of Gay Sex: An Intimate Guide for Gay Men to the Pleasures of a Gay Lifestyle,* Crown (New York City), 1977.

States of Desire: Travels in Gay America, Dutton (New York City), 1980.

Genet: A Biography, Knopf (New York City), 1993.

NOVELS

Forgetting Elena, Random House (New York City), 1973, reprinted Vintage (New York City), 1994.

Nocturnes for the King of Naples, St. Martin's (New York City), 1978.

A Boy's Own Story, Dutton, 1982, reprinted with new introduction by White, 1994.

Caracole, Dutton, 1985, reprinted, Vintage, 1996.

The Beautiful Room Is Empty, Knopf (New York City), 1988.

The Farewell Symphony, Knopf, 1997.

OTHER

Blue Boy in Black (play), produced Off-Broadway, 1963.

(With others) *Aphrodisiac* (short stories), Chatto (London), 1984.

(With Adam Mars-Jones) *The Darker Proof: Stories from a Crisis,* New American Library/Plume, 1988.

(Editor) *The Faber Book of Gay Short Fiction,* Faber & Faber (Winchester, MA), 1991.

(Compiler) *The Selected Writings of Jean Genet,* Ecco Press (New York City), 1993.

The Burning Library: Essays, Knopf, 1994.

Skinned Alive: Stories, Knopf, 1995.

Our Paris: Sketches from Memory, Knopf, 1995.

Also author of *Argument for Myth.* Contributor to anthologies, including *The Fabric of Memory: Ewa Kuryluk: Cloth Works, 1978-1987,* Northwestern University Press, 1987. Contributor of articles and reviews to *Architectural Digest, Artforum International, Home and Garden, Mother Jones, New York Times Book Review, Savvy Woman, Southwest Review,* and other periodicals. Editor, *Saturday Review* and *Horizon;* contributing editor, *Vogue.*

SIDELIGHTS: Edmund White is a master stylist who has produced acclaimed novels, intrepid and insightful nonfiction on gay society, and semi-autobiographical novels that combine the best features of fiction and nonfiction. Known as a "gay writer," White also belongs among those writers whose literary reputations transcend simplistic labels. William Goldstein explains in *Publishers Weekly,* "To call Edmund White merely a gay writer is to oversimplify his work and his intentions. Although that two-word label . . . aptly sums up White's status, the first word no doubt helps obscure the fact that the second applies just as fittingly." White's fiction in particular has garnered critical acclaim; the author has received grants from the Ingram Merrill Foundation, the Guggenheim Foundation, and the American Academy and Institute of Arts and Letters. White's studies of the gay lifestyle and changing attitudes about homosexuality in America, including the impact of AIDS on the gay community, are important contributions to contemporary social history. Though male homosexuality is the subject of his nonfiction, White offers insights into human behavior in general, according to reviewers. *Nation* contributor Carter Wilson comments, "Edmund White is to be envied not only for his productivity, . . . but because he is a gifted writer who has staked himself a distinguished claim in the rocky territory called desire."

White told *Publishers Weekly* that he is "happy to be considered a gay writer," even though that classification has resulted in some difficulties. "Since gay people have very little political representation, we have no gay spokespeople," he said. "What happens is that there is an enormous pressure placed on gay novelists because they are virtually the *only* spokespeople. The problem is that the novelist's first obligation is to be true to his own vision, not to be some sort of common denominator of public relations man to all gay people. . . . Everything is read as though it's a sort of allegory about the political dimensions of homosexuality as a general topic, rather than as a specific story about a specific person. That's understandable, because there are so few gay books, but it is regrettable because it is really an Early Stalinist view of art as propaganda." He intends his fiction to be "literary," by which he means that he hopes to attract the more serious and appreciative readers of fiction. "The market I'm going for, the kind of reader I'm looking for," he explained, "is one who is not simply looking for entertainment, but is looking for whatever we look for from art." He further explained, "I would hope that eventually my books would be good enough to be read simply as works of literature, as stories."

White's wish to have his works appreciated as serious literature seems to have been granted from the outset of his fiction-writing career. Critics praised his first novel, *Forgetting Elena,* for its satiric and insightful look at social interaction as well as for its elegant prose. A first-person narrative of an amnesia victim struggling to determine his identity and the identities of those around him, *Forgetting Elena* exposes the subtle entrapments of social hierarchy and etiquette. White told *Library Journal* that the novel's premise illustrates the "sinister" aspects of life in an artistically obsessed society. In such a culture, he explained, "Every word and gesture would . . . convey a symbolic meaning. Ordinary morality would be obscured or forgotten. People would seek the beautiful and not the good—and, perhaps, cut free from the ethics, the beautiful would turn out to be merely pretty." Setting the novel's action at a fictitious resort reminiscent of New York's Fire Island, White creates, in the words of *Nation* contributor Simon Karlinsky, "a semiology of snobbery, its complete sign system." Karlinsky feels that "what might at first seem to be merely a witty parody of a particular subculture's foibles and vagaries actually turns out to be something far more serious and profound. . . . He has produced a parable about the nature of social interaction that transcends any given period and applies to the human predicament at large."

Most critics consider *Forgetting Elena* a highly accomplished first novel. Karlinsky calls the work "an astounding piece of writing—profound, totally convincing and memorable." Alan Friedman likewise praises the book in the *New York Times Book Review,* though not without qualifications. Friedman writes, "There is something so unfailingly petty about the narrator's apprehensions . . . and something so oppressive about his preoccupations . . . that it is often difficult to be receptive to the book's genuine wonders." Friedman nevertheless concludes that this "tale of a sleuth who strives to detect the mystery of the self" is "an astonishing first novel, obsessively fussy, yet uncannily beautiful."

Larry McCaffery's introduction to an interview with White published in *Alive and Writing: Interviews* describes *Forgetting Elena* as "a hallucinogenic novel, part science fiction, part detective story, part comedy of manners. The work exudes mystery—the mystery of human desires and motives, the mystery of the signs and symbols we use to communicate those desires." In the interview, White credits Japanese literature with helping him to shape the peculiar consciousness he had while writing the novel: "One of the [Japanese] books that had a big impact on me was a tenth-century court diary called *The Pillow Book of Sei Shonagon* written by a woman who was a Heian courtier. She was the ultimate aesthete in a society dedicated to judging everything from an aesthetic point of view—in other words, morality had been replaced by aesthetics. That aesthetic overlay to everything became central to *Forgetting Elena.* . . . I was also very influenced by Susan Sontag's aesthetics when I was creating that book. In the introduction to *Against Interpretation* I seem to remember that she called a work of art a machine for creating sensation. That phrase haunted me."

White saw *Forgetting Elena* as a vehicle for "truth" as well as beauty, a mix that accounts for the book's intricate features. He told McCaffery, "Beauty is all in favor of making a story that entertains, that's well-formed, that's lively, in which there are recognizable causes and effects, in which there are decisive experiences, turning points, crucial scenes—a sequence of events that cohere to the Aristotelian notions of drama." Truth, in contrast, says White, is less orderly. The memory is selective; causes, turning points, and personalities are not clearly defined. He said, "You are not a unitary character nor is your experience unity (in fact, you are an extremely fragmented person who becomes different in almost every situation). Some of these are issues or questions that I tried to expose or dramatize in *Forgetting Elena*. I chose what I thought was an extreme metaphor for this condition: amnesia. But my narrator is an embarrassed amnesiac who doesn't want to admit to anyone that he can't remember who he is, much less who they are; he is constantly molding himself on other people's expectations. He's a skillful faker. An extreme version of any kind of social interaction."

Nocturnes for the King of Naples, White's second novel, won acclaim for its discerning treatment of human values and relationships. As John Yohalem explains in the *New York Times Book Review,* "*Nocturnes* is a series of apostrophes to a nameless, evidently famous dead lover, a man who awakened the much younger, also nameless narrator . . . to the possibility of sexual friendship. It was an experience that the narrator feels he did not justly appreciate," Yohalem continues, "and that he has long and passionately—and fruitlessly—sought to replace on his own terms." David Shields of the *Chicago Tribune* offers this assessment of the novel's impact: "Because of the speaker's final realization of the impossibility of ever finding a ground for satisfaction, a

home, this book is more than a chronicle of sorrow and regret. It becomes, rather, a true elegy in which sorrow and self-knowledge combine and transform into a higher form of insight. This higher insight is the artistic intuition of the mortality of human things and ways."

According to J. D. McClatchy in *Shenandoah,* White's "special gift is his ability to empty out our stale expectations from genres . . . and types . . . and to reimagine them in a wholly intriguing and convincing manner." While Doris Grumbach suggests in the *Washington Post Book World* that White "will seem to the careful reader to be the poet of the burgeoning homosexual literature," she also notes, "The music of White's prose is seductive. It is of course possible that a tone-deaf, a melody-indifferent reader might turn his back on White's homo-erotic narrative." However, she adds, White's prose in *Nocturnes* promises satisfaction to "the lover of good fictional writing who is open to this most subtle exploration of the many ways of love, desertion, loss, and regret."

Caracole, White's 1985 novel, goes back to an earlier century and retrieves a more elaborate fictional form. Christopher Lehmann-Haupt observes in his *New York Times* column that White has "certainly conceived a 19th century plot steeped in the conventions of romanticism" when he writes of two country lovers forcibly separated who turn to sexual escapades in a large city. The resulting story is a "puzzling melange of comic opera and sleek sensuality," says the reviewer. *New York Times Book Review* contributor David R. Slavitt describes *Caracole* as "a grand fantasy. . . . Shrewdness and self-awareness ooze from every intricate sentence, every linguistic arabesque and hothouse epigram." Slavitt concludes that *Caracole* "is, provokingly, a challenge to taste, which is likely to vary from one reader to another or even from moment to moment in the same reader."

Critics observe that each of White's books presents voices and literary strategies that differ from previous works. In the *Paris Review* interview, White commented that a writer who keeps changing his style "could be . . . defended as someone who resists the sort of packaging designed for quick product recognition and smooth consumption. Is a stylistically unpredictable writer a luxury product—or is he refusing to be a product? More subjectively, my mercurial literary personality reflects a general feeling of unreality. Like the narrator in *Forgetting Elena,* I'm an amnesiac—a guilty, not an innocent amnesiac. I keep feeling I've accomplished nothing, never written a 'real' novel. Today, when so many of my friends are dead or dying of AIDS, that feeling of unreality has been heightened. People say we should seize the day, but just *one* day turns out to be too cold (or slippery) to hold." Once concerned about the commercial success of his books, White said he writes better when not trying to "second-guess" the markets. "I have always made a point of honor to write as though I had a million dollars," he said in the *Paris Review;* "that is, I try to write in the most original way I know how, and that feels like a risk each time you do it. [French Nobel Prize winner] Andre Gide said that with each book you should lose the admirers you gained with the previous one."

As this comment suggests, White's nonfiction on gay life in America is as compelling as his fiction. *The Joy of Gay Sex: An Intimate Guide for Gay Men to the Pleasures of a Gay Lifestyle,* published in the late 1970s, attempted to make the topic less mysterious for curious heterosexuals and to provide useful information for gay men. In 1980, White published *States of Desire: Travels in Gay America.* A documentary on segments of homosexual life in fifteen major American cities, *States of Desire* contains interviews, autobiographical reminiscences, and accounts of cultural and entertainment centers for gays. According to Ned Rorem in the *Washington Post Book World,* *States of Desire* "poses as a documentary . . . on our national gay bourgeoisie. Actually it's an artist's selective vision . . . of human comportment which is and is not his own, mulled over, distilled, then spilled onto the page with a melancholy joy."

Some critics feel White's scope and objectivity are limited in *States of Desire.* Goldstein points out, "Nowhere in [the book] is there any sense of how different life is for a working-class homosexual, for a lesbian, or for a black." *New York Times Book Review* contributor Paul Cowan comments that White does not make "the promiscuous America he portrays . . . even remotely attractive to an outsider." Despite these qualifications, critics find much to applaud in *States of Desire.* John Leonard concludes in the *New York Times,* "Simply as anthropology, *States of Desire* commands attention and respect."

Village Voice contributor Richard Goldstein feels that the best aspect of the work "is White's attempt to explain the most tangible aspects of gay culture to homosexuals, who may be more confused by what they do than heterosexuals are by what they see. . . . In

its demure way, this is as didactic a treatise on homosexual experience as has ever been written." Clemons notes that if White aims to provoke heterosexuals to rethink their views on homosexuality, he also intends to stir up the gay community. For example, he challenges gays to see that persecution of drag queens and transvestites by gays who live more conventional lives reveals a contradictory latent homophobia. White also diagnoses an important rift in the gay community: a conflict between gay "moderates," who seem to desire assimilation into the American mainstream, and the "radicals," who seek social change through militant confrontation. Clemons concludes, "[White] says he hopes his book 'will enable gays and straights to imagine other lives.' Often startlingly, it accomplishes that."

The Joy of Gay Sex and *States of Desire* qualified White as one of the most prominent spokespersons for gay men in America. He knew that publishing these works would engage him in politics to some extent. He explained in a *Paris Review* interview, "It was a political act for me to sign the *The Joy of Sex* at the time. The publisher could not have cared less, but for me it was a big act of coming out. Charles Silverstein, my co-author, and I were both aware that we would be addressing a lot of people and so in that sense we were spokesmen. We always pictured our ideal reader as someone who thought he was the only homosexual in the world. *States of Desire* was an attempt to see the varieties of gay experience and also to suggest the enormous range of gay life to straight and gay people—to show that gays aren't just hairdressers, they're also petroleum engineers and ranchers and short-order cooks. Once I'd written *States of Desire* I felt it was important to show one gay life in particular depth, rather than all of these lives in a shorthand version. *A Boy's Own Story* and its sequel, *The Beautiful Room Is Empty,* grew out of that."

In addition to his accomplished fiction and nonfiction, White has produced several semi-autobiographical novels that bring together the best features of both kinds of writing, beginning with *A Boy's Own Story,* a first-person narrative of a homosexual boy's adolescence during the 1950s. As a *Harper's* reviewer describes it, *A Boy's Own Story* "is a poignant combination of the two genres . . . written with the flourish of a master stylist." The main conflict in this psychological novel is the narrator's battle against negative judgments from society and from within. Emotional turmoil related to homosexuality, though prominent in the novel, is only one difficulty among many related to coming of age, the *Harper's* reviewer observes. "[*A Boy's Own Story*] is an endearing portrait of a child's longing to be charming, popular, powerful, and loved, and of his struggles with adults, . . . told with . . . sensitivity and elegance."

More than one reviewer has called *A Boy's Own Story* a "classic" work. Comparing White to James Baldwin, Herman Wouk, and Mary McCarthy, Thomas M. Disch writes in the *Washington Post Book World* that the novel "represents the strongest bid to date by a gay writer to do for his minority experience what the writers above did for theirs—offer it as a representative, all-American instance." *New York Times Book Review* contributor Catharine R. Stimpson finds the book "as artful as [White's] earlier novels but more explicit and grounded in detail, far less fanciful and elusive. . . . Balancing the banal and the savage, the funny and the lovely, he achieves a wonderfully poised fiction." *Voice Literary Supplement* columnist Eliot Fremont-Smith concludes: "*A Boy's Own Story* seems intended to be liberating, as well as touching and clever and smart. It is something else as well: unsettling to the willing heart. This makes it a problem, with no happy solution guaranteed, which defines what's wrong with the book. But also what's right, what intrigues." Lehmann-Haupt calls the work "superior fiction," adding: "Somehow . . . Mr. White does succeed in almost simultaneously elevating and demeaning his self-history. And these extremes of epiphany and emptiness are what is most universal about this haunting Bildungsroman."

In *The Beautiful Room Is Empty,* the sequel to *A Boy's Own Story,* the narrator alternately revels in his homosexuality and rejects himself for it. Psychoanalysis and increasing surrender to sensual activity escalate the young man's battle for self-acceptance. Though his sexuality troubles him, the excitement and audacity of his experiences with gay men in public restrooms seems a needed respite from the blandness of his suburban life. While recreating these scenes, White evokes both humor and terror. The gay characters easily upstage the others in the book with their outspoken opinions, witty banter, and daring sexual exploits, while "White takes us through [the narrator's] unsentimental education like an indulgent pal, making graceful introductions, filling in with pungent details, saving his harshest judgments for himself," Vince Aletti comments in the *Voice Literary Supplement.* Sometimes the adolescent makes bold moves—as when he shouts "Gay is good!" in a Greenwich Village demonstration. At other times, he acts out his self-loathing, as when he seduces his music teacher and betrays him to the authorities. By depicting both kinds of behavior, the narrator helps White to evoke "the cautious emergence of a gay consciousness" taking place in the surrounding culture, Aletti remarks.

Some readers did not see how one could come away from *The Beautiful Room Is Empty* with a good feeling about homosexuality. In answer to these critics, White explained in a *Village Voice* interview that his role is not that of a propagandist, but that of a historian. He said, "I like to describe the way people actually are. Some rather young people don't see the historical point of *The Beautiful Room Is Empty.* . . . I was trying to point out that people were even more oppressed [in the 1960s] than they are today." Addressing the topic again in a *Publishers Weekly* interview, the author said, "I feel it wouldn't be true to the experience of the characters if I showed them gliding blissfully through, when it was obviously a painful thing coming out in a period before gay liberation." A *Time* reviewer concludes, "In the era of AIDS, White's novel is a fiercely remembered plea not to push gays back into the closet."

At a time when books by gay writers are not as widely read as he hopes they will be, White, who once had a novel rejected by twenty-two different publishers, admits to being thrilled by the recognition his writing has received. "I know I'll always be doing this," he told *Publishers Weekly,* "and I know that I'll never make a living from my writing; but that's fine. It's enough to be published. . . . I don't have very exalted notions of what a writer's life should be like." Concurrent with his career as an author, White has taught creative writing at several East Coast universities, including Johns Hopkins, Columbia, and Yale. His reviews and profiles appear frequently in *Vogue* and other magazines. He also writes travel articles, and, from his home in Paris, reports on contemporary trends in art and politics, and French social history.

Paris is hospitable toward White and other journalists who take an interest in French culture, he reports. "Maybe we're liked because there are so few of us living here," White wrote in an 1985 *Vogue* column. Paris is the second home to about half as many Americans as were living there during the 1920s when they were escaping mainstream America and prohibition. White enjoys living in Paris because it has become "*the* world clearinghouse for contemporary music, dance, theater, and video," and an important "channel for dispersing American art," he wrote in *Vogue*. He reports that as the capital becomes the home of people from many nations, it is also the place where new attitudes about effective methods of political change are becoming apparent. "The real change France is witnessing is the demise of ideology and the rise of a moderate, pragmatic politics," White observed in *Vogue*. Nicholas Wahl, who explained these changes to White, credits the new attitude to the fact that Communism never appeared attractive to the French, "and to the belated recognition that we live in a world that requires patient adjustments, not fiery gestures, and compromise, not revolution," said White.

White's interest and familiarity with French culture are evident in *Genet: A Biography,* White's study of the acclaimed French writer, Jean Genet. White spent seven years researching and writing the biography, interviewing those who knew Genet and examining Genet's literary output. He chronicles Genet's early hardships (being abandoned by his parents and becoming a ward of the state); his adolescent initiation into stealing, which became a lifelong addiction; his first burst of literary creativity during the 1940s, which resulted in five novels and secured his fame; and his turbulent personal life, marked by his homosexuality and his apparent brutish ways towards friends and lovers alike. Noting Genet's legendary habit of falsifying the events of his life, *New York Review of Books* reviewer Tony Judt commends White for attempting "to unravel the threads that Genet so assiduously knotted and crossed in his various writings and interviews."

Critical reaction to *Genet* was mostly positive, with several reviewers calling the biography a "definitive" work, in the words of *New York Times Book Review* contributor Margo Jefferson. Writing in the Chicago *Tribune Books,* Thomas McGonigle avers that "White has written a wonderfully readable account of a thoroughly repulsive individual," adding that "White brings to bear on the life of Genet a grand literary sensibility." Similarly, *Los Angeles Times Book Review* contributor Daniel Harris calls the work "an extraordinarily lucid biography" and notes that "White delights in ferreting out Genet's most compromising secrets." Some reviewers criticized White for focusing too heavily on Genet's homosexuality as a means of interpreting his life and literary output. Judt, for instance, states that occasionally White falls "victim to his own anachronistic concern with sexual preference as a key to aesthetic appreciation." Writ-

ing in the *New York Times Book Review,* Isabelle de Courtivron concurs, noting that "at times White comes perilously close to reducing his subject's complex works to an overinterpretation in light of" Genet's homosexuality. Nevertheless, comments de Courtivron, White's work "is so meticulously researched and detailed, his understanding and illumination of the works is so rich, that the book ultimately succeeds in resisting the nagging temptation of reductionism." Jefferson concludes, White "presents the life meticulously, reads Genet's work intelligently and writes beautifully." Reflecting the positive critical opinion of the book, *Genet* was awarded the National Book Critics Circle award for biography in 1994.

Continuing his role as a social historian on the homosexual experience in America, White has written several intensely personal articles on the impact of AIDS on gay life and gay writers. He told Walter Kendrick of the *Village Voice,* "I think gay male life has been reduced both by the trade press, and, unfortunately, by many gays to the single issue of AIDS. At the same time, AIDS has been used to browbeat gays, and gays embrace AIDS as a way of feeling bad about themselves. There has been a terrible loss of confidence. [In *The Beautiful Room Is Empty*] I was eager to write a fairly rousing testimonial to the importance of gay liberation."

White writes with authority about the gay liberation movement because he has been an active participant in it since the Stonewall riot in New York City in 1969. Police had raided the gay discotheque and gay men fought back in what is now seen as the official beginning of the campaign for gay rights. "The riot itself I considered a rather silly event at the time; it seemed more Dada than Bastille, a kind of romp. But I participated in that and then was active from the very beginning in gay liberation. We had these gatherings which were patterned after women's and ultimately, I think, Maoist consciousness-raising sessions. Whether or not our sessions accomplished anything for society, they were certainly useful to all of us as a tool for changing ourselves." Before that time, he explained, gay men tended to think of themselves as primarily heterosexual except for certain sexual habits—"but we weren't homosexuals as people. Even the notion of a homosexual culture would have seemed comical or ridiculous to us, certainly horrifying."

The spread of AIDS since the 1970s, he observes, has affected the way gay men see themselves. "Certainly the disease is encouraging homosexuals to question whether they want to go on defining themselves at all by their sexuality," White wrote in an *Artforum* article. "Maybe the French philosopher Michel Foucault was right in saying there are homosexual acts but not homosexual people. More concretely, when a society based on sex and expression is deeroticized, its very reason for being can vanish."

In "Residence on Earth: Living with AIDS in the '80s," an article White wrote for *Life* magazine, he observes that the general public's views of gay men has also changed over the decades: "Ten years ago gay men were perceived as playboys who put their selfish pleasures above family or community duties and responsibilities. Now they're seen as victims who have responded to a tragedy with dignity and courage. Above all, the lesbian and gay community is recognized as a *community,* one that is often angry and militant, generally well disciplined, always concerned," voluntarily raising funds and organizing support groups for AIDS sufferers, visiting the sick, and campaigning for responsible sex education.

White feels that the gay liberation movement has succeeded, in part. In *Mother Jones,* White explained that nearly two decades after the Stonewall riot, "there is a great deal more self-acceptance among gays, even a welcome show of arrogance." In addition, he wrote, "Gay men no longer look longingly over their shoulders at straight life, and they take each other seriously as mentors, buddies, sidekicks, brothers, lovers." Women have also benefited, no longer afraid that enjoying each other's company in public will lead others to suspect they are gay.

White observes in *Rolling Stone* that AIDS has caused the gay liberation movement some daunting setbacks. As he sees it, "Gay liberation opposed both the religious definition of homosexuality as sin and the medical model of homosexuality as a disease. But because of AIDS, preachers and doctors have gained back considerable ground. Many young gays are choosing to stay in the closet or to curtail almost all sexual behavior—understandable, but surely a source of frustration and bitterness." White warns that the "new moralism" brings dangers of its own, including the tendency to see gays as scapegoats and to limit their civil liberties in the attempt to impede the spread of disease.

White points out that AIDS is not the only factor that accounts for the mixed success of the gay liberation

movement. The movement has had some unanticipated side-effects. He writes in *Mother Jones,* "Gay liberation grew out of the progressive spirit of the 1960s—a strange and exhilarating blend of socialism, feminism and the human potential movement. Accordingly, what gay leaders in the late 1960s were anticipating was the emergence of the androgyne [a kind of person neither specifically masculine nor feminine], but what they got was the superbutch stud [a muscle-bound type whose homosexuality is a heightened form of masculine aggression]; what they expected was a communal hippie freedom from possessions, but what has developed is the acme of capitalist consumerism. Gays . . . consume expensive vacations, membership in gyms and discos, cars, elegant furnishings, clothes, haircuts, theater tickets and records. . . . Unfortunately, today this rampant and ubiquitous consumerism not only characterizes gay spending habits but also infects attitudes toward sexuality: gays rate each other quantitatively according to age, physical dimensions and income; and all too many gays consume and dispose of each other, as though the act of possession brought about instant obsolescence." White points out that finding a solution to this problem, as it is for the AIDS epidemic, is important not only for gays, but for all Americans.

White believes that gay writers should recognize the historical significance of the AIDS epidemic in the context of the larger culture in which they live. In a 1985 *Rolling Stone* article, White reported that the prohibitive cost of health care for many Americans and the inconsistent defense of civil liberties for gays are among the problems that have come to light as a result of AIDS. He elaborated, "The AIDS epidemic has rolled back a big rotting log and revealed all the squirming life underneath it, since it involves, all at once, the main themes of our existence: sex, death, power, money, love, hate, disease and panic. No American phenomenon has been as compelling since the Vietnam War, which itself involved most of the same themes. Although obviously a greater tragedy, the war nevertheless took place on a different continent and invited a more familiar political analysis. We knew how to protest the war. In the rancorous debates over AIDS, all the issues are fuzzy and the moral imperatives all questions." Finding the answers to these questions has been made more difficult by the speed with which attitudes about homosexuality have changed. In *Artforum,* White observed, "To have been oppressed in the '50s, freed in the '60s, exalted in the '70s, and wiped out [by AIDS] in the '80s is a quick itinerary for a whole culture to follow. For we are witnessing not just the death of individuals but a menace to an entire culture. All the more reason to bear witness to the cultural moment."

White believes gay writers have a further task ahead: "Art must compete with (rectify, purge) the media, which have thoroughly politicized AIDS in a process that is the subject of a book to be published shortly in England. It is *Policing Desire: Pornography, AIDS and the Media,* by Simon Watney. . . . To confront AIDS more honestly than the media have done, it must begin in tact, avoid humor, and end in anger." Tact is important, he says, "because we must not reduce individuals to their deaths," and "because we must not let the disease stand for other things." Humor is "grotesquely inappropriate to the occasion," since it "puts the public (indifferent when not uneasy) on cozy terms with what is an unspeakable scandal: death." He continues, "End in anger, I say, because it is only sane to rage against the dying of the light, because strategically anger is a political response, because psychologically anger replaces despondency, and because essentially anger lightens the solitude of frightened individuals."

Many of the essays in which White explores the intersection of homosexuality, culture, and AIDS are collected in *The Burning Library: Essays.* Consisting of forty pieces, many of them previously published, the collection aptly chronicles White's literary and personal odyssey from the pre-Stonewall period to the sexually liberating 1970s and into the devastation wrought by AIDS in the 1980s and 1990s. Noting the "unparalleled stylistic elegance deployed" by White in these essays, *Observer* reviewer Jonathan Keates characterizes White as being "armed with [a] . . . deep moral awareness and the . . . ability to charm the socks of the reader even while retailing unpalatable truths." Writing in the *Los Angeles Times,* Chris Goodrich calls *The Burning Library* "strikingly traditional, a writer's attempt to fathom his own identity and that of the subculture in which he works and lives."

Times Literary Supplement contributor Neil Powell claims that *The Burning Library*'s more personal essays are stronger than those in which White discusses other writers and their works. "Often in the book," comments Powell, "White's admirable capacity for sympathetic understanding not only inhibits his critical judgment but actually weakens the case being argued." Goodrich, focusing on the more personal essays, notes that White's "reflections on AIDS are uncommonly thoughtful." Keates concurs, writing that White's "own HIV-positive status might have fuelled him with accusatory hysteria and recrimination. Instead, . . . he has challenged mortality with these noble fragments."

White's concern about AIDS has also left its mark on his writing. White's stories in *The Darker Proof* zero in on the experience of AIDS in order to make use of the way fiction can minister to deep emotional needs. He told Kendrick, "AIDS is a very isolating and frightening situation. . . . To show that someone else has the same thoughts, fears, hopes—the same daily anxiety—is one of the main things fiction does." White also told Stewart Kellerman in the *New York Times Book Review* that because of the AIDS epidemic, he sees "everything as a potential last work." Now that nearly forty of his friends and former students have died from AIDS, he feels "the urge to memorialize the dead, to honor their lives," he wrote in *Artforum.* He added, "There is an equally strong urge to record one's own past—one's own *life*—before it vanishes."

White answered that urge in *Skinned Alive: Stories,* a collection of eight short stories published in 1995. Several of the stories feature "gay love and loss in the shadow of AIDS" as a central motif, comments Maxine Chernoff in a review of the work in the Chicago *Tribune Books.* In "Running on Empty," a man returns to his hometown in Texas after traveling in Europe and confronts his worsening illness. "Palace Days" offers a love triangle in which one character is dying of AIDS while another, though healthy, is coping with the recent discovery that he is HIV-positive. And in "An Oracle," a man grieving for his dead lover falls in love with a young man while traveling in Greece.

"What Edmund White conjures here is a serious, sustained look at how AIDS measures and shapes the meaning of our existence," notes *Los Angeles Times Book Review* contributor Michael Bronski. While noting that the stories dealing with AIDS are "rarely somber," *New York Times Book Review* commentator Morris Dickstein avers that "in the best stories, . . . the author sometimes gives way to a sadness that reverberates more deeply than in anything else he has written." "White is never ponderous but vastly compassionate, and has the grace to be humorous in his compassion," remarks Alberto Manguel in the *Observer.* Reviewing the work in *London Review of Books,* James Woods criticizes the parts of these stories in which White writes about sex as repetitious and unoriginal: "All one needs to do, to verify that such passages are weak stylistically, is compare them with the brilliance of White's non-sexual portraiture." Nevertheless, Woods commends "the scattered gorgeousness" in White's writing and concludes that "*Skinned Alive* shows us that for all his confusions, White has lost none of his artistry." As Chernoff observes, White's "subject is the human condition, no matter our sexual practices, and our final estrangement from each other, despite our efforts to hold on."

White believes that originality is the creative writer's foremost concern. He explained to McCaffery, "There are two ways of looking at literature. One is to feel that there is one great Platonic novel in the sky that we're all striving toward. I find that view to be very deadening, finally, and certainly it's a terrible view for a teacher or a critic to hold. The other view is that each person has a chance to write his or her own book in his or her own voice; maturing as an artist occurs when you find your own voice, when you write something that *only you* could have written. That's the view I have."

In the *Paris Review* interview White described the two impulses—toward fiction and nonfiction—between which he balances his writing: "Writers can use literature as a mirror held up to the world, or they can use writing as a consolation for life (in the sense that literature is preferable to reality). I prefer the second approach, although clearly there has to be a blend of both. If the writing is pure fantasy it doesn't connect to any of our real feelings. But if it's grim realism, that doesn't seem like much of a gift. I think literature should be a gift to the reader, and that gift is in idealization. I don't mean it should be a whitewashing of problems, but something ideally energetic. Ordinary life is *blah,* whereas literature at its best is bristling with energy."

BIOGRAPHICAL/CRITICAL SOURCES:

BOOKS

Contemporary Literary Criticism, Volume 27, Gale, 1984.
McCaffery, Larry, *Alive and Writing: Interviews,* University Press of Illinois, 1987.
White, Edmund, *States of Desire: Travels in Gay America,* Dutton, 1980.
White, Edmund, *The Beautiful Room Is Empty,* Knopf, 1988.

PERIODICALS

Advocate, October 5, 1993.
American Book Review, May, 1989.
Artforum, January, 1987.
Booklist, October 1, 1994; June 1, 1995, p. 732; November 1, 1995, p. 453.
Chicago Tribune, December 10, 1978; April 6, 1980; February 14, 1994.
Christopher Street, November 25, 1991.
Harper's, March, 1979; October, 1982; May, 1987.
House and Garden, June, 1990.
Library Journal, February 15, 1973; October 1, 1994, p. 82; June 15, 1995, p. 95; November 15, 1995, p. 92; February 1, 1996, p. 75.
Life, fall, 1989.
London Review of Books, April 17, 1986; March 3, 1988; June 10, 1993, p. 3; August 24, 1995, p. 12.
Los Angeles Times, January 12, 1994, p. C7.
Los Angeles Times Book Review, May 4, 1980; April 3, 1982; November 21, 1993, p. 1; July 16, 1995, p. 4.
Mother Jones, June, 1983.
Nation, January 5, 1974; March 1, 1980; November 13, 1982; November 16, 1985; April 9, 1988; January 3, 1994; August 28, 1995, p. 214.
New Republic, February 21, 1994.
New Statesman, March 14, 1986; January 29, 1988; June 17, 1994, p. 38.
Newsweek, April 30, 1973; February 11, 1980; January 17, 1983; November 29, 1993.
New York Review of Books, October 21, 1993, p. 15.
New York Times, January 21, 1980; December 17, 1982; September 8, 1985; March 17, 1988; December 8, 1993, p. C23.
New York Times Book Review, March 25, 1973; December 10, 1978; February 3, 1980; October 10, 1982; September 15, 1985; March 20, 1988; November 7, 1993; October 23, 1994, p. 18; July 23, 1995, p. 6; December 3, 1995, p. 50.
New York Times Magazine, June 16, 1991.
Observer, March 16, 1986; December 14, 1986; January 24, 1988; November 13, 1988; June 20, 1993; June 19, 1994; June 14, 1995.
Paris Review, fall, 1988 (interview).
Playboy, November, 1993.
Publishers Weekly, September 24, 1982 (interview); March 21, 1994, p. 8.
Punch, March 19, 1986; January 8, 1988.
Rolling Stone, December 19, 1985.
San Francisco Review of Books, winter, 1988; February/March, 1994, p. 35.
Shenandoah, Volume 30, number 1, fall, 1978.

Spectator, March 5, 1988.

Time, April 11, 1988; July 30, 1990; December 27, 1993.

Times Literary Supplement, September 5, 1980; August 19, 1983; January 22, 1988; July 1, 1994, p. 13; March 17, 1995, p. 20.

Town & Country, May, 1983.

Tribune Books (Chicago), October 24, 1993, p. 3; August 13, 1995, p. 4.

Village Voice, January 28, 1980; June 28, 1988 (interview).

Vogue, February, 1984; November, 1984; May, 1985; January, 1986; July, 1986; July, 1987.

Voice Literary Supplement, December, 1982; April, 1988; June, 1988.

Washington Post Book World, November 12, 1978; December 10, 1978; January 27, 1980; October 17, 1982; October 6, 1985; April 3, 1988.

West Coast Review of Books, Volume 14, number 1, 1988.*

*   *   *

WHITE, G(eorge) Edward 1941-

PERSONAL: Born March 19, 1941, in Northampton, MA; son of George L. (a book publisher) and Frances D. (a teacher; maiden name, McCafferty) White; married Susan Valre Davis (a lawyer), December 31, 1966; children: Alexandra Valre, Elisabeth McCafferty Davis. *Education:* Amherst College, B.A., 1963; Yale University, M.A., 1964, Ph.D., 1967; Harvard University, J.D., 1970.

ADDRESSES: Home—Charlottesville, VA. *Office*—School of Law, University of Virginia, Charlottesville, VA 22903.

CAREER: American Bar Foundation, Chicago, IL, visiting scholar, 1970-71; U.S. Supreme Court, Washington, DC, law clerk to Chief Justice Earl Warren, 1971-72; University of Virginia, Charlottesville, assistant professor, 1972-74, associate professor, 1974-76, professor of law, 1977—.

MEMBER: American Society for Legal History, Phi Beta Kappa.

AWARDS, HONORS: American Bar Association, Gavel Award Certificates of Merit, 1979, for *Patterns of American Legal Thought,* 1981, for *Tort Law*

in America: An Intellectual History, 1994, for *Justice Oliver Wendell Holmes: Law and the Inner Self,* Silver Gavel Award, 1983, for *Earl Warren: A Public Life,* James Willard Hurst Prize, 1990, for *The Marshall Court and Cultural Change, 1815-1835,* American Historical Association, Littleton-Griswold Prize for Legal History, 1994, Scribes Award, 1994, Triennial Order of the Coif Award, 1996, all for *Justice Oliver Wendell Holmes: Law and the Inner Self.*

WRITINGS:

The Eastern Establishment and the Western Experience, Yale University Press (New Haven, CT), 1968.

The American Judicial Tradition, Oxford University Press (New York City), 1976.

Patterns of American Legal Thought, Bobbs-Merrill (Indianapolis), 1978.

Tort Law in America: An Intellectual History, Oxford University Press, 1980.

Earl Warren: A Public Life, Oxford University Press, 1982.

The Marshall Court and Cultural Change, 1815-1835, Macmillan (New York City), 1988.

Justice Oliver Wendell Holmes: Law and the Inner Self, Oxford University Press, 1993.

Intervention and Detachment: Essays in Legal History and Jurisprudence, Oxford University Press, 1994.

Creating the National Pastime: Baseball Transforms Itself, Princeton University Press (Princeton, NJ), 1996.

Editor of "Studies in Legal History" series, University of North Carolina Press. Contributor to law journals.

SIDELIGHTS: G. Edward White is "one of the most productive and provocative practitioners of American legal history writing today," writes Michael R. Belknap in the *American Historical Review.* He has published books on topics encompassing many aspects of America's legal history, including top-rated biographies of Justices Earl Warren, John Marshall, and Oliver Wendell Holmes. Most recently, White has turned has analysis on the history of baseball and its transformation into America's national pastime.

In *Earl Warren: A Public Life,* White presents readers with an in-depth study of how various events in the life of the late Supreme Court chief justice may have shaped his legal philosophy and approach to the responsibilities of the Court. White takes upon himself the job of reconciling some of the circumstances of Warren's early career (such as his support for the wartime confinement of Japanese-Americans in internment camps) with his later status as one of America's most liberal Supreme Court justices. In the process the author traces the changing role of the Supreme Court in American society, "throwing fresh light on an amazing period in the . . . Court's history," according to Anthony Lewis in the *New York Times Book Review.*

Earl Warren: A Public Life is first and foremost the story of Warren himself, however, and "it is in the analysis of Warren's philosophy that White excels," writes James E. Clayton in the *Washington Post Book World.* White's portrait of Warren is that of a man for whom ethical considerations and timely interpretation carried more weight than legal precedent and scholarly abstraction. In Clayton's words, "it is a view that Warren reverted to the 19th-century practice of letting a personal sense of right and wrong determine the outcome of cases, supporting the result with any convenient legal rationale." Jerry Pacht, writing in the *Los Angeles Times Book Review,* believes that White overcomes the pitfalls associated with trying to piece together the influences that give form to the personality and ideals of a major public figure: "This is no pretentious psychobiography. White makes a serious and usually successful effort to show us the people and forces, events, ideas, plans and accidents that made Warren what he became. [His] conclusions about the genesis of Warren's attitudes, drives, and suspicions are supported by facts."

Joseph Sobran, in a *National Review* article, takes a different tack, remarking of Warren: "Liberal opinion was more than kind to him. So is White. [The author] calls Warren's premises 'broad and vague,' and so they were. White's own analysis, unfortunately, is also broad and vague." Sobran's comments are testimony to the fact that Warren remains a politically controversial figure, and Pacht asserts as much in the opening lines of his review, insisting that the book's value lies in its historical rather than political point of view: "[Warren] has been praised and vilified; simplistic explanations have been offered for his conduct. Broad and largely inapt labels have been placed on his work, his personality and his attitudes. . . . White has gone beyond the labels and given us the man."

Questions of partisan opinion aside, the real strength of *Earl Warren: A Public Life* lies not in whether, as Lewis claims, "one finishes this book with a renewed respect for Warren," but in the fact that, as Joseph L. Rauh points out in the *New Republic,* White furnishes "both Warren's supporters and detractors with a wealth of material for the continuing debate over Warren's role." Sobran identifies the immediate value of White's achievement, stating that "We haven't had a full biography until now." But it is Clayton who singles out the long-term impact of the book: "[White develops] a thesis of Warren's decision-making process with which every future Warren biographer or Supreme Court historian will have to cope."

In the 1990s, four biographies on Justice Oliver Wendell Holmes were published, including White's; Thomas C. Grey writes in the *New York Review of Books* that White's "subtle, thoughtful, and careful work seems to me the best of them." In *Justice Oliver Wendell Holmes: Law and the Inner Self,* White's work sets itself apart from other books on Holmes, writes Norman Rosenberg in *Reviews in American History,* in that "it promises to concentrate on the 'interaction' between the private and public Holmes, between his 'professional endeavors' and his 'inner self,'" while still critically assessing Holmes's legal writings. Though the work admirably places Holmes in American jurisprudence, Rosenberg maintains that it further "takes a broader view of Holmes's place in American, rather than simply American legal, history." Rosenberg asserts that by "[C]ombining careful research and thought-provoking interpretations G. Edward White's study sets a high standard against which all future legal biographies might be judged."

Largely because of Holmes' opinions on free speech, hostility to substantive due process, and acceptance of legislative reforms on economic issues, Holmes became a "jurisprudential hero to an influential generation of lawyers and legal intellectuals associated with various progressive reforms," writes Michael E. Parrish in the *American Historical Review.* Thereafter, Holmes was long lionized as a liberal and a progressive. One of White's most important accomplishments in this book is that his discussions "resituate, rather than simply debunk, earlier accounts of Holmes's progressive convictions," writes Rosenberg. According to Parrish, "As White's careful analysis makes clear, however, the Holmes of progressive imagination did not always correspond to the Holmes who decided actual cases on the Supreme Court. The progressive image of Holmes could be sustained only by ignoring the large pieces of his jurisprudence and misinterpreting others." White also properly situates some of Holmes's more now-controversial ideas. Grey points out that White "takes care to put Holmes's often horrifying pronouncements on eugenics into historical context, noting that before the Nazis permanently discredited them, [these ideas] were held among liberal reformers." Although *Justice Oliver Wendell Holmes* is "short on fresh discoveries," writes Parrish, most important is White's success at "recast[ing] the meaning of Holmes's life for a new generation" and writing "the most complete and compelling one-volume biography in the Holmes literature."

White next turned away from the legal world and to the sports world with *Creating the National Pastime: Baseball Transforms Itself*. In this work, White, Richard J. Tofel writes in the *Wall Street Journal*, "attempts to discern why baseball has enjoyed such mythic status in American culture." The book traces the development of baseball, focusing on the economic and organizational structure, from the first World Series in 1903 to various teams' relocation in 1953-54. Over the course of these five decades, though America underwent major changes, baseball seemed to stay the same. "It is Mr. White's great insight to note that this occurred by design," writes Tofel. White answers the question, posed by a contributor to *Library Journal*, "How did baseball, an urban sport originally known for its rowdiness and unwholesome image, transform itself into the mythical national pastime?" White contends that those at the "upper echelons" of the sport transformed it "to a game that simultaneously embodied America's urbanizing, commercializing future and the memory of its rural, pastoral past." A contributor to *Kirkus Reviews* writes, "as [White] meticulously demonstrates, while baseball promoted its 'anachronistic dimensions' as a rural, fresh-air sport played by apple-cheeked youths, it was able to do so, in part, by violating anti-trust laws, by implementing such unfair labor practices as the reserve clause, and by restricting its talent pool according to race."

Tofel called White's book "a solid work of history," believing it "should provide real insight into [baseball's] glorious past, and why it is no accident that we remember that past as glorious." Chris Bohjallan writes in the *Washington Post Book World*, that White's "arguments are sound and his reasoning is compelling" and that the book is "thoughtful,

scholarly and well-researched." He adds, however, that what he misses in the book is "the sort of love for the game that informs the very best baseball writing." For other readers, White's legal and historical background, represented in his writing, stands in the way of their enjoyment. Yet George F. Will contends in the *New York Times Book Review* that "Mr. White disappoints only [in an analysis made] in his final chapter."

White's writing consistently prove his "justifiably celebrated talent for close, historically sensitive readings," as Rosenberg remarks in his discussion of *Justice Oliver Wendell Holmes*. All of White's work profit from his legal mind, which is able to look at matters from a variety of angles, as well as his in-depth research, which provides a wealth of material for his readers.

BIOGRAPHICAL/CRITICAL SOURCES:

PERIODICALS

American Historical Review, October, 1995, pp. 1308-1309; December, 1995, pp. 1653-1654.
Kirkus Reviews, March 1, 1996, p. 366.
Los Angeles Times Book Review, August 1, 1982.
National Review, October 29, 1982.
New Republic, August 9, 1982.
New Yorker, August 2, 1982.
New York Review of Books, July 13, 1995, pp. 4-7.
New York Times Book Review, January 16, 1977; July 4, 1982; April 7, 1996, p. 11.
Reviews in American History, volume 23, 1995, pp. 482-487.
Wall Street Journal, August 26, 1982; July 8, 1996.
Washington Post Book World, August 1, 1982; April 21, 1996, pp. 10, 13.

*   *   *

WILMER, Dale
  See MILLER, (H.) Bill(y)

*   *   *

WILMER, Dale
  See WADE, Robert (Allison)

WIND, Herbert Warren 1916-

PERSONAL: Born August 11, 1916, in Brockton, MA; son of Max Eisen and Dora Wind. *Education:* Yale University, B.A., 1937; Cambridge University, M.A., 1939.

ADDRESSES: Home—301 East 66th St., New York, NY. *Office—New Yorker,* 25 East 43rd St., New York, NY 10036.

CAREER: Member of staff of *New Yorker* magazine, 1947-54, 1962-89, and *Sports Illustrated* magazine, 1954-60. *Military service:* U.S. Army Air Forces, 1942-46; became captain.

MEMBER: Yale Club (New York), Royal and Ancient Golf Club (St. Andrews, Scotland).

WRITINGS:

The Story of American Golf, Farrar, Straus (New York City), 1948, 3rd edition, Knopf (New York City), 1975.

(With Gene Sarazen) *Thirty Years of Championship Golf,* Prentice-Hall (New York City), 1950.

(Editor) *The Complete Golfer,* Simon & Schuster (New York City), 1954.

(Editor) *Tips from the Top,* Prentice-Hall (Englewood Cliffs, NJ), Volume I, 1955, Volume II, 1956, abridged version published as *Golf Tips from the Professionals,* Fawcett (Greenwich, CT), 1958.

(With Ben Hogan) *Five Lessons: The Modern Fundamentals of Golf,* A. S. Barnes (New York City), 1957, revised edition, Cornerstone Library (New York City), 1962.

(Editor with Peter Schwed) *Great Stories from the World of Sport,* Simon & Schuster, 1958.

On the Tour with Harry Sprague, Simon & Schuster, 1958.

The Gilded Age of Sport, Simon & Schuster, 1961.

(Editor) *The Realm of Sport: A Classic Collection of the World's Greatest Sporting Events and Personalities as Recorded by the Most Distinguished Writers,* Simon & Schuster, 1966.

(With Jack Nicklaus) *The Greatest Game of All: My Life in Golf,* Simon & Schuster, 1969.

Herbert Warren Wind's Golf Book, Simon & Schuster, 1971 (published in England as *The Lure of Golf,* Heinemann [London], 1971).

The World of P. G. Wodehouse, Praeger (New York City), 1971.

Game, Set, and Match: The Tennis Boom of the 1960's and 70's, Dutton (New York City), 1979.

Herbert Warren Wind's Golf Quiz, Golf Digest (Norwalk, CT), 1980.

Following Through, Ticknor & Fields (New York City), 1985.

SIDELIGHTS: Herbert Warren Wind is one of America's best known golf writers. Although he is no stranger to other athletic pursuits—and has published on sports as diverse as squash and ski jumping—Wind is recognized for his golf and tennis coverage, most of which made its debut in the pages of the *New Yorker* or *Sports Illustrated.* His essays for the *New Yorker's* "Sporting Scene" in particular have earned him a vast following among golf and tennis enthusiasts. Former *New York Times* columnist Arthur Daley lauded Wind for his "graceful, easy, authoritative and frequently amusing style," as made evident not only in magazine pieces but in books as well.

Wind grew up in Brockton, Massachusetts, a town with four golf courses. He began playing the game as a youngster and continued his fascination with it while studying at Yale University and abroad as a graduate student at Cambridge. He became a staff writer for the *New Yorker* after serving in World War II, moved to *Sports Illustrated* as a founding writer in 1954, and returned to the *New Yorker* and its "Sporting Scene" column in 1962. Wind, whose experiences watching tournament golf stretched back into the early decades of the twentieth century, was able to call upon a voluminous knowledge for his writing: personal friendships with some of golf's biggest names, acquaintance with the vagaries of numerous tournament courses, and a distinct and unwavering enthusiasm for the sport he has called "perhaps the most difficult of all the major games to play well."

"The best of Wind's work for *The New Yorker* takes the form of personal essays after the example of Bernard Darwin, the English golf writer who was Wind's acknowledged master," noted David Sanders in the *Dictionary of Literary Biography.* "Like Darwin, Wind excels at re-creating the 'feel' of a match, hole by hole and stroke by stroke, with history and tradition entering the account as naturally as the writer's meticulous notice of the terrain underfoot and the weather overhead."

A number of Wind's full-length books concern golf. He has edited volumes of golf writing by fellow sportswriters and the players themselves, has authored texts on how to play the game, and has served as co-author for books by some of the most famous pros, including Jack Nicklaus. "It requires an uncanny gift to describe past tournaments and give them immediacy and excitement," declared George Plimpton in a *Book World* review of *The Greatest Game of All: My Life in Golf,* by Nicklaus and Wind. "Wind can do this. . . . He is not only dedicated to golf but also to the written word, so that [his work's] fine literary quality is one of its delights." In the *San Francisco Chronicle,* Scott Newhall succinctly described Wind as "a good writer, who knows his golf history thoroughly."

BIOGRAPHICAL/CRITICAL SOURCES:

BOOKS

Dictionary of Literary Biography, Volume 171: *Twentieth Century American Sportswriters,* Gale (Detroit, MI), 1996, pp. 342-48.

PERIODICALS

Book World, June 22, 1969, p. 3; March 21, 1971, p. 1.
Chicago Sun, December 19, 1948, p. 9X.
New York Times, December 19, 1948, p. 12.
New York Times Book Review, October 29, 1961, p. 14; June 8, 1969, p. 46.
San Francisco Chronicle, December 19, 1948, p. 12.

*   *   *

WINSOR, Kathleen 1919-

PERSONAL: Born October 16, 1919, in Olivia, MN; daughter of Harold Lee (in real estate) and Myrtle Belle (Crowder) Winsor; married Robert J. Herwig, 1936 (divorced, 1946); married Artie Shaw, 1946 (a band leader; marriage ended); married Arnold Robert Krakower, 1949 (a lawyer; divorced, 1953); married Paul A. Porter (a lawyer), June 26, 1956 (died, November, 1975). *Education:* University of California, B.A., 1938.

ADDRESSES: Agent—Roslyn Targ Literary Agency, Inc., 105 West 13th St., New York, NY 10011.

CAREER: Writer. *Oakland Tribune,* Oakland, CA, reporter and receptionist; story consultant for television series *Dreams in the Dust,* 1971.

WRITINGS:

NOVELS

Forever Amber, Macmillan (New York City), 1944.
Star Money, Appleton-Century-Crofts (East Norwalk, CT), 1950.
The Lovers, Appleton-Century-Crofts, 1952.
America, with Love, Putnam (New York City), 1957.
Wanderers Eastward, Wanderers West, Random House (New York City), 1965.
Calais, Doubleday (Garden City, NY), 1979.
Jacintha, Crown (New York City), 1985.
Robert and Arabella, Crown, 1986.

ADAPTATIONS: Forever Amber was adapted as a motion picture by Twentieth Century-Fox in 1947.

SIDELIGHTS: "It wasn't such a daring book," maintains Kathleen Winsor in defense of her first novel, *Forever Amber.* "I wrote only two sexy passages, and my publishers took both of them out. They put in ellipses instead. In those days, you could solve everything with an ellipse." Regardless of both her own opinion and her publisher's attempts to cool the passionate episodes, *Forever Amber* caused a nationwide scandal and was banned in Boston, Massachusetts, as an obscene and offensive book.

A historical novel that consumed five years of research, *Forever Amber* is the story of Amber St. Claire, "that beautiful Restoration hussy who managed to take an assortment of lovers without either being struck by lightning or permanent disfigurement," related Judy Bachrach in the *Chicago Tribune.* Although held in low esteem by most critics, the book was highly successful with the general public. Within a month after its release in 1944, the book went into its second printing and the movie rights were purchased by Twentieth Century-Fox for a sum reported to exceed by several times that paid for Margaret Mitchell's *Gone with the Wind.* A year later, *Forever Amber* was into its eleventh printing.

Due to her own attractiveness, it was rumored that Winsor would herself portray the raven-haired beauty in the upcoming film, even though her contract with the studio called for a more consultative and supervisory role in the production. The general opinion at the time was that Winsor's looks played more than a minor role in promoting *Forever Amber.* Fellow author Taylor Caldwell bemoaned this situation and claimed that it worked to Winsor's disadvantage: "Her pretty face has always gotten in the way of the fact that she is one of America's most magnificent novelists."

Other reviewers, however, were not so kind in their appraisals of Winsor and *Forever Amber*. H. L. Binsse of *Commonweal*, for instance, complained that the book "possesses no slightest virtue of style, it is full of the most astounding fakery." And although *Catholic World* admitted that the "historical details are valid," it railed that "both characters and incidents seem like the stages of a prolonged sexual fantasy." This type of comment and the overemphasis on the part of critics of this aspect of the book bothered Winsor for, as she has contended, "I don't write dirty scenes. I mean I don't write medical journal, anatomical scenes. If anything, what I write is an understatement compared to the goings-on as I hear about them." L. S. Munn of the *Springfield Republican* agreed with Winsor in that there is much more to her book than merely sexual overtones: " 'Forever Amber' is not just a cloak and sword novel. Its attributes are far more substantial and inclusive." He went on to praise her writing as "florid and robust," and assess that "her characters are bawdy, and she writes with full-bodied though feminine zest for her subject and her characters." Orville Prescott of the *Yale Review*, however, condemned the book as "a crude and superficial glorification of a courtesan and the dissolute life of Restoration England."

And yet *Forever Amber* proved an overwhelming success with the general public; when released, bookstores could not keep enough books in stock to meet the enormous demand. Decades after it first appeared on the market, the book still enjoys considerable popularity. None of Winsor's later books achieved the wide readership or the notoriety of *Forever Amber*, but they did have merit in the opinion of some critics. One of her more favorably reviewed books was *America, with Love*, in which the author described a year in the life of a young girl growing up in a Western town during the 1930s. A *Library Journal* reviewer commented that while Winsor's writing style was weak, "she does have a feeling for the world of the child," and a *New York Herald Tribune Book Review* contributor took note of her "excellent ear for the rhythm and cadence of the young as they spoke in the 1930s." William Hogan, writing in the *San Francisco Chronicle*, rated *America, with Love* as "probably the best thing Kathleen Winsor has written," even as he acknowledged that it would probably never achieve the financial success of *Forever Amber*.

Christian H. Moe noted in *Twentieth-Century Romance and Historical Writers* that many of Winsor's later books utilized a heroine with the same qualities as Amber St. Claire: independent, full of sexual desire, and living outside societal norms with no regret. An exception is *Star Money*, which is distinctly autobiographical. In this novel, a beautiful authoress writes a best-selling historical novel about an irrepressible eighteenth-century woman, becomes a prominent figure in the publishing world, and then undertakes a series of affairs with famous men. That formula is repeated in *Calais*, with the central figure being an actress rather than a writer. Moe wrote: "The events are mildly interesting, but the novel lacks vigour and its characters lack verve." The critic rated *America, with Love* as the author's second-best work, but concluded: "Winsor's contributor of *Forever Amber*, with its brazen central character and its vivid historicity, stands as a significant achievement which influenced the shaping of the contemporary romance novel as a genre. It is her first novel that indicates her talent."

BIOGRAPHICAL/CRITICAL SOURCES:

BOOKS

Twentieth-Century Romance and Historical Writers, St. James Press (Detroit), 1994.

PERIODICALS

America, May 15, 1965.
Atlantic, December, 1944, p. 137; June, 1950.
Booklist, November 1, 1944.
Book Week, October 15, 1944, p. 1; May 2, 1965, p. 20.
Catholic World, January, 1945; January, 1958.
Chicago Sunday Tribune, April 16, 1950, p. 3; September 14, 1952, p. 6; October 13, 1957, p. 9.
Chicago Tribune, May 3, 1979.
Christian Science Monitor, April 12, 1950, p. 16; May 20, 1965, p. 7.
Commonweal, December 29, 1944.
Kirkus Reviews, August 1, 1952.
Library Journal, October 15, 1957.
Newsweek, May 24, 1965.
New Yorker, October 21, 1944; April 22, 1950; September 27, 1952.
New York Herald Tribune Book Review, March 30, 1947; April 16, 1950, p. 10; September 14, 1952, p. 15; October 13, 1957, p. 4.
New York Times, October 15, 1944, p. 7; April 16, 1950, p. 4; September 14, 1952, p. 28; October 20, 1957, p. 49.

New York Times Book Review, May 2, 1965, p. 5.
New York Times Magazine, August 4, 1956.
Observer, October 3, 1965.
San Francisco Chronicle, April 15, 1950; September 21, 1952, p. 21; October 14, 1957, p. 25.
Saturday Review, October 14, 1944; November 4, 1944; January 5, 1946; April 15, 1950; September 27, 1952; November 23, 1957; May 1, 1965.
Springfield Republican, October 15, 1944.
Time, April 17, 1950; September 15, 1952; October 14, 1957; April 30, 1965.
Times Literary Supplement, July 28, 1950, p. 465; October 7, 1965, p. 892.
Weekly Book Review, October 15, 1944.
Yale Review, winter, 1945.

*   *   *

WOGAMAN, J(ohn) Philip 1932-
(Philip Wogaman)

PERSONAL: Born March 18, 1932, in Toledo, OH; son of Donald Ford and Louise (Kilbury) Wogaman; married Carolyn Jane Gattis, August 4, 1956; children: Stephen Neil, Donald George, Paul Joseph, Jean Ann. *Education:* College (now University) of the Pacific, A.B., 1954; Boston University, S.T.B. 1957, Ph.D., 1960; additional study in Costa Rica.

ADDRESSES: Office—Foundry United Methodist Church, 1500 16th St. NW, Washington, DC 20036-1402.

CAREER: Ordained minister of United Methodist Church. Pastor in Marlborough, MA, 1956-58; United Methodist Church, Division of World Missions, Louisville, KY, staff member, 1960-61 (appointed to teach at Union Theological Seminary in Cuba, but unable to do so because of political developments); University of the Pacific, Stockton, CA, associate professor of Bible and social ethics and director of Pacific Center for the Study of Social Issues, 1961-66; Wesley Theological Seminary, Washington, DC, associate professor, 1966-69, professor of Christian social ethics, 1969-92, affiliated professor of Christian Ethics, 1992—, dean, 1972-83; Foundry United Methodist Church, senior minister, 1992—. Member of Committee on International Affairs, National Council of Churches. Candidate for

California State Legislature, 1964; member of California Democratic State Central Committee, 1964-66. President of Stockton Fair Housing Commission, Stockton, California, 1963-64; member of board, Suburban Maryland Fair Housing Committee, 1970.

MEMBER: American Academy of Religion, American Society of Christian Ethics (president, 1976-77).

AWARDS, HONORS: Association Theological Schools fellow, 1975.

WRITINGS:

Methodism's Challenge in Race Relations: A Study of Strategy, foreword by Edward K. Graham, Public Affairs Press (Washington, DC), 1960.
(Under the name Philip Wogaman) *Protestant Faith and Religious Liberty,* Abingdon (Nashville, TN), 1967.
(Under the name Philip Wogaman) *Guaranteed Annual Income: The Moral Issues,* Abingdon, 1968.
(Contributor) Paul Deats, editor, *Toward a Discipline of Social Ethics: Essays in Honor of Walter George Muelder,* Boston University Press (Boston), 1972.
(Editor) *The Population Crisis and Moral Responsibility,* Public Affairs Press, 1973.
A Christian Method of Moral Judgment, S.C.M. Press, 1976, Westminster (Philadelphia), 1977.
The Great Economic Debate: An Ethical Analysis, Westminster, 1977 (published in England as *Christians and the Great Economic Debate,* S.C.M. Press, 1977).
(With Paul F. McCleary) *Quality of Life in a Global Society,* Friendship (New York City), 1978.
Faith and Fragmentation: Christianity for a New Age, Fortress (Philadelphia), 1985.
Economics and Ethics, Fortress, 1986.
Christian Perspectives on Politics, Fortress, 1988.
Christian Moral Judgment, Westminster, 1989.
Making Moral Decisions, Abingdon, 1990.
Christian Ethics: An Historical Introduction, Westminster, 1993.
To Serve the Present Age: The Gift & Promise of United Methodism, Abingdon, 1995.
(Editor with Douglas M. Strong) *Readings in Christian Ethics: An Historical Sourcebook,* Westminster, 1996.

Contributor of articles and reviews to *Christian Century, South African Outlook, Religion and Life,* and other journals.

BIOGRAPHICAL/CRITICAL SOURCES:

PERIODICALS

America, June 18, 1977.
Christian Century, August 30, 1967; January 4, 1978.

* * *

WOGAMAN, Philip
  See WOGAMAN, J(ohn) Philip

* * *

WRIGHT, Charles (Penzel, Jr.) 1935-

PERSONAL: Born August 25, 1935, in Pickwick Dam, Hardin County, TN; son of Charles Penzel and Mary Castleman (Winter) Wright; married Holly McIntire, April 6, 1969; children: Luke Savin Herrick. *Education:* Davidson College, B.A., 1957; University of Iowa, M.F.A., 1963; graduate study, University of Rome, 1963-64.

ADDRESSES: Home—940 Locust Ave., Charlottesville, VA 22901-4030 *Office*—Department of English, Bryan Hall, University of Virginia, Charlottesville, VA 22903.

CAREER: University of California, Irvine, 1966-83, began as assistant professor, became professor of English; University of Virginia, Charlottesville, Souder Family Professor of English, 1983—. Fulbright lecturer in Venice, Italy, 1968-69, distinuished visiting professor, Universita Degli Studi, Florence, Italy, 1992. *Military service:* U.S. Army, Intelligence Corps, 1957-61.

MEMBER: PEN American Center, American Academy of Arts and Letters, Fellowship of Southern Writers.

AWARDS, HONORS: Fulbright scholar at University of Rome, 1963-65; Eunice Tietjens Award, *Poetry* magazine, 1969; Guggenheim fellow, 1975; Melville Cane Award, Poetry Society of America, and Edgar Allan Poe Award, Academy of American Poets, both 1976, both for *Bloodlines;* Academy-Institute Award, American Academy and Institute of the Arts, 1977;

PEN translation award, 1979; Ingram Merrill fellow, 1980 and 1993; National Book Award in poetry (co-winner), 1983, for *Country Music: Selected Early Poems;* National Book Critics Circle Award nomination in poetry, 1984, for *The Other Side of the River;* Brandeis Creative Arts Citation for poetry, 1987; Merit Medal, American Academy and Institute Arts and Letters, 1992; Ruth Lilly Poetry prize, 1993; Lenore Marshall Poetry Prize, Academy of American Poets, 1996; Wood Prize, *Poetry* magazine, 1996.

WRITINGS:

POETRY

Six Poems, David Freed, 1965.
The Dream Animal (chapbook), House of Anansi (Toronto), 1968.
Private Madrigals, limited edition, Abraxas Press (Madison, WI), 1969.
The Grave of the Right Hand, Wesleyan University Press (Middletown, CT), 1970.
The Venice Notebook, Barn Dream Press, 1971.
Hard Freight, Wesleyan University Press, 1973.
Bloodlines, Wesleyan University Press, 1975.
China Trace, Wesleyan University Press, 1977.
Colophons, limited edition, Windhover (New York City), 1977.
Wright: A Profile, with interview and critical essay by David St. John, Grilled Flowers Press, 1979.
Dead Color, limited edition, Meadow Press, 1980.
The Southern Cross, Random House (New York City), 1981.
Country Music: Selected Early Poems, Wesleyan University Press, 1982.
Four Poems of Departure, limited edition, Trace Editions, 1983.
The Other Side of the River, Random House, 1984.
Five Journals (also see below), limited edition, Red Ozier Press, 1986.
Zone Journals (includes *Five Journals*), Farrar, Straus (New York City), 1988.
The World of the Ten Thousand Things: Poems, 1980-1990, Farrar, Straus, 1990.
Chickamauga, Farrar, Straus, 1995.
Black Zodiac, Farrar, Straus, 1997.

OTHER

The Voyage, Patrician Press, 1963.
Backwater, Golem Press, 1973.
(Translator) Eugenio Montale, *The Storm,* Field Editions, 1978.
(Translator) Montale, *Motets,* Windhover, 1981.

(Translator) Dino Campana, *Orphic Songs,* Field Editions, 1984.

Halflife: Improvisations and Interviews, 1977-1987, University of Michigan Press (Ann Arbor), 1988.

Quarter Notes: Improvisations and Interviews, University of Michigan Press, 1995.

Selected writings have been recorded by the Library of Congress Archive of Recorded Poetry and Literature and The Modern Poetry Association.

SIDELIGHTS: Charles Wright's reputation has increased steadily with each poetry collection he has published. Today, he is widely regarded as one of the most important poets now living in the United States. From his early collection *The Grave of the Right Hand* to more recent books, such as *The Other Side of the River* and *Zone Journals,* Wright has worked in a style which creates a feeling of immediacy and concreteness by emphasizing objects and personal perspective. Many critics believe that Wright's childhood in rural Tennessee remains a vital force in his writing, for he shows a typically Southern concern for the past and its power. He began writing poetry while serving in Italy with the U.S. Army. While there, he "began using Ezra Pound's Italian Cantos first as a guide book to out-of-the-way places, then as a reference book and finally as a 'copy' book," *Dictionary of Literary Biography Yearbook: 1982* essayist George F. Butterick quotes the author as saying.

Ezra Pound's influence is evident in *The Grave of the Right Hand,* Wright's first major collection. These poems "have the polished clarity one would expect from a master of the plain style," *Georgia Review* contributor Peter Stitt observes. "They are obviously meant to speak to the reader, to communicate something he can share." At the same time, *The Grave of the Right Hand* is the most symbolic of all Wright's works, with images of gloves, shoes, hands, and hats recurring throughout. Through these images, the poet introduces themes that recur in all his later work: "mortality, the uses of memory, the irrepressible past, states of being, personal salvation, the correspondence between nature and the spiritual work, and, most broadly, the human condition," as Butterick describes.

Wright is credited with finding his own voice in *Hard Freight,* which Peter Meinke calls in a *New Republic* review "less Poundian, less hard-edged, than his first book, *The Grave of the Right Hand.*"

John L. Carpenter likewise applauds Wright for reaching for his own style in a *Poetry* review of *Hard Freight:* "It is less incisive and less deliberate than the first book, but it is more experimental, less ironclad and defensive." It is in this volume that the poet first exhibits his technique of creating poetry by compiling catalogs of fragmented images. It is a device which requires "that the reader assist in the creative activity," finds *Washington Post Book World* contributor Edward Kessler. "[Wright's] almost spastic writing can at times be enlivening and fascinating, like watching the changing fragments of a kaleidoscope."

This technique is not praised by all critics, however; some find it excessive. As Sally M. Gall declares in *Shenandoah:* "He frantically piles up details, images, similes, and metaphors as if sheer quantity can replace quality of perception. His catalogues can be perniciously boring rather than enlightening." But Kessler disagrees with this assessment, stating that Wright's "senses are awake, and even when he cannot quite bring his *things* of the world into a satisfying shape, his fragments are rife with suggestions. This man is feeling his way toward a personal definition."

Bloodlines continues in the same vein as *Hard Freight,* but many reviewers feel that Wright's voice is even stronger in this volume. *Yale Review* contributor J. D. McClatchy, for instance, believes that "Charles Wright has come completely home in *Bloodlines,* a book that confirms and emphasizes his reputation." Carol Muske also notes the power of this collection in *Parnassus: Poetry in Review:* "[Wright] is on the move. His poems fairly explode from the page in hurly-burly refrain, elliptical syntax, and giddy shifts that recall Hopkins." McClatchy adds that Wright "recreates not aspects but images of his past experiences—prayer meetings, sexual encounters, dreams—mingling memory and fantasy. The poems are suffused with remembered light."

Hard Freight, Bloodlines, and *China Trace* comprise what Wright thinks of as a trilogy of poetry collections. Explains Kathleen Agena in *Partisan Review,* "Like Wallace Stevens, Wright has conceived of his work as a whole. Individual poems are arresting but none of them quite has its meaning alone. The poems elucidate and comment on each other, extending and developing certain key metaphors and images." In *China Trace,* Wright again considers universal connections to the past. According to Butterick, the poet describes this collection as "a book of Chinese poems that don't sound like Chinese poems and aren't Chinese poems but are *like* Chinese poems in the sense that they give you an idea of one man's relationship to the endlessness, the ongoingness, the everlastingness of what's around him, and his relationship to it as he stands in the natural world."

Works such as *Zone Journals* and the collection *The World of the Ten Thousand Things* reflect Wright's "departure from his earlier crystalline short lyrics that aimed for inevitability of effect," Helen Vendler observes in *New Republic*. These journal poems "weave diverse thematic threads into a single autobiographical fabric" which can be read as a single work, Richard Tillinghast writes in the *New York Times Book Review*. "Freed from the stringencies of unity and closure demanded by the sort of poem most readers are used to, Mr. Wright is at liberty to spin out extended meditations that pick up, work with, lay aside and return again to landscapes, historical events and ideas." With his "subtle cadences" and "famously 'good ear,'" the critic adds, Wright "continues to reveal himself as a poet of great purity and originality."

Writing in *Poetry* about *Chickamauga,* David Baker observes that Wright uses abstractions to sustain the oblique. Of Wright's style he comments, "Almost nothing ever happens in a Charles Wright poem. This is his central act of restraint, a spiritualist's abstinence, where meditation is not absence but an alternative to action and to linear, dramatic finality." David Mason admits in the *Hudson Review* that Wright's poetry disappoints him. Mason finds that Wright's "ideas are uninteresting, his poems undramatic; his language is only intermittently charged or lyrical." He remarks, "There is plenty of meditative near-spirituality in *Chickamauga,* but it's all air and light, history without the details." According to James Longenbach in *The Yale Review,* Wright's career seems to change with *Chickamauga,* as he tries to constrain his writing. "Wright seems to feel that all he can do is spin new variations on a limited number of subjects and scenes" in *Chickamauga,* writes the critic, although the work is "a beautiful book, bearably human yet in touch with the sublime."

Agena contends that Wright's power comes from his faith in "the mad sense of language" and his willingness to abandon himself to it. She summarizes: "When Charles Wright's poems work, which is most of the time, the poetic energies seem to break the membrane of syntax, exploding the surface, reverberating in multiple directions simultaneously. It is not a linear progression one finds but rather a ricocheting, as if, at the impact of a single cue, all the words bounced into their pockets, rearranged, and displaced themselves in different directions all over again. And it seems to happen by accident, as if Wright simply sets the words in motion and they, playing a game according to their own rules, write the poem." Wright's greatest accomplishment, according to Butterick, "is the imagistic narrative. How he activates and propels the line of images . . . is his special genius, his ability to drive spirit into the matter of words." "His best work has always been founded in the hard-edged fact, not the gauze of metaphysics," William Logan summarizes in the *New York Times Book Review,* praising in particular Wright's "individuality and seriousness, his gorgeous images and taste for experiment." As a result, the critic concludes, "for twenty years, [Wright] has written to a consistently high and exacting standard."

BIOGRAPHICAL/CRITICAL SOURCES:

BOOKS

Andrews, Tom, *The Point Where All Things Meet: Essays on Charles Wright,* Oberlin College Press (Oberlin, OH), 1995.

Contemporary Authors Autobiography Series, Volume 7, Gale (Detroit), 1988.

Contemporary Literary Criticism, Gale, Volume 6, 1976, Volume 13, 1980, Volume 28, 1984.

Dictionary of Literary Biography, Volume 165: *American Poets since World War II,* fourth series, Gale, 1996.

Dictionary of Literary Biography Yearbook: 1982, Gale, 1983.

Friebert, Stuart and David Young, editors, *A Field Guide to Contemporary Poetry and Poetics,* Longman, 1980.

Ingersoll, Earl W., and others, editors, *Post-Confessionals: Conversations with American Poets of the Eighties,* Fairleigh Dickinson University Press, 1989.

Perkins, David, *A History of Modern Poetry,* Harvard University Press, 1987.

Vendler, Helen, *The Music of What Happens,* Harvard University Press, 1988.

PERIODICALS

America, April 25, 1992, p. 361.
American Poetry Review, September/October, 1982.

Antioch Review, spring, 1982; summer, 1989.

Choice, September, 1976.

Facts on File, November 4, 1993, p. 839.

Georgia Review, summer, 1978; spring, 1982.

Hudson Review, spring, 1974; autumn, 1975; spring, 1996, p. 166.

Library Journal, April 1, 1995, p. 99.

Los Angeles Times Book Review, February 7, 1982.

Michigan Quarterly Review, fall, 1978.

New Republic, November 24, 1973; November 26, 1977; January 18, 1988; August 7, 1995, p. 42.

New Yorker, October 29, 1979.

New York Times Book Review, February 17, 1974; September 7, 1975; December 12, 1982; July 1, 1984; September 4, 1988; February 24, 1991, p.18.

Parnassus: Poetry in Review, spring-summer, 1976; spring-summer, 1982.

Partisan Review, Volume 43, number 4, 1976.

Poetry, December, 1974; December, 1978; December, 1989; August, 1991, p. 280; April, 1996, p. 33.

Publishers Weekly, February 27, 1995, p. 97.

Sewanee Review, spring, 1974.

Shenandoah, fall, 1974.

Times Literary Supplement, March 1, 1985.

Washington Post Book World, May 5, 1974.

Yale Review, autumn, 1975; October, 1995, p. 144.

RECEIVED

FEB 1998

Mission College
Library